NEW PERSPECTIVES ON
Microsoft® Access® 2010

COMPREHENSIVE

Joseph J. Adamski
Grand Valley State University

Kathleen T. Finnegan

Important Information About This Printing
This printing of this book was approved to meet the official standards for the Microsoft Office Specialist Access 2010 exam. This printing includes a new Appendix B that provides:

- Information on Microsoft Office Specialist certification
- Coverage of additional skills related to the exam that are not covered in the main tutorials of this text
- A table that lists the skills for the exam and identifies where each is covered in the text

The information about the Microsoft Office Specialist exams on page viii is also new to this printing. Otherwise, the book contains the exact page-for-page content of previous printings.

COURSE TECHNOLOGY
CENGAGE Learning™

Australia • Brazil • Japan • Korea • Mexico • Singapore • Spain • United Kingdom • United States

COURSE TECHNOLOGY
CENGAGE Learning™

New Perspectives on Microsoft Access 2010, Comprehensive

Vice President, Publisher: Nicole Jones Pinard

Executive Editor: Marie L. Lee

Associate Acquisitions Editor: Brandi Shailer

Senior Product Manager: Kathy Finnegan

Product Manager: Leigh Hefferon

Product Manager: Katherine C. Russillo

Associate Product Manager: Julia Leroux-Lindsey

Editorial Assistant: Jacqueline Lacaire

Director of Marketing: Cheryl Costantini

Senior Marketing Manager: Ryan DeGrote

Marketing Coordinator: Kristen Panciocco

Developmental Editor: Jessica Evans

Content Project Manager: Jennifer Feltri

Composition: GEX Publishing Services

Art Director: Marissa Falco

Text Designer: Althea Chen

Cover Designer: Roycroft Design

Cover Art: © Veer Incorporated

Copyeditor: Camille Kiolbasa

Proofreader: Kathy Orrino

Indexer: Alexandra Nickerson

For product information and technology assistance, contact us at
Cengage Learning Customer & Sales Support, 1-800-354-9706
For permission to use material from this text or product, submit all requests online at **www.cengage.com/permissions**
Further permissions questions can be emailed to
permissionrequest@cengage.com

Some of the product names and company names used in this book have been used for identification purposes only and may be trademarks or registered trademarks of their respective manufacturers and sellers.

Microsoft and the Office logo are either registered trademarks or trademarks of Microsoft Corporation in the United States and/or other countries. Course Technology, Cengage Learning is an independent entity from the Microsoft Corporation, and not affiliated with Microsoft in any manner.

Disclaimer: Any fictional data related to persons or companies or URLs used throughout this book is intended for instructional purposes only. At the time this book was printed, any such data was fictional and not belonging to any real persons or companies.

Library of Congress Control Number: 2010932364

ISBN-13: 978-0-538-79847-1

ISBN-10: 0-538-79847-5

Course Technology
20 Channel Center Street
Boston, MA 02210
USA

Cengage Learning is a leading provider of customized learning solutions with office locations around the globe, including Singapore, the United Kingdom, Australia, Mexico, Brazil, and Japan. Locate your local office at:
international.cengage.com/global

Cengage Learning products are represented in Canada by Nelson Education, Ltd.

To learn more about Course Technology, visit **www.cengage.com/course technology**

To learn more about Cengage Learning, visit **www.cengage.com**

Purchase any of our products at your local college store or at our preferred online store **www.cengagebrain.com**

Printed in the United States of America
2 3 4 5 6 7 8 9 14 13 12 11

Preface

The New Perspectives Series' critical-thinking, problem-solving approach is the ideal way to prepare students to transcend point-and-click skills and take advantage of all that Microsoft Office 2010 has to offer.

In developing the New Perspectives Series, our goal was to create books that give students the software concepts and practical skills they need to succeed beyond the classroom. We've updated our proven case-based pedagogy with more practical content to make learning skills more meaningful to students.

With the New Perspectives Series, students understand *why* they are learning *what* they are learning, and are fully prepared to apply their skills to real-life situations.

About This Book

This book provides complete coverage of Microsoft Access 2010, and includes the following:

- Detailed, hands-on instruction of Access 2010, including creating and maintaining a database, querying a database, creating forms and reports, integrating Access with other programs, creating macros, writing VBA code, and securing a database
- Coverage of important database concepts, including guidelines for designing databases and setting field properties, defining table relationships, object dependencies, normalization, and Access naming conventions
- Exploration of new Access 2010 features, including working in Backstage view, using the Data Type gallery to add new fields, applying themes to database objects, creating navigation forms, and using the Macro Designer

New for this edition!

- Each session begins with a Visual Overview, a new two-page spread that includes colorful, enlarged screenshots with numerous callouts and key term definitions, giving students a comprehensive preview of the topics covered in the session, as well as a handy study guide.
- New ProSkills boxes provide guidance for how to use the software in real-world, professional situations, and related ProSkills exercises integrate the technology skills students learn with one or more of the following soft skills: decision making, problem solving, teamwork, verbal communication, and written communication.
- Important steps are now highlighted in yellow with attached margin notes to help students pay close attention to completing the steps correctly and avoid time-consuming rework.

System Requirements

This book assumes a typical installation of Microsoft Access 2010 and Microsoft Windows 7 Ultimate using an Aero theme. (You can also complete the material in this text using another version of Windows 7, such as Home Premium, or earlier versions of the Windows operating system. You will see only minor differences in how some windows look.) The browser used for any steps that require a browser is Internet Explorer 8.

www.cengage.com/ct/newperspectives

The New Perspectives Approach

Context

Each tutorial begins with a problem presented in a "real-world" case that is meaningful to students. The case sets the scene to help students understand what they will do in the tutorial.

Hands-on Approach

Each tutorial is divided into manageable sessions that combine reading and hands-on, step-by-step work. Colorful screenshots help guide students through the steps. **Trouble?** tips anticipate common mistakes or problems to help students stay on track and continue with the tutorial.

VISUAL OVERVIEW

Visual Overviews

New for this edition! Each session begins with a Visual Overview, a new two-page spread that includes colorful, enlarged screenshots with numerous callouts and key term definitions, giving students a comprehensive preview of the topics covered in the session, as well as a handy study guide.

PROSKILLS

ProSkills Boxes and Exercises

New for this edition! ProSkills boxes provide guidance for how to use the software in real-world, professional situations, and related ProSkills exercises integrate the technology skills students learn with one or more of the following soft skills: decision making, problem solving, teamwork, verbal communication, and written communication.

KEY STEP

Key Steps

New for this edition! Important steps are highlighted in yellow with attached margin notes to help students pay close attention to completing the steps correctly and avoid time-consuming rework.

INSIGHT

InSight Boxes

InSight boxes offer expert advice and best practices to help students achieve a deeper understanding of the concepts behind the software features and skills.

TIP

Margin Tips

Margin Tips provide helpful hints and shortcuts for more efficient use of the software. The Tips appear in the margin at key points throughout each tutorial, giving students extra information when and where they need it.

REVIEW

APPLY

Assessment

Retention is a key component to learning. At the end of each session, a series of Quick Check questions helps students test their understanding of the material before moving on. Engaging end-of-tutorial Review Assignments and Case Problems have always been a hallmark feature of the New Perspectives Series. Colorful bars and brief descriptions accompany the exercises, making it easy to understand both the goal and level of challenge a particular assignment holds.

REFERENCE

TASK REFERENCE

GLOSSARY/INDEX

Reference

Within each tutorial, Reference boxes appear before a set of steps to provide a succinct summary and preview of how to perform a task. In addition, a complete Task Reference at the back of the book provides quick access to information on how to carry out common tasks. Finally, each book includes a combination Glossary/Index to promote easy reference of material.

Our Complete System of Instruction

Coverage To Meet Your Needs

Whether you're looking for just a small amount of coverage or enough to fill a semester-long class, we can provide you with a textbook that meets your needs.

- Brief books typically cover the essential skills in just 2 to 4 tutorials.
- Introductory books build and expand on those skills and contain an average of 5 to 8 tutorials.
- Comprehensive books are great for a full-semester class, and contain 9 to 12+ tutorials.

So if the book you're holding does not provide the right amount of coverage for you, there's probably another offering available. Go to our Web site or contact your Course Technology sales representative to find out what else we offer.

CourseCasts – Learning on the Go. Always available...always relevant.

Want to keep up with the latest technology trends relevant to you? Visit our site to find a library of podcasts, CourseCasts, featuring a "CourseCast of the Week," and download them to your mp3 player at http://coursecasts.course.com.

Our fast-paced world is driven by technology. You know because you're an active participant— always on the go, always keeping up with technological trends, and always learning new ways to embrace technology to power your life.

Ken Baldauf, host of CourseCasts, is a faculty member of the Florida State University Computer Science Department where he is responsible for teaching technology classes to thousands of FSU students each year. Ken is an expert in the latest technology trends; he gathers and sorts through the most pertinent news and information for CourseCasts so your students can spend their time enjoying technology, rather than trying to figure it out. Open or close your lecture with a discussion based on the latest CourseCast.

Visit us at http://coursecasts.course.com to learn on the go!

Instructor Resources

We offer more than just a book. We have all the tools you need to enhance your lectures, check students' work, and generate exams in a new, easier-to-use and completely revised package. This book's Instructor's Manual, ExamView testbank, PowerPoint presentations, data files, solution files, figure files, and a sample syllabus are all available on a single CD-ROM or for downloading at http://www.cengage.com/coursetechnology.

Content for Online Learning

Course Technology has partnered with the leading distance learning solution providers and class-management platforms today. To access this material, visit www.cengage.com/webtutor and search for your title. Instructor resources include the following: additional case projects, sample syllabi, PowerPoint presentations, and more. For students to access this material, they must have purchased a WebTutor PIN-code specific to this title and your campus platform. The resources for students might include (based on instructor preferences): topic reviews, review questions, practice tests, and more. For additional information, please contact your sales representative.

www.cengage.com/ct/newperspectives

SAM: Skills Assessment Manager

SAM is designed to help bring students from the classroom to the real world. It allows students to train and test on important computer skills in an active, hands-on environment.

SAM's easy-to-use system includes powerful interactive exams, training, and projects on the most commonly used Microsoft Office applications. SAM simulates the Office application environment, allowing students to demonstrate their knowledge and think through the skills by performing real-world tasks, such as bolding text or setting up slide transitions. Add in live-in-the-application projects, and students are on their way to truly learning and applying skills to business-centric documents.

Designed to be used with the New Perspectives Series, SAM includes handy page references, so students can print helpful study guides that match the New Perspectives textbooks used in class. For instructors, SAM also includes robust scheduling and reporting features.

Acknowledgments

Our sincere thanks to the following reviewers for their helpful feedback and valuable insights: Matthew Alimagham, Spartanburg Community College; Steve Ganz, Western Washington University; Kristen Hockman, University of Missouri–Columbia; Ahmed Kamel, Concordia College; Jean Luoma, Davenport University; Kelly Swain, Humber College; Karen Toreson, Shoreline Community College; Raymond Yu, Douglas College; and Violet Zhang, George Brown College. Many thanks to everyone at Course Technology, especially Marie Lee for her leadership and inspiration; Brandi Shailer and Leigh Hefferon for their contributions and friendship; Kate Russillo for her guidance in this text's development; Julia Leroux-Lindsey for ensuring the quality and timely delivery of supplements; Jacqueline Lacaire for her support; and Jennifer Feltri for her outstanding management of the production process. Thanks as well to the following Manuscript Quality Assurance staff members for their diligent efforts in ensuring the quality and accuracy of this text: Christian Kunciw, MQA Supervisor; and John Freitas, Serge Palladino, Susan Pedicini, Chris Scriver, Danielle Shaw, and Teresa Storch, MQA Testers. To Jessica Evans, Developmental Editor extraordinaire—very special thanks for her commitment to excellence, incredible attention to detail, and many contributions to this book. I am grateful to have the continued support and encouragement of my parents, Ed and Mary Curran, and my two wonderful sons, Connor and Devon.
–Kathleen T. Finnegan

Thank you to all the people who guided and influenced me over the years during my educational, professional, and academic lives; specifically thanking those at Saint Francis School, Naugatuck High School, Tufts University, University of Massachusetts Amherst, United Technologies Research Laboratories, Rensselaer Polytechnic Institute, Associates Corporation of North America, and Grand Valley State University.
–Joseph J. Adamski

BRIEF CONTENTS

What is the Microsoft® Office Specialist Program?

The Microsoft Office Specialist Program enables candidates to show that they have something exceptional to offer—proven expertise in certain Microsoft programs. Recognized by businesses and schools around the world, over 4 million certifications have been obtained in over 100 different countries. The Microsoft Office Specialist Program is the only Microsoft-approved certification program of its kind.

What is the Microsoft Office Specialist Certification?

The Microsoft Office Specialist certification validates through the use of exams that you have obtained specific skill sets within the applicable Microsoft Office programs and other Microsoft programs included in the Microsoft Office Specialist Program. The candidate can choose which exam(s) they want to take according to which skills they want to validate.

The available Microsoft Office Specialist Program exams include*:

- Using Windows Vista®
- Using Microsoft® Office Word 2007
- Using Microsoft® Office Word 2007 – Expert
- Using Microsoft® Office Excel® 2007
- Using Microsoft® Office Excel® 2007 – Expert
- Using Microsoft® Office PowerPoint® 2007
- Using Microsoft® Office Access® 2007
- Using Microsoft® Office Outlook® 2007
- Using Microsoft SharePoint® 2007

The Microsoft Office Specialist Program 2010 exams will include*:

- Microsoft Word 2010
- Microsoft Word 2010 Expert
- Microsoft Excel® 2010
- Microsoft Excel® 2010 Expert
- Microsoft PowerPoint® 2010
- Microsoft Access® 2010
- Microsoft Outlook® 2010
- Microsoft SharePoint® 2010

What does the Microsoft Office Specialist Approved Courseware logo represent?

The logo indicates that this courseware has been approved by Microsoft to cover the course objectives that will be included in the relevant exam. It also means that after utilizing this courseware, you may be better prepared to pass the exams required to become a certified Microsoft Office Specialist.

For more information:

To learn more about Microsoft Office Specialist exams, visit www.microsoft.com/learning/msbc

To learn about other Microsoft approved courseware from Course Technology, visit www.cengagebrain.com

The availability of Microsoft Office Specialist certification exams varies by Microsoft program, program version and language. Visit www.microsoft.com/learning for exam availability.

TABLE OF CONTENTS

ACCESS LEVEL II TUTORIALS

Tutorial 5 Creating Advanced Queries and Enhancing Table Design

Tutorial 6 Using Form Tools and Creating Custom Forms

OBJECTIVES

- Develop file management strategies
- Explore files, folders, and libraries
- Create, name, copy, move, and delete folders
- Name, copy, move, and delete files
- Work with compressed files

Managing Your Files

Organizing Files and Folders with Windows 7

Case | *Distance Learning Company*

The Distance Learning Company specializes in distance-learning courses for people who want to gain new skills and stay competitive in the job market. Distance learning is formalized education that typically takes place using a computer and the Internet, replacing normal classroom interaction with modern communications technology. The head of the Customer Service Department, Shannon Connell, interacts with the Distance Learning Company's clients on the phone and from her computer. Shannon, like all other employees, is required to learn the basics of managing files on her computer.

In this tutorial, you'll work with Shannon to devise a strategy for managing files. You'll learn how Windows 7 organizes files and folders, and you'll examine Windows 7 file management tools. You'll create folders and organize files within them. You'll also explore options for working with compressed files.

STARTING DATA FILES

FM	→	Tutorial	Review	Case1
		Flyer.docx	Album.pptx	Art-Agenda.docx
		Map.png	Bills.xlsx	Art-Eval.docx
		Members.htm	Brochure.docx	Art-Notes.docx
		Paris.jpg	Budget.xlsx	Garden.jpg
		Proposal.docx	Photo.jpg	Inv01.xlsx
		Resume.docx	Plan.xlsx	Inv02.xlsx
		Rome.jpg	Receipt.xlsx	Inv03.xlsx
		Stationery.docx	Sales.xlsx	Sculpture.jpg

VISUAL OVERVIEW

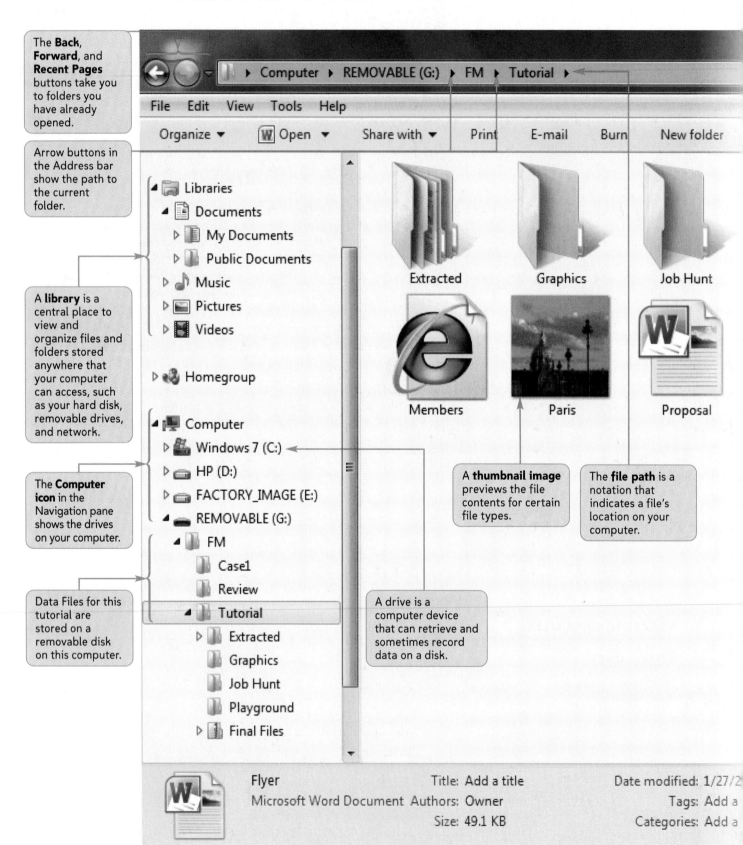

The **Back**, **Forward**, and **Recent Pages** buttons take you to folders you have already opened.

Arrow buttons in the Address bar show the path to the current folder.

A **library** is a central place to view and organize files and folders stored anywhere that your computer can access, such as your hard disk, removable drives, and network.

The **Computer** icon in the Navigation pane shows the drives on your computer.

Data Files for this tutorial are stored on a removable disk on this computer.

A **thumbnail image** previews the file contents for certain file types.

The **file path** is a notation that indicates a file's location on your computer.

A **drive** is a computer device that can retrieve and sometimes record data on a disk.

FILES IN A FOLDER WINDOW

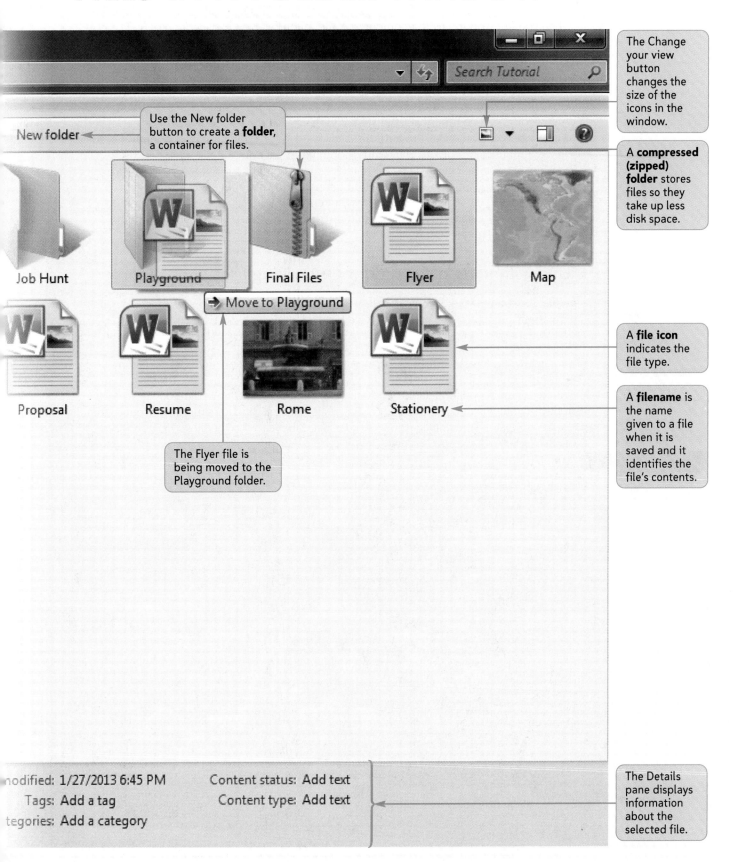

The Change your view button changes the size of the icons in the window.

Use the New folder button to create a **folder**, a container for files.

New folder

A **compressed (zipped) folder** stores files so they take up less disk space.

Job Hunt   Playground   Final Files   Flyer   Map

Move to Playground

A **file icon** indicates the file type.

Proposal   Resume   Rome   Stationery

A **filename** is the name given to a file when it is saved and it identifies the file's contents.

The Flyer file is being moved to the Playground folder.

modified: 1/27/2013 6:45 PM   Content status: Add text
    Tags: Add a tag   Content type: Add text
tegories: Add a category

The Details pane displays information about the selected file.

Organizing Files and Folders

Knowing how to save, locate, and organize computer files makes you more productive when you are working with a computer. A **file**, often referred to as a document, is a collection of data that has a name and is stored on a computer. After you create a file, you can open it, edit its contents, print it, and save it again—usually using the same program you used to create it. You organize files by storing them in folders. You need to organize files so that you can find them easily and work efficiently.

A computer can store folders and files on different types of disks, ranging from removable media—such as USB drives (also called USB flash drives), compact discs (CDs), and digital video discs (DVDs)—to **hard disks**, or fixed disks, which are permanently stored on a computer. Hard disks are the most popular type of computer storage because they provide an economical way to store many gigabytes of data.

A computer distinguishes one drive from another by assigning each a drive letter. The hard disk is usually assigned to drive C. The remaining drives can have any other letters, but are usually assigned in the order that the drives were installed on the computer—so your USB drive might be drive D or drive G.

Understanding the Need for Organizing Files and Folders

Windows 7 stores thousands of files in many folders on the hard disk of your computer. These are system files that Windows 7 needs to display the desktop, use drives, and perform other operating system tasks. To ensure system stability and to find files quickly, Windows 7 organizes the folders and files in a hierarchy, or **file system**. At the top of the hierarchy, Windows 7 stores folders and files that it needs when you turn on the computer. This location is called the **root directory**, and is usually drive C (the hard disk). The term *root* refers to a popular metaphor for visualizing a file system—an upside-down tree, which reflects the file hierarchy that Windows 7 uses. In Figure 1, the tree trunk corresponds to the root directory, the branches to the folders, and the leaves to the files.

Figure 1	Windows file hierarchy

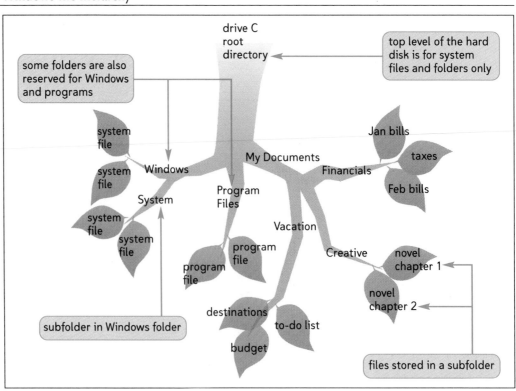

Note that some folders contain other folders. An effectively organized computer contains a few folders in the root directory, and those folders contain other folders, also called **subfolders**.

The root directory, or top level, of the hard disk is for system files and folders only—you should not store your own work here because it could interfere with Windows or a program. (If you are working in a computer lab, you might not be allowed to access the root directory.)

Do not delete or move any files or folders from the root directory of the hard disk—doing so could disrupt the system so that you can't run or start the computer. In fact, you should not reorganize or change any folder that contains installed software because Windows 7 expects to find the files for specific programs within certain folders. If you reorganize or change these folders, Windows 7 cannot locate and start the programs stored in that folder. Likewise, you should not make changes to the folder (usually named Windows) that contains the Windows 7 operating system.

Developing Strategies for Organizing Files and Folders

The type of disk you use to store files determines how you organize those files. Figure 2 shows how you could organize your files on a hard disk if you were taking a full semester of distance-learning classes. To duplicate this organization, you would open the main folder for your documents, create four folders—one each for the Basic Accounting, Computer Concepts, Management Skills II, and Professional Writing courses—and then store the writing assignments you complete in the Professional Writing folder.

| Figure 2 | Organizing folders and files on a hard disk |

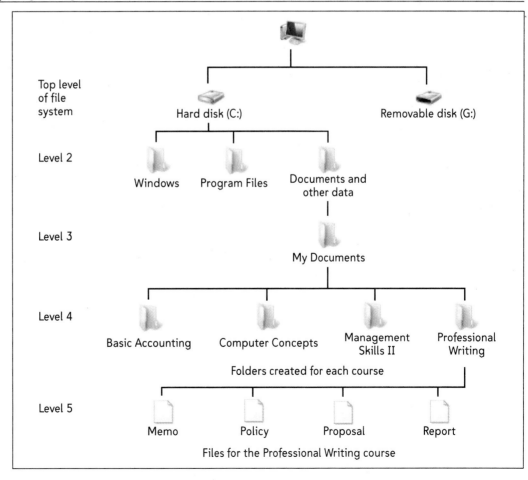

If you store your files on removable media, such as a USB drive or rewritable CD, you can use a simpler organization because you do not have to account for system files. In general, the larger the medium, the more levels of folders you should use because large media can store more files, and, therefore, need better organization. For example, if you are organizing your files on a USB drive, you could create folders in the top level of the USB drive for each general category of documents you store—one each for Courses, Creative, Financials, and Vacation. The Courses folder could then include one folder for each course, and each of those folders could contain the appropriate files.

INSIGHT

Duplicating Your Folder Organization

If you work on two computers, such as one computer at an office or school and another computer at home, you can duplicate the folders you use on both computers to simplify transferring files from one computer to another. For example, if you have four folders in your My Documents folder on your work computer, you would create these same four folders on your removable medium as well as in the My Documents folder of your home computer. If you change a file on the hard disk of your home computer, you can copy the most recent version of the file to the corresponding folder on your removable disk so the file is available when you are at work. You also then have a **backup**, or duplicate copy, of important files.

Exploring Files, Folders, and Libraries

Windows 7 provides two tools for exploring the files and folders on your computer—Windows Explorer and the Computer window. Both display the contents of your computer, using icons to represent drives, folders, and files. However, by default, each presents a slightly different view of your computer. **Windows Explorer** opens to show the contents of the Windows default libraries, making it easy to find the files you work with often, such as documents and pictures. The **Computer window** shows the drives on your computer and makes it easy to perform system tasks, such as viewing system information. You can use either tool to open a **folder window** that displays the files and subfolders in a folder.

Folder windows are divided into two sections, called panes. The left pane is the Navigation pane, which contains icons and links to locations you use often. The right pane lists the contents of your folders and other locations. If you select a folder in the Navigation pane, the contents of that folder appear in the right pane. To display the hierarchy of the folders and other locations on your computer, you select the Computer icon in the Navigation pane, and then select the icon for a drive, such as Local Disk (C:) or Removable Disk (G:). You can then open and explore folders on that drive.

TIP

Move the mouse pointer into the Navigation pane to display the expand and collapse icons.

If the Navigation pane showed all the folders on your computer at once, it could be a very long list. Instead, you open drives and folders only when you want to see what they contain. If a folder contains undisplayed subfolders, an expand icon ▷ appears to the left of the folder icon. (The same is true for drives.) To view the folders contained in an object, you click the expand icon. A collapse icon ◢ then appears next to the folder icon; click the collapse icon to hide the folder's subfolders. To view the files contained in a folder, you click the folder icon, and the files appear in the right pane. See Figure 3.

Figure 3   Viewing files in a folder window

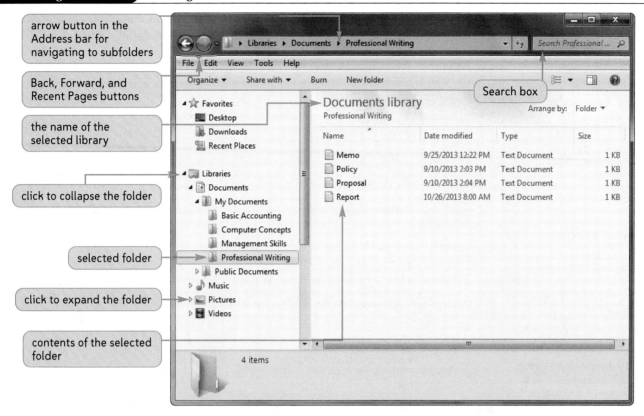

arrow button in the Address bar for navigating to subfolders

Back, Forward, and Recent Pages buttons

the name of the selected library

click to collapse the folder

selected folder

click to expand the folder

contents of the selected folder

Search box

Using the Navigation pane helps you explore your computer and orients you to your current location. As you move, copy, delete, and perform other tasks with the files in the right pane of a folder window, you can refer to the Navigation pane to see how your changes affect the overall organization.

In addition to using the Navigation pane, you can use folder windows and many dialog boxes to explore your computer in the following ways:

• Opening drives and folders in the right pane: To view the contents of a drive or folder, double-click the drive or folder icon in the right pane of a folder window.
• Using the Address bar: Use the Address bar to navigate to a different folder. The Address bar displays your current folder as a series of locations separated by arrows. Click a folder name or an arrow button to navigate to a different location.
• Clicking the Back, Forward, and Recent Pages buttons: Use the Back, Forward, and Recent Pages buttons to navigate to other folders you have already opened. After you change folders, use the Back button to return to the original folder or click the Recent Pages button to navigate to a location you've visited recently.
• Using the Search box: To find a file or folder stored in the current folder or its subfolders, type a word or phrase in the Search box. The search begins as soon as you start typing. Windows finds files based on text in the filename, text within the file, and other characteristics of the file, such as tags (descriptive words or phrases you add to your files) or the author.

Using Libraries and Folders

When you open Windows Explorer, it shows the contents of the Windows built-in libraries by default. A library displays similar types of files together, no matter where they are stored. In contrast, a folder stores files in a specific location, such as in the Professional Writing subfolder of the My Documents folder on the Local Disk (C:) drive. When you want to open the Report file stored in the Professional Writing folder, you must navigate to the Local Disk (C:) drive, then the My Documents folder, and finally the Professional Writing folder. A library makes it easier to access similar types of files. For example, you might store some music files in the My Music folder and others in a folder named Albums on your hard disk. You might also store music files in a Tunes folder on a USB drive. If the USB drive is connected to your computer, the Music library can display all the music files in the My Music, Albums, and Tunes folders. You can then arrange the files to quickly find the ones you want to open and play.

You'll show Shannon how to navigate to the My Documents folder from the Documents library.

To open the My Documents folder from the Documents library:

1. Click the **Windows Explorer** button ▇ on the taskbar. The Windows Explorer window opens, displaying the contents of the default libraries.

2. In the Libraries section of the Navigation pane, click the **expand** icon ▷ next to the Documents icon. The folders in the Documents library appear in the Navigation pane, as shown in Figure 4. The contents of your computer will differ.

Trouble? If your window displays icons in a view different from the one shown in Figure 4, you can still explore files and folders. The same is true for all the figures in this tutorial.

| Figure 4 | Viewing the contents of the Documents library |

TIP

By default, the Documents library shows all the documents located in the My Documents folder.

Documents library is expanded to display its folders

My Documents folder

Public Documents contains folders any user can access on this computer

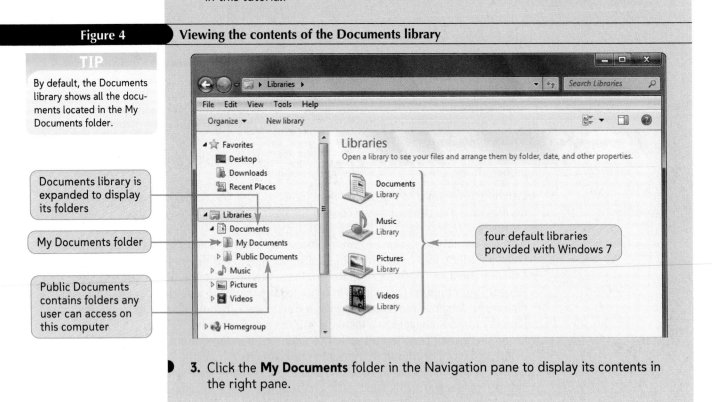

four default libraries provided with Windows 7

3. Click the **My Documents** folder in the Navigation pane to display its contents in the right pane.

Navigating to Your Data Files

To navigate to the files you want, it helps to know the file path, which leads you through the file and folder organization to your file. For example, the Map file is stored in the Tutorial subfolder of the FM folder. If you are working on a USB drive, for example, the path to this file might be as follows:

G:\FM\Tutorial\Map.png

This path has four parts, and each part is separated by a backslash (\ ):

- G: The drive name; for example, drive G might be the name for the USB drive. (If this file were stored on the hard disk, the drive name would be C.)
- FM: The top-level folder on drive G
- Tutorial: A subfolder in the FM folder
- Map.png: The full filename, including the file extension

If someone tells you to find the file G:\FM\Tutorial\Map.png, you know you must navigate to your USB drive, open the FM folder, and then open the Tutorial folder to find the Map file.

You can use any folder window to navigate to the Data Files you need for the rest of this tutorial. In the following steps, the Data Files are stored on drive G, a USB drive. If necessary, substitute the appropriate drive on your system when you perform the steps.

To navigate to your Data Files:

1. Make sure your computer can access your Data Files for this tutorial. For example, if you are using a USB drive, insert the drive into the USB port.

    Trouble? If you don't have the starting Data Files, you need to get them before you can proceed. Your instructor will either give you the Data Files or ask you to obtain them from a specified location (such as a network drive). In either case, make a backup copy of the Data Files before you start so that you will have the original files available in case you need to start over. If you have any questions about the Data Files, see your instructor or technical support person for assistance.

2. In the open folder window, click the **expand** icon ▷ next to the Computer icon to display the drives on your computer, if necessary.

3. Click the **expand** icon ▷ next to the drive containing your Data Files, such as Removable Disk (G:). A list appears below the drive name showing the folders on that drive.

4. If the list of folders does not include the FM folder, continue clicking the **expand** icon ▷ to navigate to the folder that contains the FM folder.

5. Click the **expand** icon ▷ next to the FM folder, and then click the **FM** folder. Its contents appear in the Navigation pane and in the right pane of the folder window. The FM folder contains the Case1, Review, and Tutorial folders, as shown in Figure 5. The other folders on your system might vary.

Figure 5 Navigating to the FM folder

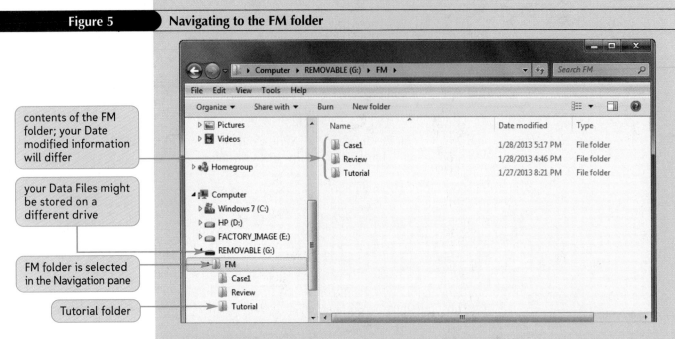

contents of the FM folder; your Date modified information will differ

your Data Files might be stored on a different drive

FM folder is selected in the Navigation pane

Tutorial folder

▶ **6.** In the Navigation pane, click the **Tutorial** folder. The files it contains appear in the right pane. To view the contents of the graphics files, you can display the files as large icons.

▶ **7.** If necessary, click the **Change your view button arrow** ▦ ▾ on the toolbar, and then click **Large Icons**. The files appear in Large Icons view in the folder window. See Figure 6.

Figure 6 Files in the Tutorial folder in Large Icons view

TIP

If you change the view of one folder, other folders continue to display files in the default Details view.

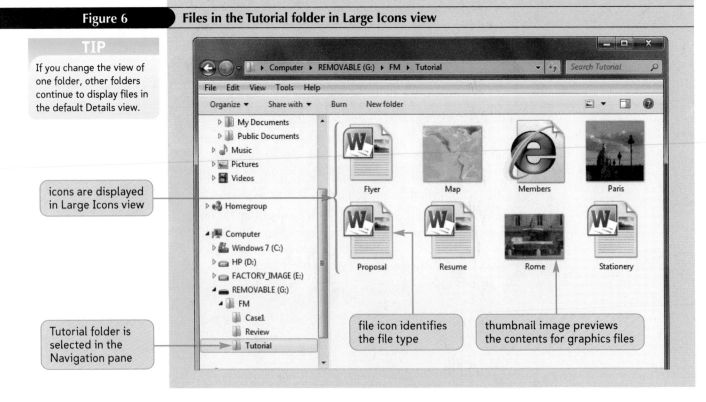

icons are displayed in Large Icons view

Tutorial folder is selected in the Navigation pane

file icon identifies the file type

thumbnail image previews the contents for graphics files

The file icons in your window depend on the programs installed on your computer, so they might be different from the ones shown in Figure 6.

Managing Folders and Files

After you devise a plan for storing your files, you are ready to get organized by creating folders that will hold your files. For this tutorial, you'll create folders in the Tutorial folder. When you are working on your own computer, you usually create folders within the My Documents folder and other standard folders, such as My Music and My Pictures.

Examine the files shown in Figure 6 again and determine which files seem to belong together. Map, Paris, and Rome are all graphics files containing pictures or photos. The Resume and Stationery files were created for a summer job hunt. The other files were created for a neighborhood association trying to update a playground.

One way to organize these files is to create three folders—one for graphics, one for the job hunt files, and another for the playground files. When you create a folder, you give it a name, preferably one that describes its contents. A folder name can have up to 255 characters, except / \ : * ? " < > or |. Considering these conventions, you could create three folders as follows:

- Graphics folder: Map, Paris, and Rome files
- Job Hunt folder: Resume and Stationery files
- Playground folder: Flyer, Proposal, and Members files

INSIGHT

Guidelines for Creating Folders

- Keep folder names short and familiar: Long names can be cut off in a folder window, so use names that are short but clear. Choose names that will be meaningful later, such as project names or course numbers.
- Develop standards for naming folders: Use a consistent naming scheme that is clear to you, such as one that uses a project name as the name of the main folder, and includes step numbers in each subfolder name, such as 01Plan, 02Approvals, 03Prelim, and so on.
- Create subfolders to organize files: If a file listing in a folder window is so long that you must scroll the window, consider organizing those files into subfolders.

Creating Folders

You've already seen folder icons in the windows you've examined. Now, you'll show Shannon how to create folders in the Tutorial folder.

REFERENCE

Creating a Folder in a Folder Window

- In the Navigation pane, click the drive or folder in which you want to create a folder.
- Click New folder on the toolbar.
- Type a name for the folder, and then press the Enter key.
or
- Right-click a folder in the Navigation pane or right-click a blank area in the folder window, point to New, and then click Folder.
- Type a name for the folder, and then press the Enter key.

You'll create the Graphics, Job Hunt, and Playground folders in your Tutorial folder.

To create folders in a folder window:

▶ **1.** Click the **New folder** button on the toolbar. A folder icon with the label *New folder* appears in the right pane. See Figure 7.

Figure 7 Creating a folder in the Tutorial folder

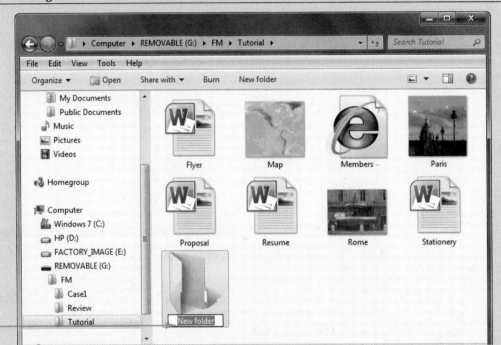

type to replace *New folder* with a folder name

Trouble? If the *New folder* name is not selected, right-click the new folder, click Rename, and then continue with Step 2.

Windows 7 uses *New folder* as a placeholder, and selects the text so that you can replace it with the name you want.

▶ **2.** Type **Graphics** as the folder name, and then press the **Enter** key. The new folder is named Graphics and is the selected item in the right pane. You'll create a second folder using a shortcut menu.

▶ **3.** Right-click a blank area near the Graphics folder, point to **New** on the shortcut menu, and then click **Folder**. A folder icon with the label *New folder* appears in the right pane with the *New folder* text selected.

▶ **4.** Type **Job Hunt** as the name of the new folder, and then press the **Enter** key.

▶ **5.** Using the toolbar or the shortcut menu, create a folder named **Playground**. The Tutorial folder contains three new subfolders.

Moving and Copying Files and Folders

If you want to place a file into a folder from another location, you can move the file or copy it. **Moving** a file removes it from its current location and places it in a new location you specify. **Copying** also places the file in a new location that you specify, but does not remove it from its current location. Windows 7 provides several techniques for moving and copying files, which you can also use to move and copy folders.

REFERENCE

Moving a File or Folder in a Folder Window

- Right-click and drag the file or folder you want to move to the destination folder.
- Click Move here on the shortcut menu.

or

- Right-click the file or folder you want to move, and then click Cut on the shortcut menu. (You can also click the file or folder and then press the Ctrl+X keys.)
- Navigate to and right-click the destination folder, and then click Paste on the shortcut menu. (You can also click the destination folder and then press the Ctrl+V keys.)

Next, you'll move the Flyer, Proposal, and Members files to the Playground folder.

To move a file using the right mouse button:

1. Point to the **Flyer** file in the right pane, and then press and hold the *right* mouse button.

2. With the right mouse button still pressed down, drag the **Flyer** file to the **Playground** folder. When the *Move to Playground* ScreenTip appears, release the button. A shortcut menu opens.

3. With the left mouse button, click **Move here** on the shortcut menu. The Flyer file is removed from the main Tutorial folder and stored in the Playground subfolder.

   Trouble? If you release the mouse button before dragging the Flyer file to the Playground folder, the shortcut menu opens, letting you move the file to a different folder. Press the Esc key to close the shortcut menu without moving the file, and then repeat Steps 1–3.

4. In the right pane, double-click the **Playground** folder. The Flyer file is in the Playground folder.

5. In the left pane, click the **Tutorial** folder to see its contents. The Tutorial folder no longer contains the Flyer file.

The advantage of moving a file or folder by dragging with the right mouse button is that you can efficiently complete your work with one action. However, this technique requires polished mouse skills so that you can drag the file comfortably. Another way to move files and folders is to use the **Clipboard**, a temporary storage area for files and information that you have copied or moved from one place and plan to use somewhere else. You can select a file and use the Cut or Copy commands to temporarily store the file on the Clipboard, and then use the Paste command to insert the file elsewhere. Although using the Clipboard takes more steps, some users find it easier than dragging with the right mouse button.

You'll move the Resume file to the Job Hunt folder next by using the Clipboard.

To move files using the Clipboard:

1. Right-click the **Resume** file, and then click **Cut** on the shortcut menu. Although the file icon is still displayed in the folder window, Windows 7 removes the Resume file from the Tutorial folder and stores it on the Clipboard.

2. In the right pane, right-click the **Job Hunt** folder, and then click **Paste** on the shortcut menu. Windows 7 pastes the Resume file from the Clipboard to the Job Hunt folder. The Resume file icon no longer appears in the folder window.

TIP

To use keyboard shortcuts to move files, click the file you want to move, press Ctrl+X to cut the file, navigate to a new location, and then press Ctrl+V to paste the file.

3. In the right pane, double-click the **Job Hunt** folder to display its contents. The Job Hunt folder now contains the Resume file.

Next, you'll move the Stationery file from the Tutorial folder to the Job Hunt folder.

4. Click the **Back** button ◀ on the Address bar to return to the Tutorial folder, right-click the **Stationery** file in the folder window, and then click **Cut** on the shortcut menu.

5. Right-click the **Job Hunt** folder, and then click **Paste** on the shortcut menu.

6. Click the **Forward** button ▶ on the Address bar to return to the Job Hunt folder. It now contains the Resume and Stationery files. See Figure 8.

Figure 8	Moving files

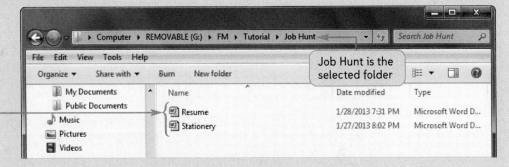

7. Click the **Back** button ◀ to return to the Tutorial folder.

You can also copy a file using the same techniques as when you move a file—by dragging with the right mouse button or by using the Clipboard. You can copy more than one file at the same time by selecting all the files you want to copy, and then clicking them as a group. To select files that are listed together in a window, click the first file in the list, hold down the Shift key, click the last file in the list, and then release the Shift key. To select files that are not listed together, click one file, hold down the Ctrl key, click the other files, and then release the Ctrl key.

REFERENCE

Copying a File or Folder in a Folder Window

- Right-click and drag the file or folder you want to move to the destination folder.
- Click Copy here on the shortcut menu.

or

- Right-click the file or folder you want to copy, and then click Copy on the shortcut menu. (You can also click the file or folder and then press the Ctrl+C keys.)
- Navigate to and right-click the destination folder, and then click Paste on the shortcut menu. (You can also click the destination folder and then press the Ctrl+V keys.)

You'll copy the three graphics files from the Tutorial folder to the Graphics folder now.

To copy files using the shortcut menu:

▶ **1.** In the Tutorial window, click the **Map** file.

▶ **2.** Hold down the **Ctrl** key, click the **Paris** file, click the **Rome** file, and then release the **Ctrl** key. Three files are selected in the Tutorial window.

▶ **3.** Right-click a selected file, and then click **Copy** on the shortcut menu.

▶ **4.** Right-click the **Graphics** folder, and then click **Paste** on the shortcut menu. Windows copies the three files to the Graphics folder.

Now you can use a different technique to copy the Proposal and Members files to the Playground folder.

To copy two files by right-dragging:

▶ **1.** Click the background of the folder window to remove the selection from the three files, hold down the **Ctrl** key, click the **Members** file, click the **Proposal** file, and then release the **Ctrl** key. The two files are selected in the Tutorial window.

▶ **2.** Point to a selected file, and then press and hold the *right* mouse button.

▶ **3.** With the right mouse button still pressed down, drag the **Members** and **Proposal** files to the **Playground** folder, and then release the mouse button. A shortcut menu opens.

▶ **4.** With the left mouse button, click **Copy here** on the shortcut menu to copy the files to the Playground subfolder.

You can move and copy folders in the same way that you move and copy files. When you do, you move or copy all the files contained in the folder.

PROSKILLS

Decision Making: Determining Where to Store Files

When you create and save files on your computer's hard disk, you should store them in subfolders. The top level of the hard disk is off-limits for your files because they could interfere with system files. If you are working on your own computer, store your files within the My Documents folder, which is where many programs save your files by default. When you use a computer on the job, your employer might assign a main folder to you for storing your work. In either case, if you simply store all your files in one folder, you will soon have trouble finding the files you want. Instead, you should create subfolders within a main folder to separate files in a way that makes sense for you.

Even if you store most of your files on removable media, such as USB drives, you still need to organize those files into folders and subfolders. Before you start creating folders, whether on a hard disk or removable disk, you need to plan the organization you will use.

Naming and Renaming Files

As you work with files, pay attention to filenames—they provide important information about the file, including its contents and purpose. A filename such as Car Sales.docx has three parts:

• Main part of the filename: The name you provide when you create a file, and the name you associate with a file

- Dot: The period (.) that separates the main part of the filename from the file extension
- File extension: Usually three or four characters that follow the dot in the filename

The main part of a filename can have up to 255 characters—this gives you plenty of room to name your file accurately enough so that you'll know the contents of the file just by looking at the filename. You can use spaces and certain punctuation symbols in your filenames. Like folder names, however, filenames cannot contain the symbols \ / ? : * " < > | because these characters have special meaning in Windows 7.

A filename might display an **extension**—three or more characters following a dot—to help you identify files. For example, in the filename Car Sales.docx, the extension *docx* identifies the file as one created by Microsoft Office Word, a word-processing program. You might also have a file called Car Sales.jpg—the *jpg* extension identifies the file as one created in a graphics program, such as Paint. Though the main parts of these file-names are identical, their extensions distinguish them as different files. You usually do not need to add extensions to your filenames because the program that you use to create the file adds the file extension automatically. Also, although Windows 7 keeps track of extensions, not all computers are set to display them.

Be sure to give your files and folders meaningful names that help you remember their purpose and contents. You can easily rename a file or folder by using the Rename command on the file's shortcut menu.

INSIGHT

Guidelines for Naming Files

The following are a few suggestions for naming your files:
- Use common names: Avoid cryptic names that might make sense now, but could cause confusion later, such as nonstandard abbreviations or imprecise names like Stuff2013.
- Don't change the file extension: When renaming a file, don't change the file extension. If you do, Windows might not be able to find a program that can open it.
- Find a comfortable balance between too short and too long: Use filenames that are long enough to be meaningful, but short enough to read easily on the screen.

Next, you'll rename the Flyer file to give it a more descriptive name.

To rename the Flyer file:

1. In the Tutorial folder window, double-click the **Playground** folder to open it.

2. Right-click the **Flyer** file, and then click **Rename** on the shortcut menu. The file-name is highlighted and a box appears around it.

3. Type **Raffle Flyer**, and then press the **Enter** key. The file now appears with the new name.

   Trouble? If you make a mistake while typing and you haven't pressed the Enter key yet, press the Backspace key until you delete the mistake, and then complete Step 3. If you've already pressed the Enter key, repeat Steps 2 and 3 to rename the file again.

   Trouble? If your computer is set to display file extensions, a message might appear asking if you are sure you want to change the file extension. Click the No button, right-click the Flyer file, click Rename on the shortcut menu, type *Raffle Flyer*, and then press the Enter key.

All the files in the Tutorial folder are now stored in appropriate subfolders. You can streamline the organization of the Tutorial folder by deleting the duplicate files you no longer need.

Deleting Files and Folders

TIP

A file deleted from removable media, such as a USB drive, does not go into the Recycle Bin. Instead, it is deleted when Windows 7 removes its icon, and cannot be recovered.

You should periodically delete files and folders you no longer need so that your main folders and disks don't get cluttered. In a folder window, you delete a file or folder by deleting its icon. When you delete a file from a hard disk, Windows 7 removes the file from the folder but stores the file contents in the Recycle Bin. The **Recycle Bin** is an area on your hard disk that holds deleted files until you remove them permanently; an icon on the desktop allows you easy access to the Recycle Bin. When you delete a folder from the hard disk, the folder and all of its files are stored in the Recycle Bin. If you change your mind and want to retrieve a file or folder deleted from your hard disk, you can use the Recycle Bin to recover it and return it to its original location. However, after you empty the Recycle Bin, you can no longer recover the files it contained.

Shannon reminds you that because you copied the Map, Paris, Proposal, Members, and Rome files to the Graphics and Playground folders, you can safely delete the original files in the Tutorial folder. As with moving, copying, and renaming files and folders, you can delete a file or folder in many ways, including using a shortcut menu.

To delete files in the Tutorial folder:

▶ 1. Use any technique you've learned to navigate to and open the **Tutorial** folder.

▶ 2. Click the **first file** in the file list, hold down the **Shift** key, click the **last file** in the file list, and then release the **Shift** key. All the files in the Tutorial folder are now selected. None of the subfolders should be selected.

Make sure you have copied the selected files to the Graphics folder before completing this step.

▶ 3. Right-click the selected files, and then click **Delete** on the shortcut menu. Windows 7 asks if you're sure you want to delete these files.

▶ 4. Click the **Yes** button to confirm that you want to delete five files.

So far, you've moved, copied, renamed, and deleted files, but you haven't viewed any of their contents. To view file contents, you can preview or open the file. When you double-click a file in a folder window, Windows 7 starts the associated program and opens the file. To preview the file contents, you can select the file in a folder window, and then click the Show the preview pane button 🔲 on the toolbar to open the Preview pane, if necessary.

Working with Compressed Files

If you transfer files from one location to another, such as from your hard disk to a removable disk or vice versa, or from one computer to another via e-mail, you can store the files in a compressed (zipped) folder so that they take up less disk space. You can then transfer the files more quickly. When you create a compressed folder, Windows 7 displays a zipper on the folder icon.

You compress a folder so that the files it contains use less space on the disk. Compare two folders—a folder named Photos that contains about 8.6 MB of files, and a compressed folder containing the same files but requiring only 6.5 MB of disk space. In this case, the compressed files use about 25 percent less disk space than the uncompressed files.

You can create a compressed folder using the Send to Compressed (zipped) folder command on the shortcut menu of one or more selected files or folders. Then you can compress additional files or folders by dragging them into the compressed folder. You can open a file directly from a compressed folder, although you cannot modify the file. To edit and save a compressed file, you must extract it first. When you **extract** a file, you create an uncompressed copy of the file in a folder you specify. The original file remains in the compressed folder.

If a different compression program, such as WinZip, has been installed on your computer, the Send to Compressed (zipped) folder command might not appear on the shortcut menu. Instead, it might be replaced by the name of your compression program. In this case, refer to your compression program's Help system for instructions on working with compressed files.

Shannon suggests that you compress the files and folders in the Tutorial folder so you can more quickly transfer them to another location.

To compress the folders and files in the Tutorial folder:

1. Select all the folders in the Tutorial folder, right-click the selected folders, point to **Send to**, and then click **Compressed (zipped) folder**. After a few moments, a new compressed folder with a zipper icon appears in the Tutorial window.

   Trouble? If the Compressed (zipped) folder command does not appear on the Send to submenu of the shortcut menu, this means that a different compression program is probably installed on your computer. Click a blank area of the Tutorial window to close the shortcut menu, and then read but do not perform the remaining steps.

2. Type **Final Files** and then press the **Enter** key to rename the compressed folder. See Figure 9.

   Trouble? If the filename is not selected after you create the compressed folder, right-click the compressed folder, click Rename on the shortcut menu, and then complete Step 2.

| Figure 9 | Creating a compressed folder |

When you compress the folders in the Tutorial folder, the original folders remain in the Tutorial folder—only copies are stored in the new compressed folder.

You open a compressed folder by double-clicking it. You can then move and copy files and folders in a compressed folder, although you cannot rename them. When you extract files, Windows 7 uncompresses and copies them to a location that you specify, preserving the files in their folders as appropriate.

To extract the compressed files:

▶ **1.** Right-click the **Final Files** compressed folder, and then click **Extract All** on the shortcut menu. The Extract Compressed (Zipped) Folders dialog box opens.

▶ **2.** Press the **End** key to deselect the path in the text box, press the **Backspace** key as many times as necessary to delete *Final Files*, and then type **Extracted**. The final three parts of the path in the text box should be *FM\Tutorial\Extracted*. See Figure 10.

| Figure 10 | Extracting compressed files |

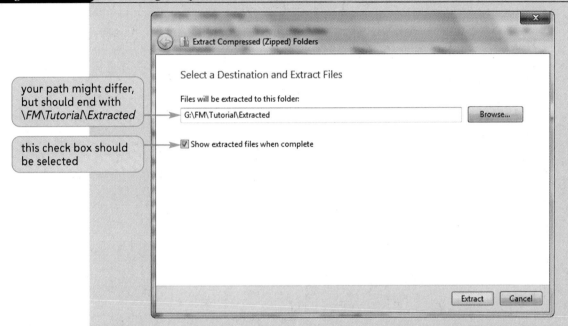

your path might differ, but should end with *FM\Tutorial\Extracted*

this check box should be selected

▶ **3.** Make sure the **Show extracted files when complete** check box is checked, and then click the **Extract** button. The Extracted folder opens, showing the Graphics, Job Hunt, and Playground folders.

▶ **4.** Open each folder to make sure it contains the files you worked with in this tutorial.

▶ **5.** Close all open windows.

Quick Check

REVIEW

1. What do you call a named collection of data stored on a disk?
2. The letter *C* is typically used for the _____ drive of a computer.
3. The term _____ refers to any window that displays the contents of a folder.
4. Describe the difference between the left and right panes of the Windows Explorer window.
5. What does the file path tell you?
6. True or False. The advantage of moving a file or folder by dragging with the right mouse button is that you can efficiently complete your work with one action.
7. What does a filename indicate?
8. Is a file deleted from a compressed folder when you extract it?

Practice the skills you learned in the tutorial.

Review Assignments

For a list of Data Files in the Review folder, see page FM 1.

Complete the following steps, recording your answers to any questions:

1. Use a folder window as necessary to find the following information:
   - Where are you supposed to store the files you use in the Review Assignments for this tutorial?
   - Describe the method you will use to navigate to the location where you save your files for this book.
   - Do you need to follow any special guidelines or conventions when naming the files you save for this book? For example, should all the filenames start with your course number or tutorial number? If so, describe the conventions.
   - When you are instructed to open a file for this book, what location are you supposed to use?
   - Describe the method you will use to navigate to this location.
2. Use a folder window to navigate to and open the **FM\Review folder** provided with your Data Files.
3. In the Review folder, create three folders: **Business**, **Marketing**, and **Project**.
4. Move the **Bills**, **Budget**, **Plan**, **Receipt**, and **Sales** files from the Review folder to the Business folder.
5. Move the **Brochure** file to the Marketing folder.
6. Copy the remaining files to the Project folder.
7. Delete the files in the Review folder (do *not* delete any folders).
8. Rename the Photo file in the Project folder as **Pond**.
9. Create a compressed (zipped) folder in the Review folder named **Final Review** that contains all the files and folders in the Review folder.
10. Extract the contents of the Final Review folder to a new folder named **Extracted**. (*Hint*: The file path will end with \FM\Review\Extracted.)
11. Locate all copies of the Budget file in the subfolders of the Review folder. In which locations did you find this file?
12. Close all open windows.
13. Submit the results of the preceding steps to your instructor, either in printed or electronic form, as requested.

Use your skills to manage files and folders for an arts organization.

Case Problem 1

For a list of Data Files in the Case1 folder, see page FM 1.

Jefferson Street Fine Arts Center   Rae Wysnewski owns the Jefferson Street Fine Arts Center (JSFAC) in Pittsburgh, and offers classes and gallery, studio, and practice space for young artists, musicians, and dancers. Rae opened JSFAC two years ago, and this year the center has a record enrollment in its classes. She hires you to teach a painting class and to show her how to manage her files on her new Windows 7 computer. Complete the following steps:

1. In the FM\Case1 folder in your Data Files, create two folders: **Invoices** and **Art Class**.
2. Move the **Inv01**, **Inv02**, and **Inv03** files from the Case1 folder to the Invoices folder.
3. In the Invoices folder, rename the Inv01 file as **Jan**, the Inv02 file as **Feb**, and the Inv03 file as **March**.
4. Move the three text documents from the Case1 folder to the Art Class folder. Rename the three documents, using shorter but still descriptive names.

5. Copy the remaining files in the Case1 folder to the Art Class folder.

6. Switch to Details view, if necessary, and then answer the following questions:
   - What is the largest file in the Art Class folder?
   - How many files in the Art Class folder are JPEG images?

7. Delete the Garden and Sculpture files from the Case1 folder.

8. Open the Recycle Bin folder by double-clicking the Recycle Bin icon on the desktop. Do the Garden and Sculpture files appear in the Recycle Bin folder? Explain why or why not. Close the Recycle Bin window.

9. Make a copy of the Art Class folder in the Case1 folder. The duplicate folder appears as Art Class – Copy. Rename the Art Class – Copy folder as **Images**.

10. Delete the text files from the Images folder.

11. Delete the Garden and Sculpture files from the Art Class folder.

12. Close all open windows, and then submit the results of the preceding steps to your instructor, either in printed or electronic form, as requested.

Use your skills to manage files for a social service organization.

CHALLENGE

Case Problem 2

There are no Data Files needed for this Case Problem.

First Call Outreach   Victor Crillo is the director of a social service organization named First Call Outreach in Toledo, Ohio. Its mission is to connect people who need help from local and state agencies to the appropriate service. Victor has a dedicated staff, but they are all relatively new to Windows 7. Because of this, they often have trouble finding files that they have saved on their hard disks. He asks you to demonstrate how to find files in Windows 7. Complete the following:

✦ EXPLORE

1. Windows 7 Help and Support includes topics that explain how to search for files on a disk without looking through all the folders. Click the Start button, click Help and Support, and then use one of the following methods to locate topics on searching for files:
   - In the Windows Help and Support window, click the Learn about Windows Basics link. Click the Working with files and folders link.
   - In the Windows Help and Support window, click the Browse Help topics link. (If necessary, click the Home icon first, and then click the Browse Help topics link.) Click the Files, folders, and libraries link, and then click Working with files and folders.
   - In the Search Help box, type **searching for files**, and then press the Enter key. Click the Working with files and folders link.

✦ EXPLORE

2. In the *In this article* section, click Finding files. Read the topic and click any *See also* or *For more information* links, if necessary, to provide the following information:
   a. Where is the Search box located?
   b. Do you need to type the entire filename to find the file?
   c. What does it mean to filter the view?

✦ EXPLORE

3. Use the Windows 7 Help and Support window to locate topics related to using libraries. Read the topics to answer the following questions:
   a. What are the names of the four default libraries?
   b. When you move, copy, or save files in the Pictures library, in what folder are they actually stored?
   c. What can you click to play all the music files in the Music library?

4. Submit the results of the preceding steps to your instructor, either in printed or electronic form, as requested.

SAM: Skills Assessment Manager

For current SAM information, including versions and content details, visit SAM Central (http://samcentral.course.com). If you have a SAM user profile, you may have access to hands-on instruction, practice, and assessment of the skills covered in this tutorial. Since various versions of SAM are supported throughout the life of this text, check with your instructor for the correct instructions and URL/Web site for accessing assignments.

ASSESS

ENDING DATA FILES

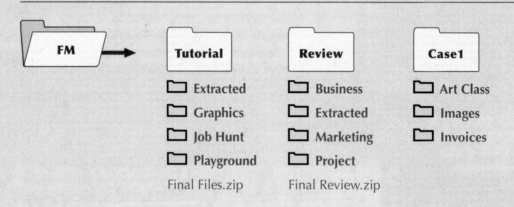

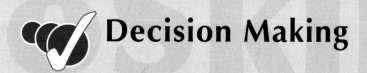 # Decision Making

Choosing the Most Efficient Organization for Your Computer Files

Decision making is choosing the best option from many possible alternatives. The alternative you select is your decision. When making a decision, you typically complete the following steps:

1. Gather information.
2. Make predictions.
3. Select the best alternative.
4. Prepare an action plan.
5. Perform tasks and monitor results.
6. Verify the accuracy of the decision.

If you are involved in making a complex decision that affects many people, you perform all six steps in the process. If you are making a simpler decision that does not affect many people, you can perform only those steps that relate to your decision.

Gather Information and Select the Best Alternative

Start by gathering information to identify your alternatives. For example, when organizing your files, you could store most of your work on your computer hard disk or on removable media, such as a USB drive or an external hard drive. Ask questions that quantify information, or use numbers to compare the alternatives. For example, how much space do you need for your files? In how many locations do you need to access the files? How often do you work with your files?

Next, ask questions that compare the qualities of the alternatives. For example, is one alternative easier to perform or maintain than another? After testing each alternative by asking both types of questions, one alternative should emerge as the best choice for you. If one option does not seem like the best alternative, continue comparing alternatives by listing the pros and cons of each.

Prepare an Action Plan

After you make a decision, prepare an action plan by identifying the steps you need to perform to put the decision into practice. One way to do this is to work backward from your final goal. If you are determining how best to manage your computer files, your final goal might be a set of folders and files organized so that you can find any file quickly. Start by listing the tasks you need to perform to meet your goal. Be as specific as possible to avoid confusion later. For example, instead of listing *Create folders* as a task, identify each folder and subfolder by name and indicate which files or types of files each folder should contain.

Next, estimate how long each task will take, and assign the task to someone. For simple decisions, you assign most tasks to yourself. If you need to use outside resources, include those in the action plan. For example, if you decide to store your files on USB drives, include a step to purchase the drives you need. If someone else needs to approve any of your tasks, be sure to include that step in the action plan. If appropriate, the action plan can also track your budget. For example, you could track expenses for a new hard disk or backup media.

ProSkills

Complete the Tasks and Monitor the Results

After you prepare an action plan and receive any necessary approvals, perform the tasks outlined in the plan. For example, create or rename the folders you identified in your action plan, and then move existing files into each folder. As you perform each step, mark its status as complete or pending, for example.

When you complete all the tasks in the action plan, monitor the results. For example, after reorganizing your files, did you meet your goal of being able to quickly find any file when you need it? If so, continue to follow your plan as you add files and folders to your computer. If not, return to your plan and determine where you could improve it.

PROSKILLS

Organize Your Files

Now that you have reviewed the fundamentals of managing files, organize the files and folders you use for course work or for other projects on your own computer. Be sure to follow the guidelines presented in this tutorial for developing an organization strategy, creating folders, naming files, and moving, copying, deleting, and compressing files. To manage your own files, complete the following tasks:

1. Use a program such as Word, WordPad, or Notepad to create a plan for organizing your files. List the types of files you work with, and then determine whether you want to store them on your hard disk or on removable media. Then sketch the folders and subfolders you will use to manage these files. If you choose a hard disk as your storage medium, make sure you plan to store your work files and folders in a subfolder of the Documents folder.
2. Use Windows Explorer or the Computer window to navigate to your files. Determine which tool you prefer for managing files, if you have a preference.
3. Create or rename the main folders you want to use for your files. Then create or rename the subfolders you will use.
4. Move and copy files to the appropriate folders according to your plan, and rename and delete files as necessary.
5. Create a backup copy of your work files by creating a compressed file and then copying the compressed file to a removable disk, such as a USB flash drive.
6. Submit your finished plan to your instructor, either in printed or electronic form, as requested.

OBJECTIVES

- Explore the programs in Microsoft Office
- Start programs and switch between them
- Explore common window elements
- Minimize, maximize, and restore windows
- Use the Ribbon, tabs, and buttons
- Use the contextual tabs, the Mini toolbar, and shortcut menus
- Save, close, and open a file
- Learn how to share files using SkyDrive
- Use the Help system
- Preview and print a file
- Exit programs

Getting Started with Microsoft Office 2010

Preparing a Meeting Agenda

Case | *Recycled Palette*

Recycled Palette, a company in Oregon founded by Ean Nogella in 2006, sells 100 percent recycled latex paint to both individuals and businesses in the area. The high-quality recycled paint is filtered to industry standards and tested for performance and environmental safety. The paint is available in both 1 gallon cans and 5 gallon pails, and comes in colors ranging from white to shades of brown, blue, green, and red. The demand for affordable recycled paint has been growing each year. Ean and all his employees use Microsoft Office 2010, which provides everyone in the company with the power and flexibility to store a variety of information, create consistent files, and share data. In this tutorial, you'll review how the company's employees use Microsoft Office 2010.

STARTING DATA FILES

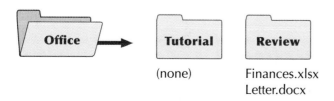

Office → Tutorial (none) Review Finances.xlsx Letter.docx

VISUAL OVERVIEW

The File tab opens **Backstage view**, which provides access to file-level options and program settings.

The **Ribbon** is the main set of commands you click to execute tasks. It is organized into tabs and groups.

The **Quick Access Toolbar** provides one-click access to commonly used commands, such as Save, Undo, and Repeat.

A **button**, or icon, provides one-click access to a command. This button underlines text.

The Ribbon is organized into tabs. Each **tab** has commands related to particular activities or tasks.

Buttons for related commands are organized on a tab in **groups**. The buttons in this group can be used to change the appearance of paragraphs.

The **insertion point** shows where characters will appear when you start to type.

The **workspace** is the area that displays the file you are working on (a Word document, an Excel workbook, and so on).

The **status bar** provides information about the program, open file, or current task or selection. It also contains buttons and other controls for working with the file and its content.

You can click a program button on the taskbar to switch between open files and programs.

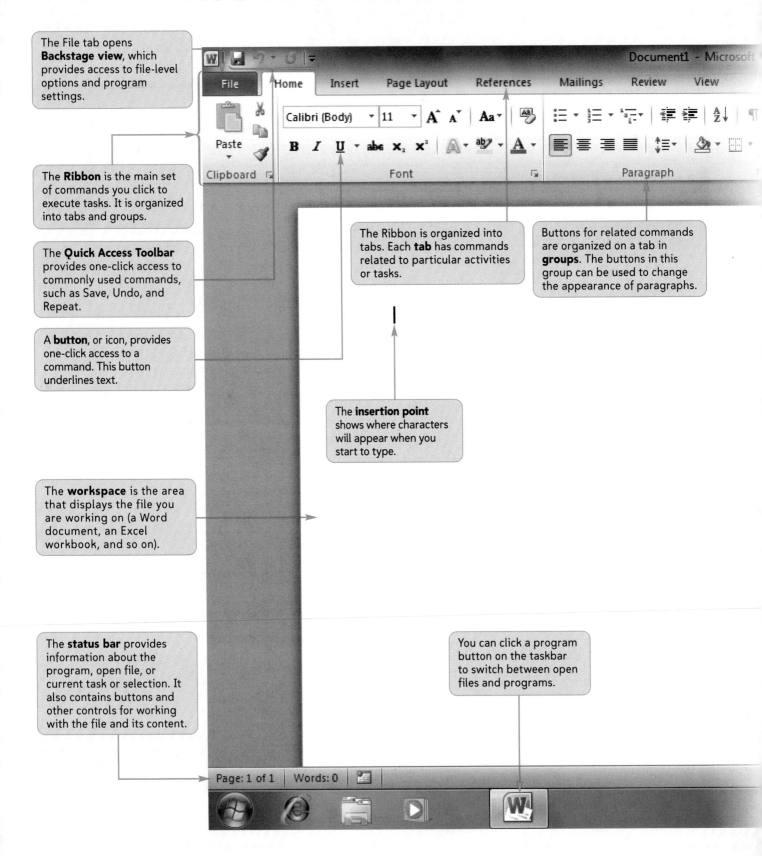

COMMON WINDOW ELEMENTS

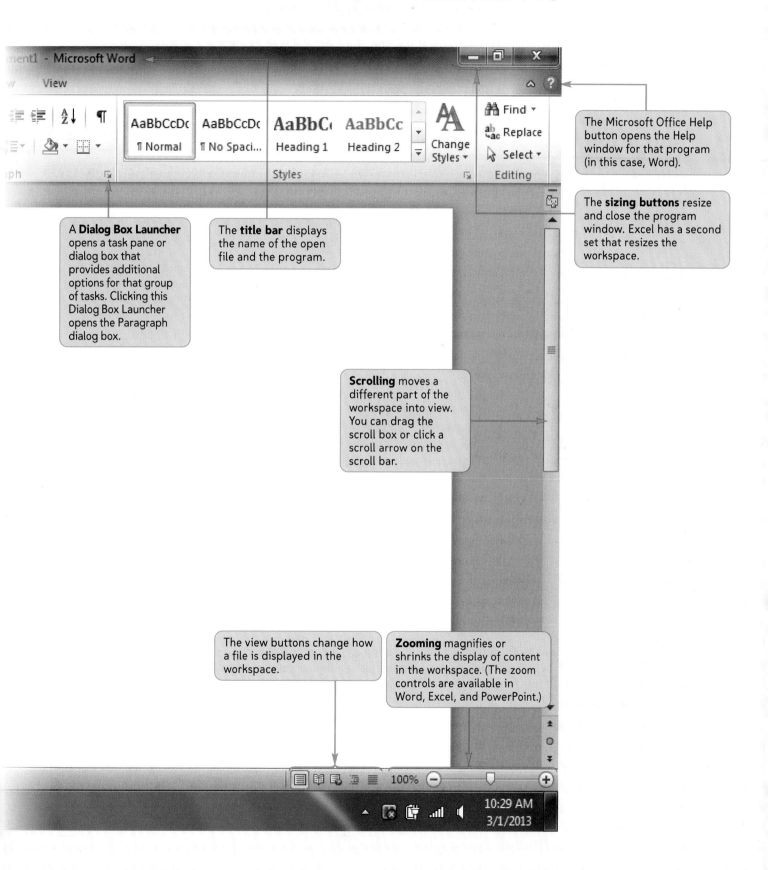

A **Dialog Box Launcher** opens a task pane or dialog box that provides additional options for that group of tasks. Clicking this Dialog Box Launcher opens the Paragraph dialog box.

The **title bar** displays the name of the open file and the program.

The Microsoft Office Help button opens the Help window for that program (in this case, Word).

The **sizing buttons** resize and close the program window. Excel has a second set that resizes the workspace.

Scrolling moves a different part of the workspace into view. You can drag the scroll box or click a scroll arrow on the scroll bar.

The view buttons change how a file is displayed in the workspace.

Zooming magnifies or shrinks the display of content in the workspace. (The zoom controls are available in Word, Excel, and PowerPoint.)

Exploring Microsoft Office 2010

Microsoft Office 2010, or **Office**, is a collection of Microsoft programs. Office is available in many suites, each of which contains a different combination of these programs. For example, the Professional suite includes Word, Excel, PowerPoint, Access, Outlook, Publisher, and OneNote. Other suites are available and can include more or fewer programs. Each Office program contains valuable tools to help you accomplish many tasks, such as composing reports, analyzing data, preparing presentations, compiling information, sending email, planning schedules, and compiling notes.

TIP

For additional information about the available suites, go to the Microsoft Web site.

Microsoft Word 2010, or **Word**, is a computer program you use to enter, edit, and format text. The files you create in Word are called **documents**, although many people use the term *document* to refer to any file created on a computer. Word, often called a word-processing program, offers many special features that help you compose and update all types of documents, ranging from letters and newsletters to reports, brochures, faxes, and even books, in attractive and readable formats. You can also use Word to create, insert, and position figures, tables, and other graphics to enhance the look of your documents. For example, the Recycled Palette employees create business letters using Word.

Microsoft Excel 2010, or **Excel**, is a computer program you use to enter, calculate, analyze, and present numerical data. You can do some of this in Word with tables, but Excel provides many more tools for recording and formatting numbers as well as performing calculations. The graphics capabilities in Excel also enable you to display data visually. You might, for example, generate a pie chart or a bar chart to help people quickly see the significance of and the connections between information. The files you create in Excel are called **workbooks** (commonly referred to as spreadsheets), and Excel is often called a spreadsheet program. The Recycled Palette accounting department uses a line chart in an Excel workbook to visually track the company's financial performance.

Microsoft Access 2010, or **Access**, is a computer program used to enter, maintain, and retrieve related information (or data) in a format known as a database. The files you create in Access are called **databases**, and Access is often referred to as a database or relational database program. With Access, you can create forms to make data entry easier, and you can create professional reports to improve the readability of your data. The Recycled Palette operations department tracks the company's inventory in an Access database.

Microsoft PowerPoint 2010, or **PowerPoint**, is a computer program you use to create a collection of slides that can contain text, charts, pictures, sound, movies, multimedia, and so on. The files you create in PowerPoint are called **presentations**, and PowerPoint is often called a presentation graphics program. You can show these presentations on your computer monitor, project them onto a screen as a slide show, print them, share them over the Internet, or display them on the Web. You can also use PowerPoint to generate presentation-related documents such as audience handouts, outlines, and speakers' notes. The Recycled Palette marketing department uses a PowerPoint slide presentation to promote its paints.

Microsoft Outlook 2010, or **Outlook**, is a computer program you use to send, receive, and organize email; plan your schedule; arrange meetings; organize contacts; create a to-do list; and record notes. You can also use Outlook to print schedules, task lists, phone directories, and other documents. Outlook is often referred to as an information management program. The Recycled Palette staff members use Outlook to send and receive email, plan their schedules, and create to-do lists.

Although each Office program individually is a strong tool, their potential is even greater when used together.

PROSKILLS

Teamwork: Integrating Office Programs

One of the main advantages of Office is **integration**, the ability to share information between programs. Integration ensures consistency and accuracy, and it saves time because you don't have to reenter the same information in several Office programs. It also means that team members can effortlessly share Office files. Team members can create files based on their skills and information that can be used by others as needed. The staff at Recycled Palette uses the integration features of Office every day, as described in the following examples:

- The accounting department created an Excel bar chart on fourth-quarter results for the previous two years, and inserted it into the quarterly financial report created in Word. The Word report includes a hyperlink that employees can click to open the Excel work-book and view the original data.
- The operations department included an Excel pie chart of sales percentages by paint colors on a PowerPoint slide, which is part of a presentation to stockholders.
- The marketing department produced a mailing to promote its recycled paints to local contractors and designers by combining a form letter created in Word with an Access database that stores the names and addresses of these potential customers.
- A sales representative merged the upcoming promotion letter that the marketing depart-ment created in Word with an Outlook contact list containing the names and addresses of prospective customers.

Even these few examples of how information from one Office program can be integrated with another illustrate how integration can save time and effort. Each team member can focus on creating files in the program best suited to convey the information he or she is responsible for. Yet, everyone can share the files, using them as needed for their specific purpose.

Starting Office Programs

You can start any Office program from the Start menu on the taskbar. As soon as the program starts, you can immediately begin to create new files or work with existing ones.

REFERENCE

Starting an Office Program

- On the taskbar, click the Start button.
- On the Start menu, click All Programs, click Microsoft Office, and then click the name of the program to start.

or

- Click the name of the program to start in the left pane of the Start menu.

You'll start Word using the Start button.

To start Word and open a new, blank document:

1. Make sure your computer is on and the Windows desktop appears on your screen.

   Trouble? If your screen varies slightly from those shown in the figures, your computer might be set up differently. The figures in this book were created while running Windows 7 with the Aero feature turned on, but how your screen looks depends on the version of Windows you are using, the resolution of your screen, and other settings.

2. On the taskbar, click the **Start** button 🔵, and then click **All Programs** to display the All Programs list.

3. Click **Microsoft Office**, and then point to **Microsoft Word 2010**. Depending on how your computer is set up, your desktop and menu might contain different icons and commands. See Figure 1.

Figure 1	Start menu with All Programs list displayed

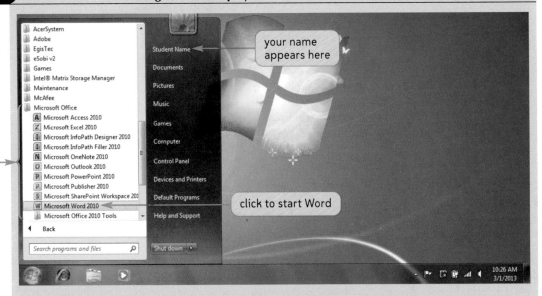

Trouble? If you don't see Microsoft Office on the All Programs list, point to Microsoft Word 2010 on the All Programs menu. If you still don't see Microsoft Word 2010, ask your instructor or technical support person for help.

4. Click **Microsoft Word 2010**. Word starts and a new, blank document opens. Refer to the Visual Overview to review the common program window elements.

   Trouble? If the Word window doesn't fill your entire screen as shown in the Visual Overview, the window is not maximized, or expanded to its full size. You'll maximize the window shortly.

You can have more than one Office program open at once. You'll use this same method to start Excel and open a new, blank workbook.

To start Excel and open a new, blank workbook:

1. On the taskbar, click the **Start** button 🏁, click **All Programs** to display the All Programs list, and then click **Microsoft Office**.

   Trouble? If you don't see Microsoft Office on the All Programs list, point to Microsoft Excel 2010 on the All Programs list. If you still don't see Microsoft Excel 2010, ask your instructor or technical support person for help.

2. Click **Microsoft Excel 2010**. Excel starts and a new, blank workbook opens. See Figure 2.

| Figure 2 | New, blank Excel workbook |

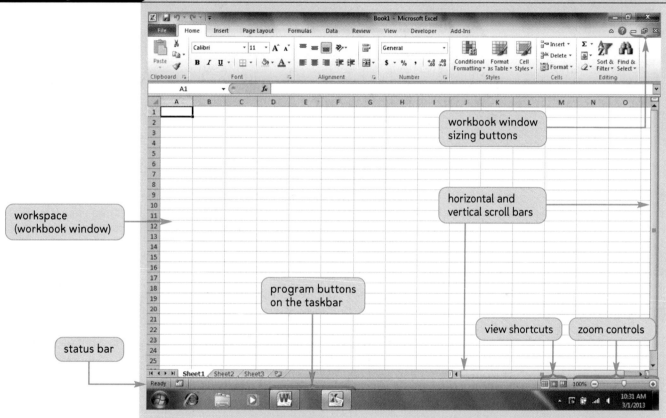

Trouble? If the Excel window doesn't fill your entire screen, the window is not maximized, or expanded to its full size. You'll maximize the window shortly.

Switching Between Open Programs and Files

Two programs are running at the same time—Word and Excel. The taskbar contains buttons for both programs. When you have two or more programs running or two files within the same program open, you can click the program buttons on the taskbar to switch from one program or file to another. When you point to a program button, a thumbnail (or small picture) of each open file in that program is displayed. You can then click the thumbnail of the file you want to make active. The employees at Recycled Palette often work in several programs and files at once.

To switch between the open Word and Excel files:

▶ **1.** On the taskbar, point to the **Microsoft Word** program button 🔲. A thumbnail of the open Word document appears. See Figure 3.

Figure 3	Thumbnail of the open Word document

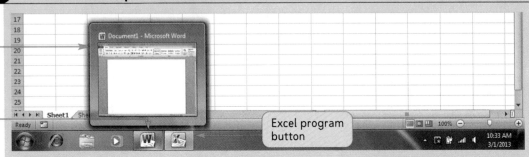

click the thumbnail that appears to make the file active

point to the Word program button

Excel program button

▶ **2.** Click the **Document1 - Microsoft Word** thumbnail. The active program switches from Excel to Word.

Exploring Common Window Elements

As you can see, many elements in both the Word and Excel program windows are the same. In fact, most Office programs have these same elements. Because these elements are the same in each program, after you've learned one program, it's easy to learn the others.

Resizing the Program Window and Workspace

There are three different sizing buttons that appear on the right side of a program window's title bar. The Minimize button 🔲, which is the left button, hides a window so that only its program button is visible on the taskbar. The middle button changes name and function depending on the status of the window—the Maximize button 🔲 expands the window to the full screen size or to the program window size, and the Restore Down button 🔲 returns the window to a predefined size. The Close button 🔲, on the right, exits the program or closes the file.

The sizing buttons give you the flexibility to arrange the program and file windows to best fit your needs. Most often, you'll want to maximize the program window and workspace to take advantage of the full screen size you have available. If you have several files open, you might want to restore down their windows so that you can see more than one window at a time, or you might want to minimize programs or files you are not working on at the moment.

To resize the windows and workspaces:

▶ **1.** On the Word title bar, click the **Minimize** button 🔲. The Word program window is reduced to a taskbar button. The Excel program window is visible again.

▶ **2.** On the Excel title bar, click the **Maximize** button 🔲 to expand the Excel program window to fill the screen, if necessary.

3. In the bottom set of Excel sizing buttons, click the **Restore Window** button. The workspace is resized smaller than the full program window. See Figure 4.

Figure 4   Resized Excel window and workspace

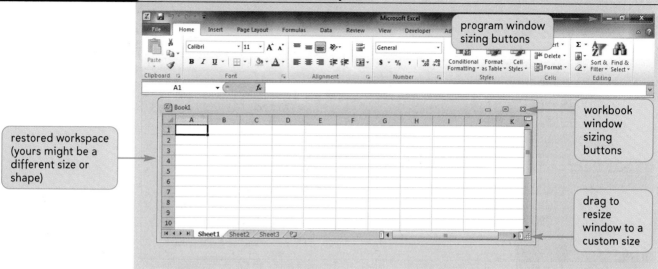

program window sizing buttons

restored workspace (yours might be a different size or shape)

workbook window sizing buttons

drag to resize window to a custom size

4. On the workbook window, click the **Maximize** button. The workspace expands to fill the program window.

5. On the taskbar, click the **Microsoft Word** program button. The Word program window returns to its previous size.

6. On the Word title bar, click the **Maximize** button if necessary to expand the Word program to fill the screen.

Switching Views

Each program has a variety of views, or ways to display the file in the workspace. For example, Word has five views: Print Layout, Full Screen Reading, Web Layout, Outline, and Draft. The content of the file doesn't change from view to view, although the presentation of the content does. In Word, for example, Print Layout view shows how the document would appear as a printed page, whereas Web Layout view shows how the document would appear as a Web page. You'll change views in later tutorials.

Zooming and Scrolling

You can zoom in to get a closer look at the content of an open document, worksheet, slide, or database report. Likewise, you can zoom out to see more of the content at a smaller size. You can select a specific percentage or size based on your file. The zoom percentage can range from 10 percent to 400 percent (Excel and PowerPoint) or 500 percent (Word). The figures shown in these tutorials show the workspace zoomed in to enhance readability. Zooming can shift part of the workspace out of view. To change which area of the workspace is visible in the program window, you can use the scroll bars. A scroll bar has arrow buttons that you can click to shift the workspace a small amount in the specified direction and a scroll box that you can drag to shift the workspace a larger amount in the direction you drag. Depending on the program and zoom level, you might see a vertical scroll bar, a horizontal scroll bar, or both.

To zoom and scroll in Word and Excel:

1. On the Word status bar, drag the **Zoom slider** ⬇ to the left until the percentage is **10%**. The document is reduced to its smallest size, which makes the entire page visible but unreadable. See Figure 5.

Figure 5	Word zoom level set to 10%

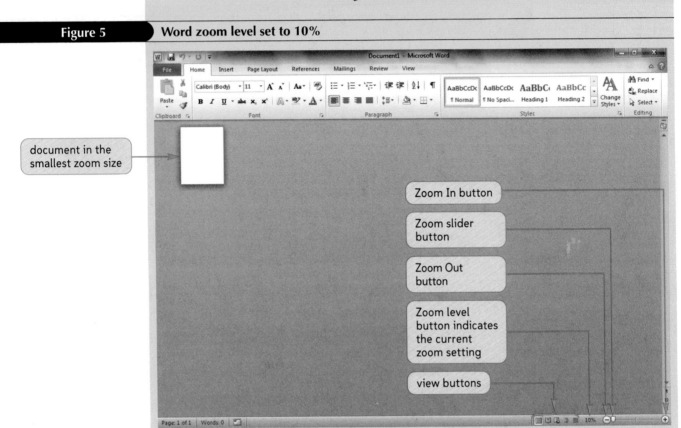

document in the smallest zoom size

Zoom In button

Zoom slider button

Zoom Out button

Zoom level button indicates the current zoom setting

view buttons

2. On the Word status bar, click the **Zoom level** button `10%`. The Zoom dialog box opens. See Figure 6.

Figure 6	Zoom dialog box

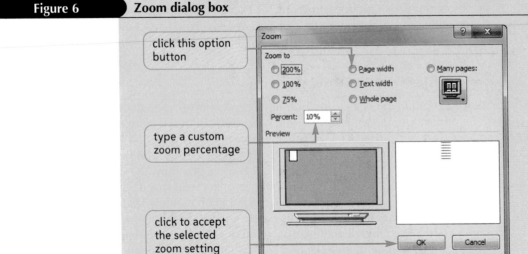

click this option button

type a custom zoom percentage

click to accept the selected zoom setting

3. Click the **Page width** option button, and then click the **OK** button. The Word document is magnified to its page width, which matches how the Word figures appear in the tutorials.

4. On the taskbar, click the **Microsoft Excel** program button. The Excel program window is displayed.

5. On the status bar, click the **Zoom In** button ⊕ twice. The worksheet is magnified to 120%, which is the zoom level that matches the Excel figures shown in the tutorials.

6. On the horizontal scroll bar, click the **right arrow** button ▶ twice. The worksheet shifts two columns to the right. Columns A and B (labeled by letter at the top of the columns) shift out of view and two other columns shift into view.

7. On the horizontal scroll bar, drag the **scroll box** all the way to the left. The worksheet shifts left to display columns A and B again.

8. On the taskbar, click the **Microsoft Word** program button. The Word program window is displayed.

Using the Ribbon

TIP

To view more workspace, click the Minimize the Ribbon button, located below the sizing buttons, to reduce the Ribbon to a single line. Click the Expand the Ribbon button to redisplay the full Ribbon.

Although the tabs on the Ribbon differ from program to program, each program has two tabs in common. The first tab on the Ribbon, the File tab, opens Backstage view. Backstage view provides access to file-level features, such as creating new files, opening existing files, saving files, printing files, and closing files, as well as the most common program options. The second tab in each program—called the Home tab—contains the commands for the most frequently performed activities, including cutting and pasting, changing fonts, and using editing tools. In addition, the Insert, Review, and View tabs appear on the Ribbon in all Office programs except Access, although the commands they include might differ from program to program. Other tabs are program specific, such as the Design tab in PowerPoint and the Datasheet Tools tab in Access.

To use the Ribbon tabs:

1. In Word, point to the **Insert** tab on the Ribbon. The Insert tab is highlighted, though the Home tab with the options for using the Clipboard and formatting text remains visible.

2. Click the **Insert** tab. The Insert tab is displayed on the Ribbon. This tab provides access to all the options for adding objects such as shapes, pages, tables, illustrations, text, and symbols to a document. See Figure 7.

Figure 7   **Insert tab on the Ribbon in Word**

Insert tab selected

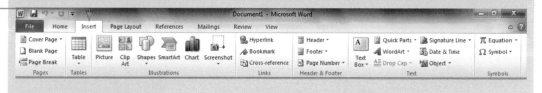

3. Click the **Home** tab. The Home tab options appear on the Ribbon.

Clicking Buttons

For the most part, when you click a button, something happens in the file. For example, the Clipboard group on the Home tab includes the Cut, Copy, Paste, and Format Painter buttons, which you can click to move or copy text, objects, and formatting.

Buttons can be **toggles**: one click turns the feature on and the next click turns the feature off. While the feature is on, the button remains colored or highlighted. For example, on the Home tab in Word, the Show/Hide ¶ button in the Paragraph group displays the nonprinting characters when toggled on and hides them when toggled off.

Some buttons have two parts: a button that accesses a command, and an arrow that opens a menu of all the commands or options available for that task. For example, the Paste button in the Clipboard group on the Home tab includes the Paste command and an arrow to access all the Paste commands and options. To select one of these commands or options, you click the button arrow and then click the command or option.

INSIGHT

How Buttons and Groups Appear on the Ribbon

The buttons and groups on the Ribbon change based on your monitor size, your screen resolution, and the size of the program window. With smaller monitors, lower screen resolutions, and reduced program windows, buttons can appear as icons without labels and a group can be condensed into a button that you click to display the group options. The figures in these tutorials were created using a screen resolution of 1024 × 768 and, unless otherwise specified, the program and workspace windows are maximized. If you are using a different screen resolution or window size, the buttons on the Ribbon might show more or fewer button names, and some groups might be reduced to a button.

You'll type text in the Word document, and then use the buttons on the Ribbon.

To use buttons on the Ribbon:

1. Type **Meeting Agenda** and then press the **Enter** key. The text appears in the first line of the document and the insertion point moves to the second line.

   Trouble? If you make a typing error, press the Backspace key to delete the incorrect letters, and then retype the text.

2. In the Paragraph group on the Home tab, click the **Show/Hide ¶** button ¶. The nonprinting characters appear in the document, and the Show/Hide ¶ button remains toggled on. See Figure 8.

Figure 8   **Button toggled on**

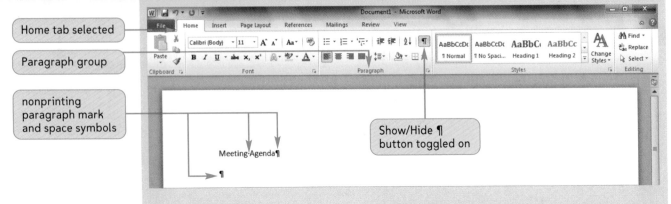

Home tab selected

Paragraph group

nonprinting paragraph mark and space symbols

Show/Hide ¶ button toggled on

Meeting·Agenda¶

Trouble? If the nonprinting characters disappear from your screen, the Show/Hide ¶ button was already on. Repeat Step 2 to show nonprinting characters.

3. Position the insertion point to the left of the word "Meeting," press and hold the left mouse button, drag the pointer across the text of the first line but not the paragraph mark to highlight the text, and then release the mouse button. All the text in the first line of the document (but not the paragraph mark ¶) is selected.

4. In the Clipboard group on the Home tab, click the **Copy** button 🖻. The selected text is copied to the Clipboard.

5. Press the ↓ key. The text is deselected (no longer highlighted), and the insertion point moves to the second line in the document.

6. In the Clipboard group on the Home tab, point to the top part of the **Paste** button 📋. Both parts of the Paste button are outlined in yellow, but the icon at the top is highlighted to indicate that it will be selected if you click the mouse button.

7. Point to the **Paste button arrow**. The button is outlined and the button arrow is highlighted.

8. Click the **Paste button arrow**. The paste commands and options are displayed. See Figure 9.

| Figure 9 | **Two-part Paste button** |

Paste button

click the button arrow to display more options and commands

Paste commands and options

---

9. On the Paste Options menu, click the **Keep Text Only** button Ⓐ. The menu closes, and the text is duplicated in the second line of the document. The Paste Options button 📋 (Ctrl) ▾ appears below the duplicated text, providing access to the same paste commands and options.

INSIGHT

Using Keyboard Shortcuts and Key Tips

Keyboard shortcuts can help you work faster and more efficiently. A **keyboard shortcut** is a key or combination of keys you press to access a feature or perform a command. You can use these shortcuts to access options on the Ribbon, on the Quick Access Toolbar, and in Backstage view without removing your hands from the keyboard. To access the options on the Ribbon, press the Alt key. A label, called a Key Tip, appears over each tab. To select a tab, press the corresponding key. The tab is displayed on the Ribbon and Key Tips appear over each available button or option on that tab. Press the appropriate key or keys to select a button.

You can also press combinations of keys to perform specific commands. For example, Ctrl+S is the keyboard shortcut for the Save command (you press and hold the Ctrl key while you press the S key). This type of keyboard shortcut appears in ScreenTips next to the command's name. Not all commands have this type of keyboard shortcut. Identical commands in each Office program use the same keyboard shortcut.

Using Galleries and Live Preview

Galleries and Live Preview let you quickly see how your file will be affected by a selection. A **gallery** is a menu or grid that shows a visual representation of the options available for a button. For example, the Bullet Library gallery in Word shows an icon of each bullet style you can select. Some galleries include a More button ▼ that you click to expand the gallery to see all the options it contains. When you point to an option in a gallery, **Live Preview** shows the results that would occur in your file if you clicked that option. To continue the bullets example, when you point to a bullet style in the Bullet Library gallery, the selected text or the paragraph in which the insertion point is located appears with that bullet style. By moving the pointer from option to option, you can quickly see the text set with different bullet styles; you can then click the style you want.

To use the Bullet Library gallery and Live Preview:

▶ 1. In the Paragraph group on the Home tab, click the **Bullets button arrow** . The Bullet Library gallery opens.

▶ 2. Point to the **check mark bullet** style ✓. Live Preview shows the selected bullet style in your document. See Figure 10.

Figure 10   Live Preview of bullet icon

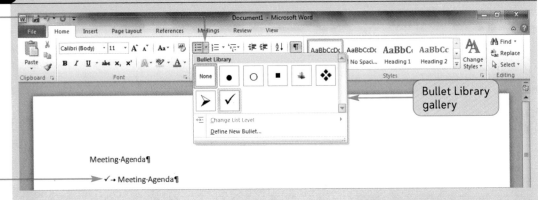

click the Bullets button arrow to open a gallery of bullet styles

Bullet Library gallery

Live Preview of the bullet style highlighted in the gallery

▶ 3. Place the pointer over each of the remaining bullet styles and preview them in your document.

▶ 4. Click the **check mark bullet** style ✓. The Bullet Library gallery closes, and the check mark bullet is added to the line, which is indented. The Bullets button remains toggled on when the insertion point is in the line with the bullet.

TIP

You can press the Esc key to close a gallery without making a selection.

▶ 5. On the second line, next to the check mark bullet, select **Meeting Agenda**. The two words are highlighted to indicate they are selected.

▶ 6. Type **Brainstorm names for the new paint colors.** to replace the selected text with an agenda item.

▶ 7. Press the **Enter** key twice to end the bulleted list.

Opening Dialog Boxes and Task Panes

The button to the right of some group names is the Dialog Box Launcher 🔲 , which opens a task pane or dialog box related to that group of tasks. A **task pane** is a window that helps you navigate through a complex task or feature. For example, you can use the Clipboard task pane to paste some or all of the items that were cut or copied from any Office program during the current work session. A **dialog box** is a window from which you enter or choose settings for how you want to perform a task. For example, the Page Setup dialog box in Word contains options to change how the document looks. Some dialog boxes organize related information into tabs, and related options and settings are organized into groups, just as they are on the Ribbon. You select settings in a dialog box using option buttons, check boxes, text boxes, and lists to specify how you want to perform a task. In Excel, you'll use the Dialog Box Launcher to open the Page Setup dialog box.

To open the Page Setup dialog box using the Dialog Box Launcher:

▶ **1.** On the taskbar, click the **Microsoft Excel** program button 🗒 to switch from Word to Excel.

▶ **2.** On the Ribbon, click the **Page Layout** tab. The page layout options appear on the Ribbon.

▶ **3.** In the Page Setup group, click the **Dialog Box Launcher**. The Page Setup dialog box opens with the Page tab displayed. See Figure 11.

| Figure 11 | Page tab in the Page Setup dialog box |

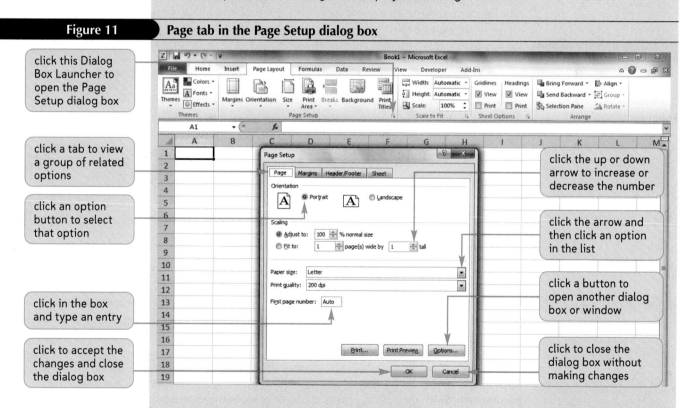

click this Dialog Box Launcher to open the Page Setup dialog box

click a tab to view a group of related options

click an option button to select that option

click in the box and type an entry

click to accept the changes and close the dialog box

click the up or down arrow to increase or decrease the number

click the arrow and then click an option in the list

click a button to open another dialog box or window

click to close the dialog box without making changes

▶ **4.** Click the **Landscape** option button. The workbook's page orientation changes to a page wider than it is long.

▶ **5.** Click the **Sheet** tab. The dialog box displays options related to the worksheet. You can click a check box to turn an option on (checked) or off (unchecked).

▶ **6.** In the Print section of the dialog box, click the **Gridlines** check box and the **Row and column headings** check box. Check marks appear in both check boxes, indicating that these options are selected.

▶ **7.** Click the **Cancel** button. The dialog box closes without making any changes to the page setup.

TIP

You can check more than one check box in a group, but you can select only one option button in a group.

Using Contextual Tools

Some tabs, toolbars, and menus come into view as you work. Because these tools become available only as you might need them, the workspace remains less cluttered. However, tools that appear and disappear as you work can take some getting used to.

Displaying Contextual Tabs

Any object that you can select in a file has a related contextual tab. An **object** is anything that appears on your screen that can be selected and manipulated, such as a table, a picture, a shape, a chart, or an equation. A **contextual tab** is a Ribbon tab that contains commands related to the selected object so you can manipulate, edit, and format that object. Contextual tabs appear to the right of the standard Ribbon tabs just below a title label. For example, Figure 12 shows the Table Tools contextual tabs that appear when you select a table in a Word document. Although contextual tabs appear only when you select an object, they function in the same way as standard tabs on the Ribbon. Contextual tabs disappear when you click elsewhere on the screen, deselecting the object. Contextual tabs can also appear as you switch views. You'll use contextual tabs in later tutorials.

| Figure 12 | Table Tools contextual tabs |

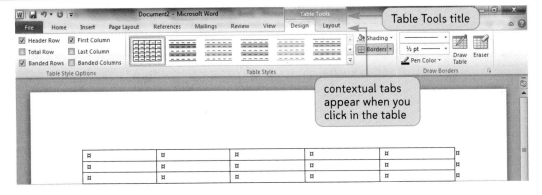

contextual tabs appear when you click in the table

Accessing the Mini Toolbar

The **Mini toolbar**, which appears next to the pointer whenever you select text, contains buttons for the most commonly used formatting commands, such as font, font size, styles, color, alignment, and indents. The Mini toolbar buttons differ in each program. A transparent version of the Mini toolbar appears immediately after you select text. When you move the pointer over the Mini toolbar, it comes into full view so you can click the appropriate formatting button or buttons. The Mini toolbar disappears if you move the pointer away from the toolbar, press a key, or click in the workspace. The Mini toolbar can help you format your text faster, but initially you might find that the toolbar disappears unexpectedly. All the commands on the Mini toolbar are also available on the Ribbon. Note that Live Preview does not work with the Mini toolbar.

You'll use the Mini toolbar to format text you enter in the workbook.

To use the Mini toolbar to format text:

1. If necessary, click cell **A1** (the rectangle in the upper-left corner of the worksheet).

2. Type **Budget**. The text appears in the cell.

3. Press the **Enter** key. The text is entered in cell A1 and cell A2 is selected.

4. Type **2013** and then press the **Enter** key. The year is entered in cell A2 and cell A3 is selected.

5. Double-click cell **A1** to place the insertion point in the cell. Now you can select the text you typed.

6. Double-click **Budget** in cell A1. The selected text appears white with a black background, and the transparent Mini toolbar appears directly above the selected text. See Figure 13.

Figure 13	Transparent Mini toolbar

Mini toolbar is transparent at first

select text to display the transparent Mini toolbar

Keep the pointer directly over the Mini toolbar; otherwise, it will disappear.

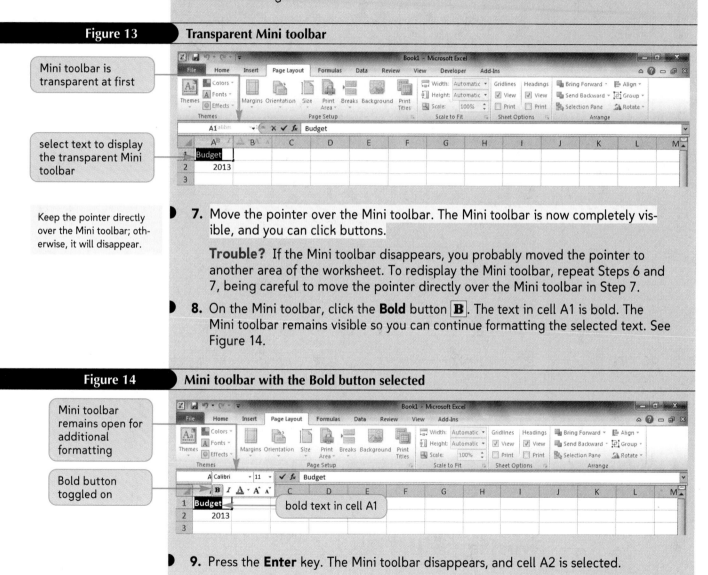

7. Move the pointer over the Mini toolbar. The Mini toolbar is now completely visible, and you can click buttons.

Trouble? If the Mini toolbar disappears, you probably moved the pointer to another area of the worksheet. To redisplay the Mini toolbar, repeat Steps 6 and 7, being careful to move the pointer directly over the Mini toolbar in Step 7.

8. On the Mini toolbar, click the **Bold** button **B**. The text in cell A1 is bold. The Mini toolbar remains visible so you can continue formatting the selected text. See Figure 14.

Figure 14	Mini toolbar with the Bold button selected

Mini toolbar remains open for additional formatting

Bold button toggled on

bold text in cell A1

9. Press the **Enter** key. The Mini toolbar disappears, and cell A2 is selected.

Opening Shortcut Menus

A **shortcut menu** is a list of commands related to a selection that opens when you click the right mouse button. Shortcut menus enable you to quickly access commands that you're most likely to need in the context of the task you're performing without using the tabs on the Ribbon. The shortcut menu includes commands that perform actions, commands that open dialog boxes, and galleries of options that provide Live Preview. The Mini toolbar also opens when you right-click. If you click a button on the Mini toolbar, the rest of the shortcut menu closes while the Mini toolbar remains open so you can continue formatting the selection. For example, you can right-click selected text to open a shortcut menu with a Mini toolbar; the menu will contain text-related commands such as Cut, Copy, and Paste, as well as other program-specific commands.

You'll use a shortcut menu to delete the content you entered in cell A1.

To use a shortcut menu to delete content:

▶ **1.** Right-click cell **A1**. A shortcut menu opens, listing commands related to common tasks you'd perform in a cell, along with the Mini toolbar. See Figure 15.

Figure 15   Shortcut menu with Mini toolbar

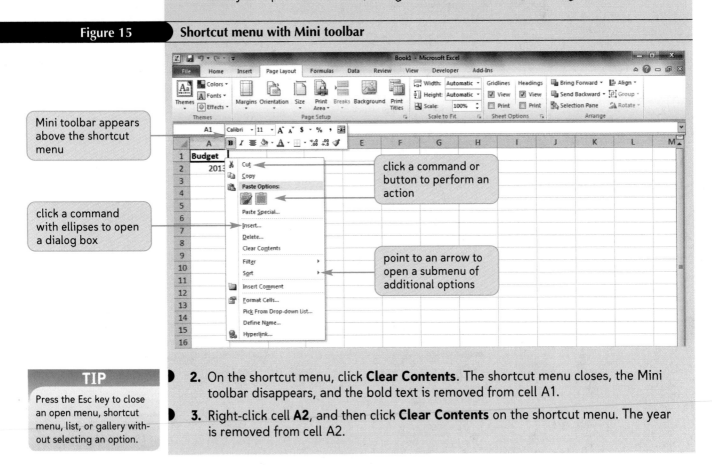

Mini toolbar appears above the shortcut menu

click a command with ellipses to open a dialog box

click a command or button to perform an action

point to an arrow to open a submenu of additional options

▶ **2.** On the shortcut menu, click **Clear Contents**. The shortcut menu closes, the Mini toolbar disappears, and the bold text is removed from cell A1.

▶ **3.** Right-click cell **A2**, and then click **Clear Contents** on the shortcut menu. The year is removed from cell A2.

Working with Files

The most common tasks you perform in any Office program are to create, open, save, and close files. All of these tasks can be done from Backstage view, and the processes for these tasks are basically the same in all Office programs. To begin working in a program, you need to create a new file or open an existing file. When you start Word, Excel, or PowerPoint, the program opens along with a blank file—ready for you to begin working on a new document, workbook, or presentation. When you start Access, the New tab in Backstage view opens, displaying options for creating a new database or opening an existing one.

Saving a File

As you create and modify an Office file, your work is stored only in the computer's temporary memory, not on a hard drive. If you were to exit the program without saving, turn off your computer, or experience a power failure, your work would be lost. To prevent losing work, save your file frequently—at least every 10 minutes. You can save files to the hard drive located inside your computer, an external hard drive, a network storage drive, or a portable storage drive such as a USB flash drive.

To save a file, you can click either the Save button on the Quick Access Toolbar or the Save command in Backstage view. If it is the first time you are saving a file, the Save As dialog box will open so that you can specify save options. You can also click the Save As command in Backstage view to open the Save As dialog box, in which you can name the file you are saving and specify a location to save it.

The first time you save a file, you need to name it. This **filename** includes a title you specify and a file extension assigned by Office to indicate the file type. You should specify a descriptive title that accurately reflects the content of the document, workbook, presentation, or database, such as "Shipping Options Letter" or "Fourth Quarter Financial Analysis." Your descriptive title can include uppercase and lowercase letters, numbers, hyphens, and spaces in any combination, but not the special characters ? " / \ < > * | and :. Each filename ends with a **file extension**, which is a period followed by several characters that Office adds to your descriptive title to identify the program in which that file was created. The default file extensions for Office 2010 are .docx for Word, .xlsx for Excel, .pptx for PowerPoint, and .accdb for Access. Filenames (the descriptive title and extension) can include a maximum of 255 characters. You might see file extensions depending on how Windows is set up on your computer. The figures in these tutorials do not show file extensions.

You also need to decide where to save the file—on which drive and in what folder. A **folder** is a container for your files. Just as you organize paper documents within folders stored in a filing cabinet, you can organize your files within folders stored on your computer's hard drive or on a removable drive such as a USB flash drive. Store each file in a logical location that you will remember whenever you want to use the file again. The default storage location for Office files is the Documents folder; you can create additional storage folders within that folder or navigate to a new location.

TIP

Office 2003 and earlier files use the extensions .doc (Word), .xls (Excel), .mdb (Access), and .ppt (PowerPoint). To save in an earlier format, click the Save as type button in the Save As dialog box and click the 97-2003 format. When you open an earlier version file in Office 2010, you can save it in the same format or the Office 2010 format.

REFERENCE

Saving a File

To save a file the first time or with a new name or location:
- Click the File tab to open Backstage view, and then click the Save As command in the navigation bar (for an unnamed file, click the Save command or click the Save button on the Quick Access Toolbar).
- In the Save As dialog box, navigate to the location where you want to save the file.
- Type a descriptive title in the File name box, and then click the Save button.

To resave a named file to the same location with the same name:
- On the Quick Access Toolbar, click the Save button.

The text you typed in the Word window needs to be saved.

To save a file for the first time:

1. On the taskbar, click the **Microsoft Word** program button . Word becomes the active program.

2. On the Ribbon, click the **File** tab. Backstage view opens with commands and tabs for creating new files, opening existing files, and saving, printing, and closing files. See Figure 16.

Figure 16	Backstage view

click the File tab to open Backstage view

click a command in the navigation bar to perform an action

click a tab in the navigation bar to display related options

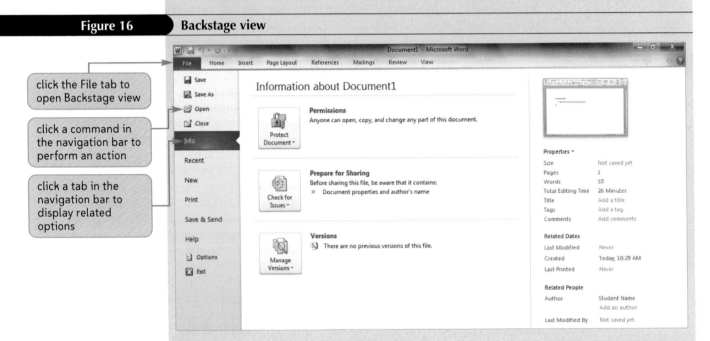

3. In the navigation bar, click the **Save As** command. The Save As dialog box opens because you have not yet saved the file and need to specify a storage location and filename. The default location is set to the Documents folder, and the first few words of the first line appear in the File name box as a suggested title.

4. In the Navigation pane along the left side of the dialog box, click the link for the location that contains your Data Files, if necessary.

   Trouble? If you don't have the starting Data Files, you need to get them before you can proceed. Your instructor will either give you the Data Files or ask you to obtain them from a specified location (such as a network drive). In either case, make a backup copy of the Data Files before you start so that you will have the original files available in case you need to start over. If you have any questions about the Data Files, see your instructor or technical support person for assistance.

5. In the file list, double-click the **Office** folder, and then double-click the **Tutorial** folder. This is the location where you want to save the document.

6. Type **Agenda** in the File name box. This descriptive filename will help you more easily identify the file. See Figure 17 (your file path may differ).

| **Figure 17** | **Completed Save As dialog box** |

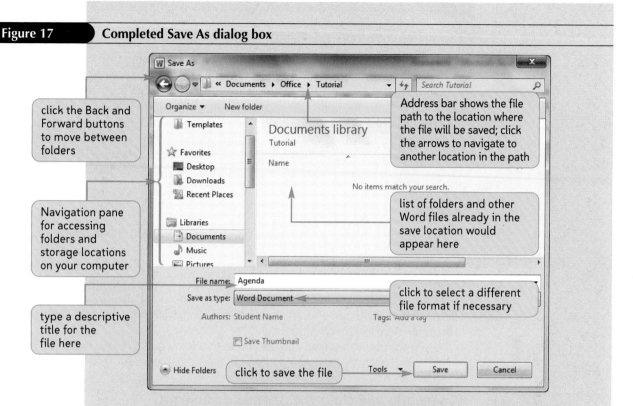

click the Back and Forward buttons to move between folders

Address bar shows the file path to the location where the file will be saved; click the arrows to navigate to another location in the path

Navigation pane for accessing folders and storage locations on your computer

list of folders and other Word files already in the save location would appear here

type a descriptive title for the file here

click to select a different file format if necessary

click to save the file

Trouble? If the .docx extension appears after the filename, your computer is configured to show file extensions. Continue with Step 7.

▶ **7.** Click the **Save** button. The Save As dialog box closes, and the name of your file appears in the Word window title bar.

The saved file includes everything in the document at the time you last saved it. Any new edits or additions you make to the document exist only in the computer's memory and are not saved in the file on the drive. As you work, remember to save frequently so that the file is updated to reflect the latest content.

Because you already named the document and selected a storage location, you don't need to use the Save As dialog box unless you want to save a copy of the file with a different filename or to a different location. If you do, the previous version of the file remains on your drive as well.

You need to add your name to the agenda. Then, you'll save your changes.

To modify and save the Agenda document:

▶ **1.** Type your name, and then press the **Enter** key. The text you typed appears on the next line.

▶ **2.** On the Quick Access Toolbar, click the **Save** button ◻. The changes you made to the document are saved in the file stored on the drive.

Saving Files Before Closing

As a standard practice, you should save files before closing them. However, Office has an added safeguard: if you attempt to close a file without saving your changes, a dialog box opens, asking whether you want to save the file. Click the Save button to save the changes to the file before closing the file and program. Click the Don't Save button to close the file and program without saving changes. Click the Cancel button to return to the program window without saving changes or closing the file and program. This feature helps to ensure that you always save the most current version of any file.

Closing a File

Although you can keep multiple files open at one time, you should close any file you are no longer working on to conserve system resources as well as to ensure that you don't inadvertently make changes to the file. You can close a file by clicking the Close command in Backstage view. If that's the only file open for the program, the program window remains open and no file appears in the window. You can also close a file by clicking the Close button in the upper-right corner of the title bar. If that's the only file open for the program, the program also closes.

You'll add the date to the agenda. Then, you'll attempt to close it without saving.

To modify and close the Agenda document:

1. Type today's date, and then press the **Enter** key. The text you typed appears below your name in the document.

2. On the Ribbon, click the **File** tab to open Backstage view, and then click the **Close** command in the navigation bar. A dialog box opens, asking whether you want to save the changes you made to the document.

3. Click the **Save** button. The current version of the document is saved to the file, and then the document closes. Word is still open, so you can create additional new files in the open program or you can open previously created and saved files.

Opening a File

When you want to open a blank document, workbook, presentation, or database, you create a new file. When you want to work on a previously created file, you must first open it. Opening a file transfers a copy of the file from the storage location (either a hard drive or a portable drive) to the computer's memory and displays it on your screen. The file is then in your computer's memory and on the drive.

REFERENCE

Opening an Existing File

- Click the File tab to open Backstage view, and then click the Open command in the navigation bar.
- In the Open dialog box, navigate to the storage location of the file you want to open.
- Click the filename of the file you want to open.
- Click the Open button.
- If necessary, click the Enable Editing button in the Information Bar.

or

- Click the File tab, and then click the Recent tab in the navigation bar.
- Click a filename in the Recent list.

Any file you open that was downloaded from the Internet, accessed from a shared network, or received as an email attachment might open in a read-only format, called **Protected View**. In Protected View, you can see the file contents, but you cannot edit, save, or print them until you enable editing. To do so, click the Enable Editing button on the Information Bar, as shown in Figure 18.

| Figure 18 | Protected View warning |

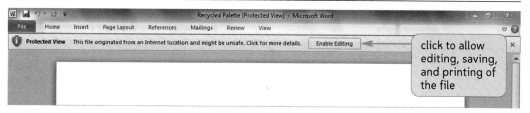

You need to print the meeting agenda you typed for Ean. To do that, you'll reopen the Agenda document.

To open the Agenda document:

1. On the Ribbon, click the **File** tab to display Backstage view.

2. In the navigation bar, click the **Open** command. The Open dialog box, which works similarly to the Save As dialog box, opens.

3. In the Open dialog box, use the Navigation pane or the Address bar to navigate to the **Office\Tutorial** folder included with your Data Files. This is the location where you saved the Agenda document.

4. In the file list, click **Agenda**. See Figure 19.

Figure 19   **Open dialog box**

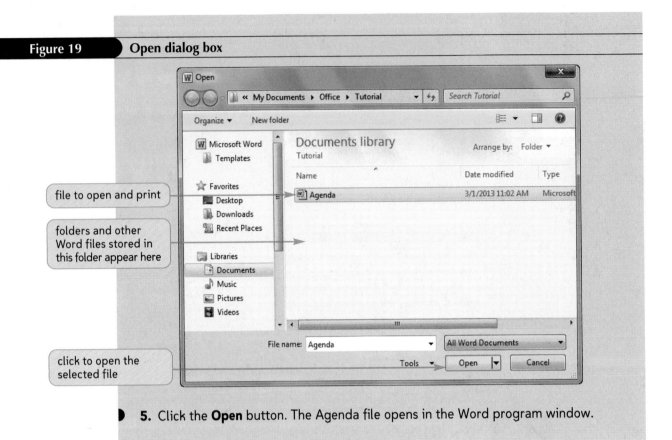

file to open and print

folders and other Word files stored in this folder appear here

click to open the selected file

5. Click the **Open** button. The Agenda file opens in the Word program window.

Sharing Files Using Windows Live SkyDrive

Often the purpose of creating a file is to share it with other people—sending it attached to an email message for someone else to read or use, collaborating with others on the same document, or posting it as a blog for others to review. You can do all of these things in Backstage view from the Save & Send tab.

When you send a file using email, you can attach a copy of the file, send a link to the file, or attach a copy of the file in a PDF or another file format. You can also save to online workspaces where you can make the file available to others for review and collaboration. The Save to Web option on the Save & Send tab in Backstage view gives you access to **Windows Live SkyDrive**, which is an online workspace provided by Microsoft; your personal workspace comes with a Public folder for saving files to share as well as a My Documents folder for saving files you want to keep private. (SkyDrive is not available for Access.) Figure 20 shows the Save to Web options on the Save & Send tab in Backstage view of Word. SharePoint is an online workspace set up by an organization, such as a school, business, or nonprofit group.

Files saved to an online workspace can be worked on by more than one person at the same time. The changes are recorded in the files with each author's name and the date of the change. A Web browser is used to access and edit the files. You choose who can have access to the files.

Figure 20   Save to Web options on the Save & Send tab

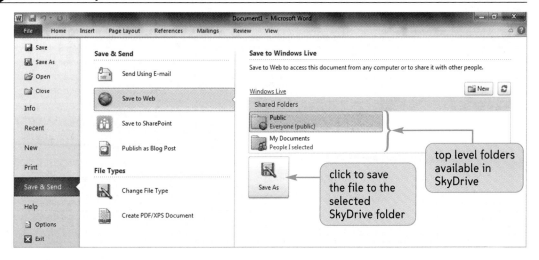

Saving a File to SkyDrive

• Click the File tab to open Backstage view, and then click the Save & Send tab in the navigation bar.
• In the center pane, click Save to Web.
• In the right pane, click the Sign In button, and then use your Windows Live ID to log on to your Windows Live SkyDrive account.

Getting Help

If you don't know how to perform a task or want more information about a feature, you can turn to Office itself for information on how to use it. This information is referred to simply as **Help**. You can get Help in ScreenTips and from the Help window.

Viewing ScreenTips

ScreenTips are a fast and simple method you can use to get information about objects you see on the screen. A **ScreenTip** is a box with descriptive text about an object or button. Just point to a button or object to display its ScreenTip. In addition to the button's name, a ScreenTip might include the button's keyboard shortcut if it has one, a description of the command's function, and, in some cases, a link to more information so that you can press the F1 key while the ScreenTip is displayed to open the Help window with the relevant topic displayed.

To view ScreenTips:

1. Point to the **Microsoft Office Word Help** button ❓. The ScreenTip shows the button's name, its keyboard shortcut, and a brief description. See Figure 21.

Figure 21 **ScreenTip for the Help button**

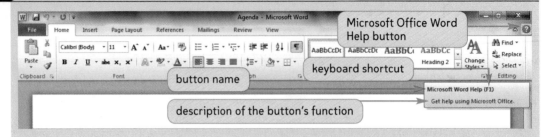

2. Point to other buttons on the Ribbon to display their ScreenTips.

Using the Help Window

For more detailed information, you can use the **Help window** to access all the Help topics, templates, and training installed on your computer with Office and available on Office.com. **Office.com** is a Web site maintained by Microsoft that provides access to the latest information and additional Help resources. For example, you can access current Help topics and training for Office. To connect to Office.com, you need to be able to access the Internet from your computer. Otherwise, you see only topics that are stored on your computer.

Each program has its own Help window from which you can find information about all of the Office commands and features as well as step-by-step instructions for using them. There are two ways to find Help topics—the search function and a topic list.

The Type words to search for box enables you to search the Help system for a task or a topic you need help with. You can click a link to open a Help topic with explanations and step-by-step instructions for a specific procedure. The Table of Contents pane displays the Help system content organized by subjects and topics, similar to a book's table of contents. You click main subject links to display related topic links. You click a topic link to display that Help topic in the Help window.

REFERENCE

Getting Help

- Click the Microsoft Office Help button (the button name depends on the Office program).
- Type a keyword or phrase in the Type words to search for box, click the Search button, and then click a Help topic in the search results list.
  or
  In the Table of Contents pane, click a "book," and then click a Help topic.
- Read the information in the Help window and then click other topics or links.
- On the Help window title bar, click the Close button.

You'll use Help to get information about printing a document in Word.

To search Help for information about printing:

1. Click the **Microsoft Office Word Help** button ⌾. The Word Help window opens.

▶ **2.** If the Table of Contents pane is not open on the left side of the Help window, click the **Show Table of Contents** button ⬔ on the toolbar to display the pane.

▶ **3.** Click the **Type words to search for** box, if necessary, and then type **print document**. You can specify where you want to search.

▶ **4.** Click the **Search button arrow**. The Search menu shows the online and local content available.

▶ **5.** If your computer is connected to the Internet, click **All Word** in the Content from Office.com list. If your computer is not connected to the Internet, click **Word Help** in the Content from this computer list.

▶ **6.** Click the **Search** button. The Help window displays a list of topics related to the keywords "print document" in the left pane. See Figure 22.

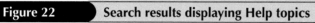

Figure 22 Search results displaying Help topics

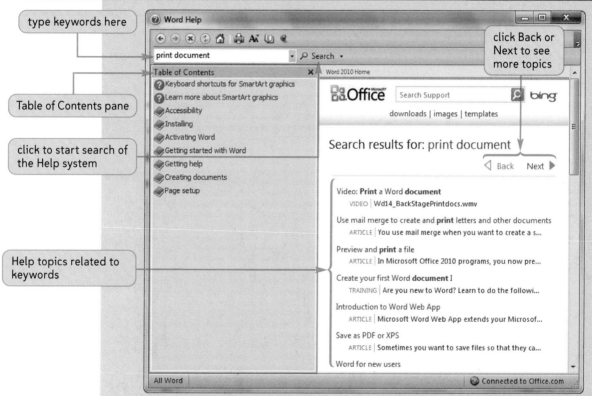

Trouble? If your search results list differs from the one shown in Figure 22, your computer is not connected to the Internet or Microsoft has updated the list of available Help topics since this book was published. Continue with Step 7.

▶ **7.** Scroll through the list to review the Help topics.

▶ **8.** Click **Preview and print a file**. The topic content is displayed in the Help window so you can learn more about how to print a document. See Figure 23.

Figure 23	Preview and print a file Help topic

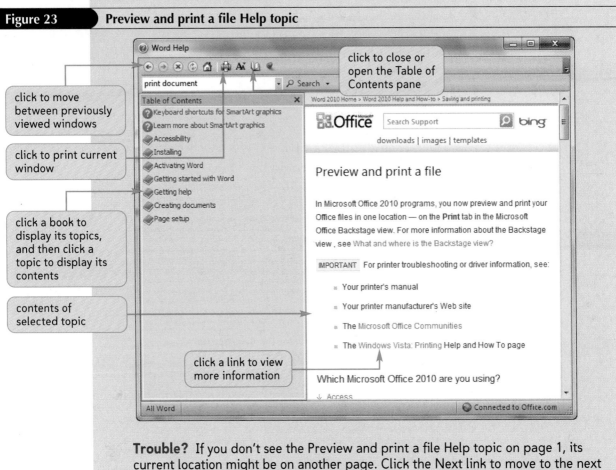

Trouble? If you don't see the Preview and print a file Help topic on page 1, its current location might be on another page. Click the Next link to move to the next page, and then scroll down to find the topic. Repeat as needed to search additional pages until you locate the topic.

▶ **9.** Read the information, click the links within this topic, and then read the additional information.

▶ **10.** On the Help window title bar, click the **Close** button to close the window.

Printing a File

At times, you'll want a paper copy of Office files. Whenever you print, you should review and adjust the printing settings as needed. You can select the number of copies to print, the printer, the portion of the file to print, and so forth; the printing settings vary slightly from program to program. You should also check the file's print preview to ensure that the file will print as you intended. This simple review will help you to avoid reprinting, which requires additional paper, ink, and energy resources.

Printing a File

- On the Ribbon, click the File tab to open Backstage view.
- In the navigation bar, click the Print tab.
- Verify the print settings and review the print preview.
- Click the Print button.

You will print the agenda for Ean.

To print the Agenda document:

1. Make sure your printer is turned on and contains paper.

2. On the Ribbon, click the **File** tab to open Backstage view.

3. In the navigation bar, click the **Print** tab. The print settings and preview appear. See Figure 24.

Figure 24   **Print tab in Backstage view**

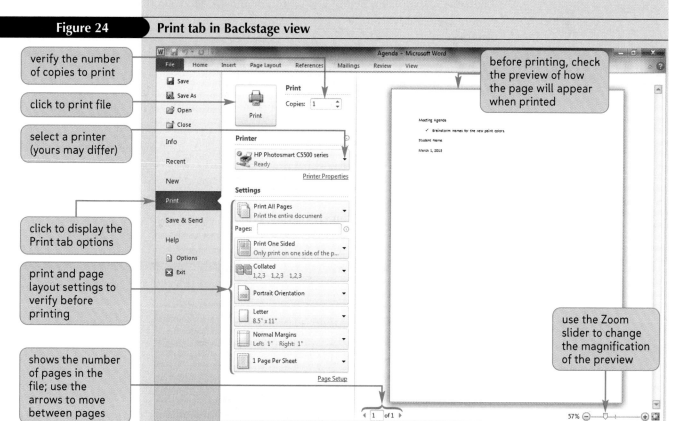

verify the number of copies to print

click to print file

select a printer (yours may differ)

click to display the Print tab options

print and page layout settings to verify before printing

shows the number of pages in the file; use the arrows to move between pages

before printing, check the preview of how the page will appear when printed

use the Zoom slider to change the magnification of the preview

4. Verify that **1** appears in the Copies box.

5. Verify that the correct printer appears on the Printer button. If it doesn't, click the **Printer** button, and then click the correct printer from the list of available printers.

6. Click the **Print** button to print the document.

Trouble? If the document does not print, see your instructor or technical support person for help.

Exiting Programs

When you finish working with a program, you should exit it. As with many other aspects of Office, you can exit programs with a button or a command. You'll use both methods to exit Word and Excel. You can use the Exit command to exit a program and close an open file in one step. If you haven't saved the final version of the open file, a dialog box opens, asking whether you want to save your changes. Clicking the Save button in this dialog box saves the open file, closes the file, and then exits the program.

To exit the Word and Excel programs:

▶ 1. On the Word title bar, click the **Close** button X. Both the Word document and the Word program close. The Excel window is visible again.

   Trouble? If a dialog box opens asking if you want to save the document, you might have inadvertently made a change to the document. Click the Don't Save button.

▶ 2. On the Ribbon, click the **File** tab to open Backstage view, and then click the **Exit** command in the navigation bar. A dialog box opens asking whether you want to save the changes you made to the workbook. If you click the Save button, the Save As dialog box opens and Excel exits after you finish saving the workbook. This time, you don't want to save the workbook.

▶ 3. Click the **Don't Save** button. The workbook closes without saving a copy, and the Excel program closes.

Exiting programs after you are done using them keeps your Windows desktop uncluttered for the next person using the computer, frees up your system's resources, and prevents data from being lost accidentally.

REVIEW

Quick Check

1. What Office program would be best to use to write a letter?
2. How do you start an Office program?
3. What is the purpose of Live Preview?
4. What is Backstage view?
5. Explain the difference between Save and Save As.
6. True or False. In Protected View, you can see file contents, but you cannot edit, save, or print them until you enable editing.
7. What happens if you open a file, make edits, and then attempt to close the file or exit the program without saving the current version of the file?
8. What are the two ways to get Help in Office?

Practice the skills you learned in the tutorial.

PRACTICE

Review Assignments

Data Files needed for the Review Assignments: Finances.xlsx, Letter.docx

You need to prepare for an upcoming meeting at Recycled Palette. You'll open and print documents for the meeting. Complete the following:

1. Start PowerPoint, and then start Excel.
2. Switch to the PowerPoint window, and then close the presentation but leave the PowerPoint program open. (*Hint*: Use the Close command in Backstage view.)
3. Open a blank PowerPoint presentation from the New tab in Backstage view. (*Hint*: Make sure Blank presentation is selected in the Available Templates and Themes section, and then click the Create button.)
4. Close the PowerPoint presentation and program using the Close button on the PowerPoint title bar; do not save changes if asked.
5. Open the **Finances** workbook located in the Office\Review folder. If the workbook opens in Protected View, click the Enable Editing button.
6. Use the Save As command to save the workbook as **Recycled Palette Finances** in the Office\Review folder.
7. In cell A1, type your name, press the Enter key to insert your name at the top of the worksheet, and then save the workbook.
8. Preview and print one copy of the worksheet using the Print tab in Backstage view.
9. Exit Excel using the Exit command in Backstage view.
10. Start Word, and then open the **Letter** document located in the Office\Review folder. If the document opens in Protected View, click the Enable Editing button.
11. Use the Save As command to save the document with the filename **Recycled Palette Letter** in the Office\Review folder.
12. Press and hold the Ctrl key, press the End key, and then release both keys to move the insertion point to the end of the letter, and then type your name.
13. Use the Save button to save the change to the Recycled Palette Letter document.
14. Preview and print one copy of the document using the Print tab in Backstage view.
15. Close the document, and then exit the Word program.
16. Submit the finished files to your instructor.

ASSESS

SAM: Skills Assessment Manager

For current SAM information, including versions and content details, visit SAM Central (http://samcentral.course.com). If you have a SAM user profile, you may have access to hands-on instruction, practice, and assessment of the skills covered in this tutorial. Since various versions of SAM are supported throughout the life of this text, check with your instructor for the correct instructions and URL/Web site for accessing assignments.

ENDING DATA FILES

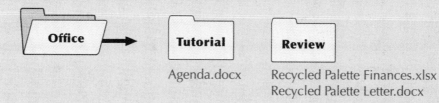

Agenda.docx   Recycled Palette Finances.xlsx
                     Recycled Palette Letter.docx

Teamwork

Working on a Team

Teams consist of individuals who have skills, talents, and abilities that complement each other and, when joined, produce synergy—results greater than those a single individual could achieve. It is this sense of shared mission and responsibility for results that makes a team successful in its efforts to reach its goals. Teams are everywhere. In the workplace, a team might develop a presentation to introduce products. In the classroom, a team might complete a research project.

Teams meet face to face or virtually. A virtual team rarely, if ever, meets in person. Instead, technology makes it possible for members to work as if everyone was in the same room. Some common technologies used in virtual teamwork are corporate networks, email, tele-conferencing, and collaboration and integration tools, such as those found in Office 2010.

Even for teams in the same location, technology is a valuable tool. For example, teams commonly collaborate on a copy of a file posted to an online shared storage space, such as SkyDrive. In addition, team members can compile data in the program that best suits the information related to their part of the project. Later, that information can be integrated into a finished report, presentation, email message, and so on.

Collaborate with Others

At home, school, or work, you probably collaborate with others to complete many types of tasks—such as planning an event, creating a report, or developing a presentation. You can use Microsoft Office to streamline many of these tasks. Consider a project that you might need to work on with a team. Complete the following steps:

1. Start Word, and open a new document, if necessary.
2. In the document, type a list of all the tasks the team needs to accomplish. If you are working with a team, identify which team member would complete each task.
3. For each task, identify the type of Office file you would create to complete that task. For example, you would create a Word document to write a letter.
4. For each file, identify the Office program you would use to create that file, and explain why you would use that program.
5. Save the document with an appropriate filename in an appropriate folder location.
6. Use a Web browser to visit the Microsoft site at *www.microsoft.com* and research the different Office 2010 suites available. Determine which suite includes all the programs needed for the team to complete the tasks on the list.
7. In the document, type which Office suite you selected and a brief explanation of why.
8. Determine how the team can integrate the different programs in the Office suite you selected to create the files that complete the team's goal or task. Include this information at the end of the Word document. Save the document.
9. Develop an efficient way to organize the files that the team will create to complete the goal or task. Add this information at the end of the Word document.
10. If possible, sign in to SkyDrive, and then save a copy of the file in an appropriate subfolder within your Public folder. If you are working with a team, have your teammates access your file, review your notes, and add a paragraph with their comments and name.
11. Preview and print the finished document, and then submit it to your instructor.

OBJECTIVES

Session 1.1
- Learn basic database concepts and terms
- Explore the Microsoft Access window and Backstage view
- Create a blank database
- Create and save a table in Datasheet view
- Enter field names and records in a table datasheet
- Open a table using the Navigation Pane

Session 1.2
- Open an Access database
- Copy and paste records from another Access database
- Navigate a table datasheet
- Create and navigate a simple query
- Create and navigate a simple form
- Create, preview, navigate, and print a simple report
- Learn how to compact, back up, and restore a database

Creating a Database

Creating a Database to Contain Customer, Contract, and Invoice Data

ACCESS

Case | *Belmont Landscapes*

Soon after graduating with a degree in Landscape Architecture from nearby Michigan State University, Oren Belmont returned to his hometown of Holland, on the shores of Lake Michigan. There, Oren worked for a local firm that provided basic landscaping services to residential customers. After several years, Oren started his own landscape architecture firm, Belmont Landscapes, which specializes in landscape designs for residential and commercial customers and numerous public agencies.

Belmont Landscapes provides a wide range of services—from site analyses and feasibility studies, to drafting and administering construction documents—for projects of various scales. Oren and his staff depend on computers to help manage all aspects of the firm's operations, including financial and information management. Several months ago the company upgraded to Microsoft Windows and **Microsoft Access 2010** (or simply **Access**), a computer program used to enter, maintain, and retrieve related data in a format known as a database. Oren and his staff want to use Access to maintain such data as information about customers, contracts, and invoices. He asks for your help in creating the necessary Access database.

STARTING DATA FILES

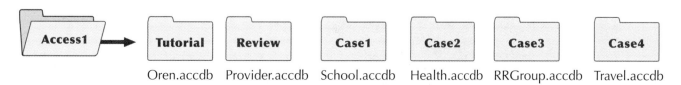

Access1 → Tutorial   Review   Case1   Case2   Case3   Case4

                Oren.accdb   Provider.accdb   School.accdb   Health.accdb   RRGroup.accdb   Travel.accdb

SESSION 1.1 VISUAL OVERVIEW

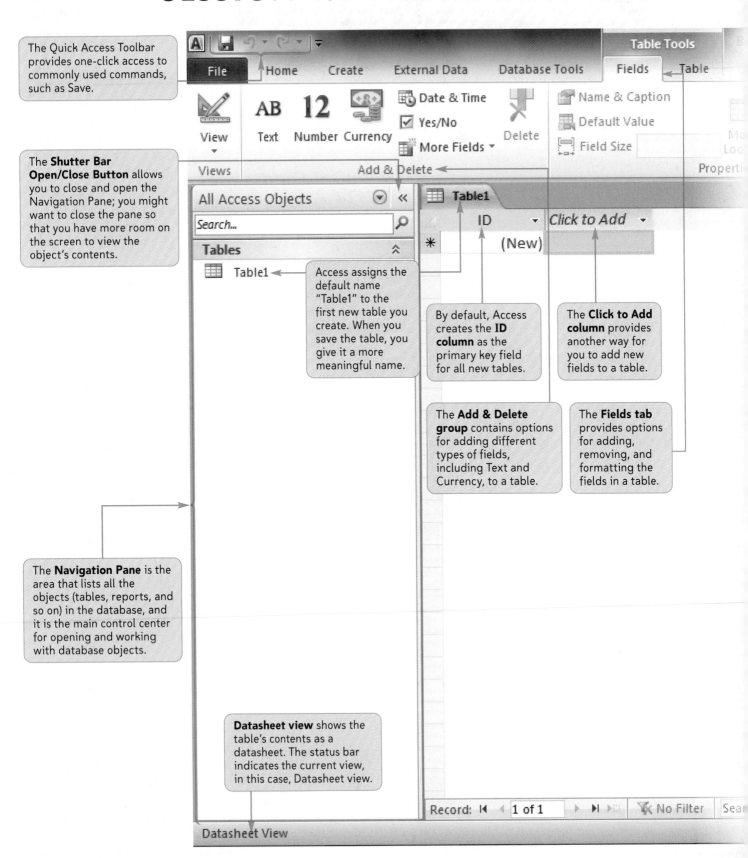

The Quick Access Toolbar provides one-click access to commonly used commands, such as Save.

The **Shutter Bar Open/Close Button** allows you to close and open the Navigation Pane; you might want to close the pane so that you have more room on the screen to view the object's contents.

Access assigns the default name "Table1" to the first new table you create. When you save the table, you give it a more meaningful name.

By default, Access creates the **ID column** as the primary key field for all new tables.

The **Click to Add column** provides another way for you to add new fields to a table.

The **Add & Delete group** contains options for adding different types of fields, including Text and Currency, to a table.

The **Fields tab** provides options for adding, removing, and formatting the fields in a table.

The **Navigation Pane** is the area that lists all the objects (tables, reports, and so on) in the database, and it is the main control center for opening and working with database objects.

Datasheet view shows the table's contents as a datasheet. The status bar indicates the current view, in this case, Datasheet view.

THE ACCESS WINDOW

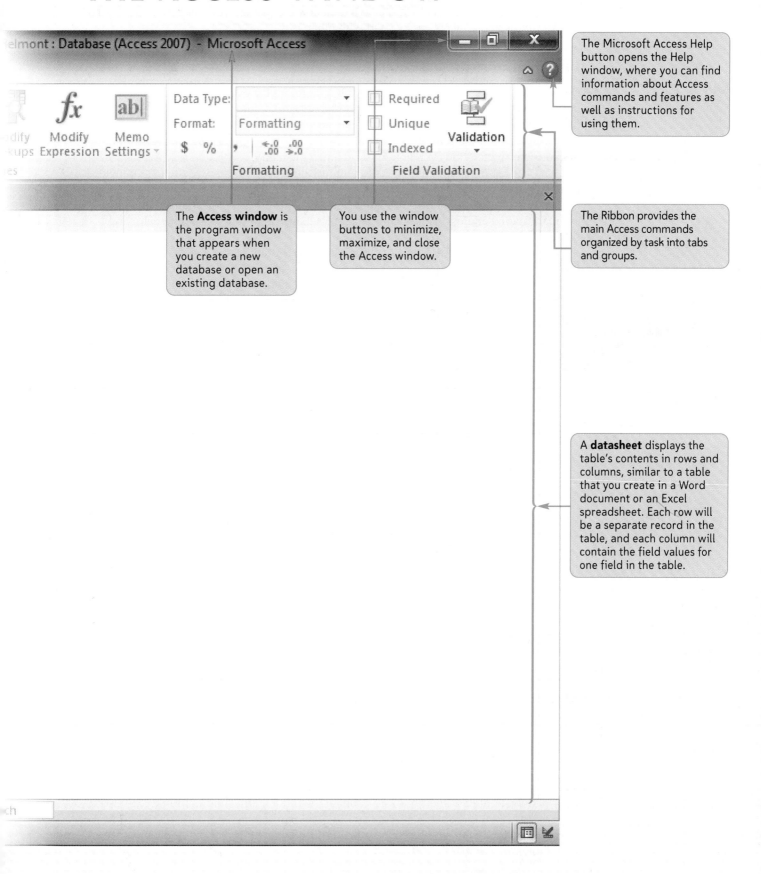

The Microsoft Access Help button opens the Help window, where you can find information about Access commands and features as well as instructions for using them.

The **Access window** is the program window that appears when you create a new database or open an existing database.

You use the window buttons to minimize, maximize, and close the Access window.

The Ribbon provides the main Access commands organized by task into tabs and groups.

A **datasheet** displays the table's contents in rows and columns, similar to a table that you create in a Word document or an Excel spreadsheet. Each row will be a separate record in the table, and each column will contain the field values for one field in the table.

Introduction to Database Concepts

Before you begin using Access to create the database for Oren, you need to understand a few key terms and concepts associated with databases.

Organizing Data

Data is a valuable resource to any business. At Belmont Landscapes, for example, important data includes customers' names and addresses and contract amounts and dates. Organizing, storing, maintaining, retrieving, and sorting this type of data are critical activities that enable a business to find and use information effectively. Before storing data on a computer, however, you must organize the data.

Your first step in organizing data is to identify the individual fields. A **field** is a single characteristic or attribute of a person, place, object, event, or idea. For example, some of the many fields that Belmont Landscapes tracks are customer ID, first name, last name, company name, address, phone number, contract amount, contract signing date, and contract type.

Next, you group related fields together into tables. A **table** is a collection of fields that describes a person, place, object, event, or idea. Figure 1-1 shows an example of a Customer table that contains the following four fields: CustomerID, FirstName, LastName, and Phone.

Figure 1-1	Data organization for a table of customers

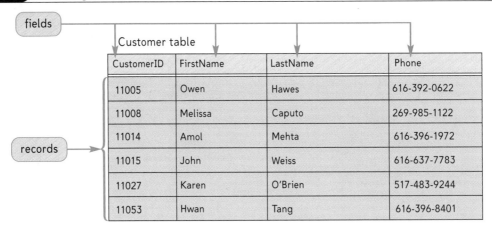

The specific value, or content, of a field is called the **field value**. In Figure 1-1, the first set of field values for CustomerID, FirstName, LastName, and Phone are, respectively: 11005; Owen; Hawes; and 616-392-0622. This set of field values is called a **record**. In the Customer table, the data for each customer is stored as a separate record. Figure 1-1 shows six records; each row of field values is a record.

Databases and Relationships

A collection of related tables is called a **database**, or a **relational database**. In this tutorial, you will create the database for Belmont Landscapes and a table named Contract to store data about contracts. In Tutorial 2, you will create two more tables, named Customer and Invoice, to store related information about customers and their invoices.

As Oren and his staff use the database that you will create, they will need to access information about customers and their contracts. To obtain this information, you must have a way to connect records in the Customer table to records in the Contract table. You connect the records in the separate tables through a **common field** that appears in both tables.

In the sample database shown in Figure 1-2, each record in the Customer table has a field named CustomerID, which is also a field in the Contract table. For example, Owen Hawes is the first customer in the Customer table and has a CustomerID field value of 11005. This same CustomerID field value, 11005, appears in three records in the Contract table. Therefore, Owen Hawes is the customer with these three contracts.

Figure 1-2   **Database relationship between tables for customers and contracts**

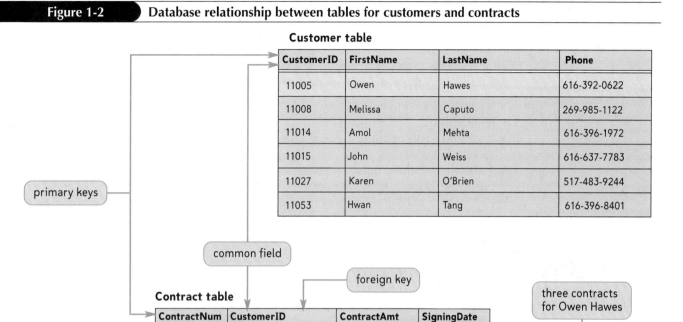

Each CustomerID value in the Customer table must be unique so that you can distinguish one customer from another. These unique CustomerID values also identify each customer's specific contracts in the Contract table. The CustomerID field is referred to as the primary key of the Customer table. A **primary key** is a field, or a collection of fields, whose values uniquely identify each record in a table. No two records can contain the same value for the primary key field. In the Contract table, the ContractNum field is the primary key because Belmont Landscapes assigns each contract a unique contract number.

When you include the primary key from one table as a field in a second table to form a relationship between the two tables, it is called a **foreign key** in the second table, as shown in Figure 1-2. For example, CustomerID is the primary key in the Customer table and a foreign key in the Contract table. Although the primary key CustomerID contains unique values in the Customer table, the same field as a foreign key in the Contract table does not necessarily contain unique values. The CustomerID value 11005, for example, appears three times in the Contract table because Owen Hawes has three contracts. Each foreign key value, however, must match one of the field values for the primary key in the other table. In the example shown in Figure 1-2, each CustomerID value in the Contract table must match a CustomerID value in the Customer table. The two tables are related, enabling users to connect the facts about customers with the facts about their contracts.

Relational Database Management Systems

To manage its databases, a company purchases a database management system. A **database management system (DBMS)** is a software program that lets you create databases and then manipulate data in them. Most of today's database management systems, including Access, are called relational database management systems. In a **relational database management system**, data is organized as a collection of tables. As stated earlier, a relationship between two tables in a relational DBMS is formed through a common field.

A relational DBMS controls the storage of databases on disk and facilitates the creation, manipulation, and reporting of data, as illustrated in Figure 1-3. Specifically, a relational DBMS provides the following functions:

- It allows you to create database structures containing fields, tables, and table relationships.
- It lets you easily add new records, change field values in existing records, and delete records.
- It contains a built-in query language, which lets you obtain immediate answers to the questions you ask about your data.
- It contains a built-in report generator, which lets you produce professional-looking, formatted reports from your data.
- It protects databases through security, control, and recovery facilities.

Figure 1-3	**Relational database management system**

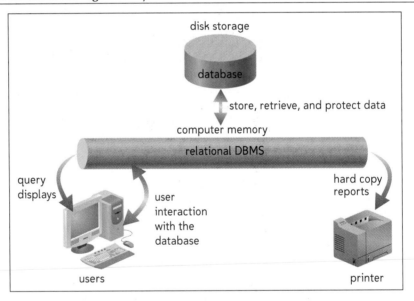

A company such as Belmont Landscapes benefits from a relational DBMS because it allows users working in different groups to share the same data. More than one user can enter data into a database, and more than one user can retrieve and analyze data that other users entered. For example, the database for Belmont Landscapes will contain only one copy of the Contract table, and all employees will use it to meet their specific requests for contract information.

Finally, unlike other software programs, such as spreadsheet programs, a DBMS can handle massive amounts of data and can be used to create relationships among multiple tables. Each Access database, for example, can be up to two gigabytes in size, can contain up to 32,768 objects (tables, queries, forms, and so on), and can have up to 255 people using the database at the same time. For instructional purposes, the databases you will create and work with throughout this text contain a relatively small number of records compared to databases you would encounter outside the classroom, which likely contain tables with very large numbers of records.

Creating a Database

Now that you've learned some database terms and concepts, you're ready to start Access and create the Belmont database for Oren.

To start Access:

1. Click the **Start** button  on the taskbar, click **All Programs**, click **Microsoft Office**, and then click **Microsoft Access 2010**. The Access program starts and opens in Backstage view. See Figure 1-4.

   Trouble? If you don't see the Microsoft Access 2010 option on the Microsoft Office menu, look for it on a different menu or as an option on the All Programs menu. If you still cannot find the Microsoft Access 2010 option, ask your instructor or technical support person for help.

Figure 1-4	Backstage view in Access

Trouble? If the Microsoft Access program window on your computer is not maximized, click the Maximize button on the program window title bar.

When you start Access, the first screen that appears is Backstage view, which is the starting place for your work in Access. Backstage view provides options for you to get information about the current database, create a new database, or open an existing database. To create a new database that does not contain any data or objects, you use the Blank database option. If the database you need to create contains objects that match those found in common databases, such as databases that store data about contacts or events, you can click Sample templates and use a template provided with Access. A **template** is a predesigned database that includes professionally designed tables, reports, and other database objects that can make it quick and easy for you to create a database. You can also search for a template and download it from Office.com.

In this case, the templates provided do not match Oren's needs for the Belmont Landscapes database, so you need to create a new, blank database from scratch.

To create the new Belmont database:

▶ 1. Make sure you have created your copy of the Access starting Data Files, and that your computer can access them.

   Trouble? If you don't have the starting Data Files, you need to get them before you can proceed. Your instructor will either give you the Data Files or ask you to obtain them from a specified location (such as a network drive). In either case, make a backup copy of the Data Files before you start so that you will have the original files available in case you need to start over. If you have any questions about the Data Files, see your instructor or technical support person for assistance.

▶ 2. Make sure the **New** tab is selected in the navigation bar, and that the **Blank database** option is selected (see Figure1-4).

Be sure to type **Belmont** or you'll create a database named Database1.

▶ 3. In the File Name box on the right side of the screen, select the default name provided by Access, and then type **Belmont**. Next you need to specify the location for the file.

▶ 4. Click the **Browse** button 📁 to the right of the File Name box. The File New Database dialog box opens.

▶ 5. Navigate to the drive that contains your Data Files.

   Trouble? If you do not know where your Data Files are located, consult with your instructor about where to save your Data Files.

▶ 6. Navigate to the **Access1\Tutorial** folder. This is the folder in which you will store the database file you create.

▶ 7. Make sure the "Save as type" box displays "Microsoft Access 2007 Databases."

   Trouble? If your computer is set up to show filename extensions, you will see the Access filename extension ".accdb" in the Save as type box.

TIP

If you don't type the filename extension, Access adds it automatically.

▶ 8. Click the **OK** button. You return to Backstage view, and the File Name box now shows the name Belmont.accdb. The filename extension ".accdb" identifies the file as an Access 2007 database.

▶ 9. Click the **Create** button. Access creates the new database, saves it to the specified drive, and then opens an empty table named Table1.

INSIGHT

Understanding the Database File Type

Access 2010 uses the .accdb file extension, which is the same file extension used for databases created with Microsoft Access 2007. To ensure compatibility between databases created with Access 2007 and Access 2010, new databases created using Access 2010 have the same file extension and file format as Access 2007 databases. This is why the File New Database dialog box provides the Microsoft Access 2007 Databases option in the "Save as type" box. In addition, the notation "(Access 2007)" appears in the title bar next to the name of an open database in Access 2010.

Refer back to the Session 1.1 Visual Overview and spend some time becoming familiar with the components of the Access window.

Creating a Table in Datasheet View

Tables contain all the data in a database and are the fundamental objects for your work in Access. There are different ways to create a table in Access, including entering the fields and records for a table directly in Datasheet view.

REFERENCE

Creating a Table in Datasheet View

- Click the Create tab on the Ribbon.
- In the Tables group, click the Table button.
- Accept the default ID primary key field with the AutoNumber data type, or rename the field and change its data type, if necessary.
- In the Add & Delete group on the Fields tab, click the button for the type of field you want to add to the table (for example, click the Text button), and then type the field name. Repeat this step to add all the necessary fields to the table.

  or

  In the table datasheet, click the Click to Add column heading, click the type of field you want to add from the list that opens, type the field name, and then press the Tab or Enter key to move to the next column in the datasheet. Repeat this step to add all the necessary fields to the table.
- In the first row below the field names, enter the value for each field in the first record, pressing the Tab or Enter key to move to the next field.
- After entering the value for the last field in the first record, press the Tab or Enter key to move to the next row, and then enter the values for the next record. Continue this process until you have entered all the records for the table.
- Click the Save button on the Quick Access Toolbar, enter a name for the table, and then click the OK button.

For Belmont Landscapes, Oren needs to track information about the company's contracts with its customers. He asks you to create the Contract table according to the plan shown in Figure 1-5.

Figure 1-5   **Plan for the Contract table**

Field	Purpose
ContractNum	Unique number assigned to each contract; will serve as the table's primary key
CustomerID	Unique number assigned to each customer; common field that will be a foreign key to connect to the Customer table
ContractAmt	Dollar amount for the full contract
SigningDate	Date on which the customer signed the contract
ContractType	Brief description of the contract

As shown in Oren's plan, he wants to store data about contracts in five fields, including fields to contain the amount of each contract, when it was signed, and the contract type. These are the most important aspects of a contract and, therefore, must be tracked. Also, notice that the ContractNum field will be the primary key for the table; each contract at Belmont Landscapes has a unique contract number, so this field is the logical choice for the primary key. Finally, the CustomerID field is needed in the Contract table as a foreign key to connect the information about contracts to customers. The data about customers and their invoices will be stored in separate tables, which you will create in Tutorial 2.

Notice the name of each field in Figure 1-5. You need to name each field, table, and other object in an Access database.

PROSKILLS

Decision Making: Naming Database Fields and Objects in Access

One of the most important tasks in creating a table is deciding what names to specify for the table's fields. Keep the following guidelines in mind when you assign field names:

- A field name can consist of up to 64 characters, including letters, numbers, spaces, and special characters, except for a period (.), exclamation mark (!), accent grave (`), and square brackets ([ ]).
- A field name cannot begin with a space.
- Capitalize the first letter of each word in a field name that combines multiple words, for example SigningDate.
- Use concise field names that are easy to remember and reference, and that won't take up a lot of space in the table datasheet.
- Use standard abbreviations, such as Num for Number, Amt for Amount, and Qty for Quantity.
- Give fields descriptive names so that you can easily identify them when you view or edit records.
- Although Access supports the use of spaces in field names (and in other object names), experienced database developers avoid using spaces because they can cause errors when the objects are involved in programming tasks.

By spending time obtaining and analyzing information about the fields in the table, and understanding the rules for naming Access fields and objects, you can determine the most appropriate object names and create a well-designed database that will be easy for others to use.

Renaming the Default Primary Key Field

As noted earlier, Access provides the ID field as the default primary key for a new table you create in Datasheet view. Recall that a primary key is a field, or a collection of fields, whose values uniquely identify each record in a table. However, according to Oren's plan, the ContractNum field should be the primary key for the Contract table. You'll begin by renaming the default ID field to create the ContractNum field.

To rename the ID field to the ContractNum field:

▶ 1. Right-click the **ID** column heading to open the shortcut menu, and then click **Rename Field**. The column heading ID is selected, so that whatever text you type next will replace it.

▶ 2. Type **ContractNum** and then click the row below the heading. The column heading changes to ContractNum and the insertion point moves to the row below the heading. See Figure 1-6.

| Figure 1-6 | ID field renamed to ContractNum |

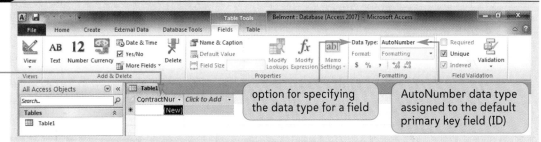

ContractNum field name entered in the column heading

option for specifying the data type for a field

AutoNumber data type assigned to the default primary key field (ID)

Trouble? If you make a mistake while typing the field name, use the Backspace key to delete characters to the left of the insertion point or the Delete key to delete characters to the right of the insertion point. Then type the correct text. To correct a field name by replacing it entirely, press the Esc key, and then type the correct text.

Trouble? The entire field name "ContractNum" might not be visible in the column heading. You'll learn how to resize columns to display the full field names later in this tutorial.

You have renamed the default primary key field, ID, to ContractNum. However, the ContractNum field still retains the characteristics of the ID field, including its data type. Your next task is to change the data type of this field.

Changing the Data Type of the Default Primary Key Field

Notice the Formatting group on the Fields tab. One of the options available in this group is the Data Type option (see Figure 1-6). Each field in an Access table must be assigned a data type. The **data type** determines what field values you can enter for the field. In this case, the AutoNumber data type is displayed. Access assigns the AutoNumber data type to the default ID primary key field because the **AutoNumber** data type automatically inserts a unique number in this field for every record. Therefore, it can serve as the primary key for any table you create.

Contract numbers at Belmont Landscapes are specific, four-digit numbers, so the AutoNumber data type is not appropriate for the ContractNum field, which is the primary key field in the table you are creating. A better choice is the **Text** data type, which allows field values containing letters, digits, and other characters, and which is appropriate for identifying numbers, such as contract numbers, that are never used in calculations. So, Oren asks you to change the data type for the ContractNum field from AutoNumber to Text.

To change the data type for the ContractNum field:

1. Make sure that the ContractNum column is selected. A column is selected when you click a field value, in which case the background color of the column heading changes (the default color is orange) and the insertion point appears in the field value. You can also click the column heading to select a column, in which case the background color of both the column heading and the field value changes (the default colors are gray and blue, respectively).

2. In the Formatting group on the Fields tab, click the **Data Type arrow**, and then click **Text**. The ContractNum field is now a Text field. See Figure 1-7.

Figure 1-7	Text data type assigned to the ContractNum field

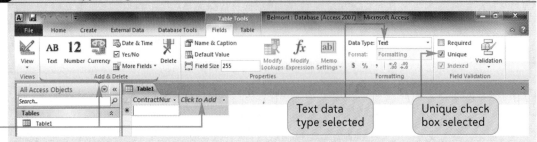

options for adding new fields to the table

Text data type selected

Unique check box selected

Note the Unique check box in the Field Validation group. This check box is selected because the ContractNum field assumed the characteristics of the default primary key field, ID, including the fact that each value in the field must be unique. No two records in the Contract table will be allowed to have the same value in the ContractNum field.

With the ContractNum field created and established as the primary key, you can now enter the rest of the fields in the Contract table.

Adding New Fields

When you create a table in Datasheet view, you can use the options in the Add & Delete group on the Fields tab to add fields to your table. You can also use the Click to Add column in the table datasheet to add new fields. (See Figure 1-7.) You'll use both methods to add the four remaining fields to the Contract table. The next field you need to add is the CustomerID field. Similar to the ContractNum field, the CustomerID field will also contain numbers that will not be used in calculations, so it should be a Text field.

To add the rest of the fields to the Contract table:

1. In the Add & Delete group on the Fields tab, click the **Text** button. Access adds a new field named "Field1" to the right of the ContractNum field. See Figure 1-8.

Figure 1-8	New Text field added to the table

new field added as the second field in the table

default name highlighted in the new field

indicates the data type of the new field

The text "Field1" is selected, so you can simply type the new field name to replace it.

2. Type **CustomerID**. The second field is added to the table. Next, you'll add the ContractAmt field. According to Oren's plan, this field will contain the dollar amount of each contract. The most appropriate data type for displaying dollar amounts is the Currency data type.

3. In the Add & Delete group, click the **Currency** button. Access adds a third field to the table, this time with the Currency data type.

4. Type **ContractAmt** to replace the highlighted name "Field1." The fourth field in the Contract table is the SigningDate field. Because this field will contain date values, you'll add a field with the Date/Time data type next—this time using the Click to Add column.

5. Click the **Click to Add** column heading. Access displays a list of available data types from which you can choose the data type for the new field you're adding.

6. Click **Date & Time** in the list. Access adds a fourth field to the table.

7. Type **SigningDate** to replace the highlighted name "Field1," and then press the **Enter** key. The Click to Add column becomes active and displays the list of field data types. The fifth and final field in the Contract table is the ContractType field, which will contain brief descriptions of the contracts. The Text data type is suitable for this field.

TIP

You can also type the first letter of a data type to select it and close the Click to Add list.

8. Click **Text** in the list, and then type **ContractType** to replace the highlighted name "Field1." All five fields are now entered for the Contract table.

   Some of the field names are not completely visible, so you need to resize the datasheet columns.

   Trouble? If you pressed the Tab or Enter key after typing the ContractType field name, press the Esc key to close the Click to Add list.

9. Place the pointer on the vertical line between the ContractNum and CustomerID field names until the pointer changes to a ✛ shape.

10. Double-click the pointer. The ContractNum column is resized and now displays the full field name.

    Trouble? If you click the arrow on the ContractNum column heading by mistake, a menu will open. Simply click the arrow again to close the menu, and then repeat Steps 9 and 10.

11. Double-click the ✛ pointer on the vertical line to the right of the CustomerID, ContractAmt, SigningDate, and ContractType column headings to resize the columns in the datasheet. When finished, click the first column for row 1. Your datasheet should now look like the one shown in Figure 1-9.

Figure 1-9 | **Table with all fields entered**

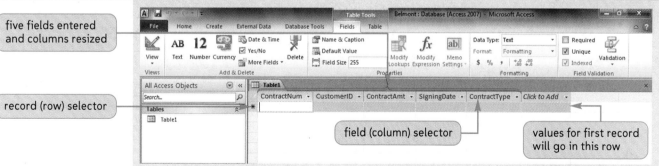

five fields entered and columns resized

record (row) selector

field (column) selector

values for first record will go in this row

The table contains three Text fields (ContractNum, CustomerID, and ContractType), one Currency field (ContractAmt), and one Date/Time field (SigningDate). You'll learn more about field data types in Tutorial 2.

As noted earlier, Datasheet view shows a table's contents in rows (records) and columns (fields). Each column is headed by a field name inside a field selector, and each row has a record selector to its left (see Figure 1-9). Clicking a **field selector** or a **record selector** selects that entire column or row (respectively), which you then can manipulate. A field selector is also called a **column selector**, and a record selector is also called a **row selector**.

Entering Records

With the fields in place for the table, you can now enter the field values for each record. Oren requests that you enter eight records in the Contract table, as shown in Figure 1-10.

| Figure 1-10 | Contract table records |

ContractNum	CustomerID	ContractAmt	SigningDate	ContractType
3011	11001	$4,000.00	2/9/2013	Residential landscape plan
3026	11038	$165,000.00	3/11/2013	Landscape plans for large-scale housing development
3012	11027	$300.00	2/18/2013	Consultation for backyard, residential
3015	11005	$1,500.00	3/1/2013	Schematic plan for backyard, residential
3022	11043	$22,000.00	4/14/2013	Landscape design for two entrances
3017	11012	$2,250.00	3/1/2013	Peer plan review for town
3023	11070	$39,000.00	3/22/2013	Renovation of large multifamily housing open space
3021	11040	$28,000.00	5/3/2013	Landscape plans for multifamily housing site

To enter records in a table datasheet, you type the field values below the column headings for the fields. The first record you enter will go in the first row (see Figure 1-9).

To enter the first record for the Contract table:

Be sure to type the numbers "0" and "1" and not the letters "O" and "l" in the field value.

1. In the first row for the ContractNum field, type **3011** (the ContractNum field value for the first record), and then press the **Tab** key. Access adds the field value and moves the insertion point to the right, in the CustomerID column. See Figure 1-11.

| Figure 1-11 | First field value entered |

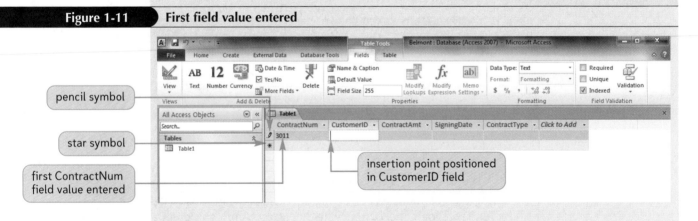

pencil symbol

star symbol

first ContractNum field value entered

insertion point positioned in CustomerID field

Trouble? If you make a mistake when typing a value, use the Backspace key to delete characters to the left of the insertion point or the Delete key to delete characters to the right of the insertion point. Then type the correct value. To correct a value by replacing it entirely, press the Esc key, and then type the correct value.

Notice the pencil symbol that appears in the row selector for the new record. The **pencil symbol** indicates that the record is being edited. Also notice the star symbol that appears in the row selector for the second row. The **star symbol** identifies the second row as the next row available for a new record.

▶ 2. Type **11001** (the CustomerID field value for the first record), and then press the **Tab** key. Access enters the field value and moves the insertion point to the ContractAmt column.

▶ 3. Type **4000** (the ContractAmt field value for the first record), and then press the **Tab** key. Notice that Access formats the field value with a dollar sign, a comma, and two decimal places—displaying it as $4,000.00—even though you did not enter the value this way. This is because the ContractAmt field has the Currency data type, which automatically formats field values in this way. You'll learn more about formatting field values later in this text.

▶ 4. Type **2/9/13** (the SigningDate field value for the first record), and then press the **Tab** key. Access displays the year as "2013" even though you entered only the final two digits of the year. This is because the SigningDate field has the Date/Time data type, which automatically formats dates with four-digit years.

Trouble? Depending on your Windows date setting, your SigningDate field values might be displayed in a different format. This difference will not cause any problems.

▶ 5. Type **Residential landscape plan** (the ContractType field value for the first record), and then press the **Tab** key. The first record is entered into the table, and the insertion point is positioned in the ContractNum field for the second record. The pencil symbol is removed from the first row because the record in that row is no longer being edited. The table is now ready for you to enter the second record. See Figure 1-12.

Figure 1-12   **Datasheet with first record entered**

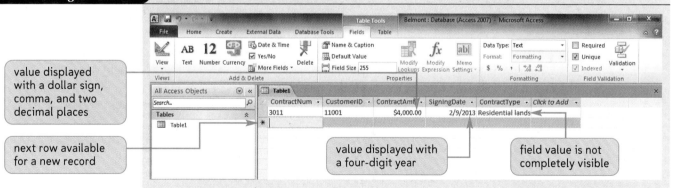

value displayed with a dollar sign, comma, and two decimal places

next row available for a new record

value displayed with a four-digit year

field value is not completely visible

Note that the ContractType field value is not completely displayed. You'll resize the table columns, as necessary, after you enter all the data.

Now you can enter the remaining seven records in the Contract table.

TIP

You can also press the Enter key instead of the Tab key to move from one field to another, and to the next row.

To enter the remaining records in the Contract table:

1. Referring to Figure 1-10, enter the values for records 2 through 8, pressing the **Tab** key to move from field to field and to the next row for a new record. Keep in mind that you do not have to type the dollar sign, comma, or decimal places in the ContractAmt values, because Access will add them automatically. Similarly, you do not have to type all four digits of the year in the SigningDate field values; you can enter only the final two digits and Access will display all four.

   Trouble? If you enter a value in the wrong field by mistake, such as entering a ContractType field value in the ContractAmt field, a menu might open with options for addressing the problem. If this happens, click the "Enter new value" option in the menu. You'll return to the field with the incorrect value highlighted, which you can then replace by typing the correct value.

   To see more of the table datasheet and the full field values, you'll close the Navigation Pane and resize the ContractType column.

2. Click the **Shutter Bar Open/Close Button** « at the top of the Navigation Pane. The Navigation Pane closes, and you can see the complete table datasheet.

3. Place the pointer on the vertical line to the right of the ContractType field name until the pointer changes to a ↔ shape, and then double-click the pointer. All the ContractType field values are now fully displayed. See Figure 1-13.

| Figure 1-13 | Datasheet with eight records entered |

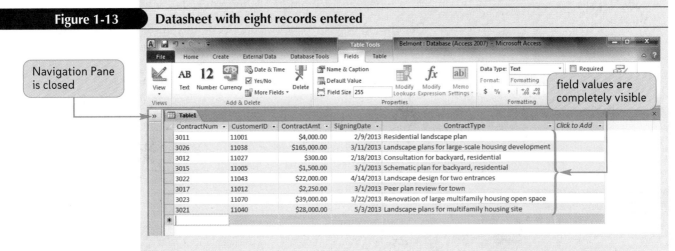

Navigation Pane is closed

field values are completely visible

ContractNum	CustomerID	ContractAmt	SigningDate	ContractType
3011	11001	$4,000.00	2/9/2013	Residential landscape plan
3026	11038	$165,000.00	3/11/2013	Landscape plans for large-scale housing development
3012	11027	$300.00	2/18/2013	Consultation for backyard, residential
3015	11005	$1,500.00	3/1/2013	Schematic plan for backyard, residential
3022	11043	$22,000.00	4/14/2013	Landscape design for two entrances
3017	11012	$2,250.00	3/1/2013	Peer plan review for town
3023	11070	$39,000.00	3/22/2013	Renovation of large multifamily housing open space
3021	11040	$28,000.00	5/3/2013	Landscape plans for multifamily housing site

Carefully compare your ContractNum and CustomerID values with those in the figure and correct any errors before continuing.

4. Compare your table to the one in Figure 1-13. If any of the field values in your table do not match those shown in the figure, you can correct a field value by clicking to position the insertion point in the value, and then using the Backspace key or Delete key to delete incorrect text. Then type the correct text and press the Enter key.

Saving a Table

The records you enter are immediately stored in the database as soon as you enter them; however, the table's design—the field names and characteristics of the fields themselves, plus any layout changes to the datasheet—are not saved until you save the table. When you save a new table for the first time, you should give it a name that best identifies the information it contains. Like a field name, a table name can contain up to 64 characters, including spaces.

Saving a Table

- Click the Save button on the Quick Access Toolbar. The Save As dialog box opens.
- In the Table Name box, type the name for the table.
- Click the OK button.

According to Oren's plan, you need to save the table with the name "Contract."

To save and name the Contract table:

1. Click the **Save** button 🖫 on the Quick Access Toolbar. The Save As dialog box opens.

2. With the default name Table1 selected in the Table Name box, type **Contract**, and then click the **OK** button. The tab for the table now displays the name "Contract," and the Contract table design is saved in the Belmont database.

Notice that after you saved and named the Contract table, Access sorted and displayed the records in order by the values in the ContractNum field because it is the primary key. If you compare your screen to Figure 1-10, which shows the records in the order you entered them, you'll see that the current screen shows the records in order by the ContractNum field values.

Oren asks you to add two more records to the Contract table. When you add a record to an existing table, you must enter the new record in the next row available for a new record; you cannot insert a row between existing records for the new record. In a table with just a few records, such as the Contract table, the next available row is visible on the screen. However, in a table with hundreds of records, you would need to scroll the datasheet to see the next row available. The easiest way to add a new record to a table is to use the New button, which scrolls the datasheet to the next row available so you can enter the new record.

To enter additional records in the Contract table:

1. If necessary, click the first record's ContractNum field value (**3011**) to make it the current record.

2. Click the **Home** tab on the Ribbon.

3. In the Records group, click the **New** button. The insertion point is positioned in the next row available for a new record, which in this case is row 9. See Figure 1-14.

Figure 1-14
Entering a new record

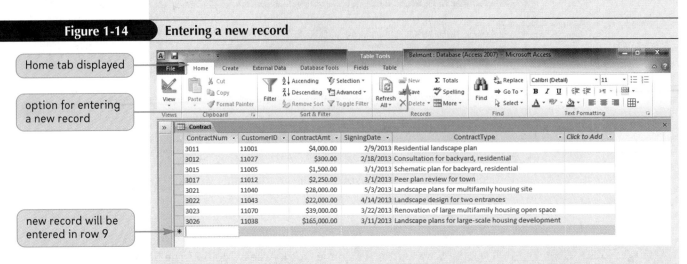

Home tab displayed

option for entering a new record

new record will be entered in row 9

4. With the insertion point in the ContractNum field for the new record, type **3020** and then press the **Tab** key.

5. Complete the entry of this record by entering each value shown below, pressing the **Tab** key to move from field to field:

CustomerID = **11055**
ContractAmt = **$6,500.00**
SigningDate = **2/19/2013**
ContractType = **Landscape design for restaurant**

6. Enter the values for the next new record, as follows, and press the **Tab** key after entering the ContractType field value:

ContractNum = **3025**
CustomerID = **11083**
ContractAmt = **$15,500.00**
SigningDate = **3/25/2013**
ContractType = **Landscape renovation for plaza**

Your datasheet should now look like the one shown in Figure 1-15.

Figure 1-15
Datasheet with additional records entered

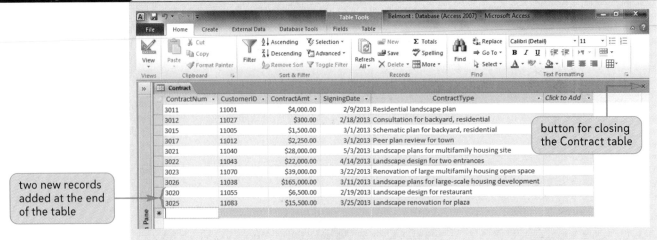

button for closing the Contract table

two new records added at the end of the table

The new records you added appear at the end of the table, and are not sorted in order by the primary key field values. For example, ContractNum 3020 should be the fifth record in the table, placed between ContractNum 3017 and ContractNum 3021. When you add records to a table datasheet, they appear at the end of the table. The records are not displayed in primary key order until you close and reopen the table, or switch between views.

7. Click the **Close 'Contract'** button ☒ on the object tab (see Figure 1-15 for the location of this button). The Contract table closes, and the main portion of the Access window is now blank because no database object is currently open.

Opening a Table

The tables in a database are listed in the Navigation Pane. You open a table, or any Access object (query, form, report), by double-clicking the object name in the Navigation Pane. Next, you'll open the Contract table so you can see the order of all the records you've entered.

To open the Contract table:

1. On the Navigation Pane, click the **Shutter Bar Open/Close Button** ⟫ to open the pane. Note that the Contract table is listed.

2. Double-click **Contract** to open the table in Datasheet view. See Figure 1-16.

Figure 1-16   **Table with 10 records entered and displayed in primary key order**

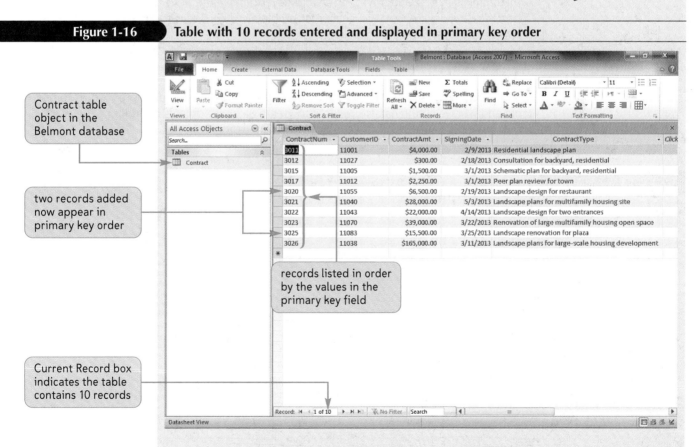

Contract table object in the Belmont database

two records added now appear in primary key order

records listed in order by the values in the primary key field

Current Record box indicates the table contains 10 records

ContractNum	CustomerID	ContractAmt	SigningDate	ContractType
3011	11001	$4,000.00	2/9/2013	Residential landscape plan
3012	11027	$300.00	2/18/2013	Consultation for backyard, residential
3015	11005	$1,500.00	3/1/2013	Schematic plan for backyard, residential
3017	11012	$2,250.00	3/1/2013	Peer plan review for town
3020	11055	$6,500.00	2/19/2013	Landscape design for restaurant
3021	11040	$28,000.00	5/3/2013	Landscape plans for multifamily housing site
3022	11043	$22,000.00	4/14/2013	Landscape design for two entrances
3023	11070	$39,000.00	3/22/2013	Renovation of large multifamily housing open space
3025	11083	$15,500.00	3/25/2013	Landscape renovation for plaza
3026	11038	$165,000.00	3/11/2013	Landscape plans for large-scale housing development

Record: 1 of 10

The two records you added, with ContractNum field values of 3020 and 3025, now appear in the correct primary key order. The table now contains a total of 10 records, as indicated by the Current Record box at the bottom of the datasheet. The **Current Record box** displays the number of the current record as well as the total number of records in the table.

Each record contains a unique ContractNum value because this field is the primary key. Other fields, however, can contain the same value in multiple records; for example, note the two values of 3/1/2013 in the SigningDate field.

3. If you are not continuing on to Session 1.2, click the **Close** button [X] on the program window title bar. Access closes the Contract table and the Belmont database, and then the Access program closes.

INSIGHT

Saving a Database

Unlike the Save buttons in other Office programs, the Save button on the Quick Access Toolbar in Access does not save the active document (database) to your disk. Instead, you use the Save button to save the design of an Access object, such as a table (as you saw earlier), or to save datasheet format changes, such as resizing columns. Access does not have a button or option you can use to save the active database.

Access saves changes to the active database to your disk automatically when you change or add a record or close the database. If your database is stored on a removable medium, such as a USB drive, you should never remove the drive while the database file is open. If you do, Access will encounter problems when it tries to save the database, which might damage the database.

Now that you've become familiar with database concepts and Access, and created the Belmont database and the Contract table, Oren wants you to add more records to the table and work with the data stored in it to create database objects including a query, form, and report. You will complete these tasks in Session 1.2.

REVIEW

Session 1.1 Quick Check

1. A(n) _____ is a single characteristic of a person, place, object, event, or idea.
2. You connect the records in two separate tables through a(n) _____ that appears in both tables.
3. The _____, whose values uniquely identify each record in a table, is called a(n) _____ when it is placed in a second table to form a relationship between the two tables.
4. The _____ is the area of the Access window that lists all the objects in a database, and it is the main control center for opening and working with database objects.
5. Which field does Access create, by default, as the primary key field for a new table in Datasheet view?
6. Which group on the Fields tab contains the options you use to add new fields to a table?
7. What does a pencil symbol at the beginning of a record represent? A star symbol?
8. Explain how the saving process in Access is different from saving in other Office programs.

SESSION 1.2 VISUAL OVERVIEW

The Forms group contains options for creating a **form**, which is a database object you use to enter, edit, and view records in a database.

The **Query Wizard** button opens a dialog box with different types of wizards that guide you through the steps to create a query. One of these, the **Simple Query Wizard**, allows you to select records and fields quickly to display in the query results.

Belmont : Database (Access

File   Home   Create   External Data   Database Tools

Application Parts ▾ | Table | Table Design | SharePoint Lists ▾ | Query Wizard | Query Design | Form | Form Design | Blank Form | Form Wi... Navigati... More Fo...

Templates   Tables   Queries   Forms

Navigation Pane

Ready

You use the options in the Tables group to create a table in Datasheet view or in Design view (which you learn about in Tutorial 2).

The Queries group contains options for creating a **query**, which is a question you ask about the data stored in a database. In response to a query, Access displays the specific records and fields that answer your question.

The **Form tool** quickly creates a form containing all the fields in the table (or query) on which you're basing the form.

The **Form Wizard** guides you through the process of creating a form.

THE CREATE TAB OPTIONS

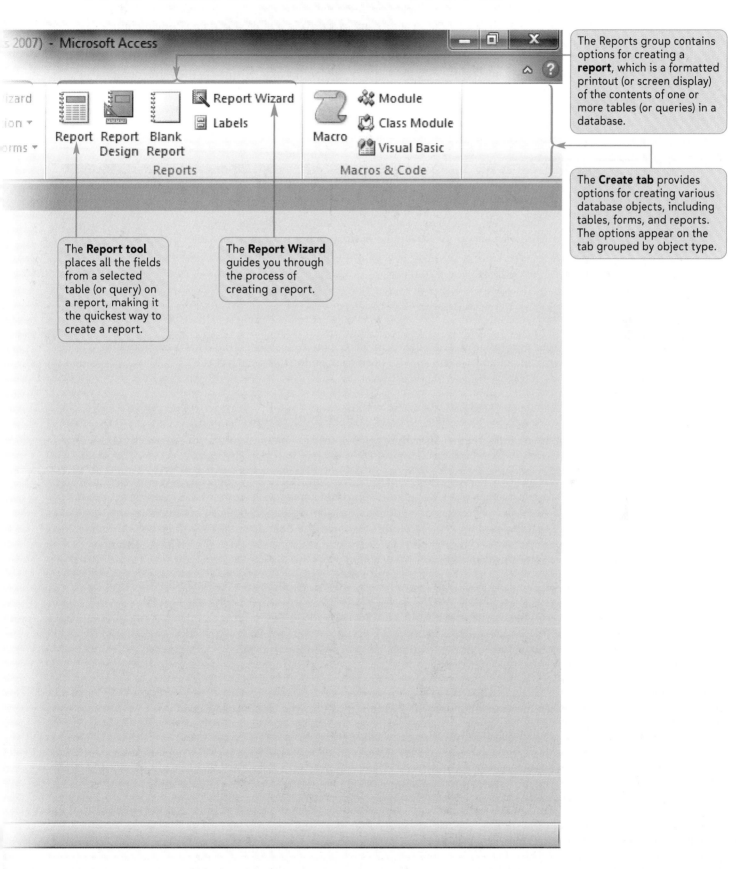

The Reports group contains options for creating a **report**, which is a formatted printout (or screen display) of the contents of one or more tables (or queries) in a database.

The **Create tab** provides options for creating various database objects, including tables, forms, and reports. The options appear on the tab grouped by object type.

The **Report tool** places all the fields from a selected table (or query) on a report, making it the quickest way to create a report.

The **Report Wizard** guides you through the process of creating a report.

Copying Records from Another Access Database

When you created the Contract table, you entered records directly into the table datasheet. There are many other ways to enter records in a table, including copying and pasting records from a table into the same database or into a different database. To use this method, however, the tables must have the same structure—that is, the tables must contain the same fields, with the same design and characteristics, in the same order.

Oren has already created a table named Agreement that contains additional records with contract data. The Agreement table is contained in a database named Oren located in the Access1\Tutorial folder included with your Data Files. The Agreement table has the same table structure as the Contract table you created.

REFERENCE

Opening a Database

- Start Access. If necessary, click the File tab to display Backstage view.
- Click the Open command in the navigation bar to display the Open dialog box.
- Navigate to the database file you want to open, and then click the file.
- Click the Open button.

Your next task is to copy the records from the Agreement table and paste them into your Contract table. To do so, you need to open the Oren database.

To copy the records from the Agreement table:

▶ **1.** If you took a break after the previous session, make sure that the Belmont database is open, and the Contract table is open in Datasheet view.

   Trouble? If you need to open the Belmont database, a Security Warning might appear below the Ribbon indicating that some active content has been disabled. Access provides this warning because some databases might contain content that could harm your computer. Because the Belmont database does not contain objects that could be harmful, you can open it safely. Click the Enable Content button next to the Security Warning.

▶ **2.** In the Navigation Pane, click the **Shutter Bar Open/Close Button** « to close the pane (if necessary) and display more of the table datasheet. To open a second database, you need to start another copy of Access.

▶ **3.** Click the **Start** button ⊕ on the taskbar, click **All Programs**, click **Microsoft Office**, and then click **Microsoft Access 2010**. The Access program opens in Backstage view. To open an existing database, you use the Open command in the navigation bar.

▶ **4.** In the navigation bar, click **Open** to display the Open dialog box.

▶ **5.** Navigate to the drive that contains your Data Files.

▶ **6.** Navigate to the **Access1\Tutorial** folder, click the database file named **Oren**, and then click the **Open** button. The Oren database opens in a second Access window. Note that the database contains only one object, the Agreement table.

   Trouble? If the Security Warning opens, click the Enable Content button to close it.

▶ **7.** In the Navigation Pane, double-click **Agreement** to open the Agreement table in Datasheet view. The table contains 55 records and the same five fields, with the same characteristics, as the fields in the Contract table. See Figure 1-17.

Figure 1-17   Agreement table in the Oren database

same fields as in the Contract table

click the datasheet selector to select all the records in the table

table contains a total of 55 records

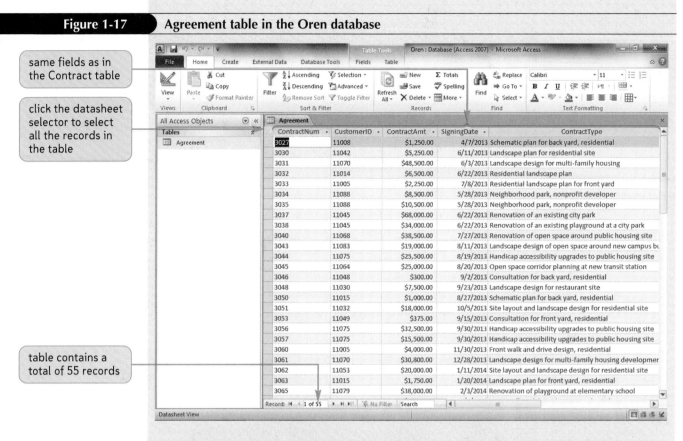

Oren wants you to copy all the records in the Agreement table. You can select all the records by clicking the **datasheet selector**, which is the box to the left of the first field name in the table datasheet (see Figure 1-17).

▶ **8.** Click the **datasheet selector** to the left of the ContractNum field. Access selects all the records in the table.

▶ **9.** In the Clipboard group on the Home tab, click the **Copy** button. All the records are copied to the Clipboard.

▶ **10.** Click the **Close 'Agreement'** button ⊠ on the object tab. A dialog box opens asking if you want to save the data you copied to the Clipboard. This dialog box opens only when you copy a large amount of data to the Clipboard.

▶ **11.** Click the **Yes** button. The dialog box closes, and then the Agreement table closes.

▶ **12.** Click the **Close** button ⊠ on the Access window title bar to close the Oren database and the second Access program window.

With the records copied to the Clipboard, you can now paste them into the Contract table.

To paste the records into the Contract table:

▶ **1.** With the Belmont database's Contract table open in Datasheet view, position the pointer on the row selector for row 11 (the next row available for a new record) until the pointer changes to a ➡ shape, and then click to select the row.

Trouble? If you have difficulty displaying the correct pointer shape, click an empty area of the table datasheet to establish the window as the active window. Then repeat Step 1.

2. In the Clipboard group on the Home tab, click the **Paste** button. The pasted records are added to the table, and a dialog box opens asking you to confirm that you want to paste all the records (55 total).

   Trouble? If the Paste button isn't active, click the ➡ pointer on the row selector for row 11, making sure the entire row is selected, and then repeat Step 2.

3. Click the **Yes** button. The dialog box closes, and the pasted records are highlighted. See Figure 1-18. Notice that the table now contains a total of 65 records—10 records that you entered and 55 records that you copied and pasted.

Figure 1-18	Contract table after copying and pasting records

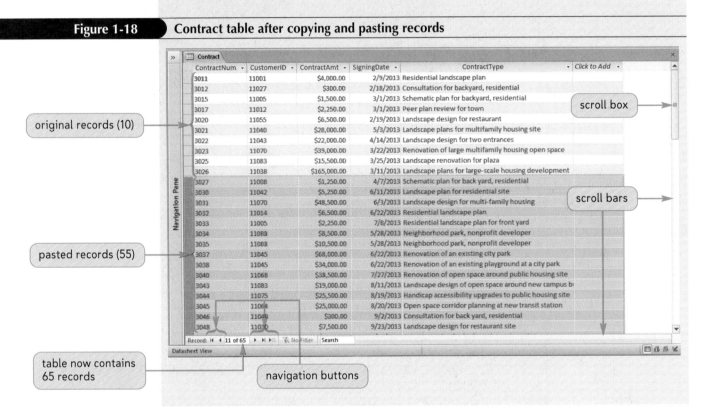

Navigating a Datasheet

The Contract table now contains 65 records, but only some of the records are visible on the screen. To view fields or records not currently visible on the screen, you can use the horizontal and vertical scroll bars shown in Figure 1-18 to navigate the data. The **navigation buttons**, shown in Figure 1-18 and also described in Figure 1-19, provide another way to move vertically through the records. The Current Record box appears between the two sets of navigation buttons and displays the number of the current record as well as the total number of records in the table. Figure 1-19 shows which record becomes the current record when you click each navigation button. Note the New (blank) record button, which works in the same way as the New button on the Home tab you used earlier to enter a new record in the table.

| Figure 1-19 | Navigation buttons |

Navigation Button	Record Selected	Navigation Button	Record Selected
⏮	First record	⏭	Last record
◀	Previous record	▶※	New (blank) record
▶	Next record		

Oren suggests that you use the various navigation techniques to move through the Contract table and become familiar with its contents.

To navigate the Contract datasheet:

TIP

You can make a field the current field by clicking anywhere within the column for that field.

1. Click the first record's ContractNum field value (**3011**). The Current Record box shows that record 1 is the current record.

2. Click the **Next record** navigation button ▶. The second record is now highlighted, which identifies it as the current record. Also, notice that the second record's value for the ContractNum field is selected, and the Current Record box displays "2 of 65" to indicate that the second record is the current record.

3. Click the **Last record** navigation button ⏭. The last record in the table, record 65, is now the current record.

4. Drag the scroll box in the vertical scroll bar (see Figure 1-18) up to the top of the bar. Notice that record 65 is still the current record, as indicated in the Current Record box. Dragging the scroll box changes the display of the table datasheet, but does not change the current record.

5. Drag the scroll box in the vertical scroll bar back down until you can see the end of the table and the current record (record 65).

6. Click the **Previous record** navigation button ◀. Record 64 is now the current record.

7. Click the **First record** navigation button ⏮. The first record is now the current record and is visible on the screen.

The Contract table now contains all the data about the customer contracts for Belmont Landscapes. To better understand how to work with this data, Oren asks you to create simple objects for the other main types of database objects—queries, forms, and reports.

Creating a Simple Query

As noted earlier, a query is a question you ask about the data stored in a database. When you create a query, you tell Access which fields you need and what criteria Access should use to select the records that will answer your question. Then Access displays only the information you want, so you don't have to navigate through the entire database for the information. In the Contract table, for example, Oren might create a query to display only those records for contracts that were signed in a specific month. Even though a query can display table information in a different way, the information still exists in the table as it was originally entered.

Oren wants to focus on the amount of each contract and the contract type. He doesn't want the list to include all the fields in the Contract table, such as CustomerID and

SigningDate. To produce this list for Oren, you'll use the Simple Query Wizard to create a query based on the Contract table.

To start the Simple Query Wizard:

▶ **1.** Click the **Create** tab on the Ribbon.

▶ **2.** In the Queries group on the Create tab, click the **Query Wizard** button. The New Query dialog box opens.

▶ **3.** Make sure **Simple Query Wizard** is selected, and then click the **OK** button. The first Simple Query Wizard dialog box opens. See Figure 1-20.

Figure 1-20 First Simple Query Wizard dialog box

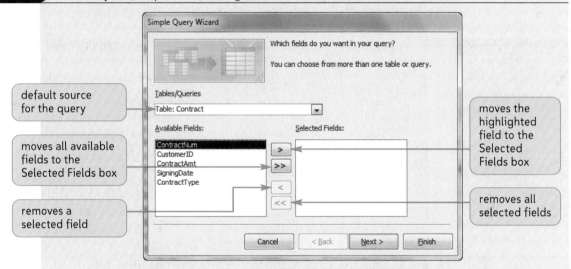

Because the Contract table is the only object in the Belmont database, it is listed in the Tables/Queries box by default. If the database contained more objects, you could click the Tables/Queries arrow and choose another table or a query as the basis for the new query you are creating. The Available Fields box lists all the fields in the Contract table.

You need to select fields from the Available Fields box to include them in the query. To select fields one at a time, click a field and then click the > button. The selected field moves from the Available Fields box on the left to the Selected Fields box on the right. To select all the fields, click the >> button. If you change your mind or make a mistake, you can remove a field by clicking it in the Selected Fields box and then clicking the < button. To remove all selected fields, click the << button.

Each Simple Query Wizard dialog box contains buttons on the bottom that allow you to move to the previous dialog box (Back button), move to the next dialog box (Next button), or cancel the creation process (Cancel button). You can also finish creating the object (Finish button) and accept the wizard's defaults for the remaining options.

Oren wants his list to include data from only the following fields: ContractNum, ContractAmt, and ContractType. You need to select these fields to include them in the query.

To create the query using the Simple Query Wizard:

TIP

You can also double-click a field to move it from the Available Fields box to the Selected Fields box.

▶ 1. Click **ContractNum** in the Available Fields box to select the field (if necessary), and then click the > button. The ContractNum field moves to the Selected Fields box.

▶ 2. Repeat Step 1 for the fields **ContractAmt** and **ContractType**, and then click the **Next** button. The second Simple Query Wizard dialog box opens and asks if you want a detail or summary query. This dialog box opens when the values in one of the fields selected for the query could be used in calculations—in this case, the ContractAmt field. Oren wants to see every field of every record and does not want to perform summary calculations on the ContractAmt field values, so you need to create a detail query.

▶ 3. Make sure the **Detail** option button is selected, and then click the **Next** button. The third, and final, Simple Query Wizard dialog box opens and asks you to choose a name (title) for your query. Access suggests the name "Contract Query" because the query you are creating is based on the Contract table. You'll change the suggested name to "ContractList."

▶ 4. Click at the end of the suggested name, use the **Backspace** key to delete the word "Query" and the space, and then type **List**. Now you can view the query results.

▶ 5. Click the **Finish** button to complete the query. Access displays the query results in Datasheet view, on a new tab named "ContractList." A query datasheet is similar to a table datasheet, showing fields in columns and records in rows—but only for those fields and records you want to see, as determined by the query specifications you select.

▶ 6. Place the pointer on the vertical line to the right of the ContractType field name until the pointer changes to a ↔ shape, and then double-click the pointer. All the ContractType field values are now fully displayed. See Figure 1-21.

Figure 1-21   Query results

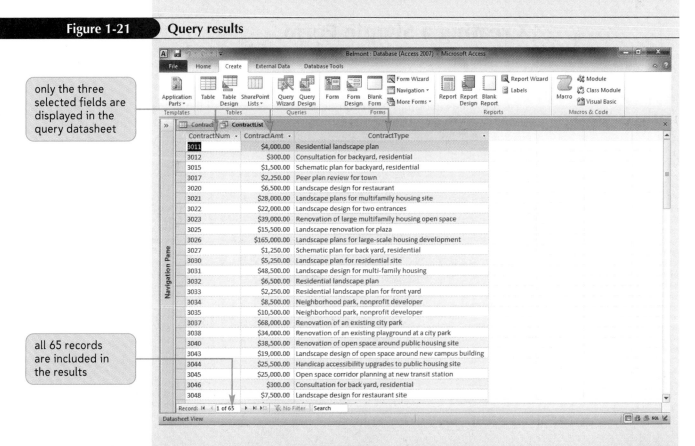

only the three selected fields are displayed in the query datasheet

all 65 records are included in the results

ContractNum	ContractAmt	ContractType
3011	$4,000.00	Residential landscape plan
3012	$300.00	Consultation for backyard, residential
3015	$1,500.00	Schematic plan for backyard, residential
3017	$2,250.00	Peer plan review for town
3020	$6,500.00	Landscape design for restaurant
3021	$28,000.00	Landscape plans for multifamily housing site
3022	$22,000.00	Landscape design for two entrances
3023	$39,000.00	Renovation of large multifamily housing open space
3025	$15,500.00	Landscape renovation for plaza
3026	$165,000.00	Landscape plans for large-scale housing development
3027	$1,250.00	Schematic plan for back yard, residential
3030	$5,250.00	Landscape plan for residential site
3031	$48,500.00	Landscape design for multi-family housing
3032	$6,500.00	Residential landscape plan
3033	$2,250.00	Residential landscape plan for front yard
3034	$8,500.00	Neighborhood park, nonprofit developer
3035	$10,500.00	Neighborhood park, nonprofit developer
3037	$68,000.00	Renovation of an existing city park
3038	$34,000.00	Renovation of an existing playground at a city park
3040	$38,500.00	Renovation of open space around public housing site
3043	$19,000.00	Landscape design of open space around new campus building
3044	$25,500.00	Handicap accessibility upgrades to public housing site
3045	$25,000.00	Open space corridor planning at new transit station
3046	$300.00	Consultation for back yard, residential
3048	$7,500.00	Landscape design for restaurant site

Record: 1 of 65   No Filter   Search

Datasheet View

The ContractList query datasheet displays the three selected fields for each record in the Contract table. The fields are shown in the order you selected them in the Simple Query Wizard, from left to right. The records are listed in order by the primary key field, ContractNum. Even though the query datasheet displays only the three fields you chose for the query, the Contract table still includes all the fields for all records.

Notice that the navigation buttons are located at the bottom of the window. You navigate a query datasheet in the same way that you navigate a table datasheet.

▶ **7.** Click the **Last record** navigation button ⏭. The last record in the query datasheet is now the current record.

▶ **8.** Click the **Previous record** navigation button ◀. Record 64 in the query datasheet is now the current record.

▶ **9.** Click the **First record** navigation button ⏮. The first record is now the current record.

▶ **10.** Click the **Close 'ContractList'** button ✕ on the object tab. A dialog box opens asking if you want to save the changes to the layout of the query. This dialog box opens because you resized the ContractType column.

▶ **11.** Click the **Yes** button to save the query layout changes and close the query.

The query results are not stored in the database; however, the query design is stored as part of the database with the name you specified. You can re-create the query results at any time by opening the query again. You'll learn more about creating and working with queries in Tutorial 3.

Next, Oren asks you to create a form for the Contract table so that Belmont Landscapes employees can use the form to enter and work with data in the table easily.

Creating a Simple Form

As noted earlier, you use a form to enter, edit, and view records in a database. Although you can perform these same functions with tables and queries, forms can present data in many customized and useful ways.

Oren wants a form for the Contract table that shows all the fields for one record at a time, with fields listed one below another in a column. This type of form will make it easier for his staff to focus on all the data for a particular contract. You'll use the Form tool to create this form quickly and easily.

To create the form using the Form tool:

▶ **1.** Make sure the Contract table is still open in Datasheet view. The table or other database object you're using as the basis for the form must either be open or selected in the Navigation Pane when you use the Form tool.

Trouble? If the Contract table is not open, click the Shutter Bar Open/Close Button ≫ to open the Navigation Pane. Then double-click Contract to open the Contract table in Datasheet view. Click the Shutter Bar Open/Close Button ≪ to close the pane.

▶ **2.** In the Forms group on the Create tab, click the **Form** button. The Form tool creates a simple form showing every field in the Contract table and places it on a tab named "Contract." Access assigns this name because the form is based on the Contract table. See Figure 1-22.

Figure 1-22	Form created by the Form tool

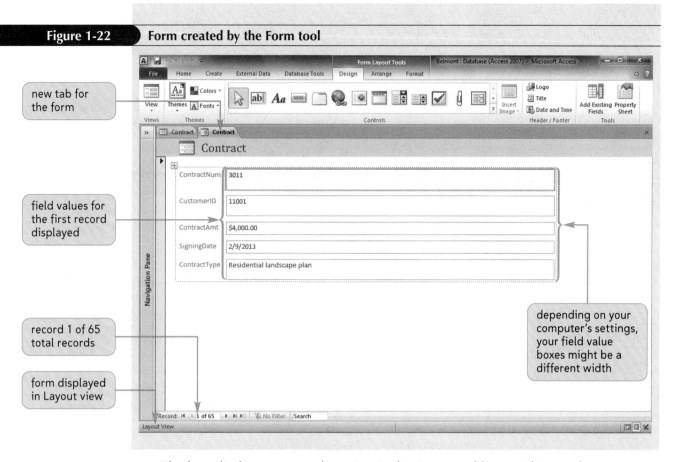

new tab for the form

field values for the first record displayed

record 1 of 65 total records

form displayed in Layout view

depending on your computer's settings, your field value boxes might be a different width

The form displays one record at a time in the Contract table, providing another view of the data that is stored in the table and allowing you to focus on the values for one record. Access displays the field values for the first record in the table and selects the first field value (ContractNum) by placing a border around the value. Each field name appears on a separate line and on the same line as its field value, which appears in a box to the right. Depending on your computer's settings, the field value boxes in your form might be wider or narrower than those shown in the figure. As indicated in the status bar, the form is displayed in Layout view. In **Layout view**, you can make design changes to the form while it is displaying data, so that you can see the effects of the changes you make immediately.

To view and maintain data using a form, you must know how to move from field to field and from record to record. Notice that the form contains navigation buttons, similar to those available in Datasheet view, which you can use to display different records in the form. You'll use these now to navigate the form; then you'll save and close the form.

To navigate, save, and close the form:

1. Click the **Next record** navigation button ▶. The form now displays the values for the second record in the Contract table.

2. Click the **Last record** navigation button ▶I to move to the last record in the table. The form displays the information for contract number 3110.

3. Click the **Previous record** navigation button ◀ to move to record 64.

4. Click the **First record** navigation button I◀ to return to the first record in the Contract table.

Next, you'll save the form with the name "ContractData" in the Belmont database. Then the form will be available for later use.

▶ **5.** Click the **Save** button 🔲 on the Quick Access Toolbar. The Save As dialog box opens.

▶ **6.** In the Form Name box, click at the end of the highlighted word "Contract," type **Data**, and then press the **Enter** key. Access saves the form as ContractData in the Belmont database and closes the dialog box. The tab containing the form now displays the name ContractData.

▶ **7.** Click the **Close 'ContractData'** button ✖ on the object tab to close the form.

After attending a staff meeting, Oren returns with another request. He would like to see the information in the Contract table presented in a more readable format. You'll help Oren by creating a report.

Creating a Simple Report

As noted earlier, a report is a formatted printout (or screen display) of the contents of one or more tables or queries. You'll use the Report tool to quickly produce a report based on the Contract table for Oren. The Report tool creates a report based on the selected table or query.

To create the report using the Report tool:

▶ **1.** With the Contract table open in Datasheet view, click the **Create** tab on the Ribbon.

▶ **2.** In the Reports group, click the **Report** button. The Report tool creates a simple report showing every field in the Contract table and places it on a tab named "Contract." Again, Access assigns this name because the object you created (the report) is based on the Contract table. See Figure 1-23.

Trouble? The records in your report might appear in a different order from the records shown in Figure 1-23. This difference will not cause any problems.

Figure 1-23   **Report created by the Report tool**

current day, date, and time displayed (yours might differ)

column headings appear in a different font color

report graphic

borders around field values

report displayed in Layout view

dotted lines show the page edges

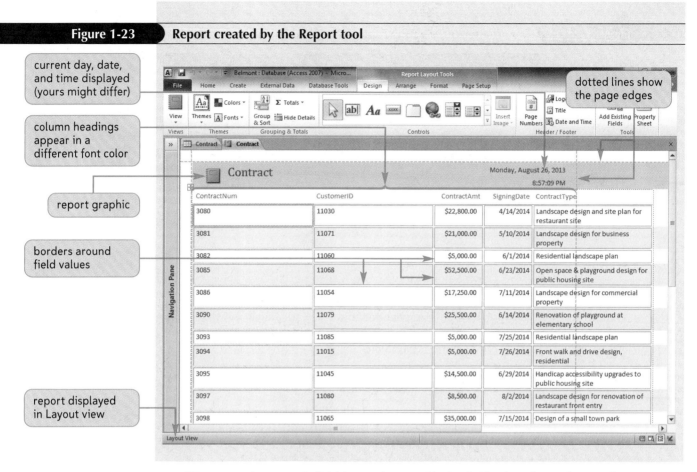

The report shows each field in a column, with the field values for each record in a row, similar to a datasheet. However, the report offers a more visually appealing format for the data, with the column headings in a different color, borders around each field value, a graphic of a report at the top left, and the current day, date, and time at the top right. Also notice the dotted horizontal and vertical lines on the top and right, respectively; these lines mark the edges of the page and show where text will print on the page.

The report needs some design changes to better display the data. The columns are much wider than necessary for the ContractNum and CustomerID fields, and the ContractType field's values and borders are not completely displayed within the page area defined by the dotted lines, which means they would not appear on the printed report. You can resize the columns easily in Layout view.

To resize the ContractNum and CustomerID columns:

1. Position the pointer on the right border of any field value in the ContractNum column until the pointer changes to a ↔ shape.

2. Click and drag the mouse to the left; dark outlines surround the field name and each field value to show the column width as you change it. Drag to the left until the column is slightly wider than the ContractNum field name.

3. Release the mouse button. The ContractNum column is now narrower, and the other four columns shifted to the left. The ContractType field, values, and borders are almost completely within the page area. See Figure 1-24.

Figure 1-24   Report after resizing the ContractNum column

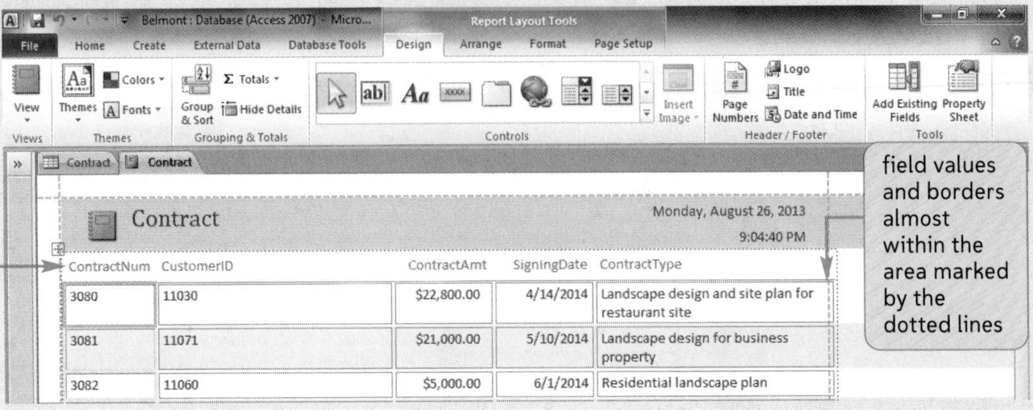

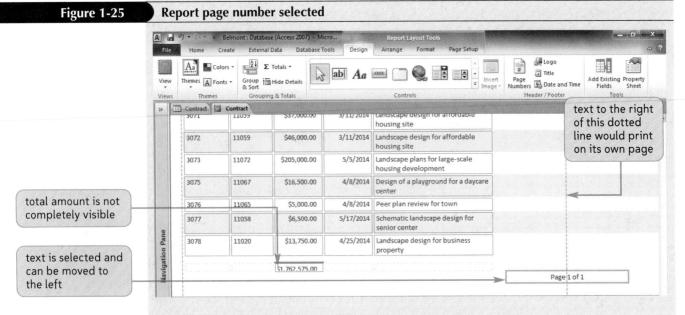

4. Click the first field value for CustomerID to establish the field as the current field.

5. Position the pointer on the right edge of the first value in the CustomerID column until the pointer changes to a ↔ shape, click and drag to the left until the column is slightly wider than its field name, and then release the mouse button. Now the entire ContractType field, values, and borders are within the report's page area.

6. Drag the scroll box on the vertical scroll bar all the way down to the bottom of the report to check its entire layout.

The Report tool automatically displays the page number at the bottom right, but the text "Page 1 of 1" appears cut off through the vertical dotted line. This will cause a problem when you print the report, so you need to move this text to the left.

7. Click anywhere on the words **Page 1 of 1**. An orange outline appears around the text, indicating it is selected. See Figure 1-25.

Figure 1-25   Report page number selected

With the text selected, you can use the keyboard arrow keys to move it.

TIP

You can also use the mouse to drag the selected page number.

8. Press the ← key repeatedly until the selected page number is to the left of the vertical dotted line (roughly 35 times). The page number text is now completely within the page area and will print on the same page as the rest of the report.

Notice the total amount shown at the end of the report for the ContractAmt field. The Report tool calculated this amount and displayed it on the report. Often, you want to include information such as summaries and totals in a report; in this case, the Report tool generated it for you automatically. However, the amount looks partially cut off at the left and bottom and might not print correctly. To be sure the entire value is displayed in the report, you'll resize the box containing it.

9. Click to select the total contract amount, **$1,762,575.00**. An orange outline surrounds the value, indicating it is selected.

10. Place the pointer on the right side of the box until the pointer changes to a ↔ shape, and then click and drag to the right just a little until the dollar sign is completely visible; then place the pointer on the bottom of the box until the pointer changes to ↕, and then click and drag down a little until the full field value is displayed. The report scrolls up after you release the mouse button. See Figure 1-26.

Figure 1-26	Report after moving the page number and resizing the total

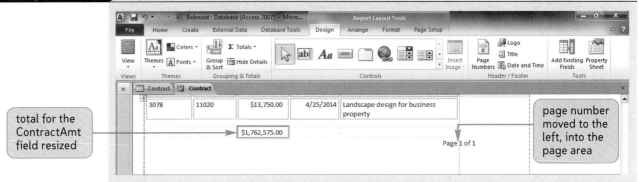

total for the ContractAmt field resized

page number moved to the left, into the page area

11. Drag the scroll box back up to redisplay the top of the report.

The report is displayed in Layout view, which doesn't show how many pages there are in the report. To see this, you need to switch to Print Preview.

To view the report in Print Preview:

1. In the Views group on the Design tab, click the **View button arrow**, and then click **Print Preview**. The first page of the report is displayed in Print Preview. See Figure 1-27.

Figure 1-27 First page of the report in Print Preview

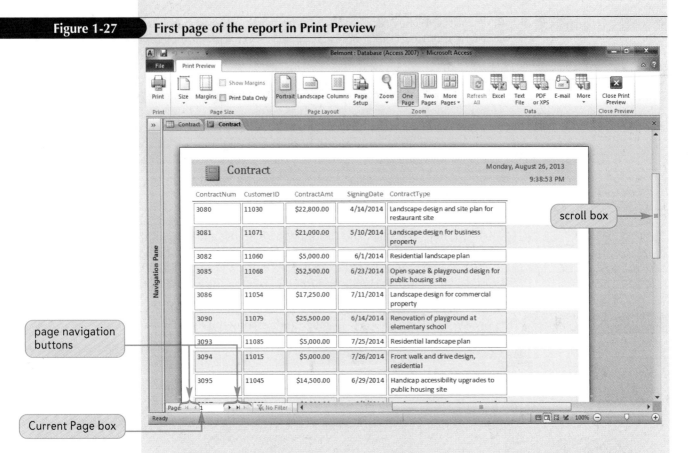

Print Preview shows exactly how the report will look when printed. Notice that Print Preview provides page navigation buttons at the bottom of the window, similar to the navigation buttons you've used to move through records in a table, query, and form.

▶ 2. Click the **Next Page** navigation button ▶ . The second page of the report is displayed in Print Preview.

▶ 3. Click the **Last Page** navigation button ▶| to move to the last page of the report.

▶ 4. Drag the scroll box in the vertical scroll bar (see Figure 1-27) down until the bottom of the report page is displayed. The notation "Page 3 of 3" appears at the bottom of the page, indicating that you are on page 3 out of a total of 3 pages in the report. Also note the total displayed for the ContractAmt field.

Trouble? Depending on the printer you are using, your report might have more or fewer pages, and some of the pages might be blank. If so, don't worry. Different printers format reports in different ways, sometimes affecting the total number of pages and the number of records printed per page.

▶ 5. Click the **First Page** navigation button |◀ to return to the first page of the report, and then drag the scroll box in the vertical scroll bar back up so that the top of the report is displayed.

Next you'll save the report as ContractDetails, and then print it.

▶ 6. Click the **Save** button 🖫 on the Quick Access Toolbar. The Save As dialog box opens.

7. In the Report Name box, click at the end of the highlighted word "Contract," and then type **Details** and press the **Enter** key. Access saves the report as ContractDetails in the Belmont database and closes the dialog box. The tab containing the report now displays the name "ContractDetails."

Printing a Report

After creating a report, you typically print it to distribute it to others who need to view the report's contents. You can print a report without changing any print settings, or display the Print dialog box and select options for printing.

REFERENCE

Printing a Report

- Open the report in any view, or select the report in the Navigation Pane.
- To print the report with the default print settings, click the File tab to display Backstage view, click the Print tab, and then click Quick Print.
  or
  To display the Print dialog box and select the options you want for printing the report, click the File tab, click the Print tab, and then click Print (or, if the report is displayed in Print Preview, click the Print button in the Print group on the Print Preview tab).

Oren asks you to print the entire report with the default settings, so you'll use the Quick Print option in Backstage view.

Note: To complete the following steps, your computer must be connected to a printer.

To print the report and then close it:

1. Click the **File** tab on the Ribbon to display Backstage view.

2. Click the **Print** tab in the navigation bar, and then click **Quick Print**. The report prints with the default print settings.

   Trouble? If your report did not print, make sure that your computer is connected to a printer, and that the printer is turned on and ready to print. Then repeat Steps 1 and 2.

3. Click the **Close 'ContractDetails'** button ☒ on the object tab to close the report.

4. Click the **Close 'Contract'** button ☒ on the object tab to close the Contract table.

You can also use the Print dialog box to print other database objects, such as table and query datasheets. Most often, these objects are used for viewing and entering data, and reports are used for printing the data in a database.

Viewing Objects in the Navigation Pane

The Belmont database now contains four objects—the Contract table, the ContractList query, the ContractData form, and the ContractDetails report. You can view and work with these objects in the Navigation Pane.

To view the objects in the Belmont database:

1. Click the **Shutter Bar Open/Close Button** ⟩⟩ on the Navigation Pane to open the pane. See Figure 1-28.

| Figure 1-28 | Belmont database objects displayed in the Navigation Pane |

specifies that all objects in the database are displayed

table icon

query icon

form icon

report icon

displays a menu with options for grouping objects in the Navigation Pane

enter text here to find objects in the database containing the search text

The Navigation Pane currently displays the default category, **All Access Objects**, which lists all the database objects in the pane. Each object type (Tables, Queries, Forms, and Reports) appears in its own group. Each database object (the Contract table, the ContractList query, the ContractData form, and the ContractDetails report) has a unique icon to its left to indicate the type of object. This makes it easy for you to identify the objects and choose which one you want to open and work with.

The arrow on the All Access Objects bar displays a menu with options for various ways to group and display objects in the Navigation Pane. The Search box enables you to enter text for Access to find; for example, you could search for all objects that contain the word "Contract" in their names. Note that Access searches for objects only in the categories and groups currently displayed in the Navigation Pane.

As you continue to build the Belmont database and add more objects to it in later tutorials, you'll learn how to use the options in the Navigation Pane.

Managing a Database

One of the main tasks involved in working with database software is managing your databases and the data they contain. By managing your databases, you can ensure that they operate in the most efficient way, that the data they contain is secure, and that you can work with the data effectively. Some of the activities involved in database management include compacting and repairing a database and backing up and restoring a database.

Compacting and Repairing a Database

Whenever you open an Access database and work in it, the size of the database increases. Further, when you delete records or when you delete or replace database objects—such as queries, forms, and reports—the space that had been occupied on the disk by the deleted or replaced records or objects does not automatically become available for other records or objects. To make the space available, you must compact the database. **Compacting** a database rearranges the data and objects in a database to decrease its file size, thereby making more space available on your disk and letting you open and close the database more quickly. Figure 1-29 illustrates the compacting process.

Figure 1-29   Compacting a database

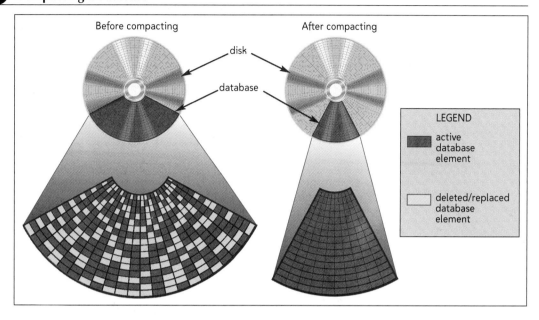

When you compact a database, Access repairs the database at the same time. In many cases, Access detects that a database is damaged when you try to open it and gives you the option to compact and repair it at that time. For example, the data in your database might become damaged, or corrupted, if you exit the Access program suddenly by turning off your computer. If you think your database might be damaged because it is behaving unpredictably, you can use the Compact & Repair Database option to fix it.

Compacting and Repairing a Database

- Make sure the database file you want to compact and repair is open.
- Click the File tab to display Backstage view.
- Make sure the Info tab is selected in the navigation bar.
- Click the Compact & Repair Database button.

Access also allows you to set an option to compact and repair a database file automatically every time you close it. The Compact on Close option is available in the Current Database section of the Access Options dialog box, which you open from Backstage view by clicking the Options command in the navigation bar. By default, the Compact on Close option is turned off.

Next, you'll compact the Belmont database manually using the Compact & Repair Database option. This will make the database smaller and cause it to use disk space more efficiently. After compacting the database, you'll close it.

To compact and repair the Belmont database:

1. Click the **File** tab on the Ribbon to display Backstage view. The Info tab in the navigation bar is selected.

   Trouble? Check with your instructor before selecting the option to compact and repair the database. If your instructor tells you not to select this option, click the Exit command in the navigation bar and skip the next two steps.

▶ **2.** Click the **Compact & Repair Database** button. Access closes Backstage view and returns to the Home tab. Although nothing visible happens on the screen, Access compacts the Belmont database, making it smaller, and repairs it at the same time.

▶ **3.** Click the **File** tab, and then click **Close Database** in the navigation bar. Access closes the Belmont database.

Backing Up and Restoring a Database

Backing up a database is the process of making a copy of the database file to protect your database against loss or damage. The Back Up Database command enables you to back up your database file from within the Access program, while you are working on your database. To use this option, click the File tab to display Backstage view, click the Save & Publish tab in the navigation bar, click Back Up Database in the Advanced section of the Save Database As pane, and then click the Save As button. In the Save As dialog box that opens, Access provides a default filename for the backup copy that consists of the same filename as the database you are backing up (for example, "Belmont"), and an underscore character, plus the current date. This filenaming system makes it easy for you to keep track of your database backups and when they were created. To restore a backup database file, you simply copy the backup from the drive on which it is stored to your hard drive, or whatever device you use to work in Access, and start working with the restored database file. (You will not actually back up the Belmont database in this tutorial.)

PROSKILLS

Problem Solving: Planning and Performing Database Backups

Experienced database users make it a habit to back up a database before they work with it for the first time, keeping the original data intact, and to make frequent backups while continuing to work with a database. Most users back up their databases on tapes, USB drives, recordable CDs or DVDs, external hard drives, or network hard drives. Also, it is recommended to store the backup copy in a different location from the original. For example, if the original database is stored on a USB drive, you should not store the backup copy on the same USB drive. If you lose the drive or the drive is damaged, you would lose both the original database and its backup copy.

If the original database file and the backup copy have the same name, restoring the backup copy might replace the original. If you want to save the original file, rename it before you restore the backup copy. To ensure that the restored database has the most current data, you should update the restored database with any changes made to the original between the time it became damaged or lost and the time you created the backup copy.

By properly planning for and performing backups, you can avoid losing data and prevent the time-consuming effort required to rebuild a lost or damaged database.

With the Contract table in place, you can continue to build the Belmont database so that Oren and his staff members can use it to store, manipulate, and retrieve important data for Belmont Landscapes. In the following tutorials, you'll help Oren complete and maintain the database, and you'll use it to meet the specific information needs of the firm's employees.

Session 1.2 Quick Check

REVIEW

1. True or False: You can copy records from any Access database table and paste them in another table.
2. A(n) _____ is a question you ask about the data stored in a database.
3. The quickest way to create a form is to use the _____.
4. To see the total number of pages in a report and navigate through the report pages, you need to display the report in _____.
5. In the Navigation Pane, each database object has a unique _____ to its left that identifies the object's type.
6. _____ a database rearranges the data and objects in a database to decrease its file size.
7. _____ a database is the process of making a copy of the database file to protect the database against loss or damage.

Practice the skills
you learned in
the tutorial using
the same case
scenario.

PRACTICE

Review Assignments

Data File needed for the Review Assignments: Provider.accdb

In the Review Assignments, you'll create a new database to contain information about
the suppliers that Belmont Landscapes works with on its landscape design projects.
Complete the following steps:

1. Create a new, blank database named **Supplier**, and save it in the Access1\Review
   folder provided with your Data Files.
2. In Datasheet view for the Table1 table, rename the default ID primary key field to
   CompanyID. Change the data type of the CompanyID field to Text.
3. Add the following 10 fields to the new table in the order shown; all of them are Text
   fields *except* InitialContact, which is a Date/Time field: **Company**, **Product**, **Address**,
   City, **State**, **Zip**, **Phone**, **ContactFirst**, **ContactLast**, and **InitialContact**. Resize the
   columns as necessary so that the complete field names are displayed. Save the table
   as **Company**.
4. Enter the records shown in Figure 1-30 in the Company table. For the first record,
   be sure to enter your first name in the ContactFirst field and your last name in the
   ContactLast field.

Figure 1-30	Company table records

CompanyID	Company	Product	Address	City	State	Zip	Phone	ContactFirst	ContactLast	InitialContact
AND225	Anderson OnSite	Site furnishings	200 Lincoln Dr	Kalamazoo	MI	49007	269-337-9266	Student First	Student Last	6/3/2012
HOL292	Holland Nursery	Plants	380 W 20th St	Holland	MI	49424	616-396-9330	Brenda	Ehlert	9/2/2013
BES327	Best Paving	Pavers	780 N Main St	Rockford	MI	49341	616-866-6364	Shirley	Hauser	2/14/2013
MID312	Midwest Lighting	Outdoor lighting	435 Central Dr	Battle Creek	MI	49014	269-979-3970	Weston	Caldwell	5/15/2012
BAC200	Backyard Structures	Play equipment	105 E 8th St	Holland	MI	49423	616-396-3989	Alan	Bastian	4/15/2012

5. Oren created a database named Provider that contains a Business table with supplier
   data. The Company table you created has the same design as the Business table.
   Copy all the records from the **Business** table in the **Provider** database (located in the
   Access1\Review folder provided with your Data Files) and paste them at the end of
   the Company table in the Supplier database.
6. Resize columns in the datasheet, as necessary, so that all the field values are completely displayed, and then save the Company table.
7. Close the Company table, and then use the Navigation Pane to reopen it. Note that
   the records are displayed in primary key order.
8. Use the Simple Query Wizard to create a query that includes the Company, Product,
   ContactFirst, ContactLast, and Phone fields (in that order) from the Company table.
   Name the query **CompanyList**, and then close the query.
9. Use the Form tool to create a form for the Company table. Save the form as
   CompanyInfo, and then close it.
10. Use the Report tool to create a report based on the Company table. In Layout
    view, resize the CompanyID, City, State, Zip, Phone, ContactFirst, ContactLast, and
    InitialContact fields so they are slightly wider than the longest entry (either the field
    name itself or an entry in the field). Also, resize the box containing the total amount
    that appears below the CompanyID column so that the amount is completely dis-
    played. Display the report in Print Preview and verify that all the fields fit across two
    pages in the report. Save the report as **CompanyDetails**, and then close it.

11. Close the Company table, and then compact and repair the Supplier database.
12. Close the Supplier database.

Case Problem 1

APPLY

Data File needed for this Case Problem: School.accdb

Pine Hill Music School   After giving private piano lessons from her home for several years, Yuka Koyama founded the Pine Hill Music School in Portland, Oregon. Because of her popularity as a music teacher, Yuka attracted top-notch students, and her school quickly established a reputation for excellence. During the past two years, other quali- fied teachers have joined Yuka to offer instruction in voice, violin, cello, guitar, percus- sion, and other instruments. As her school continues to grow, Yuka wants to use Access to keep track of information about students, teachers, and contracts. You'll help Yuka create and maintain an Access database to store data about her school. Complete the following:

1. Create a new, blank database named **Pinehill**, and save it in the Access1\Case1 folder provided with your Data Files.

2. In Datasheet view for the Table1 table, rename the default primary key ID field to **TeacherID**. Change the data type of the TeacherID field to Text.

3. Add the following five fields to the new table in the order shown; all of them are Text fields *except* HireDate, which is a Date/Time field: **FirstName**, **LastName**, **Degree**, **School**, and **HireDate**. Save the table as **Teacher**.

4. Enter the records shown in Figure 1-31 in the Teacher table. For the first record, be sure to enter your first name in the FirstName field and your last name in the LastName field.

Figure 1-31   **Teacher table records**

TeacherID	FirstName	LastName	Degree	School	HireDate
55-5310	Student First	Student Last	BA	Lewis & Clark College	4/21/2012
13-1100	Yuka	Koyama	MM	Pacific University	1/13/2012
17-1798	Richard	Jacobson	PhD	Pacific University	1/15/2012
22-0102	Andre	Dvorak	BM	University of Portland	3/3/2012
34-4506	Marilyn	Schwartz	BM	University of Portland	5/1/2012

5. Yuka created a database named School that contains a Faculty table with teacher data. The Teacher table you created has the same design as the Faculty table. Copy all the records from the **Faculty** table in the **School** database (located in the Access1\Case1 folder provided with your Data Files) and paste them at the end of the Teacher table in the Pinehill database.

6. Resize columns in the datasheet, as necessary, so that all the field values are com- pletely displayed, and then save the Teacher table.

7. Close the Teacher table, and then use the Navigation Pane to reopen it. Note that the records are displayed in primary key order.

8. Use the Simple Query Wizard to create a query that includes the FirstName, LastName, and HireDate fields (in that order) from the Teacher table. Name the query **StartDate**, and then close the query.

9. Use the Form tool to create a form for the Teacher table. Save the form as **TeacherInfo**, and then close it.

10. Use the Report tool to create a report based on the Teacher table. In Layout view, resize each field so it is slightly wider than the longest entry (either the field name itself or an entry in the field). All six fields should fit within the page area after resizing. Move the

text "Page 1 of 1" to the left so it is within the page area. Also, resize the box containing the total amount that appears below the TeacherID column so that the amount is completely displayed. Display the report in Print Preview and verify that the fields and page number appear within the page area. Save the report as **TeacherList**, print the report (only if asked by your instructor to do so), and then close it.

11. Close the Teacher table, and then compact and repair the Pinehill database.

12. Close the Pinehill database.

Apply what you learned to create a database for a business in the fitness industry.

APPLY

Case Problem 2

Data File needed for this Case Problem: Health.accdb

Parkhurst Health & Fitness Center After many years working in various corporate settings, Martha Parkhurst decided to turn her lifelong interest in health and fitness into a new business venture and opened the Parkhurst Health & Fitness Center in Richmond, Virginia. In addition to providing the usual fitness classes and weight training facilities, the center also offers specialized programs designed to meet the needs of athletes—both young and old—who participate in certain sports or physical activities. Martha's goal in establishing such programs is twofold: to help athletes gain a competitive edge through customized training, and to ensure the health and safety of all participants through proper exercises and physical preparation. Martha wants to use Access to maintain information about the members who have joined the center and the types of programs offered. She needs your help in creating this database. Complete the following steps:

1. Create a new, blank database named **Fitness**, and save it in the Access1\Case2 folder provided with your Data Files.

2. In Datasheet view for the Table1 table, rename the default primary key ID field to **ProgramID**. Change the data type of the ProgramID field to Text.

3. Add the following three fields to the new table in the order shown; all of them are Text fields *except* MonthlyFee, which is a Currency field: **ProgramType**, **MonthlyFee**, and **PhysicalRequired**. Resize the columns as necessary so that the complete field names are displayed. Save the table as **Program**.

4. Enter the records shown in Figure 1-32 in the Program table.

Figure 1-32 Program table records

ProgramID	ProgramType	MonthlyFee	PhysicalRequired
201	Junior Full (ages 13-17)	$40.00	Yes
202	Junior Limited (ages 13-17)	$30.00	Yes
203	Young Adult Full (ages 18-25)	$50.00	No
204	Young Adult Limited (ages 18-25)	$35.00	No

5. Martha created a database named Health that contains a Class table with program data. The Program table you created has the same design as the Class table. Copy all the records from the **Class** table in the **Health** database (located in the Access1\Case2 folder provided with your Data Files) and paste them at the end of the Program table in the Fitness database.

6. Resize columns in the datasheet, as necessary, so that all the field values are completely displayed, and then save the Program table.

7. Use the Simple Query Wizard to create a query that includes all the fields from the Program table. In the second Simple Query Wizard dialog box, select the Detail option. Save the query as **ProgramData**. Resize the columns in the query datasheet so that all the field values are completely displayed, if necessary, and then close the query.

8. Use the Form tool to create a form for the Program table. Save the form as **ProgramInfo**, and then close it.

9. Use the Report tool to create a report based on the Program table. In Layout view, resize the ProgramID and PhysicalRequired fields so they are slightly wider than the longest entry (either the field name itself or an entry in the field). All four fields should fit within the page area after resizing. Move the text "Page 1 of 1" to the left so it is within the page area. Also, resize the box containing the total amount that appears below the MonthlyFee column so that the amount is completely displayed. Display the report in Print Preview and verify that the fields and page number fit within the page area. Save the report as **ProgramList**, print the report (only if asked by your instructor to do so), and then close it.

10. Close the Program table, and then compact and repair the Fitness database.

11. Close the Fitness database.

Expand your skills to create a database for an agency that recycles household goods.

CHALLENGE

Case Problem 3

Data File needed for this Case Problem: RRGroup.accdb

Rossi Recycling Group   The Rossi Recycling Group is a not-for-profit agency in Salina, Kansas that provides recycled household goods to needy people and families at no charge. Residents of Salina and surrounding communities donate cash and goods, such as appliances, furniture, and tools, to the Rossi Recycling Group. The group's volunteers then coordinate with local human services agencies to distribute the goods to those in need. The Rossi Recycling Group was established by Mary and Tom Rossi, who live on the outskirts of Salina on a small farm. Mary and Tom organize the volunteers to collect the goods and store the collected items in their barn for distribution. Tom wants to create an Access database to manage information about donors, their donations, and the human services agencies. Complete the following steps:

1. Create a new, blank database named **Rossi**, and then save it in the Access1\Case3 folder provided with your Data Files.

2. In Datasheet view for the Table1 table, rename the default primary key ID field to **DonorID**. Change the data type of the DonorID field to Text.

3. Add the following four Text fields to the new table in the order shown: **Title**, **FirstName**, **LastName**, and **Phone**. Resize the columns, if necessary, so that the complete field names are displayed. Save the table as **Donor**.

4. Enter the records shown in Figure 1-33 in the Donor table. For the first record, be sure to enter your title in the Title field, your first name in the FirstName field, and your last name in the LastName field.

Figure 1-33	Donor table records

DonorID	Title	FirstName	LastName	Phone
36012	Student Title	Student First	Student Last	785-823-9275
36016	Mr.	Doug	Showers	620-793-8477
36001	Mrs.	Janis	Fendrick	785-452-8736
36020	Mrs.	JoAnn	Randolph	785-309-6540
36019	Ms.	Connie	Springen	785-452-1178

5. Tom created a database named RRGroup that contains a Contributors table with data about donors. The Donor table you created has the same design as the Contributors table. Copy all the records from the **Contributors** table in the **RRGroup** database (located in the Access1\Case3 folder provided with your Data Files) and paste them at the end of the Donor table in the Rossi database.

6. If necessary, resize the columns in the datasheet so that all the field values are completely displayed, and then save the Donor table.

7. Close the Donor table, and then use the Navigation Pane to reopen it. Note that the records are displayed in primary key order.

⊕ **EXPLORE**

8. Use the Simple Query Wizard to create a query that includes all the fields in the Donor table *except* the Title field. (*Hint*: Use the >> and < buttons to select the necessary fields.) Save the query using the name **DonorPhoneList**.

⊕ **EXPLORE**

9. The query results are displayed in order by the DonorID field values. You can specify a different order by sorting the query. Display the Home tab. Then, click the insertion point anywhere in the LastName column to make it the current field. In the Sort & Filter group on the Home tab, click the Ascending button. The records are now listed in order by the values in the LastName field. Save and close the query.

⊕ **EXPLORE**

10. Use the Form tool to create a form for the Donor table. In the new form, navigate to record 8, and then print the form *for the current record only*. (*Hint*: You must use the Print dialog box in order to print only the current record. Go to Backstage view, click the Print command, and then click Print to open the Print dialog box. Click the Selected Record(s) option button and then click the OK button to print the current record.) Save the form as **DonorInfo**, and then close it.

11. Use the Report tool to create a report based on the Donor table. In Layout view, resize each field so it is slightly wider than the longest entry (either the field name itself or an entry in the field). All five fields should fit within the page area after resizing. Move the text "Page 1 of 1" to the left so it is within the page area. Also, resize the box containing the total amount that appears below the DonorID column so that the amount is completely displayed. Display the report in Print Preview and verify that the fields and page number fit within the page area. Save the report as **DonorList**. Print the report (only if asked by your instructor to do so), and then close it.

12. Close the Donor table, and then compact and repair the Rossi database.

13. Close the Rossi database.

Case Problem 4

Data File needed for this Case Problem: Travel.accdb

GEM Ultimate Vacations As guests of a friend, Griffin and Emma MacElroy spent two weeks at a magnificent villa in the south of France. This unforgettable experience stayed with them upon returning to their home in a suburb of Chicago, Illinois. As a result, they decided to open their own agency, GEM Ultimate Vacations, which specializes in locating and booking luxury rental properties, primarily in Europe. Recently, Griffin and Emma expanded their business to include properties in Africa as well. From the beginning, Griffin and Emma used computers to help them manage all aspects of their business. They recently installed Access and now would like you to create a database to store information about guests, properties, and reservations. Complete the following:

1. Create a new, blank database named **GEM**, and then save it in the Access1\Case4 folder provided with your Data Files.

2. In Datasheet view for the Table1 table, rename the default primary key ID field to **GuestID**. Change the data type of the GuestID field to Text.

3. Add the following eight Text fields to the new table in the order shown: **GuestFirst**, **GuestLast**, **Address**, **City**, **State/Prov**, **PostalCode**, **Country**, and **Phone**. Resize the columns, if necessary, so that the complete field names are displayed. Save the table as **Guest**.

4. Enter the records shown in Figure 1-34 in the Guest table. For the first record, be sure to enter your first name in the GuestFirst field and your last name in the GuestLast field.

Figure 1-34		Guest table records						

GuestID	GuestFirst	GuestLast	Address	City	State/Prov	PostalCode	Country	Phone
201	Student First	Student Last	153 Summer Ave	Evanston	IL	60201	USA	847-623-0975
203	Tom	Davis	5003 Wilson Blvd	Chicago	IL	60603	USA	312-897-4515
206	Li	Zhu	6509 Great Rd	Gary	IN	46401	USA	219-655-8109
202	Ingrid	Gorman	207 Riverside Dr West	Windsor	ON	N9A 5K4	Canada	519-977-8577
205	Richard	Nelson	34 Settlers Dr	Tinley Park	IL	60477	USA	708-292-4441

5. Emma created a database named Travel that contains a Client table with data about guests. The Guest table you created has the same design as the Client table. Copy all the records from the **Client** table in the **Travel** database (located in the Access1\Case4 folder provided with your Data Files) and paste them at the end of the Guest table in the GEM database.

6. Resize columns in the datasheet, as necessary, so that all the field values are completely displayed, and then save the Guest table.

7. Close the Guest table, and then use the Navigation Pane to reopen it. Note that the records are displayed in primary key order.

8. Use the Simple Query Wizard to create a query that includes the following fields from the Guest table, in the order shown: GuestID, GuestLast, GuestFirst, City, and Phone. Name the query **GuestData**.

⊕ EXPLORE   9. The query results are displayed in order by the GuestID field values. You can specify a different order by sorting the query. Display the Home tab. Then, click the insertion point anywhere in the GuestLast column to make it the current field. In the Sort & Filter group on the Home tab, click the Ascending button. The records are now listed in order by the values in the GuestLast field. Save and close the query.

⊕ EXPLORE   10. Use the Form tool to create a form for the Guest table. In the new form, navigate to record 12, and then print the form *for the current record only*. (*Hint*: You must use the Print dialog box in order to print only the current record. Go to Backstage view, click the Print command, and then click Print to open the Print dialog box. Click the Selected Record(s) option button and then click the OK button to print the current record.) Save the form as **GuestInfo**, and then close it.

11. Use the Report tool to create a report based on the Guest table. In Layout view, resize each field so it is slightly wider than the longest entry (either the field name itself or an entry in the field). Move the text "Page 1 of 1" to the left so it is within the page area on the report's first page. Also, resize the box containing the total amount that appears below the GuestID column so that the amount is completely displayed. Display the report in Print Preview and notice that the columns of the report are spread across two pages. Save the report as **GuestList**.

⊕ EXPLORE   12. In the Close Preview group, click the Close Print Preview button to return to the report in Layout view. To make more room on the first page, you'll delete the Address, PostalCode, and Country columns from the report. Click anywhere in the Address column to make it active. Click the Report Layout Tools Arrange tab, and then click the Select Column button in the Rows & Columns group. Click the Home tab, and then click the Delete button in the Records group to delete the selected column. Repeat this process to delete the PostalCode and Country columns. The remaining six fields should now all fit on the report's first page.

13. Save the report, print it (only if asked by your instructor to do so), and then close it.

14. Close the Guest table, and then compact and repair the GEM database.

15. Close the GEM database.

SAM: Skills Assessment Manager

ENDING DATA FILES

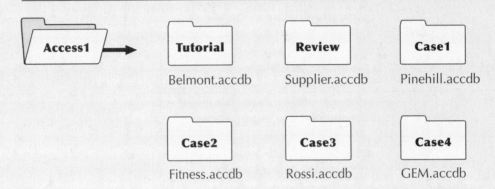

Access1 → Tutorial — Belmont.accdb

Review — Supplier.accdb

Case1 — Pinehill.accdb

Case2 — Fitness.accdb

Case3 — Rossi.accdb

Case4 — GEM.accdb

OBJECTIVES

Session 2.1
- Learn the guidelines for designing databases and setting field properties
- Modify the format of a field in Datasheet view
- Create a table in Design view
- Define fields and specify a table's primary key
- Modify the structure of a table

Session 2.2
- Import data from an Excel worksheet
- Create a table by importing an existing table structure
- Add fields to a table with the Data Type gallery
- Delete, rename, and move fields
- Add data to a table by importing a text file
- Define a relationship between two tables

Building a Database and Defining Table Relationships

Creating the Invoice and Customer Tables

Case | *Belmont Landscapes*

The Belmont database currently contains one table, the Contract table. Oren also wants to track information about the firm's customers, both residential and commercial, and the invoices sent to customers for services provided by Belmont Landscapes. This information includes such items as each customer's name and address and the invoice amount and invoice date.

In this tutorial, you'll create two new tables in the Belmont database—named Invoice and Customer—to contain the additional data Oren wants to track. You will use two different methods for creating the tables, and learn how to modify the fields. After adding records to the tables, you will define the necessary relationships between the tables in the Belmont database to relate the tables, enabling Oren and his staff to work with the data more efficiently.

STARTING DATA FILES

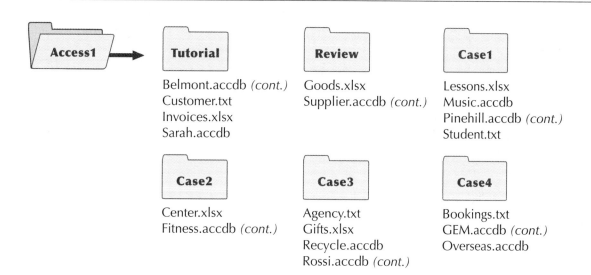

Access1 →

Tutorial

Belmont.accdb *(cont.)*
Customer.txt
Invoices.xlsx
Sarah.accdb

Review

Goods.xlsx
Supplier.accdb *(cont.)*

Case1

Lessons.xlsx
Music.accdb
Pinehill.accdb *(cont.)*
Student.txt

Case2

Center.xlsx
Fitness.accdb *(cont.)*

Case3

Agency.txt
Gifts.xlsx
Recycle.accdb
Rossi.accdb *(cont.)*

Case4

Bookings.txt
GEM.accdb *(cont.)*
Overseas.accdb

SESSION 2.1 VISUAL OVERVIEW

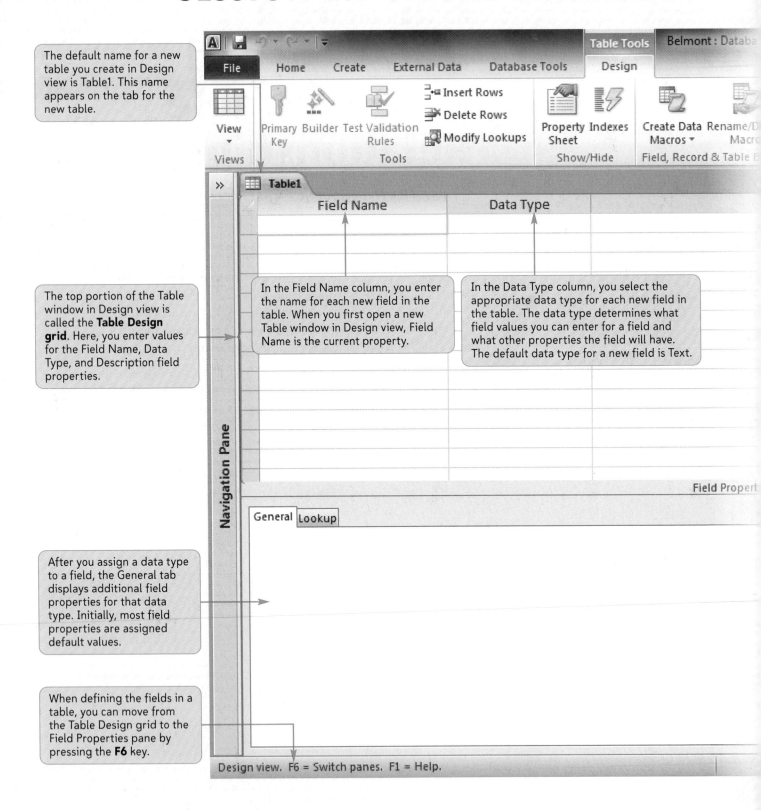

The default name for a new table you create in Design view is Table1. This name appears on the tab for the new table.

The top portion of the Table window in Design view is called the **Table Design grid**. Here, you enter values for the Field Name, Data Type, and Description field properties.

In the Field Name column, you enter the name for each new field in the table. When you first open a new Table window in Design view, Field Name is the current property.

In the Data Type column, you select the appropriate data type for each new field in the table. The data type determines what field values you can enter for a field and what other properties the field will have. The default data type for a new field is Text.

After you assign a data type to a field, the General tab displays additional field properties for that data type. Initially, most field properties are assigned default values.

When defining the fields in a table, you can move from the Table Design grid to the Field Properties pane by pressing the **F6** key.

TABLE WINDOW IN DESIGN VIEW

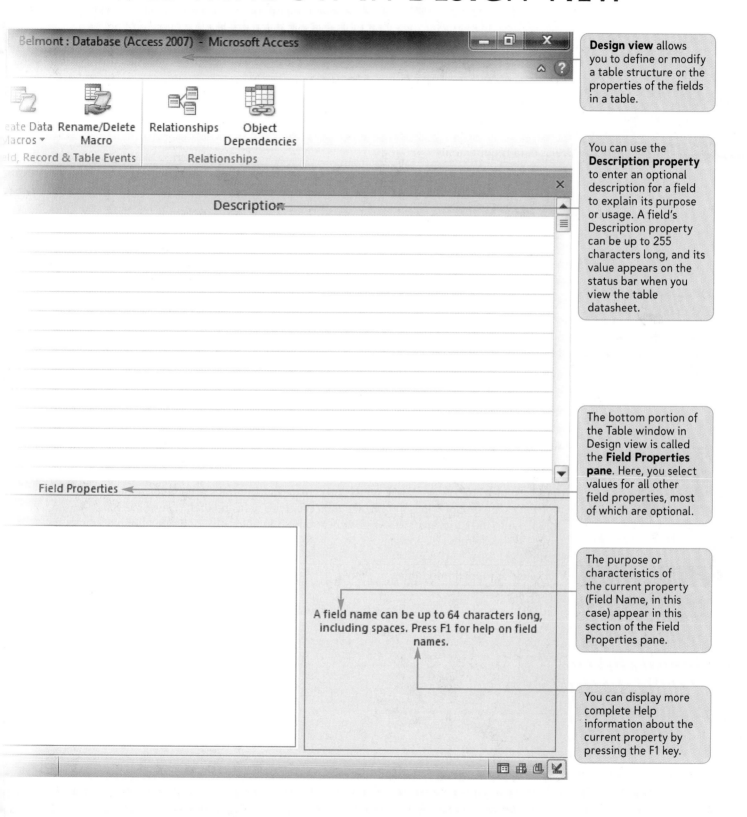

Design view allows you to define or modify a table structure or the properties of the fields in a table.

You can use the **Description property** to enter an optional description for a field to explain its purpose or usage. A field's Description property can be up to 255 characters long, and its value appears on the status bar when you view the table datasheet.

The bottom portion of the Table window in Design view is called the **Field Properties pane**. Here, you select values for all other field properties, most of which are optional.

The purpose or characteristics of the current property (Field Name, in this case) appear in this section of the Field Properties pane.

You can display more complete Help information about the current property by pressing the F1 key.

Guidelines for Designing Databases

A database management system can be a useful tool, but only if you first carefully design the database so that it meets the needs of its users. In database design, you determine the fields, tables, and relationships needed to satisfy the data and processing requirements. When you design a database, you should follow these guidelines:

- **Identify all the fields needed to produce the required information.** For example, Oren needs information about contracts, invoices, and customers. Figure 2-1 shows the fields that satisfy these information requirements.

| Figure 2-1 | Oren's data requirements |

ContractNum	ContractAmt
CustomerID	SigningDate
Company	InvoiceDate
FirstName	ContractType
LastName	Phone
Address	InvoicePaid
City	InvoiceNum
State	InvoiceAmt
Zip	

- **Organize each piece of data into its smallest useful part.** For example, Oren could store each customer's complete name in one field called CustomerName instead of using two fields called FirstName and LastName, as shown in Figure 2-1. However, doing so would make it more difficult to work with the data. If Oren wanted to view the records in alphabetical order by last name, he wouldn't be able to do so with field values such as "Tom Cotter" and "Ray Yost" stored in a CustomerName field. He could do so with field values such as "Cotter" and "Yost" stored separately in a LastName field.
- **Group related fields into tables.** For example, Oren grouped the fields related to contracts into the Contract table, which you created in Tutorial 1. The fields related to invoices are grouped into the Invoice table, and the fields related to customers are grouped into the Customer table. Figure 2-2 shows the fields grouped into all three tables for the Belmont database.

| Figure 2-2 | Oren's fields grouped into tables |

Contract table	Invoice table	Customer table
ContractNum	InvoiceNum	CustomerID
CustomerID	ContractNum	Company
ContractAmt	InvoiceAmt	FirstName
SigningDate	InvoiceDate	LastName
ContractType	InvoicePaid	Phone
		Address
		City
		State
		Zip

- **Determine each table's primary key.** Recall that a primary key uniquely identifies each record in a table. For some tables, one of the fields, such as a credit card number, naturally serves the function of a primary key. For other tables, two or more fields might be needed to function as the primary key. In these cases, the primary key is called a

composite key. For example, a school grade table would use a combination of student number and course code to serve as the primary key. For a third category of tables, no single field or combination of fields can uniquely identify a record in a table. In these cases, you need to add a field whose sole purpose is to serve as the table's primary key. For Oren's tables, ContractNum is the primary key for the Contract table, InvoiceNum is the primary key for the Invoice table, and CustomerID is the primary key for the Customer table.

- **Include a common field in related tables.** You use the common field to connect one table logically with another table. For example, Oren's Contract and Customer tables include the CustomerID field as a common field. Recall that when you include the primary key from one table as a field in a second table to form a relationship, the field is called a foreign key in the second table; therefore, the CustomerID field is a foreign key in the Contract table. With this common field, Oren can find all contracts for a particular customer; he can use the CustomerID value for a customer and search the Contract table for all records with that CustomerID value. Likewise, he can determine which customer has a particular contract by searching the Customer table to find the one record with the same CustomerID value as the corresponding value in the Contract table. Similarly, the ContractNum field is a common field, serving as the primary key in the Contract table and a foreign key in the Invoice table.

- **Avoid data redundancy.** When you store the same data in more than one place, **data redundancy** occurs. With the exception of common fields to connect tables, you should avoid data redundancy because it wastes storage space and can cause inconsistencies. An inconsistency would exist, for example, if you type a field value one way in one table and a different way in the same table or in a second table. Figure 2-3, which contains portions of potential data stored in the Customer and Contract tables, shows an example of incorrect database design that has data redundancy in the Contract table. In Figure 2-3, the Company field in the Contract table is redundant, and one value for this field was entered incorrectly, in three different ways.

| Figure 2-3 | Incorrect database design with data redundancy |

Customer table

CustomerID	Company	FirstName	LastName
11067	Blossom Day Care Center	Christina	Garrett
11068	Grand Rapids Housing Authority	Jessica	Ropiak
11070	Legacy Companies, LTD.	Michael	Faraci
11071	Blue Star Mini Golf	Vanetta	Walker
11072	Sierra Investment Company	Rodrigo	Valencia

data redundancy

Contract table

ContractNum	CustomerID	Company	ContractAmt	SigningDate
3023	11070	Legacy Company	$39,000.00	3/22/2013
3040	11068	Grand Rapids Housing Authority	$38,500.00	7/27/2013
3042	11070	Legacies Co. Limited	$48,500.00	6/3/2013
3073	11072	Sierra Investment Company	$205,000.00	5/5/2014
3081	11071	Blue Star Mini Golf	$21,000.00	5/10/2014
3085	11070	Legacy Corp. Ltd	$30,800.00	12/28/2013
3099	11067	Blossom Day Care Center	$6,500.00	7/25/2014

inconsistent data

- **Determine the properties of each field.** You need to identify the **properties**, or characteristics, of each field so that the DBMS knows how to store, display, and process the field values. These properties include the field's name, maximum number of characters or digits, description, valid values, and other field characteristics. You will learn more about field properties later in this tutorial.

The Invoice and Customer tables you need to create will contain the fields shown in Figure 2-2. Before creating these new tables in the Belmont database, you first need to learn some guidelines for setting field properties.

Guidelines for Setting Field Properties

As just noted, the last step of database design is to determine which values to assign to the properties, such as the name and data type, of each field. When you select or enter a value for a property, you **set** the property. Access has rules for naming fields and objects, assigning data types, and setting other field properties.

Naming Fields and Objects

You must name each field, table, and other object in an Access database. Access then stores these items in the database, using the names you supply. It's best to choose a field or object name that describes the purpose or contents of the field or object so that later you can easily remember what the name represents. For example, the three tables in the Belmont database will be named Contract, Invoice, and Customer because these names suggest their contents. Note that a table or query name must be unique within a database. A field name must be unique within a table, but it can be used again in another table. Refer to the ProSkills box, "Decision Making: Naming Database Fields and Objects in Access," in Tutorial 1 for a reminder of the guidelines to follow when naming fields and database objects.

Assigning Field Data Types

Each field must have a data type, which is either assigned automatically by Access or specifically by the table designer. The data type determines what field values you can enter for the field and what other properties the field will have. For example, the Invoice table will include an InvoiceDate field, which will store date values, so you will assign the Date/Time data type to this field. Then Access will allow you to enter and manipulate only dates or times as values in the InvoiceDate field.

Figure 2-4 lists the most commonly used data types in Access, describes the field values allowed for each data type, explains when you should use each data type, and indicates the field size of each data type. You can find more complete information about all available data types in Access Help.

| Figure 2-4 | Common data types |

Data Type	Description	Field Size
Text	Allows field values containing letters, digits, spaces, and special characters. Use for names, addresses, descriptions, and fields containing digits that are not used in calculations.	0 to 255 characters; default is 255
Memo	Allows field values containing letters, digits, spaces, and special characters. Use for long comments and explanations.	1 to 65,535 characters; exact size is determined by entry
Number	Allows positive and negative numbers as field values. Numbers can contain digits, a decimal point, commas, a plus sign, and a minus sign. Use for fields that will be used in calculations, except those involving money.	1 to 15 digits
Date/Time	Allows field values containing valid dates and times from January 1, 100 to December 31, 9999. Dates can be entered in month/day/year format, several other date formats, or a variety of time formats, such as 10:35 PM. You can perform calculations on dates and times, and you can sort them. For example, you can determine the number of days between two dates.	8 bytes
Currency	Allows field values similar to those for the Number data type, but is used for storing monetary values. Unlike calculations with Number data type decimal values, calculations performed with the Currency data type are not subject to round-off error.	Accurate to 15 digits on the left side of the decimal point and to 4 digits on the right side
AutoNumber	Consists of integer values created automatically by Access each time you create a new record. You can specify sequential numbering or random numbering, which guarantees a unique field value, so that such a field can serve as a table's primary key.	9 digits
Yes/No	Limits field values to yes and no, on and off, or true and false. Use for fields that indicate the presence or absence of a condition, such as whether an order has been filled or whether an invoice has been paid.	1 character
Hyperlink	Consists of text used as a hyperlink address, which can have up to four parts: the text that appears in a field or control; the path to a file or page; a location within the file or page; and text displayed as a ScreenTip.	Up to 65,535 characters total for the four parts of the Hyperlink data type

Setting Field Sizes

The **Field Size property** defines a field value's maximum storage size for Text, Number, and AutoNumber fields only. The other data types have no Field Size property because their storage size is either a fixed, predetermined amount or is determined automatically by the field value itself, as shown in Figure 2-4. A Text field has a default field size of 255 characters; you can also set its field size by entering a number from 0 to 255. For example, the FirstName and LastName fields in the Customer table will be Text fields with a size of 20 characters and 25 characters, respectively. These field sizes will accommodate the values that will be entered in each of these fields.

PROSKILLS

Decision Making: Specifying the Field Size Property for Number Fields

When you use the Number data type to define a field, you need to decide what the most appropriate Field Size setting should be for the field. You should set the Field Size property based on the largest value that you expect to store in that field. Access processes smaller data sizes faster, using less memory, so you can optimize your database's performance and its storage space by selecting the correct field size for each field. Field Size property settings for Number fields are as follows:

- **Byte:** Stores whole numbers (numbers with no fractions) from 0 to 255 in one byte
- **Integer:** Stores whole numbers from −32,768 to 32,767 in two bytes
- **Long Integer** (default): Stores whole numbers from −2,147,483,648 to 2,147,483,647 in four bytes
- **Single:** Stores positive and negative numbers to precisely seven decimal places and uses four bytes
- **Double:** Stores positive and negative numbers to precisely 15 decimal places and uses eight bytes
- **Replication ID:** Establishes a unique identifier for replication of tables, records, and other objects in databases created using Access 2003 and earlier versions and uses 16 bytes
- **Decimal:** Stores positive and negative numbers to precisely 28 decimal places and uses 12 bytes

Choosing an appropriate field size is important to optimize efficiency. For example, it would be wasteful to use the Long Integer field size for a Number field that will store only whole numbers ranging from 0 to 255 because the Long Integer field size uses four bytes of storage space. A better choice would be the Byte field size, which uses one byte of storage space to store the same values. By first gathering and analyzing information about the number values that will be stored in a Number field, you can make the best decision for the field's Field Size property and ensure the most efficient user experience for the database.

Setting the Caption Property for Fields

The **Caption property** for a field specifies how the field name is displayed in database objects, including table and query datasheets, forms, and reports. If you don't set the Caption property, Access displays the field name as the column heading or label for a field. For example, field names such as ContractAmt and SigningDate in the Contract table can be difficult to read. Setting the Caption property for these fields to "Contract Amt" and "Signing Date" would make it easier for users to read the field names and work with the database.

INSIGHT

Setting the Caption Property vs. Naming Fields

Although Access allows you to include spaces in field names, this practice is not recommended because the spaces cause problems when you try to perform more complex tasks with the data in your database. Setting the Caption property allows you to follow best field naming practices, such as not including spaces in field names, while still providing users with more readable field names in datasheets, forms, and reports.

In Tutorial 1, you created the Belmont database and the Contract table. Before you create the new tables for the database, Oren suggests that you view the formatting of the fields in the Contract table to determine if any changes are needed to improve how the data is displayed.

Changing the Format of a Field in Datasheet View

The Formatting group on the Fields tab in Datasheet view allows you to modify some formatting for certain field types. When you format a field, you change the way data is displayed, but not the actual values stored in the table. Next, you'll open the Contract table in the Belmont database to view the formatting of the fields in the table.

To view the formatting of the Contract table's fields:

1. Start Access, open the **Belmont** database you created in Tutorial 1, and make sure the Navigation Pane is open. This database file should be located in the Access1\Tutorial folder provided with your Data Files.

   Trouble? If the Security Warning is displayed below the Ribbon, click the Enable Content button.

2. In the Navigation Pane, double-click the **Contract** table to open it in Datasheet view.

3. On the Navigation Pane, click the **Shutter Bar Open/Close Button** « to close the pane and view more of the table datasheet. See Figure 2-5.

Figure 2-5   Contract table datasheet

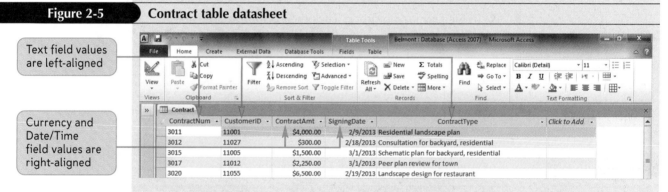

Notice that the values in the three Text fields—ContractNum, CustomerID, and ContractType—appear left-aligned within their boxes, and the values in the ContractAmt and SigningDate fields appear right-aligned. In Access, values for Text fields are left-aligned, and values for Number, Date/Time, and Currency fields are right-aligned.

The ContractAmt field contains dollar values representing the total amount of each Belmont Landscapes contract. Oren knows that these dollar amounts will never contain cents because the contracts are drawn up in whole amounts only; therefore, the two decimal places currently shown for the values are unnecessary. Further, Oren feels that the dollar signs clutter the datasheet and are also unnecessary. He asks you to modify the format of the ContractAmt field to remove the dollar signs and decimal places. You can make these changes in Datasheet view using options on the Fields tab. You'll also check the format of the SigningDate field and modify it, if necessary.

To modify the format of the ContractAmt and SigningDate fields:

1. Click the **Fields** tab on the Ribbon.

2. Click the first field value in the ContractAmt column. The options in the Formatting group indicate that this field has the Currency data type and the Currency format. See Figure 2-6.

Figure 2-6	Format of the ContractAmt field

Currency data type and Currency format

click to reduce the number of decimal places displayed

click to change the format of the field values

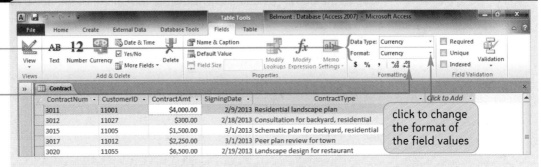

When you created the ContractAmt field in Tutorial 1, you added it as a Currency field to the table. The default format for a Currency field is the Currency format, which specifies that the values appear with dollar signs and two decimal places. You need to change this format to the Standard format, which does not display dollar signs.

3. In the Formatting group, click the **Format arrow**, and then click **Standard**. The dollar signs are removed, but the two decimal places are still displayed.

4. In the Formatting group, click the **Decrease Decimals** button ⁺⁰/.₀₀. Access decreases the decimal places by one, and the values now display only one decimal place.

5. Click the **Decrease Decimals** button ⁺⁰/.₀₀ again to remove the second decimal place and the decimal point. The ContractAmt field values are now displayed without dollar signs or decimal places. See Figure 2-7.

Figure 2-7	ContractAmt field values after modifying the format

values are now displayed without dollar signs or decimal places

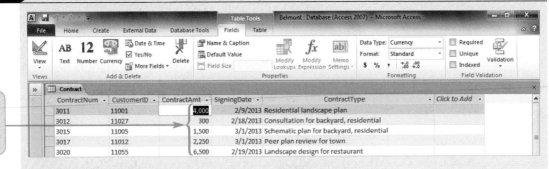

6. Press the **Tab** key to move to the SigningDate field. The Data Type option shows that this field is a Date/Time field.

By default, Access assigns the General Date format to Date/Time fields. (Even though the Format box in the Formatting group is empty, the SigningDate field has the General Date format applied to it.) The General Date format includes settings for date or time values, or a combination of date and time values. However, Oren wants *only date values* to be displayed in the SigningDate field, so he asks you to specify the Short Date format for the field.

7. In the Formatting group, click the **Format arrow**, and then click **Short Date**. See Figure 2-8.

TIP

When working with date values, you can type dates directly or click the date picker shown in Figure 2-8 to select a date from an interactive calendar.

Figure 2-8	SigningDate field after modifying the format

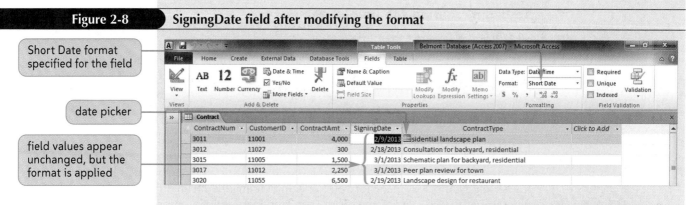

Short Date format specified for the field

date picker

field values appear unchanged, but the format is applied

Although no change is apparent in the worksheet—the SigningDate field values already appear with the Short Date setting (for example, 2/9/2013), as part of the default General Date format—the field now has the Short Date format applied to it. This ensures that only date field values, and not time or date/time values, are allowed in the field.

8. Click the **Close 'Contract'** button ⊠ on the object tab to close the table.

According to his plan for the Belmont database, Oren wants to track information about the invoices the firm sends to its customers. Next, you'll create the Invoice table for Oren—this time, working in Design view.

Creating a Table in Design View

Creating a table in Design view involves entering the field names and defining the properties for the fields, specifying a primary key for the table, and then saving the table structure. Oren documented the design for the new Invoice table by listing each field's name, data type, size (if applicable), and description, as shown in Figure 2-9.

Figure 2-9	Design for the Invoice table

Field Name	Data Type	Field Size	Description	Other
InvoiceNum	Text	4	Primary key	Caption = Invoice Num
ContractNum	Text	4	Foreign key	Caption = Contract Num
InvoiceAmt	Currency			Format = Currency
				Decimal Places = 2
				Caption = Invoice Amt
InvoiceDate	Date/Time			Format = mm/dd/yyyy
				Caption = Invoice Date
InvoicePaid	Yes/No			Caption = Invoice Paid
				Format = Yes/No

You will use Oren's design as a guide for creating the Invoice table in the Belmont database.

> **To begin creating the Invoice table:**
>
> **1.** Click the **Create** tab on the Ribbon.
>
> **2.** In the Tables group on the Create tab, click the **Table Design** button. A new table named Table1 opens in Design view. Refer to the Session 2.1 Visual Overview for a complete description of the Table window in Design view.

Defining Fields

When you first create a table in Design view, the insertion point is located in the first row's Field Name box, ready for you to begin defining the first field in the table. You enter values for the Field Name, Data Type, and Description (optional) field properties and then select values for all other field properties in the Field Properties pane. These other properties will appear when you move to the first row's Data Type box.

REFERENCE

Defining a Field in Design View

- In the Field Name box, type the name for the field, and then press the Tab key.
- Accept the default Text data type, or click the arrow and select a different data type for the field. Press the Tab key.
- Enter an optional description for the field, if necessary.
- Use the Field Properties pane to type or select other field properties, as appropriate.

The first field you need to define is the InvoiceNum field. This field will be the primary key for the Invoice table.

TIP

You can also press the Enter key to move from one property to the next in the Table Design grid.

To define the InvoiceNum field:

1. Type **InvoiceNum** in the first row's Field Name box, and then press the **Tab** key to advance to the Data Type box. The default data type, Text, appears highlighted in the Data Type box, which now also contains an arrow, and the field properties for a Text field appear in the Field Properties pane. See Figure 2-10.

Notice that the right side of the Field Properties pane now provides an explanation for the current property, Data Type.

Trouble? If you make a typing error, you can correct it by clicking to position the insertion point, and then using either the Backspace key to delete characters to the left of the insertion point or the Delete key to delete characters to the right of the insertion point. Then type the correct text.

| Figure 2-10 | Table window after entering the first field name |

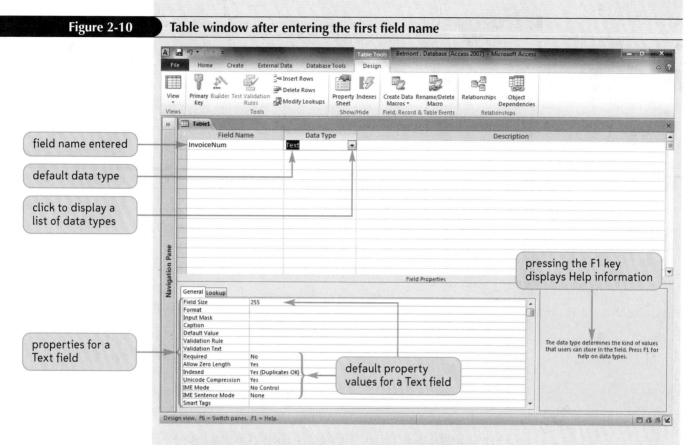

field name entered

default data type

click to display a
list of data types

properties for a
Text field

pressing the F1 key
displays Help information

default property
values for a Text field

The data type determines the kind of values
that users can store in the field. Press F1 for
help on data types.

Because the InvoiceNum field values will not be used in calculations, you will
accept the default Text data type for the field.

2. Press the **Tab** key to accept Text as the data type and to advance to the
Description box.

Next you'll enter the Description property value as "Primary key." The value you
enter for the Description property will appear on the status bar when you view the
table datasheet. Note that specifying "Primary key" for the Description property
does *not* establish the current field as the primary key; you use a button on the
Ribbon to specify the primary key in Design view, which you will do later in this
session.

3. Type **Primary key** in the Description box.

Notice the Field Size property for the field. The default setting of 255 for Text
fields is displayed. You need to change this number to 4 because all invoice numbers at Belmont Landscapes contain only four digits.

4. Double-click the number **255** in the Field Size property box to select it, and then
type **4**.

Finally, you need to set the Caption property for the field so that its name appears
with a space, as "Invoice Num."

5. Click the **Caption** property box, and then type **Invoice Num**. The definition of the first field is complete. See Figure 2-11.

Figure 2-11 | **InvoiceNum field defined**

Oren's Invoice table design (Figure 2-9) shows ContractNum as the second field. Because Oren and other staff members want to relate information about invoices to the contract data in the Contract table, the Invoice table must include the ContractNum field, which is the Contract table's primary key. Recall that when you include the primary key from one table as a field in a second table to connect the two tables, the field is a foreign key in the second table. The field must be defined in the same way in both tables.

Next, you will define ContractNum as a Text field with a field size of 4. Later in this session, you'll change the Field Size property for the ContractNum field in the Contract table to 4 so that the field definition is the same in both tables.

To define the ContractNum field:

1. In the Table Design grid, click the second row's Field Name box, type **ContractNum** in the box, and then press the **Tab** key to advance to the Data Type box.

2. Press the **Tab** key to accept Text as the field's data type. Because the ContractNum field is a foreign key to the Contract table, you'll enter "Foreign key" in the Description box to help users of the database understand the purpose of this field.

3. Type **Foreign key** in the Description box. Next, you'll change the Field Size property to 4.

4. Press the **F6** key to move to the Field Properties pane. The current entry for the Field Size property, 255, is highlighted.

5. Type **4** to set the Field Size property. Finally, you need to set the Caption property for this field.

6. Press the **Tab** key three times to move to the Caption box, and then type **Contract Num**. You have completed the definition of the second field.

The third field in the Invoice table is the InvoiceAmt field, which will display currency values, similar to the ContractAmt field in the Contract table. However, for this field, Oren wants the values to appear with two decimal places because invoice amounts might include cents. He also wants the values to include dollar signs, so that the values will be formatted as currency when they are printed in reports sent to customers.

To define the InvoiceAmt field:

1. Click the third row's Field Name box, type **InvoiceAmt** in the box, and then press the **Tab** key to advance to the Data Type box.

2. Click the **Data Type** arrow, click **Currency** in the list, and then press the **Tab** key to advance to the Description box.

   According to Oren's design (Figure 2-9), you do not need to enter a description for this field. If you've assigned a descriptive field name and the field does not fulfill a special function (such as primary key), you usually do not enter a value for the optional Description property. InvoiceAmt is a field that does not require a value for its Description property.

   Oren wants the InvoiceAmt field values to be displayed with two decimal places. The **Decimal Places property** specifies the number of decimal places that are displayed to the right of the decimal point.

TIP

You can display the arrow and the list simultaneously by clicking the right side of a box.

3. In the Field Properties pane, click the **Decimal Places** box to position the insertion point there. An arrow appears on the right side of the Decimal Places box. When you position the insertion point or select text in many Access boxes, Access displays an arrow, which you can click to display a list with options.

4. Click the **Decimal Places** arrow, and then click **2** in the list to specify two decimal places for the InvoiceAmt field values.

5. Press the **Tab** key twice to move to the Caption box, and then type **Invoice Amt**. The definition of the third field is now complete. See Figure 2-12.

| Figure 2-12 | Table window after defining the first three fields |

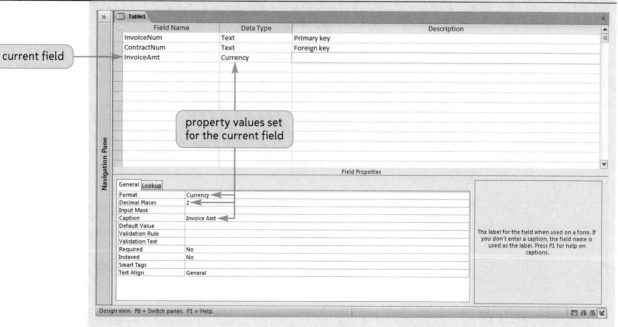

The next field you'll define in the Invoice table is InvoiceDate. This field will contain the dates on which invoices are generated for Belmont Landscapes customers. When Belmont Landscapes first draws up contracts with its customers, the firm establishes invoice dates based on the different phases of the projects. For long-term projects with multiple phases, some of these dates are months or years in the future. You'll define the InvoiceDate field using the Date/Time data type. Also, according to Oren's design (Figure 2-9), the date values should be displayed in the format mm/dd/yyyy, which is a two-digit month, a two-digit day, and a four-digit year.

To define the InvoiceDate field:

1. Click the fourth row's Field Name box, type **InvoiceDate**, and then press the **Tab** key to advance to the Data Type box.

   You can select a value from the Data Type list as you did for the InvoiceAmt field. Alternately, you can type the property value in the box or type just the first character of the property value.

2. Type **d**. The value in the fourth row's Data Type box changes to "date/Time," with the letters "ate/Time" highlighted. See Figure 2-13.

Figure 2-13 **Selecting a value for the Data Type property**

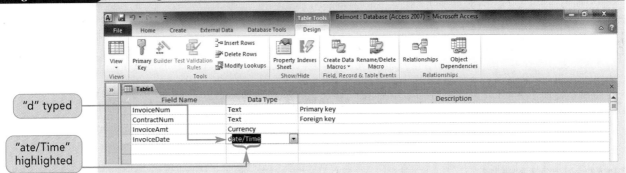

3. Press the **Tab** key to advance to the Description box. Note that Access changes the value for the Data Type property to "Date/Time."

   Oren wants the values in the InvoiceDate field to be displayed in a format showing the month, the day, and a four-digit year, as in the following example: 03/11/2013. You use the Format property to control the display of a field value.

4. In the Field Properties pane, click the right side of the **Format** box to display the list of predefined formats for Date/Time fields. As noted in the right side of the Field Properties pane, you can either choose a predefined format or enter a custom format.

   Trouble? If you see an arrow instead of a list of predefined formats, click the arrow to display the list.

   None of the predefined formats matches the exact layout Oren wants for the InvoiceDate values, so you need to create a custom date format. Figure 2-14 shows some of the symbols available for custom date and time formats.

Figure 2-14   **Symbols for some custom date formats**

TIP

A complete description of all the custom formats is available in Access Help.

Symbol	Description
/	date separator
d	day of the month in one or two numeric digits, as needed (1 to 31)
dd	day of the month in two numeric digits (01 to 31)
ddd	first three letters of the weekday (Sun to Sat)
dddd	full name of the weekday (Sunday to Saturday)
w	day of the week (1 to 7)
ww	week of the year (1 to 53)
m	month of the year in one or two numeric digits, as needed (1 to 12)
mm	month of the year in two numeric digits (01 to 12)
mmm	first three letters of the month (Jan to Dec)
mmmm	full name of the month (January to December)
yy	last two digits of the year (01 to 99)
yyyy	full year (0100 to 9999)

Oren wants the dates to be displayed with a two-digit month (mm), a two-digit day (dd), and a four-digit year (yyyy). You'll enter this custom format now.

5. Click the **Format** arrow to close the list of predefined formats, and then type **mm/dd/yyyy** in the Format box.

6. Press the **Tab** key twice to move to the Caption box, and then type **Invoice Date**. See Figure 2-15.

Figure 2-15   **Specifying the custom date format**

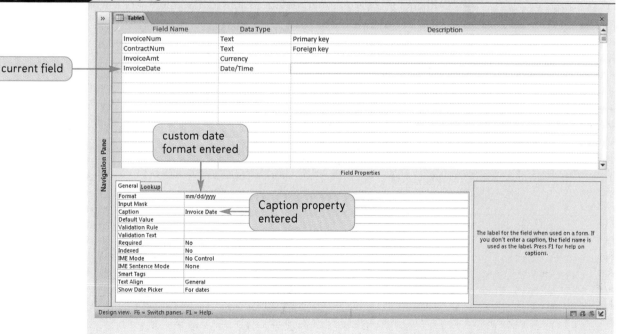

The fifth, and final, field to be defined in the Invoice table is InvoicePaid. This field will be a Yes/No field to indicate the payment status of each invoice record stored in the Invoice table. Recall that the Yes/No data type is used to define fields that store true/false, yes/no, and on/off field values. When you create a Yes/No field in a table, the default Format property is set to True/False. After setting the data type, you'll set the Format property for the InvoicePaid field to Yes/No.

To define the InvoicePaid field:

1. Click the fifth row's Field Name box, type **InvoicePaid**, and then press the **Tab** key to advance to the Data Type box.

2. Type **y**. Access completes the data type as "yes/No."

3. Press the **Tab** key to select the Yes/No data type and move to the Description box.

4. Click the **Format** box, click the **arrow** on its right side, and then click **Yes/No** to set the Format property.

5. Press the **Tab** key to move to the Caption box, and then type **Invoice Paid**.

You've finished defining the fields for the Invoice table. Next, you need to specify the primary key for the table.

Specifying the Primary Key

As you learned in Tutorial 1, the primary key for a table uniquely identifies each record in a table.

Understanding the Importance of the Primary Key

Although Access does not require a table to have a primary key, including a primary key offers several advantages:

• A primary key uniquely identifies each record in a table.

• Access does not allow duplicate values in the primary key field. For example, if a record already exists in the Contract table with a ContractNum value of 3020, Access prevents you from adding another record with this same value in the ContractNum field. Preventing duplicate values ensures the uniqueness of the primary key field.

• When a primary key has been specified, Access forces you to enter a value for the primary key field in every record in the table. This is known as **entity integrity**. If you do not enter a value for a field, you have actually given the field a **null value**. You cannot give a null value to the primary key field because entity integrity prevents Access from accepting and processing that record.

• Access stores records on disk as you enter them. You can enter records in any order, but Access displays them by default in order by the field values of the primary key. If you enter records in no specific order, you are ensured that you will later be able to work with them in a more meaningful, primary key sequence.

• Access responds faster to your requests for specific records based on the primary key.

Specifying a Primary Key in Design View

- Display the table in Design view.
- Click in the row for the field you've chosen to be the primary key to make it the active field. If the primary key will consist of two or more fields, click the row selector for the first field, press and hold down the Ctrl key, and then click the row selector for each additional primary key field.
- In the Tools group on the Design tab, click the Primary Key button.

According to Oren's design, you need to specify InvoiceNum as the primary key for the Invoice table. You can do so while the table is in Design view.

TIP

The Primary Key button works as a toggle; you can click it to remove the key symbol if you want to specify a different field as the primary key.

To specify InvoiceNum as the primary key:

1. Click in the row for the InvoiceNum field to make it the current field.

2. In the Tools group on the Design tab, click the **Primary Key** button. A key symbol appears in the row selector for the first row, indicating that the InvoiceNum field is the table's primary key. See Figure 2-16.

| Figure 2-16 | InvoiceNum field selected as the primary key |

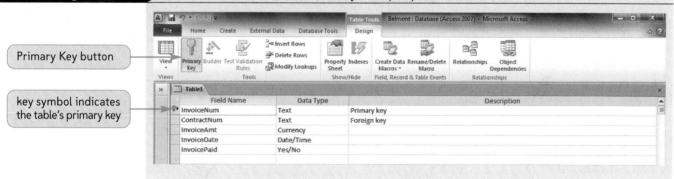

Primary Key button

key symbol indicates the table's primary key

Saving the Table Structure

The last step in creating a table is to name the table and save the table's structure. When you save a table structure, the table is stored in the database file (in this case, the Belmont database file). Once the table is saved, you can use it to enter data in the table. According to Oren's plan, you need to save the table you've defined as "Invoice."

To name and save the Invoice table:

1. Click the **Save** button 🖫 on the Quick Access Toolbar. The Save As dialog box opens.

2. Type **Invoice** in the Table Name box, and then press the **Enter** key. Access saves the Invoice table in the Belmont database. Notice that the tab for the table now displays the name "Invoice" instead of "Table1."

Modifying the Structure of an Access Table

Even a well-designed table might need to be modified. Some changes that you can make to a table's structure in Design view are changing the order of fields, adding and deleting fields, and changing field properties.

After meeting with Sarah Fisher, the office manager at Belmont Landscapes, and reviewing the structure of the Invoice table, Oren has changes he wants you to make to the table. First, he wants the InvoiceAmt field to be moved so that it appears right before the InvoicePaid field. Then, he wants you to add a new Text field, named InvoiceItem, to the table to include information about what the invoice is for, such as schematic landscape plans, construction documents, and so on. Oren would like the InvoiceItem field to be inserted between the InvoiceDate and InvoiceAmt fields.

Moving a Field

To move a field, you use the mouse to drag it to a new location in the Table Design grid. Next, you'll move the InvoiceAmt field so that it is before the InvoicePaid field.

To move the InvoiceAmt field:

▶ 1. Position the pointer on the row selector for the InvoiceAmt field until the pointer changes to a ➡ shape.

▶ 2. Click the **row selector** to select the entire InvoiceAmt row.

▶ 3. Place the pointer on the row selector for the InvoiceAmt field, click the ⬚ pointer, and then drag the ⬚ pointer to the row selector for the InvoicePaid field. See Figure 2-17.

Figure 2-17   **Moving the InvoiceAmt field in the table structure**

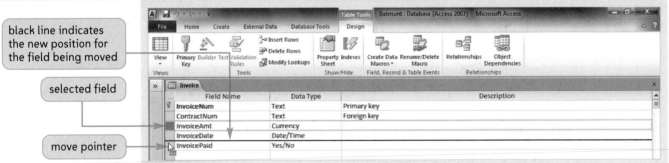

black line indicates
the new position for
the field being moved

selected field

move pointer

▶ 4. Release the mouse button. The InvoiceAmt field now appears between the InvoiceDate and InvoicePaid fields in the table structure.

   Trouble? If the InvoiceAmt field did not move, repeat Steps 1 through 4, making sure you hold down the mouse button during the drag operation.

Adding a Field

To add a new field between existing fields, you must insert a row. You begin by selecting the row below where you want the new field to be inserted.

Adding a Field Between Two Existing Fields

- In the Table window in Design view, select the row below where you want the new field to be inserted.
- In the Tools group on the Design tab, click the Insert Rows button.
- Define the new field by entering the field name, data type, optional description, and any property specifications.

Next, you need to add the InvoiceItem field to the Invoice table structure between the InvoiceDate and InvoiceAmt fields.

To add the InvoiceItem field to the Invoice table:

1. Click the **InvoiceAmt** Field Name box. You need to establish this field as the current field so that the row for the new record will be inserted above this field.

2. In the Tools group on the Design tab, click the **Insert Rows** button. Access adds a new, blank row between the InvoiceDate and InvoiceAmt fields. The insertion point is positioned in the Field Name box for the new row, ready for you to type the name for the new field. See Figure 2-18.

Figure 2-18	Table structure after inserting a row

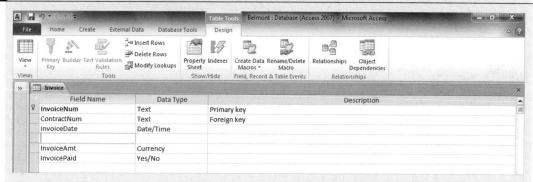

Trouble? If you selected the InvoiceAmt field's row selector and then inserted the new row, you need to click the new row's Field Name box to position the insertion point in it.

You'll define the InvoiceItem field in the new row of the Invoice table. This field will be a Text field with a field size of 40, and you need to set the Caption property to include a space between the words in the field name.

3. Type **InvoiceItem**, press the **Tab** key to move to the Data Type property, and then press the **Tab** key again to accept the default Text data type.

4. Press the **F6** key to move to the Field Size box and to select the default field size, and then type **40**.

5. Press the **Tab** key three times to move to the Caption box, and then type **Invoice Item**. The definition of the new field is complete. See Figure 2-19.

Figure 2-19 **InvoiceItem field added to the Invoice table**

new field

6. Click the **Save** button on the Quick Access Toolbar to save the changes to the Invoice table structure.

Changing Field Properties

With the Invoice table design complete, you can now go back and modify the Field Size property for the three Text fields in the Contract table. Recall that each of these fields still has the default field size of 255, which is too large for the data contained in these fields. You'll also set the Caption property for each field to include a space between the words in the field name.

To modify the Contract table's field properties:

1. Click the **Close 'Invoice'** button X on the object tab to close the Invoice table.

2. On the Navigation Pane, click the **Shutter Bar Open/Close Button** » to open the pane. Notice that the Invoice table is listed below the Contract table in the Tables section of the pane.

3. Double-click **Contract** to open the Contract table in Datasheet view. To change the Field Size property and set the Caption property, you need to display the table in Design view.

4. In the Views group on the Home tab, click the **View** button. The table is displayed in Design view with the ContractNum field selected. You need to change the Field Size property for this field to 4 because each contract number at Belmont Landscapes consists of four digits.

5. Press the **F6** key to move to and select the default setting of 255 for the Field Size property, and then type **4**. Next you need to set the Caption property for this field.

6. Press the **Tab** key three times to move to the Caption box, and then type **Contract Num**.

Next you need to set the CustomerID Field Size property to 5 because each CustomerID number at Belmont Landscapes consists of five digits. You also need to set this field's Caption property.

▶ **7.** Click the **CustomerID** Field Name box to make this the active field, press the **F6** key, type **5**, press the **Tab** key three times, and then type **Customer ID** in the Caption box.

Next you'll set the Caption property for the ContractAmt and SigningDate fields.

▶ **8.** Click the **ContractAmt** Field Name box, click the **Caption** box, type **Contract Amt**; then click the **SigningDate** Field Name box, click the **Caption** box, and then type **Signing Date**.

Finally, for the ContractType field, you will set the Field Size property to 75. This size can accommodate the longer values in the ContractType field. You'll also set this field's Caption property.

▶ **9.** Click the **ContractType** Field Name box, press the **F6** key, type **75**, press the **Tab** key three times, and then type **Contract Type**. Now you can save the modified table.

▶ **10.** Click the **Save** button 🔲 on the Quick Access Toolbar. A dialog box opens informing you that some data may be lost because you decreased the field sizes. Because you know that all of the values in the ContractNum, CustomerID, and ContractType fields include fewer characters than the new Field Size properties that you set for each field, you can ignore this message.

▶ **11.** Click the **Yes** button, and then close the Contract table.

▶ **12.** If you are not continuing to Session 2.2, click the **File** tab, and then click **Close Database** in the navigation bar to close the Belmont database.

You have created the Invoice table and made modifications to its design. In the next session, you'll add records to the Invoice table and create the Customer table in the Belmont database.

Session 2.1 Quick Check

REVIEW

1. What guidelines should you follow when designing a database?
2. What is the purpose of the Data Type property for a field?
3. The _____ property specifies how a field's name is displayed in database objects, including table and query datasheets, forms, and reports.
4. For which three types of fields can you assign a field size?
5. The default Field Size property setting for a Text field is _____.
6. In Design view, which key do you press to move from the Table Design grid to the Field Properties pane?
7. A(n) _____ value, which results when you do not enter a value for a field, is not permitted for a primary key.

SESSION 2.2 VISUAL OVERVIEW

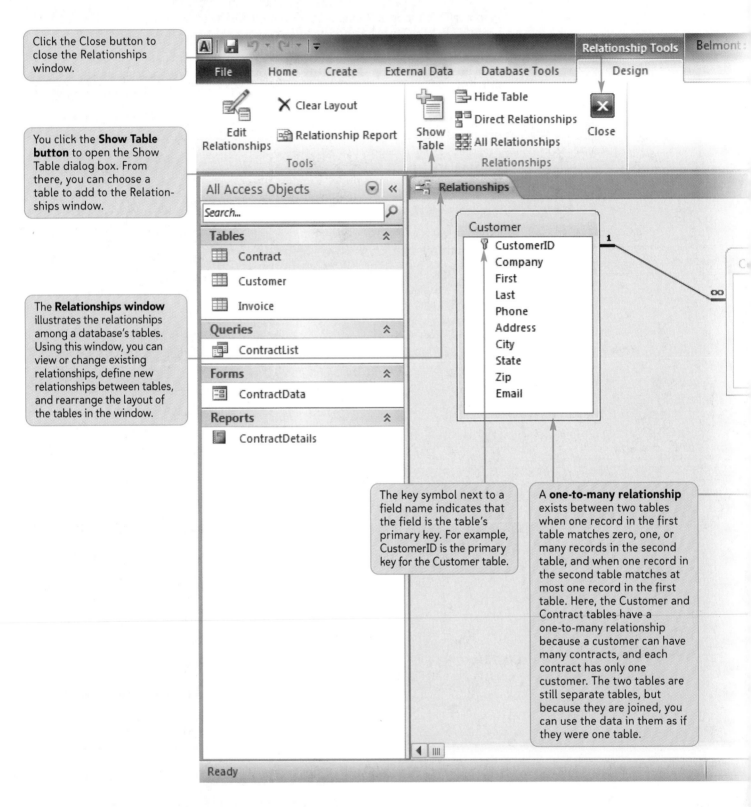

Click the Close button to close the Relationships window.

You click the **Show Table button** to open the Show Table dialog box. From there, you can choose a table to add to the Relationships window.

The **Relationships window** illustrates the relationships among a database's tables. Using this window, you can view or change existing relationships, define new relationships between tables, and rearrange the layout of the tables in the window.

The key symbol next to a field name indicates that the field is the table's primary key. For example, CustomerID is the primary key for the Customer table.

A **one-to-many relationship** exists between two tables when one record in the first table matches zero, one, or many records in the second table, and when one record in the second table matches at most one record in the first table. Here, the Customer and Contract tables have a one-to-many relationship because a customer can have many contracts, and each contract has only one customer. The two tables are still separate tables, but because they are joined, you can use the data in them as if they were one table.

TABLE RELATIONSHIPS

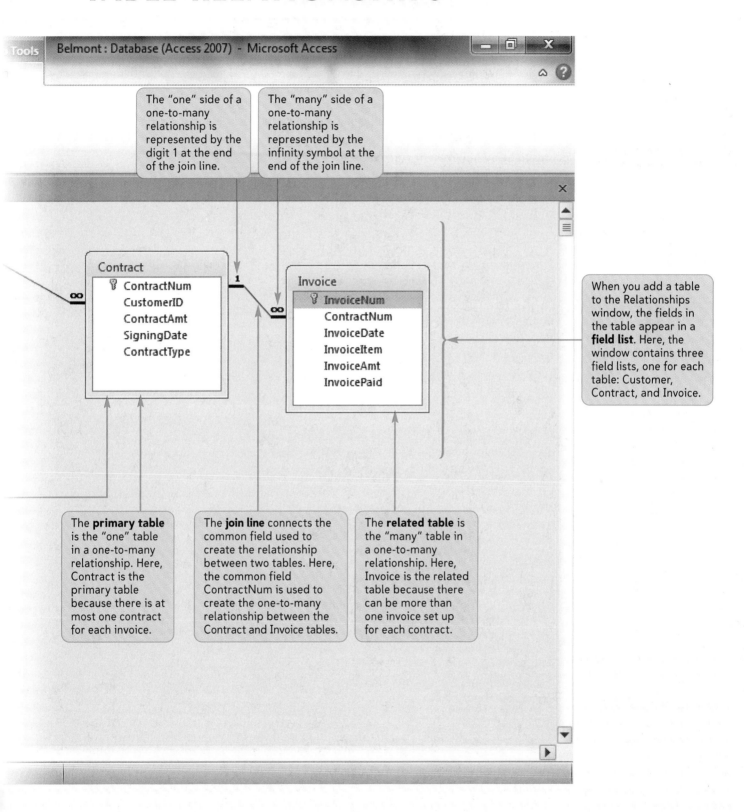

Tools   Belmont : Database (Access 2007) - Microsoft Access

The "one" side of a one-to-many relationship is represented by the digit 1 at the end of the join line.

The "many" side of a one-to-many relationship is represented by the infinity symbol at the end of the join line.

Contract
- ContractNum
- CustomerID
- ContractAmt
- SigningDate
- ContractType

Invoice
- InvoiceNum
- ContractNum
- InvoiceDate
- InvoiceItem
- InvoiceAmt
- InvoicePaid

When you add a table to the Relationships window, the fields in the table appear in a **field list**. Here, the window contains three field lists, one for each table: Customer, Contract, and Invoice.

The **primary table** is the "one" table in a one-to-many relationship. Here, Contract is the primary table because there is at most one contract for each invoice.

The **join line** connects the common field used to create the relationship between two tables. Here, the common field ContractNum is used to create the one-to-many relationship between the Contract and Invoice tables.

The **related table** is the "many" table in a one-to-many relationship. Here, Invoice is the related table because there can be more than one invoice set up for each contract.

Before you can begin to define the table relationships, as illustrated in the Session 2.2 Visual Overview, you need to finish creating the tables in the Belmont database.

Adding Records to a New Table

The Invoice table design is complete. Now, Oren would like you to add records to the table so it will contain the invoice data for Belmont Landscapes. You add records to a table in Datasheet view as you did in Tutorial 1, by typing the field values in the rows below the column headings for the fields. You'll begin by entering the records shown in Figure 2-20.

Figure 2-20	Records to be added to the Invoice table

InvoiceNum	ContractNum	InvoiceDate	InvoiceItem	InvoiceAmt	InvoicePaid
2011	3011	03/23/2013	Schematic Plan	$1,500.00	Yes
2031	3020	04/19/2013	Schematic Plan	$1,500.00	Yes
2073	3023	09/21/2015	Construction Observation	$10,000.00	No
2062	3026	09/12/2014	Permitting	$10,000.00	No

To add the first record to the Invoice table:

1. If you took a break after the previous session, make sure that the Belmont database is open, and the Navigation Pane is open.

2. In the Tables section of the Navigation Pane, double-click **Invoice** to open the Invoice table in Datasheet view.

3. Close the Navigation Pane, and then use the ↔ pointer to resize each column so that the field names are completely visible.

> Be sure to type the numbers "0" and "1" and not the letters "O" and "l" in the field value.

4. In the Invoice Num column, type **2011**, press the **Tab** key, type **3011** in the Contract Num column, and then press the **Tab** key.

   Next you need to enter the invoice date. Recall that you specified a custom date format, mm/dd/yyyy, for the InvoiceDate field. You do not need to type each digit; for example, you can type just "3" instead of "03" for the month, and you can type "13" instead of "2013" for the year. Access will display the full value according to the custom date format.

5. Type **3/23/13**, press the **Tab** key, type **Schematic Plan** in the Invoice Item column, and then press the **Tab** key. Notice that Access displays the date "03/23/2013" in the Invoice Date column.

   Next you need to enter the invoice amount for the first record. This is a Currency field with the Currency format and two decimal places specified. Because of the field's set properties, you do not need to type the dollar sign, comma, or zeroes for the decimal places; Access will display these items automatically for you.

6. Type **1500** and then press the **Tab** key. Access displays the value as "$1,500.00."

   The last field in the table, InvoicePaid, is a Yes/No field. Notice the check box displayed in the column. By default, the value for any Yes/No field is "No;" therefore, the check box is initially empty. For Yes/No fields with check boxes, you press the Tab key to leave the check box unchecked, and you press the spacebar to insert a check mark in the check box. For the record you are entering in the Invoice table, the invoice has been paid, so you need to insert a check mark in the check box.

> **TIP**
>
> The spacebar works as a toggle for Yes/No fields; you press it to insert a check mark in an empty check box and to remove an existing check mark. You can also select or deselect a check box by clicking it.

7. Press the **spacebar** to insert a check mark, and then press the **Tab** key. The values for the first record are entered. See Figure 2-21.

| Figure 2-21 | First record entered in the Invoice table |

field value displayed in the Currency format with two decimal places

field value displayed according to the custom date format

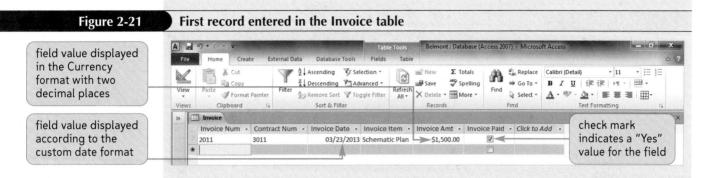

check mark indicates a "Yes" value for the field

Now you can add the remaining three records. As you do, you'll learn a shortcut for inserting the value from the same field in the previous record.

To add the next three records to the Invoice table:

▶ 1. Refer to Figure 2-20 and enter the values in the second record's Invoice Num, Contract Num, and Invoice Date columns.

Notice the value in the second record's Invoice Item column, "Schematic Plan." This value is the exact same value as in the first record. You can quickly insert the value from the same column in the previous record using the **Ctrl + '** (apostrophe) keyboard shortcut.

▶ 2. In the Invoice Item column, press the **Ctrl + '** keys. Access inserts the value "Schematic Plan" in the Invoice Item column for the second record.

▶ 3. Press the **Tab** key to move to the Invoice Amt column. Again, the value you need to enter in this column—$1,500.00—is the same as the value for this column in the previous record. So, you can use the keyboard shortcut again.

▶ 4. In the Invoice Amt column, press the **Ctrl + '** keys. Access inserts the value $1,500.00 in the Invoice Amt column for the second record.

▶ 5. Press the **Tab** key to move to the Invoice Paid column, press the **spacebar** to insert a check mark in the check box, and then press the **Tab** key. The second record is entered in the Invoice table.

▶ 6. Refer to Figure 2-20 to enter the values for the third and fourth records, using the Ctrl + ' keys to enter the value in the fourth record's Invoice Amt column. Also, for both records, the invoices have not been paid. Therefore, be sure to press the Tab key to leave the Invoice Paid column values unchecked (signifying "No").

▶ 7. Resize the columns, as necessary, so that all field values are completely visible. Then click the **Invoice Num** column for the next new record. Your table should look like the one in Figure 2-22.

| Figure 2-22 | Invoice table with four records added |

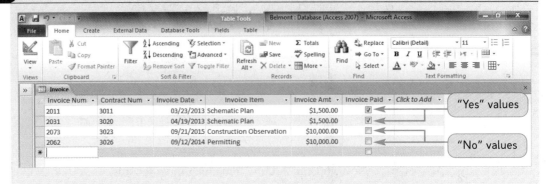

To finish entering records in the Invoice table, you'll use a method that allows you to import the data.

Importing Data from an Excel Worksheet

Often, the data you want to add to an Access table exists in another file, such as a Word document or an Excel workbook. You can bring the data from other files into Access in different ways. For example, you can copy and paste the data from an open file, or you can **import** the data, which is a process that allows you to copy the data from a source without having to open the source file.

Oren had been using Excel to track invoice data for Belmont Landscapes and already created a worksheet, named "Invoices," containing this data. You'll import this Excel worksheet into your Invoice table to complete the entry of data in the table. To use the import method, the columns in the Excel worksheet must match the names and data types of the fields in the Access table.

INSIGHT

Caption Property Values and the Import Process

When you want to import data from an Excel worksheet into an Access table, any Caption property values set for the fields in the table are not considered in the import process. For example, your Access table could have fields such as InvoiceDate and InvoiceAmt with Caption property values of Invoice Date and Invoice Amt, respectively. If the Excel worksheet you are importing has column headings such as Invoice Date and Invoice Amt, you might think that the data matches and you can proceed with the import. However, if the underlying field names in the Access table do not match the Excel worksheet column headings exactly, the import process will fail. It's a good idea to double-check to make sure that the actual Access field names—and not just the column headings displayed in a table datasheet (as specified by the Caption property)—match the Excel worksheet column headings. If there are differences, you can change the column headings in the Excel worksheet to match the Access table field names before you import the data, ensuring that the process will work correctly.

The Invoices worksheet contains the following columns: InvoiceNum, ContractNum, InvoiceDate, InvoiceItem, InvoiceAmt, and InvoicePaid. These column headings match the field names in the Invoice table exactly, so you can import the data. Before you import data into a table, you need to close the table.

To import the Invoices worksheet into the Invoice table:

1. Click the **Close 'Invoice'** button ☒ on the object tab to close the Invoice table. A dialog box opens asking if you want to save the changes to the table layout. This dialog box opens because you resized the table columns.

2. Click the **Yes** button in the dialog box.

3. Click the **External Data** tab on the Ribbon.

4. In the Import & Link group on the External Data tab, click the **Excel** button. The Get External Data - Excel Spreadsheet dialog box opens. See Figure 2-23.

Figure 2-23   Get External Data - Excel Spreadsheet dialog box

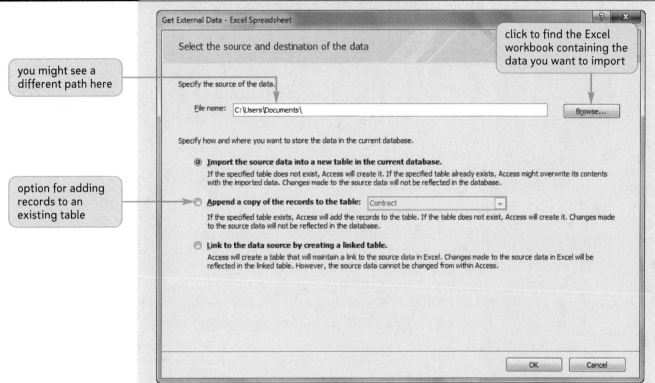

you might see a different path here

click to find the Excel workbook containing the data you want to import

option for adding records to an existing table

The dialog box provides options for importing the entire worksheet as a new table in the current database, adding the data from the worksheet to an existing table, or linking the data in the worksheet to the table. You need to add, or append, the worksheet data to the Invoice table.

5. Click the **Browse** button. The File Open dialog box opens. The Excel workbook file is named "Invoices" and is located in the Access1\Tutorial folder provided with your Data Files.

6. Navigate to the **Access1\Tutorial** folder, where your starting Data Files are stored, and then double-click the **Invoices** Excel file. You return to the dialog box.

7. Click the **Append a copy of the records to the table** option button. The box to the right of this option becomes active. Next, you need to select the table to which you want to add the data.

8. Click the **arrow** on the box, and then click **Invoice**.

9. Click the **OK** button. The first Import Spreadsheet Wizard dialog box opens. See Figure 2-24.

| Figure 2-24 | First Import Spreadsheet Wizard dialog box |

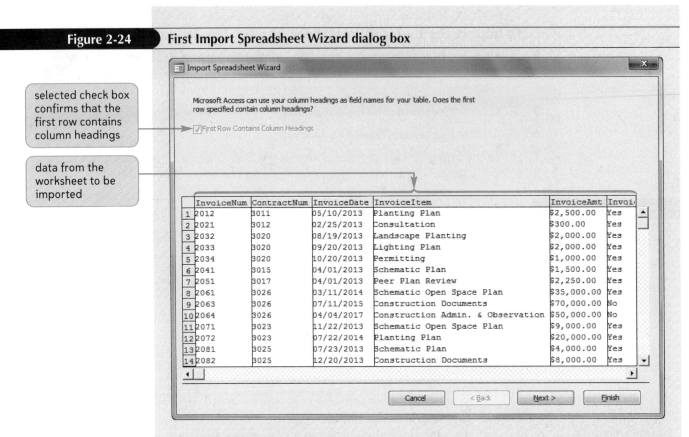

selected check box confirms that the first row contains column headings

data from the worksheet to be imported

The dialog box confirms that the first row of the worksheet you are importing contains column headings. The bottom section of the dialog box displays some of the data contained in the worksheet.

10. Click the **Next** button. The second, and final, Import Spreadsheet Wizard dialog box opens. Notice that the Import to Table box shows that the data from the spreadsheet will be imported into the Invoice table.

11. Click the **Finish** button. A dialog box opens asking if you want to save the import steps. If you needed to repeat this same import procedure many times, it would be a good idea to save the steps for the procedure. However, you don't need to save these steps because you'll be importing the data only one time. Once the data is in the Invoice table, Oren will no longer use Excel to track invoice data.

12. Click the **Close** button in the dialog box to close it without saving the steps.

The data from the Invoices worksheet has been added to the Invoice table. Next, you'll open the table to view the new records.

To open the Invoice table and view the imported data:

1. Open the Navigation Pane, and then double-click **Invoice** in the Tables section to open the table in Datasheet view.

2. Resize the Invoice Item column so that all field values are fully displayed, being sure to scroll down through the entire datasheet and repeat the resizing as necessary. When you resize a column by double-clicking the pointer on the column dividing line, you are sizing the column to its **best fit**—that is, so the column is just wide enough to display the longest visible value in the column, including the field name.

3. Press the **Ctrl+Home** keys to scroll to the top of the datasheet. Notice that the table now contains a total of 176 records—four records you entered plus 172 records imported from the Invoices worksheet. The records are displayed in primary key order by the values in the Invoice Num column. See Figure 2-25.

Figure 2-25	Invoice table after importing data from Excel

TIP

When you resize a column to its best fit, only the visible field values are affected. You must scroll down the datasheet to make sure all field values for the entire column are fully displayed, resizing as you scroll, if necessary.

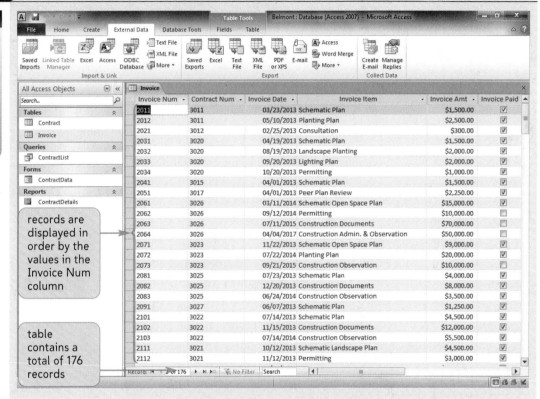

records are displayed in order by the values in the Invoice Num column

table contains a total of 176 records

4. Save and close the Invoice table, and then close the Navigation Pane.

Two of the tables—Contract and Invoice—are now complete. According to Oren's plan for the Belmont database, you need to create a third table, named "Customer," to track data about Belmont Landscapes' residential and commercial customers. You'll use a different method to create this table.

Creating a Table by Importing an Existing Table Structure

If another Access database contains a table—or even just the design, or structure, of a table—that you want to include in your database, you can easily import the table and any records it contains or import only the table structure into your database.

Oren documented the design for the new Customer table by listing each field's name; data type; and size, description, and caption (if applicable), as shown in Figure 2-26. Note that each field in the Customer table will be a Text field, and the CustomerID field will be the table's primary key.

| Figure 2-26 | Design for the Customer table |

Field Name	Data Type	Field Size	Description	Caption
CustomerID	Text	5	Primary key	Customer ID
Company	Text	50		
Last	Text	25	Contact's last name	Last Name
First	Text	20	Contact's first name	First Name
Phone	Text	14		
Address	Text	35		
City	Text	25		
State	Text	2		
Zip	Text	10		
Email	Text	50		

Sarah already created an Access database containing a Customer table design. She never entered any records into the table because she wasn't sure if the table design was complete or correct. After reviewing the table design, both Sarah and Oren agree that it contains some of the fields Oren wants to track, but that some changes are needed. So, you can import the table structure in Sarah's database to create the Customer table in the Belmont database, and then modify the imported table to produce the final table structure Oren wants.

To create the Customer table by importing the structure of another table:

▶ **1.** Make sure the External Data tab is the active tab on the Ribbon.

▶ **2.** In the Import & Link group, click the **Access** button. The Get External Data - Access Database dialog box opens. This dialog box is similar to the one you used earlier when importing the Excel spreadsheet.

▶ **3.** Click the **Browse** button. The File Open dialog box opens. The Access database file from which you need to import the table structure is named "Sarah" and is located in the Access1\Tutorial folder provided with your Data Files.

▶ **4.** Navigate to the **Access1\Tutorial** folder, where your starting Data Files are stored, and then double-click the **Sarah** database file. You return to the dialog box.

▶ **5.** Make sure the **Import tables, queries, forms, reports, macros, and modules into the current database** option button is selected, and then click the **OK** button. The Import Objects dialog box opens. The dialog box contains tabs for importing all the different types of Access database objects—tables, queries, forms, and so on. The Tables tab is the current tab.

▶ **6.** Click the **Options** button in the dialog box to see all the options for importing tables. See Figure 2-27.

Figure 2-27   **Import Objects dialog box**

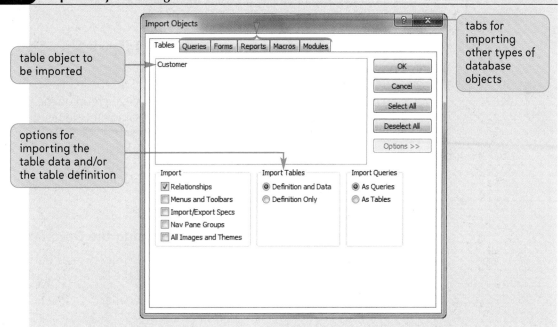

table object to be imported

options for importing the table data and/or the table definition

tabs for importing other types of database objects

Note the Import Tables section of the dialog box, which contains options for importing the definition and data—that is, the structure of the table and any records contained in the table—or the definition only. You need to import only the structure of the Customer table Sarah created.

7. On the Tables tab, click **Customer** to select this table.

8. In the Import Tables section of the dialog box, click the **Definition Only** option button, and then click the **OK** button. Access creates the Customer table in the Belmont database using the structure of the Customer table in the Sarah database, and opens a dialog box asking if you want to save the import steps.

9. Click the **Close** button to close the dialog box without saving the import steps.

10. Open the Navigation Pane and note that the Customer table is listed in the Tables section.

11. Double-click **Customer** to open the table, and then close the Navigation Pane. The Customer table opens in Datasheet view. The table contains no records. See Figure 2-28.

Figure 2-28   **Imported Customer table in Datasheet view**

The table structure you imported contains some of the fields Oren wants, but not all (see Figure 2-26); it also contains some fields Oren does not want in the Customer table. You can add the missing fields using the Data Type gallery.

Adding Fields to a Table Using the Data Type Gallery

The **Data Type gallery**, available in the Add & Delete group on the Fields tab, allows you to add a group of related fields to a table at the same time, rather than adding each field to the table individually. The group of fields you add is called a **Quick Start selection**. For example, the Address Quick Start selection adds a collection of fields related to an address, such as Address, City, State, and so on, to the table at one time.

Next, you'll use the Data Type gallery to add the missing fields to the Customer table.

To add fields to the Customer table using the Data Type gallery:

▶ 1. Click the **Fields** tab on the Ribbon. Note the More Fields button in the Add & Delete group. Clicking this button displays the Data Type gallery.

Before inserting fields from the Data Type gallery, you need to place the insertion point in the field to the right of where you want to insert the new fields. According to Oren's design, the Address field should come after the Phone field, so you need to make the next field, FaxNumber, the active field.

Make sure the correct field is active before adding new fields.

▶ 2. Click the first row in the **FaxNumber** field to make it the active field.

▶ 3. In the Add & Delete group, click the **More Fields** button. The Data Type gallery opens and displays options for different types of fields you can add to your table.

▶ 4. Scroll the gallery down so the Quick Start section is visible. See Figure 2-29.

Figure 2-29 | **Customer table with the Data Type gallery displayed**

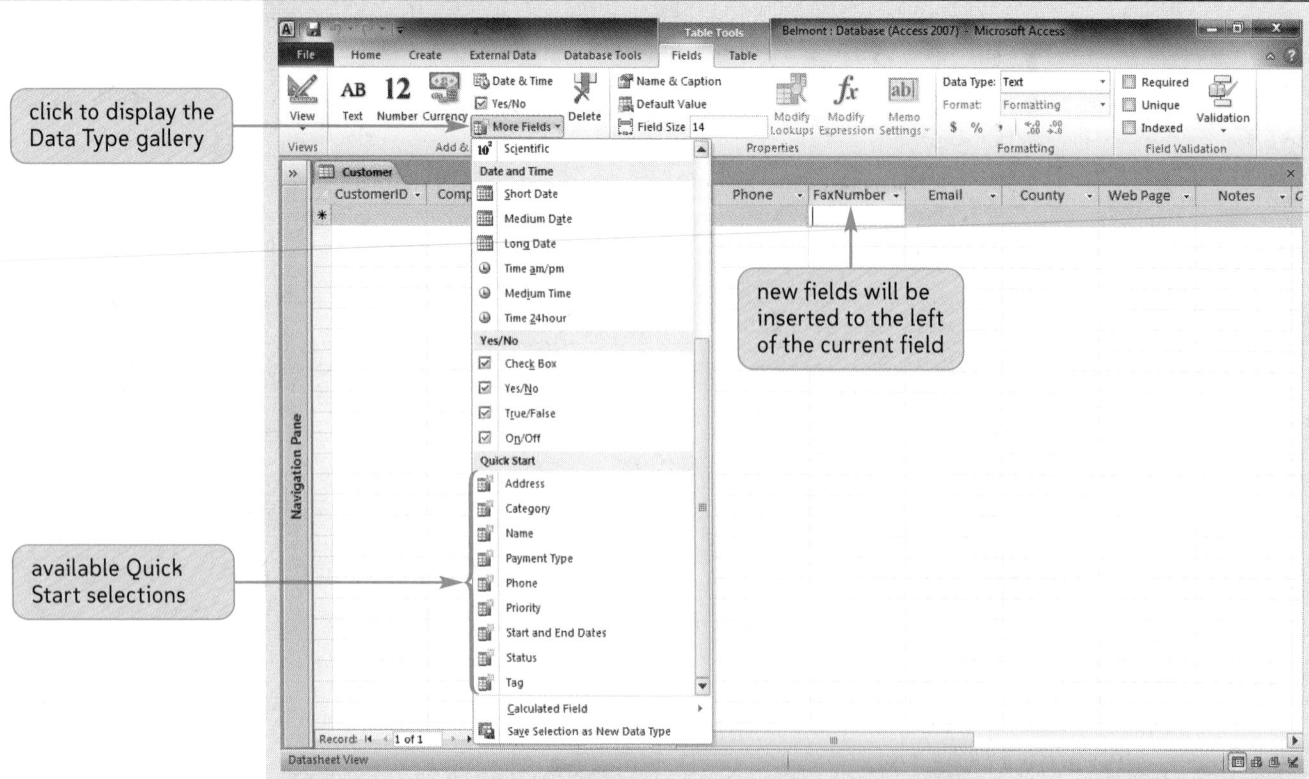

click to display the Data Type gallery

new fields will be inserted to the left of the current field

available Quick Start selections

The Quick Start section provides options that will add multiple, related fields to the table at one time. The new fields will be inserted to the left of the current field.

5. In the Quick Start section, click **Address**. Access adds five fields to the table: Address, City, State Province, ZIP Postal, and Country Region. See Figure 2-30.

Figure 2-30	Customer table after adding fields from the Data Type gallery

five fields added with Address Quick Start selection

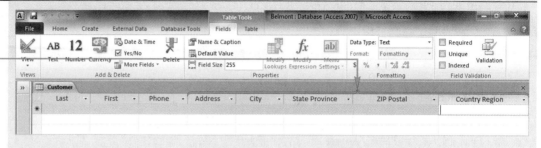

Modifying the Imported Table

Refer back to Oren's design for the Customer table (Figure 2-26). To finalize the table design, you need to modify the imported table by deleting fields, renaming fields, changing field data types, and moving some fields. You'll begin by deleting fields.

Deleting Fields from a Table Structure

After you've created a table, you might need to delete one or more fields. When you delete a field, you also delete all the values for that field from the table. So, before you delete a field you should make sure that you want to do so and that you choose the correct field to delete. You can delete fields from either Datasheet view or Design view.

REFERENCE

Deleting a Field from a Table Structure

- In Datasheet view, click the column heading for the field you want to delete.
- In the Add & Delete group on the Fields tab, click the Delete button.

or

- In Design view, click the Field Name box for the field you want to delete.
- In the Tools group on the Design tab, click the Delete Rows button.

The Address Quick Start selection added a field named "Country Region" to the Customer table. Oren doesn't need a field to store country data because all Belmont Landscapes customers are located in the United States. You'll begin to modify the Customer table structure by deleting the Country Region field.

To delete the Country Region field from the table in Datasheet view:

1. Click the first row in the **Country Region** field (if necessary).

2. In the Add & Delete group on the Fields tab, click the **Delete** button. The Country Region field is removed and the first field, CustomerID, is now the active field.

You can also delete fields from a table structure in Design view. You'll switch to Design view to delete the other unnecessary fields.

To delete the fields in Design view:

1. In the Views group on the Fields tab, click the **View** button. The Customer table opens in Design view. See Figure 2-31.

Figure 2-31 **Customer table in Design view**

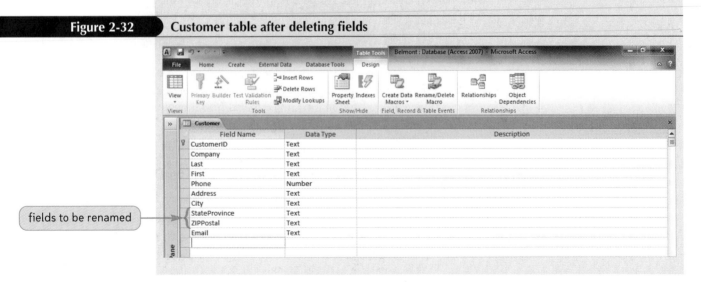

2. Click the **FaxNumber** Field Name box to make it the current field.

3. In the Tools group on the Design tab, click the **Delete Rows** button. The FaxNumber field is removed from the Customer table structure.

   You'll delete the County, Web Page, and Notes fields next. Instead of deleting these fields individually, you'll select and delete them at the same time.

4. Click and hold down the mouse button on the row selector for the **County** field, and then drag the mouse to select the **Web Page** and **Notes** fields.

5. Release the mouse button. The rows for the three fields are outlined in an orange box, meaning all three fields are selected.

6. In the Tools group, click the **Delete Rows** button. See Figure 2-32.

Figure 2-32 **Customer table after deleting fields**

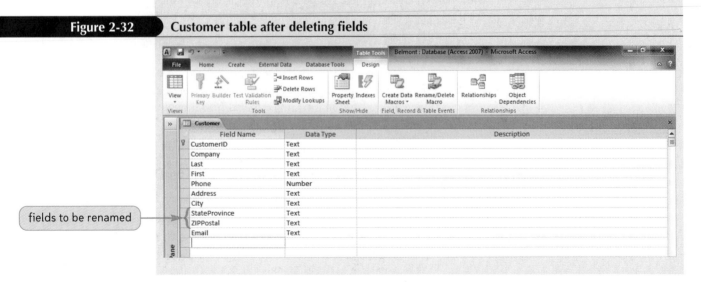

Renaming Fields in Design View

To match Oren's design for the Customer table, you need to rename the StateProvince and ZIPPostal fields. In Tutorial 1, you renamed the default primary key field, ID, in Datasheet view. You can also rename fields in Design view by simply editing the names in the Table Design grid.

To rename the fields in Design view:

1. Click to position the insertion point to the right of the word **StateProvince** in the eighth row's Field Name box, and then press the **Backspace** key eight times to delete the word "Province." The name of the eighth field is now State.

   You can also select an entire field name and then type new text to replace it.

2. In the ninth row's Field Name box, drag to select the text **ZIPPostal**, and then type **Zip**. The text you type replaces the original text. See Figure 2-33.

Figure 2-33	Customer table after renaming fields

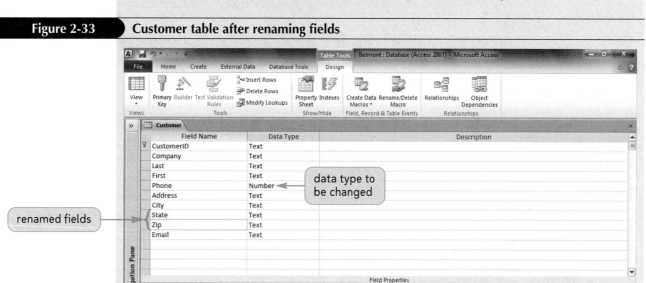

Changing the Data Type for a Field in Design View

According to Oren's plan, all of the fields in the Customer table should be Text fields. The table structure you imported specifies the Number data type for the Phone field. In Tutorial 1, you used an option in Datasheet view to change a field's data type. You can also change the data type for a field in Design view.

To change the data type of the Phone field in Design view:

1. Click the right side of the **Data Type** box for the Phone field to display the list of data types.

2. Click **Text** in the list. The Phone field is now a Text field. Note that, by default, the Field Size property is set to 255. According to Oren's plan, the Phone field should have a Field Size property of 14. You'll make this change next.

3. Press the **F6** key to move to and select the default Field Size property, and then type **14**.

Each of the remaining fields you added using the Address Quick Start selection—Address, City, State, and Zip—also has the default field size of 255. You need to change the Field Size property for these fields to match Oren's design. You'll also delete any Caption property values for these fields because the field names match how Oren wants them displayed.

To change the Field Size and Caption properties for the fields:

1. Click the **Address** Field Name box to make it the current field.

2. Press the **F6** key to move to and select the default Field Size property, and then type **35**.

   Note that the Caption property setting for this field is the same as the field name. This field doesn't need a caption, so you can delete this value.

3. Press the **Tab** key three times to move to and select the word Address in the Caption box, and then press the **Delete** key. The Caption property value is removed.

4. Repeat Steps 1 through 3 to change the Field Size property for the City field to **25** and to delete its Caption property value.

5. Change the Field Size property for the State field to **2** and delete its Caption property value.

6. Change the Field Size property for the Zip field to **10** and delete its Caption property value.

7. Click the **Save** button 🔲 on the Quick Access Toolbar to save your changes to the Customer table.

Finally, Oren would like you to set the Description and Caption properties for the CustomerID, Last, and First fields. You'll make these changes now.

To enter the Description and Caption property values:

1. Click the **CustomerID** Description box, and then type **Primary key**.

2. In the Field Properties pane, click the **Caption** box.

   After you leave the Description box, a Property Update Options button 🗷 appears below the Description box for the CustomerID field. When you change a field's property in Design view, you can use this button to update the corresponding property on forms and reports that include the modified field. For example, if the Belmont database included a form that contained the CustomerID field, you could choose to **propagate**, or update, the modified Description property in the form by clicking the Property Update Options button, and then choosing the option to make the update everywhere the field is used. The text on the Property Update Options button varies depending on the task; in this case, if you click the button, the option is "Update Status Bar Text everywhere CustomerID is used."

   Because the Belmont database does not include any forms or reports that are based on the Customer table, you do not need to update the properties, so you can ignore the button for now.

3. In the Caption box for the CustomerID field, type **Customer ID**.

4. Click the **Description** box for the Last field, and then type **Contact's last name**.

▶ 5. Click the **Caption** box, and then type **Last Name**.

▶ 6. Click the **Description** box for the First field, and then type **Contact's first name**.

▶ 7. Click the **Caption** box, and then type **First Name**. See Figure 2-34.

| Figure 2-34 | Customer table after entering descriptions and captions |

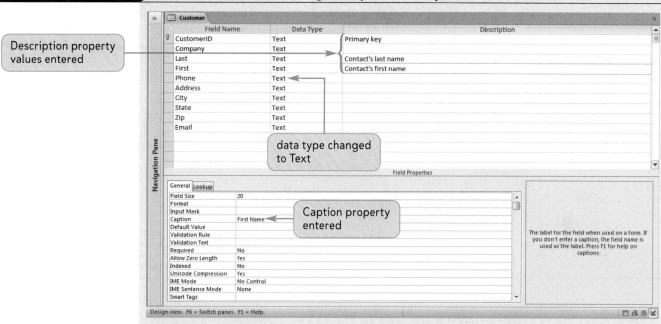

▶ 8. Click the **Save** button 🖫 on the Quick Access Toolbar to save your changes to the Customer table.

▶ 9. In the Views group on the Design tab, click the **View** button to display the table in Datasheet view.

▶ 10. Use the ↔ pointer to resize each column so that more fields are visible in the datasheet. Then click in the first row for the **Customer ID** column. See Figure 2-35.

| Figure 2-35 | Modified Customer table in Datasheet view |

After viewing the Customer table datasheet, Oren decides that he would like the First field to appear before the Last field. Earlier in this tutorial, when you created the Invoice table, you learned how to change the order of fields in Design view. Although you can move fields in Datasheet view by dragging a field's column heading to a new location, doing so rearranges only the *display* of the table's fields; the table structure is not changed. To move a field permanently, you must display the table in Design view.

To move the Last field to follow the First field:

▸ **1.** In the Views group on the Home tab, click the **View** button. The Customer table opens in Design view.

▸ **2.** Point to the row selector for the Last field so the pointer changes to a ➡ shape.

▸ **3.** Click the **row selector** to select the entire row for the Last field.

▸ **4.** Place the pointer on the row selector for the Last field, click the ⬚ pointer, and then drag the ⬚ pointer down to the line below the row selector for the First field.

▸ **5.** Release the mouse button. The Last field now appears below the First field.

▸ **6.** Click the **Save** button 🖫 on the Quick Access Toolbar to save the table, and then display the table in Datasheet view.

Trouble? If the fields in the datasheet do not appear in the same order as they did in Design view, close the Customer table, reopen it in Datasheet view, and then close the Navigation Pane. If a field that you deleted (FaxNumber, County, Web Page, or Notes) still appears in the table, close the table, open it in Design view, delete the field(s), save and close the table, open the table in Datasheet view, and then close the Navigation Pane.

With the Customer table design set, you can now enter records in it. You'll begin by entering two records, and then you'll use a different method to add the remaining records. *Note: Be sure to enter your first name and last name where indicated.*

To add two records to the Customer table:

▸ **1.** Enter the following values in the columns in the first record (these values are for a residential customer with no company name):

Customer ID = **11001**
Company = [do not enter a value; leave blank]
First Name = **[student's first name]**
Last Name = **[student's last name]**
Phone = **616-866-3901**
Address = **49 Blackstone Dr**
City = **Rockford**
State = **MI**
Zip = **49341**
Email = **student2@milocal123.com**

▸ **2.** Enter the following values in the columns in the second record, for a commercial customer:

Customer ID = **11012**
Company = **Grand Rapids Engineering Dept.**
First Name = **Anthony**
Last Name = **Rodriguez**
Phone = **616-454-9801**
Address = **225 Summer St**
City = **Grand Rapids**
State = **MI**
Zip = **49503**
Email = **arod24@gred11.gov**

▸ **3.** Close the Customer table.

Before Belmont Landscapes decided to store data using Access, Sarah managed the company's customer data in a different system. She exported that data into a text file and now asks you to import it into the new Customer table. You can import the data contained in this text file to add the remaining records to the Customer table.

Adding Data to a Table by Importing a Text File

There are many ways to import data into an Access database. So far, you've learned how to add data to an Access table by importing an Excel spreadsheet, and you've created a new table by importing the structure of an existing table. You can also import data contained in text files.

To complete the entry of records in the Customer table, you'll import the data contained in Sarah's text file. The file is named "Customer" and is located in the Access1\Tutorial folder provided with your Data Files.

To import the data contained in the Customer text file:

1. Click the **External Data** tab on the Ribbon.

2. In the Import & Link group, click the **Text File** button. The Get External Data - Text File dialog box opens. This dialog box is similar to the one you used earlier when importing the Excel spreadsheet and the Access table structure.

3. Click the **Browse** button. The File Open dialog box opens.

4. Navigate to the **Access1\Tutorial** folder, where your starting Data Files are stored, and then double-click the **Customer** file. You return to the dialog box.

5. Click the **Append a copy of the records to the table** option button. The box to the right of this option becomes active. Next, you need to select the table to which you want to add the data.

6. Click the **arrow** on the box, and then click **Customer**.

7. Click the **OK** button. The first Import Text Wizard dialog box opens. The dialog box indicates that the data to be imported is in a delimited format. A **delimited** text file is one in which fields of data are separated by a character such as a comma or a tab. In this case, the dialog box shows that data is separated by the comma character in the text file.

8. Make sure the **Delimited** option button is selected in the dialog box, and then click the **Next** button. The second Import Text Wizard dialog box opens. See Figure 2-36.

Figure 2-36 **Second Import Text Wizard dialog box**

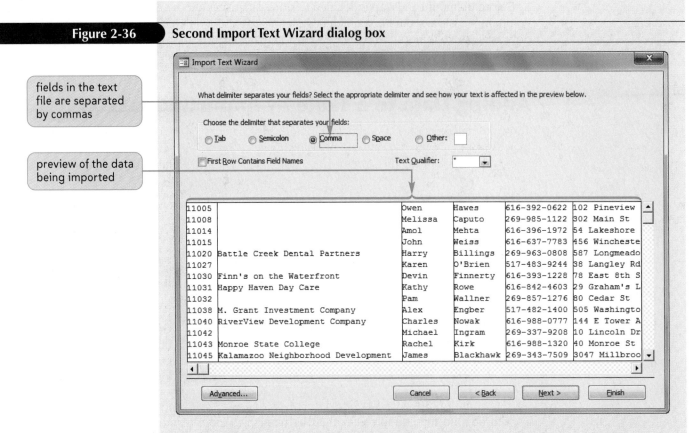

fields in the text
file are separated
by commas

preview of the data
being imported

This dialog box asks you to confirm the delimiter character that separates the
fields in the text file you're importing. Access detects that the comma character is
used in the Customer text file and selects this option. The bottom area of the dialog box provides a preview of the data you're importing.

9. Make sure the **Comma** option button is selected, and then click the **Next** button.
The third, and final, Import Text Wizard dialog box opens. Notice that the Import
to Table box shows that the data will be imported into the Customer table.

10. Click the **Finish** button. A dialog box opens asking if you want to save the import
steps. You'll only import the customer data once, so you can close the dialog box
without saving the import steps.

11. Click the **Close** button in the dialog box to close it without saving the import steps.

Oren asks you to open the Customer table in Datasheet view so he can see the results
of importing the text file.

To view the Customer table datasheet:

1. Open the Navigation Pane, and then double-click **Customer** to open the Customer
table in Datasheet view. The Customer table contains a total of 40 records.

2. Close the Navigation Pane.

▶ **3.** Resize all the columns to their best fit, scrolling the table datasheet as necessary. When finished, scroll back to display the first fields in the table. See Figure 2-37.

Figure 2-37   **Customer table after importing data from the text file**

▶ **4.** Save and close the Customer table, and then open the Navigation Pane.

The Belmont database now contains three tables—Contract, Customer, and Invoice—and the tables contain all the necessary records. Your final task is to complete the database design by defining the necessary relationships between its tables.

Defining Table Relationships

One of the most powerful features of a relational database management system is its ability to define relationships between tables. You use a common field to relate one table to another. The process of relating tables is often called performing a **join**. When you join tables that have a common field, you can extract data from them as if they were one larger table. For example, you can join the Customer and Contract tables by using the CustomerID field in both tables as the common field. Then you can use a query, form, or report to extract selected data from each table, even though the data is contained in two separate tables, as shown in Figure 2-38. In the CustomerContracts query shown in Figure 2-38, the CustomerID, Company, First, and Last fields are from the Customer table, and the ContractNum and ContractAmt fields are from the Contract table. The joining of records is based on the common field of CustomerID. The Customer and Contract tables have a type of relationship called a one-to-many relationship.

| Figure 2-38 | One-to-many relationship and sample query |

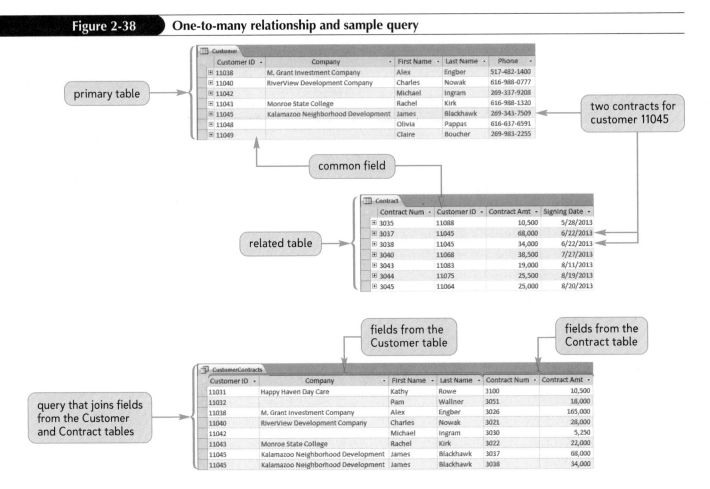

One-to-Many Relationships

As shown earlier in the Session 2.2 Visual Overview, a one-to-many relationship exists between two tables when one record in the first table matches zero, one, or many records in the second table, and when one record in the second table matches at most one record in the first table. For example, as shown in Figure 2-38, customer 11045 has two contracts in the Contract table. Other customers have one or more contracts. Every contract has a single matching customer.

Access refers to the two tables that form a relationship as the primary table and the related table. The primary table is the "one" table in a one-to-many relationship; in Figure 2-38, the Customer table is the primary table because there is only one customer for each contract. The related table is the "many" table; in Figure 2-38, the Contract table is the related table because a customer can have zero, one, or many contracts.

Problem Solving: Avoiding Inconsistent Data

Because related data is stored in two tables, inconsistencies between the tables can occur. Referring to Figure 2-38, consider the following three scenarios:

- Oren adds a record to the Contract table for a new customer, Taylor McNulty, using CustomerID 12050. Oren did not first add the new customer's information to the Customer table, so this contract does not have a matching record in the Customer table. The data is inconsistent, and the contract record is considered to be an **orphaned record**.
- In another situation, Oren changes the CustomerID in the Customer table for Kalamazoo Neighborhood Development from 11045 to 12090. Because there is no longer a customer with the CustomerID 11045 in the Customer table, this change creates two orphaned records in the Contract table, and the database is inconsistent.
- In a third scenario, Oren deletes the record for Kalamazoo Neighborhood Development, customer 11045, from the Customer table because this customer no longer does business with Belmont Landscapes. The database is again inconsistent; two records for customer 11045 in the Contract table have no matching record in the Customer table.

You can avoid these types of problems and avoid having inconsistent data in your database by specifying referential integrity (discussed next) between tables when you define their relationships.

Referential Integrity

Referential integrity is a set of rules that Access enforces to maintain consistency between related tables when you update data in a database. Specifically, the referential integrity rules are as follows:

- When you add a record to a related table, a matching record must already exist in the primary table, thereby preventing the possibility of orphaned records.
- If you attempt to change the value of the primary key in the primary table, Access prevents this change if matching records exist in a related table. However, if you choose the **Cascade Update Related Fields option**, Access permits the change in value to the primary key and changes the appropriate foreign key values in the related table, thereby eliminating the possibility of inconsistent data.
- When you attempt to delete a record in the primary table, Access prevents the deletion if matching records exist in a related table. However, if you choose the **Cascade Delete Related Records option**, Access deletes the record in the primary table and also deletes all records in related tables that have matching foreign key values.

Understanding the Cascade Delete Related Records Option

Although there are advantages to using the Cascade Delete Related Records option for enforcing referential integrity, its use does present risks as well. You should rarely select the Cascade Delete Related Records option because setting this option might cause you to inadvertently delete records you did not intend to delete. It is best to use other methods for deleting records that give you more control over the deletion process.

Defining a Relationship Between Two Tables

When two tables have a common field, you can define a relationship between them in the Relationships window (see the Session 2.2 Visual Overview). Next, you need to define a one-to-many relationship between the Customer and Contract tables, with

Customer as the primary table and Contract as the related table, and with CustomerID as the primary key in the Customer table and a foreign key in the Contract table). You'll also define a one-to-many relationship between the Contract and Invoice tables, with Contract as the primary table and Invoice as the related table, and with ContractNum as the common field (the primary key in the Contract table and a foreign key in the Invoice table).

To define the one-to-many relationship between the Customer and Contract tables:

1. Click the **Database Tools** tab on the Ribbon.

2. In the Relationships group on the Database Tools tab, click the **Relationships** button. The Show Table dialog box opens. See Figure 2-39.

Figure 2-39   Show Table dialog box

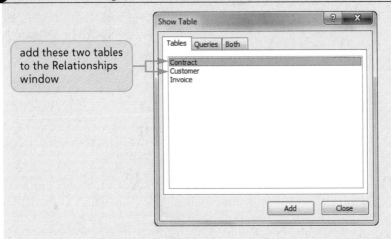

add these two tables to the Relationships window

You must add each table participating in a relationship to the Relationships window. Because the Customer table is the primary table in the relationship, you'll add it first.

TIP

You can also double-click a table in the Show Table dialog box to add it to the Relationships window.

3. Click **Customer**, and then click the **Add** button. The Customer table's field list is added to the Relationships window.

4. Click **Contract**, and then click the **Add** button. The Contract table's field list is added to the Relationships window.

5. Click the **Close** button in the Show Table dialog box to close it.

So that you can view all the fields and complete field names, you'll resize the Customer table field list.

6. Use the $\updownarrow$ pointer to drag the bottom of the Customer table field list to lengthen it until the vertical scroll bar disappears and all the fields are visible.

To form the relationship between the two tables, you drag the common field of CustomerID from the primary table to the related table. Then Access opens the Edit Relationships dialog box, in which you select the relationship options for the two tables.

7. Click **CustomerID** in the Customer field list, and then drag it to **CustomerID** in the Contract field list. When you release the mouse button, the Edit Relationships dialog box opens. See Figure 2-40.

Figure 2-40	Edit Relationships dialog box

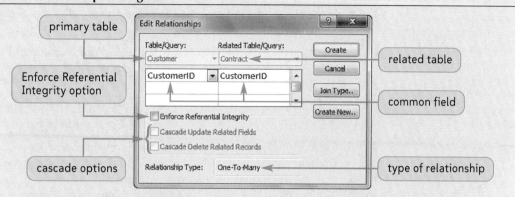

The primary table, related table, common field, and relationship type (One-To-Many) appear in the dialog box. After you click the Enforce Referential Integrity check box, the two cascade options become available. If you select the Cascade Update Related Fields option, Access will update the appropriate foreign key values in the related table when you change a primary key value in the primary table. You will not select the Cascade Delete Related Records option because doing so could cause you to delete records that you do not want to delete; this option is rarely selected.

8. Click the **Enforce Referential Integrity** check box, and then click the **Cascade Update Related Fields** check box.

9. Click the **Create** button to define the one-to-many relationship between the two tables and to close the dialog box. The completed relationship appears in the Relationships window, with the join line connecting the common field of CustomerID in each table. See Figure 2-41.

Figure 2-41	Defined relationship in the Relationships window

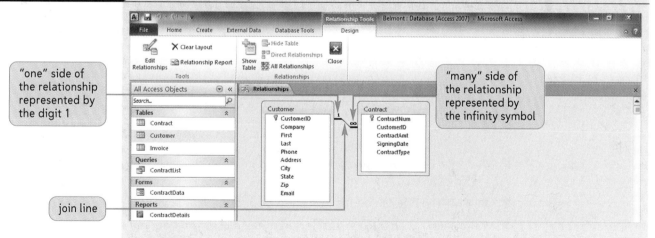

Now you need to define the one-to-many relationship between the Contract and Invoice tables. In this relationship, Contract is the primary ("one") table because there is at most one contract for each invoice. Invoice is the related ("many") table because there are zero, one, or many invoices set up for each contract, depending on how many project phases are involved for each contract.

To define the relationship between the Contract and Invoice tables:

1. In the Relationships group on the Design tab, click the **Show Table** button. The Show Table dialog box opens.

2. Click **Invoice** on the Tables tab, click the **Add** button, and then click the **Close** button to close the Show Table dialog box. The Invoice table's field list appears in the Relationships window to the right of the Contract table's field list.

    Because the Contract table is the primary table in this relationship, you need to drag the ContractNum field from the Contract field list to the Invoice field list.

3. Click and drag the **ContractNum** field in the Contract field list to the **ContractNum** field in the Invoice field list. When you release the mouse button, the Edit Relationships dialog box opens.

4. Click the **Enforce Referential Integrity** check box, and then click the **Cascade Update Related Fields** check box.

5. Click the **Create** button to define the one-to-many relationship between the two tables and to close the dialog box. The completed relationship appears in the Relationships window. See Figure 2-42.

Figure 2-42 **Both relationships defined**

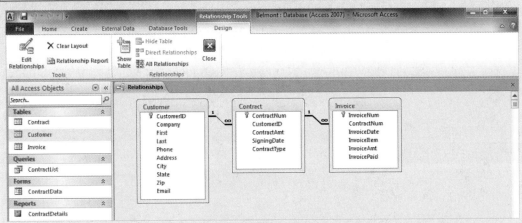

With both relationships defined, you have connected the data among the three tables in the Belmont database.

6. Click the **Save** button on the Quick Access Toolbar to save the layout in the Relationships window.

7. In the Relationships group on the Design tab, click the **Close** button to close the Relationships window.

8. Click the **File** tab on the Ribbon to display Backstage view.

9. Make sure the Info tab is selected in the navigation bar, and then click the **Compact & Repair Database** button. Access compacts and repairs the Belmont database.

10. Click the **File** tab, and then click **Close Database** to close the Belmont database.

REVIEW

Session 2.2 Quick Check

1. To insert a check mark in an empty check box for a Yes/No field, you press the _____.

2. What is the keyboard shortcut for inserting the value from the same field in the previous record into the current record?

3. _____ data is a process that allows you to copy the data from a source without having to open the source file.

4. The _____ gallery allows you to add a group of related fields to a table at the same time, rather than adding each field to the table individually.

5. What is the effect of deleting a field from a table structure?

6. A(n) _____ text file is one in which fields of data are separated by a character such as a comma or a tab.

7. The _____ is the "one" table in a one-to-many relationship, and the _____ is the "many" table in the relationship.

8. _____ is a set of rules that Access enforces to maintain consistency between related tables when you update data in a database.

Practice the skills
you learned in
the tutorial using
the same case
scenario.

PRACTICE

Review Assignments

Data Files needed for the Review Assignments: Supplier.accdb (*cont. from Tutorial 1*) **and Goods.xlsx**

In addition to tracking information about the suppliers Belmont Landscapes works with, Oren also wants to track information about their products. He asks you to create a new table in the Supplier database by completing the following steps:

1. Open the **Supplier** database, which you created and stored in the Access1\Review folder in Tutorial 1.
2. Open the **Company** table in Design view, and set the field properties as shown in Figure 2-43.

Figure 2-43 | **Field properties for the Company table**

Field Name	Data Type	Description	Field Size	Other
CompanyID	Text	Primary key	6	Caption = Company ID
Company	Text		50	Caption = Company Name
Product	Text		40	Caption = Product Type
Address	Text		35	
City	Text		25	
State	Text		2	
Zip	Text		10	
Phone	Text		14	
ContactFirst	Text		20	Caption = Contact First Name
ContactLast	Text		25	Caption = Contact Last Name
InitialContact	Date/Time			Format = Short Date
				Caption = Initial Contact Date

3. Save and close the Company table. Click the Yes button when a message appears indicating some data might be lost. Switch to Datasheet view and resize columns, as necessary, to their best fit. Then save and close the Company table.
4. Create a new table in Design view, using the table design shown in Figure 2-44.

Figure 2-44 | **Design for the Product table**

Field Name	Data Type	Description	Field Size	Other
ProductID	Text	Primary key	4	Caption = Product ID
CompanyID	Text	Foreign key	6	Caption = Company ID
ProductType	Text		35	Caption = Product Type
Price	Currency			Format = Standard
				Decimal Places = 2
Color	Text		15	
Size	Text		15	
Material	Text		30	
Weight	Number		Single	Caption = Weight in Lbs
Discount	Yes/No			Caption = Discount Offered
				Format = Yes/No

5. Specify ProductID as the primary key, and then save the table as **Product**.
6. Modify the table structure by adding a new field named **Unit** (data type: Text, field size: **15**) between the Price and Color fields. Move the Size field so that it follows the Material field.
7. Enter the records shown in Figure 2-45 in the Product table. When finished, close the Product table.

Figure 2-45	Records for the Product table

Product ID	Company ID	Product Type	Price	Unit	Color	Material	Size	Weight in Lbs	Discount Offered
5306	GEN359	Pine mulch	23.35	Cubic yard	Dark brown	Softwoods-pine			Y
5013	HOL207	Small bench	712.00	Each	Green	Steel and cast iron	8 x 2 feet	266	N

8. Use the Import Spreadsheet Wizard to add data to the Product table. The data you need to import is contained in the Goods workbook, which is an Excel file located in the Access1\Review folder provided with your Data Files.

  a. Specify the Goods workbook as the source of the data.

  b. Select the option for appending the data.

  c. Select Product as the table.

  d. In the Import Spreadsheet Wizard dialog boxes, make sure Access confirms that the first row contains column headings, and import to the Product table. Do not save the import steps.

9. Open the **Product** table in Datasheet view and resize all columns to their best fit. Then save and close the Product table.

10. Define a one-to-many relationship between the primary Company table and the related Product table. Select the referential integrity option and the cascade updates option for the relationship.

11. Save the changes to the Relationships window and close it, compact and repair the Supplier database, and then close the database.

Case Problem 1

If you have a SAM 2010 user profile, your instructor may have assigned an autogradable version of this assignment. If so, log into the SAM 2010 Web site at www.cengage.com/sam2010 to download the instructions and start files.

Data Files needed for this Case Problem: Pinehill.accdb (*cont. from Tutorial 1*), Music.accdb, Lessons.xlsx, and Student.txt

Pine Hill Music School   Yuka Koyama uses the Pinehill database to maintain information about the students, teachers, and contracts for her music school. Yuka asks you to help her build the database by updating one table and creating two new tables. Complete the following steps:

1. Open the **Pinehill** database, which you created and stored in the Access1\Case1 folder in Tutorial 1.

2. Open the **Teacher** table in Design view, and set the field properties as shown in Figure 2-46.

Figure 2-46	Field properties for the Teacher table

Field Name	Data Type	Description	Field Size	Other
TeacherID	Text	Primary key	7	Caption = Teacher ID
FirstName	Text		20	Caption = First Name
LastName	Text		25	Caption = Last Name
Degree	Text		3	
School	Text		50	
HireDate	Date/Time			Format = Short Date
				Caption = Hire Date

3. Add a new field as the last field in the Teacher table with the field name **Beginners**, the Yes/No data type, a Format property of Yes/No, and a Caption property of **Takes Beginners**.

4. Save the Teacher table. Click the Yes button when a message appears indicating some data might be lost.

5. In the datasheet, resize the Takes Beginners column to best fit, and then specify that the following teachers can take beginners: Schwartz, Eberle, Norris, Tanaka, Culbertson, and Mueller.

6. Save and close the Teacher table.

7. Yuka created a table named Student in the Music database that is located in the Access1\Case1 folder provided with your Data Files. Import the structure of the Student table in the Music database into a new table named Student in the Pinehill database. Do not save the import steps.

8. Open the **Student** table in Datasheet view, and then add the following two fields to the end of the table: **BirthDate** (Date/Time field) and **Gender** (Text field).

9. Use the Phone Quick Start selection in the Data Type gallery to add four fields related to phones between the Zip and BirthDate fields. (*Hint:* Be sure to make the BirthDate field the active field before adding the new fields.)

10. Display the Student table in Design view, delete the BusinessPhone and FaxNumber fields, and then save and close the Student table.

11. Modify the design of the Student table so that it matches the design in Figure 2-47, including the revised field names and data types.

Figure 2-47 | **Field properties for the Student table**

Field Name	Data Type	Description	Field Size	Other
StudentID	Text	Primary key	7	Caption = Student ID
LastName	Text		25	Caption = Last Name
FirstName	Text		20	Caption = First Name
Address	Text		35	
City	Text		25	
State	Text		2	
Zip	Text		10	
HomePhone	Text		14	
MobilePhone	Text		14	
BirthDate	Date/Time			Format = Short Date
				Caption = Birth Date
Gender	Text	F(emale), M(ale)	1	

12. Move the LastName field so it follows the FirstName field.

13. Save your changes to the table design, add the records shown in Figure 2-48 to the Student table, and then close the Student table.

Figure 2-48 | **Records for the Student table**

Student ID	First Name	Last Name	Address	City	State	Zip	Home Phone	Mobile Phone	Birth Date	Gender
APP7509	Sam	Applegate	15675 SW Greens Way	Portland	OR	97224	503-968-2245	503-968-0091	10/10/1996	M
BAR7544	Andrea	Barreau	7660 SW 135th Ave	Beaverton	OR	97008	503-579-2227	503-579-8754	11/28/1999	F

14. Yuka exported the student data that she was maintaining in another computer system to a text file, and she asks you to add this data to the Student table. The data you need to import is contained in the Student text file (located in the Access1\Case1 folder provided with your Data Files).

a. Specify the Student text file as the source of the data.

b. Select the option for appending the data to the table.

c. Select Student as the table.

d. In the Import Text Wizard dialog boxes, choose the option to import delimited data, to use a comma delimiter, and to import the data into the Student table. Do not save the import steps.

15. Open the **Student** table in Datasheet view, resize columns in the datasheet to their best fit (as necessary), and then save and close the table.

16. Create a new table in Design view, using the table design shown in Figure 2-49.

Figure 2-49	**Design for the Contract table**

Field Name	Data Type	Description	Field Size	Other
ContractID	Text	Primary key	4	Caption = Contract ID
StudentID	Text	Foreign key	7	Caption = Student ID
TeacherID	Text	Foreign key	7	Caption = Teacher ID
LessonType	Text		25	Caption = Lesson Type
LessonLength	Number	30 or 60 minutes	Integer	Caption = Lesson Length
LessonCost	Currency			Format = Currency Decimal Places = 0 Caption = Lesson Monthly Cost
RentalCost	Currency	Monthly rental charge for instrument		Format = Currency Decimal Places = 0 Caption = Monthly Rental Cost

17. Specify ContractID as the primary key, and then save the table using the name **Contract**.

18. Switch to Datasheet view, and then use the Start and End Dates Quick Start selection in the Data Type gallery to add two Date/Time fields between the TeacherID and LessonType fields. (*Hint:* Be sure to make the LessonType field the active field before adding the new fields.)

19. Switch to Design view, specify the Short Date format for the StartDate and EndDate fields, change the field captions to **Contract Start Date** and **Contract End Date** (respectively), and then save and close the Contract table.

⊕ **EXPLORE** 20. Use the Import Spreadsheet Wizard to add data to the Contract table. The data you need to import is contained in the Lessons workbook, which is an Excel file located in the Access1\Case1 folder provided with your Data Files.

a. Specify the Lessons workbook as the source of the data.

b. Select the option for appending the data to the table.

c. Select Contract as the table.

d. In the Import Spreadsheet Wizard dialog boxes, choose the Sheet1 worksheet, make sure Access confirms that the first row contains column headings, and import to the Contract table. Do not save the import steps.

21. Open the **Contract** table and add the records shown in Figure 2-50. (*Hint:* Use the New button in the Records group on the Home tab to add a new record.)

Figure 2-50	**Records for the Contract table**

Contract ID	Student ID	Teacher ID	Contract Start Date	Contract End Date	Lesson Type	Lesson Length	Lesson Monthly Cost	Monthly Rental Cost
3176	VAR7527	91-0178	3/21/2013	3/21/2014	Violin	30	$140	$35
3179	MCE7551	70-4490	6/1/2013	6/1/2014	Guitar	60	$200	$0

22. Resize columns in the datasheet to their best fit (as necessary), and then save and close the Contract table.

23. Define the one-to-many relationships between the database tables as follows: between the primary Student table and the related Contract table, and between the primary Teacher table and the related Contract table. Select the referential integrity option and the cascade updates option for each relationship.

24. Save the changes to the Relationships window and close it, compact and repair the Pinehill database, and then close the database.

Use the Import Spreadsheet Wizard to create a table to store data about fitness center members.

CHALLENGE

Case Problem 2

Data Files needed for this Case Problem: Fitness.accdb (*cont. from Tutorial 1*) **and Center.xlsx**

Parkhurst Health & Fitness Center Martha Parkhurst uses the Fitness database to track information about members who join the center and the programs in which each member is enrolled. She asks you to help her maintain this database. Complete the following:

1. Open the **Fitness** database, which you created and stored in the Access1\Case2 folder in Tutorial 1.

2. Open the **Program** table in Design view, and change the following field properties:

   a. ProgramID: Enter **Primary key** for the description, change the field size to **3**, and enter **Program ID** for the caption.

   b. ProgramType: Change the field size to **40** and enter **Program Type** for the caption.

   c. MonthlyFee: Change the format to **Standard** and enter **Monthly Fee** for the caption.

   d. PhysicalRequired: Change the data type to Yes/No, the Format property to Yes/No, and enter **Physical Required** for the caption.

3. Save and close the Program table. Click the Yes button when a message appears indicating some data might be lost.

✦ EXPLORE 4. Use the Import Spreadsheet Wizard to create a table in the Fitness database. As the source of the data, specify the Center workbook, located in the Access1\Case2 folder provided with your Data Files. Select the option to import the source data into a new table in the current database, and then click the OK button.

✦ EXPLORE 5. Complete the Import Spreadsheet Wizard dialog boxes as follows:

   a. Select Sheet1 as the worksheet you want to import.

   b. Accept the option specifying that the first row contains column headings.

   c. Accept the field options the wizard suggests, and do not skip any fields.

   d. Choose MemberID as your own primary key.

   e. Import the data to a table named **Member**, and do not save your import steps.

6. Open the **Member** table in Design view, and then delete the InitiationFeeWaived field.

7. Modify the design of the Member table so that it matches the design shown in Figure 2-51. (*Hint*: For Text fields, delete any formats specified in the Format property boxes.)

Figure 2-51	Design for the Member table

Field Name	Data Type	Description	Field Size	Other
MemberID	Text	Primary key	4	Caption = Member ID
ProgramID	Text	Foreign key	3	Caption = Program ID
First	Text		18	Caption = First Name
Last	Text		18	Caption = Last Name
Street	Text		30	
City	Text		24	
State	Text		2	
Zip	Text		10	
Phone	Text		14	
DateJoined	Date/Time			Format = Short Date
				Caption = Date Joined
Expiration	Date/Time	Date when membership expires		Format = Short Date
				Caption = Expiration Date
Status	Text	Active, Inactive, or On Hold	8	Caption = Membership Status

8. Save the Member table. Click the Yes button when a message appears indicating some data might be lost.

⊕ **EXPLORE**

9. The Default Value property for a field allows you to specify the value that should be entered, by default, for that field for each new record you enter in the table. Specifying a default value can save you time if most of the records you enter will include that value for the field. Set the Default Value property for the Status field to **"Active"** (including the quotation marks). Save and close the Member table.

10. Open the **Member** table in Datasheet view and confirm that the InitiationFeeWaived field was removed from the table. If not, open the table in Design view again, repeat the step to delete the InitiationFeeWaived field, and then save and close the table.

11. Add the records shown in Figure 2-52 to the Member table. (*Hint*: Use the New button in the Records group on the Home tab to add a new record.) Be sure to enter your first and last names in the appropriate fields for the first new record added. Note the default field value of "Active" in the Membership Status column as you enter the new records.

Figure 2-52	Records for the Member table

Member ID	Program ID	First Name	Last Name	Street	City	State	Zip	Phone	Date Joined	Expiration Date	Membership Status
1170	203	Student First	Student Last	40 Green Boulevard	Bon Air	VA	23235	804-323-6824	6/3/2013	12/3/2013	Active
1172	211	Ed	Curran	25 Fairway Drive	Richmond	VA	23220	804-674-0227	11/16/2013	11/16/2014	Active

12. Resize columns in the datasheet to their best fit (as necessary), and then save and close the table.

13. Define a one-to-many relationship between the primary Program table and the related Member table. Select the referential integrity option and the cascade updates option for this relationship.

14. Save the changes to the Relationships window and close it, compact and repair the Fitness database, and then close the database.

Use your skills to create and modify tables for a recycling agency.

APPLY

Case Problem 3

Data Files needed for this Case Problem: Agency.txt, Rossi.accdb (*cont. from Tutorial 1*), **Gifts.xlsx, and Recycle.accdb**

Rossi Recycling Group Tom Rossi uses the Rossi database to maintain information about the donors, agencies, and donations to his not-for-profit agency. Tom asks you to help him maintain the database by updating one table and creating two new ones. Complete the following steps:

1. Open the **Rossi** database, which you created and stored in the Access1\Case3 folder in Tutorial 1.

2. Open the **Donor** table in Design view, and change the following field properties:
   a. DonorID: Enter **Primary key** for the description, change the field size to **5**, and enter **Donor ID** for the caption.
   b. Title: Change the field size to **4**.
   c. FirstName: Change the field size to **20** and enter **First Name** for the caption.
   d. LastName: Change the field size to **25** and enter **Last Name** for the caption.
   e. Phone: Change the field size to **14.**

3. Save and close the Donor table. Click the Yes button when a message appears indicating some data might be lost.

4. Tom created a table named Agency in the Recycle database that is located in the Access1\Case3 folder provided with your Data Files. Import the structure of the Agency table in the Recycle database into a new table named Agency in the Rossi database. Do not save the import steps.

5. Open the Agency table in Datasheet view, and then delete the following fields from the table: Fax Number, Mobile Phone, and Notes.

6. Rename the ID field to **AgencyID**, and change its data type to Text.

7. Use the Address Quick Start selection in the Data Type gallery to add five fields between the First Name and Phone fields. (*Hint:* Be sure to make the Phone field the active field before adding the new fields.)

8. Switch to Design view, and then modify the Agency table so that it matches the design shown in Figure 2-53, including the field names and their order. Make sure the AgencyID field is specified as the primary key. Also, be sure to delete the CountryRegion field from the table, and delete the Caption property values for the fields added with the Address Quick Start selection.

Figure 2-53 Design for the Agency table

Field Name	Data Type	Description	Field Size	Other
AgencyID	Text	Primary key	3	Caption = Agency ID
Agency	Text		40	Caption = Agency Name
FirstName	Text		20	Caption = Contact First Name
LastName	Text		25	Caption = Contact Last Name
Address	Text		30	
City	Text		24	
State	Text		2	
Zip	Text		10	
Phone	Text		14	

9. Save your changes to the table design, add the records shown in Figure 2-54 to the Agency table, and then close the Agency table.

Figure 2-54   Records for the Agency table

Agency ID	Agency Name	Contact First Name	Contact Last Name	Address	City	State	Zip	Phone
K64	Community Development	Jerri	Clarkson	223 Penn Ave	Salina	KS	67401	785-309-3351
K82	SeniorCare Program	Todd	Groverman	718 N Walnut	McPherson	KS	67460	620-241-3668

10. Tom exported the agency data that he was maintaining in another computer system to a text file, and he asks you to add this data to the Agency table. The data you need to import is contained in the Agency text file (located in the Access1\Case3 folder provided with your Data Files).

   a. Specify the Agency text file as the source of the data.

   b. Select the option for appending the data to the table.

   c. Select Agency as the table.

   d. In the Import Text Wizard dialog boxes, choose the options to import delimited data, to use a comma delimiter, and to import the data into the Agency table. Do not save the import steps.

11. Resize columns in the Agency datasheet to their best fit (as necessary), and then save and close the table.

12. Use Design view to create a table using the table design shown in Figure 2-55.

Figure 2-55   Design for the Donation table

Field Name	Data Type	Description	Field Size	Other
DonationID	Text	Primary key	4	Caption = Donation ID
DonorID	Text	Foreign key	5	Caption = Donor ID
AgencyID	Text	Foreign key	3	Caption = Agency ID
DonationDate	Date/Time			Format = Short Date
				Caption = Donation Date
Description	Text		50	Caption = Donation Description
DonationValue	Currency	Cash amount donated or estimated value of goods donated		Format = Currency
				Decimal Places = 2
				Caption = Donation Value
Pickup	Yes/No			Caption = Pickup Required
				Format = Yes/No

13. Specify DonationID as the primary key, save the table as **Donation**, and then close the table.

EXPLORE 14. Use the Import Spreadsheet Wizard to add data to the Donation table. The data you need to import is contained in the Gifts workbook, which is an Excel file located in the Access1\Case3 folder provided with your Data Files.

   a. Specify the Gifts workbook as the source of the data.

   b. Select the option for appending the data to the table.

   c. Select Donation as the table.

   d. In the Import Spreadsheet Wizard dialog boxes, choose the Sheet1 worksheet, make sure Access confirms that the first row contains column headings, and import to the Donation table. Do not save the import steps.

15. Open the **Donation** table, and add the records shown in Figure 2-56. (Hint: Use the New button in the Records group on the Home tab to add a new record.)

Figure 2-56 **Records for the Donation table**

Donation ID	Donor ID	Agency ID	Donation Date	Donation Description	Donation Value	Pickup Required
2117	36012	K82	02/20/2013	Cash	$50.00	No
2122	36016	N33	03/22/2013	Cash	$35.00	No

16. Resize columns in the datasheet to their best fit (as necessary), and then save and close the table.

17. Define the one-to-many relationships between the database tables as follows: between the primary Donor table and the related Donation table, and between the primary Agency table and the related Donation table. Select the referential integrity option and the cascade updates option for each relationship.

18. Save the changes to the Relationships window and close it, compact and repair the Rossi database, and then close the database.

Explore some new skills to finish creating a database for a luxury rental company.

CHALLENGE

Case Problem 4

Data Files needed for this Case Problem: Bookings.txt, GEM.accdb (*cont. from Tutorial 1*), **and Overseas.accdb**

GEM Ultimate Vacations Griffin and Emma MacElroy use the GEM database to track the data about the services they provide to the clients who book luxury vacations through their agency. They ask you to help them maintain this database. Complete the following steps:

1. Open the **GEM** database, which you created and stored in the Access1\Case4 folder in Tutorial 1.

2. Open the **Guest** table in Design view and change the following field properties:
   a. GuestID: Enter **Primary key** for the description, change the field size to **3**, and enter **Guest ID** for the caption.
   b. GuestFirst: Change the field size to **20** and enter **Guest First Name** for the caption.
   c. GuestLast: Change the field size to **25** and enter **Guest Last Name** for the caption.
   d. Address: Change the field size to **32**.
   e. City: Change the field size to **24**.
   f. State/Prov: Change the field size to **2**.
   g. PostalCode: Change the field size to **10** and enter **Postal Code** for the caption.
   h. Country: Change the field size to **15**.
   i. Phone: Change the field size to **14**.

3. Save the Guest table, click the Yes button when a message appears indicating some data might be lost, resize the Guest First Name and Guest Last Name columns in Datasheet view to their best fit, and then save and close the table.

EXPLORE

4. In addition to importing the structure of an existing Access table, you can also import both the structure and the data contained in a table to create a new table. Import the Rentals table structure and data from the Overseas database into a new table in the GEM database as follows:
   a. Click the External Data tab on the Ribbon, and then click the Access button in the Import & Link group.
   b. As the source of the data, specify the Overseas database, located in the Access1\Case4 folder provided with your Data Files.

    c. Select the option button to import tables, queries, forms, reports, macros, and modules into the current database, and then click the OK button.

    d. In the Import Objects dialog box, click Rentals, click the Options button, and then make sure that the correct option is selected to import the table's data and structure (definition).

    e. Do not save your import steps.

⊕ **EXPLORE**   5. Right-click the Rentals table in the Navigation Pane, click Rename on the shortcut menu, and then enter **Property** as the new name for this table.

  6. Open the **Property** table in Design view, delete the VIP Program field, and then move the PropertyType field so that it appears between the Sleeps and Description fields. Make sure that the PropertyID field is specified as the table's primary key.

  7. Change the following properties:

    a. PropertyID: Change the data type to Text, change the field size to **4**, and enter **Property ID** for the caption.

    b. PropertyName: Enter **Property Name** for the caption.

    c. NightlyRate: Enter **Nightly Rate** for the caption.

    d. PropertyType: Enter **Property Type** for the caption.

  8. Save the modified table and then display it in Datasheet view. Resize all datasheet columns to their best fit, and then save and close the table.

  9. Use Design view to create a table using the table design shown in Figure 2-57.

Figure 2-57   **Design for the Reservation table**

Field Name	Data Type	Description	Field Size	Other
ReservationID	Text	Primary key	3	Caption = Reservation ID
GuestID	Text	Foreign key	3	Caption = Guest ID
PropertyID	Text	Foreign key	4	Caption = Property ID
StartDate	Date/Time			Caption = Start Date
EndDate	Date/Time			Caption = End Date
People	Number	Number of people in the party	Integer	
Rate	Currency	Rate per day; includes any discounts or promotions		Format = Currency
				Decimal Places = 0
				Caption = Rental Rate

  10. Specify ReservationID as the primary key, and then save the table as **Reservation**.

⊕ **EXPLORE**   11. Refer back to Figure 2-14 to review the custom date formats. Change the Format property of the StartDate and EndDate fields to a custom format that displays dates in a format similar to 11/23/13. Save and close the Reservation table.

  12. Griffin exported the reservation data that he was maintaining in another computer system to a text file, and he asks you to add this data to the Reservation table. The data you need to import is contained in the Bookings text file (located in the Access1\Case4 folder provided with your Data Files).

    a. Specify the Bookings text file as the source of the data.

    b. Select the option for appending the data to the table.

    c. Select Reservation as the table.

    d. In the Import Text Wizard dialog boxes, choose the option to import delimited data, to use a comma delimiter, and to import the data into the Reservation table.

    e. Do not save the import steps.

  13. Resize columns in the **Reservation** table datasheet to their best fit (as necessary), and then save and close the table.

14. Define the one-to-many relationships between the database tables as follows: between the primary Guest table and the related Reservation table, and between the primary Property table and the related Reservation table. Select the referential integrity option and the cascade updates option for each relationship.

15. Save the changes to the Relationships window and close it, compact and repair the GEM database, and then close the database.

SAM: Skills Assessment Manager

For current SAM information, including versions and content details, visit SAM Central (http://samcentral.course.com). If you have a SAM user profile, you may have access to hands-on instruction, practice, and assessment of the skills covered in this tutorial. Since various versions of SAM are supported throughout the life of this text, check with your instructor for the correct instructions and URL/Web site for accessing assignments.

ENDING DATA FILES

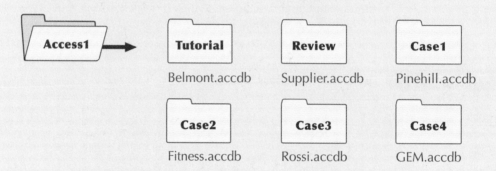

Access1 → Tutorial — Belmont.accdb

Review — Supplier.accdb

Case1 — Pinehill.accdb

Case2 — Fitness.accdb

Case3 — Rossi.accdb

Case4 — GEM.accdb

Maintaining and Querying a Database

Updating and Retrieving Information About Customers, Contracts, and Invoices

Case | *Belmont Landscapes*

At a recent meeting, Oren Belmont and his staff discussed the importance of maintaining accurate information about the firm's customers, contracts, and invoices, and regularly monitoring the business activities of Belmont Landscapes. For example, Sarah Fisher and the office staff need to make sure they have up-to-date contact information, such as phone numbers and email addresses, for all the firm's customers. They also must monitor the invoice activity to ensure that invoices are paid on time and in full. Taylor Sico, the marketing manager at Belmont Landscapes, and her marketing staff track customer activity to develop new strategies for promoting the services provided by Belmont Landscapes. In addition, Oren is interested in analyzing other aspects of the business related to contracts and finances. You can satisfy all these informational needs for Belmont Landscapes by updating data in the Belmont database and by creating and using queries that retrieve information from the database.

STARTING DATA FILES

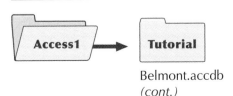

Access1	Tutorial	Review	Case1	Case2	Case3	Case4
	Belmont.accdb *(cont.)*	Supplier.accdb *(cont.)*	Pinehill.accdb *(cont.)*	Fitness.accdb *(cont.)*	Rossi.accdb *(cont.)*	GEM.accdb *(cont.)*

SESSION 3.1 VISUAL OVERVIEW

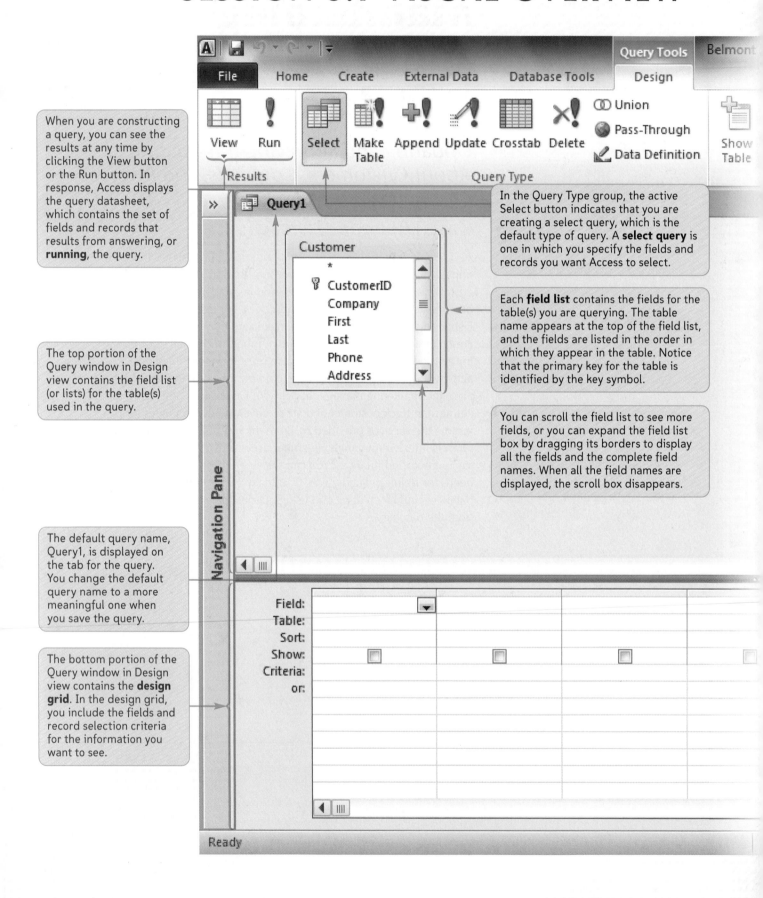

When you are constructing a query, you can see the results at any time by clicking the View button or the Run button. In response, Access displays the query datasheet, which contains the set of fields and records that results from answering, or **running**, the query.

The top portion of the Query window in Design view contains the field list (or lists) for the table(s) used in the query.

The default query name, Query1, is displayed on the tab for the query. You change the default query name to a more meaningful one when you save the query.

The bottom portion of the Query window in Design view contains the **design grid**. In the design grid, you include the fields and record selection criteria for the information you want to see.

In the Query Type group, the active Select button indicates that you are creating a select query, which is the default type of query. A **select query** is one in which you specify the fields and records you want Access to select.

Each **field list** contains the fields for the table(s) you are querying. The table name appears at the top of the field list, and the fields are listed in the order in which they appear in the table. Notice that the primary key for the table is identified by the key symbol.

You can scroll the field list to see more fields, or you can expand the field list box by dragging its borders to display all the fields and the complete field names. When all the field names are displayed, the scroll box disappears.

QUERY WINDOW IN DESIGN VIEW

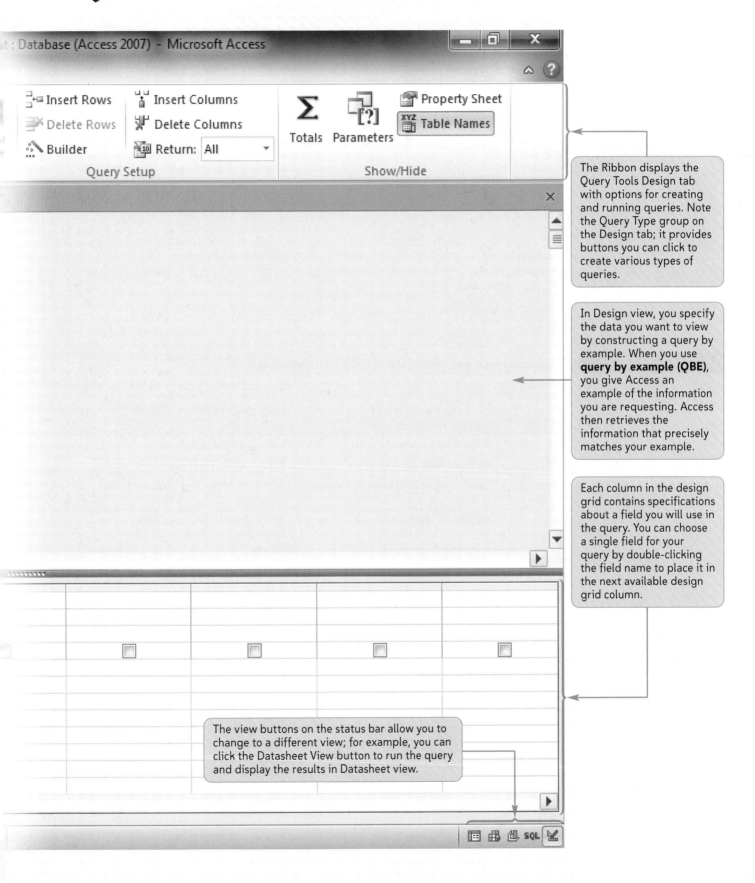

The Ribbon displays the Query Tools Design tab with options for creating and running queries. Note the Query Type group on the Design tab; it provides buttons you can click to create various types of queries.

In Design view, you specify the data you want to view by constructing a query by example. When you use **query by example (QBE)**, you give Access an example of the information you are requesting. Access then retrieves the information that precisely matches your example.

Each column in the design grid contains specifications about a field you will use in the query. You can choose a single field for your query by double-clicking the field name to place it in the next available design grid column.

The view buttons on the status bar allow you to change to a different view; for example, you can click the Datasheet View button to run the query and display the results in Datasheet view.

Updating a Database

Updating, or **maintaining**, a database is the process of adding, modifying, and deleting records in database tables to keep them current and accurate. After reviewing the data in the Belmont database, Sarah identified some changes that need to be made to the data. She would like you to modify the field values in one record in the Customer table, and then to delete a record in the Contract table.

Modifying Records

To modify the field values in a record, you must first make the record the current record. Then you position the insertion point in the field value to make minor changes or select the field value to replace it entirely. In Tutorial 1, you used the mouse with the scroll bars and the navigation buttons to navigate the records in a datasheet. You can also use keystroke combinations and the F2 key to navigate a datasheet and to select field values. The **F2 key** is a toggle that you use to switch between navigation mode and editing mode:

- In **navigation mode**, Access selects an entire field value. If you type while you are in navigation mode, your typed entry replaces the highlighted field value.
- In **editing mode**, you can insert or delete characters in a field value based on the location of the insertion point.

Figure 3-1 shows some of the navigation mode and editing mode keystroke techniques.

Figure 3-1	Navigation mode and editing mode keystroke techniques

Press	To Move the Selection in Navigation Mode	To Move the Insertion Point in Editing Mode
←	Left one field value at a time	Left one character at a time
→	Right one field value at a time	Right one character at a time
Home	Left to the first field value in the record	To the left of the first character in the field value
End	Right to the last field value in the record	To the right of the last character in the field value
↑ or ↓	Up or down one record at a time	Up or down one record at a time and switch to navigation mode
Tab or Enter	Right one field value at a time	Right one field value at a time and switch to navigation mode
Ctrl+Home	To the first field value in the first record	To the left of the first character in the field value
Ctrl+End	To the last field value in the last record	To the right of the last character in the field value

The Customer table record Sarah wants you to change is for Walker Investment Company, one of Belmont Landscapes' commercial customers. The company recently moved its office from Grand Rapids to Battle Creek, so you need to update the Customer table record with the new address and phone information.

To open the Belmont database and modify the record:

▶ **1.** Start Access and open the **Belmont** database located in the Access1\Tutorial folder.

   Trouble? If the Security Warning is displayed below the Ribbon, click the Enable Content button next to the Security Warning.

▶ **2.** Open the **Customer** table in Datasheet view. The first value for the CustomerID field, 11001, is highlighted, indicating that the table is in navigation mode.

   The record you need to modify is near the end of the table and has a CustomerID field value of 11087.

▶ **3.** Press the **Ctrl+End** keys. Access displays records from the end of the table and selects the last field value in the last record, record 40. This field value is for the Email field.

▶ **4.** Press the **Home** key. The first field value in the last record is now selected. This field value is for the CustomerID field.

▶ **5.** Press the **↑** key. The CustomerID field value for the previous record, CustomerID 11087, is selected. This record is the one you need to change.

▶ **6.** Press the **Tab** key four times to move to the Phone field and select its field value, type **269-963-0190**, press the **Tab** key, type **1752 S Main St**, press the **Tab** key, type **Battle Creek**, press the **Tab** key twice, type **49014**, and then press the **Tab** key. The changes to the record are complete. See Figure 3-2.

Figure 3-2	Table after changing field values in a record

TIP

Access saves changes to field values when you move to a new field or another record, or when you close the table. You don't have to click the Save button to save changes to field values or records.

field values changed

⊞	Russell	616-940-3380	722 Beechwood Dr	East Grand Rapids	MI	49506	srussell3@dnd57.org
⊞	Van Dousen	616-392-4629	249 W 11th St	Holland	MI	49424	jvdousen2@tulips3.com
⊞	Williams	517-337-0990	1003 Albert Ave	East Lansing	MI	48823	jwilliams94@hsc7.edu
⊞	DeSantis	616-866-4882	78 Spring St	Rockford	MI	49341	cdesantis9@milocal123.com
⊞	Phillips	616-637-5408	39 Water St	South Haven	MI	49090	ephillips8@milocal123.com
⊞	Belanger	269-963-0190	1752 S Main St	Battle Creek	MI	49014	nbelanger4@wic88.com
⊞	Kervin	616-454-3327	333 Pearl St	Grand Rapids	MI	49503	skervin3@wcpf47.org

Record: I◄ ◄ 39 of 40 ► ►I ►⚬ No Filter Search

Datasheet View

▶ **7.** Close the Customer table.

The next update Sarah asks you to make is to delete a record in the Contract table. The customer who signed contract number 3101 owns a chain of small restaurants and had planned to renovate the landscaping at each restaurant site. His plans have changed for one of these sites and he has cancelled the contract, so the record needs to be deleted. When you are maintaining database tables, you first need to find the data to change.

Finding Data in a Table

Access provides options you can use to locate specific field values in a table. Instead of scrolling the Contract table datasheet to find the contract that you need to delete—the record for contract number 3101—you can use the Find command to find the record. The **Find command** allows you to search a table or query datasheet, or a form, to locate a specific field value or part of a field value. This feature is particularly useful when searching a table that contains a large number of records.

To search for the record in the Contract table:

1. Open the **Contract** table in Datasheet view. The first field value for the ContractNum field, 3011, is selected. You need to search the ContractNum field to find the record containing the value 3101, so the insertion point is already correctly positioned in the field you want to search.

2. In the Find group on the Home tab, click the **Find** button. The Find and Replace dialog box opens. See Figure 3-3.

Figure 3-3 Find and Replace dialog box

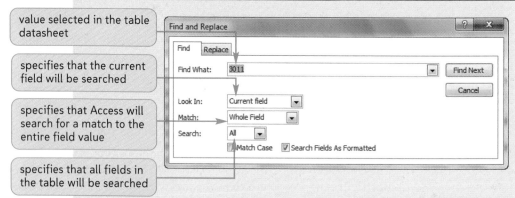

value selected in the table datasheet

specifies that the current field will be searched

specifies that Access will search for a match to the entire field value

specifies that all fields in the table will be searched

The field value 3011 appears in the Find What box because this value is selected in the table datasheet. The Look In box indicates that the current field will be searched for the value. The Match box indicates that the Find command will match the whole field value, which is correct for your search. You also can choose to search for only part of a field value, such as when you need to find all contract numbers that start with a certain value. The Search box indicates that all the records in the table will be searched for the value you want to find. You also can choose to search up or down from the currently selected record.

Trouble? Some of the settings in your dialog box might be different from those shown in Figure 3-3 depending on the last search performed on the computer you're using. If so, change the settings so that they match those in the figure.

3. Make sure the value 3011 is selected in the Find What box, type **3101** to replace the selected value, and then click the **Find Next** button. Access scrolls the datasheet to record 59 and selects the field value you specified.

4. Click the **Cancel** button to close the Find and Replace dialog box.

Deleting Records

To delete a record, you need to select the record in Datasheet view, and then delete it using the Delete button in the Records group on the Home tab, or the Delete Record option on the shortcut menu.

REFERENCE

Deleting a Record

- With the table open in Datasheet view, click the row selector for the record you want to delete.
- In the Records group on the Home tab, click the Delete button (or right-click the row selector for the record, and then click Delete Record on the shortcut menu).
- In the dialog box asking you to confirm the deletion, click the Yes button.

Now that you have found the record with contract number 3101, you can delete it. To delete a record, you must first select the entire row for the record.

To delete the record:

1. Click the row selector for the record containing the ContractNum field value **3101**, which should still be highlighted. The entire row is selected.

2. In the Records group on the Home tab, click the **Delete** button. A dialog box opens and indicates that you cannot delete the record because the Invoice table contains records that are related to ContractNum 3101. Recall that you defined a one-to-many relationship between the Contract and Invoice tables and enforced referential integrity. When you try to delete a record in the primary table (Contract), Access prevents the deletion if matching records exist in the related table (Invoice). This protection helps to maintain the integrity of the data in the database.

   To delete the record in the Contract table, you first must delete the related records in the Invoice table.

3. Click the **OK** button in the dialog box to close it. Notice the plus sign that appears at the beginning of each record in the Contract table. The **plus sign** indicates that the Contract table is related to another table—in this case, the Invoice table.

   TIP
   The plus sign changes to a minus sign for the current record when its related records are displayed.

4. Scroll the datasheet down until you see the rest of the records in the table, so that you have room to view the related records for the contract record.

5. Click the **plus sign** next to ContractNum 3101. Access displays the four related records from the Invoice table for this contract. See Figure 3-4.

Figure 3-4   Related records from the Invoice table in the subdatasheet

plus signs indicate the table is related to another table

minus sign appears when related records are displayed

subdatasheet with related records from the Invoice table

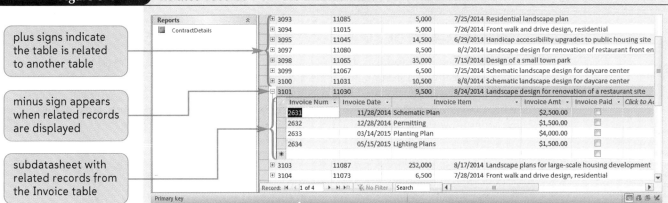

The related records from the Invoice table are displayed in a **subdatasheet**. When you first open a table that is the primary table in a one-to-many relationship, the subdatasheet containing the records from the related table is not displayed. You need to click the plus sign, also called the **expand indicator**, to display the related records in the subdatasheet. When the subdatasheet is open you can navigate and update it, just as you can using a table datasheet.

You need to delete the records in the Invoice table that are related to ContractNum 3101 before you can delete this contract record. The four Invoice table records are for invoices set up to be paid for future phases of the contract, which has now been cancelled. You could open the Invoice table and find the related records. However, an easier way is to delete them from the subdatasheet. The records will be deleted from the Invoice table automatically.

6. Click and hold the mouse button on the row selector for the first Invoice table record in the subdatasheet, drag the pointer down to select all four records, and then release the mouse button. With the four records selected, you can delete them all at the same time.

7. In the Records group on the Home tab, click the **Delete** button. Access opens a dialog box asking you to confirm the deletion of four records. Because the deletion of a record is permanent and cannot be undone, Access prompts you to make sure that you want to delete the records.

8. Click the **Yes** button to confirm the deletion and close the dialog box. The records are removed from the Invoice table, and the subdatasheet is now empty.

9. Click the **minus sign** next to ContractNum 3101 to close the subdatasheet.

Now that you have deleted all the related records in the Invoice table, you can delete the record for ContractNum 3101. You'll use the shortcut menu to do so.

Be sure to select the correct record before deleting it.

10. Right-click the row selector for the record for ContractNum **3101**. Access selects the record and displays the shortcut menu.

11. Click **Delete Record** on the shortcut menu, and then click the **Yes** button in the dialog box to confirm the deletion. The record is deleted from the table.

12. Close the Contract table.

You have finished updating the Belmont database by modifying and deleting records. Next, you'll retrieve specific data from the database to meet various requests for information about Belmont Landscapes.

Introduction to Queries

As you learned in Tutorial 1, a query is a question you ask about data stored in a database. For example, Oren might create a query to find records in the Customer table for only those customers located in a specific city. When you create a query, you tell Access which fields you need and what criteria Access should use to select the records. Access provides powerful query capabilities that allow you to do the following:

• Display selected fields and records from a table.
• Sort records.
• Perform calculations.
• Generate data for forms, reports, and other queries.
• Update data in the tables in a database.
• Find and display data from two or more tables.

Most questions about data are generalized queries in which you specify the fields and records you want Access to select. These common requests for information, such as "Which customers are located in Kalamazoo?" or "How many invoices have been paid?" are select queries. The answer to a select query is returned in the form of a datasheet. The result of a query is also referred to as a **recordset** because the query produces a set of records that answers your question.

INSIGHT

Designing Queries vs. Using a Query Wizard

More specialized, technical queries, such as finding duplicate records in a table, are best formulated using a Query Wizard. A **Query Wizard** prompts you for information by asking a series of questions and then creates the appropriate query based on your answers. In Tutorial 1, you used the Simple Query Wizard to display only some of the fields in the Contract table; Access provides other Query Wizards for more complex queries. For common, informational queries, it is easier for you to design your own query than to use a Query Wizard.

Taylor wants you to create a query to display the customer ID, company, first name, last name, city, and email address for each record in the Customer table. Her marketing staff needs this information to complete an email campaign advertising a special promotion being offered to Belmont Landscapes customers. You'll open the Query window in Design view to create the query for Taylor.

To open the Query window in Design view:

▶ **1.** Close the Navigation Pane so that more of the workspace is displayed.

▶ **2.** Click the **Create** tab on the Ribbon. Access displays the options for creating different database objects.

▶ **3.** In the Queries group, click the **Query Design** button. The Show Table dialog box opens on the Query window in Design view. See Figure 3-5.

Figure 3-5 ▶ **Show Table dialog box**

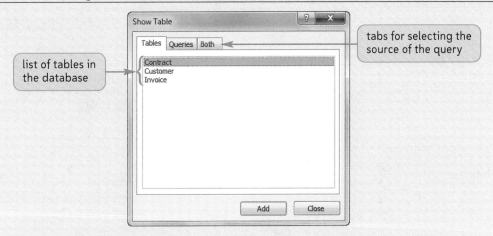

The Show Table dialog box lists all the tables in the Belmont database. You can choose to base a query on one or more tables, on other queries, or on a combination of tables and queries. The query you are creating will retrieve data from the Customer table, so you need to add this table to the Query window.

▶ **4.** Click **Customer** in the Tables list, click the **Add** button, and then click the **Close** button. Access places the Customer table's field list in the Query window and closes the Show Table dialog box.

Trouble? If you add the wrong table to the Query window, right-click the bar at the top of the field list containing the table name, and then click Remove Table on the shortcut menu. To add the correct table to the Query window, click the Show Table button in the Query Setup group on the Design tab to redisplay the Show Table dialog box, and then repeat Step 4.

Now you'll create and run Taylor's query to display selected fields from the Customer table.

Creating and Running a Query

The default table datasheet displays all the fields in the table in the same order as they appear in the table. In contrast, a query datasheet can display selected fields from a table, and the order of the fields can be different from that of the table, enabling those viewing the query results to see only the information they need and in the order they want.

Taylor wants the CustomerID, Company, First, Last, City, and Email fields from the Customer table to appear in the query results. You'll add each of these fields to the design grid. First you'll resize the Customer table field list to display all of the fields.

To select the fields for the query, and then run the query:

▶ **1.** Position the pointer on the bottom border of the Customer field list until the pointer changes to a ↕ shape, and then click and drag the pointer down until the vertical scroll bar in the field list disappears and all fields in the Customer table are displayed.

TIP

You can also use the mouse to drag a field from the field list to a column in the design grid.

▶ **2.** In the Customer field list, double-click **CustomerID** to place the field in the design grid's first column Field box. See Figure 3-6.

Figure 3-6 **Field added to the design grid**

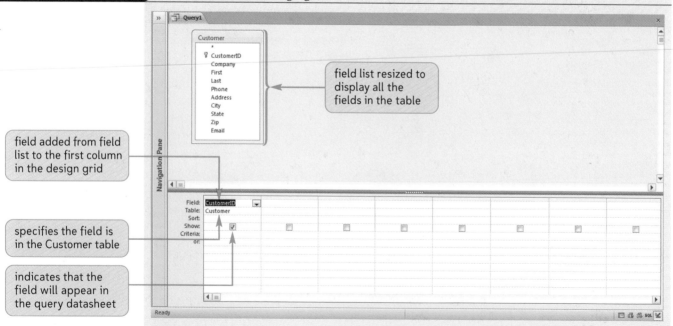

field list resized to display all the fields in the table

field added from field list to the first column in the design grid

specifies the field is in the Customer table

indicates that the field will appear in the query datasheet

In the design grid's first column, the field name CustomerID appears in the Field box, the table name Customer appears in the Table box, and the check mark in the Show check box indicates that the field will be displayed in the datasheet when you run the query. Sometimes you might not want to display a field and its values in the query results. For example, if you are creating a query to list all customers located in Lansing, and you assign the name "LansingCustomers" to the query, you do not need to include the City field value for each record in the query results—the query design only lists customers with the City field value of "Lansing." Even if you choose not to display a field in the query results, you can still use the field as part of the query to select specific records or to specify a particular sequence for the records in the datasheet.

3. Double-click **Company** in the Customer field list. Access adds this field to the second column in the design grid.

4. Repeat Step 3 for the **First**, **Last**, **City**, and **Email** fields to add these fields to the design grid in that order.

   Trouble? If you double-click the wrong field and accidentally add it to the design grid, you can remove the field from the grid. Select the field's column by clicking the pointer ↓ on the field selector, which is the thin bar above the Field box, for the field you want to delete, and then press the Delete key (or in the Query Setup group on the Design tab, click the Delete Columns button).

   Having selected the six fields for Taylor's query, you can now run the query.

5. In the Results group on the Design tab, click the **Run** button. Access runs the query and displays the results in Datasheet view. See Figure 3-7.

Figure 3-7	Datasheet displayed after running the query

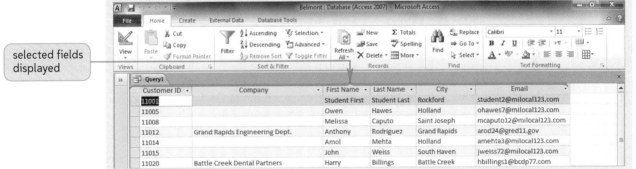

The six fields you added to the design grid appear in the datasheet in the same order as they appear in the design grid. The records are displayed in primary key sequence by CustomerID. Access selected a total of 40 records for display in the datasheet. Taylor asks you to save the query as "CustomerEmail" so that she can easily retrieve the same data again.

6. Click the **Save** button 🖫 on the Quick Access Toolbar. The Save As dialog box opens.

7. Type **CustomerEmail** in the Query Name box, and then press the **Enter** key. Access saves the query with the specified name in the Belmont database and displays the name on the tab for the query.

PROSKILLS

Decision Making: Comparing Methods for Adding All Fields to the Design Grid

If the query you are creating includes every field from the specified table, you can use one of the following three methods to transfer all the fields from the field list to the design grid:

- Click and drag each field individually from the field list to the design grid. Use this method if you want the fields in your query to appear in an order that is different from the order in the field list.
- Double-click the asterisk at the top of the field list. Access places the table name followed by a period and an asterisk (as in "Customer.*") in the Field box of the first column in the design grid, which signifies that the order of the fields is the same in the query as it is in the field list. Use this method if you don't need to sort the query or specify conditions for the records you want to select. The advantage of using this method is that you do not need to change the query if you add or delete fields from the underlying table structure. Such changes are reflected automatically in the query.
- Double-click the field list title bar to highlight all the fields, and then click and drag one of the highlighted fields to the first column in the design grid. Access places each field in a separate column and arranges the fields in the order in which they appear in the field list. Use this method when you need to sort your query or include record selection criteria.

By choosing the most appropriate method to add all the table fields to the query design grid, you can work more efficiently and ensure that the query produces the results you want.

When viewing the query results, Taylor noticed that the contact person for the RiverView Development Company is incorrect. Charles Nowak recently retired from his position, so Taylor asks you to update the record with the first name, last name, and email address of the new contact.

Updating Data Using a Query

A query datasheet is temporary and its contents are based on the criteria in the query design grid; however, you can still update the data in a table using a query datasheet. In this case, Taylor has changes she wants you to make to a record in the Customer table. Instead of making the changes in the table datasheet, you can make them in the CustomerEmail query datasheet because the query is based on the Customer table. The underlying Customer table will be updated with the changes you make.

To update data using the CustomerEmail query datasheet:

1. Locate the record with CustomerID 11040, RiverView Development Company (record 13 in the datasheet).

2. In the First Name column for this record, double-click **Charles** to select the name, and then type **Susan**.

3. Press the **Tab** key to move to and select the value in the Last Name column, and then type **Darcy**.

4. Press the **Tab** key twice to move to and select the value in the Email column, type **sdarcy33@rvdc3.com**, and then press the **Tab** key.

5. Close the CustomerEmail query, and then open the Navigation Pane. Note that the CustomerEmail query is listed in the Queries section of the Navigation Pane.

   Now you'll check the Customer table to verify that the changes you made in the query datasheet were also made in the Customer table.

▶ **6.** Open the **Customer** table in Datasheet view, and then close the Navigation Pane.

▶ **7.** For the record with CustomerID 11040 (record 13), use the **Tab** key to move through the field values. Notice that the changes you made in the query datasheet to the First Name, Last Name, and Email columns were made to the record in the Customer table.

▶ **8.** Close the Customer table.

INSIGHT

Query Datasheet vs. Table Datasheet

Although a query datasheet looks just like a table datasheet and appears in Datasheet view, a query datasheet is temporary, and its contents are based on the criteria you establish in the design grid. In contrast, a table datasheet shows the permanent data in a table. However, you can update data while viewing a query datasheet, just as you can when working in a table datasheet or form.

Sarah also wants to view specific information in the Belmont database. She would like to review the contract signing dates and amounts for customers while also viewing certain contact information for them. So, she needs to see data from both the Customer table and the Contract table at the same time.

Creating a Multitable Query

A multitable query is a query based on more than one table. If you want to create a query that retrieves data from multiple tables, the tables must have a common field. In Tutorial 2, you established a relationship between the Customer (primary) and Contract (related) tables based on the common CustomerID field that exists in both tables, so you can now create a query to display data from both tables at the same time. Specifically, Sarah wants to view the values in the City, Company, First, and Last fields from the Customer table and the SigningDate and ContractAmt fields from the Contract table.

To create the query using the Customer and Contract tables:

▶ **1.** Click the **Create** tab on the Ribbon.

▶ **2.** In the Queries group, click the **Query Design** button. Access opens the Show Table dialog box. You need to add the Customer and Contract tables to the Query window.

▶ **3.** Click **Customer** in the Tables list, click the **Add** button, click **Contract**, click the **Add** button, and then click the **Close** button. The Customer and Contract field lists appear in the Query window, and the Show Table dialog box closes.

▶ **4.** Use the ⬍ pointer to resize the Customer field list so that all the fields in the table are displayed.

The one-to-many relationship between the two tables is shown in the Query window in the same way that Access indicates a relationship between two tables in the Relationships window. Note that the join line is thick at both ends; this signifies that you selected the option to enforce referential integrity. If you had not selected this option, the join line would be thin at both ends and neither the "1" nor the infinity symbol would appear, even though the tables have a one-to-many relationship.

You need to place the City, Company, First, and Last fields (in that order) from the Customer field list into the design grid, and then place the SigningDate and ContractAmt fields from the Contract field list into the design grid. This is the order in which Sarah wants to view the fields in the query results.

5. In the Customer field list, double-click **City** to place this field in the design grid's first column Field box.

6. Repeat Step 5 to add the **Company**, **First**, and **Last** fields from the Customer table to the second through fourth columns of the design grid.

7. Repeat Step 5 to add the **SigningDate** and **ContractAmt** fields (in that order) from the Contract table to the fifth and sixth columns of the design grid. The query specifications are complete, so you can now run the query.

8. In the Results group on the Design tab, click the **Run** button. Access runs the query and displays the results in Datasheet view. See Figure 3-8.

Figure 3-8   **Datasheet for query based on the Customer and Contract tables**

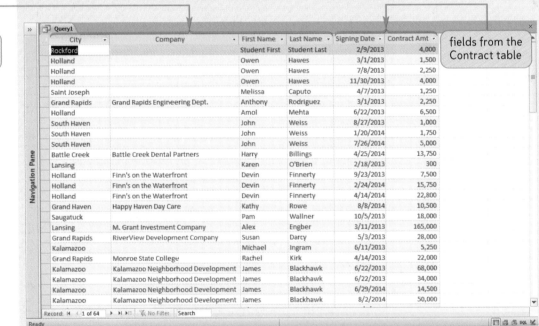

fields from the Customer table

fields from the Contract table

City	Company	First Name	Last Name	Signing Date	Contract Amt
Rockford		Student First	Student Last	2/9/2013	4,000
Holland		Owen	Hawes	3/1/2013	1,500
Holland		Owen	Hawes	7/8/2013	2,250
Holland		Owen	Hawes	11/30/2013	4,000
Saint Joseph		Melissa	Caputo	4/7/2013	1,250
Grand Rapids	Grand Rapids Engineering Dept.	Anthony	Rodriguez	3/1/2013	2,250
Holland		Amol	Mehta	6/22/2013	6,500
South Haven		John	Weiss	8/27/2013	1,000
South Haven		John	Weiss	1/20/2014	1,750
South Haven		John	Weiss	7/26/2014	5,000
Battle Creek	Battle Creek Dental Partners	Harry	Billings	4/25/2014	13,750
Lansing		Karen	O'Brien	2/18/2013	300
Holland	Finn's on the Waterfront	Devin	Finnerty	9/23/2013	7,500
Holland	Finn's on the Waterfront	Devin	Finnerty	2/24/2014	15,750
Holland	Finn's on the Waterfront	Devin	Finnerty	4/14/2014	22,800
Grand Haven	Happy Haven Day Care	Kathy	Rowe	8/8/2014	10,500
Saugatuck		Pam	Wallner	10/5/2013	18,000
Lansing	M. Grant Investment Company	Alex	Engber	3/11/2013	165,000
Grand Rapids	RiverView Development Company	Susan	Darcy	5/3/2013	28,000
Kalamazoo		Michael	Ingram	6/11/2013	5,250
Grand Rapids	Monroe State College	Rachel	Kirk	4/14/2013	22,000
Kalamazoo	Kalamazoo Neighborhood Development	James	Blackhawk	6/22/2013	68,000
Kalamazoo	Kalamazoo Neighborhood Development	James	Blackhawk	6/22/2013	34,000
Kalamazoo	Kalamazoo Neighborhood Development	James	Blackhawk	6/29/2014	14,500
Kalamazoo	Kalamazoo Neighborhood Development	James	Blackhawk	8/2/2014	50,000

Record: 1 of 64   No Filter   Search

Ready

Only the six selected fields from the Customer and Contract tables appear in the datasheet. The records are displayed in order according to the values in the CustomerID field because it is the primary key field in the primary table, even though this field is not included in the query datasheet.

Sarah plans on frequently tracking the data retrieved by the query, so she asks you to save it as "CustomerContracts."

9. Click the **Save** button on the Quick Access Toolbar. The Save As dialog box opens.

10. Type **CustomerContracts** in the Query Name box, and then press the **Enter** key. Access saves the query and displays its name on the object tab.

Sarah decides she wants the records displayed in alphabetical order by city. Because the query displays data in order by the field values in the CustomerID field, which is the primary key for the Customer table, you need to sort the records by the City field to display the data in the order Sarah wants.

Sorting Data in a Query

Sorting is the process of rearranging records in a specified order or sequence. Sometimes you might need to sort data before displaying or printing it to meet a specific request. For example, Sarah might want to review contract information arranged by the SigningDate field because she needs to know which months are the busiest for Belmont Landscapes in terms of signings. Oren might want to view contract information arranged by the ContractAmt field because he monitors the financial aspects of the business.

When you sort data in a query, you do not change the sequence of the records in the underlying tables. Only the records in the query datasheet are rearranged according to your specifications.

To sort records, you must select the **sort field**, which is the field used to determine the order of records in the datasheet. In this case, Sarah wants the data sorted by city, so you need to specify City as the sort field. Sort fields can be Text, Number, Date/Time, Currency, AutoNumber, or Yes/No fields, but not Memo, OLE object, Hyperlink, or Attachment fields. You sort records in either ascending (increasing) or descending (decreasing) order. Figure 3-9 shows the results of each type of sort for some of these data types.

Figure 3-9	Sorting results for different data types

Data Type	Ascending Sort Results	Descending Sort Results
Text	A to Z	Z to A
Number	lowest to highest numeric value	highest to lowest numeric value
Date/Time	oldest to most recent date	most recent to oldest date
Currency	lowest to highest numeric value	highest to lowest numeric value
AutoNumber	lowest to highest numeric value	highest to lowest numeric value
Yes/No	yes (check mark in check box) then no values	no then yes values

Access provides several methods for sorting data in a table or query datasheet and in a form. One of the easiest ways is to use the AutoFilter feature for a field.

Using an AutoFilter to Sort Data

TIP

You can also use the Ascending and Descending buttons in the Sort & Filter group on the Home tab to quickly sort records based on the currently selected field in a datasheet.

As you've probably noticed when working in Datasheet view for a table or query, each column heading has an arrow to the right of the field name. This arrow gives you access to the **AutoFilter** feature, which enables you to quickly sort and display field values in various ways. When you click this arrow, a menu opens with options for sorting and displaying field values. The first two options on the menu enable you to sort the values in the current field in ascending or descending order. Unless you save the datasheet or form after you've sorted the records, the rearrangement of records is temporary.

Next, you'll use an AutoFilter to sort the CustomerContracts query results by the City field.

To sort the records using an AutoFilter:

▶ **1.** Click the **arrow** on the City column heading to display the AutoFilter menu. See Figure 3-10.

Figure 3-10 Using an AutoFilter to sort records in the datasheet

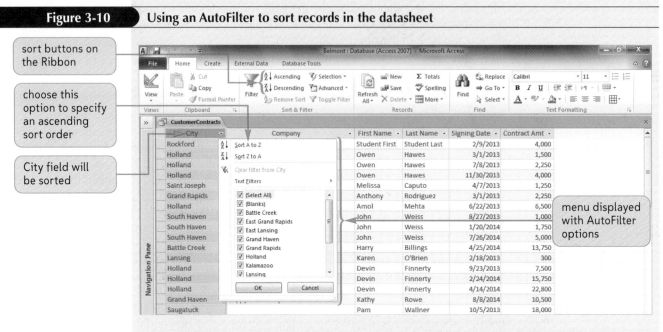

Sarah wants the data sorted in ascending order by the values in the City field, so you need to select the first option in the menu.

▶ **2.** Click **Sort A to Z**. The records are rearranged in ascending alphabetical order by city. A small, upward-pointing arrow appears on the right side of the City column heading. This arrow indicates that the values in the field have been sorted in ascending order. If you used the same method to sort the field values in descending order, a small downward-pointing arrow would appear there.

After viewing the query results, Sarah decides that she would also like to see the records arranged by the values in the ContractAmt field, so that she can identify the contracts with the largest amounts. She still wants the records to be arranged by the City field values as well. To produce the results Sarah wants, you need to sort using two fields.

Sorting Multiple Fields in Design View

Sort fields can be unique or nonunique. A sort field is **unique** if the value in the sort field for each record is different. The CustomerID field in the Customer table is an example of a unique sort field because each customer record has a different value in this primary key field. A sort field is **nonunique** if more than one record can have the same value for the sort field. For example, the City field in the Customer table is a nonunique sort field because more than one record can have the same City value.

When the sort field is nonunique, records with the same sort field value are grouped together, but they are not sorted in a specific order within the group. To arrange these grouped records in a specific order, you can specify a **secondary sort field**, which is a second field that determines the order of records that are already sorted by the **primary sort field** (the first sort field specified).

Access lets you select up to 10 different sort fields. When you use the buttons on the Ribbon to sort by more than one field, the sort fields must be in adjacent columns in the datasheet. (Note that you cannot use an AutoFilter to sort on more than one field. This method works for a single field only.) You can specify only one type of sort—either ascending or descending—for the selected columns in the datasheet. You highlight the adjacent columns, and Access sorts first by the first column and then by each remaining highlighted column in order from left to right.

TIP

The primary sort field is *not* the same as a table's primary key field. A table has at most one primary key, which must be unique, whereas any field in a table can serve as a primary sort field.

Sarah wants the records sorted first by the City field values, as they currently are, and then by the ContractAmt field values. The two fields are in the correct left-to-right order in the query datasheet, but they are not adjacent, so you cannot use the Ascending and Descending buttons on the Ribbon to sort them. You could move the City field to the left of the ContractAmt field in the query datasheet, but both columns would be sorted with the same sort order. This is not what Sarah wants—she wants the City field values sorted in ascending order so that they are in the correct alphabetical order, for ease of reference; and she wants the ContractAmt field values to be sorted in descending order, so that she can focus on the contracts with the largest amounts. To sort the City and ContractAmt fields with different sort orders, you must specify the sort fields in Design view.

In the Query window in Design view, Access first uses the sort field that is leftmost in the design grid. Therefore, you must arrange the fields you want to sort from left to right in the design grid, with the primary sort field being the leftmost. In Design view, multiple sort fields do not have to be adjacent to each other, as they do in Datasheet view; however, they must be in the correct left-to-right order.

Sorting a Query Datasheet

- In the query datasheet, click the arrow on the column heading for the field you want to sort.
- In the menu that opens, click Sort A to Z for an ascending sort, or click Sort Z to A for a descending sort.

or

- In the query datasheet, select the column or adjacent columns on which you want to sort.
- In the Sort & Filter group on the Home tab, click the Ascending button or the Descending button.

or

- In Design view, position the fields serving as sort fields from left to right.
- Click the right side of the Sort box for the field you want to sort, and then click Ascending or Descending for the sort order.

To achieve the results Sarah wants, you need to modify the query in Design view to specify the sort order for the two fields.

To select the two sort fields in Design view:

1. In the Views group on the Home tab, click the **View** button to open the query in Design view. The fields are currently in the correct left-to-right order in the design grid, so you only need to specify the sort order for the two fields.

   First, you need to specify an ascending sort order for the City field. Even though the records are already sorted by the values in this field, you need to modify the query so that this sort order, and the sort order you will specify for the ContractAmt field, are part of the query's design. Any time the query is run, the records will be sorted according to these specifications.

2. Click the right side of the **City Sort** box to display the arrow and the sort options, and then click **Ascending**. You've selected an ascending sort order for the City field, which will be the primary sort field. The City field is a Text field, and an ascending sort order will display the field values in alphabetical order.

3. Click the right side of the **ContractAmt Sort** box, click **Descending**, and then click in one of the empty text boxes to the right of the ContractAmt field to deselect the setting. You've selected a descending sort order for the ContractAmt

field, which will be the secondary sort field because it appears to the right of the primary sort field (City) in the design grid. The ContractAmt field is a Currency field, and a descending sort order will display the field values with the largest amounts first. See Figure 3-11.

Figure 3-11 **Selecting two sort fields in Design view**

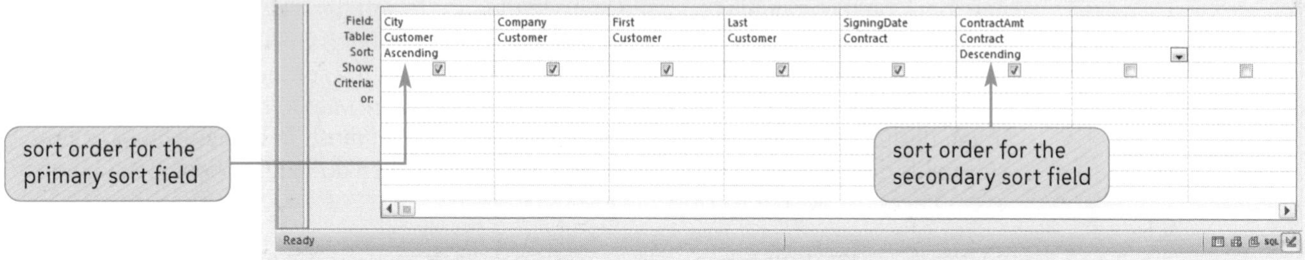

sort order for the primary sort field

sort order for the secondary sort field

You have finished your query changes, so now you can run the query and then save the modified query with the same query name.

4. In the Results group on the Design tab, click the **Run** button. Access runs the query and displays the query datasheet. The records appear in ascending order based on the values in the City field. Within groups of records with the same City field value, the records appear in descending order by the values of the ContractAmt field. See Figure 3-12.

Figure 3-12 **Datasheet sorted on two fields**

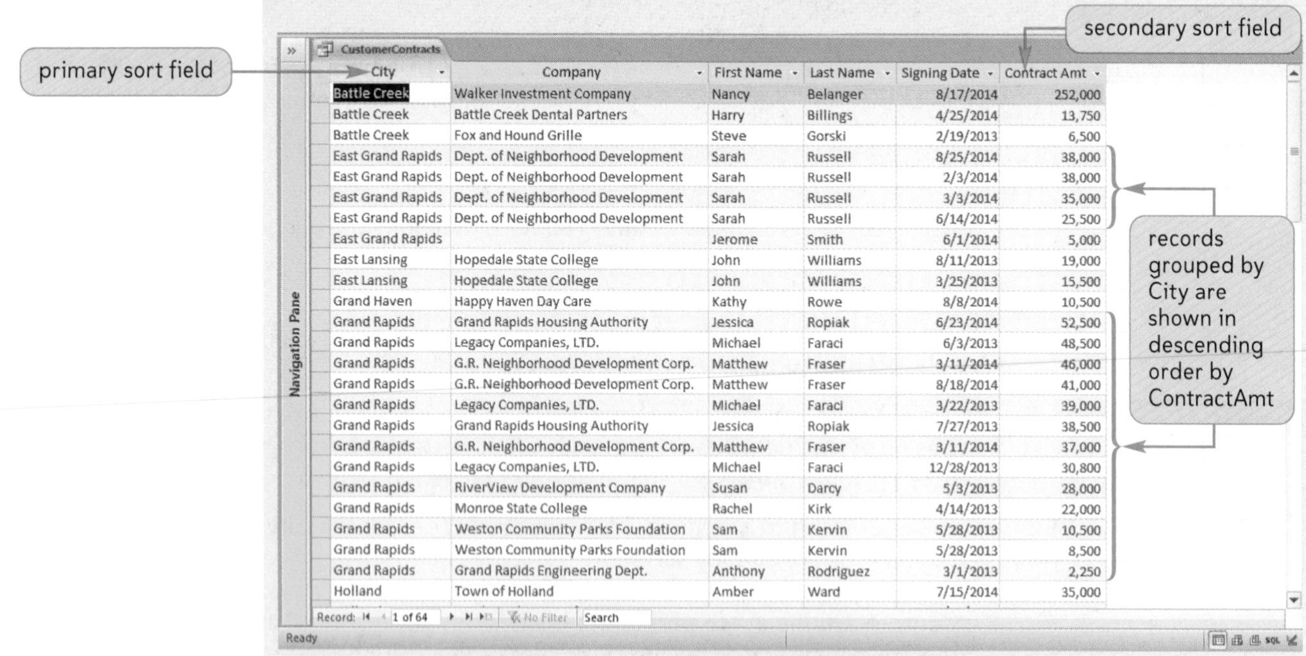

secondary sort field

primary sort field

records grouped by City are shown in descending order by ContractAmt

When you save the query, all of your design changes—including the selection of the sort fields—are saved with the query. The next time Sarah runs the query, the records will appear sorted by the primary and secondary sort fields.

5. Click the **Save** button 💾 on the Quick Access Toolbar to save the revised CustomerContracts query.

Sarah knows that Belmont Landscapes has seen an increase in business recently for customers located in the city of Grand Rapids. She would like to focus briefly on the information for customers in that city only. Also, she is interested in knowing how many contracts were signed in March because this month has sometimes been a slow month for Belmont Landscapes in terms of contract signings. Selecting only the records with a City field value of "Grand Rapids" and a SigningDate field value beginning with "3" (for the month of March) is a temporary change that Sarah wants in the datasheet, so you do not need to switch to Design view and change the query. Instead, you can apply a filter.

Filtering Data

A **filter** is a set of restrictions you place on the records in an open datasheet or form to *temporarily* isolate a subset of the records. A filter lets you view different subsets of displayed records so that you can focus on only the data you need. Unless you save a query or form with a filter applied, an applied filter is not available the next time you run the query or open the form.

The simplest technique for filtering records is Filter By Selection. **Filter By Selection** lets you select all or part of a field value in a datasheet or form, and then display only those records that contain the selected value in the field. You can also use the AutoFilter feature to filter records. When you click the arrow on a column heading, the menu that opens provides options for filtering the datasheet based on a field value or the selected part of a field value. Another technique for filtering records is to use **Filter By Form**, which changes your datasheet to display blank fields. Then you can select a value using the arrow that appears when you click any blank field to apply a filter that selects only those records containing that value.

REFERENCE

Using Filter By Selection

- In the datasheet or form, select part of the field value that will be the basis for the filter; or, if the filter will be based on the entire field value, click anywhere within the field value.
- In the Sort & Filter group on the Home tab, click the Selection button.
- Click the type of filter you want to apply.

For Sarah's request, you need to select a City field value of Grand Rapids, and then use Filter By Selection to display only those records with this value. Then you will filter the records further by selecting only those records with a SigningDate value that begins with "3" (for March).

To display the records using Filter By Selection:

1. In the query datasheet, locate the first occurrence of a City field containing the value **Grand Rapids**, and then click anywhere within that field value. (Note: Make sure you find a field value containing only "Grand Rapids," not "East Grand Rapids.")

2. In the Sort & Filter group on the Home tab, click the **Selection** button. A menu opens with options for the type of filter to apply. See Figure 3-13.

Figure 3-13 Using Filter By Selection

options for the type of filter to apply

current field is the basis for the filter

The menu provides options for displaying only those records with a City field value that equals the selected value (in this case, Grand Rapids); does not equal the value; contains the value somewhere within the field; or does not contain the value somewhere within the field. You want to display all the records whose City field value equals Grand Rapids.

3. In the Selection menu, click **Equals "Grand Rapids"**. Access displays the filtered results. Only the 13 records that have a City field value of Grand Rapids appear in the datasheet. See Figure 3-14.

Figure 3-14 Datasheet after applying the filter

click to display more options for filtering the field

datasheet displays only records with a City value of Grand Rapids

indicate that a filter has been applied to the datasheet

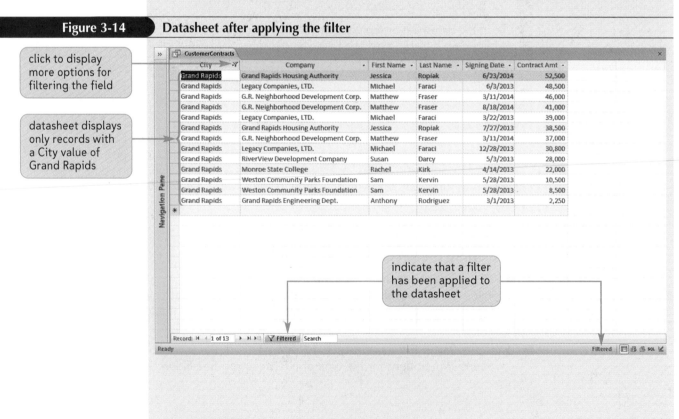

The button labeled "Filtered" to the right of the navigation buttons and the notation "Filtered" on the status bar both indicate that a filter has been applied to the datasheet. Also, notice that the Toggle Filter button in the Sort & Filter group on the Home tab is active; you can click this button or the Filtered button next to the navigation buttons to toggle between the filtered and unfiltered displays of the query datasheet. The City column heading also has a filter icon on it; you can click this icon to display additional options for filtering the field.

Next, Sarah wants to view only those records with a SigningDate value in the month of March to focus on contracts signed in that month for customers in Grand Rapids. So, you need to apply an additional filter to the datasheet.

4. In any SigningDate field value beginning with the number "3" (for the month of March), select only the first digit **3**.

5. In the Sort & Filter group, click the **Selection** button. Three filters are available based on your selection: to display only those records with a SigningDate field value that begins with 3; to display only those records with a SigningDate field value that does not begin with 3; and to display only those records with a SigningDate field value that is between two dates. If you choose the Between option, a dialog box opens in which you enter the date values that you want to use.

6. Click **Begins With 3** in the Selection menu. The second filter is applied to the query datasheet, which now shows only the four records for customers located in Grand Rapids who signed contracts in the month of March.

Now you can redisplay all the query records by clicking the Toggle Filter button, which you use to switch between the filtered and unfiltered displays.

7. In the Sort & Filter group on the Home tab, click the **Toggle Filter** button. Access removes the filter and redisplays all 64 records in the query datasheet.

8. Close the CustomerContracts query. Access asks if you want to save your changes to the design of the query—in this case, the filtered display, which is still available through the Toggle Filter button. Sarah does not want the query saved with the filter because she doesn't need to view the filtered information on a regular basis.

9. Click the **No** button to close the query without saving the changes.

10. If you are not continuing to Session 3.2, click the **File** tab, and then click **Close Database** in the navigation bar to close the Belmont database.

Session 3.1 Quick Check

REVIEW

1. In Datasheet view, what is the difference between navigation mode and editing mode?
2. What is a select query?
3. Describe the field list and the design grid in the Query window in Design view.
4. How are a table datasheet and a query datasheet similar? How are they different?
5. For a Date/Time field, how do the records appear when sorted in ascending order?
6. True or False: When you define multiple sort fields in Design view, the sort fields must be adjacent to each other.
7. A(n) _____ is a set of restrictions you place on the records in an open datasheet or form to isolate a subset of records temporarily.

SESSION 3.2 VISUAL OVERVIEW

When creating queries in Design view, you can enter criteria so that Access will display only selected records in the query results.

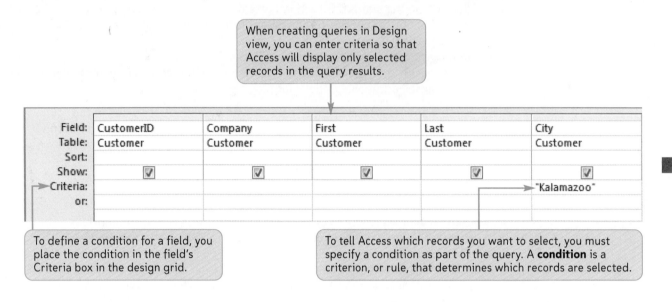

Field:	CustomerID	Company	First	Last	City
Table:	Customer	Customer	Customer	Customer	Customer
Sort:					
Show:	☑	☑	☑	☑	☑
Criteria:					"Kalamazoo"
or:					

To define a condition for a field, you place the condition in the field's Criteria box in the design grid.

To tell Access which records you want to select, you must specify a condition as part of the query. A **condition** is a criterion, or rule, that determines which records are selected.

Field:	InvoiceNum	InvoiceDate	InvoiceAmt	
Table:	Invoice	Invoice	Invoice	
Sort:				
Show:	☑	☑	☑	☐
Criteria:			> 50000	
or:				

A condition usually consists of an operator, often a comparison operator, and a value. A **comparison operator** asks Access to compare the value in a field to the condition value and to select all the records for which the condition is true.

Field:	ContractNum	ContractAmt	SigningDate	ContractType
Table:	Contract	Contract	Contract	Contract
Sort:				
Show:	☑	☑	☑	☑
Criteria:			Between #9/1/2013# And #11/30/2013#	
or:				

Most comparison operators, such as Between...And..., ask Access to select records that match a range of values for the condition—in this case, all records with dates that fall within the range shown.

SELECTION CRITERIA IN QUERIES

The results of a query containing selection criteria include only the records that meet the specified criteria.

KalamazooCustomers

Customer ID	Company	First Name	Last Name	City
11042		Michael	Ingram	Kalamazoo
11045	Kalamazoo Neighborhood Development	James	Blackhawk	Kalamazoo
11072	Sierra Investment Company	Rodrigo	Valencia	Kalamazoo
*				

The results of this query show only customers from Kalamazoo because the condition "Kalamazoo" in the City field's Criteria box specifies that Access should select records only with City field values of Kalamazoo. This type of condition is called an **exact match** because the value in the specified field must match the condition exactly in order for the record to be included in the query results.

LargeInvoiceAmts

Invoice Num	Invoice Date	Invoice Amt
2063	07/11/2015	$70,000.00
2453	05/05/2017	$85,000.00
2613	12/17/2017	$105,000.00
2614	09/30/2019	$77,000.00
*		

The results of this query show only those invoices with amounts greater than $50,000 because the condition >50000, which uses the greater than comparison operator, specifies that Access should select records only with InvoiceAmt field values over $50,000.

FallSignings

Contract Num	Contract Amt	Signing Date	Contract Type
3046	300	9/2/2013	Consultation for back yard, residential
3048	7,500	9/23/2013	Landscape design for restaurant site
3051	18,000	10/5/2013	Site layout and landscape design for residential site
3053	375	9/15/2013	Consultation for front yard, residential
3056	32,500	9/30/2013	Handicap accessibility upgrades to public housing site
3057	15,500	9/30/2013	Handicap accessibility upgrades to public housing site
3060	4,000	11/30/2013	Front walk and drive design, residential
*			

The results of this query show only those contracts that were signed in the fall of 2013 because the condition in the SigningDate's Criteria box specifies that Access should select records only with a signing date between 9/1/2013 and 11/30/2013.

Defining Record Selection Criteria for Queries

Oren wants to display customer and contract information for all customers who live in Holland, Oren's hometown. He is planning to do a special local promotion for Holland customers because Belmont Landscapes is located there, and Oren wants to increase his firm's presence in the community. For this request, you could create a query to select the correct fields and all records in the Customer and Contract tables, select a City field value of Holland in the query datasheet, and then click the Selection button and choose the appropriate filter option to filter the query results and display the information for only those customers in Holland. However, a faster way of displaying the data Oren needs is to create a query that displays the selected fields and only those records in the Customer and Contract tables that satisfy a condition.

Just as you can display selected fields from a database in a query datasheet, you can display selected records. To tell Access which records you want to select, you must specify a condition as part of the query, as illustrated in the Session 3.2 Visual Overview. A condition usually includes one of the comparison operators shown in Figure 3-15.

Figure 3-15	Access comparison operators

Operator	Meaning	Example
=	equal to (optional; default operator)	="Hall"
<>	not equal to	<>"Hall"
<	less than	<#1/1/99#
<=	less than or equal to	<=100
>	greater than	>"C400"
>=	greater than or equal to	>=18.75
Between ... And ...	between two values (inclusive)	Between 50 And 325
In ()	in a list of values	In ("Hall", "Seeger")
Like	matches a pattern that includes wildcards	Like "706*"

Specifying an Exact Match

For Oren's request, you need to create a query that will display only those records in the Customer table with the value Holland in the City field. This type of condition is an exact match because the value in the specified field must match the condition exactly in order for the record to be included in the query results. You'll create the query in Design view.

To create the query in Design view:

1. If you took a break after the previous session, make sure that the Belmont database is open and the Navigation Pane is closed.

2. Click the **Create** tab on the Ribbon.

3. In the Queries group, click the **Query Design** button. The Show Table dialog box opens. You need to add the Customer and Contract tables to the Query window.

4. Click **Customer** in the Tables list, click the **Add** button, click **Contract**, click the **Add** button, and then click the **Close** button.

5. Use the ↕ pointer to resize the Customer field list so that all the fields are displayed.

6. Add the following fields from the Customer table to the design grid in the order shown: **Company**, **First**, **Last**, **Phone**, **Address**, **City**, and **Email**.

Oren also wants information from the Contract table included in the query results.

7. Add the following fields from the Contract table to the design grid in the order shown: **ContractNum**, **ContractAmt**, **SigningDate**, and **ContractType**. See Figure 3-16.

Figure 3-16 Design grid after adding fields from both tables

The field lists for the Customer and Contract tables appear in the top portion of the window, and the join line indicating a one-to-many relationship connects the two tables. The fields you selected appear in the design grid; to see all of the fields, you need to scroll to the right using the horizontal scroll bar.

To display the information Oren wants, you need to enter the condition for the City field in its Criteria box. Oren wants to display only those records with a City field value of Holland.

To enter the exact match condition, and then save and run the query:

1. Click the **City Criteria** box, type **Holland**, and then press the **Enter** key. The condition changes to "Holland".

   Access automatically enclosed the condition you typed in quotation marks. You must enclose Text values in quotation marks when using them as selection criteria. If you omit the quotation marks, however, Access will include them automatically.

2. Click the **Save** button 🖫 on the Quick Access Toolbar to open the Save As dialog box.

3. Type **HollandCustomers** in the Query Name box, and then press the **Enter** key. Access saves the query with the specified name and displays the name on the object tab.

4. In the Results group on the Design tab, click the **Run** button. Access runs the query and displays the selected field values for only those records with a City field value of Holland. A total of 12 records is selected and displayed in the datasheet. See Figure 3-17.

Figure 3-17 Datasheet displaying selected fields and records

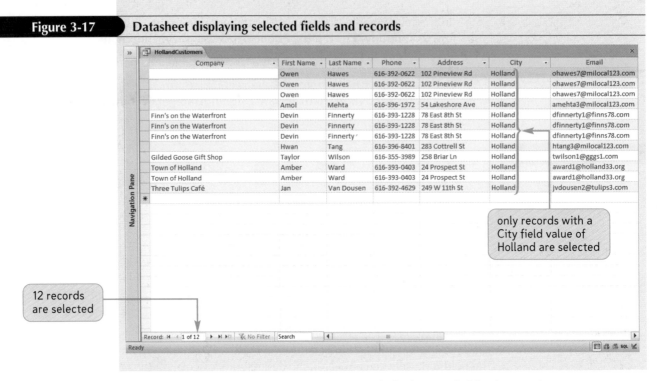

Oren realizes that it's not necessary to include the City field values in the query results. The name of the query, HollandCustomers, indicates that the query design includes all customers that are located in Holland, so the City field values are unnecessary and repetitive. Also, he decides that he would prefer the query datasheet to show the fields from the Contract table first, followed by the Customer table fields. You need to modify the query to produce the results Oren wants.

Modifying a Query

After you create a query and view the results, you might need to make changes to the query if the results are not what you expected or require. First, Oren asks you to modify the HollandCustomers query to remove the City field values from the query results.

To remove the display of the City field values:

1. In the Views group on the Home tab, click the **View** button. The HollandCustomers query opens in Design view.

   You need to keep the City field as part of the query design because it contains the defined condition for the query. You only need to remove the display of the field's values from the query results.

2. Click the **City Show** check box to remove the check mark. The query will still find only those records with the value Holland in the City field, but the query results will not display these field values.

Next, you need to change the order of the fields in the query so that the contract information is listed first.

To move the Contract table fields to precede the Customer table fields:

1. Scroll the design grid to the right so you can see all four fields from the Contract table. You need to move the ContractNum field so it becomes the first field in the query design.
2. Position the pointer on the ContractNum field selector until the pointer changes to a ⬇ shape, and then click to select the field. See Figure 3-18.

Figure 3-18 Selected ContractNum field

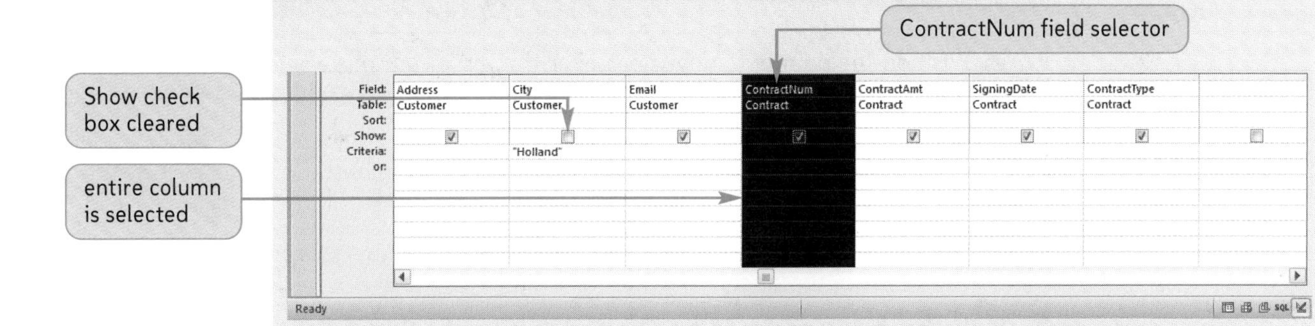

3. Position the pointer on the ContractNum field selector, and then click and drag the pointer to the left, allowing the design grid to scroll back to the left, until the vertical line to the left of the Company field is highlighted. See Figure 3-19.

Figure 3-19 Dragging the field in the design grid

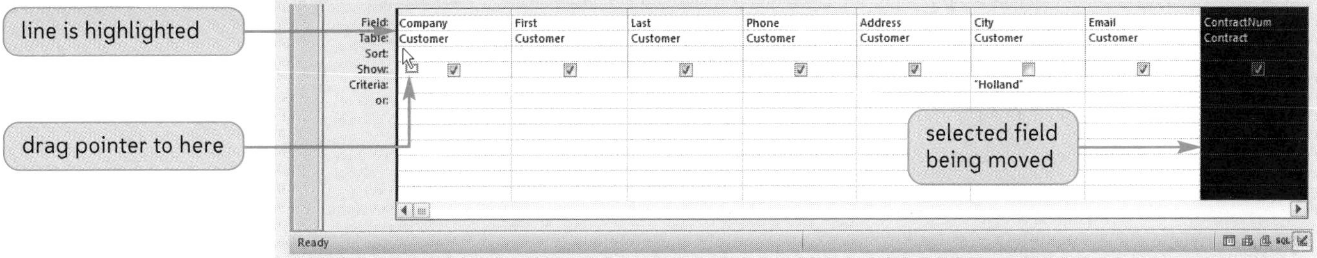

4. Release the mouse button. The ContractNum field moves to the left of the Company field.

   You can also select and move multiple fields at once.

5. Scroll back to the right to view the remaining fields in the design grid. Now you need to select and move the ContractAmt, SigningDate, and ContractType fields so that they follow the ContractNum field in the query design. To select multiple fields, you simply click and drag the mouse over the field selectors for the fields you want.
6. Click and hold the pointer ⬇ on the ContractAmt field selector, drag the pointer to the right to select the SigningDate and ContractType fields, and then release the mouse button. All three fields are now selected. See Figure 3-20.

Figure 3-20 **Multiple fields selected to be moved**

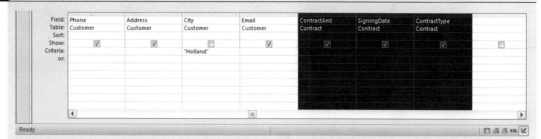

7. Position the pointer ⏳ anywhere near the top of the three selected fields, and then click and drag the pointer to the left until the vertical line to the left of the Company field is highlighted.

8. Release the mouse button. The four fields from the Contract table are now the first four fields in the query design.

   You have finished making the modifications to the query Oren requested, so you can now run the query.

9. In the Results group on the Design tab, click the **Run** button. Access displays the results of the modified query. See Figure 3-21.

Figure 3-21 **Results of the modified query**

datasheet selector

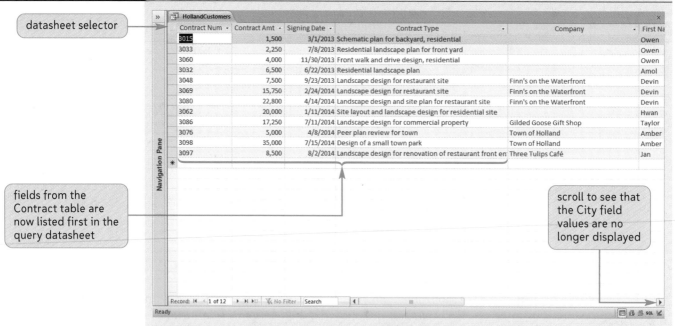

fields from the Contract table are now listed first in the query datasheet

scroll to see that the City field values are no longer displayed

Note that the City field values are no longer displayed in the query results (you need to scroll the datasheet to the right to verify this).

Oren would like to see more fields and records on the screen at one time. He asks you to change the datasheet's font size, and then to resize all the columns to their best fit.

Changing a Datasheet's Appearance

You can change the characteristics of a datasheet, including the font type and size of text in the datasheet, to improve its appearance or readability. As you learned in earlier tutorials, you can also resize the datasheet columns to view more columns on the screen at the same time. You'll change the font size from the default 11 points to 9, and then resize the datasheet columns.

To change the font size and resize the columns in the datasheet:

▶ **1.** In the Text Formatting group on the Home tab, click the **Font Size** arrow, and then click **9**. The font size for the entire datasheet changes to 9 points.

   Next, you need to resize the columns to their best fit, so that each column is just wide enough to display the longest value in the column. Instead of resizing each column individually, you'll use the datasheet selector to select all the columns and resize them at the same time.

▶ **2.** Click the **datasheet selector**, which is the box to the left of the Contract Num column heading (see Figure 3-21). All the columns in the datasheet are highlighted, indicating they are selected.

▶ **3.** Position the pointer ┿ at the right edge of any column in the datasheet, and then double-click the pointer. All the columns visible on the screen are resized to their best fit. Because only the visible columns are resized, you must scroll the datasheet to the right to make sure all field values for all columns are fully displayed, resizing as you scroll, if necessary.

▶ **4.** Scroll the datasheet to the right and verify that all columns were resized to their best fit. If necessary, resize any individual column that might not have been resized to best fit the data it contains.

▶ **5.** Scroll to the left, if necessary, so that the Contract Num column is visible, and then click any value in the Contract Num column to make it the current field. More columns are now visible in the datasheet.

TIP

Click a field value to deselect the columns before resizing an individual column.

Changing the Alternate Row Color in a Datasheet

Access uses themes to format the objects in a database. A **theme** is a predefined set of formats including colors, fonts, and other effects that enhance an object's appearance and usability. When you create a database, Access applies the Office theme to objects as you create them. By default, the Office theme formats every other row in a datasheet with a gray background color to distinguish one row from another, making it easier to view and read the contents of a datasheet. The gray alternate row color provides a subtle difference compared to the rows that have the default white row color. You can change the alternate row color in a datasheet to something more noticeable using the Alternate Row Color button in the Text Formatting group on the Home tab. Oren suggests that you change the alternate row color in the datasheet to see the effect of using this feature.

To change the alternate row color in the datasheet:

▶ **1.** In the Text Formatting group on the Home tab, click the **Alternate Row Color** button arrow ▦ ▾ to display the gallery of color choices. See Figure 3-22.

Figure 3-22   Gallery of color choices for alternate row color

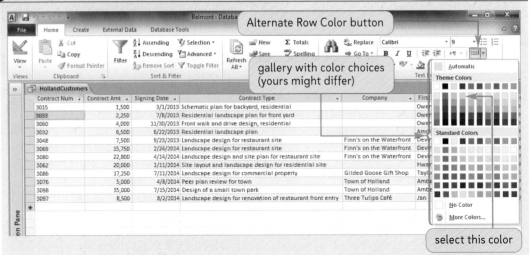

The Theme Colors section provides colors from the default Office theme, so that your datasheet's color scheme matches the one in use for the database. The Standard Colors section provides many standard color choices. You might also see a Recent Colors section, with colors that you have recently used in a datasheet. At the bottom of the gallery, you could also choose the No Color option, which sets each row's background color to white; or the More Colors option, which creates a custom color. You'll use one of the theme colors.

2. In the Theme Colors section, click the color box for **Dark Blue, Text 2, Lighter 80%** (second row, fourth color box). The alternate row color is applied to the query datasheet. See Figure 3-23.

Figure 3-23   Datasheet formatted with alternate row color

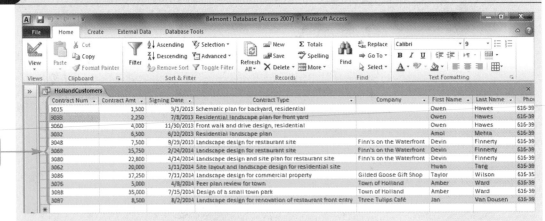

Every other row in the datasheet uses the selected theme color. Oren likes how the datasheet looks with this color scheme, so he asks you to save the query.

3. Save and close the HollandCustomers query.

After viewing the query results, Oren decides that he would like to see the same fields, but only for those records with a ContractAmt field value equal to or greater than $25,000. He is interested to know which Belmont Landscapes customers in all cities and towns have signed the largest contracts, so that he can follow up with these customers personally. To create the query that will produce the results Oren wants, you need to use a comparison operator to match a range of values—in this case, any ContractAmt value greater than or equal to $25,000.

Using a Comparison Operator to Match a Range of Values

After you create and save a query, you can double-click the query name in the Navigation Pane to run the query again. You can then click the View button to change its design. You can also use an existing query as the basis for creating another query. Because the design of the query you need to create next is similar to the HollandCustomers query, you will copy, paste, and rename this query to create the new query. Using this approach keeps the HollandCustomers query intact.

To create the new query by copying the HollandCustomers query:

▶ **1.** Open the Navigation Pane. Note that the HollandCustomers query is listed in the Queries section.

You need to use the shortcut menu to copy the HollandCustomers query and paste it in the Navigation Pane; then you'll give the copied query a different name.

▶ **2.** In the Queries section on the Navigation Pane, right-click **HollandCustomers** to select it and display the shortcut menu.

▶ **3.** Click **Copy** on the shortcut menu.

▶ **4.** Right-click the empty area near the bottom of the Navigation Pane, and then click **Paste** on the shortcut menu. The Paste As dialog box opens with the text "Copy Of HollandCustomers" in the Query Name box. Because Oren wants the new query to show the contracts with the largest amounts, you'll name the new query "LargeContractAmounts."

▶ **5.** Type **LargeContractAmounts** in the Query Name box, and then press the **Enter** key. The new query appears in the Queries section of the Navigation Pane.

▶ **6.** Double-click the **LargeContractAmounts** query to open, or run, the query. Notice that all the design changes you made to the original HollandCustomers query— decreasing the font size, resizing all the columns, and applying the alternate row color—were saved with the query.

▶ **7.** Close the Navigation Pane.

Next, you need to open the query in Design view and modify its design to produce the results Oren wants—to display only those records with ContractAmt field values that are greater than or equal to $25,000.

To modify the design of the new query:

▶ **1.** In the Views group on the Home tab, click the **View** button to display the query in Design view.

▶ **2.** Click the **ContractAmt Criteria** box, and then type **>=25000** and press the **Tab** key. See Figure 3-24.

Figure 3-24   **Criteria entered for the ContractAmt field**

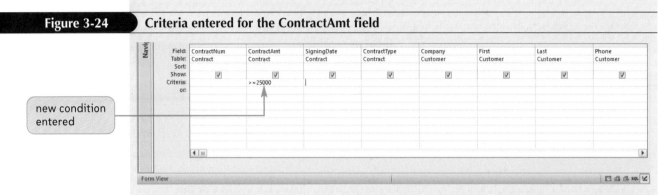

new condition entered

Form View

Trouble? If you receive an error message saying that you entered an expression containing invalid syntax, you might have typed a comma in the amount "25000". Commas are not allowed in selection criteria for Currency fields. Click the OK button to close the dialog box, delete the comma from the ContractAmt Criteria box, and then press the Tab key.

The condition specifies that a record will be selected only if its ContractAmt field value is $25,000 or greater. Before you run the query, you need to delete the condition for the City field. Recall that the City field is part of the query, but its values are not displayed in the query results. When you modified the query to remove the City field values from the query results, Access moved the field to the end of the design grid. So, you need to locate the City field, delete its condition, specify that the City field values should be included in the query results, and then move the field back to its original position following the Address field.

 3. Press the **Tab** key eight times until the condition for the City field is highlighted, and then press the **Delete** key. The condition for the City field is removed.

 4. Click the **Show** check box for the City field to insert a check mark so that the field values will be displayed in the query results.

 5. Use the ⬇ pointer to select the City field, drag the selected field to the left of the Email field, and then click in an empty box to deselect the City field. See Figure 3-25.

Figure 3-25   **Design grid after moving the City field**

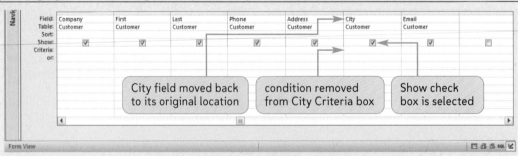

City field moved back to its original location   condition removed from City Criteria box   Show check box is selected

Form View

 6. In the Results group on the Design tab, click the **Run** button. Access runs the query and displays the selected fields for only those records with a ContractAmt field value of greater than or equal to $25,000. A total of 23 records is selected. See Figure 3-26.

Figure 3-26   **Running the modified query**

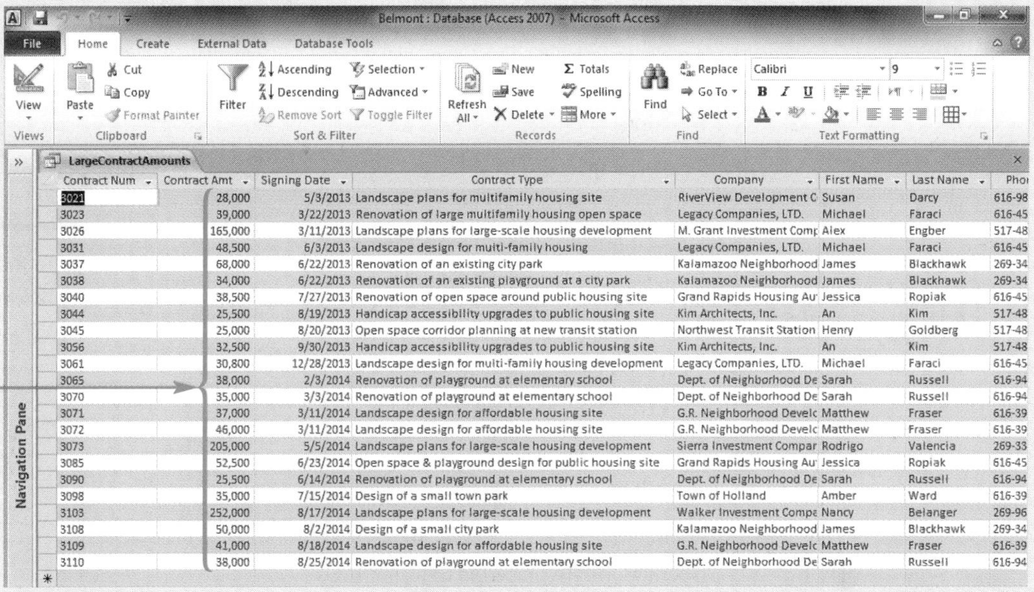

only records with a ContractAmt field value greater than or equal to 25,000 are selected

The City field values are also included in the query datasheet; you need to scroll the datasheet to the right to view them.

7. Resize the datasheet columns to their best fit, as necessary, and then save and close the LargeContractAmounts query.

Oren recently hired Steve Barry as a new consultant at Belmont Landscapes. Steve will focus primarily on customers located in Lansing. To help Steve prioritize his site visits in Lansing, Oren asks you to provide him with a list of all customers in Lansing who have signed contracts with values of greater than $25,000. To produce this list, you need to create a query containing two conditions—one for the city and another for the contract amount.

Defining Multiple Selection Criteria for Queries

Multiple conditions require you to use **logical operators** to combine two or more conditions. When you want a record selected only if two or more conditions are met, you need to use the **And logical operator**. In this case, Oren wants to see only those records with a City field value of Lansing *and* a ContractAmt field value greater than $25,000. If you place conditions in separate fields in the *same* Criteria row of the design grid, all conditions in that row must be met in order for a record to be included in the query results. However, if you place conditions in *different* Criteria rows, a record will be selected if at least one of the conditions is met. If none of the conditions are met, Access does not select the record. When you place conditions in different Criteria rows, you are using the **Or logical operator**. Figure 3-27 illustrates the difference between the And and Or logical operators.

Figure 3-27 Logical operators And and Or for multiple selection criteria

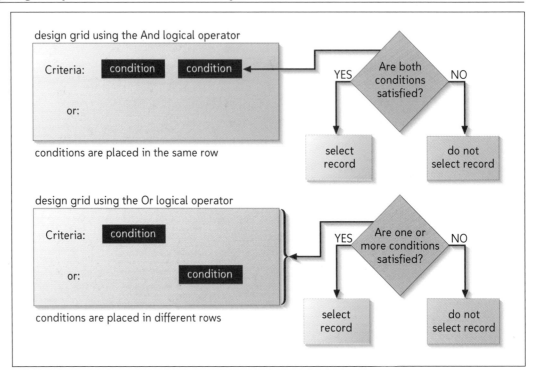

The And Logical Operator

To create the query for Oren, you need to use the And logical operator to show only the records for customers located in Lansing *and* with a contract amount greater than $25,000. You'll create a new query based on both the Customer and Contract tables to produce the necessary results. In the query design, both conditions you specify will appear in the same Criteria row; therefore, the query will select records only if both conditions are met.

To create a new query using the And logical operator:

1. Click the **Create** tab on the Ribbon.

2. In the Queries group, click the **Query Design** button.

3. Add the **Customer** and **Contract** tables to the Query window, and then close the Show Table dialog box. Resize the Customer field list to display all the field names.

4. Add the following fields from the Customer field list to the design grid in the order shown: **Company**, **First**, **Last**, **Phone**, and **City**.

5. Add the **ContractAmt** and **SigningDate** fields from the Contract table to the design grid.

   Now you need to enter the two conditions for the query.

6. Click the **City Criteria** box, and then type **Lansing**.

7. Press the **Tab** key to move to the **ContractAmt Criteria** box, type **>25000**, and then press the **Tab** key. See Figure 3-28.

| Figure 3-28 | Query to find customers in Lansing with large contracts |

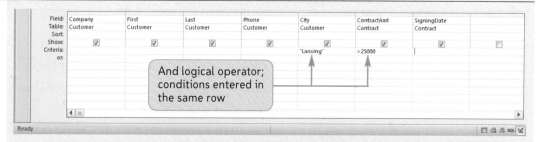

8. Run the query. Access displays only those records that meet both conditions: a City field value of Lansing and a ContractAmt field value greater than $25,000. Three records are selected for two different customers. See Figure 3-29.

| Figure 3-29 | Results of query using the And logical operator |

9. Click the **Save** button on the Quick Access Toolbar, and then save the query as **KeyLansingCustomers**.

10. Close the query. When Steve begins working at Belmont Landscapes, he can run this query to see which customers in Lansing he should contact first.

Next, Oren and Taylor meet to discuss strategies for increasing business for Belmont Landscapes. They are interested in knowing which customers signed contracts for small amounts—less than $10,000—or which contracts were signed in the first two months of 2014 because business seemed unusually slow during those months. They want to use this information for two reasons: (1) to target specific customers who signed smaller contracts with Belmont Landscapes, to determine if these customers might have additional landscaping needs; and (2) to analyze the number and type of contracts signed during these slow months so they can develop strategies for increasing contract signings in the future. To help with their planning, Oren and Taylor have asked you to produce a list of all contracts with amounts less than $10,000 or that were signed between 1/1/2014 and 3/1/2014. To create this query, you need to use the Or logical operator.

The Or Logical Operator

To create the query that Oren and Taylor requested, your query must select a record when either one of two conditions is satisfied or when both conditions are satisfied. That is, a record is selected if the ContractAmt field value is less than $10,000 *or* if the SigningDate field value is between 1/1/2014 and 3/1/2014 *or* if both conditions are met. You will enter the condition for the ContractAmt field in the Criteria row and the condition for the SigningDate field in the "or" criteria row, thereby using the Or logical operator.

To display the information Oren and Taylor want to view, you'll create a new query containing the First, Last, Company, and City fields from the Customer table; and the ContractAmt, SigningDate, and ContractType fields from the Contract table. Then you'll specify the conditions using the Or logical operator.

To create a new query using the Or logical operator:

▶ **1.** Click the **Create** tab on the Ribbon, and then click the **Query Design** button in the Queries group.

▶ **2.** Add the **Customer** and **Contract** tables to the Query window, close the Show Table dialog box, and then resize the Customer field list.

▶ **3.** Add the following fields from the Customer table to the design grid in the order shown: **First**, **Last**, **Company**, and **City**.

▶ **4.** Add the following fields from the Contract table to the design grid in the order shown: **ContractAmt**, **SigningDate**, and **ContractType**.

   Now you need to specify the first condition, <10000, in the ContractAmt field.

▶ **5.** Click the **ContractAmt Criteria** box, and then type **<10000** and press the **Tab** key.

   Because you want records selected if either of the conditions for the ContractAmt or SigningDate fields is satisfied, you must enter the condition for the SigningDate field in the "or" row of the design grid. To specify the date period for the query, you'll use the Between operator.

▶ **6.** Press the ↓ key, type **Between 1/1/2014 And 3/1/2014** in the "or" box for SigningDate, and then press the **Tab** key.

   To view the entire condition for the SigningDate field, you'll resize this field's column in the design grid.

▶ **7.** Place the pointer on the vertical line to the right of the SigningDate field selector until the pointer changes to a ✛ shape, and then double-click to increase the column width and display the entire condition in the SigningDate field. Note that Access automatically places number signs around the date values in the condition to distinguish them from the operators. See Figure 3-30.

Figure 3-30   Query window with the Or logical operator

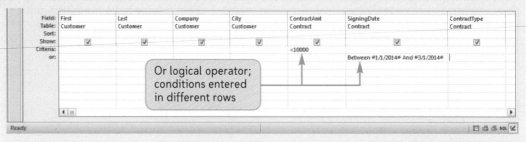

Or logical operator; conditions entered in different rows

Oren wants the list displayed in descending order by SigningDate to better analyze the data.

▶ **8.** Click the right side of the **SigningDate Sort** box, and then click **Descending**.

▶ **9.** Run the query. Access displays only those records that meet either condition: a ContractAmt field value less than $10,000 or a SigningDate field value between 1/1/2014 and 3/1/2014. Access also selects records that meet both conditions. A total of 29 records is selected. The records in the query datasheet appear in descending order based on the values in the SigningDate field. See Figure 3-31.

| Figure 3-31 | Results of query using the Or logical operator |

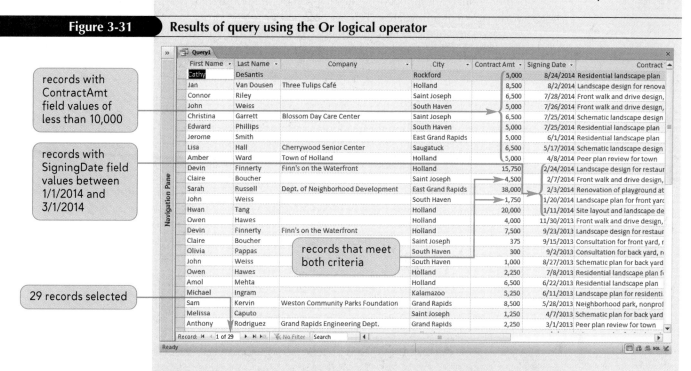

records with ContractAmt field values of less than 10,000

records with SigningDate field values between 1/1/2014 and 3/1/2014

records that meet both criteria

29 records selected

10. Save the query as **SmallContractsOrWinterSignings** and then close it.

INSIGHT

Understanding the Results of Using And vs. Or

When you use the And logical operator to define multiple selection criteria in a query, you *narrow* the results produced by the query because a record must meet more than one condition to be included in the results. When you use the Or logical operator, you *broaden* the results produced by the query because a record must meet only one of the conditions to be included in the results. This is an important distinction to keep in mind when you include multiple selection criteria in queries, so that the queries you create will produce the results you want.

Next, Oren turns his attention to some financial aspects of his business. He wants to use the Belmont database to perform calculations. He is considering imposing a 3% late fee on unpaid invoices and wants to know exactly what the late fee charges would be, should he decide to institute such a policy in the future. To produce the information for Oren, you need to create a calculated field.

Creating a Calculated Field

In addition to using queries to retrieve, sort, and filter data in a database, you can use a query to perform calculations. To perform a calculation, you define an **expression** containing a combination of database fields, constants, and operators. For numeric expressions, the data types of the database fields must be Number, Currency, or Date/Time; the constants are numbers such as .03 (for the 3% late fee); and the operators can be arithmetic operators (+ – * /) or other specialized operators. In complex expressions, you can enclose calculations in parentheses to indicate which one should be performed first. In expressions without parentheses, Access performs calculations using the following order of precedence: multiplication and division before addition and subtraction. When operators have equal precedence, Access calculates them in order from left to right.

To perform a calculation in a query, you add a calculated field to the query. A **calculated field** is a field that displays the results of an expression. A calculated field that you create with an expression appears in a query datasheet or in a form or report; however, it does not exist in a database. When you run a query that contains a calculated field, Access evaluates the expression defined by the calculated field and displays the resulting value in the query datasheet, form, or report.

To enter an expression for a calculated field, you can type it directly in a Field box in the design grid. Alternately, you can open the Zoom box or Expression Builder and use either one to enter the expression. The **Zoom box** is a dialog box that you can use to enter text, expressions, or other values. To use the Zoom box, however, you must know all the parts of the expression you want to create. **Expression Builder** is an Access tool that makes it easy for you to create an expression; it contains a box for entering the expression, an option for displaying and choosing common operators, and one or more lists of expression elements, such as table and field names. Unlike a Field box, which is too narrow to show an entire expression at one time, the Zoom box and Expression Builder are large enough to display longer expressions. In most cases, Expression Builder provides the easiest way to enter expressions because you don't have to know all the parts of the expression; you can choose the necessary elements from the Expression Builder dialog box.

REFERENCE

Using Expression Builder

- Open the query in Design view.
- In the design grid, click the Field box in which you want to create an expression.
- In the Query Setup group on the Design tab, click the Builder button.
- Use the expression elements and common operators to build the expression, or type the expression directly in the expression box.
- Click the OK button.

To produce the information Oren wants, you need to create a new query based on the Invoice table and, in the query, create a calculated field that will multiply each InvoiceAmt field value by .03 to calculate the proposed 3% late fee.

To create the new query and the calculated field:

1. Click the **Create** tab on the Ribbon, and then click the **Query Design** button in the Queries group.

   Oren wants to see data from both the Contract and Invoice tables, so you need to add these two tables to the Query window.

2. Add the **Contract** and **Invoice** tables to the Query window, and then close the Show Table dialog box. The field lists appear in the Query window, and the one-to-many relationship between the Contract (primary) and Invoice (related) tables is displayed.

3. Add the following fields to the design grid in the following order: **ContractNum** and **ContractAmt** from the Contract table; and **InvoiceItem**, **InvoicePaid**, and **InvoiceAmt** from the Invoice table.

Oren is interested in viewing data only for unpaid invoices because a late fee would apply only to them, so you need to enter the necessary condition for the InvoicePaid field. Recall that InvoicePaid is a Yes/No field. The condition you need to enter is the word "No" in the Criteria box for this field, so that Access will retrieve the records for unpaid invoices only.

▶ **4.** In the **InvoicePaid Criteria** box, type **No**. As soon as you type the letter "N," a menu appears with options for entering various functions for the criteria. You don't need to enter a function, so you can close this menu.

You must close the menu or you'll enter a function, which will cause an error.

▶ **5.** Press the **Esc** key to close the menu.

▶ **6.** Press the **Tab** key. The query name you'll use will indicate that the data is for unpaid invoices, so you don't need to include the InvoicePaid values in the query results.

▶ **7.** Click the **InvoicePaid Show** check box to remove the check mark.

▶ **8.** Save the query with the name **UnpaidInvoicesWithLateFees**.

Now you can use Expression Builder to create the calculated field for the InvoiceAmt field.

To create the calculated field:

▶ **1.** Click the blank Field box to the right of the InvoiceAmt field. This field will contain the expression.

▶ **2.** In the Query Setup group on the Design tab, click the **Builder** button. The Expression Builder dialog box opens.

TIP

You must first save and name a query in order for its fields to be listed in the Expression Categories section.

The insertion point is positioned in the large box at the top of the dialog box, ready for you to enter the expression. The Expression Categories section of the dialog box lists the fields from the query so you can include them in the expression. The Expression Elements section contains options for including other elements in the expression, including functions, constants, and operators. If the expression you're entering is a simple one, you can type it in the box; if it's more complex, you can use the options in the Expression Elements section to help you build the expression.

The expression for the calculated field will multiply the InvoiceAmt field values by the numeric constant .03 (which represents a 3% late fee).

▶ **3.** Double-click **InvoiceAmt** in the Expression Categories section. The field name is added to the expression box, within brackets and with a space following it.

Next you need to enter the multiplication operator, which is the asterisk (*), followed by the constant.

▶ **4.** Type * (an asterisk) and then type **.03**. You have finished entering the expression. See Figure 3-32.

| Figure 3-32 | Completed expression for the calculated field |

TIP

If you're not sure which operator to use, you can click Operators to display a list of available operators in the center section of the dialog box.

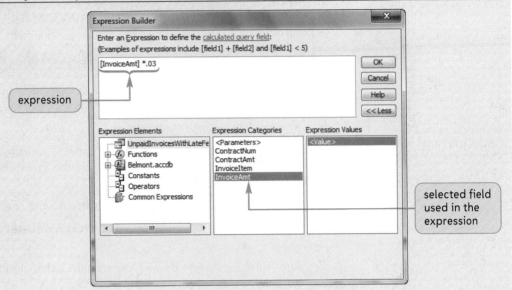

5. Click the **OK** button. Access closes the Expression Builder dialog box and adds the expression to the design grid in the Field box for the calculated field.

   When you create a calculated field, Access uses the default column name "Expr1" for the field. You need to specify a more meaningful column name so it will appear in the query results. You'll enter the name "Late Fee," which better describes the field's contents.

6. Click to the left of the text "Expr1:" at the beginning of the expression, and then press the **Delete** key five times to delete the text **Expr1**. *Do not delete the colon*; it is needed to separate the calculated field name from the expression.

7. Type **Late Fee**.

8. Run the query. Access displays the query datasheet, which contains the specified fields and the calculated field with the name "Late Fee." See Figure 3-33.

Figure 3-33   **Datasheet displaying the calculated field**

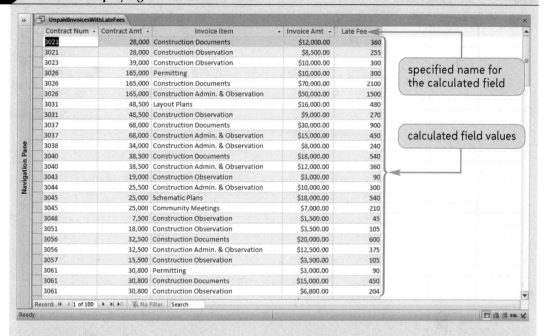

specified name for the calculated field

calculated field values

Trouble? If a dialog box opens noting that the expression contains invalid syntax, you might not have included the required colon in the expression. Click the OK button to close the dialog box, resize the column in the design grid that contains the calculated field to its best fit, change your expression to Late Fee: [Invoice Amt]*0.03 and then repeat Step 8.

The Late Fee field values are currently displayed without dollar signs and decimal places. Oren wants these values to be displayed in the same format as the InvoiceAmt field values, in case he decides to produce a report for customers showing both the invoice amounts and any imposed late fees.

Formatting a Calculated Field

You can specify a particular format for a calculated field, just as you can for any field, by modifying its properties. Next, you'll change the format of the Late Fee calculated field so that all values appear in the Currency format.

To format the calculated field:

1. Switch to Design view.

2. Right-click the **Late Fee** calculated field in the design grid to open the shortcut menu, and then click **Properties**. The Property Sheet for the calculated field opens on the right side of the window. See Figure 3-34.

Figure 3-34
Property Sheet for the calculated field

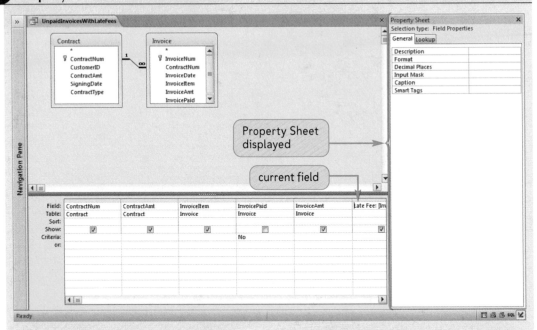

You need to change the Format property to Currency, which displays values with a dollar sign and two decimal places.

> **3.** Click the right side of the **Format** box in the Property Sheet to display the list of formats, and then click **Currency**.

> **4.** Close the Property Sheet for the calculated field, and then run the query. The amounts in the Late Fee calculated field are now displayed with dollar signs and two decimal places.

> **5.** Save and close the UnpaidInvoicesWithLateFees query.

PROSKILLS

Problem Solving: Creating Calculated Fields

The Calculated Field data type, a new data type in Access 2010, lets you store the result of an expression as a field in a table. However, database experts caution users against storing calculations in a table for several reasons. First, storing calculated data in a table consumes valuable space and increases the size of the database. The preferred approach is to use a calculated field in a query; with this approach, the result of the calculation is not stored in the database—it is produced only when you run the query—and it is always current. Second, the Calculated Field data type provides limited options for creating a calculation, whereas a calculated field in a query provides more functions and options for creating expressions. Third, including a field in a table using the Calculated Field data type limits your options if you need to upgrade the database at some point to a more robust DBMS, such as Oracle or SQL Server, that doesn't support this data type; you would need to redesign your database to eliminate this data type. Finally, most database experts agree that including a field in a table whose value is dependent on other fields in the table violates database design principles. To avoid such problems, it's best to create a query that includes a calculated field to perform the calculation you want, instead of creating a field in a table that uses the Calculated Field data type.

Oren wants to prepare a report on a regular basis that includes a summary of information about the contract amounts for Belmont Landscapes. He would like to know the minimum, average, and maximum contract amounts. He asks you to determine these statistics from data in the Contract table.

Using Aggregate Functions

You can calculate statistical information, such as totals and averages, on the records displayed in a table datasheet or selected by a query. To do this, you use the Access aggregate functions. **Aggregate functions** perform arithmetic operations on selected records in a database. Figure 3-35 lists the most frequently used aggregate functions.

Figure 3-35	Frequently used aggregate functions

Aggregate Function	Determines	Data Types Supported
Average	Average of the field values for the selected records	AutoNumber, Currency, Date/Time, Number
Count	Number of records selected	AutoNumber, Currency, Date/Time, Memo, Number, OLE Object, Text, Yes/No
Maximum	Highest field value for the selected records	AutoNumber, Currency, Date/Time, Number, Text
Minimum	Lowest field value for the selected records	AutoNumber, Currency, Date/Time, Number, Text
Sum	Total of the field values for the selected records	AutoNumber, Currency, Date/Time, Number

Working with Aggregate Functions Using the Total Row

If you want to quickly perform a calculation using an aggregate function in a table or query datasheet, you can use the Totals button in the Records group on the Home tab. When you click this button, a row labeled "Total" appears at the bottom of the datasheet. You can then choose one of the aggregate functions for a field in the datasheet, and the results of the calculation will be displayed in the Total row for that field.

Oren is interested to know the total amount of all contracts for the company. You can quickly display this amount using the Sum function in the Total row in the Contract table datasheet.

To display the total amount of all contracts in the Contract table:

1. Open the Navigation Pane, open the **Contract** table in Datasheet view, and then close the Navigation Pane.

2. In the Records group on the Home tab, click the **Totals** button. Access adds a row with the label "Total" to the bottom of the datasheet.

3. Scroll to the bottom of the datasheet to view the last records in the datasheet and the Total row. You want to display the sum of all the values in the Contract Amt column.

4. Click the **Contract Amt** column in the Total row. An arrow appears on the left side of the field.

5. Click the **arrow** to display the menu of aggregate functions. The functions displayed depend on the data type of the current field; in this case, the menu provides functions for a Currency field. See Figure 3-36.

| Figure 3-36 | Using aggregate functions in the Total row |

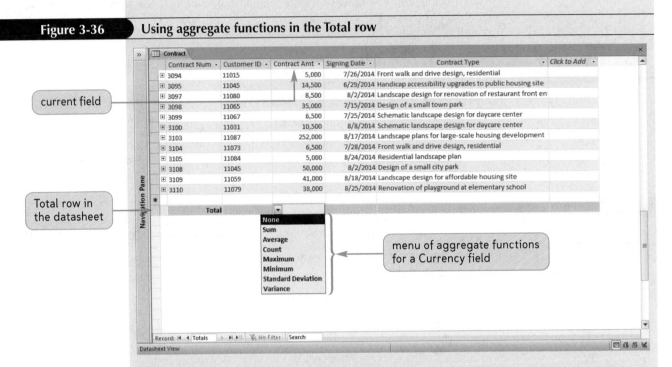

current field

Total row in the datasheet

menu of aggregate functions for a Currency field

6. Click **Sum** in the menu. Access adds all the values in the Contract Amt column and displays the total 1,753,075 in the Total row for the column.

   Oren doesn't want to change the Contract table to always display this total. You can remove the Total row by clicking the Totals button again; this button works as a toggle to switch between the display of the Total row and the results of any calculations in the row, and the display of the datasheet without this row.

7. In the Records group on the Home tab, click the **Totals** button. Access removes the Total row from the datasheet.

8. Close the Contract table without saving the changes.

Oren wants to know the minimum, average, and maximum contract amounts for the company. To produce this information for Oren, you need to use aggregate functions in a query.

Creating Queries with Aggregate Functions

Aggregate functions operate on the records that meet a query's selection criteria. You specify an aggregate function for a specific field, and the appropriate operation applies to that field's values for the selected records.

To display the minimum, average, and maximum of all the contract amounts in the Contract table, you will use the Minimum, Average, and Maximum aggregate functions for the ContractAmt field.

To calculate the minimum, average, and maximum of all contract amounts:

1. Create a new query in Design view, add the **Contract** table to the Query window, and then close the Show Table dialog box.

To perform the three calculations on the ContractAmt field, you need to add the field to the design grid three times.

▶ **2.** Double-click **ContractAmt** in the Contract field list three times to add three copies of the field to the design grid.

You need to select an aggregate function for each ContractAmt field. When you click the Totals button in the Show/Hide group on the Design tab, a row labeled "Total" is added to the design grid. The Total row provides a list of the aggregate functions that you can select.

▶ **3.** In the Show/Hide group on the Design tab, click the **Totals** button. A new row labeled "Total" appears between the Table and Sort rows in the design grid. The default entry for each field in the Total row is the Group By operator, which you will learn about later in this tutorial. See Figure 3-37.

Figure 3-37	Total row inserted in the design grid

ContractAmt field included three times in the design grid

Total row

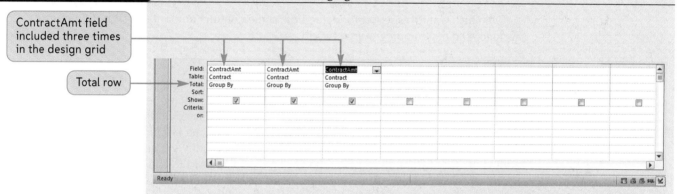

In the Total row, you specify the aggregate function you want to use for a field.

▶ **4.** Click the right side of the first column's **Total** box, and then click **Min**. This field will calculate the minimum amount of all the ContractAmt field values.

When you run the query, Access automatically will assign a datasheet column name of "MinOfContractAmt" for this field. You can change the datasheet column name to a more descriptive or readable name by entering the name you want in the Field box. However, you must also keep the ContractAmt field name in the Field box because it identifies the field to use in the calculation. The Field box will contain the datasheet column name you specify followed by the field name (ContractAmt) with a colon separating the two names.

Be sure to type the colon following the name or the query will not work correctly.

▶ **5.** Click to the left of ContractAmt in the first column's Field box, and then type **Minimum Contract Amt:** (including the colon).

▶ **6.** Click the right side of the second column's **Total** box, and then click **Avg**. This field will calculate the average of all the ContractAmt field values.

▶ **7.** Click to the left of ContractAmt in the second column's Field box, and then type **Average Contract Amt:**.

▶ **8.** Click the right side of the third column's **Total** box, and then click **Max**. This field will calculate the maximum amount of all the ContractAmt field values.

▶ **9.** Click to the left of ContractAmt in the third column's Field box, and then type **Maximum Contract Amt:**.

▶ **10.** Run the query. Access displays one record containing the three aggregate function results. The single row of summary statistics represents calculations based on all the records selected for the query—in this case, all 64 records in the Contract table.

▶ **11.** Resize all columns to their best fit so that the column names are fully displayed, and then click the field value in the first column. See Figure 3-38.

Figure 3-38 **Result of the query using aggregate functions**

▶ **12.** Save the query as **ContractAmtStatistics**.

Oren also wants his report to include the same contract amount statistics (minimum, average, and maximum) grouped by city.

Using Record Group Calculations

In addition to calculating statistical information on all or selected records in selected tables, you can calculate statistics for groups of records. For example, you can determine the number of customers in each city or the average contract amount by city.

To create a query for Oren's latest request, you can modify the current query by adding the City field and assigning the Group By operator to it. The **Group By operator** divides the selected records into groups based on the values in the specified field. Those records with the same value for the field are grouped together, and the datasheet displays one record for each group. Aggregate functions, which appear in the other columns of the design grid, provide statistical information for each group.

You need to modify the current query to add the Group By operator to the City field from the Customer table. The Group By operator will display the statistical information grouped by city for all the records in the query datasheet. To create the new query, you will save the ContractAmtStatistics query with a new name, keeping the original query intact, and then modify the new query.

To create a new query with the Group By operator:

▶ **1.** Display the ContractAmtStatistics query in Design view.

▶ **2.** Click the **File** tab to display Backstage view, and then click **Save Object As** in the navigation bar. The Save As dialog box opens, indicating that you are saving a copy of the ContractAmtStatistics query as a new query.

▶ **3.** Type **ContractAmtStatisticsByCity** to replace the highlighted name, and then press the **Enter** key. The new query is saved with the name you specified.

▶ **4.** Click the **Design** tab to return to the Query window in Design view.

You need to add the City field to the query. This field is in the Customer table. To include another table in an existing query, you open the Show Table dialog box.

▶ **5.** In the Query Setup group on the Design tab, click the **Show Table** button to open the Show Table dialog box.

▶ **6.** Add the **Customer** table to the Query window, close the Show Table dialog box, and then resize the Customer field list.

7. Drag the **City** field from the Customer field list to the first column in the design grid. When you release the mouse button, the City field appears in the design grid's first column, and the existing fields shift to the right. Group By, the default option in the Total row, appears for the City field.

8. Run the query. Access displays 12 records—one for each City group. Each record contains the City field value for the group and the three aggregate function values. The summary statistics represent calculations based on the 64 records in the Contract table. See Figure 3-39.

| Figure 3-39 | Aggregate functions grouped by City |

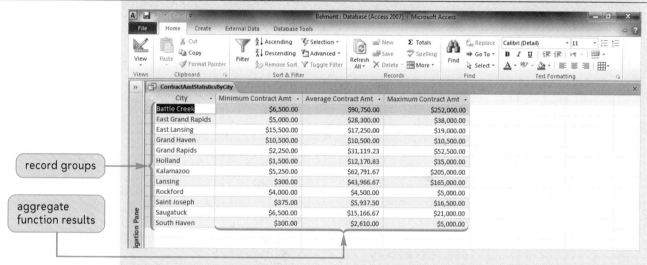

9. Save and close the query.

10. Open the Navigation Pane.

You have created and saved many queries in the Belmont database. The Navigation Pane provides options for opening and managing the queries you've created, as well as the other objects in the database, such as tables, forms, and reports.

Working with the Navigation Pane

As noted in Tutorial 1, the Navigation Pane is the main area for working with the objects in a database. As you continue to create objects in your database, you might want to display and work with them in different ways. The Navigation Pane provides options for grouping database objects in various ways to suit your needs. For example, you might want to view only the queries created for a certain table or all the query objects in the database.

The Navigation Pane divides database objects into categories, and each category contains groups. The groups contain one or more objects. The default category is **Object Type**, which arranges objects by type—tables, queries, forms, and reports. The default group is **All Access Objects**, which displays all objects in the database. You can also choose to display only one type of object, such as tables.

The default group name, All Access Objects, appears at the top of the Navigation Pane. Currently, each object type—Tables, Queries, Forms, and Reports—is displayed in a bar, and the objects related to each type are listed below the bar. To group objects differently, you can select another category by using the Navigation Pane menu. You'll try this next.

TIP

You can hide the display of a group's objects by clicking the bar for the group; click the bar again to expand the group and display its objects.

To group objects differently in the Navigation Pane:

1. At the top of the Navigation Pane, click the **All Access Objects** bar. A menu is displayed for choosing different categories and groups. See Figure 3-40.

Figure 3-40   Navigation Pane menu

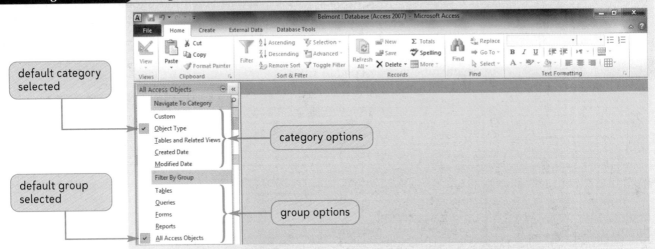

default category selected

category options

default group selected

group options

The top section of the menu provides the options for choosing a different category. The Object Type category has a check mark next to it, signifying that it is the currently selected category. The lower section of the menu provides options for choosing a different group; these options might change depending on the selected category.

2. In the top section of the menu, click **Tables and Related Views**. The Navigation Pane is now grouped into categories of tables, and each table in the database—Contract, Invoice, and Customer—is its own group. All database objects related to a table are listed below the bar containing the table's name. See Figure 3-41.

Figure 3-41   Database objects grouped by table in the Navigation Pane

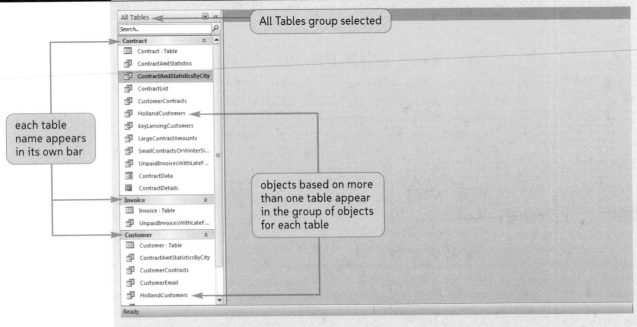

All Tables group selected

each table name appears in its own bar

objects based on more than one table appear in the group of objects for each table

Some objects appear more than once. When an object is based on more than one table, that object appears in the group for each table. For example, the HollandCustomers query is based on both the Contract and Customer tables, so it is listed in the group for both tables.

You can also choose to display the objects for only one table to better focus on that table.

▶ **3.** Click the **All Tables** bar to display the Navigation Pane menu, and then click **Customer**. The Navigation Pane now shows only the objects related to the Customer table—the table itself plus the seven queries you created that include fields from the Customer table.

▶ **4.** Click the **Customer** bar at the top of the Navigation Pane, and then click **Object Type** to return to the default display of the Navigation Pane.

▶ **5.** Compact and repair the Belmont database, and then close the database.

Trouble? If a dialog box opens and warns that this action will cause Microsoft Access to empty the Clipboard, click the Yes button to continue.

The default All Access Objects category is a predefined category. You can also create custom categories to group objects in the way that best suits how you want to manage your database objects. As you continue to build a database and the list of objects grows, creating a custom category can help you to work more efficiently with the objects in the database.

The queries you've created and saved will help Oren, Taylor, Sarah, and others to monitor and analyze the business activity of Belmont Landscapes and its customers. Now any staff member can run the queries at any time, modify them as needed, or use them as the basis for designing new queries to meet additional information requirements.

REVIEW

Session 3.2 Quick Check

1. A(n) _____ is a criterion, or rule, that determines which records are selected for a query datasheet.
2. In the design grid, where do you place the conditions for two different fields when you use the And logical operator? The Or logical operator?
3. To perform a calculation in a query, you define a(n) _____ containing a combination of database fields, constants, and operators.
4. Which Access tool do you use to create an expression for a calculated field in a query?
5. What is an aggregate function?
6. The _____ operator divides selected records into groups based on the values in a field.
7. What is the default category for the display of objects in the Navigation Pane?

Practice the skills you learned in the tutorial using the same case scenario.

PRACTICE

Review Assignments

Data File needed for the Review Assignments: Supplier.accdb (*cont. from Tutorial 2*)

Oren asks you to update some information in the Supplier database and also to retrieve specific information from the database. Complete the following:

1. Open the **Supplier** database located in the Access1\Review folder, and then click the Enable Content button next to the Security Warning, if necessary.

2. Open the **Company** table, and then change the following field values for the record with the CompanyID MID312: Address to **2250 E Riverview St**, Phone to **269-979-0700**, Contact First Name to **Aimee**, and Contact Last Name to **Gigandet**. Close the table.

3. Open the **Product** table, find the record with Product ID 5318, and then delete the record. Close the table.

4. Create a query based on the Company table. Include the following fields in the query, in the order shown: Company, ContactFirst, ContactLast, Phone, and InitialContact. Sort the query in ascending order based on the Company field values. Save the query as **ContactList**, and then run the query.

5. Use the ContactList query datasheet to update the Company table by changing the Phone field value for Genesis Garden Center to **616-456-1783**.

6. Change the alternate row color in the ContactList query datasheet to the Theme Color named Tan, Background 2, Darker 10% (second row, third column), and then save and close the query.

7. Use Design view to create a query based on the Company and Product tables. Select the Company and City fields from the Company table, and the ProductType, Price, Unit, and Discount fields from the Product table. Sort the query results in descending order based on price. Select only those records with a City field value of Holland, but do not display the City field values in the query results. Save the query as **HollandCompanies**, run the query, and then close it.

8. Use Design view to create a query that lists all products that cost more than $5,000 and are not eligible for a discount. Display the following fields from the Product table in the query results: ProductID, ProductType, Price, Unit, and Weight. (*Hint:* The Discount field is a Yes/No field that should not appear in the query results.) Save the query as **HighPricesNoDiscount**, run the query, and then close it.

9. Use Design view to create a query that lists companies located in Grand Rapids or products that cost less than $1,000. Include the Company, City, ContactFirst, and ContactLast fields from the Company table; and the ProductType, Price, and Discount fields from the Product table. Save the query as **GrandRapidsOrLowPrices**, run the query, and then close it.

10. Use Design view to create a query that lists only those products that are eligible for a discount, along with a 5% discount amount based on the current price. Include the following fields from the Product table in the query: ProductID, ProductType, and Price. (*Hint:* The Discount field is a Yes/No field that should not appear in the query results.) Save the query as **PricesWithDiscountAmounts**. Display the discount in a calculated field named **Discount Amt** that determines a 5% discount based on the Price field values. Display the results in descending order by Price. Save and run the query.

11. Modify the format of the Discount Amt field in the PricesWithDiscountAmounts query so that it uses the Standard format and two decimal places. Run the query, resize all columns in the datasheet to best fit, and then save and close the query.

12. Create a query that calculates the lowest, highest, and average prices for all products using the field names **Lowest Price**, **Highest Price**, and **Average Price**, respectively. Run the query, resize all columns in the datasheet to best fit, save the query as **PriceStatistics**, and then close it.

13. In the Navigation Pane, copy the PriceStatistics query, and then rename the copied query as **PriceStatisticsByCompany**.

14. Modify the PriceStatisticsByCompany query so that the records are grouped by the Company field in the Company table. The Company field should appear first in the query datasheet. Save and run the query, and then close it.

15. Compact and repair the Supplier database, and then close it.

Case Problem 1   If you have a SAM 2010 user profile, your instructor may have assigned an autogradable version of this assignment. If so, log into the SAM 2010 Web site at www.cengage.com/sam2010 to download the instructions and start files.

APPLY

Data File needed for this Case Problem: Pinehill.accdb (*cont. from Tutorial 2*)

Pine Hill Music School   After reviewing the Pinehill database, Yuka Koyama wants to modify some records and then view specific information about the students, teachers, and contracts for her music school. She asks you to update and then query the Pinehill database to perform these tasks. Complete the following:

1. Open the **Pinehill** database located in the Access1\Case1 folder, and then click the Enable Content button next to the Security Warning, if necessary.

2. In the **Teacher** table, change the following information for the record with TeacherID 55-5310: Degree is **BM** and Hire Date is **3/12/2012**. Close the table.

3. In the **Student** table, find the record with the StudentID HAV7535, and then delete the related record in the subdatasheet for this student. Delete the record for StudentID HAV7535, and then close the Student table.

4. Create a query based on the Student table that includes the LastName, FirstName, and MobilePhone fields, in that order. Save the query as **StudentPhoneList**, and then run the query.

5. In the results of the StudentPhoneList query, change the mobile phone number for Andrea Barreau to **503-579-2277**. Close the query.

6. Use Design view to create a query based on the Teacher and Contract tables. Display the LastName field from the Teacher table, and the StudentID, EndDate, LessonType, LessonLength, and LessonCost fields, in that order, from the Contract table. Sort in ascending order first on the teacher's last name, and then in ascending order by the StudentID. Save the query as **LessonsByTeacher**, and then run it.

7. Display Backstage view, and then save the LessonsByTeacher query as **CurrentLessons**.

8. Modify the CurrentLessons query to display all contracts that end on or after 7/1/2013. Save your changes, and then run the query.

9. Display Backstage view, and then save the CurrentLessons query as **CurrentGuitarLessons**.

10. Modify the CurrentGuitarLessons query to display only those records for guitar lesson contracts that end on or after 7/1/2013. Do not include the LessonType field values in the query results. Run and save the query.

11. In the CurrentGuitarLessons query datasheet, calculate the total monthly amount for current guitar lessons.

12. Change the alternate row color in the CurrentGuitarLessons query datasheet to the Theme Color named Purple, Accent 4, Lighter 60% (third row, eight column), and then change the font size to 12. Resize all columns in the datasheet to fit the data, and then save and close the query.

13. Compact and repair the Pinehill database, and then close it.

Follow the steps and use the figures as guides to create queries for a fitness center.

CREATE

Case Problem 2

Data File needed for this Case Problem: Fitness.accdb (*cont. from Tutorial 2*)

Parkhurst Health & Fitness Center   Martha Parkhurst needs to change a few records in the Fitness database and analyze the records for members enrolled in different programs at the fitness center. To help her perform these tasks, you'll update the Fitness database and create queries to answer her questions. Complete the following:

1. Open the **Fitness** database located in the Access1\Case2 folder, and then click the Enable Content button next to the Security Warning, if necessary.

2. In the **Member** table, find the record for MemberID 1158, and then change the Street value to **89 Mockingbird Lane** and the Phone to **804-751-1847**. Close the table.

3. In the **Program** table, find the record for ProgramID 205. In the subdatasheet, delete the related record from the Member table. Then delete the record for ProgramID 205 in the Program table. Close the table.

4. Use Design view to create a query that lists members who are required to have physical examinations. In the query results, display the First, Last, and DateJoined fields from the Member table, and the MonthlyFee field from the Program table. Sort the records in descending order by the date joined. Select records only for members required to take a physical. (*Hint:* The PhysicalRequired field is a Yes/No field that should not appear in the query results.) Save the query as **PhysicalsNeeded**, and then run the query.

5. Use the PhysicalsNeeded query datasheet to update the Member table by changing the Date Joined value for Ed Curran to **10/18/2013**.

6. Use the PhysicalsNeeded query datasheet to display the total Monthly Fee for the selected members. Save and close the query.

7. Use Design view to create a query that lists the MemberID, First, Last, DateJoined, ProgramType, and MonthlyFee fields for members who joined the fitness center between June 1 and June 30, 2013. Save the query as **JuneMembers**, run the query, and then close it.

8. Create and save the query to produce the results shown in Figure 3-42. Close the query when you are finished.

| Figure 3-42 | RichmondOnHold query results |

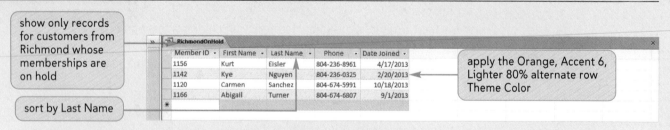

show only records for customers from Richmond whose memberships are on hold

sort by Last Name

apply the Orange, Accent 6, Lighter 80% alternate row Theme Color

EXPLORE

9. Create and save the query to produce the results shown in Figure 3-43. Close the query when you are finished.

Figure 3-43   **SelectedCities query results**

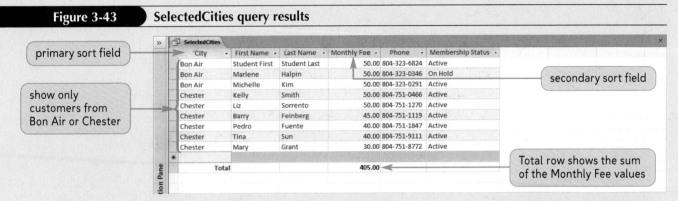

primary sort field

show only customers from Bon Air or Chester

secondary sort field

Total row shows the sum of the Monthly Fee values

⊕ **EXPLORE**   10. Create and save the query to produce results that display statistics for the MonthlyFee field, as shown in Figure 3-44. Close the query when you are finished.

Figure 3-44   **FeeStatistics query results**

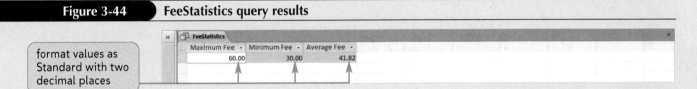

format values as Standard with two decimal places

11. In the Navigation Pane, copy the FeeStatistics query and rename the copied query **FeeStatisticsByCity**.

12. Modify the FeeStatisticsByCity query to display the same statistics grouped by City, with City appearing as the first field. (*Hint:* Add the Member table to the query.) Run the query, and then save and close it.

13. Compact and repair the Fitness database, and then close it.

Explore some new skills to create queries for a recycling agency.

CHALLENGE

Case Problem 3

Data File needed for this Case Problem: Rossi.accdb (cont. from Tutorial 2)

Rossi Recycling Group   Tom Rossi needs to modify some records in the Rossi database, and then he wants to find specific information about the donors, agencies, and donations to his not-for-profit agency. Tom asks you to help him update the database and create queries. Complete the following:

1. Open the **Rossi** database located in the Access1\Case3 folder, and then click the Enable Content button next to the Security Warning, if necessary.

2. In the **Donor** table, delete the record with DonorID 36065. (*Hint:* Delete the related record first.) Close the table.

3. Create a query based on the Agency table that includes the Agency, FirstName, LastName, and City fields, in that order. Save the query as **AgenciesByCity**, and then run it.

4. Modify the AgenciesByCity query design so that it sorts records in ascending order first by City and then by Agency. Save and run the query.

5. In the AgenciesByCity query datasheet, change the contact for the Community Development agency to **Beth Dayton**. Close the query.

6. Use Design view to create a query that displays the DonorID, FirstName, and LastName fields from the Donor table, and the Description and DonationValue fields from the Donation table for all donations over $50. Sort the query in ascending order by donation value. Save the query as **LargeDonations**, and then run the query.

7. Display Backstage view, and then save the LargeDonations query as **LargeCashDonations**.

⊕ EXPLORE 8. Modify the LargeCashDonations query to display only those records with donations valuing more than $50 in cash. Do not include the Description field values in the query results. Use the query datasheet to calculate the average cash donation. Save and close the query.

9. Use Design view to create a query that displays the AgencyID (from the Agency table), and the DonationID, DonationDate, and Description fields from the Donation table. Save the query as **SeniorDonations**, and then run the query.

10. Filter the results of the SeniorDonations query datasheet to display records for all donations to the SeniorCare Program (AgencyID K82).

⊕ EXPLORE 11. Format the datasheet of the SeniorDonations query so that it does not display gridlines, uses an alternate row Standard Color of Maroon 2, and displays a font size of 12. (*Hint*: Use the Gridlines button in the Text Formatting group on the Home tab to select the appropriate gridlines option.) Resize the columns to display the complete field names and values. Save your changes.

12. Display Backstage view, and then save the SeniorDonations query as **ComputerOrYouthDonations**.

13. Modify the ComputerOrYouthDonations query to display donations of "Computer equipment" or those to the After School Youth agency (AgencyID Y68). Sort the records in ascending order first by Description and then by AgencyID. Run, save, and then close the query.

⊕ EXPLORE 14. Use Design view to create a query (based on all three tables in the database) that displays the DonorID (Donor table), Agency, Description, and DonationValue fields for all donations that require a pickup. (*Hint:* The Pickup field is a Yes/No field that should not appear in the query results.) Save the query as **DonationsAfterPickupCharge**. Create a calculated field named **Net Donation** that displays the results of subtracting $8.75 from the DonationValue field values. Display the results in ascending order by donation value. Run the query, and then modify it to format the calculated field as Currency. Run the query again and resize the columns in the datasheet to their best fit. Save and close the query.

⊕ EXPLORE 15. Use the **Donation** table to display the sum, average, and count of the DonationValue field for all donations. Then complete the following:

    a. Specify column names of **Total Donations**, **Average Donation**, and **Number of Donations**.

    b. Save the query as **DonationStatistics**, and then run it.

    c. Modify the field properties so that the values in the Total Donations and Average Donation columns display two decimal places and the Standard format. Run the query and resize the columns in the datasheet to their best fit. Save and close the query.

    d. In the Navigation Pane, create a copy of the DonationStatistics query named **DonationStatisticsByAgency**.

    e. Modify the DonationStatisticsByAgency query to display the sum, average, and count of the DonationValue field for all donations grouped by Agency, with Agency appearing as the first field. (*Hint*: Add the Agency table to the query.) Sort the records in descending order by Total Donations. Save, run, and then close the query.

16. Compact and repair the Rossi database, and then close it.

Explore some new skills to create queries for a luxury rental company.

CHALLENGE

Case Problem 4

Data File needed for this Case Problem: GEM.accdb (*cont. from Tutorial 2*)

GEM Ultimate Vacations   Griffin and Emma MacElroy want to modify some records, and then analyze data about their clients and the luxury properties they rent. You'll help them update and query the GEM database. Complete the following:

1. Open the **GEM** database located in the Access1\Case4 folder, and then click the Enable Content button next to the Security Warning, if necessary.

2. In the **Guest** table, delete the record with a GuestID of 224, and then close the table.

3. Create a query based on the Property table that includes the PropertyName, Location, Country, NightlyRate, and PropertyType fields, in that order. Sort in ascending order based on the NightlyRate field values. Save the query as **PropertiesByRate**, and then run the query.

⊕ **EXPLORE**   4. In the results of the PropertiesByRate query, change the nightly rate for the Hartfield Country Manor property to $2,500, and then use the datasheet to display the number of properties (using the Property Type column) and the average nightly rate. Save and close the query.

5. Create a query that displays the GuestLast, City, State/Prov, ReservationID, StartDate, and EndDate fields. Save the query as **GuestTripDates**, and then run the query. Change the alternate row color in the query datasheet to the Standard Color Purple 2. In Datasheet view, use an AutoFilter to sort the query results from oldest to newest Start Date. Resize the datasheet columns to their best fit, and then save and close the query.

6. Create a query that displays the GuestLast, City, ReservationID, People, StartDate, and EndDate fields for all guests from Illinois (IL). Do not include the State/Prov field in the query results. Sort the query in ascending order by City. Save the query as **IllinoisGuests** and then run it. Resize datasheet columns to their best fit, as necessary, and then save and close the query.

⊕ **EXPLORE**   7. Create a query that displays the GuestLast, City, State/Prov, ReservationID, StartDate, and PropertyID fields for all guests who are not from Illinois or who are renting a property starting on or after July 1, 2013. (*Hint:* You must specifically type the quotation marks around the state abbreviation "IL" in the criteria.) Sort the query in descending order by StartDate. Save the query as **OutOfStateOrJuly**, and then run the query. Resize datasheet columns to their best fit, as necessary, and then save the query.

8. Display Backstage view, and then save the OutOfStateOrJuly query as **OutOfStateAndJuly**.

9. Modify the OutOfStateAndJuly query to select all guests who are not from Illinois and who are renting a property beginning on or after July 1, 2013. Sort the query in ascending order by StartDate. Run the query, and then save and close it.

10. Create a query that displays the ReservationID, StartDate, EndDate, PropertyID, PropertyName, People, and Rate fields for all reservations. Save the query as **RentalCost**. Add a field to the query named **Cost Per Person** that displays the results of dividing the Rate field values by the People field values. Display the results in descending order by Cost Per Person. Run the query. Modify the query by setting the Format property for the Cost Per Person field to Currency. Run the query, resize datasheet columns to their best fit, as necessary, and then save your changes.

11. Display Backstage view, and then save the RentalCost query as **TopRentalCost**.

⊕ **EXPLORE**   12. Modify the TopRentalCost query in Design view to display only the top five values for the Cost Per Person field. (*Hint:* Use the Return (Top Values) box in the Query Setup group on the Design tab.) Save, run, and then close the query.

13. Use the Reservation table to determine the minimum, average, and maximum rental rate values for all reservations. Then complete the following:

   a. Specify column names of **Lowest Rate**, **Average Rate**, and **Highest Rate**.

   b. Save the query as **RateStatistics**, and then run the query.

   c. In Design view, specify the Standard format and two decimal places for each column.

   d. Run the query, resize all the datasheet columns to their best fit, save your changes, and then close the query.

   e. Create a copy of the RateStatistics query named **RateStatisticsByCountry**.

   f. Revise the RateStatisticsByCountry query to display the rate statistics grouped by Country of the property, with Country appearing as the first field. Save your changes and then run and close the query.

14. Compact and repair the GEM database, and then close it.

SAM: Skills Assessment Manager

For current SAM information, including versions and content details, visit SAM Central (http://samcentral.course.com). If you have a SAM user profile, you may have access to hands-on instruction, practice, and assessment of the skills covered in this tutorial. Since various versions of SAM are supported throughout the life of this text, check with your instructor for the correct instructions and URL/Web site for accessing assignments.

ASSESS

ENDING DATA FILES

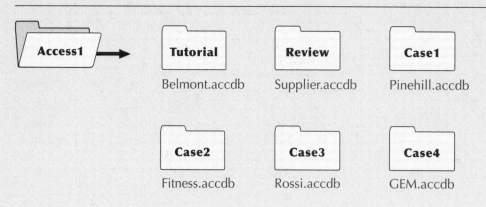

Access1 →	Tutorial	Review	Case1
	Belmont.accdb	Supplier.accdb	Pinehill.accdb
	Case2	Case3	Case4
	Fitness.accdb	Rossi.accdb	GEM.accdb

Creating Forms and Reports

Using Forms and Reports to Display Customer and Contract Data

OBJECTIVES

Session 4.1
- Create a form using the Form Wizard
- Apply a theme to a form
- Add a picture to a form
- Change the color and line type of items on a form
- Find and maintain data using a form
- Preview and print selected form records

Session 4.2
- Create a form with a main form and a subform
- Create a report using the Report Wizard
- Apply a theme to a report
- Resize fields in a report
- Insert a picture in a report
- Use conditional formatting in a report
- Preview and print a report

Case | *Belmont Landscapes*

Oren Belmont wants to continue enhancing the Belmont database to make it easier for his staff to enter, locate, and maintain data. In particular, he wants the database to include a form based on the Customer table to make it easier for employees to enter and change data about the firm's customers. He also wants the database to include a form that shows data from both the Customer and Contract tables at the same time. This form will show the contract information for each customer along with the corresponding customer data, providing a complete picture of Belmont Landscapes customers and their contracts.

In addition, Taylor Sico would like the database to include a formatted report of customer and contract data so that employees will have printed output when completing market analyses and planning strategies for selling services to customers. She wants the information to be formatted in a professional manner, to make the report appealing and easy to use.

STARTING DATA FILES

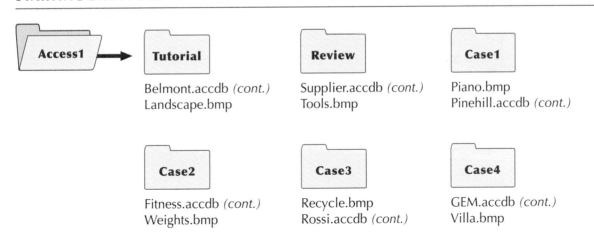

Access1 → **Tutorial**

Belmont.accdb *(cont.)*
Landscape.bmp

Review

Supplier.accdb *(cont.)*
Tools.bmp

Case1

Piano.bmp
Pinehill.accdb *(cont.)*

Case2

Fitness.accdb *(cont.)*
Weights.bmp

Case3

Recycle.bmp
Rossi.accdb *(cont.)*

Case4

GEM.accdb *(cont.)*
Villa.bmp

SESSION 4.1 VISUAL OVERVIEW

The form object's name is displayed on the tab for the form.

The form title appears at the top of the form. By default, the form object name is used as the form title, but you can edit the title to display the text you want, as done here—a space was added between the two words for readability.

With this form layout, the Columnar layout, the field captions appear in a column on the left side of the form. If captions have not been specified for the fields, the field names would appear here instead.

The navigation buttons allow you to display the first, last, next, or previous record in the form; enter a specific record number and move to that record; and create a new record.

You can add graphic elements, such as a picture, to a form to improve its appearance or add visual appeal.

The Columnar form layout displays the corresponding field values in boxes to the right of the field captions (or field names).

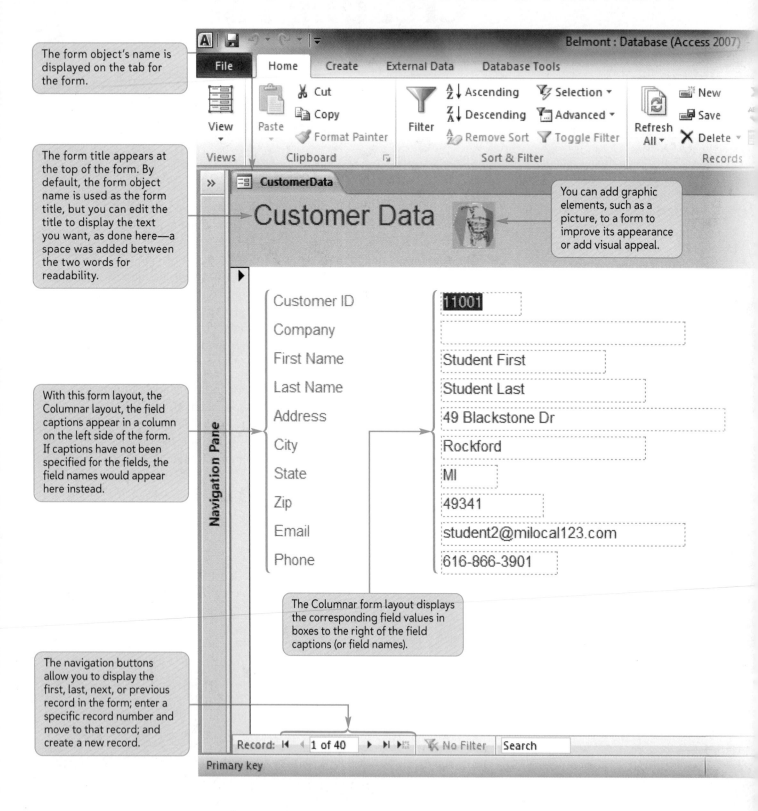

Belmont : Database (Access 2007)

File | Home | Create | External Data | Database Tools

View | Paste | Cut | Copy | Format Painter | Filter | Ascending | Descending | Remove Sort | Selection | Advanced | Toggle Filter | Refresh All | New | Save | Delete

Views | Clipboard | Sort & Filter | Records

Navigation Pane

CustomerData

Customer Data

Customer ID   11001
Company
First Name   Student First
Last Name   Student Last
Address   49 Blackstone Dr
City   Rockford
State   MI
Zip   49341
Email   student2@milocal123.com
Phone   616-866-3901

Record: ◄ ◄ 1 of 40 ► ►► ►※   No Filter   Search

Primary key

FORM DISPLAYED IN FORM VIEW

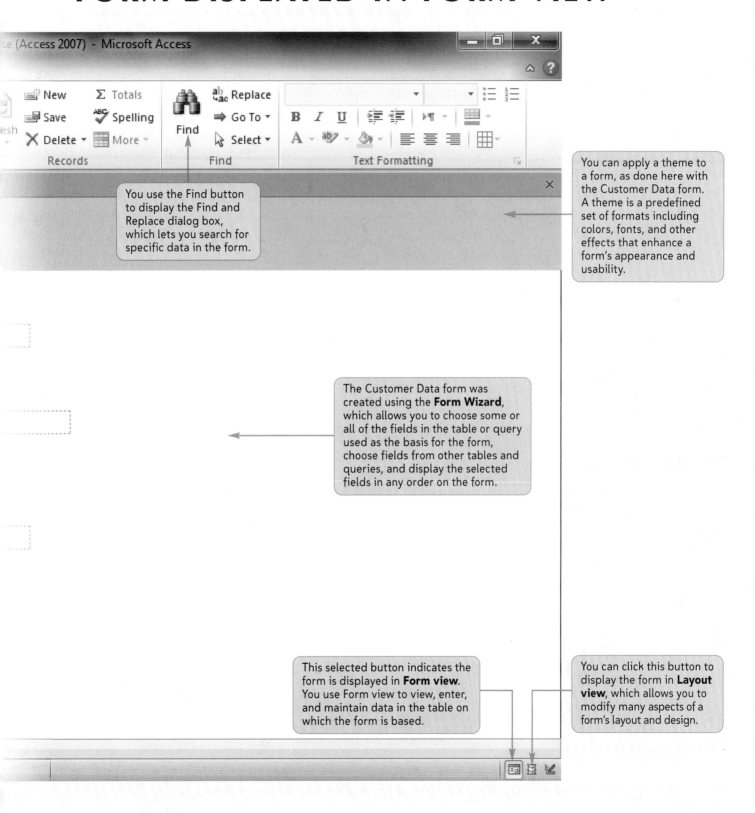

You use the Find button to display the Find and Replace dialog box, which lets you search for specific data in the form.

You can apply a theme to a form, as done here with the Customer Data form. A theme is a predefined set of formats including colors, fonts, and other effects that enhance a form's appearance and usability.

The Customer Data form was created using the **Form Wizard**, which allows you to choose some or all of the fields in the table or query used as the basis for the form, choose fields from other tables and queries, and display the selected fields in any order on the form.

This selected button indicates the form is displayed in **Form view**. You use Form view to view, enter, and maintain data in the table on which the form is based.

You can click this button to display the form in **Layout view**, which allows you to modify many aspects of a form's layout and design.

Creating a Form Using the Form Wizard

As you learned in Tutorial 1, a form is an object you use to enter, edit, and view records in a database. You can design your own forms or have Access create them for you automatically. In Tutorial 1, you used the Form tool to create the ContractData form in the Belmont database. Recall that the Form tool creates a form automatically, using all the fields in the selected table or query.

Oren asks you to create a new form that his staff can use to view and maintain data in the Customer table. To create the form for the Customer table, you'll use the Form Wizard, which guides you through the process.

To open the Belmont database and start the Form Wizard:

▶ **1.** Start Access and open the **Belmont** database located in the Access1\Tutorial folder.

Trouble? If the Security Warning is displayed below the Ribbon, click the Enable Content button next to the Security Warning.

▶ **2.** Open the Navigation Pane, if necessary. To create a form based on a table or query, you can select the table or query in the Navigation Pane first, or you can select it using the Form Wizard.

▶ **3.** In the Tables section of the Navigation Pane, click **Customer** to select the Customer table as the basis for the new form.

▶ **4.** Click the **Create** tab on the Ribbon. The Forms group on the Create tab provides options for creating various types of forms and designing your own forms.

▶ **5.** In the Forms group, click the **Form Wizard** button. The first Form Wizard dialog box opens. See Figure 4-1.

Figure 4-1 First Form Wizard dialog box

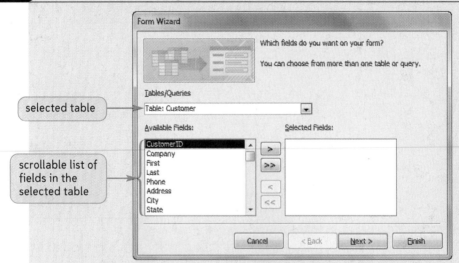

selected table

scrollable list of
fields in the
selected table

Because you selected the Customer table in the Navigation Pane before starting the Form Wizard, this table is selected in the Tables/Queries box, and the fields for the Customer table are listed in the Available Fields box.

Oren wants the form to display all the fields in the Customer table, but in a different order. He would like the Phone field to appear at the bottom of the form so that it stands out, making it easier for someone who needs to call customers to use the form and quickly identify the phone number for a customer.

To create the form using the Form Wizard:

▶ **1.** Click the `>>` button to move all the fields to the Selected Fields box. Next, you need to remove the Phone field, and then add it back as the last selected field so that it will appear at the bottom of the form.

▶ **2.** In the Selected Fields box, click the **Phone** field, and then click the `<` button to move the field back to the Available Fields box.

To add the Phone field to the end of the form, you need to highlight the last field in the list, and then move the Phone field back to the Selected Fields box.

▶ **3.** In the Selected Fields box, click the **Email** field.

▶ **4.** With the Phone field selected in the Available Fields box, click the `>` button to move the Phone field to the end of the Selected Fields box.

▶ **5.** Click the **Next** button to display the second Form Wizard dialog box, in which you select a layout for the form. See Figure 4-2.

| Figure 4-2 | Choosing a layout for the form |

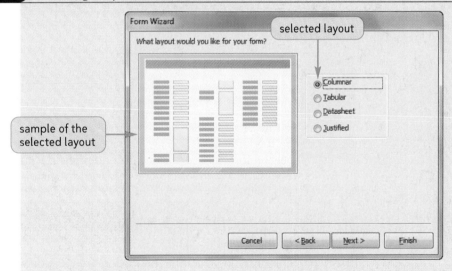

The layout choices are Columnar, Tabular, Datasheet, and Justified. A sample of the selected layout appears on the left side of the dialog box.

▶ **6.** Click each of the option buttons and review the corresponding sample layout.

The Tabular and Datasheet layouts display the fields from multiple records at one time, whereas the Columnar and Justified layouts display the fields from one record at a time. Oren thinks the Columnar layout is the appropriate arrangement for displaying and updating data in the table, so that anyone using the form can focus on just one customer record at a time.

▶ **7.** Click the **Columnar** option button (if necessary), and then click the **Next** button.

Access displays the third and final Form Wizard dialog box and shows the Customer table's name as the default form name. "Customer" is also the default title that will appear on the tab for the form.

You'll use "CustomerData" as the form name and, because you don't need to change the form's design at this point, you'll display the form.

▶ 8. Click the insertion point to the right of Customer in the text box, type **Data**, and then click the **Finish** button.

▶ 9. Close the Navigation Pane to display more of the Form window. The completed form is displayed in Form view. See Figure 4-3.

Figure 4-3 **CustomerData form in Form view**

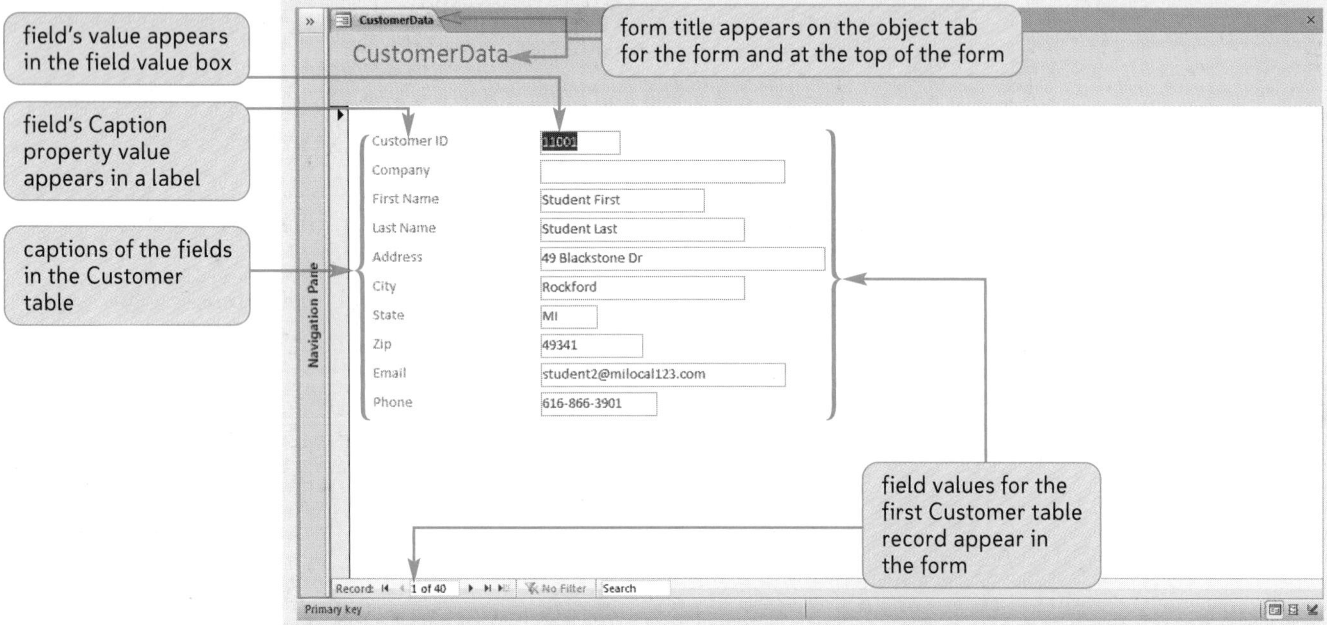

field's value appears in the field value box

field's Caption property value appears in a label

captions of the fields in the Customer table

form title appears on the object tab for the form and at the top of the form

CustomerData

Customer ID	11001
Company	
First Name	Student First
Last Name	Student Last
Address	49 Blackstone Dr
City	Rockford
State	MI
Zip	49341
Email	student2@milocal123.com
Phone	616-866-3901

field values for the first Customer table record appear in the form

Record: I◄ ◄ 1 of 40 ► ►I ►I ⚓ No Filter Search

Primary key

Notice that the title you specified for the form appears on the tab for the object and as a title on the form itself. The Columnar layout you selected places the field captions in labels on the left and the corresponding field values in boxes on the right, which vary in width depending on the size of the field. The form currently displays the field values for the first record in the Customer table.

After viewing the form, Oren decides that he doesn't like its appearance. The font used in the labels on the left is somewhat light in color and small, making them a bit difficult to read. Also, he thinks inserting a graphic on the form would add visual interest, and modifying other form elements—such as the color of certain text, the type of line used for the field value boxes, and so on—would improve the look of the form. You can make all of these changes working with the form in Layout view.

Modifying a Form's Design in Layout View

TIP

Some form design changes require you to switch to Design view, which gives you a more detailed view of the form's structure.

After you create a form, you might need to modify its design in Layout view to improve its appearance or to make the form easier to use. In Layout view, you see the form as it appears in Form view, but you can still modify the form's design; in Form view, you cannot make any design changes. Because you can see the form and its data while you are modifying the form, Layout view makes it easy for you to see the results of any design changes you make. You can continue to make changes, undo modifications, and rework the design in Layout view to achieve the look you want for the form.

The first modification you'll make to the CustomerData form is to change its appearance by applying a theme.

Applying a Theme to a Form

By default, a form you create is formatted with the Office theme, which determines the color and font used on the form. Access, like other Microsoft Office programs, provides many built-in themes, including the Office theme, making it easy for you to create objects with a unified look. You can also create a customized theme if none of the built-in themes suit your needs. To change a form's appearance, you can easily apply a new theme to it.

REFERENCE

Applying a Theme to a Form

- Display the form in Layout view.
- In the Themes group on the Design tab, click the Themes button.
- In the displayed gallery, click the theme you want to apply to all objects; or, right-click the theme to display the shortcut menu, and then choose to apply the theme to the current object only or to all matching objects.

Oren would like to see if the CustomerData form's appearance can be improved with a different theme. To apply a theme, you first need to switch to Layout view.

To apply a theme to the CustomerData form:

▶ **1.** In the Views group on the Home tab, click the **View** button. The form is displayed in Layout view. See Figure 4-4.

Figure 4-4   **Form displayed in Layout view**

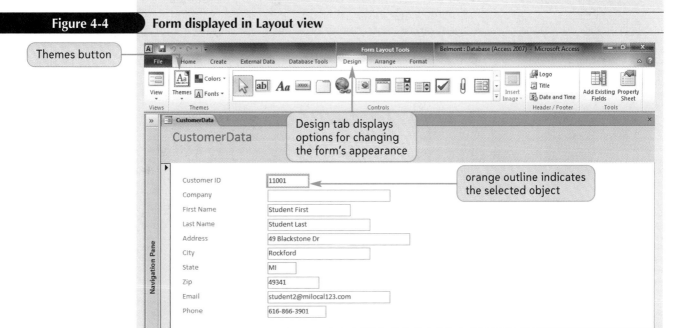

Themes button

Design tab displays options for changing the form's appearance

orange outline indicates the selected object

CustomerData

Customer ID	11001
Company	
First Name	Student First
Last Name	Student Last
Address	49 Blackstone Dr
City	Rockford
State	MI
Zip	49341
Email	student2@milocal123.com
Phone	616-866-3901

Trouble? If the Field List or Property Sheet opens on the right side of your window, close it before continuing.

You can use Layout view to modify an existing form. In Layout view, an orange outline identifies the currently selected object on the form; in this case, the field value for the CustomerID field, 11001, is selected. You need to apply a theme to the CustomerData form.

2. In the Themes group on the Design tab, click the **Themes** button. A gallery opens showing the available themes for the form. See Figure 4-5.

Figure 4-5 Themes gallery displayed

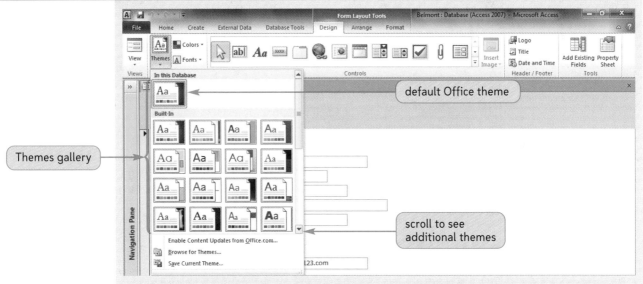

The Office theme, which is shown in the "In this Database" section and is also the first theme listed in the "Built-In" section, is the default theme currently applied in the database. Each theme provides a design scheme for the colors and fonts used in the database objects. You can point to each theme in the gallery to see its name in a ScreenTip. Also, when you point to a theme, the Live Preview feature shows the effect of applying the theme to the open object.

TIP

Themes other than the Office theme are listed in alphabetical order in the gallery.

3. Scroll through the list of themes and point to several themes to see how they would format the CustomerData form. Notice the changes in color and font type of the text, for example.

Oren likes the Perspective theme; its color in the title area at the top is more subdued than the brighter blue of the Office theme, and the theme's font is larger and easier to read. He asks you to apply this theme to the form.

4. Scroll the Themes gallery to the bottom, and then right-click the **Perspective** theme (third row from the bottom, third theme from the left). A shortcut menu opens with options for applying the theme. See Figure 4-6.

| Figure 4-6 | Shortcut menu for applying the theme |

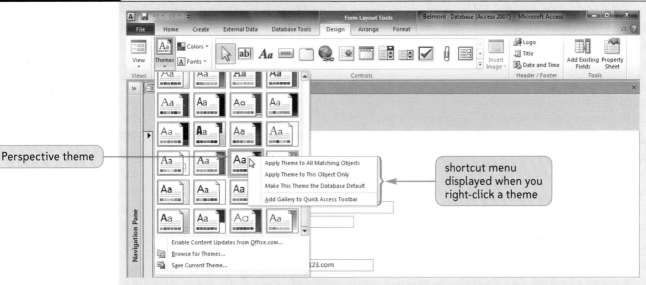

Perspective theme

shortcut menu displayed when you right-click a theme

The menu provides options for applying the theme to all matching objects—for example, all the forms in the database—or to the current object only. You can also choose to make the theme the default theme in the database, which means any new objects you create will be formatted with the selected theme. Because Oren is not sure if all forms in the Belmont database will look better with the Perspective theme, he asks you to apply it only to the CustomerData form.

Choose this option to avoid applying the theme to other forms in the database.

▸ 5. On the shortcut menu, click **Apply Theme to This Object Only**.

The gallery closes, and the Perspective theme formats the form's colors and fonts.

INSIGHT

Working with Themes

Themes provide a quick and easy way for you to format the objects in a database with a consistent look, which is a good design principle to follow. In general, all objects of a type in a database—for example, all forms—should have a consistent design. However, keep in mind that when you select a theme in the Themes gallery and choose the option to apply the theme to all matching objects or to make the theme the default for the database, Access applies it to *all* the existing forms and reports in the database as well as to new forms and reports you create. Although this ensures a consistent design, this approach can cause problems. For example, if you have already created a form or report and its design is suitable, applying a theme that includes a larger font size could cause the text in labels and field value boxes to be cut off or to extend into other objects on the form or report. The colors applied by the theme could also interfere with elements on existing forms and reports. To handle these unintended results, you would have to spend time checking the existing forms and reports and fixing any problems introduced by applying the theme. A better approach is to select the option "Apply Theme to This Object Only," available on the shortcut menu for a theme in the Themes gallery, for each existing form and report. If the newly applied theme causes problems for any individual form or report, you can then reapply the original theme to return the object to its original design.

Next, Oren asks you to add a picture to the form for visual interest. The picture, which is included on various stationery items for Belmont Landscapes—business cards, flyers, and so on—is a small graphic of a piece of landscaping equipment. You'll add this picture to the form.

Adding a Picture to a Form

A picture is one of many controls you can add and modify on a form. A **control** is an item on a form, report, or other database object that you can manipulate to modify the object's appearance. The controls you can add and modify in Layout view for a form are available in the Controls group and the Header/Footer group on the Design tab. The picture you need to add is contained in a file named Landscape.bmp, which is located in the Access1\Tutorial folder provided with your Data Files.

To add the picture to the form:

1. Make sure the form is still displayed in Layout view.

2. In the Header/Footer group on the Design tab, click the **Logo** button. The Insert Picture dialog box opens.

3. Navigate to the **Access1\Tutorial** folder provided with your Data Files, click the **Landscape** file, and then click the **OK** button. The picture appears as a selected object on top of the form's title. See Figure 4-7.

Figure 4-7 **Form with picture added**

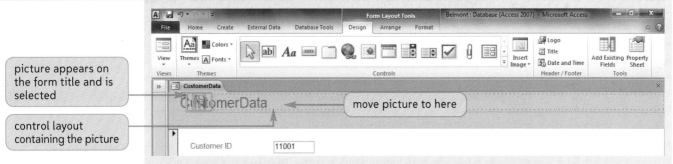

picture appears on the form title and is selected

control layout containing the picture

A solid orange outline surrounds the picture, indicating it is selected. The picture is placed in a **control layout**, which is a set of controls grouped together in a form or report so that you can manipulate the set as a single control. The dotted orange outline indicates the control layout (see Figure 4-7). The easiest way to move the picture off the form title is to first remove it from the control layout. Doing so allows you to move the picture independently.

4. Right-click the selected picture to display the shortcut menu, point to **Layout**, and then click **Remove Layout**. The picture is removed from the control layout. Now you can move the picture to the right of the form title.

5. Position the pointer ⇱ on the picture, and then click and drag the picture to the right to move it to the right of the form title.

6. When the pointer is below the button in the Controls group with the text "Aa" on it and to the right of the form's title, release the mouse button. The picture is positioned to the right of the form title.

The picture is somewhat small next to the form title, so you'll increase its size.

7. With the picture still selected, place the pointer ↕ on the bottom edge of the orange outline below the picture, and then click and drag down to increase the height of the picture (see Figure 4-8).

8. Click in a blank area on the main form (to the right of the field values) to deselect the picture. See Figure 4-8.

Figure 4-8	Form with theme applied and picture repositioned

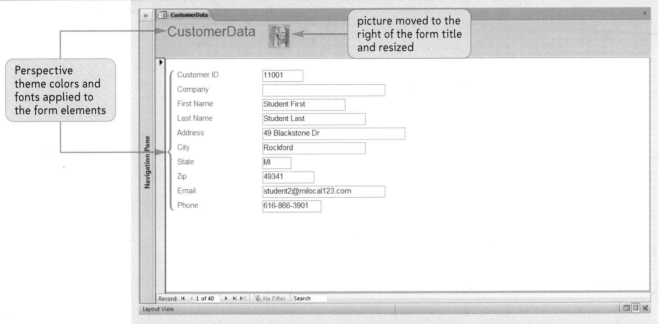

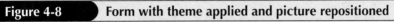

Trouble? Don't be concerned if your picture is not in the exact location or is not the same exact size as the one shown in Figure 4-8. Just make sure the picture is not blocking any part of the form title; that it appears to the right of the form title and above the main part of the form; and that it is not any larger than the shaded title area.

The addition of the picture to the form provides more color and visual interest. Next, Oren asks you to change the color of the form title to brown so that it will coordinate better with the picture next to the title.

Changing the Color of the Form Title

The Font group on the Format tab provides many options you can use to change the appearance of text on a form. For example, you can bold, italicize, and underline text; change the font, font color, and font size; and change the alignment of text. Before you change the color of the "CustomerData" title on the form to brown, you'll change the title to two words so it is easier to read.

TIP

Changing the form's title does not affect the form object name; it is still CustomerData, as shown on the object tab.

To change the form title's text and color:

1. Click the **CustomerData** form title. An orange box surrounds the title, indicating it is selected.

2. Click between the letters "r" and "D" to position the insertion point, and then press the **spacebar**. The title on the form is now "Customer Data."

▶ **3.** Click in the main form area again to deselect the title, and then click **Customer Data** to reselect the title. The orange outline appears around the words of the title.

▶ **4.** Click the **Format** tab on the Ribbon.

▶ **5.** In the Font group on the Format tab, click the **Font Color button arrow** [A ▾] to display the gallery of available colors. The gallery provides theme colors and standard colors, as well as an option for creating a custom color.

▶ **6.** In the Theme Colors palette, point to the seventh color box in the fifth row of boxes. The ScreenTip indicates this is the Brown, Accent 3, Darker 25% color.

▶ **7.** Click the **Brown, Accent 3, Darker 25%** color box.

▶ **8.** Click in a blank area of the main form to deselect the title text. The brown color is applied to the form title text, tying it to the picture on the form. See Figure 4-9.

| Figure 4-9 | Form title with new color applied |

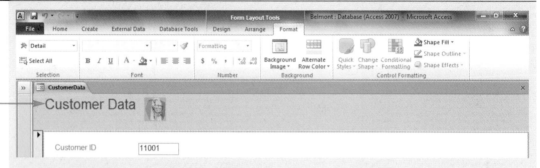

form title in a darker brown font and edited with a space between words

You have made a couple of changes to the form, and should save it now.

▶ **9.** Click the **Save** button [💾] on the Quick Access Toolbar to save the modified form.

Oren suggests a different type of line for the field value boxes. He thinks the solid line currently used on the form somewhat overshadows the field values within the boxes, and that a more subtle type of line might look better and make the field values easier to read.

Changing the Type of Line on a Form

A line on a form, such as the box around each field value, is another type of control that you can modify in Layout view. The Control Formatting group on the Format tab provides options for changing the thickness, type, and color of any line on a form. Next, you'll change the type of line for the field values boxes on the CustomerData form.

To change the type of line for the field value boxes:

▶ **1.** Click the field value **11001** for the CustomerID field. An orange outline appears around the field value box to indicate it is selected.

▶ **2.** In the Control Formatting group on the Format tab, click the **Shape Outline** button. A gallery opens with options for applying color. At the bottom of the gallery are options for modifying the line thickness and line type.

▶ **3.** Point to **Line Type** to display a submenu with various line formats, point to the **Dots** option (the fourth line type in the submenu) to display its ScreenTip, and then click the **Dots** line type.

4. Click in a blank area of the main form to deselect the box. The Customer ID field value box changes to a dotted line.

    Oren thinks the dotted line type is much better and makes the field value easier to see. He asks you to change the line type for the rest of the field value boxes on the form. To do so, you can select the remaining field value boxes and apply the new line type to all of them at the same time.

5. Click the **Company** field value box (the box is currently empty), press and hold the **Shift** key, click each remaining field value box below the Company field value box, and then release the **Shift** key. All the field value boxes except the first one should be selected; each box is outlined in orange to indicate it is selected. See Figure 4-10.

| Figure 4-10 | Form with multiple field value boxes selected |

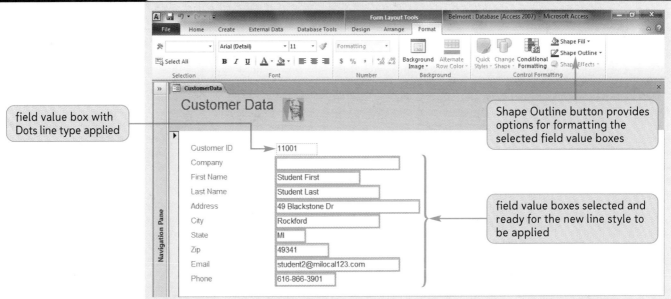

field value box with Dots line type applied

Shape Outline button provides options for formatting the selected field value boxes

field value boxes selected and ready for the new line style to be applied

6. In the Control Formatting group on the Format tab, click the **Shape Outline** button, point to **Line Type**, and then click the **Dots** option.

7. Click in a blank area of the main form to deselect the field value boxes. The line type for each box is now dotted.

8. Click the **Save** button on the Quick Access Toolbar to save the form.

9. In the bottom right section of the status bar, click the **Form View** button to display the form in Form view. Refer back to the Session 4.1 Visual Overview; your form should match the CustomerData form shown there.

Oren is pleased with the modified appearance of the form. Later, he plans to revise the existing ContractData form and make the same changes to it, so that it matches the appearance of the CustomerData form.

PROSKILLS

Written Communication: Understanding the Importance of Form Design

Similar to any document, a form must convey written information clearly and effectively. When you create a form, it's important to consider how the form will be used, so that its design will accommodate the needs of people using the form to view, enter, and maintain data. For example, if a form in a database mimics a paper form that users will enter data from, the form in the database should have the same fields in the same order as those on the paper form. This will enable users to easily tab from one field to the next in the database form to enter the necessary information from the paper form. Also, it's important to include a meaningful title on the form to identify its purpose, and to enhance the appearance of the form. A form that is visually appealing makes working with the database more user-friendly and can improve the readability of the form, thereby helping to prevent errors in data entry. Also, be sure to use a consistent design for the forms in your database whenever possible. Users will expect to see similar elements—titles, pictures, fonts, and so on—in each form contained in a database. A mix of form styles and elements among the forms in a database could lead to problems when working with the forms. Finally, make sure the text on your form does not contain any spelling or grammatical errors. By producing a well-designed and well-written form, you can ensure that users will be able to work with the form in a productive and efficient manner.

Navigating a Form

Oren wants to use the CustomerData form to view some data in the Customer table. As you saw earlier, you use Layout view to modify the appearance of a form. To view, navigate, and change data using a form, you need to display the form in Form view. As you learned in Tutorial 1, you navigate a form in the same way that you navigate a table datasheet. Also, the navigation mode and editing mode keystroke techniques you used with datasheets in Tutorial 3 are the same when navigating a form.

The CustomerData form is already displayed in Form view, so you can use it to navigate through the fields and records of the Customer table.

To navigate the CustomerData form:

1. Press the **Tab** key twice to move to the First Name field value box, and then press the **End** key to move to the Phone field value box.

2. Press the **Home** key to move back to the Customer ID field value box. The first record in the Customer table still appears in the form.

3. Press the **Ctrl+End** keys to move to the Phone field value box for record 40, which is the last record in the table. The record number for the current record appears in the Current Record box between the navigation buttons at the bottom of the form.

4. Click the **Previous record** navigation button ◀ to move to the Phone field value box in record 39.

5. Press the ↑ key twice to move to the Zip field value box in record 39.

6. Click the insertion point between the numbers "7" and "5" in the Address field value to switch to editing mode, press the **Home** key to move the insertion point to the beginning of the field value, and then press the **End** key to move the insertion point to the end of the field value.

7. Click the **First record** navigation button ⏮ to move to the Address field value box in the first record. The entire field value is highlighted because you switched from editing mode to navigation mode.

8. Click the **Next record** navigation button ▶ to move to the Address field value box in record 2, the next record.

Next, Oren asks you to display the record for the Three Tulips Café, a Belmont Landscapes customer. The paper form containing the original contact information for this customer was damaged. Oren recently contacted the owner of the café and obtained all the customer information again. Now Oren wants to use the form to view the data for this customer to make sure it is correct.

Finding Data Using a Form

As you learned in Tutorial 3, the Find command lets you search for data in a datasheet so you can display only those records you want to view. You can also use the Find command to search for data in a form. You choose a field to serve as the basis for the search by making that field the current field, and then you enter the value you want Access to match in the Find and Replace dialog box.

REFERENCE

Finding Data in a Form or Datasheet

- Open the form or datasheet, and then select the field you want to search.
- In the Find group on the Home tab, click the Find button to open the Find and Replace dialog box.
- In the Find What box, type the field value you want to find.
- Complete the remaining options, as necessary, to specify the type of search to conduct.
- Click the Find Next button to begin the search.
- Click the Find Next button to continue searching for the next match.
- Click the Cancel button to stop the search operation.

You need to find the record for the Three Tulips Café. Oren doesn't recall the CustomerID value for this customer, so you'll search for the record using the Company field.

To find the record using the CustomerData form:

1. Click in the **Company** field value box (which is empty for the current record) to establish Company as the current field. This is the field you need to search.

   Instead of searching for the entire company name, Three Tulips Café, you can search for a record that contains part of the name anywhere in the Company field value. Performing a partial search such as this is often easier than matching the entire field value and is useful when you don't know or can't remember the entire field value.

2. In the Find group on the Home tab, click the **Find** button. The Find and Replace dialog box opens. The Look In box shows that the current field (in this case, Company) will be searched. You'll search for records that contain the word "tulips" in the company name.

3. In the Find What box, type **tulips**. Note that you do not have to enter the word as "Tulips" with a capital letter "T" because the Match Case option is not selected in the Find and Replace dialog box. Access will find any record containing the word "tulips" with any combination of uppercase and lowercase letters.

4. Click the **Match** arrow to display the list of matching options, and then click **Any Part of Field**. Access will find any record that contains the word "tulips" in any part of the Company field. See Figure 4-11.

Figure 4-11 **Completed Find and Replace dialog box**

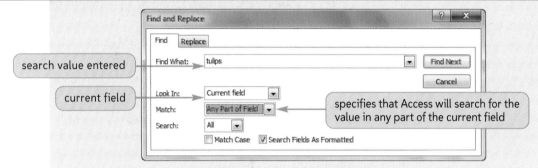

search value entered

current field

specifies that Access will search for the value in any part of the current field

5. Click the **Find Next** button. The CustomerData form now displays record 35, which is the record for the Three Tulips Café (CustomerID 11080). The word "Tulips" is selected in the Company field value box because you searched for this word. Oren reviews the information for the record and determines it is correct.

The search value you enter can be an exact value or it can include wildcard characters. A **wildcard character** is a placeholder you use when you know only part of a value or when you want to start or end with a specific character or match a certain pattern. Figure 4-12 shows the wildcard characters you can use when finding data.

Figure 4-12 **Wildcard characters**

Wildcard Character	Purpose	Example
*	Match any number of characters. It can be used as the first and/or last character in the character string.	th* finds the, that, this, therefore, and so on
?	Match any single alphabetic character.	a?t finds act, aft, ant, apt, and art
[]	Match any single character within the brackets.	a[fr]t finds aft and art but not act, ant, and apt
!	Match any character not within brackets.	a[!fr]t finds act, ant, and apt but not aft and art
-	Match any one of a range of characters. The range must be in ascending order (a to z, not z to a).	a[d-p]t finds aft, ant, and apt but not act and art
#	Match any single numeric character.	#72 finds 072, 172, 272, 372, and so on

Next, Oren wants to view the customer records for any customers with phone numbers beginning with the area code 517. He is curious to know how many customers are in cities serviced by that area code, and what the cities are. You could search for any field containing the digits 517 in any part of the field, but this search would also find records with the digits 517 in any part of the phone number. To find only those records with the 517 area code, you'll use the * wildcard character.

To find the records using the * wildcard character:

▶ **1.** Make sure the Find and Replace dialog box is still open.

▶ **2.** Click anywhere in the CustomerData form to make it active, and then press the **Tab** key eight times to move to the Phone field value box. This is the field you want to search.

▶ **3.** Click the title bar of the Find and Replace dialog box to make it active, and then drag the Find and Replace dialog box to the right so you can see the Phone field on the form. The Look In box setting is still Current field, which is now the Phone field; this is the field that will be searched.

▶ **4.** Double-click **tulips** in the Find What box to select the entire value, and then type **517***.

▶ **5.** Click the **Match** arrow, and then click **Whole Field**. Because you're using a wildcard character in the search value, you want Access to search the whole field.

With the settings you've entered, Access will find records in which any field value in the Phone field begins with the digits 517.

▶ **6.** Click the **Find Next** button. Access displays record 36, which is the first record found for a customer with the area code 517. This customer is located in East Lansing. Notice that the search process started from the point of the previously displayed record in the form, which was record 35.

▶ **7.** Click the **Find Next** button. Access displays record 8, which is the next record found for a customer with the area code 517. This customer is located in Lansing. Notice that the search process cycles back through the beginning of the records in the underlying table.

▶ **8.** Click the **Find Next** button. Access displays record 12, the third record found; this customer is also located in Lansing.

▶ **9.** Click the **Find Next** button. Access displays record 25 for another customer located in Lansing, with the area code 517.

▶ **10.** Click the **Find Next** button. Access displays record 33 for another customer located in Lansing.

▶ **11.** Click the **Find Next** button. Access displays a dialog box informing you that the search is finished.

▶ **12.** Click the **OK** button to close the dialog box. Oren notes that all customers with an area code of 517 are located in either Lansing or East Lansing.

▶ **13.** Click the **Cancel** button to close the Find and Replace dialog box.

Oren has identified some customer updates he wants you to make. You'll use the CustomerData form to update the data in the Customer table.

Maintaining Table Data Using a Form

Maintaining data using a form is often easier than using a datasheet because you can focus on all the changes for a single record at one time. In Form view, you can edit the field values for a record, delete a record from the underlying table, or add a new record to the table. You already know how to navigate a form and find specific records. Now you'll use the CustomerData form to make the changes Oren wants to the Customer table.

First, you'll update the record for the Cherrywood Senior Center. The center has a new contact person, so you need to update the first name, last name, phone number, and email address for this customer. Oren happens to know that the Cherrywood Senior Center is record 22 in the Customer table. If you know the number of the record you want to view, you can enter the number in the Current Record box to move to that record.

To change the record using the CustomerData form:

1. Click in the Current Record box at the bottom of the form, select **33**, type **22**, and then press the **Enter** key. Record 22 (Cherrywood Senior Center) is now current.

   You need to update this record with the information for the new contact person at the center, Dan Lewis.

2. In the First Name field value box, double-click **Lisa** to select the entry, and then type **Dan**.

TIP

Note that the pencil symbol appears in the upper-left corner of the form, indicating that the form is in editing mode.

3. Press the **Tab** key to move to and select the value in the Last Name field value box, and then type **Lewis**.

4. Click the insertion point before the first character in the Email field value box, press the **Delete** key seven times to delete the characters before the @ symbol, and then type **dlewis4**. The Email field value is now dlewis4@csc77.com.

5. Click the insertion point at the end of the value in the Phone field value box, press the **Backspace** key three times, and then type **890**. The Phone field value is now 269-857-1890. The updates to the record are complete. See Figure 4-13.

Figure 4-13	Customer record after changing field values

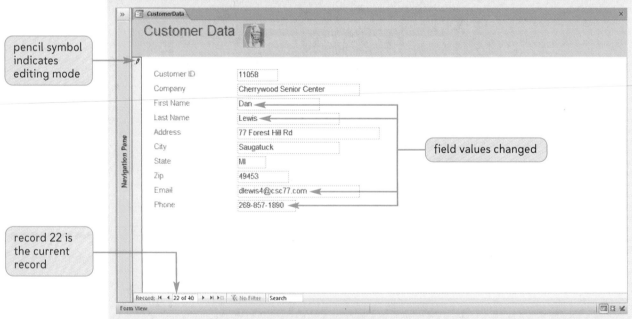

Next, Oren asks you to add a record for a new customer. The customer has not yet returned a signed contract, but Oren expects to receive the contract soon and wants to be sure the Customer table is updated first with the new customer record. You'll use the CustomerData form to add the new record.

To add the new record using the CustomerData form:

1. In the Records group on the Home tab, click the **New** button. Record 41, the next available new record, becomes the current record. All field value boxes are empty, and the insertion point is positioned in the Customer ID field value box.

2. Refer to Figure 4-14 and enter the value shown for each field. Press the **Tab** key to move from field to field.

Figure 4-14	Completed form for the new record

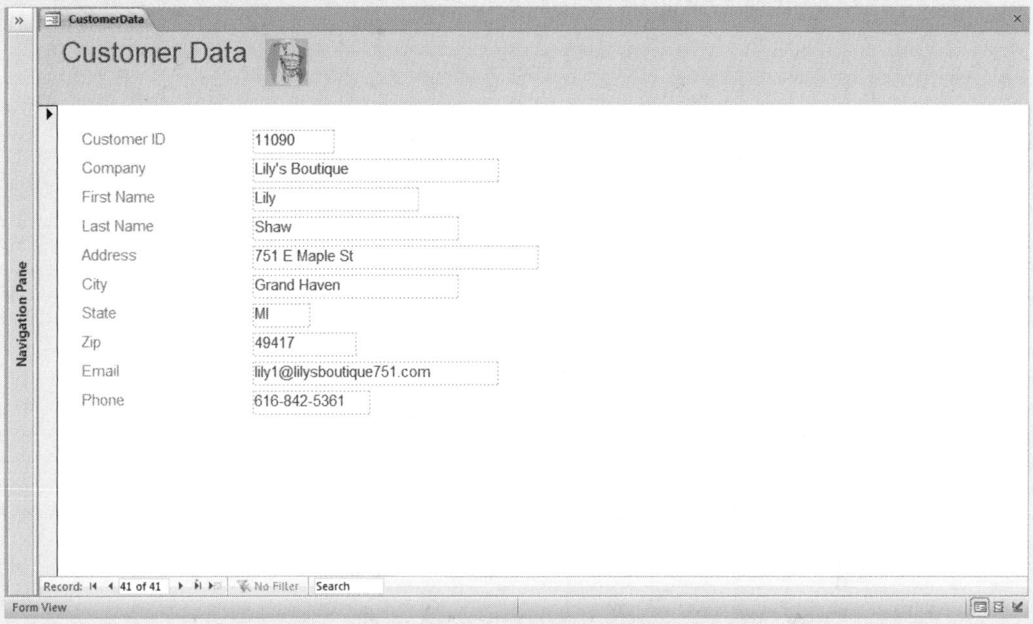

Trouble? Compare your screen with Figure 4-14. If any field value is incorrect, correct it now, using the methods described earlier for editing field values.

3. After entering the Phone field value, press the **Tab** key. Record 42, the next available new record, becomes the current record, and the record for CustomerID 11090 is saved in the Customer table.

Oren would like a printed copy of the record for the new customer only. He wants to give the printout to a staff member as a reminder to look for the new contract for this customer when it comes in.

Previewing and Printing Selected Form Records

Access prints as many form records as can fit on a printed page. If only part of a form record fits on the bottom of a page, the remainder of the record prints on the next page. Access allows you to print all pages or a range of pages. In addition, you can print the currently selected form record.

Before printing record 41, the record for Lily's Boutique, you'll preview the form record to see how it will look when printed.

To preview the form and print the data for record 41:

▶ 1. Click the **Previous record** navigation button ◀ to redisplay record 41.

▶ 2. Click the **File** tab to display Backstage view, click the **Print** tab in the navigation bar, and then click **Print Preview**. The Print Preview window opens, showing the form records for the Customer table. Notice that each record appears in its own form, and that shading is used to distinguish one record from another. See Figure 4-15.

Figure 4-15 **Form records displayed in Print Preview**

Print Preview tab contains options for viewing and printing the form and records

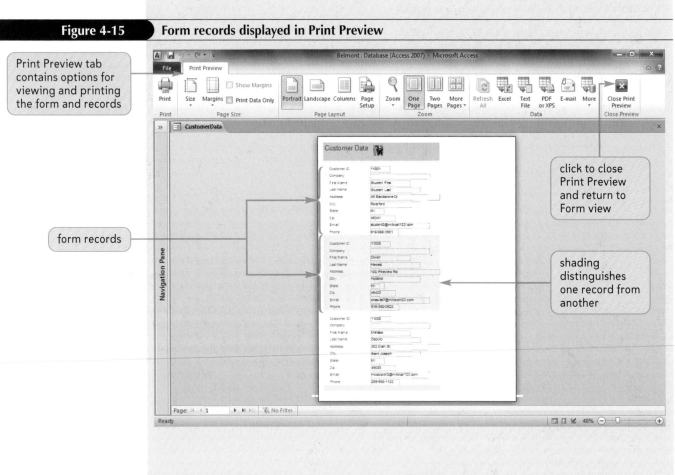

click to close Print Preview and return to Form view

form records

shading distinguishes one record from another

To print selected records, you need to close Print Preview and then use the Print dialog box.

▶ 3. In the Close Preview group on the Print Preview tab, click the **Close Print Preview** button. You return to Form view with the record for Lily's Boutique still displayed.

▶ 4. Click the **File** tab to display Backstage view again, click the **Print** tab in the navigation bar, and then click **Print**. The Print dialog box opens.

▶ 5. Click the **Selected Record(s)** option button to print the current form record (record 41).

   Trouble? Check with your instructor to be sure you should print the form; then continue to the next step. If you should not print the form, click the Cancel button, and then skip to Step 7.

▶ 6. Click the **OK** button to close the dialog box and print the selected record.

▶ 7. Close the CustomerData form.

▶ 8. If you are not continuing to Session 4.2, click the **File** tab, and then click **Close Database** in the navigation bar to close the Belmont database.

The CustomerData form will enable Oren and his staff to enter and maintain data easily in the Customer table. In the next session, you'll create another form for working with data in both the Customer and Contract tables at the same time. You'll also create a report showing data from both tables.

Session 4.1 Quick Check

REVIEW

1. Describe the difference between creating a form using the Form tool and creating a form using the Form Wizard.
2. What is a theme and how do you apply one to an existing form?
3. A(n) _____ is an item on a form, report, or other database object that you can manipulate to modify the object's appearance.
4. Which table record is displayed in a form when you press the Ctrl+End keys while you are in navigation mode?
5. Which wildcard character matches any single alphabetic character?
6. To print only the current record displayed in a form, you need to select the _____ option button in the Print dialog box.

SESSION 4.2 VISUAL OVERVIEW

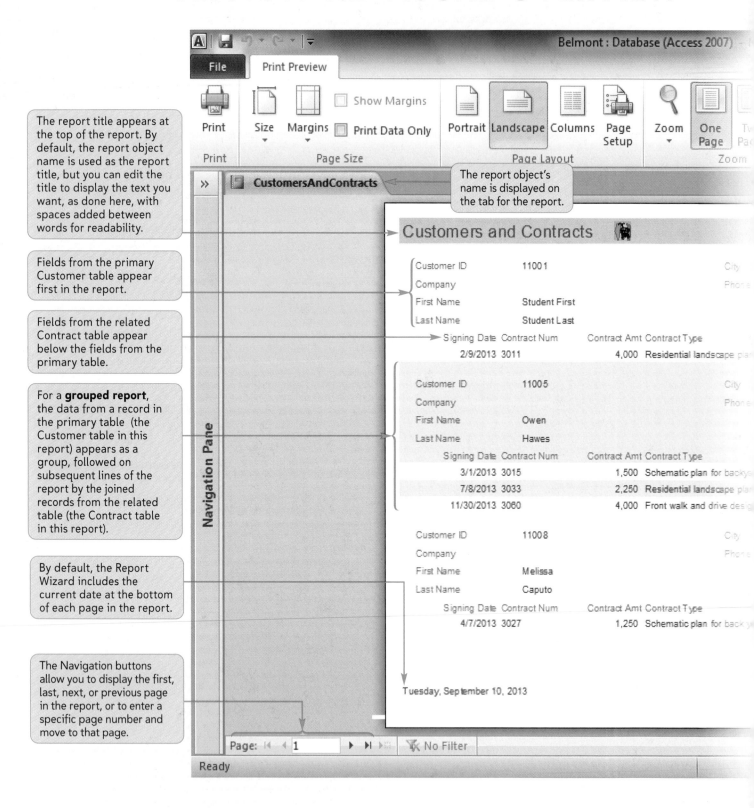

The report title appears at the top of the report. By default, the report object name is used as the report title, but you can edit the title to display the text you want, as done here, with spaces added between words for readability.

Fields from the primary Customer table appear first in the report.

Fields from the related Contract table appear below the fields from the primary table.

For a **grouped report**, the data from a record in the primary table (the Customer table in this report) appears as a group, followed on subsequent lines of the report by the joined records from the related table (the Contract table in this report).

By default, the Report Wizard includes the current date at the bottom of each page in the report.

The Navigation buttons allow you to display the first, last, next, or previous page in the report, or to enter a specific page number and move to that page.

The report object's name is displayed on the tab for the report.

REPORT IN PRINT PREVIEW

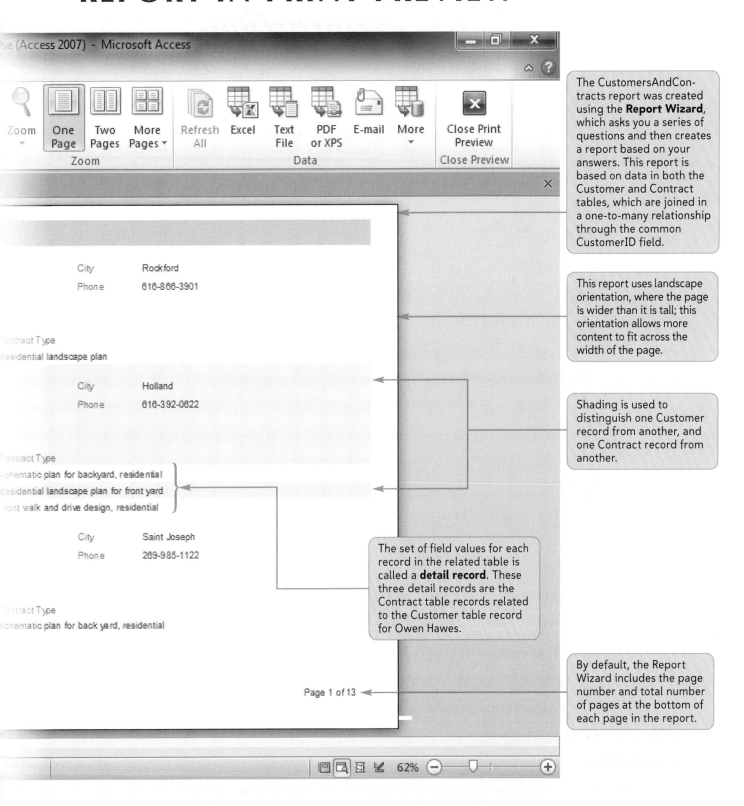

The CustomersAndContracts report was created using the **Report Wizard**, which asks you a series of questions and then creates a report based on your answers. This report is based on data in both the Customer and Contract tables, which are joined in a one-to-many relationship through the common CustomerID field.

This report uses landscape orientation, where the page is wider than it is tall; this orientation allows more content to fit across the width of the page.

Shading is used to distinguish one Customer record from another, and one Contract record from another.

The set of field values for each record in the related table is called a **detail record**. These three detail records are the Contract table records related to the Customer table record for Owen Hawes.

By default, the Report Wizard includes the page number and total number of pages at the bottom of each page in the report.

Creating a Form with a Main Form and a Subform

Before developing a report for the Belmont database, Oren would like you to create a form so that he can view the data for each customer and the customer's contracts at the same time. The type of form you need to create will include a main form and a subform. To create a form based on two tables, you must first define a relationship between the two tables. In Tutorial 2, you defined a one-to-many relationship between the Customer (primary) and Contract (related) tables, so you can now create a form based on both tables.

When you create a form containing data from two tables that have a one-to-many relationship, you actually create a **main form** for data from the primary table and a **subform** for data from the related table. Access uses the defined relationship between the tables to join them automatically through the common field that exists in both tables.

Oren and his staff will use the form when contacting customers about their contracts. The main form will contain the customer ID, company name (if any), first and last names, phone number, and email address for each customer. The subform will contain the information about the contracts for each customer. You'll use the Form Wizard to create the form.

To create the form using the Form Wizard:

▶ 1. If you took a break after the previous session, make sure that the Belmont database is open and the Navigation Pane is closed.

▶ 2. Click the **Create** tab on the Ribbon.

▶ 3. In the Forms group on the Create tab, click the **Form Wizard** button. The first Form Wizard dialog box opens.

When creating a form based on two tables, you first choose the primary table and select the fields you want to include in the main form; then you choose the related table and select fields from it for the subform.

▶ 4. If necessary, click the **Tables/Queries** arrow, and then click **Table: Customer**.

Oren wants the form to include only the CustomerID, Company, First, Last, Phone, and Email fields from the Customer table.

▶ 5. Click **CustomerID** in the Available Fields box (if necessary), and then click the ⟩ button to move the field to the Selected Fields box.

▶ 6. Repeat Step 5 for the **Company**, **First**, **Last**, **Phone**, and **Email** fields.

The CustomerID field will appear in the main form, so you do not have to include it in the subform. Otherwise, Oren wants the subform to include all the fields from the Contract table.

▶ 7. Click the **Tables/Queries** arrow, scroll the list up, and then click **Table: Contract**. The fields from the Contract table appear in the Available Fields box. The quickest way to add the fields you want to include is to move all the fields to the Selected Fields box, and then remove the only field you don't want to include (CustomerID).

TIP

The table name (Contract) is included in the CustomerID field name to distinguish it from the same field (CustomerID) in the Customer table.

▶ 8. Click the ⟩⟩ button to move all the fields in the Contract table to the Selected Fields box.

▶ 9. Click **Contract.CustomerID** in the Selected Fields box, and then click the ⟨ button to move the field back to the Available Fields box.

▶ 10. Click the **Next** button. The next Form Wizard dialog box opens. See Figure 4-16.

Figure 4-16	Choosing a format for the main form and subform

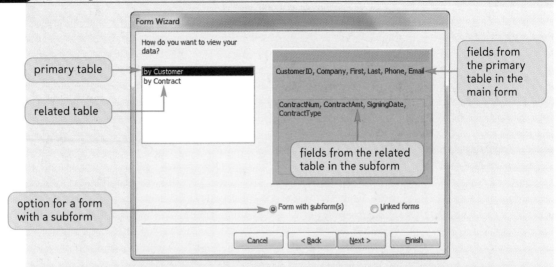

In this dialog box, the section on the left shows the order in which you will view the selected data: first by data from the primary Customer table, and then by data from the related Contract table. The form will be displayed as shown on the right side of the dialog box, with the fields from the Customer table at the top in the main form, and the fields from the Contract table at the bottom in the subform. The selected "Form with subform(s)" option button specifies a main form with a subform. The Linked forms option creates a form structure in which only the main form fields are displayed. A button with the subform's name on it appears on the main form; you can click this button to display the associated subform records.

The default options shown in Figure 4-16 are correct for creating a form with Customer data in the main form and Contract data in the subform.

To finish creating the form:

1. Click the **Next** button. The next Form Wizard dialog box opens, in which you choose the subform layout.

   The Tabular layout displays subform fields as a table, whereas the Datasheet layout displays subform fields as a table datasheet. The layout choice is a matter of personal preference. You'll use the Datasheet layout.

2. Click the **Datasheet** option button to select it (if necessary), and then click the **Next** button. The next Form Wizard dialog box opens, in which you choose titles for the main form and the subform.

   You'll use the title "CustomerContracts" for the main form and the title "ContractSubform" for the subform. These titles will also be the names for the form objects.

3. In the Form box, click the insertion point to the right of the last letter, and then type **Contracts**. The main form name is now CustomerContracts.

4. In the Subform box, delete the space between the two words so that the subform name appears as **ContractSubform**.

5. Click the **Finish** button. The completed form opens in Form view. See Figure 4-17.

Figure 4-17 Main form with subform in Form view

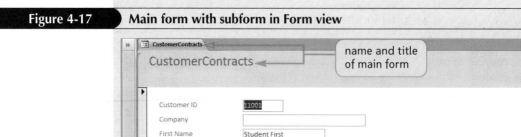

TIP

The CustomerContracts form is formatted with the default Office theme because you applied the Perspective theme only to the CustomerData form.

In the main form, Access displays the fields from the first record in the Customer table in a columnar format. The records in the main form appear in primary key order by CustomerID. CustomerID 11001 has one related record in the Contract table; this record, for ContractNum 3011, is shown in the subform, which uses the datasheet format. The main form name, "CustomerContracts," appears on the object tab and as the form title. The name of the subform appears to the left of the subform. Note that only the word "Contract" and not the complete name "ContractSubform" appears on the form. Access displays only the table name for the subform itself, but displays the complete name of the object, "ContractSubform," when you view and work with objects in the Navigation Pane. The subform designation is necessary in a list of database objects, so that you can distinguish the Contract subform from other objects, such as the Contract table; but the subform designation is not needed in the CustomerContracts form. Only the table name is required to identify the table containing the records in the subform.

You need to make some changes to the form. First, you'll edit the form title to add a space between the words so that it appears as "Customer Contracts." Then, you'll resize the subform. Oren is concerned that the subform is not wide enough to allow for all the columns to be resized and fully display their field values, especially the Contract Type column. To make these changes, you need to switch to Layout view.

To modify the CustomerContracts form in Layout view:

1. In the Views group on the Home tab, click the **View** button to switch to Layout view.

2. Click **CustomerContracts** in the blue area at the top of the form. The form title is selected.

3. Click between the letters "r" and "C" to place the insertion point, and then press the **spacebar**. The title on the form is now "Customer Contracts."

4. Click in a blank area of the form to the right of the field value boxes to deselect the title. Next, you'll increase the width of the subform.

5. Click the subform. An orange outline surrounds the subform, indicating it is selected.

6. Position the pointer on the right edge of the selected subform until the pointer changes to a ↔ shape, and then click and drag to the right approximately two inches (see Figure 4-18).

7. Use the ╋ pointer to resize each column in the subform datasheet to its best fit. Your form should now look like the one shown in Figure 4-18.

Figure 4-18	Modified form in Layout view

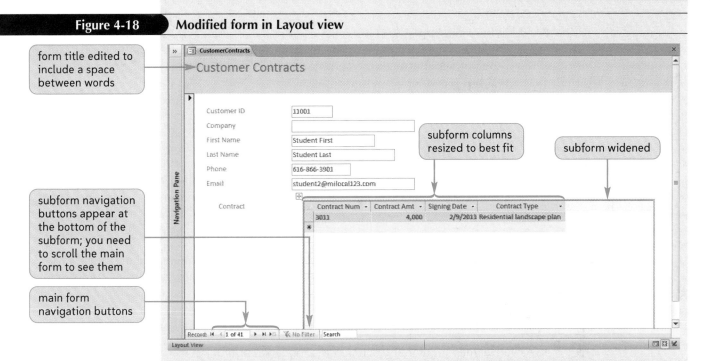

form title edited to include a space between words

subform columns resized to best fit

subform widened

subform navigation buttons appear at the bottom of the subform; you need to scroll the main form to see them

main form navigation buttons

8. Click the **Save** button on the Quick Access Toolbar to save both the main form and the subform.

9. In the Views group on the Design tab, click the **View** button to display the CustomerContracts form in Form view.

Trouble? If the fields in the main form are partially out of view, use the vertical scroll bar to scroll to the top of the form and display the fields.

The form includes two sets of navigation buttons. You use the set of navigation buttons at the bottom of the Form window to select records from the primary table in the main form (see Figure 4-18). The second set of navigation buttons is currently not visible; you need to scroll down the main form to see these buttons, which appear at the bottom of the subform. You use the subform navigation buttons to select records from the related table in the subform.

You'll use the navigation buttons to view different records.

To navigate to different main form and subform records:

1. In the main form, click the **Last record** navigation button ▶|. Record 41 in the Customer table (for Lily's Boutique) becomes the current record in the main form. The subform shows that this customer currently has no contracts; recall that you just entered this record using the CustomerData form. Oren can use the subform to enter the information for this customer's contract when he receives it, and that information will be updated in the Contract table.
2. In the main form, click the **Previous record** navigation button ◀. Record 40 in the Customer table (for Weston Community Parks Foundation) becomes the current record in the main form. The subform shows that this customer has two contracts.
3. In the main form, select **40** in the Current Record box, type **34**, and then press the **Enter** key. Record 34 in the Customer table (for Dept. of Neighborhood Development) becomes the current record in the main form. The subform shows that this customer has four contracts.
4. Double-click the pointer ✛ at the right edge of the Contract Type column in the subform, so that the complete values for this field are visible.
5. Use the vertical scroll bar for the main form to scroll down and view the bottom of the subform, if necessary. Note the navigation buttons.
6. In the subform, click the **Last record** navigation button ▶|. Record 4 in the Contract table becomes the current record in the subform.
7. Save and close the CustomerContracts form.

TIP

As you move through the form/subform, notice that some field values in the subform are not completely visible. You can resize any subform field to its best fit to fully display the field values.

You've finished your work for Oren on the forms in the Belmont database. Next, Taylor Sico asks you to create a report that she can use to prepare a new advertising campaign.

Creating a Report Using the Report Wizard

As you learned in Tutorial 1, a report is a formatted printout of the contents of one or more tables or queries in a database. In Access, you can create your own reports or use the Report Wizard to create them for you. Whether you use the Report Wizard or design your own report, you can change the report's design after you create it.

INSIGHT

Creating a Report Based on a Query

You can create a report based on one or more tables or queries. When you use a query as the basis for a report, you can use criteria and other query features to retrieve only the information you want to display in the report. Experienced Access users often create a query just so they can create a report based on that query. When thinking about the type of report you want to create, consider creating a query first and basing the report on the query, to produce the exact results you want to see in the report.

Taylor wants you to create a report that includes data from both the Customer and Contract tables, as shown in the Session 4.2 Visual Overview. Like the CustomerContracts form you just created, which includes a main form and a subform, the report will be based on both tables, which are joined in a one-to-many relationship through the common CustomerID field. You'll use the Report Wizard to create the report for Taylor.

To start the Report Wizard and select the fields to include in the report:

▶ **1.** Click the **Create** tab on the Ribbon.

▶ **2.** In the Reports group on the Create tab, click the **Report Wizard** button. The first Report Wizard dialog box opens.

As was the case when you created the form with a subform, initially you can choose only one table or query to be the data source for the report. Then you can include data from other tables or queries. You will select the primary Customer table first.

▶ **3.** If necessary, click the **Tables/Queries** arrow, and then click **Table: Customer**.

You select fields in the order you want them to appear on the report. Taylor wants the CustomerID, Company, First, Last, City, and Phone fields from the Customer table to appear on the report, in that order.

▶ **4.** Click **CustomerID** in the Available Fields box (if necessary), and then click the
    > button. The field moves to the Selected Fields box.

▶ **5.** Repeat Step 4 to add the **Company**, **First**, **Last**, **City**, and **Phone** fields to the report.

▶ **6.** Click the **Tables/Queries** arrow, scroll the list up, and then click **Table: Contract**. The fields from the Contract table appear in the Available Fields box.

The CustomerID field will appear on the report with the customer data, so you do not need to include it in the detail records for each contract. Otherwise, Taylor wants all the fields from the Contract table to be included in the report.

▶ **7.** Click the >> button to move all the fields from the Available Fields box to the Selected Fields box.

▶ **8.** Click **Contract.CustomerID** in the Selected Fields box, click the < button to move the field back to the Available Fields box, and then click the **Next** button. The second Report Wizard dialog box opens. See Figure 4-19.

| Figure 4-19 | Choosing a grouped or ungrouped report |

TIP

You can display tips for creating reports and examples of reports by clicking the "Show me more information" button.

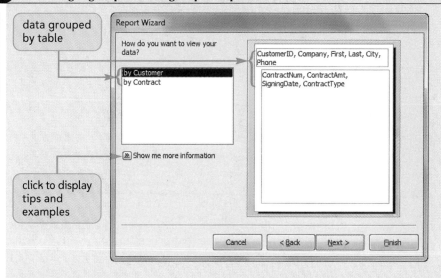

You can choose to arrange the selected data grouped by table, which is the default, or ungrouped. You're creating a grouped report; the data from a record in the Customer table will appear in a group, followed by the related records for each customer from the Contract table. An example of an ungrouped report would be a report of records from the Customer and Contract tables in order by ContractNum. Each contract and its associated customer data would appear together on one or more lines of the report; the data would not be grouped by table.

The default options shown on your screen are correct for the report Taylor wants, so you can continue responding to the Report Wizard questions.

To finish creating the report using the Report Wizard:

1. Click the **Next** button. The next Report Wizard dialog box opens, in which you choose additional grouping levels.

   Two grouping levels are shown: one for a customer's data, and the other for a customer's contracts. Grouping levels are useful for reports with multiple levels, such as those containing monthly, quarterly, and annual totals, or for those containing city and country groups. Taylor's report requires no further grouping levels, so you can accept the default options.

2. Click the **Next** button. The next Report Wizard dialog box opens, in which you choose the sort order for the detail records. See Figure 4-20.

Figure 4-20	Choosing the sort order for detail records

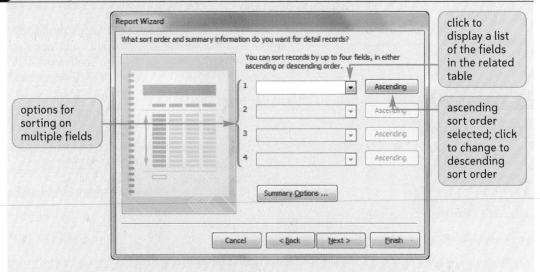

options for sorting on multiple fields

click to display a list of the fields in the related table

ascending sort order selected; click to change to descending sort order

The records from the Contract table for a customer represent the detail records for Taylor's report. She wants these records to appear in increasing, or ascending, order by the value in the SigningDate field, so that the contracts will be shown in chronological order. The Ascending option is already selected by default. To change to descending order, you click this same button, which acts as a toggle between the two sort orders. Also, you can sort on multiple fields, as you can with queries.

3. Click the **arrow** on the first box, click **SigningDate**, and then click the **Next** button. The next Report Wizard dialog box opens, in which you choose a layout and page orientation for the report. See Figure 4-21.

| Figure 4-21 | Choosing the report layout |

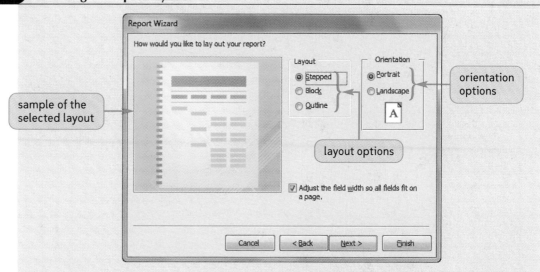

4. Click each layout option and examine each sample that appears.

   You'll use the Outline layout for Taylor's report. Also, because some of the fields in both the Customer and Contract tables contain lengthy field values, you'll change the page orientation to landscape. This will provide more space across the page to display longer field values.

5. In the Layout section, click the **Outline** option button.

6. In the Orientation section, click the **Landscape** option button, and then click the **Next** button. The final Report Wizard dialog box opens, in which you choose a report title, which also serves as the name for the report object in the database.

   Taylor wants the report title "Customers and Contracts" at the top of the report. Because the name you enter in this dialog box is also the name of the report object, you'll enter the report name as one word and edit the title on the report later.

7. In the box for the title, enter **CustomersAndContracts** and then click the **Finish** button. The Report Wizard creates the report based on your answers, saves it as an object in the Belmont database, and opens the report in Print Preview.

   To view the entire page, you need to change the Zoom setting.

8. In the Zoom group on the Print Preview tab, click the **Zoom button arrow**, and then click **Fit to Window**. The first page of the report is displayed in Print Preview.

   When a report is displayed in Print Preview, you can use the pointer to toggle between a full-page display and a close-up display of the report.

9. Click the pointer at the center of the report. The display changes to show a close-up view of the report. See Figure 4-22.

Figure 4-22 **Close-up view of the report**

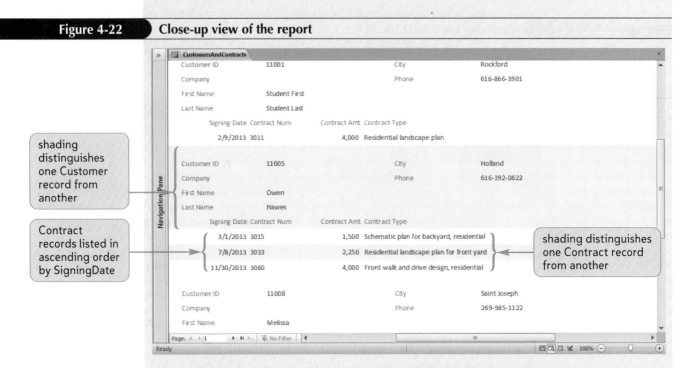

shading distinguishes one Customer record from another

Contract records listed in ascending order by SigningDate

shading distinguishes one Contract record from another

Shading is used both to distinguish one Customer record from another and, within a group of each customer's Contract records, one Contract record from another.

Trouble? Depending on your computer settings, the shading and colors used in your report might look different. This difference should not cause any problems.

The detail records for the Contract table fields appear in ascending order based on the values in the SigningDate field. Because the SigningDate field is used as the basis for sorting records, it appears as the first field in this section, even though you selected the fields in the order in which they appear in the Contract table.

▶ **10.** Use the vertical scroll bar to scroll to the bottom of the first page, checking the text in the report as you scroll. Notice the current date and page number at the bottom of the first page of the report; the Report Wizard included these elements as part of the report's design.

▶ **11.** Use the horizontal scroll bar to scroll to the right and view the page number in the footer.

Trouble? Depending on your computer's settings, the text of the page number might not be completely within the page border. If so, you'll see blank pages every other page as you complete Steps 12 and 13. You'll fix this problem shortly.

▶ **12.** Click the pointer 🔍 on the report to zoom back out, and then click the **Next Page** navigation button ▶ to move to page 2 of the report.

▶ **13.** Continue to move through the pages of the report, and then click the **First Page** navigation button ◀ to return to the first page.

Earlier, when meeting with Oren, Taylor viewed and worked with the CustomerData form. She likes how the form looks with the Perspective theme applied, and would like her report formatted with the same theme. You need to switch to Layout view to make this change.

Modifying a Report's Design in Layout View

Similar to Layout view for forms, Layout view for reports enables you to make modifications to the report's design. Many of the same options—such as those for applying a theme and changing the color of text—are provided in Layout view for reports.

Applying a Theme to a Report

The same themes available for forms are also available for reports. You can choose to apply a theme to the current report object only, or to all reports in the database. In this case, you'll apply the Perspective theme only to the CustomersAndContracts report because Taylor isn't certain if it is the appropriate theme for other reports in the Belmont database.

To apply the Perspective theme to the report:

1. On the status bar, click the **Layout View** button ⊞. The report is displayed in Layout view.

TIP

When you point to the Perspective theme, a ScreenTip displays the names of the database objects that use the theme—in this case, the CustomerData form.

2. In the Themes group on the Design tab, click the **Themes** button. The "In this Database" section at the top of the gallery shows both the default Office theme and the Perspective theme. The Perspective theme is included here because you applied it earlier to the CustomerData form.

3. At the top of the gallery, right-click the **Perspective** theme to display the shortcut menu, and then click **Apply Theme to This Object Only**. The gallery closes and the theme is applied to the report.

   The larger font used by the Perspective theme has caused both the report title text and the Contract Num field label to be cut off on the right. First, you'll fix the problem with the report title and edit the title text as well.

4. Click the **CustomersAndContracts** title at the top of the report to select it.

5. Place the pointer on the right edge of the orange outline surrounding the title, and then click and drag the ↔ pointer to the right until the title is fully displayed.

6. Click between the letters "s" and "A" in the title, press the **spacebar**, change the capital letter "A" to **a**, place the insertion point between the letters "d" and "C," and then press the **spacebar**. The title is now "Customers and Contracts."

7. Click to the right of the report title in the shaded area.

   Taylor is concerned that the larger font size of the theme might have caused other text in the report to be cut off—especially some of the Company names, which are lengthy. You need to check the report for such problems.

8. Scroll the report until you see the record for CustomerID 11045, Kalamazoo Neighborhood Development. Notice that the right part of the company name is not visible. The same is true later in the report for the record for CustomerID 11059, G.R. Neighborhood Development Corp.

To fix this problem, you need to resize the City and Phone field labels to make them smaller, allowing more room for the Company field value box, which you can then resize. You also need to resize the Contract Num field label so it is fully displayed.

Resizing a Field on a Report in Layout View

Working in Layout view, you can resize and reposition fields to improve the appearance of the report or to address the problem of some field values not being completely displayed. In the CustomersAndContracts report, you need to make space for the longer

Company field values by resizing the City and Phone field labels first, and then resizing the Company field value box. To make sure all the Company field values will fit, you should make any adjustments based on the longest company name—Kalamazoo Neighborhood Development. Then you'll resize the Contract Num field label so it is fully displayed; and finally, you'll check the page number in the footer to make sure it fits completely on the page.

To resize the field labels and field value box:

1. Make sure the Report window is still displaying the record for CustomerID 11045, Kalamazoo Neighborhood Development. To select and resize multiple fields, you use the Shift key.

2. Click the **City** field label for CustomerID 11045, press and hold the **Shift** key, and then click the **Phone** field label for the same record. Both field labels are selected and can be resized. See Figure 4-23.

Figure 4-23	Field labels selected and ready to be resized

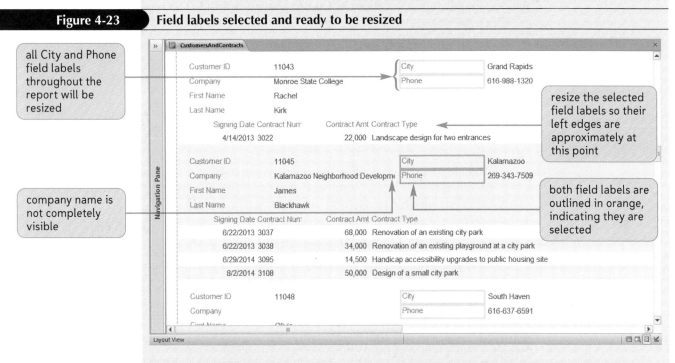

all City and Phone field labels throughout the report will be resized

resize the selected field labels so their left edges are approximately at this point

company name is not completely visible

both field labels are outlined in orange, indicating they are selected

You'll resize the field labels on their left edges, making them smaller and moving the labels closer to their corresponding field values.

3. Position the pointer ↔ on the left edge of either selected field label, and then click and drag to the right. As you drag, black outlines indicate the size of the labels.

4. Release the mouse button when the left edge of the field labels is approximately aligned with the beginning of the word "for" in the Contract Type field value box above (see Figure 4-23). The City and Phone field labels are now smaller, moving them closer to their values and making more space available for the Company field value box. Note that *all* City and Phone field labels for the entire report have been resized, not just those for the current record.

Next you'll resize the Company field value box so that the longest value (Kalamazoo Neighborhood Development) is fully displayed. This will ensure that all other company names will be completely visible in the report as well.

5. Click the Company field value **Kalamazoo Neighborhood Development** for Customer ID 11045. An orange outline appears around the field value box, indicating it is selected.

6. Position the pointer on the right side of the field value box until the pointer changes to a ↔ shape.

7. Click and drag the pointer to the right until the complete company name is visible, and then release the mouse button.

8. Click the **Contract Num** field label below the record for Customer ID 11045 to select the label, and then use the ↔ pointer to resize its right side until the field label is fully displayed. See Figure 4-24.

Figure 4-24 **Report after resizing field labels and field value boxes**

all City and Phone field labels resized and closer to their field values

Company field value is now fully displayed

Contract Num field label is now fully displayed

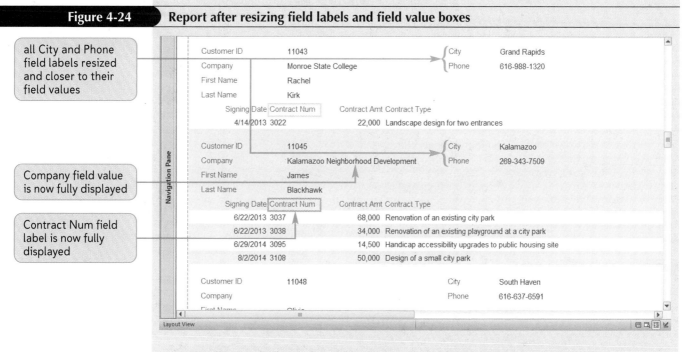

Finally, you'll check the page number in the footer to make sure the text is completely on the page.

9. Scroll the report to the bottom and to the right and view the page number text.

Trouble? If the text "Page 1 of 1" is not fully within the page border, click the text to select it, position the pointer on its right edge until the pointer changes to ↔, and then click and drag to the left until the page number text is roughly right-aligned with the text in the report.

Next, Taylor asks you to enhance the report's appearance by inserting the same picture on the CustomersAndContracts report as you included on the CustomerData form, and to change the color of the report title to the same brown color used on the form.

Changing the Title Font Color and Inserting a Picture in a Report

You can change the color of text on a report to enhance its appearance. You can also add a picture to a report for visual interest or to identify a particular section of the report. Because Taylor plans to print the report using a color printer, she asks you to change the report title color to brown and to include the Landscape picture to the right of the report title.

To change the color of the report title and insert the picture:

▶ **1.** Scroll to the top of the report, and then click the title **Customers and Contracts** to select it.

▶ **2.** Click the **Format** tab on the Ribbon. The options for modifying the format of a report are the same as those available for forms.

▶ **3.** In the Font group on the Format tab, click the **Font Color button arrow** [A ▾], and then click the **Brown, Accent 3, Darker 25%** color box (fifth row, seventh box in the Theme Colors palette). The color is applied to the report title.

Now you'll insert the picture to the right of the report title text.

▶ **4.** Click the **Design** tab on the Ribbon. Again, the options provided on this tab for reports are the same as those you worked with for forms.

▶ **5.** In the Header/Footer group on the Design tab, click the **Logo** button.

▶ **6.** Navigate to the **Access1\Tutorial** folder, and then double-click the **Landscape** file. The picture is inserted in the top-left corner of the report, partially covering the report title.

▶ **7.** Position the pointer ⁺↖ on the selected picture, and then click and drag it to the right of the report title.

▶ **8.** Release the mouse button when the pointer is to the right of the report title text and below the button in the Controls group with "Aa" on it, and then click in a blank area of the shaded bar to deselect the picture. See Figure 4-25.

Figure 4-25	Report after changing the title font color and inserting the picture

font color of the title is now brown

picture added and moved to the right of the title

Trouble? Don't be concerned if the pointer in your report is not in the exact same location as the one shown in the figure. Just make sure it is to the right of the title text and within the shaded area.

Taylor is pleased with the report's appearance and shows it to Oren. He also approves of the report's contents and design, but has one final suggestion to enhance the report. He'd like to draw attention to the contract amounts that are greater than $25,000 by formatting them with a bold, red font. Because Oren doesn't want all the contract amounts to appear in this font, you need to use conditional formatting.

Using Conditional Formatting in a Report

Conditional formatting in a report (or form) is special formatting applied to certain field values depending on one or more conditions—similar to criteria you establish for queries. If a field value meets the condition or conditions you specify, the formatting is applied to the value.

Oren would like the CustomersAndContracts report to show any contract amount that is greater than $25,000 in a bold, dark red font. This formatting will help to highlight the more significant contracts for Belmont Landscapes.

To apply conditional formatting to the ContractAmt field in the report:

▶ **1.** Make sure the report is still displayed in Layout view, and then click the **Format** tab on the Ribbon.

▶ **2.** Click the first ContractAmt field value, **4,000**, for ContractNum 3011. An orange outline appears around the field value box, and a lighter orange outline appears around each ContractAmt field value box throughout the entire report. The conditional formatting you specify will affect all the values for the field.

▶ **3.** In the Control Formatting group on the Format tab, click the **Conditional Formatting** button. The Conditional Formatting Rules Manager dialog box opens. Because you selected a ContractAmt field value box, this field is displayed in the "Show formatting rules for" box. Currently, there are no conditional formatting rules set for the selected field. You need to create a new rule.

▶ **4.** Click the **New Rule** button. The New Formatting Rule dialog box opens. See Figure 4-26.

Figure 4-26	New Formatting Rule dialog box

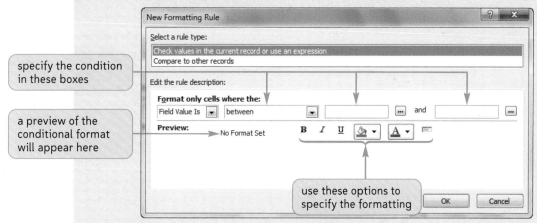

specify the condition in these boxes

a preview of the conditional format will appear here

use these options to specify the formatting

The default setting for "Select a rule type" specifies that Access will check field values and determine if they meet the condition. This is the setting you want. You need to enter the condition in the "Edit the rule description" section of the dialog box. The setting "Field Value Is" means that the conditional format you specify will be applied only when the value for the selected field, ContractAmt, meets the condition.

▶ **5.** Click the **arrow** for the box containing the word "between," and then click **greater than**. Oren wants only those contract amounts greater than $25,000 to be formatted.

▶ **6.** Press the **Tab** key to move to the next box, and then type **25000**.

7. In the Preview section, click the **Font color button arrow** 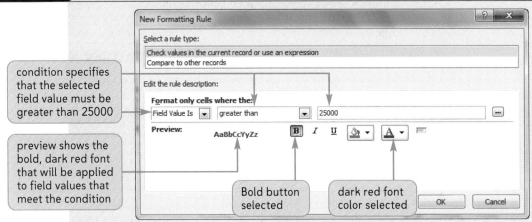, and then click the **Dark Red** color box (first color box in the last row of Standard Colors).

8. In the Preview section, click the **Bold** button **B**. The specifications for the conditional formatting are complete. See Figure 4-27.

| Figure 4-27 | Conditional formatting set for the ContractAmt field |

9. Click the **OK** button. The new rule you specified appears in the Rule section of the dialog box as Value > 25000; the Format section on the right shows the conditional formatting (dark red, bold font) that will be applied based on this rule.

10. Click the **OK** button. The conditional format is applied to the ContractAmt field values. To get a better view of the report and the formatting, you'll switch to Print Preview.

11. On the status bar, click the **Print Preview** button.

12. Move to page 9 of the report. Notice that the conditional formatting is applied only to ContractAmt field values greater than $25,000. See Figure 4-28.

| Figure 4-28 | Viewing the finished report in Print Preview |

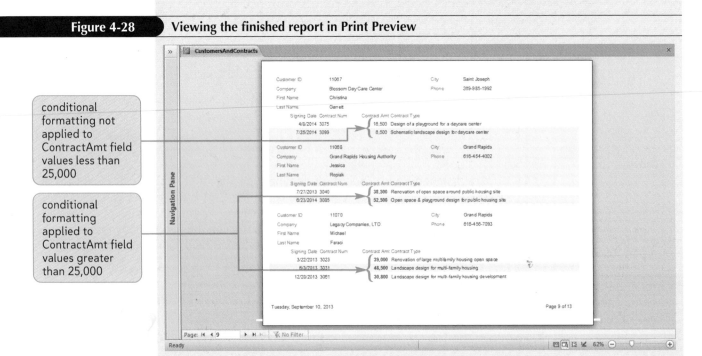

Problem Solving: Understanding the Importance of Previewing Reports

When you create a report, it is a good idea to display the report in Print Preview occasionally as you develop the report. Doing so will give you a chance to find any formatting problems or other issues so that you can make any necessary corrections before printing the report. It is particularly important to preview a report after you've made changes to its design to ensure that the changes you made have not created new problems with the report's format. Before printing any report, you should preview it so you can determine where the pages will break and make any necessary adjustments. Following this problem-solving approach will not only ensure that the final printed report looks exactly the way you want it to, but will also save you time and help to avoid wasting paper.

The report is now complete. You'll print just the first page of the report so that Oren and Taylor can view the final results and share the report design with other staff members before printing the entire report. (*Note:* Ask your instructor if you should complete the following printing steps.)

To print page 1 of the report:

▶ **1.** In the Print group on the Print Preview tab, click the **Print** button. The Print dialog box opens.

▶ **2.** In the Print Range section, click the **Pages** option button. The insertion point now appears in the From box so that you can specify the range of pages to print.

▶ **3.** Type **1** in the From box, press the **Tab** key to move to the To box, and then type **1**. These settings specify that only page 1 of the report will be printed.

▶ **4.** Click the **OK** button. The Print dialog box closes, and the first page of the report is printed.

▶ **5.** Save and close the CustomersAndContracts report.

You've created many different objects in the Belmont database. Before you close it, you'll open the Navigation Pane to view all the objects in the database.

To view the Belmont database objects in the Navigation Pane:

▶ **1.** Open the Navigation Pane and scroll down, if necessary, to display the bottom of the pane. The CustomersAndContracts report is selected because it is the object you just closed.

The Navigation Pane displays the objects grouped by type: tables, queries, forms, and reports. Notice the CustomerContracts form. This is the form you created containing a main form based on the Customer table and a subform based on the Contract table. The ContractSubform object is also listed; you can open it separately from the main form. See Figure 4-29.

Figure 4-29 **Belmont database objects in the Navigation Pane**

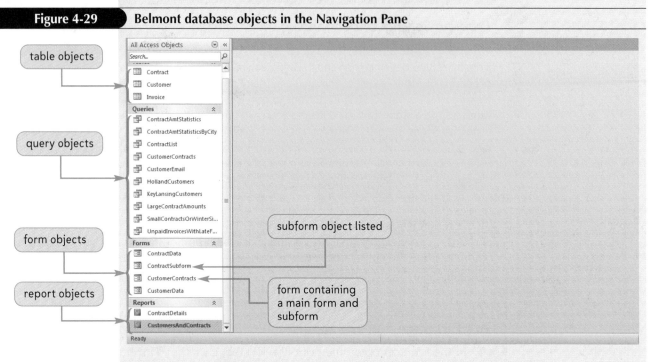

2. Compact and repair the Belmont database, and then close the database.

Oren is satisfied that the forms you created—the CustomerData form and the CustomerContracts form—will make it easier to enter, view, and update data in the Belmont database. The CustomersAndContracts report presents important information about Belmont Landscapes customers in an attractive and professional format, which will help Taylor and other staff members in their marketing efforts.

Session 4.2 Quick Check

REVIEW

1. In a form that contains a main form and a subform, what data is displayed in the main form and what data is displayed in the subform?
2. Describe how you use the navigation buttons to move through a form containing a main form and a subform.
3. When you create a report based on two tables that are joined in a one-to-many relationship, the field values for the records from the related table are called the _____ records.
4. True or False: To resize a field on a report, you first need to display the report in Design view.
5. When working in Layout view for a report, which key do you press and hold down so that you can click to select multiple fields?
6. _____ in a report (or form) is special formatting applied to certain field values depending on one or more conditions.

Practice the skills you learned in the tutorial using the same case scenario.

PRACTICE

Review Assignments

Data Files needed for the Review Assignments: Supplier.accdb (*cont. from Tutorial 3*) and Tools.bmp

Oren asks you to enhance the Supplier database with forms and reports. Complete the following steps:

1. Open the **Supplier** database located in the Access1\Review folder provided with your Data Files.

2. Use the Form Wizard to create a form based on the Product table. Select all fields for the form and the Columnar layout; specify the title **ProductData** for the form.

3. Apply the Foundry theme to the ProductData form *only*.

4. Insert the Tools picture, which is located in the Access1\Review folder provided with your Data Files, in the ProductData form. Remove the picture from the control layout, and then move the picture to the right of the form title.

5. Edit the form title so that it appears as "Product Data" (two words), and change the font color of the form title to the Tan, Accent 5, Darker 25% theme color.

6. Change the line type for the field value boxes—except the Discount Offered check box—to Dots.

7. Resize the text box for the Weight in Lbs field value so it is the same width as the Size text box above it.

8. Use the ProductData form to update the Product table as follows:

   a. Use the Find command to search for "wall" anywhere in the ProductType field and then display the record for a retaining wall (ProductID 5227). Change the Price in this record to **11.50** and the Discount Offered to **yes**.

   b. Add a new record with the following field values, leaving the Color, Material, and Weight in Lbs fields blank:

      Product ID: **5630**

      Company ID: **GEN359**

      Product Type: **Annual**

      Price: **2.90**

      Unit: **Each**

      Color: [do not enter a value]

      Material: [do not enter a value]

      Size: **1 quart**

      Weight in Lbs: [do not enter a value]

      Discount Offered: **yes**

   c. Save and close the form.

9. Use the Form Wizard to create a form containing a main form and a subform. Select all fields except Product from the Company table for the main form, and select ProductID, ProductType, Price, Unit, and Color—in that order—from the Product table for the subform. Use the Datasheet layout. Specify the title **CompaniesAndProducts** for the main form and **ProductSubform** for the subform.

10. Change the form title text to **Companies and Products**.

11. Resize the subform to the right, increasing its width by approximately two inches, and then resize all columns in the subform to their best fit, working left to right. Navigate through each record in the main form to make sure all the field values in the subform are completely displayed, resizing subform columns as necessary. Save and close the CompaniesAndProducts form.

12. Use the Report Wizard to create a report based on the primary Company table and the related Product table. Select the CompanyID, Company, ContactFirst, ContactLast, City, and Phone fields—in that order—from the Company table, and the ProductID, ProductType, Price, and Unit fields from the Product table. Do not specify any additional grouping levels, and sort the detail records in ascending order by ProductID. Choose the Outline layout and Portrait orientation. Specify the title **ProductsByCompany** for the report.

13. Change the report title text to **Products by Company**.

14. Apply the Foundry theme to the ProductsByCompany report *only*.

15. Resize the following controls in the report in Layout view, and then scroll through the report to make sure all field values are fully displayed:

    a. Resize the report title so that the text of the title, Products by Company, is fully displayed.

    b. Resize the City and Phone field labels to reduce their size from the left by roughly one half and move them closer to their field value boxes.

    c. Resize the Product ID field label on its left side, increasing its width so the label is fully displayed.

16. Change the color of the report title text to the Tan, Accent 5, Darker 25% theme color.

17. Insert the Tools picture, which is located in the Access1\Review folder provided with your Data Files, in the report. Move the picture to the right of the report title.

18. Apply conditional formatting so that the City field values equal to Lansing appear as dark red and bold.

19. Preview each page of the report, verifying that all the fields fit on the page. If necessary, return to Layout view and make changes so the report prints within the margins of the page and so that all field names and values are completely displayed.

20. Save the report, print its first page (only if asked by your instructor to do so), and then close the report.

21. Compact and repair the Supplier database, and then close it.

SAM

APPLY

Case Problem 1

If you have a SAM 2010 user profile, your instructor may have assigned an autogradable version of this assignment. If so, log into the SAM 2010 Web site at www.cengage.com/sam2010 to download the instructions and start files.

Data Files needed for this Case Problem: Pinehill.accdb (*cont. from Tutorial 3*) and Piano.bmp

Pine Hill Music School   Yuka Koyama wants to use the Pinehill database to track and view information about the classes her music school offers. She asks you to create the necessary forms and a report to help her manage this data. Complete the following:

1. Open the **Pinehill** database located in the Access1\Case1 folder provided with your Data Files.

2. Use the Form Wizard to create a form based on the Student table. Select all the fields for the form and the Columnar layout. Specify the title **StudentData** for the form.

3. Apply the Clarity theme to the StudentData form *only*.

4. Edit the form title so that it appears as "Student Data" (two words), and change the font color of the form title to the Blue-Gray, Accent 4, Lighter 40% theme color.

5. Use the Find command to display the record for Jeff Tealey, and then change the Address field value for this record to **304 Forest Ave**.

6. Use the StudentData form to add a new record to the Student table with the following field values:

    Student ID: **NEL7584**

    First Name: **Kayla**

    Last Name: **Nelson**

Address: **15540 Belleview Dr**

City: **Portland**

State: **OR**

Zip: **97229**

Home Phone: **541-563-3156**

Mobile Phone: **541-563-8882**

Birth Date: **10/13/2003**

Gender: **F**

7. Save and close the StudentData form.

8. Use the Form Wizard to create a form containing a main form and a subform. Select all the fields from the Teacher table for the main form, and select the ContractID, StudentID, and LessonType fields from the Contract table for the subform. Use the Datasheet layout. Specify the title **ContractsByTeacher** for the main form and the title **ContractSubform** for the subform.

9. Change the form title text for the main form to **Contracts by Teacher**.

10. Change the line type for the field value boxes—except the Takes Beginners check box—to Dots.

11. Resize all columns in the subform to their best fit, and then move through all the records in the main form and check to make sure that all subform field values are fully displayed, resizing the columns as necessary.

12. Save and close the ContractsByTeacher form.

13. Use the Report Wizard to create a report based on the primary Student table and the related Contract table. Select the StudentID, FirstName, LastName, and HomePhone fields from the Student table, and select all fields from the Contract table except StudentID, StartDate, and EndDate. Do not select any additional grouping levels, and sort the detail records in ascending order by ContractID. Choose the Outline layout and Landscape orientation. Specify the title **StudentContracts** for the report.

14. Apply the Clarity theme to the StudentContracts report *only*.

15. Resize the report title so that the text is fully displayed; edit the report title so that it appears as "Student Contracts" (two words); and change the font color of the title to the Blue-Gray, Accent 4, Lighter 40% theme color.

16. Resize the following controls in the report in Layout view, and then scroll through the report to make sure all field values are fully displayed:

    a. Resize the Contract ID field label on its left side, increasing its width so the label is fully displayed.

    b. Resize the Lesson Length field label on its left side, increasing its width so the label is fully displayed.

    c. Scroll to the bottom of the report and check to make sure the page number is completely within the page border. If necessary, resize the control on its right side, reducing its width so that the page number text is roughly right-aligned with the text in the report.

17. Insert the Piano picture, which is located in the Access1\Case1 folder provided with your Data Files, in the report. Move the picture to the right of the report title.

18. Apply conditional formatting so that any LessonCost field value greater than 200 appears as bold and with the Maroon 5 color applied.

19. Preview the entire report to confirm that it is formatted correctly. If necessary, return to Layout view and make changes so that all field labels and field values are completely displayed. (*Hint:* You might need to resize the Teacher ID field label so it is fully displayed; if so, resize the Contract ID field label to the left more, to make room for resizing the Teacher ID field label.) When you are finished, save the report, print its first page (only if asked by your instructor to do so), and then close the report.

20. Compact and repair the Pinehill database, and then close it.

Challenge yourself by creating and working with a form and report for a fitness center.

CHALLENGE

Case Problem 2

Data Files needed for this Case Problem: Fitness.accdb (*cont. from Tutorial 3*) and Weights.bmp

Parkhurst Health & Fitness Center Martha Parkhurst is using the Fitness database to track and analyze the business activity of the fitness center members and their programs. To make her work easier, you'll create a form and report in the Fitness database. Complete the following steps:

1. Open the **Fitness** database located in the Access1\Case2 folder provided with your Data Files.

2. Use the Form Wizard to create a form containing a main form and a subform. Select all the fields from the Program table for the main form, and select the MemberID, First, Last, and Phone fields from the Member table for the subform. Use the Tabular layout. Specify the title **ProgramMembers** for the main form and the title **MemberSubform** for the subform.

3. Apply the Slipstream theme to the ProgramMembers form *only*.

4. Edit the form title so that it appears as "Program Members" (two words), and change the font color of the form title to the Green, Accent 3, Lighter 80% theme color. Deselect the form title after changing the color.

⊕ **EXPLORE**

5. In Layout view, use the Insert Image button in the Controls group on the Design tab to insert the Weights picture, which is located in the Access1\Case2 folder provided with your Data Files. (*Hint:* In the Insert Picture dialog box, make sure the All Files option is selected in the box next to the File name box.) Click to select the picture in the dialog box, and then click the OK button. (Do *not* double-click the picture file in the dialog box.) Notice that the pointer changes to ⊕. Place this pointer below the subform name "Member" and then click to place the picture on the form. Use the ⊕ pointer to move the picture below the subform name, and then use the resizing pointers—on the sides, corners, top, and/or bottom of the picture, as needed—to resize the picture and make it smaller. Continue to move and resize the picture until it is positioned roughly one-quarter inch below the subform name "Member" and is about the same width as the subform name.

6. Save the ProgramMembers form, display the form in Form view, and then navigate to the second record in the subform for the first main record (MemberID 1110). Change the Phone field value for this record to **804-553-7986**.

7. Navigate to the ninth record in the main form, and then change the value in the Last Name column in the fourth record in the subform (MemberID 1155) to **Larsen**. Close the form.

⊕ **EXPLORE**

8. Use the Report Wizard to create a report based on the primary Program table and the related Member table. Select all fields except PhysicalRequired from the Program table, and then select the following fields from the Member table: MemberID, First, Last, City, Phone, DateJoined, and Status. In the third Report Wizard dialog box, specify the City field as an additional grouping level. Sort the detail records by DateJoined in *descending* order. Choose the Outline layout and Landscape orientation for the report. Specify the title **ProgramsAndMembers** for the report.

9. Apply the Slipstream theme to the ProgramsAndMembers report *only*.

10. Resize the report title so that the text is fully displayed; edit the report title so that it appears as "Programs and Members"; and change the font color of the title to the Green, Accent 3, Lighter 80% theme color.

11. Resize the Membership Status field label to the right, making it wider so that the label is fully displayed.

12. Scroll to the bottom of the report and check to make sure the page number is completely within the page border. If necessary, resize the control on its right side, reducing its width so that the page number text is roughly right-aligned with the text in the report.

13. Insert the Weights picture (located in the Access1\Case2 folder) in the report. Move the picture to the right of the report title. Resize the picture so that it is approximately one-inch wide.

⊕ EXPLORE 14. In the Control Formatting group on the Format tab, use the Shape Fill button to apply the Green, Accent 3, Lighter 60% theme color to the picture. (*Hint:* Make sure the picture is selected first.)

⊕ EXPLORE 15. Apply conditional formatting so that all Status field values equal to "On Hold" are formatted with an italic font and the background color Green 3. Note that you must include quotation marks around the words "On Hold" because there is a space between them.

16. Preview the report to confirm that it is formatted correctly and all field names and values are fully displayed. Save the report, print its first page (only if asked by your instructor to do so), and then close the report.

17. Compact and repair the Fitness database, and then close it.

Explore some new skills to create forms and a report for a not-for-profit agency.

CHALLENGE

Case Problem 3

Data Files needed for this Case Problem: Rossi.accdb (*cont. from Tutorial 3*) and Recycle.bmp

Rossi Recycling Group   Tom Rossi wants to work with and display data about the donations made to the Rossi Recycling Group. You'll help him by creating forms and a report in the Rossi database. Complete the following steps:

1. Open the **Rossi** database located in the Access1\Case3 folder provided with your Data Files.

2. Use the Form Wizard to create a form based on the Donation table. Select all the fields for the form and the Columnar layout. Specify the title **DonationInfo** for the form.

3. Apply the Verve theme to the DonationInfo form *only*.

4. Edit the form title so that it appears as "Donation Info" (two words), and change the font color of the form title to the Pink, Accent 2, Darker 25% theme color.

⊕ EXPLORE 5. Use the appropriate button in the Font group on the Format tab to underline the form title. Resize the title, as necessary, so that the complete title text appears on the same line.

⊕ EXPLORE 6. Use the appropriate button in the Font group on the Format tab to left-align the Donation Value field values. Save the form.

⊕ EXPLORE 7. Use the DonationInfo form to update the Donation table as follows:

a. Use the Find command to search for records that contain "tools" anywhere in the Donation Description field. Display the record with the field value Power tools, and then change the Donation Value for this record to **565**.

b. Add a new record with the following values:

Donation ID: **2219**

Donor ID: **36077**

Agency ID: **W22**

Donation Date: **12/21/2013**

Donation Description: **Toys**

Donation Value: **45**

Pickup Required: **No**

   c. Find the record with DonationID 2150, and then delete it. (*Hint:* After displaying the record in the form, you need to select it by clicking the right-pointing triangle in the bar to the left of the field labels. Then use the appropriate button in the Records group on the Home tab to delete the record. When asked to confirm the deletion, click the Yes button.) Close the form.

8. Use the Form Wizard to create a form containing a main form and a subform. Select all the fields from the Donor table for the main form, and select the DonationID, AgencyID, DonationDate, Description, and DonationValue fields from the Donation table for the subform. Use the Datasheet layout. Specify the name **DonorsAndDonations** for the main form and the title **DonationSubform** for the subform.

9. Apply the Verve theme to the DonorsAndDonations form *only*.

10. Edit the form title so that it appears as "Donors and Donations." Resize the form title so that the text fits on one line. Change the font color of the title to the Pink, Accent 2, Darker 25% theme color.

✦ **EXPLORE**   11. Use the appropriate button in the Font group on the Format tab to apply the theme color Pink, Accent 1, Lighter 80% as a background color for all the field value boxes in the main form. Then use the appropriate button in the Control Formatting group to change the outline of all the main form field value boxes to have a line thickness of 1 pt. (*Hint:* Select all the field value boxes before making these changes.)

12. Resize the subform to the right to make it as wide as possible, and then resize all columns in the subform to their best fit, *working right to left*. Navigate through each record in the main form to make sure all the field values in the subform are completely displayed, resizing subform columns as necessary. Save the form.

13. Use the appropriate wildcard character to find all records with a Phone field value that begins with the area code 316. Change the record with the Phone field value of 316-282-2226 (Donor ID 36062) to **316-282-2556**. Close the form.

✦ **EXPLORE**   14. Use the Report Wizard to create a report based on the primary Agency table and the related Donation table. Select the Agency and Phone fields from the Agency table, and select all fields except AgencyID and Pickup from the Donation table. In the third Report Wizard dialog box, select DonorID as an additional grouping level. Sort the detail records in *descending* order by DonationValue. Choose the Outline layout and Portrait orientation. Specify the name **AgenciesAndDonations** for the report.

15. Apply the Verve theme to the AgenciesAndDonations report *only*.

16. Resize the report title so that the text is fully displayed; edit the report title so that it appears as "Agencies and Donations"; and change the font color of the title to the Pink, Accent 2, Darker 25% theme color.

17. Select both the Donation Description field label and its field value box, and then resize them from the left side, making them smaller and moving them further to the right. Then select both the Donation Date field label and its field value box, and then resize them on both the left and right sides to move them further to the right and fully display their values. Finally, resize the Donation ID field label so it is fully displayed. Save the report.

18. Insert the Recycle picture, which is located in the Access1\Case3 folder provided with your Data Files, in the report. Move the picture to the right of the report title.

19. Apply conditional formatting so that any DonationValue greater than or equal to 200 is formatted as bold and with the Maroon font color.

20. Preview the report to confirm that it is formatted correctly and all field labels and field values are fully displayed. Save the report, print its first page (only if asked by your instructor to do so), and then close the report.

21. Compact and repair the Rossi database, and then close it.

With the figures provided as guides, create a form and a report for a luxury rental agency.

C R E A T E

Case Problem 4

Data Files needed for this Case Problem: GEM.accdb (*cont. from Tutorial 3*) **and Villa.bmp**

GEM Ultimate Vacations   Griffin and Emma MacElroy want to use the GEM database to track and analyze data about their clients and the luxury properties they rent. You'll help them by creating a form and a report to meet this goal. Complete the following steps:

1. Open the **GEM** database located in the Access1\Case4 folder provided with your Data Files.
2. Create the form shown in Figure 4-30.

| Figure 4-30 | Completed GuestsAndReservations form |

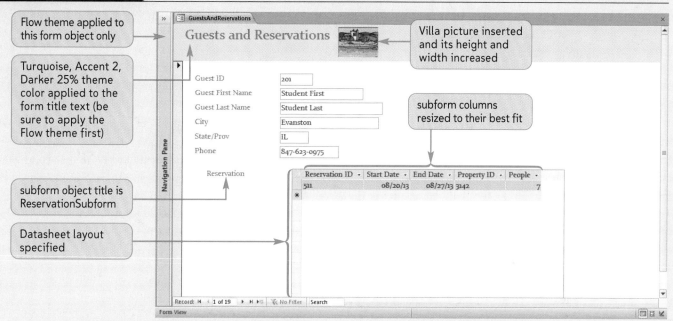

- Flow theme applied to this form object only
- Turquoise, Accent 2, Darker 25% theme color applied to the form title text (be sure to apply the Flow theme first)
- subform object title is ReservationSubform
- Datasheet layout specified
- Villa picture inserted and its height and width increased
- subform columns resized to their best fit

3. Using the form you just created, navigate to the second record in the subform for the third main record, and then change the People field value to **7**.
4. Use the Find command to move to the record for Kelly Skolnik, and then change the value in the End Date column for ReservationID 507 to **5/22/13**.
5. Use the appropriate wildcard character to find all records with a Phone field value that begins with the area code 630. Change the Phone field value of 630-442-4831 (Guest ID 230) to **630-442-5943**. Save and close the form.

⊕ **EXPLORE**

6. Use the Report Wizard to create the report shown in Figure 4-31.

   (*Hint*: To apply the background color to the field names from the Reservation table, press and hold down the Shift key and click to select the six field names, and then use the Background Color button in the Font group on the Format tab.) You might need to resize some field labels so there is white space between the field label boxes after you apply the background color.

| Figure 4-31 | Completed GuestReservations report |

Turquoise, Accent 2, Darker 25% theme color applied to the report title text

Flow theme applied to this report object only

Outline layout and Landscape orientation specified

Property ID field label resized so it is fully displayed

detail records sorted by ReservationID in ascending order

Villa picture inserted and made wider

Turquoise, Accent 2, Lighter 80% theme color applied to the field name backgrounds

Phone field value resized from the left and right to pull the values into the report and fully display them

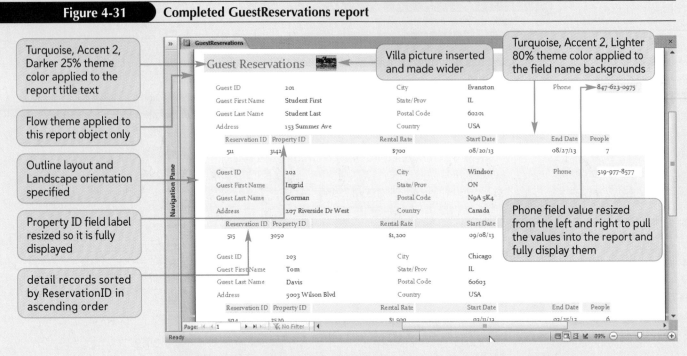

7. Scroll to the bottom of the report and check to make sure the page number is completely within the page border. If necessary, resize the control on its right side, reducing its width so that the page number text is roughly right-aligned with the text in the report.

8. Apply conditional formatting so that all People field values greater than 7 are formatted in a bold, dark red font. Save the report.

 EXPLORE

9. Preview the report so you see two pages at once. (*Hint*: Use a button on the Print Preview tab.) Check the report to confirm that all field labels and field values are fully displayed; then resize any, if necessary. Print page 1 of the report (only if asked by your instructor to do so).

10. Save and close the report, compact and repair the GEM database, and then close it.

SAM: Skills Assessment Manager

ENDING DATA FILES

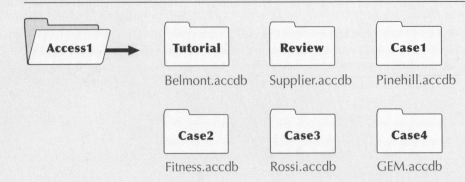

Access1	→	Tutorial	Review	Case1
		Belmont.accdb	Supplier.accdb	Pinehill.accdb
		Case2	Case3	Case4
		Fitness.accdb	Rossi.accdb	GEM.accdb

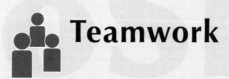

Teamwork

Working with a Team to Create a Database

Teamwork is the collaborative effort of individuals working together to achieve a goal. Most organizations rely on teams to complete work tasks, regardless of whether those teams are formal and ongoing or informally organized to achieve a specific goal. Some teams might even be virtual, such as teams that use telecommunications technologies and social networks to complete tasks from different corporate or geographical locations.

When an organization decides to use a database to manage information, the database is rarely planned, created, and maintained by a single individual. In most cases, a team of individuals is assigned to work on different stages of database development. For example, a team might research the needs of the organization, the best database management system to use to meet those needs, and the skills required of the team members to create, update, and maintain the database. Then another team might take over the task of actually creating the database and its objects, inputting the data, and installing the database on the organization's network. Finally, yet another team might conduct training sessions to teach users how to use the database to extract the data they require to perform their jobs.

Regardless of the type of database being created, the roles that individual team members play when working on a team are similar to what you might expect in any situation that requires a collaborative effort.

The Roles of Team Members

If a team is to be successful, individual members must see the value in their respective contributions and what the team as a whole gets out of each member's contribution. This means two important requirements must be met: task performance and social satisfaction. Task performance usually is handled by one or more members who are task specialists. Task specialists spend a lot of time and effort ensuring that the team achieves its goals. They initiate ideas, give opinions, gather information, sort details, and provide motivation to keep the team on track.

Social satisfaction is handled by individuals who strengthen the team's social bonds through encouragement, empathy, conflict resolution, compromise, and tension reduction. Have you ever been on a team where the tension was high, and someone stepped in to tell a joke or tried to soften the blow of criticism? That person held the role of managing social satisfaction.

Both the task specialist and social satisfaction specialist are important roles on teams. These are not the only roles, however. Other roles include team leaders, work coordinators, idea people, and critics. The roles of individual team members are not always mutually exclusive. For example, the task specialist might also be the team leader, and the idea person might also fill the social satisfaction role. As you begin working with your team in this exercise, watch how these roles are filled and how they change as your team completes its work. Perhaps you'll want to discuss upfront which role each member is comfortable filling to see how complementary your collective skill sets turn out to be. What if your team lacks a role? Then you'll need to figure out, as a team, how to move forward so you can complete your work successfully. The following are tips that everyone should respect as work on a team begins:

- Remember that everyone brings something of value to the team.
- Respect and support each other as you work toward the common goal.

ProSkills

- When criticism or questions arise, try to see things from the other person's perspective.
- If someone needs assistance, find ways to encourage or support that person so the team is not affected.
- Deal with negative or unproductive attitudes immediately so they don't damage team energy and attitude.
- Get outside help if the team becomes stuck and can't move forward.
- Provide periodic positive encouragement or rewards for contributions.

The Importance of Technology in Teamwork

Many teams now depend on technology to accomplish work tasks. For example, corporate intranets and networks, email and voice mail, texting and instant messaging, teleconferencing and software collaboration tools, social networks, and cell phones can support teamwork. Each time you work in a group, decide at the outset how the team will use different technologies to communicate and document work activities. Determine how the team will organize and combine deliverable documents or presentation materials. Use whatever technology tools make the most sense for your team, your task, and your skills.

PROSKILLS

Create a Database

Many organizations use Access to manage business data, but Access can also be a valuable tool to track personal data. For example, you might create an Access database to store information about items in a personal collection, such as CDs, DVDs, or books; items related to a hobby, such as coin or stamp collecting, travel, or family history; or items related to sports teams, theater clubs, or other organizations to which you might belong. In this exercise, you'll work with your team members to create a database that will contain information of your choice, using the Access skills and features presented in Tutorials 1 through 4. As a group, you'll choose something the team is interested in tracking, such as members and activities of a college service organization or recruiters and job opportunities at your school.

Using Templates

Access includes templates for creating databases and tables. A **database template** is a database containing predefined tables, queries, forms, and reports. A **table template** is a template containing predefined fields. Using a database or table template can save you time and effort when creating a database. For example, if the fields available in one of the table templates are similar to the data you want to store, you can use the table template to quickly create a table with the fields and field properties already created and set for you. You can then modify the table, as necessary, to suit your needs. Before you begin to create a database with your team members, review the following steps for using database and table templates.

To create a database using a database template:

1. Make sure Backstage view is displayed.
2. Click the appropriate option in the Available Templates section, or click a link in the Office.com Templates section.

3. Click the name of the template you want to use; for example, if you choose to work with a sample template, you might click the Projects Web Database template or the Tasks template.

4. Specify the name for your database and a location in which to save the database file.

5. Click the Create button (or the Download button if you are using an online template).

6. Use the resulting database objects to enter, modify, or delete data or database objects.

To create a table using a table template:

1. With your database file open, click the Create tab on the Ribbon.

2. In the Templates group, click the Application Parts button. A menu opens listing the templates provided, including table templates.

3. Click the table template you want to use.

4. Modify the resulting table as needed, by adding or deleting fields, changing field properties, and so on.

Work in a Team to Create a Database

Working with your team members, you can decide to use a database and/or table template for this exercise if the templates fit the data you want to track. Note, however, that you still need to create the additional database objects indicated in the following steps—tables, queries, forms, and reports—to complete the exercise successfully.

Note: Please be sure *not* to include any personal information of a sensitive nature in the database you create to be submitted to your instructor for this exercise. Later on, you can update the data in your database with such information for your own personal use.

1. Meet with your team to determine what data you want to track in your new Access database. Determine how many tables you need and what data will go into each table. Sketch the layout of the columns (fields) and rows (records) for each table. Also discuss the field properties for each field, so that team members can document the characteristics needed for each field as they collect data. Consider using a standard form to help each person as he or she collects the necessary data.

   Next, assign data gathering and documentation tasks to each team member and set a deadline for finishing this initial task. Consider using Excel workbooks for this task, as you can use them to import the data later when working in Access. When all the data for the fields is collected, meet again as a team to examine the data collected and determine the structure of the database you will create. Finally, assign each team member specific tasks for creating the database objects discussed in the following steps.

2. Create a new Access database to contain the data your team wants to track.

3. Create two or three tables in the database that can be joined through one-to-many relationships.

4. Using the preliminary design work done by team members, define the properties for each field in each table. Make sure to include a mix of data types for the fields (for example, do not include only Text fields in each table).

5. As a team, discuss and specify a primary key for each table.

6. Define the necessary one-to-many relationships between the tables in the database with referential integrity enforced.

7. Enter 20 to 30 records in each table. If appropriate, your team can import the data for a table from another source, such as an Excel workbook or a text file.

8. Create 5 to 10 queries based on single tables and multiple tables. Be sure that some of the queries include some or all of the following: exact match conditions, comparison operators, and logical operators.

9. For some of the queries, use various sorting and filtering techniques to display the query results in various ways. Save these queries with the sort and/or filter applied.

10. If possible, and depending on the data your team is tracking, create at least one calculated field in one of the queries.

11. If possible, and depending on the data your team is tracking, use aggregate functions to produce summary statistics based on the data in at least one of the tables.

12. Create at least one form for each table in the database. Enhance each form's appearance with pictures, themes, line colors, and so on.

13. Create at least one form with a main form and subform based on related tables in the database. Enhance the form's appearance as appropriate.

14. Create at least one report based on each table in the database. Enhance each report's appearance with pictures, themes, color, and so on.

15. Apply conditional formatting to the values in at least one of the reports.

16. Submit your team's completed database to your instructor as requested. Include printouts of any database objects, such as reports, if required. Also, provide written documentation that describes the role of each team member and his or her contributions to the team. This documentation should include descriptions of any challenges the team faced while completing this exercise and how the team members worked together to overcome those challenges.

ACCESS

OBJECTIVES

Session 5.1
- Review table and object naming standards
- Use the Like, In, Not, and & operators in queries
- Filter data using an AutoFilter
- Use the IIf function to assign a conditional value to a calculated field in a query
- Create a parameter query

Session 5.2
- Use query wizards to create a crosstab query, a find duplicates query, and a find unmatched query
- Create a top values query

Session 5.3
- Modify table designs using lookup fields, input masks, and data validation rules
- Identify object dependencies
- Review a Memo field's properties
- Designate a trusted folder

Creating Advanced Queries and Enhancing Table Design

Making the Panorama Database Easier to Use

Case | *Belmont Landscapes*

After graduating with a university degree in Landscape Architecture and then working for a firm that provides basic landscape services to residential customers, Oren Belmont started his own landscape architecture firm in Holland, Michigan. Belmont Landscapes specializes in landscape designs for residential and commercial customers and numerous public agencies. The firm provides a wide range of services—from site analyses and feasibility studies, to drafting and administering construction documents—for projects of various scales. Oren's company developed the Panorama database of customer, contract, and invoice data; and the employees use Microsoft Access 2010 (or simply Access) to manage it. The Panorama database contains tables, queries, forms, and reports that Sarah Fisher, office manager, and Taylor Sico, marketing manager, use to track customers and their landscape projects.

Oren, Sarah, and Taylor are interested in taking better advantage of the power of Access to make the database easier to use and to create more sophisticated queries. For example, Taylor wants to obtain lists of customers in certain cities, and Sarah needs a summarized list of invoice amounts by city. Sarah wants to change the design of the Customer and Contracts tables. In this tutorial, you'll modify and customize the Panorama database to satisfy these requirements.

STARTING DATA FILES

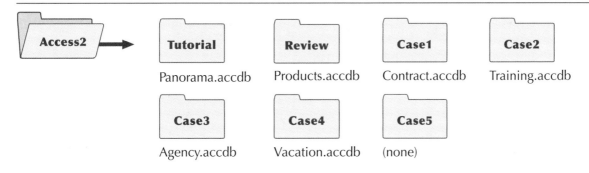

Access2 →	Tutorial	Review	Case1	Case2
	Panorama.accdb	Products.accdb	Contract.accdb	Training.accdb
	Case3	Case4	Case5	
	Agency.accdb	Vacation.accdb	(none)	

SESSION 5.1 VISUAL OVERVIEW

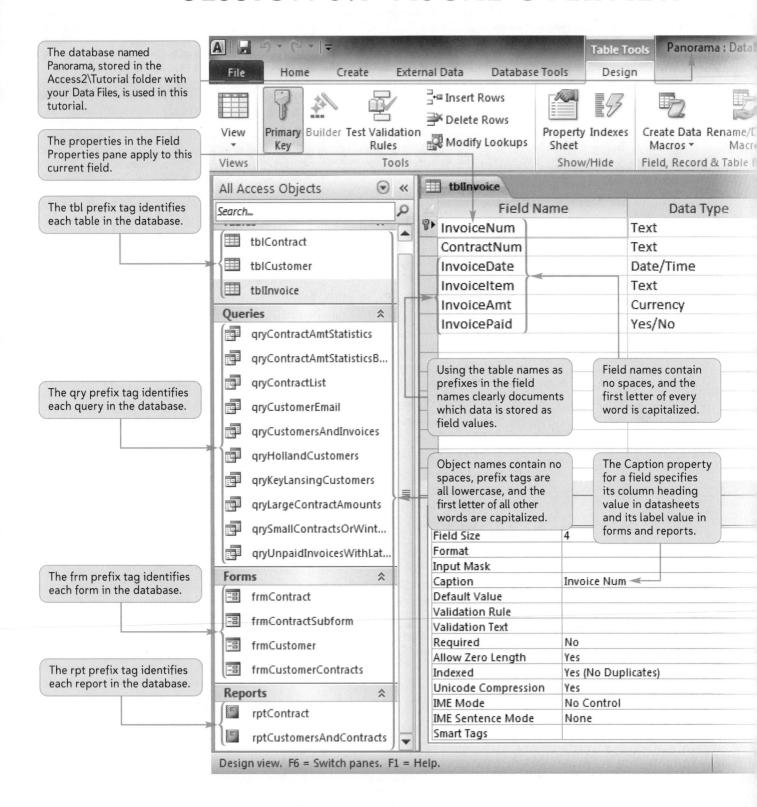

The database named Panorama, stored in the Access2\Tutorial folder with your Data Files, is used in this tutorial.

The properties in the Field Properties pane apply to this current field.

The tbl prefix tag identifies each table in the database.

The qry prefix tag identifies each query in the database.

The frm prefix tag identifies each form in the database.

The rpt prefix tag identifies each report in the database.

Using the table names as prefixes in the field names clearly documents which data is stored as field values.

Field names contain no spaces, and the first letter of every word is capitalized.

Object names contain no spaces, prefix tags are all lowercase, and the first letter of all other words are capitalized.

The Caption property for a field specifies its column heading value in datasheets and its label value in forms and reports.

DATABASE NAMING CONVENTIONS

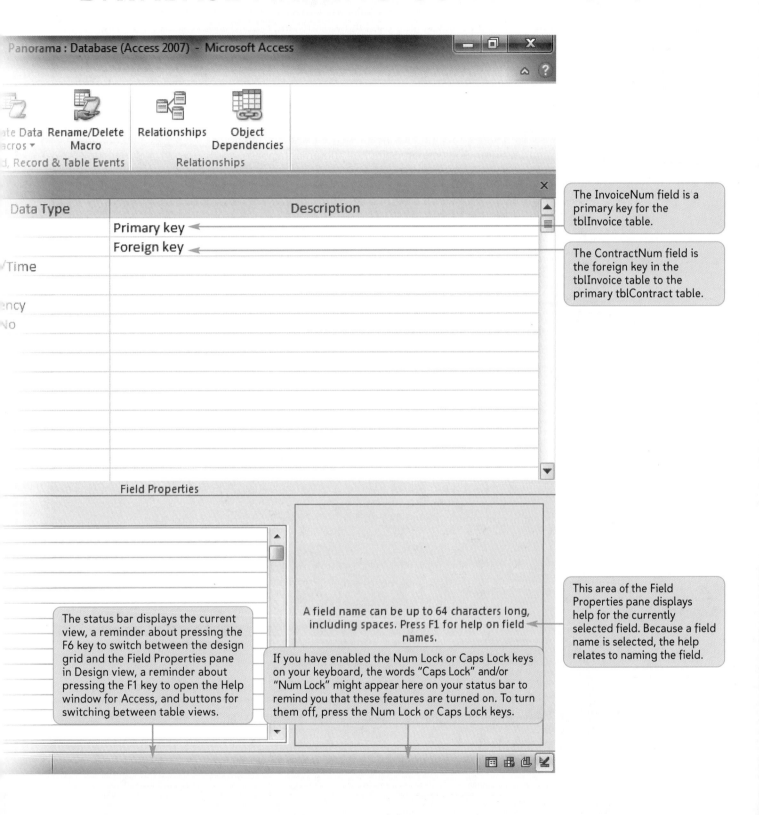

Panorama : Database (Access 2007) - Microsoft Access

ate Data | Rename/Delete Macro | Relationships | Object Dependencies
acros ▾
d, Record & Table Events | Relationships

Data Type	Description
	Primary key ←
	Foreign key ←
Time	
ency	
No	

The InvoiceNum field is a primary key for the tblInvoice table.

The ContractNum field is the foreign key in the tblInvoice table to the primary tblContract table.

Field Properties

A field name can be up to 64 characters long, including spaces. Press F1 for help on field names.

The status bar displays the current view, a reminder about pressing the F6 key to switch between the design grid and the Field Properties pane in Design view, a reminder about pressing the F1 key to open the Help window for Access, and buttons for switching between table views.

If you have enabled the Num Lock or Caps Lock keys on your keyboard, the words "Caps Lock" and/or "Num Lock" might appear here on your status bar to remind you that these features are turned on. To turn them off, press the Num Lock or Caps Lock keys.

This area of the Field Properties pane displays help for the currently selected field. Because a field name is selected, the help relates to naming the field.

Reviewing the Panorama Database

TIP

Read the Microsoft Access Naming Conventions section in the appendix titled "Relational Databases and Database Design" for more information about naming conventions.

Sarah and her staff had no previous database experience when they created the Panorama database; they simply used the wizards and other easy-to-use Access tools. As business continued to grow at Belmont Landscapes, Sarah convinced Oren that they needed to hire a computer expert to further enhance the Panorama database, and they hired Lucia Perez, who has a business information systems degree and nine years of experience developing database systems. Lucia spent a few days reviewing the Panorama database, making sure the database adhered to simple naming standards for the objects and field names to make her future work easier.

Before implementing the enhancements for Sarah and Taylor, you'll review the naming conventions for the object names in the Panorama database.

To review the object naming conventions in the Panorama database:

1. Make sure you have created your copy of the Access Data Files, and that your computer can access them.

   Trouble? If you don't have the Access Data Files, you need to get them before you can proceed. Your instructor will either give you the Data Files or ask you to obtain them from a specified location (such as a network drive). In either case, make a backup copy of the Data Files before you start so that you will have the original files available in case you need to start over. If you have any questions about the Data Files, see your instructor or technical support person for assistance.

2. Start Access, and then open the **Panorama** database in the Access2\Tutorial folder provided with your Data Files.

   Trouble? If the Security Warning is displayed below the Ribbon, click the Enable Content button next to the Security Warning.

The Navigation Pane displays the objects grouped by object type. Each object name has a prefix tag—a tbl prefix tag for tables, a qry prefix tag for queries, a frm prefix tag for forms, and a rpt prefix tag for reports. Using object prefix tags, you can readily identify the object type, even when the objects have the same base name—for instance, tblContract, frmContract, and rptContract. In addition, object names have no spaces, because other database management systems, such as SQL Server and Oracle, do not permit spaces in object and field names. If Belmont Landscapes needs to upscale to one of these other database management systems in the future, Lucia will have to do less work to make the transition.

PROSKILLS

Teamwork: Following Naming Conventions

Most Access databases have hundreds of fields, objects, and controls. You'll find it easier to identify the type and purpose of these database items when you use a naming convention or standard. Most companies adopt a standard naming convention, such as the one used for the Panorama database, so that multiple people can develop a database, troubleshoot database problems, and enhance and improve existing databases. When working on a database, a team's tasks are difficult, if not impossible, to perform if a standard naming convention isn't used. In addition, most databases and database samples on Web sites and in training books use standard naming conventions that are similar to the ones used for the Panorama database. By following the standard naming convention established by the company or organization you are a part of, you'll help to ensure smooth collaboration among all team members.

Now you'll create the queries that Sarah and Taylor need.

Using a Pattern Match in a Query

You are already familiar with queries that use an exact match or a range of values (for example, queries that use the >= or < comparison operators) to select records. Access provides many other operators for creating select queries. These operators let you create more complicated queries that are difficult or impossible to create with exact match or range of values selection criteria.

Sarah and Taylor created a list of questions they want to answer using the Panorama database:

- Which customers have the 616 area code?
- What is the customer information for customers located in Holland, Rockford, or Saugatuck?
- What is the customer information for all customers *except* those located in Holland, Rockford, or Saugatuck?
- What is the customer and contract information for contracts that have values of less than $10,000 or that were signed during the winter *and* are located in Grand Rapids or East Grand Rapids?
- What are the names of Belmont Landscapes' customers? The customer name is either the company name for nonresidential customers or the last and first names for residential customers.
- What is the customer information for customers in a particular city? For this query, the user needs to be able to specify the city.

Next, you will create the queries necessary to answer these questions. Taylor wants to view the records for all customers located in the 616 area code. She plans to travel to this area next week and wants to contact customers ahead of time to schedule appointments. To answer Taylor's question, you can create a query that uses a pattern match. A **pattern match** selects records with a value for the designated field that matches the pattern of a simple condition value, in this case, customers with the 616 area code. You do this using the Like comparison operator.

The **Like comparison operator** selects records by matching field values to a specific pattern that includes one or more of these wildcard characters: asterisk (*), question mark (?), and number symbol (#). The asterisk represents any string of characters, the question mark represents any single character, and the number symbol represents any single digit. Using a pattern match is similar to using an exact match, except that a pattern match includes wildcard characters.

To create the new query, you must first place the tblCustomer table field list in the Query window in Design view.

To create the new query in Design view:

1. If necessary, click the **Shutter Bar Open/Close Button** « at the top of the Navigation Pane to close it.

2. Click the **Create** tab on the Ribbon.

3. In the Queries group, click the **Query Design** button. Access opens the Show Table dialog box on top of the Query window in Design view.

4. Click **tblCustomer** in the Tables box, click the **Add** button, and then click the **Close** button. Access places the tblCustomer table field list in the Query window and closes the Show Table dialog box.

TIP

You can also double-click a table name to add the table's field list to the Query window.

5. Double-click the **title bar** of the tblCustomer field list to highlight all the fields, and then drag the highlighted fields to the first column's Field box in the design grid. Access places each field in a separate column in the design grid, in the same order that the fields appear in the table. See Figure 5-1.

Figure 5-1

Adding the fields for the pattern match query

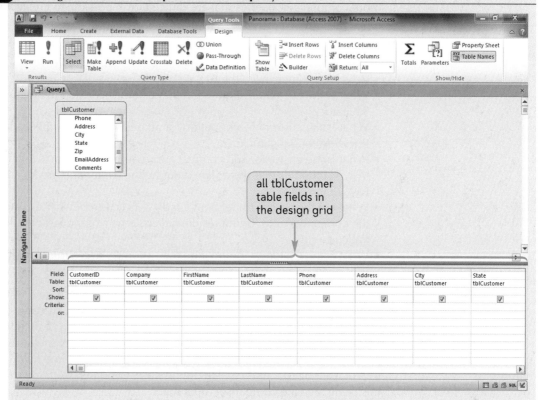

Trouble? If tblCustomer.* appears in the first column's Field box, you dragged the * from the field list instead of the highlighted fields. Press the Delete key, and then repeat Step 5.

Now you will enter the pattern match condition *Like "616*"* for the Phone field. Access will select records with a Phone field value of 616 in positions one through three. The asterisk wildcard character specifies that any characters can appear in the remaining positions of the field value.

To specify records that match the specified pattern:

1. Click the **Phone Criteria** box, and then type **L**. The Formula AutoComplete menu displays a list of functions beginning with the letter L, but the Like operator is not one of the choices in the list. You'll finish typing the condition.

2. Type **ike "616*"**. See Figure 5-2.

TIP

If you omit the Like operator, Access automatically adds it when you run the query.

| Figure 5-2 | Record selection based on matching a specific pattern |

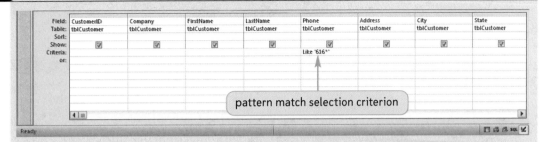

3. Click the **Save** button on the Quick Access Toolbar to open the Save As dialog box.

4. Type **qry616AreaCode** in the Query Name box, and then press the **Enter** key. Access saves the query and displays the name on the object tab.

5. In the Results group on the Design tab, click the **Run** button. The query results display the 24 records with the area code 616 in the Phone field. See Figure 5-3.

| Figure 5-3 | tblCustomer table records for area code 616 |

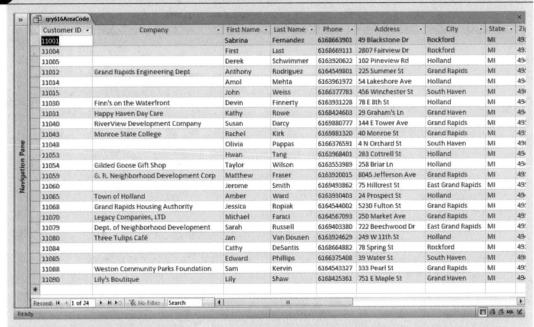

Note that Lucia removed the hyphens from the Phone field values; for example, 6168663901 in the first record used to be 616-866-3901. You'll modify the Phone field later in this tutorial to format its values with hyphens.

6. Change the second record in the table so the First Name and Last Name columns contain your first and last names.

7. Close the qry616AreaCode query.

Next, Sarah asks you to create a query that displays information about customers in Holland, Rockford, or Saugatuck. She wants a printout of the customer data for her administrative aide, who will contact these customers. To produce the results Sarah wants, you'll create a query using a list-of-values match.

Using a List-of-Values Match in a Query

A **list-of-values match** selects records whose value for the designated field matches one of two or more simple condition values. You could accomplish this by including several Or conditions in the design grid, but the In comparison operator provides an easier and clearer way to do this. The **In comparison operator** lets you define a condition with a list of two or more values for a field. If a record's field value matches one value from the list of defined values, then Access selects and includes that record in the query results.

To display the information Sarah requested, you want to select records if their City field value equals Holland, Rockford, or Saugatuck. These are the values you will use with the In comparison operator. Sarah wants the query to contain the same data as the qry616AreaCode query, so you'll make a copy of that query and modify it.

To create the query using a list-of-values match:

1. Open the Navigation Pane, then in the Queries group on the Navigation Pane, right-click **qry616AreaCode**, and then click **Copy** on the shortcut menu.

2. In the Clipboard group on the Home tab, click the **Paste** button, type **qryHollandRockfordSaugatuckCustomers** in the Query Name box, and then press the **Enter** key.

   To modify the copied query, you need to open it in Design view.

3. In the Queries group on the Navigation Pane, right-click **qryHollandRockfordSaugatuckCustomers** to select it and display the shortcut menu.

4. Click **Design View** on the shortcut menu to open the query in Design view, and then close the Navigation Pane.

   You need to delete the existing condition from the Phone field.

5. Click the **Phone Criteria** box, press the **F2** key to highlight the entire condition, and then press the **Delete** key to remove the condition.

   Now you can enter the criterion for the new query using the In comparison operator. When you use this operator, you must enclose the list of values you want to match within parentheses and separate the values with commas. In addition, for fields defined using the Text data type, you enclose each value in quotation marks, although Access adds the quotation marks if you omit them. For fields defined using the Number or Currency data type, you don't enclose the values in quotation marks.

   TIP

   After clicking in a box, you can also open its Zoom dialog box by holding down the Shift key and pressing the F2 key.

6. Right-click the **City Criteria** box to open the shortcut menu, click **Zoom** to open the Zoom dialog box, and then type **In ("Holland","Rockford","Saugatuck")**. See Figure 5-4.

Figure 5-4	Record selection based on matching field values to a list of values

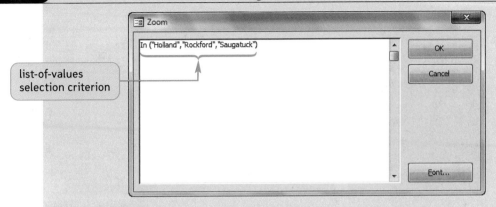

list-of-values selection criterion

7. Click the **OK** button to close the Zoom dialog box, and then save and run the query. Access displays the recordset, which shows the 13 records with Holland, Rockford, or Saugatuck in the City field.

8. Close the query.

Sarah asks her assistant to contact Belmont Landscapes customers that are not in Holland, Rockford, and Saugatuck. You can provide Sarah with this information by creating a query with the Not logical operator.

Using the Not Logical Operator in a Query

The **Not logical operator** negates a criterion or selects records for which the designated field does not match the criterion. For example, if you enter *Not "Holland"* in the Criteria box for the City field, the query results show records that do not have the City field value Holland, that is, records of all customers not located in Holland.

To create Sarah's query, you will combine the Not logical operator with the In comparison operator to select customers whose City field value is not in the list *("Holland","Rockford","Saugatuck")*. The qryHollandRockfordSaugatuckCustomers query has the fields that Sarah needs to see in the query results. Sarah doesn't need to keep the qryHollandRockfordSaugatuckCustomers query, so you'll rename and then modify the query.

To create the query using the Not logical operator:

TIP

You can rename any object type, including tables, in the Navigation Pane using the Rename command on the shortcut menu.

1. Open the Navigation Pane, then in the Queries group on the Navigation Pane, right-click **qryHollandRockfordSaugatuckCustomers**, and then click **Rename** on the shortcut menu.

2. Position the insertion point after "qry," type **Non**, and then press the **Enter** key. The query name is now qryNonHollandRockfordSaugatuckCustomers.

3. Open the **qryNonHollandRockfordSaugatuckCustomers** query in Design view, and then close the Navigation Pane.

   You need to change the existing condition in the City field to add the Not logical operator.

4. Click the **City Criteria** box, open the Zoom dialog box, click at the beginning of the expression, type **Not**, and then press the **spacebar**. See Figure 5-5.

Figure 5-5   **Record selection based on not matching a list of values**

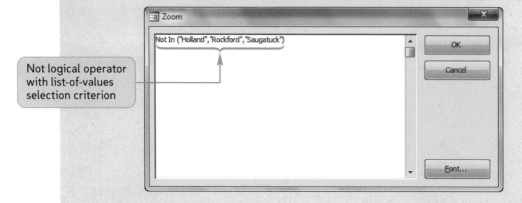

Not logical operator with list-of-values selection criterion

5. Click the **OK** button, and then save and run the query. The recordset displays only those records with a City field value that is not Holland, Rockford, or Saugatuck. The recordset includes a total of 29 customer records.

6. Scroll down the datasheet to make sure that no Holland or Rockford or Saugatuck customers appear in your results.

Now you can close and delete the query, because Sarah does not need to run this query again.

7. Close the query, and then open the Navigation Pane.

8. Right-click **qryNonHollandRockfordSaugatuckCustomers**, click **Delete** on the shortcut menu, and then click the **Yes** button when asked to confirm the query deletion. The query is permanently deleted from the database.

TIP

You can delete any object type, including tables, in the Navigation Pane using the Delete command on the shortcut menu.

You now are ready to answer Taylor's question about Grand Rapids or East Grand Rapids customers that signed contracts for less than $10,000 or that signed contracts during the winter.

Using an AutoFilter to Filter Data

Taylor wants to view the customer last and first names, company names, cities, contract amounts, signing dates, and contract types for customers in Grand Rapids or East Grand Rapids that have signed contracts for less than $10,000 or that signed contracts during the winter. The qrySmallContractsOrWinterSignings query contains the same fields Taylor wants to view. This query also uses the Or logical operator to select records if the ContractAmt field value is less than $10,000 or if the SigningDate field value is between 1/1/2014 and 3/1/2014. These are two of the conditions needed to answer Taylor's question. You could modify the qrySmallContractsOrWinterSignings query in Design view to further restrict the records selected to customers located only in Grand Rapids and East Grand Rapids. However, you can use the AutoFilter feature to choose the city restrictions faster and with more flexibility. You previously used the AutoFilter feature to sort records, and you previously used Filter By Selection to filter records. Now you'll show Taylor how to use the AutoFilter feature to filter records.

To filter the records using an AutoFilter:

1. Open the **qrySmallContractsOrWinterSignings** query in Design view, and then close the Navigation Pane.

   The *<10000* condition for the ContractAmt field selects records whose contracts amounts are less than $10,000, and the *Between #1/1/2014# And #3/1/2014#* condition for the SigningDate field selects records whose contracts were signed during the first two months of 2014. Because the conditions are in two different rows, the query uses the Or logical operator. If you wanted to answer Taylor's question in Design view, you would add a condition for the City field, using either the Or logical operator—*"Grand Rapids" Or "East Grand Rapids"*—or the In comparison operator—*In ("Grand Rapids", "East Grand Rapids")*. You'd place this condition for the City field in both the Criteria row and in the or row. The query recordset would include a record only if both conditions in either row are satisfied. Instead, you'll show Taylor how to choose the information she wants using an AutoFilter.

2. Run the query, and then click the **arrow** on the City column heading to display the AutoFilter menu. See Figure 5-6.

| Figure 5-6 | Using an AutoFilter to filter records in the query recordset |

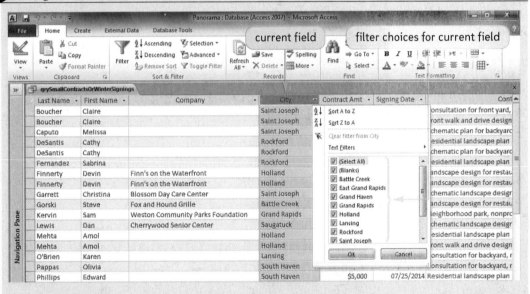

The AutoFilter menu lists all City field values that appear in the recordset. A check mark next to an entry indicates that records with that City field value appear in the recordset. To filter for selected City field values, you uncheck the cities you don't want selected and leave checked the cities you do want selected. You can click the "(Select All)" check box to select or deselect all field values. The "(Blanks)" option includes null values when checked and excludes null values when unchecked. (Recall that a null field value is the absence of a value for the field.)

3. Click the **(Select All)** check box to deselect all check boxes, click the **East Grand Rapids** check box, and then click the **Grand Rapids** check box.

   The two check boxes indicate that the AutoFilter will include only East Grand Rapids and Grand Rapids City field values.

> **4.** Click the **OK** button. Access displays the four records for customers in East Grand Rapids and Grand Rapids with small contract amounts or with winter signing dates. See Figure 5-7.

Figure 5-7	Using an AutoFilter to filter records in the query recordset

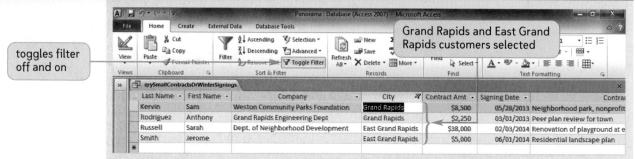

You click the Toggle Filter button in the Sort & Filter group on the Home tab to remove the current filter and display all records in the query. If you click the Toggle Filter button a second time, you reapply the filter.

> **5.** In the Sort & Filter group on the Home tab, click the **Toggle Filter** button. Access removes the filter, and all 31 records appear in the recordset.

> **6.** Click the **Toggle Filter** button. Access applies the City filter, displaying the four records for customers in East Grand Rapids and Grand Rapids.

Taylor knows how to use the AutoFilter feature and has the information she needs. You can close the query without saving your query design changes.

> **7.** Close the query without saving it.

Sarah wants to view all fields from the tblCustomer table, along with the customer name. The customer name is either the company name for nonresidential customers or the last and first names for residential customers.

Assigning a Conditional Value to a Calculated Field

Records for residential customers have nonnull FirstName and LastName field values and null Company field values in the tblCustomer table, while records for all other customers have nonnull values for all three fields. Sarah wants to view records from the tblCustomer table in order by the Company field value, if it's nonnull, and at the same time in order by the LastName and then FirstName field values, if the Company field value is null. To produce the information for Sarah, you need to create a query that includes all fields from the tblCustomer table and then add a calculated field that will display the customer name—either the Company field value or the LastName and FirstName field values, separated by a comma and a space.

To combine the LastName and FirstName fields, you'll use the expression *LastName & ", " & FirstName*. The **& (ampersand) operator** is a concatenation operator that joins text expressions. If the LastName field value is Fernandez and the FirstName field value is Sabrina, for example, the result of the expression is *Fernandez, Sabrina*.

To display the correct customer value, you'll use the IIf function. The **IIf (Immediate If) function** assigns one value to a calculated field or control if a condition is true, and a second value if the condition is false. The IIf function has three parts: a condition that is true or false, the result when the condition is true, and the result when the condition is false. Each part of the IIf function is separated by a comma. The condition you'll use is *IsNull(Company)*. The **IsNull function** tests a field value or an expression for a null value; if the field value or expression is null, the result is true; otherwise, the result is false. The expression *IsNull(Company)* is true when the Company field value is null, and is false when the Company field value is not null.

For the calculated field, you'll enter *IIf(IsNull(Company),LastName & ", " & FirstName,Company)*. You interpret this expression as: If the Company field value is null, then set the calculated field value to the concatenation of the LastName field value and the text string ", " and the FirstName field value. If the Company field value is not null, then set the calculated field value to the Company field value.

Now you are ready to create Sarah's query to display the customer name.

To create the query to display the customer name:

1. Click the **Create** tab on the Ribbon and then, in the Queries group on the Create tab, click the **Query Design** button to open the Show Table dialog box on top of the Query window in Design view.

2. Click **tblCustomer** in the Tables box, click the **Add** button, and then click the **Close** button to place the tblCustomer table field list in the Query window and close the Show Table dialog box.

   Sarah wants all fields from the tblCustomer table to appear in the query recordset and the new calculated field to appear in the first column.

3. Double-click the **title bar** of the tblCustomer field list to highlight all the fields, and then drag the highlighted fields to the second column's Field box in the design grid. Access places each field in a separate column in the design grid starting with the second column in the design grid, in the same order that the fields appear in the table.

   Trouble? If you accidentally drag the highlighted fields to the first column in the design grid, click the CustomerID Field box, and then click the Insert Columns button in the Query Setup group on the Design tab. Continue with Step 4.

4. Right-click the blank Field box to the left of the CustomerID field, and then click **Build** on the shortcut menu to open the Expression Builder dialog box.

   Sarah wants to use "Customer" as the name of the calculated field, so you'll type that name, followed by a colon, and then you'll choose the IIf function.

5. Type **Customer:** and then press the **spacebar**.

6. Double-click **Functions** in the Expression Elements (left) column, click **Built-In Functions** in the Expression Elements column, scroll down the Expression Categories (middle) column and click **Program Flow**, and then double-click **IIf** in the Expression Values (right) column. Access adds the IIf function with four placeholders to the right of the calculated field name in the expression box. See Figure 5-8.

Read the steps carefully, noting whether you should click or double-click the expression categories or expressions.

Figure 5-8   **IIf function inserted for the calculated field**

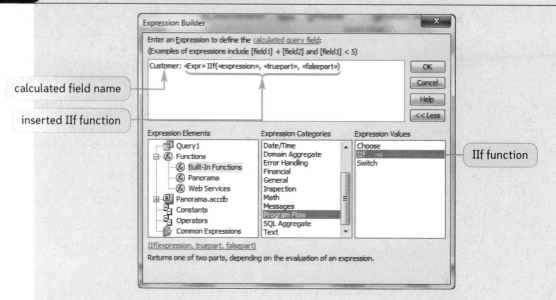

calculated field name

inserted IIf function

IIf function

The expression you will create does not need the leftmost placeholder (<<Expr>>), so you'll delete it. You'll replace the second placeholder (<<expression>>) with the condition using the IsNull function, the third placeholder (<<truepart>>) with the expression using the & operator, and the fourth placeholder (<<falsepart>>) with the Company field name.

7. Click **<<Expr>>** in the expression box, and then press the **Delete** key to delete the first placeholder.

8. Click **<<expression>>** in the expression box, click **Inspection** in the Expression Categories (middle) column, double-click **IsNull** in the Expression Values (right) column, click **<<expression>>** in the expression box, and then type **Company**. You've completed the entry of the condition in the IIf function. See Figure 5-9.

Figure 5-9   **After entering the condition for the calculated field's IIf function**

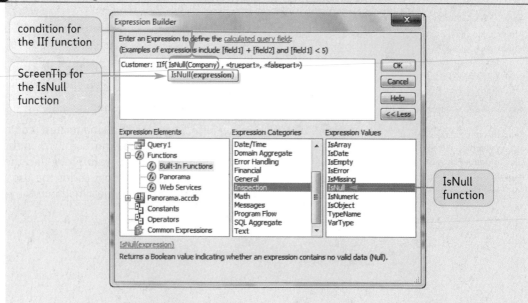

condition for
the IIf function

ScreenTip for
the IsNull
function

IsNull
function

After you typed the first letter of *Company*, the Formula AutoComplete box displayed a list of functions beginning with the letter C, and a ScreenTip for the IsNull function appeared above the box. The box closed after you typed the third letter, but the ScreenTip remains on the screen.

Instead of typing the field name of Company in the previous step, you could have double-clicked Panorama.accdb in the Expression Elements column, double-clicked Tables in the Expression Elements column, clicked tblCustomer in the Expression Elements column, and then double-clicked Company in the Expression Elements column.

Now you'll replace the fourth placeholder and then the third placeholder.

9. Click **<<falsepart>>** and then type **Company**.

10. Click **<<truepart>>**, and then type **LastName & ", " & FirstName** to finish creating the calculated field. Be sure you type a space after the comma within the quotation marks. See Figure 5-10.

TIP

The expression *[tblCustomer]![Company]*, meaning the Company field in the tblCustomer table, is the same as *Company*.

Figure 5-10	Completed calculated field

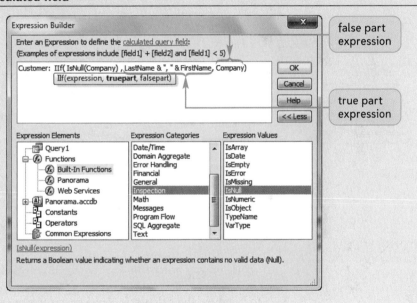

Sarah wants the query to sort records in ascending order by the Customer calculated field.

To sort, save, and run the query:

1. Click the **OK** button in the Expression Builder dialog box to close it.

2. Click the right side of the **Customer Sort** box to display the sort order options, and then click **Ascending**. The query will display the records in alphabetical order based on the Customer field values.

The calculated field name of Customer consists of a single word, so you do not need to set the Caption property for it. However, you'll review the properties for the calculated field by opening its property sheet.

3. In the Show/Hide group on the Design tab, click the **Property Sheet** button. The property sheet opens and displays the properties for the Customer calculated field. See Figure 5-11.

Figure 5-11 **Property sheet for the Customer calculated field**

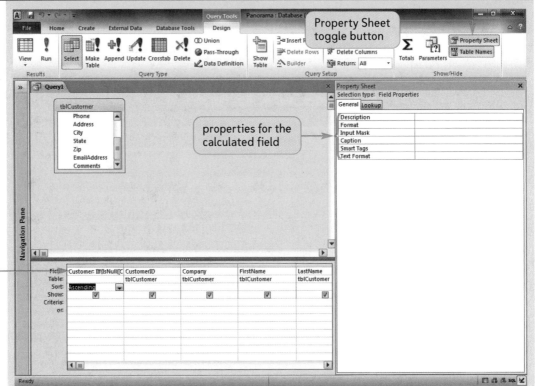

Among the properties for the calculated field, which is the current field, is the Caption property. Leaving the Caption property set to null means that the column name for the calculated field in the query recordset will be Customer, which is the calculated field name. The Property Sheet button is a toggle, so you'll click it again to close the property sheet.

4. Click the **Property Sheet** button to close the property sheet.

5. Save the query as **qryCustomersByName**, run the query, and then resize the Customer column to its best fit. Access displays all records from the tblCustomer table in alphabetical order by the Customer field. See Figure 5-12.

Figure 5-12   Completed query displaying the Customer calculated field

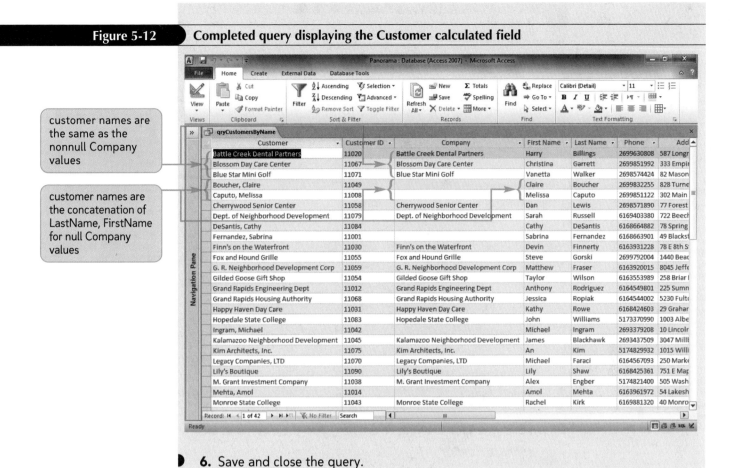

customer names are the same as the nonnull Company values

customer names are the concatenation of LastName, FirstName for null Company values

> 6. Save and close the query.

You are now ready to create the query to satisfy Sarah's request for information about customers in a particular city.

Creating a Parameter Query

Sarah's next request is for records in the qryCustomersByName query for customers in a particular city. For this query, she wants to specify the city, such as Battle Creek or Holland, when she runs the query.

To create this query, you will copy, rename, and modify the qryCustomersByName query. You could create a simple condition using an exact match for the City field, but you would need to change it in Design view every time you run the query. Alternatively, Sarah or a member of her staff could filter the qryCustomersByName query for the city records they want to view. Instead, you will create a parameter query. A **parameter query** displays a dialog box that prompts the user to enter one or more criteria values when the query is run. In this case, you want to create a query that prompts for the city and selects only those customer records with that City field value from the table. You will enter the prompt in the Criteria box for the City field. When Access runs the query, it will open a dialog box and prompt you to enter the city. Access then creates the query results, just as if you had changed the criteria in Design view.

REFERENCE

Creating a Parameter Query

- Create a select query that includes all fields to appear in the query results. Also choose the sort fields and set the criteria that do not change when you run the query.
- Decide which fields to use as prompts when the query runs. In the Criteria box for each of these fields, type the prompt you want to appear in a dialog box when you run the query, and enclose the prompt in brackets.

Now you can copy and rename the qryCustomersByName query, and then change its design to create the parameter query.

To create the parameter query based on an existing query:

1. Open the Navigation Pane, copy and then paste the qryCustomersByName query, renaming it **qryCustomersByNameParameter**.

2. Open the **qryCustomersByNameParameter** query in Design view, and then close the Navigation Pane.

   Next, you must enter the criterion for the parameter query. In this case, Sarah wants the query to prompt users to enter the city for the customer records they want to view. So, you need to enter the prompt in the Criteria box for the City field. Brackets must enclose the text of the prompt.

3. Click the **City Criteria** box, type **[Type the city:]** and then press the **Enter** key. See Figure 5-13.

Figure 5-13   **Specifying the prompt for the parameter query**

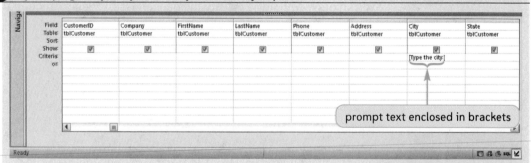

prompt text enclosed in brackets

TIP

You must enter a value that matches the spelling of a City field value in the table, but you can use either lowercase or upper-case letters.

4. Save and run the query. Access displays a dialog box prompting you for the name of the city. See Figure 5-14.

Figure 5-14   **Enter Parameter Value dialog box**

type value here

prompt

The bracketed text you specified in the Criteria box of the City field appears above a box, in which you must type a City field value. Sarah wants to see all customers in Holland.

5. Type **Holland**, press the **Enter** key, and then scroll the datasheet to the right, if necessary, to display the City field values. The recordset displays the data for the seven customers in Holland. See Figure 5-15.

Figure 5-15	Results of the parameter query

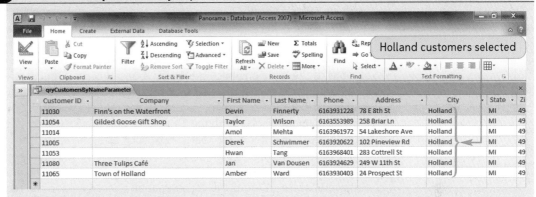

Sarah asks what happens if she doesn't enter a value in the dialog box when she runs the qryCustomersByNameParameter query. You can run the query again to show Sarah the answer to her question.

6. Switch to Design view, and then run the query. The Enter Parameter Value dialog box opens.

If you click the OK button or press the Enter key, you'll run the parameter query without entering a value for the City field criterion.

7. Click the **OK** button. Access displays no records in the query results.

When you run the parameter query and enter *Holland* in the dialog box, Access runs the query the same way as if you had entered *"Holland"* in the City Criteria box in the design grid by displaying all Holland customer records. When you do not enter a value in the dialog box, Access runs the query the same way as if you had entered *null* in the City Criteria box. Because none of the records has a null City field value, Access displays no records. Sarah asks if there's a way to display records for a selected City field value when she enters its value in the dialog box and to display all records when she doesn't enter a value.

INSIGHT

Creating a More Flexible Parameter Query

Most users want parameter queries to display the records that match their entered parameter value or to display all records when they don't enter a parameter value. To provide this functionality, you can change the Criteria box in the design grid for the specified column. For example, you could change an entry for a City field from *[Type the city:]* to *Like [Type the city:] & "*"*. That is, you can prefix the Like operator to the original criterion and concatenate the criterion to a wildcard character. When you run the parameter query with this new entry, Access will display one of the following recordsets:

- If you enter a specific City field value in the dialog box, such as *Saugatuck*, the entry is the same as *Like "Saugatuck" & "*"*, which becomes *Like "Saugatuck*"* after the concatenation operation. That is, Access selects all records whose City field values have Saugatuck in the first nine positions and any characters in the remaining positions. If the table on which the query is based contains records with City field values of Saugatuck, Access displays only those records. However, if the table on which the query is based also contains records with City field values of Saugatuck City, then Access would display both the Saugatuck and the Saugatuck City records.
- If you enter a letter in the dialog box, such as *S*, the entry is the same as *Like "S*"*, and the recordset displays all records with City field values that begin with the letter S.
- If you enter no value in the dialog box, the entry is the same as *Like Null & "*"*, which becomes *Like "*"* after the concatenation operation, and the recordset displays all records.

Now you'll modify the parameter query to satisfy Sarah's request and test the new version of the query.

To modify and test the parameter query:

> **1.** Switch to Design view.

> **2.** Click the **City Criteria** box, and then open the Zoom dialog box.

You'll use the Zoom dialog box to modify the value in the City Criteria box.

Be sure you type "*" at the end of the expression.

> **3.** Click to the left of the expression in the Zoom dialog box, type **Like**, press the **spacebar**, press the **End** key, press the **spacebar**, and then type **& "*"**. See Figure 5-16.

Figure 5-16 Modified City Criteria value in the Zoom dialog box

Now you can test the modified parameter query.

▶ **4.** Click the **OK** button to close the Zoom dialog box, save your query design changes, and then run the query.

First, you'll test the query to display customers in Saugatuck.

▶ **5.** Type **Saugatuck**, and then press the **Enter** key. The recordset displays the data for the three customers in Saugatuck.

Now you'll test the query without entering a value when prompted.

▶ **6.** Switch to Design view, run the query, and then click the **OK** button. The recordset displays all 42 original records from the tblCustomer table.

Finally, you'll test the query and enter S in the dialog box.

▶ **7.** In the Records group on the Home tab, click the **Refresh All** button to open the Enter Parameter Value dialog box, type **S**, press the **Enter** key, and then scroll to the right, if necessary, to display the City field values. The recordset displays the 10 records for customers in Saint Joseph, Saugatuck, and South Haven.

▶ **8.** Close the query.

▶ **9.** If you are not continuing on to the next session, close the Panorama database and click the **Yes** button if necessary to empty the Clipboard.

The queries you created will make the Panorama database easier to use. In the next session, you will create a top values query and use query wizards to create three additional queries.

REVIEW

Session 5.1 Quick Check

1. According to the naming conventions used in this session, you use the _____ prefix tag to identify queries.
2. Which comparison operator selects records based on a specific pattern?
3. What is the purpose of the asterisk (*) in a pattern match query?
4. When do you use the In comparison operator?
5. How do you negate a selection criterion?
6. The _____ function returns one of two values based on whether the condition being tested is true or false.
7. When do you use a parameter query?

SESSION 5.2 VISUAL OVERVIEW

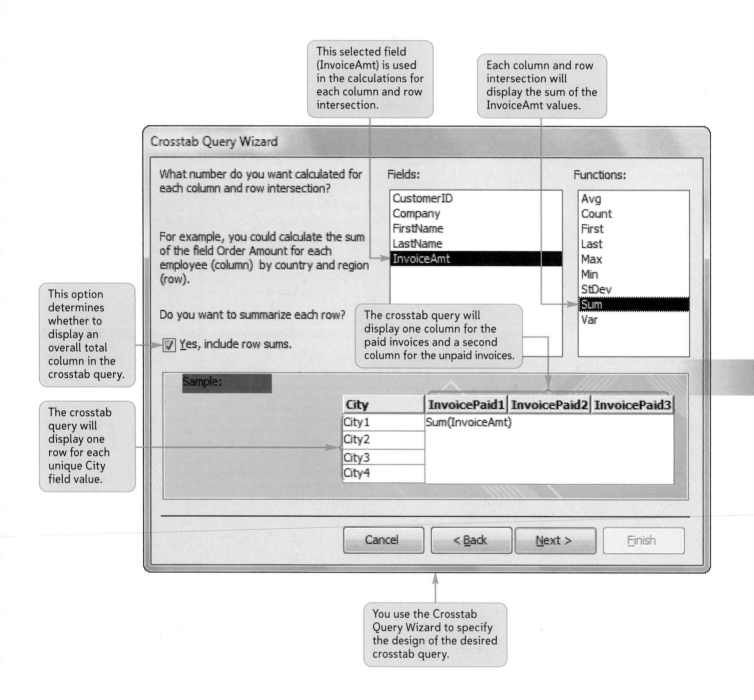

This selected field (InvoiceAmt) is used in the calculations for each column and row intersection.

Each column and row intersection will display the sum of the InvoiceAmt values.

This option determines whether to display an overall total column in the crosstab query.

The crosstab query will display one row for each unique City field value.

The crosstab query will display one column for the paid invoices and a second column for the unpaid invoices.

You use the Crosstab Query Wizard to specify the design of the desired crosstab query.

Crosstab Query Wizard

What number do you want calculated for each column and row intersection?

For example, you could calculate the sum of the field Order Amount for each employee (column) by country and region (row).

Do you want to summarize each row?

☑ Yes, include row sums.

Fields:
- CustomerID
- Company
- FirstName
- LastName
- InvoiceAmt

Functions:
- Avg
- Count
- First
- Last
- Max
- Min
- StDev
- Sum
- Var

Sample:

City	InvoicePaid1	InvoicePaid2	InvoicePaid3
City1	Sum(InvoiceAmt)		
City2			
City3			
City4			

Cancel   < Back   Next >   Finish

CREATING A CROSSTAB QUERY

These column values represent all the unique City field values.

Each column value represents the sum of all invoices (paid and unpaid) for the designated city.

Each column value represents the sum of all paid invoices for the designated city.

Each column value represents the sum of all unpaid invoices for the designated city.

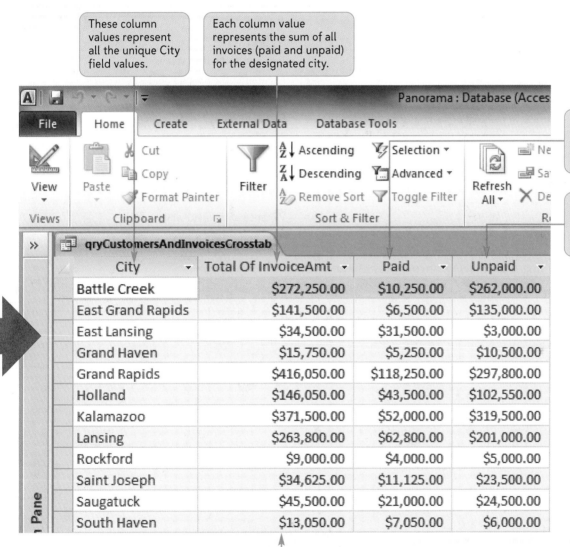

qryCustomersAndInvoicesCrosstab

City	Total Of InvoiceAmt	Paid	Unpaid
Battle Creek	$272,250.00	$10,250.00	$262,000.00
East Grand Rapids	$141,500.00	$6,500.00	$135,000.00
East Lansing	$34,500.00	$31,500.00	$3,000.00
Grand Haven	$15,750.00	$5,250.00	$10,500.00
Grand Rapids	$416,050.00	$118,250.00	$297,800.00
Holland	$146,050.00	$43,500.00	$102,550.00
Kalamazoo	$371,500.00	$52,000.00	$319,500.00
Lansing	$263,800.00	$62,800.00	$201,000.00
Rockford	$9,000.00	$4,000.00	$5,000.00
Saint Joseph	$34,625.00	$11,125.00	$23,500.00
Saugatuck	$45,500.00	$21,000.00	$24,500.00
South Haven	$13,050.00	$7,050.00	$6,000.00

A **crosstab query** performs aggregate function calculations on the values of one database field and displays the results in a spreadsheet format.

Creating a Crosstab Query

Oren wants to analyze his company's invoices by city, so he can view the paid and unpaid contract amounts for all customers located in each city. Crosstab queries use the aggregate functions shown in Figure 5-17 to perform arithmetic operations on selected records. A crosstab query can also display one additional aggregate function value that summarizes the set of values in each row. The crosstab query uses one or more fields for the row headings on the left and one field for the column headings at the top.

Figure 5-17	Aggregate functions used in crosstab queries

Aggregate Function	Definition
Avg	Average of the field values
Count	Number of the nonnull field values
First	First field value
Last	Last field value
Max	Highest field value
Min	Lowest field value
StDev	Standard deviation of the field values
Sum	Total of the field values
Var	Variance of the field values

Figure 5-18 shows two query recordsets—the recordset below (qryCustomersAndInvoices) is from a select query and the recordset on the next page (qryCustomersAndInvoicesCrosstab) is from a crosstab query based on the select query.

Figure 5-18	Comparing a select query to a crosstab query

qryCustomersAndInvoices

Customer ID	Company	First Name	Last Name	City	Invoice Amt	Invoice Paid
11001		Sabrina	Fernandez	Rockford	$1,500.00	✓
11001		Sabrina	Fernandez	Rockford	$2,500.00	✓
11027		Karen	O'Brien	Lansing	$300.00	✓
11005		Derek	Schwimmer	Holland	$1,500.00	✓
11012	Grand Rapids Engineering Dept	Anthony	Rodriguez	Grand Rapids	$2,250.00	✓
11055	Fox and Hound Grille	Steve	Gorski	Battle Creek	$1,500.00	✓
11055	Fox and Hound Grille	Steve	Gorski	Battle Creek	$2,000.00	✓
11055	Fox and Hound Grille	Steve	Gorski	Battle Creek	$2,000.00	✓
11055	Fox and Hound Grille	Steve	Gorski	Battle Creek	$1,000.00	✓
11040	RiverView Development Company	Susan	Darcy	Grand Rapids	$4,500.00	✓
11040	RiverView Development Company	Susan	Darcy	Grand Rapids	$3,000.00	✓
11040	RiverView Development Company	Susan	Darcy	Grand Rapids	$12,000.00	☐
11040	RiverView Development Company	Susan	Darcy	Grand Rapids	$8,500.00	☐
11043	Monroe State College	Rachel	Kirk	Grand Rapids	$4,500.00	✓
11043	Monroe State College	Rachel	Kirk	Grand Rapids	$12,000.00	✓
11043	Monroe State College	Rachel	Kirk	Grand Rapids	$5,500.00	✓
11070	Legacy Companies, LTD	Michael	Faraci	Grand Rapids	$9,000.00	✓
11070	Legacy Companies, LTD	Michael	Faraci	Grand Rapids	$20,000.00	✓
11070	Legacy Companies, LTD	Michael	Faraci	Grand Rapids	$10,000.00	☐
11083	Hopedale State College	John	Williams	East Lansing	$4,000.00	✓
11083	Hopedale State College	John	Williams	East Lansing	$8,000.00	✓
11083	Hopedale State College	John	Williams	East Lansing	$3,500.00	✓
11038	M. Grant Investment Company	Alex	Engber	Lansing	$35,000.00	✓
11038	M. Grant Investment Company	Alex	Engber	Lansing	$10,000.00	☐
11038	M. Grant Investment Company	Alex	Engber	Lansing	$70,000.00	☐

individual Lansing records

Lansing records with paid invoices

Lansing records with unpaid invoices

| Figure 5-18 | Comparing a select query to a crosstab query (continued) |

qryCustomersAndInvoicesCrosstab

paid invoices

unpaid invoices

one row for Lansing invoice amounts

City	Total Of InvoiceAmt	Paid	Unpaid
Battle Creek	$272,250.00	$10,250.00	$262,000.00
East Grand Rapids	$141,500.00	$6,500.00	$135,000.00
East Lansing	$34,500.00	$31,500.00	$3,000.00
Grand Haven	$15,750.00	$5,250.00	$10,500.00
Grand Rapids	$416,050.00	$118,250.00	$297,800.00
Holland	$146,050.00	$43,500.00	$102,550.00
Kalamazoo	$371,500.00	$52,000.00	$319,500.00
Lansing	$263,800.00	$62,800.00	$201,000.00
Rockford	$9,000.00	$4,000.00	$5,000.00
Saint Joseph	$34,625.00	$11,125.00	$23,500.00
Saugatuck	$45,500.00	$21,000.00	$24,500.00
South Haven	$13,050.00	$7,050.00	$6,000.00

The qryCustomersAndInvoices query, a select query, joins the tblCustomer, tblContract, and tblInvoice tables to display selected data from those tables for all invoices. The qryCustomersAndInvoicesCrosstab query, a crosstab query, uses the qryCustomersAndInvoices query as its source query and displays one row for each unique City field value. The City column in the crosstab query identifies each row. The crosstab query uses the Sum aggregate function on the InvoiceAmt field to produce the displayed values in the Paid and Unpaid columns for each City row. An entry in the Total Of InvoiceAmt column represents the sum of the Paid and Unpaid values for the City field value in that row.

PROSKILLS

Decision Making: Using Both Select Queries and Crosstab Queries

Companies use both select queries and crosstab queries in their decision making. A select query displays several records—one for each row selected by the select query—while a crosstab query displays only one summarized record for each unique field value. When management wants to analyze data at a high level to see the big picture, it might start with a crosstab query, identify which field values to analyze futher, and then look in detail at specific field values using select queries. Both select and crosstab queries serve as valuable tools in tracking and analyzing a company's business, and companies use both types of queries in the appropriate situations. By understanding how managers and other employees use the information in a database to make decisions, you can create the correct type of query to provide the information they need.

TIP

Microsoft Access Help provides more information on creating a crosstab query without using a wizard.

The quickest way to create a crosstab query is to use the **Crosstab Query Wizard**, which guides you through the steps for creating one. You could also change a select query to a crosstab query in Design view using the Crosstab button in the Query Type group on the Design tab.

Using the Crosstab Query Wizard

- In the Queries group on the Create tab, click the Query Wizard button.
- In the New Query dialog box, click Crosstab Query Wizard, and then click the OK button.
- Complete the Wizard dialog boxes to select the table or query on which to base the crosstab query, select the row heading field (or fields), select the column heading field, select the calculation field and its aggregate function, and enter a name for the crosstab query.

The crosstab query you will create, which is similar to the one shown in Figure 5-18, has the following characteristics:

- The qryCustomersAndInvoices query in the Panorama database is the basis for the new crosstab query. The base query includes the CustomerID, Company, FirstName, LastName, City, InvoiceAmt, and InvoicePaid fields.
- The City field is the leftmost column in the crosstab query and identifies each crosstab query row.
- The values from the InvoicePaid field, which is a Yes/No field, identify the rightmost columns of the crosstab query.
- The crosstab query applies the Sum aggregate function to the InvoiceAmt field values and displays the resulting total values in the Paid and Unpaid columns of the query results.
- The grand total of the InvoiceAmt field values appears for each row in a column with the heading Total Of InvoiceAmt.

Next you will create the crosstab query based on the qryCustomersAndInvoices query.

To start the Crosstab Query Wizard:

1. If you took a break after the previous session, make sure that the Panorama database is open and the Navigation Pane is closed.

   Trouble? If the Security Warning is displayed below the Ribbon, click the Enable Content button next to the Security Warning.

2. Click the **Create** tab on the Ribbon and then, in the Queries group on the Create tab, click the **Query Wizard** button. The New Query dialog box opens.

3. Click **Crosstab Query Wizard**, and then click the **OK** button. The first Crosstab Query Wizard dialog box opens.

You'll now use the Crosstab Query Wizard to create the crosstab query for Oren.

To finish the Crosstab Query Wizard:

1. Click the **Queries** option button in the View section to display the list of queries in the Panorama database, and then click **Query: qryCustomersAndInvoices**. See Figure 5-19.

Figure 5-19   **Choosing the query for the crosstab query**

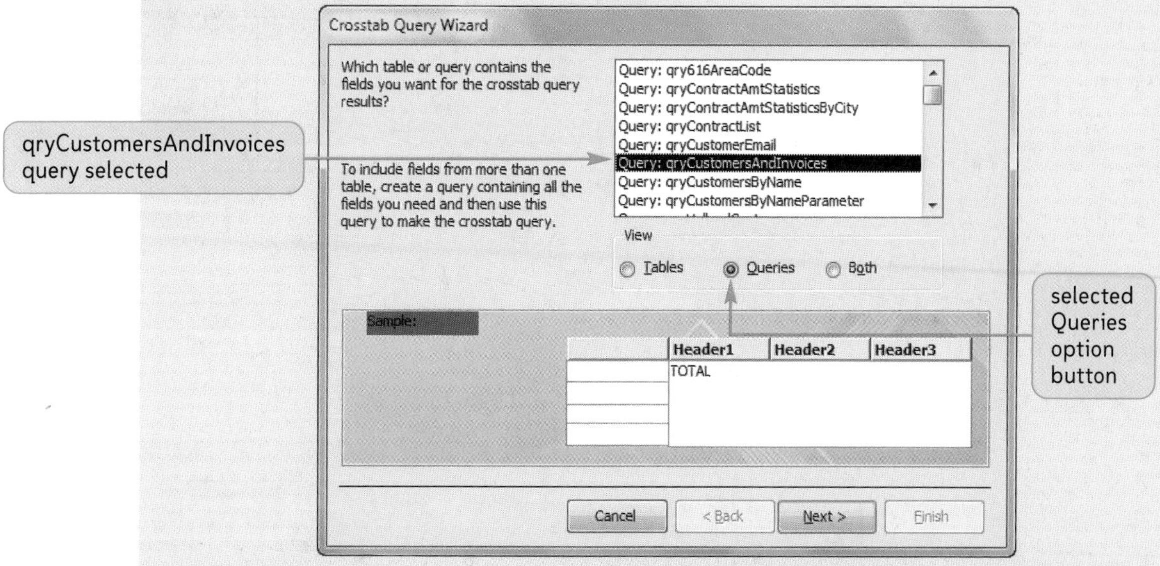

qryCustomersAndInvoices query selected

selected Queries option button

2. Click the **Next** button to open the next Crosstab Query Wizard dialog box, in which you choose the field (or fields) for the row headings. Because Oren wants the crosstab query to display one row for each unique City field value, you will select that field for the row headings.

TIP

When you select a field, Access changes the sample crosstab query in the dialog box to illustrate your choice.

---

3. In the Available Fields box, click **City**, and then click the > button to move the City field to the Selected Fields box.

4. Click the **Next** button to open the next Crosstab Query Wizard dialog box, in which you select the field values that will serve as column headings. Oren wants to see the paid and unpaid total invoice amounts, so you need to select the InvoicePaid field for the column headings.

5. Click **InvoicePaid** in the box, and then click the **Next** button.

In the next Crosstab Query Wizard dialog box, you choose the field that will be calculated for each row and column intersection and the function to use for the calculation. The results of the calculation will appear in the row and column inter-sections in the query results. Oren needs to calculate the sum of the InvoiceAmt field value for each row and column intersection.

6. Click **InvoiceAmt** in the Fields box, click **Sum** in the Functions box, and then make sure that the **Yes, include row sums** check box is checked. The "Yes, include row sums" option creates a column showing the overall totals for the values in each row of the query recordset. See Figure 5-20.

Figure 5-20 Completed crosstab query design

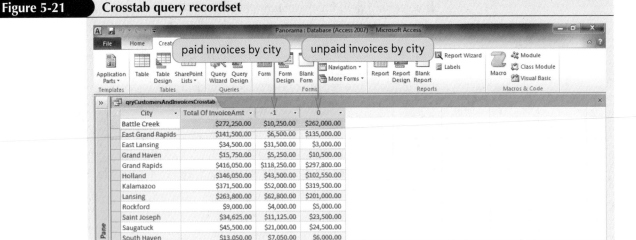

7. Click the **Next** button to open the final Crosstab Query Wizard dialog box, in which you choose the query name.

8. Click in the box, delete the underscore character so that the query name is qryCustomersAndInvoicesCrosstab, be sure the option button for viewing the query is selected, and then click the **Finish** button. Access saves the crosstab query, and then displays the query recordset.

9. Resize all the columns in the query recordset to their best fit, and then click the City field value in the first row (**Battle Creek**). See Figure 5-21.

Figure 5-21 Crosstab query recordset

City	Total Of InvoiceAmt	-1	0
Battle Creek	$272,250.00	$10,250.00	$262,000.00
East Grand Rapids	$141,500.00	$6,500.00	$135,000.00
East Lansing	$34,500.00	$31,500.00	$3,000.00
Grand Haven	$15,750.00	$5,250.00	$10,500.00
Grand Rapids	$416,050.00	$118,250.00	$297,800.00
Holland	$146,050.00	$43,500.00	$102,550.00
Kalamazoo	$371,500.00	$52,000.00	$319,500.00
Lansing	$263,800.00	$62,800.00	$201,000.00
Rockford	$9,000.00	$4,000.00	$5,000.00
Saint Joseph	$34,625.00	$11,125.00	$23,500.00
Saugatuck	$45,500.00	$21,000.00	$24,500.00
South Haven	$13,050.00	$7,050.00	$6,000.00

The query recordset contains one row for each City field value. The Total Of InvoiceAmt column shows the total invoice amount for the customers in each city. The columns labeled -1 and 0 show the total paid (-1 column) and unpaid (0 column) invoice amounts for customers in each city. Because the InvoicePaid field is a Yes/No field, by default, Access displays field values in datasheets, forms, and reports in a check box (either checked or unchecked), but stores a checked value in the database as a -1 and an unchecked value as a 0. Instead of displaying check boxes, the crosstab query displays the stored values as column headings.

Oren wants you to change the column headings of -1 to Paid and of 0 to Unpaid. You'll use the IIf function to change the column headings, using the expression *IIf (InvoicePaid,"Paid","Unpaid")*—if the InvoicePaid field value is true (because it's a Yes/No field or a True/False field), or is checked, use Paid as the column heading; otherwise, use Unpaid as the column heading. Because the InvoicePaid field is a Yes/No field, the condition *InvoicePaid* is the same as the condition *InvoicePaid = -1*, which uses a comparison operator and a value. For all data types except Yes/No fields, you must use a comparison operator in a condition.

To change the crosstab query column headings:

▶ **1.** Click the **Home** tab on the Ribbon, and then switch to Design view. The design grid has four entries. See Figure 5-22.

Figure 5-22   Crosstab query in the design grid

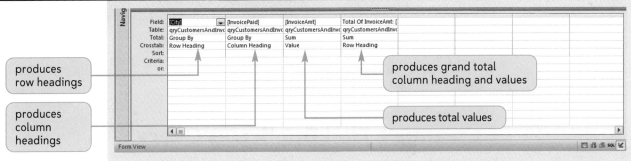

produces row headings

produces column headings

produces grand total column heading and values

produces total values

From left to right, the [City] entry produces the row headings, the [InvoicePaid] entry produces the column headings, the [InvoiceAmt] entry produces the totals in each row/column intersection, and the Total Of InvoiceAmt entry produces the row total column heading and total values. The field names are enclosed in brackets; the Total Of InvoiceAmt entry is the name of this calculated field, which displays the sum of the InvoiceAmt field values for each row.

You need to replace the Field box value in the second column with the IIf function expression to change the -1 and zero column headings to Paid and Unpaid. You can type the expression in the box, use Expression Builder to create the expression, or type the expression in the Zoom dialog box. You'll use the last method.

▶ **2.** Click the **InvoicePaid Field** box, and then open the Zoom dialog box.

▶ **3.** Delete the expression, and then type **IIf (InvoicePaid,"Paid","Unpaid")** in the Zoom dialog box. See Figure 5-23.

Figure 5-23   IIf function for the crosstab query column headings

▶ **4.** Click the **OK** button, and then save and run the query. Access displays the completed crosstab query with Paid and Unpaid as the last two column headings.

▶ **5.** Close the query, and then open the Navigation Pane.

TIP

Point to an object in the Navigation Pane to display the full object name in a ScreenTip.

In the Navigation Pane, Access uses unique icons to represent different types of queries. The crosstab query icon appears in the Queries list to the left of the qryCustomersAndInvoicesCrosstab query. This icon 🔳 looks different from the icon 🔲 that appears to the left of the other queries, which are all select queries.

INSIGHT

Using Special Database Features Cautiously

When you create a query in Design view or with a wizard, Access automatically constructs an equivalent SQL statement and saves only the SQL statement version of the query. **SQL (Structured Query Language)** is a standard language used in querying, updating, and managing relational databases. If you learn SQL for one relational DBMS, it's a relatively easy task to begin using SQL for other relational DBMSs. However, differences exist between DBMSs in their versions of SQL, somewhat like having different dialects in English, and in what additions they make to SQL. The SQL statement equivalent that Access creates for a crosstab query is one such SQL-language addition. If you need to convert an Access database to SQL-Server, Oracle, or another DBMS, crosstab queries created in Access will not work in these other DBMSs. You'd have to construct a set of SQL statements in the other DBMS to replace the SQL statement automatically created by Access. Constructing this replacement set of statements is a highly technical process that only an experienced programmer can complete, so you should use special features of a DBMS judiciously.

Next, Oren wants to identify any contracts that have the same start dates as other contracts because these are the ones that might have potential scheduling difficulties. To find the information Oren needs, you'll create a find duplicates query.

Creating a Find Duplicates Query

A **find duplicates query** is a select query that finds duplicate records in a table or query. You can create this type of query using the **Find Duplicates Query Wizard**. A find duplicates query searches for duplicate values based on the fields you select as you answer the Wizard's questions. For example, you might want to display all employers that have the same name, all students who have the same phone number, or all products that have the same description. Using this type of query, you can locate duplicates to avert potential problems (for example, you might have inadvertently assigned two different numbers to the same product), or you can eliminate duplicates that cost money (for example, you could send just one advertising brochure to all customers having the same address).

REFERENCE

Using the Find Duplicates Query Wizard

- In the Queries group on the Create tab, click the Query Wizard button.
- Click Find Duplicates Query Wizard, and then click the OK button.
- Complete the Wizard dialog boxes to select the table or query on which to base the query, select the field (or fields) to check for duplicate values, select the additional fields to include in the query results, enter a name for the query, and then click the Finish button.

You'll use the Find Duplicates Query Wizard to create and run a new query to display duplicate start dates in the tblContract table.

To create the query using the Find Duplicates Query Wizard:

▶ **1.** Close the Navigation Pane, click the **Create** tab on the Ribbon and then, in the Queries group, click the **Query Wizard** button to open the New Query dialog box.

2. Click **Find Duplicates Query Wizard**, and then click the **OK** button. The first Find Duplicates Query Wizard dialog box opens. In this dialog box, you select the table or query on which to base the new query. You'll use the tblContract table.

3. Click **Table: tblContract** (if necessary), and then click the **Next** button. Access opens the next Find Duplicates Query Wizard dialog box, in which you choose the fields you want to check for duplicate values.

4. In the Available fields box, click **StartDate**, click the [>] button to select the StartDate field as the field to check for duplicate values, and then click the **Next** button. In the next Find Duplicates Query Wizard dialog box, you select the additional fields you want displayed in the query results.

   Oren wants all remaining fields to be included in the query results.

5. Click the [>>] button to move all fields from the Available fields box to the Additional query fields box, and then click the **Next** button. Access opens the final Find Duplicates Query Wizard dialog box, in which you enter a name for the query. You'll use qryDuplicateContractStartDates as the query name.

6. Type **qryDuplicateContractStartDates** in the box, be sure the option button for viewing the results is selected, and then click the **Finish** button. Access saves the query, and then displays the 10 records for contracts with duplicate start dates. See Figure 5-24.

Figure 5-24	Query recordset for contracts with the same start dates

qryDuplicateContractStartDates

Start Date	Contract Num	Customer ID	Contract Amt	Signing Date	Contract Type
07/12/2013	3025	11083	$15,500	03/25/2013	Landscape renovation for plaza
07/12/2013	3023	11070	$39,000	03/22/2013	Renovation of large multifamily housing open space
08/17/2013	3033	11005	$2,250	07/08/2013	Residential landscape plan for front yard
08/17/2013	3021	11040	$28,000	05/03/2013	Landscape plans for multifamily housing site
03/17/2014	3068	11049	$4,500	02/07/2014	Front walk and drive design, residential
03/17/2014	3045	11064	$25,000	08/20/2013	Open space corridor planning at new transit station
06/28/2014	3077	11058	$6,500	05/17/2014	Schematic landscape design for senior center
06/28/2014	3072	11059	$46,000	03/11/2014	Landscape design for affordable housing site
10/06/2014	3105	11084	$5,000	08/24/2014	Residential landscape plan
10/06/2014	3100	11031	$10,500	08/08/2014	Schematic landscape design for daycare center

7. Close the query.

Oren now asks you to find the records for customers with no contracts. These are customers that had contracts in the past, but have chosen not to sign a contract with Belmont Landscapes in the past year. Oren wants to contact these customers to see if there are any services that the company might be able to furnish. To provide Oren with this information, you need to create a find unmatched query.

Creating a Find Unmatched Query

A **find unmatched query** is a select query that finds all records in a table or query that have no related records in a second table or query. For example, you could display all customers that have not signed recent contracts or all students who are not currently enrolled in classes. Such a query provides information for Oren to solicit business from the inactive customers and for a school administrator to contact the students to find out their future educational plans. You can use the **Find Unmatched Query Wizard** to create this type of query.

Using the Find Unmatched Query Wizard

- In the Queries group on the Create tab, click the Query Wizard button.
- Click Find Unmatched Query Wizard, and then click the OK button.
- Complete the Wizard dialog boxes to select the table or query on which to base the new query, select the table or query that contains the related records, specify the common field in each table or query, select the additional fields to include in the query results, enter a name for the query, and then click the Finish button.

Oren wants to know which customers have no open contracts. These customers are inactive, and he will contact them to determine their interest in doing further business with Belmont Landscapes. To create a list of inactive customers, you'll use the Find Unmatched Query Wizard to display only those records from the tblCustomer table with no matching CustomerID field value in the related tblContract table.

To create the query using the Find Unmatched Query Wizard:

1. In the Queries group on the Create tab, click the **Query Wizard** button to open the New Query dialog box.

2. Click **Find Unmatched Query Wizard**, and then click the **OK** button. The first Find Unmatched Query Wizard dialog box opens. In this dialog box, you select the table or query on which to base the new query. You'll use the qryCustomersByName query.

3. Click the **Queries** option button in the View section to display the list of queries, click **Query: qryCustomersByName** in the box to select this query, and then click the **Next** button to open the next Find Unmatched Query Wizard dialog box, in which you choose the table that contains the related records. You'll select the tblContract table.

4. Click **Table: tblContract** in the box (if necessary), and then click the **Next** button to open the next dialog box, in which you choose the common field for both tables. See Figure 5-25.

Figure 5-25 ▶ **Selecting the common field**

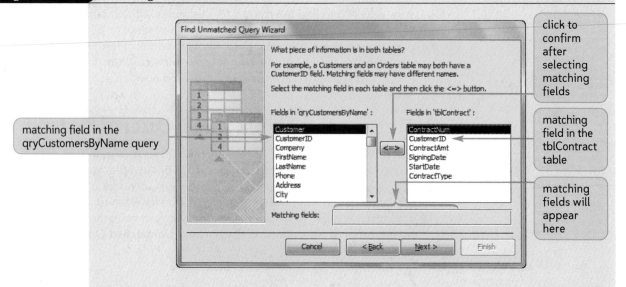

The common field between the query and the table is the CustomerID field. You need to click the common field in each box, and then click the symbol between the two boxes to join the two objects. The Matching fields box then will display CustomerID <=> CustomerID to indicate the joining of the two matching fields. If the two selected objects already have a one-to-many relationship defined in the Relationships window, the Matching fields box will join the correct fields automatically.

Be sure you click the CustomerID field in both boxes.

▶ **5.** Click **CustomerID** in the Fields in 'qryCustomersByName' box, click **CustomerID** in the Fields in 'tblContract' box, click the <=> button to connect the two selected fields, and then click the **Next** button to open the next Find Unmatched Query Wizard dialog box, in which you choose the fields you want to see in the query recordset. Oren wants the query recordset to display all available fields.

▶ **6.** Click the >> button to move all fields from the Available fields box to the Selected fields box, and then click the **Next** button to open the final dialog box, in which you enter the query name.

▶ **7.** Type **qryInactiveCustomers**, be sure the option button for viewing the results is selected, and then click the **Finish** button. Access saves the query and then displays two records in the query recordset. See Figure 5-26.

| Figure 5-26 | Query recordset displaying two customers without contracts |

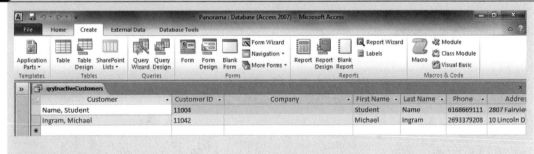

▶ **8.** Close the query.

Next, Oren wants Taylor to contact those customers who have the highest contract amounts to make sure that Belmont Landscapes is providing satisfactory service. To display the information Taylor needs, you will create a top values query.

Creating a Top Values Query

Whenever a query displays a large group of records, you might want to limit the number to a more manageable size by displaying, for example, just the first 10 records. The **Top Values property** for a query lets you limit the number of records in the query results. For the Top Values property, you can click one of the preset values from a list, or enter either an integer (such as 15, to display the first 15 records) or a percentage (such as 20%, to display the first fifth of the records), to find a specific number of records.

Suppose you have a select query that displays 45 records. If you want the query recordset to show only the first five records, you can change the query by entering a Top Values property value of either 5 or 10%. If the query contains a sort and the last record that Access can display is one of two or more records with the same value for the primary sort field, Access displays all records with that matching key value.

Taylor wants to view the same data that appears in the qryLargeContractAmounts query for customers with the highest 25% contract amounts. Based on the number or percentage you enter, a top values query selects that number or percentage of records starting from the top of the recordset. Thus, you usually include a sort in a top values query to display the records with the highest or lowest values for the sorted field. You will modify the query and then use the Top Values property to produce this information for Taylor.

To set the Top Values property for the query:

▶ **1.** Open the Navigation Pane, open the **qryLargeContractAmounts** in Datasheet view, and then close the Navigation Pane. Access displays 22 records, all with ContractAmt field values greater than $25,000, sorted in descending order by the ContractAmt field.

▶ **2.** Switch to Design view.

▶ **3.** In the Query Setup group on the Design tab, click the **Return** arrow (with the ScreenTip "Top Values"), and then click **25%**. See Figure 5-27.

Figure 5-27	Creating the top values query

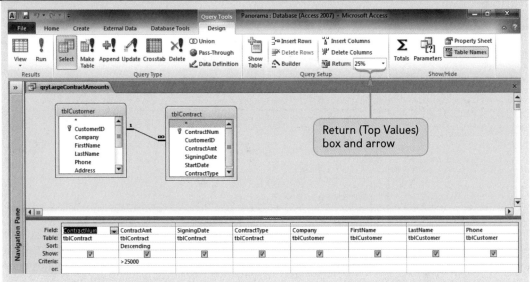

If the number or percentage of records you want to select, such as 15 or 20%, doesn't appear in the Top Values list, you can type the number or percentage in the Return box.

▶ **4.** Run the query. Access displays six records in the query recordset; these records represent the customers with the highest 25% contract amounts (25% of the original 22 records). See Figure 5-28.

| Figure 5-28 | Top values query recordset |

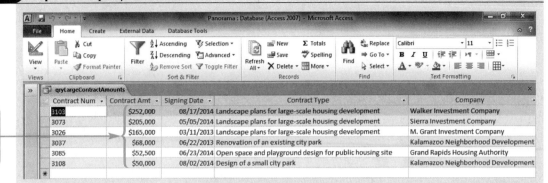

top 25% of the records selected in descending order by the ContractAmt field

Because Taylor won't need to run this query again, you won't save it.

5. Close the query without saving it.

6. If you are not continuing on to the next session, close the Panorama database, and then click the **Yes** button if necessary to empty the Clipboard.

Oren and Taylor will use the information provided by the queries you created to analyze the business and to contact customers. In the next session, you will enhance the tblCustomer and tblContract tables.

Session 5.2 Quick Check

REVIEW

1. What is the purpose of a crosstab query?
2. What are the four query wizards you can use to create a new query?
3. What is a find duplicates query?
4. What does a find unmatched query do?
5. What happens when you set a query's Top Values property?
6. What happens if you set a query's Top Values property to 2 and the first five records have the same value for the primary sort field?

SESSION 5.3 VISUAL OVERVIEW

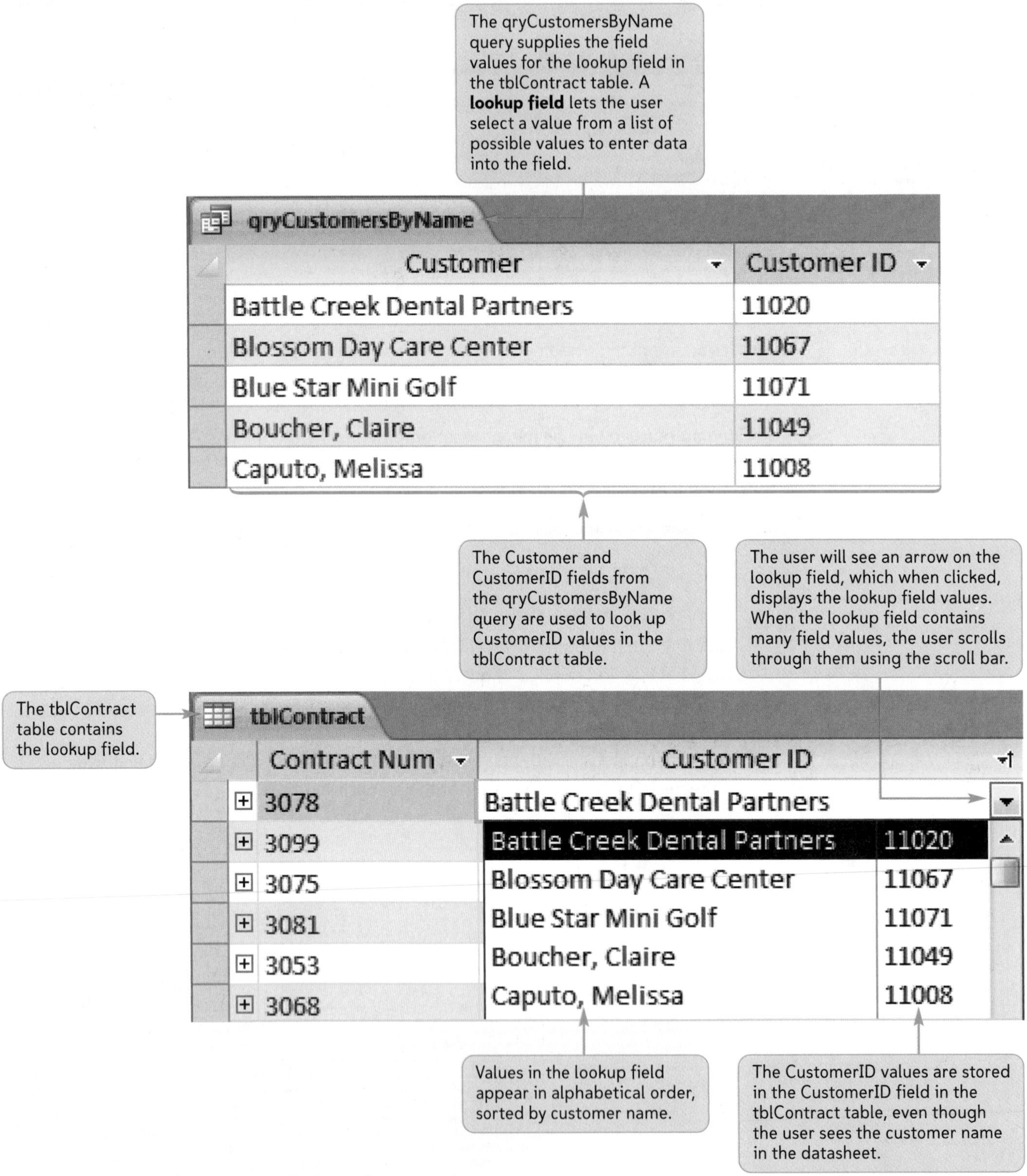

The qryCustomersByName query supplies the field values for the lookup field in the tblContract table. A **lookup field** lets the user select a value from a list of possible values to enter data into the field.

qryCustomersByName

Customer	Customer ID
Battle Creek Dental Partners	11020
Blossom Day Care Center	11067
Blue Star Mini Golf	11071
Boucher, Claire	11049
Caputo, Melissa	11008

The Customer and CustomerID fields from the qryCustomersByName query are used to look up CustomerID values in the tblContract table.

The user will see an arrow on the lookup field, which when clicked, displays the lookup field values. When the lookup field contains many field values, the user scrolls through them using the scroll bar.

The tblContract table contains the lookup field.

tblContract

Contract Num	Customer ID	
⊞ 3078	Battle Creek Dental Partners	▾
⊞ 3099	Battle Creek Dental Partners	11020
⊞ 3075	Blossom Day Care Center	11067
⊞ 3081	Blue Star Mini Golf	11071
⊞ 3053	Boucher, Claire	11049
⊞ 3068	Caputo, Melissa	11008

Values in the lookup field appear in alphabetical order, sorted by customer name.

The CustomerID values are stored in the CustomerID field in the tblContract table, even though the user sees the customer name in the datasheet.

LOOKUP FIELDS AND INPUT MASKS

The tblCustomer table contains the field that displays values with an input mask. An **input mask** is a predefined format that is used to enter and display data in a field. For example, the input mask displays a value entered as 9876543210 as 987-654-3210. The hyphens in the field value, called **literal display characters**, will not be stored in the database.

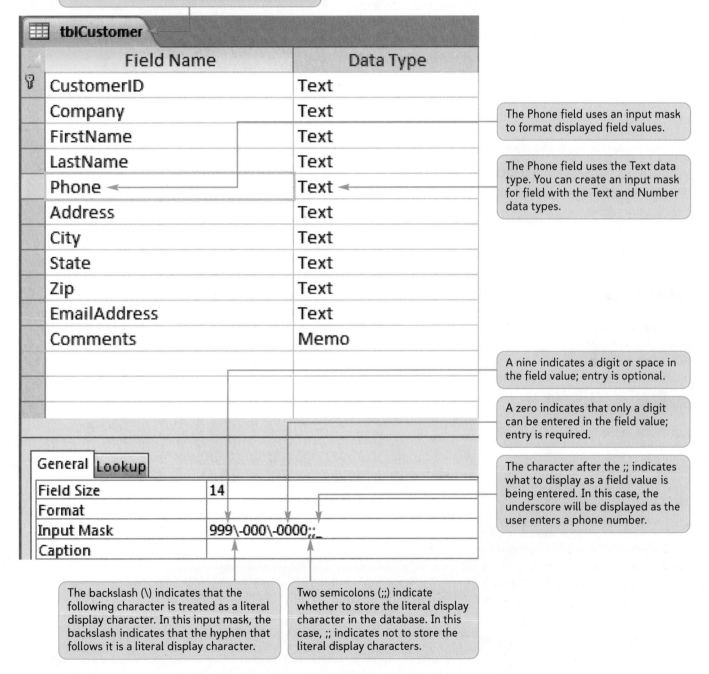

The Phone field uses an input mask to format displayed field values.

The Phone field uses the Text data type. You can create an input mask for field with the Text and Number data types.

tblCustomer

Field Name	Data Type
CustomerID	Text
Company	Text
FirstName	Text
LastName	Text
Phone	Text
Address	Text
City	Text
State	Text
Zip	Text
EmailAddress	Text
Comments	Memo

A nine indicates a digit or space in the field value; entry is optional.

A zero indicates that only a digit can be entered in the field value; entry is required.

The character after the ;; indicates what to display as a field value is being entered. In this case, the underscore will be displayed as the user enters a phone number.

General | Lookup

Field Size	14
Format	
Input Mask	999\-000\-0000;;_
Caption	

The backslash (\) indicates that the following character is treated as a literal display character. In this input mask, the backslash indicates that the hyphen that follows it is a literal display character.

Two semicolons (;;) indicate whether to store the literal display character in the database. In this case, ;; indicates not to store the literal display characters.

Creating a Lookup Field

The tblContract table in the Panorama database contains information about the contracts Belmont Landscapes has signed with its customers. Sarah wants to make entering data in the table easier for her staff. In particular, data entry is easier if they do not need to remember the correct CustomerID field values for each customer. Because the tblCustomer and tblContract tables have a one-to-many relationship, Sarah asks you to change the tblContract table's CustomerID field, which is a foreign key to the tblCustomer table, to a lookup field. As noted earlier, a lookup field lets the user select a value from a list of possible values. For the CustomerID field, the user will be able to select a customer's ID number from the list of customer names in the qryCustomersByName query rather than having to remember the correct CustomerID field value. Access will store the CustomerID in the tblContract table, but both the customer name and the CustomerID field value will appear in Datasheet view when entering or changing a CustomerID field value. This arrangement makes entering and changing CustomerID field values easier for the user and guarantees that the CustomerID field value is valid. You use a **Lookup Wizard field** in Access to create a lookup field in a table.

Sarah asks you to change the CustomerID field in the tblContract table to a lookup field. You begin by opening the tblContract table in Design view.

To change the CustomerID field to a lookup field:

▶ 1. If you took a break after the previous session, make sure that the Panorama database is open.

   Trouble? If the Security Warning is displayed below the Ribbon, click the Enable Content button next to the Security Warning.

▶ 2. If necessary, open the Navigation Pane, and then open the **tblContract** table in Design view.

▶ 3. Click the right side of the **Data Type** box for the CustomerID field to display the list of data types, and then click **Lookup Wizard**. A message box appears, warning you to delete the relationship between the tblCustomer and tblContract tables if you want to make the CustomerID field a lookup field. See Figure 5-29.

Figure 5-29 | **Warning message for an existing table relationship**

Access will use the lookup field to form the one-to-many relationship between the tblCustomer and tblContract tables, so you don't need the relationship you previously defined between the two tables.

▶ 4. Click the **OK** button, close the tblContract table, and then click the **No** button when asked if you want to save the table design changes.

▶ 5. Click the **Database Tools** tab on the Ribbon, and then in the Relationships group on the Database Tools tab, click the **Relationships** button to open the Relationships window.

▶ 6. Right-click the join line between the tblCustomer and tblContract tables, click **Delete**, and then click the **Yes** button to confirm the deletion.

Trouble? If the Delete command does not appear on the shortcut menu, click a blank area in the Relationships window to close the shortcut menu, and then repeat Step 6.

▶ **7.** Close the Relationships window.

Now you can resume changing the CustomerID field to a lookup field.

To finish changing the CustomerID field to a lookup field:

▶ **1.** Open the **tblContract** table in Design view.

▶ **2.** Click the right side of the **Data Type** box for the CustomerID field, and then click **Lookup Wizard**. The first Lookup Wizard dialog box opens.

This dialog box lets you specify a list of allowed values for the CustomerID field in a record in the tblContract table. You can specify a table or query from which users select the value, or you can enter a new list of values. You want the CustomerID values to come from the qryCustomersByName query.

▶ **3.** Make sure the option for looking up the values in another table or query is selected, and then click the **Next** button to display the next Lookup Wizard dialog box.

▶ **4.** Click the **Queries** option button in the View section to display the list of queries, click **Query: qryCustomersByName**, and then click the **Next** button to display the next Lookup Wizard dialog box. See Figure 5-30.

Figure 5-30	Selecting the lookup fields

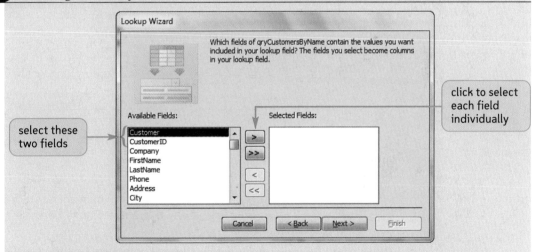

This dialog box lets you select the lookup fields from the qryCustomersByName query. You need to select the CustomerID field because it's the common field that links the query and the tblContract table. You also must select the Customer field because Sarah wants the user to be able to select from a list of customer names when entering a new contract record or changing an existing CustomerID field value.

▶ **5.** Click **Customer** (if necessary), click the ⟩ button to move the Customer field to the Selected Fields box, click **CustomerID** (if necessary), click the ⟩ button to move the CustomerID field to the Selected Fields box, and then click the

Next button to display the next Lookup Wizard dialog box. This dialog box lets you choose a sort order for the box entries. Sarah wants the entries to appear in ascending Customer order. Note that ascending is the default sort order.

▶ 6. Click the **1** arrow, click **Customer**, and then click the **Next** button to open the next dialog box.

In this dialog box, you can adjust the widths of the lookup columns. Note that when you resize a column to its best fit, Access resizes the column so that the widest column heading and the visible field values fit the column width. However, some field values that aren't visible in this dialog box might be wider than the column width, so you must scroll down the column to make sure you don't have to repeat the column resizing.

TIP

If you need to rearrange the columns in a lookup field, you can click a column heading and drag it to the left or right.

▶ 7. Click the **Customer** column selector, press and hold down the **Shift** key, click the **CustomerID** column selector to select both columns, release the **Shift** key, and then place the pointer on the right edge of the CustomerID field column heading. When the pointer changes to a ↔ shape, double-click to resize the columns to their best fit, and then scroll down the columns, and repeat the resizing as necessary. When you are finished, press **Ctrl + Home** to scroll back to the top of the Customer column. See Figure 5-31.

Figure 5-31	Adjusting the widths of the lookup columns

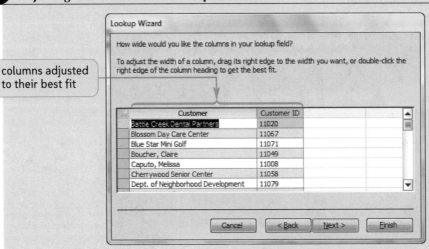

columns adjusted to their best fit

▶ 8. Click the **Next** button.

In the next dialog box, you select the field you want to store in the table. You'll store the CustomerID field in the tblContract table because it's the foreign key to the tblCustomer table.

▶ 9. Click **CustomerID** in the Available Fields box, and then click the **Next** button.

In the next dialog box, you specify the field name for the lookup field. Because you'll be storing the CustomerID field in the table, you'll accept the default field name, CustomerID.

▶ 10. Click the **Finish** button, and then save the table.

The Data Type value for the CustomerID field is still Text because this field contains text data. However, when you update the field, Access uses the CustomerID field value to look up and display in the tblContract table datasheet both the Customer and CustomerID field values from the qryCustomersByName query.

In reviewing contracts recently, Sarah noticed that the CustomerID field value stored in the tblContract table for contract number 3030 is incorrect. She asks you to test the new lookup field to select the correct field value. To do so, you need to switch to Datasheet view.

To change the CustomerID field value:

1. Switch to Datasheet view, and then resize the **CustomerID** column to its best fit.

   Notice that the Customer ID column displays Customer field values, even though the CustomerID field values are stored in the table.

2. For Contract Num 3030, click **Lily's Boutique** in the Customer ID column, and then click the **arrow** to display the list of Customer and CustomerID field values from the qryCustomersByName query. See Figure 5-32.

Figure 5-32   **List of Customer and CustomerID field values**

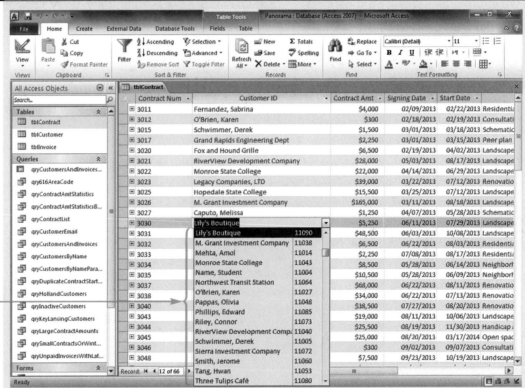

scrollable list of values for the lookup field

The customer for contract 3030 is Michael Ingram, so you need to select his entry in the list to change the CustomerID field value.

3. Scroll up the list, and then click **Ingram, Michael** to select that value to display in the datasheet and to store the CustomerID field value of 11042 in the table. The list closes and "Ingram, Michael" appears in the Customer ID column.

4. Save and close the tblContract table.

   Sarah wants you to make changes to the design of the tblCustomer table, so you'll open the table in preparation for the changes.

5. Open the **tblCustomer** table in Datasheet view, and then close the Navigation Pane.

Sarah asks you to change the appearance of the Phone field in the tblCustomer table to a standard telephone number format.

Using the Input Mask Wizard

The Phone field in the tblCustomer table is a 10-digit number that's difficult to read because it appears with none of the special formatting characters usually associated with a telephone number. For example, the Phone field value for Sabrina Fernandez, which appears as 6168663901, would be more readable in any of the following formats: 616-866-3901, 616.866.3901, 616/866-3901, or (616) 866-3901. Sarah asks you to use the (616) 866-3901 style for the Phone field.

Sarah wants the parentheses and hyphens to appear as literal display characters whenever users enter Phone field values. As noted earlier, a literal display character is a special character that automatically appears in specific positions of a field value; users don't need to type literal display characters. To include these characters, you need to create an input mask, a predefined format used to enter and display data in a field. An easy way to create an input mask is to use the **Input Mask Wizard**, an Access tool that guides you in creating a predefined format for a field. You must use the Input Mask Wizard in Design view.

To use the Input Mask Wizard for the Phone field:

▶ **1.** Switch to Design view, and then click the **Phone Field Name** box to make that row the current row and to display its Field Properties options.

▶ **2.** Click the **Input Mask** box in the Field Properties pane. A Build button ⌷⌷⌷ appears at the right edge of the Input Mask box.

▶ **3.** Click the **Build** button ⌷⌷⌷ in the Input Mask box. The first Input Mask Wizard dialog box opens. See Figure 5-33.

Figure 5-33	Input Mask Wizard dialog box

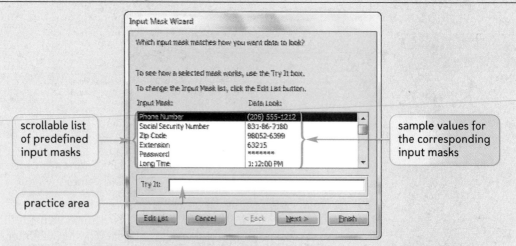

You can scroll the Input Mask box, select the input mask you want, and then enter representative values to practice using the input mask.

4. If necessary, click **Phone Number** in the Input Mask box to select it.

5. Click the far left side of the **Try It** box. (___) ____-_____ appears in the Try It box. As you type a phone number, Access replaces the underscores, which are placeholder characters.

> **Trouble?** If your insertion point is not immediately to the right of the left parenthesis, press the ← key until it is.

6. Type **9876543210** to practice entering a sample phone number. The input mask formats the typed value as (987) 654-3210.

7. Click the **Next** button. The next Input Mask Wizard dialog box opens. In it, you can change the input mask and placeholder character. Because you can change an input mask easily after the Input Mask Wizard finishes, you'll accept all wizard defaults.

8. Click the **Finish** button, and then click to the right of the value in the Input Mask box. The Input Mask Wizard creates the phone number input mask, placing it in the Input Mask box for the Phone field. See Figure 5-34.

Figure 5-34	Phone number input mask created by the Input Mask Wizard

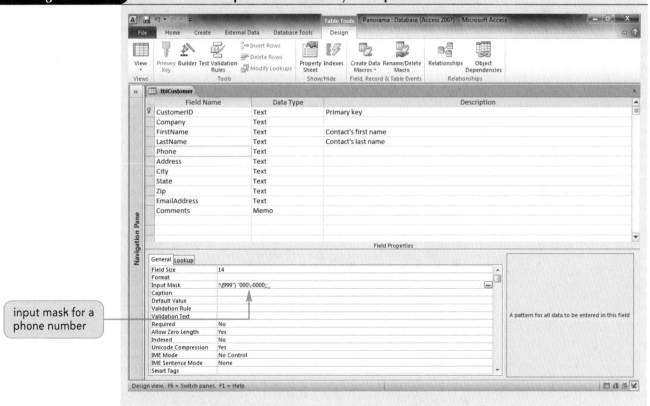

input mask for a phone number

The characters used in a field's input mask restrict the data you can enter in the field, as shown in Figure 5-35. Other characters, such as the left and right parentheses in the phone number input mask, that appear in an input mask are literal display characters.

| Figure 5-35 | Input mask characters |

Input Mask Character	Description
0	Digit only must be entered. Entry is required.
9	Digit or space can be entered. Entry is optional.
#	Digit, space, or a plus or minus sign can be entered. Entry is optional.
L	Letter only must be entered. Entry is required.
?	Letter only can be entered. Entry is optional.
A	Letter or digit must be entered. Entry is required.
a	Letter or digit can be entered. Entry is optional.
&	Any character or a space must be entered. Entry is required.
C	Any character or a space can be entered. Entry is optional.
>	All characters that follow are displayed in uppercase.
<	All characters that follow are displayed in lowercase.
"	Enclosed characters treated as literal display characters.
\	Following character treated as a literal display character. This is the same as enclosing a single character in quotation marks.
!	Input mask is displayed from right to left, rather than the default of left to right. Characters typed into the mask always fill in from left to right.
;;	The character between the first and second semicolon determines whether to store in the database the literal display characters. If left blank or a value of 1, do not store the literal display characters. If a value of 0, store the literal display characters. The character following the second semicolon is the placeholder character that will appear in the displayed input mask.

Sarah wants to view the Phone field with the default input mask.

To view and change the input mask for the Phone field:

1. Save the table, and then switch to Datasheet view. The Phone field values now have the format specified by the input mask.

Sarah decides that she would prefer to omit the parentheses around the area codes and use only hyphens as separators in the displayed Phone field values, so you'll change the input mask in Design view.

2. Switch to Design view.

The input mask is to !\(999") "000\-0000;;_. The backslash character (\) causes the character that follows it to appear as a literal display character. Characters enclosed in quotation marks also appear as literal display characters. (See Figure 5-35.)

If you omit the backslashes preceding the hyphens, Access will automatically insert them when you press the Tab key. However, Access doesn't add backslashes automatically for other literal display characters, such as periods and slashes, so it's best to always type the backslashes.

3. Change the input mask to **999\-000\-0000;;_** in the Input Mask box for the Phone field, and then press the **Tab** key.

Because you've modified a field property, the Property Update Options button appears to the left of the Input Mask property.

4. Click the **Property Update Options** button, and then click **Update Input Mask everywhere Phone is used**. The Update Properties dialog box opens. See Figure 5-36.

Figure 5-36	Update Properties dialog box

objects dependent on the Phone field

Because the frmCustomer and frmCustomerContracts forms display Phone field values from the tblCustomer table, Access will automatically change the Phone field's Input Mask property in these objects to your new input mask. This capability to update field properties in objects automatically when you modify a table field property is called **property propagation**. Although the Update Properties dialog box displays no queries, property propagation also does occur with queries automatically. Property propagation is limited to field properties such as the Decimal Places, Description, Format, and Input Mask properties.

5. Click the **Yes** button, save the table, switch to Datasheet view, and then resize the Phone column to its best fit. The Phone field values now have the format Sarah requested. See Figure 5-37.

Figure 5-37	After changing the Phone field input mask

Because Sarah wants her staff to store only standard 10-digit U.S. phone numbers for customers, the input mask you've created will enforce the standard entry and display format that Sarah desires.

Understanding When to Use Input Masks

An input mask is appropriate for a field only if all field values have a consistent format. For example, you can use an input mask with hyphens as literal display characters to store U.S. phone numbers in a consistent format of 987-654-3210. However, a multinational company would not be able to use an input mask to store phone numbers from all countries because international phone numbers do not have a consistent format. For another example, U.S. zip codes have a consistent format, and you could use an input mask of 00000#9999 to enter and display U.S. zip codes such as 98765 and 98765-4321, but you could not use an input mask if you need to store and display foreign postal codes in the same field. If you need to store and display phone numbers, zip/postal codes, and other fields in a variety of formats, it's best to define them as Text fields without an input mask so users can enter the correct literal display characters.

After the change to the Phone field's input mask, Access gave you the option to update, selectively and automatically, the Phone field's Input Mask property in other objects in the database. Sarah asks if there's an easy way to determine which objects are affected by changes made to other objects. To show Sarah how to determine the dependencies among objects in an Access database, you'll open the Object Dependencies pane.

Identifying Object Dependencies

An **object dependency** exists between two objects when a change to the properties of data in one object affects the properties of data in the other object. Dependencies between Access objects, such as tables, queries, and forms, can occur in various ways. For example, the tblContract and tblInvoice tables are dependent on each other because they have a one-to-many relationship. As another example, because the tblContract table uses the qryCustomersByName query to obtain the Customer field to display along with the CustomerID field, these two objects have a dependency. Any query, form, or other object that uses fields from the tblCustomer table is dependent on the tblCustomer table. Any form or report that uses fields from a query is directly dependent on the query and is indirectly dependent on the tables that provide the data to the query. Large databases contain hundreds of objects, so it is useful to have a way to easily view the dependencies among objects before you attempt to delete or modify an object. The **Object Dependencies pane** displays a collapsible list of the dependencies among the objects in an Access database; you click the list's expand indicators to show or hide different levels of dependencies. Next, you'll open the Object Dependencies pane to show Sarah the object dependencies in the Panorama database.

To open and use the Object Dependencies pane:

1. Click the **Database Tools** tab on the Ribbon, and then, in the Relationships group, click the **Object Dependencies** button to open the Object Dependencies pane, and then drag the left edge of the pane to the left until the horizontal scroll bar at the bottom of the pane disappears. See Figure 5-38.

Figure 5-38	After opening the Object Dependencies pane

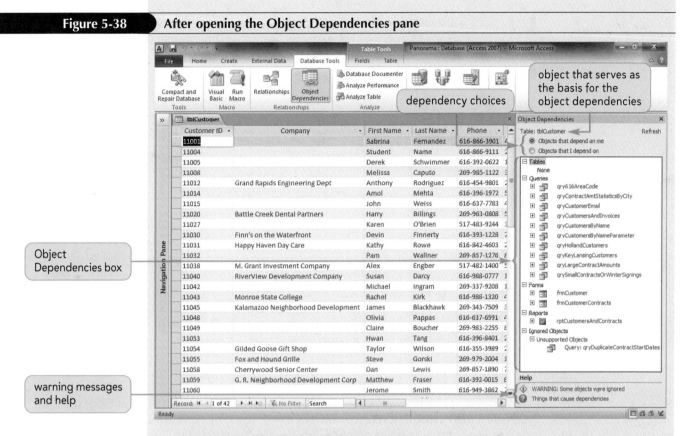

Object Dependencies box

warning messages and help

Trouble? If the "Objects that depend on me" option button is not selected, click the option button to select it.

The Object Dependencies pane displays the objects that depend on the tblCustomer table, the object name that appears at the top of the pane. If you change the design of the tblCustomer table, the change might affect objects in the pane. Changing a property for a field in the tblCustomer table that's also used by another listed object affects that other object. If the other object does not use the field you are changing, that other object is not affected.

Objects listed in the Ignored Objects portion of the box might, or might not, have an object dependency with the tblCustomer table, and you'd have to review them individually. The Help section at the bottom of the pane displays links for further information about object dependencies.

2. Click the **frmCustomer** link in the Object Dependencies pane. The frmCustomer form opens in Design view. All the fields in the form are fields from the tblCustomer table, which is why the form has an object dependency with the table.

3. Switch to Form view for the frmCustomer form. Note that the Phone field value displays using the input mask you applied to the field in the tblCustomer table. Access propagated this change from the table to the form.

4. Close the frmCustomer form, open the Navigation Pane, open the **tblContract** table in Datasheet view, and then click the **Refresh** link near the top of the Object Dependencies pane. The Object Dependencies box now displays the objects that depend on the tblContract table.

5. Click the **Objects that I depend on** option button near the top of the pane to view the objects that affect the tblContract table.

> **6.** Click the **expand indicator** ⊞ for the qryCustomersByName query in the Object Dependencies pane. The list expands to display the tblCustomer table, which is another table that the query depends upon.

> **7.** Close the tblContract table, close the Object Dependencies pane, and then save and close the tblCustomer table.

Sarah now better understands object dependencies and how to identify them by using the Object Dependencies pane.

Defining Data Validation Rules

Sarah wants to limit the entry of InvoiceAmt field values in the tblInvoice table to values greater than $10 because Belmont Landscapes does not invoice customers for balances of $10 or less. In addition, Sarah wants to make sure that a SigningDate field value entered in a tblContract table record is chronologically earlier than the StartDate field value in the same record. She's concerned that typing errors might produce incorrect query results and cause other problems. To provide these data-entry capabilities, you'll set field validation properties for the InvoiceAmt field in the tblInvoice table and set table validation properties in the tblContract table.

Defining Field Validation Rules

To prevent a user from entering an unacceptable value in the InvoiceAmt field, you can create a **field validation rule** that verifies a field value by comparing it to a constant or a set of constants. You create a field validation rule by setting the Validation Rule and the Validation Text field properties. The **Validation Rule property** value specifies the valid values that users can enter in a field. The **Validation Text property** value will be displayed in a dialog box if the user enters an invalid value (in this case, an InvoiceAmt field value of $10 or less). After you set these two InvoiceAmt field properties in the tblInvoice table, Access will prevent users from entering an invalid InvoiceAmt field value in the tblInvoice table and in all current and future queries and future forms that include the InvoiceAmt field.

You'll now set the Validation Rule and Validation Text properties for the InvoiceAmt field in the tblInvoice table.

To create and test a field validation rule for the InvoiceAmt field:

> **1.** Open the **tblInvoice** table in Design view, close the Navigation Pane, and then click the **InvoiceAmt Field Name** box to make that row the current row.

> To make sure that the only values entered in theInvoiceAmt field are greater than 10, you'll use the > comparison operator in the Validation Rule box.

> **2.** In the Field Properties pane, click the **Validation Rule** box, type **>10**, and then press the **Tab** key.

You can set the Validation Text property to a value that appears in a dialog box that opens if a user enters a value not listed in the Validation Rule box.

3. Type **Invoice amounts must be greater than 10** in the Validation Text box. See Figure 5-39.

Figure 5-39	Validation properties for the InvoiceAmt field

current field

validation properties

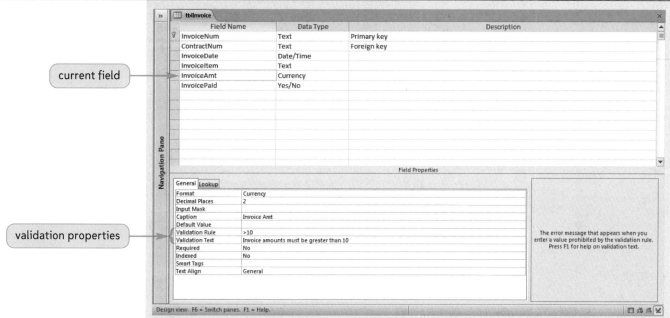

You can now save the table design changes and then test the validation properties.

4. Save the table, and then click the **Yes** button when asked if you want to test the existing InvoiceAmt field values in the tblInvoice table against the new validation rule.

Access tests the existing records in the tblInvoice table against the validation rule. If any record violates the rule, you are prompted to continue testing or to revert to the previous Validation Rule property setting. Next, you'll test the validation rule.

5. Switch to Datasheet view, select **$1,500.00** in the first row's InvoiceAmt field box, type **5**, and then press the **Tab** key. A dialog box opens containing the message "Invoice amounts must be greater than 10," which is the Validation Text property setting you created in Step 3.

6. Click the **OK** button, and then press the **Esc** key. The first row's InvoiceAmt field value again has its original value, $1,500.00.

7. Close the tblInvoice table.

Now that you've finished entering the field validation rule for the InvoiceAmt field in the tblInvoice table, you'll enter the table validation rule for the date fields in the tblContract table.

Defining Table Validation Rules

To make sure that a user enters a SigningDate field value in the tblContract table that is chronologically earlier than the record's StartDate field value, you can create a **table validation rule** that compares one field value in a table record to another field value in the same record to verify their relative accuracy. Once again, you'll use the Validation Rule and Validation Text properties, but this time you'll set these properties for the table instead of for an individual field.

To create and test a table validation rule in the tblContract table:

Be sure "Table Properties" is listed as the selection type in the property sheet.

1. Open the Navigation Pane, open the **tblContract** table in Design view, and then, in the Show/Hide group on the Design tab, click the **Property Sheet** button to open the property sheet for the table.

   To make sure that each SigningDate field value is chronologically earlier than, or less than, each StartDate field value, you'll compare the two field values in the Validation Rule box for the table.

Be sure brackets enclose each of the two field names.

2. In the property sheet, click the **Validation Rule** box, type **Si**, press the **Tab** key to select SigningDate in the AutoComplete box, type **<St**, press the **Tab** key to select StartDate in the AutoComplete box, and then press the **Tab** key.

   Trouble? If necessary, drag the left edge of the property sheet to the left until you can see the entire value in the Validation Rule box.

3. Type **The signing date must be earlier than the start date** in the Validation Text box. See Figure 5-40.

Figure 5-40 Setting table validation properties

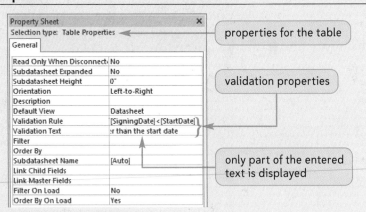

You can now test the validation properties.

4. Close the property sheet, save the table, and then click the **Yes** button when asked if you want to test the existing dates in the tblContract table against the new validation rule.

5. Close the Navigation Pane, switch to Datasheet view, click the Signing Date column value in the first record, click the **date picker** icon to the right of the date, click **27** in the calendar control to change the date to 2/27/2013, press the **Tab** key to advance to the Start Date column, and then press the **Tab** key two more times to complete your changes to the record. A dialog box opens containing the message "The signing date must be earlier than the start date," which is the Validation Text property setting you entered in Step 3.

Unlike field validation rule violations, which Access detects immediately after you finish a field entry and advance to another field, Access detects table validation rule violations when you finish all changes to the current record and advance to another record.

▶ **6.** Click the **OK** button, and then press the **Esc** key to undo your change to the Signing Date column value.

▶ **7.** Close the tblContract table.

Problem Solving: Perfecting Data Quality

It's important that you design accurate queries, forms, and reports and that you test them thoroughly. But the key to any database is the accuracy of the data stored in its tables. It's critical that the data be as error-free as possible. Most companies employ people who spend many hours tracking down and correcting errors and discrepancies in their data, and you can greatly assist and minimize their problem solving by using as many database features as possible to ensure the data is correct from the start. Among these features for fields are selecting the proper data type, setting default values whenever possible, restricting the permitted values by using field and table validation rules, enforcing referential integrity, and forcing users to select values from lists instead of typing the values. Likewise, having an arsenal of queries, such as find duplicates and top values queries, available to users will expedite the work they do to find and correct data errors.

Based on a request from Sarah, Lucia added a Memo field to the tblCustomer table, and now you'll review Lucia's work.

Working with Memo Fields

You use a Memo field to store long comments and explanations. Text fields are limited to 255 characters, but Memo fields can hold up to 65,535 characters. In addition, Text fields limit you to plain text with no special formatting, but you can define Memo fields either to store plain text similar to Text fields or to store rich text, which you can selectively format with options such as bold, italic, and different fonts and colors.

You'll review the Memo field, named Comments, that Lucia added to the tblCustomer table.

To review the Memo field in the tblCustomer table:

▶ **1.** Open the Navigation Pane, open the **tblCustomer** table in Datasheet view, and then close the Navigation Pane.

If you scroll to the right to view the Comments field, you'll no longer be able to identify which customer applies to a row because the Company, First Name, and Last Name columns will be hidden. You'll freeze those three columns so they remain visible in the datasheet as you scroll to the right.

▶ **2.** Click the **Company** column selector, press and hold down the **Shift** key, click the **Last Name** column selector, and then release the **Shift** key to select the Company, First Name, and Last Name columns.

3. In the Records group on Home tab, click the **More** button, and then click **Freeze Fields**. The three selected columns shift to the left and are now the three leftmost columns in the datasheet.

4. Scroll to the right until you see the Comments column. Notice that the Company, First Name, and Last Name columns, the three leftmost columns, remain visible. See Figure 5-41.

Figure 5-41 **Freezing three datasheet columns**

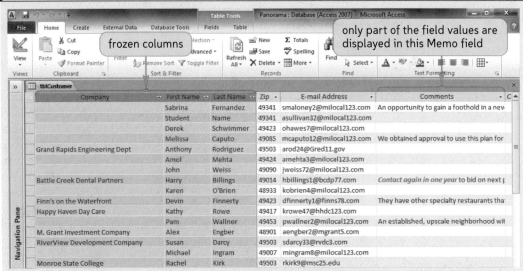

The Comments column is a Memo field that Belmont Landscapes staff members use to store notes, explanations, and other commentary about the customer. Notice that the Comments field value for Battle Creek Dental Partners displays rich text, using a bold, italic, and blue font. The Comments field values are partially hidden because the datasheet column is not wide enough. You'll view the first record's Comments field value in the Zoom dialog box.

5. Click the **Comments** box for the first record, hold down the **Shift** key, press the **F2** key, and then release the **Shift** key. The Zoom dialog box displays the entire Comments field value.

6. Click the **OK** button to close the Zoom dialog box.

INSIGHT

Table Datasheet Row and Column Resizing for Memo Fields

For Memo fields that contain many characters, you can widen the field's column to view more of its contents by dragging the right edge of the field's column selector to the right or by using the Field Width command when you click the More button in the Records group on the Home tab. However, increasing the column width reduces the number of other columns you can view at the same time. Further, for Memo fields containing thousands of characters, you can't widen the column enough to be able to view the entire contents of the field at one time across the width of the screen. Therefore, increasing the column width of a Memo field seldom makes sense.

Alternatively, you can increase the row height of a datasheet by dragging the bottom edge of a row selector down or by using the Row Height command when you click the More button in the Records group on the Home tab. Increasing the row height causes the text in a Memo field to wrap to the next line, so that you can view multiple lines at one time. Once again, however, for Memo fields containing thousands of characters, you can't increase the row height enough to ensure viewing the entire contents of the field at one time on screen. Additionally, you'd view fewer records at one time, and the row height setting for a table propagates to all queries that have an object dependency with the table. Thus, you shouldn't increase the row height of a table datasheet to accommodate a Memo field.

What is the best way to view the contents of Memo fields that contain a large number of characters? It is best to use the Zoom dialog box in a datasheet, or to use a large scrollable box on a form.

Now you'll review the property settings for the Comments field Lucia added to the tblCustomer table.

To review the property settings of the Memo field:

1. Save the table, switch to Design view, click the **Comments Field Name** box to make that row the current row, and then use the scroll bar to scroll to the bottom of the list of properties in the Field Properties pane.

2. Click the **Text Format** box in the Field Properties pane, and then click its **arrow**. The list of available text formats appears in the box. See Figure 5-42.

Figure 5-42 Viewing the properties for a Memo field

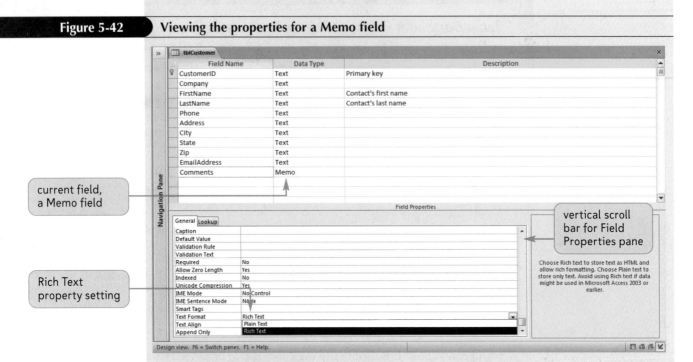

current field, a Memo field

Rich Text property setting

vertical scroll bar for Field Properties pane

Lucia set the **Text Format property** for the Comments field to Rich Text, which lets you format the field contents using the options in the Font group on the Home tab. The default Text Format property setting for a Memo field is Plain Text, which doesn't allow text formatting.

3. Click the **arrow** on the Text Format box to close the list, and then click the **Append Only** box.

The **Append Only property**, which appears at the bottom of the list of properties, tracks the changes that you make to a Memo field. The default setting of No lets you edit the Memo field value in a normal way. Setting this property to Yes also lets you edit the Memo field value in a normal way but, additionally, causes Access to keep a historical record of all versions of the Memo field value. You can view each version of the field value, along with a date and time stamp of when each version change occurred.

You've finished your review of the Memo field, so you can close the table.

4. Close the tblCustomer table.

When employees at Belmont Landscapes open the Panorama database, a Security Warning might appear below the Ribbon, and they must "enable the content" of the database before beginning their work. Sarah asks if you can eliminate this extra step when employees open the database.

Designating a Trusted Folder

A database is a file, and files can contain malicious instructions that can damage other files on your computer or files on other computers on your network. Unless you take special steps, Access treats every database as a potential threat to your computer. One such special step is to designate a folder as a trusted folder. A **trusted folder** is a folder on a drive or network that you designate as trusted and where you place databases you know are safe. When you open a database located in a trusted folder, Access treats it as a safe file and no longer displays a Security Warning. You can also place files used with other Microsoft Office programs, such as Word documents and Excel workbooks, in a trusted folder to eliminate warnings when you open them.

Because the Panorama database does not contain harmful instructions, you'll set up a trusted folder in which to store it to eliminate the security warning when a user opens the database.

To designate a trusted folder:

▶ **1.** Click the **File** tab on the Ribbon to display Backstage view, and then click **Options** in the navigation bar. The Access Options dialog box opens.

▶ **2.** In the left section of the dialog box, click **Trust Center**, click the **Trust Center Settings** button in the window on the right to open the Trust Center dialog box, and then in the left section click **Trusted Locations**. The trusted locations for your installation of Access and other trust options are displayed on the right. See Figure 5-43.

| Figure 5-43 | Designating a trusted folder |

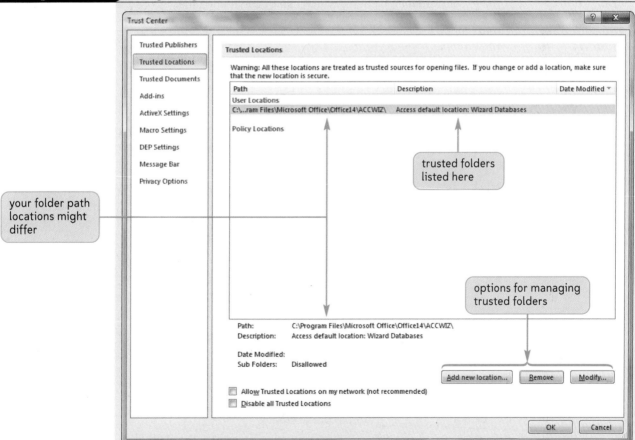

Existing trusted locations appear in the list at the top; and options to add, remove, and modify trusted locations appear at the bottom.

Trouble? Check with your instructor before adding a new trusted location. If your instructor tells you not to create a new trusted location, skip to Step 5.

▶ **3.** Click the **Add new location** button to open the Microsoft Office Trusted Location dialog box, click the **Browse** button, navigate to the Access2\Tutorial folder where your Data Files are stored, and then click the **OK** button.

You can also choose to designate subfolders of the selected location as trusted locations, but you won't select this option.

▶ **4.** Click the **OK** button. Access adds the Access2\Tutorial folder to the list of trusted locations.

▶ **5.** Click the **OK** button to close the Trust Center dialog box, and then click the **OK** button to close the Access Options dialog box.

You've created several queries and completed several table design changes, so you should compact and repair the Panorama database. Lucia doesn't use the Compact on Close option with the Panorama database because it's possible to lose the database if there's a computer malfunction when the Compact on Close operation runs. As a precaution, you'll make a backup copy of the database before you compact and repair it. Making frequent backup copies of your critical files safeguards your data from hardware and software malfunctions, which can occur at any time.

To backup and compact and repair the Panorama database:

▶ **1.** Click the **File** tab on the Ribbon, and then click the **Close Database** command to close the Panorama database.

▶ **2.** Make a backup copy of the Panorama database, preferably to a USB drive or other external medium, using a filename of Backup Panorama_date, where *date* is the current date in the format 2013-02-15, for example, if you made the backup on February 15, 2013.

▶ **3.** Make sure the Access window is the active window, and then click **Panorama.accdb** in the navigation bar. The database opens, and no Security Warning appears below the Ribbon because the database is located in the trusted location you designated.

Next, you'll compact and repair the database.

▶ **4.** Click the **File** tab on the Ribbon, and then click the **Compact & Repair Database** button.

You've finished the work requested by Belmont Landscapes, so you can close the database and exit Access.

▶ **5.** Close the Panorama database.

You've completed the table design changes to the Panorama database that will make working with it easier and more accurate.

Session 5.3 Quick Check

REVIEW

1. What is a lookup field?
2. A(n) _____ is a predefined format you use to enter and display data in a field.
3. What is property propagation?
4. Define the Validation Rule property, and give an example of when you would use it.
5. Define the Validation Text property, and give an example of when you would use it.
6. Setting a Memo field's Text Format property to _____ lets you format its contents.
7. A(n) _____ folder is a location in which you can place safe databases.

Practice the skills you learned in the tutorial using the same case scenario.

PRACTICE

Review Assignments

Data File needed for the Review Assignments: Products.accdb

In the Review Assignments, you'll create several new queries and enhance the table design in a database that contains information about the suppliers that Belmont Landscapes works with on its landscape design projects. Complete the following steps:

1. Open the **Products** database, which is located in the Access2\Review folder provided with your Data Files.

2. Modify the first record in the **tblCompany** table datasheet by changing the ContactFirstName and ContactLastName field values to your first and last names. Close the table.

3. Create a query to find all records in the tblCompany table in which the City field value starts with the letter H. Display all fields in the query recordset, and sort in ascending order by CompanyName. Save the query as **qryHSelectedCities**, run the query, and then close it.

4. Make a copy of the qryHSelectedCities query using the new name **qryOtherSelectedCities**. Modify the new query to find all records in the tblCompany table in which the City field values are not Lansing, Rockford, or Zeeland. Save and run the query, and then close it.

5. Create a query to find all records from the tblProduct table in which the Color field value is Black, White, or Grey. Use a list-of-values match for the selection criteria. Display all fields in the query recordset, and sort in descending order by Price. Save the query as **qrySelectedColors**, run the query, and then close it.

6. Create a query to display all records from the tblCompany table, selecting the CompanyName, City, and Phone fields, and sorting in ascending order by CompanyName. Add a calculated field named **ContactName** as the first column that concatenates the ContactFirstName, a space, and the ContactLastName. Set the Caption property for the ContactName field to **Contact Name**. Save the query as **qryCompanyContacts**, run the query, resize the Contact Name column to its best fit, and then save and close the query.

7. Create a parameter query to select the tblProduct table records for a Color field value that the user specifies. If the user doesn't enter a Color field value, select all records from the table. Display the ProductType, Price, Color, and DiscountOffered fields in the query recordset, sorting in ascending order by Price. Save the query as **qryColorParameter**. Run the query and enter no value as the Color field value, and then run the query again and enter **Wood** as the Color field value. Close the query.

8. Create a find duplicates query based on the tblProduct table. Select ProductType as the field that might contain duplicates, and select the ProductID, CompanyID, Price, and DiscountOffered fields as additional fields in the query recordset. Save the query as **qryDuplicateProductTypes**, run the query, and then close it.

9. Create a find unmatched query that finds all records in the tblCompany table for which there is no matching record in the tblProduct table. Display the CompanyID, CompanyName, City, Phone, ContactFirstName, and ContactLastName fields from the tblCompany table in the query recordset. Save the query as **qryCompaniesWithoutMatchingProducts**, run the query, and then close it.

10. Make a copy of the qryPricesWithDiscountAmounts query using the new name **qryTopPricesWithDiscountAmounts**. Modify the new query to use the Top Values property to select the top 25% of records. Save and run the query, and then close it.

11. In the **tblProduct** table, change the CompanyID field to a lookup field. Select the CompanyName field and then the CompanyID field from the tblCompany table; sort in ascending order by the CompanyName field, do not hide the key column, make sure the Company Name column is the leftmost column, resize the lookup columns to their best fit, select CompanyID as the field to store in the table, and accept the default label for the lookup column. View the tblProduct table datasheet, resize the Company ID column to its best fit, test the lookup field without changing a value permanently, and then save and close the table.

12. Use the Input Mask Wizard to add an input mask to the Phone field in the **tblCompany** table. The ending input mask should use periods as separators, as in 987.654.3210 with only the last seven digits required; do not store the literal display characters, if you are asked to do so. Update the Input Mask property everywhere the Phone field is used. Resize all columns in the datasheet to their best fit, test the input mask by typing over an existing Phone field value, being sure not to change the value by pressing the Esc key after you type the last digit in the Phone field.

13. Add a Memo field named **CompanyComments** as the last field in the tblCompany table. Set the Caption property to **Company Comments** and the Text Format property to Rich Text. In the table datasheet, resize the new column to its best fit, and then add your city and state in bold, italic font to the Company Comments column in the first record. Save and close the tblCompany datasheet.

14. Designate the Access2\Review folder as a trusted folder. (*Note:* Check with your instructor before adding a new trusted location.)

15. Close the Products database without exiting Access, make a backup copy of the database, and compact and repair and then close the Products database.

Use the skills you learned to work in a database for a small music school.

APPLY

Case Problem 1

Data File needed for this Case Problem: Contract.accdb

Pine Hill Music School   Yuka Koyama owns and runs the Pine Hill Music School in Portland, Oregon. She and the qualified teachers who work for her offer instruction in voice, violin, cello, guitar, percussion, and other instruments. Yuka created an Access database named Contract to store data about students, teachers, and contracts. You'll help Yuka create several new queries and make design changes to the tables. Complete the following steps:

1. Open the **Contract** database, which is located in the Access2\Case1 folder provided with your Data Files.

2. Change the first record in the **tblStudent** table datasheet so the First Name and Last Name columns contain your first and last names. Close the table.

3. Create a query to find all records in the tblStudent table in which the Phone field value begins with 541. Display the FirstName, LastName, City, and Phone fields in the query recordset; and sort in ascending order by LastName. Save the query as **qry541AreaCodes**, run the query, and then close it.

⊕ **EXPLORE**   4. Make a copy of the qryCurrentLessons query using the new name **qrySelectedLessons**. Modify the new query to delete the existing condition for the ContractEndDate field and to include a list-of-values criterion that finds all records in which the LessonType field value is Cello, Flute, or Violin. Save and run the query, and then close it.

5. Create a query to find all records in the tblStudent table in which the City field value is not equal to Portland. Display the FirstName, LastName, City, and Phone fields in the query recordset; and sort in ascending order by City. Save the query as **qryNonPortland**, run the query, and then close it.

6. Create a query to display all records from the tblTeacher table, selecting all fields, and sorting in ascending order by LastName and then in ascending order by FirstName. Add a calculated field named **TeacherName** as the second column that concatenates FirstName, a space, and LastName for each teacher. Set the Caption property for the TeacherName field to **Teacher Name**. Do not display the FirstName and LastName fields in the query recordset. Save the query as **qryTeacherNames**, run the query, resize the Teacher Name column to its best fit, and then save and close the query.

7. Create a parameter query to select the tblContract table records for a LessonType field value that the user specifies. If the user doesn't enter a LessonType field value, select all records from the table. Include all fields from the tblContract table in the query recordset. Save the query as **qryLessonTypeParameter**. Run the query and enter no value as the LessonType field value, and then run the query again and enter **Guitar** as the LessonType field value. Close the query.

⊕ EXPLORE 8. Create a crosstab query based on the tblContract table. Use the LessonType field values for the row headings, the LessonLength field values for the column headings, and the count of the ContractID field values as the summarized value, and include row sums. Save the query as **qryLessonTypeCrosstab**. Change the column heading for the row sum column to **Total Number of Lessons**, and change the column headings for the [LessonLength] columns to **Number of 30-Minute Lessons** and **Number of 60-Minute Lessons**. Resize the columns in the query recordset to their best fit, and then save and close the query.

9. Create a find duplicates query based on the tblContract table. Select StudentID and LessonType as the fields that might contain duplicates, and select all other fields in the table as additional fields in the query recordset. Save the query as **qryMultipleLessonsForStudents**, run the query, and then close it.

10. Create a find unmatched query that finds all records in the tblStudent table for which there is no matching record in the tblContract table. Display all fields from the tblStudent table in the query recordset. Save the query as **qryStudentsWithoutContracts**, run the query, and then close it.

11. In the **tblContract** table, change the TeacherID field data type to Lookup Wizard. Select the TeacherName and TeacherID fields from the qryTeacherNames query, sort in ascending order by TeacherName, resize the lookup columns to their best fit, select TeacherID as the field to store in the table, and accept the default label for the lookup column. View the tblContract table datasheet, resize the Teacher ID column to its best fit, and then save and close the table.

12. Use the Input Mask Wizard to add an input mask to the Phone field in the **tblStudent** table. The ending input mask should use periods as separators, as in 987.654.3210 with only the last seven digits required; do not store the literal display characters, if you are asked to do so. Update the Input Mask property everywhere the Phone field is used. Resize the Phone column to its best fit, test the input mask by typing over an existing Phone field value, being sure not to change the value permanently by pressing the Esc key after you type the last digit in the Phone field.

13. Define a field validation rule for the Gender field in the tblStudent table. Acceptable field values for the Gender field are F or M. Use the message "Gender values must be F or M" to notify a user who enters an invalid Gender field value. Save your table changes, test the field validation rule for the Gender field, making sure any tested field values are the same as they were before your testing, and then close the table.

14. Define a table validation rule for the **tblContract** table to verify that ContractStartDate field values precede ContractEndDate field values in time. Use an appropriate validation message. Save your table changes, test the table validation rule, making sure any tested field values are the same as they were before your testing, and then close the table.

15. Designate the Access2\Case1 folder as a trusted folder. (*Note:* Check with your instructor before adding a new trusted location.)

16. Close the Contract database without exiting Access, make a backup copy of the database, and compact and repair and then close the Contract database.

Apply your skills to work in a database for a health and fitness center.

APPLY

Case Problem 2

Data File needed for this Case Problem: Training.accdb

Parkhurst Health & Fitness Center Martha Parkhurst owns and operates the Parkhurst Health & Fitness Center in Richmond, Virginia. The center offers the usual weight training equipment and fitness classes and also offers specialized programs designed to meet the needs of athletes who participate in certain sports or physical activities. Martha created the Training database to maintain information about the members who have joined the center and the types of programs offered. To make the database easier to use, Martha wants you to create several queries and to make changes to its table design. Complete the following steps:

1. Open the **Training** database, which is located in the Access2\Case2 folder provided with your Data Files.

2. Modify the first record in the **tblMember** table datasheet by changing the First Name and Last Name column values to your first and last names. Close the table.

3. Create a query to find all records in the tblProgram table in which the MonthlyFee field value is 20, 30, or 40. Use a list-of-values match for the selection criterion, and include all fields from the table in the query recordset. Sort the query in descending order by the ProgramID field. Save the query as **qrySelectedPrograms**, run the query, and then close it.

4. Make a copy of the qrySelectedPrograms query using the new name **qrySelectedProgramsModified**. Modify the new query to find all records in the tblProgram table in which the MonthlyFee field value is not 20, 30, or 40. Save and run the query, and then close it.

5. Create a query to display all records from the tblMember table, selecting the LastName, FirstName, Street, and Phone fields, and sorting in ascending order by LastName and then in ascending order by FirstName. Add a calculated field named **MemberName** as the first column that concatenates FirstName, a space, and LastName. Set the Caption property for the MemberName field to **Member Name**. Do not display the FirstName and LastName fields in the query recordset. Create a second calculated field named **CityLine**, inserting it between the Street and Phone fields. The CityLine field concatenates City, a space, State, two spaces, and Zip. Set the Caption property for the CityLine field to **City Line**. Save the query as **qryMemberNames**, run the query, resize all columns to their best fit, and then save and close the query.

✪ EXPLORE   6. Create a query to display all matching records from the tblProgram and tblMember tables, selecting the ProgramType and MonthlyFee fields from the tblProgram table, and the FirstName and LastName fields from the tblMember table. Add a calculated field named **MonthlyFeeStatus** as the last column that equals Active if the MembershipStatus field is equal to Active and equals Not Active otherwise. Set the Caption property for the calculated field to **Monthly Fee Status**. Save the query as **qryMonthlyFeeStatus**, run the query, resize all columns to their best fit, and then save and close the query.

7. Make a copy of the qryRichmondOnHold query using the new name **qryRichmondAndChesterActive**. Modify the new query to select all records in which the City field value is Richmond or Chester and the MembershipStatus field value is Active. Save and run the query, and then close the query.

8. Create a parameter query to select the tblMember table records for a City field value that the user specifies. If the user doesn't enter a City field value, select all records from the table. Display all fields from the tblMember table in the query recordset. Save the query as **qryMemberCityParameter**. Run the query and enter no value as the City field value, and then run the query again and enter **Ashland** as the City field value. Close the query.

9. Create a crosstab query based on the qryMonthlyFeeStatus query. Use the ProgramType field values for the row headings, the MonthlyFeeStatus field values for the column headings, the sum of the MonthlyFee field values as the summarized value, and include row sums. Save the query as **qryMonthlyFeeCrosstab**, resize the columns in the query recordset to their best fit, and then save and close the query.

10. Create a find duplicates query based on the tblMember table. Select ExpirationDate as the field that might contain duplicates, and select all other fields in the table as additional fields in the query recordset. Save the query as **qryDuplicateMemberExpirationDates**, run the query, and then close it.

11. Create a find unmatched query that finds all records in the tblProgram table for which there is no matching record in the tblMember table. Select all fields from the tblProgram table. Save the query as **qryProgramsWithoutMembers**, run the query, and then close it.

12. Create a new query based on the tblMember table. Display the FirstName, LastName, Phone, ExpirationDate, MembershipStatus, and ProgramID fields, in this order, in the query recordset. Sort in ascending order by the ExpirationDate field, and then use the Top Values property to select the top 25% of records. Save the query as **qryUpcomingExpirations**, run the query, and then close it.

✪ EXPLORE 13. Use the Input Mask Wizard to add an input mask to the JoinDate field in the **tblMember** table. Select the Short Date input mask, and then modify the default Short Date input mask by changing the two slashes to dashes. Next for the JoinDate field, set the Format property to **mm-dd-yyyy** to specify the date format with dashes instead of slashes. Test the input mask by typing over an existing Join Date column value, being certain not to change the value by pressing the Esc key after you type the last digit in the Join Date column. Finally, repeat the same procedure to add the same input mask and Format property setting to the ExpirationDate field, and then save and close the table.

14. Define a field validation rule for the MonthlyFee field in the **tblProgram** table. Acceptable field values for the MonthlyFee field are values between 15 and 55. Enter the message **Value must be between 15 and 55, inclusive** so it appears if a user enters an invalid MonthlyFee field value. Save your table changes and then test the field validation rule for the MonthlyFee field; be certain the field values are the same as they were before your testing, and then close the table.

15. Define a table validation rule for the **tblMember** table to verify that JoinDate field values precede ExpirationDate field values in time. Use an appropriate validation message. Save your table changes, test the table validation rule, making sure any tested field values are the same as they were before your testing.

16. Add a Memo field named **MemberComments** as the last field in the tblMember table. Set the Caption property to **Member Comments** and the Text Format property to Rich Text. In the table datasheet, resize the new column to its best fit, and then add a comment in the Member Comments column in the first record about the types of physical activities you pursue, formatting the text with blue, italic font. Save your table changes, and then close the table.

17. Designate the Access2\Case2 folder as a trusted folder. (*Note:* Check with your instructor before adding a new trusted location.)

18. Close the Training database without exiting Access, make a backup copy of the database, and compact and repair and then close the Training database.

Explore some new skills to work with a database for a recycling agency.

CHALLENGE

Case Problem 3

Data File needed for this Case Problem: Agency.accdb

Rossi Recycling Group   The Rossi Recycling Group is a not-for-profit agency in Salina, Kansas that provides recycled household goods to needy people and families at no charge. Residents of Salina and surrounding communities donate cash and goods, such as appliances, furniture, and tools, to the Rossi Recycling Group. The group's volunteers then coordinate with local human services agencies to distribute the goods to those in need. The Rossi Recycling Group was established by Mary and Tom Rossi, who live on the outskirts of Salina on a small farm. Mary and Tom organize the volunteers to collect the goods and store the collected items in their barn for distribution. Tom has created an Access database to keep track of information about donors, their donations, and the human services agencies. He wants you to create several queries and to make changes to the table design of the database. To do so, you'll complete the following steps:

1. Open the **Agency** database, which is located in the Access2\Case3 folder provided with your Data Files.

2. Modify the first record in the **tblDonor** table datasheet by changing the Title, First Name, and Last Name column values to your title and name. Close the table.

3. Create a query to find all records in the tblDonation table in which the AgencyID field value starts with either the letter R or the letter W. Display all fields in the query recordset, and sort in descending order by DonationValue. Save the query as **qryROrWAgencyDonations**, run the query, and then close it.

4. Make a copy of the qryAgenciesByCity query using the new name **qryNonAbileneSalinaAgencies**. Modify the new query to select all records in which the City field value is not Abilene or Salina. Save and run the query, and then close it.

EXPLORE

5. The existing qryDonationsAfterPickupCharge query displays the DonorID, AgencyName, DonationDesc, and DonationValue fields for all donations that require a pickup, along with the NetDonation calculated field that displays the results of subtracting the $8.75 delivery charge from the DonationValue field value. Make a copy of the qryDonationsAfterPickupCharge query using the new name **qryNetDonations**. Modify the new query to select *all* records, to display the PickupRequired field, and to sort only in descending order by NetDonation. Also, change the NetDonation calculated field to subtract the delivery charge of $8.75 from the DonationField value when a pickup is required and to otherwise use the DonationValue field value. Save and run the query, and then close it.

6. Create a query to display all records from the tblAgency table, selecting all the fields except the ContactFirstName and ContactLastName fields, and sorting in ascending order by AgencyName. Add a calculated field named **ContactName** as the third column that concatenates ContactFirstName, a space, and ContactLastName. Set the Caption property for the ContactName field to **Contact Name**. Save the query as **qryAgencyContactNames**, run the query, resize the new column to its best fit, and then save and close the query.

7. Create a parameter query to select the tblDonation table records for a DonationDesc (donation description) field value that the user specifies. If the user doesn't enter a DonationDesc field value, select all records from the table. Display all fields from the tblDonation table in the query recordset, and sort in ascending order by DonationValue. Save the query as **qryDonationDescParameter**. Run the query and enter no value as the DonationDesc field value, and then run the query again and enter **Cash** as the DonationDesc field value. Close the query.

EXPLORE

8. Create a crosstab query based on the qryNetDonations query. Use the AgencyName field values for the row headings, the PickupRequired field values for the column headings, and the sum of the NetDonation field values as the summarized value, and include row sums. Save the query as **qryNetDonationsCrosstab**. Change the column headings for the two rightmost columns to **No Pickup** and **Pickup Required**. Change the format of the displayed values (NetDonation and Total Of NetDonation columns in Design view) to Standard with two decimal places. Resize the columns in the query recordset to their best fit, and then save and close the query.

9. Create a find duplicates query based on the qryNetDonations query. Select DonorID and AgencyName as the fields that might contain duplicates, and select the remaining fields in the query as additional fields in the query recordset. Save the query as **qryMultipleDonorDonations**, run the query, and then close it.

10. Create a find unmatched query that finds all records in the tblDonor table for which there is no matching record in the tblDonation table. Select all fields from the tblDonor table in the query recordset. Save the query as **qryDonorsWithoutDonations**, run the query, and then close it.

EXPLORE

11. Make a copy of the qryNetDonations query using the new name **qryTopNetDonations**. Modify the new query by using the Top Values property to select the top 40% of the records. Save and run the query, and then close the query.

12. Use the Input Mask Wizard to add an input mask to the Phone field in the **tblDonor** table. The ending input mask should use hyphens as separators, as in 987-654-3210 with only the last seven digits required; do not store the literal display characters, if you are asked to do so. Update the Input Mask property everywhere the Phone field is used. Test the input mask by typing over an existing Phone field value, being sure not to change the value permanently by pressing the Esc key after you type the last digit in the Phone field. Close the table.

13. Designate the Access2\Case3 folder as a trusted folder. (*Note:* Check with your instructor before adding a new trusted location.)

14. Close the Agency database without exiting Access, make a backup copy of the database, and compact and repair and then close the Agency database.

Explore some new skills to work with the data for a luxury property rental company.

CHALLENGE

Case Problem 4

Data File needed for this Case Problem: Vacation.accdb

GEM Ultimate Vacations   Griffin and Emma MacElroy own and operate their own agency, GEM Ultimate Vacations, which specializes in locating and booking luxury rental properties in Europe and Africa. To track their guests, properties, and reservations, they created the Vacation database. Griffin and Emma want you to create several queries and to make changes to the table design. To do so, you'll complete the following steps:

1. Open the **Vacation** database, which is located in the Access2\Case4 folder provided with your Data Files.

2. Modify the first record in the **tblGuest** table datasheet by changing the Guest First Name and Guest Last Name column values to your first and last names.

3. Create a query to find all records in the tblProperty table in which the PropertyName field value starts with the word Chateau. Display all fields except the Description field in the query recordset. Save the query as **qryChateauProperties**, run the query, and then close it.

4. Make a copy of the qryChateauProperties query using the new name **qryNonChateauProperties**. Modify the new query to find all records in the tblProperty table in which the PropertyName field value starts with a word other than Chateau, and sort in ascending order by PropertyName. Save and run the query, and then close it.

5. Create a query to find all records in the tblGuest table in which the City field value is Aurora, Chicago, or Crown Point. Use a list-of-values match for the selection criterion, and display all fields from the tblGuest table in the query recordset. Save the query as **qrySelectedGuests**, run the query, and then close it.

⊕ EXPLORE

6. Create a query to select all records from the tblProperty table with nightly rates of $1,700 or $2,000 in France or Italy. Display all fields except the Description field in the query recordset. Save the query as **qryFranceItalySelectedProperties**, run the query, and then close it.

7. Create a parameter query to select the tblProperty table records for a Country field value that the user specifies. If the user doesn't enter a Country field value, select all records from the table. Display all fields from the tblProperty table in the query recordset, and sort in ascending order by PropertyName. Save the query as **qryCountryParameter**. Run the query and enter no value as the Country field value, and then run the query again and enter **Scotland** as the Country field value. Close the query.

8. Create a query that contains all records from the tblGuest table and all matching records from the tblReservation table. Display all fields from the tblGuest table and all fields except GuestID from the tblReservation table. Save the query as **qryGuestsAndReservations**, run the query, and then close it. Create a crosstab query based on the qryGuestsAndReservations query. Use the City field values for the row headings, the People field values for the column headings, and the sum of the RentalRate field as the summarized value, and include row sums. Save the query as **qryReservationsCrosstab**, resize the columns in the query recordset to their best fit, and then save and close the query.

9. Create a find duplicates query based on the tblProperty table. Select Location and Country as the fields that might contain duplicates, and select the remaining fields in the table as additional fields in the query recordset. Save the query as **qryDuplicateLocations**, run the query, and then close it.

10. Create a find unmatched query that finds all records in the tblGuest table for which there is no matching record in the tblReservation table. Display the GuestFirstName, GuestLastName, City, and Phone fields from the tblGuest table in the query recordset. Save the query as **qryGuestsWithoutReservations**, run the query, and then close it.

⊕ EXPLORE 11. Modify the **qryTopRentalCost** query to use the Top Values property to select the top 30% of the records. Save and run the query, and then close it.

12. In the **tblReservation** table, change the PropertyID field data type to Lookup Wizard. Select the PropertyID, PropertyName, and Location fields from the tblProperty table, sort in ascending order by PropertyName, do not hide the key column, resize the lookup columns to their best fit, select PropertyID as the field to store in the table, and accept the default label for the look up column. View the tblReservation datasheet, resize the PropertyID column to its best fit, test the lookup field without changing a field value permanently, and then close the table.

⊕ EXPLORE 13. Open the **tblGuest** table in Design view. Change the StateProv field data type to Lookup Wizard using a list of values that you enter. In the Lookup Wizard dialog box, create two columns and type the following pairs of values: **Illinois** and **IL**, **Indiana** and **IN**, and **Ontario** and **ON**. Select Col2 as the field to store in the table, and accept the default label for the lookup column. View the tblGuest table data-sheet, test the lookup field without changing permanently field values, and then save and close the table.

⊕ EXPLORE 14. Define a field validation rule for the Bedrooms field in the **tblProperty** table. Acceptable field values for the Bedrooms field are values between 3 and 25, includ-ing those two values. Display the message **Value must be between 3 and 25** when a user enters an invalid Bedrooms field value. Save your table changes and then test the field validation rule for the Bedrooms field; be certain the field values are the same as they were before your testing.

15. Define a table validation rule for the **tblReservation** table to verify that StartDate field values precede EndDate field values in time. Use an appropriate validation message. Save your table changes, test the table validation rule, making sure any tested field values are the same as they were before your testing, and then close the table.

16. Designate the Access2\Case4 folder as a trusted folder. (*Note:* Check with your instructor before adding a new trusted location.)

17. Close the Vacation database without exiting Access, make a backup copy of the database, and compact and repair and then close the Vacation database.

Explore some new skills to create a database for an Internet service provider.

CREATE

Case Problem 5

There are no Data Files needed for this Case Problem.

Always Connected Everyday   Chris and Pat Dixon own and manage Always Connected Everyday (ACE), a successful Internet service provider (ISP) in your area. ACE provides Internet access to residential and business customers and offers a variety of access plans, from dial-up and DSL to wireless. Figure 5-44 shows the pricing options for the access plans ACE offers.

Figure 5-44	Pricing options for ACE access plans

Access Plan	Monthly	Annually	Setup Fee
Dial-up limited	$9.95		
Dial-up no e-mail	$14.95	$149.50	
Dial-up unlimited	$19.95	$199.50	
DSL pro	$29.95		$69.00
DSL turbo	$49.95		$69.00
DSL business	$89.95		$129.00
Wireless city economy	$39.95		$99.00
Wireless city basic	$49.95		$99.00
Wireless city advanced	$64.95		$109.00
Wireless city business	$99.95		$199.00
Wireless rural basic	$59.95		$109.00

Dial-up plans are available in all communities served by ACE, and DSL and wireless access are limited by a customer's proximity to DSL phone lines or wireless towers. Within each type of service—dial-up, DSL, and wireless—ACE offers low-cost plans with either slower access speeds or fewer capabilities and more expensive plans with either higher access speeds or greater service and features.

Chris and Pat need you to create a database to track their plans, customers, and service calls. The process of creating a complete database—including all fields, tables, relationships, queries, forms, and other database objects—for ACE is an enormous undertaking. You will start with just a few database components, and then you will create additional objects and functionality in subsequent tutorials.

Complete the following steps to create the database and its initial objects:

1. Read the appendix titled "Relational Databases and Database Design" at the end of this text.

2. If you are not familiar with ISPs, use your Web browser to find out more about them, so that you know common terminology and offerings. (*Hint*: You might use Wikipedia as one of your starting points.)

3. The initial database structure includes the following tables and fields:

   a. The **tblAccessPlan** table includes the fields shown in Figure 5-44, along with a primary key field, which you can define as an AutoNumber field.

   b. The **tblCustomer** table includes a unique customer account number; an optional company name; and first name, last name, address, city, state, zip, phone, access plan ID (foreign key), next billing date, and e-mail address for the customer; and the customer's user ID and password for accessing ACE's Web site.

4. Building on Step 3, for each field, determine and set its attributes, such as data type, field size, and validation rules.

5. Create the database structure using Access. Use the database name **ACE**, and save the database in the Access2\Case5 folder provided with your Data Files. Create the tables with their fields, following the naming standards used in this tutorial. Be sure to set each field's properties correctly, including the Caption property. Select a primary key for each table, use an input mask for one field, and then define the relationships between the tables.

6. For each table, create a form that you'll use to view, add, edit, and delete records in that table.

7. For tables with one-to-many relationships, create a form with a main form for the primary table and a subform for the related table.

8. Design test data for each table in the database. Your tblCustomer table should contain at least 15 records. Make sure your test data covers common situations. For example, your test data should include at least two access plans with multiple customers using the plans; at least two access plans with no customers using the plans, multiple cities, phone prefixes, and next billing dates; residential customers with no company names; and commercial customers with company names and the first and last names of the company's contact. Use your first and last names for the first record in the tblCustomer table.

9. Add the test data to your tables using the forms you created in Steps 6 and 7.

10. Open each table datasheet, and resize all datasheet columns to their best fit.

11. For the foreign key field in the tblCustomer table, change the field's data type to Lookup Wizard. If necessary, resize the lookup column in the table datasheet.

12. Create a query named **qryCustomerNames** that contains all the fields from the tblCustomer table. Add a calcualted field named **CustomerName** as the first column that is either the company name or the concatenation of the last name, a comma, a space, and the first name; set its Caption property to **Customer Name**. Sort in ascending order by CustomerName.

13. Create one parameter query, one crosstab query, and one find unmatched query, and save them using appropriate object names.

14. Designate the Access2\Case5 folder as a trusted folder. (*Note:* Check with your instructor before adding a new trusted location.)

15. Close the ACE database without exiting Access, make a backup copy of the database, and compact and repair and then close the ACE database.

SAM: Skills Assessment Manager

ASSESS

For current SAM information, including versions and content details, visit SAM Central (http://samcentral.course.com). If you have a SAM user profile, you may have access to hands-on instruction, practice, and assessment of the skills covered in this tutorial. Since various versions of SAM are supported throughout the life of this text, check with your instructor for the correct instructions and URL/Web site for accessing assignments.

ENDING DATA FILES

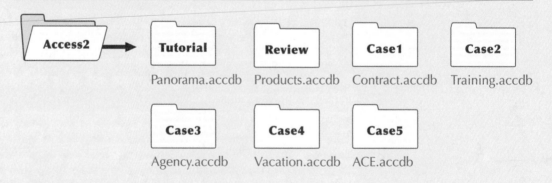

Access2 → Tutorial — Panorama.accdb

Review — Products.accdb

Case1 — Contract.accdb

Case2 — Training.accdb

Case3 — Agency.accdb

Case4 — Vacation.accdb

Case5 — ACE.accdb

Using Form Tools and Creating Custom Forms

Creating Forms for Belmont Landscapes

OBJECTIVES

Session 6.1
- Change a lookup field to a Text field
- View and print database documentation
- Create datasheet, multiple items, and split forms
- Modify a form and anchor form controls in Layout view

Session 6.2
- Plan, design, and create a custom form in Design view and in Layout view
- Select, move, align, resize, delete, and rename controls in a form
- Add a combo box to a form
- Add headers and footers to a form

Session 6.3
- Add a combo box to a form to find records
- Add a subform to a form
- Add calculated controls to a form and a subform
- Change the tab order in a form
- Improve the appearance of a form

Case | *Belmont Landscapes*

Oren Belmont hired Lucia Perez to enhance the Panorama database, and she initially concentrated on standardizing the table design and creating queries for Belmont Landscapes. Sarah Fisher and her staff created a few forms before Lucia's hiring, and Lucia's next priority is to work with Sarah to create new forms that will be more useful and easier to use.

In this tutorial, you will create new forms for Belmont Landscapes. In creating the forms, you will use many Access form customization features, such as adding controls and a subform to a form, using combo boxes and calculated controls, and adding color and special effects to a form. These features will make it easier for Sarah and her staff to interact with the Panorama database.

STARTING DATA FILES

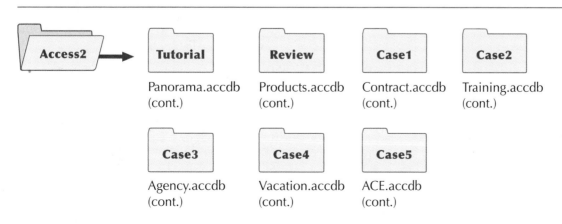

Access2 →	Tutorial	Review	Case1	Case2
	Panorama.accdb (cont.)	Products.accdb (cont.)	Contract.accdb (cont.)	Training.accdb (cont.)

Case3	Case4	Case5
Agency.accdb (cont.)	Vacation.accdb (cont.)	ACE.accdb (cont.)

SESSION 6.1 VISUAL OVERVIEW

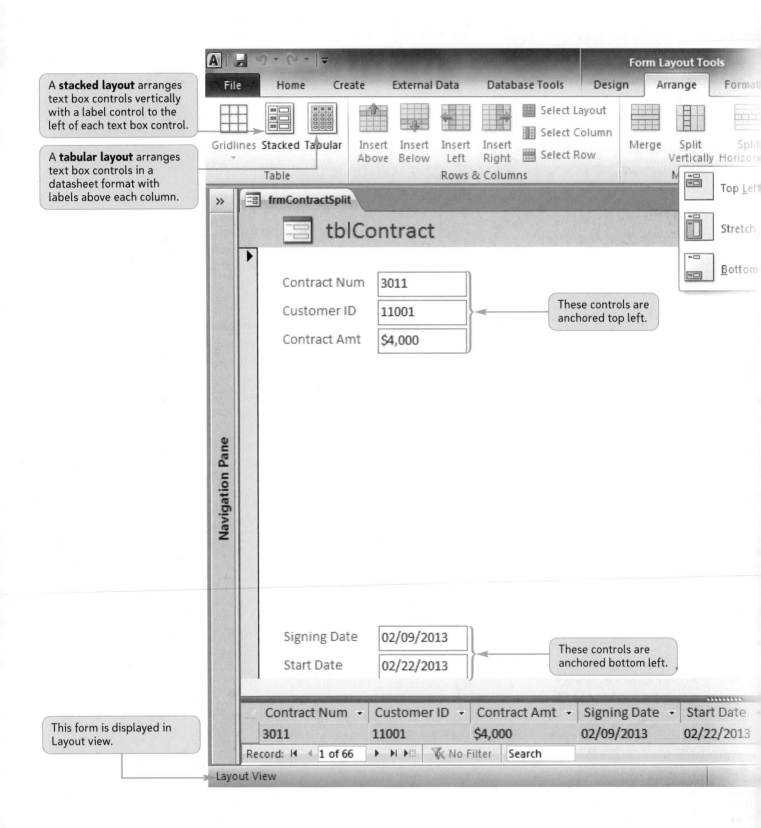

A **stacked layout** arranges text box controls vertically with a label control to the left of each text box control.

A **tabular layout** arranges text box controls in a datasheet format with labels above each column.

These controls are anchored top left.

These controls are anchored bottom left.

This form is displayed in Layout view.

ANCHORING CONTROLS

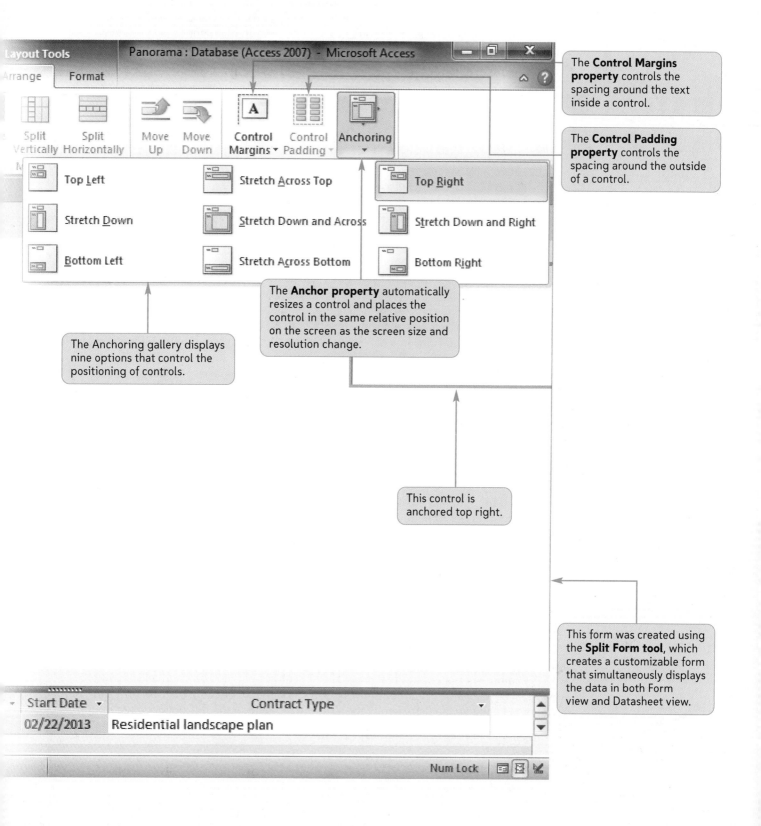

The **Control Margins property** controls the spacing around the text inside a control.

The **Control Padding property** controls the spacing around the outside of a control.

The Anchoring gallery displays nine options that control the positioning of controls.

The **Anchor property** automatically resizes a control and places the control in the same relative position on the screen as the screen size and resolution change.

This control is anchored top right.

This form was created using the **Split Form tool**, which creates a customizable form that simultaneously displays the data in both Form view and Datasheet view.

Designing Forms

You've used wizards to create forms, and you've modified a form's design in Layout view to create a custom form. To create a **custom form**, you can modify an existing form in Layout view or in Design view, or you can design and create a form from scratch in Layout view or in Design view. You can design a custom form to match a paper form, to display some fields side by side and others top to bottom, to highlight certain sections with color, or to add visual effects. Whether you want to create a simple or complex custom form, planning the form's content and appearance is always your first step.

Form Design Guidelines

When you plan a form, you should keep in mind the following form design guidelines:
- Use forms to perform all database updates because forms provide better readability and control than do table and query recordsets.
- Determine the fields and record source needed for each form. A form's **Record Source property** specifies the table or query that provides the fields for the form.
- Group related fields and position them in a meaningful, logical order.
- If users will refer to a source document while working with the form, design the form to match the source document closely.
- Identify each field value with a label that names the field, and align field values and labels for readability.
- Size the width of each text box to fully display the values it contains and also to provide a visual clue to users about the length of those values.
- Display calculated fields in a distinctive way, and prevent users from changing and updating them.
- Use default values, list boxes, and other form controls whenever possible to reduce user errors by minimizing keystrokes and limiting entries. A **control** is an item, such as a text box or command button, that you place in a form or report.
- Use colors, fonts, and graphics sparingly to keep the form uncluttered and to keep the focus on the data.
- Use a consistent style for all forms in a database.

Sarah and her staff had created a few forms and made table design changes before learning about proper form design guidelines. These guidelines recommend performing all database updates using forms. As a result, Belmont Landscapes won't use table or query datasheets to update the database, and Sarah asks if she should reconsider any of the table design changes you made to the Panorama database in the previous tutorial.

Changing a Lookup Field to a Text Field

The input mask and validation rule changes are important table design changes, but setting the CustomerID field to a lookup field in the tblContract table is an unnecessary change. A form combo box provides the same capability in a clearer, more flexible way. A **combo box** is a control that provides the features of a text box and a list box; it lets you choose a value from the list or type an entry. Before creating the new forms for Sarah, you'll change the data type of the CustomerID field in the tblContract table from a Lookup Wizard field to a Text field.

To change the data type of the CustomerID field:

1. Start Access, and then open the **Panorama** database in the Access2\Tutorial folder provided with your Data Files.

   Trouble? If the Security Warning is displayed below the Ribbon, either the Panorama database is not located in the Access2\Tutorial folder or you did not designate that folder as a trusted folder. Make sure you opened the database in the Access2\Tutorial folder, and make sure that it's designated as a trusted folder.

TIP

You can press the F11 key to open or close the Navigation Pane.

2. Open the Navigation Pane, open the **tblContract** table in Design view, and then close the Navigation Pane.

3. Click the **CustomerID** Field Name box, and then click the **Lookup** tab in the Field Properties pane. The Field Properties pane now displays the lookup properties for the CustomerID field. See Figure 6-1.

Figure 6-1   Lookup properties for the CustomerID field

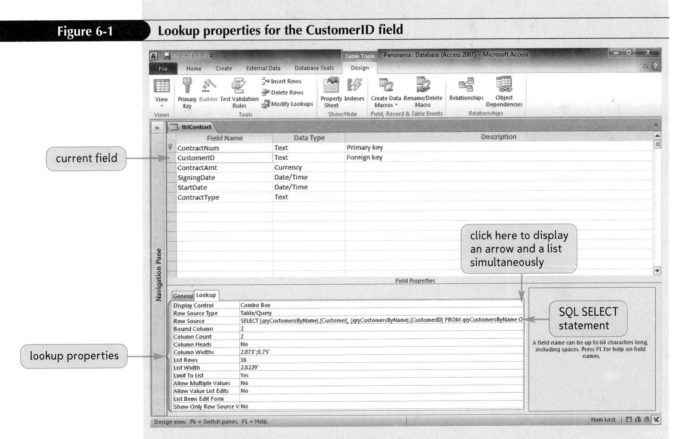

current field

click here to display
an arrow and a list
simultaneously

SQL SELECT
statement

lookup properties

Notice the **Row Source property**, which specifies the data source for a control in a form or report or for a field in a table or query. The Row Source property is usually set to a table name, a query name, or an SQL statement. For the CustomerID field, the Row Source property is set to an SQL SELECT statement. You'll learn more about SQL later in this text.

To remove the lookup feature for the CustomerID field, you need to change the **Display Control property**, which specifies the default control used to display a field, from Combo Box to Text Box.

4. Click the right side of the **Display Control** box, and then click **Text Box**. All the lookup properties in the Field Properties pane disappear, and the CustomerID field changes back to a Text field without lookup properties.

5. Click the **General** tab in the Field Properties pane and notice that the properties for a Text field still apply to the CustomerID field.

6. Save the table, switch to Datasheet view, resize the Customer ID column to its best fit, and then click one of the **Customer ID** boxes. An arrow does not appear in the Customer ID box because the field is no longer a lookup field.

7. Save the table, and then close the tblContract table.

Before you could change the CustomerID field in the tblContract table to a lookup field in the previous tutorial, you had to delete the one-to-many relationship between the tblCustomer and tblContract tables. Now that you've changed the data type of the CustomerID field back to a Text field, you'll view the table relationships to make sure that the tables in the Panorama database are related correctly.

To view the table relationships in the Relationships window:

1. On the Ribbon, click the **Database Tools** tab, and then in the Relationships group, click the **Relationships** button to open the Relationships window. See Figure 6-2.

Figure 6-2	Panorama database tables in the Relationships window

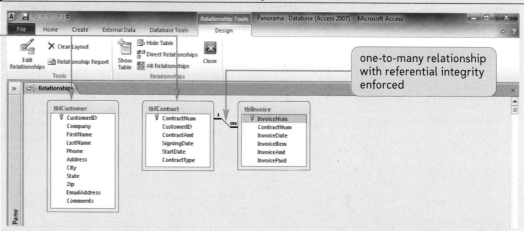

join these two tables

one-to-many relationship with referential integrity enforced

The primary tblContract table and the related tblInvoice table have a one-to-many relationship with referential integrity enforced. You need to establish a similar one-to-many relationship between the tblCustomer and tblContract tables.

2. Click **CustomerID** in the tblCustomer field list, drag it to **CustomerID** in the tblContract field list, and then release the mouse button to open the Edit Relationships dialog box.

3. Click the **Enforce Referential Integrity** check box, click the **Cascade Update Related Fields** check box, and then click the **Create** button to define the one-to-many relationship between the two tables and to close the dialog box. The join line connecting the tblCustomer and tblContract tables indicates the type of relationship (one-to-many) with referential integrity enforced (bold join line).

Sarah asks you to print a copy of the database relationships to use as a reference, and she asks if other Access documentation is available.

Printing Database Relationships and Using the Documenter

You can print the Relationships window to document the fields, tables, and relationships in a database. You can also use the **Documenter**, another Access tool, to create detailed documentation of all, or selected, objects in a database. For each selected object, the Documenter lets you print documentation, such as the object's properties and relationships, and the fields used by the object and their properties. You can use the documentation to help you understand an object and to help you plan changes to that object.

REFERENCE

Using the Documenter

- Start Access and open the database you want to document.
- In the Analyze group on the Database Tools tab, click the Database Documenter button.
- Select the object(s) you want to document.
- If necessary, click the Options button to select specific documentation options for the selected object(s), and then click the OK button.
- Click the OK button, print the documentation, and then close the Object Definition window.

Next, you'll print the Relationships window and use the Documenter to create documentation for the tblContract table. Sarah will show her staff the tblContract table documentation as a sample of the information that the Documenter provides.

To print the Relationships window and use the Documenter:

1. In the Tools group on the Design tab, click the **Relationship Report** button to open the Relationships for Panorama report in Print Preview. See Figure 6-3.

Figure 6-3	Relationships for Panorama report

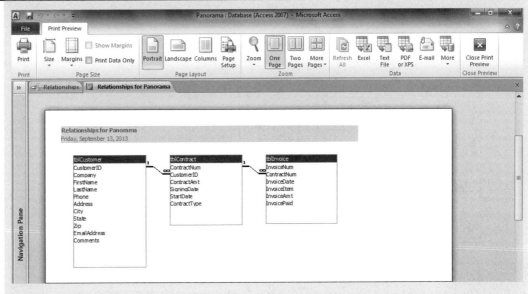

▶ **2.** In the Print group on the Print Preview tab, click the **Print** button, select your printer in the Name box (if necessary), and then click the **OK** button. Access prints the Relationships for Panorama report.

▶ **3.** Click the **Close 'Relationships for Panorama'** button ⊠ on the Relationships for Panorama tab to close the window. A dialog box opens and asks if you want to save the report. Because you can easily create the report at any time, you won't save it.

▶ **4.** Click the **No** button to close the report without saving changes, and then close the Relationships window.

Now you'll use the Documenter to create detailed documentation for the tblContract table as a sample to show Sarah.

▶ **5.** On the Ribbon, click the **Database Tools** tab. In the Analyze group, click the **Database Documenter** button, and then click the **Tables** tab (if necessary) in the Documenter dialog box. See Figure 6-4.

Figure 6-4	Documenter dialog box

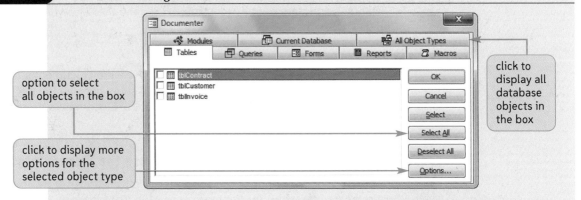

▶ **6.** Click the **tblContract** check box, and then click the **Options** button. The Print Table Definition dialog box opens on top of the Documenter dialog box. See Figure 6-5.

Figure 6-5	Print Table Definition dialog box

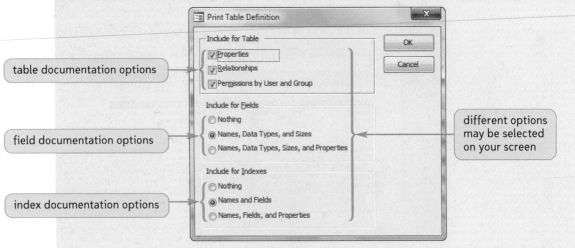

You select which documentation you want the Documenter to include for the selected table, its fields, and its indexes. Sarah asks you to include all table documentation and the second options for fields and for indexes.

7. Make sure all check boxes are checked in the Include for Table section, click the **Names, Data Types, and Sizes** option button in the Include for Fields section (if necessary), click the **Names and Fields** option button in the Include for Indexes section (if necessary), click the **OK** button, and then click the **OK** button. The Documenter dialog box closes and the Object Definition report opens in Print Preview.

8. In the Zoom group on the Print Preview tab, click the **Zoom button arrow**, and then click **Zoom 100%**.

When you need to view more of the horizontal contents of an open object, you can close the Navigation Pane. You can also minimize the Ribbon when you want to view more of the vertical contents of an open object. To minimize the Ribbon, double-click any tab on the Ribbon, or right-click a tab and then click Minimize the Ribbon on the shortcut menu. To restore the Ribbon, double-click any tab on the Ribbon, or right-click a tab and then click Minimize the Ribbon (it's a toggle option) on the shortcut menu.

TIP

If you click, instead of double-click, any tab on the minimized Ribbon, the full Ribbon appears until you click anywhere outside the Ribbon.

9. Double-click the **Print Preview** tab on the Ribbon to minimize the Ribbon, and then scroll down the report so you can see more of the report. See Figure 6-6.

Figure 6-6   Object Definition report for the tblContract table

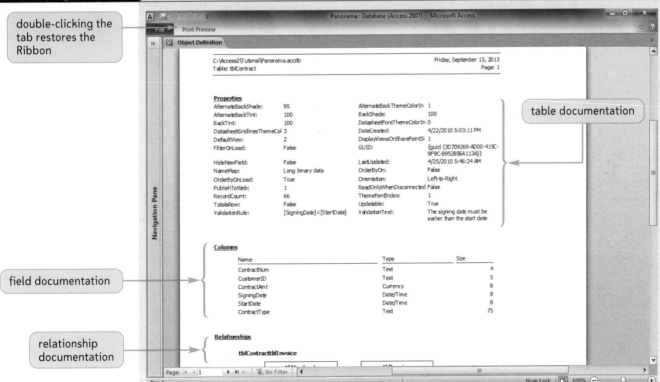

The Object Definition report displays table, field, and relationship documentation for the tblContract table.

▶ **10.** Scroll down the Object Definition report to view the remaining information in the documentation, print the documentation if your instructor asks you to do so, and then close the Object Definition report. Notice that the Navigation Pane is closed and the Ribbon is minimized.

PROSKILLS

Written Communication: Satisfying User Documentation Requirements

The Documenter produces object documentation that is useful to the technical designers, analysts, and programmers who develop and maintain Access databases and who need to understand the minutia of a database's design. Users who interact with databases have no interest in the documentation produced by the Documenter. Users need to know how to enter and maintain data using forms and how to obtain information using forms and reports, so they require special documentation that matches these needs, but this documentation isn't produced by the Documenter. Many companies assign one or more users the task of creating the documentation needed by users because they best know their company's procedures and what specific documentation users require. Databases with dozens of tables and with hundreds of other objects are complicated structures, so be sure you provide documentation that satisfies the needs of users separate from the documentation for the database developers.

Sarah and her staff will review the printout of the Relationships window and the documentation about the tblContract table and decide if they need to view additional documentation. Next, you'll create new forms for Sarah and her staff.

Creating Forms Using Form Tools

The Panorama database currently contains four forms: the frmContract form was created using the Form tool, the frmCustomer form was created using the Form Wizard, and the frmCustomerContracts main form and its frmContractSubform subform were created using the Form Wizard. Only the frmCustomer form is a custom form. Design changes that were made to the frmCustomer form in Layout view include changing its theme, changing its form title color and its line type, adding a picture, and moving a field.

Sarah wants to view the forms that she can create using other types of form tools, so she can determine if any of the forms would be helpful to her when updating the database.

Creating a Form Using the Datasheet Tool

The **Datasheet tool** creates a form in a datasheet format that contains all the fields in the source table or query. You'll use the Datasheet tool to create a form based on the tblContract table.

TIP

When you use the Datasheet tool, the record source (either a table or query) for the form must either be open or selected in the Navigation Pane.

To create the form using the Datasheet tool:

▶ **1.** Open the Navigation Pane, and then click **tblContract** (if necessary) in the Navigation Pane.

▶ **2.** Double-click the **Create** tab on the Ribbon to restore the Ribbon and to display the Create tab.

3. In the Forms group, click the **More Forms** button, and then click **Datasheet**. The Datasheet tool creates a form showing every field in the tblContract table in a datasheet format. See Figure 6-7.

Figure 6-7   **Form created by the Datasheet tool**

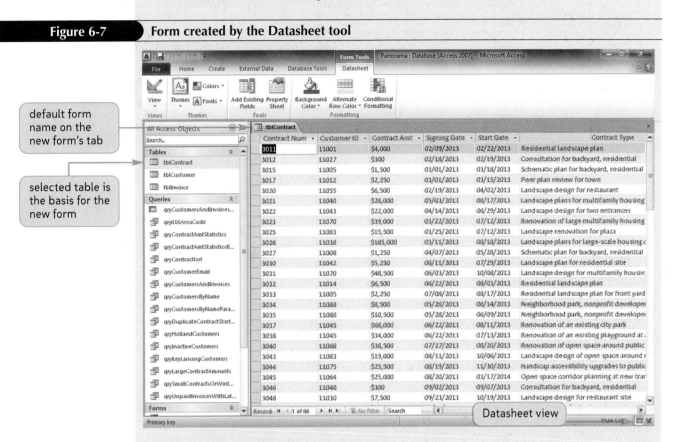

default form name on the new form's tab

selected table is the basis for the new form

Datasheet view

The new form displays all the records and fields from the tblContract table in Datasheet view and in the same format as a table or query recordset displayed in Datasheet view. On the right side of the status bar, two view icons appear, one for Datasheet view (selected) and the other for Design view. The form name, tblContract, is the same name as the table used as the basis for the form. Each table and query in a database must have a unique name. Although you could name a form or report the same as a table or query, it would cause confusion. Fortunately, using object name prefixes prevents this confusing practice, and you would change the name when you save the form.

When working with forms, you view and update data in Form view, you view and make simple design changes in Layout view, and you make simple and complex design changes in Design view. For the form created with the Datasheet tool, you'll check the available view options.

4. In the Views group on the Datasheet tab, click the **View button arrow**. See Figure 6-8.

Figure 6-8   **View options for a form created by the Datasheet tool**

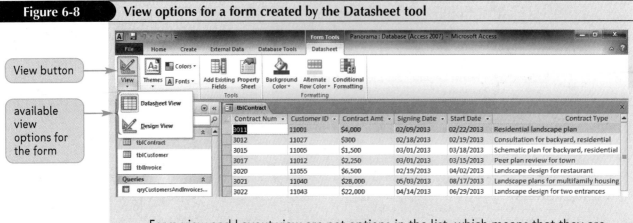

View button

available view options for the form

Form view and Layout view are not options in the list, which means that they are unavailable for this form type. Datasheet view allows you to view and update data, and Design view is the only other view option for this form.

Sarah and her staff don't have a need for a form with a datasheet format, so you won't save it.

5. Click the **View button arrow** to close the menu, and then close the form without saving it.

Next, you'll show Sarah a form created using the Multiple Items tool.

Creating a Form Using the Multiple Items Tool

The **Multiple Items tool** creates a customizable form that displays multiple records from a source table or query in a datasheet format. You'll use the Multiple Items tool to create a form based on the tblContract table.

To create the form using the Multiple Items tool:

1. Make sure that the tblContract table is selected in the Navigation Pane, and then click the **Create** tab on the Ribbon.

2. In the Forms group, click the **More Forms** button, and then click the **Multiple Items** button. The Multiple Items tool creates a form showing every field in the tblContract table and opens the form in Layout view. See Figure 6-9.

Figure 6-9 **Form created by the Multiple Items tool**

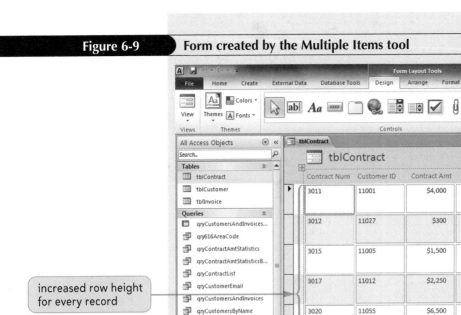

increased row height for every record

Layout view

TIP

You can click one of the view buttons on the right side of the status bar to switch to another view.

The new form displays all the records and fields from the tblContract table in a format similar to a datasheet, but the row height for every record is increased compared to a standard datasheet. Unlike a form created by the Datasheet tool, which has only Datasheet view and Design view available, a Multiple Items form is a standard form that can be displayed in Form view, Layout view, and Design view, as indicated by the buttons on the right side of the status bar.

For the form created with the Multiple Items tool, you'll check the available view options.

3. In the Views group, click the **View button arrow**. Form view, Layout view, and Design view are the available views for this form. See Figure 6-10.

Figure 6-10 **View options for a form created by the Multiple Items tool**

available view options

Sarah thinks this new form could be more useful than the form created by the Datasheet tool, but she doesn't have an immediate need for the form, so you won't save it.

▶ **4.** Click the **View button arrow** to close the menu, and then close the form without saving it.

The final form tool you'll show Sarah is the Split Form tool.

Creating a Form Using the Split Form Tool

The Split Form tool creates a customizable form that displays the data in a form in both Form view and Datasheet view at the same time. The two views are synchronized with each other at all times. Selecting a record in one view selects the same record in the other view. You can add, change, or delete data from either view. Typically, you'd use Datasheet view to locate a record, and then use Form view to update the record. You'll use the Split Form tool to create a form based on the tblContract table.

To create the form using the Split Form tool:

▶ **1.** Make sure that the tblContract table is selected in the Navigation Pane, and then click the **Create** tab on the Ribbon.

▶ **2.** In the Forms group, click the **More Forms** button, click the **Split Form** button, and then close the Navigation Pane. The Split Form tool creates a split form that opens in Layout view and displays a form with the contents of the first record in the tblContract table on the top and a datasheet of the first several records in the tblContract table on the bottom. See Figure 6-11.

Figure 6-11   Form created by the Split Form tool

form version of the form

datasheet version of the form

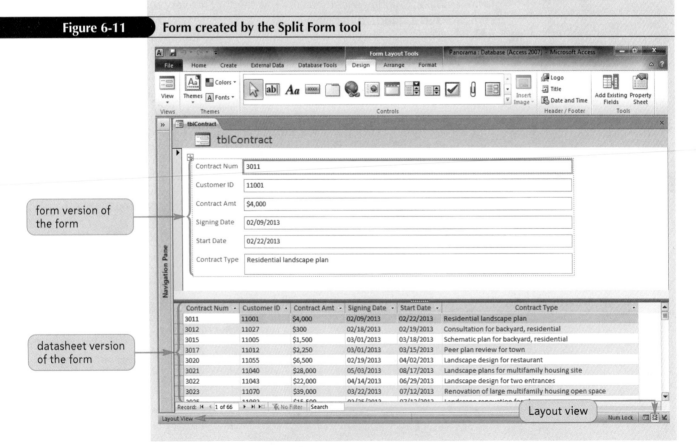

In Layout view, you can make layout and design changes to the form and layout changes to the datasheet. Sarah thinks the split form will be a useful addition to the Panorama database, and she wants you to show her the types of design modifications that are possible with a split form.

Modifying a Split Form in Layout View

You use the options on the Design tab on the Ribbon to add controls and make other modifications to the form but not to the datasheet, and you'll use these options later in this tutorial. In previous tutorials, you've shown Sarah how to use some of the form modification options on the Format tab, and you'll use other options on this tab later in this tutorial, so you won't show her any Format tab options now. Instead, you'll show her some options on the Arrange tab. For a split form, options on the Arrange tab apply only to the form and do not apply to the datasheet.

To modify the form in Layout view:

▶ **1.** Click the **Arrange** tab on the Ribbon.

The form's label and text box controls for the fields from the tblContract table are grouped in a control layout. A **control layout** is a set of controls grouped together in a form or report, so that you can manipulate the set as a single control. For example, you can move and resize all the controls in a control layout as a group—moving or resizing one control in the control layout moves or resizes all controls in the control layout. You also can rearrange fields and their attached labels within the control layout.

All the text boxes in the control layout are the same width. The first five text boxes—from the ContractNum text box to the StartDate text box—are much wider than necessary. However, if you reduce the width of any text box in a control layout, all text boxes in the control layout are also resized. Sarah wants you to reduce the width of the first five text boxes and to move and resize the ContractType label and text box.

▶ **2.** Click the **layout selector** ⊞, which is located at the top-left corner of the Contract Num label, to select all controls in the control layout. An orange outline, which identifies the controls that you've selected, appears around the labels and text boxes in the form. See Figure 6-12.

Figure 6-12   Control layout selected in the form

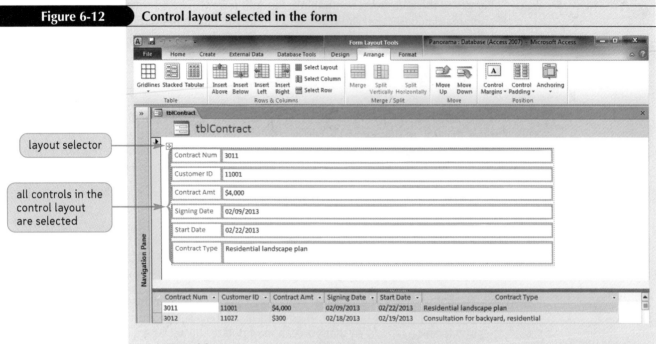

Trouble? If the layout selector wasn't visible, or if only one large orange outline appears outside the controls but not around each individual control, click the ContractNum text box, and then repeat Step 2.

Next, you'll resize the text boxes in the control layout.

3. Click the **SigningDate** text box (the text box that contains the value 02/09/2013) to deselect the control layout and select the SigningDate text box.

4. Position the pointer on the right edge of the SigningDate text box until the pointer changes to a ↔ shape, click and drag to the left until the right edge is just to the right of the SigningDate field value, and then release the mouse button. You've resized all six text boxes. See Figure 6-13.

Figure 6-13   After resizing the text boxes in the control layout

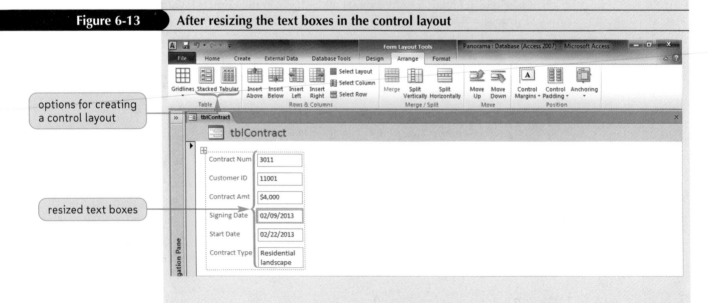

Trouble? If you resize the text boxes too far to the left, number signs appear inside the SigningDate and StartDate text boxes. Drag the right edge of the SigningDate text box slightly to the right and repeat the process until the date values are visible inside the text boxes.

The control layout for the form is a stacked layout, which arranges text box controls vertically with a label control to the left of each text box control; you click the Stacked button in the Table group to place selected controls in a stacked layout. You can also choose a tabular layout, which arranges text box controls in a datasheet format with labels above each column; you click the Tabular button in the Table group to place selected controls in a tabular layout.

You can now remove the ContractType text box and its label from the stacked layout, move the two controls, and then resize the text box.

5. Click the **ContractType** text box, hold down the **Shift** key, click the **Contract Type** label to select both controls, release the **Shift** key, right-click the **ContractType** text box to open the shortcut menu, point to **Layout**, and then click **Remove Layout**. You've removed the two selected controls from the stacked layout.

6. Make sure that the ContractType text box and its label are selected, and then drag the two controls up and to the right until their tops are aligned with the top of the ContractNum controls. See Figure 6-14. (Note: You will resize the ContractType text box in the next step.)

7. Click the **ContractType** text box so that it's the only selected control, and then drag the right edge of the control to the right and the bottom edge of the control down to the positions shown in Figure 6-14.

Figure 6-14   After moving and resizing the ContractType controls

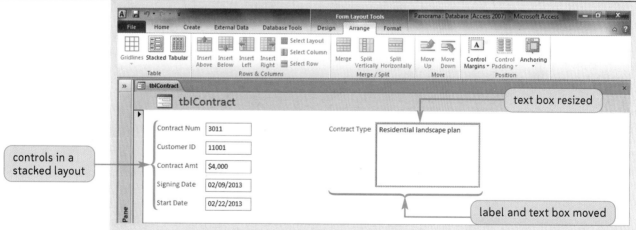

Trouble? It won't cause any problems if the two ContractType controls on your screen are in slightly different positions than the ones shown in the figure or if your ContractType text box is not exactly the same size.

You do not usually need to change the default settings for the Control Margins property, which controls the spacing around the text inside a control, and the Control Padding property, which controls the spacing around the outside of a control. However, you'll show Sarah the effects of changing these properties.

8. Click one of the controls in the stacked layout, click the **layout selector** ✛ to select all controls in the stacked layout, click the **Control Margins** button in the Position group, and then click **Medium**. The text inside the stacked layout controls moves down slightly.

▶ **9.** Click the **Control Margins** button, click **Wide** and observe the effect of this setting on the text inside the controls, click the **Control Margins** button, click **None** and observe the effect of this setting, click the **Control Margins** button, and then click **Narrow**. Narrow is the default setting for the Control Margins property.

Narrow is also the default setting for the Control Padding property.

▶ **10.** In the Position group, click the **Control Padding** button, click **Medium** and observe the change to the spacing around the controls, and then repeat for the other settings of this property, making sure you set the property to **Narrow** as your final step.

Next, you'll show Sarah how to anchor controls.

Anchoring Controls in a Form

You can design attractive forms that use the screen dimensions effectively when all the users of a database have the same sized monitors and use the same screen resolution. How do you design attractive forms when users have a variety of monitor sizes and screen resolutions? If you design a form to fit on large monitors using high screen resolutions, then only a portion of the controls in the form fit on smaller monitors with lower resolutions, forcing users to scroll the form. If you design a form to fit on smaller monitors with low screen resolutions, then the form displays on larger monitors in a small area in the upper-left corner of the screen, making the form look unattractively cramped. As a compromise, you can anchor the controls in the form. As shown in the Visual Overview for this session, the Anchor property for a control automatically resizes the control and places the control in the same relative position on the screen as the screen size and resolution change. Unfortunately, when you use the Anchor property, Access doesn't scale the control's font size to match the screen size and resolution.

Next, you'll show Sarah how to anchor controls in a form. Because all monitors at Belmont Landscapes are the same size and use the same resolution, first you'll save the split form, so that you can demonstrate anchoring and then discard the anchoring changes to the form.

To anchor controls in the form:

▶ **1.** Save the form as **frmContractSplit**.

You can't anchor individual controls in a control layout; you can only anchor the entire control layout as a group. You've already removed the ContractType controls from the stacked layout, so you can anchor them separately from the stacked layout. You'll remove the SigningDate and StartDate controls from the stacked layout, so you'll have three sets of controls to anchor—the stacked layout is one set, the ContractType controls are in the second set, and the Signing Date and StartDate controls make up the third set.

▶ **2.** Use **Shift+Click** to select the **SigningDate** and **StartDate** text boxes and labels, right-click the **SigningDate** text box, point to **Layout**, and then click **Remove Layout** to remove these two text boxes and their labels from the stacked layout.

First, you'll anchor the selected SigningDate and StartDate controls.

3. In the Position group on the Arrange tab, click the **Anchoring** button to open the Anchoring gallery. See Figure 6-15.

Figure 6-15 | **Displaying the Anchoring gallery**

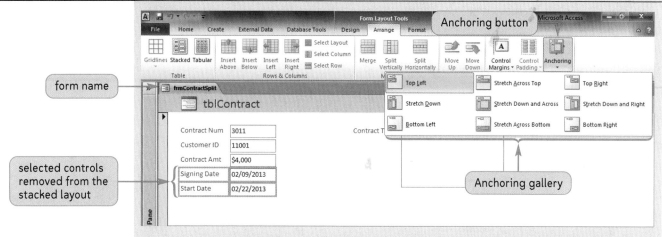

Four of the nine options in the Anchoring gallery fix the position of the selected controls in the top left (the default setting), bottom left, top right, or bottom right positions in the form. If other controls block the corner positions for controls you're anchoring for the first time, the new controls are positioned in relation to the blocking controls. The other five anchoring options resize (or stretch) and position the selected controls.

You'll anchor the SigningDate and StartDate controls in the bottom left and the ContractType controls in the top right.

4. Click **Bottom Left** in the Anchoring gallery, click the **ContractType** text box, click the **Anchoring** button, and then click **Top Right**. The SigningDate and StartDate controls shifted down, and the ContractType controls shifted to the right.

Next, you'll open the Navigation Pane, and then increase the height of the form to simulate the effect of a larger screen for the form.

5. Open the Navigation Pane. The two sets of controls on the left shift to the right because the horizontal dimensions of the form decreased from the left, and these two sets of controls are anchored to the left in the form. The ContractType controls remain in the same position in the form.

6. Position the pointer on the border between the form and the datasheet until the pointer changes to a ╪ shape, and then drag down until you see only the column headings and the first row in the datasheet. The bottom set of controls shift down, because it's anchored to the bottom, and the two sets of controls at the top remain in the same positions in the form. See Figure 6-16.

Figure 6-16 **Anchored controls in a resized form**

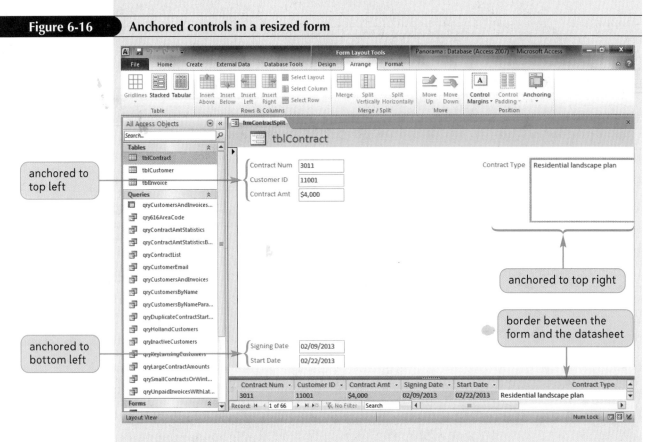

Finally, you'll show Sarah one of the anchoring options that resizes the ContractType text box as the form dimensions change.

▶ 7. Click the **ContractType** text box (if necessary), click the **Anchoring** button, and then click **Stretch Down and Right**. Because the ContractType text box is already anchored to the top right, it can't stretch any more to the right, but it does stretch down to increase the height of the text box.

▶ 8. Position the pointer on the border between the form and the datasheet until the pointer changes to a ✛ shape, and then drag up until you can see several rows in the datasheet. The bottom set of controls shifts up, and the bottom edge of the ContractType text box shifts up, reducing its height.

You've finished showing Sarah the Layout view changes to the split form, so you can close the form without saving the anchoring changes.

▶ 9. Close the frmContractSplit form without saving your design changes.

▶ 10. If you are not continuing on to the next session, close the Panorama database.

You've used form tools to create forms, and you've modified forms in Layout view. In the next session, you will continue your work with forms, concentrating on the techniques, tools, and options available in Design view.

REVIEW

Session 6.1 Quick Check

1. According to the form design guidelines, which object(s) should you use to perform all database updates?
2. The _____ property specifies the data source for a control in a form or report or for a field in a table or query.
3. What is the Documenter?
4. What is the Multiple Items tool?
5. What is a split form?
6. The _____ property for a control automatically resizes the control and places the control in the same relative position on the screen as the screen's size and resolution change.

SESSION 6.2 VISUAL OVERVIEW

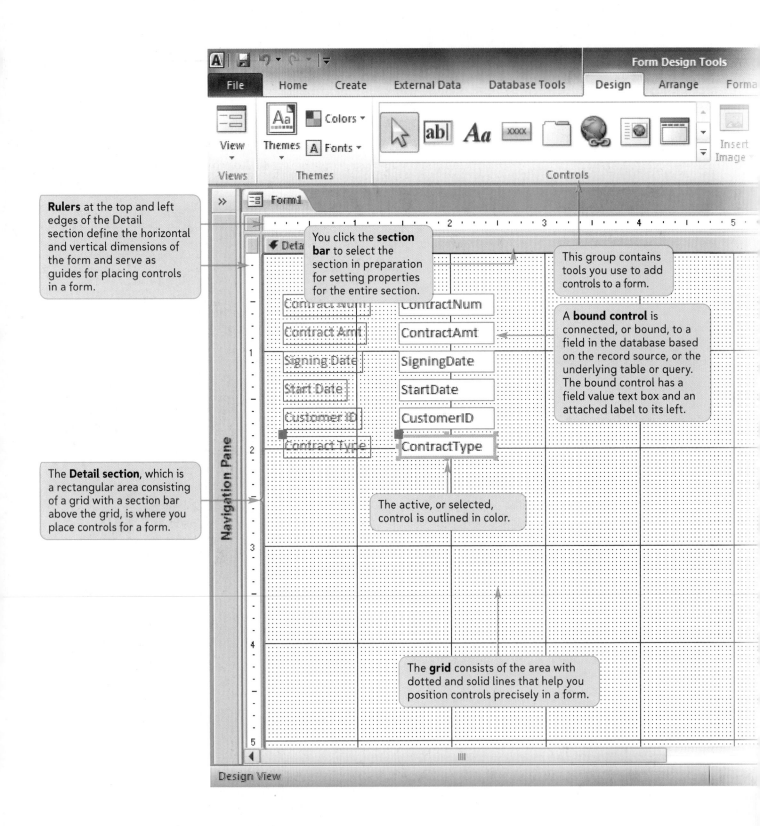

Rulers at the top and left edges of the Detail section define the horizontal and vertical dimensions of the form and serve as guides for placing controls in a form.

You click the **section bar** to select the section in preparation for setting properties for the entire section.

This group contains tools you use to add controls to a form.

A **bound control** is connected, or bound, to a field in the database based on the record source, or the underlying table or query. The bound control has a field value text box and an attached label to its left.

The **Detail section**, which is a rectangular area consisting of a grid with a section bar above the grid, is where you place controls for a form.

The active, or selected, control is outlined in color.

The **grid** consists of the area with dotted and solid lines that help you position controls precisely in a form.

FORM IN DESIGN VIEW

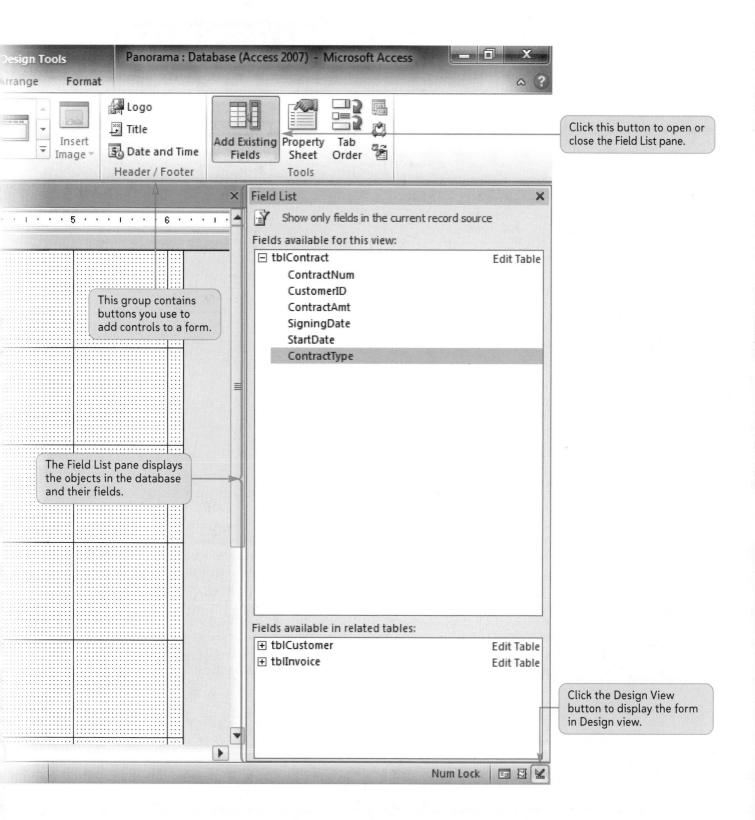

Design Tools
Arrange   Format

Panorama : Database (Access 2007) - Microsoft Access

Logo
Title
Date and Time

Header / Footer

Insert Image

Add Existing Fields

Property Sheet

Tab Order

Tools

Click this button to open or close the Field List pane.

This group contains buttons you use to add controls to a form.

Field List

Show only fields in the current record source

Fields available for this view:

⊟ tblContract   Edit Table
    ContractNum
    CustomerID
    ContractAmt
    SigningDate
    StartDate
    ContractType

The Field List pane displays the objects in the database and their fields.

Fields available in related tables:

⊞ tblCustomer   Edit Table
⊞ tblInvoice   Edit Table

Click the Design View button to display the form in Design view.

Num Lock

Planning and Designing a Custom Form

Sarah needs a form to enter and view information about Belmont Landscapes contracts and their related invoices. She wants the information in a single form, and she asks Lucia to design a form for her review.

After several discussions with Sarah and her staff, Lucia prepared a paper design for a custom form to display a contract and its related invoices. Lucia then used her paper design to create the form shown in Figure 6-17.

Figure 6-17	Lucia's design for the custom form

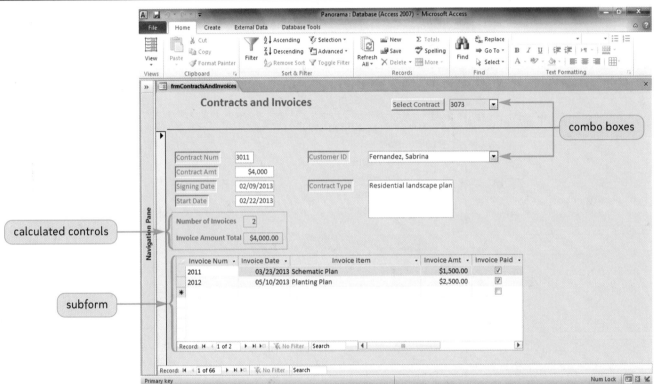

Notice that the top of the form displays a title and a combo box to select a contract record. Below these items are six field values with identifying labels from the tblContract table; these fields are the ContractNum, ContractAmt, SigningDate, StartDate, CustomerID, and ContractType fields. The CustomerID field is displayed in a combo box and the other field values are displayed in text boxes. The tblInvoice table fields appear in a subform, a separate form contained within another form. Unlike the tblContract table data, which displays identifying labels to the left of the field values in text boxes, the tblInvoice table data is displayed in datasheet format with identifying column headings above the field values. Finally, Number of Invoices and Invoice Amount Total in the main form display calculated controls based on the content of the subform.

Creating a Custom Form in Design View

To create Lucia's custom form, you could use the Form Wizard to create a basic version of the form and then customize it in Layout and Design views. However, to create Lucia's form, you would need to make many modifications to a basic form created by a wizard, so you will create the form directly in Design view. Creating forms in Design view is easy once you've done one form, and Design view allows you more control, precision, and options than creating forms in Layout view. You'll also find that you'll create forms more productively if you switch between Design view and Layout view because some design modifications are easier to make in one of the two views than in the other view.

The Form Window in Design View

You can use the Form window in Design view to create and modify forms. To create the custom form based on Lucia's design, you'll create a blank form, add the fields from the tblContract and tblInvoice tables, and then add other controls and make other form modifications.

REFERENCE

Creating a Form in Design View

- Click the Create tab on the Ribbon.
- In the Forms group, click the Blank Form button.
- Click the Design View button on the status bar.
- Make sure the Field List pane is open, and then add the required fields to the form.
- Add other required controls to the form.
- Modify the size, position, and other properties as necessary for the fields and other controls in the form.
- Save the form.

The form you'll create will be a bound form. A **bound form** is a form that has a table or query as its record source. You use bound forms for maintaining and displaying table data. **Unbound forms** are forms that do not have a record source and are usually used for forms that help users navigate among the objects in a database. Now you'll create a blank bound form based on the tblContract table.

To create a blank form in Design view:

▶ **1.** If you took a break after the previous session, make sure that the Panorama database is open and the Navigation Pane is open.

▶ **2.** Click the **Create** tab on the Ribbon and then, in the Forms group on the Create tab, click the **Blank Form** button. Access opens the Form window in Layout view.

▶ **3.** Click the **Design View** button 📐 on the status bar to switch to Design view, and then close the Navigation Pane. See Figure 6-18.

Figure 6-18 | **Blank form in Design view**

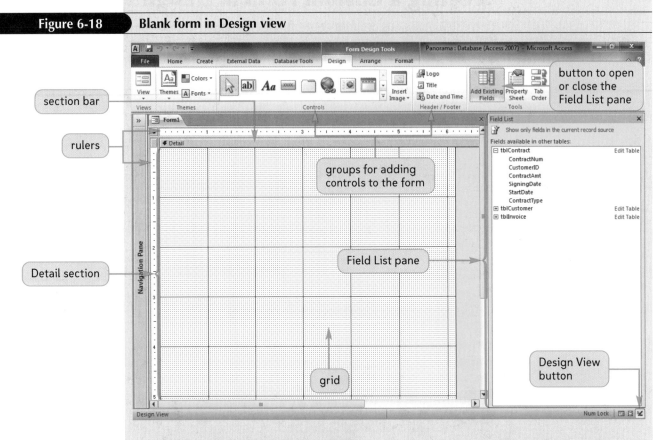

Trouble? If the Field List pane displays the "No fields available to be added to the current view" message, click the "Show all tables" link to display the tables in the Panorama database, and then click the plus sign next to tblContract in the Field List pane to display the fields in the table.

Trouble? If the tblContract table in the Field List pane is not expanded to show the fields in the table, click the plus sign next to tblContract to display the fields.

Design view contains the tools necessary to create a custom form. You create the form by placing controls in the blank form. You can place three kinds of controls in a form:

- A bound control is connected, or bound, to a field in the database based on the record source, or the underlying table or query. You use bound controls to display and maintain table field values.
- An **unbound control** is not connected to a field in the database. You use unbound controls to display text, such as a form title or instructions; to display lines, rectangles, and other objects; or to display graphics and pictures created using other software programs. An unbound control that displays text is called a **label**.
- A **calculated control** displays a value that is the result of an expression. The expression usually contains one or more fields, and the calculated control is recalculated each time any value in the expression changes.

To create a bound control, you add fields from the Field List pane to the Form window, and position the bound controls where you want them to appear in the form. To place other controls in a form or a report, you use the tools in the Controls and Header/Footer groups on the Design tab; ScreenTips are available for each control in these groups. The tools in the Controls group let you add to the form controls such as lines, rectangles, images, buttons, check boxes, and list boxes.

As noted earlier, Design view for a form contains a Detail section, which is a rectangular area consisting of a grid with a section bar above the grid. You click the section bar to select the section in preparation for setting properties for the entire section. The grid consists of the area with dotted and solid lines that help you position controls precisely in a form. In the Detail section, you place bound controls, unbound controls, and calculated controls in your form. You can change the size of the Detail section by dragging its edges. Rulers at the top and left edges of the Detail section define the horizontal and vertical dimensions of the form and serve as guides for placing controls in a form.

Your first task is to add bound controls to the Detail section for the six fields from the tblContract table.

Adding Fields to a Form

When you add a bound control to a form, Access adds a text box and, to its left, an attached label. The text box displays a field value from the record source. The attached label displays either the Caption property value for the field, if the Caption property value has been set, or the field name. To create a bound control, you first display the Field List pane by clicking the Add Existing Fields button in the Tools group on the Design tab. Then you double-click a field in the Field List pane to add the bound control to the Detail section. You can also drag a field from the Field List pane to the Detail section.

Next, you'll add bound controls to the Detail section for the six fields in the Field List pane. The Field List pane displays the three tables in the Panorama database, and the six fields in the tblContract table.

To add bound controls from the tblContract table to the grid:

▶ **1.** Double-click **ContractNum** in the Field List pane. Access adds a bound control in the Detail section of the form, removes the tblCustomer and tblInvoice tables from the "Fields available for this view" section of the Field List pane, and places the two tables in the "Fields available in related tables" section of the Field List pane.

▶ **2.** Repeat Step 1 for the **ContractAmt**, **SigningDate**, **StartDate**, **CustomerID**, and **ContractType** fields, in this order, in the Field List pane. Six bound controls—one for each of the six fields in the Field List pane—have been added in the Detail section of the form. See Figure 6-19.

Figure 6-19   Adding text boxes and attached labels as bound controls to a form

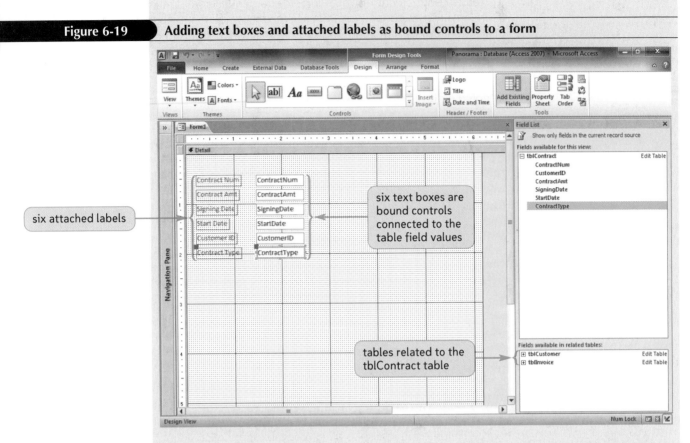

You should periodically save your work as you create a form, so you'll save the form now.

3. Click the **Save** button 🔲 on the Quick Access Toolbar. The Save As dialog box opens.

4. With the default name Form1 (your name might be different) selected in the Form Name box, type **frmContractsAndInvoices**, and then press the **Enter** key. The tab for the form now displays the form name, and the form design is saved in the Panorama database.

You've added the fields you need to the grid, so you can close the Field List pane.

5. In the Tools group on the Design tab, click the **Add Existing Fields** button to close the Field List pane.

Creating and modifying a form in Design view might seem awkward at first. With practice you will become comfortable working with custom forms.

Suggestions for Creating a Form Productively

To design a form productively, you should keep in mind the following suggestions:
- You can click the Undo button one or more times immediately after you make one or more errors or make undesired form adjustments.
- You should back up your database frequently, especially before you create new objects or customize existing objects. If you run into difficulty, you can revert to your most recent backup copy of the database.
- You should save your form after you've completed a portion of your work successfully and before you need to perform steps you've never done before. If you're not satisfied with subsequent steps, close the form without saving the changes you made since your last save, and then open the form and perform the steps again.
- You can always close the form, make a copy of the form in the Navigation Pane, and practice with the copy.
- Adding controls, setting properties, and performing other tasks in Access in the correct way should work all the time with consistent results, but in rare instances, you might find a feature doesn't work properly. If a feature you've previously used successfully suddenly doesn't work, you should save your work, close the database, make a backup copy of the database, open the database, and then compact and repair the database. Performing a compact and repair resolves most of these types of problems.

Compare your form's Detail section with Lucia's design, and notice that you need to move the ContractType bound control up and to the right. To do so, you must select and move the bound control.

Selecting, Moving, and Aligning Controls

Six text boxes now appear in the form's Detail section, one below the other. Each text box is a bound control connected to a field in the underlying table. Each text box has an attached label to its left. Each text box and attached label pair is a control in the form, and each individual text box is also a control in the form, as is each individual label. When you select a control, the control becomes outlined in orange, and eight squares, called handles, appear on its four corners and at the midpoints of its four edges. The larger handle in a control's upper-left corner is its **move handle**, which you use to move the control. You use the other seven handles, called **sizing handles**, to resize the control. When you work in Design view, controls you place in the form do not become part of a control layout, so you can individually select, move, resize, and otherwise manipulate one control without also changing the other controls. However, at any time you can select a group of controls and place them in a control layout—either a stacked layout or a tabular layout.

Selecting and Moving Controls

- Click the control to select it. To select several controls at once, press and hold down the Shift key while clicking each control. Handles appear around all selected controls.
- To move a single selected control, drag the control's move handle, which is the handle in the upper-left corner, to its new position.
- To move a group of selected controls, point to any selected control until the pointer changes to a move pointer, and then drag the group of selected controls to its new position.
- To move selected controls in small increments, press the appropriate arrow key.
- To move selected controls to the next nearest grid dot, hold down the Ctrl key and press the appropriate arrow key.

Based on Lucia's design for the custom form, you must select the ContractType bound control and move it up and to the right in the Detail section. The ContractType bound control consists of a field-value text box, labeled ContractType, and an attached label, labeled Contract Type, to its left.

To select the ContractType bound control:

1. If necessary, click the **ContractType** text box to select it. Move handles, which are the larger handles, appear on the upper-left corners of the selected text box control and its attached label. Sizing handles also appear, but only on the text box. See Figure 6-20.

Figure 6-20 | **Selecting the ContractType bound control**

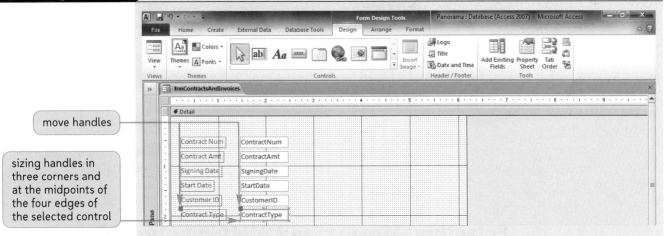

You can move a text box and its attached label together. To move them, place the pointer anywhere on the border of the text box, but not on a move handle or a sizing handle. When the pointer changes to a ⁺✥ shape, you can drag the text box and its attached label to the new location. As you move a control, an outline of the control moves on the rulers to indicate the current position of the control as you drag it. To move a group of selected controls, point to any selected control until the pointer changes to a ⁺✥ shape, and then drag the group of selected controls to its new position. You can move controls with more precision when you use the arrow keys instead of the mouse. To move selected controls in small increments, press the appropriate arrow key. To move selected controls to the next nearest grid dot, hold down the Ctrl key and press the appropriate arrow key.

You can also move either a text box or its label individually. If you want to move the text box but not its label, for example, place the pointer on the text box's move handle. When the pointer changes to a ⁺✥ shape, drag the text box to the new location. You use the label's move handle in a similar way to move only the label.

You'll now arrange the controls to match Lucia's design.

To move the ContractType bound control:

1. Position the pointer on one of the edges of the ContractType text box, but not on a move handle or a sizing handle. When the pointer changes to a ⁺✥ shape, drag the control to the right until the left edge of the highlight on the horizontal ruler is at the 3-inch mark, drag the control up until the top of the highlight on the vertical ruler is just below the top of the SigningDate bound control, and then release the mouse button. See Figure 6-21.

Figure 6-21	After moving the ContractType bound control

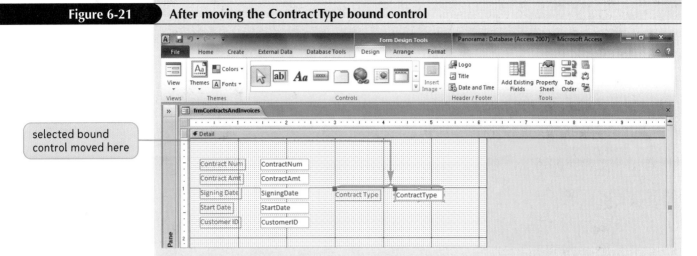

selected bound control moved here

Trouble? If you need to make major adjustments to the placement of the ContractType bound control, click the Undo button on the Quick Access Toolbar one or more times until the bound control is back to its starting position, and then repeat Step 1. If you need to make minor adjustments to the placement of the ContractType bound control, use the arrow keys.

Now you need to align the ContractType and SigningDate bound controls on their top edges. If you've selected a column of controls, you can align the left edges or the right edges of the controls. If you've selected a row of controls, you can align the top edges or the bottom edges of the controls. A fifth alignment option, To Grid, aligns selected controls with the dots in the grid. You can find the five alignment options on the Arrange tab of the Ribbon or on the shortcut menu for the selected controls. You'll use the shortcut menu to align the two bound controls. Then you'll save the modified form and review your work in Form view.

To align the ContractType and SigningDate bound controls:

1. Make sure the ContractType bound control is selected, hold down the **Shift** key, click the **Contract Type** label, click the **SigningDate** text box, click the **Signing Date** label, and then release the **Shift** key. This action selects the four controls; each selected control has an orange border.

2. Right-click one of the selected controls, point to **Align** on the shortcut menu, and then click **Top**. The four selected controls are aligned on their top edges. See Figure 6-22.

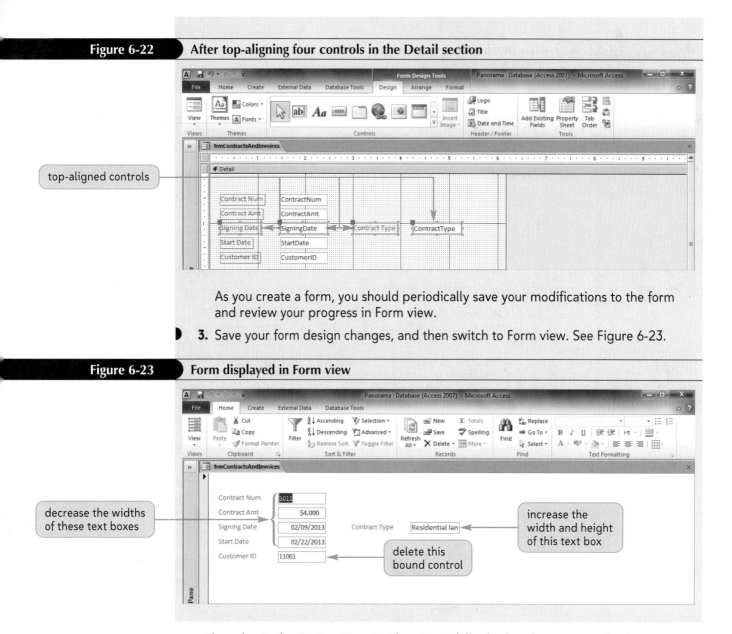

Figure 6-22 — After top-aligning four controls in the Detail section

As you create a form, you should periodically save your modifications to the form and review your progress in Form view.

3. Save your form design changes, and then switch to Form view. See Figure 6-23.

Figure 6-23 — Form displayed in Form view

The value in the ContractType text box is not fully displayed, so you need to increase the size of the text box. The widths of the other four text boxes are wider than necessary, so you'll reduce their widths. Also, the CustomerID bound control consists of a label and a text box, but the plan for the form shows a combo box for the CustomerID positioned above the ContractType bound control. You'll delete the CustomerID bound control in preparation for adding it to the form as a combo box.

Resizing and Deleting Controls

A selected control displays seven sizing handles: four at the midpoints on each edge of the control and one at each corner except the upper-left corner. Recall that the upper-left corner displays the move handle. Positioning the pointer over a sizing handle changes the pointer to a two-headed arrow; the directions in which the arrows point indicate in which direction you can resize the selected control. When you drag a sizing handle, you resize the control. As you resize the control, a thin line appears inside the sizing handle to guide you in completing the task accurately, as do the outlines that appear on the horizontal and vertical rulers.

Resizing a Control in Design View

- Click the control to select it and display the sizing handles.
- Place the pointer over the sizing handle you want, and then drag the edge of the control until it is the size you want.
- To resize selected controls in small increments, hold down the Shift key and press the appropriate arrow key. This technique applies the resizing to the right edge and the bottom edge of the control.

You'll begin by deleting the CustomerID bound control. Then you'll resize the ContractType text box, which is too narrow and too short to display ContractType field values. Then you'll resize the remaining four text boxes to reduce their widths.

To delete a bound control and resize the text boxes:

1. Switch to Design view, click an unused portion of the grid, or to the right of the grid, to deselect all controls, and then click the **CustomerID** text box to select it.

2. Right-click the **CustomerID** text box to open the shortcut menu, and then click **Delete**. The label and the text box for the CustomerID bound control are deleted.

3. Click the **ContractType** text box to select it.

4. Place the pointer on the middle-right handle of the ContractType text box. When the pointer changes to a ↔ shape, drag the right border horizontally to the right to the 6-inch mark on the horizontal ruler.

5. Place the pointer on the middle-bottom handle of the ContractType text box. When the pointer changes to a ↕ shape, drag the bottom border down to the 1.75-inch mark on the vertical ruler. See Figure 6-24.

Figure 6-24	After resizing the ContractType text box

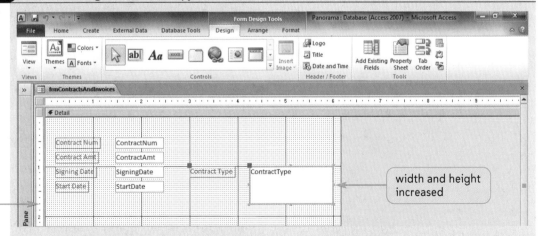

bottom of the ContractType text box aligned at the 1.75-inch mark

width and height increased

Resizing controls in Design view is a trial-and-error process, in which you resize a control in Design view, switch to Form view to observe the effect of the resizing, switch back to Design view to make further refinements to the control's size, and continue until the control is sized correctly. It's easier to resize controls in Layout view because you can see actual field values while you resize the controls. You'll resize the other four text boxes in Layout view.

6. Switch to Layout view, and then click the **ContractNum** text box (if necessary) to select it.

7. Position the pointer on the right edge of the **ContractNum** text box. When the pointer changes to a ↔ shape, drag the right border horizontally to the left until the text box is slightly wider than the field value it contains. See Figure 6-25.

The sizes of the ContractAmt, SigningDate, and StartDate text boxes will look fine if you reduce them to have the same widths, so you'll select all three text boxes and resize them as a group.

TIP

If you select a control by mistake, hold down the Shift key, and then click the selected control to deselect it.

8. Select the **ContractAmt**, **SigningDate**, and **StartDate** text boxes.

9. Position the pointer on the right edge of any of the three selected controls. When the pointer changes to a ↔ shape, drag the right border horizontally to the left until the SigningDate and StartDate text boxes are slightly wider than the field values they contain. See Figure 6-25.

| Figure 6-25 | After resizing text boxes in Layout view |

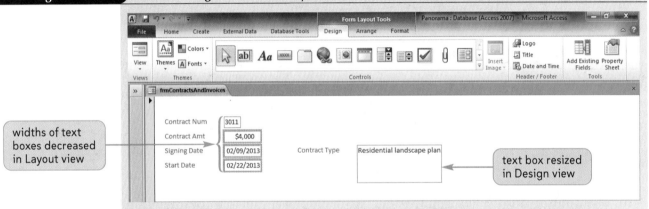

widths of text boxes decreased in Layout view

text box resized in Design view

Trouble? If you resized the text boxes too far to the left, number signs will be displayed inside the SigningDate and StartDate text boxes. Drag the right edge of the text boxes slightly to the right and repeat the process until the date values are visible inside the text boxes.

10. Navigate through the first several records to make sure the five text boxes are sized properly and display the full field values. If any text box is too small, select the text box and increase its width the appropriate amount.

11. Save your form design changes, switch to Design view, and then deselect all controls by clicking in an unused portion of the grid.

INSIGHT

Making Form Design Modifications

When you design forms and other objects, you'll find it helpful to switch frequently between Design view and Layout view. Some form modifications are easier to make in Layout view, other form modifications are easier to make in Design view, and still other form modifications can be made only in Design view. You should check your progress frequently in either Layout view or Form view, and you should save your modifications after completing a set of changes successfully.

Recall that you removed the lookup feature from the CustomerID field because a combo box provides the same lookup capability in a form. Next, you'll add a combo box for the CustomerID field to the custom form.

Adding a Combo Box to a Form

The Customer and Contract tables are related in a one-to-many relationship. The CustomerID field in the Contract table is a foreign key to the Customer table, and you can use a combo box in the custom form to view and maintain CustomerID field values more easily and accurately than using a text box. Recall that a combo box is a control that provides the features of a text box and a list box; you can choose a value from the list or type an entry.

PROSKILLS

Problem Solving: Using Combo Boxes for Foreign Keys

When you design forms, combo boxes are a natural choice for foreign keys because foreign key values must match one of the primary key values in the related primary table. If you do not use combo boxes for foreign keys, you force users to type values in the text box; when they make typing mistakes, Access rejects the values and displays frustrating non-matching error messages. Combo boxes allow users to select from a list of only valid foreign key values, so non-matching situations are eliminated. At the same time, combo boxes allow users who are skilled at data entry to more rapidly type the values, instead of using the more time-consuming technique of choosing a value from the combo box list. Whenever you use an Access feature such as combo boxes for foreign keys, it takes extra time during development to add the feature, but you save users time and improve their accuracy for the many months or years they use the database.

You use the **Combo Box tool** in Design view to add a combo box to a form. If you want help when adding the combo box, you can select one of the Control Wizards. A **Control Wizard** asks a series of questions and then uses your answers to create a control in a form or report. Access offers Control Wizards for the Combo Box, List Box, Option Group, Command Button, Subform/Subreport, and other control tools.

You will use the Combo Box Wizard to add a combo box to the form for the CustomerID field.

To add a combo box to the form:

1. In the Controls group on the Design tab, click the **More** button ⬇ to open the Controls gallery. See Figure 6-26.

Figure 6-26 | Controls gallery

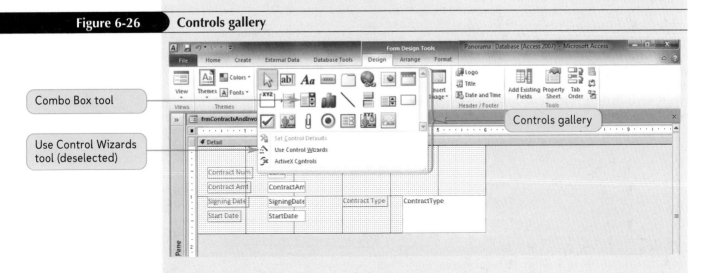

Combo Box tool

Use Control Wizards tool (deselected)

The Controls gallery contains 23 tools that allow you to add controls (such as text boxes, lines, charts, and labels) to a form. You drag a control from the Controls gallery and place it in position in the grid.

2. In the gallery, make sure the Use Control Wizards tool ⬚ is selected (with an orange background) in the Controls gallery. If the tool is not selected, click the **Use Control Wizards** tool ⬚ to select it, and then click the **More** button ⬚ to open the Controls gallery again.

3. In the Controls gallery, click the **Combo Box** tool ⬚. The Controls gallery closes. After you click the Combo Box tool or most other tools in the Controls gallery, nothing happens until you move the pointer over the form. When you move the pointer over the form, the pointer changes to a shape that is unique for the control with a plus symbol in its upper-left corner. You position the plus symbol in the location where you want to place the upper-left corner of the control.

   You'll place the combo box near the top of the form, above the ContractType bound control, and then position it more precisely after you've finished the wizard.

4. Position the + portion of the pointer three grid dots below the top of the grid and at the 4-inch mark on the horizontal ruler, and then click the mouse button. Access places a combo box control in the form and opens the first Combo Box Wizard dialog box.

   You can use an existing table or query as the source for a new combo box or type the values for the combo box. In this case, you'll use the qryCustomersByName query as the basis for the new combo box. This query includes the Customer calculated field, whose value equals the Company field value, if it's nonnull, or the concatenation of the LastName and FirstName field values in all other cases.

5. Click the **I want the combo box to get the values from another table or query** option button (if necessary), click the **Next** button to open the next Combo Box Wizard dialog box, click the **Queries** option button in the View group, click **Query: qryCustomersByName**, and then click the **Next** button. Access opens the third Combo Box Wizard dialog box. This dialog box lets you select the fields from the query to appear as columns in the combo box. You'll select the first two fields.

6. Double-click **Customer** to move this field to the Selected Fields box, double-click **CustomerID**, and then click the **Next** button. This dialog box lets you choose a sort order for the combo box entries. Lucia wants the entries to appear in ascending Customer order.

7. Click the **arrow** for the first box, click **Customer**, and then click the **Next** button to open the next Combo Box Wizard dialog box.

8. Resize the columns to their best fit, scrolling down the columns to make sure all values are visible and resizing again if they're not, and then click the **Next** button.

   In this dialog box, you select the foreign key, which is the CustomerID field.

9. Click **CustomerID** and then click the **Next** button.

   In this dialog box, you specify the field in the tblContract table where you will store the selected CustomerID value from the combo box. You'll store the value in the CustomerID field in the tblContract table.

10. Click the **Store that value in this field** option button, click its **arrow**, click **CustomerID**, and then click the **Next** button.

Trouble? If CustomerID doesn't appear in the list, click the Cancel button, press the Delete key to delete the combo box, click the Add Existing Fields button in the Tools group on the Design tab, double-click CustomerID in the Field List pane, press the Delete key to delete CustomerID, close the Field List pane, and then repeat Steps 1-10.

In this dialog box, you specify the name for the combo box control. You'll use the field name of CustomerID.

11. Type **CustomerID** and then click the **Finish** button. The completed CustomerID combo box appears in the form.

You need to position and resize the combo box control, but first you'll change the text for the attached label from CustomerID to Customer ID to match the format used for other label controls in the form. To change the text for a label control, you set the control's Caption property value.

REFERENCE

Changing a Label's Caption

- Right-click the label to select it and to display the shortcut menu, and then click Properties to display the property sheet.
- If necessary, click the All tab to display the All page in the property sheet.
- Edit the existing text in the Caption box; or click the Caption box and press the F2 key to select the current value, and then type a new caption.
- In the Tools group on the Design tab, click the Property Sheet button to close the property sheet.

Next, you'll change the text that displays in the combo box label.

To set the Caption property value for the CustomerID label:

1. Right-click the **CustomerID** label, which is the control to the left of the CustomerID text box, to select it and to display the shortcut menu, and then click **Properties** on the shortcut menu. The property sheet for the CustomerID label opens.

2. If necessary, click the **All** tab to display all properties for the selected CustomerID label.

Trouble? If the Selection type entry below the Property Sheet title bar is not "Label," then you selected the wrong control in Step 1. Click the CustomerID label to change to the property sheet for this control.

3. Click before the "ID" in the Caption box, press the **spacebar**, and then press the **Tab** key to move to the next property in the property sheet. The Caption property value should now be Customer ID and the label for the CustomerID bound control now displays Customer ID. See Figure 6-27.

TIP
After selecting a control, you can press the F4 key to open and close the property sheet for the control.

TIP
You won't see the effects of the new property setting until you select another property, select another control, or close the property sheet.

Figure 6-27   **CustomerID combo box added to the form**

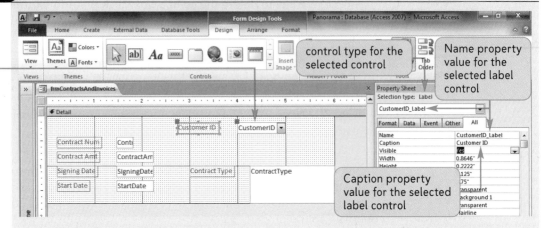

CustomerID combo box with attached label to its left

control type for the selected control

Name property value for the selected label control

Caption property value for the selected label control

Trouble? Some property values in your property sheet, such as the Width and Top property values, might differ if your label's position slightly differs from the label position used as the basis for Figure 6-27. These differences cause no problems.

The Selection type entry, which appears below the property sheet title bar, displays the control type (Label in this case) for the selected control. Below the Selection type entry in the property sheet is the Control box, which you can use to select another control in the form and then change its properties in the property sheet. Or you can simply click the control in the form to change to its properties in the property sheet. The first property in the property sheet, the **Name property**, is the property that specifies the name of a control, section, or object (CustomerID_Label in this case). The Name property value is the same as the value displayed in the Control box. For bound controls, the Name property value matches the field name. For unbound controls, Access adds an underscore and a suffix of the control type (for example, Label) to the Name property setting. For unbound controls, you can set the Name property to another, more meaningful value at any time.

TIP

Always be sure to confirm that the Selection type entry displays the correct control type and the Control box displays the correct control name.

4. Close the property sheet, and then save your design changes.

Now that you've added the combo box to the form, you can position the combo box and its attached label and resize the combo box. You'll need to view the form in Form view to determine any fine tuning necessary for the width of the combo box.

To modify the combo box in Design and Layout views:

1. Click the **CustomerID** combo box, hold down the **Shift** key, click the **Customer ID** label, and then release the **Shift** key to select both controls.

First, you'll align the CustomerID combo box and its label with the ContractType and ContractNum bound controls. You'll move the selected controls to the right, align the Customer ID and Contract Type labels on their left edges, align the CustomerID combo box and the ContractType text box on their left edges, and then align the bottom edges of the combo box and its label with the bottom edges of the ContractNum bound control.

2. Drag the selected controls to the right until the left edge of the Customer ID label is approximately one-half inch to the right of the left edge of the Contract Type label, making sure the two controls remain above the ContractNum bound control.

3. Select the **Customer ID** label and the **Contract Type** label, click the **Arrange** tab on the Ribbon, and in the Sizing & Ordering group on the Arrange tab, click the **Align** button, and then click **Left**. The selected controls are aligned on their left edges.

4. Repeat Step 3 to align the **CustomerID** combo box and the **ContractType** text box on their left edges.

5. Select the **Contract Num** label, **ContractNum** text box, **Customer ID** label, and **CustomerID** combo box, and in the Sizing & Ordering group on the Arrange tab, click the **Align** button, and then click **Bottom**. The four selected controls are aligned on their bottom edges.

6. Switch to Form view, and then click the **CustomerID** arrow to open the control's list box. See Figure 6-28.

Figure 6-28   CustomerID combo box in Form view

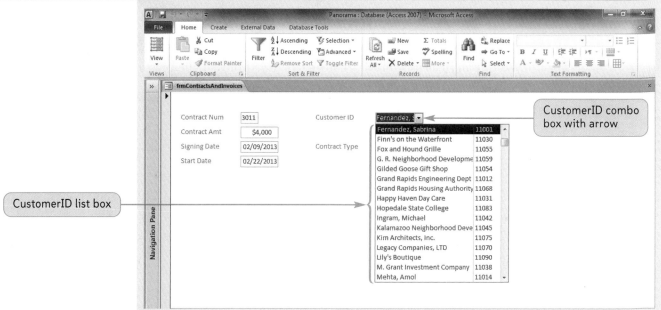

You need to widen the CustomerID combo box, so that the widest customer value in the list is displayed in the combo box. You can widen the combo box in Layout view or in Design view. Because Form view and Layout view display live data, you'll use Layout view instead of Design view to make this change because you can determine the proper width more accurately in Layout view.

7. Switch to Layout view, and then navigate to record 16. Weston Community Parks Foundation, which is the customer value for this record, is the widest value that is displayed in the combo box. You want to widen the combo box, so that the value in record 16 is completely visible.

8. Make sure that only the combo box is selected, and then pointing to the right edge, widen the combo box until the entire customer value is visible. See Figure 6-29.

Figure 6-29 **After resizing the CustomerID combo box in Layout view**

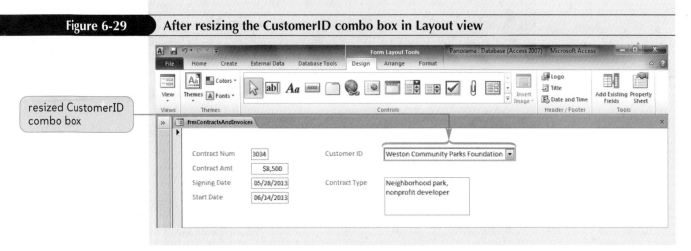

resized CustomerID combo box

Now you'll add the title to the top of the form.

Using Form Headers and Form Footers

The **Form Header** and **Form Footer sections** let you add titles, instructions, command buttons, and other controls to the top and bottom of your form, respectively. Controls placed in the Form Header or Form Footer sections remain on the screen whenever the form is displayed in Form view or Layout view; they do not change when the contents of the Detail section change as you navigate from one record to another record.

To add either a form header or footer to your form, you must first add both the Form Header and Form Footer sections as a pair to the form. If your form needs one of these sections but not the other, you can remove a section by setting its height to zero, which is the same method you would use to remove any form section. You can also prevent a section from appearing in Form view or in Print Preview by setting its Visible property to No. The **Visible property** determines if Access displays a control or section. Set the Visible property to Yes to display the control or section, and set the Visible property to No to hide it.

If you've set the Form Footer section's height to zero or set its Visible property to No and a future form design change makes adding controls to the Form Footer section necessary, you can restore the section by using the pointer to drag its bottom edge back down or by setting its Visible property to Yes.

You can add the Form Header and Form Footer sections as a pair to a form either directly or indirectly. The direct way to add these sections is to right-click the Detail section selector, and then click Form Header/Footer. This direct method is available only in Design view. The indirect way to add the Form Header and Form Footer sections in Layout view or Design view is to use one of these three buttons in the Header/Footer group on the Design tab: the Logo button, the Title button, or the Date and Time button. Clicking any of these three buttons causes Access to add the Form Header and Form Footer sections to the form and to place an appropriate control in the Form Header section. If you use the indirect method in Layout view, Access sets the Form Footer section's height to zero. In Design view, the indirect method creates a Form Footer section with the Height property set to one-quarter inch.

Adding and Removing Form Header and Form Footer Sections

- In Design view, right-click the Detail section selector, and then click Form Header/ Footer on the shortcut menu.

or

- In Layout view or Design view, click a button in the Header/Footer group on the Design tab to add a logo, title, or date and time to the form.
- To remove a Form Header or Form Footer section, drag its bottom edge up until the section area disappears or set the section's Visible property to No.

Lucia's design includes a title at the top of the form. Because the title will not change as you navigate through the form records, you will add the title to the Form Header section in the form.

Adding a Title to a Form

You'll add the title to Lucia's form in Layout view. When you add the title to the form in Layout view, Access adds the Form Header section to the form and places the title in the Form Header section. At the same time, Access adds the Page Footer section to the form and sets its height to zero.

To add a title to the form:

▶ 1. In the Header/Footer group on the Design tab, click the **Title** button. Access adds the title to the form, displaying it in the upper-left of the form and using the form name as the title.

You need to change the title. Because the title is already selected, you can type over or edit the selected title.

▶ 2. Press the **Home** key to move to the beginning of the title, press the **Delete** key three times to delete the first three characters, click before the word "And," press the **spacebar**, type the letter **a**, press the **Delete** key, press the → key twice, press the **spacebar**, and then press the **Enter** key. You've changed the title to "Contracts and Invoices." See Figure 6-30.

Figure 6-30	Title placed in the Form Header section

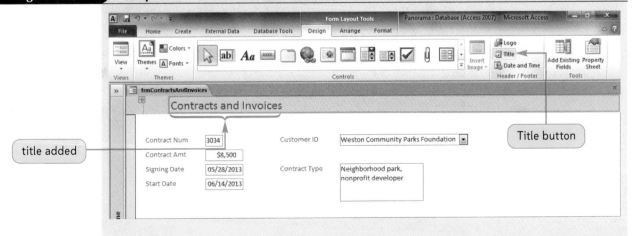

Lucia wants the title to be prominent in the form. The title is already a larger font size than the font used for the form's labels and text boxes, so you'll change the title's font weight to bold to increase its prominence.

▶ **3.** Make sure the title control is still selected, click the **Format** tab, and then in the Font group on the Format tab, click the **Bold** button **B**. The title is displayed in 18-point, bold text.

It is not obvious in Layout view that the title is displayed in the Form Header section, so you'll view the form design in Design view.

▶ **4.** Switch to Design view, and then save your design changes. The title is displayed in the Form Header section. See Figure 6-31.

Figure 6-31   Form Header and Form Footer sections in Design view

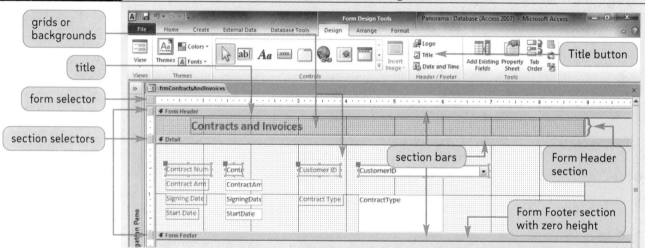

The form now contains a Form Header section that displays the title, a Detail section that displays the bound controls and combo box, and a Form Footer section that is set to a height of zero. Each section consists of a **section selector** and a section bar, either of which you can click to select and set properties for the entire section, and a grid or background, which is where you place controls that you want to display in the form. The **form selector** is the selector at the intersection of the horizontal and vertical rulers; you click the form selector when you want to select the form and set its properties. The vertical ruler is segmented into sections for the Form Header section, the Detail section, and the Form Footer section.

A form's total height includes the heights of the Form Header, Detail, and Form Footer sections. If you set the form's total height to more than the screen size, users will need to use scroll bars to view the content of your form, which is less productive for users and isn't good form design.

▶ **5.** If you are not continuing on to the next session, close the Panorama database.

So far, you've added controls to the form and modified the controls by selecting, moving, aligning, resizing, and deleting them. You've added and modified a combo box and added a title in the Form Header section. In the next session, you will continue your work with the custom form by adding a combo box to find records, adding a subform, adding calculated controls, changing form and section properties, changing control properties, and using filters.

REVIEW

Session 6.2 Quick Check

1. What is a bound form, and when do you use bound forms?
2. What is the difference between a bound control and an unbound control?
3. The _____ consists of the dotted and solid lines that appear in the Detail section to help you position controls precisely in a form.
4. The handle in a selected object's upper-left corner is the _____ handle.
5. How do you move a selected text box and its label at the same time?
6. How do you resize a control?
7. A(n) _____ control provides the features of a text box and a list box.
8. How do you change a label's caption?
9. What is the Form Header section?

SESSION 6.3 VISUAL OVERVIEW

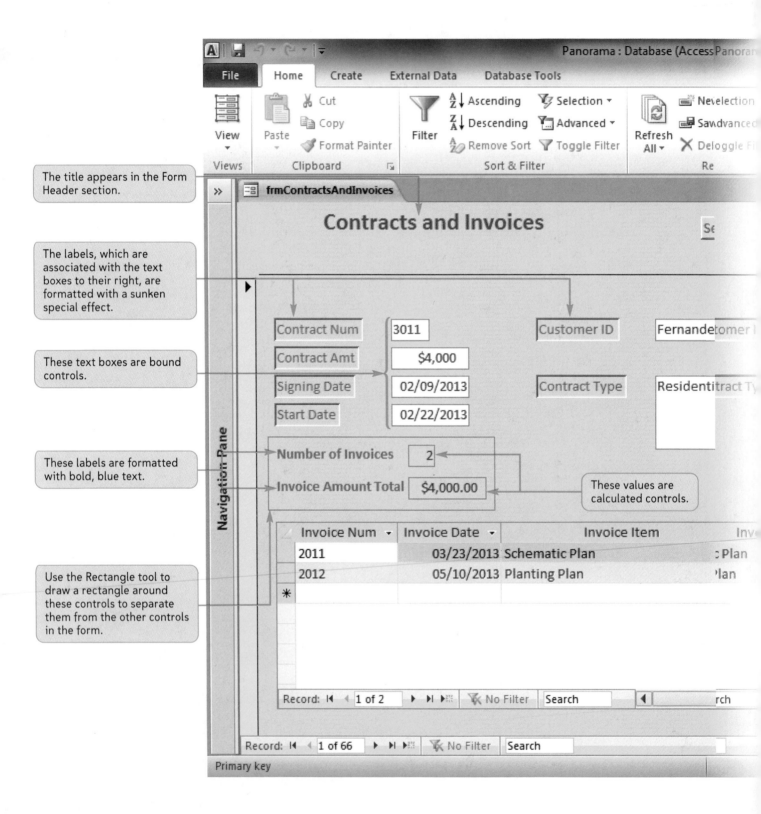

The title appears in the Form Header section.

The labels, which are associated with the text boxes to their right, are formatted with a sunken special effect.

These text boxes are bound controls.

These labels are formatted with bold, blue text.

Use the Rectangle tool to draw a rectangle around these controls to separate them from the other controls in the form.

These values are calculated controls.

CUSTOM FORM IN FORM VIEW

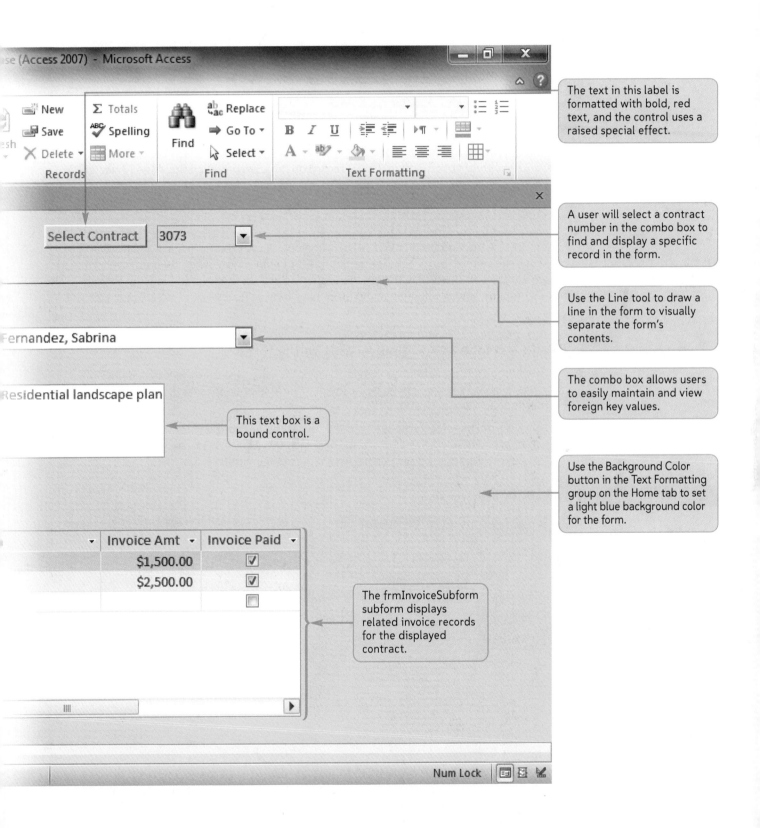

The text in this label is formatted with bold, red text, and the control uses a raised special effect.

A user will select a contract number in the combo box to find and display a specific record in the form.

Use the Line tool to draw a line in the form to visually separate the form's contents.

The combo box allows users to easily maintain and view foreign key values.

This text box is a bound control.

Use the Background Color button in the Text Formatting group on the Home tab to set a light blue background color for the form.

The frmInvoiceSubform subform displays related invoice records for the displayed contract.

Adding a Combo Box to Find Records

Most combo boxes are used to display and update data. You can also use combo boxes to find records. You will add a combo box to the Form Header section to find a specific record in the tblContract table to display in the form.

> ### Adding a Combo Box to Find Records
>
> - Open the property sheet for the form in Design view, make sure the record source is a table or query, and then close the property sheet.
> - In the Controls group on the Design tab, click the More button, click the Combo Box tool, and then click the position in the form where you want to place the control.
> - Click the third option button (Find a record on my form based on the value I selected in my combo box) in the first Combo Box Wizard dialog box, and then complete the remaining Combo Box Wizard dialog boxes.

You can use the Combo Box Wizard to add a combo box to find records in a form. However, the Combo Box Wizard provides this find option only when the form's record source is a table or query. You'll view the property sheet for the form to view the Record Source property, and you'll change the property setting, if necessary.

To add a combo box to find records to the form:

1. If you took a break after the previous session, make sure that the Panorama database is open, the frmContractsAndInvoices form is open in Design view, and the Navigation Pane is closed.

2. Click the **form selector** (located to the left of the horizontal ruler) to select the form, open the property sheet, and then click the **All** tab (if necessary). The property sheet displays the properties for the form. See Figure 6-32.

Figure 6-32	Property sheet for the form

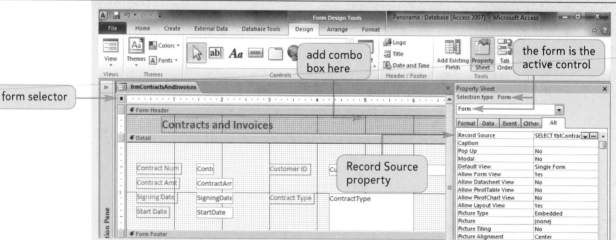

The Record Source property is set to an SQL SELECT statement. You need to change the Record Source property to a table or query, or the Combo Box Wizard will not present you with the option to find records in a form. You'll change the Record Source property to the tblContract table because this table is the record source for all the bound controls you added to the Detail section.

3. Click the **Record Source** box, press the **F2** key to select the entire property setting, type **t**, the AutoComplete feature fills in the rest of tblContract, press the **Tab** key to accept the entire entry of tblContract, and then close the property sheet.

You'll now use the Combo Box Wizard to add a combo box to the form's Form Header section to find a record in the tblContract table to display in the form.

4. In the Controls group on the Design tab, click the **More** button ⊽ to open the Controls gallery, make sure the Use Control Wizards tool ⬚ is selected in the Controls gallery, click the **Combo Box** tool ⬚, position the + portion of the pointer at the top of the Form Header section and at the 5-inch mark on the horizontal ruler (see Figure 6-32), and then click the mouse button. Access places a combo box control in the form and opens the first Combo Box Wizard dialog box.

The dialog box now displays a third option to "Find a record on my form based on the value I selected in my combo box," which you'll use for this combo box. You choose the first option, which you used for the CustomerID combo box, when you want to select a value from a list of foreign key values from an existing table or query. You choose the second option when you want users to select a value from a short fixed list of values that don't change. For example, if Belmont Landscapes wanted to include a field in the tblCustomer table to classify each customer, you could use a combo box with this second option to display a list of values such as Residential, Commercial, Nonprofit, and Government.

5. Click the **Find a record on my form based on the value I selected in my combo box** option button, and then click the **Next** button to open the next dialog box. This dialog box lets you select the fields from the tblContract table to appear as columns in the combo box. You'll select the first field.

6. Double-click **ContractNum** to move this field to the Selected Fields box, and then click the **Next** button.

7. Resize the column to its best fit, and then click the **Next** button.

In this dialog box, you specify the name for the combo box's label. You'll use Select Contract as the label.

8. Type **Select Contract**, and then click the **Finish** button. The completed unbound combo box is displayed in the form. See Figure 6-33.

Figure 6-33   **Unbound combo box added to the form**

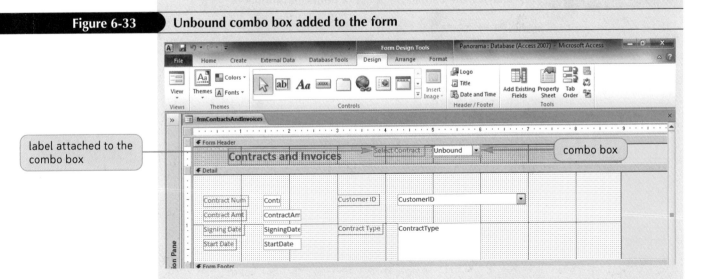

label attached to the combo box

You'll align the right edges of the two combo boxes, move the attached label closer to the combo box, and then align the bottoms of the combo box and its attached label with the bottom of the title in the Form Header section.

▶ **9.** Deselect all controls, select the two combo boxes (one in the Form Header section and the other in the Detail section), right-click one of the selected controls, point to **Align**, and then click **Right**. The two combo boxes are aligned on their right edges.

▶ **10.** Click the **Select Contract** label, point to the label's move handle, and then drag the label to the right until it is two grid dots to the left of the combo box.

▶ **11.** Select the combo box in the Form Header section, the **Select Contract** label, and the title, right-click one of the selected controls, point to **Align**, and then click **Bottom**. The three selected controls are aligned on their bottom edges. See Figure 6-34.

Figure 6-34 After aligning the combo box control and the title

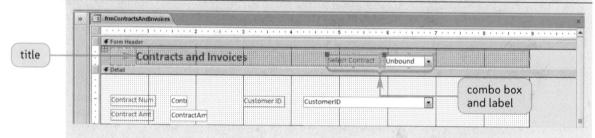

You'll save your form changes and view the new combo box in Form view.

To find contract records using the combo box:

▶ **1.** Save the form design changes, and then switch to Form view.

▶ **2.** Click the **Select Contract** combo box arrow to open the list box. See Figure 6-35.

Figure 6-35 Displaying the combo box's list of contract numbers

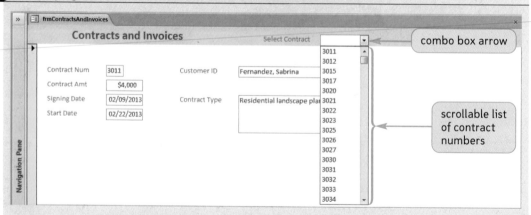

> **3.** Scroll down the list, and then click **3073**. The current record changes from record 1 to record 41, which is the record for contract number 3073.

The form design is very plain at this point with no color, special effects, or visual contrast among the controls. Before making the form more attractive and useful, you'll add the remaining controls to the form: a subform and two calculated controls.

Adding a Subform to a Form

Lucia's design for the form includes a subform that displays the related invoices for the displayed contract. The form you've been creating is the main form for records from the primary tblContract table (the "one" side of the one-to-many relationship), and the subform will display records from the related tblInvoice table (the "many" side of the one-to-many relationship). You use the **Subform/Subreport tool** in Design view to add a subform to a form. You can add the subform on your own, or you can get help adding the subform by using the SubForm Wizard.

You will use the SubForm Wizard to add the subform for the tblInvoice table records to the bottom of the form. First, you'll increase the height of the Detail section to make room for the subform.

To add the subform to the form:

> **1.** Switch to Design view.

> **2.** Place the pointer on the bottom edge of the Detail section. When the pointer changes to a ⬍ shape, drag the section's edge down until it is at the 4-inch mark on the vertical ruler.

> **3.** In the Controls group on the Design tab, click the **More** button ⬇ to open the Controls gallery, make sure the Control Wizards tool 🖾 is selected, and then click the **Subform/Subreport** tool 🖽.

> **4.** Position the + portion of the pointer in the Detail section at the 2.5-inch mark on the vertical ruler and at the 1-inch mark on the horizontal ruler, and then click the mouse button. Access places a subform control in the form's Detail section and opens the first SubForm Wizard dialog box.

TIP

Drag slightly beyond the desired ending position to expose the vertical ruler measurement, and then decrease the height back to the correct position.

You can use a table or query, or an existing form as the record source for a subform. In this case, you'll use the related tblInvoice table as the record source for a new subform.

To use the SubForm Wizard to add the subform to the form:

> **1.** Make sure the Use existing Tables and Queries option button is selected, and then click the **Next** button. Access opens the next SubForm Wizard dialog box, which lets you select a table or query as the record source for the subform and the fields from the selected table or query.

> **2.** Click the **Tables/Queries arrow** to display the list of tables and queries in the Panorama database, scroll to the top of the list, and then click **Table: tblInvoice**. The Available Fields box shows the fields in the tblInvoice table.

Lucia's form design includes all fields from the tblInvoice table in the subform, except for the ContractNum field, which you already placed in the Detail section of the form from the tblContract table.

▶ **3.** Click the ⟩⟩ button to move all available fields to the Selected Fields box, click **ContractNum** in the Selected Fields box, click the ⟨ button, and then click the **Next** button to open the next SubForm Wizard dialog box. See Figure 6-36.

Figure 6-36   Selecting the linking field

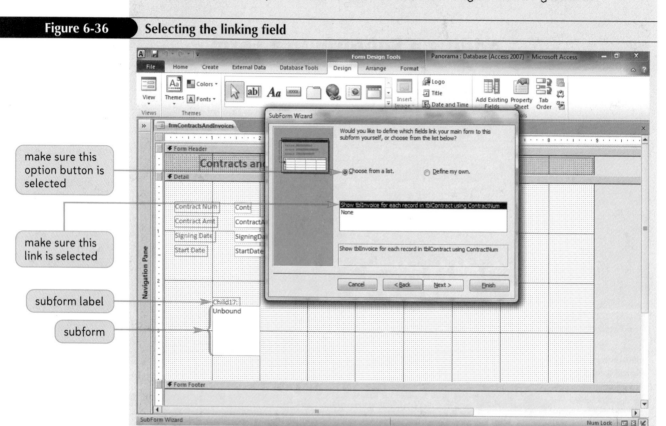

In this dialog box, you select the link between the primary tblContract table and the related tblInvoice table. The common field in the two tables, ContractNum, links the tables. Access uses the ContractNum field to display a record in the main form, which displays data from the primary tblContract table, and to select and display the related records for that contract in the subform, which displays data from the related tblInvoice table.

▶ **4.** Make sure the Choose from a list option button is selected, make sure the first link is highlighted, and then click the **Next** button. The next SubForm Wizard dialog box lets you specify a name for the subform.

▶ **5.** Type **frmInvoiceSubform** and then click the **Finish** button. Access increases the height and width of the subform in the form. The subform will display the related tblInvoice records; its label appears above the subform and displays the subform name.

▶ **6.** Deselect all controls, save your form changes, switch to Form view, and then click the **ContractNum** text box to deselect the value. See Figure 6-37.

Figure 6-37   **Viewing the subform in Form view**

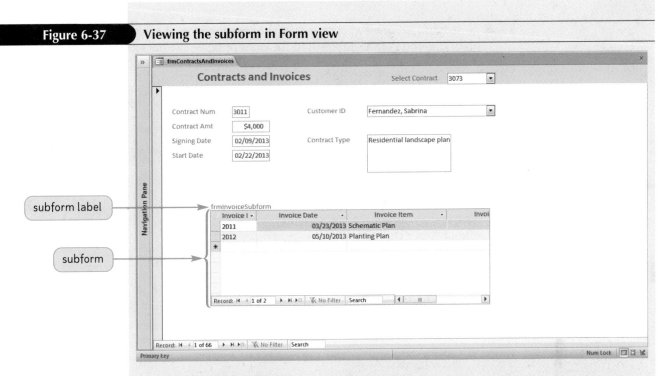

The subform displays the two invoices related to the first contract record for contract number 3011.

Trouble? If the widths of the columns in your datasheet differ or the position of your subform is different, don't worry. You'll resize all columns to their best fit and move the subform later.

After viewing the form, Lucia identifies some modifications she wants you to make. The subform is not properly sized and the columns in the subform are not sized to their best fit. She wants you to resize the subform and its columns, so that all columns in the subform are entirely visible. Also, she asks you to delete the subform label, because the label is unnecessary for identifying the subform contents. You'll use Design view and Layout view to make these changes.

To modify the subform's design:

1. Switch to Design view. Notice that in Design view, the subform data does not appear in a datasheet format as it does in Form view. That difference causes no problem; you can ignore it.

   First, you'll delete the subform label.

2. Deselect all controls (if necessary), right-click the subform label to open the shortcut menu (make sure no other controls have handles), and then click **Cut**.

   Next, you'll move the subform by aligning it with the Start Date label.

3. Click the edge of the subform to select it (an orange border and handles appear on the subform's border when the subform is selected), hold down the **Shift** key, click the **Start Date** label, and then release the **Shift** key. The subform and the Start Date label are selected, and you'll align the two controls on their left edges.

4. Right-click the **Start Date** label, point to **Align** on the shortcut menu, and then click **Left**. The two controls are aligned on their left edges. You'll resize the subform in Layout view, so you can see your changes as you make them.

5. Switch to Layout view, click the edge of the subform to select it, and then drag the right edge of the subform to the right until all five datasheet columns are fully visible.

Before resizing the columns in the subform, you'll display record 41 in the main form. The subform for this record contains the related records in the tblInvoice table with the longest field values.

6. Use the record navigation bar for the main form to display record 41, for contract number 3073, and then resize each column in the subform to its best fit.

Next, you'll resize the subform again so its width matches the width of the five resized columns.

7. Resize the subform's right edge to the left, so it is aligned with the right edge of the Invoice Paid column. See Figure 6-38.

Figure 6-38	After moving and resizing the subform

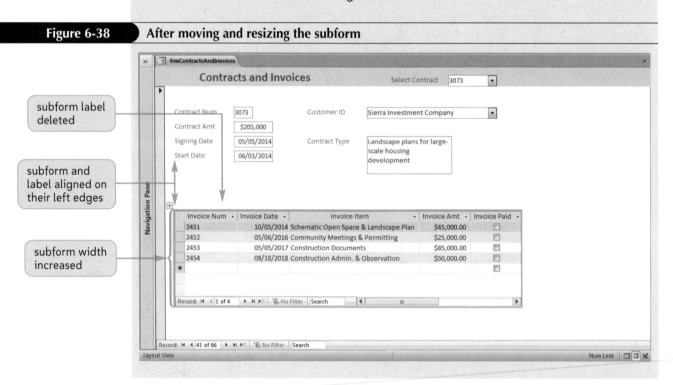

You've finished your work with the subform, and now you need to add two calculated controls to the main form.

Displaying a Subform's Calculated Controls in the Main Form

For the invoices displayed in the subform, Lucia's form design includes the display of calculated controls in the main form for the number of invoices and for the total of the invoice amounts for the related records displayed in the subform. To display these calculated controls in a form or report, you use the Count and Sum functions. The **Count function** determines the number of occurrences of an expression, and its general format as a control in a form or report is =Count(*expression*). The **Sum function** calculates the total of an expression, and its general format as a control in a form or report is =Sum(*expression*). The invoices and invoice amounts are displayed in the subform's Detail section, so you'll need to place calculated controls for the number of invoices and the total invoice amounts in the subform's Form Footer section. However, your design has these two calculated controls displayed in the main form, not in the subform. Fortunately, the subform appears in Datasheet view, and Form Headers and Footers do not appear in Datasheet view, so the subform's calculated controls will not appear in the subform. Although the calculated controls are not displayed in the subform, the calculations occur, and you can add calculated controls in the main form that reference the subform's calculated controls and display these values.

Adding Calculated Controls to a Subform's Form Footer Section

First, you'll open the subform in Design view in another window and add the calculated controls to the subform's Form Footer section.

To add calculated controls to the subform's Form Footer section:

1. Save your form design changes, switch to Design view, click the subform border to select the subform, right-click the border, and then click **Subform in New Window** on the shortcut menu. The subform opens in Design view. See Figure 6-39.

Figure 6-39   **Subform in Design view**

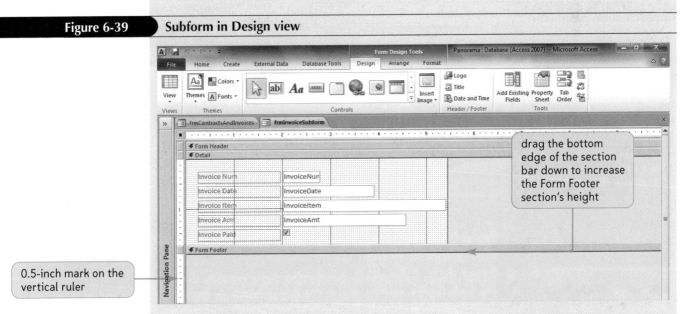

0.5-inch mark on the vertical ruler

drag the bottom edge of the section bar down to increase the Form Footer section's height

The subform's Detail section contains the tblInvoice table fields. As a subform in the main form, the fields appear in a datasheet even though the fields do not appear that way in Design view. The heights of the subform's Form Header and Form Footer sections are zero, meaning that these sections have been removed from the subform. You'll increase the height of the Form Footer section so that you can add the two calculated controls to the section.

2. Place the pointer at the bottom edge of the Form Footer section bar. When the pointer changes to a ╈ shape, drag the bottom edge of the section down to the 0.5-inch mark on the vertical ruler.

Now you'll add the first calculated control to the Form Footer section. To create the text box for the calculated control, you use the **Text Box tool** in the Controls group on the Design tab. Because the Form Footer section is not displayed in a datasheet, you do not need to position the control precisely.

3. In the Controls group on the Design tab, click the **Text Box** tool ⓐⓑ.

4. Position the + portion of the pointer near the top of the Form Footer section and at the 1-inch mark on the horizontal ruler, and then click the mouse button. Access places a text box control and an attached label control to its left in the Form Footer section.

Next, you'll set the Name and Control Source properties for the text box. Recall that the Name property specifies the name of an object or control. Later, when you add the calculated control in the main form, you'll reference the subform's calculated control value by using its Name property value. The **Control Source property** specifies the source of the data that appears in the control; the Control Source property setting can be either a field name or an expression.

TIP

You precede expressions with an equal sign to distinguish them from field names, which do not have an equal sign.

TIP

Read the Naming Conventions section in the appendix titled "Relational Databases and Database Design" for more information about naming conventions.

5. Open the property sheet for the text box in the Form Footer section (the word "Unbound" is displayed inside the text box), click the **All** tab (if necessary), select the entry in the Name box, type **txtInvoiceAmtSum** in the Name box, press the **Tab** key, type **=Sum(Inv** in the Control Source box, press the **Tab** key to accept the rest of the field name of InvoiceAmt suggested by Formula AutoComplete, type **)** (a right parenthesis), and then press the **Tab** key. InvoiceAmt is enclosed in brackets in the expression because it's a field name. See Figure 6-40.

Figure 6-40   **Setting properties for the subform calculated control**

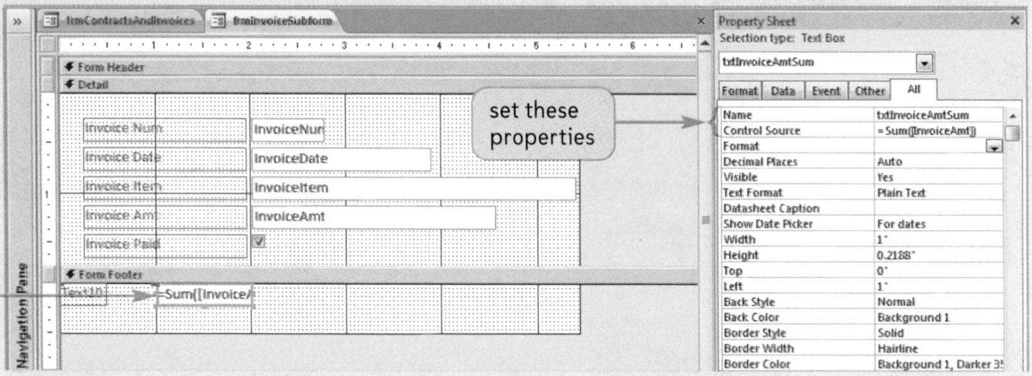

text box control set to Control Source property value

You've finished creating the first calculated control, and now you'll create the other calculated control.

TIP

In txtInvoiceAmtSum, txt identifies the control type (a text box), InvoiceAmt is the related field name, and Sum identifies the control as a summary control.

6. Repeat Steps 3 through 5, positioning the + portion of the pointer near the top of the Form Footer section and at the 4-inch mark on the horizontal ruler, setting the Name property value to **txtInvoiceNumCount**, and setting the Control Source property value to **=Count([InvoiceNum])**.

When you use the Count function, you are counting the number of displayed records—in this case, the number of records displayed in the subform. Instead of using InvoiceNum as the expression for the Count function, you could use any of the other fields displayed in the subform.

You've finished creating the subform's calculated controls, so you can close the property sheet, save your subform design changes, and return to the main form.

7. Close the property sheet, save your subform changes, and then close the subform. The active object is now the main form in Design view.

Trouble? The subform in the frmContractsAndInvoices form might appear to be blank after you close the frmInvoiceSubform form. This is a temporary effect; the subform's controls do still exist. Switch to Form view, and then back to Design view, to display the subform's controls.

8. Switch to Form view. The calculated controls you added in the subform's Form Footer section are not displayed in the subform.

9. Switch to Design view.

Next, you'll add two calculated controls in the main form to display the two calculated controls from the subform.

Adding Calculated Controls to a Main Form

The subform's calculated controls now contain a count of the number of invoices and a total of the invoice amounts. You need to add two calculated controls in the main form that reference the values in the subform's calculated controls. Because it's easy to make a typing mistake with these references, you'll use Expression Builder to set the Control Source property for the two main form calculated controls.

To add a calculated control to the main form's Detail section:

1. In the Controls group on the Design tab, click the **Text Box** tool [abl], and then add the text box and its attached label in the Detail section, clicking the + portion of the pointer at the 2-inch mark on the horizontal ruler and the 2-inch mark on the vertical ruler. Don't be concerned about positioning the control precisely because you'll resize and move the label and text box later.

2. Select the label and open the property sheet, set its Caption property to **Number of Invoices**, right-click an edge of the label to open the shortcut menu, point to **Size**, and then click **To Fit**. Don't worry if the label now overlaps the text box.

You'll use Expression Builder to set Control Source property for the text box.

3. Click the text box (the word "Unbound" is displayed inside the text box) to select it, click the **Control Source** box in the property sheet, and then click the property's **Build** button [...] to open Expression Builder.

4. Click the **expand indicator** next to frmContractsAndInvoices in the Expression Elements box, click **frmInvoiceSubform** in the Expression Elements box, scroll down the Expression Categories box, and then double-click **txtInvoiceNumCount** in the Expression Categories box. See Figure 6-41.

Figure 6-41   Text box control's expression in the Expression Builder dialog box

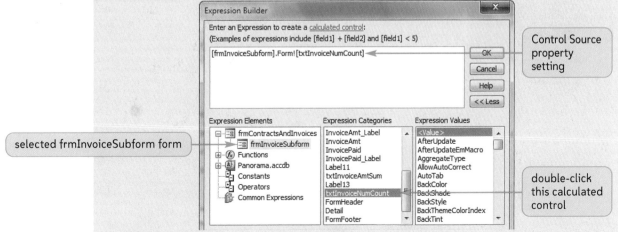

Instead of adding txtInvoiceNumCount to the expression box at the top, Access changed it to [frmInvoiceSubform].Form![txtInvoiceNumCount]. This expression asks Access to display the value of the txtInvoiceNumCount control that is located in the frmInvoiceSubform form, which is a form object.

You need to add an equal sign to the beginning of the expression.

5. Press the **Home** key, type **=** (an equal sign), and then click the **OK** button. Access closes the Expression Builder dialog box and sets the Control Source property.

Next, you'll add a second text box to the main form, set the Caption property for the label, and use Expression Builder to set the text box's Control Source property.

Be sure you resize the label to its best fit.

6. Repeat Steps 1 through 3 to add a text box to the main form, clicking the + portion of the pointer at the 5-inch mark on the horizontal ruler and the 2-inch mark on the vertical ruler, and setting the label's Caption property to **Invoice Amount Total**.

7. With the Expression Builder dialog box open for the new text box, type **=** (an equal sign), click the **expand indicator** next to frmContractsAndInvoices in the Expression Elements box, click **frmInvoiceSubform** in the Expression Elements box, scroll down the Expression Categories box, and then double-click **txtInvoiceAmtSum** in the Expression Categories box. Access changed the txtInvoiceAmtSum calculated field to the expression = [frmInvoiceSubform]. Form![txtInvoiceAmtSum].

Next, you'll save your form changes and view the form in Layout view.

8. Click the **OK** button to accept the expression and close the Expression Builder dialog box, close the property sheet, save your form changes, and then switch to Layout view. See Figure 6-42.

Figure 6-42   After adding two calculated controls

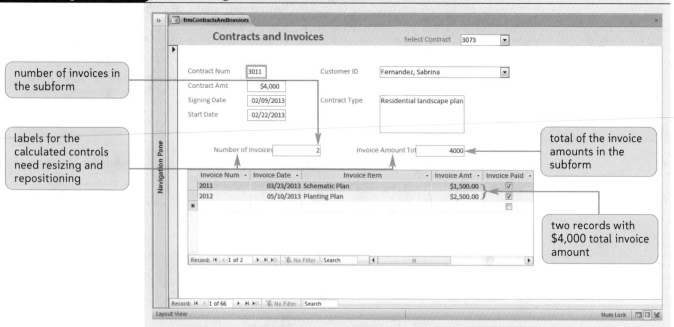

Next, you need to resize, move, and format the two calculated controls and their attached labels.

Resizing, Moving, and Formatting Calculated Controls

In addition to resizing and repositioning the two calculated controls and their attached labels, you need to change the format of the rightmost calculated control to Currency and to set the following properties for both calculated controls:

- Set the Tab Stop property to a value of No. The **Tab Stop property** specifies whether users can use the Tab key to move to a control on a form. If the Tab Stop property is set to No, users can't tab to the control.
- Set the ControlTip Text property to a value of "Calculated total number of invoices for this contract" for the leftmost calculated control and "Calculated invoice total for this contract" for the rightmost calculated control. The **ControlTip Text property** specifies the text that appears in a ScreenTip when users hold the mouse pointer over a control in a form.

Setting Properties in the Property Sheet

You can set many properties in the property sheet by typing a value in the property's box, by clicking the arrow on the property and then selecting a value from the menu, or by double-clicking the property name. If you need to set a property by typing a long text entry, you can open the Zoom dialog box and type the entry in the dialog box. You can also use Expression Builder to help you enter expressions.

Now you'll resize, move, and format the calculated controls and their attached labels, and you'll set other properties for the calculated controls.

To modify the calculated controls and their attached labels:

1. Right-click the rightmost calculated control, click **Properties** on the shortcut menu to open the property sheet, click the **All** tab in the property sheet (if necessary), set the Format property to **Currency**, and then close the property sheet. The value displayed in the calculated control changes from 4000 to $4,000.00.

   Now you'll resize the calculated controls, adjust the positions of each label and text box pair with respect to each other, and then move the controls into their final positions in the form.

2. Individually, reduce the widths of the two calculated controls from the left. See Figure 6-43.

3. Click the **Number of Invoices** label, use the → arrow key to move the label into position next to its related calculated control, repeat the process for the **Invoice Amount Total** label and its related calculated control, and then deselect all controls. See Figure 6-43.

Figure 6-43 After modifying the calculated controls and their labels

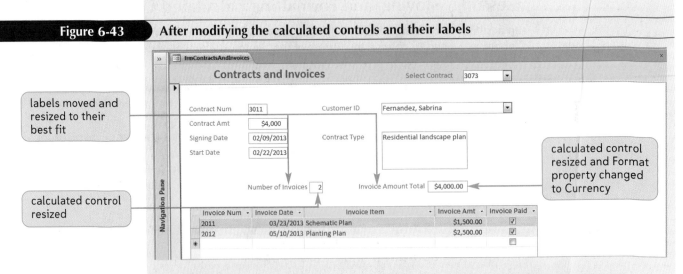

labels moved and resized to their best fit

calculated control resized

calculated control resized and Format property changed to Currency

4. Switch to Design view, Use **Shift+Click** to select the **Start Date** label, the **Number of Invoices** label, and the related text box for the Number of Invoices label, right-click one of the selected controls to open the shortcut menu, point to **Align**, click **Left** to align the labels on their left edges, press the **Shift** key, click the **Start Date** label to deselect it, release the **Shift** key, and then use the arrow key to move the **Number of Invoices** label and its related text box up to the position shown in Figure 6-44.

5. Repeat Step 4 for the **Invoice Amount Total** label and its related calculated control. See Figure 6-44.

6. Use the move handle on the top calculated control text box to move it to the right, align the two calculated control text boxes on their left edges as shown in Figure 6-44, deselect all controls, and then switch to Layout view.

TIP

In Design view you must use the move handle to move only a text box or its label, while in Layout view you can use either the move handle or the arrow keys.

Figure 6-44 After moving and aligning the calculated controls and their labels

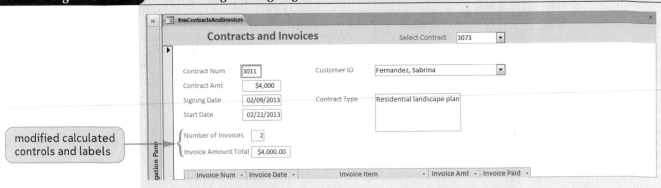

modified calculated controls and labels

7. Right-click the bottom calculated control, click **Properties** on the shortcut menu, click the **Other** tab in the property sheet, set the Tab Stop property to **No**, and then set the ControlTip Text property to **Calculated invoice total for this contract**.

8. Click the top calculated control, set the Tab Stop property to **No**, set the ControlTip Text property to **Calculated total number of invoices for this contract**, close the property sheet, save your form design changes, and then switch to Form view.

▶ **9.** Click the **Number of Invoices** text box, position the pointer on the Number of Invoices text box to display its ScreenTip, click the **Invoice Amount Total** text box, and then position the pointer on the Invoice Amount Total text box to display its ScreenTip. See Figure 6-45.

Figure 6-45

Displaying a control's ScreenTip

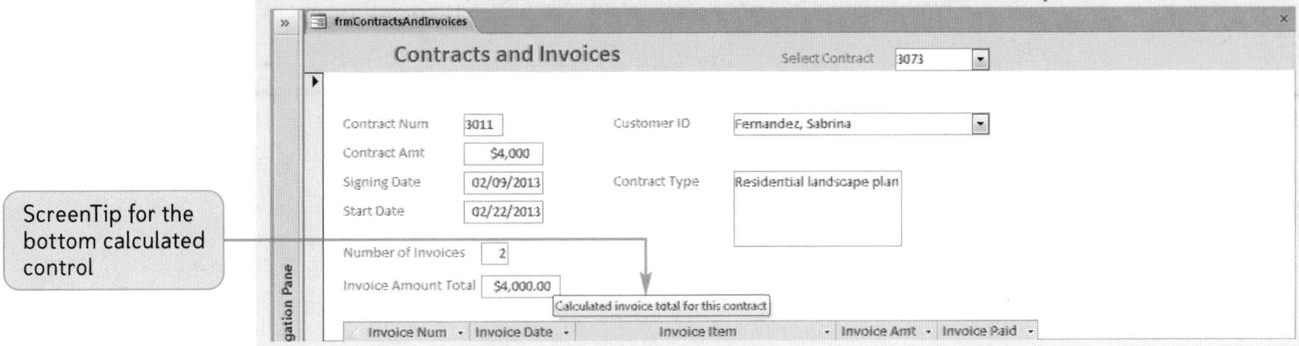

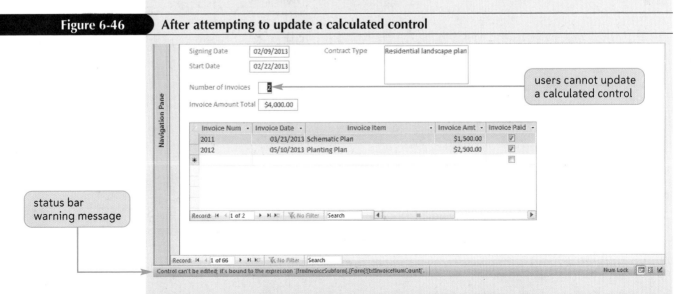

Lucia asks you to verify that users can't update the calculated controls in the main form and that users will tab in the correct order through the controls in the form.

Changing the Tab Order in a Form

Pressing the Tab key in Form view moves the focus from one control to another. **Focus** refers to the control that is currently active and awaiting user action; focus also refers to the object and record that is currently active. The order in which you move from control to control, or change the focus, in a form when you press the Tab key is called the **tab order**. Lucia wants to verify that the tab order in the main form is top-to-bottom, left-to-right. First, you'll verify that users can't update the calculated controls.

To test the calculated controls and modify the tab order:

▶ **1.** Select **2** in the Number of Invoices text box, and then press the **8** key. The Number of Invoices value remains at 2, and a message is displayed on the status bar. See Figure 6-46.

Figure 6-46

After attempting to update a calculated control

The status bar message warns you that you can't update, or edit, the calculated control because it's bound to an expression. The calculated control in the main form changes in value only when the value of the expression changes in the subform.

2. Click the **Invoice Amount Total** text box, and then press the **8** key. The value remains unchanged, and a message displays on the status bar because you cannot edit a calculated control.

Next, you'll determine the tab order of the fields in the main form. Lucia wants the tab order to be down and then across.

3. Select **3011** in the ContractNum text box, press the **Tab** key to advance to the ContractAmt text box, and then press the **Tab** key five more times to advance to the SigningDate, StartDate, ContractType, CustomerID text boxes, in order, and then to the subform.

Access sets the tab order in the same order in which you add controls to a form, so you should always check the form's tab order when you create a custom form in Layout or Design view. In this form, your testing reveals that you tab through the text boxes in a main form before tabbing through the fields in a subform. In the main form, tabbing bypasses the two calculated controls because you set their Tab Stop properties to No, and you bypass the Select Contract combo box because it's an unbound control. Also, you tab through only the text boxes in a form, not the labels.

The tab order Lucia wants for the text boxes in the main form (top-to-bottom, left-to-right) is correct for the first four text boxes (ContractNum, ContractAmt, SigningDate, and StartDate text boxes). Then you should tab from the StartDate text box to the CustomerID text box and finally to the ContractType text box, but tabbing is reversed for the last two text boxes. The default tab order doesn't match the order Lucia wants, so you'll change the tab order. You must change the tab order in Design view.

4. Switch to Design view, and then in the Tools group on the Design tab, click the **Tab Order** button. The Tab Order dialog box opens. See Figure 6-47.

Figure 6-47   **Changing the tab order for the Detail section in the main form**

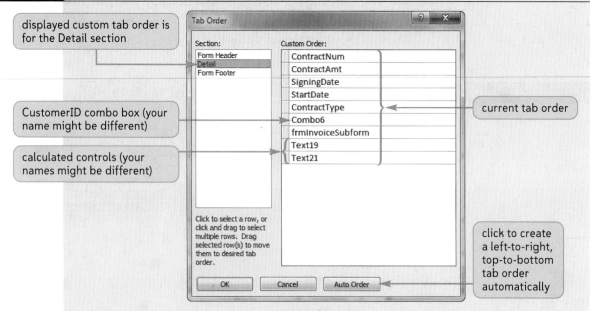

displayed custom tab order is for the Detail section

CustomerID combo box (your name might be different)

calculated controls (your names might be different)

current tab order

click to create a left-to-right, top-to-bottom tab order automatically

TIP

Setting the Name property for all your controls to meaningful names avoids having to guess which control a name references in this and similar situations.

Because you did not set the Name property for the combo box control and the calculated controls, Access assigned their names: Combo6 (your name might be different) for the CustomerID combo box, Text19 (your name might be different) for the Number of Invoices calculated control, and Text21 (your name might be different) for the Invoice Amount Total calculated control. The Auto Order button lets you create a left-to-right, top-to-bottom tab order automatically, which is not the order Lucia wants. You need to move the Combo6 entry above the ContractType entry.

▶ **5.** Click the **row selector** to the left of Combo6, and then drag the row selector above the ContractType entry. The entries are now correct and in the correct order.

▶ **6.** Click the **OK** button, save your form design changes, switch to Form view, and then tab through the controls in the main form to make sure the tab order is correct.

Trouble? If the tab order is incorrect, switch to Design view, click the Tab Order button in the Tools group on the Design tab, change your tab order in the Tab Order dialog box to match the one shown in Figure 6-47, and then repeat Step 6.

PROSKILLS

Written Communication: Enhancing Information Using Calculated Controls

For contracts with one or two invoices, it's easy for users to quickly count the number of invoices and to calculate the total invoice amount when the form doesn't display calculated controls. Similary, when students have completed few courses or when people have made few tax payments, it's easy for users to count the courses and calculate the student GPA or to count and total the tax payments. But for contracts with dozens or hundreds of invoices, for students with many courses, or for people with many tax payments, displaying summary calculated controls is mandatory. By adding a few simple calculated controls to forms and reports, you can increase the usefulness of the information presented and improve the ability of users to process the information, spot trends, and be more productive in their jobs.

You've finished adding controls to the form, but the form is plain looking and lacks visual clues for the different controls in the form. You'll complete the form by making it more attractive and easier for Sarah and her staff to use.

Improving a Form's Appearance

The frmContractsAndInvoices form has four distinct areas: the Form Header section containing the title and the Select Contract combo box, the six bound controls in the Detail section, the two calculated controls in the Detail section, and the subform in the Detail section. To visually separate these four areas, you'll increase the height of the Form Header section, add a horizontal line at the bottom of the Form Header section, and draw a rectangle around the calculated controls.

Adding a Line to a Form

You can use lines in a form to improve the form's readability, to group related information, or to underline important values. You use the **Line tool** in Design view to add a line to a form or report.

Adding a Line to a Form or Report

- Display the form or report in Design view.
- In the Controls group on the Design tab, click the More button, and then click the Line tool.
- Position the pointer where you want the line to begin.
- Drag the pointer to the position for the end of the line, and then release the mouse button. If you want to ensure that you draw a straight horizontal or vertical line, hold down the Shift key before and during the drag operation.
- To make small adjustments to the line length, select the line, hold down the Shift key, and then press an arrow key. To make small adjustments in the placement of a line, select the line, hold down the Ctrl key, and then press an arrow key.

You will add a horizontal line to the Form Header section to separate the controls in this section from the controls in the Detail section.

To add a line to the form:

▶ 1. Switch to Design view, and then drag down the bottom of the Form Header section to the 1-inch mark on the vertical ruler to make room to draw a horizontal line at the bottom of the Form Header section.

▶ 2. In the Controls group on the Design tab, click the **More** button ⊡ to open the Controls gallery, and then click the **Line** tool ◻.

▶ 3. Position the pointer's plus symbol (+) at the left edge of the Form Header section and at the 0.75-inch mark on the vertical ruler.

▶ 4. Hold down the **Shift** key, drag a horizontal line from left to right, so the end of the line ends at the 8.25-inch mark on the vertical ruler, release the mouse button, and then release the **Shift** key. See Figure 6-48.

Figure 6-48 | **Adding a line to the form**

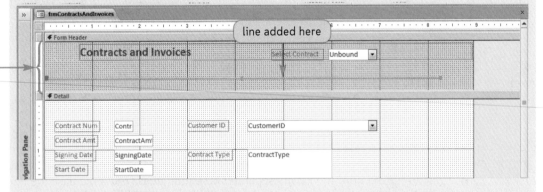

Trouble? If the line is not straight or not positioned correctly, click the Undo button on the Quick Access Toolbar, and then repeat Steps 2 through 4. If the line is not the correct length, be sure the line is selected, hold down the Shift key, and press one or more of the arrow keys until the line's length is the same as that of the line shown in Figure 6-48.

5. Drag up the bottom of the Form Header section to just below the line at the 0.75-inch mark on the vertical ruler.

6. Save your form design changes.

Next, you'll add a Rectangle around the calculated controls in the Detail section.

Adding a Rectangle to a Form

You can use a rectangle in a form to group related controls and to separate the group from other controls. You use the **Rectangle tool** in Design view to add a rectangle to a form or report.

REFERENCE

Adding a Rectangle to a Form or Report

• Display the form or report in Design view.
• In the Controls group on the Design tab, click the More button, and then click the Rectangle tool.
• Click in the form or report to create a default-sized rectangle, or drag a rectangle in the position and size you want.

You will add a rectangle around the calculated controls and their labels to separate them from the subform and from the other controls in the Detail section.

To add a rectangle to the form:

1. In the Controls group on the Design tab, click the **More** button ▾ to open the Controls gallery, and then click the **Rectangle** tool ▢.

2. Position the pointer's plus symbol (+) approximately two grid dots above and two grid dots to the left of the Number of Invoices label.

3. Drag a rectangle down and to the right until all four sides are approximately two grid dots from the two calculated controls and their labels. See Figure 6-49.

Figure 6-49	Adding a rectangle to the form

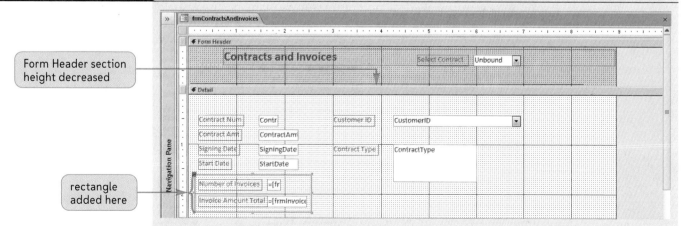

Form Header section height decreased

rectangle added here

Trouble? If the rectangle is not sized or positioned correctly, use the sizing handles to adjust its size and the move handle to adjust its position.

Next, you'll set the thickness of the rectangle's lines.

▶ 4. Click the **Format** tab; in the Control Formatting group on the Format tab, click the **Shape Outline arrow**; point to **Line Thickness** at the bottom of the gallery; click the line with the ScreenTip **1 pt** in the list; and then deselect the control.

Next, you'll add color and visual effects to the form's controls.

Modifying the Visual Effects of the Controls in a Form

Distinguishing one group of controls in a form from other groups is an important visual cue to the users of the form. For example, users should be able to distinguish the bound controls in the form from the calculated controls and from the Select Contract control in the Form Header section. You'll now modify the controls in the form to provide these visual cues. You'll start by setting font properties for the calculated control's labels.

To modify the controls in the form:

▶ 1. Select the **Number of Invoices** label and the **Invoice Amount Total** label; click the **Format** tab (if necessary); in the Font group on the Format tab, click the **Font Color button arrow** ; click the **Blue** color (row 7, column 8) in the Standard Colors palette; and then in the Font group on the Format tab, click the **Bold** button . The labels' captions now use a bold, blue font.

Next, you'll set properties for the Select Contract label in the Form Header section.

▶ 2. Select the **Select Contract** label in the Form Header section, set the label's font color to **Red** (row 7, column 2 in the Standard Colors palette), and then set the font style to bold.

Next, you'll set the label's Special Effect property to a raised effect. The **Special Effect property** specifies the type of special effect applied to a control in a form or report. The choices for this property are Flat, Raised, Sunken, Etched, Shadowed, and Chiseled.

▶ 3. Open the property sheet for the Select Contract label, click the **All** tab (if necessary), and then set the Special Effect property to **Raised**. The label now has a raised special effect, and the label's caption now uses a bold, red font.

Next, you'll set the Special Effect property for the bound control labels to a sunken effect.

▶ 4. Select the **Contract Num** label, **Contract Amt** label, **Signing Date** label, **Start Date** label, **Customer ID** label, and **Contract Type** label, set the controls' Special Effect property to **Sunken**, and then close the property sheet.

Finally, you'll set the background color of the Form Header section, the Detail section, the Select Contract combo box, and the two calculated controls. You can use the **Background Color button** in the Font group on the Design tab to change the background color of a control, section, or object (form or report).

▶ 5. Click the Form Header's section bar, and in the Font group on the Format tab, click the **Background Color button arrow** ; and then click the **Light Blue 2** color (row 3, column 5) in the Standard Colors palette. The Form Header's background color changes to the Light Blue 2 color.

▶ **6.** Click the Detail section's section bar, and in the Font Group on the Format tab, click the **Background Color** button 🖎 to change the Detail section's background color to the **Light Blue 2** color.

▶ **7.** Select the **Select Contract** combo box, **Number of Invoices** text box, and the **Invoice Amount Total** text box, set the selected controls' background color to the **Light Blue 2** color, and then deselect all controls by clicking to the right of the Detail section's grid. See Figure 6-50.

Figure 6-50 ▶ **Completed custom form in Design view**

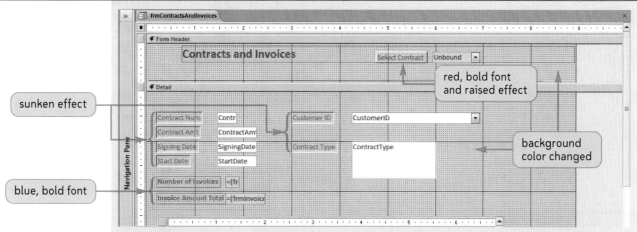

▶ **8.** Switch to Form view, and then click the **ContractNum** text box to deselect the value. The Session 6.3 Visual Overview shows the completed form.

▶ **9.** Test the form by tabbing between fields, navigating between records, and using the Select Contract combo box to find records, making sure you don't change any field values and observing that the calculated controls display the correct values.

▶ **10.** Save your form design changes, close the form, make a backup copy of the database, compact and repair the database, and then close the database.

The completed custom form will make it easier for Sarah and her staff to work with contract and invoice data in the Panorama database.

Session 6.3 Quick Check

REVIEW

1. To create a combo box to find records in a form with the Combo Box Wizard, the form's record source must be a(n) _____.
2. You use the _____ tool to add a subform to a form.
3. To calculate subtotals and overall totals in a form or report, you use the _____ function.
4. The Control Source property setting can be either a(n) _____ or a(n) _____.
5. Explain the difference between the Tab Stop property and tab order.
6. What is focus?
7. The _____ property has settings such as Raised and Sunken.

Practice the skills you learned in the tutorial using the same case scenario.

PRACTICE

Review Assignments

Data File needed for the Review Assignments: Products.accdb (*cont. from Tutorial 5*)

Sarah wants you to create several forms, including a custom form that displays and updates companies and the products they offer. You'll do so by completing the following steps:

1. Open the **Products** database located in the Access2\Review folder provided with your Data Files.

2. Remove the lookup feature from the CompanyID field in the **tblProduct** table, and resize the Company ID column in the datasheet to its best fit. Save and close the table.

3. Edit the relationship between the primary tblCompany and related tblProduct tables to enforce referential integrity and to cascade update related fields. Create the relationship report, and then save the report as **rptRelationshipsForProducts**.

4. Use the Documenter to document the qryContactList query. Select all query options; use the Names, Data Types, and Sizes option for fields; and use the Names and Fields option for indexes. Print the report produced by the Documenter.

5. Use the Datasheet tool to create a form based on the tblProduct table, and then save the form as **frmProductDatasheet**.

6. Use the Multiple Items tool to create a form based on the qryCompanyList query, and then save the form as **frmCompanyListMultipleItems**.

7. Use the Split Form tool to create a split form based on the tblProduct table, and then make the following changes to the form in Layout view:
   a. Remove the two Unit controls from the stacked layout, reduce the width of the Unit text box by about half, and then anchor the two Unit controls to the bottom left.
   b. Remove the five control pairs in the right column from the stacked layout, and then anchor the group to the bottom right.
   c. Remove the ProductType and Price control pairs from the stacked layout, move them to the top right, and then anchor them to the top right.
   d. Reduce the widths of the ProductID and CompanyID text boxes to a reasonable size.
   e. Change the title to **Product**, and then save the modified form as **frmProductSplitForm**.

8. Use Figure 6-51 and the following steps to create a custom form named **frmCompaniesWithProducts** based on the tblCompany and tblProduct tables.
   a. Place the fields from the tblCompany table at the top of the Detail section. Delete the Contact Last Name label and change the caption for the Contact First Name label to **Contact**.
   b. Move the fields into two columns in the Detail section, as shown in Figure 6-51, resizing and aligning controls, as necessary.
   c. Add the title in the Form Header section.
   d. Make sure the form's Record Source property is set to tblCompany, and then add a combo box in the Form Header section to find CompanyName field values. In the wizard steps, select the CompanyName and CompanyID fields, and hide the key column. Resize and move the control.
   e. Add a subform based on the tblProduct table, include only the fields shown in Figure 6-51, link with CompanyID, name the subform **frmPartialProductSubform**, delete the subform label, resize the columns in the subform to their best fit, and resize and position the subform.
   f. Add a calculated control that displays the number of products displayed in the subform. Set the calculated control's Tab Stop property to No, and the ControlTip Text property to **Calculated number of products**.

Figure 6-51	Products database custom form design

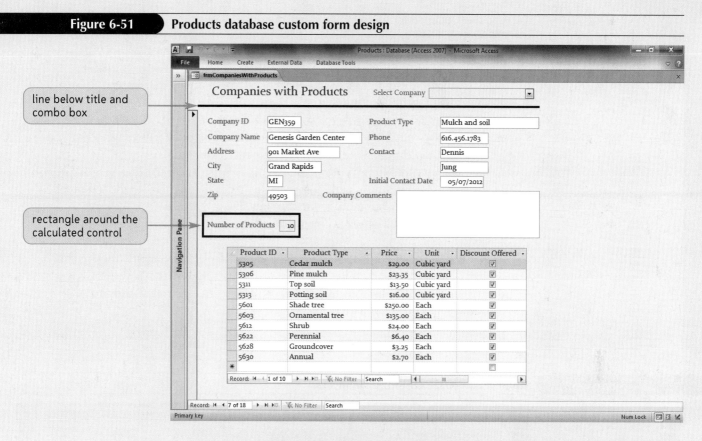

g. Add a line in the Form Header section, and add a rectangle around the calculated control and its label, setting the line thickness of both controls to the line style with the ScreenTip 3 pt. Use the Format Painter on the Format tab to paint the rectangle's color the same as the line's color.

h. In the main form, use the Black, Text 1 font color (row 1, column 2 in the Theme Colors palette) for all text boxes, and use the White, Background 1, Darker 5% fill color (row 2, column 1 in the Theme Colors palette) for the sections, the calculated control, and the Select Company combo box.

i. Make sure the tab order is top-to-bottom, left-to-right for the main form text boxes.

9. Make a backup copy of the database, compact and repair the database, and then close the database.

Apply the skills you learned in the tutorial to create a custom form.

CHALLENGE

Case Problem 1

Data File needed for this Case Problem: Contract.accdb (*cont. from Tutorial 5*)

Pine Hill Music School   Yuka wants you to create several forms, including a custom form that displays and updates the school's music contracts with students. You'll do so by completing the following steps:

1. Open the **Contract** database located in the Access2\Case1 folder provided with your Data Files.

2. Remove the lookup feature from the TeacherID field in the **tblContract** table, and then resize the Teacher ID column to its best fit. Save and close the table.

3. Define a one-to-many relationship between the primary tblTeacher table and the related tblContract table. Select the referential integrity option and the cascade updates option for this relationship.

4. Use the Documenter to document the tblContract table. Select all table options; use the Names, Data Types, and Sizes option for fields; and use the Names and Fields option for indexes. Print the report produced by the Documenter.

5. Use the Multiple Items tool to create a form based on the qryLessonsByTeacher query, change the title to **Lessons by Teacher**, and then save the form as **frmLessonsByTeacherMultipleItems**.

6. Use the Split Form tool to create a split form based on the qryLessonsByTeacher query, and then make the following changes to the form in Layout view.

   a. Reduce the widths of all six text boxes to a reasonable size.

   b. Remove the LessonType, LessonLength, and MonthlyLessonCost controls from the stacked layout, move these three controls to the right and then to the top of the form, and then anchor them to the top right.

   c. Select the MonthlyLessonCost control and its label, and then anchor them to the bottom right.

   d. Remove the ContractEndDate control from the stacked layout, and then anchor the control to the bottom left.

   e. Change the title to **Lessons by Teacher**, and then save the modified form as **frmLessonsByTeacherSplitForm**.

7. Use Figure 6-52 and the following steps to create a custom form named **frmContract** based on the tblContract table.

Figure 6-52	Contract database custom form design

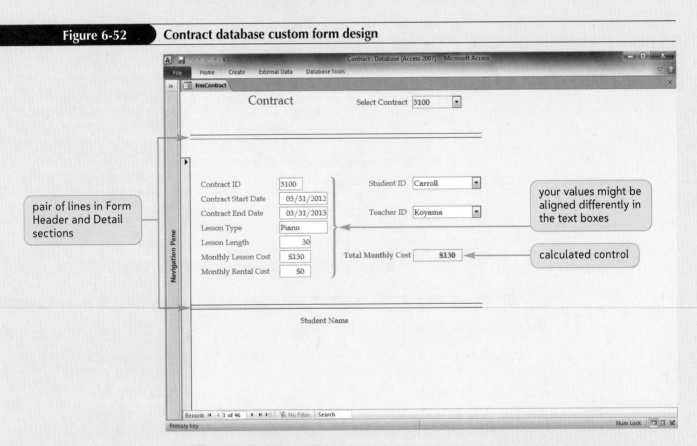

a. For the StudentID combo box, select the LastName, FirstName, and StudentID fields from the tblStudent table, in order; and sort in ascending order by the LastName field and then by the FirstName field.

b. For the TeacherID combo box, select the LastName, FirstName, and TeacherID fields from the tblTeacher table, in order; and sort in ascending order by the LastName field and then by the FirstName field.

EXPLORE

c. Make sure the form's Record Source property is set to tblContract, and then add a combo box in the Form Header section to find ContractID field values.

EXPLORE

d. Add a calculated control that displays the total of the MonthlyLessonCost and MonthlyRentalCost fields. Set the calculated control's Tab Stop property to No and format the values as currency with no decimal places.

EXPLORE

e. Add a line in the Form Header section, and then add a second line below it, and then add a second pair of lines near the bottom of the Detail section. Set the line thickness of all lines to the line setting with the ScreenTip 1 pt.

EXPLORE

f. Use the Label tool to add your name below the pair of lines at the bottom of the Detail section.

g. For the labels in the Detail section, except for the Total Monthly Cost label and the label displaying your name, use the Red font color (row 7, column 2 in the Standard Colors palette).

h. For the title, Select Contract label, and the label displaying your name, use the Dark Red font color (row 7, column 1 in the Standard Colors palette).

i. For the calculated control and its label, bold the font.

j. For the background fill color of the sections, the calculated control, and the Select Contract combo box, use the Medium Gray color (row 1, column 3 in the Standard Colors palette).

k. Make sure the tab order is top-to-bottom, left-to-right for the main form text boxes.

8. Make a backup copy of the database, compact and repair the database, and then close the database.

Use the skills you learned in the tutorial to create a custom form.

CREATE

Case Problem 2

Data File needed for this Case Problem: Training.accdb (cont. from Tutorial 5)

Parkhurst Health & Fitness Center   Martha Parkhurst wants you to create several forms, including two custom forms that display and update data in the Training database. You'll do so by completing the following steps:

1. Open the **Training** database located in the Access2\Case2 folder provided with your Data Files.

2. Use the Documenter to document the qryMemberNames query. Select all query options; use the Names, Data Types, and Sizes option for fields; and use the Names and Fields option for indexes. Print the first page of the report produced by the Documenter.

3. Use the Datasheet tool to create a form based on the tblProgram table, and then save the form as **frmProgramDatasheet**.

EXPLORE

4. Create a custom form based on the qryUpcomingExpirations query. Display all fields from the query in the form. Create your own design for the form. Add a label to the bottom of the Detail section that contains your first and last names. Change the label's font so that your name appears in bold, blue text. Change the ExpirationDate text box format so that the field value displays in bold, red text. Save the form as **frmUpcomingExpirations**.

5. Use Figure 6-53 and the following steps to create a custom form named **frmProgramsWithMembers** based on the tblProgram and tblMember tables.

Figure 6-53   Training database custom form design

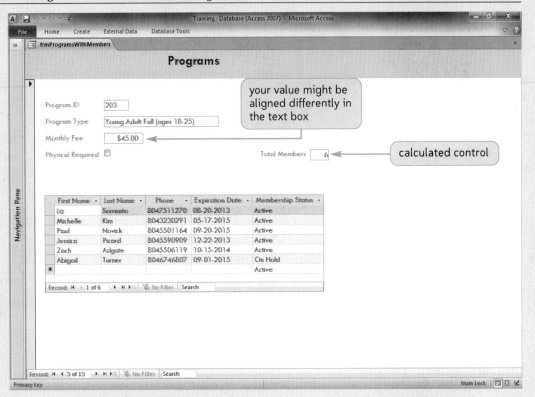

a. Selected fields from the tblMember table appear in a subform named **frmProgramMemberSubform**.

b. The calculated control displays the total number of records that appear in the subform. Set the calculated control's ControlTip Text property to **Total number of members in this program**. Set the calculated control's Tab Stop property to No.

c. Apply the Median theme to the form.

d. Save and view the form, and then print both pages for the first record.

6. Make a backup copy of the database, compact and repair the database, and then close the database.

Use the skills you learned in the tutorial to create a custom form.

CREATE

Case Problem 3

Data File needed for this Case Problem: Agency.accdb (cont. from Tutorial 5)

Rossi Recycling Group   Mary Rossi asks you to create several forms, including a custom form for the Agency database so that she can better track donations for the agency. You'll do so by completing the following steps:

1. Open the **Agency** database located in the Access2\Case3 folder provided with your Data Files.

2. Use the Documenter to document the tblDonor table. Select all table options; use the Names, Data Types, and Sizes option for fields; and use the Names and Fields option for indexes. Print the report produced by the Documenter.

3. Use the Multiple Items tool to create a form based on the qryDonorPhoneList query, change the title to **Donor Phone List**, and then save the form as **frmDonorPhoneListMultipleItems**.

4. Use the Split Form tool to create a split form based on the tblDonor table, and then make the following changes to the form in Layout view.
   a. Reduce the widths of all five text boxes to a reasonable size.
   b. Remove the FirstName, LastName, and Phone controls from the stacked layout, move them to the top right, and then anchor them to the top right.
   c. Change the title to **Donor**, and then save the modified form as **frmDonorSplitForm**.
5. Use Figure 6-54 and the following steps to create a custom form named **frmDonorDonations** based on the tblDonor and tblDonation tables.

Figure 6-54   **Agency database custom form design**

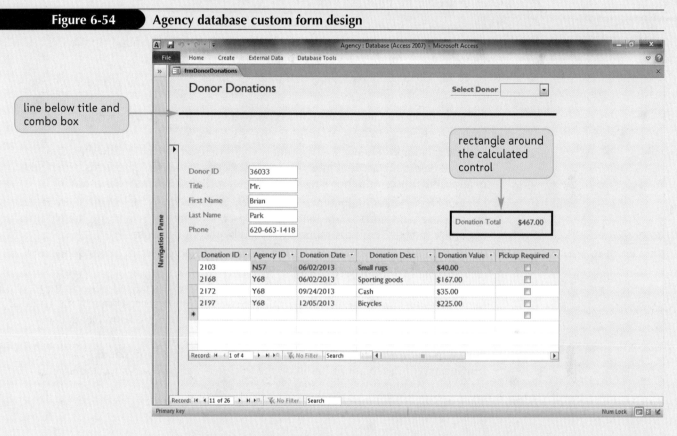

a. Add the title in the Form Header section.
b. Make sure the form's Record Source property is set to tblDonor, and then add a combo box in the Form Header section to find DonorID field values. In the wizard steps, select the DonorID field. Format the label using the Red font (row 7, column 2 in the Standard Colors palette), bold, and the Chiseled special effect.
c. Add a subform based on the tblDonation table, name the subform **frmDonorDonationSubform**, delete the subform label, and resize the columns in the subform to their best fit and resize and position the subform.

EXPLORE
d. Add a calculated control that displays the total of the DonationValue field displayed in the subform with the Currency format. Set the calculated control's Tab Stop property to No, and the Border Style property to Transparent.

EXPLORE
e. Add a line in the Form Header section, and add a rectangle around the calculated control and its label, setting the line thickness of both controls to the line style with the ScreenTip 3 pt. Set the rectangle color to Black (row 1, column 2 in the Standard Colors section) using the Shape Outline button in the Control Formatting group on the Format tab.

     f. Use the background color Aqua Blue 2 (row 3, column 9 in the Standard Colors palette) for the sections, the calculated control, and the Select Donor combo box.

     g. Make sure the tab order is top-to-bottom for the main form text boxes.

6. Make a backup copy of the database, compact and repair the database, and then close the database.

Use the skills you learned in the tutorial to create two custom forms.

CREATE

Case Problem 4

Data File needed for this Case Problem: Vacation.accdb (*cont. from Tutorial 5*)

GEM Ultimate Vacations   Griffin and Emma MacElroy want you to create several forms, including a custom form that displays and updates guest and reservation data in the Vacation database. You'll do so by completing the following steps:

1. Open the **Vacation** database located in the Access2\Case4 folder provided with your Data Files.

2. Remove the lookup feature from the PropertyID field in the **tblReservation** table. Save and close the table.

3. Edit the relationship between the primary tblProperty and related tblReservation tables to enforce referential integrity and to cascade update related fields. Create the relationship report, and then save the report as **rptRelationshipsForVacation**.

4. Use the Documenter to document the qryIllinoisGuests query. Select all query options; use the Names, Data Types, and Sizes option for fields; and use the Nothing option for indexes. Print the report produced by the Documenter.

5. Use the Datasheet tool to create a form based on the qryGuestTripDates query, and then save the form as **frmGuestTripDates**.

    ⊕ **EXPLORE**

6. Create a custom form based on the qryRentalCost query. Display all fields in the form. Use your own design for the form, but use the title **Reserved Trips** in the Form Header section, and use the Label tool to add your name to the Form Header section. Save the form as **frmRentalCost**.

7. Use Figure 6-55 and the following steps to create a custom form named **frmGuestsWithReservations** based on the tblGuest and tblReservation tables.

Figure 6-55	Vacation database custom form design

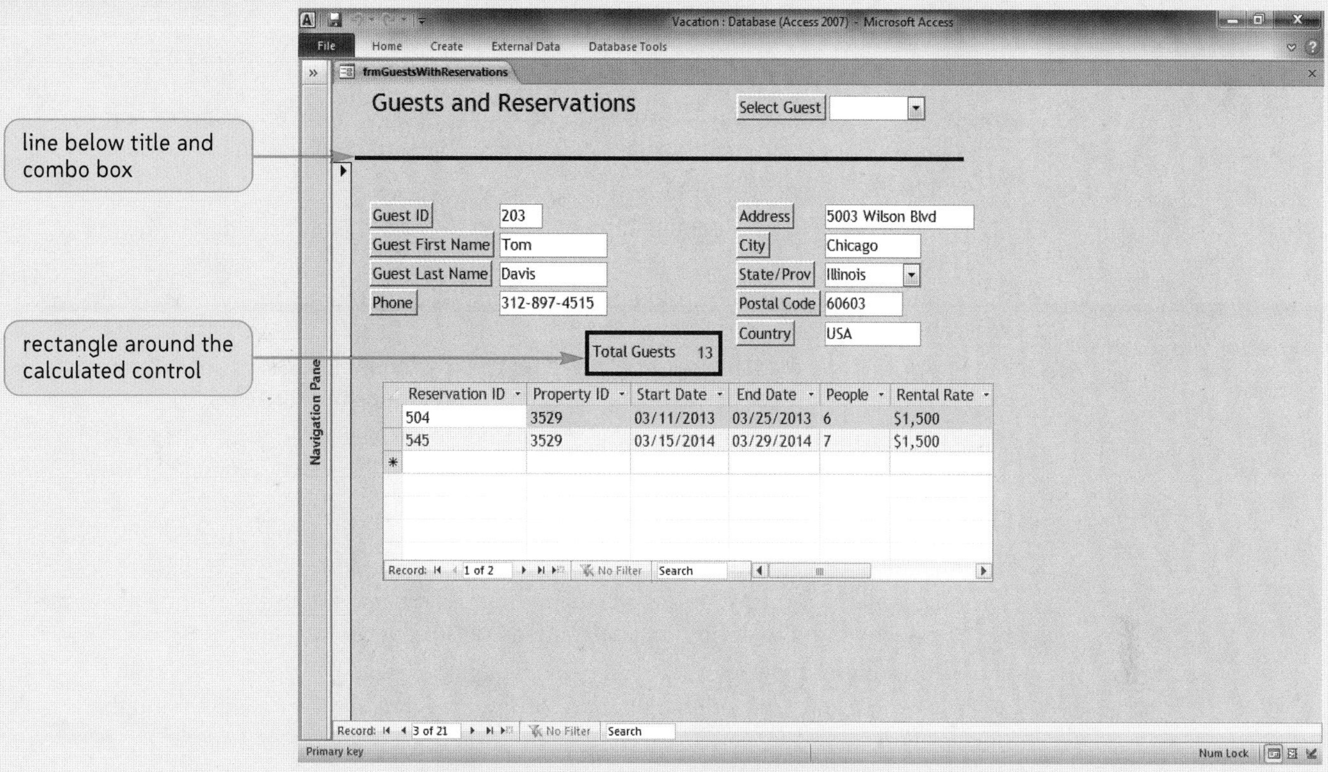

line below title and combo box

rectangle around the calculated control

a. Add the title in the Form Header section.

b. Make sure the form's Record Source property is set to tblGuest and then add a combo box in the Form Header section to find GuestID field values.

c. Add a subform based on the tblReservation table, name the subform **frmGuestsWithReservationsSubform**, delete the subform label, and resize the columns in the subform to their best fit, and then resize and position the subform.

EXPLORE   d. Add a calculated control that displays the total of the People field displayed in the subform. Set the calculated control's Tab Stop property to No, and set the calculated control's Border Style property to Transparent.

EXPLORE   e. Add a line in the Form Header section, and add a rectangle around the calculated control and its label, setting the line thickness of both controls to the line style with the ScreenTip 3 pt. Set the rectangle color to Black (row 1, column 2 in the Standard Colors section) using the Shape Outline button in the Control Formatting group on the Format tab.

EXPLORE   f. Use black font color for all controls, including the controls in the subform.

g. Use the "Pink, Text 2, Lighter 80%" fill color (row 2, column 4 in the Theme Colors palette) for the sections and the calculated control.

h. Use the Raised special effect for the labels in the Detail section, except for the calculated control label, and the Form Header section, except for the title.

i. Make sure the tab order is top-to-bottom and left-to-right for the main form text boxes.

8. Make a backup copy of the database, compact and repair the database, and then close the database.

Use the skills you learned in this tutorial to create a custom form.

CREATE

Case Problem 5

Data File needed for this Case Problem: ACE.accdb (*cont. from Tutorial 5*)

Always Connected Everyday   Chris and Pat Aquino want you to create several forms, including a custom form that displays and updates data in the ACE database. You'll do so by completing the following steps:

1. Open the **ACE** database located in the Access2\Case5 folder provided with your Data Files.
2. In Tutorial 5, you created a lookup field in the tblCustomer table. Remove the lookup feature from this field.
3. Make sure that the table relationship enforces referential integrity. Create the relationship report, and then save the report as **rptRelationshipsForACE**.
4. Use the Documenter to document one of your forms. Select all form options and use the Names option for sections and controls. Print the report produced by the Documenter.
5. In Tutorial 5, you created forms to display and update the data in the ACE database. Review these forms, and develop a consistent design strategy that you'll use to customize all the forms. Your design strategy should include the use of combo boxes for foreign keys and for searching, calculated controls, and visual effects.
6. Using your form design strategy, customize all the forms in the ACE database.
7. Make a backup copy of the database, compact and repair the database, and then close the database.

ASSESS

SAM: Skills Assessment Manager

For current SAM information, including versions and content details, visit SAM Central (http://samcentral.course.com). If you have a SAM user profile, you may have access to hands-on instruction, practice, and assessment of the skills covered in this tutorial. Since various versions of SAM are supported throughout the life of this text, check with your instructor for the correct instructions and URL/Web site for accessing assignments.

ENDING DATA FILES

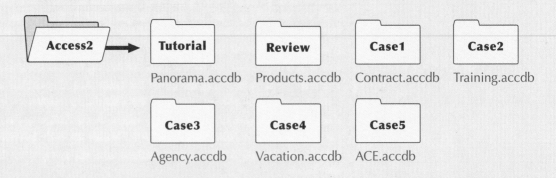

Access2 → Tutorial — Panorama.accdb
Review — Products.accdb
Case1 — Contract.accdb
Case2 — Training.accdb
Case3 — Agency.accdb
Case4 — Vacation.accdb
Case5 — ACE.accdb

TUTORIAL **7**

Creating Custom Reports

Creating Custom Reports for Belmont Landscapes

OBJECTIVES

Session 7.1
- View, filter, and copy report information in Report view
- Modify a report in Layout view
- Modify a report in Design view

Session 7.2
- Design and create a custom report
- Sort and group data in a report
- Add, move, resize, and align controls in a report
- Add lines to a report
- Hide duplicate values in a report

Session 7.3
- Add the date, page numbers, and title to a report
- Create and modify mailing labels

Case | *Belmont Landscapes*

At a recent staff meeting, Sarah Fisher indicated that she would like to make some changes to an existing report in the database. She also requested a new report that she can use to produce a printed list of all invoices for all contracts.

In this tutorial, you will modify an existing report and create the new report for Sarah. In modifying and building these reports, you will use many Access report customization features, including grouping data, calculating totals, and adding lines to separate report sections. These features will enhance Sarah's reports and make them easier to read and use.

STARTING DATA FILES

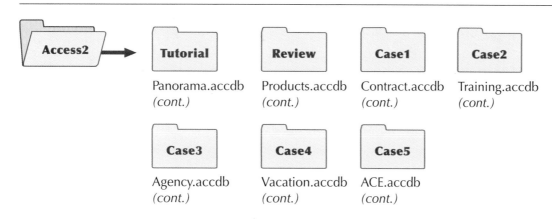

Access2 →	Tutorial	Review	Case1	Case2
	Panorama.accdb (cont.)	Products.accdb (cont.)	Contract.accdb (cont.)	Training.accdb (cont.)
	Case3	Case4	Case5	
	Agency.accdb (cont.)	Vacation.accdb (cont.)	ACE.accdb (cont.)	

SESSION 7.1 VISUAL OVERVIEW

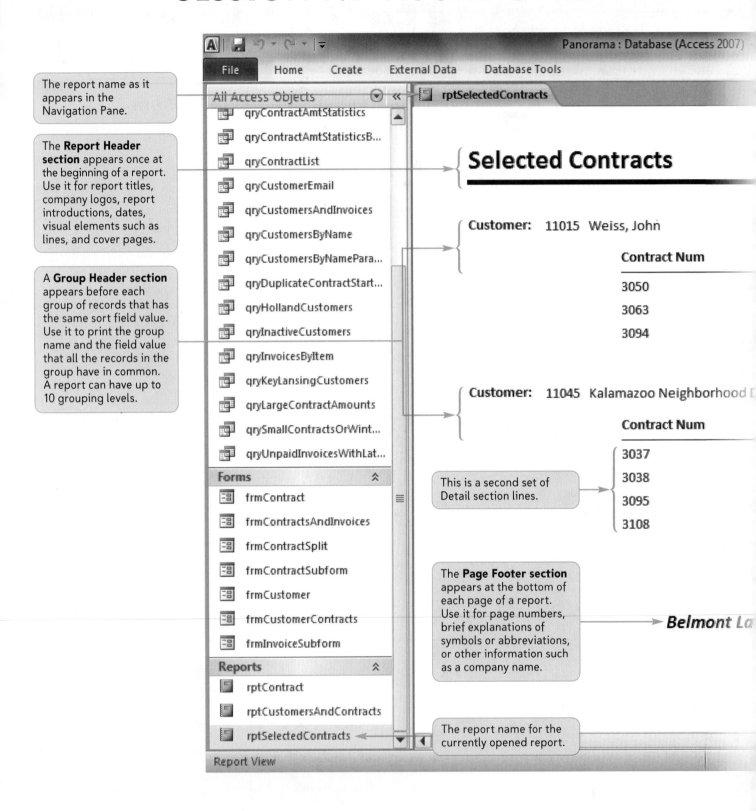

The report name as it appears in the Navigation Pane.

The **Report Header section** appears once at the beginning of a report. Use it for report titles, company logos, report introductions, dates, visual elements such as lines, and cover pages.

A **Group Header section** appears before each group of records that has the same sort field value. Use it to print the group name and the field value that all the records in the group have in common. A report can have up to 10 grouping levels.

This is a second set of Detail section lines.

The **Page Footer section** appears at the bottom of each page of a report. Use it for page numbers, brief explanations of symbols or abbreviations, or other information such as a company name.

The report name for the currently opened report.

Panorama : Database (Access 2007)

File   Home   Create   External Data   Database Tools

All Access Objects
- qryContractAmtStatistics
- qryContractAmtStatisticsB...
- qryContractList
- qryCustomerEmail
- qryCustomersAndInvoices
- qryCustomersByName
- qryCustomersByNamePara...
- qryDuplicateContractStart...
- qryHollandCustomers
- qryInactiveCustomers
- qryInvoicesByItem
- qryKeyLansingCustomers
- qryLargeContractAmounts
- qrySmallContractsOrWint...
- qryUnpaidInvoicesWithLat...

Forms
- frmContract
- frmContractsAndInvoices
- frmContractSplit
- frmContractSubform
- frmCustomer
- frmCustomerContracts
- frmInvoiceSubform

Reports
- rptContract
- rptCustomersAndContracts
- rptSelectedContracts

Report View

rptSelectedContracts

Selected Contracts

Customer: 11015 Weiss, John

Contract Num

3050

3063

3094

Customer: 11045 Kalamazoo Neighborhood D

Contract Num

3037

3038

3095

3108

Belmont La

REPORT SECTIONS

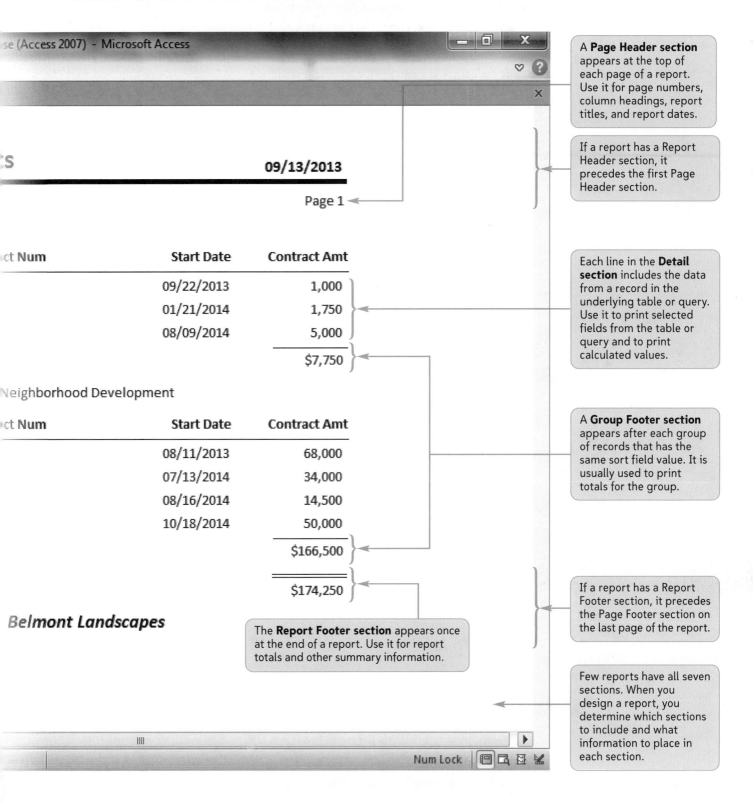

A **Page Header section** appears at the top of each page of a report. Use it for page numbers, column headings, report titles, and report dates.

If a report has a Report Header section, it precedes the first Page Header section.

Each line in the **Detail section** includes the data from a record in the underlying table or query. Use it to print selected fields from the table or query and to print calculated values.

A **Group Footer section** appears after each group of records that has the same sort field value. It is usually used to print totals for the group.

If a report has a Report Footer section, it precedes the Page Footer section on the last page of the report.

The **Report Footer section** appears once at the end of a report. Use it for report totals and other summary information.

Few reports have all seven sections. When you design a report, you determine which sections to include and what information to place in each section.

se (Access 2007) - Microsoft Access

09/13/2013

Page 1

ct Num	Start Date	Contract Amt
	09/22/2013	1,000
	01/21/2014	1,750
	08/09/2014	5,000
		$7,750

Neighborhood Development

ct Num	Start Date	Contract Amt
	08/11/2013	68,000
	07/13/2014	34,000
	08/16/2014	14,500
	10/18/2014	50,000
		$166,500
		$174,250

Belmont Landscapes

Num Lock

Customizing Existing Reports

A report is a formatted printout (or screen display) of the contents of one or more tables in a database. Although you can format and print data using datasheets, queries, and forms, reports offer greater flexibility and provide a more professional, readable appearance. For example, the staff at Belmont Landscapes can create reports from the database for billing statements and mailing labels, but they cannot use datasheets, queries, and forms for the same purposes.

Before Lucia Perez joined Belmont Landscapes to enhance the Panorama database, Sarah Fisher and her staff created two reports. Sarah used the Report tool to create the rptContract report and the Report Wizard to create the rptCustomersAndContracts report. One of Sarah's staff members modified the rptCustomersAndContracts report in Layout view by modifying the title, moving and resizing fields, changing the font color of field names, and inserting a picture. The rptCustomersAndContracts report is an example of a custom report. When you modify a report created by the Report tool or the Report Wizard in Layout view or in Design view, or when you create a report from scratch in Layout view or in Design view, you produce a **custom report**. You need to produce a custom report whenever the Report tool or the Report Wizard cannot automatically create the specific report you need, or when you need to fine-tune an existing report to fix formatting problems or to add controls and special features.

Sarah asks Lucia to review the rptContract report, make improvements to it, and demonstrate features that Sarah's staff can use when working with reports.

Viewing a Report in Report View

You can view reports on screen in Print Preview, Layout view, Design view, and Report view. You've already viewed and worked with reports in Print Preview and Layout view, and you'll find that making modifications in Design view for reports is similar to making changes in Design view for forms. **Report view** provides an interactive view of a report. You can use Report view to view the contents of a report and to apply a filter to the data in a report. You can also copy selected portions of the report to the Clipboard and use the selected data in another program.

Choosing the View to Use for a Report

You can view a report on screen using Report view, Print Preview, Layout view, or Design view. Which view you choose depends on what you intend to do with the report and its data.

- Use Report view when you want to filter the report data before printing a report, or when you want to copy a selected portion of a report.
- Use Print Preview when you want to see what a report will look like when it is printed. Print Preview is the only view in which you can navigate the pages of a report, zoom in or out, and view a **multiple-column report**, which is a report that prints the same collection of field values in two or more sets across the page.
- Use Layout view when you want to modify a report while seeing actual report data.
- Use Design view when you want to fine-tune a report's design, or when you want to add lines, rectangles, and other controls that are available only in Design view.

You'll open the rptContract report in Report view and show Sarah how she can interact with the report in this view.

To interact with the rptContract report in Report view:

▶ **1.** Start Access, and then open the **Panorama** database in the Access2\Tutorial folder provided with your Data Files.

Trouble? If the Security Warning is displayed below the Ribbon, either the Panorama database is not located in the Access2\Tutorial folder or you did not designate that folder as a trusted folder. Make sure you opened the database in the Access2\Tutorial folder, and make sure that it's designated as a trusted folder.

▶ **2.** Open the Navigation Pane, scroll down the Navigation Pane (if necessary), double-click **rptContract**, and then close the Navigation Pane. The rptContract report opens in Report view and the Navigation Pane closes.

In Report view, you can view the live version of the report prior to printing it, just as you can do in Print Preview. Unlike in Print Preview, you can apply filters to the report before printing it. You'll show Sarah how to apply filters to the rptContract report.

▶ **3.** In the first report detail line for Contract Num 3011, right-click **Residential landscape plan** in the Contract Type column to open the shortcut menu, and then point to **Text Filters**. A submenu of filter options for the Text field opens. See Figure 7-1.

Figure 7-1   **Filter options for a Text field in Report view**

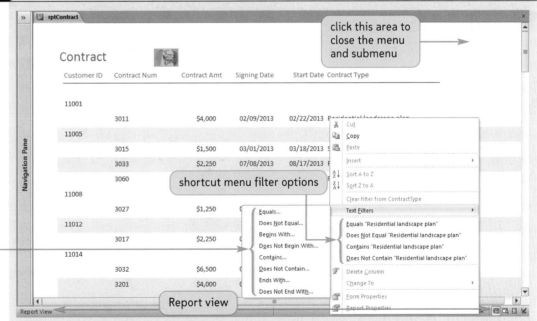

Trouble? Your Text Filters submenu will open to the left of the shortcut menu when you click the right side of the text in the Contract Type column.

The filter options that appear on the shortcut menu depend on the selected field's data type and the selected value. Because you clicked the ContractType field value without selecting a portion of the value, the shortcut menu displays filter options—various conditions using the value "Residential landscape plan"—for the entire ContractType field value. You'll close the menus and select a portion of the Contract Type column value to show Sarah a different way of filtering the report.

▶ **4.** Click a blank area in the report (see Figure 7-1) to close the menus, and in the report detail line for Contract Num 3011, double-click **Residential** in the Contract

Type column to select it, right-click **Residential**, and then point to **Text Filters** on the shortcut menu. The filter options now apply to the selected text.

Notice that the filter options on the shortcut menu and on the Text Filters submenu include options such as "Begins With" and "Does Not Begin With" because the text you selected is at the beginning of the field value in the Contract Type column.

▶ 5. Click **Contains "Residential"** on the shortcut menu. The report content changes to display only those contracts that contain the word "residential" anywhere in the Contract Type column.

▶ 6. Double-click the word **residential** in the Contract Type column for the report detail line for Contract Num 3015 to select it, right-click **residential** to open the shortcut menu, and then point to **Text Filters**. The filter options now include the "Ends With" and "Does Not End With" options because the text you selected is at the end of the field value in the Contract Type column.

Sarah wants to view only those contracts that contain the phrase "residential landscape plan" in the Contract Type column.

▶ 7. Click a blank area in the report to close the menus, and in the report detail line for Contract Num 3011, right-click **Residential landscape plan** in the Contract Type column, and then click **Equals "Residential landscape plan"** on the short-cut menu. Only the five contracts that contain the selected phrase are displayed in the report. See Figure 7-2.

| Figure 7-2 | Filter applied to the report in Report view |

report lines that match the chosen filter option

report filter has been applied

Sarah can print the filtered report, or she can select the entire filtered report or a portion of the filtered report. Then she can copy the selection to the Clipboard and paste it into another file, such as a Word document or an Excel spreadsheet. You'll show Sarah how to copy the entire filtered report to the Clipboard.

TIP

To select a portion of the report, click to the left of the top of the selection and drag down to the bottom of the selection.

▶ 8. Click to the left of the Contract title at the top of the report (but don't click in the Navigation Pane), drag down to the bottom of the report, release the mouse button to select the entire report, and then in the Clipboard group on the Home tab, point to the **Copy** button 📄. See Figure 7-3.

Trouble? If you selected nothing, you clicked above the Contract title. Make sure the mouse pointer is to the left of the Contract title, but not above it, and then repeat Step 8.

Trouble? If you selected only a portion of the report, press the Esc key to deselect your selection, and then repeat Step 8.

Figure 7-3	After selecting the filtered report in Report view

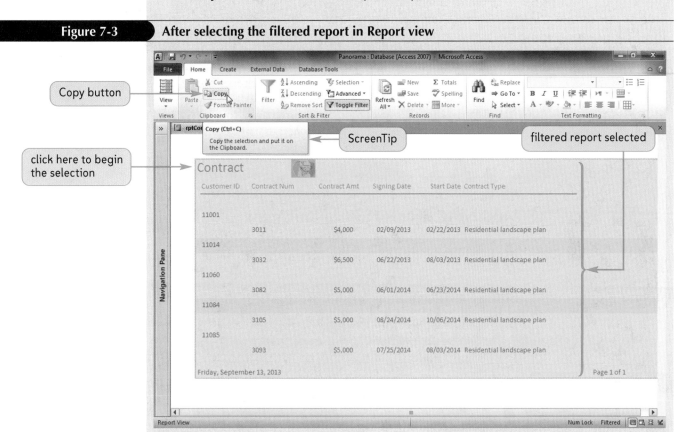

If you needed to copy the selection to the Clipboard, you would click the Copy button (see Figure 7-3). Sarah doesn't need to copy the selection, so you'll show her how to remove the filter from the report.

9. In the Sort & Filter group on the Home tab, click the **Toggle Filter** button. Access removes the filter and displays the complete report, which is still selected from the top to the bottom of the report.

10. Scroll down the report, and notice that some field values in the Contract Type column are not fully displayed and that no grand total of the ContractAmt field values is displayed at the end of the report.

Sarah wants you to modify the Contract Type column in the rptContract report so that all field values are fully displayed, while decreasing the width of other columns. She also wants you to rename some of the column headings, format the ContractAmt field values using the Standard format, resize the column headings, delete the picture from the Report Header section, remove the alternate row color from the detail and group header lines, and add a grand total of the ContractAmt field values. These changes will make the report more useful for Sarah.

PROSKILLS

Written Communication: Enhancing Reports Created by the Report Tool and the Report Wizard

Creating a report using the Report tool or the Report Wizard can save time, but you should review the report to determine if you need to make any of the following types of common enhancements and corrections:

- Change the report title from the report object name (with an rpt prefix and no spaces) to one that has meaning to the users.
- Reduce the widths of the date and page number controls, and move the controls so that they are not printed on a separate page.
- Review the report in Print Preview and, if the report displays excess pages, adjust the page margins and the placement of controls.
- Verify that all controls are large enough to fully display their values.

Some of the report adjustments you need to make are subtle ones, so you need to carefully review all report controls to ensure the report is completely readable and usable for those using the report.

Modifying a Report in Layout View

You can make the report changes Sarah wants in Layout view. Modifying a report in Layout view is similar to modifying a form in Layout view.

To view the report in Layout view:

1. On the status bar, click the **Layout View** button, and then scroll to the top of the report (if necessary). See Figure 7-4.

| Figure 7-4 | Viewing the report in Layout view |

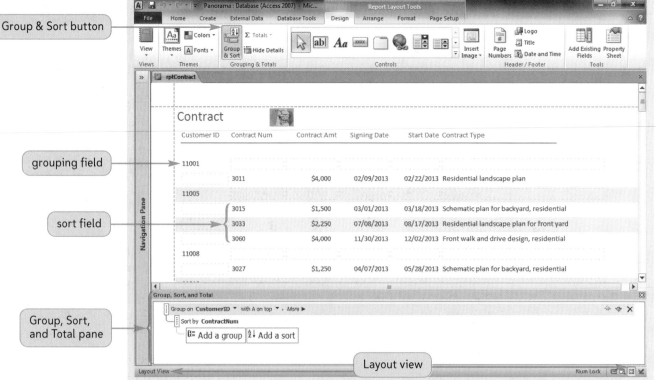

Group & Sort button

grouping field

sort field

Group, Sort, and Total pane

Layout view

Trouble? If the Group, Sort, and Total pane is not open at the bottom of the screen, click the Group & Sort button in the Grouping & Totals group on the Design tab.

TIP

You can click the Group & Sort button in the Grouping & Totals group to open and close the Group, Sort, and Total pane.

The rptContract report has a grouping field (the CustomerID field) and a sort field (the ContractNum field). At the bottom of the screen, the **Group, Sort, and Total pane** provides you with the options to modify the report's grouping fields and sort fields, and the report calculations for the groups. A **grouping field** is a report sort field that includes a Group Header section before a group of records having the same sort field value and a Group Footer section after the group of records. A Group Header section usually displays the group name and the sort field value for the group. A Group Footer section usually displays subtotals or counts for the records in that group. The rptContract report's grouping field is the CustomerID field, which is displayed in a Group Header section that precedes the set of contracts for the customer; the grouping field does not have a Group Footer section. The ContractNum field is a secondary sort key, as shown in the Group, Sort, and Total pane.

Because you don't need to change the grouping or sort fields for the report, you'll close the pane and then make Sarah's modifications to the report.

To modify the report in Layout view:

1. In the Grouping & Totals group on the Design tab, click the **Group & Sort** button to close the Group, Sort, and Total pane.

   First, you'll change the column headings for the first three columns to Cust ID, Contract#, and Amount. Sarah prefers to see all the detail data on one line, even when it means abbreviating column headings for columns whose headings are wider than the data. After reducing the column headings, you can reduce the column widths, freeing up space on the detail lines to widen the Contract Type column.

2. Double-click the **Customer ID** column heading to change to editing mode, change it to **Cust ID**, and then press the **Enter** key.

3. Repeat Step 2 to change the second column heading to **Contract#** and the third column heading to **Amount**.

   Next, you'll change the format of the field values in the Amount column to Standard.

4. Right-click any value in the **Amount** column to open the shortcut menu, click **Properties** to open the property sheet, set the Format property to **Standard**, and then close the property sheet.

   Now you'll increase the width of the Contract Type column after first reducing the widths of the first three columns.

5. Click the **Cust ID** column heading, move the pointer to the right edge of the column heading, and when the pointer changes to a ↔ shape, drag the right edge to the left. See Figure 7-5.

6. Repeat Step 5 to reduce the width of the **Contract#** column and then the width of the **Amount** column. See Figure 7-5.

Figure 7-5 After resizing columns in Layout view

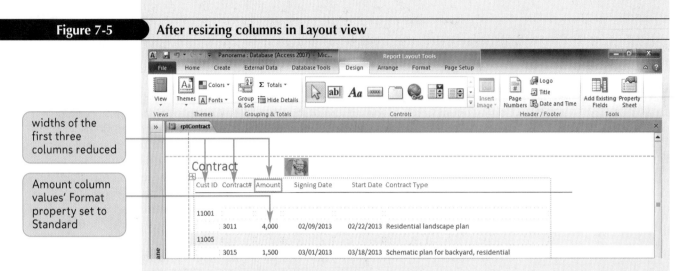

widths of the first three columns reduced

Amount column values' Format property set to Standard

▶ **7.** Scroll down the report to CustomerID 11083 and ContractNum 3043, which has the longest field value in the Contract Type column, click the **ContractType** field value for ContractNum 3043, move the pointer to the right edge of the selected value, and when the pointer changes to a ↔ shape, drag the right edge to the right until the entire field value is visible. See Figure 7-6.

Figure 7-6 After resizing columns in Layout view

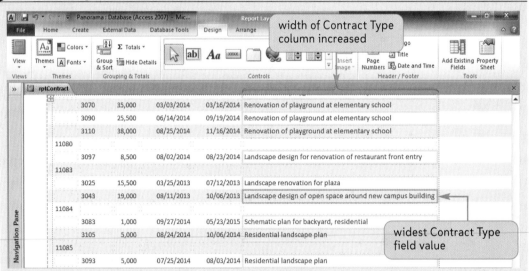

width of Contract Type column increased

widest Contract Type field value

Sarah notes that the picture at the top of the report isn't necessary, so you'll delete it.

▶ **8.** Scroll to the top of the report, right-click the picture at the top of the report to open the shortcut menu, and then click **Delete** to remove the picture.

Sarah notices the alternate row color setting in the group header and detail lines, finds it distracting, and asks you to remove this feature.

▶ **9.** Click to the left of the outer vertical dashed line to the left of 3011 in the Contract# column to select the detail lines, click the **Format** tab, in the Background group click the **Alternate Row Color arrow** to display the gallery of available colors, and then at the bottom of the gallery, click **No Color**. The alternate row color is removed from the detail lines in the report.

You've removed the alternate row color from the detail lines in the report, and next you'll remove the alternate row color from the group header lines. Because the Alternate Row Color button is now set to "No Color," you can just click the button to remove the color.

10. Click to the left of the vertical dashed line to the left of 11005 in the Cust ID column to select the group header lines, and then click the **Alternate Row Color** button in the Background group to remove the alternate row color from the group header lines.

Sarah's last change to the report is to add a grand total of the ContractAmt field values. First, you must select the Amount column or one of the values in the column.

To add a grand total to the report in Layout view:

1. In the detail line for ContractNum 3011, click **4,000** in the Amount column, click the **Design** tab, and then in the Grouping & Totals group, click the **Totals** button to display the Totals menu. See Figure 7-7.

Figure 7-7	Displaying options on the Totals menu

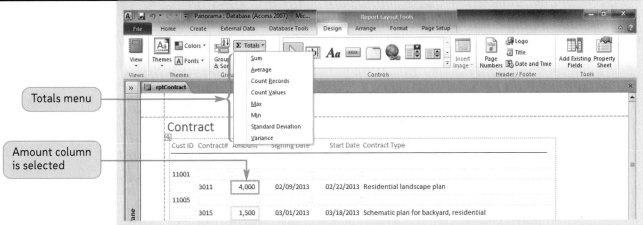

You select one of the eight aggregate functions on the Totals menu to summarize values in the selected column. To calculate and display the grand total contract amount, you'll select the Sum aggregate function.

2. Click **Sum** in the Totals menu, scroll to the bottom of the report, click **19,000** in the Amount column, and widen the Amount column to the right until the ###### changes to the correct grand total value of 1,758,075. In addition to the grand total, subtotals for each group of contracts are displayed for each CustomerID field value (19,000 for the last customer). See Figure 7-8.

Trouble? The commas in your subtotal and grand total might not be fully visible. You'll fix this problem in another step.

TIP

A text box displays pound signs when the text box is too narrow to display the full field value.

Figure 7-8	After adding subtotals and a grand total of the ContractAmt field values

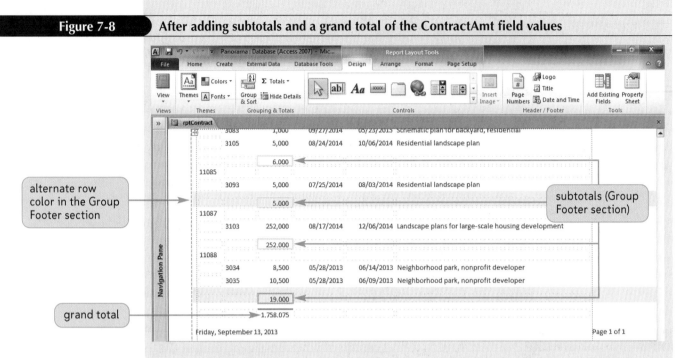

alternate row color in the Group Footer section

subtotals (Group Footer section)

grand total

When you select an aggregate function in Layout view, Access adds the results of the function to the end of the report and adds subtotals for each grouping field. Because each customer has few contracts, Sarah asks you to remove the subtotals from the report.

▶ **3.** Right-click the **19,000** subtotal to open the shortcut menu, click **Delete** to remove the subtotals, and then scroll to the end of the report. You deleted the subtotals, but the grand total still appears at the end of the report.

Although you deleted the subtotals, the Group Footer section remains, and Sarah wants you to delete the section with its alternate row color.

▶ **4.** Click to the left of the vertical dashed line on the left for one of the Group Footer lines, right-click one of the selected lines to open the shortcut menu, and then click **Delete** to remove the selected lines from the report.

Sarah notices that the commas in the grand total value are not fully visible. You'll increase the height of the grand total next.

▶ **5.** Click the grand total **1,758,075** to select it, and then use the ↕ pointer to drag the bottom edge of the grand total down slightly so the commas in the grand total are fully visible.

Sarah wants to review the rptContract report in Print Preview.

▶ **6.** Save your report changes, switch to Print Preview, and then page through the report, ending on the last page of the report.

You can use the Zoom control on the status bar to zoom in or out pointer the report view in 10% increments (using the Zoom In or Zoom Out buttons) or in variable increments (by dragging the Zoom slider control).

▶ **7.** Click the **Zoom In** button ⊕ on the status bar to increase the zoom percentage to 110%. See Figure 7-9.

Figure 7-9   **Viewing the rptContract report in Print Preview**

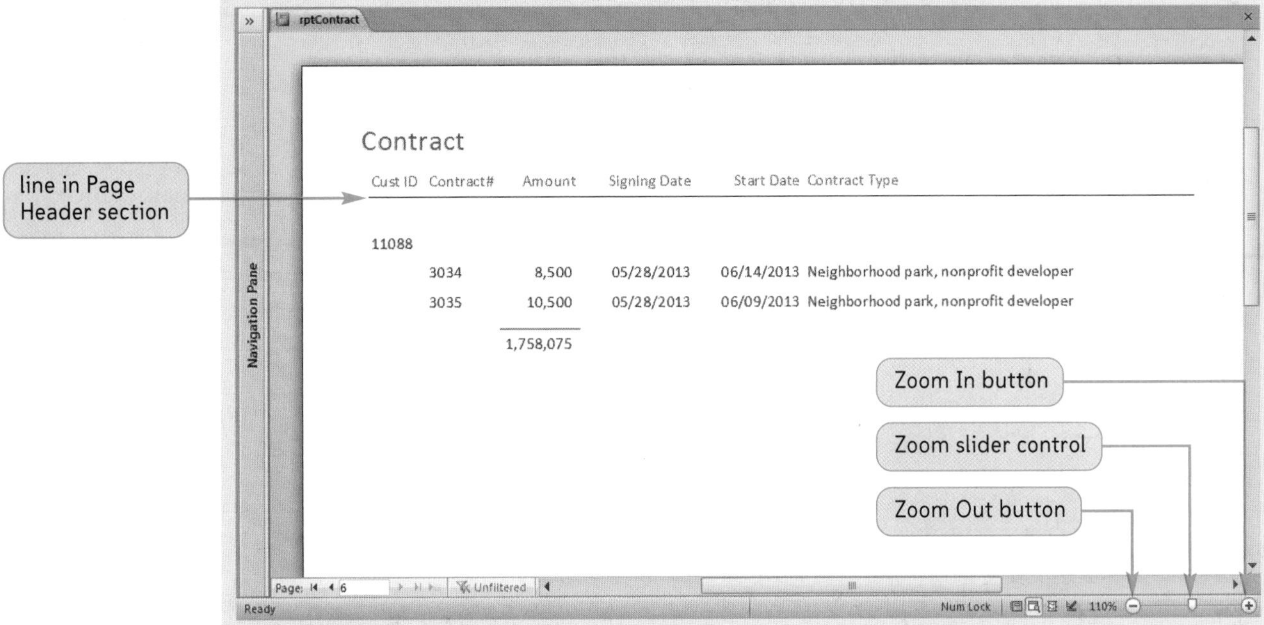

Contract

Cust ID	Contract#	Amount	Signing Date	Start Date	Contract Type
11088					
	3034	8,500	05/28/2013	06/14/2013	Neighborhood park, nonprofit developer
	3035	10,500	05/28/2013	06/09/2013	Neighborhood park, nonprofit developer
		1,758,075			

line in Page Header section

Zoom In button
Zoom slider control
Zoom Out button

Trouble? Depending on the printer you are using, the last page of your report might differ. If so, don't worry. Different printers format reports in different ways, sometimes affecting the total number of pages and the number of records printed per page.

8. Click the **Zoom Out** button ⊖ on the status bar to decrease the zoom percentage to 100%, and then close Print Preview for the report.

Sarah identifies two additional modifications she wants you to make to the report. She wants you to increase the length of the line below the column heading labels to better match the widths of the detail lines, and she wants you to move the page number at the bottom of each page to the left, so that its right edge is aligned with the right edge of ContractType text box in the Detail section.

Modifying a Report in Design View

Although you can make Sarah's modifications in Layout view, you'll make them in Design view. Design view for reports is similar to Design view for forms, which you used in Tutorial 6 to customize forms.

To view the report in Design view:

1. Switch to display the report in Design view. See Figure 7-10.

Figure 7-10 rptContract report in Design view

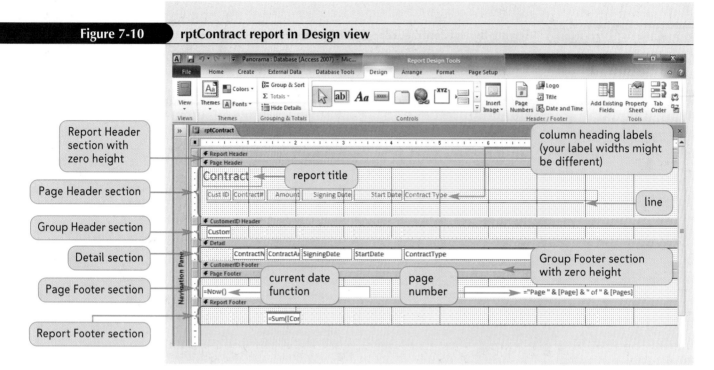

Notice that Design view for a report has most of the same components as Design view for a form. For example, Design view for forms and reports includes horizontal and vertical rulers, grids in each section, and similar buttons in the groups on the Design tab.

Design view for the rptContract report displays seven sections: the Report Header has zero height and isn't displayed in the report; the Page Header section contains the report title, column heading labels, and a horizontal line below the labels; the Group Header section (CustomerID Header) contains the CustomerID grouping field; the Detail section contains the bound controls to display the field values for each record in the record source (tblContract); the Group Footer section (CustomerID Footer) isn't displayed in the report; the Page Footer section contains the current date and the page number; and the Report Footer section contains a horizontal line above the Sum function, which calculates the grand total of the ContactAmt field values.

Refer to the Session 7.1 Visual Overview for a sample report from the Panorama database and descriptions of the seven sections in a report, all of which appear in the report shown in the Visual Overview.

To make Sarah's changes to the report, you need to extend the line control below the column headings in the Page Header section to the right, and then move the page number control in the Page Footer section to the left. Then you will align the right edges of both controls with the right edge of the ContractType text box in the Detail section.

To modify the report in Design view:

1. Click the **Page Number** text box, and then press the ← key to move the text box to the left until the right edge of the text box is to the left of the right edge of the ContractType text box in the Detail section.

2. With the Page Number text box still selected, hold down the **Shift** key, click the **ContractType** text box, and then release the **Shift** key. Both controls are now selected.

> **3.** Right-click one of the selected controls, point to **Align** on the shortcut menu, and then click **Right**. Both controls are now aligned on their right edges.

Finally, you'll extend the line in the Page Header section to the right.

> **4.** Click the **line** in the Page Header section to select the line as the current control.

> **5.** Hold down the **Shift** key, and then position the pointer on the right end of the line. When the pointer changes to a ↖ shape, drag the end of the line to the right until it is right-aligned with the Contract Type label above it, release the mouse button, and then release the **Shift** key. See Figure 7-11.

TIP

To draw or extend a straight line, press the Shift key before dragging the line and release the Shift key after releasing the mouse button.

Figure 7-11   **After modifying the rptContract report in Design view**

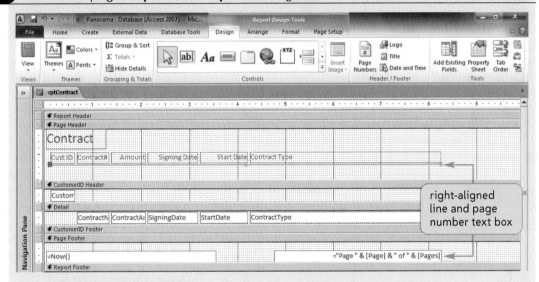

> **6.** Save your report changes, switch to Print Preview, and then scroll and page through the report, paying particular attention to the placement of the line in the Page Header section and the page number in the Page Footer section.

> **7.** Close the report.

> **8.** If you are not continuing on to the next session, close the Panorama database.

Now that you have completed the changes to the rptContract report, you'll create a custom report for Sarah in the next session.

Session 7.1 Quick Check

REVIEW

1. What is a custom report?
2. You can view a report in Report view. What other actions can you perform in Report view?
3. What is a grouping field?
4. Describe the seven sections of an Access report.

SESSION 7.2 VISUAL OVERVIEW

9/13/2013

The current date is displayed in the Page Header section of the report.

The report title is displayed in the Page Header section of the report.

Invoices by It

The Page Header section of the report displays the current date, the report title, the page number, the column headings, and a line.

Invoice Date	Customer	City
12/05/2014	Dept. of Neighborhood Development	East Grand Rapids
12/09/2014	G. R. Neighborhood Development Corp	Grand Rapids
02/16/2015	Dept. of Neighborhood Development	East Grand Rapids
02/24/2015	Dept. of Neighborhood Development	East Grand Rapids
04/18/2015	G. R. Neighborhood Development Corp	Grand Rapids

The Detail section displays the detail records.

Schematic Plans

12/22/2015	Northwest Transit Station	Lansing

The Group Header section displays the InvoiceItem field values, which are formatted in bold.

CUSTOM REPORT DESIGN

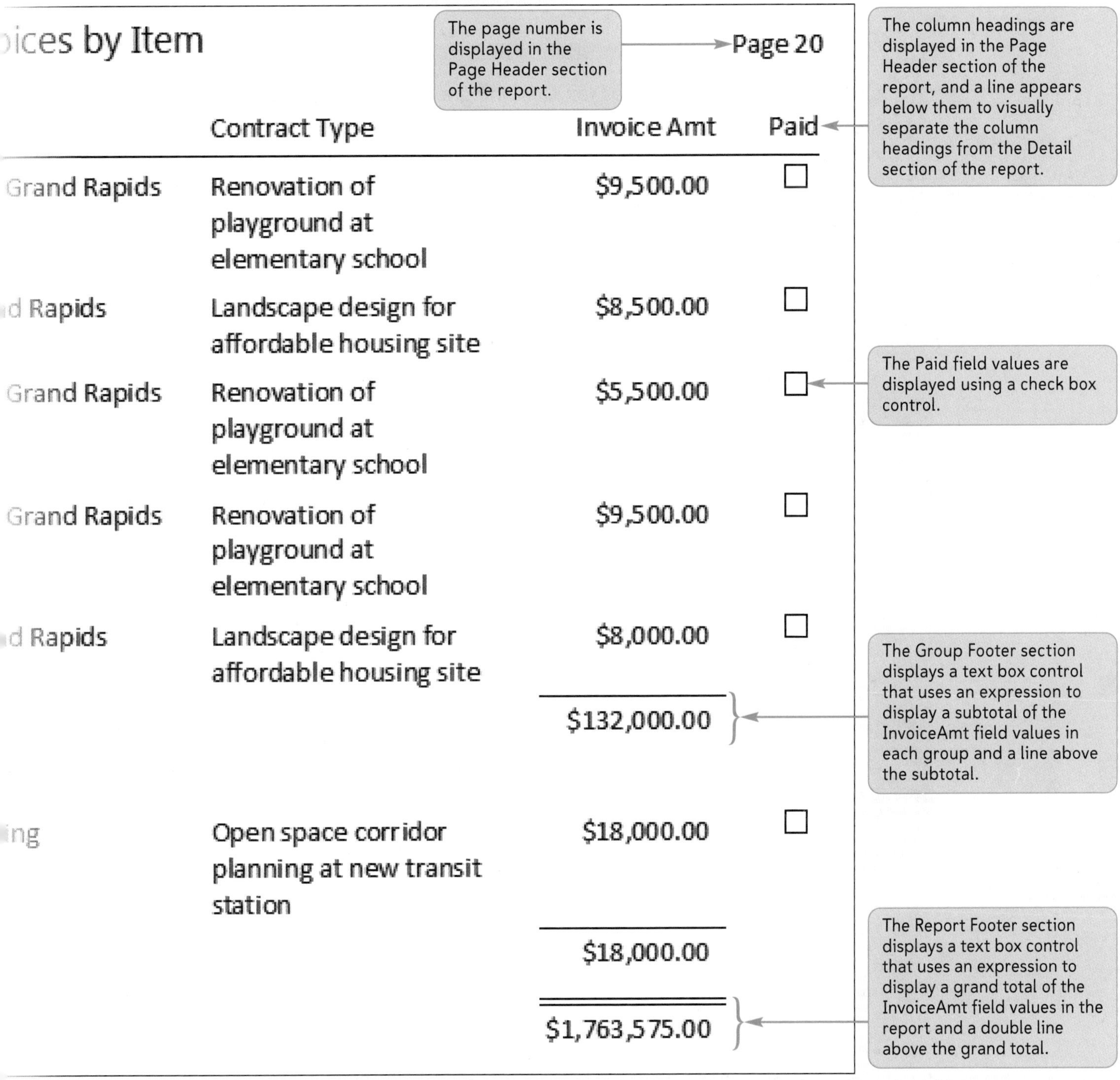

ices by Item

The page number is displayed in the Page Header section of the report. → Page 20

The column headings are displayed in the Page Header section of the report, and a line appears below them to visually separate the column headings from the Detail section of the report.

	Contract Type	Invoice Amt	Paid
Grand Rapids	Renovation of playground at elementary school	$9,500.00	☐
d Rapids	Landscape design for affordable housing site	$8,500.00	☐
Grand Rapids	Renovation of playground at elementary school	$5,500.00	☐
Grand Rapids	Renovation of playground at elementary school	$9,500.00	☐
d Rapids	Landscape design for affordable housing site	$8,000.00	☐
		$132,000.00	
ing	Open space corridor planning at new transit station	$18,000.00	☐
		$18,000.00	
		$1,763,575.00	

The Paid field values are displayed using a check box control.

The Group Footer section displays a text box control that uses an expression to display a subtotal of the InvoiceAmt field values in each group and a line above the subtotal.

The Report Footer section displays a text box control that uses an expression to display a grand total of the InvoiceAmt field values in the report and a double line above the grand total.

Designing a Custom Report

Before you create a custom report, you should first plan the report's contents and appearance.

Decision Making: Guidelines for Designing a Report

When you plan a report, you should keep in mind the following report design guidelines:
- Determine the purpose of and record source for the report. Recall that the record source is a table or query that provides the fields for a report. If the report displays detailed information (a **detail report**), such as a list of all contracts, then the report will display fields from the record source in the Detail section. If the report displays only summary information (a **summary report**), such as total contracts by city, then no detailed information appears; only grand totals and possibly subtotals appear based on calculations using fields from the record source.
- Determine the sort order for the information in the report.
- Identify any grouping fields in the report.

At the same time you are designing a report, you should keep in mind the following report formatting guidelines:
- Balance the report's attractiveness against its readability and economy. Keep in mind that an attractive, readable, two-page report is more economical than a report of three pages or more. Unlike forms, which usually display one record at a time in the main form, reports display multiple records. Instead of arranging fields vertically as you do in a form, you usually position fields horizontally across the page in a report. Typically, you single space the detail lines in a report. At the same time, make sure to include enough white space between columns so the values do not overlap or run together.
- Group related fields and position them in a meaningful, logical order. For example, position identifying fields, such as names and codes, on the left. Group together all location fields, such as street and city, and position them in their customary order.
- Identify each column of field values with a column heading label that names the field.
- Include the report title, page number, and date on every page of the report.
- Identify the end of a report either by displaying grand totals or an end-of-report message.
- Use few colors, fonts, and graphics to keep the report uncluttered and to keep the focus on the information.
- Use a consistent style for all reports in a database.

By following these report design and formatting guidelines, you create reports that make it easier for users to conduct their daily business and to make better decisions.

After working with Sarah and her staff to determine their requirements for a new report, Lucia prepared a paper design for a custom report to display invoices grouped by invoice item. Refer to the Session 7.2 Visual Overview for Lucia's design of the report.

The custom report will list the records for all invoices and will contain five sections:

- The Page Header section contains the report title ("Invoices by Item") centered between the current date on the left and the page number on the right. A horizontal line separates the column heading labels from the rest of the report page. From your work with the Report tool and the Report Wizard, you know that, by default, Access places the report title in the Report Header section and the date and page number in the Page Footer section. Sarah prefers the date, report title, and page number to appear at the top of each page, so you need to place this information in the custom report's Page Header section.
- The InvoiceItem field value from the tblInvoice table is displayed in a Group Header section.

- The Detail section contains the InvoiceDate, InvoiceAmt, and InvoicePaid field values from the tblInvoice table; the ContractType field value from the tblContract table; the City field value from the tblCustomer table; and the Customer calculated field value from the qryCustomersByName query. The detail records are sorted in ascending value by the InvoiceDate field.
- A subtotal of the InvoiceAmt field values is displayed below a line in the Group Footer section.
- The grand total of the InvoiceAmt field values is displayed below a double line in the Report Footer section.

Before you start creating the custom report, you need to create a query that'll serve as the record source for the report.

Creating a Query for a Custom Report

The data for a report can come from a single table, from a single query based on one or more tables, or from multiple tables and/or queries. Lucia's report will contain data from the tblInvoice, tblContract, and tblCustomer tables, and from the qryCustomersByName query. You'll use the Simple Query Wizard to create a query to retrieve all the data required for the custom report and to serve as the report's record source.

TIP

Create queries to serve as the record source for forms and reports. As requirements change, you can easily add fields, including calculated fields, to the queries.

To create the query using the Simple Query Wizard:

1. If you took a break after the previous session, make sure that the Panorama database is open and the Navigation Pane is closed.

2. Click the **Create** tab on the Ribbon, in the Queries group click the **Query Wizard** button, make sure **Simple Query Wizard** is selected, and then click the **OK** button. The first Simple Query Wizard dialog box opens.

   You need to select fields from the tblInvoice, tblContract, and tblCustomer tables, and from the qryCustomersByName query, in that order.

3. Select **Table: tblInvoice** in the Tables/Queries box, and then move the **InvoiceItem**, **InvoiceDate**, **InvoiceAmt**, and **InvoicePaid** fields, in that order, to the Selected Fields box.

4. Select **Table: tblContract** in the Tables/Queries box, and then move the **ContractType** field to the Selected Fields box.

5. Select **Table: tblCustomer** in the Tables/Queries box, and then move the **City** field to the Selected Fields box.

6. Select **Query: qryCustomersByName** in the Tables/Queries box, move the **Customer** calculated field to the Selected Fields box, and then click the **Next** button.

7. Make sure the **Detail (shows every field of every record)** option button is selected, and then click the **Next** button to open the final Simple Query Wizard dialog box.

   After entering the query name and creating the query, you'll need to set the sort fields for the query.

8. Change the query name to **qryInvoicesByItem**, click the **Modify the query design** option button, and then click the **Finish** button.

   The InvoiceItem field will be a grouping field, which means it's the primary sort field, and the InvoiceDate field is the secondary sort field.

9. Set the InvoiceItem Sort box to **Ascending**, set the InvoiceDate Sort box to **Ascending**, save your query changes, and then click below the field lists and above the design grid to deselect all values. The completed query contains seven fields from three tables and one query and has two sort fields, the InvoiceItem primary sort field and the InvoiceDate secondary sort field. See Figure 7-12.

Figure 7-12 | **Finished qryInvoicesByItem query in Design view**

source tables and
source query for the
qryInvoicesByItem
query

fields needed for
the custom report

primary and
secondary sort fields

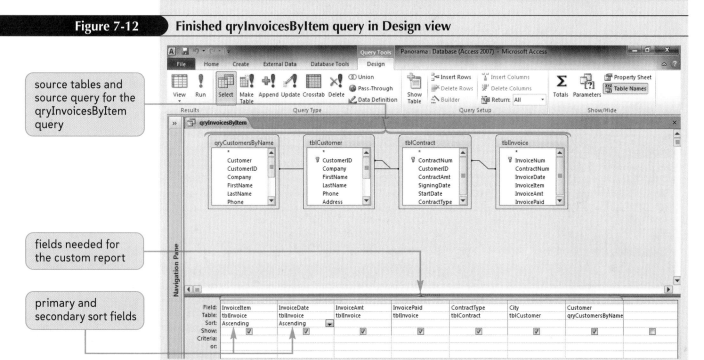

Trouble? After you've finished creating the query and close it, if you later open the query in Design view, you'll see the thicker join lines with referential integrity enforced, connecting the tblCustomer and tblContract table field lists and the tblContract and tblInvoice table field lists.

Before closing the query, you'll run it to view the query recordset.

10. Run the query, which displays 172 records, and then close the query.

You'll use the qryInvoicesByItem query as the record source for Lucia's custom report.

Creating a Custom Report

You could use the Report Wizard to create the report and then modify it to match the report design. However, because you need to customize several components of the report, you will create a custom report in Layout view, and then switch between Layout and Design view to fine-tune the report. As the first step to creating the report, you need to create a blank report in Layout view.

Creating a Blank Report in Layout View

- Click the Create tab on the Ribbon.
- In the Reports group on the Create tab, click the Blank Report button to open a blank report in Layout view.

Making Report Design Modifications

You perform operations in Layout and Design views for reports the same as you perform operations in these views for forms. These operations become easier with practice. Remember to use the Undo button, back up your database frequently, save your report changes frequently, work from a copy of the report for complicated design changes, and compact and repair the database on a regular basis. You can also display the report in Print Preview at any time to view your progress on the report.

The record source for the report will be the qryInvoicesByItem query. You'll set the record source after you create a blank report in Layout view.

To create a blank report and add bound controls in Layout view:

1. Click the **Create** tab on the Ribbon, and then in the Reports group, click the **Blank Report** button. A new report opens in Layout view with the Field List pane open. See Figure 7-13.

Figure 7-13   **Blank report in Layout view**

2. In the Tools group on the Design tab, click the **Property Sheet** button to open the property sheet for the report.

3. In the property sheet, click the **All** tab (if necessary), click the **Record Source** arrow, click **qryInvoicesByItem**, and then close the property sheet.

4. In the Tools group on the Design tab, click the **Add Existing Fields** button to open the Field List pane. The Field List pane displays the seven fields in the qryInvoicesByItem query, which is the record source for the report.

   Referring to Lucia's report design, you'll add six of the seven fields to the report in a tabular layout, which is the default control layout when you add fields to a report in Layout view.

5. Double-click **InvoiceDate** in the Field List pane, and then in order, double-click **Customer**, **City**, **ContractType**, **InvoiceAmt**, and **InvoicePaid** in the Field List pane. The six bound controls are displayed in a tabular layout in the report. See Figure 7-14.

| Figure 7-14 | After adding fields to the report in Layout view |

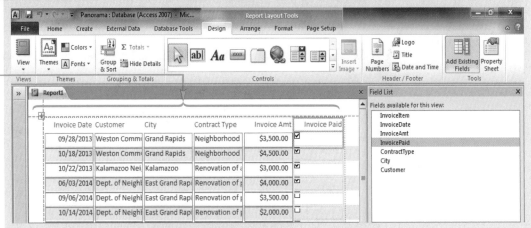

fields added in a tabular layout to the report

Trouble? If you add the wrong field to the report, click the field's column heading, press and hold the Shift key, click one of the field values in the column to select the column, release the Shift key, click the Home tab on the Ribbon, and then click the Delete button in the Records group to delete the field. If you add a field in the wrong order, click the column heading in the tabular layout, press and hold the Shift key, click one of the field values in the column, release the Shift key, and then drag the column to its correct columnar position.

You'll add the seventh field, the InvoiceItem field, as a grouping field, so you are done working with the Field List pane.

6. Close the Field List pane, and then save the report as **rptInvoicesByItem**.

Next, you'll adjust the column widths in Layout view, and then fine-tune the adjustments and the spacing between columns later in Design view. Also, because the Invoice Amt and Invoice Paid columns are adjacent, you can change the rightmost column heading to Paid without losing any meaning and to save space.

To resize and rename columns in Layout view:

1. Click **Customer** to select the column, and then drag the right edge of the control to the right to increase its width, as shown in Figure 7-15.

2. Repeat Step 1 to resize the **City** and **Contract Type** columns, as shown in Figure 7-15.

3. Double-click **Invoice Paid** in the rightmost column, delete **Invoice** and the following space, and then press the **Enter** key.

4. Drag the right edge of the **Paid** control to the left to decrease the column's width, as shown in Figure 7-15.

| Figure 7-15 | After resizing and renaming columns in Layout view |

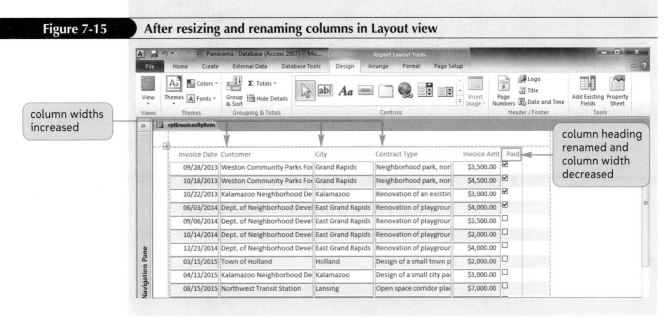

column widths increased

column heading renamed and column width decreased

According to Lucia's plan for the report (see the Session 7.2 Visual Overview), the InvoiceItem field is a grouping field that is displayed in a Group Header section. Subtotals for the InvoiceAmt field are displayed in a Group Footer section for each InvoiceItem field value.

Sorting and Grouping Data in a Report

Access lets you organize records in a report by sorting them using one or more sort fields. Each sort field can also be a grouping field. If you specify a sort field as a grouping field, you can include a Group Header section and a Group Footer section for the group. A Group Header section typically includes the name of the group, and a Group Footer section typically includes a count or subtotal for records in that group. Some reports have a Group Header section but not a Group Footer section, some reports have a Group Footer section but not a Group Header section, and some reports have both sections or have neither section.

You use the Group, Sort, and Total pane to select sort fields and grouping fields for a report. Each report can have up to 10 sort fields, and any of its sort fields can also be grouping fields.

REFERENCE

Sorting and Grouping Data in a Report

- Display the report in Layout or Design view.
- If necessary, click the Group & Sort button in the Grouping & Totals group on the Design tab to display the Group, Sort, and Total pane.
- To select a grouping field, click the Add a group button in the Group, Sort, and Total pane, and then click the grouping field in the list. To set additional properties for the grouping field, click the More button on the group field band.
- To select a sort field that is not a grouping field, click the Add a sort button in the Group, Sort, and Total pane, and then click the sort field in the list. To set additional properties for the sort field, click the More button on the sort field band.

In Lucia's report design, the InvoiceItem field is a grouping field, and the InvoiceDate field is a sort field. The InvoiceItem field value is displayed in a Group Header section, but not its label. The sum of the InvoiceAmt field values is displayed in the Group Footer section for the InvoiceItem grouping field. Next, you'll select the grouping field and the sort field and set their properties.

To select and set the properties for the grouping field and the sort field:

▶ **1.** In the Grouping & Totals group, click the **Group & Sort** button to open the Group, Sort, and Total pane.

▶ **2.** In the Group, Sort, and Total pane, click the **Add a group** button, and then click **InvoiceItem** in the list. Access adds a Group Header section to the report with InvoiceItem as the grouping field, and adds a group band in the Group, Sort, and Total pane. See Figure 7-16.

Figure 7-16   After selecting InvoiceItem as a grouping field in Layout view

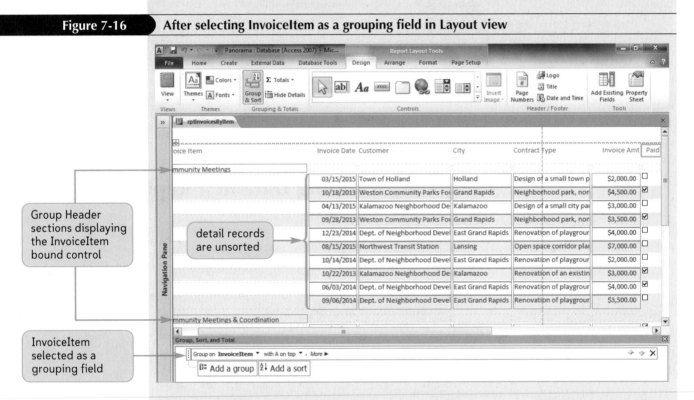

Group Header sections displaying the InvoiceItem bound control

detail records are unsorted

InvoiceItem selected as a grouping field

InvoiceItem is now a bound control in the report in a Group Header section that displays a field value text box and its attached label. The group band in the Group, Sort, and Total pane contains the name of the grouping field (InvoiceItem), the sort order ("with A on top" to indicate ascending), and the More option, which you click to display more options for the grouping field. You can click the "with A on top" arrow to change to descending sort order ("with Z on top").

Notice that the addition of the grouping field has moved the detail records to the right; you'll move them back to the left later in this tutorial. Also, notice that the detail records are unsorted, and Lucia's design specifies an ascending sort on the InvoiceDate field. Next, you'll select this field as a secondary sort field; the InvoiceItem grouping field is the primary sort field.

3. In the Group, Sort, and Total pane, click the **Add a sort** button, and then click **InvoiceDate** in the list. Access displays the detail records in ascending InvoiceDate order, and adds a sort band for the InvoiceDate field in the Group, Sort, and Total pane.

Next, you'll display all the options for the InvoiceItem grouping field, and set grouping options as shown in Lucia's report design.

4. Click ⫶ to the left of the group band to select it, and then click **More** to expand the band and display all group options. See Figure 7-17.

Figure 7-17   After expanding the group band

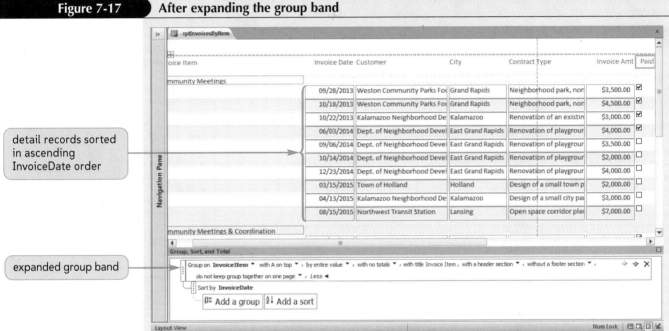

detail records sorted in ascending InvoiceDate order

expanded group band

Reviewing Lucia's report design (see the Session 7.2 Visual Overview), you need to delete the Invoice Item label, add a Group Footer section with a subtotal for the InvoiceAmt field values, add a grand total for the InvoiceAmt field values to the Report Footer section, and set the Keep Together property. The **Keep Together property** prints a group header on a page only if there is enough room on the page to print the first detail record for the group; otherwise, the group header prints at the top of the next page.

5. In the "with title Invoice Item" option, click the **Invoice Item** link to open the Zoom dialog box, press the **Delete** key to delete the expression, and then click the **OK** button. The Invoice Item label is deleted from the report, and the option in the group band changes to "with title click to add."

6. In the group band, click the **do not keep group together on one page** arrow, and then click **keep header and first record together on one page**.

7. In the group band, click **More** to expand the band (if necessary), click the **without a footer section** arrow, and then click **with a footer section**. Access adds a Group Footer section for the InvoiceItem grouping field, but the report doesn't display this new section until you add controls to it.

8. In the group band, click **More** to expand the band (if necessary), click the **with no totals** arrow to open the Totals menu, click the **Total On** arrow, click **InvoiceAmt**, make sure **Sum** is selected in the Type box, and then click the **Show Grand Total** check box. The group band collapses.

9. In the group band, click **More** to expand the band (if necessary), click the **with InvoiceAmt totaled** arrow, click the **Total On** arrow, click **InvoiceAmt**, and then click the **Show subtotal in group footer** check box. The group band collapses.

10. In the group band, click **More** to expand the band (if necessary). The group band shows the InvoiceAmt subtotals and a grand total added to the report. See Figure 7-18.

Figure 7-18 After setting properties in the group band

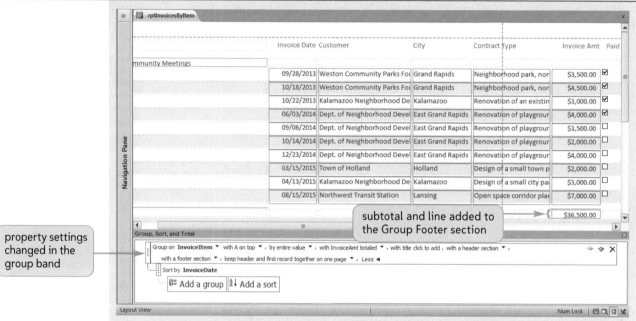

property settings changed in the group band

subtotal and line added to the Group Footer section

Similar to the sound form design strategy you followed in the previous tutorial, you should frequently save your report changes and review the report in Print Preview.

11. Save your report changes, switch to Print Preview, and review every page until you reach the end of the report—noticing in particular the details of the report format and the effects of the Keep Together property. Also, notice that because the grouping field forces the detail values to the right, the current report design prints the detail values across two pages.

Before you can move the detail values to the left onto one page, you need to remove all controls from the control layout.

To remove controls from a control layout in Layout view:

1. Switch to Layout view.

2. Click the **layout selector** ⊞, which is located at the top-left corner of the column heading line, to select the entire control layout. An orange outline, which identifies the controls that you've selected, appears around the labels and text boxes in the report.

3. Right-click one of the selected controls to open the shortcut menu, point to **Layout**, and then click **Remove Layout**.

   You'll next move all the controls to the left except for the InvoiceItem text box. You have to be careful when you move the remaining controls to the left. If you try to select all the column headings and the text boxes, you're likely to miss the subtotal and grand total controls. The safest technique is to select all controls in the report, and then remove the InvoiceItem text box from the selection. This latter step, removing individual controls from a selection, must be done in Design view because it doesn't work in Layout view.

4. Switch to Design view, click the **Format** tab, and then in the Selection group, click the **Select All** button. All controls in the report are now selected.

5. Hold down the **Shift** key, click the **InvoiceItem** text box in the InvoiceItem Header section to remove this control from the selection, and then release the **Shift** key.

6. Hold down the ← key to move the selected controls rapidly to the left edge of the report, and then release the ← key. See Figure 7-19.

Figure 7-19   After moving all controls to the left in the report

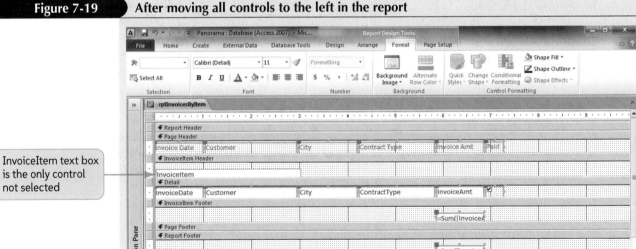

InvoiceItem text box is the only control not selected

The grand total of the InvoiceAmt field values is displayed at the end of the report, and subtotals are displayed for each unique InvoiceItem field value in the Group Footer section. It's possible for subtotals to appear in an orphaned footer section. An **orphaned footer section** appears by itself at the top of a page, and the detail lines for the section appear on the previous page. When you set the Keep Together property for the grouping field, you set it to keep the group and the first detail record together on one page to prevent an **orphaned header section**, which is a section that appears by itself at the bottom of a page. To prevent both types of orphaned sections, you'll set the Keep Together property to keep the whole group together on one page.

In addition, you need to fine-tune the sizes of the text boxes in the Detail section, adjust the spacing between columns, and make other adjustments to the current content of the report design before adding a report title, the date, and page number to the Page Header section. You'll make most of these report design changes in Design view.

Working with Controls in Design View

Compared to Layout view, Design view gives you greater control over the placement and sizing of controls, and lets you add and manipulate many more controls, but at the expense of not being able to see live data in the controls to guide you as you make changes.

The rptInvoicesByItem report has five sections: the Page Header section contains the six column heading labels, the InvoiceItem Header section (a Group Header section) contains the InvoiceItem text box, the Detail section contains the six bound controls, the InvoiceItem Footer section (a Group Footer section) contains a line and the subtotal text box, and the Report Footer section contains a line and the grand total text box.

You'll move and resize controls in the report in Design view. The Group, Sort, and Total pane is still open, so first you'll change the Keep Together property setting.

To move and resize controls in the report:

▶ 1. In the Group, Sort, and Total pane, click ⋮ to the left of the group band to select it, click **More** to expand the band and display all group options, click the **keep header and first record together on one page** arrow, and then click **keep whole group together on one page**, and then close the Group, Sort, and Total pane.

You'll start improving the report by setting the InvoiceItem text box font to bold.

▶ 2. Select the **InvoiceItem** text box in the InvoiceItem Header section, and then in the Font group on the Format tab, click the **Bold** button **B**. The InvoiceItem text box is displayed as bold text.

The report's width is approximately 16 inches, which is much wider than the width of the contents of the report, so you'll reduce its width.

▶ 3. Scroll to the right until you see the right edge of the report (the point where the dotted grid ends), move the pointer to the right edge of the report, and when the pointer changes to a ◀▶ shape, drag to the left to the 7.5-inch mark on the horizontal ruler, and then scroll to the left to display the entire report from the left (if necessary). See Figure 7-20.

| Figure 7-20 | After reducing the width of the report |

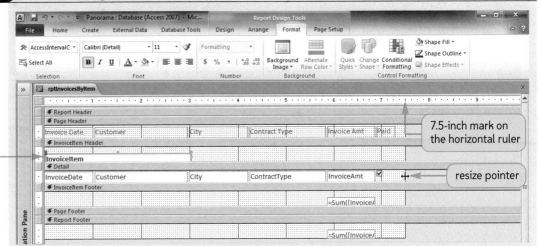

Now you'll check the report's page orientation and margins.

TIP

You usually determine page setup properties when you design a report or, as for this report, after you've placed the controls in the Detail section.

▶ **4.** Click the **Page Setup** tab on the Ribbon.

▶ **5.** In the Page Layout group, make sure the **Portrait** button is selected, click the **Page Setup** button, set the Top and Bottom margin properties to **0.7** and the Left and Right margin properties to **0.5**, and then click the **OK** button.

The text boxes in the Detail section are crowded together with little space between them. Your reports shouldn't have too much space between columns, but reports are easier to read when the columns are separated more than they are in the rptInvoicesByItem report. Sometimes the amount of spacing is dictated by the users of the report, but mostly it's the report designer's choice to make. First, you'll resize the Paid label and the InvoicePaid check box, and move them to the right.

TIP

You can resize labels and controls added with the Label tool to fit, but you can't resize text boxes to fit.

▶ **6.** Right-click the **Paid** label in the Page Header section, point to **Size**, click **To Fit**, hold down the **Shift** key, click the **InvoicePaid** check box in the Detail section, release the **Shift** key, and then move both controls to the right until the label's right edge is one column of grid dots to the left of the 7.5-inch mark on the horizontal ruler.

You'll now resize the remaining labels to fit in the Page Header section.

▶ **7.** Select the **Invoice Date** label in the Page Header section, the **Customer** label, the **City** label, the **Contract Type** label, and the **Invoice Amt** label, right-click one of the selected labels, point to **Size** on the shortcut menu, and then click **To Fit**.

Because the InvoiceAmt text box and its subtotal and grand total text boxes are Number fields, you'll align the Invoice Amt label on its right edge with the text boxes.

▶ **8.** Select the **Invoice Amt** label and the **InvoiceAmt** text box, right-click one of the selected controls, point to **Align**, and then click **Right**. See Figure 7-21.

Figure 7-21	After resizing and moving controls in Design view

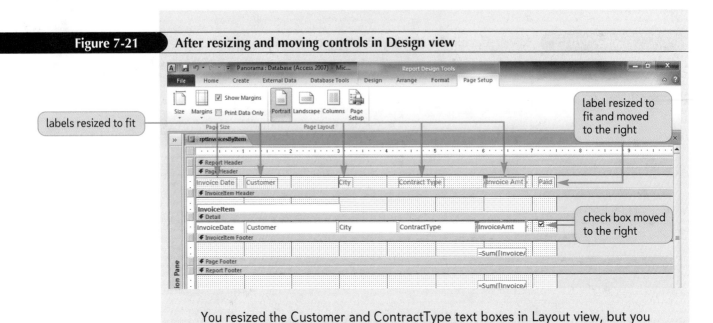

labels resized to fit

label resized to fit and moved to the right

check box moved to the right

You resized the Customer and ContractType text boxes in Layout view, but you did not resize them wide enough to display the entire field value in all cases. For the Customer and ContractType text boxes, you'll set their Can Grow property to Yes. The **Can Grow property**, when set to Yes, expands a text box vertically to fit the field value when the report is printed, previewed, or viewed in Layout and Report views.

9. Click the **Design** tab on the Ribbon, select the **Customer** and **ContractType** text boxes in the Detail section, open the property sheet, click the **Format** tab in the property sheet, scroll down the property sheet, make sure the Can Grow property is set to **Yes**, close the property sheet, and then save your report changes.

   Trouble? By default, the Can Grow property should be set to No. If the Can Grow property in your property sheet is already set to Yes, set the property to No, and then set it back to Yes.

10. Switch to Print Preview, and review every page of the report, ending on the last page of the report. See Figure 7-22.

Figure 7-22   **Reviewing the report changes in Print Preview**

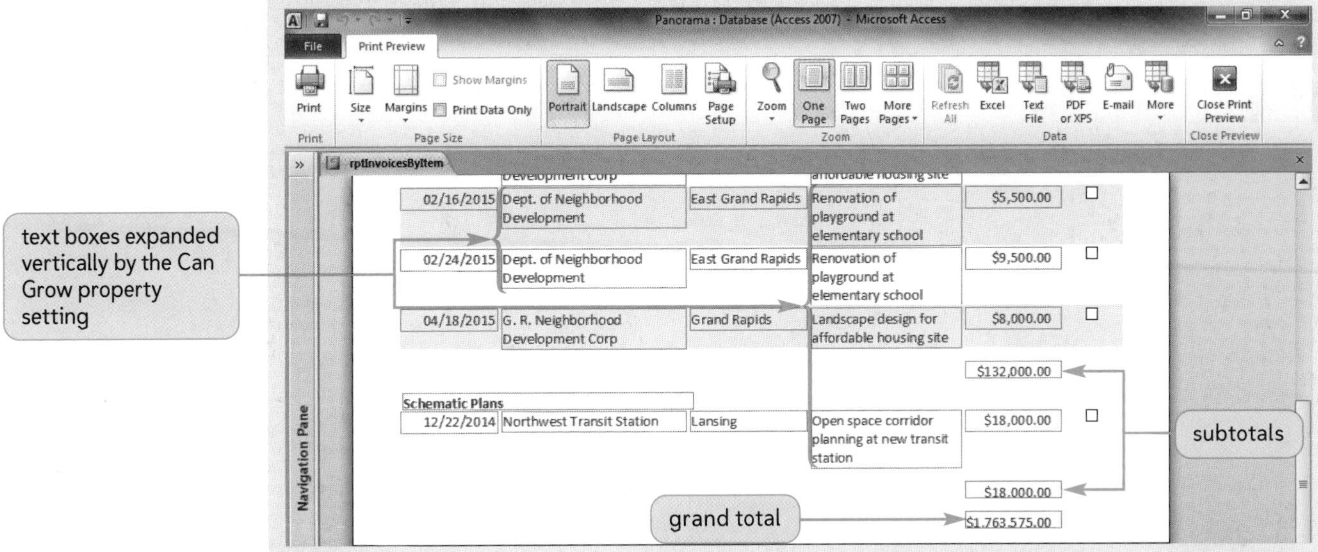

text boxes expanded vertically by the Can Grow property setting

subtotals

grand total

The groups stay together on one page, except for the groups that have too many detail lines to fit on one page. The Can Grow property correctly expands the height of the Customer and ContractType text boxes.

Also, the lines that were displayed above the subtotals and grand total are no longer displayed, and the commas in the values are not fully visible. You'll add those lines back in the report and resize the text boxes. First, Lucia thinks the borders around the text boxes and the alternate row color are too distracting, so you'll remove them from the report.

To remove the borders and alternate row color:

1. Switch to Design view.

2. Click the **Format** tab, and then in the Selection group, click the **Select All** button.

3. Right-click one of the selected controls, and then click **Properties** on the shortcut menu to open the property sheet.

4. Click the **Format** tab (if necessary) in the property sheet, click the right side of the **Border Style** box, and then click **Transparent**. The transparent setting will remove the boxes from the report by making them transparent.

5. Click the **InvoiceItem Header** section bar, click the right side of the **Alternate Back Color** box in the property sheet, and then click **No Color** at the bottom of the gallery. This setting removes the alternate row color from the InvoiceItem Header section.

   You can set the Alternate Back Color property setting to the same No Color value for the Detail and InvoiceItem Footer sections by repeating Step 5 for each section, or by selecting each section and then clicking the Alternate Row Color button on the Ribbon because the two options set the same property.

6. Click the **Detail** section bar, and then in the Background group on the Ribbon, click the **Alternate Row Color** button. The Alternate Back Color property setting in the property sheet is now set to No Color.

7. Repeat Step 6 for the **InvoiceItem Footer** section.

> **8.** Close the property sheet, save your report changes, switch to Print Preview, and review every page of the report, ending on the last page of the report. See Figure 7-23.

Figure 7-23 After removing borders and the alternate row color

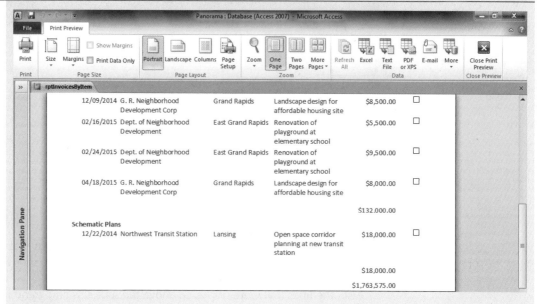

Next, you'll add lines to the report.

Adding Lines to a Report

You've used the Line tool to add lines to a form. You can also use the Line tool to add lines to a report. You'll switch to Design view and use the Line tool to add a single line above the subtotal control and a double line above the grand total control. First, you'll resize the subtotal and grand total text boxes.

To add lines to the report:

> **1.** Switch to Design view.

> **2.** In the InvoiceItem Footer section, click the text box control to select it, and then resize the control from the top so its height increases by one row of grid dots.

> **3.** Repeat Step 2 to resize the text box control in the Report Footer section.

> **4.** In the Controls group on the Design tab, click the **More** button ⊽ to open the Controls gallery.

> **5.** Click the **Line** tool ╲, position the pointer's plus symbol (+) at the upper-left corner of the subtotal text box in the InvoiceItem Footer section, hold down the **Shift** key, drag a horizontal line from left to right, so the end of the line aligns with the upper-right corner of the subtotal text box, release the mouse button, and then release the **Shift** key.

6. Click the **grand total** text box in the Report Footer section, and then press the ↓ key four times to move the control down slightly in the section, and then deselect all controls.

7. In the Controls group on the Design tab, click the **More** button ⃝, click the **Line** tool ◹, position the pointer's plus symbol (+) at the grid dot just above the upper-left corner of the grand total text box in the Report Footer section, hold down the **Shift** key, drag a horizontal line from left to right, so the end of the line aligns with the right edge of the grand total text box, release the mouse button, and then release the **Shift** key.

Next, you'll copy and paste the line in the Report Footer section, and then align the copied line into position.

8. Right-click the selected line in the Report Footer section, and then click **Copy** on the shortcut menu.

9. Right-click the **Report Footer** section bar, and then click **Paste** on the shortcut menu. A copy of the line is pasted in the upper-left corner of the Report Footer section.

10. Press the ↓ key four times to move the copied line down in the section, hold down the **Shift** key, click the original line in the Report Footer section to select both lines, release the **Shift** key, right-click the copied line to open the shortcut menu, point to **Align**, and then click **Right**. A double line is now positioned above the grand total text box.

11. Save your report changes, switch to Print Preview, and then navigate to the last page of the report. See Figure 7-24.

| Figure 7-24 | After adding lines to the report |

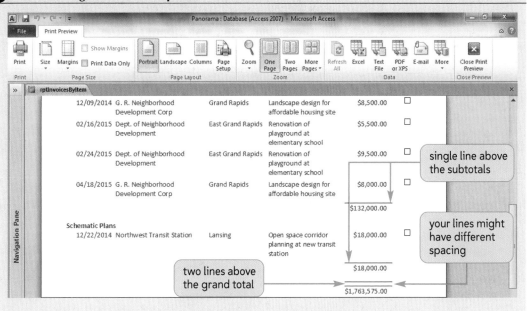

For the rptInvoicesByItem report, the InvoiceDate field is a sort field. Two or more consecutive detail report lines can have the same InvoiceDate field value. In these cases, Lucia wants the InvoiceDate field value printed for the first detail line but not for subsequent detail lines because she believes it makes the printed information easier to read.

Hiding Duplicate Values in a Report

You use the **Hide Duplicates property** to hide a control in a report when the control's value is the same as that of the preceding record in the group.

REFERENCE

Hiding Duplicate Values in a Report

- Display the report in Layout or Design view.
- Open the property sheet for the field whose duplicate values you want to hide, set the Hide Duplicates property to Yes, and then close the property sheet.

Your next design change to the report is to hide duplicate InvoiceDate field values in the Detail section. This change will make the report easier to read.

To hide the duplicate InvoiceDate field values:

1. Switch to Design view, and then click below the Report Footer grid to deselect all controls.

2. Open the property sheet for the **InvoiceDate** text box in the Detail section.

3. Click the **Format** tab (if necessary), scroll down the property sheet (if necessary), click the right side of the **Hide Duplicates** box, and then click **Yes**.

4. Close the property sheet, save your report changes, switch to Print Preview, navigate to page 5 (the actual page you view might vary depending on your printer) to the Construction Observation group to see the two invoice records for 03/30/2015. The InvoiceDate field value is hidden for the second of the two consecutive records with a 03/30/2015 date. See Figure 7-25.

TIP

For properties offering a list of choices, you can double-click the property name repeatedly to cycle through the options in the list.

Figure 7-25	Report in Print Preview with hidden duplicate values

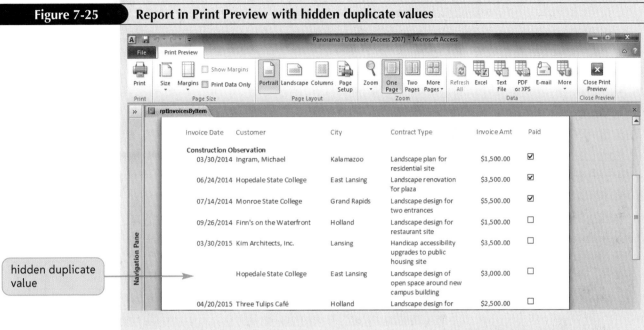

hidden duplicate value

5. If you are not continuing on to the next session, close the Panorama database.

You have completed the Detail section, the Group Header section, and the Group Footer section of the custom report. In the next session, you will complete the custom report according to Lucia's design by adding controls to the Page Header section.

REVIEW

Session 7.2 Quick Check

1. What is a detail report? a summary report?
2. The _____ property prints a group header on a page only if there is enough room on the page to print the first detail record for the group; otherwise, the group header prints at the top of the next page.
3. A(n) _____ section appears by itself at the top of a page, and the detail lines for the section appear on the previous page.
4. The _____ property, when set to Yes, expands a text box vertically to fit the field value when a report is printed, previewed, or viewed in Layout and Report views.
5. Why might you want to hide duplicate values in a report?

SESSION 7.3 VISUAL OVERVIEW

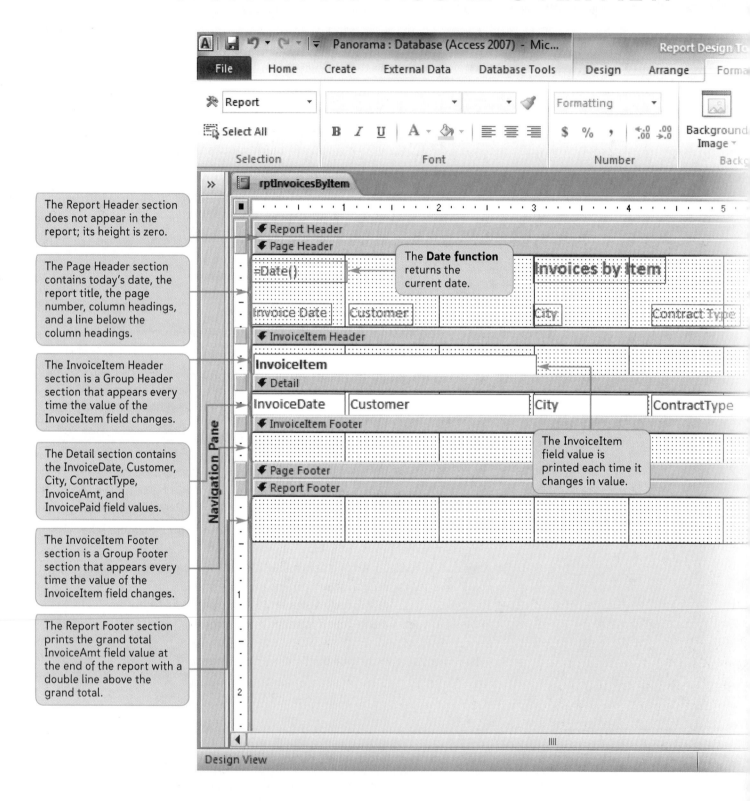

The Report Header section does not appear in the report; its height is zero.

The Page Header section contains today's date, the report title, the page number, column headings, and a line below the column headings.

The InvoiceItem Header section is a Group Header section that appears every time the value of the InvoiceItem field changes.

The Detail section contains the InvoiceDate, Customer, City, ContractType, InvoiceAmt, and InvoicePaid field values.

The InvoiceItem Footer section is a Group Footer section that appears every time the value of the InvoiceItem field changes.

The Report Footer section prints the grand total InvoiceAmt field value at the end of the report with a double line above the grand total.

The **Date function** returns the current date.

The InvoiceItem field value is printed each time it changes in value.

CUSTOM REPORT DESIGN

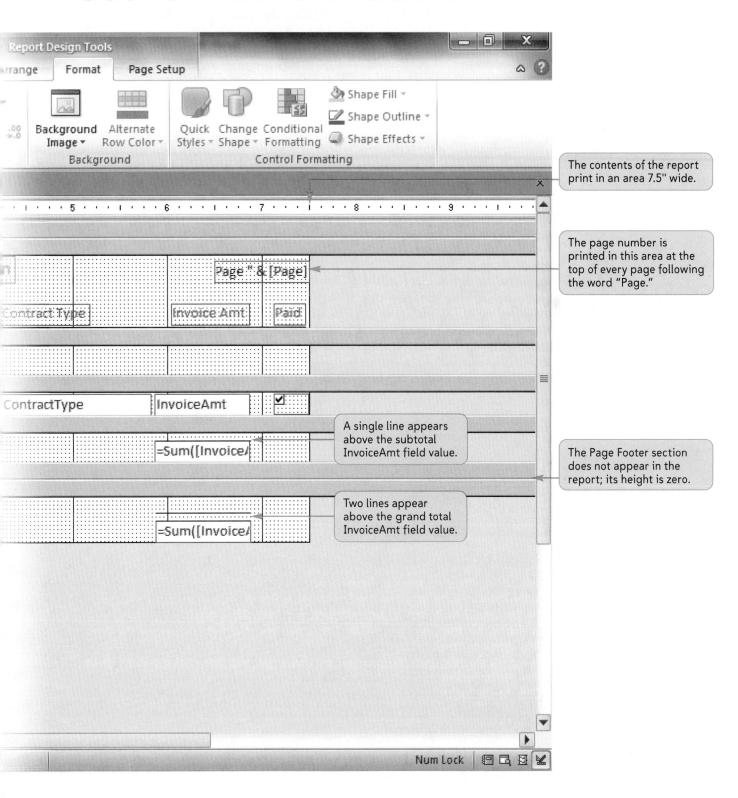

The contents of the report print in an area 7.5" wide.

The page number is printed in this area at the top of every page following the word "Page."

A single line appears above the subtotal InvoiceAmt field value.

The Page Footer section does not appear in the report; its height is zero.

Two lines appear above the grand total InvoiceAmt field value.

Adding the Date to a Report

According to Lucia's design, the rptInvoicesByItem report includes the date in the Page Header section, along with the report title, the page number, the column heading labels, and a line below the labels.

PROSKILLS

Written Communication: Placing the Report Title, Date, and Page Number in the Page Header Section

When you use the Report tool or the Report Wizard to create a report, the report title is displayed in the Report Header section and the page number is displayed in the Page Footer section. However, the date (and time) is displayed in the Report Header section when you use the Report tool and in the Page Footer section when you use the Report Wizard. Because report formatting guidelines require that all the reports in a database display controls in consistent positions, you have to move the date control for reports created by the Report tool or by the Report Wizard so the date is displayed in the same section for all reports.

Although company standards vary, a common report standard places the report title, date, and page number on the same line in the Page Header section. Using one line saves vertical space in the report compared to placing some controls in the Page Header section and others in the Page Footer section. Placing the report title in the Page Header section, instead of in the Report Header section, allows users to identify the report name on any page without having to turn to the first page. When you develop reports with a consistent format, the report users become more productive and more confident working with the information in the reports.

To add the date to a report, you can click the Date and Time button in the Header/ Footer group on the Design tab, and Access will insert the Date function in a text box without an attached label at the right edge of the Report Header section. The Date function returns the current date. The format of the Date function is =*Date()*. The equal sign (=) indicates that what follows it is an expression; *Date* is the name of the function; and the empty set of parentheses indicates a function rather than simple text.

REFERENCE

Adding the Date and Time to a Report

- Display the report in Layout or Design view.
- In the Header/Footer group on the Design tab in Design view or in Layout view, click the Date and Time button to open the Date and Time dialog box.
- To display the date, click the Include Date check box, and then click one of the three date option buttons.
- To display the time, click the Include Time check box, and then click one of the three time option buttons.
- Click the OK button.

According to Lucia's design for the report, the date appears at the left edge of the Page Header section, so you'll need to add the date to the report, and then cut the date from the Report Header section and paste it into the Page Header section.

To add the date to the Page Header section:

▶ **1.** If you took a break after the previous session, make sure that the Panorama database is open, that the rptInvoicesByItem report is open in Print Preview, and that the Navigation Pane is closed.

You can add the current date in Layout or Design view. Because you can't cut and paste controls between sections in Layout view, you'll add the date in Design view. First, you'll move the column heading labels down in the Page Header section to make room for the controls you'll be adding above them.

▶ **2.** Switch to Design view, increase the height of the Page Header section until the bottom edge of the section is at the 1-inch mark on the vertical ruler, select all six labels in the Page Header section, and then move the labels down until the tops of the labels are at the 0.5-inch mark on the vertical ruler.

Lucia's report design has a horizontal line below the labels that you'll add next.

▶ **3.** In the Controls group on the Design tab, click the **More** button ⏷, click the **Line** tool ╲, position the pointer's plus symbol (+) at the lower-left corner of the Invoice Date label in the Page Header section, hold down the **Shift** key, drag a horizontal line from left to right so the end of the line aligns with the right edge of the Paid label, release the mouse button, and then release the **Shift** key.

▶ **4.** Reduce the height of the Page Header section by dragging the bottom of the section up until it touches the bottom of the line you just added.

▶ **5.** In the Header/Footer group on the Design tab, click the **Date and Time** button to open the Date and Time dialog box, make sure the **Include Date** check box is checked and the **Include Time** check box is unchecked, and then click the third date option button. See Figure 7-26.

Figure 7-26	Completed Date and Time dialog box

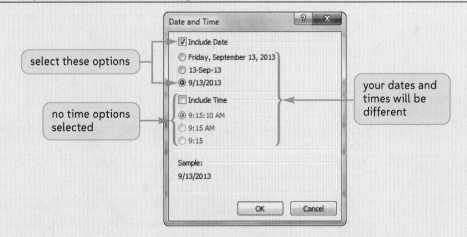

▶ **6.** Click the **OK** button. The Date function is added to the Report Header section.

▶ **7.** Click the **Date function** text box, and then click the **layout selector** ⊞ in the upper-left corner of the Report Header section. The Date function text box is part of a control layout with three additional boxes, which are empty cells. See Figure 7-27.

Figure 7-27 Date function added to the Report Header section

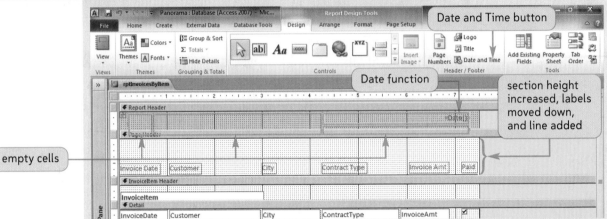

You need to remove these controls from the control layout before you work further with the Date function text box.

8. Right-click one of the selected controls, point to **Layout** on the shortcut menu, and then click **Remove Layout**. The three empty cells are deleted, and the Date function text box remains selected.

   The default size for the Date function text box must accommodate long dates and long times, so the text box is much wider than needed for the date that'll appear in the custom report. You'll decrease its width before moving it to the Page Header section.

9. Decrease the width of the Date function text box from the left to one inch total, right-click an edge of the **Date function** text box to open the shortcut menu, click **Cut** to delete the control, right-click the **Page Header** section bar to select that section and open the shortcut menu, and then click **Paste**. The Date function text box is pasted in the upper-left corner of the Page Header section.

10. Save your report changes, and then switch to Print Preview to view the date in the Page Header section. See Figure 7-28.

Figure 7-28 Viewing the date in Print Preview

TIP

Notice that the current date is displayed instead of the Date function that appears in the text box in Design view.

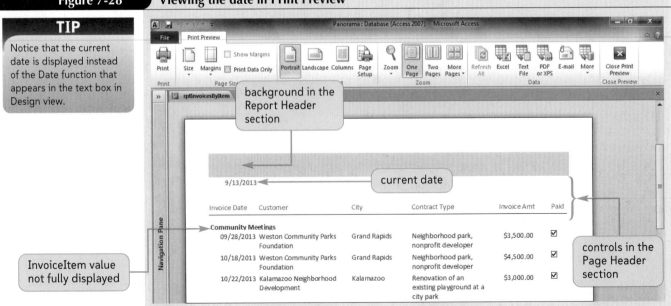

Trouble? Your year might appear with two digits instead of four digits as shown in Figure 7-28. Your date format might also differ, depending on your computer's date settings. These differences do not cause any problems.

You'll left-align the date in the text box in Design view. Also, notice that when you bolded the font in the InvoiceItem text box, you increased the size of the characters, so you need to increase the height of the text boxes to fully display all characters in the text box.

▶ **11.** Switch to Design view, make sure the Date function text box is selected, click the **Format** tab, and then in the Font group, click the **Align Text Left** button 📄.

▶ **12.** Click the **InvoiceItem** text box, and then increase the height of the text box from the top by one row of grid dots.

INSIGHT

Choosing a Theme for a Database

Access has 40 themes that you can use to set the font type and size and the color and other effects for the objects in a database. The default theme is the Office theme, which uses Calibri 11 font. You should either use the default theme or choose a theme immediately after creating the first table in the database. If you wait to choose a theme until after you've created a large number of objects in the database, the theme you choose will probably have a font different from Calibri 11, and you'll have to go back and resize the table and query datasheets and the form and report text boxes and labels.

You are now ready to add page numbers to the Page Header section. You'll also delete the empty Report Header section by decreasing its height to zero.

Adding Page Numbers to a Report

You can display page numbers in a report by including an expression in the Page Header or Page Footer section. You can click the Page Numbers button in the Header/Footer group in Layout or Design view to add a page number expression to a report. The inserted page number expression automatically displays the correct page number on each page of a report.

REFERENCE

Adding Page Numbers to a Report

- Display the report in Layout or Design view.
- In the Header/Footer group on the Design tab in Design view or in Layout view, click the Page Numbers button to open the Page Numbers dialog box.
- Select the format, position, and alignment options you want.
- Select whether you want to display the page number on the first page.
- Click the OK button to place the page number expression in the report.

Lucia's design shows the page number displayed on the right side of the Page Header section, bottom aligned with the date.

To add page numbers to the Page Header section:

▶ **1.** Delete the Report Header section by reducing its height to zero.

▶ **2.** Click the **Design** tab, and then in the Header/Footer group, click the **Page Numbers** button. The Page Numbers dialog box opens.

You use the Format options to specify the format of the page number. Lucia wants page numbers to appear as Page 1, Page 2, and so on. This is the "Page N" format option. You use the Position options to place the page numbers at the top of the page in the Page Header section or at the bottom of the page in the Page Footer section. Lucia's design shows page numbers at the top of the page.

▶ **3.** Make sure that the **Page N** option button in the Format section and that the **Top of Page [Header]** option button in the Position section are both selected.

The report design shows page numbers at the right side of the page. You can specify this placement in the Alignment box.

▶ **4.** Click the **Alignment** arrow, and then click **Right**.

▶ **5.** Make sure the **Show Number on First Page** check box is checked, so the page number prints on the first page and all other pages as well. See Figure 7-29.

Figure 7-29   **Completed Page Numbers dialog box**

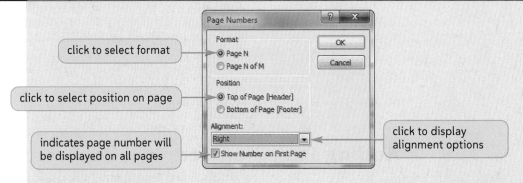

click to select format

click to select position on page

indicates page number will be displayed on all pages

click to display alignment options

▶ **6.** Click the **OK** button. The text box shown in Figure 7-30 appears in the upper-right corner of the Page Header section. The expression *="Page " & [Page]* in the text box means that the printed report will show the word "Page" followed by a space and the page number.

Figure 7-30   **Page number expression added to the Page Header section**

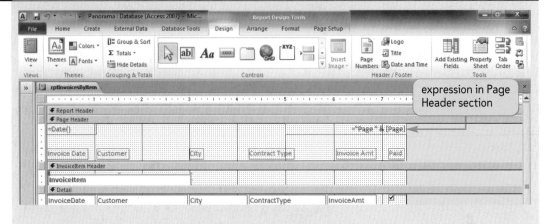

expression in Page Header section

The page number text box is much wider than needed for the page number expression that'll appear in the custom report. You'll decrease its width.

7. Click the **Page Number** text box, and then decrease its width from the left to one inch total.

8. Save your report changes, and then switch to Print Preview. See Figure 7-31.

Figure 7-31   Date and page number in the Page Header section

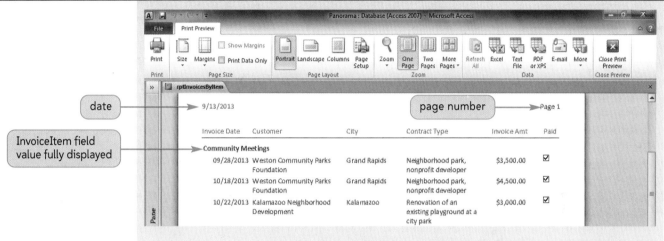

date

InvoiceItem field value fully displayed

Now you are ready to add the title to the Page Header section.

Adding a Title to a Report

Lucia's report design includes the title "Invoices by Item," which you'll add to the Page Header section centered between the date and the page number. You could use the Title button in the Header/Footer group on the Design tab to add the report title, but Access adds the title to the Report Header section, and Lucia's design positions the title in the Page Header section. It'll be easier to use the Label tool to add the title directly in the Page Header section.

To add the title to the Page Header section:

1. Switch to Design view.

2. In the Controls group on the Design tab, click the **Label** tool 𝐴𝑎, position the pointer's plus symbol (+) at the top of the Page Header section at the 3-inch mark on the horizontal ruler, and then click the mouse button. The insertion point flashes inside a narrow box, which will expand as you type the report title.

To match Lucia's design, you need to type the title as "Invoices by Item," and change its font size to 14 points and its style to bold.

3. Type **Invoices by Item**, and then press the **Enter** key.

4. Click the **Format** tab, in the Font group click the **Font Size** arrow, click **14**, and then click the **Bold** button **B**.

The Error Checking Options button ◈ appears to the left of the report title.

5. Point to the **Error Checking Options** button ◈. A ScreenTip describes the potential error. See Figure 7-32.

| Figure 7-32 | Report title in the Page Header section |

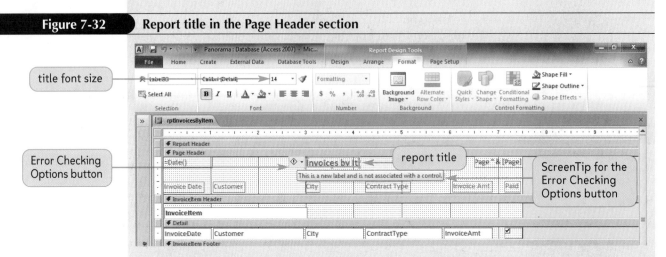

The ScreenTip indicates that the report title, which is a label control, is not associated with any bound or calculated control. Because you don't want a label that contains a report title to be associated with another control, you can ignore this potential error.

▶ **6.** Click the **Error Checking Options** button ◇, and then click **Ignore Error**.

The report title is still selected, so you can resize it to fit.

▶ **7.** Right-click an edge of the title to open the shortcut menu, point to **Size**, and then click **To Fit**.

Finally, you'll align the date, report title, and page number controls on their bottom edges.

▶ **8.** Select the date, report title, and page number controls in the Page Header section, right-click one of the selected controls, point to **Align**, and then click **Bottom**.

▶ **9.** Save your report changes. You have completed the design of the custom report. See the Session 7.3 Visual Overview.

▶ **10.** Switch to Print Preview to review the completed report, and then navigate to the top of the last page of the report to view your changes. See Figure 7-33.

| Figure 7-33 | Completed rptInvoicesByItem report in Print Preview |

11. Close the report.

Next, Sarah wants you to create mailing labels that she can use to address materials to Belmont Landscapes customers.

Creating Mailing Labels

Sarah needs a set of mailing labels printed for all customers so she can mail a marketing brochure and other materials to them. The tblCustomer table contains the name and address information that will serve as the record source for the labels. Each mailing label will have the same format: first name and last name on the first line; company name (if it exists for the customer) on the second line; address on the third line; and city, state, and zip code on the fourth line.

You could create a custom report to produce the mailing labels, but using the Label Wizard is an easier and faster way to produce them. The **Label Wizard** provides templates for hundreds of standard label formats, each of which is uniquely identified by a label manufacturer's name and number. These templates specify the dimensions and arrangement of labels on each page. Standard label formats can have between one and five labels across a page; the number of labels printed on a single page also varies. Sarah's mailing labels are Avery number C2163; each sheet has 12 1.5-inch by 3.9-inch labels arranged in two columns and six rows on the page.

Creating Mailing Labels and Other Labels

- In the Navigation Pane, click the table or query that'll serve as the record source for the labels.
- In the Reports group on the Create tab, click the Labels button to start the Label Wizard and open its first dialog box.
- Select the label manufacturer and its product number, and then click the Next button.
- Select the label font, color, and style, and then click the Next button.
- Construct the label content by selecting the fields from the record source and specifying their placement and spacing on the label, and then click the Next button.
- Select one or more optional sort fields, click the Next button, specify the report name, and then click the Finish button.

You'll use the Label Wizard to create a report to produce mailing labels for all customers.

To use the Label Wizard to create the mailing label report:

1. Open the Navigation Pane, click **tblCustomer** to make it the current object that'll serve as the record source for the labels, close the Navigation Pane, and then click the **Create** tab on the Ribbon.

2. In the Reports group, click the **Labels** button. The first Label Wizard dialog box opens and asks you to select the standard or custom label you'll use.

3. Make sure that the **English** option button is selected in the Unit of Measure section, that the **Sheet feed** option button is selected in the Label Type section, and that **Avery** is selected in the Filter by manufacturer box, and then click **C2163** in the Product number box. See Figure 7-34.

Figure 7-34 Selecting a standard label

select this Avery product number

make sure these options are selected

selected manufacturer

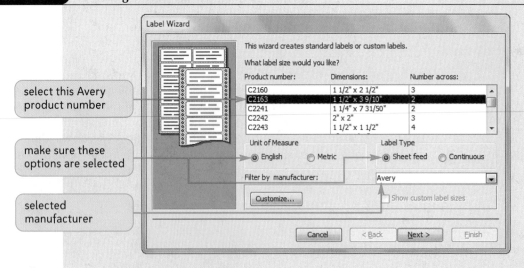

Because the labels are already filtered for the Avery manufacturer, the top box shows the Avery product number, dimensions, and number of labels across the page for each of its standard label formats. You can display the dimensions in the list in either inches or millimeters by choosing the appropriate option in the Unit of Measure section. You can also specify in the Label Type section whether the labels are on individual sheets or are continuous forms.

4. Click the **Next** button to open the second Label Wizard dialog box, in which you choose font specifications for the labels.

Sarah wants the labels to use 10-point Arial with a medium font weight and without italics or underlines. The font weight determines how light or dark the characters will print; you can choose from nine values ranging from thin to heavy.

5. If necessary, select **Arial** for the font name, **10** for the font size, and **Medium** for the font weight; make sure the Italic and the Underline check boxes are not checked and that black is the text color; and then click the **Next** button to open the third Label Wizard dialog box, from which you select the data to appear on the labels.

Sarah wants the mailing labels to print the FirstName and LastName fields on the first line; the Company field on the second line; the Address field on the third line; and the City, State, and Zip fields on the fourth line. One space will separate the FirstName and LastName fields, the City and State fields, and the State and Zip fields.

6. Click **FirstName** in the Available fields box, click the `>` button to move the field to the Prototype label box, press the **spacebar**, click **LastName** in the Available fields box (if necessary), and then click the `>` button. The braces around the field names in the Prototype label box indicate that the name represents a field rather than text that you entered.

Trouble? If you select the wrong field or type the wrong text, click the incorrect item in the Prototype label box, press the Delete key to remove the item, and then select the correct field or type the correct text.

7. Press the **Enter** key to move to the next line in the Prototype label box, and then use Figure 7-35 to complete the entries in the Prototype label box. Make sure you press the spacebar after selecting the City field and the State field.

Figure 7-35 | **Completed label prototype**

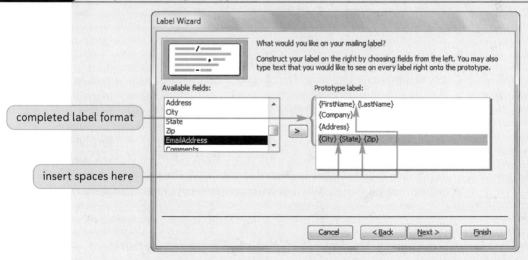

If a Company field value is null in the second line, Access moves up the third and fourth lines when you print or preview the label report to eliminate the blank line on the label.

8. Click the **Next** button to open the fourth Label Wizard dialog box, in which you choose the sort fields for the labels.

Sarah wants Zip to be the primary sort field and LastName to be the secondary sort field.

▶ 9. Scroll down the list and select the **Zip** field as the primary sort field, select the **LastName** field as the secondary sort field, and then click the **Next** button to open the last Label Wizard dialog box, in which you enter a name for the report.

▶ 10. Change the report name to **rptCustomerMailingLabels**, and then click the **Finish** button. Access saves the report as rptCustomerMailingLabels and then opens the first page of the report in Print Preview. Note that two columns of labels appear across the page. See Figure 7-36.

Figure 7-36 **Previewing the label content and sequence**

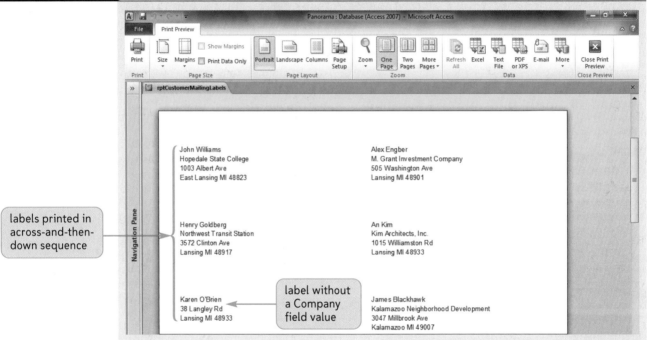

The rptCustomerMailingLabels report is a multiple-column report. The labels will be printed in ascending order by zip code and then in ascending order by last name. The first label will be printed in the upper-left corner on the first page, the second label will be printed to its right, the third label will be printed below the first label, and so on. This style of multiple-column report is the across-and-then-down layout. Instead, Sarah wants the labels to print with the "down, then across" layout—the first label is printed, the second label is printed below the first, and so on. After the bottom label in the first column is printed, the next label is printed at the top of the second column. The "down, then across" layout is also called **newspaper-style columns**, or **snaking columns**.

To change the layout to the mailing label report:

▶ 1. Switch to Design view. The Detail section, the only section in the report, is sized for a single label.

First, you'll change the layout to snaking columns.

▶ 2. Click the **Page Setup** tab on the Ribbon, click the **Page Setup** button in the Page Layout group, and then click the **Columns** tab. The Page Setup dialog box displays the column options for the report. See Figure 7-37.

| Figure 7-37 | Column options in the Page Setup dialog box |

specifies the number of column sets

option to print labels down the page

option to print labels across the page

preview of selected column layout

TIP

When you select a label using a manufacturer's name and product code, the options in the dialog box are set automatically.

The options in the Page Setup dialog box let you change the properties of a multiple-column report. In the Grid Settings section, you specify the number of column sets and the row and column spacing between the column sets. In the Column Size section, you specify the width and height of each column set. In the Column Layout section, you select between the "down, then across" and the "across, then down" layouts.

You can now change the layout for the labels.

▶ **3.** Click the **Down, then Across** option button, and then click the **OK** button.

You've finished the report changes, so you can now save and preview the report.

▶ **4.** Save your report design changes, and then switch to Print Preview. The labels appear in the snaking-columns layout.

You've finished all work on Sarah's reports.

▶ **5.** Close the report, make a backup copy of the database, and compact and repair and then close the Panorama database.

Sarah is very pleased with the modified report and the two new reports, which will provide her with improved information and help expedite her written communications with customers.

Session 7.3 Quick Check

REVIEW

1. What is the function and its format to print the current date in a report?

2. How do you insert a page number in the Page Header section?

3. Clicking the Title button in the Header/Footer group on the Design tab adds a report title to the _____ section.

4. What is a multiple-column report?

Practice the skills you learned in the tutorial using the same case scenario.

Review Assignments

Data File needed for the Review Assignments: Products.accdb (*cont. from Tutorial 6*)

Sarah wants you to create a custom report for the Products database that prints all companies and the products they offer. She also wants you to customize an existing report. You will perform the tasks for Sarah by completing the following steps:

1. Open the **Products** database located in the Access2\Review folder provided with your Data Files.
2. Modify the **rptCompanyProducts** report by completing the following steps:
   a. Delete the picture at the top of the report.
   b. Change the report title to **Belmont Supplier Products**.
   c. Remove the alternate row color from the detail lines in the report.
   d. Change the second column heading to First Name and the third column heading to Last Name, and then resize the column headings with their text boxes to make sure all values are fully visible.
   e. In the Report Footer section, add a grand total count of the number of products that appear in the report, make sure the control has a transparent border, and left-align the count with the left edge of the ContactLastName text box.
   f. Add a label that contains the text **total products** to the right of the count of the total number of products.
   g. Left-align the page number text box with the left edge of the Price text box.
3. After you've completed and saved your modifications to the rptCompanyProducts report, filter the report in Report view, selecting all records that contain the word "table" in the ProductType field. Copy the entire filtered report and paste it into a new Word document, and then change the report orientation to landscape. Save the document as **Tables** in the Access2\Review folder. Close Word, and then close the Access report without saving changes.
4. Create a query that displays the ProductType and CompanyName fields from the tblCompany table, and the ProductType, Price, and Unit fields from the tblProduct table. Sort in ascending order by the first three fields in the query, and then save the query as **qryCompanyProducts**.
5. Create a custom report based on the qryCompanyProducts query. Figure 7-38 shows a sample of the last page of the completed report. Refer to the figure as you create the report.

Figure 7-38   Products database custom report

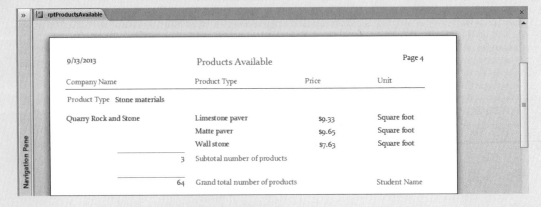

   a. Save the report as **rptProductsAvailable**.
   b. Use the ProductType field (from the tblCompany table) as a grouping field, and use the ProductType field (from the tblProduct table) as a sort field.

c. Hide duplicate values for the CompanyName field.

d. Add labels for the subtotals, the grand total, and your name.

e. Keep the whole group together on one page.

f. Remove the text box borders.

g. Remove the alternate row color from the group header and detail lines.

6. Create a mailing label report according to the following instructions:

a. Use the tblCompany table as the record source.

b. Use Avery C2160 labels, and use the default font, size, weight, and color.

c. For the prototype label, add the ContactFirstName, a space, and ContactLastName on the first line; the CompanyName on the second line; the Address on the third line; and the City, a space, State, a space, and Zip on the fourth line.

d. Sort by Zip and then by CompanyName, and then enter the report name **rptCompanyMailingLabels**.

7. Make a backup copy of the database, compact and repair, and then close the Products database.

Apply the skills you learned in the tutorial to create a custom report.

CHALLENGE

Case Problem 1

Data File needed for this Case Problem: Contract.accdb (*cont. from Tutorial 6*)

Pine Hill Music School   Yuka Koyama wants you to modify an existing report and to create a custom report and mailing labels for the Contract database. You'll do so by completing the following steps:

1. Open the **Contract** database located in the Access2\Case1 folder provided with your Data Files.

2. Modify the **rptStudentContracts** report. Figure 7-39 shows a sample of the last page of the completed report. Refer to the figure as you modify the report.

Figure 7-39	Contract database enhanced report

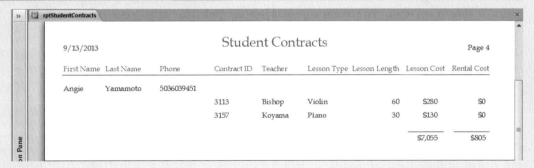

a. Delete the picture at the top of the report.

b. Center the report title.

c. Remove the alternate row color from the group header and detail lines in the report.

⊕ **EXPLORE**

d. Change the page number format from "Page n of m" to "Page n."

e. Move the date, report title, and page number to the Page Header section.

f. Add grand total controls that calculate the total monthly lesson cost and total monthly rental cost.

⊕ **EXPLORE**

g. Add a conditional formatting rule for the LessonType field to display all values of Piano in red, bold font.

3. Create a query that displays, in order, the LastName and FirstName fields from the tblTeacher table, the LessonType field from the tblContract table, the FirstName and LastName fields from the tblStudent table, and the MonthlyLessonCost and MonthlyRentalCost fields from the tblContract table. Sort in ascending order by the first three fields in the query, and then save the query as **qryTeacherLessons**.

4. Create a custom report based on the qryTeacherLessons query. Figure 7-40 shows a sample of the last page of the completed report. Refer to the figure as you create the report.

Figure 7-40 Contract database custom report

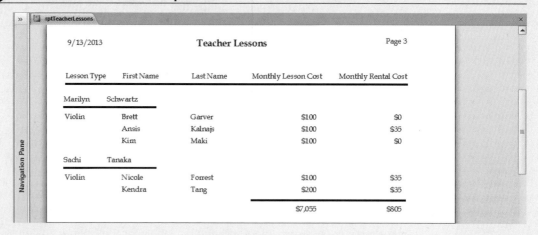

a. Save the report as **rptTeacherLessons**.

b. The LastName field (from the tblTeacher table) is a grouping field, and the FirstName field also appears in the Group Header section.

c. The LessonType field is a sort field, and the LastName field (from the tblStudent table) is a sort field.

d. Hide duplicate values for the LessonType field.

e. Use black font for all the controls, setting the lines' thickness to 3 pt.

5. Create a mailing label report according to the following instructions:

a. Use the tblStudent table as the record source.

b. Use Avery C2160 labels, use a larger font size and a heavier font weight, and use the other default font and color options.

c. For the prototype label, place FirstName, a space, and LastName on the first line; Address on the second line; and City, a space, State, a space, and Zip on the third line.

d. Sort by Zip and then by LastName, and then enter the report name **rptStudentMailingLabels**.

e. Change the mailing label layout to snaking columns.

6. Make a backup copy of the database, compact and repair, and then close the Contract database.

EXPLORE

Apply what you learned in the tutorial to create a custom report.

APPLY

Case Problem 2

Data File needed for this Case Problem: Training.accdb (*cont. from Tutorial 6*)

Parkhurst Health & Fitness Center   Martha Parkhurst wants you to create a custom report and mailing labels for the Training database. The custom report will be based on the results of a query you will create. You will create the query, the custom report, and the mailing labels by completing the following steps:

1. Open the **Training** database located in the Access2\Case2 folder provided with your Data Files.
2. Create a query that displays the ProgramID, ProgramType, and MonthlyFee fields from the tblProgram table, and the MembershipStatus, FirstName, and LastName fields from the tblMember table. Sort in ascending order by the ProgramID, MembershipStatus, and LastName fields, and then save the query as **qryProgramMembership**.
3. Create a custom report based on the qryProgramMembership query. Figure 7-41 shows a sample of the last page of the completed report. Refer to the figure as you create the report.

Figure 7-41   Training database custom report

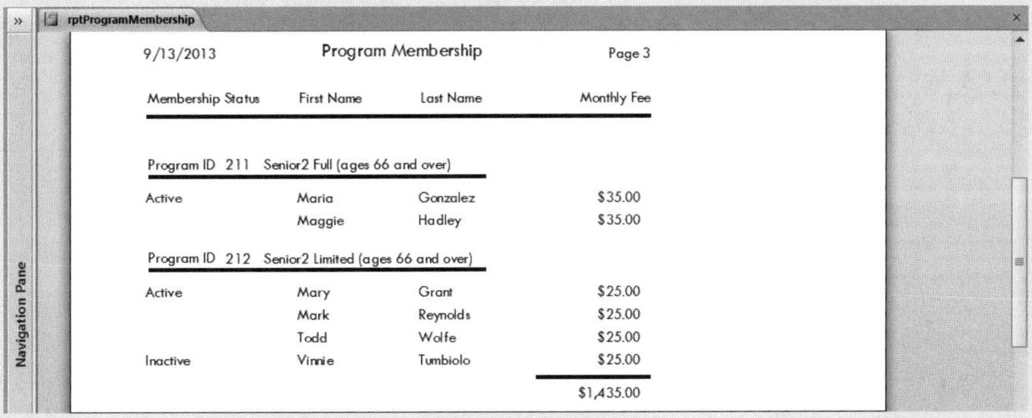

a. Save the report as **rptProgramMembership**.
b. Use the ProgramID field as a grouping field.
c. Select the MembershipStatus field as a sort field, and the LastName field as a secondary sort field.
d. Hide duplicate values for the MembershipStatus field.
e. Add the ProgramType field to the Group Header section, and then delete its attached label.
f. Keep the whole group together on one page.
g. Use black font for all the controls, and set the lines' thickness to 3 pt.
4. Use the following instructions to create the mailing labels:
a. Use the tblMember table as the record source for the mailing labels.
b. Use Avery C2160 labels, and use the default font, size, weight, and color.

c. For the prototype label, place FirstName, a space, and LastName on the first line; Street on the second line; and City, a space, State, a space, and Zip on the third line.

d. Sort by Zip and then by LastName, and then type the report name **rptMemberLabels**.

5. Make a backup copy of the database, compact and repair, and then close the Training database.

Apply what you learned in the tutorial to create a custom report.

APPLY

Case Problem 3

Data File needed for this Case Problem: Agency.accdb (*cont. from Tutorial 6*)

Rossi Recycling Group   Mary Rossi asks you to create a custom report for the Agency database so that she can better track donations made by donors and to create mailing labels. You'll do so by completing the following steps:

1. Open the **Agency** database located in the Access2\Case3 folder provided with your Data Files.

2. Create a query that displays the DonationDesc, DonationDate, and DonationValue fields from the tblDonation table, and the FirstName and LastName fields from the tblDonor table. Sort in ascending order by the DonationDesc, DonationDate, and LastName fields, and then save the query as **qryDonorDonations**.

3. Create a custom report based on the qryDonorDonations query. Figure 7-42 shows a sample of the last page of the completed report. Refer to the figure as you create the report.

Figure 7-42   Agency database custom report

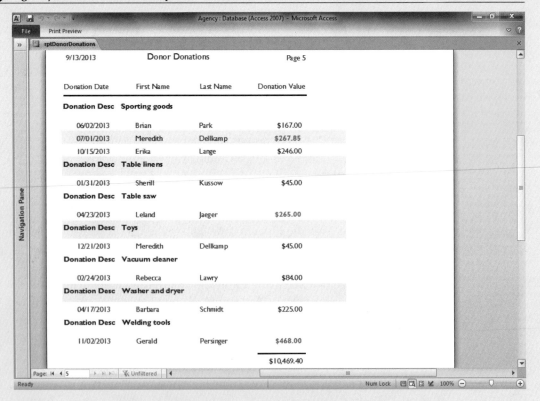

a. Save the report as **rptDonorDonations**.

b. Use the DonationDesc field as a grouping field.

c. Select the DonationDate field as a sort field, and the LastName field as a secondary sort field.

d. Hide duplicate values for the DonationDate field.

e. Use black font for all the controls, and set the lines' thickness to 2 pt.

f. Keep the whole group together on one page.

⊕ EXPLORE

g. Create a conditional formatting rule for the DonationValue field to display the value in blue, bold font when the amount is more than $250.

4. After you've created and saved the rptDonorDonations report, filter the report in Report view, selecting all records that contain the name "Park" in the LastName field. Copy the entire filtered report and paste it into a new Word document, and then change the report orientation to landscape. Save the document as **DonorPark** in the Access2\Case3 folder. Close Word, and then close the Access report without saving it.

5. Use the following instructions to create the mailing labels:

a. Use the tblAgency table as the record source for the mailing labels.

b. Use Avery C2160 labels, and use the default font, size, weight, and color.

c. For the prototype label, place ContactFirstName, a space, and ContactLastName on the first line; AgencyName on the second line; Address on the third line; and City, a space, State, a space, and Zip on the fourth line.

d. Sort by Zip and then by ContactLastName, and then type the report name **rptAgencyLabels**.

e. Change the mailing label layout to snaking columns.

6. Make a backup copy of the database, compact and repair, and then close the Agency database.

Use the skills you've learned in this tutorial to create a custom report.

CREATE

Case Problem 4

Data File needed for this Case Problem: Vacation.accdb (*cont. from Tutorial 6*)

GEM Ultimate Vacations   Griffin and Emma MacElroy want you to create a custom report and mailing labels for the Vacation database. You will create the custom report and the mailing labels by completing the following steps:

1. Open the **Vacation** database located in the Access2\Case4 folder provided with your Data Files.

2. Create a query that displays the PropertyName and Country fields from the tblProperty table, the StateProv field from the tblGuest table, and the StartDate, EndDate, and People fields from the tblReservation table. Sort in ascending order by the PropertyName, StateProv, and StartDate fields, and then save the query as **qryPropertyReservations**.

3. Create a custom report based on the qryPropertyReservations query. Figure 7-43 shows a sample of the last page of the completed report. Refer to the figure as you create the report.

| Figure 7-43 | Vacation database custom report |

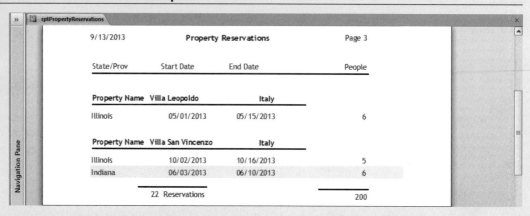

a. Save the report as **rptPropertyReservations**.

b. Use the PropertyName field as a grouping field.

c. Select the StateProv field as a sort field, and the StartDate field as a secondary sort field.

d. Hide duplicate values for the StateProv field.

e. Use black font for all the controls, and set the lines' thickness to 2 pt.

f. Keep the whole group together on one page.

EXPLORE

g. Add the Country field to the Group Header section.

4. Use the following instructions to create the mailing labels:

a. Use the tblGuest table as the record source for the mailing labels.

b. Use Avery C2163 labels, with the default font, size, weight, and color settings.

c. For the prototype label, place GuestFirstName, a space, and GuestLastName on the first line; Address on the second line; City, a space, StateProv, a space, and PostalCode on the third line; and Country on the fourth line.

d. Sort by PostalCode, then by GuestLastName, and then enter the report name **rptGuestLabels**.

e. Change the mailing label layout to snaking columns.

EXPLORE

5. Make a copy of the rptPropertyReservations report, using the name **rptPropertyReservationsSummary** for the copy. Read Access Help to find out how to create a summary report. Modify the rptPropertyReservationsSummary report as follows to create the report shown in Figure 7-44:

| Figure 7-44 | Vacation database custom summary report |

   a. Delete the column heading labels, move up the line in the Page Header section to just below the remaining controls, and then reduce the height of the section.

   b. Add subtotals for the number of reservations and number of people.

   c. Change the report to a summary report.

6. Make a backup copy of the database, compact and repair, and then close the Vacation database.

Work with the skills you've learned in the tutorial to create a custom report.

CREATE

Case Problem 5

Data File needed for this Case Problem: ACE.accdb (*cont. from Tutorial 6*)

Always Connected Everyday   Chris and Pat Dixon want you to create a custom report and mailing labels for the ACE database. You'll do so by completing the following steps:

1. Open the **ACE** database located in the Access2\Case5 folder provided with your Data Files.

2. Create a query to serve as the record source for the custom report shown in Figure 7-45, and then save the query as **qryAccessPlanCustomers**.

3. Create a custom report based on the qryAccessPlanCustomers query. Figure 7-45 shows a sample of the completed report. Refer to the figure as you create the report. Save the report as **rptAccessPlanCustomers**.

Figure 7-45   **ACE database custom report**

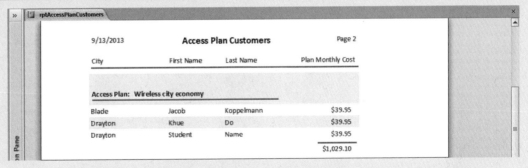

4. After you've created the rptAccessPlanCustomers report, filter the report in Report view, selecting all records that contain a specific value in the city field. Copy the entire filtered report and paste it into a new Word document. Save the document as **City** in the Access2\Case5 folder.

5. Use the tblCustomer table as the record source for the mailing labels. Choose appropriate options in the Label Wizard, change the mailing label layout to snaking columns, and save the report as **rptCustomerLabels**.

6. Make a backup copy of the database, compact and repair, and then close the ACE database.

SAM: Skills Assessment Manager

For current SAM information, including versions and content details, visit SAM Central (http://samcentral.course.com). If you have a SAM user profile, you may have access to hands-on instruction, practice, and assessment of the skills covered in this tutorial. Since various versions of SAM are supported throughout the life of this text, check with your instructor for the correct instructions and URL/Web site for accessing assignments.

ENDING DATA FILES

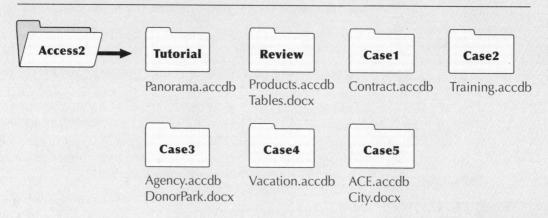

Access2 → **Tutorial**

Panorama.accdb

Review

Products.accdb
Tables.docx

Case1

Contract.accdb

Case2

Training.accdb

Case3

Agency.accdb
DonorPark.docx

Case4

Vacation.accdb

Case5

ACE.accdb
City.docx

TUTORIAL 8

Sharing, Integrating, and Analyzing Data

Importing, Exporting, Linking, and Analyzing Data in the Panorama Database

Case | *Belmont Landscapes*

Oren Belmont, Sarah Fisher, and Taylor Sico are pleased with the design and contents of the Panorama database. Oren feels that other employees would benefit from gaining access to the Panorama database and by sharing data among the different programs employees use. Oren and Sarah would also like to be able to analyze the data in the database.

In this tutorial, you will show Oren and Sarah how to import, export, link, and embed data. You will also introduce them to the charting, PivotTable, and PivotChart features of Access.

STARTING DATA FILES

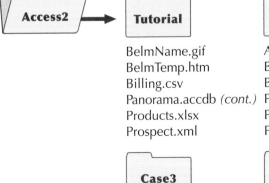

Access2 →

Tutorial
BelmName.gif
BelmTemp.htm
Billing.csv
Panorama.accdb *(cont.)*
Products.xlsx
Prospect.xml

Review
Ads.xlsx
BelmName.gif
BelmTemp.htm
Payables.csv
Payments.xml
Products.accdb *(cont.)*

Case1
Contract.accdb *(cont.)*
Instrument.csv
Room.xlsx

Case2
CreditCard.xml
ParkName.gif
ParkTemp.htm
Schedule.xlsx
Training.accdb *(cont.)*

Case3
Agency.accdb *(cont.)*
Facility.csv

Case4
Personnel.xlsx
Vacation.accdb *(cont.)*
Works.xml

Case5
ACE.accdb *(cont.)*

SESSION 8.1 VISUAL OVERVIEW

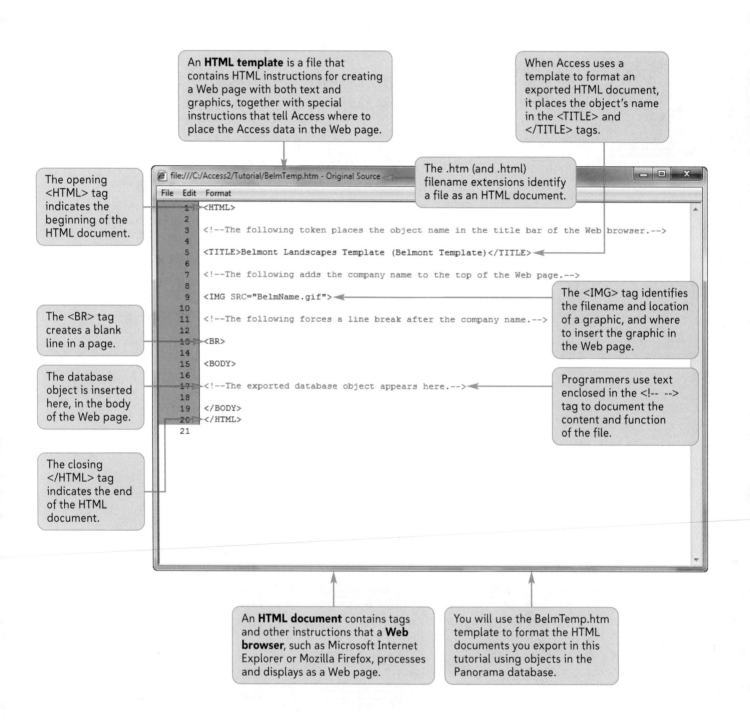

An **HTML template** is a file that contains HTML instructions for creating a Web page with both text and graphics, together with special instructions that tell Access where to place the Access data in the Web page.

When Access uses a template to format an exported HTML document, it places the object's name in the <TITLE> and </TITLE> tags.

The opening <HTML> tag indicates the beginning of the HTML document.

The .htm (and .html) filename extensions identify a file as an HTML document.

The <BR> tag creates a blank line in a page.

The <IMG> tag identifies the filename and location of a graphic, and where to insert the graphic in the Web page.

The database object is inserted here, in the body of the Web page.

Programmers use text enclosed in the <!-- --> tag to document the content and function of the file.

The closing </HTML> tag indicates the end of the HTML document.

```
file:///C:/Access2/Tutorial/BelmTemp.htm - Original Source

File   Edit   Format

1    <HTML>
2
3    <!--The following token places the object name in the title bar of the Web browser.-->
4
5    <TITLE>Belmont Landscapes Template (Belmont Template)</TITLE>
6
7    <!--The following adds the company name to the top of the Web page.-->
8
9    <IMG SRC="BelmName.gif">
10
11   <!--The following forces a line break after the company name.-->
12
13   <BR>
14
15   <BODY>
16
17   <!--The exported database object appears here.-->
18
19   </BODY>
20   </HTML>
21
```

An **HTML document** contains tags and other instructions that a **Web browser**, such as Microsoft Internet Explorer or Mozilla Firefox, processes and displays as a Web page.

You will use the BelmTemp.htm template to format the HTML documents you export in this tutorial using objects in the Panorama database.

HTML SOURCE AND WEB PAGE

The title of a Web page appears in the browser's title bar.

A **Uniform Resource Locator (URL)** identifies where the Web page is stored. A URL can be an Internet Web server or a location on a hard drive. In this case, the Web page is stored on drive C, in a subfolder named Tutorial, of the main folder named Access2. The filename of the HTML document is Crosstab.html.

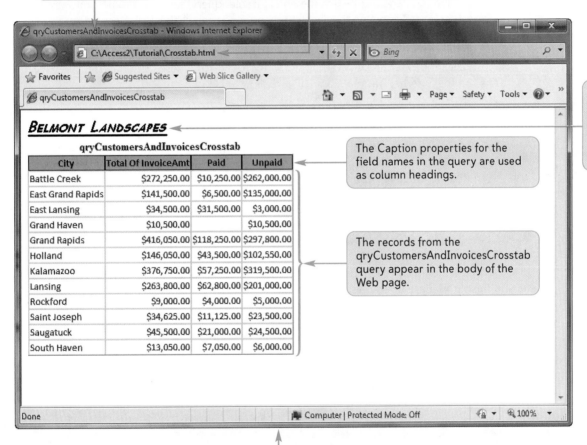

This graphic was inserted by the HTML template, using the file saved as BelmName.gif

The Caption properties for the field names in the query are used as column headings.

The records from the qryCustomersAndInvoicesCrosstab query appear in the body of the Web page.

This Web page was created using the qryCustomersAndInvoicesCrosstab query. The formatting in the Web page uses the instructions in the BelmTemp.htm template on the left.

BELMONT LANDSCAPES

qryCustomersAndInvoicesCrosstab

City	Total Of InvoiceAmt	Paid	Unpaid
Battle Creek	$272,250.00	$10,250.00	$262,000.00
East Grand Rapids	$141,500.00	$6,500.00	$135,000.00
East Lansing	$34,500.00	$31,500.00	$3,000.00
Grand Haven	$10,500.00		$10,500.00
Grand Rapids	$416,050.00	$118,250.00	$297,800.00
Holland	$146,050.00	$43,500.00	$102,550.00
Kalamazoo	$376,750.00	$57,250.00	$319,500.00
Lansing	$263,800.00	$62,800.00	$201,000.00
Rockford	$9,000.00	$4,000.00	$5,000.00
Saint Joseph	$34,625.00	$11,125.00	$23,500.00
Saugatuck	$45,500.00	$21,000.00	$24,500.00
South Haven	$13,050.00	$7,050.00	$6,000.00

Exporting an Access Query to an HTML Document

Oren wants to display the summary data in the qryCustomersAndInvoicesCrosstab query on the company's intranet so that all employees working in the office are able to access it. To store the data on the company's intranet, you'll create a Web page version of the qryCustomersAndInvoicesCrosstab query.

Creating the necessary HTML document to provide Oren with the information he wants is not as difficult as it might appear at first. You can use Access to export the query and convert it to an HTML document automatically.

REFERENCE

Exporting an Access Object to an HTML Document

- In the Navigation Pane, right-click the object (table, query, form, or report) you want to export, point to Export on the shortcut menu, and then click HTML Document.
  or
  In the Navigation Pane, click the object (table, query, form, or report) you want to export, click the External Data tab on the Ribbon, click the More button in the Export group on the External Data tab, and then click HTML Document.
- Click the Browse button in the Export – HTML Document dialog box, select the location where you want to save the file, enter the filename in the File name box, and then click the Save button.
- Click the Export data with formatting and layout check box to retain most formatting and layout information, and then click the OK button.
- If using a template, click the Select a HTML Template check box in the HTML Output Options dialog box, click the Browse button, select the location for the template, click the template filename, and then click the OK button.
- Click the OK button.

To complete the following steps, you need to use Access and a Web browser. The steps in this tutorial are written for Internet Explorer, the Web browser used at Belmont Landscapes. If you use another browser, the steps you need to complete might be slightly different.

You'll export the qryCustomersAndInvoicesCrosstab query as an HTML document.

To export the qryCustomersAndInvoicesCrosstab query as an HTML document:

▶ **1.** Start Access, and then open the **Panorama** database in the Access2\Tutorial folder provided with your Data Files.

▶ **2.** Open the Navigation Pane (if necessary), right-click **qryCustomersAndInvoicesCrosstab** to display the shortcut menu, point to **Export**, and then click **HTML Document**. The Export - HTML Document dialog box opens.

▶ **3.** Click the **Browse** button to open the File Save dialog box, navigate to the **Access2\Tutorial** folder, select the text in the File name box, type **Crosstab**, and then click the **Save** button. The File Save dialog box closes, and the Export – HTML Document dialog box is the active window. See Figure 8-1.

Figure 8-1 | **Export - HTML Document dialog box**

destination file location and filename (your file location might be different)

export options for an HTML document

click to find the destination location for the file

Export - HTML Document

Select the destination for the data you want to export

Specify the destination file name and format.

File name: C:\Access2\Tutorial\Crosstab.html   Browse...

Specify export options.

☐ **Export data with formatting and layout.**
Select this option to preserve most formatting and layout information when exporting a table, query, form, or report.

☐ **Open the destination file after the export operation is complete.**
Select this option to view the results of the export operation. This option is available only when you export formatted data.

☐ **Export only the selected records.**
Select this option to export only the selected records. This option is only available when you export formatted data and have records selected.

OK   Cancel

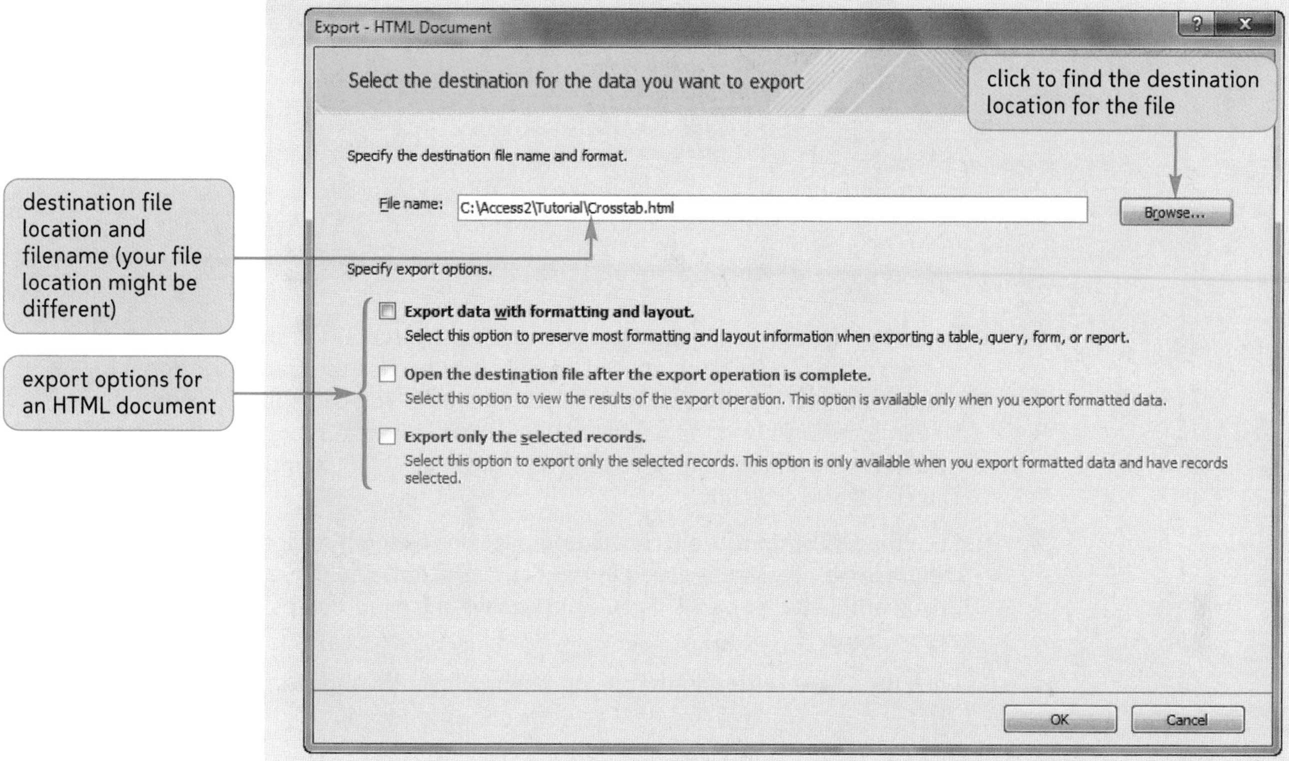

TIP

Always select the "Export data with formatting and layout" option, or the HTML document you create will be poorly formatted and difficult to read.

The dialog box provides options for exporting the data with formatting and layout, opening the exported file after the export operation is complete, and exporting selected records from the source object (available only when you select records in an object instead of the object in the Navigation Pane). You need to select the option for exporting the data with formatting and layout.

▶ 4. Click the **Export data with formatting and layout** check box to select it, and then click the **OK** button. The Export - HTML Document dialog box closes and the HTML Output Options dialog box opens.

This dialog box lets you specify an HTML template or use the default format when saving the object. Lucia used a text-editing program to create the HTML template named BelmTemp, which is shown in the Visual Overview for Session 8.1. You'll use this template to create the Crosstab HTML document. The template will automatically insert a Belmont Landscapes logo in all Web pages created with it. You need to locate Lucia's template file in your Data Files.

▶ 5. If necessary, click the **Select a HTML Template** check box to select it.

▶ 6. Click the **Browse** button to open the HTML Template to Use dialog box, navigate to the **Access2\Tutorial** folder, click **BelmTemp**, and then click the **OK** button. Access closes the HTML Template to Use dialog box, returns to the HTML Output Options dialog box, and displays the location and filename for the HTML template. See Figure 8-2.

Figure 8-2 HTML Output Options dialog box

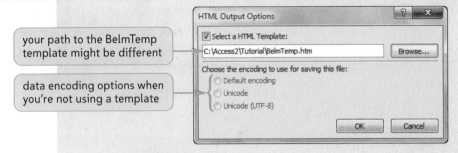

your path to the BelmTemp template might be different

data encoding options when you're not using a template

Trouble? If BelmTemp does not appear in the Access2\Tutorial folder when you open the HTML Template to Use dialog box, click the Cancel button to return to the HTML Output Options dialog box so you can specify the template filename manually. In the Select a HTML Template box, type the full path to the BelmTemp.htm file in the Access2\Tutorial folder—for example, C:\Access2\ Tutorial\BelmTemp.htm.

7. Click the **OK** button. The HTML Output Options dialog box closes, the HTML document named Crosstab is saved in the Access2\Tutorial folder, and the Export - HTML Document dialog box asks if you want to save the export steps. You won't save these export steps.

8. Click the **Close** button in the dialog box to close it without saving the steps.

Now you can view the Web page.

Viewing an HTML Document Using Internet Explorer

Oren asks to see the Web page you created. You can view the HTML document that you created using any Web browser. You'll view it using Internet Explorer.

To view the Crosstab Web page:

1. Open Windows Explorer, and then navigate to and open the **Access2\Tutorial** folder, which is where you saved the exported HTML document.

2. Right-click **Crosstab** in the file list to open the shortcut menu, click **Open with**, click **Internet Explorer**, and then click the **OK** button (if necessary). Internet Explorer starts and opens the Crosstab Web page. See the Session 8.1 Visual Overview.

Trouble? If Internet Explorer does not appear in the program list but another Web browser does appear, click the name of that browser. When you use another Web browser, your screens might look slightly different from the screen shown in the figure.

Changes that employees make to the Panorama database will not appear in the Crosstab Web page that you created because it is a **static Web page**—that is, it reflects the state of the qryCustomersAndInvoicesCrosstab query in the Panorama database at the time you created it. If data in the qryCustomersAndInvoicesCrosstab query changes, you will need to export the query as an HTML document again.

Because this static Web page is not linked to the qryCustomersAndInvoicesCrosstab query on which it is based, you cannot use your browser to make changes to its data. Before closing the Crosstab Web page, you'll try to change one of its field values.

To attempt to change a field value, and then close the browser:

▶ **1.** Double-click **Holland** in the City column for the sixth record, and then type **D**. The value of Holland remains highlighted and unchanged because the Crosstab Web page is a static page.

▶ **2.** Click the **Close** button [X] on the Internet Explorer window title bar to close it and to return to Windows Explorer.

▶ **3.** Click the **Close** button [X] on the Windows Explorer window title bar to close it and to return to Access.

Trouble? If the Access window is not active on your screen, click the Microsoft Access program button on the taskbar.

Sarah has a file containing customer billing addresses that she needs to add to the Panorama database. Instead of typing these billing addresses into new records, she asks you to import the data into the Panorama database.

Importing a CSV File as an Access Table

For most customers, the Address, City, State, and Zip fields in the tblCustomer table identify both the customer's location and billing address, which is where Belmont Landscapes sends the customer's invoices. In a few cases, however, the billing address is different from the location address; additionally, the company name used for billing purposes might be different from the company name stored in the tblCustomer table. Sarah has been maintaining an Excel workbook containing customer billing data, and she's exported the data to a CSV file. A **CSV (comma-separated values) file** is a text file in which commas separate values, and each line is a record containing the same number of values in the same positions.

REFERENCE

Importing a CSV File as an Access Table

- In the Import & Link group on the External Data tab on the Ribbon, click the Text File button to open the Get External Data - Text File dialog box.
- Click the Browse button in the dialog box, navigate to the location where the file to import is stored, click the filename, and then click the Open button.
- Click the Import the source data into a new table in the current database option button, and then click the OK button.
- In the Import Text Wizard dialog box, click the Delimited option button, and then click the Next button.
- Make sure the Comma option button is selected. If appropriate, click the First Row Contains Field Names check box to select it, and then click the Next button.
- For each field, if necessary, select the column, type its field name and select its data type, and then click the Next button.
- Choose the appropriate option button to let Access create a primary key, to choose your own primary key, or to avoid setting a primary key, click the Next button, type the table name in the Import to Table box, and then click the Finish button.

Access can import data from a CSV file directly into a database table. Sarah's CSV file is named Billing, and you'll import it as a table into the Panorama database.

To import the CSV file as an Access table:

1. Click the **External Data** tab on the Ribbon, and then in the Import & Link group, click the **Text File** button (with the ScreenTip "Import text file") to open the Get External Data - Text File dialog box.

2. Click the **Browse** button, navigate to the **Access2\Tutorial** folder, click **Billing**, click the **Open** button, and then click the **Import the source data into a new table in the current database** option button (if necessary). The selected path and filename appear in the File name box. See Figure 8-3.

Figure 8-3   **Get External Data - Text File dialog box**

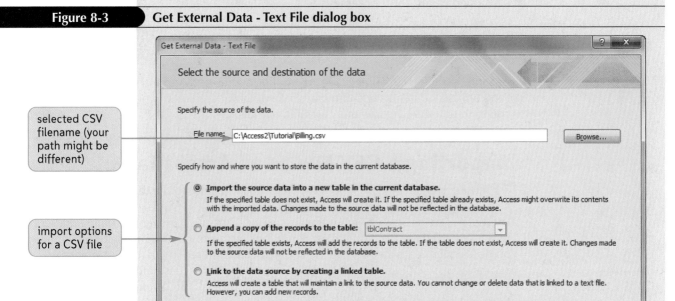

selected CSV filename (your path might be different)

import options for a CSV file

The dialog box provides options for importing the data into a new table in the database, appending a copy of the data to an existing table in the database, and linking to the source data. In the future, Sarah wants to maintain the customer billing data in the Panorama database, instead of using her Excel workbook, so you'll import the data into a new table.

3. Click the **OK** button to open the first Import Text Wizard dialog box, in which you designate how to identify the separation between field values in each line in the source data. The choices are the use of commas, tabs, or another character to separate, or delimit, the values, or the use of fixed width columns with spaces between each column. The wizard has correctly identified that values are delimited by commas.

4. Click the **Next** button to open the second Import Text Wizard dialog box, in which you verify the delimiter for values in each line. See Figure 8-4.

Figure 8-4   Verifying the delimiter for values in the CSV file

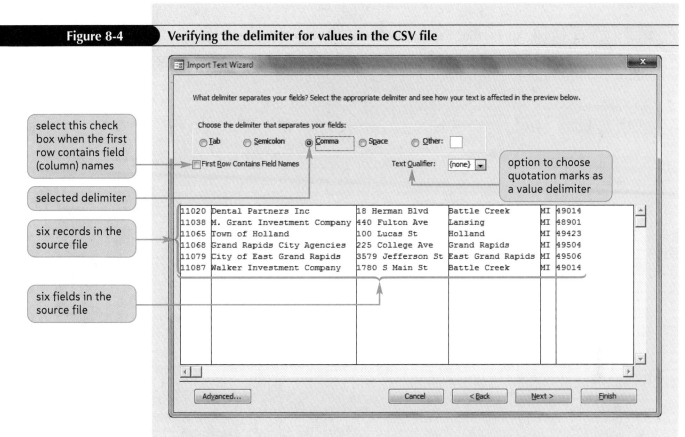

select this check box when the first row contains field (column) names

selected delimiter

six records in the source file

six fields in the source file

The CSV source file contains six records with six fields in each record. A comma serves as the delimiter for values in each line, so the Comma option button is selected. The first row in the source file contains the first record, not field names, so the First Row Contains Field Names check box is not checked. If the source file uses either single or double quotation marks to enclose values, you would click the Text Qualifier arrow to choose the appropriate option.

5. Click the **Next** button to open the third Import Text Wizard dialog box, in which you enter the field name and set other properties for the imported fields. You will import all fields from the source file and use the default data type and indexed settings for each field, except for the first field's data type.

6. Type **CustomerID** in the Field Name box, click the **Data Type** arrow, click **Text** in the list, and then click **Field2** in the table list. CustomerID (partially hidden) is the heading for the first column in the table list, and the second column is selected.

7. Repeat Step 6 for the rightmost five columns, making sure Text is the data type for all fields, typing **BillingCompany**, **BillingAddress**, **BillingCity**, **BillingState**, and **BillingZip** in the Field Name box. See Figure 8-5.

Figure 8-5 | **After setting field names for the six fields in the source file**

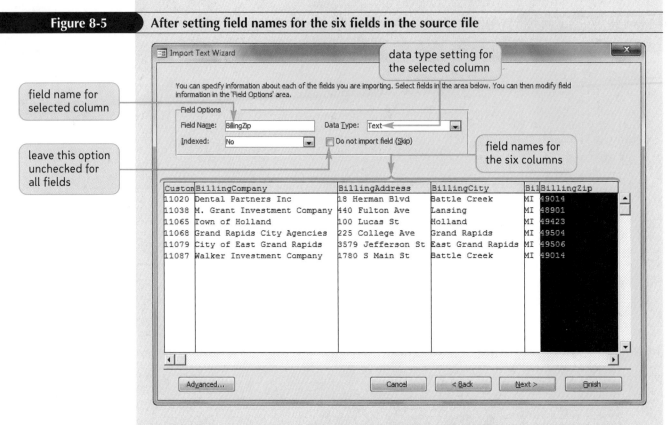

> **8.** Click the **Next** button to open the fourth Import Text Wizard dialog box, in which you select the primary key for the imported table. CustomerID, the first column, will be the primary key. When you select this column as the table's primary key, Access will delete the ID column it created.

> **9.** Click the **Choose my own primary key** option button, make sure **CustomerID** appears in the box for the option, click the **Next** button, type **tblCustomerBilling** as the table name in the Import to Table, click the **I would like a wizard to analyze my table after importing the data** check box to select it, and then click the **Finish** button. An Import Text Wizard dialog box opens asking if you want to analyze the table.

After importing data and creating a new table, you can use the Import Text Wizard to analyze the imported table. When you choose this option, you start the Table Analyzer.

Analyzing a Table with the Table Analyzer

TIP

Read the Normalization section in the appendix titled "Relational Databases and Database Design" for more information about normalization and third normal form.

The **Table Analyzer** analyzes a single table and, if necessary, splits it into two or more tables that are in third normal form. The Table Analyzer looks for redundant data in the table. When the Table Analyzer encounters redundant data, it removes redundant fields from the table and then places the redundant fields in new tables.

To use the Table Analyzer to analyze the imported table:

TIP

You can start the Table Analyzer directly by clicking the Database Tools tab, and then clicking the Analyze Table button in the Analyze group.

1. Click the **Yes** button to close the dialog box and to open the first Table Analyzer Wizard dialog box. The diagram and explanation in this dialog box describe the problem when duplicate data is stored in a table.

2. Click the first **Show me an example** button 🔊, read the explanation, close the example box, click the second **Show me an example** button 🔊, read the explanation, close the example box, and then click the **Next** button to open the second Table Analyzer Wizard dialog box. The diagram and explanation in this dialog box describe how the Table Analyzer solves the duplicate data problem.

3. Click the first **Show me an example** button 🔊, read the explanation, close the example box, click the second **Show me an example** button 🔊, read the explanation, close the example box, and then click the **Next** button to open the third Table Analyzer Wizard dialog box. In this dialog box, you choose whether to let the wizard decide which fields go in what tables, if the table is not already normalized. You'll let the wizard decide.

4. Make sure the **Yes, let the wizard decide** option button is selected, and then click the **Next** button. A message box informs you that the wizard does not recommend splitting the table because the table is normalized and does not contain redundant data.

5. Click the **Cancel** button to close the message box, exit the wizard, and return to the Get External Data - Text File dialog box, in which you are asked if you want to save the import steps. You don't need to save these steps because you're importing the data only this one time.

6. Click the **Close** button to close the dialog box.

The tblCustomerBilling table is now listed in the Tables section in the Navigation Pane. You'll open the table to verify the import results.

To open the imported tblCustomerBilling table:

1. Double-click **tblCustomerBilling** in the Navigation Pane to open the table datasheet, resize all columns to their best fit, and then click **11020** in the first row in the CustomerID column to deselect all values. See Figure 8-6.

| Figure 8-6 | **Imported tblCustomerBilling table datasheet** |

2. Save and close the table.

Sarah has some additional data that she wants to import into the Panorama database. The data is stored in XML format.

Using XML

Belmont Landscapes has contacts in the building trade industry and gets customer leads from builders when they sell new homes. One of the builders has stored data about several prospective customers available to Sarah in an XML document, which she wants to add to the Panorama database. **XML** (**Extensible Markup Language**) is a programming language that is similar in format to HTML, but is more customizable and suited to the exchange of data between different programs. Unlike HTML, which uses a fixed set of tags to describe the appearance of a Web page, developers can customize XML to describe the data it contains and how that data should be structured.

Decision Making: Exchanging Data Between Programs

XML files are used to exchange data between companies, and they are also used to exchange data between programs within a company. For example, you can store data either in an Excel workbook or in an Access table or query, depending on which program works best for the personnel working with the data and the business requirements of the company. Because the XML file format is a common file format for Excel and Access, whenever the data is needed in the other program, you can export the data as an XML file and import the file into the other program. You should consider the needs of the users and the characteristics of the programs they use when deciding the best means for exchanging data between programs.

Importing an XML File as an Access Table

Access can import data from an XML file directly into a database table. Sarah's XML file is named Prospect, and you'll import it as a table into the Panorama database.

REFERENCE

Importing an XML File as an Access Table

- In the Import & Link group on the External Data tab on the Ribbon, click the XML File button to open the Get External Data - XML File dialog box.
- Click the Browse button, navigate to the location for the XML file, click the XML file-name, and then click the Open button.
- Click the OK button in the Get External Data - XML File dialog box, click the table name in the Import XML dialog box, click the appropriate option button in the Import Options section, and then click the OK button.
- Click the Close button.

  or

  If you need to save the import steps, click the Save import steps check box, enter a name for the saved steps in the Save as box, and then click the Save Import button.

Now you will import the Prospect XML document as an Access database table.

To import the XML document as an Access table:

1. Click the **External Data** tab on the Ribbon (if necessary), and then in the Import & Link group, click the **XML File** button (with the ScreenTip "Import XML file"). The Get External Data - XML File dialog box opens.

2. Click the **Browse** button, navigate to the **Access2\Tutorial** folder, click **Prospect**, and then click the **Open** button. The selected path and filename now appear in the File name box.

3. Click the **OK** button. The Import XML dialog box opens. See Figure 8-7.

Figure 8-7   **Import XML dialog box**

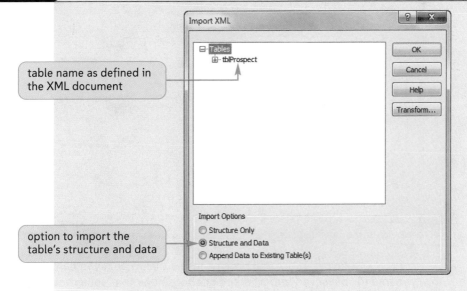

table name as defined in the XML document

option to import the table's structure and data

From the XML file, you can import only the table structure to a new table, import the table structure and data to a new table, or append the data in the XML file to an existing table. You'll import the table structure and data to a new table named tblProspect.

4. Make sure the **Structure and Data** option button is selected, click **tblProspect** in the box, and then click the **OK** button. The Import XML dialog box closes, and the last Get External Data - XML File dialog box is displayed.

Before reviewing the imported table, you'll save the import steps.

Saving and Running Import Specifications

If you need to repeat the same import procedure many times, you can save the steps for the procedure and expedite future imports by running the saved import steps without using a wizard. Because the builder intends to send Sarah additional lists of prospective customers in the future, you'll save the import steps for Sarah.

To save and run the XML file import steps:

1. Click the **Save import steps** check box to select it. The dialog box displays additional options for the save operation. See Figure 8-8.

Figure 8-8 Saving the import steps

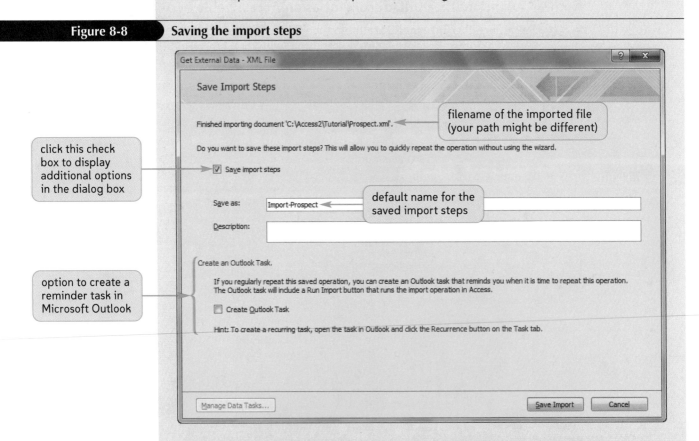

After displaying additional options in the dialog box, you can accept the default name for the saved import steps or choose one that you create, and you can enter an optional description. If the import will occur on a set schedule, you can also create a reminder task in Microsoft Outlook. You'll accept the default name for the saved steps, and you won't enter a description or schedule an Outlook task.

TIP

The table name is tblProspect, not Prospect, because the table name is tblProspect within the XML file.

2. Click the **Save Import** button. The import steps are saved as Import-Prospect, the Get External Data - XML File dialog box closes, the tblProspect table is imported into the Panorama database, and the table is now listed in the Navigation Pane.

You'll now show Sarah how she can run the saved steps when she receives customer prospects from the builder in the future.

3. In the Import & Link group on the External Data tab, click the **Saved Imports** button. The Manage Data Tasks dialog box opens. See Figure 8-9.

Figure 8-9   **Manage Data Tasks dialog box**

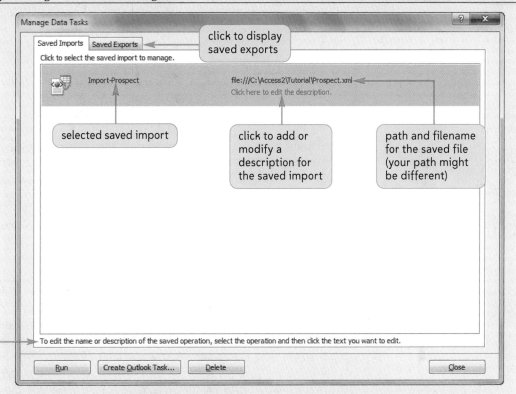

instructions for editing the saved import name or description

In this dialog box, you can change the saved import name, add or change its description, create an Outlook task for the saved import, run a saved import, or delete a saved import. You can also manage any saved export by clicking the Saved Exports tab. You'll add a description for the saved procedure and review the list of saved exports.

4. Click the **Click here to edit the description** text to open a box that contains the insertion point, type **Builder's XML file of customer prospects**, click an unused portion of the orange selection band to close the box and accept the typed description, and then click the **Saved Exports** tab. You have not saved any export steps, so no saved exports are displayed.

5. Click the **Close** button to close the Manage Data Tasks dialog box.

6. Double-click the **tblProspect** table in the Navigation Pane to open the table datasheet, close the Navigation Pane, resize all columns to their best fit, and then click **12001** in the first row in the CustomerID column to deselect all values. See Figure 8-10.

Figure 8-10   **Imported tblProspect table datasheet**

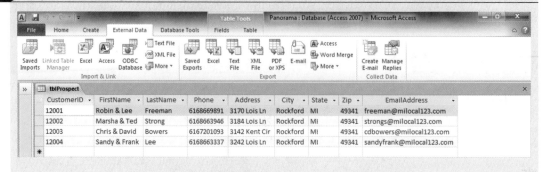

> **7.** Save and close the table.

Sarah next asks you to export the tblInvoice table as an XML file.

Exporting an Access Table as an XML File

Belmont Landscapes uses an accounting package that accepts the data in XML files as input for making accounting entries. Sarah wants to test this capability by exporting the tblInvoice table as an XML file and giving the XML file to the company's accounting manager for testing with the accounting package.

REFERENCE

Exporting an Access Object as an XML File

- Right-click the object (table, query, form, or report) in the Navigation Pane, point to Export, and then click XML File.
  or
  Click the object (table, query, form, or report) in the Navigation Pane. In the Export group on the External Data tab, click XML File button.
- Click the Browse button in the Export - XML File dialog box, navigate to the location where you will save the XML file, and then click the Save button.
- Click the OK button in the dialog box, select the options in the Export XML dialog box or click the More Options button and select the options in the expanded Export XML dialog box, and then click the OK button.
- Click the Close button.
  or
  If you need to save the export steps, click the Save export steps check box, enter a name for the saved steps in the Save as box, and then click the Save Export button.

You can now export the tblInvoice table as an XML file.

To export the tblInvoice table as an XML file:

> **1.** Open the Navigation Pane, right-click **tblInvoice** in the Navigation Pane, point to **Export** on the shortcut menu, and then click **XML File**. The Export - XML File dialog box opens.

> **2.** Click the **Browse** button, navigate to the **Acess2\Tutorial** folder, change the name in the File name box to **Invoice**, and then click the **Save** button. The selected path and filename now appear in the File name box in the Export - XML File dialog box.

3. Click the **OK** button. The Export XML dialog box opens.

Clicking the More Options button in the Export XML dialog box expands the dialog box and lets you view and change detailed options for exporting a database object to an XML file.

4. Click the **More Options** button to reveal detailed export options in the Export XML dialog box. See Figure 8-11.

Figure 8-11 — **Data tab in the Export XML dialog box**

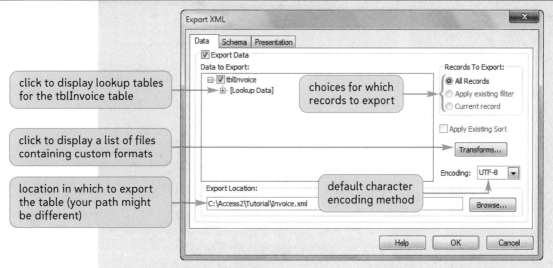

The Export Data check box, the Export Location box, and the Records To Export option group display the selections you made in the previous step. You're exporting all records from the tblInvoice table, including the data in the records and the structure of the table, to the Invoice.xml file in the Access2\Tutorial folder. The encoding option determines how characters will be represented in the exported XML file. The encoding choices are UTF-8, which uses 8 bits to represent each character, and UTF-16, which uses 16 bits to represent each character. You can also click the Transforms button if you have a special file that contains instructions for changing the exported data.

The accounting package doesn't have a transform file and requires the default encoding, but Sarah wants to review the tables that contain lookup data.

5. Click the plus box to the left of [Lookup Data]. The tblContract table contains lookup data because it's the primary table in the one-to-many relationship with the related tblInvoice table. The accounting package requirements don't include any lookup data from the tblContract table, so make sure the tblContract check box is not checked.

The Data tab settings are correct, so you'll verify the Schema tab settings.

▶ **6.** Click the **Schema** tab. See Figure 8-12.

Schema tab in the Export XML dialog box

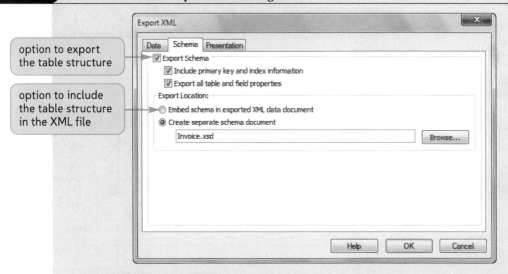

option to export the table structure

option to include the table structure in the XML file

Along with the data from the tblInvoice table, you'll be exporting its table structure, including information about the table's primary key, indexes, and table and field properties. You can include this information in a separate **XSD** (**XML Structure Definition**) file, or you can embed the information in the XML file. The accounting package expects a single XML file, so you'll embed the structure information in the XML file.

▶ **7.** Click the **Embed schema in exported XML data document** option button to select that option and to dim the "Create separate schema document" option, and then click the **Presentation** tab. See Figure 8-13.

Presentation tab in the Export XML dialog box

option to export formatting instructions

TIP

Unlike HTML, XML provides no formatting information. An XSL file provides formatting instructions so that a browser or another program can display the XML data file in a readable way.

The Presentation tab options let you export a separate **XSL** (**Extensible Stylesheet Language**) file containing the format specifications for the tblInvoice table data. The accounting package will import the tblInvoice table data directly into its computer program, which contains its own formatting instructions, so you will not export an XSL file.

▶ **8.** Make sure that the **Export Presentation (HTML 4.0 Sample XSL)** check box is not checked, and then click the **OK** button. Access closes the Export XML dialog box, exports the data in the tblInvoice table as an XML file in the Access2\Tutorial folder, and returns you to the final Export - XML File dialog box.

Sarah plans to make further tests exporting the tblInvoice table as an XML file, so you'll save the export steps.

INSIGHT

Importing and Exporting Data

You've imported data from an Excel workbook and a text file (.txt extension) in Tutorial 2 and from a text file (.csv extension) and an XML file in this tutorial. Additional Access options include importing an object from another Access database, importing data from other databases (dBASE and ODBC databases such as SQL Server), and importing an HTML document, an Outlook folder, or a SharePoint list.

In addition to exporting Access objects as an XML file or an HTML document, Access includes options for exporting data to another Access database, other databases (ODBC database or dBASE), an Excel workbook, a text file, a Word document, a SharePoint list, or a PDF or XPS file. You can also "export" table or query data to Word's mail merge feature, or export an object to an e-mail message.

The steps you follow for all import and export options work similar to the import and export steps you've used in this tutorial and in Tutorial 2. For example, to save an object as an XPS file, right-click the name of the object you want to export in the Navigation Pane, point to Export on the shortcut menu, click PDF or XPS, navigate to the folder where you want to store the file, click the Save as type arrow, click XPS Document, click the Publish button, and then click the Close button.

Saving and Running Export Specifications

Saving the steps to export the tblInvoice table as an XML file will save time and eliminate errors when Sarah repeats the export procedure. You'll save the export steps and then show Sarah how to run the saved export steps.

To save and run the XML file export steps:

▶ **1.** Click the **Save export steps** check box. The dialog box displays additional options for the save operation.

The dialog box has the same options you saw earlier when you saved the XML import steps. You'll enter a description, and you won't create an Outlook task because Sarah will be running the saved export steps on an as needed basis.

2. In the Description box, type **XML file accounting entries from the tblInvoice table**. See Figure 8-14.

Figure 8-14　　Saving the export steps

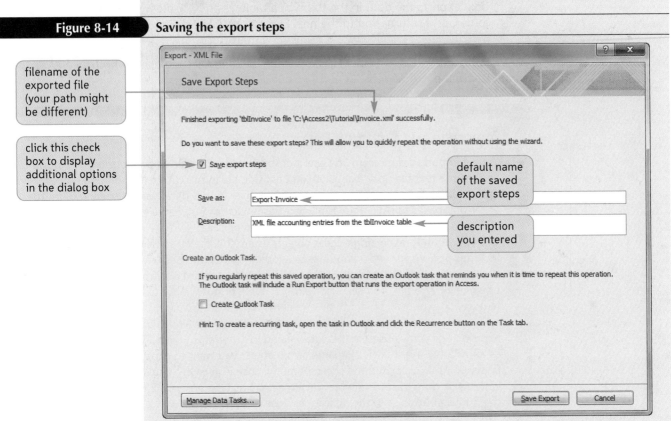

filename of the exported file (your path might be different)

click this check box to display additional options in the dialog box

default name of the saved export steps

description you entered

---

3. Click the **Save Export** button. The export steps are saved as Export-Invoice, the Export - XML File dialog box closes, and the tblInvoice table is exported as an XML file named Invoice.

You'll now show Sarah how she can run the saved steps.

4. Click the **External Data** tab on the Ribbon (if necessary), and in the Export group, click the **Saved Exports** button. The Manage Data Tasks dialog box opens. See Figure 8-15.

Figure 8-15   **Manage Data Tasks dialog box**

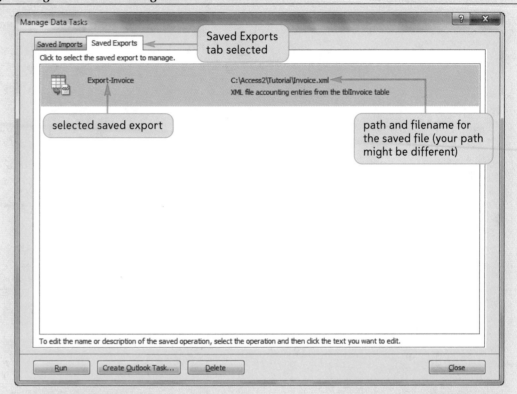

5. Click the **Run** button. The saved procedure runs, and a message box opens, asking if you want to replace the existing XML file you created earlier.

6. Click the **Yes** button to replace the existing XML file. A message box informs you that the export was completed successfully.

7. Click the **OK** button to close the message box, and then click the **Close** button to close the Manage Data Tasks dialog box.

8. If you are not continuing on to the next session, close the Panorama database.

You've imported and exported data, analyzed a table's design, and saved and run import and export specifications. In the next session, you will analyze data by working with a chart, PivotTable, PivotChart, and linked data, and you will add a tab control to a form.

REVIEW

Session 8.1 Quick Check

1. What is HTML?
2. What is an HTML template?
3. What is a static Web page?
4. What is a CSV file?
5. What is the Table Analyzer?
6. _____ is a programming language that describes data and its structure.

SESSION 8.2 VISUAL OVERVIEW

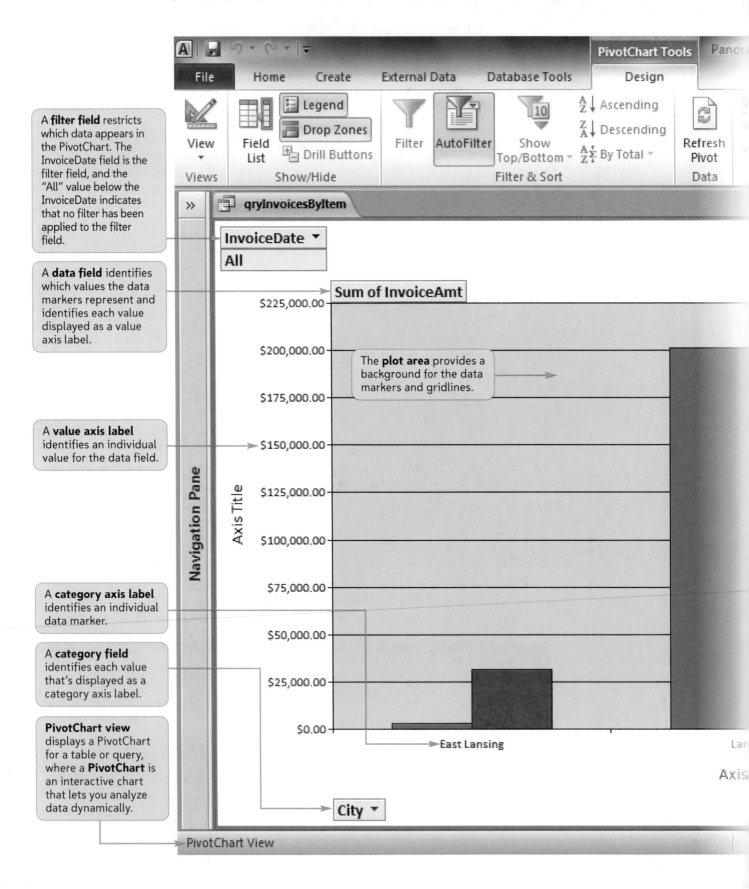

A **filter field** restricts which data appears in the PivotChart. The InvoiceDate field is the filter field, and the "All" value below the InvoiceDate indicates that no filter has been applied to the filter field.

A **data field** identifies which values the data markers represent and identifies each value displayed as a value axis label.

A **value axis label** identifies an individual value for the data field.

A **category axis label** identifies an individual data marker.

A **category field** identifies each value that's displayed as a category axis label.

PivotChart view displays a PivotChart for a table or query, where a **PivotChart** is an interactive chart that lets you analyze data dynamically.

The **plot area** provides a background for the data markers and gridlines.

qryInvoicesByItem

InvoiceDate ▼
All

Sum of InvoiceAmt

$225,000.00
$200,000.00
$175,000.00
$150,000.00
$125,000.00
$100,000.00
$75,000.00
$50,000.00
$25,000.00
$0.00

East Lansing

Axis Title

City ▼

Navigation Pane

PivotChart View

PivotChart Tools

Panor

File   Home   Create   External Data   Database Tools   Design

View   Field List   Legend   Drop Zones   Drill Buttons   Filter   AutoFilter   Show Top/Bottom   Ascending   Descending   By Total   Refresh Pivot

Views   Show/Hide   Filter & Sort   Data

FILTERED PIVOTCHART

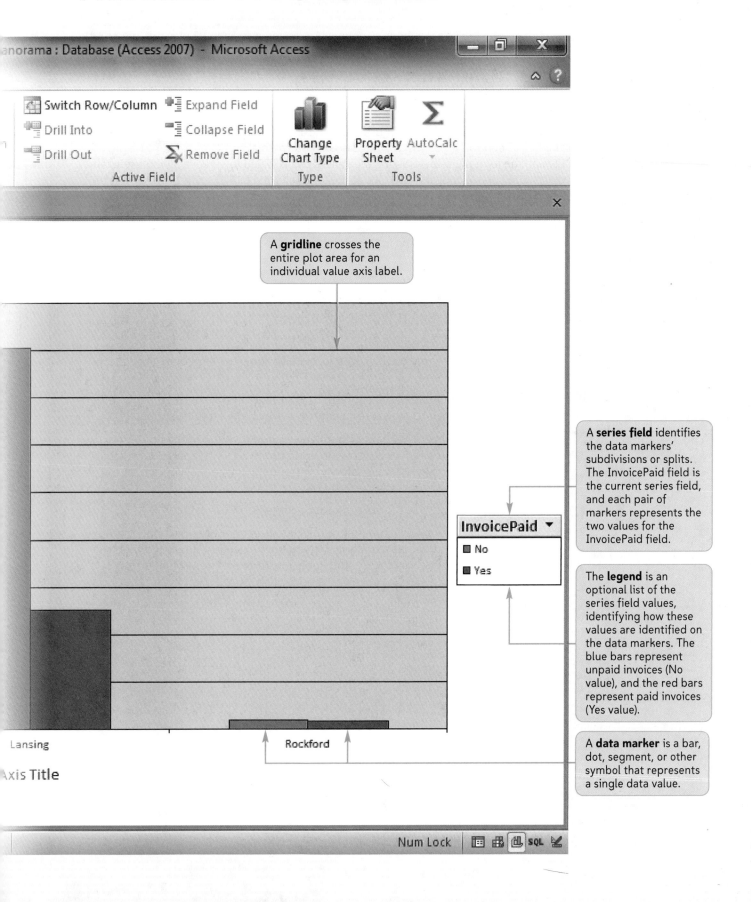

Creating a Multi-page Form Using a Tab Control

Sarah wants you to enhance the frmContractsAndInvoices form to display two pages—with the form on one page, and a chart on the other page—to create a multi-page form. The first page will contain the frmInvoiceSubform subform that is currently positioned at the bottom of the frmContractsAndInvoices form. The second page will contain a chart showing the invoice amounts for the invoices associated with the displayed contract.

You can create a multi-page form in two ways: use the **Page Break tool** to insert a page break control in the form, or use the **Tab Control tool** to insert a control that's called a tab control. If you insert a page break control in a form, users can move between the form pages by pressing the Page Up and Page Down keys. If you use a tab control, the control appears with tabs at the top, with one tab for each page. Users can switch between pages by clicking the tabs.

To expedite placing the subform in the tab control, you'll cut the subform from the form, add the tab control, and then paste the subform into the left tab on the tab control. You need to perform these steps in Design view.

To add the tab control to the form:

▶ 1. If you took a break after the previous session, make sure that the Panorama database is open and the Navigation Pane is open.

▶ 2. Open the **frmContractsAndInvoices** form in Design view, and then close the Navigation Pane.

▶ 3. Right-click the top edge of the subform control to open the shortcut menu, and then click **Cut** to delete the subform control and place it on the Clipboard.

   Trouble? If you do not see Subform in New Window as one of the options on the shortcut menu, you did not click the top edge of the subform control correctly. Right-click the top edge of the subform control until you see this option on the shortcut menu, and then click Cut.

▶ 4. In the Controls group on the Design tab, click the **Tab Control** tool 🔲.

▶ 5. Position the + portion of the pointer in the Detail section three grid dots from the left edge of the grid and at the 2.5-inch mark on the vertical ruler, and then click the mouse button. Access places a tab control with two pages in the form.

▶ 6. Right-click in the middle of the tab control, and when an orange outline appears inside the tab control, click **Paste** on the shortcut menu. The subform is pasted in the tab control. See Figure 8-16.

Figure 8-16 **Subform on the tab control in the Detail section**

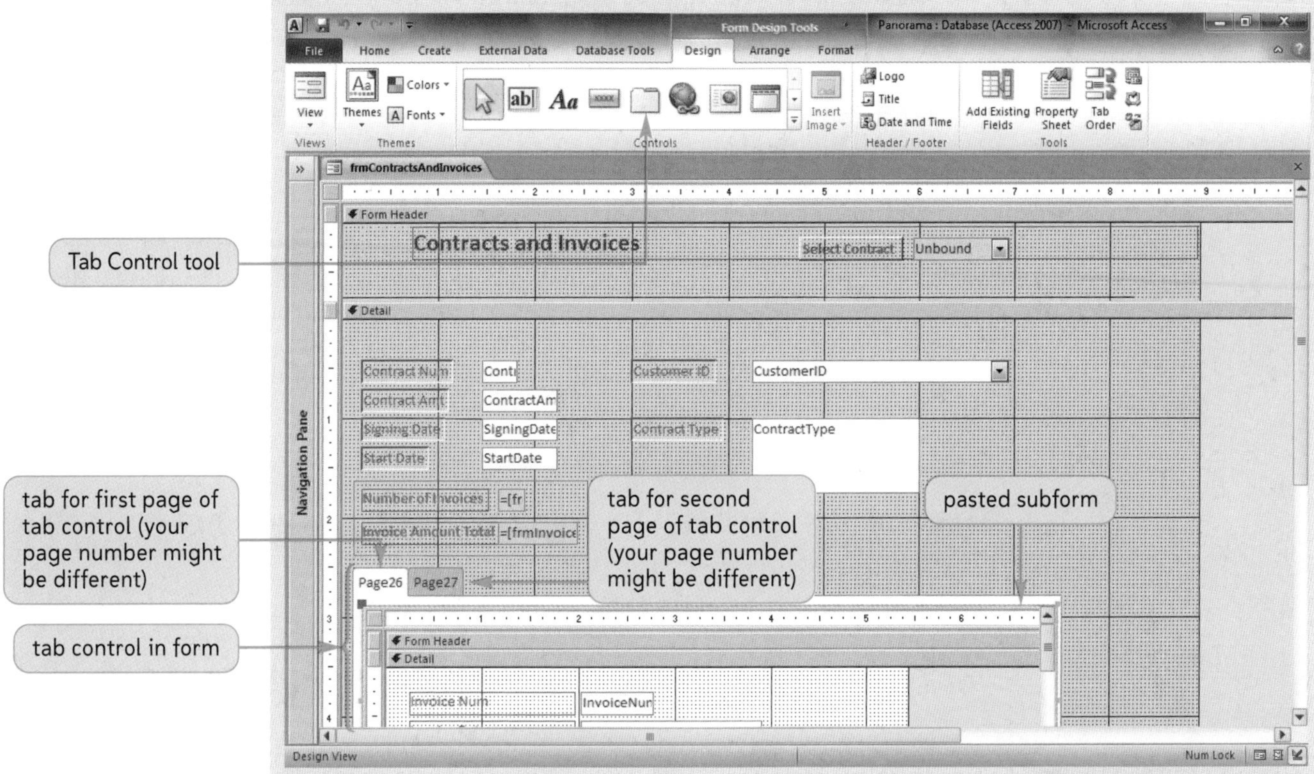

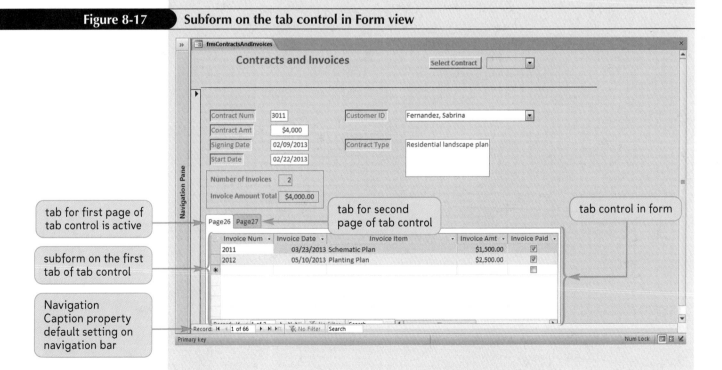

Tab Control tool
tab for first page of tab control (your page number might be different)
tab control in form
tab for second page of tab control (your page number might be different)
pasted subform
Contracts and Invoices

7. Switch to Form view, and then click **3011** in the ContractNum text box to deselect all controls. The left tab, which represents the first page in the tab control, is the active tab. See Figure 8-17.

Figure 8-17 **Subform on the tab control in Form view**

tab for first page of tab control is active
subform on the first tab of tab control
Navigation Caption property default setting on navigation bar
tab for second page of tab control
tab control in form
Contracts and Invoices

The subform is now displayed on the first page of the tab control and its design is the same as it was before you cut and pasted it to the tab control.

8. Click the **right tab** of the tab control to display the second page, which is empty because you haven't added any controls to it yet.

After viewing the form in Form view, Sarah asks you to edit the labels for the tabs in the tab control, so they indicate the contents of each page. Also, Sarah's staff finds the two sets of navigation buttons confusing—they waste time determining which set of navigation buttons applies to the subform and which to the main form. You'll set the Navigation Caption property for the main form and the subform. The **Navigation Caption property** lets you change the navigation label from the word "Record" to another value. Because the main form displays data about contracts and the subform displays data about invoices, you'll change the Navigation Caption property for the main form to "Contract" and for the subform to "Invoice."

To change the captions for the tabs and the navigation buttons:

1. Switch to Design view.

2. Click the **form selector** for the main form to select the form control in the main form, open the property sheet to display the properties for the selected form control, click the **All** tab (if necessary), click the **Navigation Caption** box, and then type **Contract**. See Figure 8-18.

Figure 8-18   **Setting the Navigation Caption property for the main form**

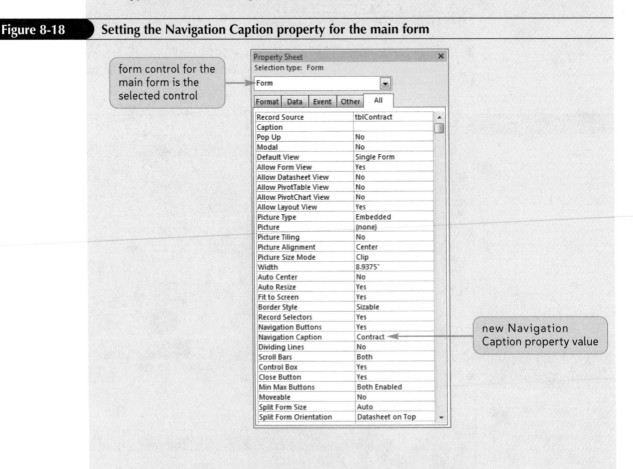

form control for the main form is the selected control

Property Sheet	
Selection type: Form	
Form	
Format	Data	Event	Other	**All**	
Record Source	tblContract
Caption	
Pop Up	No
Modal	No
Default View	Single Form
Allow Form View	Yes
Allow Datasheet View	No
Allow PivotTable View	No
Allow PivotChart View	No
Allow Layout View	Yes
Picture Type	Embedded
Picture	(none)
Picture Tiling	No
Picture Alignment	Center
Picture Size Mode	Clip
Width	8.9375"
Auto Center	No
Auto Resize	Yes
Fit to Screen	Yes
Border Style	Sizable
Record Selectors	Yes
Navigation Buttons	Yes
Navigation Caption	Contract
Dividing Lines	No
Scroll Bars	Both
Control Box	Yes
Close Button	Yes
Min Max Buttons	Both Enabled
Moveable	No
Split Form Size	Auto
Split Form Orientation	Datasheet on Top

new Navigation Caption property value

▶ **3.** Click the **form selector** for the subform to select the subform, click the **form selector** for the subform again to select the form control in the subform and display the properties for the selected form control, click the **Navigation Caption** box, and then type **Invoice**. Navigation buttons don't appear in Design view, so you won't see the effects of the Navigation Caption property settings until you switch to Form view.

▶ **4.** Click the **left tab** in the subform, click the **left tab** in the subform again to select it, type **Invoice Data** in the Caption box on the property sheet, and then press the **Tab** key. The Caption property value now appears in the left tab. See Figure 8-19.

Figure 8-19   **Setting the Caption property for the left tab**

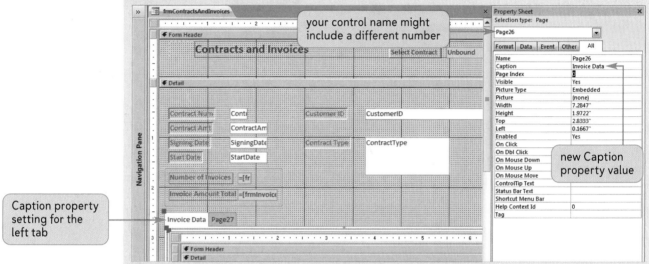

▶ **5.** Click the **right tab** in the subform to select it, type **Invoice Chart** in the Caption box, and then close the property sheet.

▶ **6.** Save your form design changes, switch to Form view, click **3011** in the ContractNum text box to deselect all controls, and then scroll to the bottom of the form. The tabs and the navigation buttons now display the new caption values. See Figure 8-20.

Figure 8-20 **Subform on the tab control in Form view**

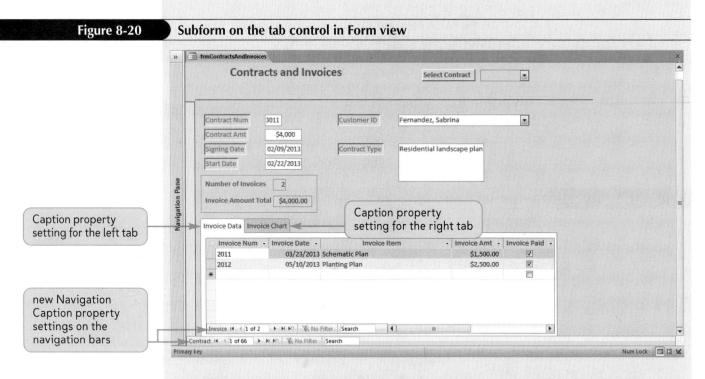

The tab control's height has increased the form's height, so you no longer can view the entire form on screen without scrolling. You can either decrease the tab control's height, or view the form with a minimized Ribbon. Until you finish the contents of the right tab, you won't decide which approach works best.

Sarah wants you to add a simple chart to the second page of the tab control.

Integrating Access with Other Programs

When you create a form or report in Access, you include more than just the data from the record source table or query. You've added controls such as lines, rectangles, tab controls, and graphics in your forms and reports to improve their appearance and usability. You can also add charts, drawings, and other objects to your forms and reports, but Access doesn't have the capability to create them. Instead, you create these other objects using other programs and then place them in a form or report using the appropriate integration method.

When you integrate information between programs, the program containing the original information, or object, is called the **source program**, and the program in which you place the information created by the source program is called the **destination program**. Access offers three ways for you to integrate objects created by other programs.

- **Importing**. When you import an object, you include the contents of a file in a new table or append it to an existing table, or you include the contents of the file in a form, report, or field. For example, in Tutorial 2 you added a picture to a form, or imported it into the form, and in this tutorial you imported CSV and XML files as new tables in the Panorama database. The imported picture is a file with a .bmp extension that was created by a graphics program, and the CSV and XML files were created by other programs. After importing an object, it no longer has a connection to the program that created it. Any subsequent changes you make to the object using the source program are not reflected in the imported object.

- **Embedding**. When you embed an object in a form, report, or field, you preserve its connection to the source program, which enables you to edit the object, if necessary, using the features of the source program. Any changes you make to the object are reflected only in the form, report, or field in which it is embedded; the changes do not affect the original object in the file from which it was embedded. Likewise, if you start the source program outside Access and make any changes to the original object, these changes are not reflected in the embedded object.
- **Linking**. When you link an object to a form, report, or field, you include a connection in the destination program to the original file maintained by the source program; you do not store data from the file in the destination program. Any changes you make to the original file using the source program are reflected in the linked file version in the destination program.

PROSKILLS

Decision Making: Importing, Embedding, and Linking Data

How do you decide which method to use when you need to include in an Access database data that is stored in another file or format? When you intend to use Access to maintain the data and no longer need an updated version of the data with the source program, you can import a file as a new table or append the records in the file to an existing table. You link to the data when the source program will continue to maintain the data in the file, and you need to use an updated version of the file at all times in the destination program. When linking to the data, you can also maintain the data using the destination program, and the source program will always use the updated version of the file.

For objects in forms or reports, you import an object (such as a picture) when you want a copy of the object in your form or report and you don't intend to make any changes to the object. You embed or link an object when you want a copy of the object in your form or report and you intend to edit the object using the source program in the future. You embed the object when you do not want your edits to the object in the destination program to affect any other copies of the object used by other programs. You link the object when you want your edits to the object in the destination program to affect the object used by other programs.

The decision to import, embed, or link to data depends on how you will use the data in your database, and what connection is required to the original data. You should carefully consider the effect of changes to the original data and to the copied data before choosing which method to use.

Sarah wants you to embed a chart on the second page of the tab control.

Embedding a Chart in a Form

The Chart Wizard in Access helps you to embed a chart in a form or report. The chart is actually created by another program, Microsoft Graph, but the Chart Wizard does the work of embedding the chart. After embeddng the chart in a form or report, you can edit it using the Microsoft Graph program.

REFERENCE

Embedding a Chart in a Form or Report

- In the Controls group on the Design tab in Design view, click the More button, and then click the Chart tool.
- Position the + portion of the pointer where you want to position the upper-left corner of the chart, and then click the mouse button to start the Chart Wizard.
- Select the record source, fields, and chart type.
- Edit the chart contents, and select the fields that link the object and chart, if necessary.
- Enter a chart title, select whether to include a legend, and then click the Finish button.

The tblInvoice table contains the information needed for the chart Sarah wants you to include in the form's right tab in the tab control.

To add a chart in the tab control and start the Chart Wizard:

1. Switch to Design view, and then click the **Invoice Chart** tab on the tab control, if necessary.

2. In the Controls group on the Design tab, click the **More** button ⊽, click the **Chart** tool 📊, and then move the pointer to the tab control. When the pointer is inside the tab control, the rectangular portion of the tab control you can use to place controls is filled in black.

3. Position the + portion of the pointer in the upper-left corner of the black portion of the tab control, and then click the mouse button. Access places a chart control in the form and opens the first Chart Wizard dialog box, in which you select the source record for the chart.

Sarah wants the chart to provide her staff with a simple visual display of the relative proportions of the invoice amounts for the invoices for the currently displayed contract. You'll use the tblInvoice table as the record source for the chart and select the InvoiceDate and InvoiceAmt fields as the fields to use in the chart.

To create the chart with the Chart Wizard:

1. Click **Table: tblInvoice** in the box, and then click the **Next** button to display the second Chart Wizard dialog box.

2. Select the **InvoiceDate** and the **InvoiceAmt** fields, and then click the **Next** button to display the third Chart Wizard dialog box, in which you choose the chart type.

3. Click the **Pie Chart** button (row 4, column 1) to select the pie chart as the chart type to use for Sarah's chart. See Figure 8-21.

TIP

The box on the right displays a brief description of the selected chart type.

Figure 8-21   Selecting the chart type

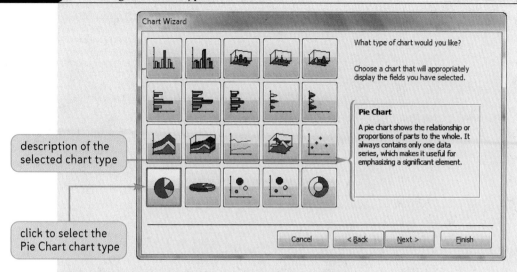

description of the selected chart type

click to select the Pie Chart chart type

4. Click the **Next** button to display the next Chart Wizard dialog box, in which you preview the chart and modify the data and its placement in the chart. Because visualizing the chart from the displayed preview is difficult, you'll use the default layout based on the two selected fields. You can easily modify the chart after you create it.

5. Click the **Next** button to display the next Chart Wizard dialog box, in which you choose the fields that link records in the main form (the main form uses the tblContract table as its record source) to records in the chart (the chart uses the tblInvoice table as its record source). ContractNum is the common field linking these two tables, and you can use that field as the linking field even though you didn't select it as a field for the chart.

6. Click the **Next** button to display the final dialog box, in which you enter the title that will appear at the top of the chart and choose whether to include a legend in the chart.

7. Type **Invoices for this Contract**, make sure the **Yes, display a legend** option button is selected, and then click the **Finish** button. The completed chart appears in the tab control.

You'll view the form in Form view, where it's easier to assess the chart's appearance.

8. Save your form design changes, switch to Form view, scroll down to the bottom of the form (if necessary), navigate to record 5 in the main form, notice the four contracts displayed in the subform, click the **Invoice Chart** tab to display the chart, and then scroll down to the bottom of the form (if necessary). See Figure 8-22.

Figure 8-22 **Embedded chart in Form view**

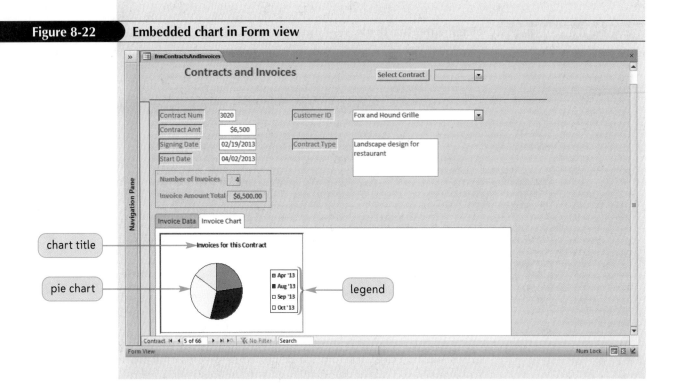

Linking Record Sources

The record source for a primary main form must have a one-to-many relationship to the record source for a related subform or chart. The subform or chart object has its Link Master Fields property set to the primary key in the record source to the main form and its Link Child Fields property set to the foreign key in the record source to the subform or chart.

After viewing the chart, Sarah decides it needs some modifications. She wants you to change the chart type from a pie chart to a bar chart, remove the legend, and modify the chart's background color. You'll make these changes by switching to Design view, and then you'll start Microsoft Graph so you can edit the chart.

To edit the chart using Microsoft Graph:

If Chart Object doesn't appear on the shortcut menu, right-click the edge until it does.

1. Switch to Design view, right-click an edge of the chart object to open the shortcut menu, point to **Chart Object**, and then click **Open**. Microsoft Graph starts and displays the chart. See Figure 8-23.

Figure 8-23   **Editing the chart with Microsoft Graph**

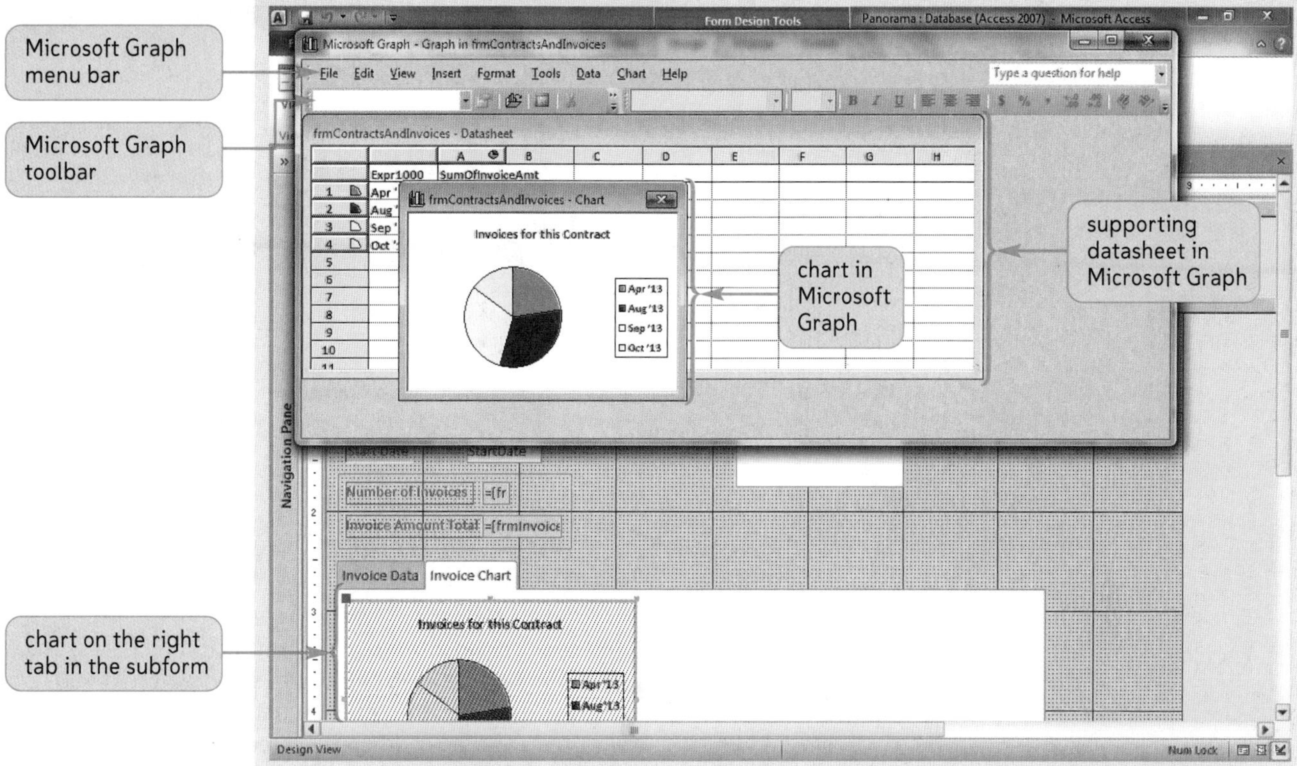

- Microsoft Graph menu bar
- Microsoft Graph toolbar
- chart in Microsoft Graph
- supporting datasheet in Microsoft Graph
- chart on the right tab in the subform

Microsoft Graph is the source program that the Chart Wizard used to create the chart. Because the chart was embedded in the form, editing the chart object starts Graph and allows you to edit the chart using the Graph menu bar and toolbar. In addition to displaying the selected chart, the Graph window displays a datasheet, which contains the data on which the chart is based. You'll now make Sarah's chart changes using Graph.

2. Click **Chart** on the Graph menu bar, click **Chart Type** to open the Chart Type dialog box, and then click **Column** in the Chart type box to display the types of column charts. See Figure 8-24.

Figure 8-24 **Chart Type dialog box**

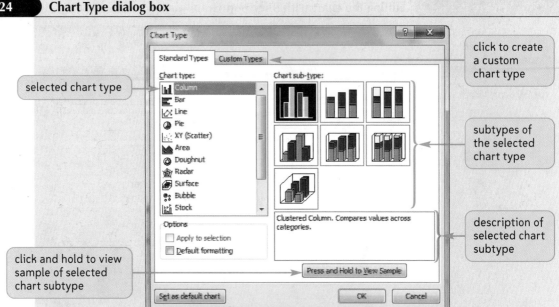

The column chart is the selected chart type, and the clustered column chart is the default chart subtype (row 1, column 1). A description of the selected chart sub-type appears below the chart subtypes. You can create a custom chart by click-ing the Custom Types tab. If you click and hold down the Press and Hold to View Sample button, you'll see a sample of the selected subtype.

3. Click the **Press and Hold to View Sample** button to view a sample of the chart, release the mouse button, and then click the **OK** button to close the dialog box and change the chart to a column chart in the Graph window and in the form.

4. Click **Chart** on the Graph menu bar, click **Chart Options** to open the Chart Options dialog box, click the **Legend** tab to display the chart's legend options, click the **Show legend** check box to clear it, and then click the **OK** button. The legend is removed from the chart object in the Graph window and in the form.

To change the color or other properties of a chart control—the chart background (or chart area), axes, labels to the left of the y-axis, labels below the x-axis, or data markers (columnar bars for a column chart)—you need to double-click the control.

5. In the Chart window, double-click one of the blue data markers inside the chart to open the Format Data Series dialog box, and then click the orange box (row 2, column 2) in the color palette in the Area section. See Figure 8-25.

TIP

A data marker is a bar, dot, segment, or other symbol that represents a single data value.

Figure 8-25   **Format Data Series dialog box**

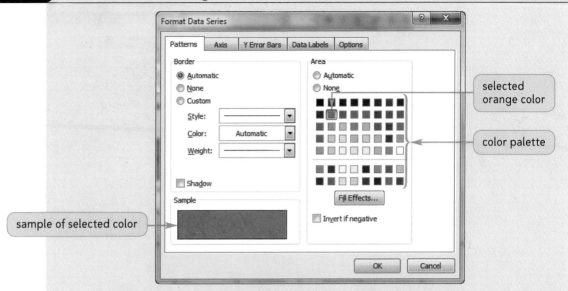

The sample color in the dialog box changes to orange to match the selected color in the color palette.

▶ **6.** Click the **OK** button to close the dialog box and to change the color of the data markers in the chart in the Graph window and in the form to orange.

▶ **7.** In the Chart window, double-click the white chart background to the left of the title to open the Format Chart Area dialog box, click the light orange box (row 5, column 2) in the color palette in the Area section, and then click the **OK** button. The chart's background color changes from white to light orange in the chart in the Graph window and in the form.

▶ **8.** Click **File** on the Graph menu bar, and then click **Exit & Return to frmContractsAndInvoices** to exit Graph and return to the form.

▶ **9.** Save your form design changes, switch to Form view, double-click the **Home** tab to minimize the Ribbon, navigate to record 5 in the main form, and then click the **Invoice Chart** tab to display the chart. See Figure 8-26.

Figure 8-26	**Completed chart in Form view**

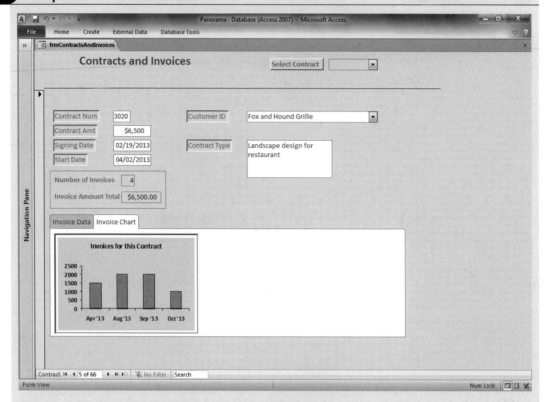

10. Close the form, and then double-click the **Home** tab to restore the Ribbon.

Sarah wants to know if Access has other charting and data analysis tools. You'll show her how to create a PivotTable and a PivotChart.

Creating and Using a PivotTable

Sarah wants to be able to analyze data in a flexible way. You can use PivotTables to provide the flexible analysis that Sarah needs. A **PivotTable** is an interactive table that lets you analyze data dynamically. You can use a PivotTable to view and organize data from a database, look for summary or detail information, and dynamically change the contents and organization of the table. Figure 8-27 shows a PivotTable.

Figure 8-27 **Sample PivotTable**

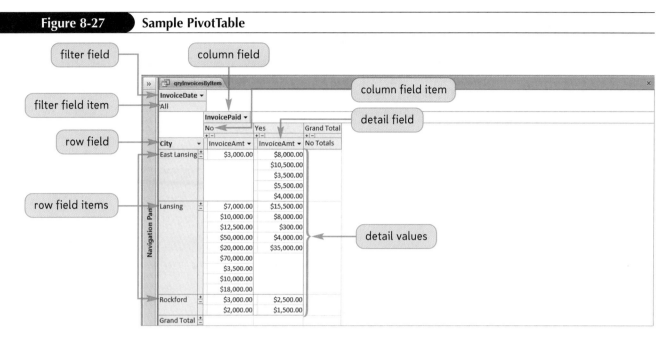

A PivotTable contains the following basic components:

- The **total/detail area**, consisting of a **detail field** and **detail values**, provides details and optional totals from a database table or query. In Figure 8-27, the detail field is the InvoiceAmt field from the tblInvoice table, and the detail values are the InvoiceAmt field values.
- The **row area**, consisting of a **row field** and **row field items**, provides row groupings in the PivotTable. In Figure 8-27, the row field is the City field from the tblCustomer table, and the row field items are the City field values.
- The **column area**, consisting of a **column field** and **column field items**, provides column groupings in the PivotTable. In Figure 8-27, the column field is the InvoicePaid field from the tblInvoice table, and the column field items are the InvoicePaid field values.
- The **filter area**, consisting of a **filter field** and **filter field items**, lets you restrict which data appears in the PivotTable. In Figure 8-27, the filter field is the InvoiceDate field from the tblInvoice table, and the filter field item is "All" dates, which means that all InvoiceDate field values are represented in the PivotTable.
- All the PivotTable areas—detail area, row area, column area, and filter area—can have multiple fields with multiple field items.

When you work with PivotTables, you use another program, the **Office PivotTable Component**, which is one of the **Office Web Components** that are part of Office 2010. Therefore, you can use PivotTables with other programs such as Excel. You can create PivotTables with Access tables and queries; the PivotTable view with these Access objects provides this capability.

Creating a PivotTable

Sarah wants to analyze invoice amounts by city and by invoice date in various ways. You'll create a PivotTable using the qryInvoicesByItem query to let her perform this analysis.

To create a PivotTable using a query:

1. Open the Navigation Pane, open the **qryInvoicesByItem** query datasheet to display the 172 records in the query, close the Navigation Pane, right-click the **qryInvoicesByItem** tab, and then click **PivotTable View** to switch to PivotTable view. See Figure 8-28.

Figure 8-28 PivotTable view for the qryInvoicesByItem query

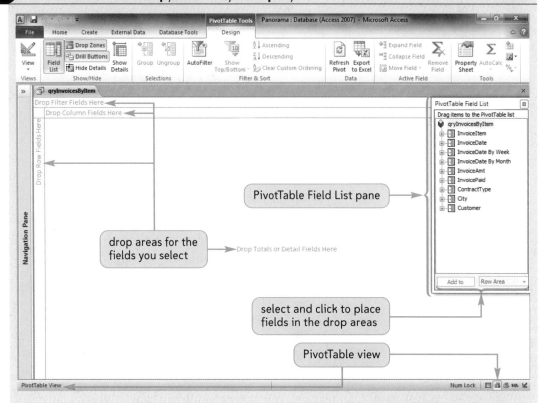

To create a PivotTable, you click a field in the PivotTable Field List pane to select it, and then drag it to one of the four drop areas—row, column, filter, or total/detail—or click the Add to button at the bottom of the PivotTable Field List pane after selecting one of the four drop areas in the list to the right of the Add to button.

Sarah wants to use the InvoicePaid field as the column field, the City field as the row field, the InvoiceDate field as the filter field, and the InvoiceAmt field as the detail field.

2. Click **InvoiceDate** in the PivotTable Field List pane, click the **Add to arrow** at the bottom of the PivotTable Field List pane, click **Filter Area** in the list, and then click the **Add to** button. Access places the InvoiceDate field and its field values in the filter drop area.

    Trouble? If you receive an error when you try to add a field to the PivotTable, switch to Design view, right-click the qryInvoicesByItem tab, click PivotTable View on the shortcut menu, and then repeat Step 2.

3. Repeat Step 2 to add the **City** field to the row drop area, the **InvoicePaid** field to the column drop area, and the **InvoiceAmt** field to the detail drop area. The four selected fields are bold in the PivotTable Field List pane and appear as components in the PivotTable. See Figure 8-29.

| Figure 8-29 | After adding the four fields to the PivotTable |

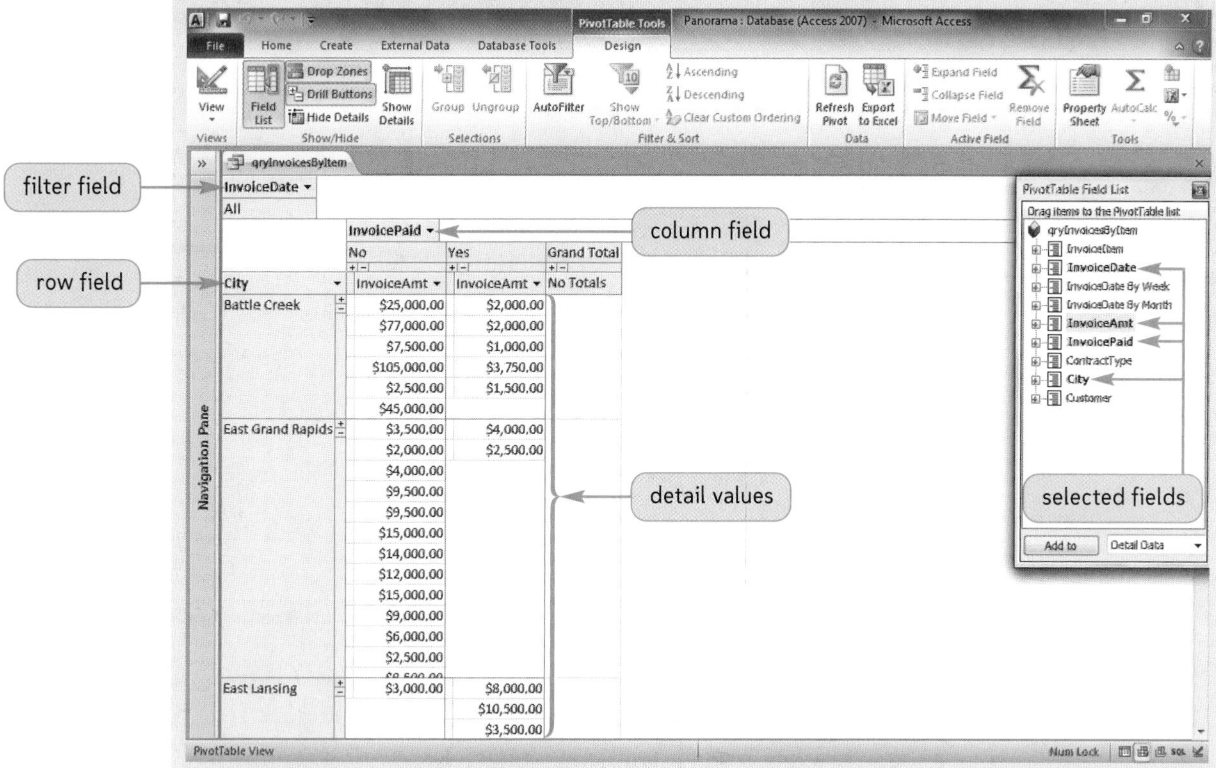

The PivotTable displays all the InvoiceAmt field values from the source query organized by city and invoice status (unpaid or paid).

4. Close the PivotTable Field List pane.

Sarah can filter the PivotTable using one or more of the four selected fields. She can also add total fields and hide the detail values in the PivotTable.

Filtering and Summarizing Data in a PivotTable

A **total field** summarizes values from a source field. For example, Sarah can add subtotals and a grand total of the InvoiceAmt field values to the PivotTable. You'll show Sarah how to filter data in the PivotTable and how to add subtotals by city and a grand total for the InvoiceAmt field values.

To filter data and add a total field in a PivotTable:

1. Click the **City** arrow, click the **All** check box to clear all the selections, click the **East Lansing** check box, click the **Lansing** check box, click the **Rockford** check box, and then click the **OK** button. Access applies the City filter and displays total invoice amounts for the three selected cities. See Figure 8-30.

TIP

You've applied a filter to the row field. In a similar way, you can apply filters to the column, filter, and detail fields.

Figure 8-30 Filtering data for three cities

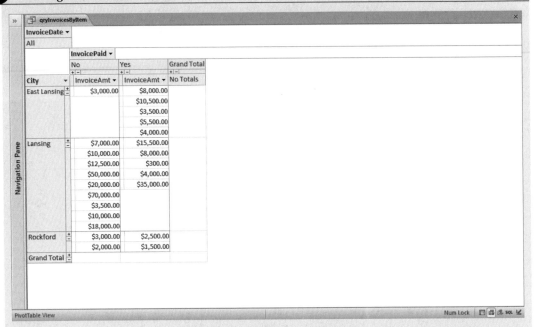

The applied City filter displays all the InvoiceAmt field values from the source query for the cities of East Lansing, Lansing, and Rockford.

2. Click one of the **InvoiceAmt** column heading labels to select the InvoiceAmt columns in the PivotTable; in the Tools group on the Design tab, click the **AutoCalc** button, click **Sum**, and then click to the right of the PivotTable to deselect all values. Access adds a new row for each city in the PivotTable that displays the city's InvoiceAmt total and a new row at the bottom of the PivotTable that displays the grand total for the displayed InvoiceAmt values. See Figure 8-31.

| Figure 8-31 | After adding the total field to the PivotTable |

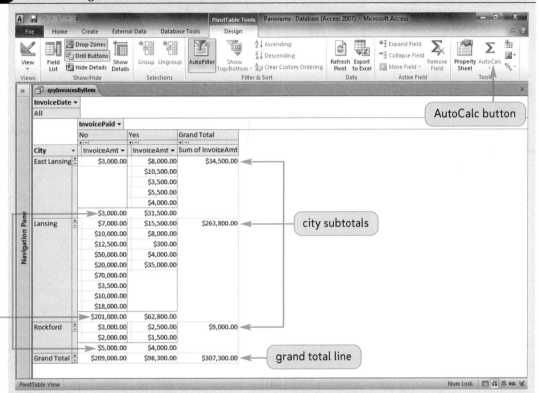

city subtotals

AutoCalc button

grand total line

total field rows displaying subtotals by city of unpaid and paid invoices

3. In the Show/Hide group on the Design tab, click the **Hide Details** button. Access hides the detail lines and displays only the subtotal and grand total lines in the PivotTable. See Figure 8-32.

| Figure 8-32 | Subtotals and grand totals displayed in the PivotTable |

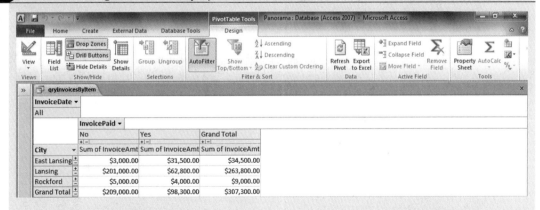

4. In the Show/Hide group on the Design tab, click the **Show Details** button. Access shows the detail lines and the subtotal and grand total lines in the PivotTable for the cities of East Lansing, Lansing, and Rockford.

Sarah asks if you can display the filtered PivotTable data in a chart. You'll switch to PivotChart view to satisfy Sarah's request.

Creating a PivotChart

Office 2010 provides the **Office PivotChart Component** to assist you in adding a chart to a table or query. Using the Office PivotChart Component, you can create a PivotChart, an interactive chart that provides capabilities similar to a PivotTable. You can open a table or query, switch to PivotChart view, add fields to the PivotChart's drop areas, just as you did when you created the PivotTable, and then filter the data in the PivotChart. See the Session 8.2 Visual Overview for an example of a filtered PivotChart. When you create a PivotChart, you can switch to PivotTable view to view and further filter the charted data in a PivotTable. Likewise, after creating a PivotTable, you can switch to PivotChart view to view and further filter the tabular data in a PivotChart.

You'll switch to PivotChart view to show Sarah the PivotChart of the PivotTable data.

To switch to PivotChart view:

▶ 1. Right-click the **qryInvoicesByItem** tab, click **PivotChart View** on the shortcut menu to switch to PivotChart view, close the Chart Field List (if necessary), and then in the Show/Hide group, click the **Legend** button to display the legend. See the Session 8.2 Visual Overview to become familiar with the contents of the PivotChart for the qryInvoicesByItem query.

Next, you'll show Sarah how to modify the PivotChart. First, Sarah wants to change the City filter to display data for Grand Rapids, Holland, Kalamazoo, and Lansing.

To modify the PivotChart:

▶ 1. Click the **City** arrow, click the **East Lansing** check box to clear it, click the **Rockford** check box to clear it, click the **Grand Rapids** check box to select it, click the **Holland** check box to select it, click the **Kalamazoo** check box to select it, and then click the **OK** button. Access applies the City filter, displays total invoice amounts for the four selected cities, and changes the scale of the horizontal axis and its value axis labels. See Figure 8-33.

Figure 8-33   After changing the City filter

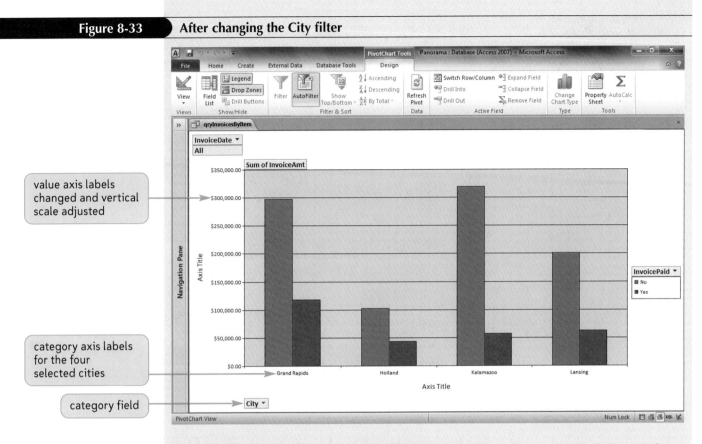

value axis labels changed and vertical scale adjusted

category axis labels for the four selected cities

category field

Sarah wants to change the PivotChart from a column chart to a bar chart, and she wants to change the colors of the data markers.

2. Click in the white portion of the chart (if necessary) to deselect any chart control, and then in the Type group on the Design tab, click the **Change Chart Type** button, click **Bar** in the left list, and then click the **Stacked Bar** chart (row 1, column 2) in the right list. The chart changes from a clustered column chart to a stacked bar chart.

3. In the chart, click the red data marker for Grand Rapids, hold down the **Shift** key, click the red data marker for Grand Rapids a second time, and then release the **Shift** key. All red data markers are now selected, and any property change you make in the Properties dialog box will apply to all four red data markers.

4. Click the **Border/Fill** tab in the Properties dialog box, click the **Fill Color** button, and then click the **DodgerBlue** color (row 3, column 4) in the color palette. The four selected data markers change to the selected DodgerBlue color. See Figure 8-34.

5. Repeat Steps 3 and 4, selecting the other four data markers (the leftmost data marker in each set), and clicking the **Tomato** color (row 8, column 13), and then click the **Fill Color** button to display the color palette. The four selected data markers change to the Tomato color. See Figure 8-34.

Figure 8-34   **After changing the chart type and data marker colors**

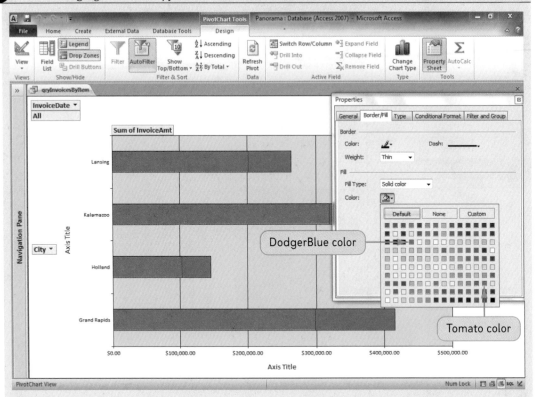

> **6.** Close the Properties dialog box, save your PivotTable and PivotChart changes, and then close the query.

> **7.** Open the Navigation Pane, open the **qryInvoicesByItem** query datasheet to display the 172 records in the query, switch to PivotChart view to display the saved PivotChart, switch to PivotTable view to display the saved PivotTable, and then close the query.

Sarah's staff mainatins an Excel workbook that tracks the products Belmont Landscapes has used for its landscaping projects. Sarah want to use the product data in the Panorama database.

Linking Data from an Excel Worksheet

Sarah's staff has extensive experience working with Excel and prefers to maintain the landscaping product data in the Products workbook using Excel. However, Sarah needs to reference the product data in the Panorama database, and the data she's referencing must always be the current version of the worksheet data. Importing the Excel workbook data as an Access table would provide Sarah with data that's quickly out of date unless she repeats the import steps each time the data in the Excel workbook changes. Because Sarah doesn't need to update the product data in the Panorama database, you'll link to the workbook from the database. When the staff changes the Products workbook, the changes will be reflected automatically in the linked version of the database table. At the same time, Sarah won't be able to update the product data from the Panorama database, which ensures that only the staff members responsible for maintaing the workbook can update the data.

You'll now link to the data in the workbook.

To link to the data in the Excel workbook:

1. Click the **External Data** tab on the Ribbon, and then in the Import & Link group, click the **Excel** button (with the ScreenTip "Import Excel spreadsheet"). The Get External Data - Excel Spreadsheet dialog box opens.

2. Click the **Browse** button, navigate to the **Access2\Tutorial** folder, click **Products**, click the **Open** button, and then click the **Link to the data source by creating a linked table** option button. The selected path and filename now appear in the File name box, and you've set the option to link to the data instead of importing or appending the data. See Figure 8-35.

Figure 8-35	Linking to data in an Excel workbook

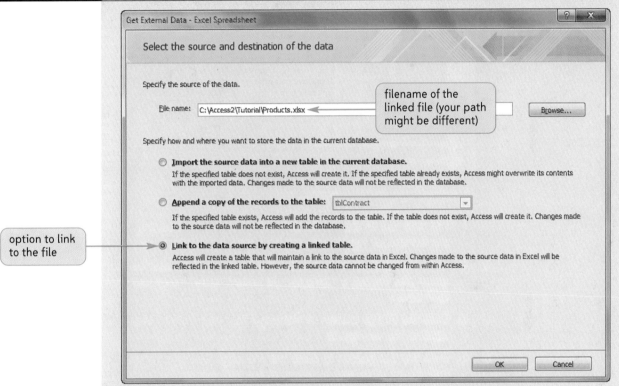

3. Click the **OK** button. The Link Spreadsheet Wizard dialog box opens. See Figure 8-36.

Figure 8-36	Linking to data in an Excel worksheet

checked box will use the first row in the worksheet as column heading names

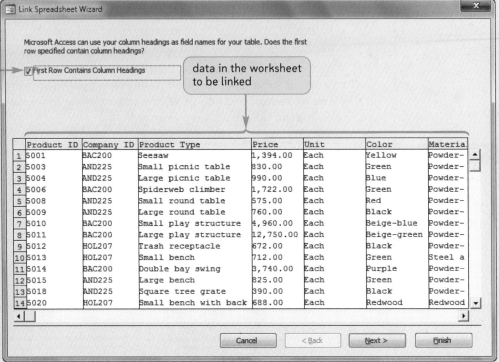

data in the worksheet to be linked

The first row in the worksheet contains column heading names, and each row in the worksheet represents the data about a single product.

4. Click the **Next** button to open the final Link Spreadsheet Wizard dialog box, in which you choose a name for the linked table. You'll use the default table name tblProduct.

5. Click the **Finish** button. A message box informs you that you've created a linking table to the workbook.

6. Click the **OK** button to close the message box and complete the linking steps. The tblProduct table now appears in the Navigation Pane. The icon to the left of the table name 🔗 identifies the table as a linked table.

You can open and view the tblProduct table and use fields from the linked table in queries, forms, and reports, but you can't update the products data using the Panorama database. You can update the products data only from the Excel workbook.

Next, you'll show Sarah how the workbook and the linked table interact.

To update the Excel workbook and view the data in the linked table:

1. Open Windows Explorer, navigate to and open the **Access2\Tutorial** folder, right-click **Products**, and then open the file using **Microsoft Excel**. The Products workbook opens and displays the tblProduct worksheet.

   Trouble? If you attempt to open the table in Access before you open the workbook in Excel, you'll get an error message and won't be able to open the workbook. Make sure you always open the workbook or other source file before you open a linked table.

▶ **2.** Click the **Microsoft Access** program button on the taskbar to switch to the Panorama database, and then open the **tblProduct** datasheet. The fields and records in the tblProduct table display the same data as the tblProduct worksheet.

▶ **3.** Select **Yellow** in the first record's Color column, and then type **G**. A warning sound chimes, the message "This Recordset is not updateable" is displayed on the status bar, and the value is not changed.

   Trouble? The Yellow value might change to another color value. Don't be concerned because this is a temporary aberration.

▶ **4.** Click the **Microsoft Excel** program button on the taskbar to switch to the Products workbook, select **Yellow** in cell F2, type **Green**, and then press the **Enter** key. The value in cell F2 changes from Yellow to Green.

▶ **5.** Click the **Microsoft Access** program button on the taskbar to switch to the Panorama database. The first row's Color field value is now Green because this is the updated value in the worksheet.

   When the Excel workbook and the linked Access table are open at the same time, you must first close the linked table in Access before closing the Excel workbook, or Access will display error values in the linked file.

   You've completed your work for Sarah and her staff.

▶ **6.** Close the tblProduct table in Access.

▶ **7.** Click the **Microsoft Excel** program button on the taskbar to switch to the Products workbook, save your worksheet change, and then exit Excel.

▶ **8.** Make a backup copy of the database, compact and repair the Panorama database, and then close the database.

Knowing how to create charts, PivotTables, and PivotCharts and how to link to data maintained by other programs will make it easier for Sarah and her staff to anlayze their operations and to work efficiently in managing data.

REVIEW

Session 8.2 Quick Check

1. The _____ property lets you change the default navigation label from the word "Record" to another value.

2. When you use the Microsoft Graph program to create and change charts in a form or report, you must _____ the chart.

3. What is a PivotTable?

4. Within a PivotTable you can choose fields from the field list to be a column field, a row field, a detail field, or a(n) _____ field.

5. In a PivotChart, the _____ field identifies which values are shown as value axis labels.

6. You can show or hide a legend for the _____ field in a PivotChart.

Practice the skills you learned in the tutorial to integrate data.

PRACTICE

Review Assignments

Data Files needed for the Review Assignments: Ads.xlsx, BelmName.gif, BelmTemp.htm, Payables.csv, Payments.xml, and Products.accdb (*cont. from Tutorial 7*)

Sarah wants you to integrate the data in the Products database with other programs and she wants to be able to analyze the data in the database. You'll help her achieve these goals by completing the following steps:

1. Open the **Products** database located in the Access2\Review folder provided with your Data Files.

2. Export the qryCompanyList query as an HTML document to the Access2\Review folder, using the HTML template file named BelmTemp, which is located in the Access2\Review folder, and saving the file as **Company**. Do not save the export steps.

3. Import the CSV file named Payables, which is located in the Access2\Review folder, as a new table in the database. Use the names in the first row as field names, use Currency as the data type for the numeric fields, choose your own primary key, name the table **tblPayable**, run the Table Analyzer, and record the Table Analyzer's recommendation. Do not save the import steps.

4. Import the data and structure from the XML file named Payments, which is located in the Access2\Review folder, as a new table named **tblPayments** in the database. Save the import steps, and then rename the table **tblPayment**.

5. Export the tblCompany table as an XML file named **Company** to the Access2\Review folder; do not create a separate XSD file. Save the export steps.

6. Link to the Ads workbook, which is located in the Access2\Review folder, using **tblAd** as the table name. Change the cost of the flyer for Ad Num 5 to **$300** and save the workbook.

7. Modify the **frmCompaniesWithProducts** form in the following ways:
   a. Add a tab control to the bottom of the Detail section, and place the existing subform on the first page of the tab control.
   b. Change the caption for the left tab to **Product Data** and for the right tab to **Product Chart**.
   c. Change the caption for the main form's navigation buttons to **Company** and for the subform's navigation buttons to **Product**.
   d. Add a chart to the second page of the tab control. Use the tblProduct table as the record source, select the ProductType, Price, and Unit fields, use the 3-D Column Chart type, include a legend, and use **Products Offered** as the chart title.
   e. Change the chart to a Clustered Column chart, and change the blue colored data markers to pink.

8. Open the **tblPayment** table and create a PivotTable with PaymentAmt as the detail field, PaymentDate as the column field, CompanyID as the row field, and PaymentID as the filter field. Add subtotals and a grand total for the PaymentAmt field values.

9. Switch to PivotChart view. Filter the CompanyID field, selecting BAC200, BEL273, and CHE802, make sure the legend is displayed, and then save the table.

10. Make a backup copy of the database, compact and repair the Products database, and then close the database.

Apply the skills you learned in the tutorial to integrate data.

APPLY

Case Problem 1

Data Files needed for this Case Problem: Contract.accdb (*cont. from Tutorial 7*), **Instrument.csv, and Room.xlsx**

Pine Hill Music School   Yuka wants you to integrate the data in the Contract database with other programs, and she wants to be able to analyze the data in the database. You'll help her achieve these goals by completing the following steps:

1. Open the **Contract** database located in the Access2\Case1 folder provided with your Data Files.

✪ EXPLORE

2. Export the rptTeacherLessons report as an HTML document with a filename of **Less** to the Access2\Case1 folder; do not use a template or save the export steps. Use your Web browser to open the **Less** HTML document. Then scroll to the bottom of the page; use the First, Previous, Next, and Last links to navigate through the document.

3. Import the CSV file named Instrument, which is located in the Access2\Case1 folder, as a new table in the database. Use the names in the first row as field names, set the third column's data type to Currency and the other fields' data type to Text, choose your own primary key, name the table **tblInstrument**, run the Table Analyzer, and record the Table Analyzer's recommendation, but do not accept the recommendation. Do not save the import steps.

4. Export the tblTeacher table as an XML file named **Teacher** to the Access2\Case1 folder; do not create a separate XSD file. Save the export steps.

5. Link to the Room workbook, which is located in the Access2\Case1 folder, using **tblRoom** as the table name. Add a new record to the Room workbook as follows: Room Num **5**, Rental Cost **$25**, and Type **Private**.

6. Open the **qryLessonsByTeacher** query, and create a PivotTable with MonthlyLessonCost as the detail field, LessonType as the column field, LastName as the row field, and LessonLength as the filter field. Filter the LessonType field, selecting Guitar, Piano, and Saxophone. Add subtotals and a grand total for the MonthlyLessonCost field values.

7. Switch to PivotChart view. Display the legend (if necessary), change the color of the Saxophone data markers to yellow, and then save the query.

8. Make a backup copy of the database, compact and repair the Contract database, and then close the database.

Use the skills you learned in the tutorial to integrate data.

APPLY

Case Problem 2

Data Files needed for this Case Problem: CreditCard.xml, ParkName.gif, ParkTemp.htm, Schedule.xlsx, and Training.accdb (*cont. from Tutorial 7*)

Parkhurst Health & Fitness Center   Martha Parkhurst wants you to integrate the data in the Training database with other programs, and she wants to be able to analyze the data in the database. You'll help her achieve these goals by completing the following steps:

1. Open the **Training** database located in the Access2\Case2 folder provided with your Data Files.

2. Export the qryPhysicalsNeeded query as an HTML document to the Access2\Case2 folder using a filename of **Physicals** and using the HTML template file named ParkTemp, which is located in the Access2\Case2 folder. Save the export steps.

⊕**EXPLORE**

3. Export the rptProgramMembership report as an HTML document with a filename of **Program** to the Access2\Case2 folder; do not use a template or save the export steps. Use your Web browser to open the **Program** HTML document. Then scroll to the bottom of the page; use the First, Previous, Next, and Last links to navigate through the document.

4. Import the the data and structure from the XML file named CreditCard, which is located in the Access2\Case2 folder, as a new table. Rename the table as **tblCreditCard**. Save the import steps.

5. Export the tblProgram table as an XML file named **Program** to the Access2\Case2 folder; do not create a separate XSD file. Save the export steps.

6. Link to the Schedule workbook, which is located in the Access2\Case2 folder, using **tblSchedule** as the table name. For ClassID 301, change the ClassDay value to **F**.

7. Modify the **frmProgramsAndMembers** form in the following ways:

   a. Add a tab control to the bottom of the Detail section, and place the existing subform on the first page of the tab control.

   b. Change the caption for the left tab to **Member Data** and for the right tab to **Member Chart**.

   c. Change the caption for the main form's navigation buttons to **Program** and for the subform's navigation buttons to **Member**.

   d. Add a chart to the second page of the tab control. Use the tblMember table as the record source, select the ProgramID and MembershipStatus fields, use the Column Chart chart type, include a legend, and use **Membership Status** as the chart title.

   e. Change the color of the right data marker (or the middle data marker, depending on whether you see two or three data markers) to red.

8. Open the **qryMonthlyFeeStatus** query and create a PivotTable with MonthlyFee as the detail field, MonthlyFeeStatus as the column field, LastName as the row field, and ProgramType as the filter field. Add subtotals and a grand total of the MonthlyFee values, hide the details, and filter the ProgramType field to display only programs for juniors.

9. Switch to PivotChart view for the qryMonthlyFeeStatus query. Change the chart type to Clustered Bar, display the legend, change the data markers to colors of your choice, and then save the query.

10. Make a backup copy of the database, compact and repair the Training database, and then close the database.

Use the skills you learned in the tutorial to integrate data.

CHALLENGE

Case Problem 3

Data Files needed for this Case Problem: Agency.accdb (*cont. from Tutorial 7*) and Facility.csv

Rossi Recycling Group   Mary Rossi wants you to integrate the data in the Agency database with other programs, and she wants to be able to analyze the data in the database. You'll help her achieve these goals by completing the following steps:

1. Open the **Agency** database located in the Access2\Case3 folder provided with your Data Files.

2. Export the qryNetDonationsCrosstab query as an HTML document named **Crosstab** to the Access2\Case3 folder; do not use a template. Save the export steps.

⊕**EXPLORE**

3. Export the frmDonation form as an HTML document named **Donation** to the Access2\Case3 folder; do not use a template or save the export steps. Use your Web browser to open the HTML document and review its contents.

⊕ **EXPLORE**

4. Import the CSV file named Facility, which is located in the Access2\Case3 folder, as a new table in the database. Use the Text data type for all fields, choose your own primary key, name the table **tblTemporary**, and run the Table Analyzer. Accept the Table Analyzer's recommendations, rename the tables as **tblStorage** and **tblFacility**, make sure each table has the correct primary key, and let the Table Analzyer create a query. Do not save the import steps. Review the tblTemporary query, review the tblTemporary table (it might be named tblTemporary_OLD), and then review the tblStorage and tblFacility tables.

5. Export the tblDonation table as an XML file named **Donation** to the Access2\Case3 folder; do not create a separate XSD file. Save the export steps.

6. Modify the **frmDonorDonations** form in the following ways:

   a. Add a tab control to the bottom of the Detail section, and place the existing sub-form on the first page of the tab control.

   b. Change the caption for the left tab to **Donation Data** and for the right tab to **Donation Chart**.

   c. Change the caption for the main form's navigation buttons to **Donor** and for the subform's navigation buttons to **Donation**.

   d. Add a chart to the second page of the tab control. Use the tblDonation table as the record source; select the AgencyID, DonationValue, PickupRequired, and DonationDate fields; use the 3-D Column Chart type; include a legend; and use **Donations by Agency** as the chart title.

   e. Change the chart to a Clustered Bar chart, and change the color of the maroon data marker to red.

7. Open the **qryNetDonations** query and create a PivotTable with NetDonation as the data field, AgencyName as the column field, DonationDesc as the row field, and PickupRequired as the filter field. Filter the DonationDesc field to display only cash donations.

8. Switch to PivotChart view. Filter the AgencyName by removing the first five agencies, leaving the data for five agencies in the chart, display the legend, change the chart type to Clustered Bar, and then save the query.

9. Make a backup copy of the database, compact and repair the Agency database, and then close the database.

Use the skills you learned in the tutorial to analyze data.

C R E A T E

Case Problem 4

Data Files needed for this Case Problem: Personnel.xlsx, Vacation.accdb (*cont. from Tutorial 7*), **and Works.xml**

GEM Ultimate Vacations   Griffin and Emma MacElroy want you to integrate the data in the Vacation database with other programs, and they want to be able to analyze the data in the database. You'll help them achieve these goals by completing the following steps:

1. Open the **Vacation** database located in the Access2\Case4 folder provided with your Data Files.

2. Export the qryPropertiesByRate query as an HTML document named **Property** to the Access2\Case4 folder; do not use a template. Save the export steps.

3. Import the data and structure from the XML file named Works, which is located in the Access2\Case4 folder, as a new table in the database. Rename the table as **tblWork**. Save the import steps.

4. Export the qryPropertyReservations query as an XML file named **Property** to the Access2\Case4 folder; do not create a separate XSD file. Do not save the export steps.

5. Link to the Personnel workbook, which is located in the Access2\Case4 folder, using **tblPersonnel** as the table name. Change the name in the fourth record from Edward Leary to **Marie Leary**.

6. Modify the **frmGuestsWithReservations** form in the following ways:

   a. Add a tab control to the bottom of the Detail section, and place the existing subform on the first page of the tab control.

   b. Change the caption for the left tab to **Reservation Data** and for the right tab to **Reservation Chart**.

   c. Change the caption for the main form's navigation buttons to **Guest** and for the subform's navigation buttons to **Reservation**.

   d. Add a chart to the second page of the tab control. Use the tblReservation table as the record source, select the StartDate, PropertyID, and RentalRate fields, use the Column Chart chart type, include a legend, and use **Reservations** as the chart title.

⊕ EXPLORE 7. Open the **qryGuestsAndReservations** query, and create a PivotTable with RentalRate as the detail field, StateProv as the column field, the Quarters component of the StartDate By Month entry in the PivotTable Field List as the row field, and PropertyID as the filter field. Add subtotals and a grand total of the RentalRate field, and then hide the details.

8. Switch to PivotChart view. Display the legend, change the green color to yellow, and then save the query.

9. Make a backup copy of the database, compact and repair the Vacation database, and then close the database.

Use the skills you learned in this tutorial to integrate data.

C R E A T E

Case Problem 5

Data File needed for this Case Problem: ACE.accdb (*cont. from Tutorial 7*)

Always Connected Everyday   Chris and Pat Aquino want you to integrate the data in the ACE database with other programs, and they want to be able to analyze the data in the database. You'll help them achieve these goals by completing the following steps:

1. Open the **ACE** database located in the Access2\Case5 folder provided with your Data Files.

2. Export the tblAccessPlan table as an HTML document named **Plan** to the Access2\Case5 folder; do not use a template or save the import steps.

⊕ EXPLORE 3. Export the rptAccessPlanCustomers report as an HTML document named **Customers** to the Access2\Case5 folder; do not use a template or save the export steps. Use your Web browser to open and review the HTML document.

4. Export the tblCustomer table as an XML file named **Customer** to the Access2\Case5 folder; do not create a separate XSD file. Save the export steps.

5. Modify one of the existing forms or create a new form so that the form uses a tab control. Change the caption for the navigation buttons, and set the captions for the tab labels.

6. For one of the existing queries (or a new query you create), create a PivotTable, add subtotals and a grand total, apply a filter, and hide details. In PivotChart view, display the legend and make any other appropriate changes.

7. Make a backup copy of the database, compact and repair the ACE database, and then close the database.

SAM: Skills Assessment Manager

For current SAM information, including versions and content details, visit SAM Central (http://samcentral.course.com). If you have a SAM user profile, you may have access to hands-on instruction, practice, and assessment of the skills covered in this tutorial. Since various versions of SAM are supported throughout the life of this text, check with your instructor for the correct instructions and URL/Web site for accessing assignments.

ENDING DATA FILES

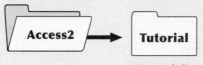

Tutorial

Crosstab.html
Invoice.xml
Panorama.accdb
Products.xlsx

Review

Ads.xlsx
Company.html
Company.xml
Products.accdb

Case1

Contract.accdb
Less.html
LessPage2.html
LessPage3.html
Room.xlsx
Teacher.xml

Case2

Physicals.html
Program.html
ProgramPage2.html
ProgramPage3.html
Program.xml
Schedule.xlsx
Training.accdb

Case3

Agency.accdb
Crosstab.html
Donation.html
Donation.xml

Case4

Personnel.xlsx
Property.html
Property.xml
Vacation.accdb

Case5

ACE.accdb
Customer.xml
Customers.html
CustomersPage2.html
Plan.html

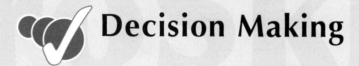

Decision Making

Deciding When to Create a Personal Database

Decision making is a process of choosing between alternative courses of action. When you make decisions, you normally follow these steps:

1. Gather information relevant to the decision
2. Consider viable alternatives
3. Select the best alternative
4. Prepare an implementation action plan
5. Take action and monitor results
6. Verify the accuracy of the decision

For some decisions, you might combine some steps, and you might even skip steps for the simplest decisions.

Gathering Information, Considering Alternatives, and Selecting the Best Alternative

To complete this ProSkills exercise, you'll create a personal database with any content of your choice. To get you started, however, you'll follow through the decision-making steps in creating a sample database. For example, you might now, or in the future, be charged with tracking volunteers and their jobs for a service organization or other entity that requires coordination of a large group of people. The first step in decision making—gathering relevant information—starts with the choice of how to organize the people and their jobs. For example, if your information shows that each person completes only one job, few people are involved in the process, and volunteers all report to the same coordinator, then you could use a Word document or an Excel workbook to manage the volunteers and their jobs. Documents and workbooks are easy to use for most people and can store the data you need in a useful and efficient format.

However, what if your information shows a very large number of volunteers, and many volunteers work in multiple jobs and report to more than one coordinator? Consider the efforts of a volunteer coordinator for parents who volunteer at a local elementary school. Some parents volunteer their time in multiple classrooms (one classroom for each of their children); others volunteer as needed in ways that contribute to fundraising efforts, leadership, and special events such as school plays or concerts. When the relevant information changes so that one parent is no longer completing only one job and no longer reporting to a single coordinator, managing the data in a Word document or Excel workbook becomes problematic—having multiple worksheets or documents to list all of the volunteers, jobs, and coordinators is almost guaranteed to result in problems related to data redundancy, data anomalies, and errors.

When making the decision to use a database to manage your data, at first you might find that some data exists in another format, such as in an Excel workbook. After considering the data that you have already collected (such as in a workbook) or data that you will collect in the future, consider the types of decisions you need to make. These decisions might include determining whether a database will effectively and efficiently manage your data, deciding which DBMS you will use, and evaluating the ability of users to manage and use the database to get the information they need. These decisions usually have an immediate impact—the decision to use a DBMS has an upfront cost, requires someone with knowledge of database development and the selected DBMS to create it, and involves training users to access the database. It's also important to consider the long-term impact of your decision, such as whether future volunteer coordinators will have the ability and interest to continue using the DBMS you selected. In other words, part of the decision-making process needs to consider the impact of your decision both now and in the future. Being able to predict an organization's short-term and long-term needs can be difficult, but it's important to consider many possible outcomes when making your decision.

Preparing an Implementation Action Plan

Once you have made the choice to use a DBMS, determine the steps you need to take to design and create the database. The first step is to analyze the data you have collected or will collect and start compiling it into tables. Then, you can begin identifying the primary and foreign keys in the tables to create the relationships between those tables. Finally, you can determine the field properties in anticipation of making data entry easier and reducing the likelihood of errors. For example, you might use the Default Value property to enter a city or state field value if all of your volunteers reside in the same geographic area, or use the AutoNumber data type to assign a primary key value to a table automatically when there is no natural primary key available.

Taking Action and Monitoring Results

The next step in decision making involves implementation, which includes creating the database, defining the tables, and entering the data. After designing and installing the database, you need to make decisions about the types of queries, forms, and reports to create to produce the data in the format that users need. After implementation, you should make decisions about how the database will be updated so it remains current and ready for any future decisions you need to make.

Verifying the Accuracy of the Decision

At the end of your decision-making process, review your steps and evaluate how well they worked. Did you discover data you wish you had originally collected and stored in the database, but didn't have available? How did that limitation affect your ability to make a good decision? What changes do you need to make to your database so that it will provide better information for future decisions? As you review your decisions, be sure to document any changes you need to make to enhance or reorganize the database so it provides greater usefulness for future decisions.

PROSKILLS

Create a Personal Database

Most businesses use databases for decision making, and you can also use databases to track data in your personal life. Examples of personal database use include tracking personal collections, such as songs or books; hobby data, such as crafts or antiques; or items related to sports teams, theater clubs, or other organizations to which you might belong. In this exercise, you'll use Access to create a database that will contain information of your choice, using the Access skills and features you've learned in these tutorials.

Note: Please be sure *not* to include any personal information of a sensitive nature in the database you create to be submitted to your instructor for this exercise. Later on, you can update the data in your database with such information for your own personal use.

1. Consider your personal interests and activities, school-related functions, and work-related duties, and select from them one set of requirements that includes data that is best tracked using a DBMS. (If you completed Tutorials 1-4 of this book and the ProSkills Exercise at the end of Tutorial 4, you can use and enhance the database you've already created, and you can skip this step and the next step.) Make sure the data is sufficiently complex that a Word document or Excel workbook would not be viable alternatives to store and manage the data.

2. Create a new Access database to contain the data you want to track. The database must include two or more tables that you can join through one-to-many relationships. Define the properties for each field in each table. Make sure you include a mix of data types for the fields (for example, do not include only Text fields in each table). Specify a primary key for each table, define the table relationships with referential integrity enforced, and enter records in each table.

3. Create queries that include at least the following: pattern query match, list-of-values match, parameter, crosstab, find duplicates, find unmatched, and the use of a conditional value in a calculated field.

4. For one or more fields, apply an input mask and specify field validation rules.

5. Create a split form and modify the form.

6. Create a custom form that uses at least the following: combo box for a lookup, combo box to find records, subform, lines and rectangles, and a tab control. Add one or more calculated controls to the main form based on the subform's calculated control(s), and add a chart, if appropriate. Check the main form's tab order, and improve the form's appearance.

7. Create a custom report that uses at least the following: grouping field, sort field(s), lines, and rectangles. Hide duplicates; and add the date, page numbers, and a report title.

8. Export two or more objects in different formats, and save the step specifications.

9. Create a PivotTable and PivotChart for one of the tables or queries.

10. Designate a trusted folder, make a backup copy of the database, and compact and repair the database.

11. Submit your completed database to your instructor as requested. Include printouts of any database objects, if required. Also, prepare a document that addresses the specific data you selected to store and track and why a DBMS was the best alternative choice.

TUTORIAL **9**

Using Action Queries and Advanced Table Relationships

Enhancing User Interaction with the Holland Database

OBJECTIVES

Session 9.1
- Create an action query to create a table
- Create action queries to append, delete, and update data

Session 9.2
- Define many-to-many and one-to-one relationships between tables
- Learn about joining tables
- Join a table using a self-join
- View and create indexes for tables

Case | *Belmont Landscapes*

After graduating with a university degree in Landscape Architecture and then working for a firm that provides basic landscape services to residential customers, Oren Belmont started his own landscape architecture firm in Holland, Michigan. Belmont Landscapes specializes in landscape designs for residential and commercial customers and numerous public agencies. The firm provides a wide range of services—from site analyses and feasibility studies, to drafting and administering construction documents—for projects of various scales. Oren's company developed the Holland database of customer, contract, invoice, employee, and assignment data; and the employees use Microsoft Access 2010 (or simply Access) to manage it. Lucia Perez, the company's database expert and developer, has been enhancing the Holland database containing tables, queries, forms, and reports that Sarah Fisher, office manager, and Taylor Sico, marketing manager, use to track customers and their landscape projects. Oren, Sarah, and Taylor have asked you to continue enhancing the database by creating some advanced queries and integrating more tables into the database.

STARTING DATA FILES

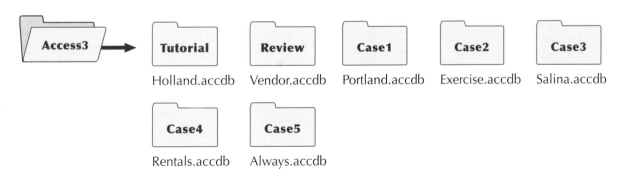

Access3 → Tutorial — Holland.accdb
Review — Vendor.accdb
Case1 — Portland.accdb
Case2 — Exercise.accdb
Case3 — Salina.accdb

Case4 — Rentals.accdb
Case5 — Always.accdb

SESSION 9.1 VISUAL OVERVIEW

The selected Make Table button indicates this query is a **make-table query**, which is an action query that creates a new table by copying records from one or more existing tables.

The design grid for a make-table query contains the same elements as the design grid for a select query.

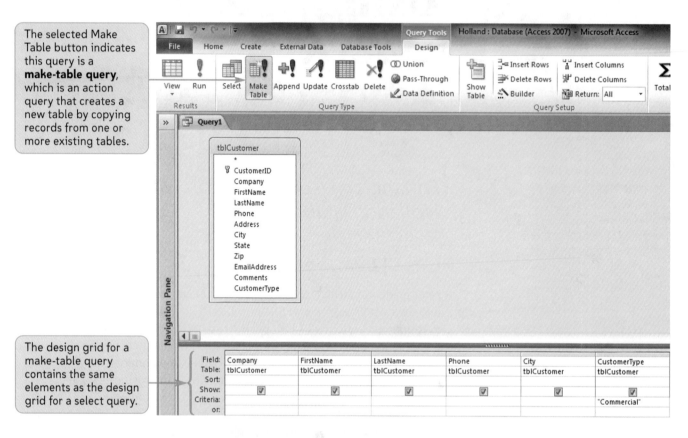

Field:	Company	FirstName	LastName	Phone	City	CustomerType
Table:	tblCustomer	tblCustomer	tblCustomer	tblCustomer	tblCustomer	tblCustomer
Sort:						
Show:	☑	☑	☑	☑	☑	☑
Criteria:						"Commercial"
or:						

The selected Append button indicates this query is an **append query**, which is an action query that adds records from existing tables or queries to the end of another table.

For an append query, the Append To row replaces the Show row. The Append To row identifies the fields that the query will append to the designated table.

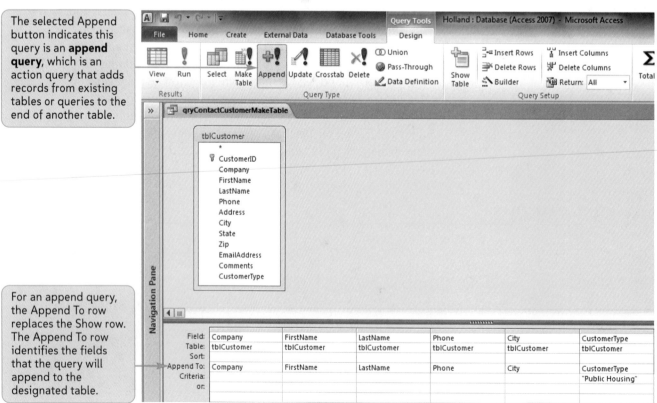

Field:	Company	FirstName	LastName	Phone	City	CustomerType
Table:	tblCustomer	tblCustomer	tblCustomer	tblCustomer	tblCustomer	tblCustomer
Sort:						
Append To:	Company	FirstName	LastName	Phone	City	CustomerType
Criteria:						"Public Housing"
or:						

ACTION QUERIES

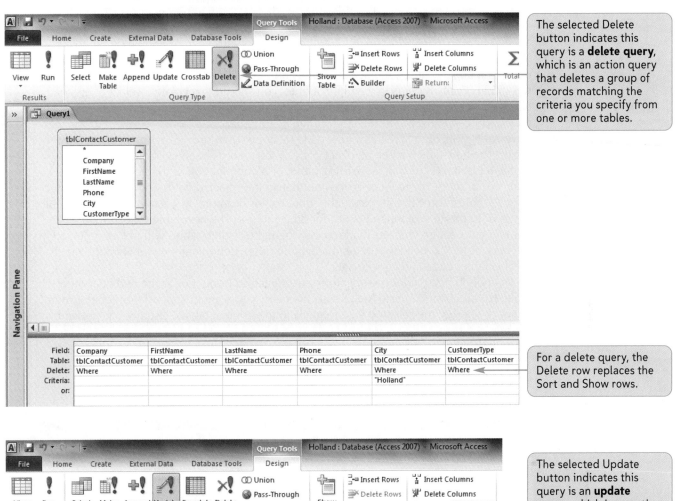

The selected Delete button indicates this query is a **delete query**, which is an action query that deletes a group of records matching the criteria you specify from one or more tables.

For a delete query, the Delete row replaces the Sort and Show rows.

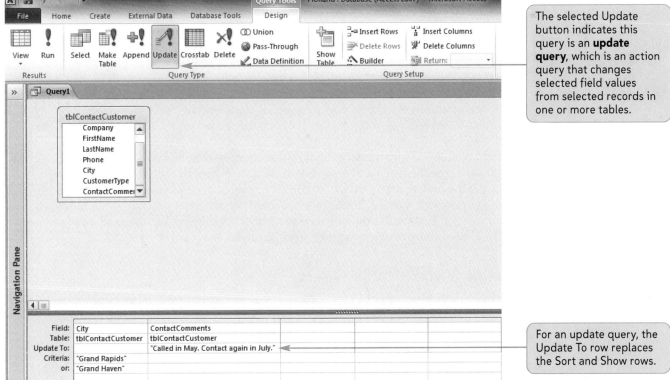

The selected Update button indicates this query is an **update query**, which is an action query that changes selected field values from selected records in one or more tables.

For an update query, the Update To row replaces the Sort and Show rows.

Action Queries

Queries can do more than display answers to the questions you ask; they can also perform actions on the data in the tables in your database. An **action query** is a query that adds, changes, or deletes multiple table records at a time. For example, Sarah can use an action query to delete all paid invoices from the previous year. As shown on the Visual Overview for Session 9.1, Access provides four types of action queries: the make-table query, the append query, the delete query, and the update query. Because action queries modify many records in a table at a time, you should first create a select query that chooses the records you need to update. After you confirm that the query works correctly, you can convert it to the appropriate action query.

A make-table query creates a new table by copying records from one or more existing tables. The new table can be an exact copy of the records in an existing table, a subset of the fields and records in an existing table, or a combination of the fields and records from two or more tables. Access does not delete the selected fields and records from the existing tables. You can use make-table queries, for example, to create backup copies of tables or to create customized tables for others to use. The new table reflects data at a point in time; future changes made to the original (existing) tables will not be reflected in the new table. You need to run the make-table query periodically if you want the newly created table to contain current data.

An append query adds records from existing tables or queries to the end of another table. For an append query, you choose the fields you want to append from one or more tables or queries; the selected data remains in the original tables. Usually you append records to history tables. A **history table** contains data that is no longer needed for current processing but that you might need to reference in the future.

A delete query deletes a group of records matching the criteria you specify from one or more tables. You choose which records you want to delete by entering selection criteria. Deleting records removes them permanently from the database.

An update query changes selected field values from selected records in one or more tables. You choose the fields and records you want to change by entering the selection criteria and the update rules. You can use update queries, for example, to increase the salaries of selected employee groups by a specified percentage or to change the billing dates of selected customers from one date to another. Update queries are particularly valuable in performing multiple updates to large tables.

Creating a Make-Table Query

Taylor wants to call all commercial customers. These customers have the largest contracts with Belmont Landscapes, and she wants to contact them to discuss their projects and assess the possibility for further work. She asks you to create a new table containing the Company, FirstName, LastName, Phone, City, and CustomerType fields from the tblCustomer table for all customers whose CustomerType field value is Commercial. She wants to create a new table so she can modify it by adding notes that she will take when she calls the commercial customers. By creating a new table, Taylor won't need to worry about disrupting or changing the data in any existing tables or in any objects on which those existing tables are based.

You can create the new table for Taylor by using a make-table query that uses fields from the tblCustomer table in the Holland database. When you run a make-table query, you create a new table. The records in the new table are based on the records in the query's underlying tables. The fields in the new table will have the data type and field size of the fields in the query's underlying tables. The new table does not preserve the primary key designation or field properties such as the format or lookup properties.

REFERENCE

Creating a Make-Table Query

- Create a select query with the necessary fields and selection criteria.
- In the Results group on the Design tab, click the Run button to preview the results.
- Switch to Design view to make any necessary changes to the query. When the query is correct, click the Make Table button in the Query Type group on the Design tab.
- In the Make Table dialog box, type the new table name in the Table Name box. Make sure the Current Database option button is selected to include the new table in the current database; or, click the Another Database option button and enter the database name in the File Name box. Then click the OK button.
- Click the Run button, and then click the Yes button to confirm the creation of the new table.

Now you can create the new table using a make-table query. You'll base the make-table query on the tblCustomer table to enter the fields and records that Taylor wants in the new table.

To create and run the select query based on the tblCustomer table:

1. Make sure you have created your copy of the Access Data Files, and that your computer can access them.

   Trouble? If you don't have the Access Data Files, you need to get them before you can proceed. Your instructor will either give you the Data Files or ask you to obtain them from a specified location (such as a network drive). In either case, make a backup copy of the Data Files before you start so that you will have the original files available in case you need to start over. If you have any questions about the Data Files, see your instructor or technical support person for assistance.

2. Start Access, open the **Holland** database in the Access3\Tutorial folder provided with your Data Files, and then click the **Enable Content** button next to the Security Warning.

   You can eliminate the Security Warning by designating the Access3\Tutorial folder as a trusted folder.

3. Click the **File** tab on the Ribbon to display Backstage view, and then click **Options** in the navigation bar to open the Access Options dialog box.

4. In the left section of the dialog box, click **Trust Center**, click the **Trust Center Settings** button in the window on the right to open the Trust Center dialog box, and then in the left section, click **Trusted Locations**. The trusted locations for your installation of Access and other trust options are displayed on the right.

   Trouble? Check with your instructor before adding a new trusted location. If your instructor tells you not to create a new trusted location, click the Cancel button, click the Cancel button again, and then skip to Step 6.

5. Click the **Add new location** button to open the Microsoft Office Trusted Location dialog box, click the **Browse** button, navigate to the **Access3\Tutorial** folder where your Data Files are stored, click the **OK** button, click the **OK** button to add the Access3\Tutorial folder to the list of trusted locations, click the **OK** button to close the Trust Center dialog box, and then click the **OK** button to close the Access Options dialog box.

6. Make sure the Navigation Pane is closed, click the **Create** tab on the Ribbon and then, in the Queries group, click the **Query Design** button. Access opens the Show Table dialog box on top of the Query window in Design view.

7. Click **tblCustomer** in the Tables box, click the **Add** button, and then click the **Close** button. Access places the tblCustomer table field list in the Query window and closes the Show Table dialog box.

8. Drag down the bottom of the tblCustomer field list to display all its fields, double-click **Company**, double-click **FirstName**, double-click **LastName**, double-click **Phone**, double-click **City**, and then double-click **CustomerType** to add these six fields to the design grid.

Next, you'll enter the CustomerType field's selection criterion of Commercial.

9. Click the **CustomerType Criteria** box, type **Commercial**, and then press the **Tab** key. The condition changes to "Commercial". See Figure 9-1.

Figure 9-1	Select query on which to base the make-table query

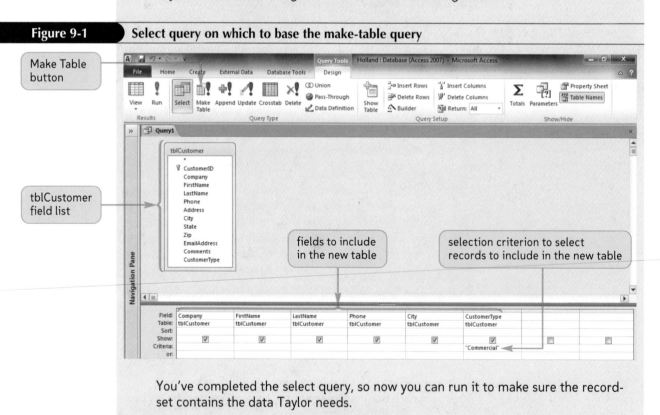

You've completed the select query, so now you can run it to make sure the record-set contains the data Taylor needs.

10. Run the query. The query recordset shows the 14 records for commercial customers.

Now that you have the correct select query, you can change the query to a make-table query.

To change the query type, and then run and save the make-table query:

▶ **1.** Switch to Design view, and then in the Query Type group on the Design tab, click the **Make Table** button. Access opens the Make Table dialog box, in which you enter the name of the new table and designate the database to be used to store the table. See Figure 9-2.

Figure 9-2	Make Table dialog box

enter the new table name here

option to create the new table in the Holland database

option to create the new table in another database

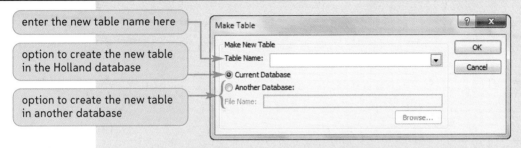

▶ **2** In the Table Name box, type **tblContactCustomer**, make sure the **Current Database** option button is selected so that the new table will be added to the Holland database, and then click the **OK** button.

Now that you have created and tested the query, you can run it to create the tblContactCustomer table. After you run the query, you can save it, and then you can view the new table.

▶ **3.** Run the query. Access opens a dialog box indicating that you are about to paste 14 rows into a new table. Because you are running an action query, which alters the contents of the database, Access gives you the opportunity to cancel the operation, if necessary, or to confirm it.

▶ **4.** Click the **Yes** button. Access closes the dialog box, runs the make-table query to create the tblContactCustomer table and continues displaying the query in Design view.

▶ **5.** Save the query as **qryContactCustomerMakeTable**, close the query, and then open the Navigation Pane. The qryContactCustomerMakeTable query appears in the Queries list with a special icon indicating that it is a make-table query. See Figure 9-3.

| Figure 9-3 | Query type icons in the Navigation Pane |

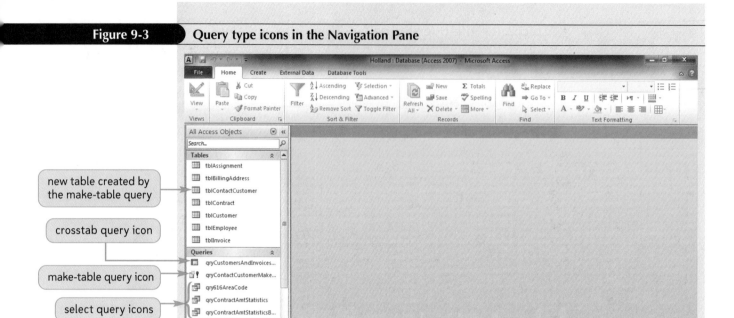

new table created by the make-table query

crosstab query icon

make-table query icon

select query icons

You can now open the tblContactCustomer table to view the results of the make-table query.

6. Open the **tblContactCustomer** table in Datasheet view, resize all datasheet columns to their best fit, and then click the first row's **Company** field value to deselect all values. See Figure 9-4.

| Figure 9-4 | tblContactCustomer table datasheet |

The tblContactCustomer table includes the Company, FirstName, LastName, Phone, City, and CustomerType fields for commercial customers. Make-table queries do not transfer Caption property settings to the created tables. Other field properties that do not transfer include Decimal Places, Default Value, Format, Input Mask, Validation Rule, and Validation Text.

7. Save your datasheet changes, and then close the table.

Taylor can now make any necessary changes to the tblContactCustomer table records when she contacts customers without affecting the tblCustomer table in the Holland database.

Creating an Append Query

Taylor has decided to expand the list of customers that she will call to include public housing customers, which also have large contracts with Belmont Landscapes. She asks you to add these new records to the tblContactCustomer table. You could make this change by modifying the selection criterion in the qryContactCustomerMakeTable query to select customers with CustomerType field values of Public Housing. If you ran this modified query, however, you would overwrite the existing tblContactCustomer table with a new table. If Taylor had made any changes to the existing tblContactCustomer table records, creating a new table would overwrite these changes, as well.

Instead, you will modify the qryContactCustomerMakeTable query to select only public housing customers and change the query to an append query. When you run this new query, the selected records will be appended to the records in the existing tblContactCustomer table.

You can now modify the qryContactCustomerMakeTable query to create the append query you'll use to include the additional customer data Taylor wants in the tblContactCustomer table.

To create the append query:

1. Open the **qryContactCustomerMakeTable** query in Design view, and then close the Navigation Pane.

   You'll change the selection criterion to Public Housing.

2. Click the **CustomerType Criteria** box, press the **F2** key to highlight the entire condition, type **Public Housing**, and then press the ↓ key. The condition changes to "Public Housing". See Figure 9-5.

| Figure 9-5 | Changing the selection criterion |

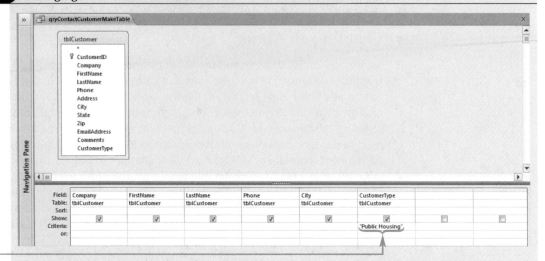

changed condition

Before you can run the query to append the records to the tblContactCustomer table, you have to change the query type to an append query. It is always a good idea to test an action query before you run it, so you will first change the query type to a select query and run it to make sure the correct records are selected. Then you will change the query type to an append query and run it to append the new records to the tblContactCustomer table.

3. In the Query Type group on the Design tab, click the **Select** button.

4. Run the query. The query recordset shows the two records for public housing customers.

These two records are the additional records you will append to the tblContactCustomer table. Now that the results show that the query is correct, you can change the query type to an append query.

5. Switch to Design view, and then in the Query Type group on the Design tab, click the **Append** button. Access opens the Append dialog box, in which you select the name of the new table to which you want to append the data and designate the database to be used to store the table.

6. Make sure **tblContactCustomer** appears in the Table Name box and that the **Current Database** option button is selected, and then click the **OK** button. Access replaces the Show row in the design grid with the Append To row. See the Session 9.1 Visual Overview.

The Append To row in the design grid identifies the fields that the query will append to the designated table. The Company, FirstName, LastName, Phone, City, and CustomerType fields are selected and will be appended to the tblContactCustomer table, which already contains these same six fields for commercial customers.

You can now run and then save the append query.

To run and save the append query:

1. Run the query. Access opens a dialog box warning you that you are about to append two rows.

2. Click the **Yes** button to acknowledge the warning. Access closes the dialog box, runs the append query, adds the two records to the tblContactCustomer table, and continues displaying the Query window in Design view.

3. Click the **File** tab on the Ribbon, and then click **Save Object As** in the navigation bar to open the Save As dialog box.

4. Change the entry in the Save box to **qryContactCustomerAppend**, click the **OK** button, and then click the **Home** tab on the Ribbon. Access saves the query with the new name, which now appears in the Navigation Pane with a special icon that identifies the query as an append query.

5. Close the query.

   Next, you'll open the tblContactCustomer table to make sure that the two records were appended to the table.

6. Open the Navigation Pane, open the **tblContactCustomer** table datasheet, and then click the first row's **Company** field value to deselect all values. See Figure 9-6.

| Figure 9-6 | tblContactCustomer table datasheet after appending records |

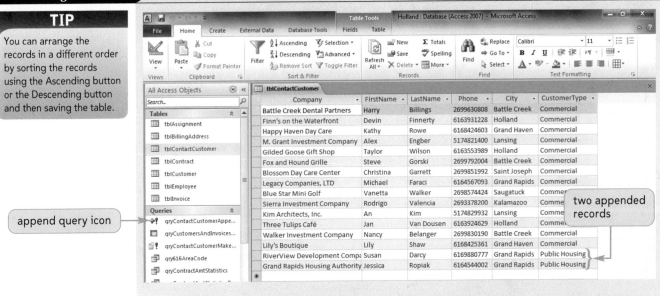

The new records have been added to the tblContactCustomer table. Because the tblContactCustomer table does not have a primary key, the new records appear at the end of the table.

7. Close the table, and then close the Navigation Pane.

Creating a Delete Query

Taylor has contacted all the customers in the tblContactCustomer table that are located in the city of Holland. She asks you to delete these records from the tblContactCustomer table so that the table contains only those records for customers she has not yet contacted. You can either delete the table records individually or create a delete query to remove them all at once.

REFERENCE

Creating a Delete Query

- Create a select query with the necessary fields and selection criteria.
- In the Results group on the Design tab, click the Run button to preview the results.
- Switch to Design view to make any necessary changes to the query. When the query is correct, click the Delete button in the Query Type group on the Design tab. Access replaces the Show and Sort rows in the design grid with the Delete row.
- Click the Run button, and then click the Yes button to confirm deleting the records.

You'll create a delete query to delete the Holland customers in the tblContactCustomer table. First, you'll create a select query to choose the correct records and run the query to verify you're selecting the correct records. Then you'll change the query to a delete query and run it.

To create the delete query:

1. Click the **Create** tab on the Ribbon and then, in the Queries group on the Create tab, click the **Query Design** button, add the **tblContactCustomer** table field list to the Query window, and then close the Show Table dialog box.

2. Double-click the title bar of the tblContactCustomer field list to select all the fields in the table, drag the pointer from the highlighted area of the field list to the design grid's first column Field box, and then release the mouse button. Access adds all the fields to the design grid.

3. Click the **City Criteria** box, type **Holland**, and then press the **Tab** key. Access changes the criterion to "Holland" and will select only the records with a City field value of Holland when you run the query.

4. Run the query, and then click the first row's **Company** field value to deselect all values. The query results display the three records with City field values of Holland. The select query is correct. See Figure 9-7.

| Figure 9-7 | Three records to be deleted |

Trouble? If your query did not select the correct three records, switch to Design view, correct the selection criterion, and then run the query again.

Now that you have verified that the correct records are selected, you can change the query to a delete query.

5. Switch to Design view, and then in the Query Type group on the Design tab, click the **Delete** button. In the design grid, Access replaces the Sort and Show rows with the Delete row. See the Session 9.1 Visual Overview.

6. Run the query. Access opens a dialog box warning that you are about to delete three rows.

7. Click the **Yes** button to close the dialog box and run the delete query. Access deletes the three records in the tblContactCustomer table and continues to display the Query window in Design view. Because you'll need to run this query only once, you won't save it.

8. Close the query, and then click the **No** button when Access asks if you want to save it.

   You can now open the tblContactCustomer table to verify that the records have been deleted.

9. Open the Navigation Pane, open the **tblContactCustomer** table in Datasheet view, and then click the first row's **Company** field value to deselect all values. The table contains 13 records, and the Holland records were correctly deleted. See Figure 9-8.

Figure 9-8	tblContactCustomer table after deleting three records

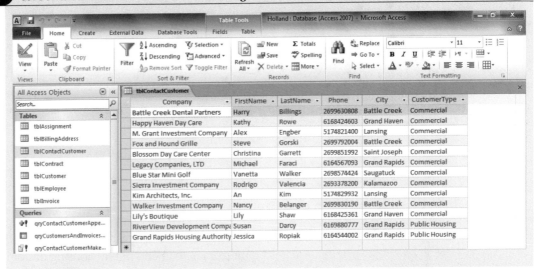

Taylor wants you to add a field named ContactComments to the tblContactCustomer table in which she can keep notes about the calls she makes. You can add the field to the tblContactCustomer table without affecting the objects in the Holland database because the table was created only to meet Taylor's specific need to contact commercial and public housing customers.

To add the new ContactComments field to the tblContactCustomer table:

1. Switch to Design view.

   You'll set the new field's data type to Memo, so that Taylor is not limited to 255 characters of data in the field, which would be the case with the Text data type.

2. Click the **Field Name** box below the CustomerType field, type **ContactComments**, press the **Tab** key, type the letter **m**, and then press the **Tab** key to select the Memo data type.

> **3.** Press the **F6** key to position the insertion point in the Format property in the Field Properties pane, press the **Tab** key, and then type **Contact Comments** in the Caption box. You've completed adding the ContactComments field to the table. See Figure 9-9.

| Figure 9-9 | ContactComments field added to the tblContactCustomer table |

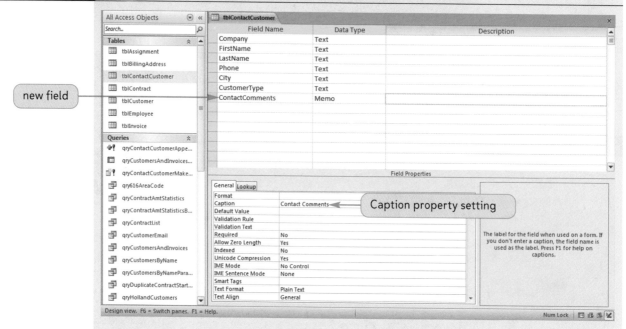

> **4.** Save your table structure changes, close the table, and then close the Navigation Pane.

Taylor has contacted the commercial and public housing customers in Grand Rapids and Grand Haven, and she wants to update the ContactComments field in the tblContactCustomer table with the same comments for all Grand Rapids and Grand Haven records. She could type the comments in the ContactComments field for one of the records, and then copy and paste the comments to the other records. However, performing these steps takes time and could result in updating a wrong record or missing one of the records. Instead, you'll create an update query.

Creating an Update Query

Recall that an update query changes selected field values and records in one or more tables.

REFERENCE

Creating an Update Query

- Create a select query with the necessary fields and selection criteria.
- In the Results group on the Design tab, click the Run button to preview the results.
- Switch to Design view to make any necessary changes to the query. When the query is correct, click the Update button in the Query Type group on the Design tab. Access replaces the Show and Sort rows in the design grid with the Update To row.
- Type the updated values in the Update To boxes for the fields you want to update.
- Click the Run button, and then click the Yes button to confirm changing the records.

Now you can create an update query to update the ContactComments field in the tblContactCustomer table for records with City field values of Grand Haven or Grand Rapids.

To create the update query:

1. Click the **Create** tab and then, in the Queries group, click the **Query Design** button, add the **tblContactCustomer** table field list to the Query window, and then close the Show Table dialog box.

   You will select the City and ContactComments fields for the query results. The City field lets you select records for customers in particular cities. The ContactComments field is the field Taylor needs to update.

2. In the tblContactCustomer field list, double-click the **City** and **ContactComments** to add these fields to the design grid, scrolling down the field list as necessary.

3. Click the **City Criteria** box, type **Grand Rapids**, press the ↓ key, and then type **Grand Haven** in the or box. Access will select a record only if the City field value is Grand Rapids or Grand Haven.

4. Run the query. The query recordset displays five records, each one with a City field value of Grand Rapids or Grand Haven. The select query is correct.

   Now that you have verified that the correct records are selected, you can change the query to an update query.

> **TIP**
>
> For complicated expressions, use Expression Builder. For lengthy expressions, use the Zoom dialog box.

5. Switch to Design view, and then in the Query Type group on the Design tab, click the **Update** button. In the design grid, Access replaces the Sort and Show rows with the Update To row.

   You tell Access how you want to change a field value for the selected records by entering an expression in the field's Update To box. An expression is a calculation resulting in a single value. You can type a simple expression directly into the Update To box.

> **TIP**
>
> For text expressions with quotation marks, you need to type the quotation marks twice. For example, to enter the expression *A "text" expression*, type "A""text"" expression".

6. Click the **ContactComments Update To** box, type **"Called in May. Contact again in July."** (be sure to type the quotation marks), and then drag the right edge of the ContactComments column to the right to display the entire expression value. See the Session 9.1 Visual Overview.

7. Run the query. Access opens a dialog box warning you that you are about to update five rows in the tblContactCustomer table.

8. Click the **Yes** button to close the dialog box and run the update query. Access updates the ContactComments field values for customers in Grand Rapids or Grand Haven and leaves the Query window in Design view open.

   You are finished updating the tblContactCustomer table, so you can close the query without saving it.

9. Close the query, and then click the **No** button when Access asks if you want to save it.

Now you can view the tblContactCustomer table to see the results of the update operation.

To view the updated tblContactCustomer table:

1. Open the Navigation Pane, open the **tblContactCustomer** table in Datasheet view, close the Navigation Pane, resize the **Contact Comments** column to its best fit, and then click the first row's **Company** field value to deselect all values. The ContactComments field values for customers in Grand Rapids or Grand Haven have been updated correctly. See Figure 9-10.

Figure 9-10 **tblContactCustomer table with updated ContactComments field values**

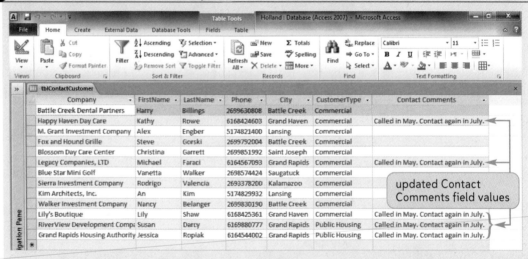

updated Contact Comments field values

2. Save your table datasheet changes, close the table, and then open the Navigation Pane.

PROSKILLS

Decision Making: Deleting Action Queries

You usually create an action query and run it for a special purpose, and in most cases, you need to run the query only once. If you create and run an action query, and then save it, you might accidentally run it again. Doing so would result in the update of tables in unintended ways. Therefore, after you've run an action query, you shouldn't save it in your database to prevent users from running it by mistake.

Because you saved the make-table and append queries after you ran them, you'll delete them now.

To delete the action queries:

▶ **1.** Right-click **qryContactCustomerAppend** in the Queries list, click **Delete** on the shortcut menu, and then click the **Yes** button to confirm the deletion.

   Trouble? The ScreenTip for an action query might display the query name, the type of action query (such as "Append"), plus the name of the table name it affects. The query name is correct as displayed in the Navigation Pane.

▶ **2.** Repeat Step 1 to delete the **qryContactCustomerMakeTable** query.

▶ **3.** If you are not continuing on to the next session, close the Holland database.

Taylor can now use action queries in her future work with the Holland database. In the next session, you'll learn about the different types of relationships you can create between tables, and view and create indexes to increase a database's efficiency.

REVIEW

Session 9.1 Quick Check

1. What is an action query?
2. What precautions should you take before running an action query?
3. What is the difference between a make-table query and an append query?
4. What does a delete query do?
5. What does an update query do?
6. How does the design grid change when you create an update query?

SESSION 9.2 VISUAL OVERVIEW

The tblInvoice table contains one record for each invoice billed for work performed by Belmont Landscapes employees, and is one of the two primary tables in the many-to-many relationship.

The tblAssignment table contains two assignment records for invoice 2612.

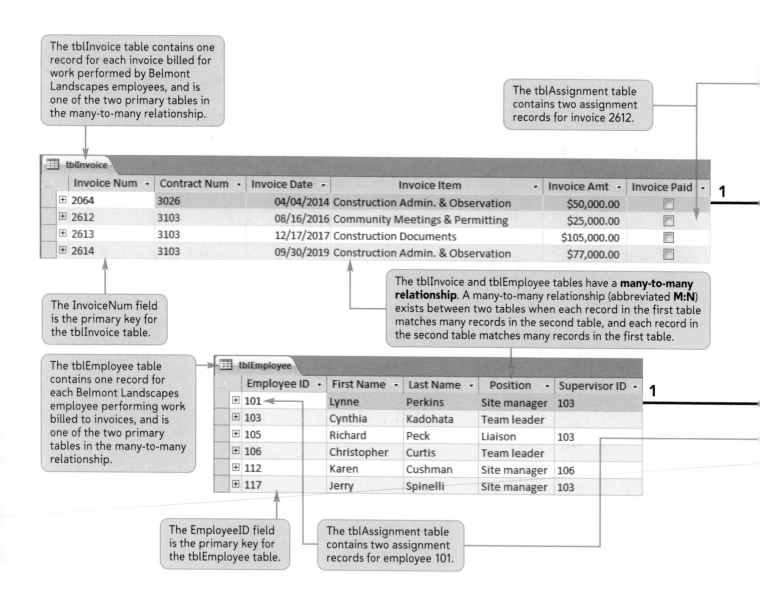

tblInvoice

Invoice Num	Contract Num	Invoice Date	Invoice Item	Invoice Amt	Invoice Paid
⊞ 2064	3026	04/04/2014	Construction Admin. & Observation	$50,000.00	☐
⊞ 2612	3103	08/16/2016	Community Meetings & Permitting	$25,000.00	☐
⊞ 2613	3103	12/17/2017	Construction Documents	$105,000.00	☐
⊞ 2614	3103	09/30/2019	Construction Admin. & Observation	$77,000.00	☐

The InvoiceNum field is the primary key for the tblInvoice table.

The tblInvoice and tblEmployee tables have a **many-to-many relationship**. A many-to-many relationship (abbreviated **M:N**) exists between two tables when each record in the first table matches many records in the second table, and each record in the second table matches many records in the first table.

The tblEmployee table contains one record for each Belmont Landscapes employee performing work billed to invoices, and is one of the two primary tables in the many-to-many relationship.

tblEmployee

Employee ID	First Name	Last Name	Position	Supervisor ID
⊞ 101	Lynne	Perkins	Site manager	103
⊞ 103	Cynthia	Kadohata	Team leader	
⊞ 105	Richard	Peck	Liaison	103
⊞ 106	Christopher	Curtis	Team leader	
⊞ 112	Karen	Cushman	Site manager	106
⊞ 117	Jerry	Spinelli	Site manager	103

The EmployeeID field is the primary key for the tblEmployee table.

The tblAssignment table contains two assignment records for employee 101.

MANY-TO-MANY RELATIONSHIP

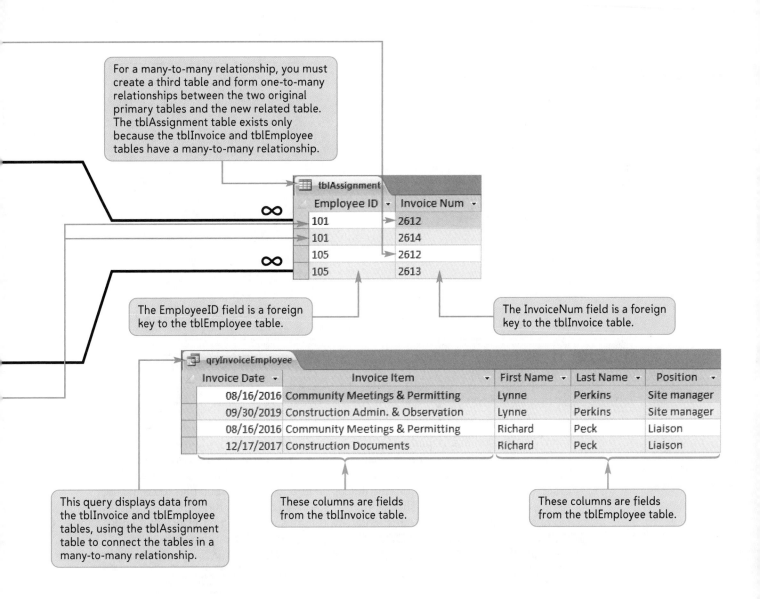

For a many-to-many relationship, you must create a third table and form one-to-many relationships between the two original primary tables and the new related table. The tblAssignment table exists only because the tblInvoice and tblEmployee tables have a many-to-many relationship.

tblAssignment

Employee ID	Invoice Num
101	2612
101	2614
105	2612
105	2613

The EmployeeID field is a foreign key to the tblEmployee table.

The InvoiceNum field is a foreign key to the tblInvoice table.

qryInvoiceEmployee

Invoice Date	Invoice Item	First Name	Last Name	Position
08/16/2016	Community Meetings & Permitting	Lynne	Perkins	Site manager
09/30/2019	Construction Admin. & Observation	Lynne	Perkins	Site manager
08/16/2016	Community Meetings & Permitting	Richard	Peck	Liaison
12/17/2017	Construction Documents	Richard	Peck	Liaison

This query displays data from the tblInvoice and tblEmployee tables, using the tblAssignment table to connect the tables in a many-to-many relationship.

These columns are fields from the tblInvoice table.

These columns are fields from the tblEmployee table.

Relationships Between Database Tables

A one-to-many relationship (abbreviated as 1:M) exists between two tables when each record in the primary table matches zero, one, or more records in the related table, and when each record in the related table matches at most one record in the primary table. For example, Figure 9-11 shows a one-to-many relationship between portions of the tblCustomer and tblContract tables and also shows a sample query based on the two tables. (Most examples in this session use portions of tables for illustrative purposes.) Customer 11065 has two contracts, customers 11038 and 11087 have one contract, and customer 11004 has zero contracts. The first four contracts each have a single matching customer based on the CustomerID foreign key values. The fifth contract with a ContractNum value of 3110 has a null CustomerID foreign key value. Permitted foreign key values are governed by referential integrity, which is the rule that requires each non-null foreign key value to match a primary key value in the primary table.

Figure 9-11	One-to-many relationship and sample query

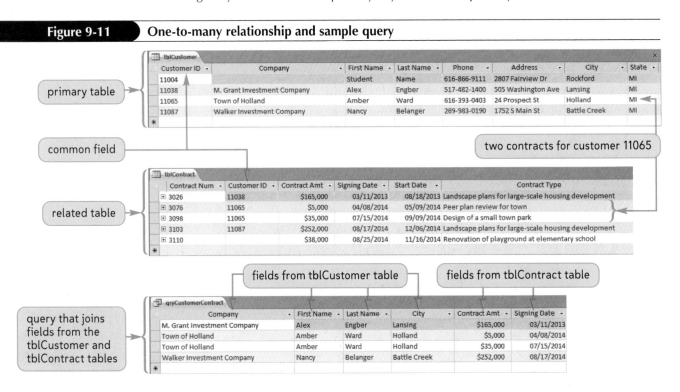

You use the common field, the CustomerID field, to form the one-to-many relationship between the tblCustomer and tblContract tables. When you join the two tables based on CustomerID field values, you can extract data from them as if they are one larger table. For example, you can join the tblCustomer and tblContract tables to create the qryCustomerContract query shown in Figure 9-11. In the qryCustomerContract query, the Company, First Name, Last Name, and City columns are from the tblCustomer table, and the Contract Amt and Signing Date columns are from the tblContract table.

In addition to one-to-many relationships between tables, you can also relate tables through many-to-many and one-to-one relationships.

Many-to-Many Relationships

In the Holland database, an invoice can represent work performed by many employees, and each employee can work on many invoiced projects, so the tblInvoice and tblEmployee tables have a many-to-many relationship, as shown in the Session 9.2 Visual Overview.

When you have a many-to-many relationship (abbreviated as M:N) between two tables, you must create a third table and form one-to-many relationships between the two original primary tables and the new related table. For instance, the tblAssignment table, shown in the Session 9.2 Visual Overview, exists only because the tblInvoice and tblEmployee tables have a many-to-many relationship. Each record in the tblAssignment table contains two foreign keys: the EmployeeID field is a foreign key that allows you to join the tblEmployee table to the tblAssignment table; and the InvoiceNum field is a foreign key that allows you to join the tblInvoice table to the tblAssignment table. For example, the first record in the tblAssignment table represents Community Meetings & Permitting work for InvoiceNum 2612 that was performed by Lynne Perkins with EmployeeID 101. Lynne Perkins, who has EmployeeID 101, appears in two records in the tblAssignment table that represent work she performed for invoices 2612 and 2614. Also, InvoiceNum 2612 appears in two tblAssignment table records, each for a different employee: Lynne Perkins and Richard Peck. The primary key of the tblAssignment table is a composite key, consisting of the combination of the EmployeeID and InvoiceNum fields. Each pair of values in this primary key is unique.

PROSKILLS

Decision Making: Identifying Many-to-Many Relationships

Although one-to-many relationships are the most common type of table relationship, many-to-many relationships occur frequently, and most databases have one or more many-to-many relationships. For example, in a college database, a student takes more than one class, and each class has more than one student enrolled; a course has many prerequisites and can be the prerequisite to many courses. In a pharmacy database, a medication is prescribed to many customers, and a customer can take many medications. In an airline database, a flight has many passengers, and a passenger can take many flights. In a publisher database, an author writes many books, and a book can have multiple authors. In a manufacturing database, a manufactured product consists of many parts, and a part can be a component in many manufactured products. In a film database, a movie has many actors, and each actor appears in many movies.

Common one-to-many relationships can turn into many-to-many relationships when circumstances change. For example, a department in an organzation has many employees, and an employee usually works in a single department. However, an instructor can have a joint appointment to two departments, and some companies hire employees and split their time between two departments. You must carefully analzye each situation and design your table relationships to handle the specific requirements for today and for the future.

When you join tables that have a many-to-many relationship, you can extract data from them as if they were one larger table. For example, you can join the tblInvoice and tblEmployee tables to create the qryInvoiceEmployee query shown in the Session 9.2 Visual Overview. In the tblAssignment table, the EmployeeID field joins the tblEmployee and tblAssignment tables, and the InvoiceNum field joins the tblInvoice and tblAssignment tables. In the qryInvoiceEmployee query, the Invoice Date and Invoice Item columns are from the tblInvoice table, and the First Name, Last Name, and Position columns are from the tblEmployee table. The first record in the query recordset shows data from the second record in the tblInvoice table, joined with data from the matching first record in the tblEmployee table. These two records are joined through the first record in the tblAssignment table.

One-to-One Relationships

A **one-to-one relationship** (abbreviated as **1:1**) exists between two tables when each record in the first table matches at most one record in the second table, and each record in the second table matches at most one record in the first table. Most relationships between tables are either one-to-many or many-to-many; the primary use for one-to-one relationships is as entity subtypes. An **entity subtype** is a table whose primary key is a foreign key to a second table and whose fields are additional fields for the second table. For example, the tblCustomer table and the tblBillingAddress table, which is an entity subtype, have a one-to-one relationship, as shown in Figure 9-12.

Figure 9-12	tblCustomer and tblBillingAddress tables with a 1:1 relationship

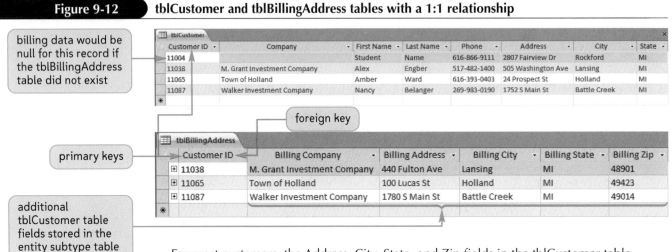

- billing data would be null for this record if the tblBillingAddress table did not exist
- foreign key
- primary keys
- additional tblCustomer table fields stored in the entity subtype table

For most customers, the Address, City, State, and Zip fields in the tblCustomer table identify both the customer's location and billing address, which is where Belmont Landscapes sends the customer's invoices. In a few cases, however, the billing address is different from the location address; additionally, the customer name used for billing purposes might be different from the customer name in the tblCustomer table. There are two ways to handle these two sets of names and addresses. The first way is to add the BillingCompany, BillingAddress, BillingCity, BillingState, and BillingZip fields to the tblCustomer table. For those customers having a different billing name and address, you store the appropriate values in these billing fields. For those customers having identical location and billing names and addresses, leave these billing fields null.

As shown in Figure 9-12, the second way to handle the two sets of addresses is to create the entity subtype named tblBillingAddress. In the tblBillingAddress table, the CustomerID field, which is the primary key, is also a foreign key to the tblCustomer table. A record appears in the tblBillingAddress table only for those customers having a differ-ent billing name and address. All billing data appears only in the tblBillingAddress table.

When you join tables that have a one-to-one relationship, you can extract data from them as if they were one larger table. For example, you can join the tblCustomer and tblBillingAddress tables to create the qryBillingAddressData query shown in Figure 9-13.

Figure 9-13	Query results produced by joining tables having a 1:1 relationship

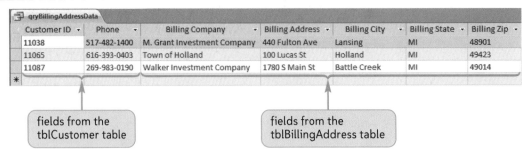

- fields from the tblCustomer table
- fields from the tblBillingAddress table

The CustomerID field joins the tblCustomer and tblBillingAddress tables. In the query, the Customer ID and Phone columns are from the tblCustomer table; and the Billing Company, Billing Address, Billing City, Billing State, and Billing Zip columns are from the tblBillingAddress table. Only the three customers that have records in the tblBillingAddress table—because they have different billing addresses—appear in the qryBillingAddressData query recordset.

Next, you'll define a many-to-many relationship between the tblInvoice and tblEmployee tables, and a one-to-one relationship between the tblCustomer and tblBillingAddress tables.

Defining M:N and 1:1 Relationships Between Tables

Similar to how you define one-to-many relationships, you define many-to-many and one-to-one relationships in the Relationships window. First, you'll open the Relationships window and define the many-to-many relationship between the tblInvoice and tblEmployee tables. You'll define a one-to-many relationship between the tblInvoice and tblAssignment tables, with tblInvoice as the primary table, tblAssignment as the related table, and InvoiceNum as the common field (the primary key in the tblInvoice table and a foreign key in the tblAssignment table). Next, you'll define a one-to-many relationship between the tblEmployee and tblAssignment tables, with tblEmployee as the primary table, tblAssignment as the related table, and EmployeeID as the common field (the primary key in the tblEmployee table and a foreign key in the tblAssignment table).

To define a many-to-many relationship between the tblInvoice and tblEmployee tables:

1. If you took a break after the previous session, make sure that the Holland database is open.

2. Close the Navigation Pane (if necessary), click the **Database Tools** tab on the Ribbon, and then in the Relationships group on the Database Tools tab, click the **Relationships** button to open the Relationships window.

3. In the Relationships group on the Design tab, click the **Show Table** button to open the Show Table dialog box, double-click **tblAssignment** to add the tblAssignment field list to the Relationships window, double-click **tblBillingAddress** to add the tblBillingAddress field list to the Relationships window, double-click **tblEmployee** to add the tblEmployee field list to the Relationships window, and then close the Show Table dialog box.

4. Drag the field list title bars of the field lists for the tblBillingAddress, tblInvoice, tblEmployee, and tblAssignment tables as shown in Figure 9-14.

Figure 9-14	After adding three table field lists to the Relationships window

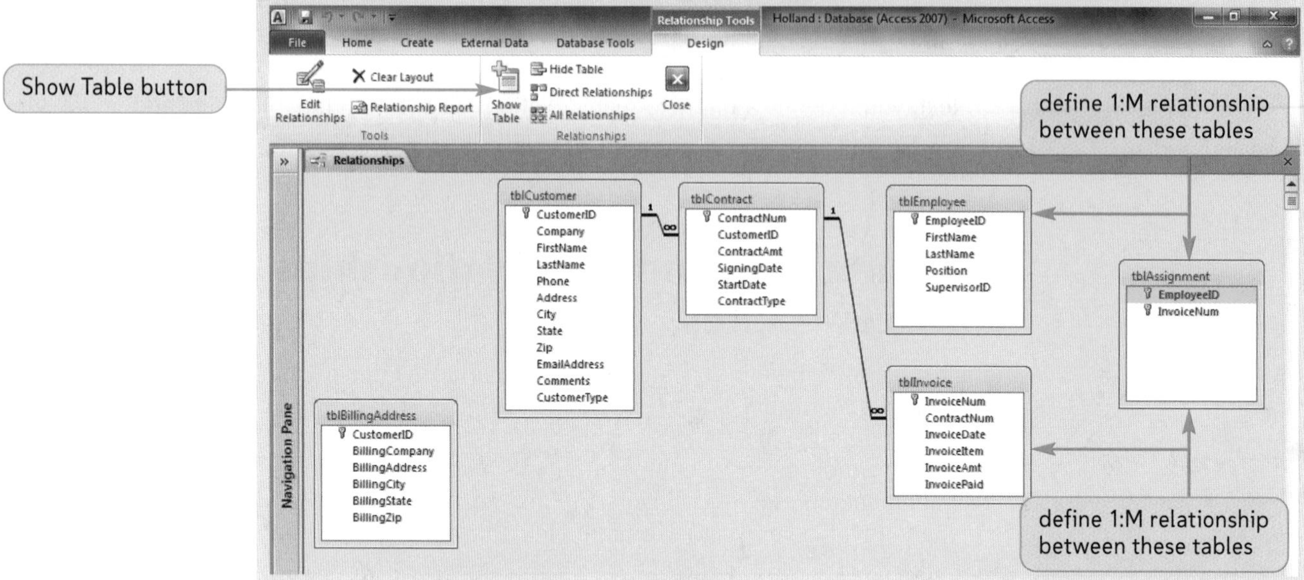

First, you'll define the one-to-many relationship between the tblInvoice and tblAssignment tables.

5. Click **InvoiceNum** in the tblInvoice field list, and drag it to **InvoiceNum** in the tblAssignment field list. When you release the mouse button, the Edit Relationships dialog box opens.

The primary table, related table, and common field appear at the top of the dialog box. The type of relationship, One-To-Many, appears at the bottom of the dialog box. When you click the Enforce Referential Integrity check box, the two cascade options become available. If you select the Cascade Update Related Fields option, Access will change the appropriate foreign key values in the related table when you change a primary key value in the primary table. If you select the Cascade Delete Related Records check box, when you delete a record in the primary table, Access will delete all records in the related table that have a matching foreign key value. You'll enforce referential integrity and cascade updates to related fields, but you won't cascade deletions to related records.

6. Click the **Enforce Referential Integrity** check box, and then click the **Cascade Update Related Fields** check box. You have now selected all the necessary relationship options.

7. Click the **Create** button to close the dialog box and define the one-to-many relationship between the two tables. The completed relationship appears in the Relationships window.

8. Repeat Steps 5 through 7 to define the one-to-many relationship between the primary tblEmployee table and the related tblAssignment table, using EmployeeID as the common field. See Figure 9-15.

Figure 9-15   **M:N relationship defined between the tblInvoice and tblEmployee tables**

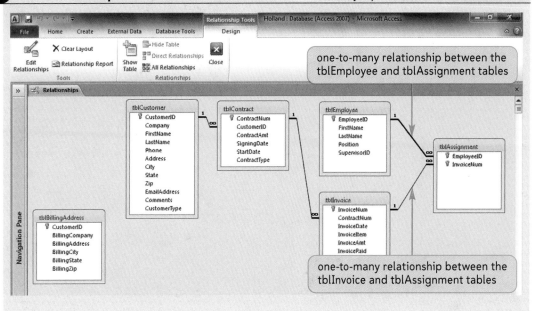

Now you'll define a one-to-one relationship between the tblCustomer and tblBillingAddress tables.

To define a one-to-one relationship between the tblCustomer and tblBillingAddress tables:

1. Click **CustomerID** in the tblCustomer field list, and drag it to **CustomerID** in the tblBillingAddress field list. When you release the mouse button, the Edit Relationships dialog box opens.

   The primary table, related table, and common field appear at the top of the dialog box. The type of relationship, One-To-One, appears at the bottom of the dialog box.

2. Click the **Enforce Referential Integrity** check box, click the **Cascade Update Related Fields** check box, and then click the **Create** button to define the one-to-one relationship between the two tables and close the dialog box. The completed relationship appears in the Relationships window. See Figure 9-16.

Figure 9-16 **1:1 relationship defined between the tblCustomer and tblBillingAddress tables**

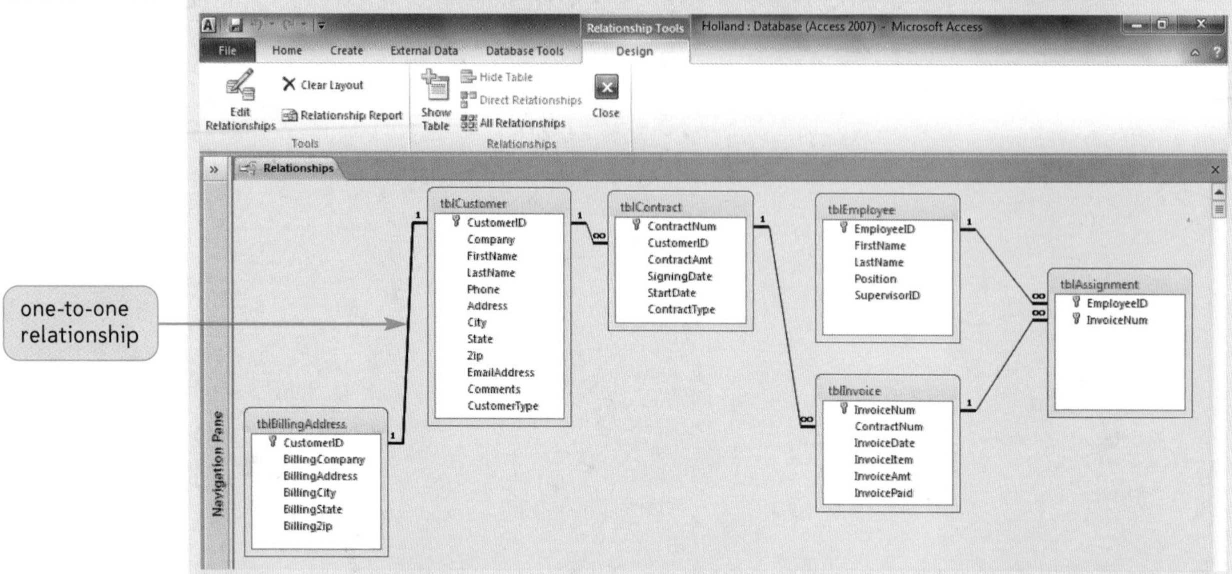

Both sides of the relationship have the digit 1 at the ends of their join lines to indicate a one-to-one relationship between the two tables. The thick join line indicates that you've chosen to enforce referential integrity in the relationship.

3. Save your relationship changes.

The tblEmployee table contains data about the workers at Belmont Landscapes who work directly on landscaping projects and whose efforts on the projects are billed to customer invoices. Sarah asks you to create a select query to display the employees in the tblEmployee table and their supervisors. The select query you'll create will require a special join using the tblEmployee table.

Joining Tables

The design of the Holland database includes a one-to-many relationship between the tblCustomer and tblContract tables using CustomerID as the common field, which allows you to join the two tables to create a query based on data from both tables. The type of join you have used so far is an inner join. Two other types of joins are the outer join and the self-join.

Inner and Outer Joins

An **inner join** is a join in which the DBMS selects records from two tables only when the records have the same value in the common field that links the tables. For example, in a database containing a table of student information and a table of class information, an inner join would show all student records that have a matching class record and all class records that have a matching student record. In the Holland database, CustomerID is the common field for the tblCustomer and tblContract tables. As shown in Figure 9-17, the results of a query based on an inner join of these two tables include only those records that have a matching CustomerID value. The record in the tblCustomer table with a Customer ID column value of 11004 is not included in the query recordset because it fails to match a record with the same Customer ID column value in the tblContract table. (That customer has no current contracts.) Also, the record in the tblContract table with a Contract Num column value of 3110 is not included in the query recordset because it has a null Customer ID column value. (Perhaps the clerk entering the contract in the Holland database wasn't sure which customer signed that contract and left the field value null.) Because primary key values can't be null, records with null foreign key values do not appear in a query recordset based on an inner join. You usually use an inner join whenever you perform a query based on more than one table; it is the default join you have used to this point.

| Figure 9-17 | Example of an inner join |

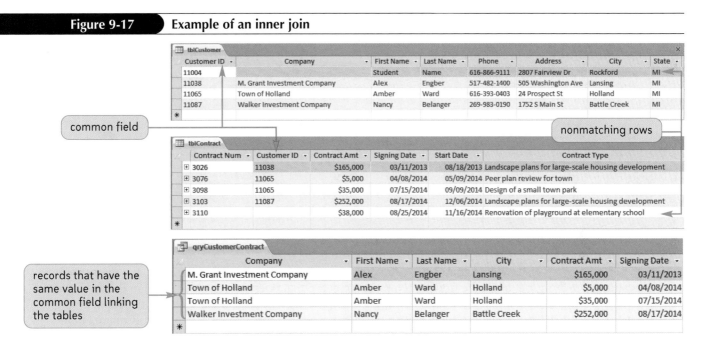

An **outer join** is a join in which the DBMS selects *all* records from one table and only those records from a second table that have matching common field values. For example, in a database containing a student table and a class table, an outer join would show all students whether or not the students are enrolled in a class, and another outer join would show all classes whether or not there are any students enrolled in them. In the Holland database, you would use this kind of join if you wanted to see, for example, all records from the tblCustomer table and also any and all matching records from the tblContract table. Figure 9-18 shows an outer join for the tblCustomer and tblContract tables. All records from the tblCustomer table appear in the query recordset, along with only matching records from the tblContract table. Notice that the first record from the tblCustomer table for Customer ID 11004 appears even though it does not match a record in the tblContract table. The record in the tblContract table with Contract Num 3110 does not appear in the query recordset, however, because it does not match a record in the tblCustomer table.

Figure 9-18	Example of an outer join

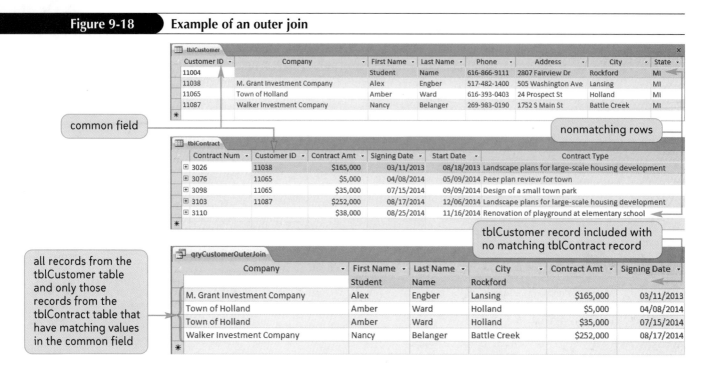

common field

nonmatching rows

tblCustomer record included with no matching tblContract record

all records from the tblCustomer table and only those records from the tblContract table that have matching values in the common field

Another example of an outer join using the tblCustomer and tblContract tables is shown in Figure 9-19. All records from the tblContract table appear in the query record-set, even the Contract Num 3110 record that does not match a record in the tblCustomer table. The Customer ID 11004 record from the tblCustomer table does not appear in the query recordset, however, because it does not match a record in the tblContract table.

Figure 9-19	Another example of an outer join

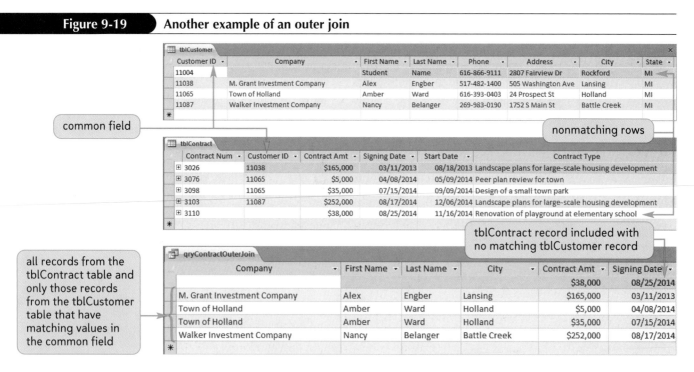

common field

nonmatching rows

tblContract record included with no matching tblCustomer record

all records from the tblContract table and only those records from the tblCustomer table that have matching values in the common field

Inner joins are the default join type, but you can change the join type between two tables to be an outer join. You'll show Sarah how she can view the join type between the tblCustomer and tblContract tables and how she can change the default join type.

To view the join type between the tblCustomer and tblContract tables:

▶ **1.** Right-click the join line between the tblCustomer and tblContract tables, and then click **Edit Relationship** on the shortcut menu to open the Edit Relationships dialog box.

Trouble? If right-clicking the join line does not work, click the join line, and then click the Edit Relationships button in the Tools group on the Design tab.

▶ **2.** Click the **Join Type** button in the dialog box to open the Join Properties dialog box. See Figure 9-20.

Figure 9-20   Join Properties dialog box

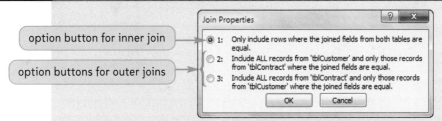

In the Join Properties dialog box, the first option button is selected, indicating that the join type between the tblCustomer and tblContract tables is an inner join. You would click the second or third option button to establish an outer join between the two tables. You'd select the second option when you want to select all records from the tblCustomer table and any matching records from the tblContract table based on the CustomerID common field. You'd select the third option when you want to select all records from the tblContract table and any matching records from the tblCustomer table based on the CustomerID common field.

When you change the join type between two tables in the Relationships window, every new query based on the two tables uses the join type you selected in the Join Properties dialog box. Existing queries based on the two tables continue to use the join type that was in effect at the time you created the query.

Sarah wants to continue to use an inner join for all queries based on the tblCustomer and tblContract tables.

▶ **3.** Click the **Cancel** button to close the Join Properties dialog box without making any changes, click the **Cancel** button to close the Edit Relationships dialog box without making any changes, and then close the Relationships window.

Self-Joins

A table can also be joined with itself; this join is called a **self-join**. A self-join can be either an inner or outer join. For example, you would use this kind of join if you wanted to see records from the tblEmployee table together with information about each employee's supervisor. Figure 9-21 shows a self-join for the tblEmployee table. In this case, the self-join is an inner join because records appear in the query results only if the SupervisorID field value matches an EmployeeID field value. To create this self-join, you would add two copies of the tblEmployee table to the Query window in Design view, and then join the SupervisorID field of one tblEmployee table to the EmployeeID field of the other tblEmployee table.

| Figure 9-21 | Example of a self-join |

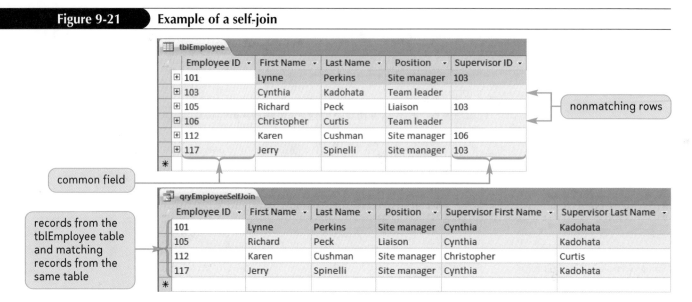

In Figure 9-21, the query results show the record for each employee in the tblEmployee table and the supervisor for that employee. The supervisor information also comes from the tblEmployee table through the SupervisorID field. The join for the query is an inner join, so only employees with nonnull SupervisorID field values appear in the query recordset.

To create a select query to display the employees in the tblEmployee table and their supervisors, you need to create a self-join.

Creating a Self-Join

You need to create a query to display the employees and their supervisors in the tblEmployee table. This query requires a self-join. To create the self-join, you need to add two copies of the tblEmployee field list to the Query window in Design view, and then add a join line from the EmployeeID field in one field list to the SupervisorID field in the other. The SupervisorID field is a foreign key that matches the primary key field EmployeeID. You can then create a query to display employee information from one copy of the table and supervisor information from the other copy of the table.

REFERENCE

Creating a Self-Join

- Click the Create tab on the Ribbon.
- In the Queries group on the Create tab, click the Query Design button.
- In the Show Table dialog box, double-click the table for the self-join, double-click the table a second time, and then click the Close button.
- Click and drag the primary key field from one field list to the foreign key field in the other field list.
- Right-click the join line between the two tables, and then click Join Properties to open the Join Properties dialog box.
- Click the first option button to select an inner join, or click the second option button or the third option button to select an outer join, and then click the OK button.
- Select the fields, specify the selection criteria, select the sort options, and set other properties as appropriate for the query.

Now you'll create the self-join query to display employees and their supervisors.

To create the self-join query:

1. Click the **Create** tab on the Ribbon, and then in the Queries group, click the **Query Design** button to open the Show Table dialog box on top of the Query window in Design view.

2. Double-click **tblEmployee** to add the tblEmployee field list to the Query window.

3. Double-click **tblEmployee** again to add a second copy of the tblEmployee field list to the Query window, and then click the **Close** button. Access identifies the left field list as tblEmployee and the right field list as tblEmployee_1 to distinguish the two copies of the table.

   You will now create a join between the two copies of the tblEmployee table by linking the EmployeeID field in the tblEmployee field list to the SupervisorID field in the tblEmployee_1 field list. The SupervisorID field is a foreign key that matches the primary key field EmployeeID.

4. Click and drag the **EmployeeID** field from the tblEmployee field list to the **SupervisorID** field in the tblEmployee_1 field list. Access adds a join line between the two fields. You can verify that this is an inner join query by opening the Join Properties dialog box.

5. Right-click the join line between the two tables, click **Join Properties** on the shortcut menu to open the Join Properties dialog box, and then click **tblEmployee** in the Left Table Name box to deselect all controls. See Figure 9-22.

Figure 9-22 | **Join Properties dialog box**

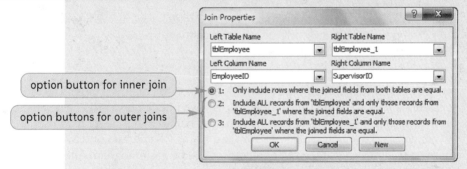

The first option button is selected, indicating that this is an inner join. Because the inner join is correct, you can close the dialog box and then add the necessary fields in the design grid.

6. Click the **Cancel** button, and then double-click the following fields (in order) from the tblEmployee_1 field list: **EmployeeID**, **FirstName**, **LastName**, and **Position**.

7. Double-click the following fields (in order) from the tblEmployee field list: **FirstName** and **LastName**.

8. Run the query, and then click the first row's **Employee ID** field value to deselect all values. Access displays the query recordset with six fields and 12 records. See Figure 9-23.

Figure 9-23   **Initial self-join on the tblEmployee table**

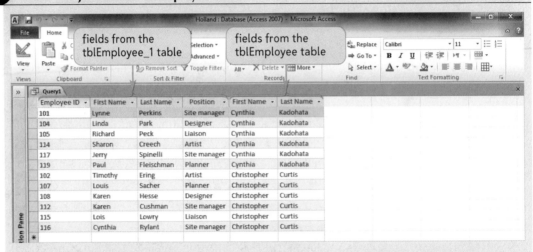

The query recordset displays all employees and their supervisors with the exception of the records for Cynthia Kadohata and Christopher Curtis because their records contain null SupervisorID field values. (They are supervisors of the other employees and do not have assigned supervisors.) Remember that an inner join doesn't display records from the second table unless it contains a matching value in the common field. In the tblEmployee_1 table, the SupervisorID field values for Cynthia Kadohata and Christopher Curtis are null, so the inner join doesn't select their records in the tblEmployee table.

Trouble? If your query results do not match Figure 9-23, switch to Design view, and review the preceding steps to make any necessary corrections to your query design. Then run the query again.

Access displays 12 of the 14 records from the tblEmployee table. The records for Cynthia Kadohata and Christopher Curtis have null SupervisorID field values; therefore, their records are not displayed. Two column names in the query recordset are "First Name," and two column names are "Last Name." Sarah asks you to rename the two right-most columns so that the query recordset will be easier to read. After you set the Caption property for the two rightmost fields, the column names in the query recordset will be, from left to right, Employee ID, First Name, Last Name, Position, Supervisor First Name, and Supervisor Last Name. You'll also sort the query in increasing EmployeeID order.

To set the Caption property for two query fields and sort the query:

▶ **1.** Switch to Design view.

▶ **2.** Click the sixth column's **Field** box, in the Show/Hide group on the Design tab, click the **Property Sheet** button, and then set the Caption property to **Supervisor Last Name**.

▶ **3.** Click the fifth column's **Field** box, and then set the Caption property to **Supervisor First Name**.

▶ **4** Close the property sheet, click the right side of the **EmployeeID Sort** box to display the sort order options, and then click **Ascending**.

▶ **5.** Save the query as **qryEmployeeSupervisors**, run the query, resize all columns to their best fit, and then click the first row's **Employee ID** field value to deselect all values. The query recordset displays the new names for the fifth and sixth columns. See Figure 9-24.

| Figure 9-24 | Final self-join on the tblEmployee table |

query Caption property settings for these columns

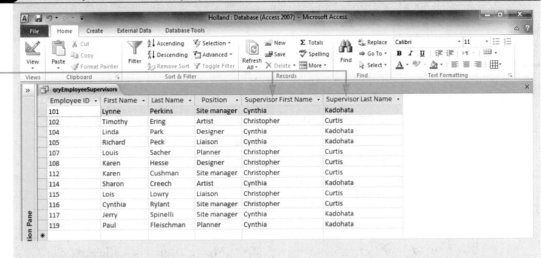

▶ **6.** Save and close the query.

Sarah asks you if her staff's work will take longer as the Holland database grows in size with the addition of more table records. Specifically, she wants to know if queries will take longer to run. You tell her that using indexes will help make her queries run faster.

Using Indexes for Table Fields

Suppose you need to find all the pages in a book that discuss a specific topic. The fastest, most accurate way to perform your search is to look up the topic in the book's index. In a similar fashion, you can create indexes for fields in a table, so that Access can quickly locate all the records in a table that contain specific values for one or more fields. An **index** is a list that relates field values to the records that contain those field values.

Access automatically creates and maintains an index for a table's primary key. For example, the tblInvoice table in the Holland database includes an index for the InvoiceNum field, which is the table's primary key. Conceptually, as shown in Figure 9-25, Access identifies each record in the tblInvoice table by its record number, and the InvoiceNum index has two columns. The first column contains an InvoiceNum value, and the second column contains the record number in the tblInvoice table for that InvoiceNum value. For instance, InvoiceNum 2063 in the index has a record number value of 4; and record number 4 in the tblInvoice table contains the data for InvoiceNum 2063.

tblInvoice table with index for the InvoiceNum field

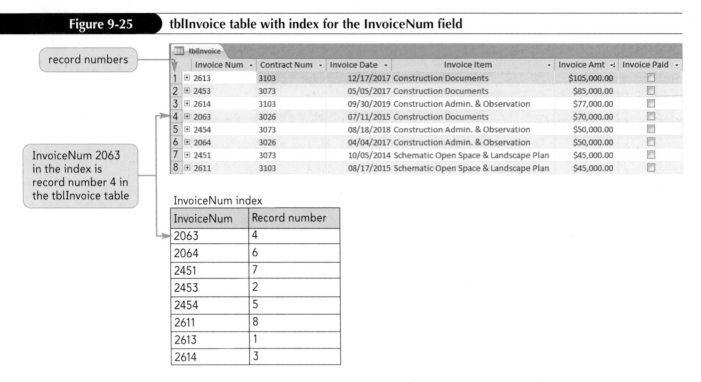

Because InvoiceNum values in the tblInvoice table are unique, each row in the InvoiceNum index has a single record number. When you or Access create indexes for non-primary-key fields, however, the indexes may contain multiple record numbers in a row. Figure 9-26 illustrates a ContractNum index for the tblInvoice table. Because ContractNum is a foreign key in the tblInvoice table (a contract can have many invoices), each ContractNum entry in the index can be associated with many record numbers in the tblInvoice table. For instance, ContractNum 3026 in the index has record number values of 4 and 6, and record numbers 4 and 6 in the tblInvoice table contain the invoice data for ContractNum 3026.

tblInvoice table with index for the ContractNum field

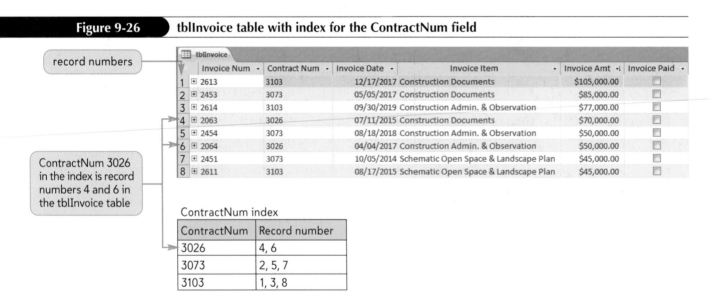

If an index exists for the ContractNum field in the tblInvoice table, queries that use ContractNum as a sort field or as a selection criterion will run faster.

Tradeoffs of Using Indexes

With small tables, the increased speed associated with indexes is not readily apparent. In practice, tables with hundreds of thousands or millions of records are common. In such cases, the increase in speed is dramatic. In fact, without indexes, many database operations in large tables would not be practical because they would take too long to complete. Why the speed difference in these cases? To sort or select records from a large table without an index, Access must make numerous accesses to disk storage to retrieve table records because the entire table can't fit in computer memory. In contrast, indexes are usually small enough to fit completely in computer memory, and Access sorts and selects records based on indexes with minimal need to access disk storage. Because accessing disk storage is very slow and performing operations in computer memory is very fast, using indexes in large tables is faster.

The speed advantage of using an index must be weighed against two disadvantages: the index adds disk storage requirements to the database, and it takes time to update the index as you add and delete records. Except for primary key indexes, you can add and delete indexes at any time. Thus, you can add an index if you think searching and querying would be faster as the number of records in the database increases. You can also delete an existing index if you later deem it to be unnecessary.

Viewing Existing Indexes

You can view the existing indexes for a table by opening the table in Design view.

View a Table's Existing Indexes

- Open the table in Design view.
- To view an index for a single field, click the field, and then view the Indexed property in the Field Properties pane.
- To view all the indexes for a table or to view an index consisting of multiple fields, click the Indexes button in the Show/Hide group on the Design tab.

Sarah wants to view the indexes for the tblAssignment table.

To view the indexes for the tblAssignment table:

1. Open the Navigation Pane, and then open the **tblAssignment** table in Design view.

2. In the Show/Hide group on the Design tab, click the **Indexes** button to open the Indexes: tblAssignment dialog box, drag the dialog box to the position shown in Figure 9-27, and then click **PrimaryKey** in the Index Name box to deselect all values. See Figure 9-27.

Figure 9-27 Indexes for the tblAssignment table

3. Close the Indexes: tblAssignment dialog box, and then close the table.

Because the EmployeeID field was selected when you opened the Indexes dialog box, the properties in the Field Properties pane pertained to this field. In particular, the Indexed property value of No for the EmployeeID field specifies there's no index for this field.

In the Indexes: tblAssignment dialog box, the properties in the Index Properties pane apply to the selected PrimaryKey index, which consists of the table's composite key of the EmployeeID and InvoiceNum fields. Because InvoiceNum in the dialog box's second row does not have an Index Name property value, both EmployeeID and InvoiceNum make up the PrimaryKey index. Access automatically created the PrimaryKey index when the table was created and the EmployeeID and InvoiceNum fields were designated as the table's composite key. The properties for the PrimaryKey index indicate that this index is the primary key index (Primary property setting of Yes), and that values in this index must be unique (Unique property setting of Yes)—that is, each EmployeeID and InvoiceNum pair of field values must be unique. The Ignore Nulls property setting of No means that records with null values for the EmployeeID field or InvoiceNum field are included in the index, but this setting is ignored because the Yes setting for the Primary property doesn't allow either field to have a null value.

Default Automatic Indexes

Access automatically creates an index for the primary key field in a table. In addition, Access automatically creates an index for any field name that contains the following letter sequences: *code*, *ID*, *key*, or *num*. You can add, change, and delete from this list of letter sequences to manage the automatic indexes created in a database. To do so, click the File tab on the Ribbon, click Options in the navigation bar, and then click Object Designers. In the Table design view section, the AutoIndex on Import/Create box displays, by default, *ID;key;code;num*. Modify the entries in the AutoIndex on Import/Create box if you want a different list of letter sequences that Access will use to automatically create indexes for the fields in your tables.

Over the past few weeks, Sarah's staff has been monitoring the performance of the Holland database by timing how long it takes to run queries. She wants her staff to let her know if the performance changes over the next several days as a result of creating an index for the City field in the tblCustomer table. Many queries use the City field as a sort field or selection criterion, and adding an index might speed up those queries.

Creating an Index

You can create an index for a single field in the Indexes dialog box or by setting its Indexed property in Design view. However, for a multiple-field index, you must create the index in the Indexes dialog box.

Creating an Index

- Open the table in Design view.
- To create an index for a single field, click the field, and then set the Indexed property in the Field Properties pane.
- To create an index consisting of multiple fields, click the Indexes button in the Show/Hide group on the Design tab, enter a name for the index in the Index Name box, select the fields in the Field Name box, and then set other properties as necessary for the index.

Next, you'll create an index for the City field in the tblCustomer table by setting the field's Indexed property.

To create an index for the City field in the tblCustomer table:

1. Open the **tblCustomer** table in Design view, and then in the Show/Hide group on the Design tab, click the **Indexes** button to open the Indexes: tblCustomer dialog box.

2. Make sure the dialog box is positioned as shown in Figure 9-28, click the **tblCustomer** tab to make the Table window the active window, and then click **City** in the Field Name column to make it the current field. See Figure 9-28.

Figure 9-28 Indexes for the tblCustomer table

indexes created by Access when CustomerID was selected as the primary key

current field

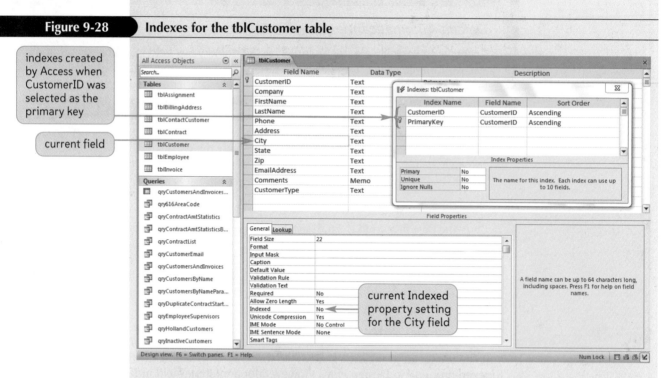

current Indexed property setting for the City field

Access created two indexes when CustomerID was selected as the primary key: the PrimaryKey index because the field is the primary key, and the CustomerID index because the field name has an ID suffix. No other indexes exist for the tblCustomer table. You'll create an index for the City field allowing duplicates because the same City field value can appear in many records in the tblCustomer table.

3. Click the right side of the **Indexed** property in the Field Properties pane, click **Yes (Duplicates OK)**, and then click the **Indexed** property box to deselect the value. An index for the City field is created with duplicate values allowed. Setting the Indexed property automatically created the City index in the Indexes: tblCustomer dialog box. See Figure 9-29.

Figure 9-29 After creating the City index

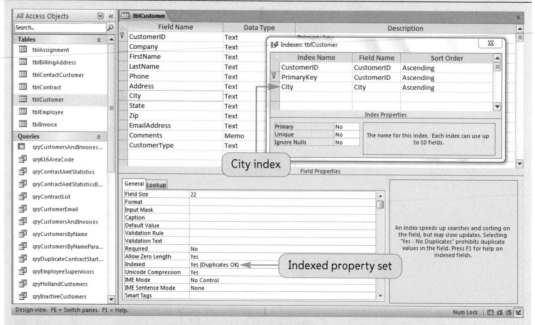

City index

Indexed property set

▶ **4.** Close the dialog box, save your table design changes, and then switch to Datasheet view.

▶ **5.** Change the second record in the table so the First Name and Last Name columns contain your first and last names.

▶ **6.** Close the table, make a backup copy of the database, compact and repair the Holland database, and then close the database.

The work you completed with table relationships, table and query joins, and indexes will make it much easier for Sarah and her staff to enter, retrieve, and view information in the Holland database.

Session 9.2 Quick Check

REVIEW

1. What are the three types of relationships you can define between tables?
2. What is an entity subtype?
3. What is the difference between an inner join and an outer join?
4. What is a self-join?
5. What is an index?
6. Figure 9-30 lists the field names from two tables: tblDepartment and tblEmployee.

Figure 9-30	Fields for the tblDepartment and tblEmployee tables

tblDepartment	tblEmployee
DepartmentID	EmployeeSSN
DepartmentName	EmployeeName
PhoneNumber	DepartmentID
	Salary
	SupervisorSSN

a. What is the primary key for each table?
b. What type of relationship exists between the two tables?
c. Is an inner join possible between the two tables? If so, give one example of an inner join.
d. Is an outer join possible between the two tables? If so, give one example of an outer join.
e. Is a self-join possible for one of the two tables? If so, give one example of a self-join.

Practice the skills you learned in the tutorial using the same case scenario.

PRACTICE

Review Assignments

Data File needed for the Review Assignments: Vendor.accdb

The Vendor database contains data about Belmont Landscapes suppliers and their products, and the invoices from the suppliers and the payments made by Belmont Landscapes to the suppliers. The database also contains queries, forms, and reports. Sarah wants you to define relationships between the tables and to create some new queries for her. To meet these requests, complete the following steps:

1. Open the **Vendor** database located in the Access3\Review folder provided with your Data Files.

2. Designate the Access3\Review folder as a trusted folder. (*Note:* Check with your instructor before adding a new trusted location.)

3. Modify the first record in the **tblCompany** table datasheet so the Contact First Name and Contact Last Name columns contain your first and last names. Close the table.

4. Define a many-to-many relationship between the tblInvoice and tblPayment tables, using the tblInvoicePayment table as the related table. Define a one-to-one relationship between the primary tblCompany table and the related tblCompanyCreditLine table. Select the referential integrity option and the cascade updates option for the relationships.

5. Create a make-table query based on the tblProduct table, selecting the ProductID, CompanyID, ProductType, Price, Unit, Material, and DiscountOffered fields, and selecting only those records that contain the word **steel** anywhere in the Material field value. Use **tblProductSpecial** as the new table name, store the table in the current database, and then run the query.

6. Modify the make-table query to create an append query that selects only those records containing the word **iron** anywhere in the Material field value. Append the records to the tblProductSpecial table, run the query, and then close the query without saving it.

7. Suppliers are offering a 10% discount off the regular price for all products in the tblProductSpecial table. Create an update query to select all records in the tblProductSpecial table, decrease the Price field values by 10%, run the query, and then close the query without saving it. (*Hint*: Use the expression **0.9*[Price]**.)

8. Create a delete query that deletes all records in the tblProductSpecial table in which the ProductType field value starts with the word **small**. Run the query, and then close the query without saving it. Open the tblProductSpecial table, resize all columns to their best fit, and then save and close the table.

9. Create an outer join between the tblCompany and tblInvoice tables, selecting all records from the tblCompany table and any matching records from the tblInvoice table. Display the CompanyName, City, Phone, ContactFirstName, and ContactLastName from the tblCompany table, and the InvoiceDate and InvoiceAmt fields from the tblInvoice table. Save the query as **qryCustomerInvoiceOuterJoin**, and then run and close the query.

10. Open the **tblProductSpecial** table in Design view, specify the primary key, add an index that allows duplicates for the CompanyID field, and then save and close the table.

11. Make a backup copy of the database, compact and repair the Vendor database, and then close the database.

Apply the skills you learned to create action queries for a music school.

APPLY

Case Problem 1

Data File needed for this Case Problem: Portland.accdb

Pine Hill Music School   Yuka Koyama owns and runs the Pine Hill Music School in Portland, Oregon. She and the qualified teachers who work for her offer instruction in voice, violin, cello, guitar, percussion, and other instruments. Yuka created an Access database named Portland to store data about students, teachers, contracts, instruments, and credit cards. The tblStudent table contains data about the students taking lessons, the tblTeacher table contains data about the lesson instructors, the tblCreditCard table contains data about the credit cards used to pay the monthly fees for lessons, the tblContract table contains data about the student contracts, the tblInstrument table contains data about the instruments students can rent, and the tblInstrumentContract table contains data about the contracts that have instrument rental agreements. Yuka asks you to define table relationships and create some new queries for her. To do so, complete the following steps:

1. Open the **Portland** database located in the Access3\Case1 folder provided with your Data Files.

2. Designate the Access3\Case1 folder as a trusted folder. (*Note:* Check with your instructor before adding a new trusted location.)

3. Change the first record in the **tblStudent** table datasheet so the First Name and Last Name columns contain your first and last names. Close the table.

4. Define a many-to-many relationship between the tblContract and tblInstrument tables, using the tblInstrumentContract table as the related table. Define a one-to-one relationship between the primary tblStudent table and the related tblCreditCard table. Select the referential integrity option and the cascade updates option for the relationships.

5. Create a make-table query based on the qryLessonsByTeacher query, selecting all fields from the query and only those records where the LessonType field value is **Cello**, **Piano**, **Violin**, or **Voice**. Use **tblSpecialLesson** as the new table name, store the table in the current database, and then run the query.

6. Modify the make-table query to create an append query that selects only those records where the LessonType field value is **Guitar**. Append the records to the tblSpecialLesson table, run the query, and then close the query without saving it.

7. Create an update query to select all records in the tblSpecialLesson table where the LessonLength field value is **60**, changing the field value to **55**. Run the query, and then close the query without saving it.

8. Create a delete query that deletes all records in the tblSpecialLesson table in which the ContractEndDate field value is less than **7/1/2013**. Run the query, and then close the query without saving it. Open the **tblSpecialLesson** table, resize all columns to their best fit, and then save and close the table.

9. Create an outer join between the tblStudent and tblCreditCard tables, selecting all records from the tblStudent table and any matching records from the tblCreditCard table. Display the FirstName and LastName fields from the tblStudent table, and the FirstName, LastName, and CreditRelationship fields from the tblCreditCard table. Change the column names for the FirstName and LastName fields from the tblCreditCard table to **Credit First Name** and **Credit Last Name**. Save the query as **qryStudentCreditCardOuterJoin**, run the query, resize all columns to their best fit, and then save and close the query.

⊕ EXPLORE   10. Create a self-join based on the tblTeacher table with the TeacherID field as the primary key and Coordinator as the foreign key. Select the TeacherID, FirstName, LastName, and HireDate fields from the related table (the table that has the Coordinator field connected to the join line), and the FirstName and LastName fields from the primary table. The column names in the query recordset should be **Teacher ID**, **First Name**,

Last Name, **Hire Date**, **Coordinator First Name**, and **Coordinator Last Name**, respectively. Use an outer join on the related table. Run the query, resize all columns to their best fit, save the query as **qryTeacherSelfJoin**, and then close the query.

11. Open the **tblSpecialLesson** table in Design view, add an index that allows duplicates for the StudentID field, and then save and close the table.

12. Make a backup copy of the database, compact and repair the Portland database, and then close the database.

Apply what you learned to manage the data for a fitness center.

APPLY

Case Problem 2

Data File needed for this Case Problem: Exercise.accdb

Parkhurst Health & Fitness Center   Martha Parkhurst owns and operates the Parkhurst Health & Fitness Center in Richmond, Virginia. The center offers the usual weight training equipment and fitness classes and offers specialized programs designed to meet the needs of athletes who participate in certain sports or physical activities. Martha created the Exercise database to maintain information about the members who have joined the center and the types of programs and classes the center offers. The tblClass table contains data about members and the scheduled classes they take, the tblCreditCard table contains data about members' credit cards, the tblMember table contains data about members, the tblProgram table contains data about training programs offered to members, and the tblSchedule table contains data about each scheduled class. The database also contains several other objects, including queries, forms, and reports. Martha wants you to define a many-to-many relationship between the tblMember and tblSchedule tables, create a one-to-one relationship between the tblMember and tblCreditCard tables, and create several new queries. To do so, complete the following steps:

1. Open the **Exercise** database located in the Access3\Case2 folder provided with your Data Files.

2. Designate the Access3\Case2 folder as a trusted folder. (*Note:* Check with your instructor before adding a new trusted location.)

3. Modify the first record in the **tblMember** table datasheet so the First Name and Last Name columns contain your first and last names. Close the table.

4. Define a many-to-many relationship between the tblMember and tblSchedule tables, using the tblClass table as the related table. Define a one-to-one relationship between the primary tblMember table and the related tblCreditCard table. Select the referential integrity option and the cascade updates option for the relationships.

5. Create a make-table query based on the tblMember table, selecting all fields from the table except the Street, City, and State fields, and only those records where the MembershipStatus field value is **On Hold**. Use **tblSpecialMember** as the new table name, store the table in the current database, and then run the query.

6. Modify the make-table query to create an append query based on the tblMember table (selecting all fields from the table except the Street, City, and State fields) and that selects only those records where the MembershipStatus field value is **Inactive**. Append the records to the tblSpecialMember table, run the query, and then close the query without saving it.

7. Create an update query to select all records in the tblSpecialMember table in which the Zip field value is **23058**, changing the MemberComments field value to **Create a special program**. Run the query, and then close the query without saving it.

8. Create a delete query that deletes all records in the tblSpecialMember table where the ProgramID field value equals **207**. Run the query, and then close the query without saving it. Open the **tblSpecialMember** table, resize all columns to their best fit, and then save and close the table.

9. Create an outer join between the tblMember and tblCreditCard tables, selecting all records from the tblMember table and any matching records from the tblCreditCard table. Display all fields from the tblMember table, and the CardNum and ExpDate fields from the tblCreditCard table. Save the query as **qryMemberCreditCardOuterJoin**, and then run and close the query.

✦ **EXPLORE**   10. Add an index that allows duplicates named **JoinDate** to the **tblMember** table, delete the ProgramID index, and then save and close the table.

11. Make a backup copy of the database, compact and repair the Exercise database, and then close the database.

Apply what you learned to manage a database for a recycling agency.

APPLY

Case Problem 3

Data File needed for this Case Problem: Salina.accdb

Rossi Recycling Group   The Rossi Recycling Group is a not-for-profit agency in Salina, Kansas that provides recycled household goods to needy people and families at no charge. Residents of Salina and surrounding communities donate cash and goods, such as appliances, furniture, and tools, to the Rossi Recycling Group. The group's volunteers then coordinate with local human services agencies to distribute the goods to those in need. The Rossi Recycling Group was established by Mary and Tom Rossi, who live on the outskirts of Salina on a small farm. Mary and Tom organize the volunteers to collect the goods and store the collected items in their barn for distribution. Tom has created an Access database to keep track of information about donors, their donations, and the human services agencies. The tblDonor table contains data about people who donate cash or goods, the tblAgency table contains data about the human services agencies, the tblDonation table contains data about the donations people make, the tblFacility table contains data about the buildings used to temporarily store donated goods, the tblStorage table contains data about the storage locations in the facilities, and the tblDonationStorage table contains data about the location of stored goods. The database also contains other objects, such as queries, forms, and reports. Tom wants you to define table relationships and create several new queries. To do so, you'll complete the following steps:

1. Open the **Salina** database located in the Access3\Case3 folder provided with your Data Files.

2. Designate the Access3\Case3 folder as a trusted folder. (*Note:* Check with your instructor before adding a new trusted location.)

3. Modify the first record in the **tblDonor** table datasheet so the Title, First Name, and Last Name columns contain your title and name. Close the table.

4. Define a one-to-many relationship between the primary tblFacility table and the related tblStorage table. Define a many-to-many relationship between the tblDonation and tblStorage tables, using the tblDonationStorage table as the related table. Select the referential integrity option and the cascade updates option for the relationships.

5. Create a make-table query based on the tblDonation table, selecting all fields from the table and only those records where the DonationDesc field value is **Cash**. Use **tblSpecialDonation** as the new table name, store the table in the current database, and then run the query.

6. Modify the make-table query to create an append query that selects only those records where the DonationDesc field value is **Computer equipment**. Append the records to the **tblSpecialDonation** table, run the query, and then close the query without saving it.

7. Create an update query to select all records in the tblSpecialDonation table in which the AgencyID field value equals **Y68**, changing the AgencyID field value to **N57**. Run the query, and then close the query without saving it.

8. Create a delete query that deletes all records in the **tblSpecialDonation** table in which the DonationValue field value is less than **$50**. Run the query, and then close the query without saving it. Open the **tblSpecialDonation** table, resize all columns to their best fit, and then save and close the table.

9. Create an outer join between the tblAgency and tblDonation tables, selecting all records from the tblAgency table and any matching records from the tblDonation table. Display the AgencyID and AgencyName fields from the tblAgency table, and the DonationID, DonationDate, and DonationValue fields from the tblDonation table. Save the query as **qryAgencyDonationOuterJoin**, and then run and close the query.

10. Add an index named **City** that allows duplicate values to the **tblAgency** table, and then save and close the table.

11. Make a backup copy of the database, compact and repair the Salina database, and then close the database.

Apply what you learned to manage data for a property rental company.

APPLY

Case Problem 4

Data File needed for this Case Problem: Rentals.accdb

GEM Ultimate Vacations   Griffin and Emma MacElroy own and operate their own agency, GEM Ultimate Vacations, which specializes in locating and booking luxury rental properties in Europe and Africa. To track their guests, properties, and reservations, they created the Rentals database. The tblReservation table contains data about scheduled vacations by their client guests, the tblGuest table contains data about guests, the tblProperty table contains data about the available luxury rental properties, the tblPersonnel table contains data about the people who manage the properties, and the tblWork table contains data about the management personnel assigned to each property. The database also contains several other objects, including queries, forms, and reports. Griffin and Emma want you to define a many-to-many relationship between the tblProperty and tblPersonnel tables, and to create several new queries. To do so, complete the following steps:

1. Open the **Rentals** database located in the Access3\Case4 folder provided with your Data Files.

2. Designate the Access3\Case4 folder as a trusted folder. (*Note:* Check with your instructor before adding a new trusted location.)

3. Modify the first record in the **tblGuest** table so the Guest First Name and Guest Last Name columns contain your first and last names.

4. Define a many-to-many relationship between the tblProperty and tblPersonnel tables, using the tblWork table as the related table. Select the referential integrity option and the cascade updates option for the relationships.

5. Create a make-table query based on the tblGuest and tblReservation tables, selecting the GuestFirstName, GuestLastName, and City fields from the tblGuest table and the StartDate, EndDate, and RentalRate fields from the tblReservation table. Select those records with a City field value of **Chicago**. Save the table as **tblSelectedReservation** in the current database, and then run the query.

6. Modify the make-table query to create an append query that selects those records with a city field value of **Aurora** or **Evanston** and appends the selected records to the tblSelectedReservation table. Run the query, and then close the query without saving it.

7. Create a delete query that deletes all records from the tblSelectedReservation table in which the RentalRate field value is less than **$1,000**. Run the query, and then close the query without saving it. Open the **tblSelectedReservation** table, resize all columns to their best fit, and then save and close the table.

8. Create an outer join between the tblGuest and tblReservation tables, selecting all records from the tblGuest table and any matching records from the tblReservation table. Display the GuestFirstName, GuestLastName, and City fields from the tblGuest table, and the PropertyID and RentalRate fields from the tblReservation table. Save the query as **qryGuestReservationOuterJoin**, and then run and close the query.

⊕ EXPLORE

9. Create a self-join based on the tblPersonnel table with the PersonID field as the primary key and Manager as the foreign key. Select the PersonID, FirstName, and LastName fields from the related table (the table that has the Manager field connected to the join line), and the PersonID, FirstName, and LastName fields from the primary table. The column names in the query recordset should be **Person ID**, **First Name**, **Last Name**, **Manager ID**, **Manager First Name**, and **Manager Last Name**, respectively. Use an inner join. Run the query, resize all columns to their best fit, save the query as **qryPersonnelSelfJoin**, and then close the query.

⊕ EXPLORE

10. Add an index named **Location** to the **tblGuest** table that consists of the StateProv and City fields and uses the default property settings, delete the PostalCode index, and then save and close the table.

11. Make a backup copy of the database, compact and repair the Rentals database, and then close the database.

Explore some new skills to manage and update a database for an ISP.

CREATE

Case Problem 5

Data File needed for this Case Problem: Always.accdb

Always Connected Everyday   Chris and Pat Dixon own and manage Always Connected Everyday (ACE), a successful Internet service provider (ISP) in your area. ACE provides Internet access to residential and business customers and offers a variety of access plans, from dial-up and DSL to wireless. Within each type of service—dial-up, DSL, and wireless—ACE offers low-cost plans with either slower access speeds or fewer capabilities and more expensive plans with either higher access speeds or greater service and features.

To keep track of their business, Chris and Pat have developed the Always database. The database has two tables: the tblAccessPlan table contains data about the plans they offer commercial and residential customers, and the tblCustomer contains data about their customers. The database also contains several queries, forms, and reports.

Chris and Pat want you to add two new tables to the database to keep track of their business's service calls. Also, they want you to define a many-to-many relationship and to create several new queries. To help them with their requests, complete the following steps:

1. Open the **Always** database located in the Access3\Case5 folder provided with your Data Files.

2. Designate the Access3\Case5 folder as a trusted folder. (*Note:* Check with your instructor before adding a new trusted location.)

3. Use your first and last names for the first record in the tblCustomer table.

4. Create the following tables:

   a. The **tblService** table includes a unique service ID (AutoNumber data type), a service description, and a service rate (Currency data type).

   b. The **tblServiceCall** table includes a unique service call ID (AutoNumber data type), the customer account number, service ID, and service date.

5. Define a many-to-many relationship between the tblCustomer and tblService tables, using the tblServiceCall table as the related table. Select the referential integrity option and the cascade updates option for the relationships.

6. Design test data for the tblService and tblServiceCall tables, and then add the test data to the tables. Your tblService table should contain at least 10 records, and your tblServiceCall table should contain at least 12 records.

7. Create a make-table query based on the tblCustomer table, selecting the CustomerAcctNum, CompanyName, FirstName, LastName, City, and AccessPlanID fields from the table. Select those records with a City field value of **Blade** or **Drayton**. Save the table as **tblSelectedCustomer** in the current database. Run the query, and then switch to Design view.

8. Modify the make-table query to create an append query that selects those records with a city field value of **Brunson** and appends the selected records to the tblSelectedCustomer table. Run the query, and then close the query without saving it.

9. Create an update query to select all records in the tblSelectedCustomer table in which the AccessPlanID field value equals **4**, changing the AccessPlanID field value to **5**. Run the query, and then close the query without saving it.

10. Create a delete query that deletes all records from the tblSelectedCustomer table in which the AccessPlanID field value equals **7**. Run the query, and then close the query without saving it. Open the **tblSelectedCustomer** table, resize all columns to their best fit, and then save and close the table.

11. Create an outer join between the tblAccessPlan and tblCustomer tables, selecting all records from the tblAccessPlan table and any matching records from the tblCustomer table. Display the AccessPlanID, AccessPlan, and PlanMonthlyCost fields from the tblAccessPlan table, and the CompanyName, FirstName, and LastName fields from the tblCustomer table. Save the query as **qryPlanCustomerOuterJoin**, and then run and close the query.

 EXPLORE 12. Add an index that allows duplicates named **Zip** to the **tblCustomer** table, delete the UserID index, and then save and close the table.

13. Make a backup copy of the database, compact and repair the Always database, and then close the database.

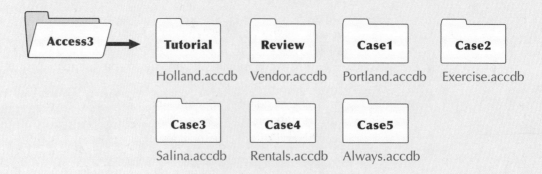
ENDING DATA FILES

Access3 →

Tutorial
Holland.accdb

Review
Vendor.accdb

Case1
Portland.accdb

Case2
Exercise.accdb

Case3
Salina.accdb

Case4
Rentals.accdb

Case5
Always.accdb

Automating Tasks with Macros

Creating a User Interface for the Holland Database

OBJECTIVES

Session 10.1
- Run and add actions to macros
- Single step a macro
- Create a submacro
- Add a command button to a form
- Attach a macro to a command button

Session 10.2
- Create an unbound form
- Add a list box to a form
- Use an SQL statement to fill a list box with object names
- Create multiple macros for a form
- Create a navigation form

Case | *Belmont Landscapes*

At a recent office automation conference, Lucia Perez, the database developer for Belmont Landscapes, saw several database applications developed by database designers. The designers' applications used several advanced Access features to automate and control how a user interacts with Access. One of these features allowed the designers to create a custom user interface for a database. This interface made it much easier for inexperienced users to access the database, and it minimized the chance that an unauthorized user could change the design of any database object.

Lucia would like to implement a similar user interface for the Holland database. She would like the interface to display specific forms and reports, and all the queries in the database, so that the users can select the object they want to work with from the interface. This interface will make it much easier for employees to use the Holland database, and it will reduce the chance that they will make undesirable changes to the design of these database objects.

STARTING DATA FILES

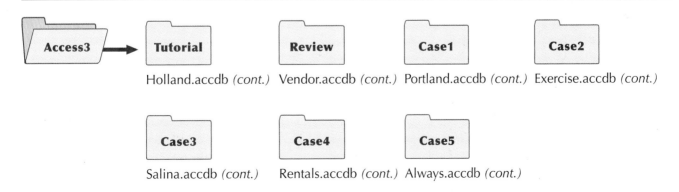

Access3 → Tutorial — Holland.accdb *(cont.)*

Review — Vendor.accdb *(cont.)*

Case1 — Portland.accdb *(cont.)*

Case2 — Exercise.accdb *(cont.)*

Case3 — Salina.accdb *(cont.)*

Case4 — Rentals.accdb *(cont.)*

Case5 — Always.accdb *(cont.)*

SESSION 10.1 VISUAL OVERVIEW

Click the Single Step button to **single step**, which executes one macro action at a time, pausing between actions.

The **Action Catalog button** is a toggle to open and close the Action Catalog pane. The **Action Catalog** lists all actions by category and all macros in the database.

Click the Run button to execute the open macro.

Click the Convert Macros to Visual Basic button to create a Visual Basic version of the macro.

The *mcr* prefix tag identifies the object as a macro. Read the Naming Conventions section in the appendix titled "Relational Databases and Database Design" at the end of this book for more information about naming conventions.

An optional comment in a macro starts and ends with "/*" and "*/" and appears in a green font.

The **OpenForm action** opens a specified form in a specified view. An **action** is an instruction to Access to perform an operation, such as opening a form or displaying a query.

Arguments are additional facts Access needs to execute an action.

The **MessageBox action** displays a message box containing a warning or informational message.

The **Beep action** produces a beep tone through the computer's speakers.

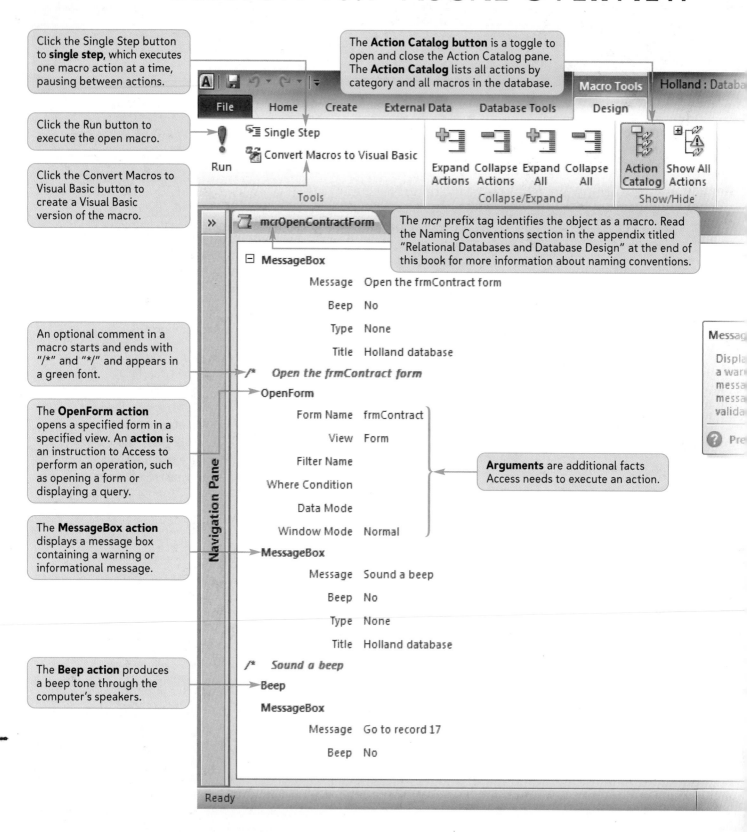

MACRO DESIGNER

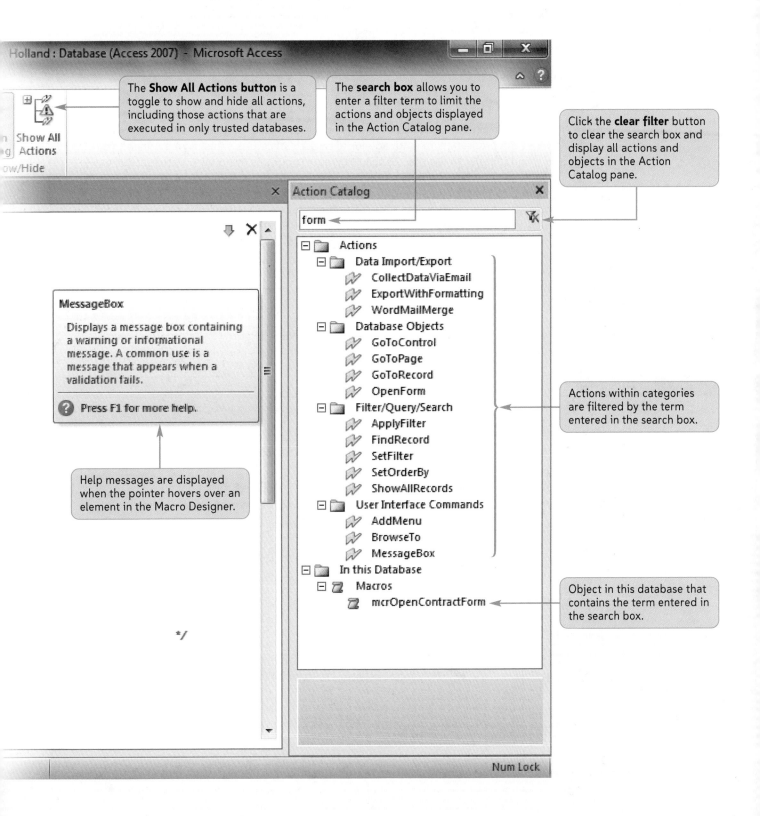

Holland : Database (Access 2007) - Microsoft Access

The **Show All Actions button** is a toggle to show and hide all actions, including those actions that are executed in only trusted databases.

The **search box** allows you to enter a filter term to limit the actions and objects displayed in the Action Catalog pane.

Click the **clear filter** button to clear the search box and display all actions and objects in the Action Catalog pane.

Show All Actions
ow/Hide

Action Catalog

form

MessageBox

Displays a message box containing a warning or informational message. A common use is a message that appears when a validation fails.

? Press F1 for more help.

Help messages are displayed when the pointer hovers over an element in the Macro Designer.

Actions
- Data Import/Export
  - CollectDataViaEmail
  - ExportWithFormatting
  - WordMailMerge
- Database Objects
  - GoToControl
  - GoToPage
  - GoToRecord
  - OpenForm
- Filter/Query/Search
  - ApplyFilter
  - FindRecord
  - SetFilter
  - SetOrderBy
  - ShowAllRecords
- User Interface Commands
  - AddMenu
  - BrowseTo
  - MessageBox
- In this Database
  - Macros
    - mcrOpenContractForm

Actions within categories are filtered by the term entered in the search box.

Object in this database that contains the term entered in the search box.

*/

Num Lock

Introduction to Macros

Lucia plans to automate some of the processing in the Holland database, initially by using macros and then later by using Visual Basic for Applications code. A **macro** is an action, or a set of actions, that you want Access to perform automatically for you. Macros automate repetitive tasks, such as opening forms, printing selected form records, and running queries.

INSIGHT

Deciding When to Use Macros and VBA

Access lets you automate most tasks using either macros or Visual Basic for Applications (VBA), the programming language for Microsoft Office programs. As a beginner, you will find it easier to use macros than to create programs using VBA. With macros, you simply select a series of actions from a list to create a macro that does what you want it to do. To use VBA, you need to understand the VBA command language well enough to be able to write your own code. VBA does provide advantages over using macros, such as better error-handling capabilities and making your application easier to change. Macros, however, are useful for small applications and for simple tasks, such as opening and closing objects. Additionally, you cannot use VBA to assign actions to a specific key or key combination or to open an application in a special way, such as displaying a user interface. For these types of actions, you must use macros.

When you use Access, over 80 actions are available; Figure 10-1 describes several frequently used Access actions. None of the action names contains spaces.

Figure 10-1   **Frequently used Access actions**

Action	Description
ApplyFilter	Applies a filter to a table, form, or report to restrict or sort the records in the recordset
Beep	Produces a beep tone through the computer's speakers
CloseWindow	Closes the specified window, or the active window if none is specified
FindRecord	Finds the first record, or the next record if the action is used again, that meets the specified criteria
GoToControl	Moves the focus to a specified field or control on the active datasheet or form
MessageBox	Displays a message box containing a warning or informational message
OpenForm	Opens a form in the specified view
QuitAccess	Exits Microsoft Access
RunMacro	Runs a macro
SelectObject	Selects a specified object so you can run an action that applies to the object
SendKeys	Sends keystrokes to Microsoft Access or another active program

Running a Macro

Lucia had never used Access macros, so she created a macro with multiple actions as a practice exercise after she returned from the conference. Before you begin creating the final macros Lucia wants, you'll run Lucia's first macro, named mcrOpenContractForm, which performs multiple actions using the frmContract form. You can reference and run a macro from within a form or report, or you can run an existing macro directly.

Directly Running an Existing Macro

- With the Macro Designer open, click the Run button in the Tools group on the Design tab on the Ribbon.

  or

  In the Macro group on the Database Tools tab on the Ribbon, click the Run Macro button, select the macro name in the Macro Name list in the Run Macro dialog box, and then click the OK button.

  or

  In the Macros group in the Navigation Pane, right-click the macro name, and then click Run on the shortcut menu.

You'll use the shortcut menu to run the mcrOpenContractForm macro.

To run the mcrOpenContractForm macro:

1. Start Access, and then open the **Holland** database in the Access3\Tutorial folder provided with your Data Files.

   Trouble? If the Security Warning is displayed below the Ribbon, either the Holland database is not located in the Access3\Tutorial folder or you did not designate that folder as a trusted folder. Make sure you opened the database in the Access3\Tutorial folder, and make sure that it's a trusted folder.

2. Make sure the Navigation Pane is open, scroll down the Navigation Pane (if necessary), right-click **mcrOpenContractForm** in the Macros group, and then click **Run** on the shortcut menu. A message box opens. See Figure 10-2.

| Figure 10-2 | Using a macro action to open a message box |

Opening the message box is the first action Lucia added to the mcrOpenContractForm macro. A **message box** is a special dialog box that contains a message and a command button, but no options. The message box remains on the screen until you click the OK button. This message box specifies that the next macro action will open the frmContract form. When you click the OK button, the message box closes, and the macro resumes with the next action. Lucia added this message box and other message boxes to the macro so that she could more easily observe the macro's actions as she experimented with the macro. With macros you create for working databases, you don't include message boxes between steps as Lucia did in her macro.

> **3.** Click the **OK** button. The next two actions in the mcrOpenContractForm macro are performed: the frmContract form opens, and the second message box opens. See Figure 10-3.

Figure 10-3   **Second and third actions in the mcrOpenContractForm macro**

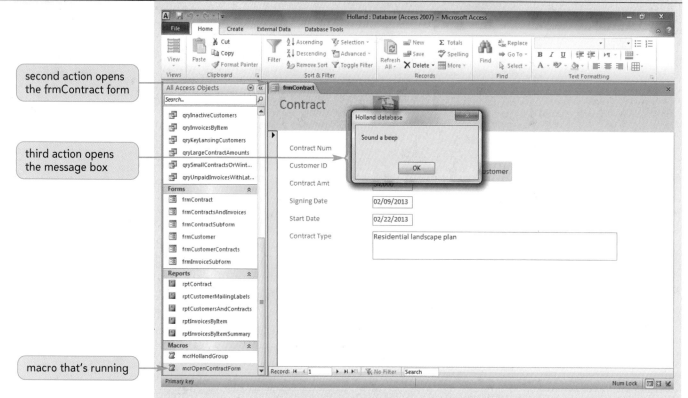

second action opens
the frmContract form

third action opens
the message box

macro that's running

> **4.** Click the **OK** button. A beep sounds, and the third message box opens. These are the fourth and fifth actions in the mcrOpenContractForm macro.
>
>   **Trouble?** If your computer doesn't have speakers, you won't hear the beep sound. If you do hear the beep, its sound varies depending on your computer and its settings.
>
> **5.** Click the **OK** button, and then drag the message box title bar to the right so you can view the values in the form's text boxes. The frmContract form now displays record 17 for ContractNum 3035. These are the sixth and seventh actions in the mcrOpenContractForm macro.
>
> **6.** Click the **OK** button. The frmContract form closes, and the mcrOpenContractForm macro ends.

Lucia suggests that you add some actions to the mcrOpenContractForm macro to learn about the Macro Designer and how to modify an existing macro.

Adding Actions to a Macro

To modify the mcrOpenContractForm macro, you need to open the Macro Designer for the macro. To open the Macro Designer, you'll open the macro in Design view.

To open the Macro Designer:

▶ **1.** Right-click **mcrOpenContractForm** in the Navigation Pane, click **Design View** on the shortcut menu, and then close the Navigation Pane. The Macro Designer displays the mcrOpenContractForm macro. See Figure 10-4.

Figure 10-4	Macro Designer

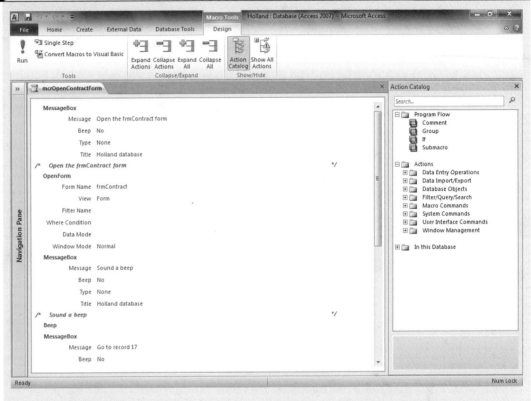

The **Macro Designer** allows you create and modify macros. See the Session 10.1 Visual Overview for descriptions and explantions of the Macro Designer components.

A MessageBox action is the first action in the macro, and the action is followed by the four arguments needed by the action. For example, the MessageBox action needs the wording of the message to be displayed in the message box and the title bar's name as arguments. When a macro contains a MessageBox action, the macro doesn't proceed to the next action until users click the OK button, so they have as much time as they need to read and react to the message box.

The MessageBox action requires four arguments: Message, Beep, Type, and Title, described as follows:

- The Message argument contains the text that will appear in the message box when it is displayed.
- The Beep argument is either Yes or No to specify whether a beep will sound when the message box opens.
- The Type argument determines which icon, if any, appears in the message box to signify the critical level of the message. The icon choices are None (no icon), Critical (⊗), Warning? (❓), Warning! (⚠), and Information (ℹ).
- The Title argument contains the word(s) that will appear in the message box title bar.

You'll add two actions, the MessageBox and FindRecord actions, to the mcrOpenContractForm macro between the GoToRecord and the last MessageBox actions. For the FindRecord action, you'll find the record for ContractNum 3040. You use the **FindRecord action** to find the first record, or the next record if the action is used again, that meets the criteria specified by the FindRecord arguments.

To add two actions to the mcrOpenContractForm macro:

1. In the Collapse/Expand group on the Design tab, click the **Collapse Actions** button to hide all the detailed argument lines in the macro. Only the lines for the actions and comments now appear in the macro.

   Below the last action in the macro is the Add New Action box, which you use to add actions to the end of the macro. You'll select the MessageBox action in the box, set its arguments, and then move it above the current last MessageBox action.

2. Click the **Add New Action** arrow to display the list of actions, scroll down the list, and then click **MessageBox**. The list closes, MessageBox becomes the new action with four arguments, and two arguments are set with default values. See Figure 10-5.

Figure 10-5	After adding the MessageBox action

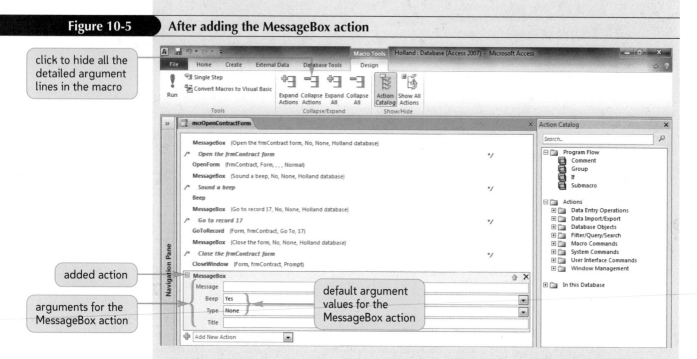

You'll enter values for the Message and Title arguments, change the Beep argument value from Yes to No, and retain the default Type argument value of None. If you hover the mouse pointer on the MessageBox line or on any argument line, a ScreenTip displays a brief explanation of the action or argument. You can also use Help to learn about specific actions and their arguments, and about macros in general.

3. Click the **Message** box (if necessary), type **Find contract 3040**, press the **Tab** key, click the **Beep** arrow, click **No**, press the **Tab** key twice, and then type **Holland database** in the Title box. See Figure 10-6.

Figure 10-6   **Completed MessageBox action**

move the new MessageBox action to here

MessageBox   (Go to record 17, No, None, Holland database)

↗ **Go to record 17**   */

GoToRecord   (Form, frmContract, Go To, 17)

MessageBox   (Close the form, No, None, Holland database)

↗ **Close the frmContract form**   */

CloseWindow   (Form, frmContract, Prompt)

⊟ MessageBox   Move up button

   Message   Find contract 3040

   Beep   No   argument values typed here

   Type   None

   Title   Holland database

✦ Add New Action

Data Entry Operations
Data Import/Export
Database Objects
Filter/Query/Search
Macro Commands
System Commands
User Interface Commands
Window Management

In this Database

You now need to move the new MessageBox action three positions up in the macro because it needs to be above the two actions and one comment that precede it.

TIP

Use the Move down button to move actions down in the macro.

4. On the MessageBox line, click the **Move up** button 🔼 three times to move the action to its correct position. Nine lines of actions and comments are now above the new MessageBox action, and two actions and one comment are now below the action.

You'll now add the FindRecord action to the macro. You could add the FindRecord action to the bottom of the macro and move it up three positions as you did for the MessageBox action. Instead, you'll search for the action in the Action Catalog pane, and then drag it to its correct position in the macro. First, you'll collapse the MessageBox action.

5. In the Collapse/Expand group on the Design tab, click the **Collapse Actions** button to hide all the detailed argument lines in the MessageBox action.

6. In the Action Catalog pane, click the **search** box, and then type **find**. Access displays a filtered list of actions containing the search term of *find*.

7. In the Action Catalog pane, drag **FindRecord** to the macro immediately below the newly added MessageBox action until a colored line appears just below the MessageBox action. See Figure 10-7.

Figure 10-7   **Dragging the FindRecord action to the macro**

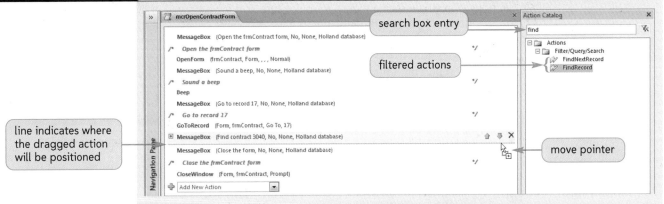

line indicates where the dragged action will be positioned

mcrOpenContractForm

MessageBox   (Open the frmContract form, No, None, Holland database)

↗ **Open the frmContract form**   */

OpenForm   (frmContract, Form, , , , Normal)

MessageBox   (Sound a beep, No, None, Holland database)

↗ **Sound a beep**   */

Beep

MessageBox   (Go to record 17, No, None, Holland database)

↗ **Go to record 17**   */

GoToRecord   (Form, frmContract, Go To, 17)

⊞ MessageBox   (Find contract 3040, No, None, Holland database)

MessageBox   (Close the form, No, None, Holland database)

↗ **Close the frmContract form**   */

CloseWindow   (Form, frmContract, Prompt)

✦ Add New Action

search box entry — find

filtered actions

Action Catalog

Actions
Filter/Query/Search
FindNextRecord
FindRecord

move pointer

8. Release the mouse button to add the FindRecord action to the macro. The FindRecord action has seven arguments.

Trouble? If you drag the wrong action or drag the action to the wrong location, delete the action by clicking the Delete button to the right of the Move up and Move down buttons, and then repeat Steps 7 and 8.

You need to set the Find What argument to a value of 3040. You'll accept the defaults for the other action arguments.

▶ **9.** Click the **Find What** box (if necessary), type **3040**, and then click the minus box ⊟ to the left of FindRecord to hide all the detailed argument lines for the action.

Finally, you'll add a comment above the FindRecord action.

▶ **10.** In the Action Catalog pane, click the **clear filter** button 🔻 to remove the filter and display the entries in the box, drag **Comment** to the macro immediately above the FindRecord action, type **Find contract 3040** in the Comment box, and then click an empty area at the bottom of the Macro Designer to close the Comment box and complete your macro changes. See Figure 10-8.

Figure 10-8	After adding two actions to the macro

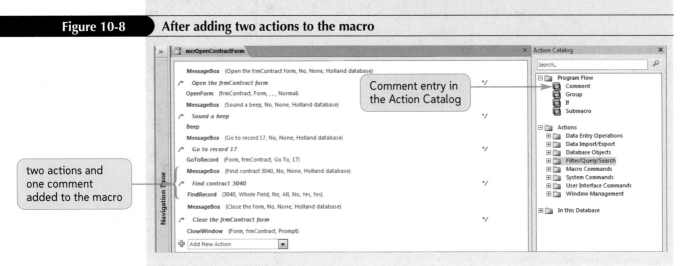

When you create complicated macros with many actions, you'll find it useful to run through a macro one step at a time.

Single Stepping a Macro

The macro single step feature executes a macro one action at a time, pausing between actions. You single step a macro to make sure you have placed actions in the right order and with the correct arguments. If you have problems with a macro, you can use single step to find the causes of the problems and to determine their proper corrections. The Single Step button in the Tools group on the Design tab is a toggle you use to turn single stepping on and off. Once you turn on single stepping, it stays on for all macros until you turn it off.

REFERENCE

Single Stepping a Macro

- In the Macro Designer, click the Single Step button in the Tools group on the Design tab.
- Click the Run button in the Tools group on the Design tab.
- In the Macro Single Step dialog box, click the Step button to execute the next action, click the Stop All Macros button to stop the macro, or click the Continue button to execute all remaining actions in the macro and turn off the single step process.

To get a clearer understanding of the effects of the actions in the mcrOpenContractForm macro, you can single step through it. First, you need to save your macro changes.

To save the macro changes and then single step through it:

▶ **1.** Click the **Save** button 🖫 on the Quick Access Toolbar to save your macro design changes.

▶ **2.** Click the **Single Step** button in the Tools group on the Design tab to turn on the single step feature.

▶ **3.** Click the **Run** button in the Tools group on the Design tab. The Macro Single Step dialog box opens. See Figure 10-9.

| Figure 10-9 | Macro Single Step dialog box |

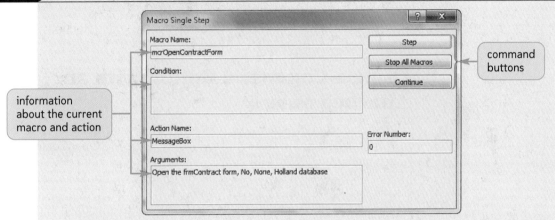

Trouble? If the first message box opens instead of the Macro Single Step dialog box, then you turned off single stepping in Step 2 when you clicked the Single Step button. Click the OK button to run through the end of the macro, and then repeat Steps 2 and 3.

When you single step through a macro, Access opens the Macro Single Step dialog box before performing each action. This dialog box shows the macro's name and the action's condition, name, and arguments. The action will be executed or not executed, depending on whether the condition is true or false. The three command buttons let you step through the macro one action at a time, stop the macro and return to the Macro Designer, or continue by executing all remaining actions without pausing. If you click the Continue button, you also turn off single stepping.

▶ **4.** Click the **Step** button. Access runs the first action (MessageBox). Because the MessageBox action pauses the macro, the Macro Single Step dialog box remains hidden until you click the OK button in the message box.

▶ **5.** Click the **OK** button to close the message box. The Macro Single Step dialog box shows the macro's second action (OpenForm).

▶ **6.** Click the **Step** button. Access runs the second action by opening the frmContract form and shows the macro's third action (MessageBox) in the Macro Single Step dialog box.

▶ **7.** Continue clicking the **Step** button and the **OK** button until you see the "Find contract 3040" message box, making sure you read the Macro Single Step dialog box carefully and observe the actions that occur. At this point, record 17 is the current record in the frmContract form.

8. Click the **OK** button, and then click the **Step** button. The FindRecord action runs, record 20 for ContractNum 3040 is now the current record in the frmContract form, and the Macro Single Step dialog box shows the macro's last MessageBox action.

9. Click the **Step** button, click the **OK** button, and then click the **Step** button. The Macro Single Step dialog box closes automatically after the last macro action is completed; the last macro action closes the frmContract form.

You've finished your work with Lucia's macro, and can turn off the single step feature.

10. Click the **Design** tab on the Ribbon, click the **Single Step** button in the Tools group to turn off single step feature, and then click the **Close 'mcrOpenContractForm'** button ☒ to close the macro.

Lucia suggests you next review a macro she created for the frmContract form.

Using a Command Button with an Attached Macro

Lucia created a macro that she associated with, or attached to, a command button on the frmContract form that you just opened using the mcrOpenContractForm macro. A **command button** is a control on a form that starts an action, or a set of actions, when you click it. You can also add a command button to a form to execute a set of actions. To add a command button to a form, you open the form in Design view and use the Button tool in the Controls group on the Design tab. After adding the command button to the form and while still in Design view, you attach a macro with the desired actions to the command button. Then, when a user clicks the command button, the macro's actions are executed.

Lucia asks you to use the View Customer command button on the frmContract form to see how the macro attaches to the command button, and then to view the macro.

To use the View Customer command button:

1. Open the Navigation Pane, open the **frmContract** form in Form view to display the frmContract form for the first contract with ContractNum 3011 and CustomerID 11001, click **3011** in the Contract Num text box to deselect all values, and then close the Navigation Pane. See Figure 10-10.

Figure 10-10   **View Customer command button on the frmContract form**

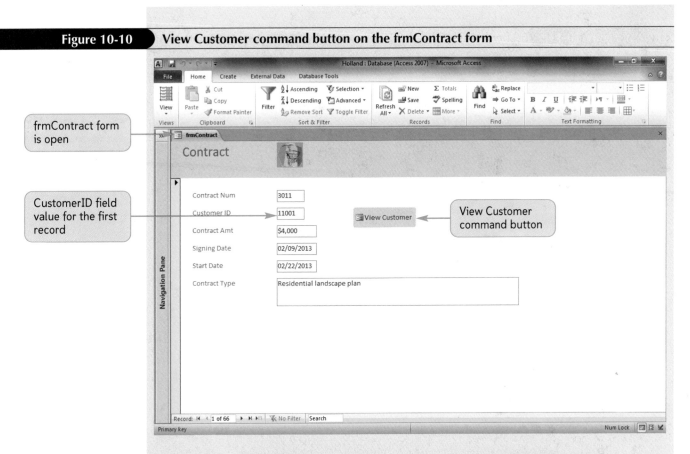

2. Click the **View Customer** command button, and then click **11001** in the Customer ID text box to deselect all values. The frmContract form remains open, and the frmCustomer form opens for CustomerID 11001. The frmCustomer form is the active form. See Figure 10-11.

Figure 10-11   After opening the frmCustomer form with the View Customer command button

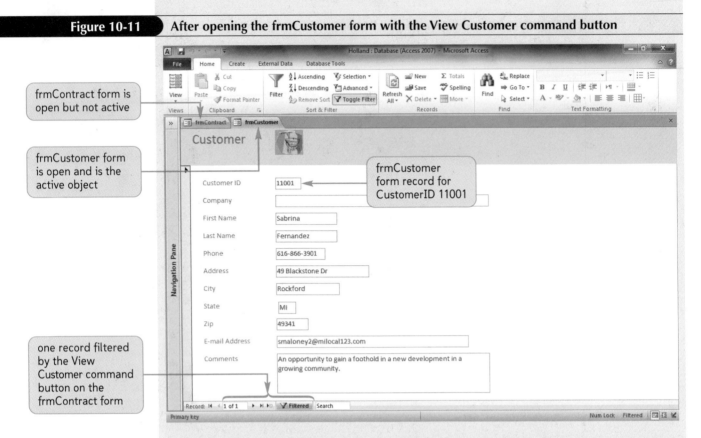

frmContract form is open but not active

frmCustomer form is open and is the active object

frmCustomer form record for CustomerID 11001

one record filtered by the View Customer command button on the frmContract form

Clicking the View Customer command button triggered an attached macro that opened the frmCustomer form. The record displayed in the frmCustomer form is for the customer (CustomerID 11001) who signed the contract displayed in the frmContract form. The text "Record 1 of 1 (Filtered)" that appears around the navigation buttons in the frmCustomer form indicates that you can view only the record for CustomerID 11001 in the frmCustomer form at this point.

▶ 3. Close the frmCustomer form, click the **Next record** navigation button ▶ to move to record 2 in the frmContract form for ContractNum 3012 and CustomerID 11027, and then click the **View Customer** command button. The frmCustomer form opens for CustomerID 11027.

▶ 4. Close the frmCustomer form. The frmContract form is now the active object.

Clicking the View Customer command button is an event, and the opening of the frmCustomer form is controlled by setting an event property.

Events

An **event** is a state, condition, or occurrence detectable by Access. For example, events occur when you click a command button on a form, when you use the mouse to position the pointer on a form, or when you press a key to choose an option. In your work with Access, you've initiated hundreds of events on forms, controls, records, and reports without any special effort. For example, three form events are: Open, which occurs when you open a form; Activate, which occurs when the form becomes the active window; and Close, which occurs when you close a form and the form is removed from the screen. Each event has an associated event property. An **event property** specifies how an object responds when an event occurs. For example, each form has OnOpen, OnActivate, and OnClose event properties associated with Open, Activate, and Close events, respectively.

Event properties appear in the property sheet when you create forms and reports. Unlike most properties you've used previously in property sheets, event properties do not have an initial value. If an event property contains no value, it means the event property has not been set. In this case, Access takes no *special action* when the associated event occurs. For example, if a form's OnOpen event property is not set and you open the form, then the Open event occurs (the form opens), and no *special action* occurs beyond the opening of the form. You can set an event property value to a macro name, and Access will execute the macro when the event occurs. For example, you could write a macro that automatically selects a particular field in a form when you open it. You can also create a group of statements using VBA code and set the event property value to the name of that group of statements. Access will then execute the group of statements, or **procedure**, when the event occurs. Such a procedure is called an **event procedure**.

When you clicked the View Customer command button on the frmContract form, the Click event occurred and triggered an attached macro. The View Customer command button contains an OnClick event property setting, which you will examine next.

To view the OnClick event property setting for the View Customer command button:

1. Switch to Design view, right-click the **View Customer** command button, click **Properties** on the shortcut menu to open the property sheet, and then click the **Event** tab (if necessary) in the property sheet.

2. Right-click the **On Click** box, click **Zoom** on the shortcut menu to open the Zoom dialog box, and then click to the right of the selected text to deselect it. See Figure 10-12.

Figure 10-12 | Macro attached to the OnClick event property

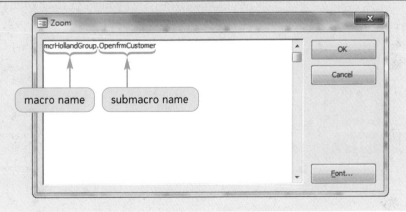

The OnClick event property value shown in the Zoom dialog box is *mcrHollandGroup.OpenfrmCustomer*. This is an example of a reference to a submacro in a macro.

Submacros

If you need to create several related macros, you can create them as submacros in a single macro instead of creating them as separate macros. A **submacro** is a complete macro with a Submacro header within a macro. Using submacros allows you to consolidate related macros and to manage large numbers of macros. For example, if a form's design uses command buttons to open a form with a related record and to print the related record displayed in the form, you can create one macro for the form that contains two submacros—one submacro to open the form, and a second submacro to print the related record. Because you created the macro specifically for the form object, you can store all the submacros you need in a single macro. When a macro contains a submacro, a period separates the macro name from the submacro name. For the OnClick event property value shown in Figure 10-12, for example, mcrHollandGroup is the macro name, and OpenfrmCustomer is the submacro name. When you click the View Customer command button on the frmContract form, Access processes the actions contained in the OpenfrmCustomer submacro, which is located in the mcrHollandGroup macro.

You'll now close the Zoom dialog box, and then open the Macro Designer from the property sheet.

To open the mcrHollandGroup macro in the Macro Designer:

▶ 1. Click the **Cancel** button in the Zoom dialog box to close it. In the property sheet for the selected View Customer command button (named cmdViewCustomer, where *cmd* is a prefix tag to identify a command button control), the On Click box contains an arrow and a Build button to its right. See Figure 10-13.

| **Figure 10-13** | OnClick event property value for the View Customer command button |

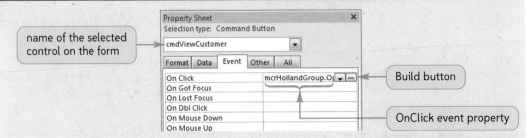

You click the On Click arrow if you want to change the current macro to a different macro, and you click the Build button if you want to use the Macro Designer to view or change the existing macro. The Build button is also called the **Macro Builder** when you use it to work with macros.

▶ 2. Click the **Build** button […] on the right side of the On Click box. The Macro Designer opens and displays the mcrHollandGroup macro and the OpenfrmCustomer submacro. See Figure 10-14.

| **Figure 10-14** | Macro Designer displaying the mcrHollandGroup macro and its submacro |

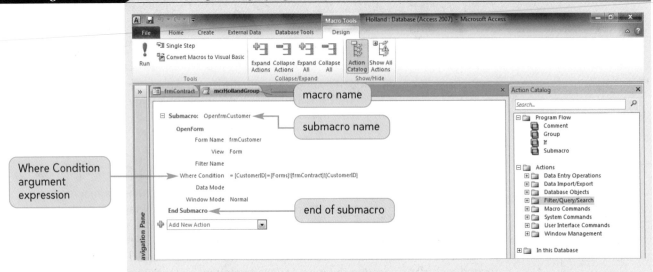

The mcrHollandGroup macro consists of one submacro that starts with the Submacro statement and ends with the End Submacro statement. These statements are not actions; they are control statements to identify the beginning and end of a submacro. If a macro contains several submacros, each submacro starts with a Submacro statement and ends with an End Submacro statement.

The OpenfrmCustomer submacro consists of a single action, OpenForm, which opens the frmCustomer form (the **Form Name argument** value is frmCustomer). The other OpenForm action arguments are as follows:

- The **View argument** specifies the view in which to open the object. For forms, you can specify Form, Design, Print Preview, Datasheet, PivotTable, PivotChart, or Layout view.
- The **Filter Name argument** specifies the name of a query, or a filter that was saved as a query, that will be used to sort or filter the object's records. When the submacro does not use a filter, the Filter Name argument is blank.
- The **Where Condition argument** specifies an expression or SQL statement that will be used to select records to display in the form. You'll learn more about SQL statements later in this tutorial.
- The **Data Mode argument** specifies the form's data-entry options. Allowable settings for this argument are Add (users can add new records but can't change or delete existing records), Edit (users can change and delete existing records and can add new records), and Read Only (users can only view records). If you don't select an argument value, Edit is the default setting.
- The **Window Mode argument** specifies the form's window characteristics. Allowable settings for this argument are Normal (the form opens as it normally would from the Navigation Pane), Hidden (the form opens but is not visible), Icon (the form opens minimized as a small title bar at the bottom of the screen), and Dialog (the form opens as a dialog box). Normal is the default setting.

The Where Condition argument value in Figure 10-14 specifies which record appears in the frmCustomer form when you open the form by clicking the View Customer button. The Where Condition argument value contains the expression =[CustomerID]=[Forms]! [frmContract]![CustomerID]. In simple terms, the expression asks Access to find the record in the frmCustomer form with the same CustomerID as the current record in the frmContract form. The expression, however, is complex. The OpenForm action in the macro opens the frmCustomer form; the value [CustomerID] to the left of the equal sign determines which record will be displayed in the frmCustomer form. What is this CustomerID value? It's the same as (equal sign) the CustomerID that appears in the current frmContract form record ([Forms]![frmContract]![CustomerID] to the right of the equal sign). To the right of the equal sign, [Forms] identifies the object collection, such as forms or queries. Next, [frmCustomer] identifies the name of the specific object within the object collection—in this case, frmCustomer. Finally, [CustomerID] identifies the specific control within the specified object—in this case, the CustomerID field in the frmCustomer form.

Now that you've seen a macro that's attached to a command button, Lucia asks you to add a command button to the frmContract form, and then to attach a new macro to the command button. Users want to be able to print the current record in the frmContract form by clicking a command button on the form. Lucia created the mcrHollandGroup macro to group together all the submacros in the Holland database. Because the Macro Designer is already open for the mcrHollandGroup macro, you'll add a submacro to it to print the current record.

Adding a Submacro

To print the contents of a form's current record, normally you have to click the File tab on the Ribbon to display Backstage view, click Print, click Selected Record(s), and then click the OK button—a process that takes four steps and several seconds. Instead of following this process, you can create a command button on the form, create a macro that prints the contents of a form's current record, and then attach the macro to the command button on the form. To print the form's current record, you'd simply click the command button.

First, you'll add a submacro to the mcrHollandGroup macro. You'll use the SelectObject and RunMenuCommand actions for the new submacro. The **SelectObject action** selects a specified object so that you can run an action that applies to the object. The **RunMenuCommand action** selects and runs a command on the Ribbon. The specific argument you'll use with the RunMenuCommand action is the **PrintSelection argument**, which prints the selected form record. You'll use the submacro name PrintSelectedRecord when you add it to the mcrHollandGroup macro. Because macros and submacros are database objects, you follow the naming conventions for database objects when naming macros and submacros. These naming conventions include using descriptive object names so that the object's function is obvious, capitalizing the first letter of each word in the name, and excluding spaces from the name.

REFERENCE

Adding a Submacro

- Open the macro in the Macro Designer.
- Click the Add New Action arrow, click Submacro, and then type the submacro name in the Submacro box.
- Click the Add New Action arrow above the End Submacro statement, click the action you want to use, and then set the action's arguments.
- If the submacro consists of more than one action, repeat the previous step for each action.
- Add comments as needed to the submacro to document the submacro's function or provide other information.
- Save the macro.

You'll now add the PrintSelectedRecord submacro to the mcrHollandGroup macro.

To add the PrintSelectedRecord submacro to the mcrHollandGroup macro:

TIP

You can also type the first few letters of the action until the full action name appears, and then press the Tab key to select the action.

1. Click the minus box ⊟ to the left of Submacro OpenfrmCustomer to collapse the actions and arguments for the submacro.

2. Click the **Add New Action** arrow to display the list of actions and control statements, click **Submacro**, and then type **PrintSelectedRecord** in the Submacro box. The Submacro and End Submacro statements are added to the macro, and the Add New Action box appears between these two statements. See Figure 10-15.

| Figure 10-15 | Adding a new submacro |

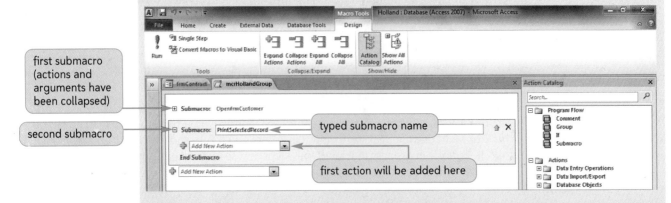

first submacro (actions and arguments have been collapsed)

second submacro

typed submacro name

first action will be added here

You need to select the SelectObject action and set its arguments.

3. Between the Submacro and End Submacro statements, click the **Add New Action** arrow, scroll down the list, and then click **SelectObject**. The SelectObject action is added to the PrintSelectedRecord submacro. This action has three arguments. The first argument, Object Type, specifies the type of database object to select. The second argument, Object Name, specifies the name of the object to open.

You need to open a form named frmContract, so you'll set these arguments first.

4. Click the **Object Type** arrow, click **Form**, click the **Object Name** arrow, and then click **frmContract**. Because the form will be open when you run the macro, you'll leave the In Database Window argument set to No.

You'll next select the RunMenuCommand action and set its arguments. The RunMenuCommand action lets you add a command available on the Ribbon to a submacro. The Command argument in this submacro lets you select the command. In this case, the Command argument is named PrintSelection.

5. Below the SelectObject action, click the **Add New Action** arrow, scroll down the list, click **RunMenuCommand**, click the **Command** arrow, scroll down the list, and then click **PrintSelection**.

You've completed the second action. You'll add another SelectObject action to the submacro to return control back to the frmContract form after printing the selected record to make the form the active object.

6. Below the RunMenuCommand action, click the **Add New Action** arrow, scroll down the list, click **SelectObject**, set the Object Type argument to **Form**, and then set the Object Name argument to **frmContract**. You've finished adding the three actions to the PrintSelectedRecord submacro. See Figure 10-16.

| Figure 10-16 | After adding three actions to the PrintSelectedRecord submacro |

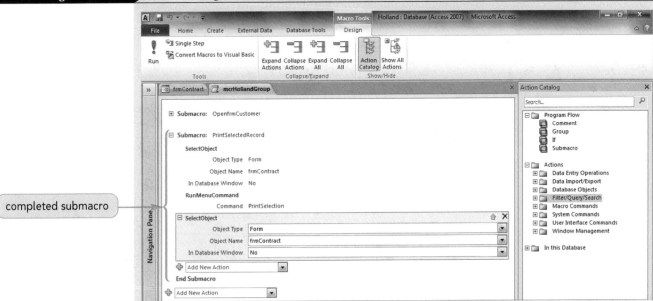

completed submacro

7. Save your macro design changes, and then close the Macro Designer. The frmContract form is the active object.

Next, you'll add a command button to the frmContract form. After you attach the PrintSelectedRecord macro to the command button, you'll be able to click the command button to print the current frmContract form record.

Adding a Command Button to a Form

In Design view for a form, you use the Button tool in the Controls group on the Design tab to add a command button to a form. If the Use Control Wizards tool is selected when you click the Button tool, the Command Button Wizard guides you through the process of adding the command button. Instead, you'll add the command button directly to the frmContract form without using the wizard. Then you'll set the command button's properties using its property sheet.

To add a command button to the frmContract form:

1. Close the property sheet.

2. Click the **Design** tab, click the **More** button ⏷ in the Controls group, and then make sure the **Use Control Wizards** tool ⚒ in the Controls group on the Design tab is not selected.

   Trouble? If the Use Control Wizards tool has an orange background, click it to disable the control wizards, and then continue with Step 3.

3. In the Controls group on the Design tab, click the **Button** tool ▭.

4. Move the pointer over the Detail section, and when the pointer's plus symbol (+) is positioned in the Detail section at the 1.5-inch mark on the horizontal ruler and the 2.75-inch mark on the vertical ruler, click the mouse button. Access adds a command button to the form. See Figure 10-17.

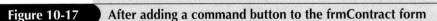

Figure 10-17   **After adding a command button to the frmContract form**

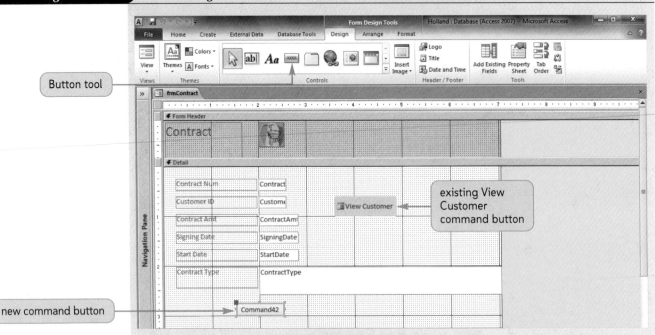

Trouble? If the Command Button Wizard dialog box opens, click the Cancel button to close it, click the Use Control Wizards tool in the Controls group on the Design tab to deselect it, and then repeat Steps 3 and 4.

> **Trouble?** The command button on your screen might show a different number in its label, depending on how you completed the previous steps. This difference will not affect the command button or macro. Just continue with the tutorial.

You can now attach the PrintSelectedRecord submacro to the command button.

Attaching a Submacro to a Command Button

You created the PrintSelectedRecord submacro and added the command button to the frmContract form. You'll attach the submacro to the command button's OnClick property so that the submacro is executed when the command button is clicked.

To attach the PrintSelectedRecord submacro to the command button:

▶ **1.** Make sure the command button is selected, and in the Tools group on the Design tab, click the **Property Sheet** button to open the property sheet, and then, if necessary, click the **Event** tab in the property sheet.

▶ **2.** Click the **On Click** arrow in the property sheet to display the macros list, and then click **mcrHollandGroup.PrintSelectedRecord**.

> **Trouble?** If your property sheet isn't wide enough to display the macro names, drag the left edge of the property sheet to the left to widen it, and then repeat Step 2.

You can change the text that appears on the command button (also known as the command button's label or caption) by changing its Caption property, you can replace the text with a picture by setting its Picture property, or you can include both text and a picture. Lucia wants you to place a picture of a printer on the command button and to display text on the command button.

▶ **3.** Click the **Format** tab in the property sheet, click the **Picture** box, and then click the **Build** button ⋯ that appears on the right side of the Picture box. The Picture Builder dialog box opens. See Figure 10-18.

Figure 10-18 | **Picture Builder dialog box**

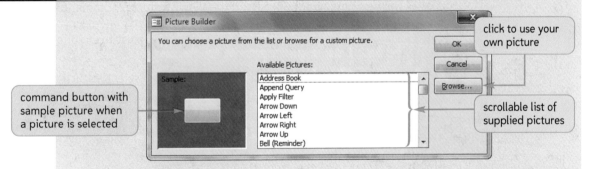

The Picture Builder dialog box contains an alphabetical list of pictures supplied with Access. You can scroll the list and select one of the pictures, or you can click the Browse button to select your own picture. When you select a picture, a sample of the picture appears on the command button in the Sample box on the left.

▶ **4.** Scroll down the Available Pictures box, and then click **Printer**. A printer picture appears on the command button in the Sample box.

5. Click the **OK** button. The Picture Builder dialog box closes, and the printer picture appears on the command button in the form.

6. Click the **Caption** box in the property sheet, press the **F2** key to select the Caption property value, type **Print selected record**, and then press the **Tab** key.

   The **Picture Caption Arrangement property** specifies how a command button's Caption property value is arranged in relation to the picture placed on the command button. The choices are No Picture Caption, General, Top, Bottom, Left, and Right.

7. Click the **Picture Caption Arrangement** arrow, and then click **Bottom**.

   The command button is not tall enough or wide enough to display the picture and caption, so you'll resize it.

8. Use the middle-bottom sizing handle and the middle-right sizing handle to increase the width and height of the command button so it looks like the one shown in Figure 10-19.

Figure 10-19	Command button with picture and caption

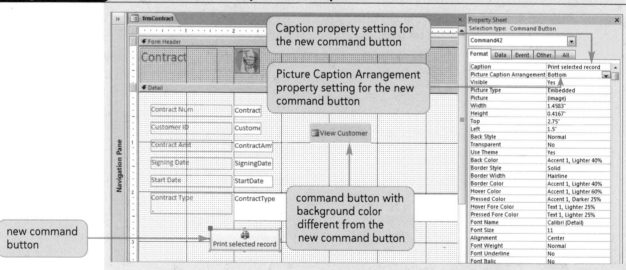

The new command button and the View Customer command button have different background colors. Lucia wants the colors to match, so you'll change the new command button's background color. The simplest technique is to copy and paste the Back Color property settings for the controls.

9. Click the **View Customer** command button to select it, click the **Back Color** box in the property sheet, press the **F2** key to select the value, press **Ctrl+C** to copy the selection, click the **Print selected record** command button, click the **Back Color** box in the property sheet, press the **F2** key, press **Ctrl+V** to paste the copied property setting, and then press the **Tab** key. The two command buttons now have the same gray background color.

Next, you'll save the frmContract form and test the command button.

To save the form and test the command button:

▶ **1.** Close the property sheet, save your form design changes, and then switch to Form view.

▶ **2.** Click the **Last record** navigation button ▶ on the Contract navigation bar to move to the last contract record for ContractNum 3201.

▶ **3.** Click the **Print selected record** command button on the form to open the Print dialog box. Notice that the submacro correctly set the print range to print the selected record.

▶ **4.** Click the **OK** button to print the last contract record. The submacro correctly returned control to the frmContract form after the record was printed.

▶ **5.** Close the form.

▶ **6.** If you are not continuing on to the next session, close the Holland database.

You've now completed your initial work with macros. Next, you'll start to develop the user interface for the Holland database. You'll create a form that contains a list box to display the queries in the Holland database, use an SQL statement to select the values for the list box, and then add command buttons to the form.

REVIEW

Session 10.1 Quick Check

1. What is a macro?
2. What is the Macro Designer?
3. What does the MessageBox action do?
4. What are you trying to accomplish when you single step through a macro?
5. What is an event property?
6. What is the purpose of the Where Condition argument for the OpenForm action?
7. How do you change the picture on a command button?

SESSION 10.2 VISUAL OVERVIEW

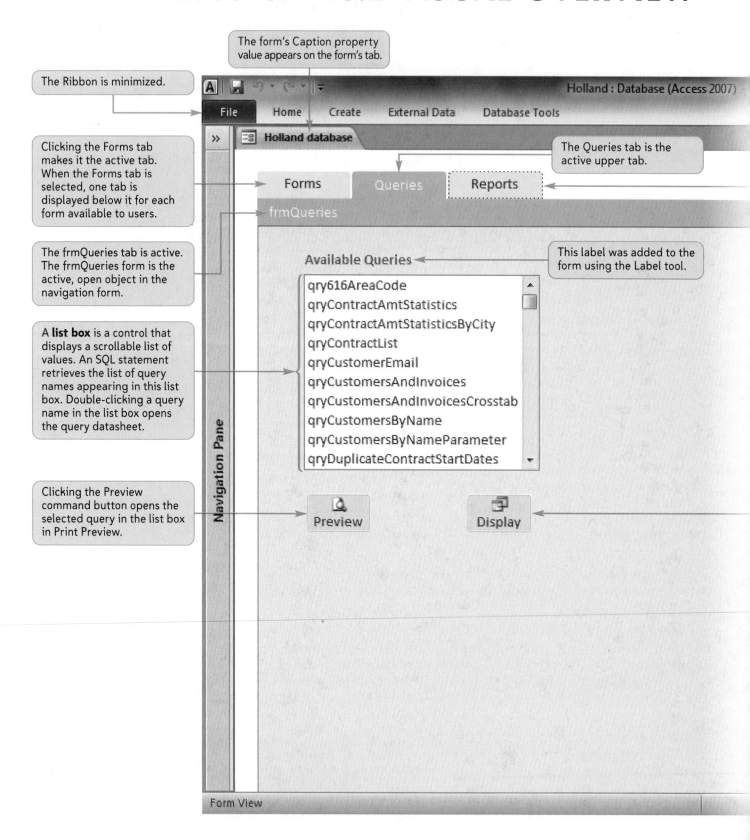

The form's Caption property value appears on the form's tab.

The Ribbon is minimized.

Holland : Database (Access 2007)

File   Home   Create   External Data   Database Tools

» Holland database

Clicking the Forms tab makes it the active tab. When the Forms tab is selected, one tab is displayed below it for each form available to users.

The Queries tab is the active upper tab.

Forms   Queries   Reports

frmQueries

The frmQueries tab is active. The frmQueries form is the active, open object in the navigation form.

Available Queries

This label was added to the form using the Label tool.

A **list box** is a control that displays a scrollable list of values. An SQL statement retrieves the list of query names appearing in this list box. Double-clicking a query name in the list box opens the query datasheet.

qry616AreaCode
qryContractAmtStatistics
qryContractAmtStatisticsByCity
qryContractList
qryCustomerEmail
qryCustomersAndInvoices
qryCustomersAndInvoicesCrosstab
qryCustomersByName
qryCustomersByNameParameter
qryDuplicateContractStartDates

Navigation Pane

Clicking the Preview command button opens the selected query in the list box in Print Preview.

Preview   Display

Form View

NAVIGATION FORM

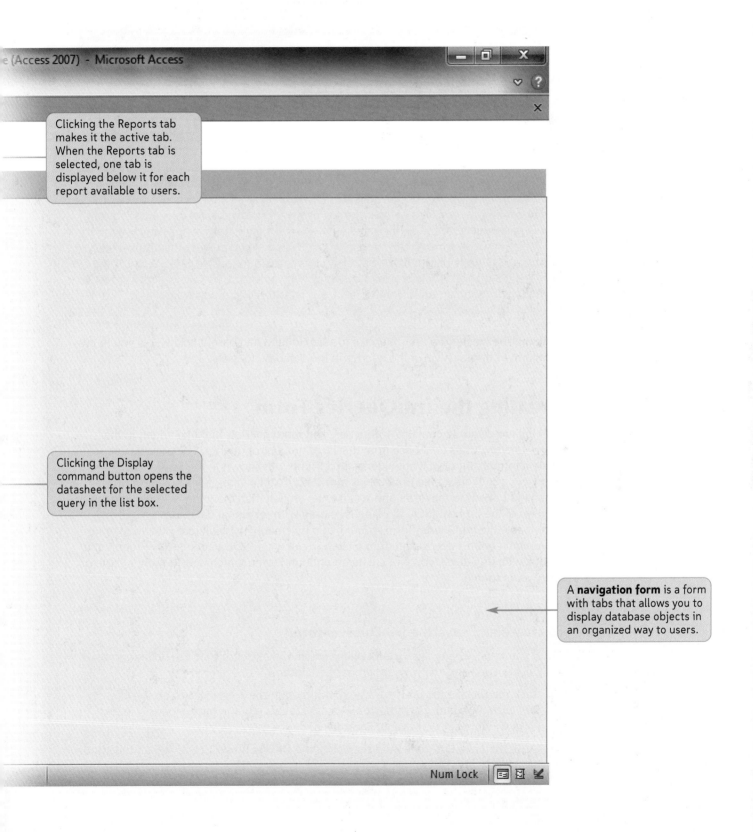

> Clicking the Reports tab makes it the active tab. When the Reports tab is selected, one tab is displayed below it for each report available to users.

> Clicking the Display command button opens the datasheet for the selected query in the list box.

> A **navigation form** is a form with tabs that allows you to display database objects in an organized way to users.

Designing a User Interface

A **user interface** is what you see and use when you communicate with a computer program. Lucia wants to provide a simple user interface for the Holland database.

PROSKILLS

Problem Solving: Restricting Access to Database Objects and Prohibiting Design Changes

Database users need to be able to add, change, and delete data, but they should make these updates using forms and special queries, such as action queries. Users should not directly update data using table datasheets. Users also need to review and print information from a database using reports, forms, and queries. Finally, users should not be allowed to change the design of any database object or the design of the user interface. You need to create a user interface that meets all these needs and restrictions. When users open a database, you should present them with a form that allows them to choose among the available forms, reports, and queries and to navigate from one object to another object as they perform their work. At the same time, you must limit users to this controlled user interface and prevent them from circumventing it, so that you prevent them from changing any aspect of the design of the database. By considering the needs of the users and by using the features and tools provided by the DBMS, you ensure users can work productively with a database and ensure the integrity of the data stored in the database.

Before she creates the user interface for the Holland database, Lucia wants you to create a form to display a list of the queries in the database to users.

Creating the frmQueries Form

The Holland database contains 18 queries, and more queries might be added in the future. To allow users to choose from this large number of queries, Lucia wants you to create a form that'll display the queries in a list box. As shown in the Session 10.2 Visual Overview, you'll create the frmQueries form. You'll add a label, a list box, and two command buttons to the form, and you'll enter an SQL statement that will provide the contents of the list box. (SQL is a language used with relational databases.)

To create the frmQueries form, you'll begin by creating a blank form. Because none of the form controls needs data from a table or query (an SQL statement will supply the list box with its values), you will create an unbound form, which does not use a table or query as its source.

To create and save the frmQueries form:

▶ **1.** If you took a break after the previous session, make sure that the Holland database is open and the Navigation Pane is closed.

▶ **2.** Click the **Create** tab on the Ribbon, and then in the Forms group on the Create tab, click the **Blank Form** button. Access creates a blank form, opens it in the Form window in Layout view, and opens the Field List pane.

▶ **3.** Close the Field List pane, and then click the **Design View** button on the status bar to switch to Design view.

▶ **4.** Click the **Save** button on the Quick Access Toolbar, type **frmQueries** in the Form Name box, and then press the **Enter** key.

Before adding any controls to the form, you need to set the overall form properties so that the form matches Lucia's design. You will set the Caption property to "Queries," which is the value that will appear on the form's tab when you open the form. You will also set the Shortcut Menu, Record Selectors, Navigation Buttons, and Close Button properties to No because Lucia doesn't want the form to include these features. Figure 10-20 shows the form property settings you will use to create the frmQueries form for Lucia.

Figure 10-20   **frmQueries form properties**

Property	Setting	Function
Caption	Queries	Value that appears on the form's object tab when the form is open
Close Button	No	Disables the display of the Close button on the form's object tab
Navigation Buttons	No	Disables the display of navigation buttons at the bottom of the form
Record Selectors	No	Disables the display of a record selector on the left side of the form
Shortcut Menu	No	Disables the display of the shortcut menu when a user right-clicks the form

Setting Form Properties for Unbound Forms

All the objects you've created and used so far are standard objects in which users need to navigate from record to record, or from page to page in the case of reports, and to perform other operations such as copying data and closing the object. For unbound forms, users do not need to perform any of these operations, so you should set the appropriate form properties to remove these features from the form. This means removing the navigation buttons and record selectors, and preventing users from opening the shortcut menu. In addition, Lucia's plans for the user interface will not require users to close the unbound form, so you should also remove the Close button from the form.

You'll use the property sheet to set the form properties shown in Figure 10-20.

To set the properties for the unbound form:

1. Right-click the **form selector**, which is the box immediately to the left of the horizontal ruler, and then click **Properties** on the shortcut menu to open the form's property sheet.

2. If necessary, click the **Format** tab in the property sheet to display the Format page of the property sheet.

   You can now set the Caption property for the form. The Caption property value will appear on the tab when the form is displayed.

3. Click the **Caption** box, and then type **Queries**.

   Next, you'll set the Record Selectors property so that a record selector will not be displayed on the left side of the form. Because the form does not display any records, there's no need to include a record selector.

4. Double-click **Yes** in the Record Selectors box to change the property setting from Yes to No.

   You'll now set the remaining form properties.

5. Scrolling as necessary, set the Navigation Buttons property to **No**, set the Close Button property to **No**, click the **Other** tab in the property sheet, and then set the Shortcut Menu property to **No**.

6. Close the property sheet, and then save your form design changes.

Now that you have set the form's properties, you can add a label and a list box to it. The label will identify the list box for the user, and the list box will display the list of queries in the Holland database. You will not use the Control Wizards tool for the list box because you'll be using an SQL statement to provide the query names for the list box.

Adding a List Box to a Form

The list box in the frmQueries form will display the list of queries that the user can preview or view. Clicking the name of a query selects it, and then the user can click one of the command buttons to preview or view the query. Double-clicking a query name in the list box also will open the query datasheet.

REFERENCE

Adding a List Box to a Form

- Switch to Design view, if necessary.
- If necessary, click the More button in the Controls group on the Design tab, and then click the Use Control Wizards tool to select or deselect it, depending on whether you want to use the wizard.
- Click the More button in the Controls group on the Design tab, and then click the List Box tool.
- Position the pointer's plus symbol (+) where you want to place the upper-left corner of the list box, and then click the mouse button.
- If you use the List Box Wizard, complete the dialog boxes to choose the source of the list, select the fields to appear in the list box, select a sort order, size the columns, and select the label.
- If you do not use the List Box Wizard, set the Row Source property and size the list box.

First, you'll add the label "Available Queries" to the form. Then you'll add the list box to display the list of queries in the database.

To add the label to the form:

1. In the Controls group on the Design tab, click the **Label** tool $\boxed{Aa}$.

2. Position the pointer in the Detail section; when the pointer's plus symbol (+) is positioned at the 0.5-inch mark on the horizontal ruler and the 0.25-inch mark on the vertical ruler, click the mouse button. A small label box containing an insertion point opens in the form.

3. Type **Available Queries** and then press the **Enter** key.

Lucia wants the label to stand out more, so you'll make the label bold, and then resize the label box.

4. Click the **Format** tab on the Ribbon, in the Font group click the **Bold** button **B**, right-click the **label** to open the shortcut menu, point to **Size**, and then click **To Fit**.

Now you can add the list box to the form.

To add the list box to the form:

1. Click the **Design** tab on the Ribbon, click the **More** button ⊡ in the Controls group, and then make sure the **Use Control Wizards** tool ⬚ in the Controls group is not selected.

   Trouble? If the Use Control Wizards tool has an orange background, click it to disable the control wizards, and then continue with Step 2.

2. In the Controls group, click the **More** button ⊡, if necessary, to open the Controls gallery, and then in the Controls group on the Design tab, click the **List Box** tool ⊞.

3. Move the pointer over the Detail section, and when the pointer's plus symbol (+) is positioned in the row of grid dots below the left edge of the Available Queries label box, click the mouse button. Access adds a list box to the form. See Figure 10-21.

| Figure 10-21 | Form's design after adding the label and list box |

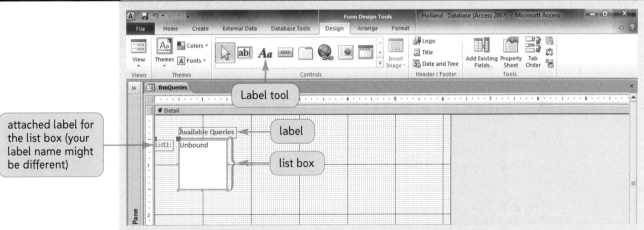

attached label for the list box (your label name might be different)

Trouble? If your list box is sized or positioned differently, resize it or move it until it matches the list box shown in Figure 10-21.

You can now save the form and then check your progress by switching to Form view.

4. Save your form design changes, and then switch to Form view. See Figure 10-22.

| Figure 10-22 | **frmQueries form displayed in Form view** |

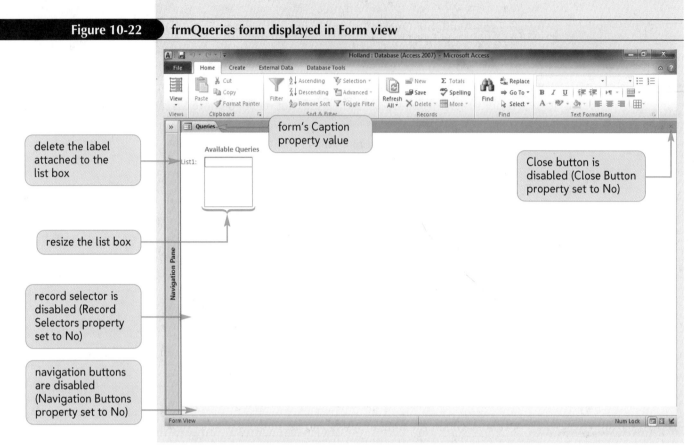

After viewing the form, Lucia asks you to make two changes to it. Because the form already includes the label "Available Queries," the label attached to the list box is unnecessary. Lucia asks you to delete this label. She'd also like you to resize the list box by making it taller and wider so that it will accommodate the list of queries better.

To delete the label attached to the list box and resize the list box:

 1. Switch to Design view.

 2. Right-click the **label** attached to the list box to open the shortcut menu, and then click **Cut** to delete it.

 3. Click the **list box** to select it.

 4. Use the middle-right sizing handle to drag the right border of the list box to the 3-inch mark on the horizontal ruler, use the middle-bottom sizing handle to drag the bottom border of the list box to the 2.5-inch mark on the vertical ruler, and then save your form design changes.

You now can enter the SQL statement that will provide the query names for the list box.

Using SQL

SQL (Structured Query Language) is a standard language used in querying, updating, and managing relational databases. Every full-featured relational DBMS has its own version of the current standard SQL. If you learn SQL for one relational DBMS, it's a relatively easy task to begin using SQL for other relational DBMSs. When you work with two or more relational DBMSs, which is the case in most companies, you'll learn that few differences exist among the various SQL versions.

Much of what Access accomplishes behind the scenes is done with SQL. Whenever you create a query, for example, Access automatically constructs an equivalent SQL statement. When you save a query, Access saves the SQL statement version of the query.

Viewing an SQL Statement for a Query

When you are working in Design view or viewing a query recordset, you can see the SQL statement that is equivalent to your query by switching to SQL view.

REFERENCE

Viewing an SQL Statement for a Query

- Open the query in Datasheet view or Design view.
- Click the SQL View button on the status bar, right-click the object tab and click SQL View on the shortcut menu, or click the View button arrow in the Views group (in Datasheet view) or in the Results group (in Design view) and click SQL View.

Next, you'll examine the SQL statements that are equivalent to two existing queries: qryContractList and qryCustomersAndInvoices.

To view the SQL statement for the qryContractList query:

1. Open the Navigation Pane, open the **qryContractList** query datasheet, and then close the Navigation Pane. The query displays 66 records from the tblContract table. The columns displayed are Contract Num, Contract Amt, and Contract Type.

2. Right-click the **qryContractList** object tab to open the shortcut menu, click **SQL View** to display the query in SQL view, and then click an unused portion of the window to deselect the SQL statement. See Figure 10-23.

Figure 10-23   **SQL view for the qryContractList query**

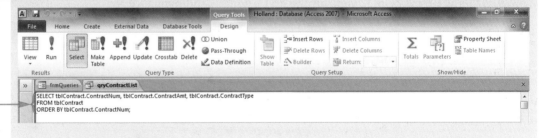

SQL statement

```
SELECT tblContract.ContractNum, tblContract.ContractAmt, tblContract.ContractType
FROM tblContract
ORDER BY tblContract.ContractNum;
```

SQL uses the **SELECT statement** to define what data it retrieves from a database and how it presents the data. For the work you've done so far, the options on the Ribbon, in dialog boxes, and on the property sheet have sufficed. If you learn SQL to the point where you can use it efficiently, you will be able to enter your own SELECT and other SQL statements in SQL view. If you work with more complicated databases, you might find that you need the extra power of the SQL language to implement your database strategies fully.

The rules that SQL uses to construct a statement similar to the SELECT statement shown in Figure 10-23 are summarized as follows:

- The basic form of an SQL SELECT statement is: SELECT-FROM-WHERE-ORDER BY. After SELECT, list the fields you want to display. After FROM, list the tables used in the query. After WHERE, list the selection criteria. After ORDER BY, list the sort fields.
- If a field name includes a space or special symbol, enclose the field name in brackets. Because the Holland database does not use field names with spaces or special symbols, you don't have to enclose its field names in brackets. However, if your database has field names such as *Contract Type*, then you would use [Contract Type] in an SQL statement.
- Precede a field name with the name of its table by connecting the table name to the field name with a period. For example, you would enter the ContractNum field in the tblContract table as *tblContract.ContractNum*.
- Separate field names and table names by commas, and end the statement with a semicolon.

The SQL statement shown in Figure 10-23 selects the ContractNum, ContractAmt, and ContractType fields from the tblContract table; the records are sorted in ascending order by the ContractNum field. The SQL statement does not contain a WHERE clause, so the recordset will include all records from the tblContract table when the query is run.

You can enter or change SQL statements directly in SQL view. If you enter an SQL statement and then switch to Design view, you will see its equivalent in the design grid.

Next, you'll examine the SQL statement for the qryCustomersAndInvoices query.

To view the SQL statement for the qryCustomersAndInvoices query:

1. Close the qryContractList query, open the Navigation Pane, open the **qryCustomersAndInvoices** query in Design view, and then close the Navigation Pane. The query selects data from the tblCustomer, tblContract, and tblInvoice tables and does not sort the records. The fields included in the query design are CustomerID, Company, FirstName, LastName, City, InvoiceAmt, and InvoicePaid.

2. In the Results group on the Design tab, click the **View** button arrow, click **SQL View** to change to SQL view, and then click an unused portion of the window to deselect the SQL statement. See Figure 10-24.

Figure 10-24 | **SQL view for the qryCustomersAndInvoices query**

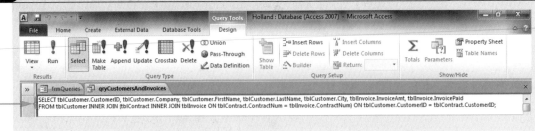

SQL statement

```
SELECT tblCustomer.CustomerID, tblCustomer.Company, tblCustomer.FirstName, tblCustomer.LastName, tblCustomer.City, tblInvoice.InvoiceAmt, tblInvoice.InvoicePaid
FROM tblCustomer INNER JOIN (tblContract INNER JOIN tblInvoice ON tblContract.ContractNum = tblInvoice.ContractNum) ON tblCustomer.CustomerID = tblContract.CustomerID;
```

The SELECT statement for this query is similar to the one shown in Figure 10-23, except for the INNER JOIN clause. The INNER JOIN clause selects records from the two tables only when the records have the same value in the common field that links the tables. The syntax for this clause is to type INNER JOIN between the two table names, followed by ON, and then followed by the names of the fields serving as the common field, connected by an equal sign. (Access uses the ON clause here instead of the standard SQL WHERE clause.)

The SQL SELECT statements mirror the query options you viewed in Design view. In effect, every choice you make in Design view is reflected as part of the SQL SELECT statement. Viewing the SQL statements generated from queries that you design is an effective way to begin learning SQL.

To close the query and return to the frmQueries form:

▶ **1.** Close the query. The frmQueries form in Design view is now the active object.

You now can enter the SQL statement that will provide the query names for the list box.

Using an SQL Statement for a List Box

You'll use an SQL SELECT statement to retrieve the list of query names from one of the Access system tables. **System tables** are special tables maintained by Access that store information about the characteristics of a database and about the structure of the objects in a database. Although system tables do not appear in the Navigation Pane, you can retrieve information from system tables using SELECT statements. One of the system tables, the **MSysObjects table**, keeps track of the names, types, and other characteristics of every object in a database. The Name and Type fields are the two MSysObjects table fields you'll use in the SELECT statement. The Name field contains a query name when the Type field value is 5, as shown in Figure 10-25.

Figure 10-25	MSysObjects table Type field values

Object Type	Type Field Value in MSysObjects Table
Table	1
Query	5
Form	-32768
Report	-32764
Macro	-32766
Module	-32761

Access creates its own queries to handle many tasks for you; each of these queries has a name that begins with the tilde (~) character. Because you want to exclude these special system queries from the list box, you'll also need to use the Left function in your SELECT statement. The **Left function** provides the first character(s) in a text string. The format of the Left function is *Left(text string, number of characters)*. You'll use *Left([Name],1)* to retrieve the first character of the Name field. To include only those queries whose names do not begin with the ~ character, you'll use the expression *Left([Name],1)<>"~"*. In this expression, the <> operator is the not equal operator. Access interprets this expression as "the first character of the Name field does not equal the ~ character." Figure 10-26 shows the Zoom dialog box, which contains the complete SELECT statement that you will use to select the list of query names.

Figure 10-26   **SELECT statement for the list box**

TIP

SQL is case insensitive, but typing SQL keywords in uppercase makes the statements more readable.

The **Row Source property** specifies the data source, such as a table, a query, or an SQL statement, to a list box and to other controls, so you'll enter the SELECT statement as the value for the list box's Row Source property.

To set the Row Source property for the list box:

1. Right-click the **list box** to open the shortcut menu, click **Properties** to open the property sheet, and then click the **Data** tab (if necessary).

2. Right-click the **Row Source** box to open the shortcut menu, and then click **Zoom**. The Zoom dialog box opens.

Compare your SQL statement to the one in Step 3, and make any necessary changes before continuing to Step 4.

3. Type **SELECT [Name] FROM MSysObjects WHERE [Type]=5 And Left([Name],1)<>"~" ORDER BY [Name];** in the Zoom dialog box (be sure to type the semicolon at the end of the statement).

4. Click the **OK** button to close the Zoom dialog box.

5. Close the property sheet, save your form design changes, and then switch to Form view. The queries in the database now appear in alphabetical order in the list box. See Figure 10-27.

Figure 10-27   **Completed list box**

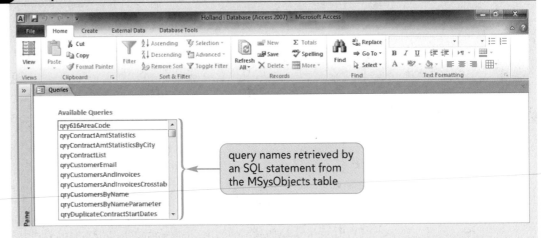

query names retrieved by an SQL statement from the MSysObjects table

Trouble? If a syntax-error message appears, click the OK button, switch to Design view, right-click the list box, click Properties, right-click the Row Source box, and then click Zoom. Correct the SELECT statement until it's the same as the statement shown in Figure 10-26, click the OK button, and then repeat Step 5.

You can now add command buttons to the form.

Adding Command Buttons to a Form

First, you will add the Preview command button to the form. You can add a command button to a form by placing the button directly on the form or by using the Use Control Wizards tool. If you use the Use Control Wizards tool, you can attach a standard Access action (such as opening a specific query or closing a window) or a macro to the button. Because the query to be opened in Print Preview will depend on the query the user has selected in the list box, you'll attach a macro to the command button's On Click property after you've added both command buttons and added a macro to the form.

To add the Preview command button to the form:

▶ **1.** Switch to Design view, make sure the **Use Control Wizards** tool ⬚ in the Controls group on the Design tab is deselected, and then in the Controls group on the Design tab, click the **Button** tool ⬚.

▶ **2.** Position the pointer in the Detail section; when the pointer's plus symbol (+) is positioned at the 2.75-inch mark on the vertical ruler and one grid dot from the left edge of the list box, click the mouse button. Access adds a command button to the form.

▶ **3.** If necessary, open the property sheet for the command button.

　　You can now change the default text that appears on the command button to the word "Preview" and add the Print Preview picture.

▶ **4.** In the property sheet, click the **Format** tab (if necessary), set the Caption property to **Preview**, click the **Picture** box, and then click the **Build** button ⬚ to the right of the Picture box. The Picture Builder dialog box opens.

▶ **5.** Scroll down the Available Pictures box, and then click **Preview**. A Print Preview picture appears on the command button in the Sample box.

▶ **6.** Click the **OK** button to close the Picture Builder dialog box and to place the Print Preview picture on the command button.

▶ **7.** Click the **Picture Caption Arrangement** box, click its **arrow**, and then click **Bottom**.

　　Lucia wants you to change the background color of the command button because it's too pale.

▶ **8.** Click the **Back Color** box, click its **Build** button ⬚, in the Standard Colors section click the **Dark Blue 1** color (row 2, column 4), and then close the property sheet.

▶ **9.** Use the middle-bottom sizing handle and the middle-right sizing handle to increase the height and decrease the width of the command button, and then click to the right of the grid to deselect the command button. See Figure 10-28.

Figure 10-28   After adding the Preview command button to the form

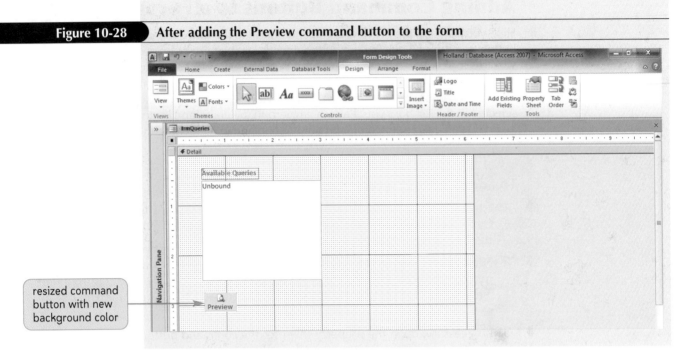

resized command button with new background color

Instead of repeating the steps to add the command button for viewing a query recordset, you'll copy the first command button and paste it in the Detail section. After moving the copied button into position, you can change the text and picture on it.

To add the Display command button to the form:

▶ **1.** Right-click the **Preview** command button, and then click **Copy** on the shortcut menu.

▶ **2.** Right-click the **Detail** section bar, and then click **Paste** on the shortcut menu. Access adds a copy of the command button in the upper-left corner of the Detail section.

▶ **3.** Move the new command button into position to the right of the original command button, and then deselect all controls. See Figure 10-29.

Figure 10-29   After pasting and repositioning a copy of the command button

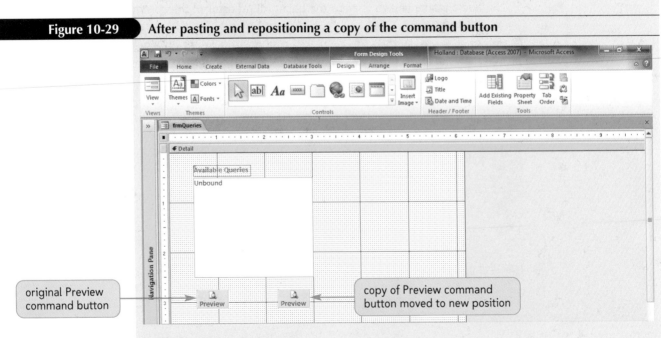

original Preview command button

copy of Preview command button moved to new position

4. Open the property sheet for the new command button, set the Caption property to **Display**, and then set the Picture property to the **MS Access Query**.

5. Save your form design changes.

Before creating the macros for the form and for the command buttons to open the query selected by the user, you'll set the Name property for the list box. It's a good idea to give meaningful names to controls on your forms for easy identification later, so you will enter the name lstQueryList for the list box control, where *lst* (the word *list* without its second letter) is a prefix tag to identify a list box control. You'll also set the background color of the Detail section and the list box.

To set the Name property for the list box and to set background colors:

1. Click the **list box** to make it the active control.

2. Click the **All** tab in the property sheet, select the value in the Name box, and then type **lstQueryList** in the Name box.

3. Click the **Back Color** box in the property sheet, click its **Build** button ⟨...⟩, and then in the Theme Colors section click the **White, Background 1** color (row 1, column 1).

4. Click the **Detail** section bar, and then set the section's Back Color property to **White, Background 1, Darker 5%** (row 2, column 1 in the Theme Colors section).

5. Save your form design changes, and then switch to Form view to display the completed frmQueries form. See Figure 10-30.

| Figure 10-30 | Completed frmQueries form |

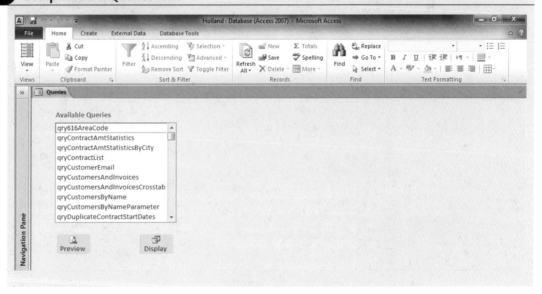

You now can create the macros for the frmQueries form.

Creating the Macros for the frmQueries Form

Lucia wants Access to highlight the first query name in the list box when the frmQueries form first opens, by placing the focus on it. Then, when a user double-clicks a query name in the list box or selects a query name and then clicks the Display command button, the selected query should open in Datasheet view. Finally, when a user selects a query name in the list box and then clicks the Preview command button, the selected query should open in Print Preview. You'll attach macros to the On Click property for the two command buttons, and you'll attach a macro to the On Dbl Click property for the list box. But first you'll attach a macro to the On Load property for the form to highlight the first query name in the list box when the form opens.

The **Load event** occurs when Access opens a form. When you attach a macro to the Load event through the forms's On Load property, Access will process the actions in the macro each time the form is opened. You'll add two actions to the macro. First, you'll use the GoToControl action to move the focus to the list box; however, this action does not set the focus to any specific query name in the list box. You'll use the SendKeys action to send the down arrow keystroke to the list box; Access responds to the SendKeys action by highlighting the first query name in the list box. The end result of these two actions is that when the user opens the frmQueries form, the first query name is highlighted and has the focus.

To create the macro for the On Load property:

▶ **1.** Switch to Design view, click the **Event** tab in the property sheet, click the **On Load** box, and then click its **Build** button ⋯ . The Choose Builder dialog box opens. See Figure 10-31.

Figure 10-31   **Choose Builder dialog box**

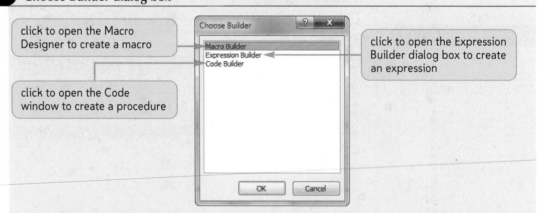

click to open the Macro Designer to create a macro

click to open the Expression Builder dialog box to create an expression

click to open the Code window to create a procedure

The Choose Builder dialog box presents three choices for setting the property value. You can attach a macro to the event property (Macro Builder), set the property to an expression (Expression Builder), or attach a VBA procedure to the event property (Code Builder).

You'll attach a macro to the event property.

▶ **2.** Make sure **Macro Builder** is selected, and then click the **OK** button to open the Macro Designer.

▶ **3.** Click the **Add New Action** arrow to display the list of actions, and then click **GoToControl**. The list closes, and GoToControl becomes the new action with one argument.

4. Type **lst** and then press the **Tab** key to select the AutoComplete box's value of lstQueryList, which is the Name property setting for the list box.

The second and final action you need to add is the SendKeys action.

5. Click the **Add New Action** arrow, scroll down the list, notice that the SendKeys action doesn't appear in the list, click the **Add New Action** arrow to close the list, and then point to the **Show All Actions** button in the Show/Hide group on the Design tab to display the button's ScreenTip. See Figure 10-32.

Figure 10-32   Creating the macro for the form's On Load property

macro for the
frmQueries form's
On Load property

first action in
the macro

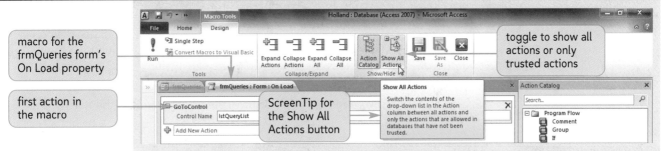

By default, Access displays only trusted actions, but you can display all actions by clicking the Show All Actions button. Because the SendKeys action is not a trusted action, you'll display all actions.

6. In the Show/Hide group on the Design tab, click the **Show All Actions** button, click the **Add New Action** arrow, scroll down the list, and then click **SendKeys**. The list closes, and SendKeys becomes the new action with two arguments. The Keystrokes value of *{Down}* represents the down arrow keystroke, and Wait value of *No* will not pause the macro when it runs.

7. Type **{Down}** in the Keystrokes box to complete the macro. See Figure 10-33.

Figure 10-33   Completed macro for the form's On Load property

Unsafe
Action icon

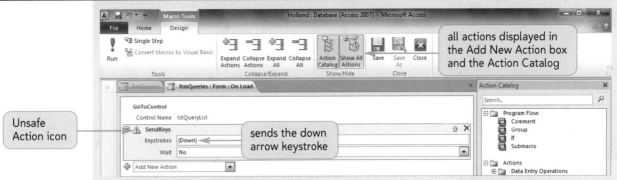

8. Point to the icon to the left of the SendKeys action. The icon's ScreenTip of "Unsafe Action" identifies that the action isn't a trusted action.

9. Save the macro, and then close the Macro Designer to return to the frmQueries form in Design view.

You'll now create the macros for the Preview and Display command buttons and the list box.

To create the macros for the command buttons and the list box:

1. Click the **Preview** command button, click the **On Click** box (if necessary), click its **Build** button ... to open the Choose Builder dialog box, and then click the **OK** button to open the Macro Designer.

   When users click the Preview command button, the query selected in the list box should open in Print Preview.

2. Click the **Add New Action** arrow, scroll down the list, and then click **OpenQuery**. The list closes, and OpenQuery becomes the new action with three arguments.

3. In the Query Name box, type **=**. The Query Name arrow to the right of the Query Name box changes to the Expression Builder button.

4. Click the **Expression Builder** button 📐 to open the Expression Builder dialog box, double-click **lstQueryList** in the Expression Categories column, and then click the **OK** button to close the dialog box. The expression = *[lstQueryList]* now appears in the Query Name box.

5. Click the **View** arrow, and then click **Print Preview** to complete the macro. See Figure 10-34.

| Figure 10-34 | Completed macro for the Preview command button |

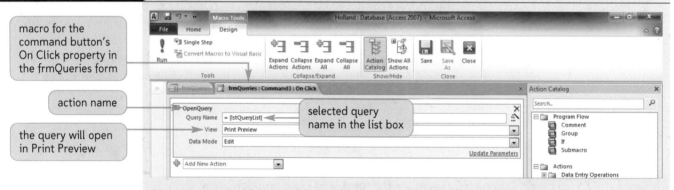

Because you did not set the Name property for the command buttons, the tab displays the default name of Command3 (your name might be different).

6. Save the macro, and then close the Macro Designer.

   You'll next create the macro for the Display command button.

7. Repeat Steps 1 to 5 for the Display command button, setting the View property for the OpenQuery action to **Datasheet**. See Figure 10-35.

| Figure 10-35 | Completed macro for the Display command button |

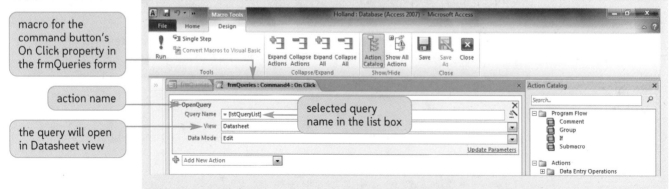

> **8.** Save the macro, and then close the Macro Designer.

> **9.** Click the **list box**, click the **On Dbl Click** box, click its **Build** button [...] to open the Choose Builder dialog box, and then click the **OK** button to open the Macro Designer.

> **10.** Repeat Steps 2 to 6, setting the View property for the OpenQuery action to **Datasheet**.

> **11.** Close the property sheet, save your form changes, and then switch to Form view.

You have finished creating the macros for the form. Next, you will test the list box and the command buttons.

Testing the frmQueries Form

After creating a custom form, you should test the form in Form view. For the frmQueries form, you need to double-click a query name in the list box to make sure the query datasheet opens. You also need to scroll the list box, click a query name, and then click the Display command button to make sure the query datasheet opens, and also click the Preview command button to make sure the query opens in Print Preview.

To test the form's design:

> **1.** Double-click a query name in the list box to verify that the correct query datasheet opens, and then close the query to make the frmQueries form the active object.

> **2.** Repeat Step 1 for a few more query names in the list box, making sure you scroll the list.

> **3.** Click a query name in the list box, click the **Preview** command button to verify that the correct query opens in Print Preview, and then close the Print Preview window to make the frmQueries form the active object.

> **4.** Repeat Step 3 for a few more query names in the list box, making sure you scroll the list.

> **5.** Click a query name in the list box, click the **Display** command button to verify that the correct query datasheet opens, and then close the query to make the frmQueries form the active object.

> **6.** Repeat Step 5 for a few more query names in the list box, making sure you scroll the list.

> Because the frmQueries form's Close button is disabled, you need to switch to Design view, which still has an enabled Close button, to close the form, or you can close the form by using the shortcut menu for the form object's tab.

> **7.** Right-click the **Queries** tab, and then click **Close** on the shortcut menu.

You've completed the custom frmQueries form. Next, Lucia wants you to create the navigation form for the Holland database.

Creating a Navigation Form

TIP

Navigation forms replace switchboards, which were available with all previous versions of Access.

Lucia wants to restrict the access users have to the Holland database to the queries that'll be displayed in the frmQueries form, and to selected forms and reports. To control how users interact with the database, she wants you to create a navigation form that provides users access to only those database objects. A navigation form is a form with tabs that allows you to display database objects in an organized way to users. Access has six predefined layouts for a navigation form with the layouts differing in the placement of tabs and subtabs. Lucia wants you to use the Horizontal Tabs, 2 Levels layout for the navigation form.

To create the navigation form:

▸ **1.** Click the **Create** tab on the Ribbon.

▸ **2.** In the Forms group, click the **Navigation** button. The Navigation gallery opens. See Figure 10-36.

| **Figure 10-36** | **Displaying the Navigation gallery** |

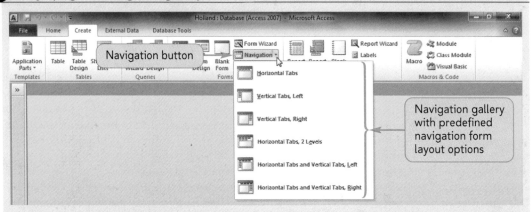

▸ **3.** Click **Horizontal Tabs, 2 Levels** in the gallery, and then close the Field List pane. The navigation form with the default title of "Navigation Form" opens in Layout view. See Figure 10-37.

| **Figure 10-37** | **Initial navigation form** |

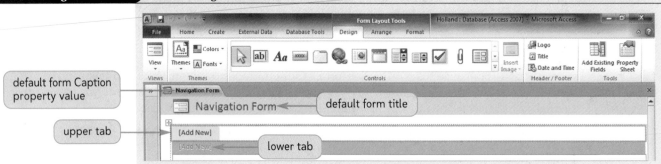

TIP

You must enter tab names and drag objects to the navigation form in Layout view.

Because the navigation form won't display data from the database, it will be an unbound form. You'll enter names for the upper tabs of Forms, Reports, and Queries. You'll then drag the forms and reports that Lucia wants to include in the navigation form from the Navigation Pane to the lower tabs.

To add names and objects to the navigation form:

▶ **1.** Click the upper **[Add New]** tab, type **Forms**, and then press the **Enter** key. Forms is the name on the first tab, and a second tab appears to its right.

> **Trouble?** If you need to correct or change a tab name, click the name, edit the name, and then press the Enter key.

▶ **2.** Click the upper **[Add New]** tab to the right of the Forms tab, type **Queries**, and then press the **Enter** key.

▶ **3.** Click the upper **[Add New]** tab to the right of the Queries tab, type **Reports**, and then press the **Enter** key.

You'll next drag form and report objects from the Navigation Pane to the lower tabs. As you drag the objects, their names are added to the tabs.

TIP

You can drag only forms and reports to tabs in a navigation form.

▶ **4.** Open the Navigation Pane, click the **Forms** tab in the navigation form, and then drag the **frmContract** form from the Navigation Pane to the lower [Add New] tab. The frmContract form opens in the first tab below the Forms tab, and the tab displays the form's name.

> **Trouble?** If you drag the wrong object to a tab, right-click the tab, click Delete on the shortcut menu, and then drag the correct object to the tab.

TIP

You can rearrange the order of objects on the lower tabs by dragging the name from its current tab to its new tab.

▶ **5.** Drag the **frmContractsAndInvoices** form from the Navigation Pane to the [Add New] tab to the right of the frmContract tab, and then drag the **frmCustomer** form from the Navigation Pane to the next [Add New] tab to the right. You've added the three forms Lucia wants users to work with in the Holland database. See Figure 10-38.

Figure 10-38	After dragging three forms to the navigation form

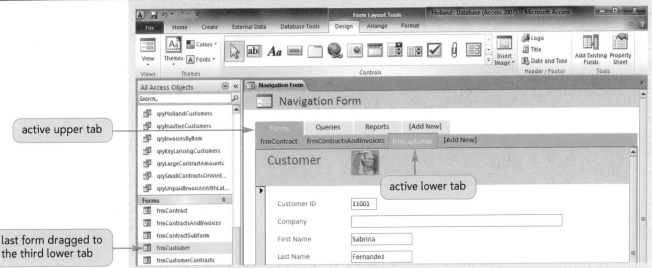

Next, you'll drag objects from the Navigation Pane to the lower tabs below the Queries and Reports tabs.

▶ **6.** Click the **Queries** tab at the top of the navigation form, and then drag the **frmQueries** form from the Navigation Pane to the [Add New] tab below the Queries tab.

7. Click the **Reports** tab at the top of the navigation form, and then drag from the Navigation Pane to the lower tabs, in order, the **rptContract** report, the **rptCustomerAndContracts** report, and the **rptInvoicesByItem** report. Notice that each report opens as you drag it to the form.

8. Close the Navigation Pane. You've finished adding objects to the navigation form. See Figure 10-39.

Figure 10-39   After dragging all required objects to the navigation form

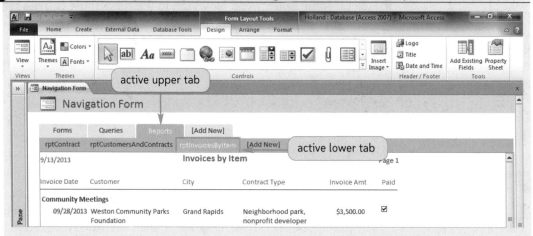

Lucia asks you to delete the picture at the top of the form, delete the form title, set the form's Caption property to "Holland database," and then save the form.

9. Right-click the **picture** at the top of the form, click **Delete** on the shortcut menu, right-click the **form title**, and then click **Delete** on the shortcut menu.

10. Save the form as **frmNavigation**, switch to Design view, open the property sheet for the form, click the **Format** tab (if necessary), and then set the Caption property to **Holland database**.

11. Switch to Form view, and then minimize the Ribbon. See Figure 10-40.

| Figure 10-40 | Completed navigation form |

form's Caption property value

picture and form title deleted

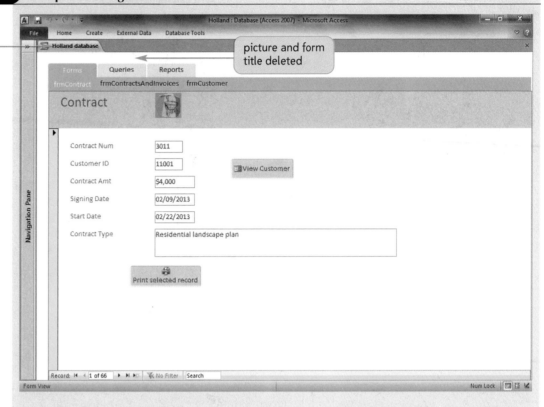

12. Navigate through the navigation form by clicking each upper tab and each of its lower tabs.

> **Trouble?** When you open the navigation form, it also opens every object on the lower tabs. When you click a tab below the Forms tab, you need to click a blank area of the form to place the focus in the first field in the record. When you click the Queries tab, the Load event does not occur for the frmQueries form because the frmQueries form was previously loaded when the navigation form opened it. You need to click a query in the Available Queries list box before you click one of the command buttons on the form.

13. Save and close the form, restore the Ribbon, make a backup copy of the database, compact and repair the Holland database, and then close the database.

Lucia has further changes to make to the navigation form, and you'll make these changes in later tutorials.

Session 10.2 Quick Check

REVIEW

1. What is a list box control?
2. What are system tables?
3. What is the Row Source property?
4. When does the Load event occur?
5. What is a navigation form?

Review Assignments

Data File needed for the Review Assignments: Vendor.accdb (*cont. from Tutorial 9*)

Lucia wants you to create a user interface for the Vendor database. To help with this request, complete the following steps:

1. Open the **Vendor** database located in the Access3\Review folder provided with your Data Files.

2. Design and create a form named **frmQueries** that has the following components and characteristics:

   a. Use the text **Holland Queries** on the form's tab.

   b. Add a list box with a Name property value of **lstQueryList** that displays all the query names contained in the Vendor database, excluding those that start with a "~" character. To place the query names in the list box, use an SQL SELECT statement to retrieve the query names from the MSysObjects table, and display the queries in alphabetical order. Delete the label attached to the list box, and widen the list box to approximately 2.5 inches.

   c. Add the label **Queries Available**, formatted with a 12-point, bold font, above the list box.

   d. Add two command buttons below the list box. The left command button displays the Preview icon above the word **Preview**, and the right command button displays the MS Access Query icon above the word **Display**. Double-clicking a query name has the same effect as selecting a query name in the list box and clicking the right command button. Both events cause Access to display the query datasheet for the selected query. Clicking the left command button opens the selected query in Print Preview.

   e. Create macros for the form (when the form loads move the focus to the first query name in the list box), the list box (when a user double-clicks a query name), and both command buttons (when a user clicks a command button).

   f. Set the background color of the Detail section to Maroon 2 in the Standard Colors section and the background color of the list box to Maroon 1, and then disable the form's shortcut menu, record selectors, and navigation buttons.

   g. Test the form.

3. Create a navigation form named **frmNavigation**, using the Horizontal Tabs, 2 Levels layout, that includes the following tab names and objects:

   a. Use **Forms** as the name for the left tab, and place the following forms below it, in order: frmCompany, frmProduct, and frmCompaniesWithProducts.

   b. Use **Queries** as the name for the second tab, and place the frmQueries form below it.

   c. Use **Reports** as the name for the third tab, and place the following reports below it, in order: rptCompany, rptCompanyProducts, and rptProductsAvailable.

   d. Delete the navigation form's picture and title, and change the tab name to **Vendor database**.

   e. Test the navigation form.

4. Make a backup copy of the database, compact and repair the Vendor database, and then close the database.

Use the skills you learned in the tutorial to create a new user interface.

APPLY

Case Problem 1

Data File needed for this Case Problem: Portland.accdb (*cont. from Tutorial 9*)

Pine Hill Music School   Yuka Koyama wants the Portland database to include an easy-to-use interface. To help Yuka with her request, complete the following steps:

1. Open the **Portland** database located in the Access3\Case1 folder provided with your Data Files.

2. Design and create a form named **frmQueries** that has the following components and characteristics:

   a. Use the text **Portland Queries** on the form's tab.

   b. Add a list box with a Name property value of **lstQueryList** that displays all the query names contained in the Portland database, excluding those queries that start with a "~" character. To place the query names in the list box, use an SQL SELECT statement to retrieve the query names from the MSysObjects table, and display the queries in alphabetical order. Delete the label attached to the list box, and widen the list box to approximately 2.5 inches.

   c. Add the label **Select a query**, formatted with Calibri 12-point, bold font, above the list box.

   d. Add two command buttons below the list box. The left command button displays the Preview icon above the word **Preview**, and the right command button displays the MS Access Query icon above the word **Display**. Double-clicking a query name has the same effect as selecting a query name in the list box and clicking the right command button. Both events cause Access to display the query datasheet for the selected query. Clicking the left command button opens the selected query in Print Preview.

   e. Create macros for the form (when the form loads move the focus to the first query name in the list box), the list box (when a user double-clicks a query name), and both command buttons (when a user clicks a command button).

   f. Set the background color of the Detail section to Brown 3 in the Standard Colors section and the background color of the list box to Brown 2, and then disable the form's shortcut menu, record selectors, and navigation buttons.

   g. Test the form.

3. Create a navigation form named **frmNavigation**, using the Horizontal Tabs, 2 Levels layout, that includes the following tab names and objects:

   a. Use **Forms** as the name for the left tab, and place the following forms below it, in order: frmContract, frmStudent, frmTeacher, and frmTeachersAndContracts.

   b. Use **Queries** as the name for the second tab, and place the frmQueries form below it.

   c. Use **Reports** as the name for the third tab, and place the following reports below it, in order: rptStudentContracts, rptTeacher, rptTeacherLessons, and rptStudentMailingLabels.

   d. Delete the navigation form's picture and title, and change the tab name to **Portland database**.

   e. Test the navigation form.

4. Make a backup copy of the database, compact and repair the Portland database, and then close the database.

Use the skills you learned in the tutorial to create a new user interface.

APPLY

Case Problem 2

Data Files needed for this Case Problem: Exercise.accdb (*cont. from Tutorial 9*)

Parkhurst Health & Fitness Center   To make the Exercise database easier to use, Martha Parkhurst wants you to create a user interface for it. To help Martha with her request, complete the following steps:

1. Open the **Exercise** database located in the Access3\Case2 folder provided with your Data Files.

2. Design and create a form named **frmQueries** that has the following components and characteristics:

   a. Use the text **Exercise Queries** on the form's tab.

   b. Add a list box with a Name property value of **lstQueryList** that displays all the query names contained in the Exercise database, excluding those queries that start with a "~" character. To place the query names in the list box, use an SQL SELECT statement to retrieve the query names from the MSysObjects table, and display the queries in alphabetical order. Delete the label attached to the list box, and widen the list box to approximately 2.75 inches.

   c. Add the label **Select a query**, formatted with Century Gothic 12-point, bold font, above the list box.

   d. Add two command buttons below the list box. The left command button displays the Preview icon above the word **Preview**, and the right command button displays the MS Access Query icon above the word **Display**. Double-clicking a query name has the same effect as selecting a query name in the list box and clicking the right command button. Both events cause Access to display the query datasheet for the selected query. Clicking the left command button opens the selected query in Print Preview.

   e. Create macros for the form (when the form loads, move the focus to the first query name in the list box), the list box (when a user double-clicks a query name), and both command buttons (when a user clicks a command button).

   f. Set the background color of the Detail section to Aqua Blue 2 in the Standard Colors section and the background color of the list box to Aqua Blue 1, and then disable the shortcut menu, record selectors, and navigation buttons.

   g. Test the form.

3. Create a navigation form named **frmNavigation**, using the Horizontal Tabs, 2 Levels layout, that includes the following tab names and objects:

   a. Use **Forms** as the name for the left tab, and place the following forms below it, in order: frmProgram, frmProgramsWithMembers, and frmUpcomingExpirations.

   b. Use **Queries** as the name for the second tab, and place the frmQueries form below it.

   c. Use **Reports** as the name for the third tab, and place the following reports below it, in order: rptProgram, rptProgramAndMembers, and rptProgramMembership.

   d. Delete the navigation form's picture and title, and change the tab name to **Exercise database**.

   e. Test the navigation form.

4. Make a backup copy of the database, compact and repair the Exercise database, and then close the database.

Apply what you learned in the tutorial to create a new user interface.

APPLY

Case Problem 3

Data File needed for this Case Problem: Salina.accdb (*cont. from Tutorial 9*)

Rossi Recycling Group   Mary and Tom Rossi want the Salina database to include an easy-to-use user interface. To help them with their request, complete the following steps:

1. Open the **Salina** database located in the Access3\Case3 folder provided with your Data Files.

2. Design and create a form named **frmQueries** that has the following components and characteristics:

   a. Use the text **Salina Queries** on the form's tab.

   b. Add a list box with a Name property value of **lstQueryList** that displays all the query names contained in the Salina database, excluding those queries that start with a "~" character. To place the query names in the list box, use an SQL SELECT statement to retrieve the query names from the MSysObjects table, and display the queries in alphabetical order. Delete the label attached to the list box, and widen the list box to approximately 2.5 inches.

   c. Add the label **Choose a query**, formatted with a 14-point, bold font, above the list box.

   d. Add two command buttons below the list box. The left command button displays the Preview icon above the word **Preview**, and the right command button displays the MS Access Query icon above the word **Display**. Double-clicking a query name has the same effect as selecting a query name in the list box and clicking the right command button. Both events cause Access to display the query datasheet for the selected query. Clicking the left command button opens the selected query in Print Preview.

   e. Create macros for the form (when the form loads, move the focus to the first query name in the list box), the list box (when a user double-clicks a query name), and both command buttons (when a user clicks a command button).

   f. Set the background color of the Detail section to Light Gray 2 in the Standard Colors section and the background color of the list box to Light Gray 1, and then disable the form's shortcut menu, record selectors, and navigation buttons.

   g. Test the form.

3. Create a navigation form named **frmNavigation**, using the Horizontal Tabs, 2 Levels layout, that includes the following tab names and objects:

   a. Use **Forms** as the name for the left tab, and place the following forms below it, in order: frmDonation, frmDonor, and frmDonorDonations.

   b. Use **Queries** as the name for the second tab, and place the frmQueries form below it.

   c. Use **Reports** as the name for the third tab, and place the following reports below it, in order: rptAgenciesAndDonations, rptDonor, and rptDonorDonations.

   d. Delete the navigation form's picture and title, and change the tab name to **Salina database**.

   e. Test the navigation form.

4. Make a backup copy of the database, compact and repair the Salina database, and then close the database.

Case Problem 4

Data File needed for this Case Problem: Rentals.accdb (*cont. from Tutorial 9*)

GEM Ultimate Vacations Griffin and Emma MacElroy want you to create a user-friendly interface for the Rentals database. To help them with their request, complete the following steps:

1. Open the **Rentals** database located in the Access3\Case4 folder provided with your Data Files.

2. Design and create a form named **frmQueries** that has the following components and characteristics:

   a. Use the text **Rentals Queries** on the form's tab.

   b. Add a list box with a Name property value of **lstQueryList** that displays all the query names contained in the Rentals database, excluding those queries that start with a "~" character. To place the query names in the list box, use an SQL SELECT statement to retrieve the query names from the MSysObjects table, and display the queries in alphabetical order. Delete the label attached to the list box, and widen the list box to approximately 2.5 inches.

   c. Add the label **Select a query**, formatted with an 12-point, bold font, above the list box.

   d. Add two command buttons below the list box. The left command button displays the Preview icon below the word **Preview**, and the right command button displays the MS Access Query icon below the word **Display**. Double-clicking a query name has the same effect as selecting a query name in the list box and clicking the right command button. Both events cause Access to display the query datasheet for the selected query. Clicking the left command button opens the selected query in Print Preview.

   e. Create macros for the form (when the form loads, move the focus to the first query name in the list box), the list box (when a user double-clicks a query name), and both command buttons (when a user clicks a command button).

   f. Set the background color of the Detail section to Light Gray 1 in the Standard Colors section and the background color of the list box to Aqua Blue 1 in the Standard Colors section, and then disable the form's shortcut menu, record selectors, and navigation buttons.

   g. Test the form.

3. Create a navigation form named **frmNavigation**, using the Horizontal Tabs, 2 Levels layout, that includes the following tab names and objects:

   a. Use **Forms** as the name for the left tab, and place the following forms below it, in order: frmGuest, frmGuestsWithReservations, and frmRentalCost.

   b. Use **Queries** as the name for the second tab, and place the frmQueries form below it.

   c. Use **Reports** as the name for the third tab, and place the following reports below it, in order: rptGuest, rptGuestReservations, and rptPropertyReservations.

   d. Delete the navigation form's picture and title, and change the tab name to **Rentals database**.

   e. Test the navigation form.

4. Make a backup copy of the database, compact and repair the Rentals database, and then close the database.

Explore some new skills to create a user interface for an Internet service provider.

CREATE

Case Problem 5

Data File needed for this Case Problem: Always.accdb (*cont. from Tutorial 9*)

Always Connected Everyday   Chris and Pat Dixon want you to create a user interface for the Always database. To help them with their request, complete the following steps:

1. Open the **Always** database located in the Access3\Case5 folder provided with your Data Files.

2. Design and create a form named **frmQueries** that has the following components and characteristics:

   a. Use the text **Always Queries** on the form's tab.

   b. Add a list box with a Name property value of **lstQueryList** that displays all the query names contained in the Always database, excluding those queries that start with a "~" character. To place the query names in the list box, use an SQL SELECT statement to retrieve the query names from the MSysObjects table, and display the queries in alphabetical order. Delete the label attached to the list box, and widen the list box to approximately 2.25 inches.

   c. Add the label **Choose a query**, formatted with an 12-point, bold font, above the list box.

   d. Add two command buttons below the list box. The left command button displays the Preview icon below the word **Preview**, and the right command button displays the MS Access Query icon below the word **Display**. Double-clicking a query name has the same effect as selecting a query name in the list box and clicking the right command button. Both events cause Access to display the query datasheet for the selected query. Clicking the left command button opens the selected query in Print Preview.

   e. Create macros for the form (when the form loads, move the focus to the first query name in the list box), the list box (when a user double-clicks a query name), and both command buttons (when a user clicks a command button).

   f. Set the background color of the Detail section to Purple 1 in the Standard Colors section and the background color of the list box to Maroon 1 in the Standard Colors section, and then disable the form's shortcut menu, record selectors, and navigation buttons.

   g. Test the form.

3. Create a navigation form named **frmNavigation**, using the Horizontal Tabs, 2 Levels layout, that includes the following tab names and objects:

   a. Use **Forms** as the name for the left tab, and place the following forms below it, in order: frmCustomer, frmAccessPlans, and frmAccessPlansAndCustomers.

   b. Use **Queries** as the name for the second tab, and place the frmQueries form below it.

   c. Use **Reports** as the name for the third tab, and place the rptAccessPlanCustomers report below it.

   d. Delete the navigation form's picture and title, and change the tab name to **Always database**.

   e. Test the navigation form.

4. Make a backup copy of the database, compact and repair the Always database, and then close the database.

SAM: Skills Assessment Manager

For current SAM information, including versions and content details, visit SAM Central (http://samcentral.course.com). If you have a SAM user profile, you may have access to hands-on instruction, practice, and assessment of the skills covered in this tutorial. Since various versions of SAM are supported throughout the life of this text, check with your instructor for the correct instructions and URL/Web site for accessing assignments.

ENDING DATA FILES

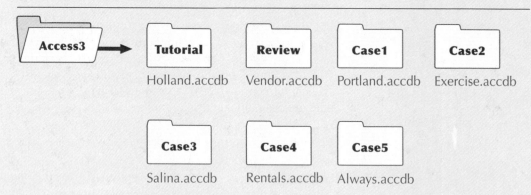

Access3 →

Tutorial
Holland.accdb

Review
Vendor.accdb

Case1
Portland.accdb

Case2
Exercise.accdb

Case3
Salina.accdb

Case4
Rentals.accdb

Case5
Always.accdb

TUTORIAL **11**

Using and Writing Visual Basic for Applications Code

ACCESS

Creating VBA Code for the Holland Database

OBJECTIVES

Session 11.1
- Learn about Function procedures (functions), Sub procedures (subroutines), and modules
- Review and modify an existing subroutine in an event procedure
- Create a function in a standard module
- Test a procedure in the Immediate window

Session 11.2
- Create event procedures
- Compile and test functions, subroutines, and event procedures
- Hide text and change display colors

Case | *Belmont Landscapes*

Lucia Perez and Sarah Fisher are pleased with your progress in developing the user interface for the Holland database. Next, Lucia and Sarah want you to modify the frmCustomerContracts, frmCustomer, and frmContractsAndInvoices forms to make data entry easier and to highlight important information on them. To make these modifications, you will write Visual Basic for Applications code to perform the necessary operations.

STARTING DATA FILES

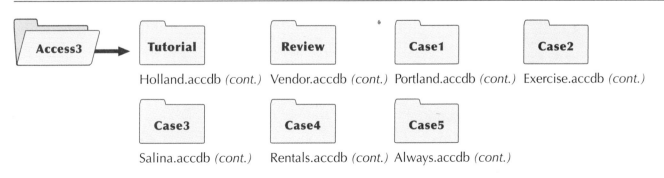

Access3 → Tutorial — Holland.accdb *(cont.)*

Review — Vendor.accdb *(cont.)*

Case1 — Portland.accdb *(cont.)*

Case2 — Exercise.accdb *(cont.)*

Case3 — Salina.accdb *(cont.)*

Case4 — Rentals.accdb *(cont.)*

Case5 — Always.accdb *(cont.)*

SESSION 11.1 VISUAL OVERVIEW

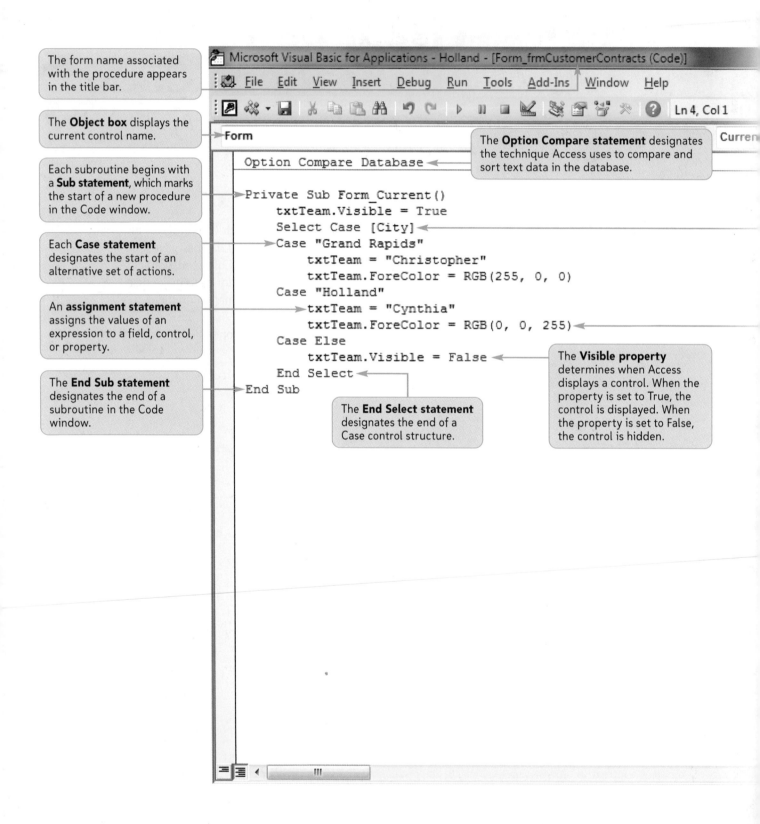

The form name associated with the procedure appears in the title bar.

The **Object box** displays the current control name.

Each subroutine begins with a **Sub statement**, which marks the start of a new procedure in the Code window.

Each **Case statement** designates the start of an alternative set of actions.

An **assignment statement** assigns the values of an expression to a field, control, or property.

The **End Sub statement** designates the end of a subroutine in the Code window.

Microsoft Visual Basic for Applications - Holland - [Form_frmCustomerContracts (Code)]

File   Edit   View   Insert   Debug   Run   Tools   Add-Ins   Window   Help

Ln 4, Col 1

Form

Curren

```
Option Compare Database

Private Sub Form_Current()
    txtTeam.Visible = True
    Select Case [City]
    Case "Grand Rapids"
        txtTeam = "Christopher"
        txtTeam.ForeColor = RGB(255, 0, 0)
    Case "Holland"
        txtTeam = "Cynthia"
        txtTeam.ForeColor = RGB(0, 0, 255)
    Case Else
        txtTeam.Visible = False
    End Select
End Sub
```

The **Option Compare statement** designates the technique Access uses to compare and sort text data in the database.

The **Visible property** determines when Access displays a control. When the property is set to True, the control is displayed. When the property is set to False, the control is hidden.

The **End Select statement** designates the end of a Case control structure.

VBA CODE WINDOW

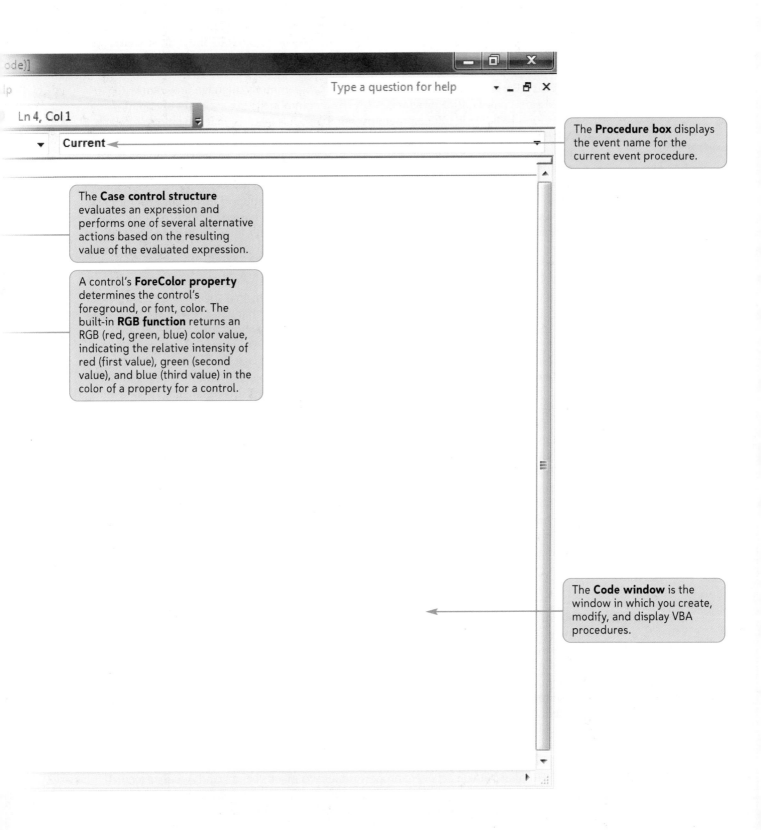

ode)]

lp
                                                   Type a question for help

Ln 4, Col 1

Current

The **Procedure box** displays the event name for the current event procedure.

The **Case control structure** evaluates an expression and performs one of several alternative actions based on the resulting value of the evaluated expression.

A control's **ForeColor property** determines the control's foreground, or font, color. The built-in **RGB function** returns an RGB (red, green, blue) color value, indicating the relative intensity of red (first value), green (second value), and blue (third value) in the color of a property for a control.

The **Code window** is the window in which you create, modify, and display VBA procedures.

Introduction to Visual Basic for Applications

Your next task in the development of the Holland database is to add a procedure to ensure proper capitalization of data entered using the frmCustomer form. Lucia wants to make sure that all values entered in this form's State field will be stored in the tblCustomer table using uppercase letters. She asks you to modify the form so that it will automatically convert any lowercase letters entered in the State field to uppercase. To accomplish this objective, you will use Visual Basic for Applications.

Visual Basic for Applications (VBA) is the programming language provided with Access and other Office programs. VBA has a common syntax and a set of common features for all Microsoft Office programs, but it also has features that are unique for each Microsoft Office program due to each program's different structure and components. For example, because Access has fields, tables, queries, forms, other objects, tab controls, subforms, and other controls that are unique to Access, VBA for Access has features that support these particular components. In contrast, because Microsoft Excel does not have these same Access components, VBA for Excel does not support them, but VBA for Excel does support cells, ranges, and worksheets—three of the basic structures of Excel. The fundamental VBA skills you learn for one of the Microsoft Office programs transfer to any other Microsoft Office program, but to become proficient with VBA in another program, you first need to master its unique aspects.

When you use a programming language, such as VBA, you write a set of instructions to direct the computer to perform specific operations in a specific order, similar to writing a set of instructions for a recipe or an instruction manual. The Visual Overview for Session 11.1 shows the VBA Code window with instructions for Access to use in the frmCustomerContracts form. The process of writing instructions in a programming language is called **coding**. You write the VBA instructions, each of which is called a **statement**, to respond to an event that occurs with an object or control in a database. A language such as VBA is, therefore, called both an **event-driven language**—an event in the database triggers a set of instructions—and an **object-oriented language**—each set of instructions operates on objects in the database. Your experience with macros, which are also event-driven and object-oriented, should facilitate your learning of VBA. Although you must use macros if you need to assign actions to a specific keyboard key or key combination, you can use VBA for everything else you normally accomplish with macros. VBA provides advantages over using macros, such as better error-handling features and easier updating capabilities. You can also use VBA in situations that macros do not handle, such as creating your own set of statements to perform special calculations, verifying a field value based on the value of another field or set of fields, or dynamically changing the color of a form control when a user enters or views a specific field value.

Events

Recall from Tutorial 10 that an event is a state, condition, or action that Access recognizes. For example, events occur when you click a field or command button on a form, open an object, change a field value in a form, or press a key. Each event has an associated event property that specifies how an object responds when an event occurs. For example, each report has an OnOpen event property that specifies what happens when a user opens the report and triggers the Open event, and each form control has an OnClick event property that specifies what happens when a user clicks the control and triggers the Click event. Event properties appear in the property sheet for forms, reports, and controls. By default, event properties are not set to an initial value, which means that no special action takes place when the event occurs.

In Tutorial 10, you set event property values to macro names and Access executed the macros when those events occurred. You can also create a group of statements using VBA code and set an event property value to the name of that group of statements. Access then executes the group of statements, or procedure, when the event occurs.

Such a procedure is called an event procedure. Access has over 60 events and associated event properties. Figure 11-1 describes some frequently used Access events. Each event (such as the AfterUpdate event) has an associated event property (AfterUpdate) and event procedure (ContractNum_AfterUpdate for the AfterUpdate event procedure for the ContractNum control).

Figure 11-1	Frequently used Access events

Event	Description
AfterUpdate	Occurs after changed data in a control or a record is updated
BeforeUpdate	Occurs before changed data in a control or a record is updated
Click	Occurs when a user presses and then releases a mouse button over a control in a form
Current	Occurs when the focus moves to a record, making it the current record, or when a form is refreshed or requeried
DblClick	Occurs when a user presses and releases the left mouse button twice over a control in a form within the double-click time limit
Delete	Occurs when a user performs some action, such as pressing the Delete key, to delete a record, but before the record is actually deleted
GotFocus	Occurs when a form or a form control receives the focus
Load	Occurs when a form is opened and its records are displayed
MouseDown	Occurs when a user presses a mouse button
NoData	Occurs after Access formats a report for printing that has no data (the report is bound to an empty recordset), but before the report is printed. Use this event to cancel the printing of a blank report.
Open	Occurs when a form is opened, but before the first record is displayed. For reports, the event occurs before a report is previewed or printed.

Procedures

When you work with VBA, you code a group of statements to perform a set of operations or calculate a value, and then you attach the group of statements to the event property of an object. Access then executes (or runs or **calls**) these statements every time the event occurs for that object or control. Each group of statements is called a procedure. The two types of procedures are Function procedures and Sub procedures.

A **Function procedure**, or **function**, performs operations, returns a value, accepts input values, and can be used in expressions (recall that an expression is a calculation resulting in a single value). For example, some of the Holland database queries use built-in Access functions, such as Sum, Count, and Avg, to calculate a sum, a record count, or an average. To meet Lucia's request, you will create a function named CapAll by entering the appropriate VBA statements. The CapAll function will accept the value entered in a field text box—in this case, the State field—as an input value, capitalize all characters of the field value, and then return the changed field value to be stored in the database and displayed in the field text box.

A **Sub procedure**, or **subroutine**, performs operations and accepts input values, but does not return a value and cannot be used in expressions. Most Access procedures are subroutines because you need the procedures to perform a series of actions or operations in response to an event. Later in this tutorial, you will create a subroutine that displays a message in the frmContractsAndInvoices form only when the contract start date is earlier than a specified date.

Modules

You store a group of related procedures together in an object called a **module**. Figure 11-2 shows the structure of a typical module.

Figure 11-2   **Structure of a VBA module and its procedures**

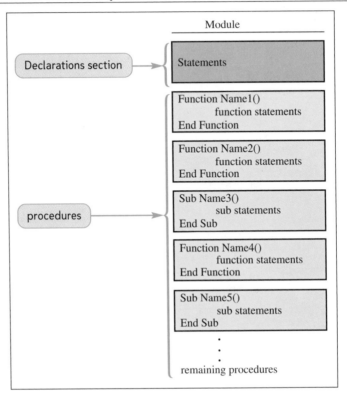

Each module starts with a **Declarations section**, which contains statements that apply to all procedures in the module. One or more procedures, which follow the Declarations section and which can be a mixture of functions and subroutines, constitute the rest of the module. The two basic types of modules are standard modules and class modules.

A **standard module** is a database object that is stored in memory with other database objects (queries, forms, and so on) when you open the database. You can use the procedures in a database's standard modules from anywhere in the database—even from procedures in other modules. A procedure that more than one object can use is called a **public procedure**. For example, the CapAll procedure that you will create capitalizes all letters in the value passed to it. Although you are creating this procedure specifically to work with State field values, you will place it in a standard module and make it public. You could then use the CapAll procedure for any object in the database. All standard modules are listed under the Modules bar in the Navigation Pane.

A **class module** is usually associated with a particular form or report. When you create the first event procedure for a form or report, Access automatically creates an associated form or report class module. When you add additional event procedures to the form or report, Access adds them to the class module for that form or report. Each event procedure in a class module is a **local procedure**, or a **private procedure**, which means that only the form or report for which the class module was created can use the event procedure.

Using an Existing Procedure

Before creating the CapAll procedure for Lucia, you'll use an existing procedure that Lucia created in the class module for the frmCustomerContracts form. Sarah has assigned Cynthia, a staff supervisor, and her team to work with Holland customers and Christopher, another staff supervisor, and his team to work with Grand Rapids customers. The procedure in the class module for the frmCustomerContracts form displays Cynthia's name in blue in a text box to the right of the City field text box for Holland customers and Christopher's name in red for Grand Rapids customers. For customers in other cities, the text box is made invisible.

You'll navigate the frmCustomerContracts form to observe the effects of the procedure.

To navigate a form that uses a VBA procedure:

1. Start Access, and then open the **Holland** database in the Access3\Tutorial folder provided with your Data Files.

2. Open the Navigation Pane (if necessary), open the **frmCustomerContracts** form in Form view, and then close the Navigation Pane. For the first record for Sabrina Fernandez, no value is displayed to the right of the City field text box because the City field value is neither Grand Rapids nor Holland.

3. Select the record number **1** in the Current Record box between the Customer navigation buttons, type **3**, press the **Enter** key, and then click the **CustomerID** text box to deselect all values. The frmCustomerContracts form displays record 3 for Derek Schwimmer. Because he is a Holland customer, "Cynthia" appears in a blue font to the right of the City field text box. See Figure 11-3.

| Figure 11-3 | Using an existing VBA procedure |

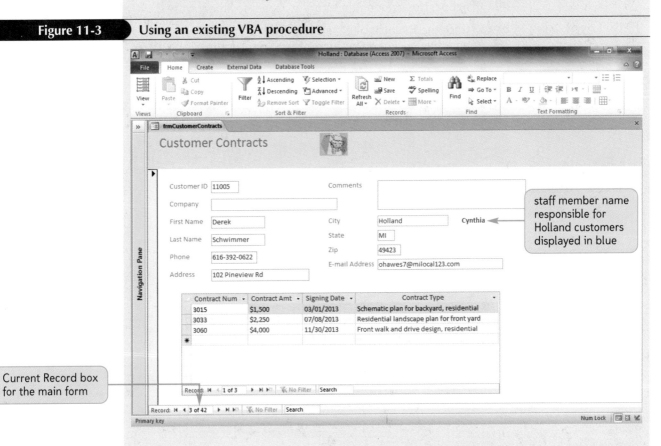

staff member name responsible for Holland customers displayed in blue

Current Record box for the main form

4. Click the Customer **Next record** navigation button ▶ twice to display record 5 for Grand Rapids Engineering Dept, which is a Grand Rapids customer. "Christopher" appears in a red font to the right of the City field text box.

Sarah asks you to change the red color for the display of "Christopher" to black so that it doesn't appear to be a warning and so it blends in better with the form.

Displaying an Event Procedure

TIP

"Focus" refers to the control that is currently active and awaiting user interaction; focus also refers to the object and record that are currently active.

The VBA procedure that controls the display of the staff member's name and its color for each record is in the class module for the frmCustomerContracts form. Access processes the statements in the procedure when you open the frmCustomerContracts form and also when the focus leaves one record and moves to another. Because the **Current event** occurs when a form opens and when the focus moves to another record, the VBA procedure is associated as an event procedure with the form's **OnCurrent property**.

To change the color of the display of "Christopher" from red to black, you'll modify the event procedure for the form's OnCurrent property. First, you'll switch to Design view, and then you'll display the event procedure.

To display the event procedure for the form's OnCurrent property:

1. Switch to Design view.

2. Right-click the **form selector** to display the shortcut menu, and then click **Properties** to open the property sheet for the form.

3. Click the **Event** tab (if necessary) to display the Event page of the property sheet, and then click the **On Current** box. See Figure 11-4.

Figure 11-4 **Event properties for the frmCustomerContracts form**

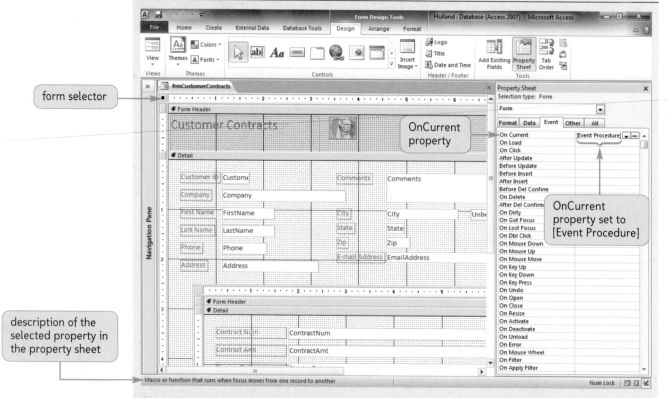

The OnCurrent property is set to [Event Procedure], indicating that Access calls a VBA procedure when the Current event occurs. You'll click the Build button to display the procedure.

4. Click the **Build** button 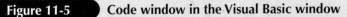 to the right of the On Current box. The Code window opens in the Visual Basic window. See Figure 11-5.

Figure 11-5	Code window in the Visual Basic window

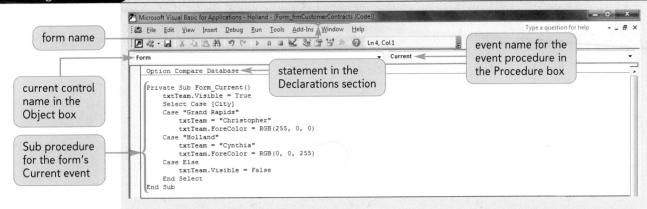

form name

current control name in the Object box

Sub procedure for the form's Current event

statement in the Declarations section

event name for the event procedure in the Procedure box

```
Option Compare Database
Private Sub Form_Current()
    txtTeam.Visible = True
    Select Case [City]
    Case "Grand Rapids"
        txtTeam = "Christopher"
        txtTeam.ForeColor = RGB(255, 0, 0)
    Case "Holland"
        txtTeam = "Cynthia"
        txtTeam.ForeColor = RGB(0, 0, 255)
    Case Else
        txtTeam.Visible = False
    End Select
End Sub
```

Trouble? If other windows appear in your Visual Basic window, click their Close buttons to close them.

Trouble? If your Code window opens in a restored window, maximize it.

The program you use to create and modify VBA code is called the **Visual Basic Editor** (**VBE**, or **editor** for short), and the **Visual Basic window** is the program window that opens when you use VBE. The Code window is the window in which you create, modify, and display specific VBA procedures. You can have as many Code windows open as you have modules in the database. In the Code window, the Object box (the upper-left box) indicates the current control (Form), and the Procedure box (the upper-right box) indicates the event name (Current) for the event procedure you are viewing.

All event procedures are subroutines. A horizontal line visually separates each procedure in the Code window. Each subroutine begins with a Sub statement and ends with an End Sub statement. The Sub statement includes the **scope** of the procedure (private or public), the name of the procedure (for example, Form_Current, which means the Current event for the form control), and opening and closing parentheses.

Notice the Option Compare statement in the Declarations section above the horizontal line. The Option Compare statement designates the technique Access uses to compare and sort text data. The default method "Database," as shown in Figure 11-5, means that Access compares and sorts letters in normal alphabetical order, using the language settings specified for Access running on your computer.

The remaining statements in the Form_Current procedure shown in Figure 11-5 use only two controls in the form: the City field from the tblCustomer table; and txtTeam, which is the text box control that displays "Cynthia" or "Christopher" when it's visible. Based on the City field value, the statements in the procedure do the following:

- If the City field value is "Grand Rapids," then set txtTeam to "Christopher" and set its font color to red.
- If the City field value is "Holland," then set txtTeam to "Cynthia" and set its font color to blue.
- If the City field has any other value, then hide the txtTeam control.

The statements from the *Select Case [City]* statement to the *End Select* statement are an example of a control structure. A **control structure** is a set of VBA statements that work together as a unit. The Case control structure is a conditional control structure; it evaluates an expression—the value of the City field, in this case—and then performs one of several alternative actions based on the resulting value (or condition) of the evaluated expression. Each Case statement, such as *Case "Grand Rapids"* and *Case Else*, designates the start of an alternative set of actions.

Statements such as *txtTeam = "Christopher"* are assignment statements. An assignment statement assigns the value of an expression—Christopher, in this case—to a field, control, or property—the txtTeam control, in this case.

Because a property is associated with a control, you use the general form of *ControlName.PropertyName* to specify a property for a control. An assignment statement such as *txtTeam.ForeColor = RGB(255, 0, 0)*, for example, assigns a value to the txtTeam's ForeColor property. A control's ForeColor property determines the control's foreground, or font, color. The expression in this assignment statement uses a built-in VBA function named RGB. The RGB function returns an RGB (red, green, blue) color value, indicating the relative intensity of red (first value), green (second value), and blue (third value) in the color of a property for a control. Figure 11-6 displays a list of some common colors and the red, green, and blue values for the RGB function that produces those colors. Each color component value must be in the range 0 through 255. Instead of using the RGB function for the eight colors shown in Figure 11-6, you can use one of the VBA constants (vbBlack, vbBlue, vbCyan, vbGreen, vbMagenta, vbRed, vbWhite, or vbYellow). A **VBA constant** is a predefined memory location that is initialized to a value that doesn't change. For example, *txtTeam.ForeColor = vbRed* and *txtTeam.ForeColor = RGB(255, 0, 0)* set the color of the txtTeam control to red. You must use the RGB function when you want colors that differ from the eight colors shown in Figure 11-6.

Figure 11-6   **RGB function values for some common colors**

Color	Red Value	Green Value	Blue Value	VBA Constant
Black	0	0	0	vbBlack
Blue	0	0	255	vbBlue
Cyan	0	255	255	vbCyan
Green	0	255	0	vbGreen
Magenta	255	0	255	vbMagenta
Red	255	0	0	vbRed
White	255	255	255	vbWhite
Yellow	255	255	0	vbYellow

The Visible property determines when Access displays a control. Access displays a control when its Visible property is True, and hides the control when its Visible property is False. The *txtTeam.Visible = True* statement, which Access processes before the *Select Case [City]* statement, displays the txtTeam control. Because Sarah doesn't want the txtTeam control to appear for cities other than Grand Rapids and Holland, the *txtTeam.Visible = False* statement hides the txtTeam control when the City field value doesn't equal one of the two cities.

Modifying an Event Procedure

Because Sarah wants you to change the red color for the display of "Christopher" to black, with a RGB function value of (0, 0, 0), you'll modify the first set of RGB function values in the event procedure. Then you'll close the Visual Basic window and save and test your modifications.

To modify, save, and test the event procedure:

▶ **1.** Double-click **255** in the first RGB function, and then type **0**. The RGB function is now RGB (0, 0, 0).

▶ **2.** Click the **Save** button 🖫 on the Standard toolbar to save your change, and then click the **Close** button ▬▬✗▬ on the Visual Basic window title bar to close it and return to the Form window in Design view.

▶ **3.** Close the property sheet, save your form design changes, and then switch to Form view.

▶ **4.** Navigate to record 5 for Grand Rapids Engineering Dept. The text "Christopher" displays in black to the right of the City field text box. Your modification to the event procedure was completed successfully.

▶ **5.** Close the frmCustomerContracts form.

You've completed your modifications to the event procedure. Next, you'll create the CapAll function.

Creating Functions in a Standard Module

Sarah wants you to create a VBA procedure for the frmCustomer form that will automatically convert the values entered in the State field to uppercase. That is, if a user enters "mi" as the state, the procedure should automatically convert it to "MI." Sarah feels that this function will make data entry easier and reduce the number of data-entry errors. Users might not always be consistent about capitalizing entries in the State field, and using this procedure to capitalize entries will ensure consistency.

To accomplish this change, you will first create a simple function, named CapAll, that accepts a **string** (text) input value and returns that string with all letters converted to uppercase. You create the function by typing the statements in the Code window. Then you will create an event procedure that calls the CapAll function whenever the user enters a value in the State field using the frmCustomer form.

Whenever a user enters or changes a field value in a control or in a form and changes the focus to another control or record, Access automatically triggers the **AfterUpdate event**, which, by default, simply accepts the new or changed entry. However, you can set the AfterUpdate event property of a control to a specific event procedure in order to have something else happen when a user enters or changes the field value. In this case, you need to set the State field's AfterUpdate event property to [Event Procedure], and then code an event procedure to call the CapAll function. Calling the CapAll function will cause the entry in the State field to be converted to uppercase letters before storing it in the database.

You will use the CapAll function with the frmCustomer form, so you could add it to the class module for that form. Adding the function to the class module for the frmCustomer form would make it a private function; that is, you could not use it in other forms or database objects. Because you might use the CapAll function in other forms in the Holland database, you'll instead place the CapAll function in a new standard module named basHollandProcedures (*bas* is a standard prefix for modules). Generally, when you enter a procedure in a standard module, it is public, and you can use it in event procedures for any object in the database.

To create a new standard module, you'll begin by opening the Code window.

To create a new standard module:

1. Click the **Create** tab on the Ribbon.

2. In the Macros & Code group on the Create tab, click the **Module** button. A new Code window opens in the Visual Basic window. See Figure 11-7.

Figure 11-7 **Creating a new standard module**

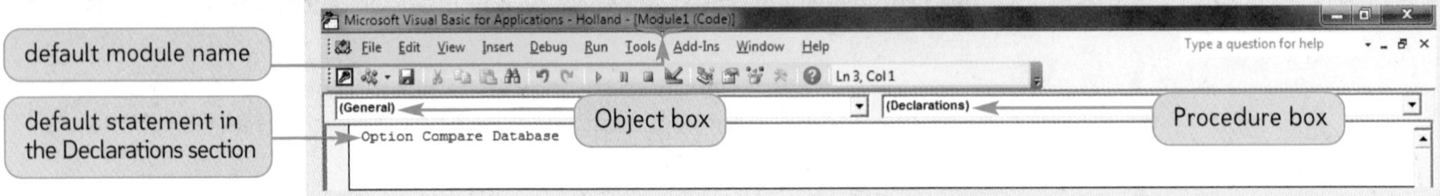

default module name

default statement in the Declarations section

Object box

Procedure box

Trouble? If other windows appear in your Visual Basic window, click their Close buttons to close them.

In the Code window for the new standard module, the Procedure box displays the Declarations section as the current procedure in the module. Access automatically includes the Option Compare statement in the Declarations section of a new module. The CapAll function is a simple function that does not require additional statements in the Declarations section.

Creating a Function

Each function begins with a **Function statement** and ends with an **End Function statement**. Access visually separates each procedure in the Code window with a horizontal line. You can view a procedure's statements by selecting the procedure name from the Procedure box.

The CapAll function begins with the statement *Function CapAll(FValue)*. CapAll is the function name and FValue is used as a placeholder for the input value in the function definition. When the user enters a value for the State field in the frmCustomer form, that value will be passed to the CapAll function and substituted for FValue in the function definition. A placeholder like FValue is called a **parameter**. The value passed to the function and used in place of the parameter when the function is executed is called an **argument**. In other words, the value passed to the function is the argument, which is assigned to the parameter named FValue.

INSIGHT

VBA Naming Rules

All VBA function names, Sub procedure names, argument names, and other names you create must conform to the following rules:

- They must begin with a letter.
- They cannot exceed 255 characters.
- They can include letters, numbers, and the underscore character (_). You cannot use a space or any punctuation characters.
- They cannot contain keywords, such as Function, Sub, Case, and Option, that VBA uses as part of its language.
- They must be unique; that is, you can't declare the same name twice within the same procedure.

You'll enter the CapAll function in the Code window and then test it. Then you'll attach it to an event procedure for the frmCustomer form. You now can start entering the CapAll function.

To start a new function:

1. With the insertion point two lines below the Option Compare statement, type **Function CapAll(FValue)** and then press the **Enter** key. The editor displays a horizontal line that visually separates the new function from the Declarations section. See Figure 11-8.

| Figure 11-8 | Starting a new function |

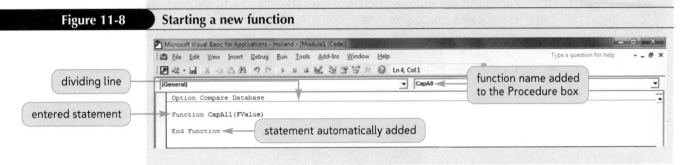

dividing line

entered statement

function name added to the Procedure box

statement automatically added

The function name CapAll now appears in the Procedure box. The editor automatically added the End Function statement and moved the insertion point to the beginning of the blank line between the Function and End Function statements, where you will enter the procedure statements. The editor displays the reserved words Function and End Function in blue. The function name and the parameter name appear in black.

The CapAll function will consist of a single executable assignment statement that you will place between the Function and End Function statements. You'll enter the following assignment statement: *CapAll = UCase(FValue)*. The value of the expression, which is UCase(FValue), will be assigned to the function, which is CapAll.

The expression in the assignment statement uses a built-in Access function named UCase. The **UCase function** accepts a single string argument as input, converts the value of the argument to uppercase letters, and then returns the converted value. The assignment statement assigns the converted value to the CapAll function. Figure 11-9 illustrates this process.

| Figure 11-9 | Evaluation of the assignment statement |

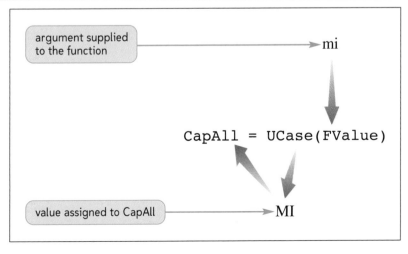

argument supplied to the function → mi

CapAll = UCase(FValue)

value assigned to CapAll → MI

Before entering the assignment statement, you will add a comment line to explain the procedure's purpose. You can include comments anywhere in a VBA procedure to describe what the procedure or a statement does to make it easier for you and other programmers to identify the purpose of statements in your code. You begin a comment with the word Rem (for "Remark") or with a single quotation mark ('). VBA ignores anything following the word Rem or the single quotation mark on a single line.

PROSKILLS

Problem Solving: Commenting and Indenting VBA Code

Different people can use multiple approaches to solving a problem, so you should use comments in a VBA procedure to explain the purpose of the procedure and to clarify any complicated programming logic used. Most companies have documentation standards that specify the types of comments that should be included in each procedure. These standards typically require comments that identify the name of the original creator of the procedure, the purpose of the procedure, and a history of changes made to the procedure by whom and for what purpose.

VBA does not require statements to be indented in procedures. However, experienced programmers indent statements to make procedures easier to read and maintain. Pressing the Tab key once indents the line four spaces to the right, which is a sufficient amount of indentation, and pressing the Shift+Tab key combination or the Backspace key once moves the insertion point four spaces to the left. As an example of indenting statements, you left align Select Case and End Select statements to clearly show the start and end of the Case control structure, and indent the statements between them four spaces. Commenting and indenting your procedures will help you recall the logic of the procedures you created months or years ago, and will help others understand your work.

To add a comment and statement to the function:

1. Press the **Tab** key.

2. Type **'Capitalize all letters of a field value** and then press the **Enter** key.

Notice that the editor displays the comment in green and indents the new line. After entering the comment line, you can enter the assignment statement, which is the executable statement in the function that performs the actual conversion of the argument to uppercase.

3. Type **CapAll = UCase(**. The editor provides assistance as you enter the statement. After you type UCase and the opening parenthesis, the editor displays a Quick Info banner with a reminder that UCase accepts a single string argument. See Figure 11-10.

Figure 11-10	Entering the CapAll function in the Code window

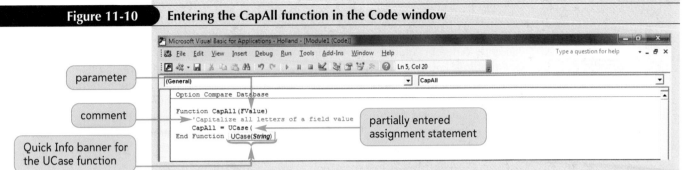

parameter

comment

Quick Info banner for the UCase function

partially entered assignment statement

Trouble? If the Quick Info banner does not open, click Tools on the menu bar, click Options, click the Editor tab, click the Auto Quick Info check box to select it, and then click the OK button.

You'll now finish typing the assignment statement.

4. Type **FValue)** to finish the assignment statement.

The editor scans each statement for errors when you press the Enter key or change the focus to another statement. Because the function is complete and you want the editor to scan the line you just entered for errors, you must move the insertion point to another line.

5. Press the ↓ key to move the insertion point to the next line. Because Access finds no errors, the insertion point continues to blink on the last line.

You have finished entering the function, so you'll save it before continuing with your work.

Saving a Function

When you click the Save button in the Visual Basic window, the editor saves the module and its procedures. If you are entering a long procedure, it's a good idea to save your work periodically.

To save the module:

1. Click the **Save** button 🔲 on the Standard toolbar, type **basHollandProcedures** in the Module Name box, and then press the **Enter** key. The editor saves the module and places the new module name in the title bar.

Before making the changes to the frmCustomer form so that the CapAll function automatically acts on every entry in the State field, you can test the function using the Immediate window.

TIP

VBA functions that you create won't run if the database is not trusted. One way to designate the database as trusted is by opening it from a trusted folder.

Testing a Procedure in the Immediate Window

When you finish entering a VBA statement, the editor checks the statement to make sure its syntax is correct. Although you may have entered all procedure statements with the correct syntax, the procedure may still contain logic errors. A **logic error** occurs when the procedure produces incorrect results. For example, the CapAll function would have a logic error if you typed mi and the function changed it to ml, Mi, or anything other than the correct result of MI. Even the simplest procedure can contain errors. Be sure to test each procedure thoroughly to ensure that it does exactly what you expect it to do in all situations.

When working in the Code window, you can use the **Immediate window** to test VBA procedures without changing any data in the database. In the Immediate window, you can enter different values to test the procedure you just entered. To test a procedure, type the *Print* keyword or a question mark (?), followed by the procedure name and the value you want to test in parentheses. For example, to test the CapAll function in the Immediate window using the test word mi, type *?CapAll("mi")* and then press the Enter key. Access executes the function and prints the value returned by the function (you expect it to return MI). Note that you must enclose a string of characters within quotation marks in the test statement.

REFERENCE

Testing a Procedure in the Immediate Window

- In the Code window, click View on the menu bar, and then click Immediate Window to open the Immediate window.
- Type a question mark (?), the procedure name, and the procedure's arguments in parentheses. If the argument contains a string of characters, enclose the argument in quotation marks.
- Press the Enter key and verify the displayed answer.

Now you can use the Immediate window to test the CapAll function.

To test the CapAll function in the Immediate window:

1. Click **View** on the menu bar, and then click **Immediate Window**. The editor opens the Immediate window across the bottom of the screen and places the insertion point inside the window.

   The Immediate window allows you to run individual lines of VBA code for **debugging** (testing). You will use the Immediate window to test the CapAll function.

2. Type **?CapAll("mi")** and then press the **Enter** key. The editor executes the function and prints the function result, MI, on the next line. See Figure 11-11.

Figure 11-11 CapAll function executed in the Immediate window

result of executing the function

function call statement

```
Immediate
?CapAll("mi")
MI
```

Trouble? If Access displays a dialog box with an error message, click the OK button in the dialog box, correct the error in the Immediate window, and then press the Enter key. If the function does not produce the correct output (MI), correct the CapAll function statements in the Code window, save your changes, click a blank line in the Immediate window, and then repeat Step 2.

To test the CapAll function further, you could enter several other test values, retyping the entire statement each time. Instead, you'll select the current test value, type another value, and then press the Enter key.

3. Double-click the characters **mi** in the first line of the Immediate window.

▶ **4.** Type **mI** and then press the **Enter** key. The editor executes the function and prints the function result, MI, on the next line.

▶ **5.** Repeat Steps 3 and 4 two more times, using **Mi** and then **MI** as the test values. The editor prints the correct values, MI and MI.

▶ **6.** Click the **Close** button ☒ on the Immediate window title bar to close it, and then click the **Close** button ☐ ☒ ☐ on the Visual Basic window title bar to return to the Access window.

▶ **7.** If you are not continuing on to the next session, close the Holland database.

Your initial test of the CapAll function is successful. In the next session, you'll modify the frmCustomer form to call the CapAll function for the State field.

REVIEW

Session 11.1 Quick Check

1. Why is Visual Basic for Applications called an event-driven, object-oriented language?
2. What is an event procedure?
3. What are the differences between a Function procedure and a Sub procedure?
4. Describe the two different types of modules.
5. The _____ of a procedure is either private or public.
6. What can you accomplish in the Immediate window?

SESSION 11.2 VISUAL OVERVIEW

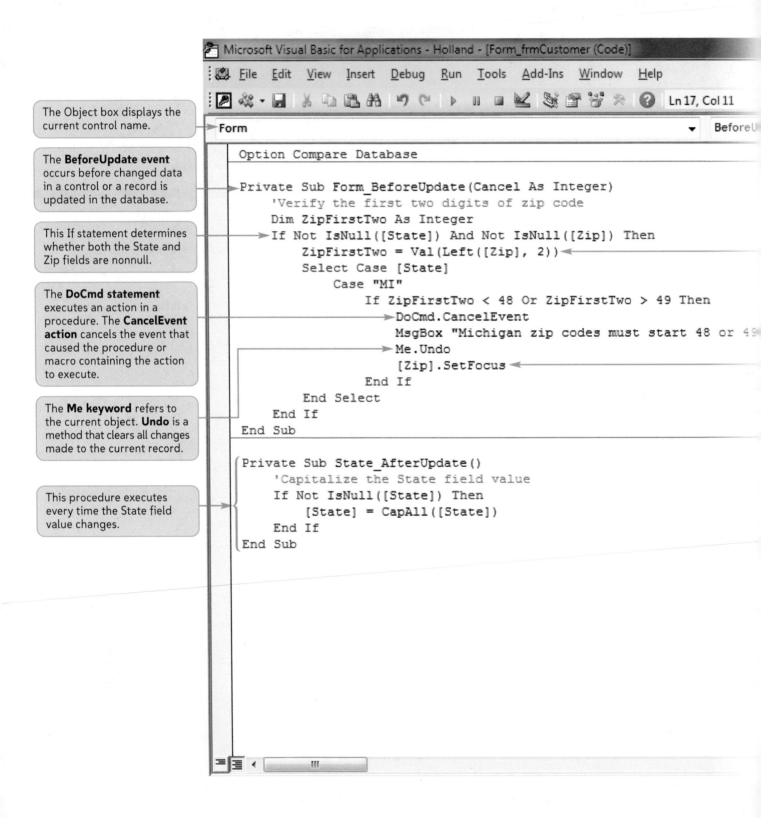

The Object box displays the current control name.

The **BeforeUpdate event** occurs before changed data in a control or a record is updated in the database.

This If statement determines whether both the State and Zip fields are nonnull.

The **DoCmd statement** executes an action in a procedure. The **CancelEvent action** cancels the event that caused the procedure or macro containing the action to execute.

The **Me keyword** refers to the current object. **Undo** is a method that clears all changes made to the current record.

This procedure executes every time the State field value changes.

Microsoft Visual Basic for Applications - Holland - [Form_frmCustomer (Code)]

File   Edit   View   Insert   Debug   Run   Tools   Add-Ins   Window   Help

Ln 17, Col 11

Form   BeforeU

```
Option Compare Database

Private Sub Form_BeforeUpdate(Cancel As Integer)
    'Verify the first two digits of zip code
    Dim ZipFirstTwo As Integer
    If Not IsNull([State]) And Not IsNull([Zip]) Then
        ZipFirstTwo = Val(Left([Zip], 2))
        Select Case [State]
            Case "MI"
                If ZipFirstTwo < 48 Or ZipFirstTwo > 49 Then
                    DoCmd.CancelEvent
                    MsgBox "Michigan zip codes must start 48 or 49
                    Me.Undo
                    [Zip].SetFocus
                End If
        End Select
    End If
End Sub

Private Sub State_AfterUpdate()
    'Capitalize the State field value
    If Not IsNull([State]) Then
        [State] = CapAll([State])
    End If
End Sub
```

EVENT PROCEDURE

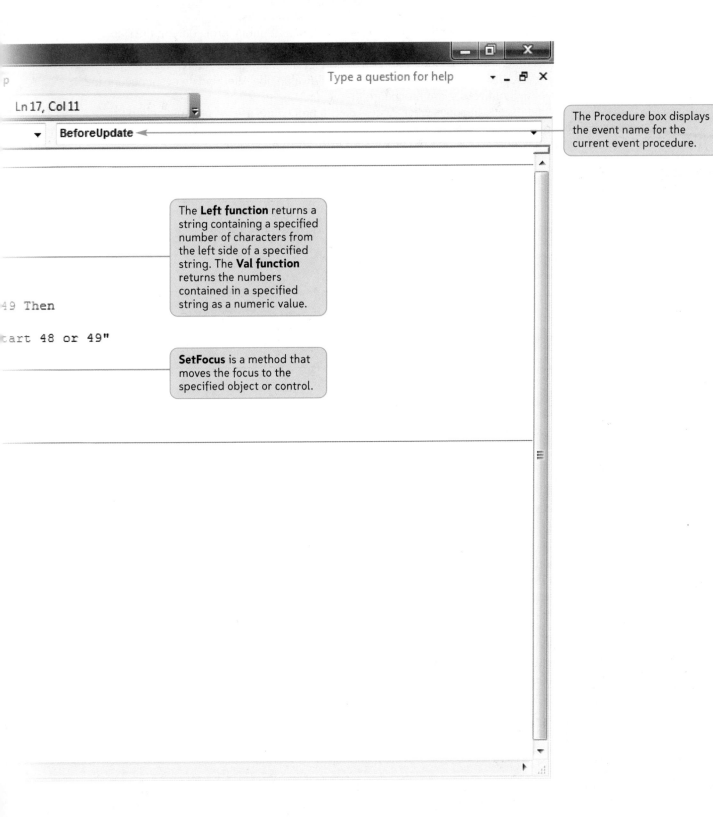

Type a question for help

Ln 17, Col 11

BeforeUpdate

The Procedure box displays the event name for the current event procedure.

The **Left function** returns a string containing a specified number of characters from the left side of a specified string. The **Val function** returns the numbers contained in a specified string as a numeric value.

49 Then

art 48 or 49"

SetFocus is a method that moves the focus to the specified object or control.

Creating an Event Procedure

Recall that when you add a procedure to a form or report, Access automatically creates a class module for that form or report. Each of these procedures is called an event procedure; Access runs a procedure when a specific event occurs.

Now that you have created the CapAll function as a public procedure in the standard module named basHollandProcedures, you can create an event procedure for the frmCustomer form to call the CapAll function for the State field's AfterUpdate event. Whenever a user enters or changes a State field value, the AfterUpdate event occurs and Access will run your event procedure.

What exactly happens when Access calls a procedure? There is an interaction between the calling statement and the function statements as represented by a series of steps. Figure 11-12 shows the process for the CapAll procedure.

| Figure 11-12 | Process of executing a function |

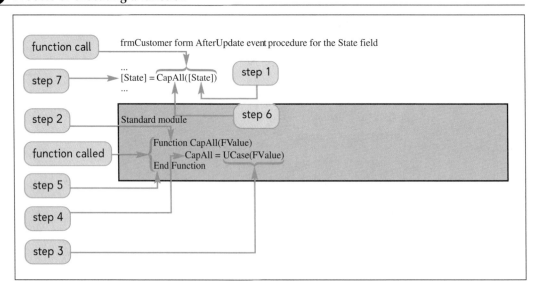

The steps in Figure 11-12 are numbered in the order in which they occur as Access processes the statement and the function. Access goes through the following steps:

- Step 1. The call to the function CapAll passes the value of the argument [State]. This is the value of the State field that is entered or changed by the user.
- Step 2. The function CapAll begins, and the parameter FValue receives the value of [State].
- Step 3. FValue is changed to uppercase.
- Step 4. The value of CapAll is set equal to the result of Step 3.
- Step 5. The function CapAll ends.
- Step 6. The value of CapAll is returned to the point of the call to the function.
- Step 7. The value of [State] is set equal to the returned value of CapAll.

Although it looks complicated, the general function process is simple. The statement contains a function call. When the statement is executed, Access performs the function call, executes the function, returns a single value to the original statement, and completes that statement's execution. Study the steps in Figure 11-12 and trace their sequence until you understand the complete process.

Designing an Event Procedure

Whenever a user enters a new value or modifies an existing value in the State field in the frmCustomer form, Sarah wants Access to execute the CapAll function to ensure that all State field values appear in uppercase letters. After a user changes a State field value, the AfterUpdate event automatically occurs. You can set the AfterUpdate event property to run a macro, call a built-in Access function, or execute an event procedure. Because you want to call your user-defined function from within the event procedure, you'll set the AfterUpdate event property to [Event Procedure], and then add the VBA statements needed to use the CapAll function.

All event procedures are subroutines. Access automatically adds the Sub and End Sub statements to an event procedure. All you need to do is place the statements between the Sub and End Sub statements. Figure 11-13 shows the completed event procedure. The following text describes the parts of the procedure.

Figure 11-13	AfterUpdate event procedure for the State field

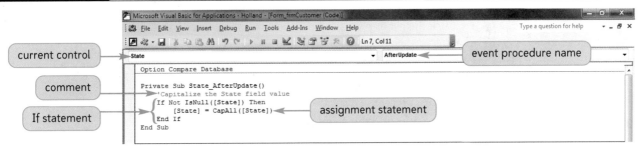

Access names each event procedure in a standard way, using the name of the control, an underscore (_), and the event name. No parameters are passed to an event procedure, so Access places nothing in the parentheses following the name of the subroutine.

A user might delete an existing State field value, so that it contains no value, or becomes null. In this case, calling the function accomplishes nothing. The procedure is designed to call the CapAll function only when a user changes the State field to a value that is not null. The If statement screens out the null values. In its simplest form, an **If statement** executes one of two groups of statements based on a condition, similar to common English usage. For example, consider the English statements, "If I work the night shift, then I'll earn extra spending money. Otherwise, I'll go to the movies, and I'll dip into my savings." In these sentences, the two groups of statements come before and after the "otherwise," depending on the condition, "if I work the night shift." The first group of statements consists of the clause "I'll earn extra spending money." This clause is called the **true-statement group** because it's what happens if the condition ("I work the night shift") is true. The second group of statements contains "I'll go to the movies, and I'll dip into my savings." This clause is called the **false-statement group** because it is what happens if the condition is false. VBA uses the keyword *If* to precede the condition. The keyword *Then* precedes the true-statement group and the keyword *Else* precedes the false-statement group. The general syntax of a VBA If statement is:

```
If condition Then
    true-statement group
[Else
    false-statement group]
End If
```

Access executes the true-statement group when the condition is true and the false-statement group when the condition is false. In this statement's syntax, the bracketed portions are optional. Therefore, you must omit the *Else* and its related false-statement group when you want Access to execute a group of statements only when the condition is true.

> **TIP**
>
> If the name of the control contains spaces or special characters, Access substitutes underscores for them in the event procedure name.

In Figure 11-13, the If statement uses the VBA **IsNull function**, which returns True when the State field value is null and False when it is not null. The *Not* in the If statement is the same logical operator you've used previously to negate an expression. So, Access executes the statement *[State] = CapAll([State])* only when the State field value is not null.

You are ready to make your changes to the frmCustomer form.

Adding an Event Procedure

To add an event procedure to the State field's AfterUpdate event property, you need to open the frmCustomer form in Design view.

REFERENCE

Adding an Event Procedure to a Form or Report

- Open the form or report in Design view, select the control whose event property you want to set, open the property sheet for the control, and then click the Event tab in the property sheet.
- Click the event property box, click its Build button, click Code Builder in the Choose Builder dialog box, and then click the OK button.
- Enter the subroutine statements in the Code window.
- Compile the procedure, fix any statement errors, and then save the event procedure.

You can now add the event procedure to the frmCustomer form.

To add the event procedure to the frmCustomer form:

1. If you took a break after the previous session, make sure that the Holland database is open.

2. Open the Navigation Pane, and then open the **frmCustomer** form in Design view.

3. Right-click the **State** text box to select it and to display the shortcut menu, click **Properties** to open the property sheet, and then, if necessary, click the **Event** tab in the property sheet. Access displays only the event properties in the property sheet. You need to set the AfterUpdate property for the State text box.

4. Click the **After Update** box, click the **Build** button [...] to the right of the After Update box to open the Choose Builder dialog box, click **Code Builder**, and then click the **OK** button. The Code window opens in the Visual Basic window. See Figure 11-14.

Figure 11-14 | Starting a new event procedure in the Code window

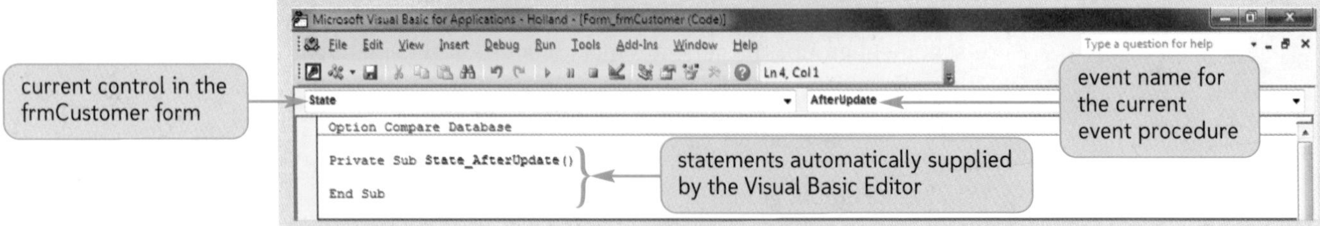

current control in the frmCustomer form

event name for the current event procedure

statements automatically supplied by the Visual Basic Editor

```
Option Compare Database

Private Sub State_AfterUpdate()

End Sub
```

Trouble? If the Object box does not display the State control, close the Visual Basic window, delete "[Event Procedure]" from the After Update box in the property sheet, click the State text box control on the form, and then repeat Step 4.

5. Enter the statements shown in Figure 11-15. Use the Tab key to indent the lines as shown in the figure, press the Enter key at the end of each line, and press the Backspace key to move one tab stop to the left. Compare your screen with Figure 11-15, and make any necessary corrections.

Figure 11-15   **Completed event procedure**

```
Private Sub State_AfterUpdate()
    'Capitalize the State field value
    If Not IsNull([State]) Then
        [State] = CapAll([State])
    End If
End Sub
```

Trouble? If your event procedure contains errors, correct them by highlighting the errors and typing the corrections. Use the Backspace or Delete keys to delete characters.

Before saving the event procedure, you'll compile it.

Compiling Modules

The VBA programming language is not your native language, nor is it the computer's native language. Although you can learn VBA and become fluent in it, computers cannot understand or learn VBA. For a computer to understand the statements in your VBA modules, Access must translate the statements into a form that it can run. The process of translating modules from VBA to a form your computer understands is called **compilation**; you say that you **compile** the module when you translate it.

When you run a procedure for the first time, Access compiles it for you automatically and opens a dialog box only when it finds syntax errors in the procedure. If it finds an error, Access does not translate the procedure statements. If no errors are detected, Access translates the procedure and does not display a confirmation.

INSIGHT

Compiling Procedures

You also can compile a procedure at any time as you enter it by clicking the Compile command on the Debug menu in the Visual Basic window. In response, Access compiles the procedure and all other procedures in all modules in the database. It's best to compile and save your modules after you've made changes to them, to make sure they don't contain syntax errors. If you don't compile a procedure when you first create it or after you've changed it, Access will compile the procedure when the first user opens the form or report that uses the procedure, and the user could encounter a syntax error and be unable to use the form or report. You don't want users to experience these types of problems, so follow the sound strategy of compiling and fully testing all procedures.

You'll now compile the procedures in the Holland database and save the class module for the frmCustomer form.

To compile the procedures in the Holland database and save the class module:

▶ **1.** Click **Debug** on the menu bar, and then click **Compile Holland**. Access compiles all the modules in the Holland database. Because you have no syntax errors, Access translates the VBA statements and returns control to the Visual Basic window.

   Trouble? If Access identifies any errors in your code, correct the errors and repeat Step 1.

▶ **2.** Save your module changes, close the Visual Basic window, and then close the property sheet.

You have created the function and the event procedure and have set the event property. Next, you'll test the event procedure to make sure it works correctly.

Testing an Event Procedure

You need to display the frmCustomer form in Form view and test the State field's event procedure by entering a few different test State field values in the first record of the form. Moving the focus to another control on the form or to another record triggers the AfterUpdate event for the State field and executes your attached event procedure. Because the CapAll function is attached only to the frmCustomer form, the automatic capitalization of State field values is not in effect when you enter them in the tblCustomer table or in any other object in the Holland database.

To test the event procedure:

▶ **1.** Switch to Form view.

▶ **2.** Select the **State** field value (MI), type **mi** in the State text box, and then press the **Enter** key. Access executes the AfterUpdate event procedure for the State field and changes the State field value to "MI." See Figure 11-16.

Figure 11-16 **frmCustomer form after executing the event procedure**

▶ **3.** Repeat Step 2 three more times, entering **Mi**, then **mI**, and finally **MI** in the State text box. Access displays the correct value "MI" each time.

Sarah wants you to create a more complicated function for the Zip field in the frmCustomer form.

Adding a Second Procedure to a Class Module

Sarah has found that her staff makes frequent errors when entering Michigan zip codes, whose first two digits start 48 through 49, because they tend to transpose the first two digits. She asks you to create a procedure that will verify that Michigan zip codes are in the correct range when her staff updates the Zip field in the frmCustomer form. For this procedure, you will use an event procedure attached to the BeforeUpdate event for the frmCustomer form. The BeforeUpdate event occurs before changed data in a control or a record is updated. You'll use the form's BeforeUpdate event for this new procedure because you want to find data-entry errors for Michigan zip codes and alert users to the errors before the database is updated.

Designing the Field Validation Procedure

Figure 11-17 shows the procedure that you will create to verify Michigan zip codes. You've already seen several of the statements in this procedure in your work with the CapAll function and with the form's Current event.

Figure 11-17   **Zip validation procedure**

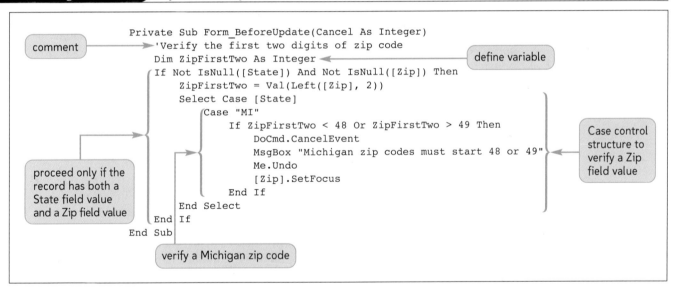

```
                          Private Sub Form_BeforeUpdate(Cancel As Integer)
comment                   'Verify the first two digits of zip code
                          Dim ZipFirstTwo As Integer          ← define variable
                          If Not IsNull([State]) And Not IsNull([Zip]) Then
                              ZipFirstTwo = Val(Left([Zip], 2))
                              Select Case [State]
                                  Case "MI"
                                      If ZipFirstTwo < 48 Or ZipFirstTwo > 49 Then
                                          DoCmd.CancelEvent
                                          MsgBox "Michigan zip codes must start 48 or 49"
                                          Me.Undo
                                          [Zip].SetFocus
                                      End If
                              End Select
                          End If
                          End Sub
```

comment

define variable

proceed only if the record has both a State field value and a Zip field value

Case control structure to verify a Zip field value

verify a Michigan zip code

The Sub and End Sub statements begin and end the subroutine. As specified in the Sub statement, the subroutine executes when the form's BeforeUpdate event occurs. Within parentheses in the Sub statement, *Cancel As Integer* defines Cancel as a parameter with the Integer data type. VBA has data types that are different from the Access data types you've used to define table fields, but each Access data type is equivalent to one of the VBA data types. For example, the Access Number data type with an Integer field size is the same as the VBA Integer data type, and the Access Text data type is the same as the VBA String data type. Figure 11-18 shows the primary VBA data types.

Figure 11-18   **Primary VBA data types**

Data Type	Stores
Boolean	True/False values
Byte	Integer values from 0 to 255
Currency	Currency values from –922,337,203,685,477.5808 to 922,337,203,685,477.5807
Date	Date and time values from 1 January 100 to 31 December 9999
Decimal	Non-integer values with 0 to 28 decimal places
Double	Non-integer values from $-1.79769313486231*10^{308}$ to $-4.94065645841247*11^{-324}$ for negative values, from $4.94065645841247*11^{-324}$ to $1.79769313486232*10^{308}$ for positive values, and 0
Integer	Integer values from –32,768 to 32,767
Long	Integer values from –2,147,483,648 to 2,147,483,647
Object	Any object reference
Single	Non-integer values from $-3.402823*10^{38}$ to $-1.401298*11^{-45}$ for negative values, from $1.401298*11^{-45}$ to $3.402823*10^{38}$ for positive values, and 0
String	Text values up to 2 billion characters in length
Variant	Any numeric or string data type

When an event occurs, Access performs the default behavior for the event. For some events, such as the BeforeUpdate event, Access executes the event procedure or macro before performing the default behavior. Thus, if something is wrong and the default behavior should not occur, you can cancel the default behavior in the event procedure or macro. For this reason, Access automatically includes the Cancel parameter for the BeforeUpdate event.

The second procedure statement, which starts with a single quotation mark, is a comment. The third statement, *Dim ZipFirstTwo As Integer*, declares the Integer variable named ZipFirstTwo that the subroutine uses. A **variable** is a named location in computer memory that can contain a value. If you use a variable in a module, you must explicitly declare it in the Declarations section or in the procedure where the variable is used. You use the **Dim statement** to declare variables and their associated data types in a procedure. The subroutine will assign the first two digits of a zip code (the Zip field) to the ZipFirstTwo variable, and then will use the variable when verifying that a Michigan zip code begins in the correct range.

The procedure should not attempt to verify records that contain null field values for the State field and the Zip field. To screen out these conditions, the procedure uses the fourth procedure statement, *If Not IsNull([State]) And Not IsNull([Zip]) Then*, which pairs with the last *End If* statement. The If statement determines whether both the State and Zip fields are nonnull. If both conditions are true (both fields contain values), then Access executes the next statement in the procedure. If either condition is false, then Access executes the paired End If statement, and the following End Sub statement ends the procedure without the execution of any other statement.

The fifth procedure statement, *ZipFirstTwo = Val(Left([Zip], 2))*, uses two built-in VBA functions, the Val function and the Left function, to assign the first two digits of the Zip field value to the ZipFirstTwo variable. The Left function returns a string containing a specified number of characters from the left side of a specified string. In this case, the Left function returns the leftmost two characters of the Zip field value. The Val function returns the numbers contained in a specified string as a numeric value. In this case, the Val function returns the leftmost two characters of the Zip field value as an integer value.

You encountered the Case control structure previously in the frmCustomerContracts form's Current event procedure. For the BeforeUpdate event procedure, the *Select Case [State]* statement evaluates the State field value. For State field values equal to

MI (Michigan zip codes), the next If statement is executed. For all other State field values, nothing further in the procedure is executed; Access performs the default behavior, and control returns back to the form for further processing. The procedure uses the Case control structure because although Sarah wants the procedure to verify the first two digits of only Michigan zip codes for now, she might want to expand the procedure in the future to verify the first two digits of zip codes for other states, as Belmont Landscapes expands its business.

Because valid Michigan zip codes start 48 through 49, invalid numeric values for the Zip field are less than 48 or greater than 49. The next VBA statement, *If ZipFirstTwo < 48 Or ZipFirstTwo > 49 Then*, is true only for invalid Michigan zip codes. When the If statement is true, the next four statements are executed. When the If statement is false, nothing further in the procedure is executed, Access performs the default behavior, and control returns back to the form for further processing.

The first of the four VBA statements that executes for invalid Michigan zip codes is the DoCmd statement. The DoCmd statement executes an action in a procedure. The *DoCmd.CancelEvent* statement executes the CancelEvent action. The CancelEvent action cancels the event that caused the procedure or macro containing the action to execute. In this case, Access cancels the BeforeUpdate event and does not update the database with the changes to the current record. In addition, Access cancels subsequent events that would have occurred if the BeforeUpdate event had not been canceled. For example, because the form's BeforeUpdate event is triggered when you move to a different record, the following events are triggered when you move to a different record, in the order listed: BeforeUpdate event for the form, AfterUpdate event for the form, Exit event for the control with the focus, LostFocus event for the control with the focus, RecordExit event for the form, and Current event for the form. When the CancelEvent action executes, all these events are canceled and the focus remains with the record being edited.

TIP

The macro MessageBox action is the same as the VBA MsgBox statement.

The second of the four VBA statements that are executed for invalid Michigan zip codes is the MsgBox statement. The *MsgBox "Michigan zip codes must start 48 or 49"* statement displays its message in a message box that remains on the screen until the user clicks the OK button. The message box appears on top of the frmCustomer form so the user can view the changed field values in the current record.

For invalid Michigan zip codes, after the user clicks the OK button in the message box, the *Me.Undo* statement is executed. The Me keyword refers to the current object, in this case the frmCustomer form. Undo is a method that clears all changes made to the current record in the frmCustomer form, so that the field values in the record are as they were before the user made current changes. A **method** is an action that operates on specific objects or controls.

Finally, for invalid Michigan zip codes, the *[Zip].SetFocus* statement is executed. SetFocus is a method that moves the focus to the specified object or control. In this case, Access moves the focus to the Zip field in the current record in the frmCustomer form.

Adding a Second Event Procedure

After designing the procedure to verify Michigan zip codes, you can now add an event procedure for the frmCustomer form's BeforeUpdate event property. Access will execute the event procedure whenever field values in a record are entered or updated.

To add the event procedure for the frmCustomer form's BeforeUpdate event:

 1. Switch to Design view.

TIP

Horizontal lines separate the Option Compare statement from the new procedure and from the AfterUpdate event procedure you entered earlier.

TIP

As you enter statements for the procedure, remember that capitalization is important in all statements so that your code is readable and maintainable.

2. Right-click the **form selector** to display the shortcut menu, and then click **Properties** to open the property sheet for the form.

3. If necessary, click the **Event** tab in the property sheet.

4. Click the **Before Update** box, click the **Before Update** arrow, click **[Event Procedure]**, and then click the **Build** button ⟦...⟧ to the right of the Before Update box. The Code window, which contains new Private Sub and End Sub statements, opens in the Visual Basic window.

5. Press the **Tab** key, and then type the subroutine statements exactly as shown in Figure 11-19. Press the Enter key after you enter each statement, press the Tab key to indent lines as necessary, and press the Backspace key to move the insertion point one tab stop to the left. When you are finished, your screen should look like Figure 11-19.

Figure 11-19	Event procedure for the frmCustomer form's BeforeUpdate event

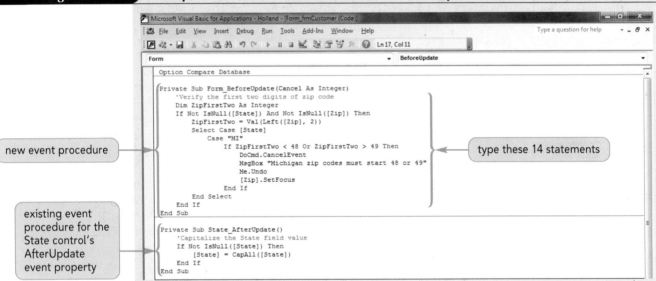

new event procedure

type these 14 statements

existing event procedure for the State control's AfterUpdate event property

6. Click **Debug** on the menu bar, and then click **Compile Holland**. Access compiles all the modules in the Holland database.

   Trouble? If the editor finds an error, it highlights the error and opens a dialog box with a message describing the nature of the error. Click the OK button and then change the highlighted error by comparing your entries with those shown in Figure 11-19. Then repeat Step 6 to scan the statements for errors again and to compile the module.

7. Save your class module changes.

8. Close the Visual Basic window to return to the Form window, close the property sheet, and then close the Navigation Pane.

You can now test the event procedure. To do so, you'll switch to Form view for the frmCustomer form and test the form's BeforeUpdate event procedure by entering valid and invalid Zip field values.

To test the form's BeforeUpdate event procedure:

1. Switch to Form view. Access displays record 1 for Sabrina Fernandez. The first two digits of the Zip field value, 49, represent a valid Michigan zip code in the range that starts 48 or 49.

2. Select **49341** in the State text box, type **98765**, press the **Tab** key to move to the Email Address text box, and then click the **Next record** navigation button ▶ to move to the next record. Access executes the BeforeUpdate event procedure for the frmCustomer form, determines that the Michigan zip code's first two digits are incorrect, and displays the message box you included in the procedure. See Figure 11-20.

> **TIP**
>
> You must navigate to another record, not to another field, to trigger the form's BeforeUpdate event procedure.

Figure 11-20 After the frmCustomer form's BeforeUpdate event procedure detects an error

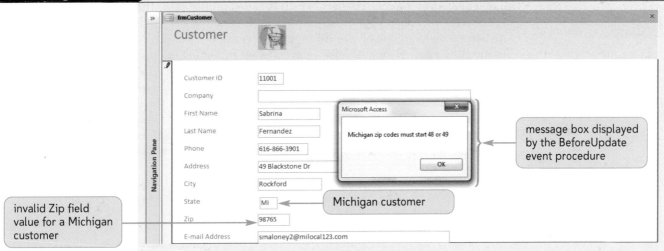

invalid Zip field value for a Michigan customer

Michigan customer

message box displayed by the BeforeUpdate event procedure

While the message box is open, the updated Zip field value of 98765 remains on screen for you to review.

3. Click the **OK** button. The message box closes, the Undo method changes the Zip field value to 49341 (its original value), and the SetFocus method moves the focus to the Zip text box.

Next, you'll change the Zip field value to 49999, which is a valid Michigan zip code.

4. Change the Zip field value to **49999**, and then click the **Next record** navigation button ▶ to move to the next record. The form's BeforeUpdate event procedure verifies that the zip code is a valid value for a Michigan customer, and the focus moves to the Zip text box in the next record.

5. Click the **Previous record** navigation button ◀ to move to the first record, change the State field value to **TX**, change the Zip field value to **98765**, and then press the **Next record** navigation button ▶ to move to the next record. The form's BeforeUpdate event procedure checks zip codes only for Michigan, so the focus moves to the Zip text box in the next record.

Next, you'll change the first record's State field value to MI and the Zip field value to 49341, which are the original values for the record.

6. Click the **Previous record** navigation button ◀ to move to the first record, and then change the State field value to **MI** and the Zip field value to **49341**.

Sarah has one more procedure she wants you to create for the frmCustomer form.

Changing the Case of a Field Value

Sarah wants to make it easier for users to enter a company name when using the frmCustomer form, so she asks you to create a procedure that will automatically convert the case of letters entered in the Company field. This procedure will capitalize the first letter of each word in the field and change all other letters to lowercase. You'll use an event procedure attached to the AfterUpdate event for the Company field to perform this automatic conversion. For example, if a user enters "monroe sTate College" as the Company field value, the event procedure will correct the field value to "Monroe State College."

You'll use the StrConv function in the event procedure to perform the conversion. The **StrConv function** converts the letters in a string to all uppercase letters or to all lowercase letters, or converts the first letter of every word in the string to uppercase letters and all other letters to lowercase letters, which is called proper case. The statement you'll use in the event procedure is: *Company = StrConv(Company, vbProperCase)*. The StrConv function's second argument, the **vbProperCase constant**, is a VBA constant that specifies the conversion of the first letter in every word in a string to uppercase letters and the conversion of all other letters to lowercase letters. Recall that the CapAll function you created earlier in this tutorial used the statement *CapAll = UCase(FValue)* to capitalize every character in a string. Instead, you could have used the statement *CapAll = StrConv(FValue, vbUpperCase)* to accomplish the same result. Other VBA constants you can use with the StrConv function are the **vbUpperCase constant**, which specifies the conversion of the string to all uppercase letters, and the **vbLowerCase constant**, which specifies the conversion of the string to all lowercase letters.

Next, you'll create the AfterUpdate event procedure for the Company field in the frmCustomer form to perform the automatic conversion of entered and updated Company field values.

To add the event procedure for the Company field's AfterUpdate event:

▶ 1. Switch to Design view.

▶ 2. Right-click the **Company** text box to display the shortcut menu, and then click **Properties** to open the property sheet for the control.

▶ 3. If necessary, click the **Event** tab in the property sheet.

▶ 4. Click the **After Update** box, click the **After Update** arrow, click **[Event Procedure]**, and then click the **Build** button ··· to the right of the After Update box. The Code window, which contains new Private Sub and End Sub statements, opens in the Visual Basic window. The Code window also contains two other event procedures defined in the form's class module, one event procedure for the form's BeforeUpdate event, and the other event procedure for the State field's AfterUpdate event.

▶ 5. Press the **Tab** key, and then type the subroutine statements exactly as shown in Figure 11-21.

| Figure 11-21 | Event procedure for the Company control's AfterUpdate event |

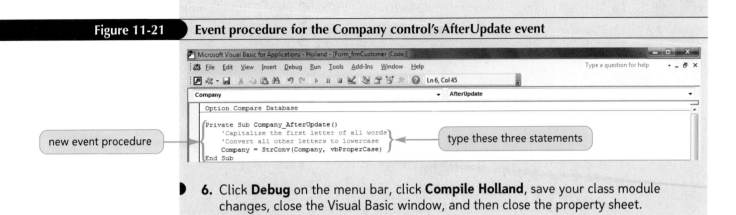

6. Click **Debug** on the menu bar, click **Compile Holland**, save your class module changes, close the Visual Basic window, and then close the property sheet.

You can now test the event procedure. To do so, you'll view the frmCustomer form in Form view and test the Company field's event procedure by entering different Company field values.

To test the new event procedure:

1. Switch to Form view, and then press the **Tab** key to move to the Company text box for the first record, for Sabrina Fernandez. This record does not display a Company field value.

    You'll test the new event procedure by entering Company field values in record 1, making sure the field value is null when you finish testing.

2. Type **test company name** and then press the **Enter** key. Access executes the AfterUpdate event procedure for the Company field and changes the Company field value to "Test Company Name".

3. Press the ↑ key to select the Company field value.

4. Repeat Steps 2 and 3 two more times, entering **sECond test namE** (correctly changed to "Second Test Name"), and then entering **THIRD TEST NAME** (correctly changed to "Third Test Name").

5. Press the ↑ key to select the Company field value, press the **Delete** key to remove the Company field value, and then close the form.

Hiding a Control and Changing a Control's Color

Sarah wants you to add a message to the frmContractsAndInvoices form that will remind her staff when a contract record should be considered for archiving and deletion from the tblContract table. Specifically, when the start date is prior to the year 2014, Sarah wants the StartDate field value displayed in red; all other StartDate field values should be displayed in black. She also wants to display a message to the right of the StartDate text box in red only when the contract is a candidate for archiving and deletion. The red font will help to draw attention to these contracts. See Figure 11-22.

Figure 11-22   **Purge message and red StartDate field value in frmContractsAndInvoices form**

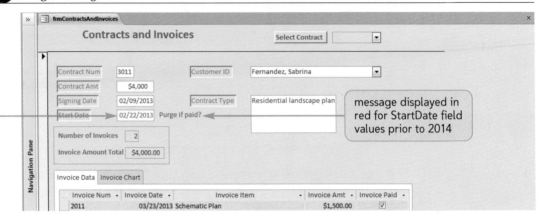

In the frmContractsAndInvoices form, you will add a label to the right of the StartDate text box that will display the text "Purge if paid?" in red. Because Sarah wants the text to appear only when the StartDate field has a value of less than 1/1/2014, you will change the label's Visible property during execution. You will also change the foreground color of the value in the StartDate text box to red when the StartDate field value is less than 1/1/2014 and to black for all other dates.

Because the change to the Visible property takes place during execution, you will add code to the Current event procedure in the frmContractsAndInvoices form. To set a property in a Visual Basic statement, you enter the object name followed by the property name, separating the two names with a period. For example, if the label name for the message is lblPurgeMsg, then the statement *lblPurgeMsg.Visible = False* hides the label on the form.

PROSKILLS

Problem Solving: Reusing Code from Other Sources

Creating your first few VBA procedures from scratch is a daunting task. To get started, you should take advantage of the available resources that discuss various ways of designing and programming commonly encountered situations. These resources include the sample databases available from Microsoft, Access VBA books, periodicals, Web sites that provide sample code, and Access Help. These resources contain sample procedures and code segments, often with commentary about what the procedures and statements accomplish and why. However, when you create a procedure, you are responsible for knowing what it does, how it does it, when to use it, how to enhance it in the future, and how to fix it when problems occur. If you simply copy statements from another source without thoroughly understanding them, you won't be able to enhance or fix the procedure in the future. In addition, you might overlook better ways to accomplish the same thing—better because the procedure would run faster or would be easier to enhance. In some cases, the samples you find might be flawed, so that they won't work properly for you. The time you spend researching and completely understanding sample code will pay dividends in your learning experience to create VBA procedures.

First, you'll add a label to the frmContractsAndInvoices form that will display a message in red for values that have a StartDate field value of less than 1/1/2014. For all other dates, the label will be hidden.

To add the label to the frmContractsAndInvoices form:

1. Open the Navigation Pane, open the **frmContractsAndInvoices** form in Design view, and then close the Navigation Pane.

2. In the Controls group on the Design tab, click the **Label** button Aa.

3. Position the pointer in the Detail section; when the center of the pointer's plus symbol is positioned two grid dots to the right of the StartDate text box and just below the top of the StartDate text box, click the mouse button.

4. Type **Purge if paid?** and then press the **Enter** key. The new label box appears in the form and displays the Error Checking Options button. See Figure 11-23.

Figure 11-23	Label box added to the form

Error Checking Options button

Trouble? If you do not see the Error Checking Options button, error checking is disabled in Access. Click the File tab on the Ribbon, click Options in the navigation bar, click Object Designers, scroll down the page, click the Enable error checking check box to add a check mark to it, click the OK button, click a blank area in the form, and then click the "Purge if paid?" label box. Continue with Step 5.

5. Position the pointer on the **Error Checking Options** button ⧉. The message, "This is a new label and is not associated with a control," appears. Because the new label should not be associated with a control, you'll choose to ignore this error.

6. Click the **Error Checking Options button arrow** ⧉ ▾, and then click **Ignore Error**. The Error Checking Options button disappears.

7. Hold down the **Shift** key, click the **StartDate** text box to select this control and the label box, release the **Shift** key, right-click one of the selected controls, point to **Align**, and then click **Top** to align both controls on their top edges.

Trouble? If the Error Checking Options button appears, click the Error Checking Options button arrow, and then click Dismiss Error.

You'll now set the label's Name and ForeColor properties, and add the Current event procedure to the frmContractsAndInvoices form.

To set the label's properties and add the Current event procedure to the form:

1. Deselect all controls, right-click the **Purge if paid?** label to display the shortcut menu, and then click **Properties** to open the property sheet.

TIP

The *lbl* (the consonants in the word "label") prefix tag identifies a label control.

  2. Click the **All** tab (if necessary), select the value in the **Name** box (if necessary), and then type **lblPurgeMsg**.

     You can now set the ForeColor property for the label so that the message is displayed in red.

  3. Click the **Fore Color** box, and then click the **Build** button [...] to the right of the Fore Color box. Access opens a color gallery.

  4. Click the **Red** box (row 7, column 2 in the Standard Colors palette), and then press the **Enter** key. Access sets the ForeColor property value to the code for red (#ED1C24). Notice that Access changed the foreground (font) color of the "Purge if paid?" label to red.

     You'll now enter the event procedure for the form's Current event. Access will execute this event procedure whenever the frmContractsAndInvoices form is opened or the focus moves from one record to another.

  5. Click the **form selector**, scroll down the property sheet to the On Current box, click the **On Current** box, click the **On Current** arrow, click **[Event Procedure]**, and then click the **Build** button [...]. Access opens the Code window in the Visual Basic window, displaying the Sub and End Sub statements.

  6. Press the **Tab** key, and then type the Sub procedure statements exactly as shown in Figure 11-24.

Figure 11-24	Current event procedure for the frmContractsAndInvoices form

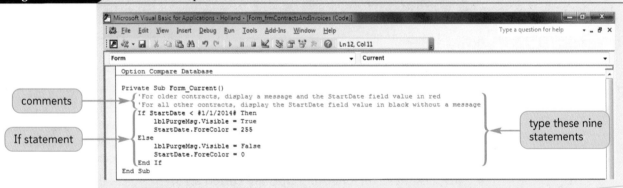

The form's Current procedure uses an If statement to determine whether the current value of the StartDate field is less than 1/1/2014. If the current value of the StartDate field is less than 1/1/2014, the procedure sets the lblPurgeMsg control's Visible property to True (which means the "Purge if paid?" message will appear in the frmContractsAndInvoices form), and it sets the StartDate control's ForeColor property to 255 (red). If the current value of the StartDate field is greater than 1/1/2014, the procedure sets the lblPurgeMsg control's Visible property to False, hiding the message in the form, and sets the StartDate control's ForeColor property to 0 (black).

  7. Click **Debug** on the menu bar, and then click **Compile Holland**. Access compiles all the modules in the Holland database.

  8. Save your class module changes, close the Visual Basic window, and then close the property sheet.

You'll now test the frmContractsAndInvoices form's Current event procedure.

To test the Current event procedure for the frmContractsAndInvoices form:

1. Switch to Form view. Access displays the first record for ContractNum 3011, whose start date is prior to 1/1/2014. The "Purge if paid?" message appears in red, as does the StartDate field value of 02/22/2013.

   Trouble? If Access displays a dialog box indicating a run-time error, Access could not execute the event procedure. Click the Debug button in the dialog box. Access displays the event procedure in the Code window and highlights the line containing the error. Check the statements carefully and make sure that they are exactly like those shown in Figure 11-24. Make the necessary changes, compile the module, save the module, and then close the Code window. Then repeat Step 1.

2. Click the Contract **Last record** navigation button ▶| to display record 66 for ContractNum 3201, whose start date is after 1/1/2014. The "Purge if paid?" message does not appear, and the StartDate field value is displayed in black.

3. Close the form, make a backup copy of the database, compact and repair the Holland database, and then close the database.

Lucia and Sarah are pleased with the VBA modifications to the forms. Next, they want you to make access to the Holland database more secure, and they want you to make the final enhancements to the database and the user interface. In the next tutorial, you'll complete your work with the Holland database.

Session 11.2 Quick Check

REVIEW

1. The VBA _____ statement executes one of two groups of statements based on a condition.
2. What happens when you compile a module?
3. What is the purpose of the Dim statement?
4. The _____ function returns the numbers contained in a specified string as a numeric value.
5. What is the purpose of the DoCmd statement?
6. What is a method?
7. What is a VBA constant?
8. You can use the UCase function or the _____ function to convert a string to all uppercase letters.
9. What does the Visible property determine?
10. What does the ForeColor property determine?

PRACTICE

Review Assignments

Data File needed for the Review Assignments: Vendor.accdb (*cont. from Tutorial 10*)

Lucia asks you to continue your work on the Vendor database by enhancing the appearance of the frmCompaniesWithProducts form. To help with this request, complete the following steps:

1. Open the **Vendor** database located in the Access3\Review folder provided with your Data Files.
2. Create a procedure for the **frmCompaniesWithProducts** form to convert CompanyName field values to proper case—capitalize the first letter of each word, and convert all other letters to lowercase. Test the procedure, and then close the form.
3. Create a procedure for the **frmProduct** form to do the following:
   a. Display the Price field value in red when the value is greater than $1,000 and in black for other values.
   b. Display the message **high price** to the left of the Price text box in bold, red text. Display the message only when the Price field value is greater than $1,000.
   c. Test the procedure, and then save and close the form.
4. Make a backup copy of the database, compact and repair the Vendor database, and then close the database.

APPLY

Case Problem 1

Data File needed for this Case Problem: Portland.accdb (*cont. from Tutorial 10*)

Pine Hill Music School   Yuka Koyama wants you to continue your work on the Portland database by enhancing the frmTeachersAndContracts and frmContract forms. To help Yuka with her request, complete the following steps:

1. Open the **Portland** database located in the Access3\Case1 folder provided with your Data Files.
2. Create a procedure for the **frmTeachersAndContracts** form to convert School field values to proper case—capitalize the first letter of each word, and convert all other letters to lowercase. Test the procedure, and then close the form.

⊕ **EXPLORE**

3. Create a procedure for the **frmContract** form to do the following:
   a. Display the LessonType field value in a bold, blue text when the value is "Voice" and in normal, black text for all other values. (*Hint*: Use the FontBold property.)
   b. Display the message **No instrument** to the right of the LessonType text box in bold, blue text only when the LessonType field value is "Voice".
   c. Test the procedure, and then save your form changes.
4. Make a backup copy of the database, compact and repair the Portland database, and then close the database.

Explore some new skills to enhance a form by creating procedures.

CHALLENGE

Case Problem 2

Data File needed for this Case Problem: Exercise.accdb (*cont. from Tutorial 10*)

Parkhurst Health & Fitness Center   Martha Parkhurst asks you to continue your work on the Exercise database by creating a new form and enhancing its accuracy and appearance. To help Martha with her request, complete the following steps:

1. Open the **Exercise** database located in the Access3\Case2 folder provided with your Data Files.
2. Use the Form tool to create a form named **frmMemberInfo** using the tblMember table as the source table. Create a procedure for the frmMemberInfo form to convert City field values to proper case—capitalize the first letter of each word, and convert all other letters to lowercase. Test the procedure.

✪ **EXPLORE**   3. Create a procedure to verify Phone field values in the frmMemberInfo form by doing the following:
   a. For a State field value of VA, the first three digits of the Phone field value must equal 703 or 804. If the Phone field value is invalid, display an appropriate message, cancel the event, undo the change, and move the focus to the Phone field.
   b. No special action is required for other Phone field values.
   c. Test the procedure, and then save your form changes.

✪ **EXPLORE**   4. Create a procedure for the frmMemberInfo form to do the following:
   a. Display the word **Current** to the right of the MemberID text box in bold, magenta text only when the MembershipStatus field value is Active. Otherwise, display the word **Review** in bold, blue text. (*Hint*: Remove all controls from the control layout before resizing the MemberID text box and adding the label for the message. Use the Caption property in your VBA code, and make sure you enclose Caption property settings in quotation marks.)
   b. Test the modified form, and then save your form changes.
5. Make a backup copy of the database, compact and repair the Exercise database, and then close the database.

Apply what you learned in the tutorial to enhance a form's function and appearance.

APPLY

Case Problem 3

Data File needed for this Case Problem: Salina.accdb (*cont. from Tutorial 10*)

Rossi Recycling Group   Mary and Tom Rossi want you to continue working on the Salina database by enhancing the appearance of the frmDonorDonations form. To help them with their request, complete the following steps:

1. Open the **Salina** database located in the Access3\Case3 folder provided with your Data Files.

✪ **EXPLORE**   2. Create a procedure for the **frmDonorDonations** form to do the following:
   a. Display the calculated field value (the donation total) in bold, red text when the value is greater than $500 and in regular, black text otherwise. (*Hint*: Use the FontBold property.)
   b. Display the message **Large donation** above the calculated field text box in bold, red text only when the calculated field value is greater than $500.
   c. Test the procedure, and then save your form design changes.
3. Make a backup copy of the database, compact and repair the Salina database, and then close the database.

Apply what you learned in the tutorial to enhance a form's function and appearance.

APPLY

Case Problem 4

Data File needed for this Case Problem: Rentals.accdb (*cont. from Tutorial 10*)

GEM Ultimate Vacations   Griffin and Emma MacElroy ask you to continue your work on the Rentals database by enhancing the frmGuest form's accuracy and appearance. To help them with their request, complete the following steps:

1. Open the **Rentals** database located in the Access3\Case4 folder provided with your Data Files.

2. Create a procedure for the **frmGuest** form to convert new Country field values to all uppercase letters. Test the procedure.

⊕ **EXPLORE**

3. Add the message **Trips of a Lifetime!** to the frmGuest form. Display the message in 14-point, bold, orange text and position it above and to the right of the GuestID text box. Display the message only when the GuestFirstName and GuestLastName field values equal your first and last names. (*Hint*: Make sure you enclose your first and last names in quotation marks in your VBA code.) Save your form changes, and then test the procedure.

4. Make a backup copy of the database, compact and repair the Rentals database, and then close the database.

Explore some new skills to enhance the function and appearance of a form.

CHALLENGE

Case Problem 5

Data File needed for this Case Problem: Always.accdb (*cont. from Tutorial 10*)

Always Connected Everyday   Chris and Pat Dixon ask you to continue your work on the Always database by enhancing and improving the frmAccessPlansAndCustomers form. To help them with their request, complete the following steps:

1. Open the **Always** database located in the Access3\Case5 folder provided with your Data Files.

⊕ **EXPLORE**

2. Modify the **frmAccessPlansAndCustomers** form by doing the following:

   a. Display the PlanMonthlyCost field value in bold, blue text when the value is greater than $50 and in regular, black text for all other values. (*Hint*: Use the FontBold property.)

   b. Display the message **Premium Customer** to the right of the PlanMonthlyCost text box in bold, blue text only when the PlanMonthlyCost field value is greater than $50.

   c. Test the procedure, and then save your form changes.

⊕ **EXPLORE**

3. Modify the frmAccessPlansAndCustomers form by doing the following:

   a. To the right of the rectangle that encloses the Number of Customers calculated field, add a new calculated field that displays the product of the PlanMonthlyCost value and Number of Customers calculated field value. Use the label **Monthly Income for Plan** and display the label and calculated field values in bold, blue text. Format the calculated field as Currency with two decimal places.

   b. Perform the Monthly Income for Plan calculation and display the label and calculated field value only when the Number of Customers calculated field value is not zero.

   c. Test the modified procedure, and then save your form changes.

4. Make a backup copy of the database, compact and repair the Always database, and then close the database.

SAM: Skills Assessment Manager

For current SAM information, including versions and content details, visit SAM Central (http://samcentral.course.com). If you have a SAM user profile, you may have access to hands-on instruction, practice, and assessment of the skills covered in this tutorial. Since various versions of SAM are supported throughout the life of this text, check with your instructor for the correct instructions and URL/Web site for accessing assignments.

ENDING DATA FILES

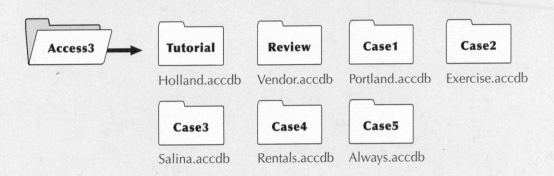

Access3 → Tutorial — Holland.accdb

Review — Vendor.accdb

Case1 — Portland.accdb

Case2 — Exercise.accdb

Case3 — Salina.accdb

Case4 — Rentals.accdb

Case5 — Always.accdb

Managing and Securing a Database

Administering the Holland Database

OBJECTIVES

Session 12.1
- Filter data in a table and a form
- Save a filter as a query and apply the saved query as a filter
- Create a subquery
- Create a multivalued field

Session 12.2
- Create an Attachment field
- Use an AutoNumber field
- Save a database as a previous version
- Analyze a database's performance
- Link a database to a table in another database
- Use the Linked Table Manager
- Split a database
- Encrypt a database with a password
- Set database properties and startup options
- Create an ACCDE file

Case | *Belmont Landscapes*

Lucia Perez and Sarah Fisher have planned training sessions for staff members to learn how to use the Holland database. These training sessions are scheduled to begin right after you finalize the Holland database. Your remaining work will address advanced Access features, such as multivalued fields and Attachment fields, and Sarah's concerns about database management, database security, and the database's overall performance. You'll also set database properties and startup options to complete the development of the Holland database.

ACCESS

STARTING DATA FILES

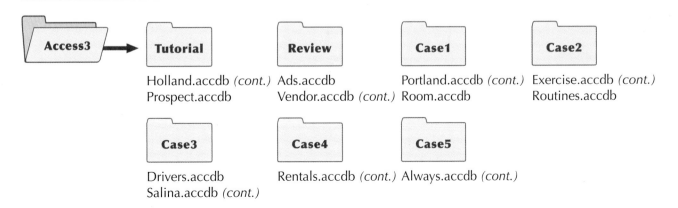

Access3 → **Tutorial**
Holland.accdb *(cont.)*
Prospect.accdb

Review
Ads.accdb
Vendor.accdb *(cont.)*

Case1
Portland.accdb *(cont.)*
Room.accdb

Case2
Exercise.accdb *(cont.)*
Routines.accdb

Case3
Drivers.accdb
Salina.accdb *(cont.)*

Case4
Rentals.accdb *(cont.)*

Case5
Always.accdb *(cont.)*

SESSION 12.1 VISUAL OVERVIEW

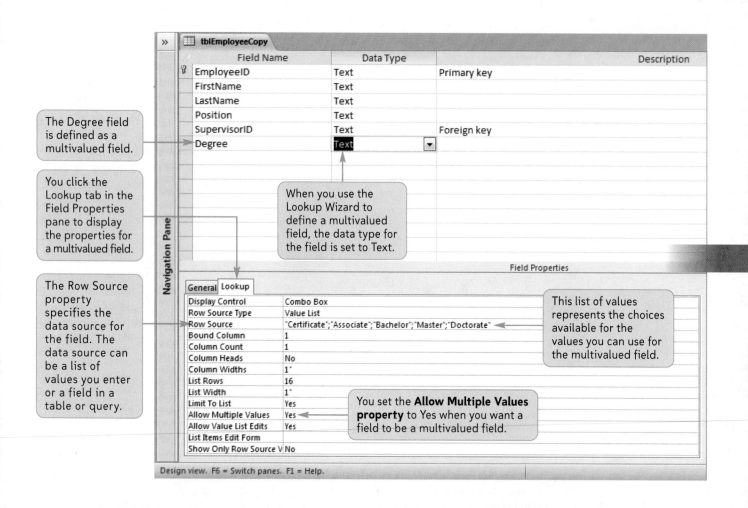

The Degree field is defined as a multivalued field.

You click the Lookup tab in the Field Properties pane to display the properties for a multivalued field.

The Row Source property specifies the data source for the field. The data source can be a list of values you enter or a field in a table or query.

When you use the Lookup Wizard to define a multivalued field, the data type for the field is set to Text.

This list of values represents the choices available for the values you can use for the multivalued field.

You set the **Allow Multiple Values property** to Yes when you want a field to be a multivalued field.

MULTIVALUED FIELDS

The Degree field is a **multivalued field**, which is a lookup field that allows you to store more than one value in a field in each record.

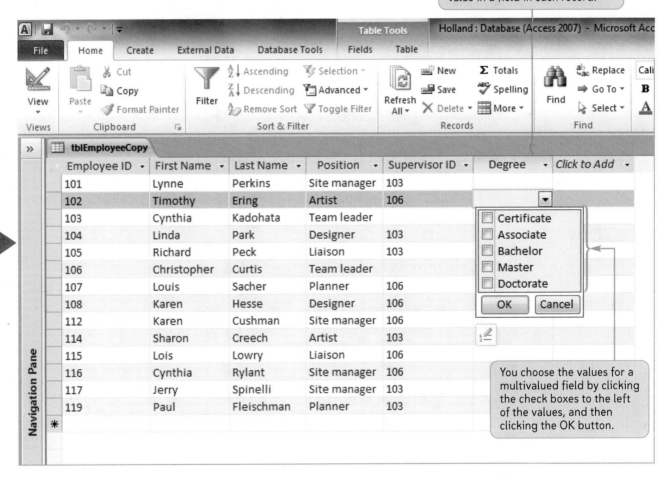

You choose the values for a multivalued field by clicking the check boxes to the left of the values, and then clicking the OK button.

Filtering Data

Sarah has two new filtering requests. She wants to see all contracts with May start dates using the tblContract table datasheet, and then she wants to view all residential customers in Rockford and Holland using the tblCustomer table.

A filter is a set of criteria you place on the records in an open form or datasheet to isolate a subset of the records temporarily. A filter is similar to a query, but it applies only to the open form or datasheet. If you want to use a filter at another time, you can save the filter as a query.

Four filter tools let you specify and apply filters in a form or datasheet: AutoFilter, Filter By Selection, Filter By Form, and Advanced Filter/Sort. With the first three tools, you specify the filter directly in the form or datasheet. An AutoFilter filters records that contain one of the selections displayed in a menu of values and context-sensitive choices for the selected field. Filter By Selection filters records that equal or contain (or do not equal or do not contain) a selected value in a field. Filter By Form filters records that match multiple selection criteria using the same Access logical and comparison operators used in queries. After applying one of these filter tools, you can use the Sort Ascending or Sort Descending buttons in the Sort & Filter group on the Home tab to rearrange the records, if necessary.

Advanced Filter/Sort lets you specify multiple selection criteria and specify a sort order for selected records in the Filter window, in the same way you specify record selection criteria and sort orders for a query in Design view.

Using an AutoFilter in a Table Datasheet

Although Sarah has used filters with a query datasheet and a form, she's never used a filter with a table datasheet. You'll show Sarah how to create a filter to display all contracts with May start dates in the tblContract table datasheet.

To filter records in the tblContract table datasheet:

▶ 1. Start Access, and then open the **Holland** database in the Access3\Tutorial folder provided with your Data Files.

▶ 2. Open the Navigation Pane (if necessary), open the **tblContract** table in Datasheet view, and then close the Navigation Pane.

▶ 3. Click the **arrow** on the Start Date column heading to open the AutoFilter menu, point to **Date Filters** to open a submenu of context-sensitive options, and then point to **All Dates In Period** to open an additional submenu. See Figure 12-1.

| Figure 12-1 | AutoFilter menu and submenus for a date field |

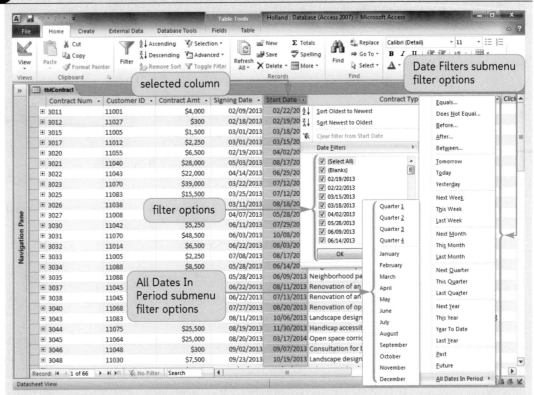

The Start Date menu displays all the values that appear in the Start Date column; you use the Start Date menu when you want to select specific values for the filter. The Date Filters submenu displays filter options that apply to a Date field, and the All Dates In Period submenu displays additional filter options for a Date field.

4. In the All Dates In Period submenu, click **May**. Only the six records with May start dates are displayed in the recordset.

If you save a table with an applied filter, the filter is saved, and you can reapply the filter anytime you open the table datasheet.

5. Save and close the table.

6. Open the Navigation Pane, open the **tblContract** table datasheet to display all 66 records, and then click the **Toggle Filter** button (with the ScreenTip "Apply Filter") in the Sort & Filter group on the Home tab. Access applies the StartDate filter, displaying the six records with May start dates.

7. Close the table.

Next, you'll use Filter By Form to produce the other results Sarah wants.

Filter By Form

You can use Filter By Form to display only those records for residential customers in Holland and Rockford.

Selecting Records Using Filter By Form

- Open the table or query datasheet, or the form in Form view.
- In the Sort & Filter group on the Home tab, click the Advanced button, and then click Filter By Form.
- Enter a simple selection criterion or an And condition in the first datasheet or form, using the text boxes for the appropriate fields.
- If there is an Or condition, click the Or tab and enter the Or condition in the second datasheet or form. Continue to enter Or conditions on separate datasheets or forms by using the Or tab.
- In the Sort & Filter group on the Home tab, click the Toggle Filter button (with the ScreenTip "Apply Filter").

To answer Sarah's question, the multiple selection criteria you will enter are: Holland *and* Residential *or* Rockford *and* Residential.

To select the records using Filter By Form:

▶ **1.** Open the **tblCustomer** datasheet to display the 42 records in the recordset, and then close the Navigation Pane.

▶ **2.** In the Sort & Filter group on the Home tab, click the **Advanced** button, click **Filter By Form** to display a blank datasheet, and then press the **Tab** key until both the City and Customer Type columns are visible. See Figure 12-2.

Figure 12-2	Blank form for Filter By Form option

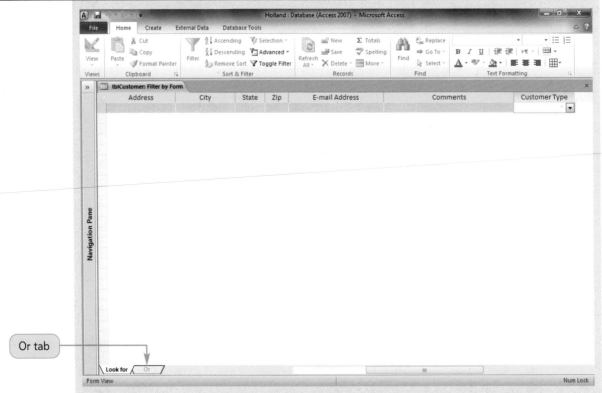

Or tab

On the blank datasheet, you specify multiple selection criteria by entering conditions in the text boxes for the fields in a record. If you enter criteria in more than one field, you create the equivalent of an And condition—Access selects any record that matches all criteria. To create an Or condition, you enter the criteria for the first part of the condition in the field on the first ("Look for") blank datasheet, and then click the Or tab to display a new blank datasheet. You enter the criteria for the second part of the condition on the second ("Or") blank datasheet. Access selects any record that matches all criteria on the Look for datasheet or all criteria on the Or datasheet.

For a criterion, you can select a value from the list of values in a text box, or you can use a comparison operator (such as <, >=, <>, and Like) and a value, similar to conditions you enter in the query design grid.

3. Click the **City** box, click the **City** arrow, and then click **Holland**. Access adds the criterion "Holland" to the City box.

4. Click the **Customer Type** box, click the **Customer Type** arrow, and then click **Residential**. Access adds the criterion "Residential" to the Customer Type box.

   You specified the logical operator (And) for the condition "Holland" And "Residential". To add the rest of the criteria, you need to display the Or blank datasheet.

TIP

Notice that a third tab, also labeled "Or," is now available in case you need to specify another Or condition.

5. Click the **Or** tab to display a second blank datasheet. The insertion point is in the Customer Type box.

6. Click the **Customer Type** arrow, and then click **Residential**.

7. Click the right side of the **City** box to display the list, click **Rockford**, and then click the **City** box to deselect all values. The filter now contains the second And condition: "Rockford" And "Residential". See Figure 12-3.

Figure 12-3   **Completed filter using Filter By Form option**

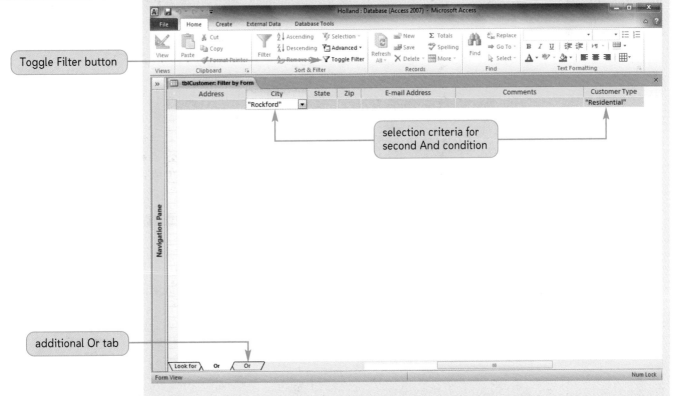

Toggle Filter button

selection criteria for second And condition

additional Or tab

Combined with the Look for conditions, you now have the Or conditions and the complete Filter By Form conditions.

▶ 8. In the Sort & Filter group, click the **Toggle Filter** button (with the ScreenTip "Apply Filter"), click the **Customer ID** box to deselect all values, and then scroll to the right until both the City and Customer Type columns are visible. Access applies the filter, displays the six records that match the selection criteria, and displays "Filtered" in the navigation bar. See Figure 12-4.

Figure 12-4   **First record that matches the Filter By Form criteria**

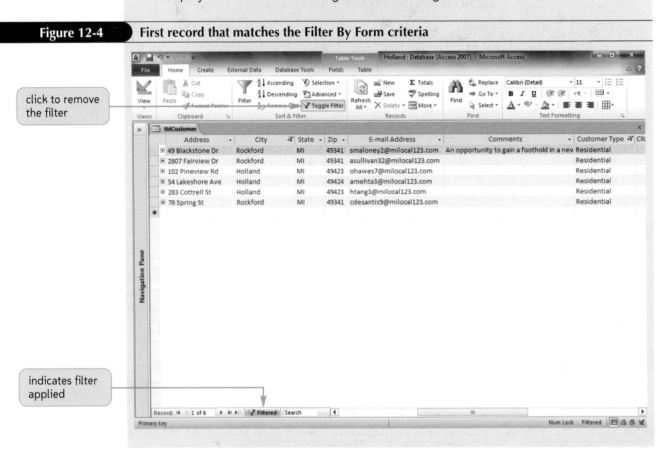

Now that you have defined the filter, you can save it as a query, so that Sarah can easily view the information in the future.

Saving a Filter as a Query

When you save a filter as a query, you can reuse the filter in the future by opening the saved query.

REFERENCE

Saving a Filter as a Query

- Create a filter using Filter By Selection, Filter By Form, or Advanced Filter/Sort.
- If you applied the filter using Filter By Form, click the Advanced button, and then click Filter By Form.
- In the Sort & Filter group on the Home tab, click the Advanced button, and then click Save As Query.
- Type the name for the query, and then press the Enter key.

Next, you'll save the filter as a query named qryHollandRockfordResidentialFilter.

To save the filter as a query:

1. In the Sort & Filter group on the Home tab, click the **Advanced** button, and then click **Filter By Form**. Access displays the datasheet with the selection criteria.

2. In the Sort & Filter group, click the **Advanced** button, and then click **Save As Query**. The Save As Query dialog box opens.

3. Type **qryHollandRockfordResidentialFilter** in the Query Name box, and then press the **Enter** key. Access saves the filter as a query in the Holland database and closes the dialog box.

   Now you can clear the selection criteria, close the Filter by Form window, and return to Datasheet view.

4. In the Sort & Filter group, click the **Advanced** button, and then click **Clear Grid**. Access removes the selection criteria from the filter datasheet.

5. Close the Filter by Form window to return to Datasheet view for the tblCustomer table.

6. In the Sort & Filter group, click the **Toggle Filter** button (with the ScreenTip "Remove Filter"), click the **Advanced** button, and then click **Clear All Filters**. The recordset displays 42 records and the recordset has no filters.

   Next, you'll leave the datasheet open while you open the qryHollandRockfordResidentialFilter query in Design view.

7. Open the Navigation Pane, open the **qryHollandRockfordResidentialFilter** query in Design view, and then close the Navigation Pane. In the design grid, the first And condition ("Holland" And "Residential") appears in the Criteria row, the second And condition ("Rockford" And "Residential") appears in the or row, and the Or condition combines the first And condition with the second And condition. See Figure 12-5.

| Figure 12-5 | Filter saved as a query in Design view |

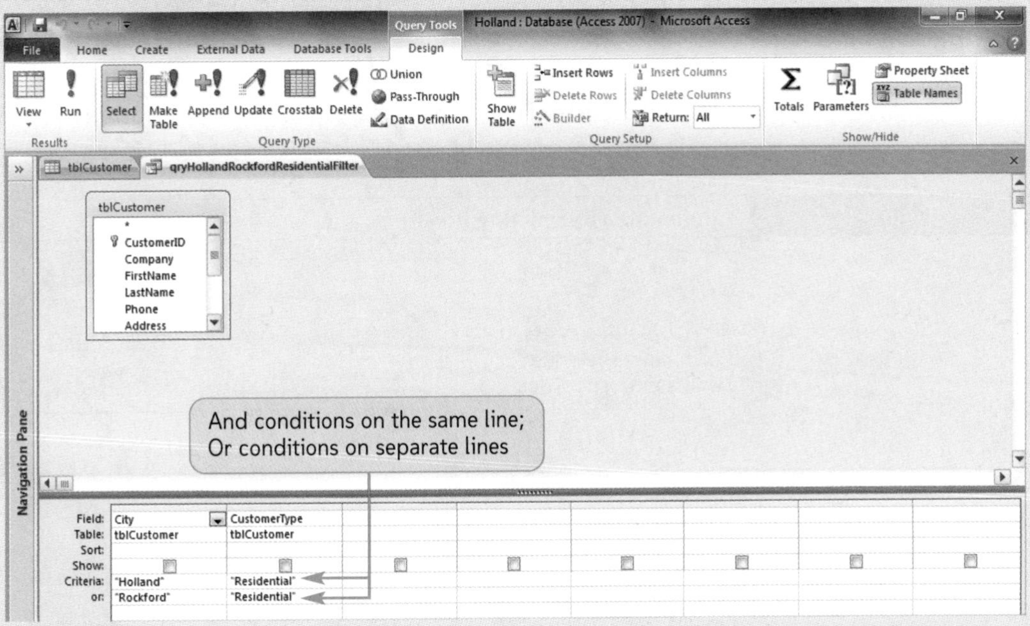

And conditions on the same line; Or conditions on separate lines

8. Run the query to display the six records that satisfy the selection criteria, close the query, close the table, and then click the **No** button when asked if you want to save the table design changes because you don't want to save the filter with the table.

The next time Sarah wants to view the records selected by the filter, she can apply the qryHollandRockfordResidentialFilter query to the tblCustomer table.

Applying a Filter Saved as a Query

To see how to apply a query as a filter to a table, you will open the tblCustomer table and apply the qryHollandRockfordResidentialFilter query as a filter.

REFERENCE

Applying a Filter Saved as a Query

- Open the table to which you want to apply the filter in Datasheet view.
- In the Sort & Filter group on the Home tab, click the Advanced button, and then click Filter By Form.
- In the Sort & Filter group, click the Advanced button, and then click Load from Query.
- In the Applicable Filter dialog box, click the query you want to apply as a filter, and then click the OK button.
- In the Sort & Filter group on the Home tab, click the Toggle Filter button (with the ScreenTip "Apply Filter") to apply the filter.

To apply the qryHollandRockfordResidentialFilter query as a filter, you'll first need to open the tblCustomer table.

To apply the filter saved as a query:

1. Open the Navigation Pane, and then open the **tblCustomer** table datasheet.

2. In the Sort & Filter group, click the **Advanced** button, and then click **Filter By Form**. Access displays a blank datasheet.

3. In the Sort & Filter group, click the **Advanced** button, and then click **Load from Query**. Access opens the Applicable Filter dialog box. See Figure 12-6.

Figure 12-6 Applicable Filter dialog box

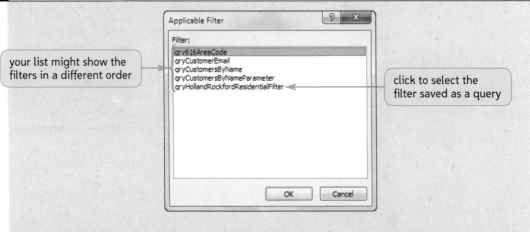

your list might show the filters in a different order

click to select the filter saved as a query

▶ **4.** Click **qryHollandRockfordResidentialFilter** in the Filter box, and then click the **OK** button. Access loads the saved query into the Filter by Form window.

▶ **5.** In the Sort & Filter group, click the **Toggle Filter** button. Access applies the filter and displays the six filtered records in the datasheet.

▶ **6.** Click the **Advanced** button, click **Clear All Filters**, and then close the table without saving your design changes.

Lucia wants to show you how to modify the qryHollandRockfordResidentialFilter query to use a subquery.

Creating a Subquery

When you create a query using an SQL SELECT statement, you can place a second SELECT statement inside it; this second inner query is called a **subquery**. Access runs the subquery first, and then Access uses the results of the subquery to run the outer query.

To view the qryHollandRockfordResidentialFilter query in SQL view:

▶ **1.** Open the **qryHollandRockfordResidentialFilter** query in Design view, and then close the Navigation Pane. In the design grid, the first And condition ("Holland" And "Residential") appears in the Criteria row, the second And condition ("Rockford" And "Residential") appears in the or row, and the Or condition combines the first And condition with the second And condition.

▶ **2.** In the Results group on the Design tab, click the **View button arrow**, click **SQL View**, and then click an unused portion of the window to deselect the SQL SELECT statement. See Figure 12-7.

Figure 12-7   **SQL statement for the qryHollandRockfordResidentialFilter query**

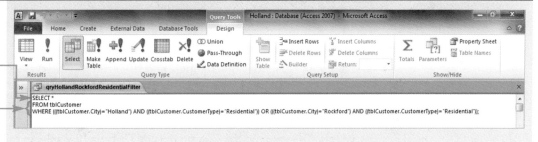

selects all fields from the record source

selection criteria

SELECT * FROM tblCustomer selects all fields from the tblCustomer table in the order in which they appear in the table. The WHERE clause specifies the selection criteria: records with a City field value of Holland and a CustomerType field value of Residential, or records with a City field value of Rockford and a CustomerType field value of Residential.

To modify the query to use a subquery, you'll retain the *SELECT * FROM tblCustomer* portion of the SQL statement to select all fields from the tblCustomer table in the order in which they appear in the table, and you'll change the selection criteria as shown in Figure 12-8. The *WHERE CustomerType="Residential"* will select residential customers, and the *AND CustomerID IN* completes the outer query to select those records with

CustomerID values that satisfy the subquery. The And logical operator specifies that a record will be selected when both the CustomerType="Residential" and the CustomerID is among those selected by the subquery. *SELECT CustomerID FROM tblCustomer WHERE City="Holland" OR City="Rockford"* is the subquery, selecting CustomerID field values for Holland and Rockford customers. The subquery is enclosed in parentheses, and a semicolon terminates the entire SELECT statement.

Figure 12-8	SQL SELECT statement using a subquery

```
SELECT *
FROM tblCustomer
WHERE CustomerType="Residential"
AND CustomerID IN
(SELECT CustomerID
FROM tblCustomer
WHERE City="Holland" OR City="Rockford");
```

Now you'll change the query to use a subquery.

To change the query to use a subquery:

1. Select the word **WHERE** and the text to the end of the statement (the semicolon), and then type the last five lines shown in Figure 12-8 to change the SQL SELECT statement to use a subquery. See Figure 12-9.

Figure 12-9	SQL statement using a subquery

type these lines

subquery

2. Save your query design changes, and then run the query. Access displays the same six records you viewed earlier before changing the query design to use a subquery.

3. Switch to Design view, and then click the first column's **Field** box to deselect all values. The value in the CustomerType Criteria box selects records for residential customers, and the value in the CustomerID Criteria box is a subquery that selects Holland and Rockford customers. See Figure 12-10.

Figure 12-10	Query using a subquery in the Design window

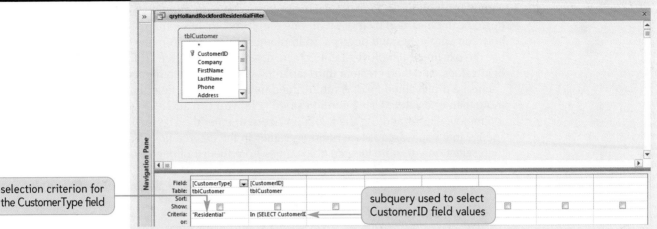

selection criterion for the CustomerType field

subquery used to select CustomerID field values

It's unclear from looking at the two columns in the design grid that all fields are displayed from the tblCustomer table.

4. In the Show/Hide group on the Design tab, click the **Property Sheet** button to display the properties for the query. See Figure 12-11.

Figure 12-11	Properties for the query

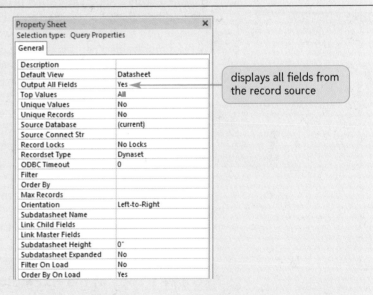

displays all fields from the record source

The Output All Fields property setting of Yes specifies that Access displays all fields from the record source, the tblCustomer table, without these fields being added to the design grid.

5. Close the property sheet, close the query, and then click the **Yes** button if you're asked to save changes to the query design.

Lucia wants to experiment with two advanced features of Access 2010: multivalued fields and Attachment fields.

Using Multivalued Fields

Sarah wants to keep track of the degrees, such as Associate, Bachelor, and Master, earned by employees. Because each employee can earn more than one degree, and each degree can be earned by more than one employee, there's a many-to-many relationship between employees and degrees. To implement this many-to-many relationship, you'd use the existing tblEmployee table, create a separate tblDegree table to store the Degree field values, and then create a third table to tie together the other two tables. Instead, you can use a multivalued field. A multivalued field is a lookup field that allows you to store more than one value. Using a multivalued field, you can add a Degree field to the tblEmployee table and use the Lookup Wizard to enter the Degree field values and specify that you want to store multiple values in the Degree field. Sarah and her staff can then select one or more Degree field values from the list of degrees.

INSIGHT

Using Multivalued Fields

When you define a multivalued field in a table, Access does not actually store values in the field in that table. Instead, Access stores the values in hidden, system tables in a many-to-many relationship with the table. Access manages, manipulates, and displays the data to make it appear as if the data was stored in the multivalued field in the table.

Users with limited Access and database experience are the intended audience for multivalued fields because understanding the concepts of many-to-many relationships and creating them are difficult for beginning or casual database users. Experienced database users avoid multivalued fields and implement many-to-many relationships in the traditional way you learned earlier in this book because they have total control over the data and are not limited as they would be with multivalued fields. One of the limitations of multivalued fields is that you can't sort records in queries, forms, and reports, except in special circumstances, based on the values stored in the multivalued field. Also, multivalued fields do not convert properly to a database managed by a DBMS such as SQL Server or Oracle. If you need to convert the Access database to another DBMS in the future, you'd have to change the multivalued field to many-to-many relationships, which is a change that's much more difficult at that point than if you had avoided using a multivalued field from the beginning.

Lucia wants to experiment with the multivalued field feature without modifying the existing tables and relationships, so you'll make a copy of the tblEmployee table and experiment with the copied version of the table.

To create a copy of the tblEmployee table:

1. Open the Navigation Pane, then in the Navigation Pane, right-click **tblEmployee** to open the shortcut menu, and then click **Copy**.

2. In the Clipboard group on the Home tab, click the **Paste** button to open the Paste Table As dialog box, and then click the **Table Name** box to deselect all values. See Figure 12-12.

Figure 12-12   Paste Table As dialog box

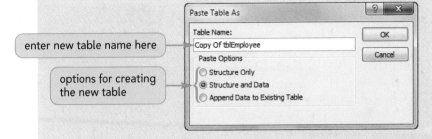

enter new table name here

options for creating
the new table

When you copy a table to create a new table, you can use the design of the table without copying its data (Structure Only), use the design and copy the data from the table (Structure and Data), or add the data to an existing table (Append Data to Existing Table).

You'll create the new table using the design and data from the tblEmployee table.

3. Change the name in the Table Name box to **tblEmployeeCopy**, make sure the **Structure and Data** option button is selected, and then click the **OK** button. Access creates a new table named tblEmployeeCopy that contains the same structure and data as the tblEmployee table.

Now you can add the multivalued field to the tblEmployeeCopy table.

To add a multivalued field to the tblEmployeeCopy table:

1. Open the **tblEmployeeCopy** table in Design view, and then close the Navigation Pane.

2. Click the **Field Name** box in the blank row below the SupervisorID field, type **Degree**, press the **Tab** key, click the **Data Type** arrow, and then click **Lookup Wizard**. The first Lookup Wizard dialog box opens.

   You'll type the Degree field values instead of obtaining them from a table or query.

3. Click the **I will type in the values that I want** option button, and then click the **Next** button to open the second Lookup Wizard dialog box, in which you'll type the Degree field values.

4. Click the **Col1** box in the first row, type **Certificate**, press the **Tab** key, type **Associate**, press the **Tab** key, type **Bachelor**, press the **Tab** key, type **Master**, press the **Tab** key, and then type **Doctorate**. These are the five values that users can choose from for the Degree multivalued field. See Figure 12-13.

Figure 12-13 **Values for the Degree multivalued field**

type these values

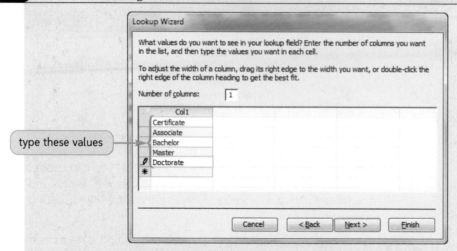

5. Click the **Next** button to open the last Lookup Wizard dialog box, and then click the **Allow Multiple Values** check box to add a check mark to it. See Figure 12-14.

Figure 12-14 **Specifying a multivalued field**

use the default label value

click to check this box to select a multivalued field

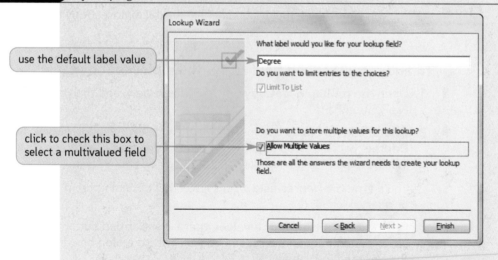

You'll accept the default label name of Degree for the field. When you click the Allow Multiple Values check box to place a check mark in it, you are specifying that you want the Degree field to be a multivalued field.

6. Click the **Finish** button to complete the definition of the Degree field as a lookup field that allows multiple values, or a multivalued field.

7. Click the **Lookup** tab in the Field Properties pane. The Degree field has its Row Source property set to the five values you typed in one of the Lookup Wizard dialog boxes, and the Allow Multiple Values property has been set to Yes. See Figure 12-15.

Figure 12-15   After defining the Degree field as a multivalued field

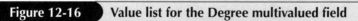

new field

If you forget to select the Allow Multiple Values check box when you use the Lookup Wizard, you can change to Design view and set the Allow Multiple Values property for the field to Yes to change the field to a multivalued field. If you need to add values in the future to the multivalued field, you can add them to the Row Source property.

8. Save your table design changes, and then switch to Datasheet view.

9. Click the right side of the **Degree** box for record 2 (Timothy Ering) to open the value list for the field. See Figure 12-16.

Figure 12-16   Value list for the Degree multivalued field

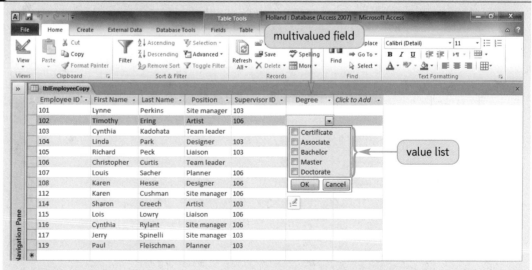

▶ **10.** Click the **Associate** check box, and then click the **OK** button.

▶ **11.** Repeat Steps 9 and 10 for record 4 (Linda Park), selecting **Associate**, **Bachelor**, and **Master**, and for record 5 (Richard Peck), selecting **Bachelor**, resize the Degree column to its best fit, and then click the **Degree** box for record 5 to deselect all values. Records 2 (Timothy Ering) and 5 (Richard Peck) have one value selected for the Degree field, and record 4 (Linda Park) has three values selected for the Degree field. See Figure 12-17.

TIP

In the Sort & Filter group, the Ascending and Descending buttons are dimmed because you can't sort records based on multivalued fields.

Figure 12-17   After selecting values for the multivalued field

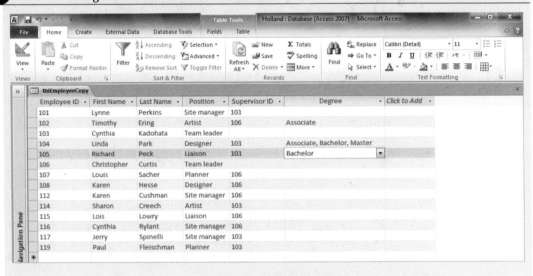

Lucia wants you to create queries to display all field values from the tblEmployeeCopy table to see how Access displays multivalued field values.

To create queries to display the Degree multivalued field:

▶ **1.** Save and close the tblEmployeeCopy table, click the **Create** tab on the Ribbon, and then in the Queries group on the Create tab, click the **Query Wizard** button to open the New Query dialog box.

▶ **2.** Make sure the **Simple Query Wizard** option is selected, click the **OK** button to open the Simple Query Wizard dialog box, select all fields from the tblEmployeeCopy table, click the **Next** button, change the query title to **qryEmployeeCopy**, click the **Finish** button, and then click the first row's Employee ID column value to deselect all values. Access displays 16 records in the query recordset. See Figure 12-18.

Figure 12-18   **Query that displays the Degree multivalued field**

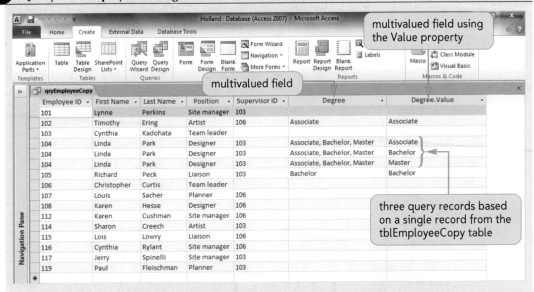

Trouble? The rightmost column heading on your screen might be the equivalent tblEmployeeCopy.Degree.Value instead of Degree.Value, indicating the Degree field in the tblEmployeeCopy table. This difference does not affect the contents of the column.

The six fields from the tblEmployeeCopy table are displayed in seven columns in the query recordset because the Degree field is displayed in two columns: the Degree column and the Degree.Value column. The Degree column displays field values exactly as they appear in the tblEmployeeCopy table; all values for the Degree multivalued field, such as those for Linda Park, are displayed in one row in the query. The Degree.Value column displays the Degree multivalued field in expanded form so that each value appears in a separate row in the query. *Degree.Value* identifies the Degree field and the Value property for the Degree field.

In queries that contain a multivalued field, you should display the field in a single column, not in two columns, with values appearing as they are in the table or in expanded form. You can eliminate the extra column by deleting it, by clearing its Show check box in Design view, or by selecting just one of the two fields in the Simple Query Wizard when you select the fields for the query.

3. Click the **Home** tab on the Ribbon, notice that the Ascending and Descending buttons in the Sort & Filter group on the Ribbon are active, click the first row's **Degree** box, notice that the Ascending and Descending buttons are dimmed, and then click the first row's **Degree.Value** box. The Ascending and Descending buttons are active and you can sort records in the query based on the values in the Degree.Value column.

Next, you'll review the query design.

4. Switch to Design view, and then drag down the bottom of the tblEmployeeCopy field list to show all values in the list. See Figure 12-19.

Figure 12-19 Design of the query containing the Degree multivalued field

collapse indicator for the multivalued field

Value property appended to the Degree multivalued field

Degree multivalued field

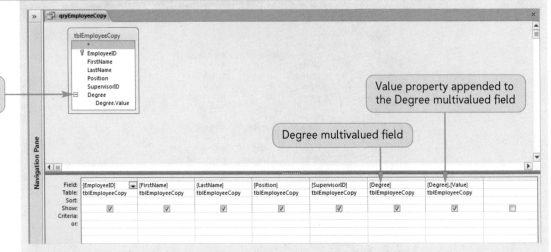

The Degree field in the tblEmployeeCopy field list has a collapse indicator to its left that you can click to hide the Degree.Value entry below it. The rightmost column in the design grid, [Degree].[Value], uses the Value property for the Degree field. Using the **Value property** with a multivalued field displays the multivalued field in expanded form so that each value is displayed in a separate row.

You'll delete the [Degree] column from the query design, retaining the [Degree].[Value] column and setting its Caption property, and then you'll save the query with a new name.

5. Right-click the **column selector bar** for the [Degree] column to highlight the column and open the shortcut menu, and then click **Cut**.

6. Open the property sheet for the [Degree].[Value] column, set the Caption property to **Degree**, and then close the property sheet.

7. Click the **File** tab on the Ribbon, click **Save Object As** to open the Save As dialog box, change the query name to **qryEmployeeCopyValue**, click the **OK** button, click the **Home** tab, switch to Datasheet view, and then resize the Degree column to its best fit. Access displays 16 records in the query recordset.

8. Save the query datasheet change, and then close the query.

9. Open the Navigation Pane, open the **qryEmployeeCopy** query in Design view, close the Navigation Pane, delete the **Degree.Value** column, save the query, and then run the query. Access displays the 14 records from the tblEmployeeCopy table and displays the Degree multivalued field values in one row.

10. Close the query, and if you are not continuing on to the next session, close the Holland database.

In the next session, Lucia wants you to experiment with Attachment fields using the tblEmployeeCopy table.

REVIEW

Session 12.1 Quick Check

1. Filter By _____ filters records that match multiple selection criteria using the same Access comparison operators used in queries.
2. You can save a filter as a(n) _____ and reuse the filter by opening the saved object.
3. What is a subquery?
4. What is a multivalued field?
5. You use the _____ property to display a multivalued field in expanded form so that each value is displayed in a separate row in a query.

SESSION 12.2 VISUAL OVERVIEW

The Current Database page in the Access Options dialog box displays options that apply only to the currently open database.

The **Application Title property** specifies the name for the database that appears in the Access window title bar. You'll set it to "Holland Release 1."

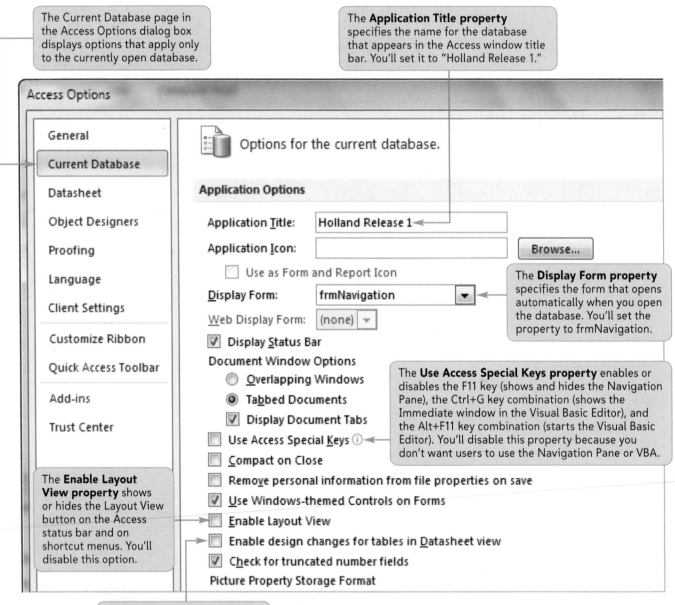

Access Options

| General |
| **Current Database** |
| Datasheet |
| Object Designers |
| Proofing |
| Language |
| Client Settings |
| Customize Ribbon |
| Quick Access Toolbar |
| Add-ins |
| Trust Center |

Options for the current database.

Application Options

Application Title: Holland Release 1

Application Icon: [   ] Browse...

☐ Use as Form and Report Icon

Display Form: frmNavigation ▼

Web Display Form: (none) ▼

☑ Display Status Bar

Document Window Options
- ○ Overlapping Windows
- ◉ Tabbed Documents
- ☑ Display Document Tabs

☐ Use Access Special Keys ⓘ

☐ Compact on Close

☐ Remove personal information from file properties on save

☑ Use Windows-themed Controls on Forms

☐ Enable Layout View

☐ Enable design changes for tables in Datasheet view

☑ Check for truncated number fields

Picture Property Storage Format

The **Display Form property** specifies the form that opens automatically when you open the database. You'll set the property to frmNavigation.

The **Use Access Special Keys property** enables or disables the F11 key (shows and hides the Navigation Pane), the Ctrl+G key combination (shows the Immediate window in the Visual Basic Editor), and the Alt+F11 key combination (starts the Visual Basic Editor). You'll disable this property because you don't want users to use the Navigation Pane or VBA.

The **Enable Layout View property** shows or hides the Layout View button on the Access status bar and on shortcut menus. You'll disable this option.

The **Enable design changes for tables in Datasheet view property** allows you to change a table's design in Datasheet view. You'll disable this option.

DATABASE PROPERTIES

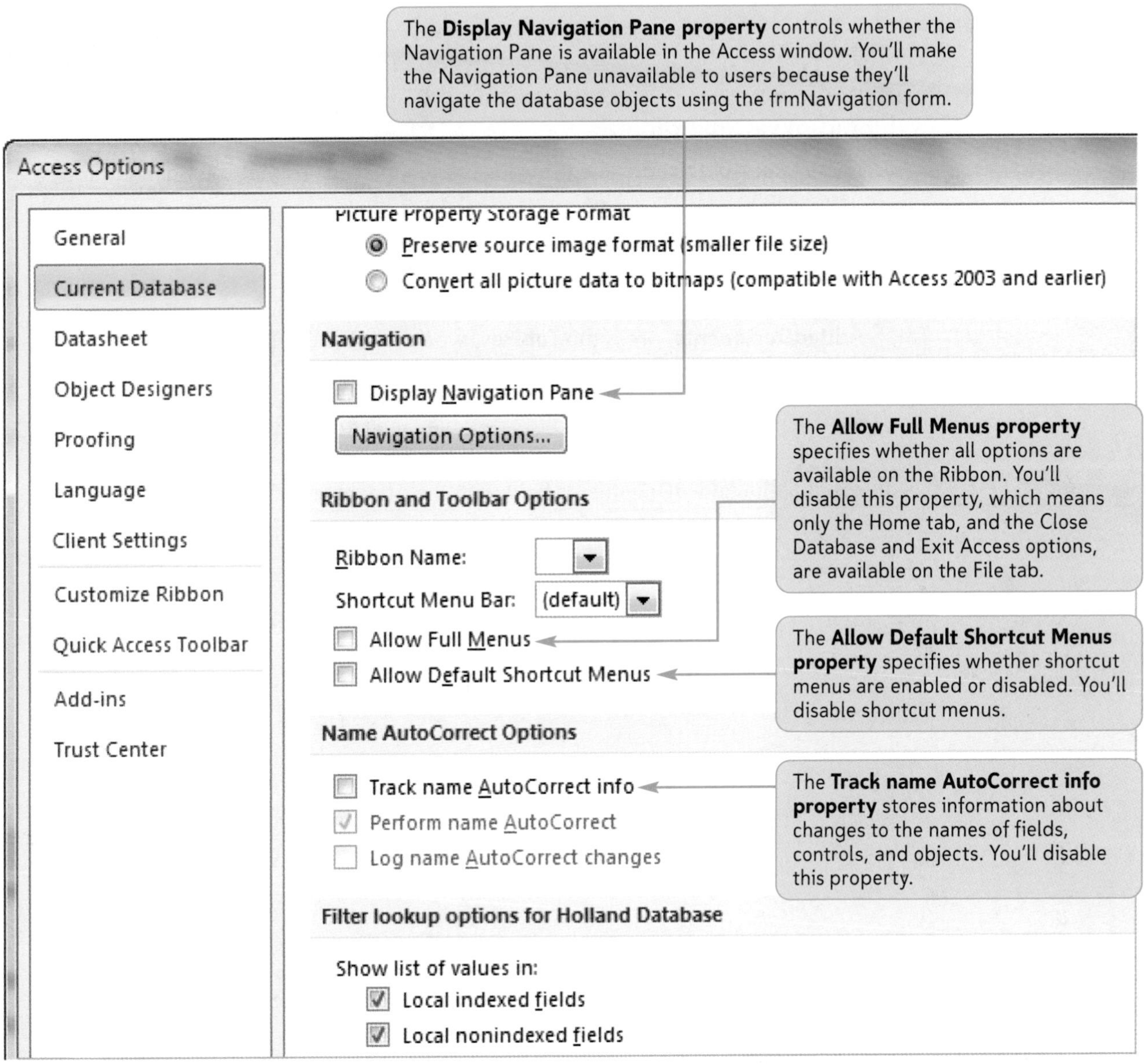

The **Display Navigation Pane property** controls whether the Navigation Pane is available in the Access window. You'll make the Navigation Pane unavailable to users because they'll navigate the database objects using the frmNavigation form.

Access Options

| General |
| Current Database |
| Datasheet |
| Object Designers |
| Proofing |
| Language |
| Client Settings |
| Customize Ribbon |
| Quick Access Toolbar |
| Add-ins |
| Trust Center |

Picture Property Storage Format
- ◉ Preserve source image format (smaller file size)
- ○ Convert all picture data to bitmaps (compatible with Access 2003 and earlier)

Navigation

☐ Display Navigation Pane

[Navigation Options...]

Ribbon and Toolbar Options

Ribbon Name: [▼]
Shortcut Menu Bar: (default) [▼]
☐ Allow Full Menus
☐ Allow Default Shortcut Menus

The **Allow Full Menus property** specifies whether all options are available on the Ribbon. You'll disable this property, which means only the Home tab, and the Close Database and Exit Access options, are available on the File tab.

The **Allow Default Shortcut Menus property** specifies whether shortcut menus are enabled or disabled. You'll disable shortcut menus.

Name AutoCorrect Options

☐ Track name AutoCorrect info
☑ Perform name AutoCorrect
☐ Log name AutoCorrect changes

The **Track name AutoCorrect info property** stores information about changes to the names of fields, controls, and objects. You'll disable this property.

Filter lookup options for Holland Database

Show list of values in:
☑ Local indexed fields
☑ Local nonindexed fields

Creating an Attachment Field

In addition to storing data such as text, numbers, and dates in a database, you can attach external files such as Excel workbooks, Word documents, and images, similar to how you attach external files to email messages. You use the **Attachment data type** to attach one or more attachments to a table record. Access stores attachments in compressed form to minimize file size and maximize disk space usage.

Lucia wants you to add a field with the Attachment data type to the tblEmployeeCopy table.

To add a new field with the Attachment data type to the tblEmployeeCopy table:

▶ 1. If you took a break after the previous session, make sure that the Holland database is open.

▶ 2. Open the Navigation Pane (if necessary), open the **tblEmployeeCopy** table in Design view, and then close the Navigation Pane.

▶ 3. Click the **Field Name** box for the blank row below the Degree field, type **AddedDocuments**, press the **Tab** key, type **at**, press the **Tab** key to select Attachment as the data type, press the **F6** key to switch to the Caption box in the Field Properties pane, and then type **Added Documents**. You've completed adding the AddedDocuments field to the table. See Figure 12-20.

| Figure 12-20 | After adding the AddedDocuments field with the Attachment data type |

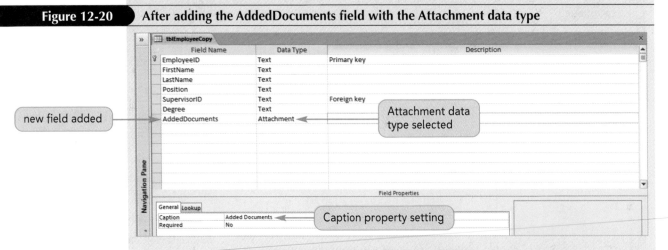

▶ 4. Save your table design changes, switch to Datasheet view, resize the Added Documents column to its best fit, click the first row's **Employee ID** box to deselect all values, and then save your datasheet format changes. See Figure 12-21.

Figure 12-21   Attachment field displayed in the table datasheet

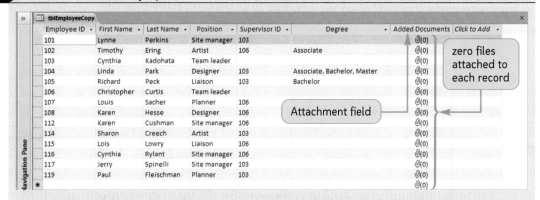

Employee ID	First Name	Last Name	Position	Supervisor ID	Degree	Added Documents	Click to Add
101	Lynne	Perkins	Site manager	103		◐(0)	
102	Timothy	Ering	Artist	106	Associate	◐(0)	
103	Cynthia	Kadohata	Team leader			◐(0)	
104	Linda	Park	Designer	103	Associate, Bachelor, Master	◐(0)	
105	Richard	Peck	Liaison	103	Bachelor	◐(0)	
106	Christopher	Curtis	Team leader			◐(0)	
107	Louis	Sacher	Planner	106		◐(0)	
108	Karen	Hesse	Designer	106		◐(0)	
112	Karen	Cushman	Site manager	106		◐(0)	
114	Sharon	Creech	Artist	103		◐(0)	
115	Lois	Lowry	Liaison	106		◐(0)	
116	Cynthia	Rylant	Site manager	106		◐(0)	
117	Jerry	Spinelli	Site manager	103		◐(0)	
119	Paul	Fleischman	Planner	103		◐(0)	

zero files attached to each record

Attachment field

Each AddedDocuments field value displays an attachment icon in the shape of a paper clip followed by a number in parentheses that indicates the number of files attached in that field for the record. You've not attached any files, so each record displays zero file attachments.

Lucia asks you to create a Word document, an Excel workbook, and a PowerPoint presentation, so she can experiment with attaching files in the Added Documents column.

▶ 5. Start Word, save the blank document that opens as **Perkins1** in the Access3\Tutorial folder, exit Word, start Excel, save the blank workbook that opens as **Perkins2** in the Access3\Tutorial folder, exit Excel, start PowerPoint, save the blank presentation that opens as **Perkins3** in the Access3\Tutorial folder, and then exit PowerPoint.

▶ 6. Make sure the tblEmployeeCopy table is open in Datasheet view, right-click the first row's **Added Documents** box to open the shortcut menu, and then click **Manage Attachments** to open the Attachments dialog box.

You'll add all three files you created as attachments to the first row's AddedDocuments field.

▶ 7. Click the **Add** button to open the Choose File dialog box, navigate to the Access3\Tutorial folder, click **Perkins1**, and then click the **Open** button to add the Perkins1.docx file to the Attachments dialog box.

▶ 8. Click the **Add** button to open the Choose File dialog box, click **Perkins2**, hold down the **Ctrl** key, click **Perkins3**, release the **Ctrl** key, and then click the **Open** button. The three files you've added now appear in the Attachments dialog box. See Figure 12-22.

Figure 12-22   Attachments dialog box

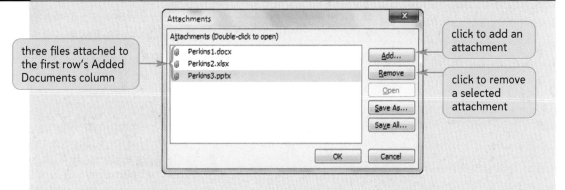

three files attached to the first row's Added Documents column

click to add an attachment

click to remove a selected attachment

▶ **9.** Click the **OK** button to close the dialog box. The table datasheet now indicates that three files (as noted by the 3 in parentheses) are attached to the AddedDocuments field in the first record.

Next, you'll open one of the files attached in the first record, detach one of the attached files, and export an attached file.

To open, export, and detach files attached in a table field:

▶ **1.** Right-click the first row's **AddedDocuments** box to open the shortcut menu, and then click **Manage Attachments** to open the Attachments dialog box.

▶ **2.** Click **Perkins2.xlsx** in the Attachments list, and then click the **Open** button. Excel starts and opens the Perkins2 workbook.

▶ **3.** Exit Excel.

▶ **4.** Click **Perkins1.docx** in the Attachments list, and then click the **Remove** button. Access removes the Perkins1 document from the Attachments list and detaches the Perkins1 document from the first row's AddedDocuments field.

TIP

The Perkins1 document remains in the Access3\Tutorial folder because detaching a file doesn't delete it.

▶ **5.** Click **Perkins3.pptx** in the Attachments list, click the **Save As** button to open the Save Attachment dialog box, type **Perkins3 Export.pptx** in the File name box, make sure the Access3\Tutorial folder is the current destination folder, and then click the **Save** button. Access exports the Perkins3 presentation with the name Perkins3 Export and saves it in the Access3\Tutorial folder.

▶ **6.** Click the **OK** button to close the Attachments dialog box. Because you removed the Perkins1 file as an attachment in the first record, the Added Documents column for the first record now shows that there are two attachments.

Lucia wants you to add an AutoNumber field to the tblEmployeeCopy table.

Using an AutoNumber Field

TIP

Read the Natural, Artificial, and Surrogate Keys section in the appendix titled "Relational Databases and Database Design" for more information about AutoNumber fields and primary keys.

When you create a table in Datasheet view, Access assigns the AutoNumber data type to the default ID primary key field because the AutoNumber data type automatically inserts a unique number in this field for every record in the table. Therefore, it can serve as the primary key for any table you create. When defining a field with the AutoNumber data type, you can specify sequential numbering or random numbering, either of which guarantees a unique field value for every record in the table.

You'll add an AutoNumber field to the tblEmployeeCopy table.

To add an AutoNumber field to the tblEmployeeCopy table:

▶ **1.** Switch to Design view, right-click the **row selector** for the EmployeeID field to open the shortcut menu, and then click **Insert Rows**. Access adds a blank row above the EmployeeID row. You'll add the AutoNumber field to this new first row in the table design.

▶ **2.** Click the first row's **Field Name** box, type **EmployeeNum**, press the **Tab** key, type **a**, press the **Tab** key to accept AutoNumber as the data type, press the **F6** key to switch to the Field Properties pane, press the **Tab** key three times to navigate to the Caption box, and then type **Employee Num** in the Caption box. You've finished adding the EmployeeNum field to the table. See Figure 12-23.

Figure 12-23   **After adding the EmployeeNum field with the AutoNumber data type**

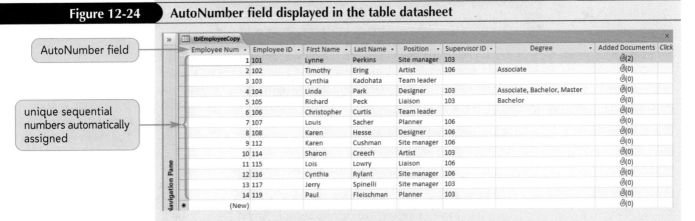

new field added

Field Name	Data Type	Description
EmployeeNum	AutoNumber	
EmployeeID	Text	Primary key
FirstName	Text	
LastName	Text	
Position	Text	
SupervisorID	Text	Foreign key
Degree	Text	
AddedDocuments	Attachment	

AutoNumber data type selected

Field Properties

General | Lookup

Field Size	Long Integer
New Values	Increment
Format	
Caption	Employee Num
Indexed	Yes (Duplicates OK)
Smart Tags	
Text Align	General

sequential numbering will be used

Caption property setting

The label for the field when used on a form. If you don't enter a caption, the field name is used as the label. Press F1 for help on captions.

The default New Values property setting of Increment specifies that sequential numbering will be used for the AutoNumber field. The other New Values property value you can select is Random.

3. Save your table design changes, switch to Datasheet view, resize the first column to its best fit, and then click the first row's **Employee Num** box to deselect all values. The new EmployeeNum field is displayed as the first column in the table, and Access automatically assigned unique sequential numbers to the EmployeeNum field for the 14 records in the table. See Figure 12-24.

Figure 12-24   **AutoNumber field displayed in the table datasheet**

AutoNumber field

unique sequential numbers automatically assigned

Employee Num	Employee ID	First Name	Last Name	Position	Supervisor ID	Degree	Added Documents
1	101	Lynne	Perkins	Site manager	103		(2)
2	102	Timothy	Ering	Artist	106	Associate	(0)
3	103	Cynthia	Kadohata	Team leader			(0)
4	104	Linda	Park	Designer	103	Associate, Bachelor, Master	(0)
5	105	Richard	Peck	Liaison	103	Bachelor	(0)
6	106	Christopher	Curtis	Team leader			(0)
7	107	Louis	Sacher	Planner	106		(0)
8	108	Karen	Hesse	Designer	106		(0)
9	112	Karen	Cushman	Site manager	106		(0)
10	114	Sharon	Creech	Artist	103		(0)
11	115	Lois	Lowry	Liaison	106		(0)
12	116	Cynthia	Rylant	Site manager	106		(0)
13	117	Jerry	Spinelli	Site manager	103		(0)
14	119	Paul	Fleischman	Planner	103		(0)
(New)							(0)

Lucia wants to review the property settings for the Position field in the tblEmployeeCopy table.

4. Switch to Design view, and then click the **Field Name** box for the Position field to display its properties. See Figure 12-25.

Figure 12-25   **Property settings for the Position field**

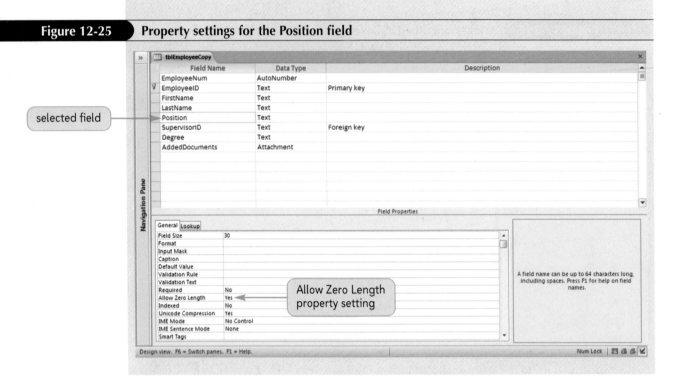

The Position field's Required property is set to No, which means field value entries are optional. The Allow Zero Length property is set to Yes, which is the default setting for Text fields and Memo fields. When its **Allow Zero Length property** is set to Yes, a field can store a zero length string value.

INSIGHT

Setting the Allow Zero Length Property to No

For a Text or Memo field, there is a difference between how you specify a null field value and a zero length value and how Access interprets the two values. You specify a zero length value in a Text or a Memo field by typing two consecutive double quotation marks (" "), and you specify a null value by entering no value. When you view a value for a Text or Memo field that has its Allow Zero Length property set to Yes, you can't determine if the field value has been set to null or has a zero length value because both field values look the same—the absence of a visible value.

However, Access treats the two values differently. If you run a query to display all records in the table that have a null value in the field using the IsNull function, only the records with a null field value appear in the query recordset; the records with a zero length value in the field do not appear. And if you change the query to display all records that have a nonnull value, the records with a zero length value in the field appear in the query recordset, which often raises questions by users about why those records are displayed. A typical user doesn't understand the distinction between a null value and a zero length value and doesn't need to make this distinction, so you should set the Allow Zero Length property to No for Text and Memo fields.

Sarah has a previous version of Access on her home computer and wonders if she can open the Holland database on that computer.

Saving an Access Database as a Previous Version

The default file format for databases you create in Access 2010 uses the .accdb filename extension, and is referred to as the Access 2007 file format because it was introduced with Access 2007. None of the versions of Access prior to Access 2007 can open a database that has the .accdb filename extension. However, you can save an .accdb database to a format that is compatible with previous versions of Access—specifically, to a format that is compatible with Access 2000 or to a format that is compatible with Access 2002-2003; both have the .mdb filename extension. For people who don't have Access 2010 or 2007 but do have one of the previous versions of Access, saving the database to a previous version allows them to use the database. Unfortunately, when an Access 2007 file format database uses features such as multivalued and Attachment fields, you cannot save the database in a previous version.

To save an Access 2007 file format database as a previous version, you would complete the following steps (note that you will not actually save the database now):

1. Make sure that the database you want to save is open and all database objects are closed, and that the database does not contain any multivalued fields, Attachment fields, or any other features that are included only in Access 2007 file-formatted databases.
2. Click the File tab on the Ribbon to display Backstage view, click Save & Publish in the navigation bar, click Save Database As, and then click Access 2002-2003 Database or click Access 2000 Database, depending on which file format you want to use.
3. Click the Save As button. In the Save As dialog box, navigate to the folder where you want to save the file, enter a name for the database in the File name box, and then click the Save button.

Next, Lucia asks you to analyze the performance of the Holland database.

Analyzing Database Performance with the Performance Analyzer

Lucia wants the Holland database to respond as quickly as possible to user requests, such as running queries and opening reports. You'll use the Performance Analyzer to check the performance of the Holland database. The **Performance Analyzer** is an Access tool that you can use to optimize the performance of an Access database. You select the database objects you want to analyze for performance and then run the Performance Analyzer. The Performance Analyzer lists three types of analysis results: recommendation, suggestion, and idea. Access can complete the recommendation and suggestion optimizations for you, but you must implement the idea optimizations. Analysis results include changes such as those related to the storage of fields and the creation of indexes and relationships.

REFERENCE

Using the Performance Analyzer

- Start Access and open the database you want to analyze.
- In the Analyze group on the Database Tools tab on the Ribbon, click the Analyze Performance button.
- Select the object(s) you want to analyze, and then click the OK button.
- Select the analysis result(s) you want the Performance Analyzer to complete for you, and then click the Optimize button.
- Note the idea optimizations and perform those optimizations, as appropriate.
- Click the Close button.

You'll use the Performance Analyzer to optimize the performance of the Holland database.

To use the Performance Analyzer to optimize the performance of the Holland database:

▶ 1. Save and close the tblEmployeeCopy table.

▶ 2. Click the **Database Tools** tab on the Ribbon, and then in the Analyze group, click the **Analyze Performance** button. The Performance Analyzer dialog box opens. See Figure 12-26.

Figure 12-26 Performance Analyzer dialog box

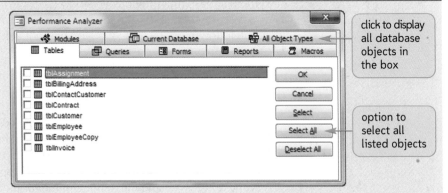

Lucia wants you to analyze every object in the Holland database.

▶ 3. Click the **All Object Types** tab, and then click the **Select All** button. All objects in the Holland database appear in the box, and all of them are now selected.

▶ 4. Click the **OK** button. The Performance Analyzer analyzes all the objects in the Holland database and, after a few moments, displays its analysis results. See Figure 12-27.

Figure 12-27 Performance Analyzer analysis results

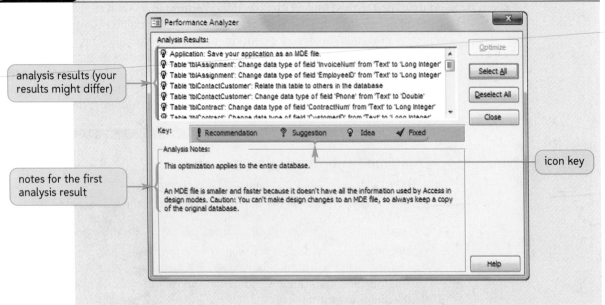

Trouble? The contents of the Analysis Results box on your screen might be different from those shown in Figure 12-27, depending on how you've completed the steps in the previous tutorials.

Most of the analysis results are in the idea category, which means that you have to implement them yourself. You should consider all idea analysis results, but more important now are the recommendation and suggestion analysis results, which the Performance Analyzer can complete for you automatically.

▶ 5. Click several entries in the Analysis Results box, and read each entry and its analysis notes.

You'll let the Performance Analyzer automatically create a relationship between the tblEmployee table and itself because the table has a one-to-many relationship based on the EmployeeID field as the primary key and the SupervisorID field as the foreign key.

▶ 6. Scroll the Analysis Results box as necessary, click the **Table 'tblEmployee': Relate to table 'tblEmployee'** analysis result (its icon is a green question mark) to select it, and then click the **Optimize** button. Access creates a relationship between the tblEmployee table and itself, and the icon for the selected analysis result changes to a blue check mark to indicate a "Fixed" status.

▶ 7. Click the **Close** button to close the dialog box.

Next, you'll open the Relationships window to view the new relationship created by the Performance Analyzer.

To view the relationship created by the Performance Analyzer:

▶ 1. Click the **Database Tools** tab on the Ribbon, and then in the Relationships group, click the **Relationships** button to open the Relationships window. See Figure 12-28.

Figure 12-28   tblEmployee table one-to-many relationship

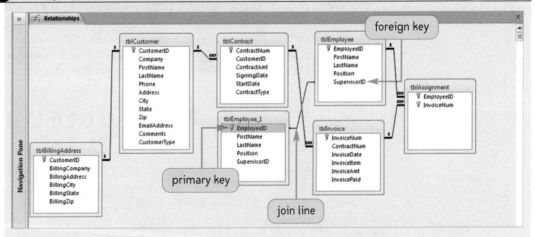

Trouble? The field lists in the Relationships window might be in different positions from what is shown in Figure 12-28. This difference causes no problems.

The Performance Analyzer added a second copy of the tblEmployee table (named tblEmployee_1) and a join line between the tblEmployee and tblEmployee_1 tables to the Relationships window. The join line connects the primary table (tblEmployee_1) to the related table (tblEmployee) using the EmployeeID field as the primary key and the SupervisorID field as the foreign key. You'll use the Edit Relationships dialog box to view the join properties for the relationship.

2. Right-click the join line between the tblEmployee_1 and tblEmployee tables, and then click **Edit Relationship** on the shortcut menu to open the Edit Relationships dialog box. See Figure 12-29.

Figure 12-29   **Edit Relationships dialog box for the new relationship**

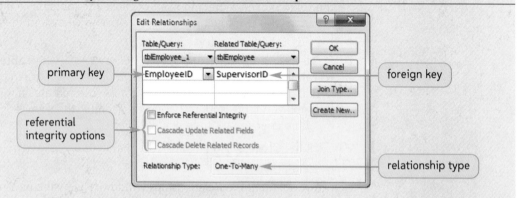

The referential integrity options are not selected, so you'll select them now for the new one-to-many relationship.

3. Click the **Enforce Referential Integrity** check box, click the **Cascade Update Related Fields** check box, and then click the **OK** button to close the dialog box.

4. Close the Relationships window, and then click the **Yes** button, if necessary, to save your changes.

Taylor Sico, marketing manager, has the responsibility at Belmont Landscapes for maintaining a separate database named Prospect in which she stores information about potential customers. Sarah wants to retrieve the data in the tblProspect table in the Prospect database from within the Holland database. To provide Sarah with access to this table, you'll create a link to the tblProspect table in the Holland database.

Linking Tables and Using the Linked Table Manager

You'll provide Sarah and other users of the Holland database with access to the tblProspect table by using a linked table in the Holland database. A **linked table** is a table that is stored in a file outside the open database and that can be updated from the open database. You can retrieve and update (add, change, and delete) records in a linked table, but you can't change its structure. From the Holland database, you'll be able to update the tblProspect table as a linked table, but you won't be able to change its structure. However, from the Prospect database, Taylor will be able to update the tblProspect table *and* change its structure. You can link a database to data stored in Excel worksheets, HTML documents, text files, other Access databases, and databases created by other DBMSs, such as SQL Server, Paradox, and dBASE. Although Access works faster with its own tables than it does with linked tables, you must use linked tables when you need access to data maintained in another Access database or by other programs.

REFERENCE

Linking to a Table in Another Access Database

- Click the External Data tab on the Ribbon.
- In the Import & Link group on the External Data tab, click the Access button (with the ScreenTip "Import Access database").
- Click the Link to the data source by creating a linked table option button.
- Click the Browse button, select the folder and file containing the linked data, and then click the Open button.
- Click the OK button, select the table(s) in the Link Tables dialog box, and then click the OK button.

You'll link to the tblProspect table in the Prospect database from the Holland database.

To link to the tblProspect table in the Prospect database:

1. Click the **External Data** tab on the Ribbon, and then in the Import & Link group, click the **Access** button (with the ScreenTip "Import Access database") to open the Get External Data - Access Database dialog box.

2. Click the **Link to the data source by creating a linked table** option button, and then click the **Browse** button to open the File Open dialog box.

3. Navigate to the Access3\Tutorial folder, click **Prospect**, and then click the **Open** button to close the File Open dialog box and return to the Get External Data - Access Database dialog box. The path and file you selected now appear in the File name box.

4. Click the **OK** button. Access opens the Link Tables dialog box. See Figure 12-30.

| Figure 12-30 | Link Tables dialog box |

click to select this table in the Prospect database

5. Click **tblProspect** in the Tables box, and then click the **OK** button. The Link Tables dialog box closes, and you return to the Access window. A small blue arrow appears to the left of the tblProspect table icon in the Navigation Pane to identify the tblProspect table as a linked table.

Lucia informs Sarah that she'll be reorganizing the company network folders soon and might move the Prospect database to a different folder. Sarah asks if moving the Prospect database would cause a problem for the linked tblProspect table. You'll use the Linked Table Manager to show Sarah how to handle this situation. The **Linked Table Manager** is an Access tool you use to change the filename or disk location for linked tables in an Access database. When you use Access to link to data in another file, Access stores the file's location (drive, folder, and filename) in the database and uses the stored location to connect to the linked data. If you change the file's location, you can use the Linked Table Manager to change the stored file location, or **refresh the link**, in the Access database.

Using the Linked Table Manager

- In the Navigation Pane, right-click the linked table name, and then click Linked Table Manager on the shortcut menu.
  or
  In the Import & Link group on the External Data tab, click the Linked Table Manager button.
- Click the check box(es) for the linked table(s) you want to refresh, and then click the OK button.
- Navigate to the linked table location, click the filename, and then click the Open button.
- Click the OK button, and then close the Linked Table Manager dialog box.

Next, you'll move the Prospect database to a different folder, and then you'll use the Linked Table Manager to refresh the link to the tblProspect table in the Holland database.

To move the Prospect database and refresh the link to the tblProspect table:

1. Use Windows Explorer to move the **Prospect** database from the Access3\Tutorial folder to the Access3 folder.

2. In the Navigation Pane, right-click **tblProspect** to open the shortcut menu, and then click **Linked Table Manager**. The Linked Table Manager dialog box opens. See Figure 12-31.

Figure 12-31 Linked Table Manager dialog box

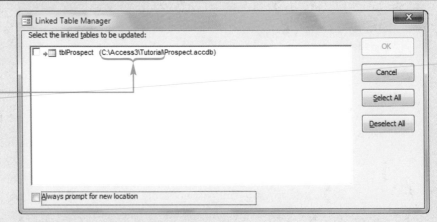

original disk location of the Prospect database (yours might differ)

The tblProspect table is the only linked table, so it's the only table listed. The Access3\Tutorial folder provided with your Data Files, which is the original disk location of the Prospect database, is listed as the current disk location for the tblProspect table.

> **3.** Click the **Select All** button, and then click the **OK** button. The Select New Location of tblProspect dialog box opens.

> **4.** Navigate to the **Access3** folder, click **Prospect** in the file list, and then click the **Open** button. A dialog box informs you that all selected linked tables were successfully refreshed.

> **5.** Click the **OK** button to close the dialog box. The Linked Table Manager dialog box now displays the Access3 folder as the current disk location of the linked tblProspect table.

> **6.** Close the Linked Table Manager dialog box.

Next, you'll open the tblProspect table to show Sarah how she can update it as a linked table from the new disk location.

To update the tblProspect table and view its design in the Holland database:

> **1.** Open the **tblProspect** table in Datasheet view, and then close the Navigation Pane. The tblProspect table datasheet displays four records.

> First, you'll add a new record to the tblProspect table.

> **2.** Click the **New (blank) record** navigation button [▶*], type **12005** in the Customer ID column, press the **Tab** key, type **Gail** in the First Name column, press the **Tab** key, type **Browning** in the Last Name column, press the **Tab** key, type **616-888-1231** in the Phone column, press the **Tab** key, type **3200 Kent Cir** in the Address column, press the **Tab** key, type **Rockford** in the City column, press the **Tab** key, type **MI** in the State column, press the **Tab** key, type **49341** in the Zip column, and then press the **Tab** key twice.

> Next, you'll switch to Design view to show Sarah that she can't change the design of the tblProspect table from the Holland database.

> **3.** Switch to Design view. A dialog box informs you that the tblProspect table is a linked table and has some properties that you cannot modify.

> **4.** Click the **Yes** button to close the dialog box and switch to Design view. The CustomerID field is the current field, and the Help message in the Field Properties pane indicates that you can't change the Field Name property value for linked tables. See Figure 12-32.

Figure 12-32   Linked table in Design view

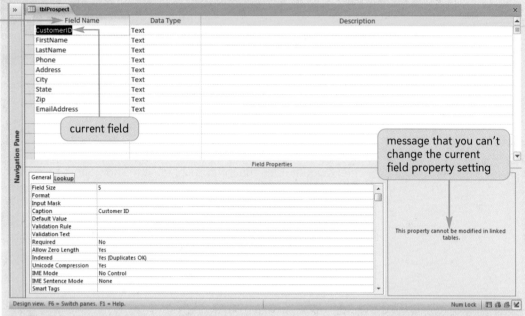

5. Press the **F6** key to highlight the Field Size property in the Field Properties pane. The Help message indicates that you can't change the Field Size property.

6. Press the **Tab** key to position the insertion point in the Format box. The normal Help message for the Format property appears, so you can change this field property.

7. Close the table.

Now you'll open the Prospect database to show Sarah the new record in the tblProspect table that you added from the Holland database. Then you'll delete that record and view the table in Design view.

To update the tblProspect table and view its design in the Prospect database:

1. Start another instance of Access, and then open the **Prospect** database located in the Access3 folder on the drive where you are storing your Data Files.

   Trouble? If the Security Warning is displayed below the Ribbon, click the Enable Content button next to the Security Warning.

2. Open the Navigation Pane (if necessary), open the **tblProspect** table datasheet, and then click the **row selector** for record 5. The record for Gail Browning, which you added to the tblProspect linked table in the Holland database, appears as record 5 in the tblProspect table in the Prospect database.

3. In the Records group on the Home tab, click the **Delete** button, and then click the **Yes** button to delete record 5.

4. Switch to Design view. Because the tblProspect table is not a linked table in the Prospect database, the Help message in the Field Properties pane does not warn you that you can't change the Field Name property. You can make any design changes you want to the tblProspect table in the Prospect database.

5. Close the tblProspect table, and then exit Access.

Sarah wants to know what would happen if she deletes the linked tblProspect table in the Holland database. You'll delete the linked tblProspect table in the Holland database to show her that Access deletes the link to the tblProspect table but does not delete the tblProspect table in the Prospect database.

To delete the linked tblProspect table in the Holland database:

1. Open the Navigation Pane, right-click **tblProspect** in the Navigation Pane to open the shortcut menu, and then click **Delete**. A dialog box asks you if you want to remove the link to the tblProspect table. See Figure 12-33.

| **Figure 12-33** | Dialog box that opens when attempting to delete a linked table |

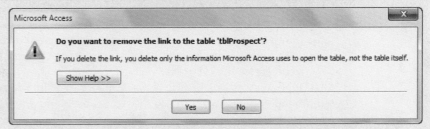

The dialog box confirms that you'll delete only the link to the tblProspect table, not the tblProspect table in the Prospect database.

2. Click the **Yes** button. Access deletes the link to the tblProspect table, and the tblProspect table no longer appears in the Navigation Pane for the Holland database.

Sarah now understands how to link to Taylor's tblProspect table and to other data if she needs to do so in the future.

Sarah wants to create several queries for the Holland database, but she doesn't want the user interface for other users to be cluttered with queries they won't need to use. She asks if there's a way for her to have a special user interface to access the data in the Holland database.

Using the Database Splitter

Users might want to customize their own versions of the user interface, while accessing the same central table data. The **Database Splitter** is an Access tool that splits an Access database into two files: one file contains the tables, and the other file contains the queries, forms, reports, and other database objects. Although a single master copy of the file containing the tables is stored and accessed, users can have their own copies of the other file and add their own queries, reports, and other objects to handle their processing needs. Each file created by the Database Splitter is an Access database. The database that contains the tables is called the **back-end database**; and the database that contains the other objects, including the user interface, is called the **front-end database**.

After you split a database, when users open a front-end database, the objects they open use data in the tables in the back-end database. Because the tables in the front-end database are linked tables that are stored in the back-end database, the front-end database contains the physical disk locations of the tables in the back-end database. You can move the front-end database to a different disk location without affecting the physical connections to the back-end database. However, if you move the back-end database to a different disk location, you'll need to use the Linked Table Manager to change the physical disk locations of the back-end database's tables in the front-end database.

PROSKILLS

Decision Making: Splitting a Database

People who develop databases and sell them to multiple companies usually split their databases. When a developer delivers a split database, the initial back-end database does not include the company's data, and the initial front-end database is complete as created by the developer. Companies use the front-end database to update their data in the back-end database, but they do not modify the front-end database in any way. Periodically, the database developer improves the front-end database by modifying and adding queries, reports, and other objects without changing the structure of the tables. In other words, the developer changes the front-end database, but does not change the back-end database. The developer gives its client companies replacement front-end databases, which continue to work with the back-end database that contains the company's data. This entire process is illustrated in Figure 12-34, which follows this ProSkills box.

Splitting a database also lets you place the files on different computers. You can place the front-end database on each user's computer, and the back-end database on a network server that users access through their front-end databases; this arrangement distributes the workload across the network. Finally, as a company grows, it might need a more powerful DBMS such as Oracle, SQL Server, DB2, or MySQL. You could retain the original Access front-end database and replace the Access back-end database with a new non-Access back-end database, which is an easier task than replacing all database objects.

Because splitting an Access database causes minimal disruption to a company's database processing as you periodically enhance the user interface and because splitting provides greater flexibility for future growth, you should always develop your databases with splitting in mind.

Figure 12-34 **Split Access database**

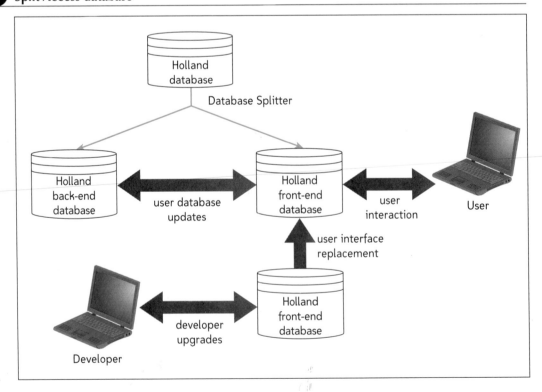

Using the Database Splitter

- Make a backup copy of the database that you want to split.
- Start Access and open the database you want to split.
- Click the Database Tools tab on the Ribbon, and then in the Move Data group, click the Access Database button.
- Click the Split Database button, select the drive and folder for the back-end database, type a name for the database in the File name box, and then click the Split button.
- Click the OK button.

You'll use the Database Splitter to split the Holland database into two files. As a precaution, you'll make a backup copy of the database before you split the database.

To use the Database Splitter:

▶ **1.** Close the Holland database without exiting Access, make a backup copy of the Holland database, and then open the **Holland** database.

▶ **2.** Click the **Database Tools** tab on the Ribbon, and then in the Move Data group, click the **Access Database** button. The Database Splitter dialog box opens. See Figure 12-35.

Figure 12-35   Database Splitter dialog box

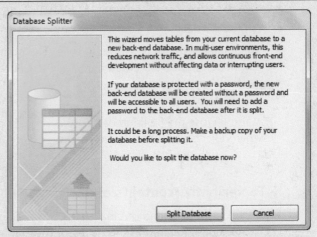

▶ **3.** Click the **Split Database** button. The Create Back-end Database dialog box opens. The back-end database will contain the tables from the Holland database. You'll use the default filename (Holland_be with the .accdb extension) for the back-end database.

▶ **4.** Navigate to the **Access3\Tutorial** folder (if necessary), and then click the **Split** button. After a few moments, a dialog box informs you that the database was successfully split.

▶ **5.** Click the **OK** button to close the dialog boxes, and then scroll up to the top of the Navigation Pane, if necessary. See Figure 12-36.

| Figure 12-36 | Linked tables in the Holland database |

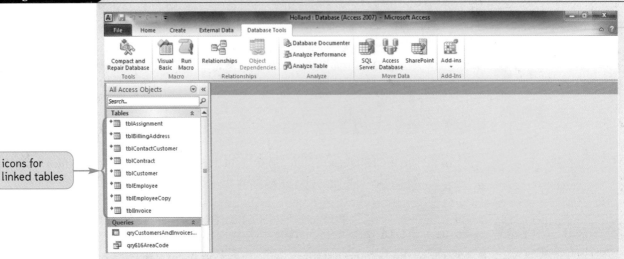

icons for linked tables

Each table in the Holland database has an icon next to its name indicating that there's a link to that table in another file. The tables are no longer stored in the Holland database; they are stored in the Holland_be database file you just created with the Database Splitter.

You can use the linked tables as if they were stored in the Holland database, except you cannot change a table's design from the Holland database. You have to close the Holland database and open the Holland_be database to change a table's design.

▶ **6.** Scroll down the Navigation Pane. The queries, forms, reports, macros, and modules you've created appear in the Navigation Pane and are still stored in the Holland database.

You'll close the Holland database and then open the Holland_be database to verify which objects are stored in the back-end database.

To verify the contents of the back-end database:

▶ **1.** Close the Holland database without exiting Access, and then open the **Holland_be** database located in the Access3\Tutorial folder. The tables from the Holland database appear in the Navigation Pane with their usual icons, indicating the tables are now stored in the Holland_be database. No other objects exist in the Holland_be database.

▶ **2.** Open the **tblInvoice** table in Design view. You can modify the design of the tables in the Holland_be database because they are stored in that database; they are not linked as they are in the Holland database.

▶ **3.** Close the table, close the Holland_be database without exiting Access, and then open the **Holland** database.

Next, Lucia wants you to make access to the Holland database more secure.

Securing an Access Database

Security refers to the protection of a database against unauthorized access, either intentional or accidental. Access provides encryption and passwords as two of its security features.

Encryption translates the data in a database to a scrambled format that's indecipherable to a word processor or other program and stores it in an encrypted format. If unauthorized users attempt to bypass Access and get to the data directly, they will see only the encrypted version of the data. However, users accessing the data using Access will have no problem working with the data. When a user stores or modifies data in an encrypted database, Access will encrypt the data before updating the database. **Decrypting** a database reverses the encryption. Once you've encrypted a database, you can use Access to decrypt it. Before a user retrieves encrypted data using Access, the data will be decrypted and presented to the user in the normal format. If your encrypted database takes longer to respond to requests as it gets larger, you might consider decrypting it to improve its responsiveness.

To prevent access to a database by an unauthorized user through Access, you can assign a password to the database. A **password** is a string of characters assigned to a database that users must enter before they can open the database. As long as the password is known only to authorized users of the database, unauthorized access to the database is prevented. It's best if you use a password that's easily remembered by authorized users, but is not obvious and easily guessed by others.

Lucia wants to restrict access to the Holland database to authorized employees at Belmont Landscapes and also wants to prevent people from using other programs to access the data in the Holland database. Access provides a single option to encrypt a database and set a password at the same time.

REFERENCE

Encrypting a Database and Setting a Password

- Start Access, click the File tab on the Ribbon, and then click Open in the navigation bar.
- Select the drive and folder that contains the database, and then click the database name.
- Click the Open button arrow, and then click Open Exclusive.
- Click the File tab, and then click the Encrypt with Password button.
- Type the password in the Password box, type the same password in the Verify box, press the Enter key, and then click the OK button in the message box.

The way you usually open an Access database allows **shared access** of the database with others; that is, two or more users can open and use the same database at the same time. When you set a password for the Holland database, you need to open the database with exclusive access. When you open an Access database with **exclusive access**, you prevent other users from opening and using the database at the same time. You must open the database with exclusive access in order to set a password, so that you can guarantee that only one copy of the database is open when you set the password.

You'll now encrypt the Holland database and set the password for it to X83yK34.

To encrypt and set the password for the Holland database:

1. Close the Holland database without exiting Access.

2. Click **Open** in the navigation bar. The Open dialog box opens.

3. Navigate to the **Access3\Tutorial** folder (if necessary), click **Holland** in the list (if necessary), and then click the **Open button arrow**. See Figure 12-37.

Figure 12-37 Opening a database with exclusive access

selected database

options for opening
a database

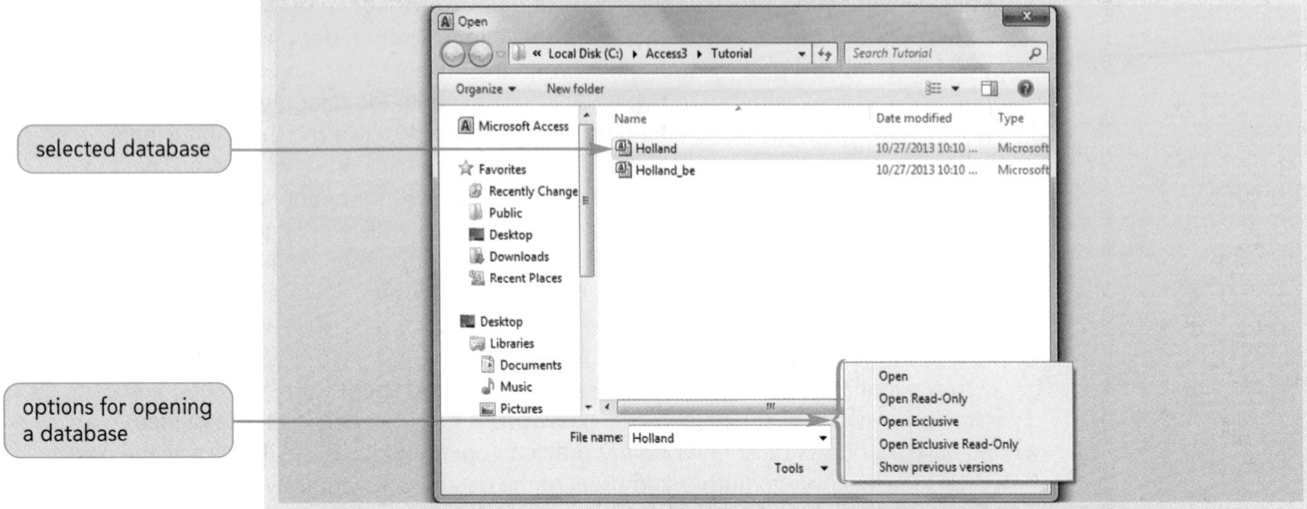

Clicking the Open option in the list opens the selected database with shared
access for both reading and updating, whereas clicking the Open Read-Only
option opens the selected database with shared access for reading only. **Reading**
includes any database action that does not involve updating the database, such
as running queries (but not action queries) and viewing table records. Actions
that are prohibited when you open a database as read-only (because they involve
updating the database) include changing the database design and updating table
records. The other two open options in the Open list open the selected database
with exclusive access for reading and updating (Open Exclusive) or for reading
only (Open Exclusive Read-Only). The Show previous versions option displays previous versions of databases in the selected disk and folder location.

4. Click **Open Exclusive**. The Holland database opens.

5. Click the **File** tab on the Ribbon, and then click the **Encrypt with Password** button. The Set Database Password dialog box opens. See Figure 12-38.

Figure 12-38 Set Database Password dialog box

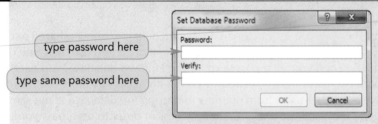

type password here

type same password here

You must type the password twice: once in the Password box, and again in the
Verify box. Passwords are case-sensitive, so you must type the same password in
both boxes. Because the password is stored in the database, you cannot open the
database if you forget the password.

TIP

Passwords are more
secure when they consist
of a mixture of numbers
and both lowercase and
uppercase letters.

6. Type **X83yK34** in the Password box, press the **Tab** key, type **X83yK34** in the
Verify box, and then press the **Enter** key. A message warns you that row-level
locking will be ignored. See Figure 12-39.

Trouble? If a dialog box opens, asking you to verify the new password by retyping it in the Verify box, click the OK button, type X83yK34 in the Verify box, and
then press the Enter key.

Figure 12-39	Row-level locking warning message

When multiple users update the database at the same time, Access uses row-level locking to prevent inconsistencies with the updates. **Locking** denies access by other users to data while Access processes one user's updates to the database. **Row-level locking** denies access by other users to the table rows one user is in the process of updating; other users can update the database simultaneously as long as the rows they need to update are not being updated, and therefore not being locked, by other users at the same time.

▶ **7.** Click the **OK** button in the message box. The message box closes and the Set Database Password dialog box closes, and then Access sets the Holland database password to X83yK34 and encrypts the database.

Next, you'll close and reopen the Holland database to verify that the password has been set. Then you'll unset, or remove, the password.

REFERENCE

Unsetting a Database Password

- Start Access, click the File tab on the Ribbon, and then click Open in the navigation bar.
- Select the drive and folder that contains the database, and then click the database name.
- Click the Open button arrow, and then click Open Exclusive.
- Click the File tab, and then click the Decrypt Database button.
- Type the password in the Password box, and then press the Enter key.

Unsetting a password cancels the password protection for the database and also decrypts the database. After unsetting the password, you can encrypt the database again and set a new password.

To test and unset the password for the Holland database:

▶ **1.** Close the Holland database without exiting Access.

Because you'll be unsetting the password, you need to open the Holland database with exclusive access.

▶ **2.** Open the **Holland** database with exclusive access. The Password Required dialog box opens. See Figure 12-40.

Figure 12-40 **Password Required dialog box**

type password here

3. Type **x83yk34** (all lowercase letters) in the Enter database password box, and then press the **Enter** key. A dialog box opens, warning you that you did not enter a valid password.

4. Click the **OK** button, type **X83yK34** in the Enter database password box, and then press the **Enter** key. The Holland database opens.

   You'll now unset the password. When you unset the password, you also decrypt the database.

5. Click the **File** tab on the Ribbon, and then click the **Decrypt Database** button. The Unset Database Password dialog box opens. See Figure 12-41.

Figure 12-41 **Unset Database Password dialog box**

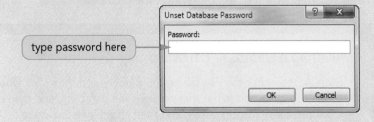

type password here

6. Type **X83yK34** in the Password box, and then press the **Enter** key.

   The next time you open the Holland database, you won't be asked to enter a password because you've unset it.

Sarah is pleased with the changes you have made. As a final enhancement to the user interface, she asks you to set Access to open the navigation form you created in Tutorial 10 automatically when a user opens the Holland database.

Setting the Database Properties and Startup Options

TIP

To bypass the startup options that you set, press and hold down the Shift key when you open the database, or after entering the password in an encrypted database.

Access lets you specify certain actions, called **startup options**, that take place when a database opens. For example, you can specify the name that appears in the Access window title bar, prevent users from using the Navigation Pane, or specify a form that is automatically opened when you open a database.

Sarah wants users to be able to open the Holland database and have the navigation form you created in Tutorial 10 open automatically. In this way, users won't need to use the Navigation Pane to access the navigation form.

Setting the Database Properties and Startup Options

- Open the database, click the File tab, and then click Options in the navigation bar.
- In the Access Options dialog box, click Current Database in the left section.
- Set the database properties and startup options, and then click the OK button. Most options will take effect the next time the database is opened.

See the Session 12.2 Visual Overview for a description of the database properties and startup options you'll set for the Holland database. In addition, you'll disable the **Enable error checking property**, which checks for design errors in forms and reports and alerts you to errors by displaying the Error Checking Options button. Unlike all the other properties, which appear on the Current Database page in the Access Options dialog box, the Enable error checking property appears on the Object Designers page in the Access Options dialog box.

Setting Database Properties and Startup Options

After you've developed and split a database and turned it over to its users, you've completed the design and creation of all fields and objects. Users don't need to change the design, so you should disable any Access property or feature that allows them to change the design. For this reason, you should and will disable the following properties: Use Access Special Keys, Enable Layout View, Enable design changes for tables in Datasheet view, Allow Full Menus, Allow Default Shortcut Menus, Track name AutoCorrect info, and Enable error checking.

When your database design includes a navigation form, you should display the navigation form when the database opens (set the Display Form property); therefore, users do not need the Navigation Pane (disable the Display Navigation Pane property).

Before you set the database properties and startup options, you'll set one of the basic properties that provides documentation about the Holland database. You'll also create a custom property to document the Holland database.

Setting Database Documentation Properties

- Open the database, click the File tab, and then click the View and edit database properties link in the right section of the window.
- Click the Custom tab.
- To set an existing property, scroll the Name list, click the property in the Name list, type the property setting in the Value box, and then click the Add button.
- To create a new property, type the property name in the Name box, select the data type in the Type box, type the property value in the Value box, and then click the Add button.
- Click the OK button.

Now you'll set the Checked by property and create a new property named Platform, which you'll use to document the operating system used on your computer.

To set the Checked by property and create the Platform property in the Holland database:

1. Click the **File** tab on the Ribbon, and then click the **View and edit database properties** link in the right section to open the Holland.accdb Properties dialog box.

2. Click the **Custom** tab, click **Checked by** in the Name box, and then click the **Value** box. See Figure 12-42.

Figure 12-42	**Setting a database property**

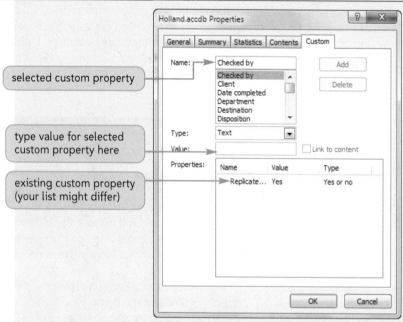

selected custom property

type value for selected custom property here

Value:

existing custom property (your list might differ)

3. Type your full name in the Value box, and then click the **Add** button. The Checked by property is added to the list of custom properties.

Next, you'll create the custom property named Platform.

4. Type **Platform** in the Name box, type **Windows 7** (or your operating system) in the Value box, and then click the **Add** button to add the Platform custom property to the list of custom properties.

5. Click the **OK** button.

You can now finish developing the Holland database by setting the database properties and startup options.

To set the database properties and startup options in the Holland database:

1. Click the **Options** button in the navigation bar to open the Access Options dialog box.

2. In the left section of the dialog box, click **Current Database** to display the list of options for the current database.

3. Type **Holland Release 1** in the Application Title box, click the **Display Form** arrow, and then click **frmNavigation**.

4. Scrolling as necessary, click the following check boxes to disable (uncheck) the properties: **Use Access Special Keys**, **Enable Layout View**, **Enable design changes for tables in Datasheet view**, **Display Navigation Pane**, **Allow Full Menus**, **Allow Default Shortcut Menus**, and **Track name AutoCorrect info**. See the Session 12.2 Visual Overview.

5. In the left section of the dialog box, click **Object Designers** to display the list of options for creating and modifying database objects, and then scroll to the bottom of the dialog box. See Figure 12-43.

Figure 12-43   Error checking options in the Access Options dialog box

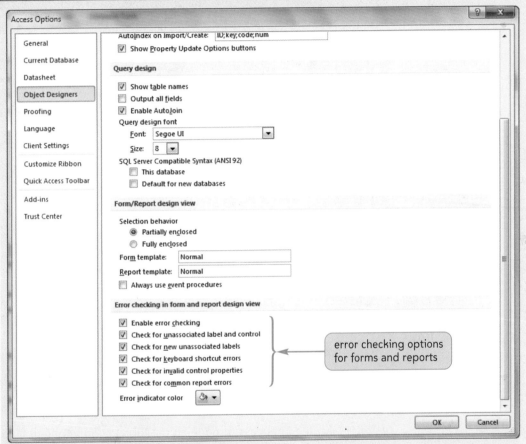

6. If necessary, click the **Enable error checking** check box to clear it and disable all error checking options.

   Trouble? If the Error checking check box does not contain a check mark, continue on to the next step.

7. Click the **OK** button to close the Access Options dialog box. A dialog box informs you that you must close and reopen the Holland database for the options you selected to take effect.

8. Click the **OK** button to close the dialog box.

To test the database properties and startup options, you need to close and reopen the Holland database.

TIP

Unlike the other database properties, which apply only to the current database, the Enable error checking property applies to all databases.

To test the database properties and startup options:

▶ **1.** Close the Holland database without exiting Access.

▶ **2.** Click **Holland.accdb** in the navigation bar to open the **Holland** database. See Figure 12-44.

Figure 12-44   Holland database user interface

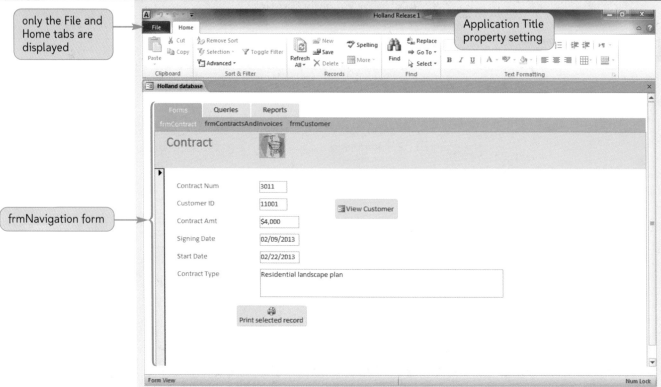

only the File and Home tabs are displayed

Application Title property setting

frmNavigation form

Access opens the Holland database, opens the frmNavigation form, disables the Navigation Pane, displays a restricted Ribbon with only the File and Home tabs, and displays "Holland Release 1" in the Access window title bar.

Now you can make one final test of the Holland database user interface.

▶ **3.** Make one final pass through all the tabs to verify that all features work properly on the Holland database user interface.

Trouble? When you click the Queries tab, the Load event does not occur for the frmQueries form because the frmQueries form was previously loaded when the navigation form opened it. You need to click a query in the Available Queries box before you click one of the command buttons on the form, or you will receive an error.

▶ **4.** As a final test, click the **File** tab, and then click **Exit** in the navigation bar to close the database and exit Access.

Before completing your work with the Holland database, Sarah asks you to research another Access security feature—creating an ACCDE file.

Saving a Database as an ACCDE File

If a database contains VBA code, you can save an ACCDE file version of the database to prevent people from viewing or changing the VBA code. Saving an Access database as an **ACCDE file**, which has the .accde extension instead of the .accdb extension for a normal Access database, compiles all VBA modules, removes all editable VBA source code, and compacts the resulting database. The database and its VBA code continue to run as normal, but users cannot view or edit the VBA code. Also, users can't view, modify, or create forms, reports, or modules in Design view, nor can they import or export forms, reports, or modules. Because an ACCDE file limits database design changes to tables and queries, saving a database as an ACCDE file is best suited to a front-end database. You should keep a backup copy of the complete front-end database in case you need to modify the database design. To save a database as an ACCDE file, follow these steps:

1. Open the database you want to save as an ACCDE file.
2. Click the File tab on the Ribbon, click Save & Publish in the navigation bar, and then click Make ACCDE.
3. Click the Save As button. In the Save As dialog box, type the name for the file in the File name box, navigate to the location where you want to store the file, and then click the Save button.

Because the Holland database has very few VBA modules, you won't save the Holland database as an ACCDE file.

Your work with the Holland database is now complete. Lucia and Sarah review the final user interface, security measures, and database management tools with the staff, and they agree that the database will fully satisfy the company's requirements.

REVIEW

Session 12.2 Quick Check

1. Access stores attachments in _____ form to minimize file size and maximize disk space usage.
2. You can specify sequential numbering or random numbering for a(n) _____ field.
3. What is the Performance Analyzer?
4. When do you use the Linked Table Manager?
5. What is the Database Splitter?
6. _____ refers to the protection of a database against unauthorized access, either intentional or accidental.
7. What is a startup option?

Practice the skills you learned in the tutorial using the same case scenario.

PRACTICE

Review Assignments

Data Files needed for the Review Assignments: Ads.accdb and Vendor.accdb (*cont. from Tutorial 11*)

Lucia asks you to complete your work with the user interface for the Vendor database. To meet this request, complete the following steps:

1. Open the **Vendor** database located in the Access3\Review folder provided with your Data Files.

2. Open the **tblProduct** table datasheet, use an AutoFilter to filter records using the Unit field for values of Linear foot and Square foot, and then save and close the table.

3. Use Filter By Form with the **frmCompaniesAndProducts** form to select all records in which the city is Grand Rapids or Kalamazoo and the initial contact date is before January 1, 2013. Apply the filter, save the filter as a query named **qryCityDateFilter**, clear all filters, and then close the form.

4. Create a query named **qryProductSubquery** that selects all fields from the tblProduct table for all products that weigh more than 100 pounds. Switch to SQL view, add a subquery that selects all products whose color is green, run the query, and then save and close the query.

5. Add a multivalued field to the end of the **tblInvoice** table, defining permitted values of **Courier**, **Email**, **Fax**, and **USPS**, and naming the field **Transmitted**. Save the table, and then add the following values to the field in the table datasheet: for record 11—Email and USPS, for record 16—Courier, and for record 17—Fax and USPS. Close the table.

6. Use the Simple Query Wizard to create a query named **qryInvoiceValue** that displays all fields from the tblInvoice table; for the Transmitted field, display only the version of the field that uses the Value property and change its Caption property setting to **Transmitted**. Save and close the query.

7. Add an Attachment field named **ProductFiles** to the end of the **tblProduct** table, using a Caption property setting of **Product Files**. Create two Excel workbooks named **First Last_1** and **First Last_2**, substituting your first name for *First* and your last name for *Last* and storing them in the Access3\Review folder. Attach both workbooks to the ProductFiles field for record 5 in the tblProduct table, and then close the table.

8. Add an AutoNumber field named **ProductNum** to the beginning of the **tblProductSpecial** table, using a Caption property setting of **Product Num** and a New Values property setting of Random. Save and close the table.

9. Use the Performance Analyzer to analyze the entire Vendor database, but do not implement any of the analysis results. How many analysis results of the recommendation type did the Performance Analyzer find? Of the suggestion type? Of the idea type? Close the Performance Analyzer dialog box.

10. Link to the tblAd table in the Ads database located in the Access3\Review folder. Use Windows Explorer to move the Ads database to the Access3 folder, and then use the Linked Table Manager to refresh the link to the tblAd table. Open the **tblAd** table in Datasheet view, and then add a new record to the table: Ad Num **7**, Ad Date **9/13/2013**, Ad Cost **$227.60**, and Placed **Newspaper**.

11. Close the Vendor database without exiting Access, create a copy of the Vendor database in the Access3\Review folder, and then rename the copy as **Sellers**. Open the **Vendor** database in the Access3\Review folder, and then use the Database Splitter to split the Vendor database. Use the default name for the back-end database and store it in the Access3\Review folder.

12. Encrypt the Vendor database and set the password to **k2Everest**.

13. Set the same database properties and startup options for the Vendor database that you set in Tutorial 12 for the Holland database, using a value of **Vendor for Belmont Landscapes** for the Application Title property. (*Note:* Do not close and reopen the database after setting the database properties and startup options.)

14. Set the Client custom property to your school name, and then create a new custom property named **Course name**, setting its value to the name of the course for which you're using this book.

15. Compact and repair the Vendor database, exit Access, open the **Vendor** database, test all the navigation options, and then exit Access.

Apply what you learned to complete the database for a small music school.

APPLY

Case Problem 1

Data Files needed for this Case Problem: Portland.accdb (*cont. from Tutorial 11*) and Room.accdb

Pine Hill Music School   Yuka Koyama wants you to complete your work with the user interface for the Portland database. To meet her request, complete the following steps:

1. Open the **Portland** database located in the Access3\Case1 folder provided with your Data Files.

2. Open the **tblContract** table datasheet, use an AutoFilter to filter records using the LessonType field for values of Guitar, Piano, and Violin, and then save and close the table.

3. Use Filter By Form with the **frmStudent** form to select all records in which the city is Cornelius or Portland and the gender is F. Apply the filter, save the filter as a query named **qryCityGenderFilter**, and then close the form.

⊕ **EXPLORE**

4. Create a query named **qryInstrumentSubquery** that contains the following fields, in order, from the tblContract table: LessonType, StudentID, ContractStartDate, ContractEndDate, and MonthlyRentalCost. Sort in ascending order by LessonType and then by ContractStartDate. Select only those records with a MonthlyRentalCost value not equal to zero. Switch to SQL view, add a subquery to the existing query that selects all students who play the guitar, run the query, and then save and close the query.

5. Add a multivalued field to the end of the **tblTeacher** table, defining permitted values of **Band**, **Group**, and **Solo**, and naming the field **LessonSize** with a Caption property value of **Lesson Size**. Save the table, and then add the following values to the field in the table datasheet: for record 1—Solo; for record 2—Solo; for record 3—Band and Group; for record 4—Band, Group, and Solo; and for record 5—Solo. Resize the Lesson Size column to its best fit, and then save and close the table.

6. Use the Simple Query Wizard to create a query named **qryTeacherMultivalued** that displays all fields from the tblTeacher table; for the LessonSize field, display only the version of the field that displays multiple values in a text box. Resize the Lesson Size column to its best fit, and then save and close the query.

7. Add an Attachment field named **PressRelease** to the end of the **tblTeacher** table, using a Caption property setting of **Press Release**. Create two Notepad documents named **Reese_1** and **Reese_2**, and store them in the Access3\Case1 folder. Attach both documents to the PressRelease field for record 12 in the tblTeacher table, resize the Press Release column to its best fit, and then save and close the table.

8. Add an AutoNumber field named **SpecialNum** to the beginning of the **tblSpecialLesson** table, using a Caption property setting of **Special Num** and a New Values property setting of Increment. Specify the SpecialNum field as the primary key. Resize the Special Num column to its best fit in the datasheet, and then save and close the table.

9. Use the Performance Analyzer to analyze the entire Portland database. How many analysis results of the recommendation type did the Performance Analyzer find? Of the suggestion type? Of the idea type? Use the Performance Analyzer to implement any suggestion task, and perform any subsequent task(s) required due to implementing the suggestion(s). Close the Performance Analyzer dialog box.

10. Link to the tblRoom table in the Room database located in the Access3\Case1 folder. Use Windows Explorer to move the Room database to the Access3 folder, and then use the Linked Table Manager to refresh the link to the tblRoom table. Open the **tblRoom** table in Datasheet view, and then add a new record to the table: Room Num **2**, Rental Cost **$75**, and Room Type **Group**. Close the table.

11. Close the Portland database without exiting Access, create a copy of the Portland database in the Access3\Case1 folder, and then rename the copy as **Oregon**. Open the **Portland** database in the Access3\Case1 folder, and then use the Database Splitter to split the Portland database. Use the default name for the back-end database and store it in the Access3\Case1 folder.

12. Encrypt the Portland database and set the password to **4Lhotse4**.

13. Set the same database properties and startup options for the Portland database that you set in Tutorial 12 for the Holland database, using a value of **Portland Final** for the Application Title property. (*Note:* Do not close and reopen the database after setting the database properties and startup options.)

14. Set the Date completed custom property to today's date, and then create a new custom property named **My location**, setting its value to your home town or city.

15. Compact and repair the Portland database, exit Access, open the **Portland** database, test all the navigation options, and then exit Access.

Apply what you learned to complete the database for a health and fitness center.

APPLY

Case Problem 2

Data Files needed for this Case Problem: Exercise.accdb (*cont. from Tutorial 11*) and Routines.accdb

Parkhurst Health & Fitness Center   Martha Parkhurst asks you to complete your work with the user interface for the Exercise database. To meet her request, complete the following steps:

1. Open the **Exercise** database located in the Access3\Case2 folder provided with your Data Files.

2. Open the **tblMember** table datasheet, use an AutoFilter to filter records using the MembershipStatus field for values of Inactive and On Hold, and then save and close the table.

3. Use Filter By Form with the **frmMemberInfo** form to select all records in which the city is Ashland or Richmond and the membership status is Active. Apply the filter, save the filter as a query named **qryCityStatusFilter**, and then close the form. (*Hint:* You should close the Navigation Pane.)

⊕ EXPLORE

4. Make a copy of the qryJuneMembers query, naming it **qryJuneMembersSubquery**. Switch to SQL view, add a subquery to the existing query that selects all ProgramID field values that have a monthly fee of $25. Save and close the query.

5. Add an Attachment field named **MemberAttachment** to the end of the **tblMember** table, using a Caption property setting of **Member Attachment**. Create two Notepad documents named **Picard_1** and **Picard_2**, and store them in the Access3\Case2 folder. Attach both documents to the MemberAttachment field for record 11 in the tblMember table, resize the Member Attachment column to its best fit, and then save and close the table.

6. Add an AutoNumber field named **MemberNum** to the beginning of the **tblSpecialMember** table, using a Caption property setting of **Member Num** and a New Values property setting of Random. Specify the MemberNum field as the primary key. Resize the Member Num column to its best fit in the datasheet, and then save and close the table.

7. Use the Performance Analyzer to analyze the entire Exercise database, but do not implement any of the analysis results. How many analysis results of the recommendation type did the Performance Analyzer find? Of the suggestion type? Of the idea type? Close the Performance Analyzer dialog box.

8. Link to the **tblRoutine** table in the **Routines** database located in the Access3\Case2 folder. Use Windows Explorer to move the Routines database to the Access3 folder, and then use the Linked Table Manager to refresh the link to the tblRoutine table. Open the **tblRoutine** table in Datasheet view, and then add a new record to the table: Routine ID **130**, and Routine Desc **Yoga**.

9. Close the Exercise database without exiting Access, create a copy of the Exercise database in the Access3\Case2 folder, and then rename the copy as **InShape**. Open the **Exercise** database in the Access3\Case2 folder, and then use the Database Splitter to split the Exercise database. Use the default name for the back-end database and store it in the Access3\Case2 folder.

10. Encrypt the Exercise database and set the password to **10Annapurna01**.

11. Set the same database properties and startup options for the Exercise database that you set in Tutorial 12 for the Holland database, using a value of **Final Exercise** for the Application Title property. (*Note:* Do not close and reopen the database after setting the database properties and startup options.)

12. Set the Owner custom property to your first and last name, and then create a new custom property named **Nickname**, setting its value to your nickname (or the version of your first name you use when introducing yourself).

13. Compact and repair the Exercise database, exit Access, open the **Exercise** database, test all the navigation options, and then exit Access.

Apply what you learned to complete a database for a recycling business.

APPLY

Case Problem 3

Data Files needed for this Case Problem: Drivers.accdb and Salina.accdb (*cont. from Tutorial 11*)

Rossi Recycling Group   Mary and Tom Rossi want you to complete your work with the user interface for the Salina database. To meet their request, complete the following steps:

1. Open the **Salina** database located in the Access3\Case3 folder provided with your Data Files.

2. Open the **tblDonation** table datasheet, use an AutoFilter to filter records using the PickupRequired field for values of Yes, and then save and close the table.

3. Use Filter By Form with the **frmDonation** form to select all records in which the agency ID is R15 or W22 and the donation description is Cash. Apply the filter, save the filter as a query named **qryAgencyDescFilter**, and then close the form.

⊕ **EXPLORE**

4. Make a copy of the qryNetDonations query, naming it **qryNetDonationsSubquery**. Switch to SQL view, add a subquery to the existing query that selects all DonationID field values for which a pickup is required. Save and close the query.

5. Add a multivalued field to the end of the **tblDonor** table, defining permitted values of **Donor**, **Driver**, **Speaker**, and **Volunteer**, and naming the field **DonorType** with a Caption property value of **Donor Type**. Save the table, and then add the following values to the field in the table datasheet: for record 1—Donor and Volunteer; for record 2—Donor and Driver; for record 3—Donor, Driver, Speaker, and Volunteer; and for record 4—Volunteer. Resize the Donor Type column to its best fit, and then save and close the table.

6. Create a query named **qryDonorValue** that displays all fields from the tblDonor table; for the DonorType field, display only the version of the field that uses the Value property and change its Caption property setting to **Donor Type**. Resize the Donor Type column to its best fit in the datasheet, and then save and close the query.

7. Add an Attachment field named **AgencyFiles** to the end of the **tblAgency** table, using a Caption property setting of **Agency Files**. Create two Notepad documents named **Baker_1** and **Baker_2** and store them in the Access3\Case3 folder. Attach both documents to the AgencyFiles field for record 3 in the tblAgency table, and then close the table.

8. Add an AutoNumber field named **DonationNum** to the beginning of the **tblSpecialDonation** table, using a Caption property setting of **Donation Num** and a New Values property setting of Increment. Specify the DonationNum field as the primary key. Resize the Donation Num column to its best fit in the datasheet, and then save and close the table.

9. Use the Performance Analyzer to analyze the entire Salina database, but do not implement any of the analysis results. How many analysis results of the recommendation type did the Performance Analyzer find? Of the suggestion type? Of the idea type? Close the Performance Analyzer dialog box.

10. Link to the tblDriver table in the Drivers database located in the Access3\Case3 folder. Use Windows Explorer to move the Drivers database to the Access3 folder, and then use the Linked Table Manager to refresh the link to the tblDriver table.

11. Close the Salina database without exiting Access, create a copy of the Salina database in the Access3\Case3 folder, and then rename the copy as **Kansas**. Open the **Salina** database in the Access3\Case3 folder, and then use the Database Splitter to split the Salina database. Use the default name for the back-end database and store it in the Access3\Case3 folder.

12. Encrypt the Salina database and set the password to **mT888T**.

13. Set the same database properties and startup options for the Salina database that you set in Tutorial 12 for the Holland database, using a value of **Salina Donations** for the Application Title property. (*Note:* Do not close and reopen the database after setting the database properties and startup options.)

14. Set the Status custom property to **Salina version 1**, and then create a new custom property named **Milestone**, setting its value to **Completed**.

15. Compact and repair the Salina database, exit Access, open the **Salina** database, test all the navigation options, and then exit Access.

Apply what you learned to complete the database for a luxury property rental company.

APPLY

Case Problem 4

Data File needed for this Case Problem: Rentals.accdb (*cont. from Tutorial 11*)

GEM Ultimate Vacations Griffin and Emma MacElroy ask you to complete your work with the user interface for the Rentals database. To meet their request, complete the following steps:

1. Open the **Rentals** database located in the Access3\Case4 folder provided with your Data Files.

2. Open the **tblPersonnel** table datasheet, use an AutoFilter to filter records using the JobTitle field for values of Finance Manager and Staff Manager, and then save and close the table.

⊕ EXPLORE

3. Use Filter By Form with the **tblProperty** table to select all records in which the country is France or Italy and the property type is Villa. Apply the filter, save the filter as a query named **qryCountryPropertyFilter**, and then save and close the table. (*Hint:* You might have to close the Navigation Pane and widen the table before filtering.)

⊕ EXPLORE

4. Make a copy of the qryGuestData query, naming it **qryGuestDataSubquery**. Switch to SQL view, add a subquery to the existing query that selects all GuestID field values for guests from Chicago or Gary. Save and close the query.

5. Add an Attachment field named **AddedFiles** to the end of the **tblPersonnel** table, using a Caption property setting of **Added Files**. Create two Notepad documents named **Leary_1** and **Leary_2** and store them in the Access3\Case4 folder. Attach both documents to the AddedFiles field for record 4 in the tblPersonnel table, and then close the table.

6. Add an AutoNumber field named **GuestNum** to the beginning of the **tblSelectedReservation** table, using a Caption property setting of **Guest Num** and a New Values property setting of Increment. Specify the GuestNum field as the primary key. Save and close the table.

7. Use the Performance Analyzer to analyze the entire Rentals database, but do not implement any of the analysis results. How many analysis results of the recommendation type did the Performance Analyzer find? Of the suggestion type? Of the idea type? Use the Performance Analyzer to implement any suggestion task, and perform any subsequent task(s) required due to implementing the suggestion(s). Close the Performance Analyzer dialog box.

8. Close the Rentals database without exiting Access, create a copy of the Rentals database in the Access3\Case4 folder, and then rename the copy as **Illinois**. Open the **Rentals** database in the Access3\Case4 folder, and then use the Database Splitter to split the Rentals database. Use the default name for the back-end database and store it in the Access3\Case4 folder.

9. Encrypt the Rentals database and set the password to **9NangaParbat9**.

10. Set the same database properties and startup options for the Rentals database that you set in Tutorial 12 for the Holland database, using a value of **Rentals European** for the Application Title property. (*Note:* Do not close and reopen the database after setting the database properties and startup options.)

11. Set the Language custom property to **English**, and then create a new custom property named **State completed**, setting its value to the full name of the state where you currently live.

12. Compact and repair the Rentals database, close the Rentals database without exiting Access, open the **Rentals** database, test all the navigation options, and then exit Access.

Apply what you learned to complete the database for an Internet service provider.

APPLY

Case Problem 5

Data Files needed for this Case Problem: Always.accdb (*cont. from Tutorial 11*)

Always Connected Everyday   Chris and Pat Dixon ask you to complete your work with the user interface for the Always database. To meet their request, complete the following steps:

1. Open the **Always** database located in the Access3\Case5 folder provided with your Data Files.

2. Open the **tblServiceCall** table datasheet, use an AutoFilter to filter records using the ServiceID field for values of 3 and 8, and then save and close the table.

3. Use Filter By Form with the **frmCustomer** form to select all records in which the city is Drayton and the access plan ID is 3 or 7. Apply the filter, save the filter as a query named **qryCityPlanFilter**, and then close the form.

⊕ EXPLORE

4. Make a copy of the qryCustomerNames query, naming it **qryCustomerNamesSubquery**. Switch to SQL view, add a subquery to the existing query that selects all CustomerAcctNum field values for customers in the cities of Blade or Brunson. Save and close the query.

5. Add a multivalued field to the end of the **tblServiceCall** table, defining permitted values of **Chet**, **Donna**, and **Kent**, and naming the field **ServiceName** with a Caption property value of **Service Name**. Save the table, and then add the following values to the field in the table datasheet: for record 10—Donna, for record 11—Chet and Kent, for record 12—Kent, and for record 13—Donna. Resize the Service Name column to its best fit, and then save and close the table.

6. Use the Simple Query Wizard to create a query named **qryServiceCallValue** that displays all fields from the tblServiceCall table; for the ServiceName field, display only the version of the field that uses the Value property and change its Caption property setting to **Service Name**. Resize the Service Name column to its best fit, and then save and close the query.

7. Add an AutoNumber field named **CustomerNum** to the beginning of the **tblSelectedCustomer** table, using a Caption property setting of **Customer Num** and a New Values property setting of Increment. Specify the CustomerNum field as the primary key. Resize the Customer Num column in the table datasheet to its best fit, and then save and close the table.

8. Use the Performance Analyzer to analyze the entire Always database, but do not implement any of the analysis results. How many analysis results of the recommendation type did the Performance Analyzer find? Of the suggestion type? Of the idea type? Close the Performance Analyzer dialog box.

9. Close the Always database without exiting Access, create a copy of the Always database in the Access3\Case5 folder, and then rename the copy as **Provider**. Open the **Always** database in the Access3\Case5 folder, and then use the Database Splitter to split the Always database. Use the default name for the back-end database and store it in the Access3\Case5 folder.

10. Encrypt the Always database and set the password to **3Kanchenjunga3**.

11. Set the same database properties and startup options for the Always database that you set in Tutorial 12 for the Holland database, using a value of **Always Internet Provider** for the Application Title property. (*Note:* Do not close and reopen the database after setting the database properties and startup options.)

12. Compact and repair the Always database, exit Access, open the **Always** database, test all the navigation options, and then exit Access.

SAM Assessment and Training

ENDING DATA FILES

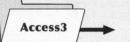

Access3 → **Tutorial**

Ads.accdb
Drivers.accdb
Prospect.accdb
Room.accdb
Routines.accdb

Tutorial

Holland.accdb
Holland_be.accdb
Perkins1.docx
Perkins2.xlsx
Perkins3.pptx
Perkins3 Export.pptx

Review

First Last_1.xlsx
First Last_2.xlsx
Sellers.accdb
Vendor.accdb
Vendor_be.accdb

Case1

Oregon.accdb
Portland.accdb
Portland_be.accdb
Reese_1.txt
Reese_2.txt

Case2

Exercise.accdb
Exercise_be.accdb
InShape.accdb
Picard_1.txt
Picard_2.txt

Case3

Baker_1.txt
Baker_2.txt
Kansas.accdb
Salina.accdb
Salina_be.accdb

Case4

Illinois.accdb
Leary_1.txt
Leary_2.txt
Rentals.accdb
Rentals_be.accdb

Case5

Always.accdb
Always_be.accdb
Provider.accdb

Written Communication

Writing Clear and Effective Database Documentation

The steps in developing a database include gathering all the data and processing requirements, analyzing the requirements, organizing the requirements, designing the database, documenting the database, and then creating the database. Notice that you prepare the documentation before you create the database because the documentation serves both as a blueprint for the database you will create and as a reference for users after the database is completed. In other words, database documentation must effectively convey to the database developers the technical details developers need to create the database, and convey to the users the data and processing requirements users need to perform their jobs using the database.

Having identified the dual audience for the database documentation; having gathered, analyzed, and organized the requirements; and having designed the database, you are ready to write the database documentation. Unlike writing business documents, essays, and other narrative documents in which you usually need to persuade or to present a point of view, you should write database documentation in a factual manner that accurately presents the data, processing, and technical requirements. It's helpful to prepare a draft of the database documentation and to schedule multiple review cycles. During the review cycles, you select database developers and users to read the documentation, provide feedback by pointing out errors, omissions, and other problems with the documentation, and then you revise the documentation and release it again for further review.

PROSKILLS

Document a Personal Database

Throughout this book, you have learned how to use Access to develop and manage a database. The appendix at the end of this book, titled "Relational Databases and Database Design," includes additional content about designing tables, examining the keys used in those tables, creating entity-relationship diagrams to describe the tables and their relationships, and setting integrity constraints. In this ProSkills exercise, you'll use a word processor or Access to design a database that will manage the data of your choice. You can choose any situation that interests you. For example, you might design a database based on your work experience, your involvement with a club or program at your school, your participation or interest in sports or a hobby, or something that you need to organize in your personal life. Be sure to choose a situation that contains enough variation so that you can design at least five to eight tables that are related to each other with at least one many-to-many and at least one one-to-one relationship.

Note: Please be sure *not* to include any personal information of a sensitive nature in the database you create to be submitted to your instructor for this exercise. Later on, you can update the data in your database with such information for your own personal use.

1. Read the appendix titled "Relational Databases and Database Design," which appears at the end of this book.

ProSkills

2. Identify each entity (table) in the database that you are designing. Your database should have at least five to eight tables. For each table, list the fields and their attributes, such as data types, field sizes, and validation rules. Place the set of tables in third normal form and identify all primary, alternate, and foreign keys. You can document these tables using a word processor or by using Access. If you use a word processor for your design, make sure that your work clearly indicates each table and the fields it contains, the attributes for each field, and the keys. If you use Access for your design, create the tables by defining each table's fields and field attributes, specify the primary key for each table, and establish the table relationships in the Relationships window.

3. Draw an entity-relationship diagram showing the entities and the relationships between the entities. Your database should have at least one many-to-many relationship and at least one one-to-one relationship.

4. For each table in the database, represent the functional dependencies and determinants in a bubble diagram or by using the shorthand representation shown in the appendix (that lists the determinant, followed by an arrow and the dependent fields).

5. Submit your completed database design to your instructor as requested.

ACCESS

OBJECTIVES

- Change field properties
- Add fields to a table
- Enter data in a table
- Create table relationships
- Create select, parameter, and crosstab queries
- Create a form using the Form Wizard
- Create calculated controls in a form
- Create a custom report
- Create an unbound form
- Create macros
- Create a navigation form
- Set database properties and startup options

In this case you will use skills you learned in the following tutorials:

- Tutorials 1-10 and 12 (startup options only)

Enhancing an Investment Club Database

Case | *Nest Egg Investment Club*

Barbara and Neal Hennessey and some friends recently formed an investment club. Researching investment clubs on the Web, Barbara found the National Association of Investors Corporation (NAIC) site. Established in 1951, NAIC is a nonprofit organization founded to educate investment clubs and individual investors. Following guidelines recommended by NAIC, the club members chose Nest Egg as their club name, prepared and approved a partnership agreement and a set of bylaws, registered their club, obtained the club's tax ID, and established an online brokerage account to handle the club's investments.

The club decided to meet monthly and to set monthly dues at $200. The 15 permanent club members, each having one vote for all club matters, include 13 individuals and two couples for a total of 17 individuals. Each of the 15 members can contribute $200 monthly (a participation level of 1) or $400 monthly (a participation level of 2), but the participation level does not affect the voting rule of one vote per member.

The online brokerage account will track the club's investments, but Felicia Rodriquez, the club treasurer, has created a database to handle club accounting for monthly dues and for any future withdrawals. Felicia's database consists of two tables, tblMember and tblContribution. Figure 1 shows the structure of the tblMember table, which stores data about each club member. Each tblMember table record contains a member ID number and each member's first name, last name, address, phone, join date, and participation level (the Level field).

STARTING DATA FILES

AddCases

NestEgg.accdb

Figure 1 **Structure of the tblMember table**

Field Name	Data Type	Properties
MemberID	AutoNumber	Description: Primary key
		Caption: Member ID
FirstName	Text	Field Size: 15
		Caption: First Name
LastName	Text	Field Size: 15
		Caption: Last Name
Address	Text	Field Size: 32
Phone	Text	Field Size: 14
JoinDate	Date/Time	Format: mm/dd/yyyy
		Caption: Join Date
Level	Number	Description: Participation level used to determine the member's monthly dues
		Field Size: Byte
		Decimal Places: 0

Figure 2 shows the structure of the tblContribution table, which contains one record for each monthly dues payment. PaymentID is the table's primary key. MemberID is a foreign key in the tblContribution table, and the tblMember table will have a one-to-many relationship with the tblContribution table. The other fields in the tblContribution table are PaidDate and InvestmentAmt.

Figure 2 **Structure of the tblContribution table**

Field Name	Data Type	Properties
PaymentID	Number	Description: Primary key
		Caption: Payment ID
		Field Size: Long Integer
		Decimal Places: 0
MemberID	Number	Description: Foreign key
		Field Size: Long Integer
		Decimal Places: 0
		Caption: Member ID
PaidDate	Date/Time	Format: mm/dd/yyyy
		Caption: Paid Date
InvestmentAmt	Currency	Decimal Places: 2
		Caption: Investment Amt

Felicia wants to create special queries, forms, and reports in the database to help her manage club accounting. To help Felicia finish her work with the database, complete the following steps:

1. Make sure you have created your copy of the Access Data Files and stored them in a trusted folder, and that your computer can access them. Start Access, and then open the **NestEgg** database located in the AddCases folder.

2. Review the **tblMember** and **tblContribution** tables to become familiar with their structures and data. If you are unfamiliar with any property setting, use the Access Help system for an explanation of that property.

3. For the tblContribution table, specify PaymentID as the primary key and resize all datasheet columns to their best fit. For the tblMember table, add a validation rule for the Level field to store only values equal to 1 or 2, add an appropriate validation text message, and then add the following new Text fields between the Address and Phone fields: **City** (Field Size **24**), **StateProv** (Field Size **2** and caption of **State/Prov**), and **PostalCode** (Field Size **10** and caption of **Postal Code**).

4. Modify the first record in the tblMember table datasheet by entering your name, city, state or province (two-character postal abbreviation), postal code (zip code), and phone number; enter phone numbers in 987-654-3210 format. For the last four records, enter the same city, state or province, postal code, and phone area code but enter different phone numbers. Select a second city, state or province, postal code, and phone area code, and then enter these values in records 2-6, using five different phone numbers. Finally, select a third city, state or province, postal code, and phone area code, and then enter these values in records 7-11, using five different phone numbers. Resize all datasheet columns to their best fit.

5. Define a one-to-many relationship between the primary tblMember table and the related tblContribution table, using MemberID as the common field, enforcing referential integrity, and selecting the Cascade Update Related Fields option. Resize the tblMember field list so that all fields are visible, and then create and print the Relationships for NestEgg report but do not save it.

6. Export the tblMember table as an XML file named **Member** to the AddCases folder; do not create a separate XSD file. Save the export steps.

7. Create and save a query named **qryDistantMembers** that displays the FirstName, LastName, Address, City, StateProv, PostalCode, and Phone fields for all members not living in the same city where you live in ascending order by LastName. Print the query recordset in landscape orientation after testing and saving the query.

8. Create and save a query named **qryMarch17Contributions** that displays the FirstName, LastName, Phone, and InvestmentAmt fields for all contributions made on 3/17/2013 in ascending order by LastName. Print the query recordset after testing and saving the query.

9. Create and save a query named **qryInvestmentTotalsByMember** that displays each member's first name, last name, and total investment amount. For the calculated field, use the name **TotalInvested** and a Caption value of **Total Invested**. Sort in descending order by total investment amount, and resize all columns to best fit. Print the query recordset after testing and saving the query. Modify the query by deleting the FirstName and LastName fields, adding the PaidDate field as the first field in the query, sorting in ascending order by PaidDate (and not by the investment total), and then saving the query as **qryInvestmentTotalsByDate**. Print the query recordset.

10. Create and save a parameter query named **qryLevelParameter** that displays the FirstName, LastName, Phone, JoinDate, and Level fields in ascending order by LastName for a Level field value that the user enters. If the user doesn't enter a field value, select and display all records. After creating and saving the query, run the query and enter **2** as the Level field value. Print the query results.

⊕ EXPLORE 11. Create a crosstab query that uses PaidDate field values for the row headings, Level field values for the column headings, and the sum of the InvestmentAmt field as the summarized value. (*Hint:* Create a query named **qryInvestmentAmounts** that contains the three fields you need for the crosstab query.) Save the query as **qryInvestmentAmountsCrosstab**, resize the columns in the query recordset to their best fit, and then save and print the query recordset.

⊕ EXPLORE 12. Use the Form Wizard to create a form containing a main form and a subform. Select all the fields from the tblMember table for the main form, and select all fields except MemberID from the tblContribution table for the subform. Use the Tabular layout.

Specify the title **frmContributionsByMember** for the main form and the title **frmContributionSubform** for the subform. Change the text in the main form's title control to **Contributions by Member**, and then adjust the widths of the text box controls in the main form to size them for the data they display. Select the Phone, JoinDate, and Level text box and label controls, and then move them to the right and then up in the main form. Delete the subform label, move the subform up close to the bottom boxes in the main form, and then reduce the widths of the columns in the subform. Open the subform in a new window in Design view, move the three boxes in the Form Header to the top of the section, reduce the height of the section to the bottom of the boxes, and then save the subform changes. Reduce the height of the subform in Layout view (see Figure 3). Change the caption on the record navigation bar for the main form to **Member** and for the subform to **Contribution**. Print only the first main form record and its subform records.

⊕ **EXPLORE** 13. Create a copy of the frmContributionsByMember form, and use **frmContributionsByMemberModified** as the new form's name. Modify the new form by adding a calculated control, as shown in Figure 3, that displays the sum of the InvestmentAmt field values that appear in the subform. (*Hint:* Set the Visible property for the Form Footer section in the subform to No.) Set the calculated control's Format property to Currency, set its ControlTip Text property to **Calculated total investment amount**, and set its Tab Stop property to No. Print only the first main form record and its subform records.

| **Figure 3** | **Modified Contributions by Member form** |

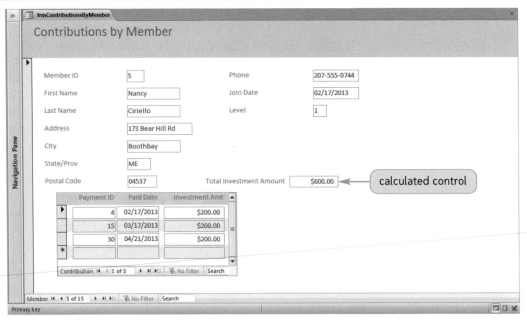

14. Create the custom Contributions by Date report shown in Figure 4. The report contains Page Header, Detail, PaidDate Footer, and Report Footer sections. Sort the detail records in ascending order by the PaidDate field, and then in ascending order by the LastName field. Hide duplicate values for the PaidDate field. Calculate and print totals of the InvestmentAmt field for each PaidDate field value and in grand total. The color used in the lines, title, and label controls is Black in the Standard Colors section, and the line thickness is 3 pt. Save the report as **rptContributionsByDate**. Print the report.

Figure 4   Contributions by Date report

Contributions by Date

Page 2 of 2

Paid Date	First Name	Last Name	Phone	Level	Investment Amt
04/21/2013	Kathy & Bob	Bakanas	510-555-2000	1	$200.00
	Francine	Barnes	604-555-4848	2	$400.00
	Kevin	Bioski	207-555-7811	1	$200.00
	Nancy	Ciriello	207-555-0744	1	$200.00
	Shawn	Erickson	604-555-9033	1	$200.00
	Thomas	Evensen	207-555-7144	2	$400.00
	Maureen	Heller	207-555-0101	1	$200.00
	Barbara & Neal	Hennessey	510-555-9786	2	$400.00
	Student	Name	512-555-6487	2	$400.00
	Lee	Nguyen	604-555-3856	1	$200.00
	Peter	O'Rourke	510-555-8631	1	$200.00
	Naomi	Ramos	207-555-8986	1	$200.00
	Felicia	Rodriguez	604-555-8733	1	$200.00
	Yonglei	Tao	510-555-3010	1	$200.00
	Marsha	Van Ry	510-555-7011	2	$400.00
					$4,000.00
					$11,000.00

15. Create a form named **frmQueries** that has the following components and characteristics:

   a. Use the text **NestEgg Queries** on the form's tab.

   b. Add a list box with a Name property value of **lstQueryList** that displays all the query names contained in the NestEgg database, excluding those queries that start with a "~" character. To place the query names in the list box, use an SQL SELECT statement to retrieve the query names from the MSysObjects table, and display the queries in alphabetical order. Delete the label attached to the list box, widen the list box to approximately 2.5 inches, and set its height to approximately one inch.

   c. Add the label **Select a query**, formatted with Calibri 12-point, black, bold font, above the list box.

   d. Add two command buttons below the list box. The left command button displays the Preview icon above the word **Preview**, and the right command button displays the MS Access Query icon above the word **Display**. Double-clicking a query name has the same effect as selecting a query name in the list box and clicking the right command button. Both events cause Access to display the query datasheet for the selected query. Clicking the left command button opens the selected query in Print Preview.

   e. Create macros for the form (when the form loads, move the focus to the first query name in the list box), the list box (when a user double-clicks a query name), and both command buttons (when a user clicks a command button).

   f. Set the background color of the Detail section to the Green 1 color in the Standard Colors section and the background color of the list box to the Light Gray 1 color in the Standard Colors section, and then disable the form's shortcut menu, record selectors, and navigation buttons. Set the width of the Detail section to five inches, and set its height to three inches.

   g. Test the form.

16. Create a navigation form named **frmNavigation**, using the Horizontal Tabs, 2 Levels layout, that includes the following tab names and objects:

    a. Use **Forms** as the name for the left tab, and place the frmContributionsByMemberModified form below it.

    b. Use **Queries** as the name for the second tab, and place the frmQueries form below it.

    c. Use **Reports** as the name for the third tab, and place the rptContributionsByDate report below it.

    d. Delete the navigation form's picture and title, and change the tab name to **NestEgg database**.

    e. Test the navigation form.

17. Make a backup copy of the database, and then compact and repair the NestEgg database.

18. Set the database properties for the **NestEgg** database so the frmNavigation form opens when the database is opened, to set startup options to disable features as appropriate for a database that uses a navigation form, and to change the database name in the title bar to **Nest Egg Investment Club**.

19. Close the NestEgg database to activate the database startup options, open the database, test the navigation form options, and then exit Access.

ENDING DATA FILES

AddCases

NestEgg.accdb
Member.xml

ADDITIONAL CASE **2**

OBJECTIVES

- Change field properties
- Create a new table
- Enter data in a table
- Create table relationships
- Create select, query wizard, parameter, and crosstab queries
- Create forms using wizards and customize forms
- Create calculated controls in a form
- Create a custom report
- Create an unbound form
- Create macros
- Create a navigation form
- Set database properties and startup options

In this case you will use skills you learned in the following tutorials:
- Tutorials 1-11 and 12 (startup options only)

Tracking Parking Permits and Violations

ACCESS

Case | *Tophill College*

Sandy Tatoian is the office manager in the Public Safety department at Tophill College. Among her responsibilities, Sandy coordinates issuing parking permits to staff, faculty, and students, and processing citations for on-campus parking violations. Reductions in the college budget have forced her department to reduce the number of part-time student workers. As a result, the department is experiencing an increase in the backlog for processing citations and parking permit requests. After discussing the problem with her supervisor, Sandy meets with Pat Davis, a database analyst in the college computer center.

Pat questions Sandy about her requirements and agrees to design a database to reduce her workload and to help her gain better control over her coordination responsibilities. Sandy explains that parking permits are issued to students, faculty, and staff for their vehicles. The permit is affixed to the windshield in the lower corner on the driver's side. Each parking permit request form includes the parking permit number, the vehicle license plate number, and the person's name. With each issued permit, a person receives a brochure that describes the campus parking regulations and the fines for parking violations.

The Public Safety department employs a patrol force that enforces the campus parking regulations. The patrol force issues citations for parking violations. Each citation includes the citation number, the date and time of the violation, and a description of the violation. For vehicles with permits, the citation includes the permit number and the license plate number. For vehicles without permits, the citation includes the license plate number but not the permit number. Sandy's staff also tracks payments for the fines levied with the citations.

Pat's initial database contains three tables: tblPermit, tblCitation, and tblPayment. Figure 5 shows the structure of the tblPermit table, which stores data about each parking permit issued to students,

STARTING DATA FILES

AddCases

NoPark.bmp
Tophill.accdb

faculty, and staff. Each tblPermit table record contains a permit number, the vehicle license plate number, and the permit holder's name.

| Figure 5 | Structure of the tblPermit table |

Field Name	Data Type	Properties
PermitNum	Text	Description: Primary key; unique number issued to an individual's vehicle Field Size: 5 Caption: Permit Num
LicensePlateNum	Text	Description: License plate number of the vehicle issued the permit Field Size: 8 Caption: License Plate Num
OwnerFirst	Text	Description: Vehicle owner's first name Field Size: 15 Caption: Owner First
OwnerLast	Text	Description: Vehicle owner's last name Field Size: 15 Caption: Owner Last

Figure 6 shows the structure of the tblCitation table, which contains one record for each issued citation. Each tblCitation record contains the citation number, date, and time; the vehicle license plate number; the violation code; and the permit number, if a permit is visible on the front windshield.

| Figure 6 | Structure of the tblCitation table |

Field Name	Data Type	Properties
CitationNum	Text	Description: Primary key; unique number assigned to a citation for a parking violation Field Size: 6 Caption: Citation Num
CitationDate	Date/Time	Description: Issue date for the citation Format: mm/dd/yyyy Caption: Citation Date
CitationTime	Date/Time	Description: Issue time for the citation Format: Medium Time Caption: Citation Time
PermitNum	Text	Description: Null if the vehicle has no visible permit Field Size: 5 Caption: Permit Num
LicensePlateNum	Text	Description: Vehicle license plate number Field Size: 8 Caption: License Plate Num
ViolationCode	Text	Description: Violation code for the parking infraction Field Size: 2 Caption: Violation Code

Figure 7 shows the structure of the tblPayment table, which contains one record for each parking violation payment. Each tblPayment record contains a unique payment ID, the payment amount and date, and the number of the citation to which the payment applies.

| Figure 7 | Structure of the tblPayment table |

Field Name	Data Type	Properties
PaymentID	AutoNumber	Description: Primary key; unique number assigned to a parking violation payment
		Caption: Payment ID
PaymentAmt	Currency	Description: Amount paid
		Format: Currency
		Decimal Places: 2
		Caption: Payment Amt
PaymentDate	Date/Time	Description: Payment date
		Format: mm/dd/yyyy
		Caption: Payment Date
CitationNum	Text	Description: Citation to which the payment applies
		Field Size: 6
		Caption: Citation Num

Pat turns the completed database design over to Sandy, who wants to create special queries, forms, and reports in the database to help her manage parking permits and violations. To help Sandy finish her work with the database, complete the following steps:

1. Make sure you have created your copy of the Access Data Files and stored them in a trusted folder, and that your computer can access them. Start Access, and then open the **Tophill** database located in the AddCases folder.

2. Review the **tblPermit**, **tblCitation**, and **tblPayment** tables to become familiar with their structures and data, and then resize all columns to best fit the data they contain. If you are unfamiliar with any property setting, use the Access Help system for an explanation of that property.

3. The tblCitation table contains a two-character ViolationCode field. Design and create a new table to store the violation codes, descriptions, and fine amounts, using the field names **ViolationCode**, **ViolationDesc**, and **FineAmt**, making ViolationCode the primary key, and setting the Caption property and other field properties to appropriate values. Save the table as **tblViolation**, add the eight records shown in Figure 8 to the table, resize all datasheet columns to their best fit, and then print the tblViolation table recordset.

Figure 8   tblViolation table records

ViolationCode	ViolationDesc	FineAmt
BE	Improper Parking Building Entrance	$20
EM	Expired Meter	$15
HA	Improper Parking Handicapped Area	$75
OA	Improper Parking Other Areas	$20
RA	Improper Parking Reserved Area	$50
RD	Improper Parking Roadway	$15
SD	Improper Parking Service Drive	$17
WL	Improper Parking Walk/Lawn	$22

4. Modify the first record in the tblPermit table datasheet by entering your name in the Owner First and Owner Last columns.

5. Add all four tables to the Relationships window, make sure all fields are visible in the field lists, and then define the three one-to-many relationships. Enforce referential integrity, and select the Cascade Update Related Fields option for each relationship. Rearrange the field lists as appropriate so that join lines don't cross field lists, save your design, and then create and print the Relationships for Tophill report but do not save it.

6. Create and save a query named **qryCollegeCitations** that displays, in order, all fields from the tblCitation table, and the OwnerFirst and OwnerLast fields from the tblPermit table. Sort in ascending order by OwnerLast as the first sort field, OwnerFirst as the second sort field, CitationDate as the third sort field, and CitationTime as the fourth sort field. Print the query recordset in landscape orientation after testing and saving the query, but don't close the query.

7. Save the qryCollegeCitations query as **qryAllCitations**, and then modify the new query to use an outer join to include all records from the tblCitation table and the matching records from the tblPermit table. Print the query recordset in landscape orientation after testing and saving the query, and then close the query.

8. Export the data with formatting and layout in the qryAllCitations query to an Excel workbook named **Citations** in the AddCases folder. Save the export steps.

9. Create and save a query named **qryTotalPaymentsByDate** that displays the PaymentDate field and the sum of the PaymentAmt field from the tblPayment table. For the total field, use a Caption value of **Total Payments**. Sort the query in ascending order by PaymentDate. Resize all datasheet columns to their best fit, and then print the query recordset after testing and saving the query.

10. Create a find duplicates query based on the tblCitation table. Select LicensePlateNum as the field that might contain duplicates, and select all the other fields in the table as additional fields in the query recordset. Save the query as **qryVehiclesWithMultipleCitations**, and then view and print the query recordset.

11. Make a copy of the qryAllCitations query, save the copy as **qryAllCitationsParameter**, and then modify the new query to display records for a ViolationCode field value that the user enters. If the user doesn't enter a field value, select and display all records. After modifying and saving the query, run the query and enter **HA** as the ViolationCode field value. Print the query recordset in landscape orientation.

EXPLORE 12. Make a copy of the qryAllCitations query, save the copy as **qryAllCitationsWithoutPermits**, and then modify the new query to display only those records that have a null PermitNum field value. After modifying and saving the query, run the query and print the query results in landscape orientation.

13. Create a crosstab query that uses the tblCitation table. Select the CitationDate field values for the row headings, ViolationCode field values for the column headings,

and the count of the CitationNum field as the summarized value. Save the query as **qryCitationCrosstab**, use a Caption value of **Total Citations** for the Count Row Heading column, resize the columns in the query recordset to their best fit, print the query results, and then save and close the query.

14. Create and save a query named **qryCitationsAndPayments** that displays, in order, all fields from the tblCitation table, and the PaymentID, PaymentAmt, and PaymentDate fields from the tblPayment table. Include all records from the tblCitation table and only the matching records from the tblPayment table. Sort in ascending order by CitationNum. Use the Totals row in the query datasheet to add a count of the number of citations in the Citation Num column, a count of the number of payments in the Payment ID column, and a total of the payment amounts in the Payment Amt column. Print the query recordset in landscape orientation after testing and saving the query.

15. Use the Form Wizard to create a form containing the main form and subform shown in Figure 9. Select all the fields from the tblPermit table for the main form, and select the appropriate fields from the qryCitationsAndPayments query for the subform. Use the Tabular layout. Save the main form as **frmPermitsAndCitations** and the subform as **frmCitationsAndPaymentsSubform**. Change the text in the main form's title control to **Permits and Citations**. Delete the subform label, resize the widths of the columns in the subform, and adjust the width and height of the subform as necessary. Change the caption on the record navigation bar for the main form to **Permit** and for the subform to **Citation**. Make sure the tab order in the main form is top-to-bottom and the tab order in the subform is left-to-right. Modify the form by adding the Total Payments calculated control that displays the total PaymentAmt field values from the subform. (*Hint:* Set the Visible property for the Form Footer section in the subform to No.) Print only main form record 29 and its subform records.

Figure 9	Permits and Citations form

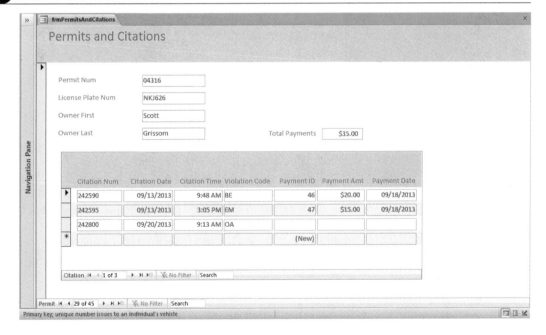

16. Create a blank form and add all fields from the tblCitation table to it, except for the ViolationCode field, in a Stacked layout. Add the ViolationCode field to the form as a combo box control that displays values from the tblViolation table. Display all three fields from the tblViolation table, sort the records in ascending order by ViolationCode, do not hide the key column, resize all columns to their best fit, store values in the ViolationCode field, and use the label **Violation Code**. Resize the text

boxes and the combo box as appropriate for the displayed values, and so the text box and combo box controls do not overlap the label controls. Save the form as **frmCitation**, and then print only the last form record.

17. Create the report shown in Figure 10, which is based on the qryCitationsAndPayments query, and save it as **rptCitationsAndPayments**. Use landscape orientation, and increase the report width to at least 9.5 inches. Add the title, date, time, and picture (which is saved in the AddCases folder as NoPark.bmp) to the Report Header section. Print the first page of the report.

Figure 10   **Citations and Payments report**

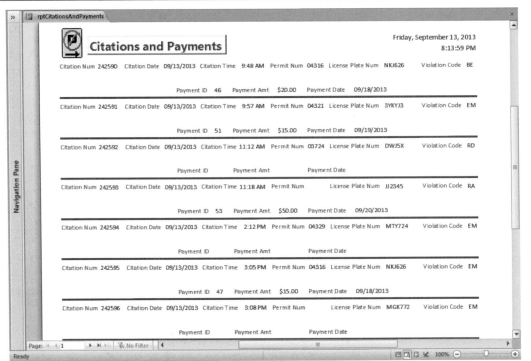

🔄 **EXPLORE** 18. Make a copy of the rptCitationsAndPayments report, and save the copy as **rptCitationsAndPaymentsModified**. Modify the new report to suppress the printing of the three controls that are based on the tblPayment table when the PaymentID control value is null. (*Hint:* Use the Detail section's Format event, and use assignment statements for all the labels and text boxes in the Detail section similar to *Me![control name].Visible = True/False*, where *Me* refers to the open form, and *True/False* means to select the appropriate property setting. The controls are suppressed only when you print the report or view the report in Print Preview.) After modifying and saving the report, print the first page of the report.

19. Create a form named **frmQueries** that has the following components and characteristics:

    a. Use the text **Tophill Queries** on the form's tab.

    b. Add a list box with a Name property value of **lstQueryList** that displays all the query names contained in the NestEgg database, excluding those queries that start with a "~" character. To place the query names in the list box, use an SQL SELECT statement to retrieve the query names from the MSysObjects table, and display the queries in alphabetical order. Delete the label attached to the list box, widen the list box to approximately 2.5 inches, and set its height to approximately one inch.

    c. Add the label **Available Queries**, formatted with Calibri 12-point, black, bold font, above the list box.

d. Add two command buttons below the list box. The left command button displays the Preview icon above the word **Preview**, and the right command button displays the MS Access Query icon above the word **Display**. Double-clicking a query name has the same effect as selecting a query name in the list box and clicking the right command button. Both events cause Access to display the query datasheet for the selected query. Clicking the left command button opens the selected query in Print Preview.

e. Create macros for the form (when the form loads, move the focus to the first query name in the list box), the list box (when a user double-clicks a query name), and both command buttons (when a user clicks a command button).

f. Disable the form's shortcut menu, record selectors, and navigation buttons. Set the width of the Detail section to 3.5 inches, and set its height to three inches.

g. Test the form.

20. Create a navigation form named **frmNavigation**, using the Horizontal Tabs, 2 Levels layout, that includes the following tab names and objects:

a. Use **Forms** as the name for the left tab, and place the following forms below it, in order: frmCitation and frmPermitsAndCitations.

b. Use **Queries** as the name for the second tab, and place the frmQueries form below it.

c. Use Reports as the name for the third tab, and place the rptCitationsAndPaymentsModified below it.

d. Delete the navigation form's picture and title, and change the tab name to **Tophill database**.

e. Test the navigation form.

21. Make a backup copy of the database, and then compact and repair the Tophill database.

22. Set the database properties for the **Tophill** database so the frmNavigation form opens when the database is opened, to set startup options to disable features as appropriate for a database that uses a navigation form, and to change the database name in the title bar to **Tophill College**.

23. Close the Tophill database to activate the database startup options, open the database, test the navigation form options, and then exit Access.

ENDING DATA FILES

AddCases

Citations.xlsx
Tophill.accdb

OBJECTIVES

- Design a database and draw its entity-relationship diagram
- Create the tables and relationships for the database
- Create forms to maintain the database
- Design and enter test data for the database
- Create queries and reports from the database
- Create a navigation form
- Set database properties and startup options

In this case you will use skills you learned in the following tutorials:

- Tutorials 1-7, 9-11, 12 (startup options only), and the "Relational Databases and Database Design" appendix

Internship Program for Journey College

ACCESS

Case | *Journey College*

Journey College provides students in the northern New Jersey area with opportunities for professional development and field study through its internship program, which is administered by the Office of Internships and Field Experience. Students complement their courses with a structured training experience provided by qualified professionals in selected fields. Internships are offered in many different areas, including law, counseling, government, administration, public relations, communications, health care, software engineering, and marketing.

The college recently hired Maria Senn as its new Internship Coordinator. She is eager to make information about the sponsoring agencies, potential internships, and current student interns more readily available to her office and to the students who qualify for the program. Maria's most ambitious project is to develop a database for the internship program to help meet these goals. The database will allow potential interns to view the internships that meet the criteria they specify. Maria asks Robert Mendes, an information systems major working in the Office of Internships and Field Experience, to help her design and develop the database.

Maria first outlines the steps in the internship program process for Robert:

- Identify and document the available internships.
- Arrange for student intern placements.
- Assign and track student interns.

As the first step in the internship program process, Maria receives a letter or phone call from a potential sponsoring agency. After some discussions, a sponsoring agency proposes an internship possibility and fills out the Agency/Internship Information form shown in Figure 11.

STARTING DATA FILES

AddCases

(none)

Figure 11   Agency/Internship Information form

```
                    AGENCY/INTERNSHIP INFORMATION

                          AGENCY INFORMATION

NAME OF AGENCY     _____

DEPARTMENT         _____

ADDRESS            _____
                   Street

                   _____
                   City                        State        Zip

CONTACT            _____  PHONE _____


                        INTERNSHIP INFORMATION

TITLE              _____

DESCRIPTION OF     _____
DUTIES             _____
                   _____

ORIENTATION &      _____
TRAINING           _____
                   _____

ACADEMIC           _____
BACKGROUND         _____
REQUIRED           _____

SUPERVISOR         _____  PHONE _____

Office Use
Agency ID          _____
Internship ID      _____
Category           _____
```

Many agencies offer more than one type of internship possibility. For each possible internship, the agency fills out a separate form and assigns one person as the contact for all internship questions and problems. In addition, each internship lists a supervisor who will work with the student intern. The internship remains active until the agency notifies the Office of Internships and Field Experience that the internship is filled or no longer available.

Maria assigns a four-digit Agency ID to each new agency and a three-digit Internship ID to each new internship using sequential numbers. She also classifies each internship into a category that helps students identify internships that are related to their academic major or interests. For example, a student might be interested in health care, accounting, social service, or advertising.

A copy of each Agency/Internship Information form is placed in reference books in the Office of Internships and Field Experience. Students browse through these books to find internships that interest them. If an internship interests a student, the student copies the information about the internship and contacts the sponsoring agency directly to request an interview.

When a student gets an internship, the student and agency establish a Learning Contract, outlining the goals to be accomplished during the internship. The student then fills out the Student Internship form, shown in Figure 12, to provide basic personal information for the office files.

Figure 12   Student Internship form

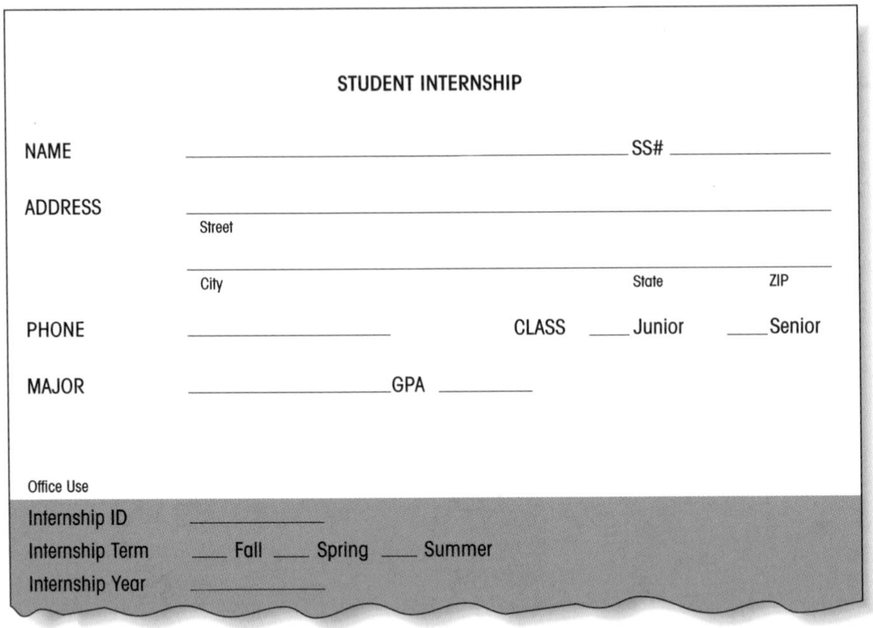

STUDENT INTERNSHIP

NAME _____ SS# _____

ADDRESS _____
         Street

         _____
         City   State   ZIP

PHONE _____   CLASS ____ Junior ____ Senior

MAJOR _____ GPA _____

Office Use

Internship ID   _____

Internship Term   ____ Fall ____ Spring ____ Summer

Internship Year   _____

Maria enters the Internship ID and year on the Student Internship form and checks the term for the internship. Next, a clerk enters information from the form into a word processor to prepare lists of current interns and internships, and then prints and places the form in a binder.

Maria and Robert determine that getting these two forms into an Access database is their first priority, and then they will work on creating several new reports. The first report, shown in Figure 13, lists all student interns alphabetically by last name for a selected term. In order to identify the student interns who should be included in the report, the system prompts the user for the term and year.

Figure 13   Student Interns report

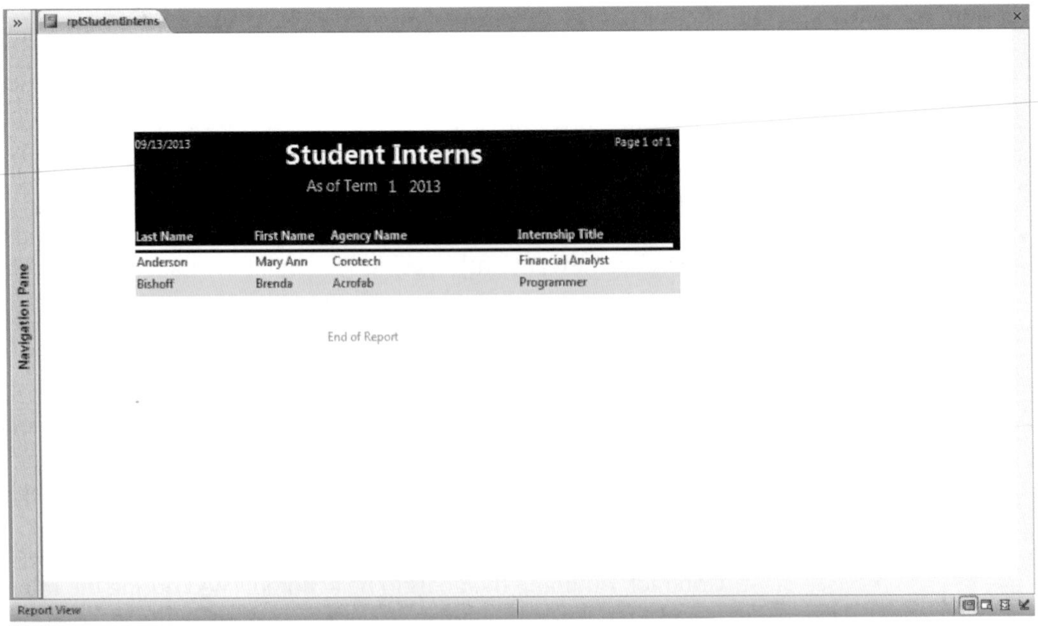

rptStudentInterns

09/13/2013   Page 1 of 1

Student Interns
As of Term 1   2013

Last Name	First Name	Agency Name	Internship Title
Anderson	Mary Ann	Corotech	Financial Analyst
Bishoff	Brenda	Acrofab	Programmer

End of Report

Report View

A second new report lists all agencies in the database alphabetically by agency name. Figure 14 shows this report.

Figure 14	Internship Agencies report

The Internships by Category report, shown in Figure 15, lists internships grouped by category. The staff will use this report when talking with students about the internship program.

Figure 15	Internships by Category report

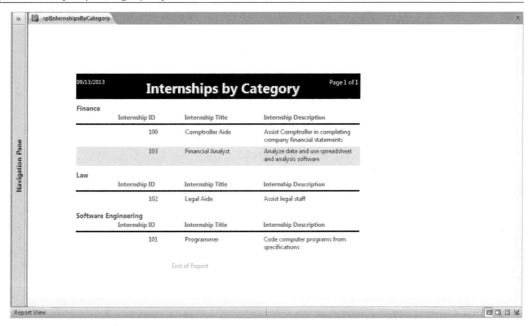

At the end of an internship, the intern's supervisor evaluates the intern's work experience, using an evaluation form mailed from the Office of Internships and Field Experience. Maria needs mailing labels addressed to the supervisor of each intern for the current term and year. The mailing labels should contain the supervisor's name on the first line; the agency name on the second line; the agency's street address on the third line; and the agency's city, state, and zip code on the fourth line. Maria wants the labels sorted by agency name.

To create the database, complete the following steps:

1. Read the appendix titled "Relational Databases and Database Design," which appears at the end of this book.

⊕ **EXPLORE**   2. Identify each entity (table) in the database for the internship system.

⊕ **EXPLORE**   3. Draw an entity-relationship diagram showing the entities and the relationships between the entities.

⊕ **EXPLORE**   4. Design the database for the internship system. For each table, list the fields and their attributes, such as data types, field sizes, and validation rules. Place the set of tables in third normal form and identify all primary, alternate, and foreign keys.

5. Use Access to create the **Journey** database in the AddCases folder with your Data Files. Be sure to define relationships between appropriate tables.

⊕ **EXPLORE**   6. Create and save forms to maintain data on agencies, internships, student interns, and any other tables in your database structure. The forms should be used to view, add, edit, and delete records in the database.

7. Create test data for each table in the database and add the test data, using the forms you created in Step 6.

8. Create and save the **rptStudentInterns** report, the **rptInternshipAgencies** report, and the **rptInternshipsByCategory** report. The reports shown in Figures 13 through 15 are guides—improve them as you see fit. Then create the **rptMailingLabels** report to create mailing labels for agencies using a label of your choice.

9. Design, create, and save a form that a student can use to view internships for a selected category. Display one internship at a time on the screen. For each internship, display the category, internship ID, title, description of duties, orientation and training, academic background, agency name, department, agency address, contact name, and contact phone. Provide an option to print the current record displayed on the screen.

10. Design, create, and save a navigation form to coordinate the running of the internship system.

11. Set the database properties so the frmNavigation form opens when the database is opened, to set startup options to disable features as appropriate for a database that uses a navigation form, and to change the database name in the title bar to **Journey College Internships**.

12. Test all features of the internship system.

ENDING DATA FILES

AddCases

Journey.accdb

APPENDIX **A**

OBJECTIVES

- Learn the characteristics of a table
- Learn about primary, candidate, alternate, composite, and foreign keys
- Study one-to-one, one-to-many, and many-to-many relationships
- Learn to describe tables and relationships with entity-relationship diagrams and with a shorthand method
- Study database integrity constraints for primary keys, referential integrity, and domains
- Learn about determinants, functional dependencies, anomalies, and normalization
- Understand the differences among natural, artificial, and surrogate keys
- Learn about naming conventions

Relational Databases and Database Design

ACCESS

This appendix introduces you to the basics of database design. Before trying to master this material, be sure you understand the following concepts: data, information, field, field value, record, table, relational database, common field, database management system (DBMS), and relational database management system (RDBMS).

STARTING DATA FILES

There are no starting Data Files needed for this appendix.

Tables

A relational database stores its data in tables. A **table** is a two-dimensional structure made up of rows and columns. The terms table, **record** (row), and **field** (column) are the popular names for the more formal terms **relation** (table), **tuple** (row), and **attribute** (column), as shown in Figure A-1.

Figure A-1   **A table (relation) consisting of records and fields**

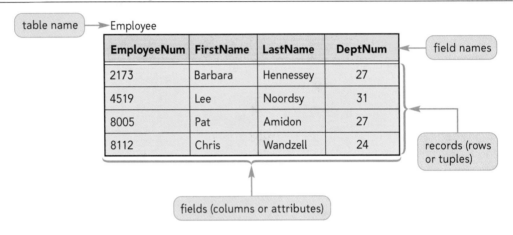

The Employee table shown in Figure A-1 is an example of a relational database table, a two-dimensional structure with the following characteristics:

- Each row is unique. Because no two rows are the same, you can easily locate and update specific data. For example, you can locate the row for EmployeeNum 8005 and change the FirstName value, Pat, the LastName value, Amidon, or the DeptNum value, 27.
- The order of the rows is unimportant. You can add or view rows in any order. For example, you can view the rows in LastName order instead of EmployeeNum order.
- Each table entry contains a single value. At the intersection of each row and column, you cannot have more than one value. For example, each row in Figure A-1 contains one EmployeeNum value, one FirstName value, one LastName value, and one DeptNum value.
- The order of the columns is unimportant. You can add or view columns in any order.
- Each column has a unique name called the **field name**. The field name allows you to access a specific column without needing to know its position within the table.
- Each row in a table describes, or shows the characteristics of, an **entity**. An entity is a person, place, object, event, or idea for which you want to store and process data. For example, EmployeeNum, FirstName, LastName, and DeptNum are characteristics of the employees of a company. The Employee table represents all the employee entities and their characteristics. That is, each row of the Employee table describes a different employee of the company using the characteristics of EmployeeNum, FirstName, LastName, and DeptNum. The Employee table includes only characteristics of employees. Other tables would exist for the company's other entities. For example, a Department table would describe the company's departments and a Position table would describe the company's job positions.

Knowing the characteristics of a table leads directly to a definition of a relational database. A **relational database** is a collection of tables (relations).

Note that this book uses singular table names, such as Employee and Department, but some people use plural table names, such as Employees and Departments. You can use either singular table names or plural table names, as long as you consistently use the style you choose.

Keys

Primary keys ensure that each row in a table is unique. A **primary key** is a column, or a collection of columns, whose values uniquely identify each row in a table. In addition to being *unique*, a primary key must be *minimal* (that is, contain no unnecessary extra columns) and must not change in value. For example, in Figure A-2 the State table contains one record per state and uses the StateAbbrev column as its primary key.

Figure A-2 **A table and its keys**

State

StateAbbrev	StateName	EnteredUnionOrder	StateBird	StatePopulation
CT	Connecticut	5	American robin	3,518,288
MI	Michigan	26	robin	9,969,727
SD	South Dakota	40	pheasant	812,383
TN	Tennessee	16	mockingbird	6,296,254
TX	Texas	28	mockingbird	24,782,302

alternate keys — StateName, EnteredUnionOrder
primary key — StateAbbrev

Could any other column, or collection of columns, be the primary key of the State table?

- Could the StateBird column serve as the primary key? No, because the StateBird column does not have unique values (for example, the mockingbird is the state bird of more than one state).
- Could the StatePopulation column serve as the primary key? No, because the StatePopulation column values change periodically and are not guaranteed to be unique.
- Could the StateAbbrev and StateName columns together serve as the primary key? No, because the combination of these two columns is not minimal. Something less, such as the StateAbbrev column by itself, can serve as the primary key.
- Could the StateName column serve as the primary key? Yes, because the StateName column has unique values. In a similar way, you could select the EnteredUnionOrder column as the primary key for the State table. One column, or a collection of columns, that can serve as a primary key is called a **candidate key**. The candidate keys for the State table are the StateAbbrev column, the StateName column, and the EnteredUnionOrder column. You choose one of the candidate keys to be the primary key, and each remaining candidate key is called an **alternate key**. The StateAbbrev column is the State table's primary key in Figure A-2, so the StateName and EnteredUnionOrder columns become alternate keys in the table.

Figure A-3 shows a City table containing the fields StateAbbrev, CityName, and CityPopulation.

Figure A-3	A table with a composite key

primary key

City

StateAbbrev	CityName	CityPopulation
CT	Hartford	124,062
CT	Madison	18,803
CT	Portland	9,551
MI	Lansing	119,128
SD	Madison	6,482
SD	Pierre	13,899
TN	Nashville	569,462
TX	Austin	757,688
TX	Portland	16,490

What is the primary key for the City table? The values for the CityPopulation column periodically change and are not guaranteed to be unique, so the CityPopulation column cannot be the primary key. Because the values for each of the other two columns are not unique, the StateAbbrev column alone cannot be the primary key and neither can the CityName column (for example, there are two cities named Madison and two cities named Portland). The primary key is the combination of the StateAbbrev and CityName columns. Both columns together are needed to identify—uniquely and minimally—each row in the City table. A multiple-column primary key is called a **composite key** or a **concatenated key**.

The StateAbbrev column in the City table is also a foreign key. A **foreign key** is a column, or a collection of columns, in one table in which each column value must match the value of the primary key of some table or must be null. A **null** is the absence of a value in a particular table entry. A null value is not blank, nor zero, nor any other value. You give a null value to a column value when you do not know its value or when a value does not apply. As shown in Figure A-4, the values in the City table's StateAbbrev column match the values in the State table's StateAbbrev column. Thus, the StateAbbrev column, the primary key of the State table, is a foreign key in the City table. Although the field name StateAbbrev is the same in both tables, the names could be different. However, all experts use the same name for a field stored in two or more tables to broadcast clearly that they store similar values.

| Figure A-4 | StateAbbrev as a primary key (State table) and a foreign key (City table) |

primary key (State table)

State

StateAbbrev	StateName	EnteredUnionOrder	StateBird	StatePopulation
CT	Connecticut	5	American robin	3,518,288
MI	Michigan	26	robin	9,969,727
SD	South Dakota	40	pheasant	812,383
TN	Tennessee	16	mockingbird	6,296,254
TX	Texas	28	mockingbird	24,782,302

composite primary key (City table)

City

foreign key

StateAbbrev	CityName	CityPopulation
CT	Hartford	124,062
CT	Madison	18,803
CT	Portland	9,551
MI	Lansing	119,128
SD	Madison	6,482
SD	Pierre	13,899
TN	Nashville	596,462
TX	Austin	757,688
TX	Portland	16,490

A **nonkey field** is a field that is not part of the primary key. In the two tables shown in Figure A-4, all fields are nonkey fields except the StateAbbrev field in the State and City tables and the CityName field in the City table. *Key* is an ambiguous word because it can refer to a primary, candidate, alternate, or foreign key. When the word key appears alone, however, it means primary key and the definition for a nonkey field consequently makes sense.

Relationships

In a database, a table can be associated with another table in one of three ways: a one-to-many relationship, a many-to-many relationship, or a one-to-one relationship.

One-to-Many Relationship

The Department and Employee tables, shown in Figure A-5, have a one-to-many relationship. A **one-to-many relationship** (abbreviated **1:M** or **1:N**) exists between two tables when each row in the first table (sometimes called the **primary table**) matches many rows in the second table and each row in the second table (sometimes called the **related**

table) matches at most one row in the first table. "Many" can mean zero rows, one row, or two or more rows. The DeptNum field, which is a foreign key in the Employee table and the primary key in the Department table, is the common field that ties together the rows of the two tables. Each department has many employees; and each employee works in exactly one department or hasn't been assigned to a department, if the DeptNum field value for that employee is null.

| Figure A-5 | A one-to-many relationship |

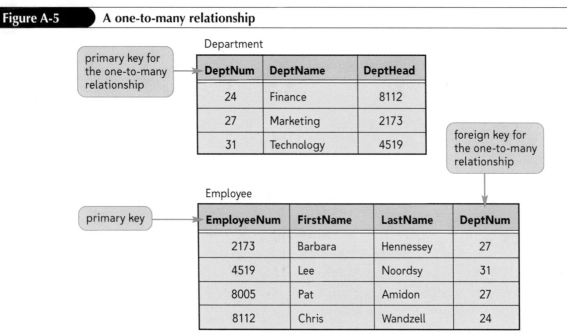

Many-to-Many Relationship

In Figure A-6, the Employee table (with the EmployeeNum field as its primary key) and the Position table (with the PositionID field as its primary key) have a many-to-many relationship. A **many-to-many relationship** (abbreviated as **M:N**) exists between two tables when each row in the first table matches many rows in the second table and each row in the second table matches many rows in the first table. In a relational database, you must use a third table (often called an **intersection table**, **junction table**, or **link table**) to serve as a bridge between the two many-to-many tables; the third table has the primary keys of the two many-to-many tables as its primary key. The original tables now each have a one-to-many relationship with the new table. The EmployeeNum and PositionID fields represent the primary key of the Employment table that is shown in Figure A-6. The EmployeeNum field, which is a foreign key in the Employment table and the primary key in the Employee table, is the common field that ties together the rows of the Employee and Employment tables. Likewise, the PositionID field is the common field for the Position and Employment tables. Each employee has served in many different positions within the company over time, and each position in the company has been filled by many different employees over time.

| Figure A-6 | A many-to-many relationship |

Employee

primary key
(Employee
table)

EmployeeNum	FirstName	LastName	DeptNum
2173	Barbara	Hennessey	27
4519	Lee	Noordsy	31
8005	Pat	Amidon	27
8112	Chris	Wandzell	24

Position

primary key
(Position table)

PositionID	PositionDesc	PayGrade
1	Director	45
2	Manager	40
3	Analyst	30
4	Clerk	20

composite key of the
intersection table

Employment

foreign keys related
to the Employee and
Position tables

EmployeeNum	PositionID	StartDate	EndDate
2173	2	12/14/2011	
4519	1	04/23/2013	
4519	3	11/11/2007	04/22/2013
8005	3	06/05/2012	08/25/2013
8005	4	07/02/2010	06/04/2012
8112	1	12/15/2012	
8112	2	10/04/2011	12/14/2012

One-to-One Relationship

In Figure A-5, recall that there's a one-to-many relationship between the Department table (the primary table) and the Employee table (the related table). Each department has many employees, and each employee works in one department. The DeptNum field in the Employee table serves as a foreign key to connect records in that table to records with matching DeptNum field values in the Department table.

Furthermore, each department has a single employee who serves as the head of the department, and each employee either serves as the head of a department or simply works in a department without being the department head. Therefore, the Department and Employee tables not only have a one-to-many relationship, but these two tables also have a second relationship, a one-to-one relationship. A **one-to-one relationship** (abbreviated **1:1**) exists between two tables when each row in each table has at most one matching row in the other table. As shown in Figure A-7, each DeptHead field value in the Department table represents the employee number in the Employee table of the employee who heads the department. In other words, each DeptHead field value in the Department table matches exactly one EmployeeNum field value in the Employee table. At the same time, each EmployeeNum field value in the Employee table matches at most one DeptHead field value in the Department table—matching one DeptHead field value if the employee is a department head, or matching zero DeptHead field values if the employee is not a department head. For this one-to-one relationship, the EmployeeNum field in the

Employee table and the DeptHead field in the Department table are the fields that link the two tables, with the DeptHead field serving as a foreign key in the Department table and the EmployeeNum field serving as a primary key in the Employee table.

Some database designers might use EmployeeNum instead of DeptHead as the field name for the foreign key in the Department table because they both represent the employee number for the employees of the company. However, DeptHead better identifies the purpose of the field and would more commonly be used as the field name.

Figure A-7	A one-to-one relationship

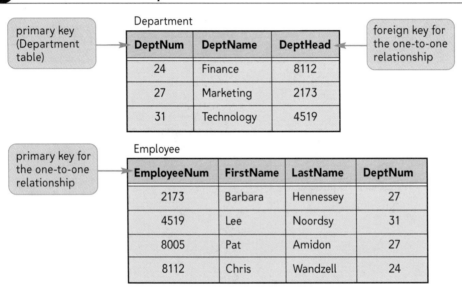

primary key (Department table)

Department

DeptNum	DeptName	DeptHead
24	Finance	8112
27	Marketing	2173
31	Technology	4519

foreign key for the one-to-one relationship

primary key for the one-to-one relationship

Employee

EmployeeNum	FirstName	LastName	DeptNum
2173	Barbara	Hennessey	27
4519	Lee	Noordsy	31
8005	Pat	Amidon	27
8112	Chris	Wandzell	24

Entity Subtype

Suppose the company awards annual bonuses to a small number of employees who fill director positions in selected departments. As shown in Figure A-8, you could store the Bonus field in the Employee table because a bonus is an attribute associated with employees. The Bonus field would contain either the amount of the employee's bonus (record 4 in the Employee table) or a null value for employees without bonuses (records 1 through 3 in the Employee table).

Figure A-8	Bonus field added to the Employee table

Employee

EmployeeNum	FirstName	LastName	DeptNum	Bonus
2173	Barbara	Hennessey	27	
4519	Lee	Noordsy	31	
8005	Pat	Amidon	27	
8112	Chris	Wandzell	24	$20,000

nulls for these Bonus field values

Bonus field value for the fourth record

Figure A-9 shows an alternative approach, in which the Bonus field is placed in a separate table, the EmployeeBonus table. The EmployeeBonus table's primary key is the EmployeeNum field, and the table contains one row for each employee earning a bonus. Because some employees do not earn a bonus, the EmployeeBonus table has fewer rows than the Employee table. However, each row in the EmployeeBonus table has a matching row in the Employee table, with the EmployeeNum field serving as the common field; the EmployeeNum field is the primary key in the Employee table and is a foreign key in the EmployeeBonus table.

| Figure A-9 | Storing Bonus values in a separate table, an entity subtype |

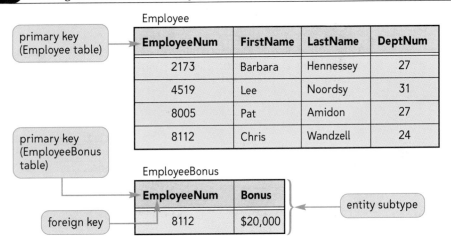

The EmployeeBonus table, in this situation, is called an **entity subtype**, a table whose primary key is a foreign key to a second table and whose fields are additional fields for the second table. Database designers create an entity subtype in two situations. In the first situation, some users might need access to all employee fields, including employee bonuses, while other employees might need access to all employee fields except bonuses. Because most DBMSs allow you to control which tables a user can access, you can specify that some users can access both tables and that other users can access the Employee table but not the EmployeeBonus table, keeping the employee bonus information hidden from the latter group. In the second situation, you can create an entity subtype when a table has fields that could have nulls, as was the case for the Bonus field stored in the Employee table in Figure A-8. You should be aware that database experts are currently debating the validity of the use of nulls in relational databases, and many experts insist that you should never use nulls. This warning against nulls is partly based on the inconsistent way different RDBMSs treat nulls and partly due to the lack of a firm theoretical foundation for how to use nulls. In any case, entity subtypes are an alternative to the use of nulls.

Entity-Relationship Diagrams

A common shorthand method for describing tables is to write the table name followed by its fields in parentheses, underlining the fields that represent the primary key and identifying the foreign keys for a table immediately after the table. Using this method, the tables that appear in Figures A-5 through A-7 and Figure A-9 are described in the following way:

Department (<u>DeptNum</u>, DeptName, DeptHead)
   Foreign key: DeptHead to Employee table
Employee (<u>EmployeeNum</u>, FirstName, LastName, DeptNum)
   Foreign key: DeptNum to Department table
Position (<u>PositionID</u>, PositionDesc, PayGrade)
Employment (<u>EmployeeNum</u>, <u>PositionID</u>, StartDate, EndDate)
   Foreign key: EmployeeNum to Employee table
   Foreign key: PositionID to Position table
EmployeeBonus (<u>EmployeeNum</u>, Bonus)
   Foreign key: EmployeeNum to Employee table

Another popular way to describe tables *and their relationships* is with entity-relationship diagrams. An **entity-relationship diagram (ERD)** shows a database's entities and the relationships among the entities in a symbolic, visual way. In an ERD, an entity and a table are equivalent. Figure A-10 shows an entity-relationship diagram for the tables that appear in Figures A-5 through A-7 and Figure A-9.

Figure A-10	**An entity-relationship diagram (ERD)**

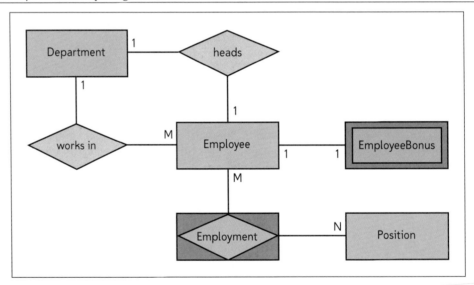

ERDs have the following characteristics:

- Entities, or tables, appear in rectangles, and relationships appear in diamonds. The entity name appears inside the rectangle, and a verb describing the relationship appears inside the diamond. For example, the Employee rectangle is connected to the Department rectangle by the "works in" diamond and is read: "an employee works in a department."
- The 1 by the Department entity and the M by the Employee entity identify a one-to-many relationship between these two entities. In a similar manner, a many-to-many relationship exists between the Employee and Position entities and one-to-one relationships exist between the Department and Employee entities and between the Employee and EmployeeBonus entities.

- A diamond inside a rectangle defines a composite entity. A **composite entity** is a relationship that has the characteristics of an entity. For example, Employment connects the Employee and Position entities in a many-to-many relationship and acts as an entity by containing the StartDate and EndDate fields, along with the composite key of the EmployeeNum and PositionID fields.
- An entity subtype, for example, EmployeeBonus, appears in a double rectangle and is connected without an intervening diamond directly to its related entity, Employee.

You can also show fields in an ERD by placing each individual field in a bubble connected to its entity or relationship. However, typical ERDs have large numbers of entities and relationships, so including the fields might confuse rather than clarify the ERD.

Integrity Constraints

A database has **integrity** if its data follows certain rules; each rule is called an **integrity constraint**. The ideal is to have the DBMS enforce all integrity constraints. If a DBMS can enforce some integrity constraints but not others, the other integrity constraints must be enforced by other programs or by the people who use the DBMS. Integrity constraints can be divided into three groups: primary key constraints, foreign key constraints, and domain integrity constraints.

- One primary key constraint is inherent in the definition of a primary key, which says that the primary key must be unique. The **entity integrity constraint** says that the primary key cannot be null. For a composite key, none of the individual fields can be null. The uniqueness and nonnull properties of a primary key ensure that you can reference any data value in a database by supplying its table name, field name, and primary key value.
- Foreign keys provide the mechanism for forming a relationship between two tables, and referential integrity ensures that only valid relationships exist. **Referential integrity** is the constraint specifying that each nonnull foreign key value must match a primary key value in the primary table. Specifically, referential integrity means that you cannot add a row with an unmatched foreign key value. Referential integrity also means that you cannot change or delete the related primary key value and leave the foreign key orphaned. In some RDBMSs, if you try to change or delete a primary key value, you can specify one of these options: restricted, cascades, or nullifies. If you specify **restricted**, the DBMS updates or deletes the value only if there are no matching foreign key values. If you choose **cascades** and then change a primary key value, the DBMS changes the matching foreign key values to the new primary key value, or, if you delete a primary key value, the DBMS also deletes the matching foreign key rows. If you choose **nullifies** and then change or delete a primary key value, the DBMS sets all matching foreign key values to null.
- Recall that a domain is a set of values from which one or more fields draw their actual values. A **domain integrity constraint** is a rule you specify for a field. By choosing a data type for a field, you impose a constraint on the set of values allowed for the field. You can create specific validation rules for a field to limit its domain further. As you make a field's domain definition more precise, you exclude more and more unacceptable values for the field. For example, in the State table, shown in Figures A-2 and A-4, you could define the domain for the EnteredUnionOrder field to be a unique integer between 1 and 50 and the domain for the StateBird field to be any name containing 25 or fewer characters.

Dependencies and Determinants

Tables are related to other tables. Fields are also related to other fields. Consider the modified Employee table shown in Figure A-11. Its description is:

Employee (<u>EmployeeNum</u>, <u>PositionID</u>, LastName, PositionDesc, StartDate, HealthPlan, PlanDesc)

Figure A-11	A table combining fields from three tables

primary key

Employee

EmployeeNum	PositionID	LastName	PositionDesc	StartDate	HealthPlan	PlanDesc
2173	2	Hennessey	Manager	12/14/2011	B	Managed HMO
4519	1	Noordsy	Director	04/23/2013	A	Managed PPO
4519	3	Noordsy	Analyst	11/11/2007	A	Managed PPO
8005	3	Amidon	Analyst	06/05/2012	C	Health Savings
8005	4	Amidon	Clerk	07/02/2010	C	Health Savings
8112	1	Wandzell	Director	12/15/2012	A	Managed PPO
8112	2	Wandzell	Manager	10/04/2011	A	Managed PPO

The modified Employee table combines several fields from the Employee, Position, and Employment tables that appeared in Figure A-6. The EmployeeNum and LastName fields are from the Employee table. The PositionID and PositionDesc fields are from the Position table. The EmployeeNum, PositionID, and StartDate fields are from the Employment table. The HealthPlan and PlanDesc fields are new fields for the Employee table, whose primary key is now the combination of the EmployeeNum and PositionID fields.

In the Employee table, each field is related to other fields. To determine field relationships, you ask "Does a value for a particular field give me a single value for another field?" If the answer is Yes, then the two fields are related. For example, a value for the EmployeeNum field determines a single value for the LastName field, and a value for the LastName field depends on the value of the EmployeeNum field. In database discussions, the word *functionally* is used, as in: "EmployeeNum functionally determines LastName" and "LastName is functionally dependent on EmployeeNum." In this case, EmployeeNum is called a determinant. A **determinant** is a field, or a collection of fields, whose values determine the values of another field. A field is functionally dependent on another field (or a collection of fields) if that other field is a determinant for it.

You can graphically show a table's functional dependencies and determinants in a **bubble diagram**; a bubble diagram is also called a **data model diagram** and a **functional dependency diagram**. Figure A-12 shows the bubble diagram for the Employee table shown in Figure A-11.

| **Figure A-12** | **A bubble diagram for the modified Employee table** |

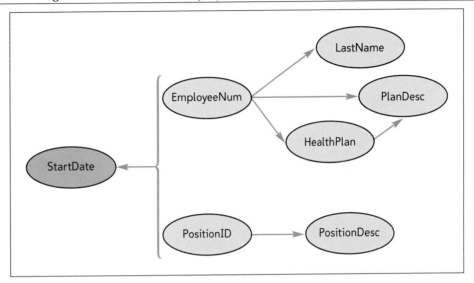

You can read the bubble diagram in Figure A-12 as follows:

- The EmployeeNum field is a determinant for the LastName, HealthPlan, and PlanDesc fields.
- The PositionID field is a determinant for the PositionDesc field.
- The StartDate field is functionally dependent on the EmployeeNum and PositionID fields together.
- The HealthPlan field is a determinant for the PlanDesc field.

Note that EmployeeNum and PositionID together is a determinant for the StartDate field and for all fields that depend on the EmployeeNum field alone and the PositionID field alone. Some experts include these additional fields and some don't. The previous list of determinants does not include these additional fields.

An alternative way to show determinants is to list the determinant, a right arrow, and then the dependent fields, separated by commas. Using this alternative, the determinants shown in Figure A-12 are:

EmployeeNum → LastName, HealthPlan, PlanDesc
PositionID → PositionDesc
EmployeeNum, PositionID → StartDate
HealthPlan → PlanDesc

Only the StartDate field is functionally dependent on the table's full primary key, the EmployeeNum and PositionID fields. The LastName, HealthPlan, and PlanDesc fields have partial dependencies because they are functionally dependent on the EmployeeNum field, which is part of the primary key. A **partial dependency** is a functional dependency on part of the primary key, instead of the entire primary key. Does another partial dependency exist in the Employee table? Yes, the PositionDesc field has a partial dependency on the PositionID field.

Because the EmployeeNum field is a determinant of both the HealthPlan and PlanDesc fields, and the HealthPlan field is a determinant of the PlanDesc field, the HealthPlan and PlanDesc fields have a transitive dependency. A **transitive dependency** is a functional dependency between two nonkey fields, which are both dependent on a third field.

How do you know which functional dependencies exist among a collection of fields, and how do you recognize partial and transitive dependencies? The answers lie with the questions you ask as you gather the requirements for a database application. For each field and entity, you must gain an accurate understanding of its meaning and relationships in the context of the application. **Semantic object modeling** is an entire area of study within the database field devoted to the meanings and relationships of data.

Anomalies

When you use a DBMS, you are more likely to get results you can trust if you create your tables carefully. For example, problems might occur with tables that have partial and transitive dependencies, whereas you won't have as much trouble if you ensure that your tables include only fields that are directly related to each other. Also, when you remove data redundancy from a table, you improve that table. **Data redundancy** occurs when you store the same data in more than one place.

The problems caused by data redundancy and by partial and transitive dependencies are called **anomalies** because they are undesirable irregularities of tables. Anomalies are of three types: insertion, deletion, and update.

To examine the effects of these anomalies, consider the modified Employee table that is shown again in Figure A-13.

| Figure A-13 | A table with insertion, deletion, and update anomalies |

primary key

Employee

EmployeeNum	PositionID	LastName	PositionDesc	StartDate	HealthPlan	PlanDesc
2173	2	Hennessey	Manager	12/14/2011	B	Managed HMO
4519	1	Noordsy	Director	04/23/2013	A	Managed PPO
4519	3	Noordsy	Analyst	11/11/2007	A	Managed PPO
8005	3	Amidon	Analyst	06/05/2012	C	Health Savings
8005	4	Amidon	Clerk	07/02/2010	C	Health Savings
8112	1	Wandzell	Director	12/15/2012	A	Managed PPO
8112	2	Wandzell	Manager	10/04/2011	A	Managed PPO

- An **insertion anomaly** occurs when you cannot add a record to a table because you do not know the entire primary key value. For example, you cannot add the new employee Cathy Corbett with an EmployeeNum of 3322 to the Employee table if you do not know her position in the company. Entity integrity prevents you from leaving any part of a primary key null. Because the PositionID field is part of the primary key, you cannot leave it null. To add the new employee, your only option is to make up a PositionID field value, until you determine the correct position. This solution misrepresents the facts and is unacceptable, if a better approach is available.

- A **deletion anomaly** occurs when you delete data from a table and unintentionally lose other critical data. For example, if you delete EmployeeNum 2173 because Hennessey is no longer an employee, you also lose the only instance of HealthPlan B in the database. Thus, you no longer know that HealthPlan B is the "Managed HMO" plan.
- An **update anomaly** occurs when you change one field value and either the DBMS must make more than one change to the database or else the database ends up containing inconsistent data. For example, if you change a LastName, HealthPlan, or PlanDesc field value for EmployeeNum 8005, the DBMS must change multiple rows of the Employee table. If the DBMS fails to change all the rows, the LastName, HealthPlan, or PlanDesc field now has different values in the database and is inconsistent.

Normalization

Database design is the process of determining the content and structure of data in a database in order to support some activity on behalf of a user or group of users. After you have determined the collection of fields users need to support an activity, you need to determine the precise tables needed for the collection of fields and then place those fields into the correct tables. Crucial to good database design is understanding the functional dependencies of all fields; recognizing the anomalies caused by data redundancy, partial dependencies, and transitive dependencies when they exist; and knowing how to eliminate the anomalies. Failure to eliminate anomalies leads to data redundancy and can cause data integrity and other problems as your database grows in size.

The process of identifying and eliminating anomalies is called **normalization**. Using normalization, you start with a collection of tables, apply sets of rules to eliminate anomalies, and produce a new collection of problem-free tables. The sets of rules are called **normal forms**. Of special interest for our purposes are the first three normal forms: first normal form, second normal form, and third normal form. First normal form improves the design of your tables, second normal form improves the first normal form design, and third normal form applies even more stringent rules to produce an even better design. Note that normal forms beyond third normal form exist; these higher normal forms can improve a database design in some situations but won't be covered in this section.

First Normal Form

Consider the Employee table shown in Figure A-14. For each employee, the table contains EmployeeNum, which is the primary key; the employee's first name, last name, health plan code and description; and the ID, description, pay grade, and start date of each position held by the employee. For example, Barbara Hennessey has held one position, while the other three employees have held two positions. Because each entry in a table must contain a single value, the structure shown in Figure A-14 does not meet the requirements for a table, or relation; therefore, it is called an **unnormalized relation**. The set of fields that includes the PositionID, PositionDesc, PayGrade, and StartDate fields, which can have more than one value, is called a **repeating group**.

Repeating groups of data in an unnormalized Employee table

repeating group

Employee

EmployeeNum	PositionID	FirstName	LastName	PositionDesc	PayGrade	StartDate	HealthPlan	PlanDesc
2173	2	Barbara	Hennessey	Manager	40	12/14/2011	B	Managed HMO
4519	1 3	Lee	Noordsy	Director Analyst	45 30	04/23/2013 11/11/2007	A	Managed PPO
8005	3 4	Pat	Amidon	Analyst Clerk	30 20	06/05/2012 07/02/2010	C	Health Savings
8112	1 2	Chris	Wandzell	Director Manager	45 40	12/15/2012 10/04/2011	A	Managed PPO

First normal form addresses this repeating-group situation. A table is in **first normal form (1NF)** if it does not contain repeating groups. To remove a repeating group and convert to first normal form, you expand the primary key to include the primary key of the repeating group, forming a composite key. Performing the conversion step produces the 1NF table shown in Figure A-15.

After conversion to 1NF

primary key

Employee

EmployeeNum	PositionID	FirstName	LastName	PositionDesc	PayGrade	StartDate	HealthPlan	PlanDesc
2173	2	Barbara	Hennessey	Manager	40	12/14/2011	B	Managed HMO
4519	1	Lee	Noordsy	Director	45	04/23/2013	A	Managed PPO
4519	3	Lee	Noordsy	Analyst	30	11/11/2007	A	Managed PPO
8005	3	Pat	Amidon	Analyst	30	06/05/2012	C	Health Savings
8005	4	Pat	Amidon	Clerk	20	07/02/2010	C	Health Savings
8112	1	Chris	Wandzell	Director	45	12/15/2012	A	Managed PPO
8112	2	Chris	Wandzell	Manager	40	10/04/2011	A	Managed PPO

The alternative way to describe the 1NF table is:

Employee (EmployeeNum, PositionID, FirstName, LastName, PositionDesc, PayGrade, StartDate, HealthPlan, PlanDesc)

The Employee table is now a true table and has a composite key. The table, however, suffers from insertion, deletion, and update anomalies. (As an exercise, find examples of the three anomalies in the table.) The EmployeeNum field is a determinant for the FirstName, LastName, HealthPlan, and PlanDesc fields, so partial dependencies exist in the Employee table. It is these partial dependencies that cause the anomalies in the Employee table, and second normal form addresses the partial-dependency problem.

Second Normal Form

A table in 1NF is in **second normal form (2NF)** if it does not contain any partial dependencies. To remove partial dependencies from a table and convert it to second normal form, you perform two steps. First, identify the functional dependencies for every field in the table. Second, if necessary, create new tables and place each field in a table, so that the field is functionally dependent on the entire primary key, not part of the primary key. If you need to create new tables, restrict them to ones with a primary key that is a subset of the original composite key. Note that partial dependencies occur only when you have a composite key; a table in first normal form with a single-field primary key is automatically in second normal form.

First, identifying the functional dependencies leads to the following determinants for the Employee table:

EmployeeNum → FirstName, LastName, HealthPlan, PlanDesc
PositionID → PositionDesc, PayGrade
EmployeeNum, PositionID → StartDate
HealthPlan → PlanDesc

The EmployeeNum field is a determinant for the FirstName, LastName, HealthPlan, and PlanDesc fields. The PositionID field is a determinant for the PositionDesc and PayGrade fields. The HealthPlan field is a determinant for the PlanDesc field. The composite key EmployeeNum and PositionID is a determinant for the StartDate field. Performing the second step in the conversion from first normal form to second form produces the three 2NF tables shown in Figure A-16.

Figure A-16	After conversion to 2NF

Employee

primary key →

EmployeeNum	FirstName	LastName	HealthPlan	PlanDesc
2173	Barbara	Hennessey	B	Managed HMO
4519	Lee	Noordsy	A	Managed PPO
8005	Pat	Amidon	C	Health Savings
8112	Chris	Wandzell	A	Managed PPO

Position

primary key →

PositionID	PositionDesc	PayGrade
1	Director	45
2	Manager	40
3	Analyst	30
4	Clerk	20

primary key

Employment

EmployeeNum	PositionID	StartDate
2173	2	12/14/2011
4519	1	04/23/2013
4519	3	11/11/2007
8005	3	06/05/2012
8005	4	07/02/2010
8112	1	12/15/2012
8112	2	10/04/2011

The alternative way to describe the 2NF tables is:

Employee (<u>EmployeeNum</u>, FirstName, LastName, HealthPlan, PlanDesc)
Position (<u>PositionID</u>, PositionDesc, PayGrade)
Employment (<u>EmployeeNum</u>, <u>PositionID</u>, StartDate)
    Foreign key: EmployeeNum to Employee table
    Foreign key: PositionID to Position table

All three tables are in second normal form. Do anomalies still exist? The Position and Employment tables show no anomalies, but the Employee table suffers from anomalies caused by the transitive dependency between the HealthPlan and PlanDesc fields. (As an exercise, find examples of the three anomalies caused by the transitive dependency.) That is, the HealthPlan field is a determinant for the PlanDesc field, and the EmployeeNum field is a determinant for the HealthPlan and PlanDesc fields. Third normal form addresses the transitive-dependency problem.

Third Normal Form

A table in 2NF is in **third normal form (3NF)** if every determinant is a candidate key. This definition for 3NF is referred to as **Boyce-Codd normal form (BCNF)** and is an improvement over the original version of 3NF. What are the determinants in the Employee table? The EmployeeNum and HealthPlan fields are the determinants; however, the EmployeeNum field is a candidate key because it's the table's primary key, and the HealthPlan field is not a candidate key. Therefore, the Employee table is in second normal form, but it is not in third normal form.

To convert a table to third normal form, remove the fields that depend on the non-candidate-key determinant and place them into a new table with the determinant as the primary key. For the Employee table, the PlanDesc field depends on the HealthPlan field, which is a non-candidate-key determinant. Thus, you remove the PlanDesc field from the table, create a new HealthBenefits table, place the PlanDesc field in the HealthBenefits table, and then make the HealthPlan field the primary key of the HealthBenefits table. Note that only the PlanDesc field is removed from the Employee table; the HealthPlan field remains as a foreign key in the Employee table. Figure A-17 shows the database design for the four 3NF tables.

Figure A-17   After conversion to 3NF

Employee

primary key →

EmployeeNum	FirstName	LastName	HealthPlan
2173	Barbara	Hennessey	B
4519	Lee	Noordsy	A
8005	Pat	Amidon	C
8112	Chris	Wandzell	A

HealthBenefits

primary key →

HealthPlan	PlanDesc
A	Managed PPO
B	Managed HMO
C	Health Savings

Position

primary key

PositionID	PositionDesc	PayGrade
1	Director	45
2	Manager	40
3	Analyst	30
4	Clerk	20

primary key

Employment

EmployeeNum	PositionID	StartDate
2173	2	12/14/2011
4519	1	04/23/2013
4519	3	11/11/2007
8005	3	06/05/2012
8005	4	07/02/2010
8112	1	12/15/2012
8112	2	10/04/2011

The alternative way to describe the 3NF relations is:

HealthBenefits (HealthPlan, PlanDesc)
Employee (EmployeeNum, FirstName, LastName, HealthPlan)
   Foreign key: HealthPlan to HealthBenefits table
Position (PositionID, PositionDesc, PayGrade)
Employment (EmployeeNum, PositionID, StartDate)
   Foreign key: EmployeeNum to Employee table
   Foreign key: PositionID to Position table

The four tables have no anomalies because you have eliminated all the data redundancy, partial dependencies, and transitive dependencies. Normalization provides the framework for eliminating anomalies and delivering an optimal database design, which you should always strive to achieve. You should be aware, however, that experts sometimes denormalize tables to improve database performance—specifically, to decrease the time it takes the database to respond to a user's commands and requests. Typically, when you denormalize tables, you combine separate tables into one table to reduce the need for the DBMS to join the separate tables to process queries and other informational requests. When you denormalize a table, you reintroduce redundancy to the table. At the same time, you reintroduce anomalies. Thus, improving performance exposes a database to potential integrity problems. Only database experts should denormalize tables, but even experts first complete the normalization of their tables.

Natural, Artificial, and Surrogate Keys

When you complete the design of a database, your tables should be in third normal form, free of anomalies and redundancy. Some tables, such as the State table (see Figure A-2), have obvious third normal form designs with obvious primary keys. The State table's description is:

State (<u>StateAbbrev</u>, StateName, EnteredUnionOrder, StateBird, StatePopulation)

Recall that the candidate keys for the State table are StateAbbrev, StateName, and EnteredUnionOrder. Choosing the StateAbbrev field as the State table's primary key makes the StateName and EnteredUnionOrder fields alternate keys. Primary keys such as the StateAbbrev field are sometimes called natural keys. A **natural key** (also called a **logical key** or an **intelligent key**) is a primary key that consists of a field, or a collection of fields, that is an inherent characteristic of the entity described by the table and that is visible to users. Other examples of natural keys are the ISBN (International Standard Book Number) for a book, the SSN (Social Security number) for a U.S. individual, the UPC (Universal Product Code) for a product, and the VIN (vehicle identification number) for a vehicle.

Is the PositionID field, which is the primary key for the Position table (see Figure A-17), a natural key? No, the PositionID field is not an inherent characteristic of a position. Instead, the PositionID field has been added to the Position table only as a way to identify each position uniquely. The PositionID field is an **artificial key**, which is a field that you add to a table to serve solely as the primary key and that is visible to users.

Another reason for using an artificial key arises in tables that allow duplicate records. Although relational database theory and most experts do not allow duplicate records in a table, consider a database that tracks donors and their donations. Figure A-18 shows a Donor table with an artificial key of DonorID and with the DonorFirstName and DonorLastName fields. Some cash donations are anonymous, which accounts for the fourth record in the Donor table. Figure A-18 also shows the Donation table with the DonorID field, a foreign key to the Donor table, and the DonationDate and DonationAmt fields.

Donor

DonorID	DonorFirstName	DonorLastName
1	Christina	Chang
2	Franco	Diaz
3	Angie	Diaz
4		Anonymous
5	Tracy	Burns

primary key

Donation

DonorID	DonationDate	DonationAmt
1	10/12/2013	$50.00
1	09/30/2014	$50.00
2	10/03/2014	$75.00
4	10/10/2014	$50.00
4	10/10/2014	$50.00
4	10/11/2014	$25.00
5	10/13/2014	$50.00

duplicate records

What is the primary key of the Donation table? No single field is unique, and neither is any combination of fields. For example, on 10/10/2014, two anonymous donors (DonorID value of 4) donated $50 each. You need to add an artificial key, DonationID for example, to the Donation table. The addition of the artificial key makes every record in the Donation table unique, as shown in Figure A-19.

Donation

artificial key

DonationID	DonorID	DonationDate	DonationAmt
1	1	10/12/2013	$50.00
2	1	09/30/2014	$50.00
3	2	10/03/2014	$75.00
4	4	10/10/2014	$50.00
5	4	10/10/2014	$50.00
6	4	10/11/2014	$25.00
7	5	10/13/2014	$50.00

The descriptions of the Donor and Donation tables now are:

Donor (<u>DonorID</u>, DonorFirstName, DonorLastName)
Donation (<u>DonationID</u>, DonorID, DonationDate, DonationAmt)
   Foreign key: DonorID to Donor table

For another common situation, consider the 3NF tables you reviewed in the previous section (see Figure A-17) that have the following descriptions:

HealthBenefits (<u>HealthPlan</u>, PlanDesc)
Employee (<u>EmployeeNum</u>, FirstName, LastName, HealthPlan)
   Foreign key: HealthPlan to HealthBenefits table
Position (<u>PositionID</u>, PositionDesc, PayGrade)
Employment (<u>EmployeeNum</u>, <u>PositionID</u>, StartDate)
   Foreign key: EmployeeNum to Employee table
   Foreign key: PositionID to Position table

Recall that a primary key must be unique, must be minimal, and must not change in value. In theory, primary keys don't change in value. However, in practice, you might have to change EmployeeNum field values that you incorrectly entered in the Employment table. Further, if you need to change an EmployeeNum field value in the Employee table, the change must cascade to the EmployeeNum field values in the Employment table. Also, changes to a PositionID field value in the Position table must cascade to the Employment table. For these and other reasons, many experts add surrogate keys to their tables. A **surrogate key** (also called a **synthetic key**) is a system-generated primary key that is hidden from users. Usually you can use an automatic numbering data type, such as the Access AutoNumber data type, for a surrogate key. Figure A-20 shows the four tables with surrogate keys added to each table.

Figure A-20 Using surrogate keys

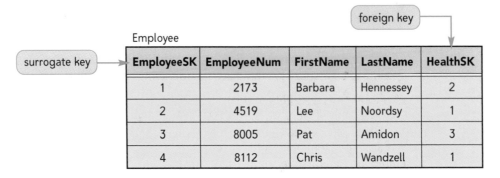

Employee

EmployeeSK	EmployeeNum	FirstName	LastName	HealthSK
1	2173	Barbara	Hennessey	2
2	4519	Lee	Noordsy	1
3	8005	Pat	Amidon	3
4	8112	Chris	Wandzell	1

HealthBenefits

HealthSK	HealthPlan	PlanDesc
1	A	Managed PPO
2	B	Managed HMO
3	C	Health Savings

Position

PositionID	PositionDesc	PayGrade
1	Director	45
2	Manager	40
3	Analyst	30
4	Clerk	20

Employment

EmploymentSK	EmployeeSK	PositionID	StartDate
1	1	2	12/14/2011
2	2	1	04/23/2013
3	2	3	11/11/2007
4	3	3	06/05/2012
5	3	4	07/02/2010
6	4	1	12/15/2012
7	4	2	10/04/2011

The HealthSK field replaces the HealthPlan field as a foreign key in the Employee table, and the EmployeeSK field replaces the EmployeeNum field in the Employment table. When you change an incorrectly entered EmployeeNum field value in the Employee table, you don't need to cascade the change to the Employment table. When you change an incorrectly entered HealthPlan field value in the HealthBenefits table, you don't need to cascade the change to the Employee table.

As you design a database, you should *not* consider the use of surrogate keys, and you should use an artificial key only for the rare table that has duplicate records. At the point when you implement a database, you might choose to use artificial and surrogate keys, but be aware that database experts debate their use and effectiveness. Some of the trade-offs between natural and surrogate keys that you need to consider are:

- Use surrogate keys to avoid cascading updates to foreign key values. Surrogate keys can also replace lengthier foreign keys when those foreign keys reference composite fields.
- You don't need a surrogate key for a table whose primary key is not used as a foreign key in another table because cascading updates is not an issue.
- Tables with surrogate keys require more joins than do tables with natural keys. For example, if you need to know all employees with a HealthPlan field value of A, the surrogate key in Figure A-20 requires that you join the Employee and HealthBenefits tables to answer the question. Using natural keys as shown in Figure A-17, the HealthPlan field appears in the Employee table, so no join is necessary.
- Although surrogate keys are meant to be hidden from users, they cannot be hidden from users who create SQL statements and use other ad hoc tools.
- Because you need a unique index for the natural key and a unique index for the surrogate key, your database size is larger and index maintenance takes more time when you use a surrogate key. On the other hand, a foreign key using a surrogate key is usually smaller than a foreign key using a natural key, especially when the natural key is a composite key, so those indexes are smaller and faster to access for lookups and joins.

Microsoft Access Naming Conventions

In the early 1980s, Microsoft's Charles Simonyi introduced an identifier naming convention that became known as Hungarian notation. Microsoft and other companies use this naming convention for variable, control, and other object naming in Basic, Visual Basic, and other programming languages. When Access was introduced in the early 1990s, Stan Leszynski and Greg Reddick adapted Hungarian notation for Microsoft Access databases; their guidelines became known as the Leszynski/Reddick naming conventions. In recent years, the Leszynski naming conventions, the Reddick naming conventions, and other naming conventions have been published. Individuals and companies have created their own Access naming conventions, but many are based on the Leszynski/Reddick naming conventions, as are the naming conventions covered in this section.

An Access database can contain thousands of objects, fields, controls, and other items, and keeping track of their names and what they represent is a difficult task. Consequently, you should use naming conventions that identify the type and purpose of each item in an Access database. You can use naming conventions that identify items generally or very specifically.

For objects, include a prefix tag to identify the type of object, as shown in Figure A-21. In each example in Figure A-21, the final object name consists of a three-character tag prefixed to the base object name. For example, the form name of frmEmployeesAndPositions consists of the frm tag and the EmployeesAndPositions base form name.

Figure A-21   Object naming tags

Object type	Tag	Example
Form	frm	frmEmployeesAndPositions
Macro	mcr	mcrSwitchboard
Module	bas	basCalculations
Query	qry	qryEmployee
Report	rpt	rptEmployeesAndPositions
Table	tbl	tblEmployee

The tags in Figure A-21 identify each object type in general. If you want to identify object types more specifically, you could expand Figure A-21 to include tags such as fsub for a subform, qxtb for a crosstab query, tlkp for a lookup table, rsub for a subreport, and so on.

For controls in forms and reports, a general naming convention uses lbl as a prefix tag for labels and ctl as a prefix tag for other types of controls. For more specific naming conventions for controls, you'd use a specific prefix tag for each type of control. Figure A-22 shows the prefix tag for some common controls in forms and reports.

Figure A-22   Control naming tags

Control type	Tag
Check box	chk
Combo box	cbo
Command button	cmd
Image	img
Label	lbl
Line	lin
List box	lst
Option button	opt
PivotTable	pvt
Rectangle	shp
Subform/Subreport	sub
Text box	txt

Some database developers use a prefix tag for each field name to identify the field's data type (for example, dtm for Date/Time, num for Number, and chr for Text or Character), others use a prefix tag for each field name to identify in which table the field is located (for example, emp for the Employee table and pos for the Position table), and still others don't use a prefix tag for field names.

You might use suffix tags for controls that might otherwise have identical names. For example, if you have two text boxes in a form for calculated controls that display the average and the sum of the OrderAmt field, both could legitimately be named txtOrderAmt unless you used suffix tags to name them txtOrderAmtAvg and txtOrderAmtSum.

You should ensure that any name you use does not duplicate a property name or any keyword Access reserves for special purposes. In general, you can avoid property and keyword name conflicts by using two-word field, control, and object names. For example, use StudentName instead of Name, and use OrderDate instead of Date to avoid name conflicts.

All database developers avoid spaces in names, mainly because spaces are not allowed in server DBMSs, such as SQL Server, Oracle, and DB2. If you are prototyping a Microsoft Access database that you'll migrate to one of these server DBMSs, or if future requirements might force a migration, you should restrict your Access identifier names so that they conform to the rules common to them all. Figure A-23 shows the identifier naming rules for Access, SQL Server, Oracle, and DB2.

| Figure A-23 | Identifier naming rules for common database management systems |

Identifier naming rule	Access	SQL Server	Oracle	DB2
Maximum character length	64	30	30	30
Allowable characters	Letters, digits, space, and special characters, except for period (.), exclamation point (!), accent grave ('), and square brackets ([ ])	Letters, digits, dollar sign ($), underscore (_), number symbol (#), and at symbol (@)	Letters, digits, dollar sign ($), underscore (_), and number symbol (#)	Letters, digits, at symbol (@), dollar sign ($), underscore (_), and number symbol (#)
Special rules		No spaces; first character must be a letter or at symbol (@)	No spaces; first character must be a letter; stored in the database in uppercase	No spaces; first character must be a letter, at symbol (@), dollar sign ($), or number symbol (#); stored in the database in uppercase

PRACTICE

Review Assignments

1. What are the formal names for a table, for a row, and for a column? What are the popular names for a row and for a column?
2. What is a domain?
3. What is an entity?
4. What is the relationship between a primary key and a candidate key?
5. What is a composite key?
6. What is a foreign key?
7. Look for an example of a one-to-one relationship, an example of a one-to-many relationship, and an example of a many-to-many relationship in a newspaper, magazine, book, or everyday situation you encounter. For each one, name the entities and select the primary and foreign keys.
8. When do you use an entity subtype?
9. What is a composite entity in an entity-relationship diagram?
10. What is the entity integrity constraint?
11. What is referential integrity?
12. What does the cascades option, which is used with referential integrity, accomplish?
13. What are partial and transitive dependencies?
14. What three types of anomalies can be exhibited by a table, and what problems do they cause?
15. Figure A-24 shows the Employee, Position, and Employment tables with primary keys EmployeeNum, PositionID, and both EmployeeNum and PositionID, respectively. Which two integrity constraints do these tables violate and why?

Figure A-24   Integrity constraint violations

Employee

EmployeeNum	FirstName	LastName	HealthPlan
2173	Barbara	Hennessey	B
4519	Lee	Noordsy	A
8005	Pat	Amidon	C
8112	Chris	Wandzell	A

Position

PositionID	PositionDesc	PayGrade
1	Director	45
2	Manager	40
3	Analyst	30
4	Clerk	20

Employment

EmployeeNum	PositionID	StartDate
2173	2	12/14/2011
4519	1	04/23/2013
4519		11/11/2007
8005	3	06/05/2012
8005	4	07/02/2010
8112	1	12/15/2012
9876	2	10/04/2011

16. The State and City tables, shown in Figure A-4, are described as follows:
    State (StateAbbrev, StateName, EnteredUnionOrder, StateBird, StatePopulation)
    City (StateAbbrev, CityName, CityPopulation)
         Foreign key: StateAbbrev to State table
    Add the field named CountyName for the county or counties in a state containing the city to this database, justify where you placed it (that is, in an existing table or in a new one), and draw the entity-relationship diagram for all the entities. Counties for some of the cities shown in Figure A-4 are Travis and Williamson counties for Austin TX; Hartford county for Hartford CT; Clinton, Eaton, and Ingham counties for Lansing MI; Davidson county for Nashville TN; Hughes county for Pierre SD; and Nueces and San Patricio counties for Portland TX.

17. Suppose you have a table for a dance studio. The fields are dancer's identification number, dancer's name, dancer's address, dancer's telephone number, class identification number, day that the class meets, time that the class meets, instructor name, and instructor identification number. Assume that each dancer takes one class, each class meets only once a week and has one instructor, and each instructor can teach

more than one class. In what normal form is the table currently, given the following alternative description?

Dancer (<u>DancerID</u>, DancerName, DancerAddr, DancerPhone, ClassID, ClassDay, ClassTime, InstrName, InstrID)

Convert this relation to 3NF and represent the design using the alternative description method.

18. Store the following fields for a library database: AuthorCode, AuthorName, BookTitle, BorrowerAddress, BorrowerName, BorrowerCardNumber, CopiesOfBook, ISBN (International Standard Book Number), LoanDate, PublisherCode, PublisherName, and PublisherAddress. A one-to-many relationship exists between publishers and books. Many-to-many relationships exist between authors and books and between borrowers and books.

a. Name the entities for the library database.

b. Create the tables for the library database and describe them using the alternative method. Be sure the tables are in third normal form.

c. Draw an entity-relationship diagram for the library database.

19. In the database shown in Figure A-25, which consists of the Department and Employee tables, add one record to the end of the Employee table that violates both the entity integrity constraint and the referential integrity constraint.

Figure A-25   **Creating integrity constraint violations**

Department

DeptID	DeptName	Location
M	Marketing	New York
R	Research	Houston
S	Sales	Chicago

Employee

EmployeeID	EmployeeName	DeptID
1111	Sue	R
2222	Pam	M
3333	Bob	S
4444	Chris	S
5555	Pat	R
6666	Meg	R

20. Consider the following table:

    Patient (PatientID, PatientName, BalanceOwed, DoctorID, DoctorName,
        ServiceCode, ServiceDesc, ServiceFee, ServiceDate)

    This is a table concerning data about patients of doctors at a clinic and the services the doctors perform for their patients. The following dependencies exist in the Patient table:

    PatientID → PatientName, BalanceOwed

    DoctorID → DoctorName

    ServiceCode → ServiceDesc, ServiceFee

    PatientID, DoctorID, ServiceCode → PatientName, BalanceOwed, DoctorName,
        ServiceDesc, ServiceFee, ServiceDate

    a. Based on the dependencies, convert the Patient table to first normal form.

    b. Next, convert the Patient table to third normal form.

21. Suppose you need to track data for mountain climbing expeditions. Each member of an expedition is called a climber, and one of the climbers is named to lead an expedition. Climbers can be members of many expeditions over time. The climbers in each expedition attempt to ascend one or more peaks by scaling one of the many faces of the peaks. The data you need to track includes the name of the expedition, the leader of the expedition, and comments about the expedition; the first name, last name, nationality, birth date, death date, and comments about each climber; the name, location, height, and comments about each peak; the name and comments about each face of a peak; comments about each climber for each expedition; and the highest height reached and the date for each ascent attempt by a climber on a face with commentary.

    a. Create the tables for the expedition database and describe them using the alternative method. Be sure the tables are in third normal form.

    b. Draw an entity-relationship diagram for the expedition database.

22. What is the difference among natural, artificial, and surrogate keys?

23. Why should you use naming conventions for the identifiers in a database?

ENDING DATA FILES

There are no ending Data Files for this appendix.

OBJECTIVES

- Learn about the Microsoft Office Specialist certification program
- Work in Backstage view to save database objects
- Hide, unhide, and unfreeze fields
- Change the page size and orientation of a report
- Apply application parts
- Split, merge, insert, and move controls
- Apply quick styles to and modify the shape of command buttons and tabs
- Apply background images
- Add hyperlinks to forms and reports
- Convert a macro to Visual Basic

Microsoft Office Specialist Certification Skills

This appendix provides information about the Microsoft Office Specialist certification program and the benefits of achieving certification. The appendix also presents coverage of additional skills related to the Microsoft Office Specialist exam for Microsoft Access 2010 that are not covered in the main tutorials of this text. Finally, the appendix includes a grid showing where the skills for the Access 2010 exam are covered in this text.

STARTING DATA FILES

AppendixB

Seasonal.accdb

What Is Microsoft Office Specialist Certification?

Certification is a growing trend in the Information Technology industry whereby a software or hardware company devises and administers exams for users that enable them to demonstrate their ability to use the software or hardware effectively. By passing a certification exam, users prove their competence and knowledge of the software or hardware to prospective employers and colleagues.

The Microsoft Office Specialist program is the only comprehensive, performance-based certification program approved by Microsoft to validate desktop computer skills using the Microsoft Office 2010 programs, including Microsoft Access. The program provides computer program literacy, measures proficiency, and identifies opportunities for skill enhancement. Successful candidates receive a certificate that sets them apart from their peers in the competitive job market. The certificate is a valuable credential, recognized worldwide as proof that an individual has the desktop computing skills needed to work productively and efficiently. Certification is a valuable asset to individuals who want to begin or advance their computer careers.

The Microsoft Office Specialist exams are developed, marketed, and administered by Certiport, Inc., a company that has an exclusive license from Microsoft. Exams must be taken at an authorized Certiport Center, which administers exams in a quiet room with the proper hardware and software and has trained personnel to manage and proctor the exams.

Go to www.microsoft.com/learning/en/us/certification/mos.aspx#certifications to access the Microsoft Office Specialist Certification page, as shown in Figure B-1.

| Figure B-1 | Microsoft Office Specialist Certification page |

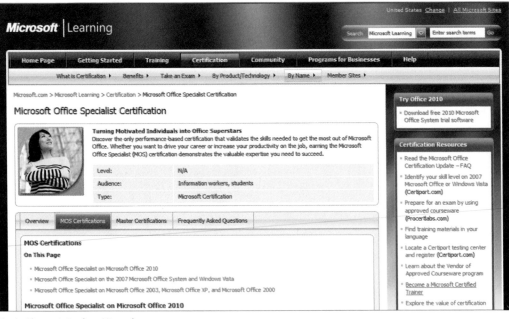

Used with permission from Microsoft.

TIP

For more information about the exams, view the FAQ documents at www.microsoft.com/certification or www.certiport.com/portal.

Benefits of Achieving Certification

Achieving Microsoft Office Specialist certification in one or several of the Microsoft Office 2010 programs can be beneficial to you and your current or prospective employer. Earning certification acknowledges that you have the expertise to work with Microsoft Office programs. Individuals who are Microsoft Office Specialist certified report increased competence and productivity with Microsoft Office programs, as well as increased credibility with their employers, coworkers, and clients. Certification sets you apart in today's competitive job market, bringing employment opportunities, greater earning potential and career advancement, and increased job satisfaction.

Certification can help you increase your productivity within your current job and is a great way to enhance your skills without taking courses to obtain a new degree. Another benefit of Microsoft certification is that you gain access to a member website, career-building tools, and training. More information about the certification series can be located on the Certiport web site at www.certiport.com/portal, as shown in Figure B-2.

Figure B-2	Certification information on the Certiport site

Courtesy of Certiport, Inc. www.certiport.com

Certification Process

TIP

Course Technology publishes a multitude of Microsoft Office 2010 products that you can use for self-study. Visit www. cengagebrain.com to view the options. You can also purchase the texts directly from this site.

The steps to successfully completing Microsoft Office Specialist (Core) Certification for Microsoft Access are outlined below. The core-level user should be able to create professional-looking documents for a variety of business, school, and personal situations. The core-level user should be able to use about 80% of the features of the program. Note that the Web addresses shown throughout might change. If you cannot find what you're looking for, go to the main site (www.microsoft.com or www.certiport.com) to search for a topic.

1. Find an authorized testing center near you using the Certiport Center locator at www.certiport.com/Portal/Pages/LocatorView.aspx.
2. Prepare for the exam by selecting the method that is appropriate for you, including taking a class or purchasing self-study materials.
3. Take a practice test (recommended) before taking the exam. To view the practice tests available, go to www.certiport.com/portal. Follow the online instructions for purchasing a voucher and taking the practice test.
4. Contact the Certiport Center and make an appointment for the exam you want to take. Check the organization's payment and exam policies. Purchase an exam voucher at www.certiport.com/portal. Go to the Certiport Center to take the test, and bring a printout of the exam voucher, your Certiport username and password, and a valid picture ID.
5. You will find out your results immediately. If you pass, you will receive your certificate two to three weeks after the date of the exam.

If you do not pass, refunds will not be given. But keep in mind that the exams are challenging and do not become discouraged. If you purchased a voucher with a retake, a second chance to take the exam might be all you need to pass. Check your Certiport Center's exam retake policies for more information.

Saving Database Objects

When you are working in Backstage view in Access, the Save Object As command allows you to save the current object as another object of the same type, such as saving a query with a new name to create another query, or as an object of a different type. For example, you can save a form as a report.

To use the Save Object As command to create a new query based on an existing query:

1. Start Access and open the **Seasonal** database located in the AppendixB folder provided with your Data Files. If the Security Warning opens, click the Enable Content button to close it.

2. In the Navigation Pane, click the **Shutter Bar Open/Close Button** ⟩⟩ to open the pane. The list of database objects appears.

3. In the Queries section of the Navigation Pane, click the **qryHighWageAmounts** query to select it.

    Trouble? If you double-clicked the query by mistake, the query opens in Datasheet view. Close the query and continue with the steps.

    Now you'll switch to Backstage view to create a new query by saving the selected query, qryHighWageAmounts, with a new name.

4. Click the **File** tab to display Backstage view.

5. In the navigation bar, click the **Save Object As** command to open the Save As dialog box. See Figure B-3.

Figure B-3   Save As dialog box

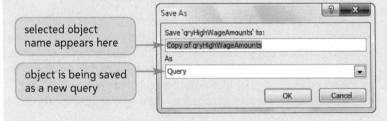

Because the qryHighWageAmounts query is selected in the Navigation Pane, the dialog box displays its name as the object being saved. Note that the As box shows the type of new object being saved—in this case, another query.

6. Replace the highlighted text in the Save to box with the new name **qryHighWageAmountsCT**. You're creating a new query that will show the high wage amounts in the state of Connecticut.

7. Click the **OK** button, and then click the **Home** tab to return to the view of the Seasonal database and its objects. Notice that a new query named qryHighWageAmountsCT appears below the selected qryHighWageAmounts query in the Navigation Pane.

8. Right-click the **qryHighWageAmountsCT** query, and then click **Design View** on the shortcut menu to open the new query in Design view.

9. Scroll the query design grid to the right, and then enter the condition **"CT"** in the Criteria box for the StateProv field. The query will now retrieve records that meet both conditions: a Wage field value greater than or equal to 17 and a StateProv field value of CT.

10. Save and run the query. The results show only the three records with high wage amounts in the state of Connecticut.

11. Close the qryHighWageAmountsCT query.

Hiding and Unhiding Fields

When you are viewing a table or query datasheet in Datasheet view, you might want to remove certain fields from the displayed datasheet to focus on the data you're interested in viewing. The **Hide Fields** command allows you to remove the display of one or more fields, and the **Unhide Fields** command allows you to redisplay any hidden fields.

To hide and unhide fields in a datasheet:

1. In the Navigation Pane, double-click the **tblEmployer** table to open it in Datasheet view.

2. Close the Navigation Pane. To focus the display of the datasheet on the employer and contact data, you can hide the fields related to the employer's address.

3. Right-click the **Address** field name, and then click **Hide Fields** on the shortcut menu. The Address field is no longer displayed in the datasheet. You can also select and hide multiple fields at one time.

4. Click and drag to select the following four field names: **City**, **State/Prov**, **Postal Code**, and **Country**.

5. Right-click any of the selected field names to display the shortcut menu, and then click **Hide Fields**. All five fields related to the employer's address are now hidden.

   To redisplay hidden fields, you use the Unhide Fields command on the shortcut menu.

6. Right-click any field name to display the shortcut menu, and then click **Unhide Fields**. The Unhide Columns dialog box opens. See Figure B-4.

Figure B-4	Unhide Columns dialog box

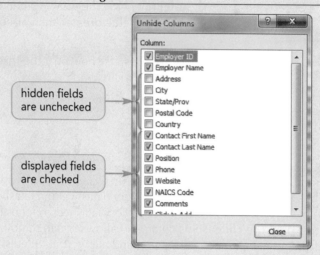

All currently displayed fields are checked in this dialog box, and all hidden fields are unchecked. To redisplay them, you simply click their check boxes to select them.

▶ **7.** Click the check box for each of the following fields: **Address**, **City**, **State/Prov**, **Postal Code**, and **Country**. As you click each check box, the selected field is redisplayed in the datasheet.

▶ **8.** Click the **Close** button to close the Unhide Columns dialog box.

▶ **9.** Right-click any field name to display the shortcut menu. Notice the Freeze Fields and Unfreeze All Fields options. In Tutorial 5 you used the Freeze Fields option to freeze the first three columns of a table. You'd use the Unfreeze All Fields option to unfreeze all columns that you previously froze in a table or query.

▶ **10.** Close the tblEmployer table without saving changes to its layout.

Changing the Page Size and Orientation of a Report

You can modify many layout and formatting aspects of an Access report to suit the data, including the page size and orientation, using options available on the Print Preview tab.

To change the page size and orientation of a report:

▶ **1.** Open the Navigation Pane, and then double-click the **rptEmployerPositions** report in the Report section of the Navigation Pane to open it in Print Preview.

▶ **2.** In the Page Size group on the Print Preview tab, click the **Size** button arrow to display the menu of available page sizes, and then click **Executive**. The report layout changes to fit the smaller page size.

   Trouble? If you do not see the Executive option on the Size menu, select another size option that has dimensions of approximately 7.25 × 10.5.

3. In the Page Layout group, click the **Landscape** button to change the orientation of the report from portrait to landscape. The page is now wider than it is tall.

4. In the Close Preview group, click the **Close Print Preview** button to close the report.

Applying Application Parts

An **application part** is a template containing objects that can be added to an existing database. The template can contain a single object or multiple objects, including relationships. You use the Application Parts gallery to view and add predefined and user-defined templates. You can add your own user-defined template as an application part, so that it'll appear in the Application Parts gallery. To do so, you modify a copy of your existing database until it contains only the objects needed in the template, and then you save and publish it as a template in Backstage view by doing the following:

1. In the navigation bar of Backstage view, click the Save & Publish tab, click Template in the Save Database As pane, and then click the Save As button to open the Create New Template from This Database dialog box.
2. Enter an appropriate name for the template in the Name box, enter an appropriate description in the Description box, click the Application Part check box to specify you also want to create an application part, and then click the Include Data in Template check box to include the data in the Seasonal database in the template. See Figure B-5.

Figure B-5	Create New Template from This Database dialog box

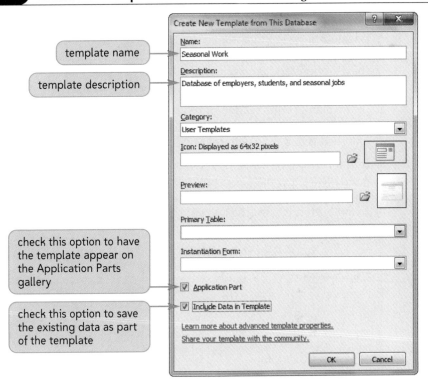

template name

template description

check this option to have the template appear on the Application Parts gallery

check this option to save the existing data as part of the template

3. Click the OK button to create the template, and then click the OK button to close the confirmation message.

You can view the available application parts in the Application Parts gallery and apply one of them to the Seasonal database.

To view and apply an application part:

1. Click the **Create** tab on the Ribbon, and then click the **Application Parts** button in the Templates group to display the Application Parts gallery. See Figure B-6.

Figure B-6   Application Parts gallery

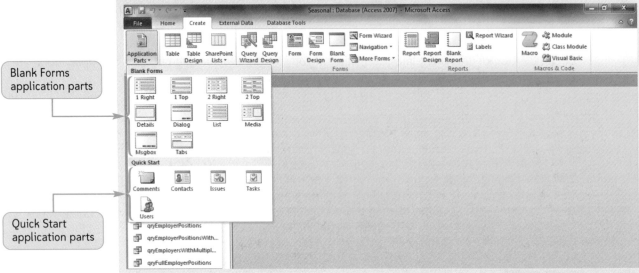

Blank Forms application parts

Quick Start application parts

TIP

If user-defined templates are saved as application parts, they appear in the User Templates section of the gallery. You click a template to add its objects and data to a database.

Predefined templates appear in the Quick Start section of the gallery. You'd click one of the options in this section if you wanted to add the objects from the selected template to an open database. The options in the Blank Forms section of the gallery are application parts consisting of single blank forms; clicking one of these options adds the selected blank form to the currently open database. You'll add one of the blank forms to the Seasonal database.

2. In the Blank Forms section of the Application Parts gallery, click the **1 Right** button. Access adds a form, named SingleOneColumnRightLabels, that will display one record at a time with text boxes to the right of attached labels.

3. In the Navigation Pane, double-click the **SingleOneColumnRightLabels** form. The open form contains four preset labels with text boxes to their right, the default form title of *Form Title*, a command button to save the current record, and a command button to save the current record and then close the form.

4. Close the form.

Manipulating Controls in Forms and Reports

You perform design tasks in Access in the same way whether you are designing a form or a report. The following are some examples:

- In Tutorial 4 you applied conditional formatting to a field in a report, and you can apply conditional formatting to a field in a form in the same way by clicking the field in Layout view, clicking the Conditional Formatting button in the Control Formatting group on the Format tab, clicking the New Rule button, and then filling in the entries in the New Formatting Rule dialog box.
- In Tutorial 6 you added a combo box (drop down) to a form, and you can add a combo box to a report in the same way. In Design view, click the Combo Box tool in the Controls gallery on the Design tab, and then select or enter options in the Combo Box Wizard dialog boxes.
- In Tutorial 8 you learned that you can add a page break to a form by using the Page Break tool, and you can use the same tool in the same way to add a page break to a report. To do so, display the report in Design view, and then click the Insert Page Break button ▦ in the Controls group on the Design tab. Then click the pointer in the location where you want the page break to occur. A short line appears where you click, indicating the location of the page break.
- In Tutorial 8 you embedded a chart (graph) into a form using the Chart Wizard, and you can use the Chart Wizard in the same way to embed a chart in a report.
- In Tutorial 6 you changed the tab order for the controls in a form, and you can change the tab order for the controls in a report in the same way by clicking the Tab Order button in the Tools group on the Design tab in Design view, and then rearranging the controls in the correct order in the Tab Order dialog box.
- In Tutorial 6 you modified the padding and margins for controls in a form, and you can modify the padding and margins in the same way in a report. In Design view, click the Control Padding button and the Control Margins button in the Position group on the Arrange tab.
- In Tutorial 4 you found specific data in a form, and you can find specific data in the same way in a report by clicking the Find button in the Find group on the Home tab, and then selecting or entering entries in the Find dialog box.
- In Tutorial 6 you learned to align controls in a form, and you can align controls to the nearest dots in the design grid in the same way in a report by right-clicking the selected controls, pointing to Align on the shortcut menu, and then clicking To Grid.

You can also split, merge, insert, and move selected controls in forms and reports.

To split, merge, insert, and move controls in forms and reports:

1. In the Navigation Pane, open the **SingleOneColumnRightLabels** form in Layout view, and then click the **Arrange** tab. See Figure B-7.

Figure B-7	Arrange tab for forms and reports

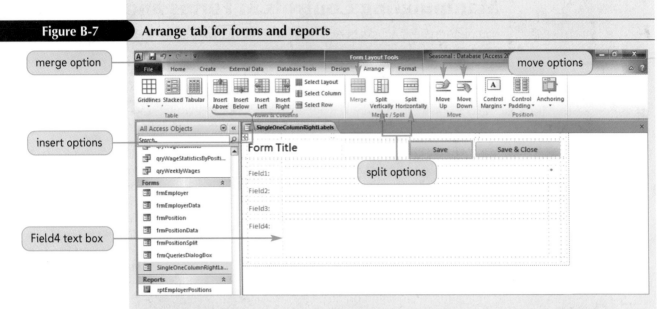

merge option

move options

insert options

Field4 text box

split options

The Arrange tab has options that allow you to insert, split, merge, and move selected controls in a form or report.

▶ **2.** Click the **Field4** text box, and then click the **Insert Above** button in the Rows & Columns group. Access inserts a new text box and attached label above the Field4 text box and label.

▶ **3.** With the Field4 text box still selected, click the **Split Horizontally** button in the Merge/Split group. Access splits the Field4 text box horizontally into two equal-sized text boxes.

▶ **4.** Select both **Field4** text boxes, and then click the **Merge** button in the Merge/Split group. Access merges the two text boxes into a single text box.

▶ **5.** Select the **Field4** text box and its attached label, and then click the **Move Up** button in the Move group. Access moves the selected control up in the control layout.

You can also change the appearance of command buttons and tabs on forms and reports by applying quick styles and by changing their shapes.

To apply quick styles to command buttons and to change their shapes:

▶ **1.** Select the **Save** command button and the **Save & Close** command button, click the **Format** tab, and then click the **Quick Styles** button in the Control Formatting group to display the Quick Styles gallery. See Figure B-8.

Figure B-8   **Quick Styles gallery**

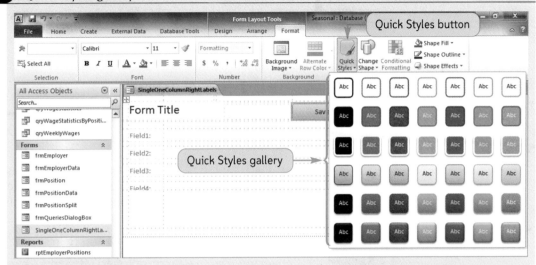

The Quick Styles gallery contains 42 styles you can apply to selected command buttons and tabs.

2. Click the **Intense Effect – Purple, Accent 4** button (row 6, column 5) to change the color of the two selected command buttons to purple.

3. With both command buttons still selected, click the **Change Shape** button in the Control Formatting group to display the Change Shape gallery, and then click the **Oval** button (row 3, column 2). The shape of both command buttons changes to an oval shape.

4. Close the form without saving your design changes.

You can apply a background image to forms and reports by doing the following:

1. In Design view or Layout view, click the Format tab.
2. In the Background group, click the Background Image button.
3. Browse to the folder that contains the background image, click the image filename, and then click the OK button.

You can also add a hyperlink to a form or report by doing the following:

1. In Design view, click the Design tab.
2. In the Controls group, click the Hyperlink button 🌐 to open the Insert Hyperlink dialog box.
3. In the Link to pane, select the source of the hyperlink: Existing File or Web Page, Object in This Database, E-mail Address, or Hyperlink Builder.
4. Based on your choice in the previous step, complete the displayed options in the dialog box, and then click the OK button.

Converting a Macro to Visual Basic

Most people find it easier to learn to use macros than to use Visual Basic. As a way to ease into learning to use Visual Basic, you can create a macro, convert the macro to Visual Basic, and then study the resulting Visual Basic module.

To convert a macro to Visual Basic:

1. Open the **mcrEmployerData** macro in Design view.

2. In the Tools group on the Design tab, click the **Convert Macro to Visual Basic** button.

3. In the Convert macro: mcrEmployerData dialog box, make sure the **Add error handling to generated functions** check box and the **Include macro comments** check box are both checked, click the **Convert** button, and then click the **OK** button to close the confirmation message box.

4. Close the Visual Basic window (if necessary), and then close the macro.

5. Open the **Converted Macro – mcrEmployerData** module in Design view.

6. Read through the module, and then close the Visual Basic window.

7. Close the database.

ENDING DATA FILES

AppendixB

Seasonal.accdb

Microsoft Office Specialist: Access 2010 Certification Skills Reference

Managing the Access Environment

Skill	Pages Where Covered
Create and manage a database	
Use Save Object As	AC B4
Use Open	AC 24
Use Save and Publish	AC 40, AC 639, AC 659
Use Compact & Repair Database	AC 38–AC 40
Use Encrypt with Password commands	AC 651–AC 653
Create a database from a template	AC 7, AC 214–AC 215
Set Access options	AC 632–AC 633, AC 654–AC 658
Configure the Navigation Pane	
Rename objects	AC 225
Delete objects	AC 226
Set Navigation options	AC 37–AC 38, AC 155–AC 157
Apply Application Parts	
Use Blank Forms	AC B7–AC B8
Use Quick Start	AC B7–AC B8
Use user templates	AC B7–AC B8

Building Tables

Skill	Pages Where Covered
Create tables	
Create tables in Design View	AC 50–AC 51, AC 59–AC 67
Create and modify fields	
Insert a field	AC 69, AC 485–AC 486
Delete a field	AC 83–AC 84
Rename a field	AC 85
Hide or Unhide fields	AC B5–AC B6
Freeze or Unfreeze fields	AC 267–AC 268, AC B6
Modify data types	AC 11–AC 12, AC 85
Modify the field description	AC 61–AC 62
Modify field properties	AC 85–AC 87
Sort and filter records	
Use Find	AC 113–AC 114, AC 179–AC 181
Use Sort	AC 123–AC 126, AC 231, AC 381–AC 383
Use Filter commands	AC 127–AC 129, AC 226–AC 228, AC 614–AC 621

Skill	Pages Where Covered
Set relationships	
Define Primary Keys	AC 52–AC 53, AC 66–AC 67, AC A3
Use Primary Keys to create Relationships	AC 4–AC 5, AC 72–AC 73, AC 91–AC 96, AC 254–AC 255, AC 290, AC 490–AC 498
Edit Relationships	AC 254–AC 255, AC 290, AC 501
Import data from a single data file	
Import source data into a new table	AC 76–AC 81
Append records to an existing table	AC 89–AC 90
Import data as a linked table	AC 642–AC 647

Building Forms

Skill	Pages Where Covered
Create forms	
Use the Form Wizard	AC 22, AC 167–AC 170
Create a Blank Form	AC 309
Use Form Design Tools	AC 30–AC 31, AC 294–AC 298
Create Navigation forms	AC 560–AC 563
Apply Form Design options	
Apply a Theme	AC 167, AC 171–AC 173, AC 399
Add bound controls	
Text box	AC 337–AC 338
Drop down	AC 319–AC 324, AC 330–AC 332
Format Header/Footer	AC 324–AC 326
View Code	AC 572–AC 573, AC 578–AC 579, AC 588–AC 589, AC 598
Convert Macros to Visual Basic	AC B12
View Property Sheet	AC 321–AC 322, AC 338
Add Existing Fields	AC 311–AC 312
Apply Form Arrange options	
Use the Table functions	
Insert	AC B9–AC B10
Merge	AC B9–AC B10
Split	AC B9–AC B10
Move table	AC B9–AC B10
Reposition/Format controls	
Anchor	AC 302–AC 304
Padding	AC 301–AC 302
Margins	AC 301–AC 302
Apply Form Format options	
Reformat Font in form	AC 326, AC 341, AC 348–AC 349
Apply background image to form	AC B11
Apply Quick Styles to controls in form	AC B10–AC B11
Apply conditional formatting in form	AC 201–AC 202, AC B9

Creating and Managing Queries

Skill	Pages Where Covered
Construct queries	
Create Select query	AC 27–AC 29, AC 118–AC 120, AC 121–AC 126, AC 221–AC 226, AC 233–AC 236, AC 246–AC 250
Create Make Table query	AC 476–AC 479
Create Append query	AC 481–AC 483
Create Crosstab query	AC 238–AC 246
Manage source tables and relationships	
Use the Show Table command	AC 117–AC 118
Use Remove Table command	AC 503
Create ad hoc relationships	AC 502–AC 503
Manipulate fields	
Add field	AC 118–AC 120, AC 222
Remove field	AC 119, AC 134
Rearrange fields	AC 135–AC 136
Use Sort and Show options	AC 123–AC 126, AC 134
Calculate totals	
Use the Total row	AC 151–AC 152
Use Group By	AC 152–AC 155
Generate calculated fields	
Perform calculations	AC 145–AC 150, AC 245
Use the Zoom box	AC 146, AC 245
Use Expression Builder	AC 146–AC 148, AC 229–AC 231

Designing Reports

Skill	Pages Where Covered
Create reports	
Create a Blank Report	AC 379
Use Report Design Tools	AC 32–AC 33, AC 362–AC 407
Use the Report Wizard	AC 192–AC 195
Apply Report Design options	
Apply a Theme	AC 197
Add calculated controls	
Total report records	AC 369–AC 370, AC 381–AC 384
Group report records	AC 381–AC 384
Add bound/unbound controls	
Text box	AC 337–AC 338
Hyperlink	AC B11
Drop down	AC 319–AC 324, AC 330–AC 332, AC B9
Graph	AC 445–AC 451, AC B9
Insert page break	AC 440, AC B9

Skill	Pages Where Covered
Header/Footer	
Insert page number	AC 399–AC 401
Insert logo	AC 200
Reorder tab function	AC 343–AC 345, AC B9
Apply Report Arrange options	
Use the Table functions	
Insert	AC B9–AC B10
Merge	AC B9–AC B10
Split	AC B9–AC B10
Move table	AC B9–AC B10
Reposition/Format records	
Padding	AC 301–AC 302, AC B9
Margins	AC 301–AC 302, AC B9
Align report outputs to grid	AC 315–AC 316, AC 399, AC 402, AC B9
Apply Report Format options	
Rename label in a report	AC 197
Apply background image to report	AC B11
Change shape in report	AC B10–AC B11
Apply conditional formatting in report	AC 201–AC 202
Apply Report Page Setup options	
Change page Size	AC B6–AC B7
Change page orientation	AC B6–AC B7
Sort and filter records for reporting	
Use the Find command	AC 113–AC 114, AC 179–AC 181, AC B9
Use the Sort command	AC 381–AC 384
Use Filter commands	AC 363–AC 365
Use view types	AC 363

GLOSSARY/INDEX

Note: Boldface entries include definitions.

SPECIAL CHARACTERS

\~(backslash), AC 253, AC 260
> (greater than operator), AC 132, AC 260
< (less than operator), AC 132, AC 260
<> (not equal to operator), AC 132
! (exclamation point), AC 180, AC 260
" (quotation mark), AC 260
" (quotation marks), AC 487
(pound sign), AC 180, AC 260
& (ampersand), AC 118, AC 260
* (asterisk), AC 180, AC 181
+ (plus sign), AC 115
- (hyphen), AC 180
= (equal sign), AC 132, AC 338
>= (greater than or equal to operator), AC 132
<= (less than or equal to operator), AC 132
? (question mark), AC 180, AC 260
[] (square brackets), AC 180
; (semicolon), AC 253, AC 260

A

.accdb file extension, AC 8

ACCDE file A special version of an Access database that runs as a normal database, but its VBA code can't be viewed or edited. Also, you can't view, modify, or create forms, reports, or modules in Design view, and you can't import or export forms, reports, or modules. The ACCDE file has an .accde extension instead of the usual .accdb extension. AC 659

Access. *See* Microsoft Access 2010

Access naming rule, AC A27

Access Options dialog box, AC 657

Access window The program window that appears when you start the Access program to create a new database or open an existing database. AC 3

action An instruction to Access to perform an operation. AC 520

Action Catalog Lists all actions by category and all macros in a database. AC 520

Action Catalog button A toggle to open and close the Action Catalog pane. AC 520

action query A query that adds, changes, or deletes multiple table records at a time. AC 474–489
append, AC 474, AC 481–483
changing query type, AC 479
delete, AC 475, AC 483–486
deleting, AC 488–489

make-table, AC 474, AC 476–480
update, AC 475, AC 486–488

Add & Delete group A group on the Fields tab in Table Datasheet view that contains options for adding different types of fields to a table. AC 2

Advanced Filter/Sort A form and datasheet tool that lets you specify multiple selection criteria and specify a sort order for selected records in the Filter window, in the same way you specify record selection criteria and sort orders for a query in Design view. AC 614

AfterUpdate event An event that occurs after changed data in a control or a record is updated. AC 575, AC 581

aggregate function A function that performs an arithmetic operation on selected records in a database. AC 151–155
calculations for groups of records, AC 154–155
creating queries with, AC 152–154
Total row, AC 151–152

aligning controls, AC 315–316

All Access Objects The default category in the Navigation Pane; it lists all the objects in the database grouped by type (tables, queries, forms, reports, and so on). AC 38, AC 155–157

Allow Default Shortcut Menus property A database property that specifies whether shortcut menus are enabled or disabled. AC 633

Allow Full Menus property A database property that specifies whether all options are available on the Ribbon. AC 633

Allow Multiple Values property A property that allows you to store more than one value in a field when the property is set to Yes. AC 612

Allow Zero Length property A property that allows you to store a zero length string value in a field when the property is set to Yes. AC 638

alternate key A candidate key that was not chosen to be the primary key. AC A3

ampersand (&), input masks, AC 260

ampersand (&) operator A concatenation operator that joins text expressions. AC 228

Anchor property A form control property that automatically resizes the control and places the control in the same relative position on the screen as the screen size and resolution change. AC 276

anchoring controls in a form, AC 302–304

And logical operator The logical operator you use in a query when you want a record selected only if two or more conditions are met. AC 141, AC 142–143, AC 145

anomalies Undesirable irregularities of tables caused by data redundancy and by partial and transitive dependencies. Anomalies are of three types: insertion, deletion, and update. AC A14–A15

Append Only property A field property for a Memo field that lets you edit the field value and, when set to Yes, causes Access to keep a historical record of all versions of the field value. You can view each version of the field value, along with a date and time stamp of when each version change occurred. AC 270

append query An action query that adds records from existing tables or queries to the end of another table. AC 474, AC 481–483

Applicable Filter dialog box, AC 620–621

application part, AC B7

Application Title property A database property that specifies the name for a database that appears in the Access window title bar. AC 632

ApplyFilter action, AC 522

argument (for VBA) A value passed to a VBA function and used in place of a parameter when the function is executed. AC 582

arguments (for an action) Additional facts Access needs to execute an action. AC 520

artificial key A field that you add to a table to serve solely as the primary key and that is visible to users. AC A21–A23

Ascending button, AC 123

assignment statement A VBA statement that assigns the value of an expression to a field, control, or property. AC 572

asterisk (*), wildcard character, AC 180, AC 181

Attachment data type A data type used to attach one or more files to a table record. Access stores the attachments in compressed form to minimize file size and maximize disk space usage. AC 634–636

Attachments dialog box, AC 635–636

attribute The formal term for a column in a relation (table). AC A2

AutoFilter An Access feature, available by clicking the arrow to the right of a field name in Datasheet view for a table or query, that enables you to quickly sort and display the field's values in various ways. AC 123–124, AC 226–228

automatic index, default, AC 509

AutoNumber An Access data type that automatically assigns a unique number to a record. AC 11, AC 55, AC 636–638

B

back-end database A database that contains the tables that are needed for an application. AC 647

TASK REFERENCE

TASK	PAGE #	RECOMMENDED METHOD
Access, start	AC 7	Click 🟦, click All Programs, click Microsoft Office, click Microsoft Access 2010
Action, add to a macro	AC 526	In the Macro Designer, click the Add New Action arrow, click the action
Action, add to a macro by dragging	AC 527	In the Macro Designer, find the action in the Action Catalog, click and drag the action to the desired location in the macro
Action, find in Action Catalog	AC 527	Click the search box, type the action to find
Aggregate functions, use in a datasheet	AC 151	Open table or query in Datasheet view, in Records group on Home tab click Totals button, click Total field row arrow, click function
Aggregate functions, use in a query	AC 153	Display the query in Design view, click Totals button in the Show/Hide group on the Query Tools Design tab
Append query, create	AC 481	*See* Reference box: Creating an Append Query
AutoFilter, use in a table or query datasheet	AC 227	Click arrow on column heading, click filter option
Calculated field, add to a query	AC 146	*See* Reference box: Using Expression Builder
Caption, change for a form's navigation bar	AC 442	Click the form selector, open the property sheet, type the value in the Navigation Caption box, press Enter
Caption, change for a label	AC 321	*See* Reference box: Changing a Label's Caption
Caption, set for a form	AC 545	Right-click the form selector, click the Format tab, click the Caption box, type caption name
Chart, edit with Microsoft Graph	AC 448	In Design view, right-click the chart's edge, point to Chart Object, click Open, make desired changes, click File, click Exit & Return
Chart, embed in a form or report	AC 446	*See* Reference box: Embedding a Chart in a Form or Report
Color, change an object's background	AC 348	Click the object, click 🖌️▾ arrow, click the desired color
Column, resize width in a datasheet	AC 13	Double-click ↔ on the right border of the column heading
Combo box, add to a form	AC 330	*See* Reference box: Adding a Combo Box to Find Records
Command button, add to a form	AC 538	Click Design tab, click ▾, make sure 🖉 is not selected, click ▭ in Controls group on Design tab, position the pointer in the form, click the mouse button
Compressed folder, create	FM 18	In a folder window, select the files and folders to be compressed, right-click the selection, point to Send to, click Compressed (zipped) folder, type a folder name, press Enter
Compressed folder, extract all files and folders from	FM 19	Right-click the compressed folder, click Extract All
Compressed folder, open	FM 18	Double-click the compressed folder
Control layout, remove control from in a form	AC 301	In Layout view, right-click the control, point to Layout, click Remove Layout
Control tip property, set for a form control	AC 342	In Layout view, right-click the control, click Properties, click Other tab, type the tip in the ControlTip Text property, press Enter
Control, anchor in a form	AC 302	In Layout view, select the control to anchor, click Arrange tab, click Anchoring button in Position group, click option in gallery

TASK	PAGE #	RECOMMENDED METHOD
Control, apply special effect to	AC 348	Select the control, open property sheet, set the Special Effect property
Control, delete	AC 317	Right-click the control, click Delete
Control, move in a form	AC 313	*See* Reference box: Selecting and Moving Controls
Control, resize in a form	AC 317	*See* Reference box: Resizing a Control in Design View
Control, select	AC 313	*See* Reference box: Selecting and Moving Controls
Controls, align selected	AC 315	Right-click one of the selected controls, point to Align, click desired alignment
Crosstab query, create	AC 242	*See* Reference box: Using the Crosstab Query Wizard
CSV file, import as an Access table	AC 423	*See* Reference box: Importing a CSV File as an Access Table
Data, find	AC 179	*See* Reference box: Finding Data in a Form or Datasheet
Data, group in a report	AC 381	*See* Reference box: Sorting and Grouping Data in a Report
Data, sort in a report	AC 381	*See* Reference box: Sorting and Grouping Data in a Report
Data Type gallery, add fields to a table with	AC 82	Click Fields tab, click More Fields in Add & Delete group, click field or Quick Start selection to add
Database, compact and repair	AC 39	*See* Reference box: Compacting and Repairing a Database
Database, compact on close	AC 39	Click File tab, click Options, click Current Database, click Compact on Close
Database, create a blank	AC 7	Start Access, click Blank database, type the database name, select the drive and folder, click OK, click Create
Database, decrypt	AC 653	*See* Reference box: Unsetting a Database Password
Database, encrypt	AC 651	*See* Reference box: Encrypting a Database and Setting a Password
Database, save as a previous version	AC 639	Open the database to save and close all open objects, click the File tab, click Save & Publish, click Save Database As, click the desired Access format, click Save As, choose the destination folder and enter the database name, click Save
Database, save as an ACCDE file	AC 659	Open the database, click the File tab, click Save & Publish, click Make ACCDE, click Save As, type database name, select the destination folder, click Save
Database, split	AC 649	*See* Reference box: Using the Database Splitter
Database, open	AC 24	*See* Reference box: Opening a Database
Database documentation, set	AC 655	*See* Reference box: Setting Database Documentation Properties
Database properties, set	AC 655	*See* Reference box: Setting the Database Properties and Startup Options
Datasheet view for tables, switch to	AC 87	In the Views group on the Table Tools Design tab, click the View button
Date and time, add to a report	AC 396	*See* Reference box: Adding the Date and Time to a Report
Design view, switch to	AC 70	In the Views group on the Home tab, click the View button
Delete query, create	AC 484	*See* Reference box: Creating a Delete Query
Documenter, use	AC 291	*See* Reference box: Using the Documenter
Duplicate values, hide	AC 392	*See* Reference box: Hiding Duplicate Values in a Report
Event procedure, add to a form or report	AC 592	*See* Reference box: Adding an Event Procedure to a Form or Report
Event procedure, display an existing	AC 578	Open the property sheet for the control or object, click the Event tab, click the event property box, click [...]

TASK	PAGE #	RECOMMENDED METHOD
Excel worksheet, link data from	AC 460	Click External Data tab, click Excel button in Import & Link group, click Browse, select the workbook, click Open, click Link to the data source by creating a linked table, click OK, follow the steps in the Link Spreadsheet Wizard
Export steps, save	AC 435	Click Save export steps check box in Export dialog box, enter description, click Save Export
Field, add to a form or report	AC 311	In Design view, click Add Existing Fields button in Tools group, click the record source, double-click the field
Field, add to a table	AC 69	*See* Reference box: Adding a Field Between Two Existing Fields
Field, define in a table	AC 60	*See* Reference box: Defining a Field in Design View
Field, delete from a table	AC 83	*See* Reference box: Deleting a Field from a Table Structure
Field, move to a new location in a table	AC 88	Display the table in Design view, click the field's row selector, drag the field with the pointer
Field property change, update	AC 86	Click 🔁, select the option for updating the field property
File, attach to a record using an Attachment field	AC 635	Right-click the record's Attachment field, click Manage Attachments, click Add, select the file to attach, click Open, click OK
File, close	OFF 22	Click File tab, click Close
File, copy	FM 14	*See* Reference box: Copying a File or Folder in a Folder Window
File, delete	FM 17	Right-click the file, click Delete
File, detach from a record's Attachment field	AC 636	Right-click the record's Attachment field, click Manage Attachments, select the file to detach, click Remove, click OK
File, export from a record's Attachment field	AC 636	Right-click the record's Attachment field, click Manage Attachments, select the file to export, click Save As, type the filename and choose the destination folder, click Save, click OK
File, move	FM 13	*See* Reference box: Moving a File or Folder in a Folder Window
File, open	OFF 22	*See* Reference box: Opening an Existing File
File, open from a record's Attachment field	AC 636	Right-click the record's Attachment field, click Manage Attachments, select the file to open, click Open
File, print	OFF 29	*See* Reference box: Printing a File
File, rename	FM 16	Right-click the file, click Rename, type the new filename, press Enter
File, save	OFF 19	*See* Reference box: Saving a File
File, save to SkyDrive	OFF 24	*See* Reference box: Saving a File to SkyDrive
File, switch between open	OFF 7	Point to program button on taskbar, click thumbnail of file to make active
Files, select multiple	FM 14	Hold down the Ctrl key and click files
Files, view in Large Icons view	FM 10	Click 📋 ▾, click Large Icons
Filter, apply to a form from a saved query	AC 620	*See* Reference box: Applying a Filter Saved as a Query
Filter, save as a query	AC 618	*See* Reference box: Saving a Filter as a Query
Filter By Form, use to select records	AC 616	*See* Reference box: Selecting Records Using Filter By Form
Filter By Selection, activate	AC 127	*See* Reference box: Using Filter By Selection

TASK	PAGE #	RECOMMENDED METHOD
Lookup field, create	AC 254	Click the Data Type arrow, click Lookup Wizard, specify your choices in the Lookup Wizard dialog boxes
Macro, run an existing	AC 523	*See* Reference box: Directly Running an Existing Macro
Macro, single step	AC 528	*See* Reference box: Single Stepping a Macro
Mailing labels, create	AC 404	*See* Reference box: Creating Mailing Labels and Other Labels
Make-table query, create	AC 477	*See* Reference box: Creating a Make-Table Query
Memo field, change properties of	AC 269	Display the table in Design view, select the Memo field, click the Text Format box or click the Append Only box
Module, compile	AC 594	Click Debug, click Compile *database name*
Module, create	AC 582	In the Macros & Code group on the Create tab, click the Module button
Module, save	AC 585	Click [save icon], type module name, press Enter
Multiple-column report, modify	AC 406	In Design view, click Page Setup tab, click Page Setup button, click the Columns tab, set the column options, click OK
Multivalued field, create in a table	AC 625	In Design view, enter the field name, choose the Lookup Wizard data type, select the method for looking up field values and choose the appropriate Lookup Wizard options, select the Allow Multiple Values check box, finish the Lookup Wizard
My Documents folder, open	FM 8	In a folder window, click [▷] next to Libraries in the Navigation pane, click [▷] next to Documents, click My Documents
Navigation form, create	AC 560	In the Forms group on the Create tab, click the Navigation button, choose desired navigation form in gallery
Navigation form, drag form or report to	AC 561	Open the Navigation Pane, open the navigation form in Layout view, drag object from Navigation Pane to desired tab on navigation form
Object, open	AC 19	Double-click the object in the Navigation Pane
Object, save	AC 17	Click [save icon], type the object name, click OK
Object dependencies, identify	AC 262	Click Database Tools tab, click Object Dependencies button in Relationships group, click the object, click [+]
Office program, exit	OFF 30	Click [X]
Office program, start	OFF 5	*See* Reference box: Starting an Office Program
Office program, switch between open	OFF 7	Click program button on taskbar to make active
Padding, change in a form control	AC 302	In Layout view, click the control, click Arrange tab, click Control Padding button in Position group, click the desired setting
Page numbers, add to a report	AC 399	*See* Reference box: Adding Page Numbers to a Report
Parameter query, create	AC 234	*See* Reference box: Creating a Parameter Query
Password, set a database	AC 651	*See* Reference box: Encrypting a Database and Setting a Password
Password, unset a database	AC 653	*See* Reference box: Unsetting a Database Password
Performance Analyzer, use	AC 639	*See* Reference box: Using the Performance Analyzer
Picture, add to or change on a command button	AC 539	Open the property sheet for the command button, click the Picture box, click [...], select the picture, click OK
Picture, insert in a form	AC 200	In Layout view, click Design tab, click Logo button in the Header/Footer group, select the picture file, click OK

TASK	PAGE #	RECOMMENDED METHOD
Picture caption, add to a command button	AC 540	Open the property sheet for the command button, click the Caption box, press F2, type desired caption
Picture caption, change location of on a command button	AC 540	Open the property sheet for the command button, click the Picture Caption Arrangement arrow, click the desired setting
PivotChart, add to a table or query	AC 458	Open the table or query in Datasheet view, right-click the object tab, click PivotChart View, drag the fields from the Field List pane into the PivotChart
PivotTable, add a total field	AC 455	Click a detail field's column heading, click Design tab, click AutoCalc button in Tools group, click an aggregate option
PivotTable, add to a table or query	AC 453	Open the table or query in Datasheet view, right-click the object tab, click PivotTable View, drag the fields from the Field List pane into the PivotTable
PivotTable, show or hide details	AC 457	Click Design tab, click Show Details or Hide Details in Show/Hide group
Preview pane, open	FM 17	In a folder window, click [icon]
Primary key, specify	AC 67	*See* Reference box: Specifying a Primary Key in Design View
Program window, maximize	OFF 8	Click [icon]
Program window, minimize	OFF 8	Click [icon]
Program window, restore down	OFF 8	Click [icon]
Property sheet, open	AC 149	Right-click the object or control, click Properties
Property sheet, open or close for a field or control	AC 232	Select the field or control, click Design tab, click Property Sheet button in Show/Hide group
Procedure, test in the Immediate Window	AC 586	*See* Reference box: Testing a Procedure in the Immediate Window
Query datasheet, sort	AC 125	*See* Reference box: Sorting a Query Datasheet
Query, define	AC 117	Click the Create tab, click the Query Design button in the Queries group
Query, run	AC 119	Double-click query in Navigation Pane or, in Results group on Query Tools Design tab, click Run button
Query results, sort	AC 125	*See* Reference box: Sorting a Query Datasheet
Quick Start selection, add	AC 82	Click Fields tab, click More Fields in Add & Delete group, click Quick Start selection
Record, add new	AC 17	In the Records group on the Home tab, click the New button
Record, delete	AC 115	*See* Reference box: Deleting a Record
Record, move to first	AC 27	Click [icon]
Record, move to last	AC 27	Click [icon]
Record, move to next	AC 27	Click [icon]
Record, move to previous	AC 27	Click [icon]
Records, print selected in a form	AC 184	Click File tab, click Print in navigation bar, click Print, click Selected Record(s), click OK
Records, redisplay all after filter	AC 129	In Sort & Filter group on Home tab, click the Toggle Filter button

TASK	PAGE #	RECOMMENDED METHOD
Rectangle, add to a form or report	AC 347	*See* Reference box: Adding a Rectangle to a Form or Report
Report, create a custom	AC 379	*See* Reference box: Creating a Blank Report in Layout View
Report, filter in Report view	AC 363	Right-click the value to filter, point to Text Filters, click filter option
Report, print	AC 37	*See* Reference box: Printing a Report
Report, print specific pages of	AC 203	Click File tab, click Print in navigation bar, click Print, click Pages, enter number of pages to print in From and To boxes, click OK.
Report, select and copy data in Report view	AC 364	Click the top of the selection, drag to the end of the selection, click Home tab, click 📋 in Clipboard group
Report Wizard, activate	AC 193	Click Create tab, click Report Wizard button in Reports group, choose the table or query for the report, select fields, click Next
Saved export, run	AC 435	Click External Data tab, click Saved Exports button in Export group, click the saved export, click Run
Saved import, run	AC 430	Click External Data tab, click Saved Imports button in Import & Link group, click the saved import, click Run
Self-join, create	AC 502	*See* Reference box: Creating a Self-Join
Sort, specify ascending in datasheet	AC 123	Click a column heading arrow, click Sort A to Z
Sort, specify descending in datasheet	AC 123	Click a column heading arrow, click Sort Z to A
Spacing, change in a form control	AC 301	In Layout view, click the control, click Arrange tab, click Control Margins button in Position group, click the desired setting
SQL statement, use for a list box	AC 552	Open the property sheet for the list box, click the Data tab, right-click the Row Source box, click Zoom, enter the SQL statement, click OK
SQL statement, view	AC 549	*See* Reference box: Viewing an SQL Statement for a Query
Startup options, set for a database	AC 655	*See* Reference box: Setting the Database Properties and Startup Options
Subform, open in a new window	AC 337	Right-click the subform border, click Subform in New Window
Subform/Subreport Wizard, activate	AC 333	Click Design tab, click ▾ in Controls group, make sure 🔧 is selected, click 📇, click in the grid at the upper-left corner for the subform/subreport
Submacro, add to a macro	AC 536	*See* Reference box: Adding a Submacro
Submacro, attach to a command button	AC 539	Open the property sheet for the command button, click the Event tab, click the arrow for the event property box, click submacro name
Tab Control, add to a form	AC 440	Click Design tab, click Tab Control tool in Controls group, click in the grid at the upper-left corner for the tab control
Tab order, change in a form	AC 343	In Design view, click the Design tab, click Tab Order button in Tools group, drag the rows into the desired order, click OK
Tab Stop property, change for a form control	AC 342	In Layout view, right-click the control, click Properties, click Other tab, set the Tab Stop property
Table, analyze	AC 426	Select the table, click Database Tools tab, click Analyze Table button in Analyze group
Table, create in Datasheet view	AC 9	*See* Reference box: Creating a Table in Datasheet View
Table, link to in another Access database	AC 643	*See* Reference box: Linking to a Table in Another Access Database

TASK	PAGE #	RECOMMENDED METHOD
Table, open in a database	AC 19	Double-click the table in the Navigation Pane
Table, save in a database	AC 17	*See* Reference box: Saving a Table
Template, use an HTML	AC 421	Click the Export data with formatting and layout check box in the Export - HTML Document dialog box, click the Select a HTML Template check box, click Browse, select template, click OK
Theme, apply to a form	AC 171	*See* Reference box: Applying a Theme to a Form
Title, add to a form or report	AC 325	In Header/Footer group, click Title button, type the title, press Enter
Top values query, create	AC 249	In the Query Setup group on the Design tab, enter the number of or percentage of records to select in the Return (Top Values) box
Total, calculate in a report	AC 369	In Layout view, click any value in the column to calculate, click Design tab, click Totals button in Grouping & Totals group, click desired function
Trusted folder, create	AC 270	Click File tab, click Options, click Trust Center, click Trust Center Settings, click Trusted Locations, click Add new location, click Browse, navigate to the desired folder, click OK four times
Update query, create	AC 487	*See* Reference box: Creating an Update Query
Validation Rule property, set	AC 264	Display the table in Design view, select the field, enter the rule in the Validation Rule box
Validation Text property, set	AC 265	Display the table in Design view, select the field, enter the text in the Validation Text box
Workspace, scroll	OFF 9	Click arrow button on scroll bar or drag scroll box
Workspace, zoom	OFF 9	Drag the Zoom slider
XML file, export an Access object to an	AC 432	*See* Reference box: Exporting an Access Object as an XML File
XML file, import as an Access table	AC 429	*See* Reference box: Importing an XML File as an Access Table